HANDBOOK OF

Research on Teaching Literacy Through the Communicative and Visual Arts

VOLUME II

HANDBOOK OF RESEARCH ON TEACHING LITERACY THROUGH THE COMMUNICATIVE AND VISUAL ARTS

VOLUME II

EDITED BY JAMES FLOOD

SHIRLEY BRICE HEATH

DIANE LAPP

New York London

Lawrence Erlbaum Associates
Taylor & Francis Group
270 Madison Avenue
New York, NY 10016

Lawrence Erlbaum Associates
Taylor & Francis Group
2 Park Square
Milton Park, Abingdon
Oxon OX14 4RN

Lawrence Erlbaum Associates is an imprint of Taylor & Francis Group, an Informa business

Printed in the United States of America on acid-free paper
10 9 8 7 6 5 4 3 2 1

International Standard Book Number-13: 978-0-8058-5700-9 (Softcover) 978-0-8058-5699-6 (Hardcover)

Library of Congress Cataloging-in-Publication Data

Handbook of research on teaching literacy through the communicative and visual arts / James Flood, Shirley Brice Heath, and Diane Lapp, editors.
p. cm.
Includes index.
ISBN 0-8058-5379-0
1. Communication--Study and teaching--Research--Handbooks, manuals, etc. I. Flood, James. II. Heath, Shirley Brice. III. Lapp, Diane.
P91.3.H36 1996

302.2'07--dc20
96-31706 CIP

Visit the Taylor & Francis Web site at
http://www.taylorandfrancis.com

and the LEA and Routledge Web site at
http://www.routledge.com

CONTENTS

Part II

METHODS OF INQUIRY IN THE COMMUNICATIVE, VISUAL, AND PERFORMATIVE ARTS

Part IV

INTO THE LANGUAGE ARTS CLASSROOM THROUGH THE VISUAL AND COMMUNICATIVE ARTS

NOTE TO READERS

The title of the *Handbook of Research on Teaching Literacy Through the Communicative and Visual Arts, Volume II* remains the same as that of *Volume I* (1997). Titles of multi-volume handbooks can never reflect the changes that fields undergo between volumes, and librarians, scholars, and bibliographic services need continuity in titles of series. Readers of *Volume II* (2007) will be very aware that in the past decade visual and *performative* have come to be almost synonymous with *communicative*, and *literacy research* has come to encompass much more than decoding and encoding of verbal material. Moreover, *literacy* is now rarely spoken of in the singular or without prefatory descriptors such as *multi-modal*. Along with the marked shift to visual and *performative* in the decade between the two volumes has come the widespread recognition that teachers and students have to become *learners together*. Therefore, *Volume II*, far more than *Volume I*, speaks of the research and practice in the technologies that have vastly expanded our meanings and uses of literacy and demonstrates the extent to which these technologies originate and evolve through the skills and interests of the young. This volume captures learning beyond and between the niches of formal education and narrates some of the technological advances that integrate music and movement into the visual, verbal, and performative dimensions of literacies.

PREFACE

Much has changed since the publication in 1997 of the first volume of the *Handbook of Research on Teaching Literacy Through the Communicative and Visual Arts.* This second volume could have carried many different titles in an attempt to convey some of these changes. For example, one title might have been *Handbook of Literacy Research: Visual, Communicative, and Performative Arts.* Such a title, along with others that readers might construct, connotes far more than might seem to be the case at first glance. Any *Handbook* that includes *literacy* in its title will have to reflect the accelerating prominence of the *visual* and *performative* dimensions of *reading, comprehending,* and *interpreting*; almost any form of communication goes beyond reliance on simply the *verbal* channel.

Complexities and multiplicities do not stop with the addition of modes, channels, and layers of symbol systems embedded within different forms of literacies. The worlds of advertising, entertainment, and education now rely on multiple technologies. Greeting cards talk, sing, project animation, and sometimes they offer printed messages as well. Children's "books" come not just in pages between book covers, but through the aural performance of "books on tape"; the visual worlds of television, film, photographic exhibitions; and the performative possibilities offered by clothing and toys. Children and young people produce their own books and magazines, ranging from sequels to young adult novels to graphic novels to 'zines, blogs, and dialogues across personal websites.

These rapidly expanding technologies and means of production and reception of communication mean that *teaching literac(ies)* has become a misnomer. *Learning* takes prominence over teaching, for the speed and directions of technological developments outpace the ability of any literacy instructor to claim expertise in more than a few.

Therefore every classroom is likely to contain a range of experts on the potential of different technologies for supporting verbal representations through visual and performative means. Knowledge and skills truly have to be distributed. Age, status, and credentials—long-standing markers of "the teacher"—now need the complementarity of diverse experiences, dedicated time for exploration, and risk-tasking with new technologies that "the student" offers. A presumption dominant through much of the history of formal education has been that teachers teach and learners learn; at no point in human history have we been more aware than we are today that *we must all be learners and teachers.* Those who undertake research on the ever-widening topic of *literacy* have to take this tenet to be fundamental in their work.

Several other changes fundamental to the study of literacy have come about since 1997. A decade later, when we consider visual learning and "visual literacies," we immediately encounter confusion, for these terms have become enmeshed with ideas that surround "multimodal literacies" or "multi-literacy(ies)." The perspective that dominates throughout this *Handbook* is that "literacies" refers to media and means of transmission dependent on combinations of iconic images, symbolic systems, and conventions of presentation and interpretation.

A further clarification is necessary, for the terms *literacies* and *arts* are often conflated, no doubt, in part because the term *language arts* tends to refer to early learning of reading and writing verbal language. Yet it is important to distinguish between *language* or *literacy arts* and those *arts* that result from intentional acts of composition and carry values—religious, aesthetic, or ideological—that extend beyond the pragmatic or informational. These arts often complement and even spring from *literate* sources. Yet within many cultures, they also stand on their own and are, in fact, widely assumed to be those art forms encompassed within the expression "art for art's sake."

Those forms of literacy referred to as *visual* have the special characteristic of depending for their expression on material forms that exist outside the human body. These range from paintings to architectural models, from jewelry to costume, from illuminated manuscripts to sculpture, from print to illustration, from video graphics to schematic diagrams. Visual literacies have through the ages combined several of these forms.

The term *communicative arts,* used in the title of this *Handbook* as well as broadly within education, refers to means of transmission that rely primarily on language—either oral or visual (as in Sign Language representation) or in scripted/written form. Some regard music as a special case of the communicative arts, for all music carries meaning, and its form may or may not be recorded in some kind of permanent or quasi-permanent form.

In many ways, those literacies and arts included in the descriptor *performative* embrace both visual and communicative arts and yet also operate as a subset of the communicative arts. These are heavily dependent on visual literacies (e.g., programs, scripts, choreographic or musical notation). The fundamental means of transmission for the performative arts is the human body (as in dance and drama) or its extension (as in puppetry or in the playing of musical instruments). Performative arts generally take place as one-time-only unique experiences; though the "same" play script may be repeated across the ages, each performance is unique to an individual, group, or company and to specific combinations of spatial and temporal limits.

Terms such as "technical," "electronic," "digital," or "interactive technological" often tend to cluster around only certain of the visual, communicative, or performative arts. Yet we must remember that technology has entered each means of transmission to complement, reproduce, and play within and from all of the arts and our many different forms of literacies.

Historically, two functions of all the forms and means of literacies have held constant: their exchange value and their resource for the building of community and the reinforcing of memory. Through all literacies, meaning is conveyed and received (therefore ideally "exchanged") by means of reciprocal engagement based on mutually perceived needs. Essential within all means of literacy is their power to remind individuals of their communal membership and of their own past experiences as well as their power to project themselves and their ideas and intentions into the future. Remembering together ensures affirmation of social membership, as does joint creative activity, often stimulated by an in-the-moment visual and narrative experience.

This *Handbook* takes up the persistent capacity of humans to depend in their production and reception of information and social values on the fusion of visual, communicative, and performative channels working in combination and persistently with evolving technologies. In 1997, terms such as *blogs* and *vpods* had not yet been coined, and no one spoke of a "Digital Divide." Today educators have become painfully aware of this divide that signifies separations of knowledge between those of different ages as well as chasms of opportunity and access that result from economic differences across families, regions, and nations. In this volume we provide a glimpse into some of the literacy challenges these divisions present now and in the future for learning both within and beyond formal education.

Many of the changes predicted in the 1997 volume of the *Handbook* have come about. Educators feel keenly the changes in their students that result from their ever- widening means of access to information. Children and young people now engage in accepted practices foreign to their elders, and their quest for learning environments of high participation and considerable risk seems never-ending.

Yet other predictions made nearly a decade ago have not come through. Primary among these is the relative absence of attention to full integration of arts media into school life. Voluminous rhetoric about such integration has no match in evidence that educators truly believe in the fact that literate skills and competencies across multiple literacies depend on media beyond print. A second prediction that has little or no trace of influence among educators (and holds only modest interest for literacy researchers) is any sustained linkage between classroom lessons and community-based organizational learning grounded in experiential opportunities. The British and Australians have come closest to generating widespread approval of more involvement in the arts and greater engagement with community or civic learning; yet their efforts have yet to match the stated goals of policymakers and business/community leaders. Within the United States and across Europe, some local governments have struggled to make learning environments extend beyond homework monitoring in after-school programs. Yet without national and state support, these programs lack sustainability and the critically needed integration with core bodies of information and sets of skills that can be learned only within formal schooling. Moreover, adults and children alike in many nations have few opportunities to engage with interactive technologies, and their literacy artifacts often consist of a single chalkboard and perhaps a few slates. Within post-industrial nations, equity of access is far from universal, and the commercial drive behind new hardware and software promises no let-up in the association of opportunity-to-learn with economic resources of individual families.

But almost regardless of economic standing, students in post-industrial nations no longer see school, formal instruction, textbooks, libraries, or worksheets as sources of "real" learning or even as their primary or essential means of education or opportunity. The Digital Divide, so astutely predicted by many researchers in the first volume, has indeed come to be a tangible reality, and it is felt nowhere more keenly than within schools. Around the world, many young people spend most of their discretionary time in a sea of blogs, on-line-communication through instant messaging and text messaging, cell phones with seemingly endless visual capability, and chatrooms and graphic novels that leave most adults in wonderment. For students with the economic means, these technologies of the quick, short, and instrumental dominate their out-of-school experiences. In the persistent hope of keeping control and of transmitting facts and of instilling deeper learning, schools ban these technologies during class lessons and, in many instances, on school grounds. Unless young people have extensive family modeling and encouragement, their engagement with and respect for extended printed texts or depth of knowledge across curricular subject areas do not stand up to their fascination with what they think of as "real" learning.

To capture these and other dichotomies, some researchers have used the metaphor of the differences between immigrant and natives to describe the phenomenon of adults born before and after 1983. The digital natives were literally born into high tech cribs; they speak, view and listen to digital language with the ease of first language learners. The immigrants, however, speak digital with an accent that manifests itself with fussing over cell phone routines, laboring over text messaging, and holding steadfastly to reading and writing of extended texts as the dominant means of achieving "literacy."

The chasm between the two groups grows by the minute. It seems almost impossible for adults, whether as parents or as professional educators, to bridge the increasing number of gaps between their skills and those of the young. Yet all adults will increasingly face the need to accept and to understand the visual, communicative, and performative means of conveying information previously transmitted through language in printed form. Currently, these "arts" constitute the core components of what many term "multi-literacies" or "multimodal literacies." It is critical to note that most dictionaries include within their first definition of *art(s)* the core feature of: "skill acquired by experience, study, or observation (Webster 2003)." Literacy educators have come to accept this idea of the "arts" within the term "language arts" and, more recently, with "graphic arts."

However, this *Handbook* and its authors go further than this broad simple notion of the *arts*. Here we explore how the arts most often viewed as resulting from conscious composition and specialized skills work within those proficiences previously linked with the "language arts." Art forms, such as painting, sculpture, drama, dance, singing, and playing a musical instrument, result from their creators' commitment to the creation of aesthetic objects or events. These forms of communication call for interpretation and integration of past knowledge with new information, just as print does. Yet within the history of formal schooling, consciously aesthetic art forms (aside from literature) have fallen away from the integration into everyday learning that they have held since the beginning of human history. The rise of "fine arts" and their association in the Western world with wealth accumulation of families and state systems contributed to the sense that these art forms were no longer essential to the human spirit and instrumental roles in daily life. This *Handbook* carries the strong suggestion throughout that art forms—visual, communicative, and performative—belong together and must not be pulled apart in our considerations of what achieving "literacy" means.

Throughout history, these arts have reflected and promoted the distribution of knowledge and skills as well as the affirmation of ideologies and beliefs. Today we see both this distribution and affirmation in the out-of-school learning lives of young people who share with one another their values about interactive technologies, as well as their acquired insights into innovative ways of doing this or that with one or another piece of technology. By so doing, they accelerate their learning as well as their commitment to staying connected.

The new knowledge world of today's children and young people, including young adults, can best be characterized as "experiential learning together" through sharing and cooperation. As we research our students' places of learning, we are only beginning to understand their changing perceptions about how to obtain, assess, use, complement, ignore, and "unlearn" information and skills. Moreover, we know very little about their views of what "literacy" means and what such a label might do for them or their friends. For most young people, print plays very little role—beyond instrumental purposes—in their lives. Extended texts, in particular, figure in almost no way in their own daily lives or, for many, in the everyday existence of their parents. What their grandparents might have done with novels, biographies, daily national newspapers, religious texts, or treatises on gardening seems centuries away from their values and experiences. Print is there for many children today—even in homes where books, magazines, daily newspapers, and children's literature exist—only as supplement to visual renderings of information. For some, print may have no conscious place in their literacy development, since diagrams, graphic arts, and performative events dominate. DVDs and television programs may "come with" books, but the visual, bodily movement, musical, and dramatic versions of children's "programs" and "stories" carry far greater influence than their printed counterparts. Many parents see interpretation of a character's motivation rendered by a three-year old through dance and song as much more compelling than their sustained engagement with illustrations and a string of words in a book. As a consequence, "reading" is increasingly becoming "printless" through toys, video programming, and interactive technologies.

Ubiquitous societal changes come through both the loss and the multiplication of types of literacies in the learning lives of all of us. Newspapers, so prominent in the lives of most adults thirty-five years of age and older, now teeter on the brink of collapse. Video arcades and hand-held video games have given way to more complex computerized games for individuals and collaborative teams. Television technologies, as well as those associated with DVD's and storage of music, promise immediate radical changes in hardware, powers of adaptation, and degrees of interactivity. The speed of such changes, as well as their unpredictable directions, makes it impossible for any *Handbook* to claim objectivity, comprehensiveness, or complete balance. Yet we have tried throughout the sections of this volume to accept and to manage realistically the fact that this *Handbook* cannot be everything for everyone. We consciously include research that renders the voices of young people. Yet we also acknowledge the painful and challenging, though promising, changes that much within this volume will mean for adults. Both young and old will continue to be pushed and pulled by rapid and often dramatic changes in information access and speed. How we accept, adapt, adopt, and learn from these makes all the difference. This volume presents a wide range of views that reflects a host of ways to study, use, and reflect on the instrumental and philosophical dimensions of living and learning to the fullest extent possible with the literacies of the visual, communicative, and performative arts.

STRUCTURE OF THE BOOK

We have invited leading literacy researchers from all over the world (England, Italy, the United Arab Emirates, Switzerland, Germany, Australia, Canada, and the United States) to write chapters. Though we know that we are venturing into an emerging field with astounding complexities, we are also confident that scholars around the world understand much about the ways that children (and indeed all of us) learn from the visual, communicative, and performative worlds around us. Having made this claim, we also fully realize that many questions remain to be answered, and we do not yet know enough to pose some questions that will, no doubt, emerge as most important in the decades ahead.

Many of the issues discussed in this Preface have been raised in this volume. Part I, Historical and Theoretical Foundations, edited by Renee Hobbs, presents some of the historical and theoretical foundations of learning literacy through the visual, communicative, and performative arts. This section includes topics such as: examination of continuities and contradictions between school and contemporary culture; the construction of photographic meaning; the history of the book and the reconstruction of media literacy.

The issue of inquiry into the visual, communicative, and performative arts continues to confound many researchers, because the "tried and true" methods of the past simply do not work effectively when we set out to understand the complex phenomena, technological and interactive, of new symbol and sign systems that affect the teaching of literacy. Topics in Part II, Methods of Inquiry in the Communicative, Visual, and Performative Arts, edited by Donna Alvermann, Margaret Hagood and Leslie Rush, include literacy in a multimodal environment of communication: case studies; ethnographies; transformative representations in literacy; and the impact of policies, local and national, on research methodology.

Part III, Family and Communicative Contexts in the Communicative, Visual, and Performing Arts, edited by Victoria Chou and Pamela Konkol, focuses on family and community contexts for learning literacy. In this section our authors focus on the critical issue of young people creating and working with numerous channels of transmission for their literacies and their identities. Their creative work both in and out-of-school figures prominently in this section with examinations of: youth radio, internet communication forms, comic books; and their innovations in forms that raise new challenges to existing notions of literacy.

Part IV, Into the Language Arts Classroom Through the Visual and Communicative Arts, edited by Nancy Roser and Dorothy Strickland, includes papers on making sense of multimodal materials in classrooms. Topics include: children's visual meaning-making; dramatic play; digital storytelling; film; writing; standards in the arts; and response to literature.

In addition to these four sections, we have retained the feature of "Voices from the Field"—the view of practitioners and artists alike—from the 1997 *Handbook* which has again been edited by Deborah Wooten and Bernice Cullinan. However, in recognition of the fact that increasingly we are all "in the field"—inquiring and practicing at the same time, in Volume II we scatter these "voices" throughout the four sections. These speak of music, picture book biographies, several types of arts in classroom life, as well as the truth about nonfiction.

The entire volume speaks to our sense of the urgent need to inquire, value, and incorporate into our own ways of knowing and doing the visual, communicative, and performative arts in their centrality to literacy education. Through all of these challenges must be a sustained and consistent focus on equity, with a vigilant awareness that generalizations based only on the lives of the privileged and the economically secure seriously endanger freedoms fundamental to the human spirit. On these core values critical to learning and literacy rests the future of investigating, analyzing, assessing, and transmitting the what and how of learning.

CONTRIBUTORS

Malik Ali is a doctoral student in the English Department at University of California, Berkeley. He focuses on 20th-century American literature and biographical studies. His research interest is also in the intersections between music and literature. This focus was initially established when he taught high school in Northern California. At present, he conducts research and presents lectures about the novelist and essayist Ralph Ellison and the cultural critic Anatole Broyard.

Marino C. Alvarez is professor of literacy at Tennessee State University, and a senior research scientist with the Center of Excellence in Information Systems at TSU directing the Exploring Minds Project with teachers and students electronically communicating using the Exploring Minds Network he authored. He has served on national committees and editorial advisory boards and is Past President of the College Reading Association and Past Chair of the Action Research Special Interest Group of the American Educational Research Association. He is the recipient of both the Teacher-of-the-Year and Distinguished Researcher-of-the-Year Awards at TSU. He is coauthor of *The Art of Educating with V Diagrams* (2005).

Donna E. Alvermann is Distinguished Research Professor of Language and Literacy Education at the University of Georgia, where she teaches doctoral seminars on theory and research related to young people's literacies (digital, visual, and print). From 1992 to 1997, she codirected the National Reading Research Center, funded by the U.S. Department of Education. Her coauthored/coedited books include *Content Reading and Literacy: Succeeding in Today's Diverse Classrooms* (5th ed.), *Reconceptualizing the Literacies in Adolescents' Lives* (2nd ed.), Popular *Culture in the Classroom: Teaching and Researching Critical Media Literacy*, and *Adolescents and Literacies in a Digital World.* A Past President of the National Reading Conference (NRC), cochair of the International Reading Association's Commission on Adolescent Literacy (1997–2000), and member of the 2009 NAEP Reading Framework, she currently edits *Reading Research Quarterly* and serves on the Adolescent Literacy Advisory Group of the Alliance for Excellent Education. She was elected to the International Reading Association Reading Hall of Fame in 1999, and she is the recipient of NRC's Oscar Causey Award for Outstanding Contributions to Reading Research.

Evelyn Arizpe is a Research Fellow at the Faculty of Education, University of Glasgow. She has lectured and published in the areas of literacy, gender, and children's literature both in Mexico and in the United Kingdom. She is coauthor of *Children Reading Pictures: Interpreting Visual Texts* (2003) and *Reading Lessons from the Eighteenth Century: Mothers, Children and Texts* (2006). Her current research is on literacy and multicultural communities in Scotland.

Bolota Asmerom is a graduate student in education at University of California, Berkeley. His research interests focus on the academic and athletic experiences of Black Immigrants and African Americans. He is currently conducting research and volunteering at University of California, Berkeley's Athletic Study Center. He is also in the process of developing an athletic program focused on academic achievement and health for a local alternative high school.

Steven Z. Athanases is Associate Professor in the School of Education at University of California, Davis, where he chairs the campus Graduate Group in Education. He studies diversity and equity in English teaching and teacher education and has taught courses on response to culturally diverse literature, research on discussion and dramatic performance in schools, and teacher inquiry and teacher education research. He has studied and taught performance theory and practice, and for eight years directed high school productions of original student writing. His recent articles have appeared in *Teachers College Record*, *Teaching and Teacher Education*, *Journal of Curriculum Studies*, and *Multicultural Education*, and he coedited *Mentors in the Making: Developing New Leaders for New Teachers* with B. Achinstein (2006). He received the Distinguished Research Award from the Association of Teacher Educators in 2006.

Rick Ayers is a doctoral student in the Language, Literacy, and Culture program of University of California, Berkeley Graduate School of Education. He has taught high school for 11 years and is cofounder of the Communication Arts and Sciences program at an urban, public California high school. He is coeditor of the series *Between Teacher and Text*, Teachers College Press, and of the book *Zero Tolerance: Resisting the Drive for Punishment in our Schools, A Handbook for Parents, Students, Educators and Citizens* (2001). He is coauthor of *Great Books for High School Kids: A Teacher's Guide to Books That Can Change Teens' Lives* (2004), and author of *Working, a Teaching Guide* (2000).

Lawrence Baines is interested in creative approaches to teaching and living. Currently, he is Associate Dean at The University of Toledo and teaches courses in writing and research. He has written 60 articles, several works of fiction, and 6 books including *How to Get a Life* (2004), a unique book of short biographies, and *Multisensory Learning* (2006), a book that describes guerilla tactics for getting adolescents to read and write like they mean it.

Molly Bang is the author/illustrator of over 30 picture books for children ranging from folk tales to books on sewage treatment and how sunlight becomes electricity. For many years, she has also explored picture making with both adults and children which led to the writing of *Picture This*, her analysis of how the most simple and basic elements of picture structure affect our emotions.

Cary Bazalgette worked at the British Film Institute for nearly 30 years, having previously been a teacher of English and filmmaking in London secondary schools. She has written and edited a number of pioneering classroom resources for media education and has published and spoken widely on this topic in the U.K. and in 22 countries around the world. She was Head of BFI Education from 1999–2006, leading the BFI's commitment to developing new approaches to teaching and learning about the moving image media, particularly for the 3–14 age group, and helping to gain a higher profile for this area of education at policy level, nationally and internationally. Following 18 months as the BFI's Education Policy Adviser, she is now working as a freelance researcher, writer, trainer and consultant specializing in media literacy and in children's media.

Michael Bitz is a Senior Research Associate at Teachers College, Columbia University, where he received his EdD in 1998. He is the founding director of The Comic Book Project (www.ComicBookProject.org), an arts-based literacy initiative that has impacted thousands of children nationwide. Bitz has published results of his practice and research in *Art Education* and *The Journal of Adolescent & Adult Literacy*. His work has been featured by the national media including *The Washington Post* and *National Public Radio*. In 2005, Dr. Bitz was a research grantee of the Robert Bowne Foundation and was awarded the Distinguished Alumni Early Career Award from Teachers College.

Randy Bomer is a member of the education faculty at The University of Texas at Austin, where he teaches courses about research, theory, and pedagogy in literacy education. His research focuses on the material and social processes of K–12 classrooms in which students are reading and writing and on the role of literacy in education for democracy. He is the author of *Time for Meaning: Crafting Literate Lives in Middle and High School* and *For a Better World: Reading and Writing for Social Action* as well as numerous articles. A past president of the National Council of Teachers of English, Bomer is also involved in research and advocacy about education policy.

Karen Boran directs research and evaluation for the Chicago Teachers' Center of Northeastern Illinois University. Her current research examines the relationship between literacy coaches and urban teachers as they collaborate in the design, implementation, and assessment of thematic standards-based units. Other recent research explored the roles that music, movement, and drawing play in the writing development of bilingual primary students. Her previous experience includes managing high school literacy (reading and English) for the Chicago Public Schools.

Aliki Brandenberg has written and illustrated over 55 books for children (fiction and nonfiction) and illustrated 150 by other authors. Her books have been translated into 14 languages. She travels regularly to speak at many schools in the United States as well as international schools in Africa, China, India, and Europe. One of her recent books, *Ah Music!* (2003), drew her deep into a subject that has been central to her life since her Greek American childhood. Aliki lives in London.

Cynthia Brock is Associate Professor in Literacy Studies at the University of Nevada, Reno. Her research interests include studying the literacy learning of children at the upper elementary level who are English learners. She also studies the process of teaching preservice and in-service teachers to teach literacy to children who are English learners in mainstream classrooms. Finally, she studies the process of teaching teachers to engage in teacher research.

Karen Bromley is a Distinguished Teaching Professor in the School of Education at Binghamton University, SUNY, where she is Director of Graduate Studies and the America Reads Program and teaches literacy courses. Her research interests include classroom practices and strategies for improving reading and writing. She was a third grade teacher and reading specialist in New York and Maryland, and has written articles for professional journals and several books for teachers; *Stretching Students' Vocabulary, Graphic Organizers: Visual Strategies for Active Learning, 50 Graphic Organizers for Reading, Writing and More, Journaling, Language Arts: Exploring Connections,* 3rd ed., and *Webbing with Literature,* 2nd ed.

Pamela U. Brown is Associate Professor of curriculum studies at Oklahoma State University and serves as codirector of the OSU Writing Project. Her research interests include teacher research, autonomy, diversity, and critical media literacy. She uses critical theory as a basis for her writing and encourages teacher advocacy to make professional knowledge public. Her years as a social studies teacher inform her work, and she is committed to the importance of classroom interactions as situated within a complex web of cultural issues. As coeditor of an NSSE yearbook on media literacy she writes of the "shadow curriculum," the largely hidden though pervasive marketing to both students and teachers in U.S. schools.

David Bruce is Assistant Professor at Kent State University in the department of Teaching, Leadership and Curriculum studies. Prior to earning his PhD, David taught high school English and media studies. His primary interests of research and teaching deal with reading and composing with video, particularly the way in which students and teachers can use print and video to complement each other. He serves as President of the Ohio Council of Teachers of English Language Arts (OCTELA) and as Director for the Commission on Media for the National Council of Teachers of English (NCTE).

Rod Case is Assistant Professor in the TESOL program at the University of Nevada, Reno. He holds a PhD in Literacy Education with a focus on TESOL from Washington State University. His area of interest is the connection between language acquisition and identity. He teaches courses in Second Language Acquisition, Curriculum Development, ESL Methods, and Language Assessment.

Kelly Chandler-Olcott, a former high school English and social studies teacher, is Associate Professor in the Reading & Language Arts Center at Syracuse University where she directs the English Education program and teaches courses in English methods and content literacy. Her research interests include adolescents' technology-mediated literacy practices, content literacy, and teacher research. Her most recent book is *Tutoring Adolescent Literacy Learners: A Guide for Volunteers* (2005).

Julie Cheville is Assistant Professor of Literacy Education in the School of Education and Human Development at the University of Maine. Her book and journal articles examine how learning is constituted by embodied activity and urge researchers to expand sociocultural investigations of literacy to include concern for spatial semiosis. For her critique of automated scoring technologies, she received the NCTE Edwin A. Hopkins Award and for her impact on teaching she received the New Jersey Governor's Award in Arts Education.

Victoria Chou has served as Dean of the College of Education at University of Illinois at Chicago since 1996. Prior to her deanship, she was a classroom teacher, a reading specialist, a teacher educator, and a reading researcher. With her colleagues at UIC, she seeks to develop a model "Great Cities" school of education that is relevant and responsive to the third largest school district in the country. She has secured numerous grants to support the preparation and professional development of excellent teachers for high-poverty, predominantly minority schools. She chairs UIC's Council on Teacher Education and the governing board of the National Teachers Academy-Professional Development School. From 1997–2005, she cochaired the steering committee of the Consortium on Chicago School Research.

S. D. Collins is Assistant Professor of Literacy at Tennessee Technological University. His research interests are the lived experiences of practicing writers as well the literacy habits of preservice and in-service teachers. Before becoming a professor, he facilitated writer and reader workshops for middle school students at the Tennessee School for the Deaf. He serves on the National Council of Teachers of English's Promising Young Writers Advisory Board and reviews articles for NCTE's *English Journal*. He also is on the editorial review board for the International Reading Association's *Journal of Adolescent and Adult Literacy*.

Bernice E. Cullinan, Professor Emeritus at New York University, is known both nationally and internationally for her work in children's literature. She has written over 30 books on literature for classroom teachers and librarians, including *Literature and the Child* (6th ed.), *Poetry Lessons to Dazzle and Delight*, and *Three Voices: Invitation to Poetry Across the Curriculum*. She is Editor in Chief of *Wordsong*, the poetry imprint of Boyds Mills Press, a Highlights for Children company, and has collected poems written by the recipients of the National Council of Teachers of English Award for Poetry in *A Jar of Tiny Stars*. She served as president of the International Reading Association, was inducted into the International Reading Association Reading Hall of Fame and The Ohio State University Hall of Fame, and was selected as the recipient of the Arbuthnot Award for Outstanding Teacher of Children's Literature. She lives in New York City.

Erica Deiparine-Sugars is Director of Education at Just Think. As program director of the Department of Education funded Media Education, Arts, and Literacy (MEAL) program, Erica works with teachers in underresourced middle schools to integrate the key concepts of media literacy and hands-on creative production. She received her BA in Communications with a dual major in Sociology from the University of Notre Dame and her MFA in Film with a focus in Documentary Production from Columbia College Chicago. She cofounded the Asian American Association at Notre Dame, and later served on the planning board of the Asian Alumni Association. Erica's background includes independent, commercial, and educational projects as well as directing morning news for the NBC affiliate in Austin, Texas. Previously, Erica served as Program Director for Community TV Network, a youth media non-profit in Chicago.

Anne Haas Dyson is a former teacher of young children and currently a Professor of Education at the University of Illinois at Urbana-Champaign. Previously she was on the faculties of Michigan State University, the University of California, Berkeley, where she was a recipient of the campus Distinguished Teaching Award, and the University of Georgia. She studies the childhood cultures and literacy learning of young schoolchildren. Among her recent publications are *Social Worlds of Children Learning to Write in an Urban Primary School*, which was awarded NCTE's David Russell Award for Distinguished Research, *Writing Superheroes,* and *The Brothers and Sisters Learn to Write: Popular Literacies in Childhood and School Cultures*. She recently coauthored a book *On the Case*, on interpretive case study methods.

A. Jonathan Eakle is Assistant Professor at The Johns Hopkins University Graduate Division of Education where he directs its literacy programs and teaches cross-cultural studies and reading. His research addresses how young people use multiple literacies for learning, pleasure, and resistance in classrooms and out-of-school settings, creativity, museum literacy practices, and designs and applications of novel research methodologies. Eakle is founder and Director of The Johns Hopkins University Reading Clinic, Principal Investigator of literacy-related grants, and an editor of literacy publications. He is trained in fine arts, sciences, and education, publishes in research journals, and presents his work to international and national audiences.

Patricia A. Edwards is Professor of Language and Literacy in the Department of Teacher Education at Michigan State University, where she teaches graduate courses in reading and language arts. She is a recognized national authority on family literacy and the role of families in the process of learning to read and write. Her books include *A Path to Follow: Learning to Listen to Parents* (1999) and *Children Literacy Development: Making it Happen Through School, Family, Community Involvement* (2004). She served on the Board of Directors of the

International Reading Association (1998–2001) and now serves as the President of the National Reading Conference (NRC). Edwards holds a PhD in reading education from the University of Wisconsin-Madison and has taught at Grambling State University, Louisiana Tech University, and Louisiana State University.

John F. Else currently heads Action Outcomes, a consulting and evaluation firm. He is founder and President Emeritus of the Institute for Social and Economic Development (ISED), a nonprofit organization focused on economic and asset development with low-income people. Most recently, he headed its consulting and research subsidiary. Previously he was an Associate Professor of social policy, planning, and research at the University of Iowa.

Damiano Felini is Lecturer in Education at the State University of Parma, where he teaches "Pedagogia dei media." His research centers on the theory of media literacy, both from a historical and cross-cultural point of view. He copublished *Pedagogia dei media* (2004), *Primi passi nella media education* (2006), the first Italian curriculum in media literacy education for primary schools, and *Organizzazione e fantasia* (2006), about some experiences of creative media literacy education in Italy, Austria, and Germany. Felini holds a PhD in Education from the Catholic University of Milan.

Douglas Fisher is Professor of Language and Literacy Education in the Department of Teacher Education at San Diego State University and the former Director of Professional Development for the City Heights Educational Collaborative. He is the recipient of an International Reading Association Celebrate Literacy Award as well as a Christa McAuliffe award for excellence in teacher education. He has published numerous articles on reading and literacy, differentiated instruction, and curriculum design as well as books, such as *Improving Adolescent Literacy: Strategies at Work* and *Language Arts Workshop: Purposeful Reading and Writing Instruction*. He has taught a variety of courses in SDSU's teacher-credentialing program as well as graduate-level courses on English language development and literacy. He has also taught classes in English, writing, and literacy development to public school students.

JoEllen Fisherkeller is Associate Professor in the Department of Culture and Communication at New York University. She teaches undergraduate and graduate courses and conducts research in the areas of youth and media cultures, media education, and cultural learning. Her publications cross the disciplines of communication, culture, and education, including her book, *Growing Up in TV Culture: Everyday Learning Among Young Adolescents* (2002).

James Flood was Distinguished Professor of Education at San Diego State University. He taught in preschool, elementary, and secondary schools and was a language arts supervisor. He was also a Fulbright scholar at the University of Lisbon in Portugal and the President of the National Reading Conference. Dr. Flood chaired and cochaired IRA, NCTE, NCRLL, and NRC committees. Dr. Flood taught graduate courses at SDSU. He coauthored and coedited many articles, columns, texts, handbooks and children's materials on reading and language arts issues. These included *Teaching Reading to Every Child* (4th ed.); *Content Area Reading and Learning* (3rd ed.); *Handbook of Research on Teaching the English Language Arts* (2nd ed.); *Handbook of Research on Visual, Communicative, and Performative Arts* (Vol. 1 & 2). He was named Outstanding Teacher Educator in the Department of Teacher Education and Distinguished Research Lecturer from SDSU's Graduate Division of Research. He was inducted into both California's and the International Reading Halls of Fame. Dr. Flood, a former coeditor of *The California Reader*, was a member of the Board of Directors of the International Reading Association.

Nancy Frey is Associate Professor of Literacy in the School of Teacher Education at San Diego State University. Before joining the university faculty, Nancy was a teacher in the Broward County (FL) Public Schools, where she taught students at the elementary and middle school level. She is a recipient of the Christa McAuliffe award for excellence in teacher education from the American Association of State Colleges and Universities. Her research interests include reading and literacy, assessment, intervention, and curriculum design, and she was a finalist for the International Reading Association's Outstanding Dissertation Award. She has coauthored books on literacy such as *Improving Adolescent Literacy: Strategies at Work* and *Language Arts Workshop: Purposeful Reading and Writing Instruction*, both published by Pearson Merrill Prentice Hall. She teaches a variety of courses in SDSU's teacher-credentialing program on elementary and secondary literacy in content area instruction and supporting students with diverse learning needs.

Lee Galda is Professor of Children's and Adolescent Literature at the University of Minnesota where she teaches and advises undergraduate, masters, and doctoral students. She has written extensively on children's and adolescent literature, and is coauthor of *Literature and the Child*, now in its sixth edition, and coauthor of *Reading and Responding in the Middle Grades*. Her research has focused on children's narrative development, including how they develop their responses to the literature they read.

Colleen P. Gilrane is Associate Professor of Theory and Practice in Teacher Education at the University of Tennessee. Her teaching and research interests focus on working with teachers to create communities in which all learners have access to literacy that is rich, joyful, and powerful.

Jan Greenberg is the author of seven novels for young readers and ten books on art and architecture, including pictures books and biographies. Her awards include the Norman A. Sugerman Award for Biography, a Boston Globe-Horn Book Honor Book, American Library Association Notable and Best Book, New York Times Notable Book, and a Parenting Best Book of the Year. *Heart to Heart: New Poems Inspired by Twentieth Century Art* is a 2002 Printz Honor Award Book for Young Adults. *Vincent Van Gogh: Portrait of an Artist* (Greenberg & Jordan) and *Action Jackson* (Greenberg & Jordan) are both Robert F. Sibert Honor Award books of 2002 and 2003 for distinguished informational books. She holds a BA degree from Washington University and an MAT degree from Webster University. She lives in St. Louis.

Margaret C. Hagood is Assistant Professor in the Department of Early Childhood, Elementary, and Middle Grades in the School of Education at the College of Charleston. She teaches undergraduate and graduate courses in early childhood, elementary, and middle grade literacies, focusing on sociocultural and poststructural theories relevant to new literacies. She is the primary researcher for the Center of the Advancement of New Literacies in Middle Grades, studying how middle grades educators and students understand new literacies and utilize out-of-school literacies to improve their literacy performance in teaching and learning in school settings.

Shirley Brice Heath is a linguistic anthropologist whose research centers on language socialization of children and young people learning outside of schools. She has written extensively on youth organizations, especially those dedicated to the arts, sports, and community service, and she has also studied the effects on underresourced schools of long-term partnerships with local artists. She is the producer and director of several documentaries on youth organizations, most notably *ArtShow* (2000) shown on PBS and BBC. She lectures internationally on studios, rehearsals, and laboratories as learning environments and the importance in the sciences and the arts of learning through observation and collaborative performance.

Renee Hobbs is Associate Professor of communication at Temple University, where she directs the Media Education Lab. She has created award-winning curriculum materials for K–12 English language arts educators and has conducted research to examine the impact of media literacy on adolescent development. Her book, *Teaching the Media in High School* (2007) examines a school district in New Hampshire, which integrated media literacy into the high school English program. She holds an EdD from Harvard Graduate School of Education.

Barbara Kapinus is a Senior Policy Analyst and Program Consultant for the National Education Association where she works on projects and publications in literacy, high school improvement, assessment, and policy. She has worked on several assessment projects including the National Assessment of Educational Progress in both reading and writing, the Programme for International Student Assessment, the Progress in International Reading Literacy Study and several state reading assessments. In addition to her assessment work, she has taught in public schools. She has served on the editorial board of all the International Reading Association journals. Her research and publications have been in the areas of comprehension, assessment, and vocabulary.

Barbara Kiefer is the Charlotte S. Huck Professor of Children's Literature at The Ohio State University. Originally trained in art education, she taught grades one, two, four, and five in several regions of the U.S and in overseas schools. She received her PhD in Language, Literature, and Reading from The Ohio State University in 1982. She has studied and written extensively about children's response to literature, particularly the art of the picture book. She served as the elected chair of the year 2000 Caldecott Award Committee of the American Library Association and was a member of the 1988 Caldecott Award Committee. She is the author of *The Potential of Picturebooks: From Visual Literacy to Aesthetic Understanding* and *Charlotte Huck's Children's Literature,* 9th edition.

William Kist is Associate Professor at Kent State University, Stark Campus. He has been a middle school and high school English teacher, a language arts and social studies curriculum coordinator, and a consultant and trainer for school districts across the United States. Kist has over 30 national and international conference presentations and some 20 published articles to his credit, including his book *New Literacies in Action: Teaching and Learning in Multiple Media* (2005), which has been chosen as a National Council of Teachers of English Select Book. A member of NCTE's Commission on Media, Kist has also worked as a video/film producer and musician. He is the recipient of an Ohio Educational Broadcasting Network Commission (OEBIE) Honorable Mention and a regional Emmy Award nomination for outstanding achievement in music composition. Kist has just finished writing and directing an independent feature film, *Summer's Journey*, and is developing an original screenplay, *Field Trip*, to be filmed as an independent feature in 2007.

Pamela J. Konkol, a former high school journalism teacher and program associate at the University of Illinois at Chicago, is Assistant Professor of Teacher Education at Concordia University. Although her interest in teacher identity, culture, community, and ethics finds a home in the broader contexts of philosophy of education and social foundations, her publications have crossed into the areas of educational policy and leadership issues as well. Her doctoral work at UIC focused on a critical examination of the potential and possibilities of a shared "ethos," "creed," or "oath" for teachers that would be both philosophically supportable and practically useful. In addition to her teaching and research endeavors, she serves as a member of the editorial board of the *Journal on Educational Controversy.*

Gunther Kress is Professor of Education/English at the Institute of Education, University of London. He has a specific interest in the interrelations in contemporary texts of different modes of communication (writing, image, speech, music, and gesture) and their effects on shapes of knowledge and forms of learning, and in the changes and their effects and consequences brought by the shift in the media of communication from the page to the screen. Some of his recent books are *Reading Images: The Grammar of Graphic Design* (1996); *Multimodal Discourse: The Modes and Media of Contemporary Communication* (2001); *Before Writing: Rethinking the Paths to Literacy* (1997); *Early Spelling: Between Convention and Creativity* (2000); *Literacy in the New Media Age* (2003); *Multimodal Teaching and Learning: The Rhetorics of the Science Classroom* (2002); edited, with Carey Jewitt, *Multimodal Literacy* (2003); and *English in Urban Classrooms* (2004).

Diane Lapp, Distinguished Professor of Education in the Department of Teacher Education at San Diego State University, has taught in elementary and middle schools. Her major areas of research and instruction have been of issues related to struggling readers and their families who live in urban settings. Dr. Lapp, who directs and teaches field-based preservice and graduate programs and courses, continues to team teach in public school classrooms. Dr. Lapp has coauthored and coedited many articles, columns, texts, handbooks and children's materials on reading and language arts issues. These include the following: *Teaching Reading to Every Child* (4th ed.), a reading methods textbook; *Content Reading Instruction* (3rd ed.); *The Handbook of Research in Teaching the English Language Arts* (2nd ed); and *Handbook of Research on Visual, Communicative and Performative Arts* (Vol. 1 & 2). She has also chaired and cochaired several IRA and NRC committees. She is currently the cochair of IRA's Early Literacy Commission. Her many educational awards include being named as the Outstanding Teacher Educator and Faculty Member in the Department of Teacher Education at SDSU, the Distinguished

Research Lecturer from SDSU's Graduate Division of Research, an inducted member of the California and the International Reading Association Halls of Fame and IRA's 1996 Outstanding Teacher Educator of the Year. Dr. Lapp is the coeditor of California's literacy journal *The California Reader*.

Cynthia Lewis is Professor of English Education at the University of Minnesota, Twin Cities. Her research focuses on the literacy practices of adolescents, digital literacies, the social politics of response to literature, and classroom discourse. Her books include *Literary Practices as Social Acts: Power, Status, and Cultural Norms in the Classroom* (2001).

Guofang Li is Assistant Professor in the Department of Learning and Instruction at the University of Buffalo Graduate School of Education. She is the author of *Culturally Contested Pedagogy* (2005), a study of the literacy battles between mainstream teachers and Asian immigrant parents. Her research interests are in the area of second language and literacy education, family and community literacy, and multicultural education.

Andrea A. Lunsford is Louise Hewlett Nixon Professor of English and Humanities and the Director of the Program in Writing and Rhetoric at Stanford University, where she teaches courses on the history and theory of rhetoric, cultures of writing, and literacy. Her current research includes a national study of patterns of error in student writing and a five-year longitudinal study of student writers at Stanford.

Jabari Mahiri is Associate Professor of Education at University of California, Berkeley. His research is on the literacy learning of youth, particularly African American students, in schools and outside of them. He is author of *Shooting for Excellence: African American and Youth Culture in New Century Schools* (1998), and editor of *What They Don't Learn in School: Literacy in the Lives of Urban Youth* (2004). His forthcoming book is *Teaching in New Times: Bridging Diversity and Achievement*. He is a senior scholar for the National Urban Alliance for Effective Education and a long-standing board member of the Bay Area Coalition of Equitable Schools.

Yolanda J. Majors is Assistant Professor of Curriculum and Instruction in the College of Education, University of Illinois at Chicago, where she focuses her research on adult/adolescent literacy, curriculum instruction, and multicultural education. Majors has published several articles in *Pedagogy, Culture and Society; Anthropology and Education Quarterly; Journal of Adolescent and Adult Literacy;* and *Mind, Culture and Activity*.

Jackie Marsh is Reader in Education at the University of Sheffield, where she teaches masters and doctoral students. Jackie is involved in research that examines the role and nature of popular culture, media, and new technologies in early childhood literacy, both in- and out-of-school contexts. Recent books include the edited volume, *Popular Culture, Media and New Technologies in Early Childhood* (2005) and the coauthored book, *Making Literacy Real: Theories and Practices for Teaching and Learning* (2005).

Mary Massie is Senior Literacy Specialist at the Chicago Teachers' Center of Northeastern Illinois University, where she designs and implements grant-funded professional development and research programs in teaching reading, writing, and arts integration pre-K through 12. Recent projects include: Roots of Language and Literacy (an Early Reading First demonstration project); an Advanced Reading Development Demonstration Project in Chicago elementary schools; the Arts for Learning Lessons Project with Young Audiences, Inc.; High School Matters, a content area literacy joint project of GEAR UP Chicago and National-Louis University; and a case study on differentiated literacy instruction in a bilingual fifth grade classroom.

Nan L. McDonald is Professor of Music at San Diego State University. Her research and writing focuses on the incorporation of music, dance, theatre, and visual arts into the general K–12 curriculum with particular emphasis toward the enhancement of student literacy skills. She is a national program author and clinician for Silver Burdett Music's *Making Music, 2005 K–8 series*. She has coauthored *Developing Arts Loving Readers* (2002) and *Teaching Literacy Through the Arts* (2006).

Anne McGill-Franzen is Professor at the University of Tennessee, College of Education, Health and Human Sciences, Department of Theory and Practice in Teacher Education, and Director of the Reading Center. She is co-PI on a federally funded research study of ways to mitigate summer reading loss, particularly among children in communities with few literacy resources.

Gwendolyn Michele Thompson McMillon is Assistant Professor of Literacy in the Department of Reading & Language Arts at Oakland University in Rochester, Michigan. Her research, which has appeared in several journals and edited books, focuses on examining literacy experiences of African American children at school and at church. She recently received a Title II Teacher Quality Improvement Grant entitled *Whom Are We Serving? Building on Students' Home and Community Literacy Experiences to Improve Literacy Teaching and Learning in Urban Schools*.

Andrew L. Mendelson is Associate Professor in the Department of Journalism in the School of Communications and Theater at Temple University. He has written extensively on the ways people understand the world through photographs, examining various psychological and social factors that affect viewers' interpretations. His teaching connects closely with this research, focusing on visual literacy and documentary photography. He holds a PhD in Journalism from the Missouri School of Journalism.

Alan Michel is the director of HOME, Inc., a Boston nonprofit organization that teaches video production and media analysis to educators and youth to foster confident, creative, individuals with the ability to think for themselves. His work in media and teen empowerment has won citations from the National Council on Family Relations, Telly Awards and the National Federation of Local Cable Programmers. He is a former board member of the National Association of Educational Communications and Technology's Media Production Division and is a founding member of the Alliance for a Media Literate America (AMLA).

Stacy J. Miller is Assistant Professor of Secondary English Education at Indiana University of Pennsylvania. She is the coauthor of the forthcoming text: *From Preservice to Inservice: Unpacking the Loaded Teacher Matrix-Negotiating Space and Time Between University and Secondary English Language Arts Classrooms.* She is a social justice educator who mentors preservice teachers to develop and negotiate their professional teaching identities. Her research interests are in making meaning of teacher identity through space-time theories, critical literacy, and hybridity theories. As a consumer of popular culture and a published SLAM poet, and teaching a wide range of methods course, she integrates popular culture and postcontemporary literacies into her teacher methods courses. A former high school English teacher, her article, *Shattering Images of Violence in Young Adult Literature,* was selected article of the year 2005 in the *English Journal.*

Suzanne M. Miller is Associate Professor of English Education at the University at Buffalo, SUNY, where she directs the New Literacies Group. Her research centers on the social and cognitive influences of transformative literacy teaching, curricula, and programs on teacher/student learning and school change, with special focus on literature and arts integration. In the monograph *Why Multimodal Literacies?* (2006), she summarizes her work with Grade 5–12 urban teachers in the City Voices, City Visions Digital Video Composing program in classes across the curriculum.

Elizabeth Birr Moje is an Arthur F. Thurnau Professor of Literacy, Language, and Culture in Educational Studies at the University of Michigan, Ann Arbor, and a Faculty Associate in the University's Institute for Social Research. Moje teaches undergraduate and graduate courses in secondary and adolescent literacy, cultural theory, and qualitative research methods. Her research interests revolve around the intersection between the literacies and texts youth are asked to learn in the disciplines and the literacies and texts they engage outside of school. Moje also studies how youth construct cultures and enact identities via their literacy practices outside of school. Moje is coeditor the forthcoming book from LEA, *Identity, Agency, and Power: New Directions in Sociocultural Research on Literacy.*

Kelly Moore is a literacy resource specialist at Health Sciences High and Middle College, a charter school, within the San Diego Unified School District. She is a former classroom teacher, having spent several years teaching in the primary grades. At her current school site, Dr. Moore collaborates with teachers from all grade levels on literacy staff development, beginning teacher support, and student teacher supervision. Additionally, Dr. Moore teaches undergraduate and masters courses at San Diego State University in the areas of literacy and curriculum and instruction. She is the coauthor of several articles and two texts: *Teaching Literacy in First Grade* and *Designing Responsive Curriculum: Planning Lessons That Work.*

Barbara Moss is Professor of Education at San Diego State University whose research centers on uses of informational texts in the classroom. She has written on a variety of topics related to informational texts, including middle graders' responses to informational texts, first graders' retellings of informational texts, as well as strategies for helping English learners comprehend this text type. She has been a classroom teacher at every level from first through twelfth grade and a reading supervisor. She regularly works as a consultant to school districts and is presently conducting research related to children's comprehension of visual features of informational texts.

Lorri Neilsen is an ethnographer, researcher, and poet whose work in literacy has focused on women's writing, research through the arts, aesthetics, and lyric inquiry. The author and editor of nine books of essays, scholarly writing, research, poetry, and creative nonfiction, Lorri has taught at Mount Saint Vincent University in Halifax since 1986. In her current role as Halifax Poet Laureate, she works with new Canadians and community organizations to further awareness of the arts in daily life. A citizen actor and sometime visual artist, she lectures and offers workshops across Canada and internationally to promote the aesthetics of academic inquiry. Her poetry is published under the name Lorri Neilsen Glenn.

Christine C. Pappas is Professor of Curriculum and Instruction, Literacy, and Language in the College of Education at the University of Illinois at Chicago. Her research interests include classroom-based teaching and learning in integrated, multimodal, curriculum in urban settings, most recently on the integration of science and literacy; collaborative university-school action research; classroom discourse; and children's development and understanding of various genres and multimodal texts (especially informational).

A. D. Pellegrini is Professor of Psychological Foundations of Education in the Department of Educational Psychology, University of Minnesota, Twin Cities. He has research interests in methodological issues in the general area of human development, with specific interests in direct observations. His substantive interests are in the development of play and dominance. He is a Fellow of the American Psychological Association and has been awarded a Fellowship from the British Psychological Society.

Julie Pennington is Assistant Professor in Literacy Studies in the Department of Educational Specialties at the University of Nevada, Reno. Her research interests include literacy instruction for young children, exploring the relationship between literacy and race, and critical perspectives in qualitative methodology. She is the author of *The Colonization of Literacy Education* from Peter Lang publications.

Jacqueline T. Pham is a sophomore at Stanford University who is currently vacillating between conflicting desires to pursue the lovely intricacies of the English language and the mysteries of the frontal cortex. During summer 2006, she interned at Cornell University's Weill Medical College where she worked on developmental neurobiology research. She is an avid fan of Neil Gaiman and other graphic novelists.

Doreen M. Piano is Assistant Professor of English at the University of New Orleans where she teaches courses in rhetorical theory, the teaching of writing, and feminist studies. Her research focuses on youth cultures, third wave feminism, and rhetorical theory. Previous publications include "Resisting Subjects: The Politics of Spectacular Style in Women's Subcultural Production" in *The Post Subcultures Reader* and "Leaving Las Vegas: The Prostitute as a Site of Abjection" in *Exclusions in Feminist Thought: Challenging the Boundaries of Womanhood.*

Ian Pumpian is Professor of Educational Leadership at San Diego State University, the former Executive Director of the City Heights Educational Collaborative, and the Director of Urban Education

Projects. He is the coauthor *of Challenging the Classroom Standard Through Museum-Based Education* and numerous articles on urban school improvement. He is the recipient of the Robert Gaylord Ross award for contributions to education and teaches classes in educational leadership, school improvement, and school change.

Victoria J. Risko is Professor of Language, Literacy, and Culture at Peabody College of Vanderbilt University. Her research centers on prospective teachers' reflection practices, instructional practices for culturally and linguistically diverse students, text comprehension, uses of multimedia cases for teacher education, and uses of multimedia environments for anchoring interdisciplinary curriculum in elementary and middle schools. She is a former member of the board of directors of the International Reading Association and former president of the College Reading Association.

Bernard R. Robin is Associate Professor in the Instructional Technology Program at the University of Houston's College of Education. He teaches courses on the educational uses of digital photography, digital storytelling, digital video, and project-based multimedia. He frequently works with art museums to design and develop large-scale educational websites and has published a large body of work on the educational use of digital media and emerging technologies. Dr. Robin is a coauthor of the book, *The Educator's Guide to the Web* and is the founder and executive editor of the *Texas Journal of Distance Learning*. In addition, he currently serves as the Vice President for the Digital Storytelling Committee of the Society for Technology and Teacher Education.

Cathy Roller is the Director of Research and Policy at the International Reading Association, works with IRA's Board of Directors to develop research-based position statements on a variety of topics in reading. Current and recent projects include the development of *Standards for Middle and High School Literacy Coaches* in collaboration with associations representing core content areas; a review of literature, as part of a Teacher Education Task Force, and *No Child Left Behind: A Survey of Its Impact on IRA Members*. Previously, she was a Professor of Curriculum and Instruction at the University of Iowa and she directed the Summer Residential Reading Clinic while at Iowa. Roller was involved in education programs in Zimbabwe during the mid-1980s.

Elana Yonah Rosen is cofounder and Executive Director of Just Think, a 501(c) delivering programs and professional development in school, after school and online environments primarily in underserved communities locally, national and abroad. With over 20 years experience in media and education, Elana is a former producer with KQED-TV, a contributing writer for the Center for Investigative Reporting, and senior associate with the George Lucas Educational Foundation, Elana serves as a board member of the first national media education membership organization in the U.S., the Alliance for a Media Literate America (AMLA), and sits on the board of Kimya Institute and Envision Schools. She received an Emmy nomination for the documentary, *Czeslaw Milosz: A Poet Remembers*, and is the coauthor of the media literacy education guidebook, *Changing the World Through Media Education*.

Nancy Roser is Professor of Language and Literacy Studies and the Flawn Professor of Early Childhood in the College of Education at the University of Texas at Austin. A former elementary teacher, she now teaches undergraduate elementary reading and language arts, and graduate courses in teaching the English language arts and children's literature. Her research centers on the instructional support that surrounds children's literature in classrooms. A recent coauthored book is *What a Character! Character Study as a Guide to Literary Meaning Making*.

Leslie S. Rush is Assistant Professor of English education in the Department of Secondary Education at the University of Wyoming in Laramie, Wyoming. A former high school English teacher, she teaches courses in English methods, adolescent literacy, and young adult literature; she also supervises secondary English preservice teachers during their student teaching semester. Leslie's research interests include multigenre writing, multiliteracies, and the work of literacy coaches with secondary content area teachers. Leslie also serves as the technology liaison for the Wyoming Writing Project and is involved in the work of Professional Learning Communities in the state of Wyoming.

Rachel Salas is Assistant Professor in the School of Education at the University of North Carolina at Greensboro, where she teaches courses in language arts, children's literature and English as a Second Language teaching methods. Her research focuses on the literacy environment and instruction provided to culturally and linguistically diverse students in schools.

Gretchen Schwarz is Professor in Curriculum Studies at Oklahoma State University. Formerly a high school German and English teacher, she has also worked with the secondary English education program and still works with the OSU Writing Project. She teaches graduate courses in curriculum, teaching, research, and media literacy. She has published in the field of media literacy and is currently doing research on graphic novels.

Allison Lindsay Scott is a doctoral student in the School Psychology program at University of California, Berkeley. Her research and professional focus is on the academic achievement of African American students and factors affecting academic performance. Her specific research interests include culturally relevant teaching and curriculum and parental involvement within African American families. She has worked in a variety of schools and agencies serving low-income populations, and she is currently involved with the formulation and implementation of special education services at a local alternative high school.

Kimberly Sheridan is Assistant Professor in the College of Education and Human Development and the College of Visual and Performing Arts at George Mason University. From 2001–2006, she was a Research Specialist on the Studio Thinking Project at Harvard University's Project Zero, studying teaching, learning and assessment in the visual arts. She is a coauthor of the book, *Studio Thinking: How Visual Arts Teaching Can Promote Disciplined Habits of Mind*. She received her doctorate in Human Development and Psychology from Harvard University Graduate School of Education. Her research focuses on the intersection of cognition and the arts.

Lawrence R. Sipe is Associate Professor in the Reading/Writing/Literacy program of the Graduate School of Education at the University of Pennsylvania, where he teaches courses in literature written for children and adolescents. He has taught in a one-room school; a multigrade (K–2) independent school, and has been a coordinator of language arts and early childhood education for a small school district in Newfoundland, Canada. His research is concerned with young children's understanding of picture storybooks, and the ways they make meaning from both the text and pictures in these books. He is also interested in the ways the arts and literacy can be combined in exciting ways to integrate school curricula.

Kim Slack, who has over 20 years experience developing curriculum for a variety of audiences and in many different topics, has a Masters in Education from Harvard University, and a BS from the University of Massachusetts. He has developed media literacy curriculum for Boston Public Schools as part of HOME Inc.'s partnership with the school system and has coached teachers in curriculum development and media literacy instruction as well as conducting professional development training. Kim has also developed and taught programs in leadership, team building, and collaboration skills for school superintendents, principals, teachers and parents and has also developed instructional materials for many businesses, government and nonprofit organizations.

Elisabeth Soep is Education Director and Senior Producer at Youth Radio in the San Francisco Bay Area, where she collaborates with young media artists on stories for local and national outlets, including National Public Radio. Her research, which has appeared in several national and international journals, focuses on youth learning and cultural production beyond classroom walls. She coedited *Youthscapes: The Popular, the National, the Global* (2005), a volume on youth culture and globalization. Soep holds a PhD in education from Stanford University and has taught at San Francisco State University and the University of California, Berkeley.

Dorothy S. Strickland is the Samuel DeWitt Proctor Professor of Education at Rutgers, the State University of New Jersey. A former classroom teacher, reading consultant, and learning disabilities specialist, she is a past president of both the International Reading Association and the IRA Reading Hall of Fame. She received IRA's Outstanding Teacher Educator of Reading Award. She was the recipient of the National Council of Teachers of English Award as Outstanding Educator in the Language Arts and the National-Louis University Ferguson Award for Outstanding Contributions to Early Childhood Education. She was a member of the panel that produced *Becoming a Nation of Readers, Preventing Reading Difficulties in Young Children, The Rand Report, Reading for Understanding,* and the National Early Literacy Panel. Her latest publications include *Learning About Print in Preschool Settings; Bridging the Literacy Achievement Gap, Grades 4–12;* and *Improving Reading Achievement Through Professional Development.*

Morag Styles is a Research Fellow at the Faculty of Education, University of Cambridge.

Edward T. Sullivan, formerly a young adult specialist with the New York Public Library, is now a school librarian in Knoxville, Tennessee and the series editor for *Scarecrow Press Guides to Children's and Young Adult Literature.* He served three years on the board of the Young Adult Library Services Association. Ed also serves on editorial advisory boards of several professional journals. He has published over two hundred articles, author interviews, bibliographies, and reviews in such journals as *The ALAN Review, Book Links, Booklist, English Journal, Library Media Connection, Multicultural Review, School Library Journal,* and *Voices of Youth Advocates.* He is the author of two professional books for librarians and teachers, *The Holocaust in Literature for Youth: A Guide and Resource Book* (1999) and *Reaching Reluctant Young Adult Readers: A Handbook for Librarians and Teachers* (2002). His first book for young people, *The Ultimate Weapon: The Race to Build the Atomic Bomb,* was published in 2006 by Holiday House.

Robert J. Tierney, Dean of the Faculty of Education at the University of British Columbia, has contributed to research discussions particularly in the areas of teaching, reading comprehension, reading–writing relationships, multiliteracies, literacy assessment and educational reform. He has been the Past President of the National Reading Conference, past chair of the Research Assembly for the National Council for Teachers of English and past editor of the Reading Research Quarterly. He has served on several panels for the United States Office of Education, international agencies and a number of corporations including publishing and media groups. During his tenure in the United States, he has been a member of the Faculties of the University of Arizona, the University of Illinois, Harvard University, and the University of California, Berkeley, and The Ohio State University.

Kit Tisdale is an independent scholar who lives and writes in Maryville, Tennessee. She holds a PhD in Educational Psychology from the University of Georgia. Her academic interests include poststructural theories, disability studies, and qualitative research methodologies. She is involved in disability rights efforts within her community. In particular, she is involved with local awareness groups and parent and professional training and support. She has a special interest in accessible and integrated outdoor play spaces for children and in how accessibility relates to urban planning.

James Trier is Assistant Professor of English Education at the University of North Carolina at Chapel Hill. He is interested in investigating critical methods to engage pre-service teachers in theoretical explorations of various important educational issues by considering—simultaneously, in juxtaposition—academic and popular culture texts. Among his publications are the following articles: "Inquiring Into 'Techniques of Power' With Preservice Teachers Through the 'School Film' *The Paper Chase*" (*Teaching and Teacher Education*); "Exploring the Concept of 'Habitus' With Preservice Teachers Through the Use of Popular School Films" (*Interchange*); "Detournement as Pedagogical Praxis" (*Taboo: The Journal of Culture and Education*); "'Sordid Fantasies': Reading Popular 'Inner-City' School Films as Racialized Texts with Preservice Teachers" (*Race, Ethnicity and Education*); and others. Trier is also the editor of the "Media Literacy" department for the *Journal of Adolescent and Adult Literacy*, and in this role, he contributes a bimonthly column on media literacy.

Renate Valtin is Professor of Education at Humboldt University, Berlin, Germany. Her research, which has appeared in many books and national and international journals, includes literacy development, dyslexia, social cognition, and primary school education. In

2000, she was elected to the International Reading Association's Reading Hall of Fame. She is member of the German team of PIRLS 2001 and 2006 and president of the German Association of Reading and Writing. Presently she serves as chair of the PISA PIRLS Task Force of the International Reading Association.

Lalitha Vasudevan is Assistant Professor of Technology and Education at Teachers College, Columbia University. She received a PhD in education from the University of Pennsylvania where she studied the stories, literacy practices, and technology engagements of adolescent boys. Her current research explores education in the lives of urban youth outside the school walls, in between institutional spaces, and across new literacies and technologies. She is also coeditor of a volume of essays titled *Media, Learning, and Sites of Possibility* that critically examines the integration of media and technologies in teaching/learning spaces with youth.

Jeffrey D. Wilhelm is Professor of English Education at Boise State University and the founding director of the Boise State Writing Project. His research agenda centers on engagement in reading, and assisting reluctant and struggling readers through various modalities such as drama, visual art, technology, and inquiry contexts. He is the author or coauthor of 14 books about literacy education, including *You Gotta BE the Book* (winner of the NCTE Promising Research Award) and *Reading Don't Fix No Chevys* (winner of the David H. Russell Award for Distinguished Research in English Education).

Jennifer Lynn Wolf is Lecturer in Education at the Graduate School of Education at Stanford University, where she teaches courses in Young Adult Literature, drama, and language arts teaching methods. Her research centers in learning environments and behaviors that adolescents choose in their leisure time. In 2003, she authored with Jan Mandell, *Acting, Learning, and Change: Creating Original Plays With Adolescents*, a longitudinal study of youth theatre bridging school and community. Using the pictorial arts, she created a similar bridging program in the 1990s that was featured in the award-winning documentary for PBS entitled *ArtShow,* which was released in 2000. She has taught high school English and drama for fifteen years in the public schools of California.

Robert Wollach works in Europe, primarily in Switzerland, as arts director, film editor, and script designer for film productions related to the lives of young people. He served as arts director for a documentary based on the 2006 World Cup Soccer Games in Germany. He studied Modern Culture and Media at Brown University and has written and directed several short films, as well as a 90-minute independent production entitled "Waves in Empty Spaces."

S. E. Woodson is Associate Professor of Theatre and Film at Arizona State University, where she teaches in the Theatre for Youth MFA and PhD programs. Her research and creative interests focus on the social construction of childhood through performance, representational ethics, children's media environments, and the group creation and performance of original work. She is the artistic director of the *Place: Vision & Voice* program, a community-based digital storytelling, and performance program for youth. *PVV* artworks have been showcased internationally and nationally through multiple venues including television and film festivals. Two of the pieces created are held in the collections of the Huhugum Heritage Center and the Smithsonian Museum for the American Indian, Film Collection.

Deborah A. Wooten is Assistant Professor of Literacy in the Theory and Practice in Teacher Education Department at The University of Tennessee. Before joining the university faculty, Deborah taught in urban and rural public elementary classrooms for twenty-three years where she created the Writing and Sharing Connections teaching and learning methodology. Her research focuses on historical and metacognitive thinking through the Connections process at the elementary level. She is the author of *Valued Voices: An Interdisciplinary Approach to Teaching and Learning* as well as numerous chapters and articles on quality teaching methodology. At UT, she teaches primarily graduate courses in reading and children's literature.

Christopher Worthman teaches literacy courses in the School of Education at DePaul University in Chicago. He also facilitates critical literacy programs for teenage parents. His study of youth theatre in an urban setting, *"Just Playing the Part": Engaging Adolescents in Drama and Literacy*, was published in 2002.

Jane Yolen is the author of almost 300 books, including *Owl Moon, The Devil's Arithmetic,* and *How Do Dinosaurs Say Goodnight?* The books range from rhymed picture books and baby board books, through middle grade fiction, poetry collections, nonfiction, to novels and story collections for young adults and adults. She has 30 books under contract and waiting to come out, most of them already written. Her books and stories have won an assortment of awards—two Nebulas, a World Fantasy Award, a Caldecott, the Golden Kite Award, three Mythopoeic awards, two Christopher Medals, a nomination for the National Book Award, and the Jewish Book Award, among others. She is also the winner (for body of work) of the Kerlan Award and the Catholic Library's Regina Medal. Five colleges and universities have given her honorary doctorates.

Jacqueline Love Zeig, a doctoral candidate in reading at the University of Florida, has developed summer school interventions for children at risk of failure. Jacqueline's dissertation revisits the First R study of the 1960s and more recently, the Baumann et al. (1998) survey of reading methods and materials used in elementary classrooms. Her focus is on the reported pedagogy and curricula presently being used by teachers in Florida schools, with emphasis on instruction for struggling readers.

Part I

HISTORICAL AND THEORETICAL FOUNDATIONS

Renee Hobbs
TEMPLE UNIVERSITY

Humans are irrepressible communicators. A writer for the *New York Times* recently estimated that, from the days of Sumerian clay tablets until today, humans have created at least 32 million books, 750 million articles and essays, 25 million songs, 500 million images, 500,000 movies, 3 million videos, TV shows, and short films, and 100 billion public Web pages (Kelly, 2006). For young people growing up in the 21st century, this ever-expanding array of texts creates important challenges and opportunities both in and out of school. The chapters in Part I examine the historical, theoretical, and policy dimensions of an expanding conceptualization of literacy, one that includes the symbol systems of language, image, performance, and digital technologies of communication and expression.

Authors in Part I explore the historical factors that have contributed to make visual and digital texts ubiquitous, and they examine the ways that educators and policy makers have responded to this challenge. A number of important controversies and tensions are emerging as literacy is positioned within a global culture that is replete with digital technologies. New tools and technologies enable every individual to be both a reader and a writer using an ever-expanding number of modes of expression. In these chapters, the process of meaning making is examined in light of visual media, media production, and the interactive technologies of gaming and online communication, revealing new dimensions and issues that link literacy to inquiry from the fields of education, communication, media studies, social psychology, cultural studies, art history, and public policy. The next generation of literacy scholars and educators will need a broad perspective to realize the benefits and avoid the drawbacks that may result from an expanded perspective on literacy.

REFERENCE

Kelly, K. (2006, May 14). Scan this book! *New York Times Magazine,* p. 43.

1

VISION FOR LEARNING: HISTORY, THEORY, AND AFFIRMATION

Shirley Brice Heath
STANFORD UNIVERSITY

Robert Wollach
BROWN UNIVERSITY

Try an experiment. Pick up any newspaper, turn to any television channel, or listen to any radio station. In the news reports of any of these media, check off every reference to *vision, visual, seeing, display, appeared,* and other terms similar in meaning. This activity undertaken as an "experiment" will allow you to recognize the ubiquity of references in the media to the dependence of understanding and communicating on our metaphorical use of concepts surrounding vision.

Western society is and has been cut through with the idea that *visual learning*, including observation of performances, provides the most fundamental and efficient channel for information transfer. These essential facts about vision have held through human history. The capacity for vision came well before the biological development of language, and as the capacity for communication through oral symbol systems evolved, the visual functioned as primary reinforcement of meaning transfer in verbal and performative communication and of memory retention.[1]

This chapter looks at a few examples of the power of the visual to stimulate spontaneous verbal communication and to support conveyance across time and space of shared memories. In the first section of this chapter (as in the opening portion of the *Handbook*), we take an historical view on learning, exchanging, and belonging through all the arts that constitute "multimodal literacies." We look at two historical cases to illustrate how visual learning undergirds many of the functions, goals, and channels of literacies. These cases, drawn from the Middle Ages, may seem far-fetched in conception and vastly different from contemporary digital technologies. Yet with these, we lay the groundwork that will enable us to see just how persistent are key social continuities in patterns of interdependence that tie the visual with the communicative and performative.

In the second section, we support this interdependence through evidence from current work in evolutionary biology and the neurosciences. Theories and findings from these fields are extending what we know about the neural operations that support our capacities for envisioning, embodying, or articulating knowledge, wisdom, skills, and information.

The third and final section of this chapter threads several key themes from the prior two sections through selected aspects of current advances in videogames. We take these up because of their rapid rise to near universality in the postindustrial world and their foreshadowing of technological and social trends in the arts that challenge long-standing views about individual learning, the role of play, and the primacy of *texts* in literacy. Examined here in close detail is the affirmative value of communal membership carried out by engaging through multiparty video games in collaborative visual and performative design.

The chapter closes with the challenge of keeping a Janus-like consciousness—looking back to history and forward to what we still

[1] Any discussion of visual learning should take into account how that which has been learned about the key role of vision relates to the blind, particularly those who are blind from birth. However, so few studies exist of the development of perceptual performance and verbalizable metaknowledge of such individuals that generalizations are impossible. For those individuals who become severely impaired beyond childhood, a growing body of knowledge is influencing the world of art and the representations of art forms in museums. See, for example, the discussion of the exhibition Blind at the Museum, presented at the Berkeley Museum in 2005 and headlined by the blind photographer, Alice Wingwall.

have to learn about how the brain works from and with visual and embodied learning (Kosslyn & Osherson, 1995; LeDoux, 2002; Levin, 2004). Moreover, aspects of today's modes of visual learning parallel in several ways features and purposes prominent in the Middle Ages. This basic acknowledgment carries unending ramifications for our perspectives on *literacy* and its rapidly evolving dependence on intertwined layering of graphic design, role-playing, symbol systems, and music.

LOOKING BACK

Choices abound of where to look for the origins of the fundamental roles of the visual conveyance of meaning (whether with or without accompanying print or script representations). We can start with cartography, account ledgers, or judicial and constitutional documents. Or we can begin with the earliest recorded accounts of dramatic productions—those performed by traveling minstrels and mime artists, or within the liturgical cycle plays of the Church, or the spectacular pageant wagons that moved from town to town to celebrate particular historical events (Beadle, 1994). From even the shadowy beginnings we have of the earliest theater, we know that the iconography of architecture, dress, and adornments of civic life found its way into the spectacle of these plays as well as into the sculpted, painted, and stained-glass images of pictorial arts in churches and governmental buildings. It is in the merger of spectacle, narrative, and religious and economic history that we begin to look at the visual basis of literacy.

Because of its close associations with the beginnings of the book in the Western world, we start our historical sweep with a brief look at *illumination.* On this topic, we have not only ample documentation of process but also physical products that provide insight into the multiple ways in which humans have long created and valued pictorial support for music, oral and written language, and the performing arts. Illumination has its primary historical association with manuscripts. Yet, long before the manuscripts and books of the Middle Ages came scrolls, produced in support of political and legal matters, as well as calendrical records, or commercial transactions and religious participation. By providing possibilities for longer preservation and for wider distribution, illuminated manuscripts and books enabled those who could afford to sponsor or own them to ensure for their families or civic units that memories of events, places, and people continued beyond the span of a single generation.[2]

Manuscript books began in the third century and continued primarily as a monastic and court industry through the 12th century. From the 13th century forward, the commercial book trade took over their production. It was during medieval times, however, that *illumination* came to be a term that referred to any ornament that was perceived as making a text *legible*, that is, read or deciphered easily. Borders, fancy pen work, or pictures to be read in co-ordination with the text or to elaborate initial letters would be considered legibility enhancements. All of these first drew the reader's eye into the text and then deepened the meanings of the written words.

For example, in choral texts provided for some cathedrals in Europe, these illuminations took the form of *miniatures* and rendered within a single quintessential scene an entire narrative. Stories such as those that surround the Nativity, the Last Supper, Crucifixion, and the Resurrection, or even such specific scenes as the visit of Mary Magdalene and the other Mary (Mother of James) to the sepulcher would be called forth within each miniature created within the text of the music. These stories would be known to listeners and readers as scriptural narratives told and read from pulpits, but also rendered visually in lead glass windows, paintings, friezes, and frescoes on the walls of private chapels and churches and cathedrals. These separate illuminations or *miniatures* are termed such both for their small size and for their power to reflect in the tiniest of scale the magnificence of scriptural messages and the intricacy of natural wonders (such as that of a single flower at the height of its bloom or a magnificent peacock in full display).

Two aspects of literacy carried within illuminations, including miniatures, merit special attention for their continuity. Yet both aspects rarely receive attention in contemporary studies of how reading works. First is the fact that these visual (largely pictorial) aids to legibility and learning affirmed the collective social and shared-knowledge membership of those using the illuminated manuscripts or books. Second is the expansive force that such small intricate visual renderings carried.

To demonstrate this first aspect, we consider in some detail illuminated choir books in their support role for the religious services' liturgy (Carli, n.d.). As noted above, the miniatures pictured scenes that, in most cases, immediately conveyed a particular Biblical story. But the miniatures related also to the music and liturgy used for particular celebrations and rituals within the Church calendar. For example, the Sundays leading up to and following Epiphany (when the wise men are said to have been told of the birth of Jesus) have special music. Embedded within the musical score would be miniatures of key scenes within this particular story or renderings in exquisite detail of some item (e.g., one of the gifts brought by the wise men) that symbolizes the event.

For the second aspect, we also use the miniatures included within choir books of Gregorian music. Deep within the details of these miniatures were messages discernible to choir members and carrying musical, as well as symbolic, significance. Gregorian music is based on certain modalities (e.g., tetrachord, hexachord, and octachord), and at this important level, the miniatures could carry within them symbols to indicate to the singers (in advance of the chords within the musical text itself) the modality of, for example, the response to come following certain prayers.

The point here is that the deepening or expansive power of the miniatures was carried not only in the *general association* of a certain story with a particular seasonal ritual celebration but also within *details of adornment* around the single scene of the miniature. For example, a miniature including a certain number of angels with a particular combination of musical instruments and choristers would convey the message of *octachord,* perceived to be a portrayal of "perfection" in form and harmony. This modality of Gregorian music would be further reinforced in its "perfection" by the fact that the story behind the scene conveyed in one of the accompanying miniatures would be interpreted as embodying perfection itself—for example, the Virgin Mary being taken up into Heaven (Carli, n.d, pp. 43–44).

Critical for understanding the multiplying effects of illuminations is a sense of not only the associations they carried to music and writ-

[2] Treatises abound of nearly every aspect of the details, processes, and ideologies behind and within illuminated manuscripts. Accessible references drawn upon in this discussion include Alexander (1994); Backhouse (1997); Camille (1992); Gumbert (1990); Hindman (1991); Hindman, Camille, Rose, and Watson (2001); and Watson (2003). Specialized works treat the inclusion of miniatures in choral books (e.g., Carli, n.d.).

ten and spoken texts, but also the many forms these illuminations could assume. Some were decorative initials that carried within them one or two scenes that conveyed entire stories. These initial letters (that usually opened portions of extended scripted or printed texts) held within their curves and crevices details that conveyed Biblical scenes from the Old and New Testaments: Abraham's readying his son Isaac as sacrifice, the shaming of King David by the prophet Nathan, or the clearing of the tables of money changers in the tabernacle.

But forms of scripts changed during the Middle Ages. Therefore, the scribes who created the illuminations could choose the type of script that might afford more or less room for internal additions—distant craggy mountains, angels or cherubs, cityscapes, and so forth. These often bore no relation to any accompanying textual materials. Scribes also had borders and frames, as well as ornamental flourishes within the pages, as "extra" hooks and corners. Within borders, scribes sometimes created frames of narrative that in their sequencing told a particular story not necessarily associated with Biblical texts. (Both frames and borders of illuminated texts foreshadowed today's storyboards and comic strips in their linear portrayals of narratives.)

Borders and frames, more often than not, particularly in medieval manuscript books prepared for noble households or for doctors, lawyers, bureaucrats, and merchants, also pictured flowers, fruits, insects, and birds, along with traditional grotesques. String foliage, appearing as sprays of flowers or climbing vines, enclosed these creatures as secondary ornaments. It is significant that until the eighteenth century, the term *vignette* meant "border," and, in fact, portraitures, histories, and vignettes were combined in the designs of medieval books (Watson, 2003, p. 35). Also within these borders, as well as within some large ornamented initials, were quintessential scenes of everyday life: the hard-working peasant woman home from collecting firewood and scolding her lazy husband.

Though illuminated manuscripts are generally thought of as strictly religious, their art often portrayed grotesque animals and figures that bear no connection to religious content. By introducing the play of humor or satire, illuminations multiplied the interpretive meanings a reader or parishioner could carry in his or her attitude in relation to a Biblical scripture. Playful monkeys, grotesque figures covering their ears, or hybrid figures blending fantastical creatures with half bodies of humans could convey attitudes ranging from cynical to incredulous. Reversals of the realities of everyday life, such as hares chasing dogs, also bore evidence that scribes chose to include in their art their own thinking beyond the rigid, given, or strictly "textual." These scribes introduced into their work what today might be considered obscene or bawdry illustrations, showing the persistent inclination of humans to subvert conventional hierarchies.

The role of play for extended meanings, through both the fantastic and the everyday, but often in association with the noble and the godly, continues in another historical selection to illustrate the value of reading in, with, and through the visual, dramatic, and performative. In the city of Ferrara is the residence Palazzo Schifanoia, its earliest portions dating from 1385 and built by a prince of the Este family (whose members were the regional counterparts of the Medici family of Florence). Gentlemen of all of the four families of greatest wealth in Italy at this time had multiple residences, and at least one of these was often designated a "pleasure house" or "delizia." In Ferrara, the Palazzo Schifanoia (drawn from *schivar la noia* or "away with boredom") was a place of entertainment and recreation designed to enable those who handled the business of the day (from governing to hunting to cultural event organizing) to rest, play, and be entertained.[3]

On the second floor of the Estes *delizia*, two well-known local artists created a 96 metre fresco within the *salone dei mesi* or "room of the months." Portrayed within the fresco are three levels depicting allegories of the months of the year through scenes of life of the Estes family in everyday and business or courtly life (bottom level), the work of the particular season by peasants and city dwellers alike (middle level), and mythological figures—all of whom are pictured returning in triumph from battle (upper-most level). The 12 months are represented by their astrological association for the most part; gods of Roman mythology also appear in each of the months portrayed.

Remarkable in the reading of these three levels is their dependence on small details for conveyance of symbolic meanings, story continuities, sexual innuendoes, and peculiarities specific to certain families, topographical features of the region, or particular occupations. For example, in the section painted for the month of April, the upper layer shows Venus in a chariot drawn by swans. Kneeling before her and in chains is the figure of Mars. Among the gods, both triumph and defeat are reflected.

Playing about the chariot of Venus are numerous rabbits, and in the background behind her chariot, three graces appear along with numerous groups of young people in amorous attitudes. Nature is clearly bursting forth. More than the abundance of the spring season comes through in this one level; in the subsequent levels, the rabbits and swans reappear, along with a court jester, nobles returning from a hunt, and ladies standing by to watch it all.

Cutting across this triple layering of meanings to be held within each month are certain icons, utterly predictable as well as deviously hidden, but always serving the role of linguistic connectors or particles that indicate "as in" or "in comparison with" or "in contrast to." Two key points stand out in any close analysis of this rendering of the interdependence of visual, performative, and verbal literacies:

- Some of those who read the frescoes in this house built to relieve boredom and to offer rest would not have been practiced readers of linear verbal texts, either with or without illuminations. Instead, their "reading" of these complex visual images would have to have come about through their having listened to and no doubt been told repeatedly the tales that went along with the history of each of the gods depicted within each of the 12 months, as well as meanings associated with particular astrological alignments.
- Moreover, many visitors to the room of the months of the Palazzo Schifanoia would have taken part in the work of the various seasons. They would have visited the Castle of the Este family, where they could view similar scenes of everyday life

[3] Beyond local residents and specialists in the arts, the frescoes of the buildings created by the Este family in Ferrara have achieved little acclaim, and reproductions are difficult to obtain. Information used here comes from direct observation and consultation in 2006 with local historians and historical sources. The primary buildings with art of note are the Castello Estense (dating from 1385), the cathedral of Ferrara (dating from 1135) and its museum, and the Palazzo Schifanoia (dating from 1385; see the tourist publication *Ferrara: The Estense city*, DiFrancesco & Borella, n.d.).

> in each month in stone friezes on the building's walls. They would also have taken part in dramatic festivals that served as rites of seasonal intensification within the city. These involved the pageantry of flags, horses, armor, elaborate costuming for horses and riders, elevated stages within the city's market centers, and banners throughout the city. Within the details of the accoutrements of the pageantry would have been the icons, characters, colors, and details portrayed also within the frescoes and friezes.

Here in architecture, pictorial art, iconography, and drama, as in the illuminated manuscripts, meaning came alive, carried by details and patterns of repetition. Viewers could link all of these in one way or another to their own daily civic life as well as to imagined worlds.[4] In every horse, every nobleman, and every ripple of a flag, the shifts of markings, alignment of buildings, and alternations of colors conveyed significant differences of meaning.

The reading of frescoes, friezes, pageantry, and the hearing of Biblical, Classical, and civic texts, along with participation in the vibrant life of the close connections between city and countryside in the seasons mattered. All of these in combination affirmed civic membership for individuals living in a specific place and time. To understand life fully was to see oneself in visual arts in the company of the great, both distant and close to one's own existence. Rites of intensification and rites of passage, such as those of seasonal festivals or holy days, depended on the interplay of dramatic, musical, and visual arts along with the verbal. The combination brought the familiar of the labor, laughs, and contradictions of the everyday close up, while also reminding listeners and viewers—from lords to peasants, from clerics to parishioners—of what they knew in common. Above all were the gods and the government, and both could experience supreme triumphs and great failures.

SEEING, THINKING, AND SAYING

Perhaps the fundamental tenet that ties vision and learning together restates a view that philosophers have long held: perception amounts to intelligent decision making. Fundamentally, "perceptions are prediction, never entirely certain, *hypotheses* of what may be out there" (Gregory, 1997, p. 5). All visual art forms push interpreters toward some sense of connection and completion, because the brain is merely *representing* some selected features of the world. The eye's images come to us as useless until and unless we can go beyond the sensed evidence to look into the future with some awareness of prediction or possibility. We have to remember that we all "behave to the present by anticipation of what is likely to happen, rather than from immediate stimuli" (Gregory, 1997, p. 11). Critical to understanding what is to come is then not what is current information, but experiential and stored information fed by sensory stimuli within the present moment and used to create hypotheses toward the future. In essence, what we see in any moment both feeds into and enables past memory, and it activates and enables our sense of ourselves as actors moving with agency into the future.

We speak easily of "seeing ourselves" within a film, painting, or play. When we do so, we generally refer to our perception that the current art form represents our own past actions or feelings in some way, but we have relatively little understanding of how this kind of visual metacognition works or the ways in which we realize that representations do not copy or reproduce the world, but instead become material we use to represent to ourselves our own perceptions. These we recreate and manipulate visually and linguistically, for our perceptions are our obligatory filter on the world. These filters work in large part with regard for our intentions (Malle, Moses, & Baldwin, 2001) that guide us in focusing our attention. There is "no conscious perception without attention" (Mack & Rock, 1998).

Evolutionary biologists and neuroscientists help us understand why connecting, completing, and especially moving the past into the future matter so much to us in our efforts to read and to interpret symbol systems and icons. Archaeologists and biologists working together with the same recovered evidence continue to confirm that, for example, in our earliest evidence of art, the portrayal of *roles* was critical (Donald, 1991; Houston, 2006). As human beings evolved, their altered social and physical environments forced an increasing range of social roles and hence of language use and capacities for taking on multiple perspectives as individuals performed to meet the growing number of societal needs (Deacon, 1997). *Performance* implies agentry, which in turn holds possibilities of action envisioned as part of our perceptions of ourselves in the world around us.

The visual and performative arts bring viewers and participants into identification within scenes, for these scenes enact metaphorically what neuroscientists describe in the action of mirror neurons in the brain. Observed action that another individual takes stimulates the viewer to do—or to think of him or herself as doing—the same. In this way, the viewer of a painting, dance, or drama becomes an agent in interaction with the work of art (Turner, 2006). This markedness is driven by the awareness on the part of all individuals of their role in the future replication or replaying of the current moment for the instructional, mentoring, or modeling function that such actions will have on others.

Children learn to *see, do,* and *be* simultaneously in their play, for here they enact and embody roles they take on for themselves; they shed those roles that others assign them (e.g., that of *child, student,* or *pupil*). In the roles they assume in play, as well as in their own created and visual arts, children learn to project consequences and subsequent actions, issue strings of words, and extend themselves in their imaginations beyond the current visual field (Gallese, 2000; Mathews, 2003). Later learning challenges have to be met through honing the powers of attentiveness, memory storage, and capacity to connect, correlate, and conceptualize with appropriate relevance. The more practice and engagement with the forms of participation and viewing that call for projection into possibilities, the more learners store for connection with new information (Gopnik & Meltzoff

[4] These aspects of the representation of human activity receive examination in the work of Meoni (2005). Here the analysis is of the fresco cycle in Siena's Palazzo Pubblico. The overall image of this fresco is that of the "Allegory of Good Government," and one portion portrays the "effects of good government," while another depicts the "effects of bad government." Notable is the fact that the "good" contains a continuum and a layering of life from the highly domestic to the intensely ceremonial, legal, and governmental and extends in reach from the inner city to the countryside. The interdependence of peasant and royal, men and women, young and old, commercial and religious, civic and recreational shows through in every details. The "bad government" portrayal, on the other hand, contains relatively little detail, and a sense of vibrancy is missing, as is the stretch of continuity and the delicacy of the interweaving of life from city to country.

1998; Heath, 2000). The more positive the rewards for appropriate connection, the more habit building and creative these behaviors become. Today developmentalists understand that engagement across a range of roles early in life, through middle childhood, and into adolescence critically supports later language development (Heath, 2006). Evidence from neuroscience is mounting that multiple and varied opportunities to role-play and to sustain visual focus and attentiveness enhance language development. In particular, these occasions give practice for taking creative jumps and seeking reconciliation among disjuncture and disparities. We may best capture this idea by thinking of the visual speaking brain.

Central here is work that continues to attempt to understand the "mind reading" or theory of mind capacity of humans (Baron-Cohen, 1995). When we try to understand both when and how this endowment of humans came into being (both in the evolutionary process and in the development of a young child), we have to give substantial attention to ways that humans detect the intentions of others through eye gaze, mutual tuning in, and other shared attention mechanisms (Carey, Perrett, & Oram, 1997). Many today still believe the old idea that an image of the visual world is impressed on the retina and then transmitted for reception and actual "seeing" to one part of the visual brain and then interpreted by another cortical area of the brain. But well before the end of the 20th century, neurobiologists were able to tell us that the brain, in a sense, dissects the visual scene, and vision, therefore, is organized through a highly efficient modular system that makes seeing and thinking almost inseparable. The brain has many visual areas, and each group of these areas looks at different attributes of a visual scene (e.g., form, line, color, motion). Within and across these areas, specialized areas distribute visual signals (Zeki, 1993, 1999). It stands to reason that these signals in association must then connect with the memory storage areas of the brain. If verbal communication is involved, as it must be when perceptions have to be verbally shared with others or even for inner voice, the visual areas then link with those portions of the brain responsible for language in highly specific ways.

We have known for some time that responses to pictures are predicated in large part on underlying mental structures that we draw upon not only to decipher or decode visual images, but also to encode these for access in short-term and working memory. What we are only now beginning to understand are the regularities of pattern, for example, in neuronal spiking for the simplest of visual feats (Rieke, Warland, de Ruyter van Steveninck, & Bialek, 1997). The limits of PET or fMRI images, as well as EEG and MEG, and of cerebral blood flow, are well known to us. Yet, we are very far from identifying neural substrates necessary to build image schemas of particular sorts or connections. We understand that given the complexities of vision, and certainly those of language reception and production, we will never be able to say just how it might be that sustained visual focus, role playing, *and* verbal explication or narration (in either inner speech or spoken language) work together in the dynamism of completion that is indispensable to human perception.

Yet neuroscientists increasingly work together to sort out two complementary strategies currently believed to help explain, among many things, just how we read ourselves as we read the arts—from the visual to the performative and the verbal. *Individual* neurons are certainly tuned to particular arrays and combinations of visual input activity. These neurons establish explicit representations of those constellations of features that selectively converge in hierarchically structured architectures. This kind of work of individual neurons allows rapid processing as well as quick recall of frequently observed and experienced input. A second kind of work of the brain amounts to *temporary linkage or association* of neurons that work in functionally coherent constellations that represent as a whole a particular content. Here each participating neuron carries one of the elementary features of the composite perceptual object. This strategy allows for flexibility of the neurons, for a particular neuron can take part in different assemblies at different times. We have no limits to the dynamic and rapid association of neurons in ever-changing constellations, and thus we are able to cope with particularly unpredictable and highly complex information.

The role of the visual system within this processing is intimately linked with the "acting" capabilities of humans. When we see an object or scene and consciously image that visual information through enactment, we thereby activate other parts of the human system. This conscious imaging is termed *perceptual* by some scientists and is believed to be the essence of all conscious awareness (Metzinger, 2000).

> The best current interpretation of the visual scene in humans is to produce the best current interpretation of the visual scene in the light of past experience, either of ourselves or of our ancestors . . . and to make this interpretation directly available . . . to the parts of the brain that plan possible voluntary motor outputs of one sort or another, including speech. (Crick & Koch, 2000, p. 103)

Though we may never know why or how vision supports the verbal and the performative or enactive, some key points are becoming clear with each year of research in the neurosciences. Seeing, imaging, and perceiving, or much mental visual activity that we consider essential to "thinking," "understanding," or "enabling" relies on attending and acting, seeing and doing. In other words, we have to play along in order to know.

THE SOCIAL GAMES OF LEARNING

For literacy researchers reading this chapter, the usual inclination with regard to the visual, communicative, and performative arts is to think of contemporary events—not to return to the Middle Ages or to contemplate the internal workings of the brain. Indeed, the majority of chapters in the *Handbook* speak almost exclusively of here and now practical combinations of visual, communicative, and performative technologies, arts, and activities that constitute multimodal literacies. In the closing section of this chapter, we do the same by considering a particular type of social game—one that many regard as *the* wave of the future. But we look at this *new* wave with an unexpected twist, for we argue that it is in fact a replay of its counterparts that go back at least to the Middle Ages.

Video arcades entered the pastime of children and adolescents in the 1980s; players would stand together at a single machine or station and watch one another play, sometimes switching off, so that more than one player could benefit from the fee paid per game or for a specific period of time with one or more stations. Within the span of a few years, however, these table-size video games morphed into handheld individual games, in which an individual player competed against the preprogramming of the device itself or one's own prior record.

By the end of the first decade of the 21st century, the appeal of video games quickly spread beyond children and adolescents to adults, making the video game industry's size comparable to that of the music industry. Industries behind video games and those that generate films began to battle for dominance in terms of gross revenue and consumer commitment. The individual video game gradually lost popularity, ironically, through the broad potential evidenced in the internet for social communication, cross-connected, multiply layered, ongoing, and instantaneous readings. While the popular media viewed the youth market as driving innovation, the business needs of the global economy weighed in far more heavily (Beck & Mitchell, 2004). The shrinking of the world demanded that interactive technology speed up and improve ways to network ideas, people, and places through visual images *and* verbal exchange and with an ever-widening range of graphic supports (e.g., computer modeling, global positioning systems, and meteorological and economic forecasting).

As these technologies developed, each accelerated the possibilities for and from visual learning with social enactment. As these accelerations and advancements in combination of possibilities happened, demand increased for multiple-layered information sourcing and creative input into games. We use here as a prime example of an innovation reflecting these features multiplayer video games, known as MMORPGs (massively multiplayer online role-playing games) or MMORLGs (massively multiplayer online real-life/rogue-like games). These have brought certain practices of playing both "back from" the Middle Ages and forward to an age of interconnectivity and creativity that still lies well outside either the imagination or our most expansive theories of learning.

Online video games have transformed the initially "isolationist" practice of video gaming into a hitherto unparalleled socializing experience. First available late in the first decade of the 21st century, online video games known as MMORPGs create entire virtual universes in which players from around the world can evolve and interact. These virtual spaces range from fantastic magical lands (as in the game *Everquest*, one of the first and most popular MMORPGs that has a sequel *Everquest 2*) to futuristic environments resembling complex science-fiction universes (such as *Planetside* and *Earth and Beyond*). Others provide worlds inspired by popular fiction narratives (such as the movie inspired *The Matrix Online* and *Star Wars Galaxies*) or more traditional, realistic settings replicating either mythology-based historical periods (*Dark Age of Camelot*) or the present (*The Sims Online*).

Possibilities for creating virtual realities multiply through the social interactivity of these MMORPGs. In essence, each player creates his or her own virtual characters, also called an *avatar,* and controls this avatar within a game's concocted universe. Over long periods of time (often years), an avatar can evolve in almost infinitely diverse ways (gaining new abilities, items, knowledge), ultimately reflecting the *unique* individual experience of the player it represents within the virtual world. In light of this kind of creative power, the avatars of online video gaming move into their creators' and players' imaginations, stimulating and simulating human desires and capabilities for having power over other creatures and indeed of environments (Yee, 2006).

In some respects, the MMORPG offers an original form of role-playing. Within conventional role-playing (such as that of mentally healthy children/adults *pretending* to be, or *playing at being* someone/something in a given context), the *play* ends as does the game or the theatrical event. Those who have been playing roles suspend their *act* and resume the *real* of their "true" selves. However, through online role-playing in MMORPGs, the player's avatar continues to exist even when the player is *not* actively in the game. In other words, online video games engender everlasting virtual "space-times" that suggestively coexist with reality.

These simulated space-times exist exclusively online, each player accessing them through an internet connection. Notably, users must generally pay a fee (often monthly) to keep playing the game (about $10 per month). The justification of such maintenance fees (that contrast with the one time only payment required to purchase traditional video games) lies in the fact that software developers must maintain and update the game's servers. Indeed, huge amounts of memory are required for these artificial spaces to operate continuously 24 hours a day, seven days a week. Thus, software companies have dedicated servers that host all the critical, preestablished data, as well as the constantly changing information that results from players' interaction with the virtual environment. Furthermore, these imaginary places, always accompanied by defining fictitious backgrounds (histories, characters, even laws of nature), tend to be moderated by the software developers. For example, a world-changing event might be introduced into the game, such as the discovery of a new galaxy in a science-fiction game; such an event then calls for modifications to what we may consider the context, scenery, or background of the game's world. Moreover, significant additions/modifications spawn "add-ons" (also known as "expansion packs"). These separate programs complement or expand the original virtual universes and perpetuate a game's lifespan. These add-ons require that the original game has been preinstalled, so they are truly added to the prior game, creating a kind of history internal to the interactive game world.

The MMORPGs massiveness spills into reality in discernible ways, affecting how individuals spend their money and time and manage the rhythm of their lives. Most video game experts agree that the reach of MMORPGs stretches far beyond the realm of *hyperreality.* More and more individuals and groups therefore encourage and facilitate critical discourse about online video games and the problematic "spaces" they encompass in players' lives.

Yet others point out ways in which these games include "real" diversity. Because players generally do not know the "real" identity of other players, the usual socially constructed differentiations that distance adult from child, male from female, handicapped from able-bodied, or one ethnicity from another disappear. In the world of MMORPGs, 40-year-olds seamlessly interact with preteens and teenagers. In these hyperreal spaces, people evolve, communicate, and undertake tasks together without regard for age, sex, race, or religion. Often, player collaborations are simply joint attempts at progressing within the video game, taking on progressively more complex challenges in groups to increase the chances of success. They eventually share then the rewards of the accomplished expeditions with members of a given group; in essence, the majority of each player's actions in the game's universe are motivated by the desire to improve one's avatar continuously. In effect, every player begins his or her virtual life within an online video game as a "nobody," a character template among a limited number of templates, endowed with no more than a unique nickname. This name distinguishes the individual from all other game characters. But the player seeks to become a "somebody" through his or her avatar by accumulating upgrades, experience points, monetary units, and all kinds of possessions that make the avatar more powerful, respectable, recognizable, and most of all, more central to the virtual universe.

But here, aspects of the hierarchical nature of power from the "real" world reveal themselves, for certain players possess more powerful characters than others. Those who are more powerful keep pushing the artificial space-time forward, and they instigate changes that shape the structure of the virtual world. The dominant avatars are those of players who spend the most time playing the video game and are thus more skilled, knowledgeable, and organized than the relatively less experienced gamers. The more the player *actively* interacts in the virtual space (the more he or she plays the game), the more meaningful the rewards. The less active players constantly remain a step behind, powerless to influence the virtual universe in any significant way without following more experienced leaders. Indeed, the majority of players find their virtual avatars perpetually chasing after the power of higher ranked players. Concurrently, even those players with the most highly evolved avatars perseveringly modify them in the hope of upholding their status, persistently unstable and constantly threatened. Even in these interactive, virtual worlds, the ideals of power and identity, along with the desire for transcendental selfhood, seem to remain both in the everyday world and in what is seen as the highest layer. (Here we recall triumphant Venus with Mars at her feet in the fresco of the Palazzo Schifanoia.) Moving ahead depends on one's observations of details of behavior and attitude among the avatars as well as ways to imagine ways to change the world to make these behaviors and attitudes work against power accumulation.

The realms proposed by MMORPGs seem capable of providing environments that stimulate the imaginations of both the young and the old. Metaphorically, this and other virtual realities represent an extended playground that allows relatively "free" play without the "real" constraints of socially constructed identities and powers. Building on ideas originally formulated by Jacques Derrida (1976), online video games delineate an original playground that *plays* on the "deconstruction-prone" characteristics of the already *unstable* signifiers of language. In this way, the virtual playground's effects on cultural systems of meaning eerily echo the playful mockery of children—always a highly specialized form of imitation (Sutton-Smith, 1997). The virtual space generated by MMORPGs *playfully* removes existing power relations affiliated with real-world differentiations along the lines of age, gender, and race, as well as between work and play.

In an essential way, MMORPG universes present an additional feature that makes participation within them deeply felt as reading. When any player begins an interactive experience within the virtual space-time, the MMORPG accords him or her a *tabula rasa* on which to write new rules of operation, personal character, dimensions of competence, and plot lines. Here one is reading and writing simultaneously, and being a passive player is not possible, for at all times, one has to identify with one or more roles taken unto and into the self. MMORPGs create and sustain continuously stages upon which the scripts, characters, direction of action, and plays of emotion, power, and identity move with limitless possibilities. Each player's interaction with the virtual universe and its avatars carries risk at every point, making the rush of excitement highly personalized and definable by specific unique moves within the game. As a result, the type of role-playing "performed" by subjects in an MMORPG tends to have relatively high stakes in comparison to other contemporary passive or risk predictable games. The player knows he or she is subject only to the current game world's core elements (such as the impact of interstellar travel in a game such as *Star Wars Galaxies*). Yet in contrast to other modern practices involving role-playing, MMORPGs offer almost unlimited freedom for redefining the core elements that dominate or delineate the context of the virtual world. But with any such redefinition, each player's interaction with the fantastic world must become even more detail driven and detail sensitive than ever before, because the complexities and possibilities within the world will only multiply and diverge from prior "rules" or "givens."

It is here that MMORPGs come in for critique, as do their engineers. Some observers suggest that those who have created MMORPGs lack concern for the social and cultural implications of the kind of immersive experience that these games create. They remove players from "true" emotional consequences, just as some would argue all games do. Observers have long noted that players of all ages find appeal in games and activities that involve the relative absence of actual harmful physical consequences. Consequently, readers and game players gravitate to animation, cartoons, and science fiction. Emotions in any of these forms can be "played out" through creatures and scenarios that do not require the kind of "caring" about other human beings in "true-life" situations expected through the reading of novels, poetry, or dramas. But MMORPGs, in their very social nature and allowance for the creation of avatars that carry identities and abilities "given" by the players who "own" them, stand on the border between being close and distant. Players cannot escape either the response or the responsibility for what happens to their avatars, while at the same time, they need not feel nor will they themselves ever experience the happenings of the virtual world. There the "normal" rules of consequences, cause and effect, or sequencing do not apply. Yet, the intensification of basic role-playing operated by MMORPGs produce more than superficial involvement that can be turned on and off at will. As players engage in the complex, elaborate, and intimate "playing at being," they and their avatars create and follow a performative script that both escapes and reflects the tensions of real social (though not physical or bodily) life.

A variant on the MMORPG concept deserves special mention. In 2004, the United Nations World Food Program introduced a computer video game on hunger around the world. Introduced at a children's book fair in Bologna, Italy, Food Force (http://www.food-force.com) immediately drew so many players, the Web site kept crashing until the World Food Program revamped it to take the tens of thousands of hits. One of a small and relatively new category of peace games, Food Force puts its players in negotiating positions and allows them to do airdrops and to drive convoys through terrain filled with land mines. The goal here is to bring players together in a peace game within the realities of the far-reaching effects of violence, competition, and rebel confrontations (Rosenberg, 2005).

"NOTHING NEW UNDER THE SUN . . .?"

It is probably safe to say that every culture has some variation on the Biblical text from Ecclesiastes: "What has been will be again, what has been done will be done again; there is nothing new under the sun. . . ." (Ecclesiastes 1:9–14 NIV). As a deeply human phenomenon, "playing along" by seeing, being, and doing puts one into the imperative of role relationships and social hierarchies, struggle and quiet peace, feast and famine. Success in every social game begins with focused attention to detailed manipulations of scenes, character reflections, and contextual interactions and evolves into actions and communications. The point here is that, whether in the Middle Ages or the 21st century, developing a sense of self now and in terms of possibilities for the future demands an understanding of the interdependence of the highest and the lowest in social terms, the seemingly unattainable achievements—such as those of triumphant gods—as well as the most mundane routines of the everyday. Doing so comes to us most intimately in the plays of meaning made possible through multimodal literacies—whether those of illuminated manuscripts and frescoes in the Middle Ages or MMORPGs in the 21st century.

Why is it that of multimodal literacies we can rightfully say "nothing new under the sun . . .?" As human beings, we are hard wired to learn through making and interpreting symbol systems visually, linguistically, and performatively. Making meaning for us comes through seeing, communicating, *and* acting together; our neuronal capacities insist on this interdependence. Our oldest forms of artifactual and artistic evidence make this persistent and essential gift of being human clear. Moreover, through this interdependence and our facility with representational means, we have for millennia built communities, reinforced and transmitted our shared memories, inspired creativity, and opened more and more creative possibilities of interpretation. Seeing is fundamental to our thinking and speaking as humans who depend on images and image making for our cognitive and social existence.

MMORPGs bear within them the mix of otherworld, the everyday, and the realities of hierarchies of power found in illuminated manuscripts and frescoes of the Middle Ages. All these forms similarly both build upon and challenge our notions of experience and the exchange possible through images in interaction with talking, writing, and acting. One of the ultimate ironies of imaging devices akin to videogames is that only through these have we been able to see the ways in which the neurons of the brain spike, its dendrites connect, and its blood flows. These devices tell us not only how we think but also "how images think" (Burnett, 2004). This kind of imaging offers a vantage point from which we can probe more deeply and analyze more carefully just how it is that seeing opens communication and agency.

Such learning makes possible the continuous experimentation of creating, reading, and interpreting symbol systems that reach back into history long before us and will stretch well into the future. In this continuum, the forms of reading and writing that humans create, interpret, and act with and against matter most. But achievement with these depends essentially on images and the visual learning these provide "in the head" and as components and complements of language, theatre, and dance. Images do not simply give us representations of the world. They are the foundation of our understanding of ourselves as thinkers and as players—ever moving between realism and fantasy, across contexts and continuities (Kress, 2004).

REFERENCES

Alexander, J. J. G. (Ed.). (1994). *The painted page: Italian Renaissance book illumination*, 1450–1550. New York: FDC Publishers.

Backhouse, J. (1997). *The illuminated page: Ten centuries of manuscript painting in the British Library*. London: Thames & Hudson.

Baron-Cohen, S. (1995). *Mindblindness: An essay on autism and theory of mind*. Cambridge, MA: MIT Press.

Beadle, R. (Ed.). (1994). *Medieval English theatre*. New York: Cambridge University Press.

Beck, J. C., & Wade, M. (2004). *Got game: How the gamer generation is reshaping business forever*. Boston: Harvard Business School Press.

Burnett, R. (2004). *How images think*. Cambridge, MA: MIT Press.

Camille, M. (1992). *Image on the edge: The margins of medieval art*. London: TRC Publications.

Carey, A. R., Perrett, R., & Oram, M. (1997). Recognizing, understanding, and reproducing action. In F. Boller, & J. Grafman (Eds.), *Handbook of Neuropsychology* (Vol. 11, pp. 111–129). Philadelphia: Elsevier Science.

Carli, E. (n.d.). *The choir book miniatures for Siena Cathedral*. Florence, Italy: I.F.I. Editions.

Crick, F., & Koch, C. (2000). The unconscious homunculus. In T. Metzinger (Ed.), *Neural correlates of consciousness* (pp. 103–110). Cambridge, MA: MIT Press.

Deacon, T. W. (1997). *The symbolic species: The co-evolution of language and the brain*. New York: W. W. Norton & Company.

Derrida, J. (1976). *Of grammatology* (G. Spivak, Trans.). London: Johns Hopkins Press.

Di Francesco, C., & Borella, M. (n.d.). *Ferrara: The Estense City*. Bologna, Italy: Italcards.

Donald, M. (1991). *Origins of the modern mind*. Cambridge, MA: Harvard University Press.

Gallese, V. (2000). The acting subject: Toward the neural basis of social cognition. In T. Metzinger (Ed.), *Neural correlates of consciousness* (pp. 325–334). Cambridge, MA: MIT Press.

Gopnik, A., & Meltzoff, A. N. (1997). *Words, thoughts, and theories*. Cambridge, MA: MIT Press.

Gregory, R. L. (1997). *Eye and brain: The psychology of seeing*. Princeton, NJ: Princeton University Press.

Gumbert, J. P. (1990). *The Dutch and their books in the manuscript age*. London: Oxford University Press.

Heath, S. B. (2000). Seeing our way into learning. *Cambridge Journal of Education*, 30(1), 121–132.

Heath, S. B. (2006). Dynamics of completion. In M. Turner (Ed.), *The artful mind* (pp. 149–176). New York: Oxford University Press.

Hindman, S. (Ed.). (1991). *Printing the written word: The social history of books*, 1450–1520. Ithaca, NY: Cornell University Press.

Hindman, S. Camille, M., Rowe, N., & Watson, R. (2001). *Manuscript illumination in the modern age*. Evanston, IL: Northwestern University Press.

Houston, S. D. (2006). Impersonation, dance, and the problem of spectacle among the classic Maya. In T. Inomata, & L. S. Cohen (Eds.), *Archaeology of performance: Theatres of power, community, and politics* (pp. 135–155). New York: Rowman and Littlefield.

Kosslyn, S. M., & Osherson, D. N. (Eds.). (1995). *Visual cognition* (Vol. 2). Cambridge, MA: MIT Press.

Kress, G. (2004). *Literacy in the new media age*. London: Routledge.

LeDoux, J. (2002). *Synaptic self: How our brains become who we are*. New York: Viking Penguin.

Levin, D. T. (Ed.). (2004). *Thinking and seeing: Visual metacognition in adults and children*. Cambridge, MA: MIT Press.

Mack, A., & Rock, I. (1998). *Inattentional blindness*. Cambridge, MA: MIT Press.

Malle, B. F., Moses, L. J., & Baldwin, D. A. (Eds.). (2001). *Intentions and intentionality: Foundations of social cognition*. Cambridge, MA: MIT Press.

Matthews, J. (2003). *Drawing and painting: Children and visual representation* (2nd ed.). Thousand Oaks, CA: Sage.

Meoni, M. L. (2005). *Utopia and reality in Ambrogio Lorenzetti's good government*. Florence, Italy: Edizioni IFI.

Metzinger, T. (Ed.). (2000). *Neural correlates of consciousness*. Cambridge, MA: MIT Press.

Rieke, F., Warland, D., de Ruyter van Stevenick, R., & Bialeck, W. (1997). *Spikes: Exploring the neural code*. Cambridge, MA: MIT Press.

Rosenberg, T. (2005, December 30). *What Lara Croft would look like if she carried rice bags*. New York Times, p. A26.

Sutton-Smith, B. (1997). *The ambiguity of play*. Cambridge, MA: Harvard University Press.

Turner, M. (Ed.). (2006). *The artful mind*. New York: Oxford University Press.

Watson, R. (2003). *Illuminated manuscripts and their makers*. London: V&A Publications.

Yee, N. (2006). *The Daedalus project*. Retrieved June, 2006, from http://www.nickyee,com/daedalus

Zeki, S. (1993). *A vision of the brain*. Cambridge, MA: Oxford University Press.

Zeki, S. (1999). *Inner vision: An exploration of art and the brain*. New York: Oxford University Press.

2

MULTIMEDIA PRODUCTION AS COMPOSITION

David L. Bruce
KENT STATE UNIVERSITY

> If our children are to be able to navigate their lives through this multimedia culture, they need to be fluent in "reading" and "writing" the language of images and sounds just as we have always taught them to "read" and "write" the language of printed communications. (Thoman & Jolls, 2005, p. 180)

As multimedia becomes more prominent in our culture and schools, it offers the opportunity for challenging and expanding traditional concepts of literacy. This is true not only in reading media texts but also in writing them. There are a number of multimedia authoring tools that deal with various combinations of still and motion, sound and image, and text and graphics. This article will examine the compositional aspects of multimedia through the lens of video.

Why video? It is still the dominant medium with which all students are familiar in reading, particularly in forms of TV and movies. In speaking about the emergent conventions of film, Langer (1953) stated that "this new art [film] . . . seems to be omnivorous, able to assimilate the most diverse materials and turn them into elements of its own. . . . It swallows everything: dancing, skating, drama, panorama, cartooning, music . . ." (p. 412). In terms of production, video is both an established and emergent modality. It is the former because it has existed in the form of TV production for decades. However, the digital technology has allowed the processes and products of video—as well as its accessibility—to be completely changed.

Video also encompasses numerous modalities. Working with video, in Langer's terminology, "swallows" all of the following: movement, various aspects of audio (ambient sound, sound effects, voice-overs, music) text, graphics, audio, still images, moving images, special effects, and transitions. In essence, most of what is possible in all forms of multimedia can be accomplished with video.

Tyner (1998) addressed the broad modalities of multimedia as, "the ability of digital tools to collapse sight, sound, and motion with relative ease accelerates experimentation with the convergence of aesthetic form and structure from different media" (p. 39). While Tyner was speaking more broadly toward all digital media, her assessment can certainly be applied directly to video.

This chapter will position video in the broader field of media literacy and address how it is both read and written. The latter is explored through the terms of production and composition. In addition, parallels to the field of print composition studies are discussed as a means of explaining potential teaching and research issues.

THE PRIVILEGE OF READING

Inherent in the following media literacy definition is reading and writing with various media "to access, analyze, evaluate and communicate messages in a variety of forms" (Aufderheide, 1993, p. xx). Ideally, writing and reading are complementary processes (Scholes, 1985) and should be integrated as much as possible. Thoman and Jolls (2005) stated, "When *analysis* is combined with creative *production*, theory unites with application, thereby allowing students to discover and express their learning in an interconnected and natural process" (p. 188, emphasis added).

Yet a disconnect has occurred in that reading media has been favored over writing media. For instance, over the past four decades much has been written about reading the media (Buckingham, 1992; Considine, 1997; Costanzo, 1984; Foster, 1979; Krueger & Christel, 2001; Masterman, 1980, 1985; Monaco, 1981; Teasely & Wilder, 1997) as a form of text that can be read and interpreted much in the same way as print texts.

Comparatively less has been written about media writing. Referencing the reading and writing aspects of media literacy, Schwarz (2005) stated, "Some would take exception to the definition for not emphasizing media *creation* enough" (p. 11). The heavier emphasis on reading (as opposed to writing) is not something that has occurred only within the field of media literacy. In a similar manner with print literacy, reading has long been privileged over writing in terms of status and funding (Brandt, 2001).

Despite the imbalanced emphasis on reading, the field of media literacy has recently moved toward a corrective call for the inclusion of writing with media. In the 2005 Yearbook of The National

Society for the Study of Education (NSSE), a number of articles focused on media literacy studies mentioned the necessity and challenge of assessing "the role of media production in the media literacy curriculum" (Schwarz, 2005, p. 237). The Media Literacy On-Line Project indicated that, in addition to learning to understand media codes, "media literacy also aims to provide students with the ability to create media products" (Center for Advanced Technology, 1997). Zettl (1998) stated, "media literacy does not mean just greater competence in 'reading,' that is, decoding media messages, but also in 'writing'—encoding them" (p. 82). Others (Buckingham, 1998; Grahame, 1991; Thoman & Jolls, 2005; Tyner, 1998) have emphasized the complementary nature of the two processes, asserting that with media texts students who write them become better readers.

Professional organizations have also focused attention on media writing. When it came out with its new K–12 competency standards, the National Communication Association (1998) included in its Media Literacy strand "the ability to use media to communicate to specific audiences" (p. 3). The National Council of Teachers of English (NCTE) passed the Resolution on Composing with Nonprint Media at its 2003 conference, which stated,

> Resolved, that the National Council of Teachers of English
>
> - encourage preservice, inservice, and staff development programs that will focus on new literacies, multimedia composition, and a broadened concept of literacy;
> - encourage research and develop models of district, school, and classroom policies that would promote multimedia composition;
> - encourage integrating multimedia composition in English language arts curriculum and teacher education, and in refining related standards at local, state, and national levels;
> - renew the commitment expressed in the 1983 Resolution on Computers in English and Language Arts to achieve equity of access to the full range of composing technologies.

One repercussion from that resolution was the establishment of a task force to help guide NCTE regarding information and policy for multimodal composition (R. Bomer, personal communication, May 8, 2005).

PRODUCTION VERSUS REPRODUCTION

There are a number of benefits for writing with media, as the process motivates the alienated and the underachieving and empowers students as media producers. Writing with media also helps students,

- Shape and express meaning;
- Engage in collaborative problem solving as well as discussion opportunities;
- Represent ideas in verbal, visual or graphic forms;
- Develop creativity;
- Frame individual representations of reality and/or self-expression;
- Present final products to authentic audiences;
- Capitalize on the visual aspects of thinking and learning;
- Make connections to mental storehouses of media images.

(Bragg, 2002; Bruce, 2004; Brunner & Tally, 1999; Ferguson, 1981; Goodman, 2003; Hobbs, 2005; Tyner, 1998).

Despite potential benefits of composing with media, there are some valid concerns. Within the field of media literacy, there exists a division of attitudes toward video production (Hobbs, 1998). One facet of the controversy deals with students' poor replication of professional standards. Masterman (1980) claimed that student video productions would become part of the "endless wilderness of third-rate imitative 'pop'-shows, embarrassing video dramas, and derivative documentaries" (p. 140) that were already part of the television landscape.

A further extension of the replication argument stated that as students' learned models of professional productions, they would be more concerned with production skills than the content of what is being produced. Denski (1991) emphasized, "in the case of media production, these skills include equipment operation and general indoctrination into the techniques of classical or dominant entertainment production" (p. 6). Lewis and Jhally (1998) stated that such replication of professional models will "seduce" the student producers to focus on only the professionals' "aesthetic or technical prowess" (p. 115). They continued bleakly, "at best, teaching production as purely a set of technical skills leads to an analytical immersion rather than a critical distance" (p. 115).

The concern is that students will be unwitting transmitters of cultural inequity through the thoughtless replication of professional productions (Masterman, 1985). In a damning indictment, Denski (1991) stated that media production courses, particularly at the university level have "trained a generation of media (re)production students and (value maintenance) engineers [and] must be asked to examine the wider and unavoidable political dimensions of their efforts" (p. 6).

Those critical of media production as cultural reproduction argue that any video production that students make should be for real audiences, creating critical or oppositional texts to the mainstream media. Lewis and Jhally (1998) stated that video production can be a valid part of the media literacy curriculum as long as the projects are "not so much copying the medium as exploring its potential" (p. 116). They suggested that this will happen by having groups and/or students who often "feel marginalized by mainstream media" (p. 116) tell their stories and experiences—stories that are often unheard or ignored by traditional media outlets.

However, others within the field of media literacy disagree that students are blindly reproducing dominant media when they write with media. Buckingham (1998) stated,

> Studies of classroom practice have challenged the earlier view that practical production necessarily entails the mindless imitation of dominant media. On the contrary, students' uses of popular media forms and genres frequently display a clear understanding of media language, and a form of ironic distance that is at least potentially critical. (p. 40).

Buckingham, Fraser and Sefton-Green (2000) continued the antireplication argument, stating, "we do not believe that the best way of developing students' conceptual understanding of the media lies in requiring them to produce 'radical' or 'oppositional' texts—even assuming that we could agree about what those might be" (p.151). They stated that rather than subjecting students to highly controlled, often-decontextualized production activities, "students need to be given opportunities to experiment with the technology in less-constrained ways, to revise and 'redraft' their work, and to learn from their own mistakes" as well as "regular and frequent engagement with production throughout the course" (Buckingham, et al., 2000, p. 151).

Meyrowitz' (1998) notion of *media grammar literacy* seems to be the balance between the media replication arguments. He defined media grammar literacy as "the notion that media are languages with distinct grammars" and he urged that teachers "highlight the need to be literate in media production variables" (p. 106). He felt that this literacy occurred when students were able to "manipulate the variables skillfully in one's own media productions, understanding what cultural and institutional forces tend to encourage some uses of grammar variables rather than others, and recognizing that responses to production variables may vary individually and culturally" (pp. 99–100).

PRODUCTION VERSUS COMPOSITION

Arguments regarding cultural replication aside, the issue of "production" also should be of concern. While the terms production and composition are often used synonymously in reference to writing, the two terms are not necessarily the same. Since we use language in ways to define and describe, the terminology becomes important. Production—the word most associated with writing with media—has connotations of a factory-line, a conveyer belt of piece-by-piece assemblage. It follows that students need only to follow a series of sequential steps to create their intended project.

An example of media writing-as-production activities was described by Grahame (1991), who advocated a series of isolated technical projects that are tied to the media studies but have strict guidelines and limitations from a production standpoint. She argued for rigorous student planning processes in highly controlled (and somewhat limited) production activities so that students develop "a greater respect for the processes of production and a less reverent attitude to the end product" (p. 156).

Instead of production to describe media writing, a more appropriate term might be composition. Even though this term is more often associated with print literacy, composition speaks broadly to authoring, no matter what form the final product takes. Hobson (1998) emphasized, "the composing processes across different media are similar; the basic algorithms are not as disconnected as we in the verbal fields believe" (p. 140).

Smagorinsky (2002) defined composition as "the act by which people make things that have meaning or use for them" (p. 10). He detailed a list of compositional acts that, among other things, include "the use of an appropriate tool or set of tools, and an understanding of the conventions and genres within which one is working and an understanding of the effects of breaking these conventions" (p. 10). Composition, then, empowers students to be authors—writers and composers—of work. The process is inherently more complex and recursive than production. This is not to say that student media compositions should not be referenced as productions. However, the naming act of composition should be our paradigmatic lens through which to reference student media work.

It is not a leap to see how video production had developed an assembly connotation. Media production has a one-step-at-a-time association due to the technology that originally drove it. Until roughly ten years ago, video production could be compared to writing using a typewriter (Reilly, 1998). When typing a paper, the page is built together in a concrete form, word by word, line by line, paragraph by paragraph. Only by using correcting tape or fluid could minor surface errors of print code be changed. Revision with a typewriter meant marking up a final copy and retyping it to make necessary changes. Likewise, linear editing required that the video be created in a similar sequential manner. While changes could be made, substantive edits would require starting the production over.

To continue the analogy, the more recent nonlinear editing systems were like word processors. The latter enabled the storage and manipulation of text. The process of composing a paper was no longer constrained to the limitations of the typewriter. Likewise, computer-based editors allowed for the storage and manipulation of video and audio text. Brunner and Tally (1999) stated that the "digital medium made it easier to experiment and to concentrate on analyzing the effect of the reordering rather than on the mechanics of rewriting" (p. 146).

LINEAR STAGES

Despite the changes made in the technology pertaining to video, the way in which it has been studied has largely described the linear steps by which students created it. In fact, much of the research dealing with video composition has utilized a priori categories from print literacy that explain the writing process. For example, Kenyon's (1996) research of students using video identified 16 sequential steps that the students went through in putting their productions together. Those video production steps were placed into the categories of prewriting, drafting, revision, and publication. Likewise, Lobdell (1997) made comparisons between video and print such as prewriting (preproduction), drafting (camera work), and revision (postproduction work).

Reilly's (1998) study placed the students' production process into three stages that are similar to traditional filmmaking and video production: "pre-production, which includes preparation, review, and editing of the idea and script, production—shooting the video, and post-production, involving editing, special effects, sound work and credits" (p. 93).

A clear example of such a prescriptive model (Zettl, 1984) defined video production in terms of (a) the shooting phase, (b) the review phase, (c) the decision-making phase and (d) the operational phase. Zettl (1998) later refined the video production process calling it the "effect-to-cause production model" (p. 7). He advocated examining the desired final result and working backwards (figuring out production elements by which that result could be achieved), moving through the actual production aspects (preproduction, production, and postproduction) before finally arriving at evaluation, by which the producer examines the degree of success of his or her product. The effect-to-cause model takes various compositional components such as audience, logistics, and process into consideration. However, embedded within the model, the process of production (pre, during, post) is set forth like a linear step process.

Clearly, there is good reason for those comparisons to writing process phases. Working with video does entail a stage-like aspect to the process. What is missing in those production descriptions, however, is the *recursive* processes we find in print composition studies that originated the terminology. Despite the nonlinear technology through which videos can now be produced, the traditional models for explaining and teaching video production have tended to follow a linear framework.

It may be that, thus far, the research in the field has been examining video productions *as* productions. The focus has tended to be less on the compositional acts of creating video, and more on the final product itself. It may be beneficial to frame further research as a study of the composition acts of student videos rather than production results of student videos.

RECURSIVE STAGES

Studies in print literacy may provide valuable guidance to the field of media literacy. Dyson and Warshauer-Freedman (2003) stated,

> In the past 2 decades researchers shifted their attention from studies of pieces of writing, the written products, to studies of 'how you do it,' of writers' composing processes. They investigate what writers think about and the decisions they make, in essence how they manage the complex task of putting thoughts on paper. (p. 974)

Hayes and Flowers (1980) created a schematic detailing how composition was not a series of sequential steps, but rather a series of nonsequential subprocesses that the writer used. Dyson and Warshauer-Freeman (2003) described written composition as "consisting of several main processes—planning, transcribing text, reviewing—that do not occur in any fixed order. Thought in writing is not linear but jumps from process to process in an organized way which is largely determined by the individual writer's goals" (p. 975). Hillocks (1986) stated that we need to "view composing as involving a variety of plans and subprocesses which are brought to bear throughout the composing process as they are needed" (p. 27).

The traditional stage model of prewriting through publishing, "though seeming to provide a convenient instructional scheme for writing, is not a valid representation of how writing processes actually work" (Farnan & Dahl, 2003, p. 995). Writing-stage descriptions become problematic in that they "model the growth of the written product, not the inner process of the person producing it" (Flower & Hayes, 1981, p. 367). Hillocks (1986) wrote that "even these stages are not discrete, that they are frequently interrupted by other processes" (p. 28).

In a similar manner, if researchers in the field of media literacy were to broaden their research focus to consider students' compositional processes, we might move away from the paradigm of linear production models. And there are good indications that this shift is starting to take place. Connections are being made between the nonlinear capabilities of the technology and the process by which those media compositions are created. Not only does multimedia writing "require a new set of authoring skills" (Brunner & Tally, 1999, p. 125) but also both the products and process of editing changes through the students' use of nonlinear editing equipment (Stafford, 1995).

Holzwarth and Maurer (2001) reported that students found comfort in the knowledge that at any point in the process changes could be made to their video. The researchers stated that the students "arranged different sequences on the editing screen, and discovered how they could change the meaning by putting sequences into different context" (p. 191). Goodman (2003) stated that the students in his study found that the final version of "their story is linear, following the structured stages of video production. But there is a nonlinear aspect to the tale, consisting of the learning process that constantly interrupts the description of how the students created their video" (p. 65).

MULTIMEDIA COMPOSITION CONSIDERATIONS

What should be the guiding teaching and research considerations for multimedia composition? The following example can be a model of the symbiotic nature of research-informing pedagogy. It deals with the approach instructors might take when introducing video equipment for student use. The Video Culture project that Holzwarth and Maurer (2001) studied did not teach the production process in a prescribed preproduction, production, postproduction mode that other researchers have documented. Instead, the participants learned through discovery with some technical input from the instructors. The participants experienced some frustration with their lack of production expertise, but they were able to learn in a spirit of play through trial and error. In Kenyon's (1996) study, the participants also learned in such a manner and reported levels of frustration as well. The research findings of both reports might suggest that a "discovery approach" (or trial and error) may not be the most effective manner in teaching production techniques to students. The benefits of student discovery and "happy mistakes" may be outweighed by high levels of student frustration, particularly with those who feel threatened by technology.

A parallel may be drawn between the critical mass of research with media composition and print literacy studies. Hawisher (1989), drawing upon the studies done by Kuhn, claimed that computer and composition studies were just moving out of the preparadigm stage—where many studies tended to be inconclusive and the same research territory is covered again and again—after a decade plus of studies and research. A similar arc seems to be happening in media literacy. Research in video composition appears to be at the beginning of a preparadigm phase because so few studies have been done.

Print composition studies have a deeply researched background and can inform the study of those composition processes that students use with nonlinear video. In addition, media literacy researchers studying video composition may deepen the quality of their research inquiries by drawing upon the voluminous studies conducted on the use of computers in print composition.

One such clear example from the latter is how word processors changed the way writing could be taught. A great attribute of the word processor that researchers touted was its capacity to store a draft so that students would not have the "tedium of recopying the draft" (Dudley-Marling & Oppenheimer, 1990, p. 33). Computers enhanced "drafting and revision by removing the drudgery of repetitive text production" (Selfe, 1990, p. 193). Teachers who *integrated* the word processing technology into the classroom were "teaching a new way of thinking about and working with writing—a way of thinking of text as fluid and movable, a way of thinking about communication as dynamic and purposeful" (Rodrigues & Rodrigues, 1994, p. 398).

Technology itself is not a pedagogical panacea for good student writing. A number of researchers (Bridwell, Nancarrow, & Ross, 1984; Grejda & Hannafin, 1992; Rodrigues & Rodrigues, 1989) have suggested that writing—rather than the word processor—remain the focus of both teaching and research. Selfe (1990) stressed that teachers should not forget what they know about teaching reading and writing in exchange for technology information because "we are teachers of English first and computer specialists second" (p. 200). Thus, a guiding research pitfall that those in media literacy can learn from print literacy studies is to avoid a "techno-centric" approach (Hawisher, 1989) in the research question (i.e. What is the effect of the computer on . . .). This is important because the phrasing of such a question "attributes far too much power to computers rather than how writers or literacy teachers might use computers" (Hawisher & Selfe, 1998, p. 5).

The best possible scenario for the fields of print and media literacy would be one where, in complementary fashion, multimedia findings might also guide print studies. For example, I have found (in teaching many hundreds of people how to edit) that creating videos becomes a powerful metaphor to both students and teachers for what writing processes are like. Those who struggle with print conventions—and they are legion—somehow do not seem to grapple with those parallel processes in video. As with print, composing a video involves brainstorming, drafting, revision, and publication phases, yet also involves recursive, complex processes. Students who struggle with print composition processes have exhibited those same broad compositional skills through the medium of video (Bruce, in press). I have seen numerous students who struggle with print composing "get" the function/purpose of the parallel process in video. Media literacy, then, might help provide guidance for print composition studies to make those writing processes more visible.

CONCLUSION

Since video contains a plethora of modalities and opportunities for student expression, the field of media literacy needs to reconsider the importance of multimedia composition. To do so, we must move from the production mentality—both in terms of activities and descriptions—to a compositional perspective. And while the technology advances are opening new venues for research and teaching, the focus should remain on how the students are able to utilize those applications for their literacy development. This chapter detailed some of the many parallels between media and print literacy. If the two fields are perceived as complementary, not competing, we can provide students with the opportunity to read and write broadly in both print and nonprint forms. By providing students aesthetic opportunities to experience a wide variety of texts, we will, in Maxine Greene's (1995) words, "allow them to read and to name, to write and to rewrite their own lived worlds" (p. 147).

REFERENCES

Aufderheide, P. (1993). *Media literacy: A report of the national leadership conference on media literacy.* Aspen, CO: Aspen Institute.

Bragg, S. (2002). Wrestling in woolly gloves: Not just being critically media literate. *Journal of Popular Film and Television, 30*(1), 41–52.

Brandt, D. (2001). *Literacy in American lives.* New York: Cambridge University Press.

Bridwell, L., Nancarrow, P., & Ross, D. (1984). The writing process and the writing machine: Current research on word processors relevant to the teaching of composition. In R. Beach & L. Bridwell (Eds.), *New directions in composition research: Perspectives in writing research* (pp. 381–398). New York: Guilford Press.

Bruce, D. (2004). Visualizing success: Using video composition in the classroom. *Ohio Journal of English Language Arts, 44*(1), 51–56.

Bruce, D. (in press). *Visualizing literacy: Building bridges with media.* Reading & Writing Quarterly.

Brunner, C., & Tally, W. (1999). *The new media literacy handbook: An educator's guide to bringing new media into the classroom.* New York: Anchor Books.

Buckingham, D. (1992). English and media studies: Making the difference. *English Quarterly, 25,* 8–13.

Buckingham, D. (1998). Media education in the UK: Moving beyond protectionism. *Journal of Communication, 48,* 33–43.

Buckingham, D., Fraser, P., & Sefton-Green, J. (2000). Making the grade: Evaluating student production in media studies. In J. Sefton-Green & R. Sinker (Eds.), *Evaluating creativity: Making and learning by young people* (pp. 129–153). London: Routledge.

Center for Advanced Technology, College of Education, University of Oregon. (1997). *Media literacy online project.* Retrieved October 18, 2002, from http://interact@uoregon.edu/medialit/homepage/

Considine, D. (1997). Media literacy: A compelling component of school reform and restructuring. In R. Kubey (Ed.), *Media literacy in the information age* (pp. 215–235). New Brunswick, NJ: Transaction.

Costanzo, W. (1984). *Double exposure: Composing through writing and film.* Upper Montclair, NJ: Boynton/Cook Publishers.

Costanzo, W. (1992). *Reading the movies: Twelve great films on video and how to teach them.* Urbana, IL: NCTE.

Denski, S. (1991). Critical pedagogy and media production: The theory and practice of the video documentary. *Journal of Film and Video, 43,* 3–17.

Dudley-Marling, C., & Oppenheimer, J. (1990). The introduction of word processing into a grade 7/8 writing program. *Journal of Research on Computing in Education, 23,* 28–44.

Dyson, A., & Warshauer-Freedman, S. (2003). In J. Flood, D. Lapp, J. Squire, & J. Jensen (Eds.), *Handbook of research on teaching the English language arts* (2nd ed; pp. 967–992). Mahwah, NJ: Lawrence Erlbaum.

Farman, N., & Dahl, K. (2003). Children's writing: Research and practice. In J. Flood, D. Lapp, J. Squire, & J. Jensen (Eds.), *Handbook of research on teaching the English language arts* (2nd ed; pp. 993–1007). Mahwah, NJ: Lawrence Erlbaum.

Flower, L., & Hayes, J. (1981). A cognitive process theory of writing. *College Composition and Communication, 32,* 365–87.

Ferguson, B. (1981). Practical work and pedagogy. *Screen Education, 38,* 41–55.

Foster, H. (1979). *The new literacy: The language of film and television.* Urbana, IL: NCTE.

Goodman, S. (2003). *Teaching youth media: A critical guide to literacy, video production, and social change.* New York: Teachers College Press.

Grahame, J. (1991). The production process. In D. Lusted (Ed.), *The media studies book: A guide for teachers* (pp. 146–170). London: Routledge.

Greene, M. (1995). *Releasing the imagination: Essays on education, the arts, and social change.* San Francisco: Jossey-Bass.

Grejda, G., & Hannafin, M. (1992). Effects of word processing on sixth graders' holistic writing and revisions. *Journal of Educational Research, 85,* 144–149.

Hawisher, G. (1989). Research and recommendations for computers and composition. In G. Hawisher & C. Selfe (Eds.), *Critical perspectives on computers and composition instruction* (pp. 44–69). New York: Teachers College Press.

Hawisher, G., & Selfe, C. (1998). Reflections on computers and composition studies at the century's end. In I. Snyder (Ed.), *Page to screen: Taking literacy into the electronic era* (pp. 3–19). London: Routledge.

Hayes, J. R., & Flower, L. S. (1980). Identifying the organization of writing processes. In L. Gregg & E. Steinberg (Eds.), *Cognitive processes in writing* (pp. 3–30). Hillsdale, NJ: Lawrence Erlbaum Associates.

Hillocks, G. (1986). *Research on written composition: New directions for teaching.* Urbana, IL: NCTE/ERIC.

Hobbs, R. (1998). The seven great debates in the media literacy movement. *Journal of Communication, 48*, 16–32.

Hobbs, R. (2005). Media literacy and the K–12 content areas. In G. Schwarz & P. Brown (Eds.), *Media literacy: Transforming curriculum and teaching, the 104th yearbook of the National Society for the Study of Education*, Part I (pp. 74–99). Malden, MA: Blackwell.

Hobson, E. (1998). Drawing students into writing: A faculty development workshop. In P. Childers, E. Hobson, & J. M. (Eds.), *ARTiculating: Teaching writing in a visual world* (pp. 137–147). Portsmouth, NH: Boynton/Cook.

Holzwarth, P., & Maurer, B. (2001). Aesthetic creativity, reflexivity and the play with meaning: A video culture case study. *Journal of Educational Media, 26*, 185–202.

Kenyon, J. (1996). Media literacy and adolescent education: Curriculum goals assessment. Dissertation Abstracts International. (UMI No. 9635988).

Krueger, E., & Christel, M. (2001). *Seeing and believing: How to teach media literacy in the English classroom*. Portsmouth, NH: Boynton/Cook.

Langer, S. (1953). *Feeling and form*. New York: Charles Scribner's Sons.

Lewis, J., & Jhally, S. (1998). The struggle over media literacy. *Journal of Communication, 48*, 109–120.

Lobdell, J. (1997). Hands–on video: A multimedia approach to multiple literacies in the middle school. Dissertation Abstracts International. (UMI No. 9803101).

Meyrowitz, J. (1998). Multiple media literacies. *Journal of Communication, 48*, 96–108.

Monaco, J. (1981). *How to read a film: The art, technology, language, history and theory of film and media*. New York: Oxford University Press.

Masterman, L. (1980). *Teaching about television*. London: Macmillan.

Masterman, L. (1985). *Teaching the media*. London: Comedia.

National Communication Association. (1998). The speaking, listening, and media standards and competency statements for K–12 education. Retrieved October 17, 2002 from http://www.natcom.org/instruction/k12

National Council of Teachers of English (NCTE). (2003). Position statement: On composing with nonprint media. Retrieved April 13, 2004, from http://www.ncte.org/about/over/positions/category/media/11419.htm

Reilly, B. (1998). New media and new literacies: Understanding the culture of a high school video production classroom. Dissertation Abstracts International. (UMI No. 9902212)

Rodrigues, D., & Rodrigues, R. (1989). In C. Selfe, D. Rodgrigues, & W. Oates (Eds.), *Computers in English and the language arts: The challenge of teacher education*. Urbana, IL: National Council of Teachers of English.

Rodrigues, D., & Rodrigues, R. (1994). How word processing is changing our teaching: New technologies, new approaches, new challenges. In G. Tate, E. Corbett, & N. Myers (Eds.), *The writing teacher's sourcebook* (3rd ed; pp. 391–399). New York: Oxford University Press.

Scholes, R. (1985). *Textual power: Literacy theory and the teaching of English*. New Haven, CT: Yale University Press.

Schwarz, G. (2005). Overview: What is media literacy, who cares, and why. In G. Schwarz & P. Brown (Eds.), *Media literacy: Transforming curriculum and teaching, the 104th yearbook of the National Society for the Study of Education*, Part I (pp. 5–17). Malden, MA: Blackwell.

Schwarz, G. (2005). Obstacles, challenges, and potential: Envisioning the future. In G. Schwarz & P. Brown (Eds.), *Media literacy: Transforming curriculum and teaching, the 104th yearbook of the National Society for the Study of Education*, Part I (pp. 229–250). Malden, MA: Blackwell.

Selfe, C. (1990). English teachers and the humanization of computers: Networking communities of readers and writers. In G. Hawisher & A. Soter (Eds.), *On literacy and its teaching: Issues in English education* (pp. 190–205). Albany, NY: State University of New York.

Smagorinsky, P. (2002). *Teaching English through principled practice*. Upper Saddle River, NJ: Merrill Prentice Hall.

Stafford, R. (1995). *Nonlinear editing and visual literacy*. London: BFI Publishing.

Teasley, A., & Wilder, A. (1997). *Reel conversations: Reading films with young adults*. Portsmouth, NH: Boynton/Cook.

Thoman, E., & Jolls, T. (2005). Media literacy education: Lessons from the Center for Media Literacy. In G. Schwarz & P. Brown (Eds.), *Media literacy: Transforming curriculum and teaching: The 104th yearbook of the National Society for the Study of Education*, Part I (pp. 180–205). Malden, MA: Blackwell.

Tyner, K. (1998). *Literacy in a digital world: Teaching and learning in the age of information*. Mahwah, NJ: Lawrence Erlbaum.

Zettl, H. (1984). *Television production handbook*. (4th ed.). Belmont, CA: Wadsworth Publishing Company.

Zettl, H. (1998). *Video basics 2*. Belmont, CA: Wadsworth.

• 3 •

CROSSING THE BRIDGE: LITERACY BETWEEN SCHOOL EDUCATION AND CONTEMPORARY CULTURES

Damiano Felini

STATE UNIVERSITY OF PARMA (ITALY)

Reading and writing are two activities specific to human beings: animals do not read or write. From the beginning of human civilization until today, the concept of literacy has always been changing together with the ideas of culture and of the learned human with his or her social necessities of education, school goals and politics, and with the changes of communication languages and systems. Literacy must be examined from two points of view: the development of the human communication systems and, as a consequence, the emerging necessity to improve competencies in reading and writing texts. The latter view takes into consideration the role that school education plays today and considers its present difficulties and its mission in handing down knowledge and culture. In this essay, I first outline the reasons for the gap between school and mass media that several theories have highlighted and the features of the consequent education philosophies based on the idea of contrast and fight. Then, I argue that media literacy can be the foundation on which it is possible to build a positive and fruitful relationship between media culture and school education. Going through the history of the concept of literacy and taking into consideration the media literacy theories will show how media literacy practices not only function for education and cultural growth but also have important significance in human growth.

SCHOOL AND MEDIA CULTURE: THE REASONS FOR THE GAP

The everyday talk of common people reveals diverse opinions about the relationship among children, school, and TV (or media in general). Naïve perspectives on the relationship are necessary for parents, educators and politicians to explain and justify their experiences and opinions about the role of media in daily life. For example, it is not unusual to hear people say, "If TV didn't exist, families would talk more," "Children don't play anymore because they're busy watching TV," or "Ignorance is widespread due to TV programs." Although they are assumptions, these naïve theories work in a collective sense as a way to create conceptions of society and mass media and their educational functions of media socialization (Caron & Caronia, 2000).

Pedagogical traditions have highlighted the distance between school and media, with their own cultures, logics, and methods of handing down knowledge. In particular, it is impossible for the media to bend to the traditional logics of education and school and, as a result, media systems have been understood as alternatives for socialization. Since the 1970s, above all in Europe, the idea of a *parallel school* exercised great appeal because it evoked the idea of media consumption as a site for learning and, at the same time, the lack of connection between school and the media, exactly as the parallel lines are (Fulchignoni, 1972; Genovesi, 1981; Porcher, 1974; Postman, 1985). As Porcher (1974) noted,

> The *parallel school* is made up of a series of channels thanks to which pupils (and the whole audience) can get, outside school, news, knowledge, a sort of education in different fields. The instruments of the parallel school are the ones of mass communication, that is *mass media*: press, comics, radio, cinema and, above all, television. These new education channels, not controlled by teachers, are often used by pupils. Any opinion you can express towards them, the pedagogic problem they propose cannot be ignored. We want to know whether the school and the parallel school will continue to ignore each other, to behave as if they were enemies or they will form an alliance. In any case, the problem cannot be ignored by teachers. (p. 5)

The gap between school education and media culture is exactly the starting point of this essay because we are convinced of the persistence of this idea if not in literature, at least as a naïve theory. For this reason, it is important to understand the causes of such a deep dichotomy, which can be traced back to four contradictions:

1. *Fatigue versus amusement.* School has always been characterized by a long and demanding training period of learning and improving one's knowledge, which would otherwise be impossible. On the other hand, media culture, mostly based on images, does not include teaching and is characterized by amusement, *loisir*, and frivolity. In other words, we could oppose the educational austerity of school and the cultural hedonism of media.
2. *The primacy of images.* If, on the one hand, school culture is based on presenting elaborate concepts and abstractions through more or less formal speeches, then the language of images is by nature unable to obey and follow the cause and effect law or to communicate abstractions since it manages only to arrange images and frames in sequence, one after the other. The paratactic style of audiovisual communication was seen, before the theory of *brainframes* (de Kerckhove, 1991), as one of the possible causes of the change, if not the reduction, of the cognitive capabilities of young people.
3. *High culture versus popular culture.* While school is officially a repository of humane and scientific studies, fields which are well-established, "classic," and meant for a limited circle of people, mass media is popularized as an "easy" culture addressed to everybody, which lacks high-level contents and is considered a *divertissement d'ilotes* (for more about the contrast between high culture and pop culture, see Barthes, 1957; Eco, 1964; Hall & Whannel, 1964).
4. *Relativism versus control.* School culture refers mainly to the transmission of fixed knowledge, recognized in scientific subjects controlled by the Academy. It aims to hand down a well-established, validated, certain knowledge in an organic and structured way. Conversely, media culture is a fast-changing, dynamic, and relative culture where every opinion and position has validity.

It is not surprising that the history of media pedagogy has been a history of conflict when drawing on the aforementioned conception of the relation between school and media culture. There are two different historically and ideologically situated antithetical versions: the "right-wing" and the "left-wing" perspectives. The former is represented by Neil Postman (1979) in his book, *Teaching as a Conserving Activity.* He put forward a homeostatic theory of the educational process with two assumptions: first, the mass media are children's "first curriculum" in terms of both the amount of time spent and the efficacy of handing down and inculcating messages; second, this "first curriculum" has caused a reduction of young people's logical abstractive and linguistic competences. If this is true, school should play the role of a "cultural thermostat" since it has always aimed at revealing the main tendencies in culture and opposing them with any educational philosophy. In this way, the teleological vision of pedagogy, according to which education has to direct its efforts to reach a certain anthropologic ideal, is denied. On the contrary, the aim of education lies in preserving culture and the society where it is put into effect.

Against the culture of entertainment spread by electronic media, Postman (1979) wrote that the traditional school system should be preserved and appreciated because of its values of continuity, socialization experience, social order, hierarchy, deferred satisfaction, and individuality. As for school subjects, Postman insisted on a return to the literary tradition of the humanities, underlining the importance of correct spelling, lexical enrichment, rhetoric, and argumentative abilities. The gap between this curriculum and the media curriculum is plain and clear, and the author is fully aware of it (Postman, 1979).

Unlike Porcher (1974), who hoped that the future of school to be "a meeting between the parallel lines" that could be realized thanks to the choice of audiovisual aids and of other learning technologies, Postman (1979) did not want a compromise between the two cultures of school and mass media, which he considered intrinsically and inevitably antithetical. The introduction of media into schools is surely to be hoped, not as mere learning aids, but as textual samples to analyze. American proponents of media education propose the creation of a school subject—similar to media literacy—which has media as the subject matter of its teaching. It would aim at helping children and adolescents to understand the world of mass media and its technologies, the speed and spread of information, and the media's influence on thoughts, social behaviors, and values. Thus, the main goal is *media ecology*, which countervails their influences through a rational and critical meditation on themselves. Inevitably, according to Postman's point of view, a metaphor for the use of media in school is the creation of an Indian reservation, where it is possible to hide and regulate the media so that it cannot influence education in general, but can be easily controlled. In this way, media is not a precious gift to preserve, but an enemy to keep in check.

In contrast to such a conservative framework, neo-Marxism inspired media pedagogy has a more progressive slant. The Frankfurt School, as embodied in the work of Horkheimer and Adorno (1969), interpreted mass media as a *cultural industry*, an enormous system aimed at creating and imposing role models, needs, and new outlooks. Its principal characteristics were the mass production of cultural objects whose aesthetic value was lost by addressing an individual whose originality is unknown and occupying people's amusement and recreation spaces. The general effect was one of mass alienation together with other alienation that people suffered because of the devaluation of human production. From this perspective, mass media were seen as a means able to rouse a dialectic comparison and a cultural opposition among several class forces.

Confirmed by Althusser (1970), this theory considered mass media as a superstructural system that, by popularizing models and values, established a space for the conservation of the system and thus, a sort of ideology in the Marxist meaning of the word. So, against mass media, the cultural elite developed an attitude of low opinion and regarded the media as a "mass culture," fostering a middle-class prejudice toward them. Critics accused the bourgeoisie of using the mass media for the social control of the working class.

From this perspective, some educators have developed what Valeri and Betti (1976) called "alternative information." This alternative perspective was presented as enhancing global education by fostering "young people's critical thinking education, [that is] to help them to uncover the mechanisms that work in the system with manipulative and repressive aims. So it served as means to guide them by a precise critical analysis of messages, to define the function stated by media inside a classist system" (Valeri & Betti, 1976, p. 33). It is for this reason that Valeri and Betti criticized the commonly used way of introducing media into the school, which they define as a "bleaching operation," a narrow form of critical analysis that dwells only upon contents such as violence, immorality, vulgarity, and horror, or at the most, advertising and propaganda. In their opinions, such an approach to education becomes a sterile activity that sinks into political indifference because denouncing mass media culture only strengthens all the other messages and the overall culture of the cultural industry. The teachers who have these attitudes may be partly responsible for a behavior of "political indifference or conformism or proper conservative will, all attitudes that, anyway, are precious supports for the middle-class system" (Valeri & Betti, 1976, pp. 44–45).

From a critical perspective, education aimed at teaching aesthetics—the philosophical sense of educating to recognize and contemplate beauty—loses significance by being "bourgeois" and misleading as to the social-political needs of today. On the contrary, education that involves students in the production of media messages is stimulating because, according to social dialectic, people's approval of the techniques for creating media products (audiovisual, radio, and written products), and the organizational methods of networks is a meaningful occasion to test opposition to the oligarchic control of mass media; in addition, such work may renew the meaning of both technique and manual ability, overcoming the simplicity of *learning by doing*, which is pursued by the supporters of active teaching.

The diverse perspectives of Postman (1979) and Valeri and Betti (1976) exemplified the two diverse forms of tension in the field. Some educators continue to view the media as useless, even antithetical, to the proper processes and functions of education in handing down values and the cultural heritage of humanity. Other educators insist that a more active role must be inculcated in students to enable them to culturally oppose the distortion of information carried out by media for political reasons and to understand the roots of cultural and political alienation.

In Great Britain, where media education has been developing for many years, this tension is also evident. Halloran and Jones (1992) introduced the concept of the *inoculation approach*, the most traditional approach towards media education. It is traditional both from a chronological perspective, since it traces back to the 1930s and the early 1960s in this geographical context, and from the modern media literacy theorists' points of view, who consider it completely outdated (Buckingham, 2003), all the more so because it draws inspiration from a media theory—so-called bullet theory of media influence (Lasswell, 1938), a theoretical perspective that has lost credibility.

From this point of view, media education has had to play the role of a vaccine that serves to inoculate the population to immunize them from the harmful effects of the media. Indeed, in England, the first and longest phase in media education's development, lasting from the early 1930s to the early 1960s, was mainly a defensive and paternalistic movement whose function was to introduce popular forms into the classroom only in order to dismiss them as commercial, manipulative, and derivative—the culture of the machine—in comparison with more traditional "high" cultural forms. Media education was, thus, in its earliest manifestation, education *against* the media. Its function to encourage pupils to develop discrimination, fine judgment, and taste by grasping the basic differences between the timeless values of authentic "high" culture (in which teachers were themselves initiated) and the debased, anticultural values of largely commercial mass media (Masterman, 1997).

The inoculation approach is seen by English scholars as the first and already outdated phase of the historical evolution of media literacy education. But by looking around the world, it is clear that these tensions cannot be regarded as completely outdated. For instance, unlike other fields of pedagogic science that deal with a value in itself (the human being, the child, the family), media pedagogy, although it has gotten rid of some prejudices towards the mass media, continues to present a sort of opposition towards them. Educators instinctively continue to critically assess the impact and consequences of media upon children's growth and education.

Even beyond this positive and "critical" function of the tension between different ideas about media education, in the last 20 years media educators throughout Europe, the Americas, and Asia have been looking for an encounter instead of a clash. Even though parallel lines travel close to each other and never meet, educators and scholars have done their best to make them cross and cover part of the way together. But there is still an unresolved question: What is the conceptual cornerstone on which we can foster the meeting between school and media culture? One of the most interesting attempts to answer this question has emerged within the worldwide movement of media education among those who have embraced the idea of expanding the concept of literacy.

Pedagogical Background for the Concept of Literacy

The English word *literacy* means the ability to read and write, and corresponds to the Italian word *alfabetizzazione*, the French *alphabétisation*, the Spanish *alfabetización*, and the German *Alphabetisierung*. In western countries of the 19th century, a literate person was able to read and write his or her first name and surname. Today, according to UNESCO, literacy means being able to understand and write down a short composition about everyday life events. Moreover, the concept of *functional literacy*, though it has been criticized, has broadened the definition of literacy, linking the learning of language comprehension and expression abilities to the solution of concrete problems that humans face in everyday life, that range from family and social experiences to concerns of life and health (Faure, 1972). The concept of literacy cannot be considered static: Throughout the years, it has experienced a progressive redefinition, which is necessary due to changing social-cultural conditions of humankind and the understanding of these changes. This redefinition of the concept of literacy has gone towards a gradual enlargement (Buckingham, 1993; Hobbs, 1997; Tyner, 1998; Watts Pailliotet & Mosenthal, 2000).

Above all, Freire's (1971) studies gave prominence to the social and political meaning of literacy. Drawing from his experience with poor people in Brazil, Freire combined the words *literacy, conscientization,* and *liberation* of the oppressed, so that the acquisition of reading and writing abilities was connected to giving meaning to reality and becoming aware of one's role in society. According to Freire, process of conscientization means the passage from a situation of intransitivity (stagnation and refusal to change), to transitivity, which cultivates the will to change the established power relations in society, and by expropriation not only of all possessions but also of personal dignity and the role in community. In this way, literacy has a liberatory direction because it aims to provide people with the proper cognitive instruments to become aware of their situations and to make change.

Beyond these expanded interpretations of literacy for social change, we have to recognize the great conceptual importance which characterizes the use of the word *literacy*, as it is popularly used to mean basic education in any field, often as a reaction to some level of ignorance in the population. Considering the diffusion and the plural use of the word literacy in the American education, Considine (2000) listed, with a good deal of irony, different literacies that are commonly referred to in contemporary society: health literacy, cultural literacy (an approach that reinforces the dominant ideology of Western civilization), multicultural literacy, media literacy, information literacy, cyberliteracy, and even Amish literacy.

From One Literacy to Multiple Literacies

If we dwell upon the constitutive link between literacy and language, we can easily realize that the posttypographic world we live in has a multiplicity of languages, all simultaneously used, which change the concept of literacy. Watts Pailliotet and Mosenthal (2000) moved from the assumption that "multiple forms of representation inherent in mass media texts profoundly impact thinking processes, educational products, and the ways we represent and perceive the world," to suggest the development of "new definitions of the theory of literacy, practice, study, and policy" (pp. xxi–xxii). For media literacy educators, the concept of literacy benefits from the meaning of a metaphor on one side and the power of an umbrella concept on the other.

Using the term *media literacy* to show the connections between the study of language and the study of communication technologies has caused confusion because there are considerable differences between print literacy and the skills required to comprehend a visual media text, particularly in the area of decoding and comprehension (Desmond, 1977). Meyrowitz (1998) shared this opinion, arguing that "understanding visual symbols has nothing to do with literacy: [. . . the first one] has no linguistic symbols to decode, no letters to recognize, no grammatical rules to master" (p. 103). Moreover, Desmond (1997) claimed the word *literacy* should be accepted in a wide, metaphorical sense bearing in mind its explicative power and its ability to take on a multiplicity of functions connected to language. It is for this reason that Tyner (1998) regarded literacy as an umbrella concept that can help us to understand "the wide range of real and perceived literacy needs for contemporary times" and for this reason, she introduces *multiliteracies*, a word which is intentionally plural" (pp. 62–63).

The concept of multiliteracies has had a great success because it goes well with the theory of multiple intelligences, developed by Howard Gardner (1983). The theory of multiple intelligences was appreciated all over the world for its ability to explain and promote differences in cognitive styles. Under the brim of this umbrella concept, the diverse forms of literacy required by contemporary culture and new technology can be seen as strictly connected, not as fragments of a literacy once united, but as a whole series of distinct and, at the same time, interrelated and overlapping competencies.

Tyner (1998) distinguished between tool literacies and literacies of representation. Some of the multiliteracies are connected to specific technologies and specific representational forms and structures of mass media; this implies that there may be teachable concepts both in terms of reading (analysis/understanding) and writing (production/expression). Thus, the multiliteracies theory has the merit of putting these learning subjects in relationships potentially to create a common conceptual foundation that avoids regarding them as distinct agglomerates of knowledge and abilities. Hobbs (2006) proposed a taxonomy that links, in operational terms, the different intervening fields of media literacy, visual literacy, information literacy, and critical literacy. Each of these expanded perspectives on literacy can encourage educators to link linguistic learning to the diverse other communication competencies required for today's youth.

Defining Media Competence

Recent studies have begun to provide scientific evidence to favor teaching literacy through the communicative arts. I refer to the *transferability* of learned abilities from one field to the other which is always invoked but never proved. In other words, one of the justifications of media literacy is that the abilities of analyzing messages and communicating with media instruments, once learned by studying popular texts, can be applied directly to different contexts. For instance, literacy skills from one genre, such as print, could be applied to other genres of audiovisual media, television, or film. In reality, the transferability of literacy knowledge had always been either taken for granted or supported depending on teachers' and educators' experiences. Only recently, some experimental research has tested this principle empirically and rigorously, finding that when the analysis of media texts is included in a traditional class, students' reading comprehension and writing skills improve (Hobbs & Frost, 1999; 2003).

These kinds of studies, still at the onset, are particularly interesting for several reasons. One reason is that such studies highlight the relations between media literacy and other school subjects, demonstrating the validity of media literacy curricula to school teachers and administrators. In this way media literacy becomes not only an activity that motivates students, but it is a formative process that can really teach something to students, so it strengthens basic abilities that are transferable. Moreover, these studies give an empirical confirmation to the idea of multiliteracies, demonstrating the transferability of abilities and of some analysis categories (genre, point of view, message target, etc.). It is shown that reading and writing abilities in different media formats is founded on a series of common skills and that traditional literacy, strictly connected to the reading and writing of the alphabetic code, can be seen in continuity with the other literacies of representation that Tyner (1998) described.

When conceptualizing *media competence*, as media literacy is commonly identified in Europe, three families of concepts are evident: understanding, critical viewing, and producing messages (Felini, 2004). Each of these is linked to specific typologies of educational activities that promote their development.

Understanding
This includes the ability to understand media messages, the mass communication system, and the logics of production and reception. This understanding is linked not only to the intratextual (semiological) dimension but also to the political and economics contexts in which media communication takes shape. This series of skills is connected above all to the cognitive dimension and develops through educational activities which involve textual analysis and gaining knowledge about media systems.

Critical viewing
This includes the ability to meditate on our own method of media consumption and that of others. This series of skills can be strengthened using educational methodologies that encourage reflection on media use habits, uses and motivations, content choices and behaviors.

Media production
This includes the ability to create messages in different media formats (press, video, radio, comics, hypertexts, Web pages) to express opinions and take part in the community life. This series of skills is linked both to the cognitive dimension but also to operating abilities and cooperation. A typical educational activity is a media production workshop where collaborative work includes brainstorming, message design, development, and performance.

Another sound definition of literacy skills is the one proposed by the Aspen Institute's National Leadership Conference on Media Literacy, which pointed out the following four areas: decode, evaluate, analyze, and communicate (Aufderheide, 1997).

To sum up, we can underline how reflections about literacy made in the last decade fostered an expansion that took into account (a) how human communication is a phenomenon that is organic and diversified at the same time because it both respects constant and transferable laws and it takes place through a multiplicity of forms and instruments; and (b) how it is possible to blend rich literary tradition and Western culture into the symbolic and emotional nature of the new media forms, in order to overcome the separation between life in and out of school that today sets up students for failure.

As shown in Fig. 3.1, the expansion of the concept of literacy has developed into three distinct axes. First, new language teaching methods have been added to the traditional alphabetic dimension that has taken into consideration the new tools, instruments and several different representational forms (x-axis). Second, other and more complex abilities such as message analysis, research, evaluation, and production have been added to reading and writing skills, skills that have been important since ancient times (y-axis). Lastly, visual, audiovisual, digital, and hypertextual forms—belonging both to high culture and mass culture—have been added to written text, which previously was the focus of literacy because visual texts were presumed to be easy to understand (z-axis). Today, the space for literacy has been widening, influencing all the possible channels of human communication.

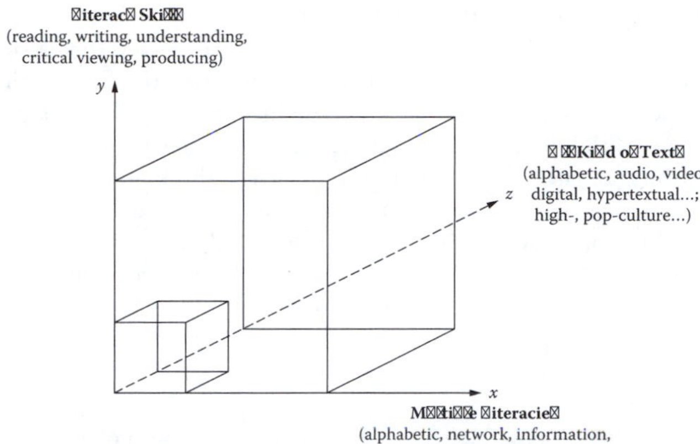

If you ask teachers, educators, or scholars why media literacy should be fostered, the most common answers are linked the widespread diffusion of mass media in contemporary society. Children's and adolescents' lives are marked and molded by media, and there is a widely perceived need to start young generations off on understanding different modes of communication besides print (imagery, interactivity, hypertextuality). These kinds of justifications circulate, on a more sophisticated level, even among experts. For example, Masterman (1985) provided the following seven reasons for the importance of media literacy: (a) the high rate of media consumption and the saturation of contemporary societies by the media; (b) the ideological importance of the media, and their influence as consciousness industries; (c) the growth in the management and manufacture of information and its dissemination by the media; (d) the increasing penetration of media into our central democratic processes; (e) the increasing importance of visual communication and information in all areas; (f) the importance of educating students to meet the demands of the future; and (g) the fast-growing national and international pressures to privatise information (p. 2).

There seems to be a general excess of causal explanations common among the researchers that justify the importance of media literacy, and this is absolutely necessary. But reasons are missing from a pedagogical perspective, which requires planning subjects for educational purposes that inspire a hopeful future for man and society. Media literacy, thus, aims at the development of specific skills that make up what we have named media competence. However, it lends itself to reaching wider objectives that put it, in fact, within a context of meanings consistent with the traditional learning outcomes of formal instruction in the arts and humanities: "Media literacy is, first of all, an educational action in its proper meaning since its objectives, steeped in humanism, aim at bringing up more autonomous and clear people" (Giroux, as cited in Piette, 1996, p. 8).

In a synthetic way, six areas of connection between media literacy education and the human growth can be indicated with a further rationale for the teaching of media literacy in schools:

Critical thinking education
According to most literature about media education, teaching literacy through the media is a useful practice to develop critical

thinking. Even if Piette (1996) revealed the sometimes confused notion of critical thinking contained in media literacy curricula, teaching literacy through the media improves critical thinking, both in the sense of *convergent thinking* (including analyzing the message content, finding underlying values, deconstructing an argument) and in the sense of *divergent thinking* (such as thinking differently compared to the masses and expressing original opinions). Critical thinking education is also linked to moral education because expressing a positive or negative judgment about a media message implies the reference to a personal and valid belief, that is, in the very end, a moral value.

Democracy and civic participation

The link among the literacy, democracy, and wealth of a nation has been perfectly expressed by many thinkers and educators since the modern age. Participation in community life is not possible today if we are not able to read what happens in the world and to write our ideas not only through the press but also through other kinds of media. Two assumptions about media production activities in the classroom support the development of youth civic participation. First, educators must prevent adolescents from simply copying the most banal formats of mass media texts only because they are more fashionable than traditional school reports. Secondly, to develop civic participation, adolescents' media productions must have a real audience, not only a familial and school audience. Partnerships with local media can give pupils the possibility of being listened to by their whole community. Listening to young people is a good exercise for the community too.

Health education

Health teachers, particularly in the United States, are among the most active media literacy teachers. Media messages often emphasize body image and social and personal behaviors that could impair or improve healthy decision making. Analyzing these kinds of messages may provide youth with protective and preparatory skills (Office of National Drug Control Policy, 2001).

Development of gender identity

Media literacy can be useful to introduce the theme of gender identities into children's and adolescents' classes; for example, demystifying the stereotypes about gender roles, exploring different tastes boys and girls may have about media consumption (Alvermann, Moon, & Hagood, 1999), or simulating different roles and identities through chat rooms.

Aesthetic education

Ugliness is invading our world, and we are not able yet to recognize what is beautiful and what is ugly. Sometimes, media are responsible for this situation. Teaching the media is an occasion to develop an understanding of aesthetics, not only the psychological perception of colors, proportions, manipulation, as the Anglo-Saxon tradition states (Messaris, 1994), but developing the sense of beauty according to the philosophical European tradition (Gennari, 1994).

The perspective outlined so far allow us to define two important themes. The first theme is how studies about the history of literacy introduced the idea of *restricted literacy* (Roggero, 1999). For different reasons depending on the historical period, a more or less numerous part of the population did not receive a basic education. Restricted literacy implies a split competency. One who learned how to read and write could not be thought to be able to read and write everything because his or her ability was limited to certain types of texts. For example, during the 18th century Germany and England, spelling books which educated people how to read were printed in with Gothic type, but not in Roman type, of which books of the high learned were printed. People could learn how to read the printed characters but not the handwritten ones, which prevented them from understanding common documents such as leases, receipts, letters, or wills, which in fact were handwritten. As a consequence, people were neither fully illiterate nor literate but had gradations and levels of literacy that enabled them to function more or less competently in society (Graff, 1987).

Beyond the good intentions of 19th-century popular school policies, today a similar phenomenon occurs: People can be literate, but in a restricted sense. The multiplicity of textual typologies, linguistic codes, and transmission channels can prevent people from developing their literacy skills in a comprehensive way and so they cling only to traditional processes and texts that they understand. In this case, it can be useful to highlight briefly some priorities:

- Promoting the spread of the concept of multiliteracies, making sure that it cannot remain patrimony only to scholars but that it is spread to school administrators and teachers
- Experimenting with taxonomies of educational standards and indicators regarding the whole spectrum of multiliteracies. This aim is not easy to reach—recent and reliable international research, such as the Programme for International Student Assessment (PISA, 2003) of OECD have widened the spectrum of reading skills, but not of textual typologies, remaining linked to written alphabetic text
- Developing literacy curricula based on the principle of multiliteracies for the whole span of compulsory school attendance
- Assuming that media literacy programs are not only the benefit for a limited number of students attending high-class schools, but they should be placed at all schools' and students' disposal. Without community-wide implementation, the risk is a "literacy divide" depending on socioeconomic class

One dangerous possibility must be considered: Literacy education through the media arts could appear to be just a routine set of skills linked to reading and writing in several media formats or, even worse, only a pretext to make getting in contact with texts of different genres pleasant for young people. We have to remember that media are the culture of the 21st century. Today, this makes media literacy a very important element of what has been named "liberal education" (Maritain, 1943; Smith, 2002), the general education that leads us into the cultural production of civilization. This education opportunity must be available to everyone. Media literacy belongs to the field of liberal education for three reasons: (a) It teaches the process of semiotic analysis (and in this sense it is an education that makes learning anything else easier); (b) it enables learners to get to know the content of contemporary culture and even the production, spread, and fruition that characterize it (all in all, it is another way of studying history, sociology, or anthropology of the group we belong to); and (c) it goes well with the development of the human personality in all of its aspects. Based on these assumptions, we can add another series of guidelines:

- Regarding media literacy education as a study of symbol systems, of language, and of cultural phenomena
- Applying media literacy curricula to content with cultural depth, including the exploration of media messages that consider social issues (democracy; worldwide conflicts; city and rural lifestyles; nature and environment), cultural issues (cultural diversity; beauty; religion and spirituality; scientific discoveries; the meaning of life) and personal issues (self and body image; relationships with others; happiness, money and success)
- Supplying teachers with cultural training and an educational competence aiming above all at strengthening adolescents' ability to think critically about themselves and their realities

CONCLUSION

The world around us continues to unfold and a new future is going to open its doors, even though it remains nearly completely unknown to adults. Who will explain it to young generations? I would like to end this essay with this question because, among the most obscure and confused elements that mark the gap between generations, it appears that youth seem to benefit in a far more immediate way from technologies and media than the people who are older do. Like Robinson Crusoe, a lot of youth manage quite well to dominate and tame the strangeness of their realities, creating meaningful island habitats without much need of the (more or less) experienced guides who may introduce them to the obscure secrets of the contemporary world, media, and communication technologies, too. To conclude, media literacy education is to be seen as a little like a bet that adults have with children and adolescents (and maybe even themselves) about the best ways to thrive in a culture saturated with mass media technologies and messages. As island guides to an unknowable future, we are colearners with students; as a result, we cannot not teach these things in an exhaustive and systematic way. But as guides, we can help create situations for meaningful in-depth analysis, the discovery of meaning, critical analysis of texts, and self-reflexive communication.

(Translation by Ines Sala, MA, and revision by the author)

REFERENCES

Althusser, L. (1970). Idéologie et appareils idéologiques d'Etat [Ideology and the Ideological Systems of the State]. *Le Pensée, 151,* 3–38.

Alvermann, D. E., Moon, J. S., & Hagood, M. C. (1999). *Popular culture in the classroom.* Newark, DE: International Reading Association.

Aufderheide, P. (1997). Media literacy: From a report of the national leadership conference on media literacy. In R. Kubey (Ed.), *Media literacy in the information age: Current perspectives* (pp. 79–86). New Brunswick, NJ: Transaction Publishers.

Barthes, R. (1957). *Mythologies.* Paris: Éditions du Seuil.

Buckingham, D. (1993). *Changing literacies: Media education and modern culture.* London: Tufnell.

Buckingham, D. (2003). *Media education: Literacy, learning and contemporary culture.* Cambridge, U.K.: Polity Press.

Caron, A. H., & Caronia, L. (2000). Contents in context: A study on Canadian family discourse about media practices in the home. In C. von Feilitzen, & U. Carlsson (Eds.), *Children in the new media landscape* (pp. 313–331). Nordicom, Göteborg: International Clearinghouse, UNESCO.

Considine D. M. (2000). Media literacy as evolution and revolution: In the culture, climate, and context of American education. In A. Watts Pailliotet, & P. B. Mosenthal (Eds.), *Reconceptualizing literacy in the media age* (pp. 299–327). Stamford, CT: Jai Press.

Desmond, R. (1997). Media literacy in the home: Acquisition versus deficit Models. In R. Kubey (Ed.), *Media literacy in the information age: Current perspectives* (pp. 323–343). New Brunswick, NJ: Transaction Publishers.

Eco, U. (1964). *Apocalittici e integrati: comunicazioni di massa e teorie della cultura di massa[Apocalyptic and Integrated: Mass Communications and Theories of the Popular Culture].* Milan: Bompiani.

Faure, E. (1972). *Learning to be: The world of education today and tomorrow.* Paris: UNESCO.

Felini, D. (2004). *Pedagogia dei media: Questioni, percorsi e sviluppi [Media Pedagogy. Issues, Pathways, and Perspectives].* Brescia, Italy: La Scuola.

Felini, D., & Weyland B. (2007). *Media education tra organizzazione e fantasia [Media literacy between organization and creativity].* Trento, Italy: Erickson.

Freire, P. (1971). *Pedagogia do oprimido [Pedagogy of the Oppressed].* Rio de Janeiro, Brazil: Paz Terra.

Fulchignoni, E. (1972). *L'immagine nell'era cosmica [The Image in the Cosmic Era].* Rome: Armando.

Gardner, H. (1983). *Frames of mind: The theory of multiple intelligences.* New York: Basic Books.

Gennari, M. (1994). *L'educazione estetica [Esthetic Education].* Milan: Bompiani.

Genovesi, G. (1981). *Scuola parallela e mass media [Parallel School and Mass Media].* Florence: La Nuova Italia.

Graff, H. J. (1987). *The legacies of literacy: Continuities and contradictions in Western culture and society.* Bloomington, IN: Indiana University Press. [AQ3]

Hall, S., & Whannel, P. (1964). *The popular arts.* London: Hutchinson.

Halloran, J. D., & Jones, M. (1992). The inoculation approach. In M. Alvarado, & O. Boyd Barret (Eds.), *Media education: An introduction* (pp. 10–13). London: British Film Institute.

Hobbs, R. (1997). Expanding the concept of literacy. In R. Kubey (Ed.), *Media literacy in the information age: Current perspectives* (pp. 163–183). New Brunswick, NJ: Transaction Publishers.

Hobbs, R. (2006) Multiple visions of multimedia literacy: Emerging areas of synthesis. In M. McKenna, L. Labbo, R. Kieffer, & D. Reinking (Eds.), *Handbook of Literacy and Technology* (pp. 15–28). Mahwah, NJ: Lawrence Erlbaum Associates.

Hobbs, R., & Frost, R. (1999). Instructional practices in media literacy education and their impact on students' learning. *New Jersey Journal of Communication, 6*(2), 123–148.

Hobbs, R., & Frost, R. (2003). Measuring the acquisition of media literacy skills. *Reading Research Quarterly, 38*(3), 330–355.

Horkheimer, M., & Adorno, T. W. (1969). *Dialektik der Aufklärung [Dialectic of Enlightenment].* Frankfurt, Germany: Fischer Verlag.

de Kerckhove, D. (1991). *Brainframes: Technology, mind and business.* Utrecht, The Netherlands: Bosch & Keuning.

Lasswell, H. D. (1938). *Propaganda technique in the World War.* New York: Peter Smith.

Maritain, J. (1943). *Education at the crossroads.* New Haven: Yale University Press.

Masterman, L. (1985). *Teaching the media.* London: Comedia.

Masterman, L. (1997). A rationale for media education. In R. Kubey (Ed.), *Media literacy in the information age: Current perspectives* (pp. 15–68). New Brunswick, NJ: Transaction Publishers.

Messaris, P. (1994). *Visual literacy: Image, mind, and reality.* Boulder, CO: Westview Press.

Meyrowitz, J. (1998). Multiple media literacies. *Journal of Communication, 48*(1), 76–83.

Office of National Drug Control Policy. (2001). *Helping youth navigate the media age: A new approach to drug prevention.* Washington, DC: National Youth Anti-Drug Media Campaign.

Piette, J. (1996). *Éducation aux médias et fonction critique [Media Education and Critical Thinking].* Paris: L'Harmattan.

Porcher, L. (1974). *L'éducation parallèle [The Parallel Education].* Paris: Larousse.

Postman, N. (1979). *Teaching as a conserving activity.* New York: Delacorte.

Postman, N. (1985). *Amusing ourselves to death.* New York: Viking.

Programme for International Student Assessment. (2003). The PISA 2003 assessment framework. *OECD.* Retrieved May 5, 2006, from http://www.pisa.oecd.org

Roggero, M. (1999). *L'alfabeto conquistato [The Conquered Alphabet].* Bologna, Italy: Il Mulino.

Smith, B. (Ed.). (2002). *Liberal education in a knowledge society.* Chicago: Open Court.

Tyner, K. (1998). *Literacy in a digital world: Teaching and learning in the age of information.* Mahwah, NJ: Lawrence Erlbaum Associates.

Valeri, M., & Betti, C. (1976). *I mass media e l'educazione: Per un'interpretazione alternativa dei messaggi dei media [Education and Mass Media: Towards an Alternative Interpretation of Media Messages].* Florence: Le Monnier.

Watts Pailliotet, A., & Mosenthal, P. B. (Eds.). (2000). *Reconceptualizing literacy in the media age.* Stamford, CT: JAI Press.

4

THE CONSTRUCTION OF PHOTOGRAPHIC MEANING

Andrew L. Mendelson
TEMPLE UNIVERSITY

People learn much about the world through photographs. Photographs show people what war is like, what social ills look like, and what products to buy. Photographs tell people whom to look up to and whom to despise; they identify leaders, heroes, and enemies. They bring people together in celebration and mourning. Indeed, no aspect of life seems uninfluenced by photographs.

Yet the sheer ubiquity of photographs conceals their constructed nature. People look at images daily, sometimes for less than a few milliseconds, seldom stopping to puzzle over them, to think about how and what they say. Photographs are assumed to simply be surface records of things that exist(ed), requiring little if any interpretation. Contrast this treatment with that of written and spoken language, which schoolchildren the world over (and politicians, for that matter) studiously parse for meaning. Photographs are assumed transparent, obvious, and representative of reality. They are merely windows to the world, revealing just the object itself. As Barthes (1981) stated, "It is as if the photograph always carries its referent with itself" (p. 5).

The meaning of photographs is far from simple, however. The seeming effortlessness and transparency masks a much more involved process, much of which occurs before the photograph appears in front of viewers. Some of this process lies within the head of the viewer, existing independently of any individual image. The photograph, thus, has many potential meanings depending on the production, viewing context, and the viewer. In essence, photographs are the ultimate quote out of context, needing a viewer at a specific time in history to fill in the blanks. Sekula (1984) stated it most clearly when he said, "In other words, the photograph, as it stands alone, presents merely the possibility of meaning" (p. 7). So, how do photographs come to mean what they do? What is involved in understanding an image?

Scholars have discussed the production and reception of photographs in a wide variety of fields and disciplines, including cultural studies, cognitive psychology, mass communications, anthropology, art history, and American studies. Each of these treatments has yielded important insights about the nature of photographs and the ways in which people construct meaning from them. The purpose of this chapter is to synthesize, for literacy scholars and educators, a growing body of research on photographs and their meaning into a single model of how meaning is created from images—what I call the sociohistorical model of photographic meaning (see Fig. 4.1). This model is intended to apply to all photographs, including those from the areas of fine art, documentary, photojournalism, family or personal, and advertising, and I will draw on photography examples from these categories. Each of these categories often blurs in its distinctiveness, placing emphasis on different aspects of the model. As a tool, this model provides educators and researchers ways of relating seemingly disparate studies of photographic meaning. Further, this model will foster understanding of the highly constructed nature of photographs, by parsing the many factors that influence the meaning of a photograph.

MEANING IN PHOTOGRAPHY

Figure 4.1 shows a model of photographic meaning that is influenced by multiple factors, some of which are involved prior to the creation of the actual image and others that come into play once the photograph is created and viewed. Meaning is the end product of the interplay of numerous factors. Meaning is ultimately the interaction of a photograph and a viewer while the photograph is a product of a producer and a subject, all set within a specific context.

The model expands upon ideas presented by Byers (1966), S. Hall (1993), and Scherer (1975, 1992), who argued that to understand photographs three aspects must be examined: the photographer, subject, and viewer. This model elaborates and expands on this tripartite relationship by including the photograph's context of presentation and other intermediary influences in the process. It also draws on semiotic concepts suggesting that meaning is based on the photographer's choices of the subject, compositional elements for inclusion

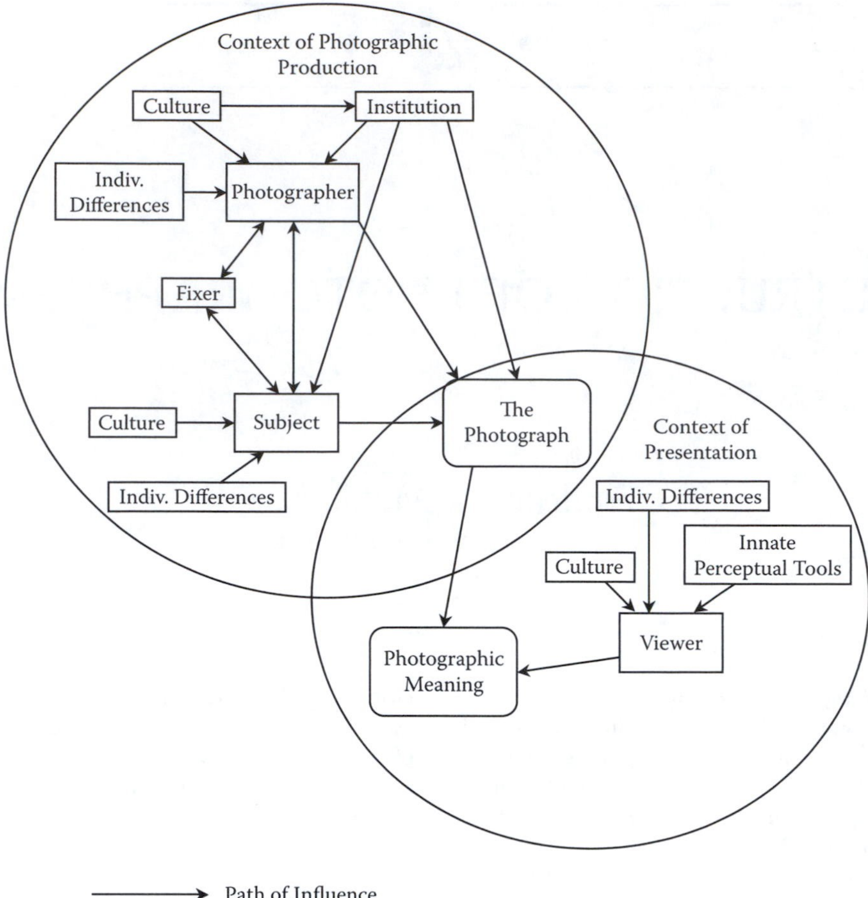

FIGURE 4.1. A sociohistorical model of photographic meaning

within the frame, and the way these various choices are combined (Barthes, 1967; Fiske, 1990).

Further, this model builds on ideas presented by Shoemaker and Reese (1996), who suggested that the production of mediated messages is influenced by a variety of factors including individual reporters, institutional factors, norms and routines, external influences, and cultural and ideological influences. The model expands on Shoemaker and Reese by examining not just the influences on the producer, but also on the subject and viewer, all of which impact meaning. Each node of the model is influenced by multiple factors, using a multilevel approach to understand the meaning of photographs, drawing explicit connections between cultural and psychological influences.

Viewers of photographs are active in the construction of their meanings (Hall, S., 1997). Meaning does not exist solely in the image itself, to which viewers passively respond; nor does it lie totally within the viewer's mind. There are limits to polysemy (the condition where there is more than one meaning for a text), as Condit argued (1989), since meanings are somewhat constrained by the production of the image. Neuman, Just, and Crigler (1992) argued, "Construction emphasizes the importance of the medium of communication, including the historical, structural, and technological character of media institutions" (pp. 17–18).

Finally, the model assumes that the ability to interpret photographs is not entirely learned or completely innate. As Messaris (1994) argued, specific knowledge of visual communication is not necessary to understand images. Even object recognition is part of the meaning process, but knowledge does enhance appreciation of visual media and changes the realm of possible interpretations.

The explication of the model begins by examining its left side, considering the elements that underlie the production of a photograph, the range of photographic choices available to a photographer, and the ways these influence meaning.

THE PRODUCTION OF A PHOTOGRAPH

The Photographer

The first node of the model focuses on the individual photographer and his or her influence on the meaning of the photograph. The romantic image of a lone photographer making art independent of any influence is hardly the case. Though the photographer pushes the button to make a photograph, he or she actually represents the confluence of sociological, cultural, institutional, and individual differences before and after the image is made. These factors affect the choice of subjects, the way they are photographed, and the potential meaning received by viewers. Culture and the individual cannot be separated because culture is internalized as an individual's "way of seeing," a process that occurs automatically with little conscious thought (Berger, J., 1972).

The style and approach to photography varies between photographers, depending on their background, beliefs, and demographic differences including gender, race, class, and age. All of these factors affect their perception of the world, and thus, their photographs. Much biographical work examines the relationship between such individual differences and the resulting photographs (e.g., Goldberg, 1987; Morrisroe, 1995; Whelan, 1985). For instance, two photographers, Dorthea Lange and Ansel Adams, documented the Japanese internment camp Manzanar during World War II in very different ways (Ohrn, 1977). Lange was trained as a portrait photographer and became one of the preeminent social documentary photographers, whereas Adams was one of the greatest landscape photographers, producing stunning images of places of natural beauty. Their attitudes differed toward internment. Lange was vehemently opposed to the internment, while Adams saw it as a necessary, though unfortunate, precaution. Their resulting images of the camps are quite different. Adams attempted to situate the camps in a geographic context. His shots show grand vistas, suggesting almost a resort experience, or possibly a more isolating experience with internees not actually able to enjoy the setting. Lange focused more on individual suffering and upheaval, showing families uprooted by a country they thought was theirs. These two approaches illustrate different senses of the internment camp.

Another factor affecting the photographic product is a photographer's preconceived ideas of a subject. Coles (1997) discussed his own work, saying that he focused on positive qualities of his poor Black subjects, sanctifying their existences. On the other hand, he stated, "On the White side of the tracks, however, I had considerable less trouble acknowledging the less attractive side of human nature" (p. 58). Preconceived ideas of a subject are both individual and cultural, as stereotypes circulate within a society (Hall, S., 1997).

Beyond biographical and individual differences, photographers work within systems that have well-established standards, conventions, and constraints of what constitutes good photography (Becker, 1983; Rosemblum, 1978). Photographers learn these conventions of photography through both on the job training and education. Even the institution of the family sets norms and practices for snapshots, in terms of who is photographed, how they are posed, who makes the photographs, and which events are documented (Chalfen, 1987). Bourdieu (1990) argued that the range of acceptable subjects to be photographed is highly dependent on class and culture. Thus, photographers in all contexts are limited in their autonomy and in the choices they make.

In mass media, for example, photography happens under the auspices of large media companies that are composed of layers of people, including editors, art directors, and gallery owners, who decide the content of the photograph, its style, and which photograph(s) are published (Lutz & Collins, 1993; Newton, 2001; Rosenblum, 1978; Shoemaker, 1991). The institutional context also influences the amount of time and money available for the photographer, which in turn affects the resulting photographs. Often, the choice of photograph(s) made available to the public occurs in the absence of the photographer and certainly without input of the subject. For example, a newspaper photographer submits a selection of images for an assignment to a photo editor, who selects the appropriate image(s) to run with a story. If time allows, some consultation may occur. But under deadline pressure, the photographer may actually never even see any of his or her photographs until they are published.

In addition to the photographers, decision makers have beliefs about the content and composition of photographs. For example, journalism has definitions of newsworthiness that affect the choice of subject, stylistic conventions that define a "good" news photograph, and time requirements that affect the conditions under which photographs are produced. News photography is highly conventional in terms of content and composition (Hall, S., 1973; Rosenblum, 1978), but can depend on conventions for a specific newspaper (content) and norms of photographing the subject (composition; Hagaman, 1996). Candid images are preferred over posed ones; little evidence of the photographer's presence should be visible (Becker, 1985; Schwartz, D., 1999). Ethical issues have generally required that photographs should not be staged in any way. Roy Stryker, who directed the U.S. government's documentation of the Great Depression as director of the Farm Security Administration's Historical Section, established highly detailed shooting scripts for his photographers, predefining the content of those photographs (Lesy, 2002). In J. Berger and Mohr's (1982) example of a photograph of Tito, the late Yugoslavian leader, editors did not use the photograph because he did not look enough like a Communist dictator, but as times changed and views toward Tito changed, this picture later become publishable in Western magazines.

Individual media institutions also set standards for the range of manipulation: Today, most photographic production is digital, and technological manipulation in photography is common. Advertising, journalism, fine art, and even family photography have different standards regarding the use of photo editing software to change or create the content of photographs. Retouching has long been the norm in advertising imagery. Likewise, art photographers have often created images by combining several negatives (see the work of Jerry Uelsmann and Oscar Gustav Rejlander). Journalists, in contrast, have been more concerned about the potential effects of such manipulation on credibility and authenticity.

A last level of influence working through the photographer and the institution is culture. Culture influences photographers' perception of themselves and others (Barthes, 1972, 1977; Berger, J., 1972). Cultural ways of seeing can dictate the types of subject matter appropriate to record and the manner in which it is recorded. Gans (1979) discussed the values that affect the way U.S. news stories are framed, often focusing on small town pastoralism, altruistic democracy, responsible capitalism, and ethnocentrism. These values appear neutral, as if the definitions of news flow naturally from the world, but they confirm power relations and reinforce cultural ways of seeing.

Examples of cultural influence include famed photojournalist Robert Capa, who documented the birth of Israel, recapitulating Zionist myths of the Holy Land (Mendelson & Smith, in press). Likewise, British and French photographers in the mid-19th-century recorded aspects of the Holy Land that spoke to and reconfirmed each of their respective views of the world and religion (Nir, 1985). Culture also influences the conventions used to construct visual messages. In their ground-breaking study of Navajo filmmakers, Worth and Adair (1997) argued that there were clear differences in the construction of films and the composition of shots based on structure of Navajo language, principles of behavior within the culture, and aspects of emphasis within the culture, such as the importance of walking, a theme which appears throughout the Navajo imagery. Earlier artistic conventions within a culture inform photography as well, influencing, for example, the style of early photographic portraits and landscapes (Berger, J., 1972). Mendelson (2004b) argued that Norman Rockwell's cover art for publications such as *Saturday Evening Post* influenced the way in which modern news photographers record moments for newspaper feature photographs. The way of seeing is dependent on the visual norms established within this culture.

Thus, individual differences, institutional conventions, and cultural norms affect both the content and composition of photographs, and, ultimately, the received meaning of an image. Photographs are as much a construction as are their verbal counterparts—they are not mere mechanical recordings.

The Subject

One of the important aspects of photographs, unlike other visual art forms, is that the subject exists or has existed. The fact that the subject was or is real lends photographs much of their power and meaning. While this existential reality of subjects has changed somewhat in the digital age, where content can be created and manipulated, for the most part this notion is still true. As Szarkowski (1966) stated, "The first thing that the photographer learned was that photography dealt with the actual. . . . The subject and the picture were not the same thing, although they would afterwards seem so" (p. 8).

The subject matter of a photograph can influence the photograph's content. Human subjects, for instance, are not necessarily passive before camera lens, there is a range of control that they have. People are unaware they are being photographed, are not in control of the situation, or are highly conscious of how they want to be portrayed and control this. The mere presence of a camera can cause people to change the way they present themselves. Goffman (1959) suggested that people are constantly thinking about self-presentation, trying to appear in ways that show them positively. Barthes (1981) noticed that he would adjust himself when he sat before a camera: "I instantaneously make another body for myself, I transform myself in advance into an image" (p. 10). Subjects have different motivations for being photographed. For example, celebrities desire publicity as well as control over their images, and elite celebrities have control over time, place, and style of the photographs (Mendelson, 2005). Another example is that in some cases Native American subjects chose the props and their dress, sometimes even those of other tribes, in order to create a desired look (Scherer, 1975).

The subject can also cue the photographer to aspects that are more worthy of being recorded. *National Geographic Magazi*ne photographer Jodi Cobb (personal communication, 2003) suggested that subjects often have their own agendas for being photographed. Many of Cobb's Saudi women subjects were interested in being photographed without the veil, something a Saudi photographer would not or could not do. Subjects can significantly change the look and meaning of a photograph when they have control of the photographic situation.

Previous experience with photographers can also affect how subjects act before a camera. An unusual example is the reaction of people with little or no exposure to photography. Carpenter (1975) recounted the reactions by tribesmen in New Guinea to their first exposure cameras. They were often confused by the process and the results, though they eventually were able to recognize themselves. Coles (1997) presented cases where subjects in Appalachia were tired of being treated as mere objects to be documented. Subjects are often aware of the stereotypical way they are presented. Such awareness can lead to resistance by posing in unexpected ways or refusing to be portrayed at all.

There are cultural differences that influence subjects, and in particular, their attitudes toward photography. Nir (1995) argued that being photographed was a new experience, often violating local norms, for natives of the Holy Land. Still, some subjects agreed to be photographed, even suggesting poses and locations, clearly co-operating with the photographers. In addition, people internalize ways of posing which are culturally determined. Byers (1966) cited the example of young girls quickly learning how to pose in gender appropriate ways based on parental cues or media exposure (see Milgram, 1977). Moreover, media play a role in communicating norms of how to act in front of camera, including where, when, and how to pose, especially in response to times of grief, disaster, and celebration (Kitch, 2005). Finally, posing before a camera often involves unconscious actions, as when many visitors smiled as they had their photograph taken at the site of the World Trade Center—an automatic response to the camera.

Photographer-Subject Interaction

The process of photography is interactive, as Newton (2001) stated, "In a photographic relationship, photographer and subject exchange and negotiate resources ranging from smiles to power" (p. 39). Central to this interaction is power, which S. Hall (1997) believed to be a dynamic process, constantly in negotiation. Many argue that the photographer will always have greater power over the subject and the final image (e.g., Beloff, 1983; Denzin, 1986), with Sontag (1977) referring to photography as a predatory act. Edwards (1992) argued that an understanding persists of power relations regarding race that existed in colonial contexts still persist today in understanding the meaning of photographs. Power is borne out in the way people pose before the camera, their appearances, and the labels ascribed to them. Because the final use of a photograph is usually outside the subject's control, ultimate power of representation does reside with the photographer and an institution (Milgram, 1977).

Nonetheless, the subject-photographer relationship varies from situation to situation. Newton (2001) presented a typology of photographic behavior between subject and photographer, ranging from what she referred to as "visual embrace" to "visual rape," representing a continuum of control, purposes, and interaction between the two entities. The interaction can certainly be altered through technology. Through the use of telephoto lenses, a subject may not even be aware of being photographed. In this case, the power lies totally with the photographer.

A subject is influenced not only by the power of the photographer, but also by the perceived power of the institution that the photographer represents. The clout of a national magazine such as *Time* or *Newsweek* or even a local paper can influence subjects to act differently than they might for an unaffiliated photographer or a family member.

Race, class, and gender (among other demographic variables) also affect the interaction of a subject with a photographer, and these factors have historically been linked to significant power imbalances. For example, *National Geographic* photographers have often been criticized for exhibiting dominance over Third World subjects in portraying them as exotic others. At the same time, race and gender offer different ways of seeing the world, and can open (or shut) doors to various subjects. For instance, *National Geographic* magazine photographer Jodi Cobb (personal communication, 2003) discussed how being a woman opened doors to subjects like Geisha and Saudi women, subjects that were not available to male photographers. Thus, the photographic act is a process of negotiation, rapport building, and the relationship between a photographer and subject. The amount of time and the way in which it is spent in relationship building affects the content and style of the photograph, and, ultimately, its meaning.

Fixer/Translator

Standing between photographer and subject are informants or fixers—individuals (or organizations) who assist a photographer in gaining access to subjects. This additional player adds another level of complexity and power to the interactive act of photography. Coles (1997) discussed how James Agee and Walker Evans, when documenting the effects of the Depression for their book *Let Us Now Praise Famous Men* were brought to sharecroppers' homes by their landlords. The subjects may have agreed to be photographed for fear of losing their land. Other examples of this intervening power brokerage might be a village elder asking tribe members to be photographed, or parents allowing children to be photographed.

Publicists of celebrities and politicians can both provide and deny access to their clients, affecting the conditions under which their clients are photographed. Planned political events limit the perspectives and content recordable by photographers. In wartime, the government can control photographers by setting access and censorship rules, limiting the content and exhibition of photographs (Mendelson & Smith, 1995; Moeller, 1989).

Fixers often serve as translators both of language and culture. They can direct photographers toward elements of the culture the fixer believes are significant and away from elements they would rather not stress.

The Context of Photographic Production

The last factor influencing the production of the photograph is the context of the photographic act, which Barrett (2000) referred to as the original context. The photographer and subject interact within a specific time and place (Edwards, 1992; Scherer, 1975; Tagg, 1988). Photographs can suggest a time period and also are informed by knowledge of a time period.

Stott (1973) analyzed the historical context that produced the Farm Security Administration photographs in the 1930s. He argued that a documentary mindset was part of the time. Numerous people sought to make vivid the experiences of those less fortunate in society in order to bring about change through photography, film, and also fiction and nonfiction writing.

Another example is the opening sequence of Leni Reifenstahl's Nazi propaganda film, *Triumph of the Will*, which revealed a plane descending through the clouds, then landing to deposit Hitler before throngs of adoring followers in Nuremburg. The choice of the plane was not just a heavenly symbol, but also a symbol suggesting Hitler's drive to advance Germany technologically. The airplane had served as a symbolic element of technology in his earlier campaign for the Presidency in 1932.

Another historical factor focuses on photographers' attitudes toward photography. For example, journalistic standards requiring that photographers not stage or set up any photograph have not always existed. Civil War photographers often moved bodies around to create more dramatic imagery. A body from the Battle of Gettysburg appears in at least two different Alexander Gardner photographs.

A photographer is limited by the photographic equipment and processes available in a certain time period. In the 1800s, improvements in chemistry, from the daguerreotype to the wet plate to the dry plate, allowed photographers to be more spontaneous in their shooting (Carlebach, 1992, 1997; Taft, 1938). The aesthetics and content of early photographs were highly driven by the technology of the day. Slow exposures, the need to prepare the photographic plates immediately before making the photograph, and processing the exposed plate immediately after exposure limited the range of subjects that could be recorded. Further, long exposures required stiff unnatural poses that prevented movement during exposure.

The invention of roll film and handheld cameras, such as the Kodak, put photography into the hands of many more people, expanding not only the content of photographs but also the look and style. No longer would photographers have to be wealthy and highly skilled or dependent on large, bulky equipment and dangerous, complicated chemical processes. No longer would subjects have to be willing to sit patiently before the camera (Jay, 1984). For the first time, candid photographs could be made with the subject unaware. The ability to photograph an unaware subject expanded further with the invention of lightweight cameras such as the Ermanox, Leica, and Nikon, starting in the 1920s and the invention of longer lenses. Photographs could be taken from great distances away, without any interaction with the subject, enhancing the voyeuristic nature of photography (Sontag, 1977).

Lighter weight cameras and small lenses allow photographers to be both physically and emotionally close to their subjects, capturing intimate moments that reveal positive and negative aspects of human existence. In the case of documentary photography, the intimacy created between subject and photographer crosses the line between reportage and advocacy, permitting the photographer to more clearly take a position for or against an issue. For example, small cameras and wide-angle lenses allow Donna Ferrato to document domestic violence from an often uncomfortably close quarter, revealing both the perpetrators and the victims.

More recently, digitization has provided new ways of creating visual media, in addition to more easily and seamlessly producing effects of analog photography, such as removing content, combining materials from other negatives, and changing the color of an image. Digitization allows the creation of content from scratch, requiring no negatives or referent to return to (Ritchin, 1999). Digital photographs no longer have a perceived existential connection to the "real world." Ritchin (1999) even argued that digital imagery represents a new medium (see also Wells, 2003).

Photographic Choices

A variety of conscious and unconscious choices of photographers, patrons, editors, subjects, informants, culture, and equipment affect the construction of photographs. At a basic level of meaning, the selected subject matter is given central importance. The subject has been deemed worthy of being recorded and observed. Further, the choice of one subject over another frames our understanding of an event. Thus, it is necessary to consider content that was *not* chosen for inclusion in the photograph (Fiske, 1990; Szarkowski, 1966; Trachtenberg, 1989; van Leeuwen, 2001).

Meaning is suggested by the relationships between and among these choices. Numerous studies have analyzed the patterns of subject matter, both in its presence and absence. For example, studies of advertisements demonstrate a reliance on a thin female body type, one that does not represent most women's bodies and that can lead to unrealistic body expectations. Goffman (1979) also argued that women are more often posed with expressions and gestures that emphasize the subjects' psychological detachment or childishness. Other studies show that African Americans are disproportionately absent, based on actual population size, in media content such as films and advertisements, and when they are portrayed, studies suggest it is often in stereotypical patterns as criminals, sidekicks, and buffoons (Bogle, 1997; Entman & Rojecki, 2000). Similar studies have shown limited and stereotyped portrayal of women in news photographs (Luebke, 1989) and conventional portrayals of politicians (Moriarty & Garramone, 1986) and athletes (Hagaman, 1993).

Although subject matter may be considered the most important part aspect a photograph, compositional choices also affect meaning. Compositional choices are, in essence, the adjectives of the nouns of subject matter. Three groups of compositional features will be discussed. A first group of compositional features focus on the vantage point of the photographer, including the choice of subject-camera distance, horizontal camera angle, and vertical camera angle (Messaris, 1994; Szarkowski, 1966). Varying these parameters through the physical position of the photographer or lens choice can affect perception of the subject matter. Camera-subject distance, for example, can range from extreme close-ups, that emphasize drama, intimacy, or threat, to an extreme long shot, where a vast area is included within the frame of the photograph. Horizontal camera angles range from a photograph taken straight on to one taken from the back of a subject. Here, a subject that is turned toward the camera appears more open to the viewers' understanding. Vertical camera angles range from a photograph taken from straight above (a birds-eye view), to eye level, looking straight at a subject, to a low-angle shot, looking up at the subject. Low camera angles make a subject look more powerful, while high camera angles make a subject look weak. The photographer can also alter whether the subject is seen parallel, perpendicular, or skewed in relation to the horizon: tilting the frame edge of a photograph creates more visual tension (Zettl, 1999).

The second group of features focuses on the formal features and graphic elements in the photograph. Photographers use graphics such as shapes, lines, and curves, to link objects in the frame and to create a sense of direction, orienting viewers and helping them decide where the action starts, how it progresses, and where it ends. The use of lines draws viewers toward the focal point of the picture. Moreover, the dominant use of vertical lines can suggest dignity, horizontal lines serenity, diagonal lines motion and depth, and curves grace and beauty (Fox & Kerns, 1961; Hoy, 1986; Kerns, 1980; Lewis, 1995).

Photographers also can frame a subject with an object in the foreground, alter the amount of subject matter in focus and compose their picture around shapes or patterns (Fox & Kerns, 1961; Kerns, 1980; Lewis, 1995). These compositional tools create visual interest through similarity and contrast, as well as creating unity and organization within a photograph. Patterns create emphasis and organization by building visual connections, while visual contrast can add tension and comparison (Clements & Rosenfeld, 1974; Dondis, 1973).

Light is also a graphic and symbolic compositional element in photographs. Light can be applied from a variety of directions and with different intensities. Such choices place emphasis on different aspects of a subject and produce different moods and meanings (Feinberg, 1970; Fox & Kerns, 1961; Keene, 1995; Kobre, 2004; Metallinos, 1996). Lighting can be used to build a sense of depth and texture (Berger, A. A., 1998; Zettl, 1999).

A third set of compositional features focus on the location of the center of interest within a frame. Instructional books on photography insist that the major subject of interest should never be in the center of the frame because a centered subject tends to be static and boring (Geraci, 1984; Hoy, 1986). A compositional guide to aid photographers is the "rule of thirds," where the frame is divided into three equal parts vertically and horizontally (Lewis, 1995). The rule says that subjects should be placed on one of the lines or at their junctions in order to create a more dynamic photograph (Kerns, 1980). Elements pushed to the bottom of the frame appear less powerful or smaller, while the opposite is true for elements pushed to the top.

Lastly, balance is a formal feature that focuses on the distribution of elements within the frame. There are two basic forms of balance: symmetrical and asymmetrical. Symmetrical balance is the arranging of elements in equal proportion around a center axis, which typically occurs when the subject is centered in the frame. Such formal organization tends to be seen as quiet and a bit boring. In contrast, asymmetrical balance occurs when elements of different visual weights are played off each other, creating a dynamic interaction (Arnheim, 1974; Clements & Rosenfeld, 1974; Dondis, 1973).

THE CONTEXT OF PRESENTATION

The time, place, manner, and culture in which the photograph is seen (as opposed to those in which it was produced) affect the meaning of all photographs (Barthes, 1981; Sekula, 1984), and context influences viewing, as "Today we see the art of the past as nobody saw it before. We actually perceive it in a different way" (Berger, J., 1972, p. 16). For example, in the mid- to late-19th-century, it was not uncommon for families to have photographs taken of children who died young. Since most people did not own cameras, it would be the only visual representation they would have. Today, a viewer would probably see these same images as shocking or revolting.

Krauss (1989) argued that the realm in which a photograph is seen creates a unique "discursive space" (p. 195), one that cues specific ideas within the viewer, but at the same time, limits ideas about other areas of knowledge. A mugshot viewed in a newspaper seldom raises questions of ethical or aesthetic importance, while the same image in an art gallery might.

Finnegan (2003) examined the various contexts in which Farm Security Administration photographs of the Great Depression appeared. She argued that each of these contexts in which these photographs circulated, including fine art magazines, social reform magazines, and general audience magazines, affected the possible interpretations of the photograph and thus the interpretations of the Great Depression. A variety of contexts made certain interpretations about poverty more available.

Another example is the rise of photographic stock agencies, which allows photographs taken for one purpose to be purchased later for uses in entirely different contexts. For example, a documentary photograph of a geisha originally appearing in a news magazine can be resold to promote a Japanese restaurant. The potential meaning of this single photograph is shifted when viewed in these different contexts. In the former case, the Geisha is a named individual, while in the latter, she is an anonymous symbol of Japanese authenticity.

The way a communication event is defined affects how a viewer will process and perceive it. A photograph presented as fictional or authentic, or as "art" or "news" will be interpreted differently, as Worth and Gross (1982) noted, "The assessment of an event as natural or symbolic determines whether we use an interpretive strategy which we shall call attribution, or an interpretative strategy which we shall call communicational inference" (p. 135). Emotional and cognitive responses to photographs vary depending on whether viewers thought they were news or fictional (Mendelson & Papacharissi, 2005).

Photographs are highly ambiguous, revealing many possible stories. Accompanying text passages can also serve to "anchor" or narrow the meanings perceivable in photographs (Barthes, 1977), directing readers to a preferred reading (Fiske, 1990; Hall, S., 1973), as "It is a very common practice for the captions to news photographs to tell us, in words, exactly how the subject's expression ought to be read" (Hall, S., 1973, p. 178). S. Hall (1973) discussed an example of the power of captions to shape a reader's interpretation of a news event, using the case of the resignation of a British politician. One paper labeled him as angry, while another referred to him as tragic. As he argued, "Here the caption selects and prefers one of the possible readings, then amplifies it" (p. 177). The photographer does not always choose the words that accompany and frame a photograph; captions are often rewritten by editors.

Texts can also serve to keep the subjects of a photograph at a distance by not providing a name. The subject becomes merely a symbol of a larger group. Edwards (1990) analyzed the prevalence of "type" photographs within anthropology and other scientific domains in the mid- to late-1800s. They were usually of anonymous individuals to show the essential qualities not of a person but of a racial or ethnic group. On the other hand, texts can provide a name, thus helping viewers to relate to the subject as a known individual. Likewise, the titling of a fine art photograph can shape the way it is perceived.

The layout of photographs on a newspaper page, including the placement, sizing, headlines, text, and captions creates different levels of emphasis for viewers, directing the eye to dwell longer on certain parts of the page. Layout can also create comparisons between photographs by, for example, juxtaposing on the same page before and after images. Multiple images can add together to form a larger meaning than could a single photograph. This is what Hicks (1952) called the "third effect" as he explained, "Under this principle, when two selected pictures are brought together, their individual effects are combined and enhanced by the reader's interpretative and evaluative reaction" (p. 34). The social documentary photographer Lewis Hine argued that it was a large volume of photographs of child labor, for example, that brought about social change.

The format of a photograph, including its size, shape, and whether it is color or black and white can affect how a subject is viewed. Black and white photographs are often used in journalism to demonstrate documentary authenticity (Grainge, 1999). In advertising, black and white images are used to represent products considered to be classic or high status. An example of the influence of size is photographer Andreas Gursky's massive prints (7′ × 11′) of highly detailed locations, such as the Tokyo Stock Exchange. These works speak quite differently when seen large in a gallery rather than as a reproduction in a book or magazine: Their power and meaning are greatly diminished in smaller formats.

THE INTERPRETATION OF THE PHOTOGRAPH

Until now, this chapter has focused on influences that occur in the production and presentation of the photograph. Yet the photograph and its context are only raw materials to be mined for meaning by a viewer. The photograph is necessary but not sufficient to understanding the received meaning, which exists in the mind of the viewer, as S. Hall (1997) stated, "There is no one, true meaning. Meaning 'floats.' It cannot be finally fixed" (p. 228). More specifically, meaning is not fixed until the viewer's background, experiences, and knowledge are taken into consideration. Like photographers, viewers are surrounded by layers of influence.

A photograph stands for the subject represented (the denotative level of meaning) and the higher level meanings associated with the subject matter (the connotative level of meaning; Barthes, 1967, 1972, 1977; Fiske, 1990). The meanings associated with different subjects and the way the subjects are photographed are both culturally and individually based.

The denotative meaning is based on object recognition, something people can do quite quickly. Even the gist of a photograph can be formed in a few hundred milliseconds (Biederman, Rabinowitz, Glass, & Stacey, 1974; Loftus, 1976; Mandler & Johnson, 1976; Rayner & Pollatsek, 1992), recognition is based on prior experience with, or knowledge of, the subject matter. While learning and recognizing subject matter is individually determined, it is important to remember that certain types of subjects circulate more frequently than others within a culture or geographic location.

Connotative meanings, however, transcend mere object recognition. These meanings are "the layer of broader concepts, ideas and values which the represented people, places and things stand for" (van Leeuwen, 2001, pp. 96–97; see also Barthes, 1967, 1972, 1977; Hall, S., 1973). Photographs signify because people draw from stored associated meanings based on prior experiences (Barthes, 1977; Berger, J., 1972). Culture influences the connotative meaning attached to a subject and being part of a culture means seeing the world in similar ways according to cultural myths and ideology (Barthes, 1972; Hall, S., 1997). These cultural ways of seeing obstruct the constructed nature of photographs, making certain meanings appear to be the only way to interpret a photograph, even the meanings of gestures, poses, and expressions are highly culture bound (Byers, 1966).

The connotative meanings are automatically, and often unconsciously, activated because of a close connection between denotative and connotative meanings through reinforcement. For instance, research on stereotypes shows that negative concepts of minorities are called up automatically when viewing a photograph and can affect future decision making (Devine, 1989; Fazio et al., 1995). To move beyond such automatic reactions requires critical thinking and cognitive effort.

Cultures also have different notions about the nature of photography. Different cultures believe that photographs reveal the true nature of a subject; that photographs are infallible (Trachtenberg, 1989; Wright, 1992). Such a cultural belief affects the extent to which viewers interpret photographs as subjective views of the world. As Tagg (2001) argued, placing the production of a photograph within a historical context is not enough: "We must historicise the spectator, or. . . we must also take care to specify to whom and under what conditions . . . images would appear 'realistic'" (p. 89).

While some aspects of visual processing are learned, others seem to be based solely on biological and developmental characteristics. Messaris (1994) outlined a series of processing factors that seem consistent across all adults. For example, the ability to recognize depth in and derive meaning from a two dimensional image seems to be part of our visual system and does not have to be learned. Many compositional features, such as camera angle and camera subject distance, are analogous to real-life physical circumstances. Perceiving a subject as weak because he or she was photographed from above is not a learned response, but innate to the way we visually process the world. Further, the effect of the perceived closeness of a subject to a viewer is analogously related to a viewer's sense of social distance (Hall, E., 1966).

Viewers' stages of physical and mental development also affect their understanding of photographs. For example, the ability to distinguish fiction from reality, and to identify the genre or purpose of a photograph changes as people age (Messaris, 1994; Messaris & Gross, 1977). Further, people also differ in their predisposition for processing visual and verbal material, and this affects their perceptions of photographs. A person's visual-learning orientation affects the amount of time he or she spends looking at visual messages, the amount he or she learns from them, and the perceptions of them (Mendelson, 2004a).

Although innate perceptual features of the viewer are important factors in creating meaning, differences in learning and experience also play a role. Learning facilitates an awareness of visual manipulation and an appreciation of an artist's skill (Barrett, 2000; Messaris, 1994). Viewers can learn to slow down the processing of photographs, moving from automatic processing to controlled processing. Knowledge of the production process affects how people understand images. This knowledge may include photographic techniques and conventions (Messaris, 1994), knowledge of the photographer (Barrett, 2000), and knowledge of the time, place, and subject matter. While such knowledge does not necessarily lead to "more correct" interpretations, it does lead to different, and perhaps more complex, interpretations. Based on acquired knowledge, people look for different aspects of photographs when interpreting and evaluating them (Barrett, 2000). For example, photojournalism students perceive photographs differently from non-photo students, making finer, more complex distinctions based on their experiences in visual storytelling (Mendelson & Ognianova, 1997). Sekula (1984), in discussing Stieglitz's *Equivalent* photographs, argued that viewers would have to be aware of the metaphoric nature of these images to be able "to invest the photograph with a meaning appropriate to Stieglitz's expectations" (p. 15). Experience with other images enhances meaning as well. Helmers and Hill (2004, p. 5) stated,

> One of the ways that images may communicate to us is through intertextuality, the recognition and referencing of images from one scene to another. If the reader is unaware of the precursors, the image will have a different meaning, or no meaning at all.

A specific case of intertextuality is referred to by B. Schwartz (1998) as "frame images," pictorial representations that organize understandings of present events "by aligning them with well-understood and affecting events of the past" (p. 6). Such knowledge of intertextuality operates at both at a cultural and individual level. Certain images, through their frequent circulation within a society, create a common visual language.

Thus, though the visual raw material is the same, differences in culture and individuality leads to seeing different meanings in photographs. The same factors influencing the way viewers process photographs also affect viewers when they become producers of or subjects in images. The factors that influence viewing seamlessly become the factors that influence producing and posing. In this way, the model becomes cyclical.

CONSTRUCTED PHOTOGRAPHIC MEANING

While it seems that meaning ultimately lies within the viewer, it is the end product of a cascade of events that began before the photograph was taken. These events are shaped by the psychology, culture, and innate perceptual tools influencing the photographer and the subject, the interaction between the photographer and subject, and the particular historical and viewing context. Thus, for any one viewer viewing a specific photograph in a specific context, the range of meaning is highly constrained. The limited range of meaning harkens back to Condit's (1989) argument on the limits of polysemy and S. Hall's (1993) emphasis on preferred ways of reading texts. It is difficult for a viewer to move outside these consecutive and overlapping constraints, and the meaning a person perceives in an image seems obvious and natural, therefore, additional cognitive effort is necessary to push beyond the initial way of seeing the photograph.

As a pedagogical device, the sociohistorical model of photographic meaning is useful for challenging students to think critically about visual texts. Students can investigate the cultural, sociological, institutional, historical, and psychological paths of influence and how alterations in these factors could affect meaning. Such analysis can then extend visual literacy and understanding into the realm of verbal literacy through written exposition on photography. Clearly, there is not one way to understand the meaning derived from a photograph; as the model depicts, photographs are complex and highly constructed products, influenced in their conception and perception by a host of interacting variables.

REFERENCES

Arnheim, R. (1974). *Art and visual perception: A psychology of the creative eye.* Berkeley, CA: University of California Press.

Barrett, T. (2000). *Criticizing photographs: An introduction to understanding images* (3rd ed.). Mountain View, CA: Mayfield Publishing Company.

Barthes, R. (1967). *Elements of semiology.* New York: The Noonday Press.

Barthes, R. (1972). *Mythologies.* New York: Hill and Wang.

Barthes, R. (1977). *Image—Music—Text.* New York: Hill and Wang.

Barthes, R. (1981). *Camera lucida: Reflections on photography.* New York: Hill and Wang.

Becker, H. S. (1983). *Art worlds.* Berkeley, CA: University of California Press.

Becker, H. S. (1985). Visual sociology, documentary photography, and photojournalism: It's (almost) all a matter of context. *Visual Sociology, 10*(1–2), 5–14.

Beloff, H. (1983). Social interaction in photographing. *Leonardo, 16*(3), 165–171.

Berger, A. A. (1998). *Seeing is believing: An introduction to visual communication.* Mountain View, CA: Mayfield Publishing Co.

Berger, J. (1972). *Ways of seeing.* London: BBC.

Berger, J., & Mohr, J. (1982). *Another way of telling.* New York: Vintage Books.

Biederman, I., Rabinowitz, J. C., Glass, A. L., & Stacey, E. W., Jr. (1974). On the information extracted from a glance at a scene. *Journal of Experimental Psychology, 103,* 597–600.

Bogle, D. (1997). *Toms, coons, mulattoes, mammies & bucks: An interpretative history of Blacks in American films.* New York: Continuum.

Bourdieu, P. (1990). *Photography: A middle-brow art.* Stanford, CA: Stanford University Press.

Byers, P. (1966). Cameras don't take pictures. *Columbia University Forum, 95*(1), 27–31.

Carlebach, M. L. (1992). *The origins of photojournalism in America.* Washington, DC: Smithsonian Institution Press.

Carlebach, M. L. (1997). *American photojournalism comes of age.* Washington, DC: Smithsonian Institution Press.

Carpenter, E. (1975). The tribal terror of self-awareness. In P. Hockings (Ed.), *Principles of visual anthropology* (pp. 451–461). The Hague, The Netherlands: Mouton Publishers.

Chalfen, R. (1987). *Snapshot versions of life.* Bowling Green, OH: Bowling Green State University Popular Press.

Clements, B., & Rosenfeld, D. (1974). *Photographic composition.* Englewood Cliffs, NJ: Prentice-Hall.

Coles, R. (1997). *Doing documentary work.* New York: Oxford University Press.

Condit, C. M. (1989). The rhetorical limits of polysemy. *Critical Studies in Mass Communication, 6*(2), 103–122.

Denzin, N. K. (1986). Reflections on the ethnographer's camera. *Current Perspectives in Social Theory, 7,* 105–123.

Devine, P. G. (1989). Stereotypes and prejudice: Their automatic and controlled components. *Journal of Personality and Social Psychology, 56*(1), 5–18.

Dondis, D. A. (1973). *A primer of visual literacy.* Cambridge, MA: The MIT Press.

Edwards, E. (1990). The image as anthropological document: Photographic "types:" The pursuit of method. *Visual Anthropology, 3,* 235–258.

Edwards, E. (1992). *Anthropology and photography, 1860–1920.* New Haven, CT: Yale University Press.

Entman, R. M., & Rojecki, A. (2000). *The Black image in the White mind.* Chicago: The University of Chicago Press.

Fazio, R. H., Jackson, J. R., Dunton, B. C., & Williams, C. J. (1995). Variability in automatic activation as an unobtrusive measure of racial attitudes: A bona fide pipeline. *Journal of Personality and Social Psychology, 69*(6), 1013–1027.

Feinberg, M. (1970). *Techniques of photojournalism.* New York: Wiley-Interscience.

Finnegan, C. A. (2003). *Picturing poverty: Print culture and FSA photographs.* Washington, DC: Smithsonian Books.

Fiske, J. (1990). *Introduction to communication studies.* London: Routledge.

Fox, R., & Kerns, R. (1961). *Creative news photography.* Ames, IA: Iowa State University Press.

Gans, H. J. (1979). *Deciding what's news: A study of CBS Evening News, NBC Nightly News, Newsweek and Time.* New York: Vintage Books.

Geraci, P. C. (1984). *Photojournalism: New images in visual communication.* Dubuque, IA: Kendall/Hunt Publishing Company.

Goffman, E. (1959). *The presentation of self in everyday life.* Garden City, NY: Doubleday.

Goffman, E. (1979). *Gender advertisements.* Cambridge, MA: Harvard University Press.

Goldberg, V. (1987). *Margaret Bourke-White: A biography.* Reading, MA: Addison-Wesley Publishing Company.

Grainge, P. (1999). Time's past in the present: Nostalgia and the black and white image. *Journal of American Studies, 33*(3), 383–392.

Hagaman, D. (1993, Fall). The joy of victory, the agony of defeat: Stereotypes in newspaper sports feature photographs. *Visual Sociology, 8,* 48–66.

Hagaman, D. (1996). *How I learned not to be a photojournalist.* Lexington, KY: The University of Kentucky Press.

Hall, E. (1966). *The hidden dimension.* Garden City, NY: Anchor Books.

Hall, S. (1973). The determinations of news photographs. In S. Cohen, & J. Young (Eds.), *The manufacture of news: Social problems, deviance, and the mass media* (pp. 176–190). London: Constable.

Hall, S. (1993). Encoding, decoding. In S. During (Ed.), *The cultural studies reader* (pp. 90–103). London: Routledge.

Hall, S. (1997). The spectacle of the 'other'. In S. Hall (Ed.), *Representation: Cultural representations and signifying practices* (pp. 223–279). London: Sage Publications.

Helmers, M., & Hill, C. A. (2004). Introduction. In C. A. Hill, & M. Helmers (Eds.), *Defining visual rhetorics* (pp. 1–24). Mahwah, NJ: Lawrence Erlbaum Associates.

Hicks, W. (1952). *Words and pictures: An introduction to photojournalism.* New York: Harper & Brothers.

Hoy, F. P. (1986). *Photojournalism: The visual approach.* Englewood Cliffs, NJ: Prentice-Hall.

Jay, B. (1984). The photographer as aggressor. In D. Featherstone (Ed.), *Observations: Essays on documentary photography* (pp. 7–24). Carmel, CA: The Friends of Photography.

Keene, M. (1995). *Practical photojournalism: A professional guide.* Boston: Focal Press.

Kerns, R. L. (1980). *Photojournalism: Photography with a purpose.* Englewood Cliffs, NJ: Prentice-Hall.

Kitch, C. (2005). *Pages from the past: History and history in American magazines.* Chapel Hill, NC: The University of North Carolina Press.

Kobre, K. (2004). *Photojournalism: The professional's approach.* Burlington, MA: Focal Press.

Krauss, R. (1989). Photography's discursive spaces. In R. Bolton (Ed.), *The contest of meaning: Critical histories of photography* (pp. 287–301). Cambridge, MA: The MIT Press.

Lesy, M. (2002). *Long time coming: A photographic portrait of America, 1935–1943.* New York: Norton.

Lewis, G. (1995). *Photojournalism: Content & technique.* Madison, WI: Brown & Benchmark.

Loftus, G. R. (1976). A framework for a theory of picture recognition. In R. A. Monty, & J. W. Senders (Eds.), *Eye movements and psychological processes* (pp. 499–513). Hillsdale, NJ: Lawrence Erlbaum Associates.

Luebke, B. F. (1989). Out of focus: Images of women and men in newspaper photographs. *Sex Roles, 20,* 121–133.

Lutz, C. A., & Collins, J. L. (1993). *Reading National Geographic.* Chicago: The University of Chicago Press.

Mandler, J. M., & Johnson, N. S. (1976). Some of the thousand words a picture is worth. *Journal of Experimental Psychology: Human Learning and Memory, 2,* 529–540.

Mendelson, A. L. (2004a). For whom is a picture worth a thousand words: Effects of the visualizing cognitive style and attention on processing of news photos. *Journal of Visual Literacy, 24*(1), 85–105.

Mendelson, A. L. (2004b). Slice-of-life moments as visual "truth": Norman Rockwell, feature photography, and American values in pictorial journalism. *Journalism History, 29*(4), 166–178.

Mendelson, A. L. (2005, May). *Image is everything: Celebrities, the paparazzi and the practice of journalism.* Paper presented at the International Communication Association annual conference, New York City.

Mendelson, A. L., & Ognianova, E. (1997, May). *Dimensions of picture judgment by photo- and non-photojournalism students: A reconciliation of the visual literacy debate.* Paper presented at the International Communication Association annual conference, Montreal, Canada.

Mendelson, A. L., & Papacharissi, Z. (2005, August). *Reality vs. fiction: How defined realness affects cognitive & emotional responses to photographs.* Paper presented to the Association for Education in Journalism and Mass Communication annual conference, San Antonio, Texas.

Mendelson, A. L., & Smith, C. Z. (1995). Part of the team: Life photographers and their symbiotic relationship with the military during World War II. *American Journalism, 12,* 276–289.

Mendelson, A. L., & Smith, C. Z. (in press). Visions of a new state: Israel as mythologized by Robert Capa. *Journalism Studies.*

Messaris, P. (1994). *Visual literacy: Image, mind, & reality.* Boulder, CO: Westview Press.

Messaris, P., & Gross, L. (1977). Interpretations of a photographic narrative by viewers in four age groups. *Studies in the Anthropology of Visual Communication, 4*(2), 99–111.

Metallinos, N. (1996). *Television aesthetics: Perceptual, cognitive, and compositional bases.* Hillsdale, NJ: Lawrence Erlbaum Associates.

Milgram, S. (1977). The image freezing machine. In S. Milgram (Ed.), *The individual in a social world: Essays and experiments* (pp. 339–350). Reading: MA: Addison-Wesley.

Moeller, S. D. (1989). *Shooting war: Photography and the American experience of combat.* New York: Basic Books.

Moriarty, S. E., & Garramone, G. M. (1986). A study of newsmagazine photographs of the 1984 Presidential campaign. *Journalism Quarterly, 63,* 728–734.

Morrisroe, P. (1995). *Mapplethorpe: A biography.* New York: Random House.

Neuman, W. R., Just, M. R., & Crigler, A. N. (1992). *Common knowledge: News and the construction of political meaning.* Chicago: The University of Chicago Press.

Newton, J. H. (2001). *The burden of visual truth: The role of photojournalism in mediating reality.* Mahwah, NJ: Lawrence Erlbaum Associates.

Nir, Y. (1985). Cultural predispositions in early photography: The case of the Holy Land. *Journal of Communication, 34,* 32–50.

Nir, Y. (1995). Photographic representation and social interaction: The case of the Holy Land. *History of Photography, 19*(3), 185–194.

Ohrn, K. B. (1977). What you see is what you get: Dorothea Lange and Ansel Adams at Manzanar. *Journalism History, 4*(1), 14–22, 32.

Rayner, K., & Pollatsek, A. (1992). Eye movements and scene perception. *Canadian Journal of Psychology, 46,* 342–376.

Ritchin, F. (1999). *In our own image: The coming revolution in photography.* New York: Aperture.

Rosenblum, B. (1978). Style as social process. *American Sociological Review, 43,* 422–438.

Scherer, J. C. (1975). You can't believe your eyes: Inaccuracies in photographs of North American Indians. *Studies in the Anthropology of Visual Communication, 2*(2), 67–79.

Scherer, J. C. (1992). The photographic document: Photographs as primary data in anthropological enquiry. In E. Edwards (Ed.), *Anthropology and photography, 1860–1920* (pp. 32–41). New Haven, CT: Yale University Press.

Schwartz, B. (1998). Frame images: Towards a semiotics of collective memory. *Semiotica, 121*(1/2), 1–40.

Schwartz, D. (1999). Objective representation: Photographs as facts. In B. Brennen, & H. Hardt (Eds.), *Picturing the past: Media, history, and photography* (pp. 158–181). Urbana, IL: University of Illinois Press.

Sekula, A. (1984). *Photography against the grain: Essays and photo works 1973–1983.* Halifax, Nova Scotia: The Press of the Nova Scotia College of Art and Design.

Shoemaker, P. J. (1991). *Gatekeeping.* Newbury Park, CA: Sage Publications.

Shoemaker, P. J., & Reese, S. D. (1996). *Mediating the message: Theories of influences on mass media content.* White Plains, NY: Longman.

Sontag, S. (1977). *On photography.* New York: Farrar, Straus, and Giroux.

Stott, W. (1973). *Documentary expression and Thirties America.* Chicago: The University of Chicago Press.

Szarkowski, J. (1966). *The photographer's eye.* New York: The Museum of Modern Art.

Taft, R. (1938). *Photography and the American scene.* New York: Dover Publications.

Tagg, J. (1988). *The burden of representation: Essays on photographies and histories.* Amherst, MA: The University of Massachusetts Press.

Tagg, J. (2001). The currency of the photograph (1978). In M. Alvarado, E. Buscombe, & R. Collins (Eds.), *Representation and photography: A screen education reader* (pp. 87–118). New York: Palgrave.

Trachtenberg, A. (1989). *Reading American photographs: Images as history, Mathew Brady to Walker Evans.* New York: Hill and Wang.

van Leeuwen, T. (2001). Semiotics and iconography. In T. van Leeuwen, & C. Jewitt (Eds.), *Handbook of visual analysis* (pp. 92–118). London: Sage Publications.

Wells, L. (2003). *The photography reader.* London: Routledge.

Whelan, R. (1985). *Robert Capa: A biography.* New York: Knopf.

Worth, S., & Adair, J. (1997). *Through Navajo eyes: An exploration in film, communication and anthropology.* Albuquerque, NM: University of New Mexico Press.

Worth, S., & Gross, L. (1982). Symbolic strategies. In L. Gross (Ed.), *Studying visual communication* (pp. 134–147). Philadelphia: University of Pennsylvania Press.

Wright, T. (1992). Photography: Theories of realism and convention. In E. Edwards (Ed.), *Anthropology and photography, 1860–1920* (pp. 18–31). New Haven, CT: Yale University Press.

Zettl, H. (1999). *Sight, sound, motion: Applied media aesthetics.* Belmont, CA: Wadsworth.

• 5 •

CONSTRUCTING, PERFORMING, AND READING REPRESENTATIONS OF YOUTH AND CHILDHOOD

S.E. *Woodson*
ARIZONA STATE UNIVERSITY

> "You have told me stories," Jerold complained. "It isn't the same thing as information."
>
> "Oh, but it is," the cat said, "If you know how to listen."
>
> —Jane Yolen

There is a key similarity shared between children's theater practitioners and literacy specialists: an elemental belief in the power of story. Both fields acknowledge that humans live inside networks of stories, stories we tell ourselves, stories we tell others, and stories we are told. Stories hold power. Stories help us structure our lives and solve problems; they highlight some virtues over others, suggesting general models for how "the good life is to be conducted" (Fleischacker 1994, pp. 72–73). In the end, these narrative nests provide us with an architecture of how to be human, to practice power, and to develop individuality. Both fields also are engaged in exploring the boundaries of story—how stories are created, communicated, understood, decoded, contextualized, or decontextualized—exposing the master narratives hidden deep within them and investigating how stories can contribute to the creation of a more just and equitable society. This is a process that that both fields label as "literacy" and in particular "critical literacy." There are key differences between the fields of children's theater and literacy education, however, that can illuminate theoretical paradigms, suggesting blind spots within both fields as well as directions for future research. In this essay, I explore this divergence with an eye toward presenting key performance concepts that can contribute to the circulation of research and discussion on critical literacy traditions. In particular, I explore the construction of childhood as a performative process coconstructed by both adults and children.

The children's theater and educational drama field is not a monolithic entity but rather a diverse group of practices and traditions that can be generally categorized along questions of who, what, where, when, and how. Who is the intended audience? Who are the artist/producers? Who funds the production, and who pays for the tickets? What is produced? Asking where performance occurs is perhaps a misleading question. More apropos is asking where theater does not occur. "When" relates deeply to contextual questions as to the function of art in cultural and society. Finally, "how" ranges across culture and performance traditions incorporating the improvisational performance of everyday living, oral storytelling, and traditional dance theater, fully produced realistic theater, and multimedia performance collage. What these diverse practices share are a common set of theoretical beliefs as outlined by Grady (2003):

1. A belief in the efficacy of artistic engagement
2. Faith in the productivity of production
3. A solemn regard for reflection (p. 68)

Although Grady was writing about only one type of theater practice, these three iterations effectively capture effective practices within the field.

CONSTRUCTING AND PERFORMING CHILDHOOD

Childhood is not a universal. Unlike gender or race, childhood is a temporary and temporal classification; however, it can be understood in much the same manner—as sets of power relationships revolving around different axes. Humans, indeed most species, must necessarily experience biological immaturity, but childhood is the manner in which a society understands and expresses that physical reality. Viewed in this light, the child becomes a metaphor—a pattern of meaning—and childhood can be conceived of as "culturally specific sets of ideas and philosophies, attitudes and practices"

(James & Prout, 1990, p. 1). Such an approach decenters traditional "common-sense" reasoning that naturalizes children, and "indicates that the child . . . is made present through a variety of forms of discourse" (Jenks, 1996, p. 32).

As a scholar, an artist, and an educator, I have been studying childhood and the social performance of childhood for many years. And childhood is a contested site. For one, childhood is intimately associated with the family and conceptualizations of "family" have been undergoing polemical politicization. This is not a recent phenomenon however carried out by the religious right or advocates of gay marriage. Throughout the 18th century, dominant thought concerning the family, and therefore children, altered connected at a deep level to the "more general revolt against tyranny and patriarchy . . . closely linked to political developments and [Enlightenment] thought" (Reinier, 1996, p. 2). Stone (1977) labeled this evolution of thought in the 18th century the rise of "affective individualism." As a contested site, childhood exposes the tensions between ideologies of liberalism—focused on promoting individual rights—and that of communitarianism, or the belief that individual rights are not privileged to the good.

Postmodern studies of the child and of childhood acknowledge that children themselves participate in defining their own stories—constructing a place within their cultural spheres. Children have and practice agency. They are not empty vessels (tabula rasa) waiting to filled by adult knowledge. Corsaro (1997) reminded us, "Children are active, creative social agents who produce their own unique children's cultures while simultaneously contributing to the production of adult societies" (p. 4). In a process he called "interpretive reproduction," Corsaro pointed out, "Children do not simply imitate or internalize the world around them. They strive to interpret or make sense of their culture and to participate in it. In attempting to make sense of the adult world, children come to collectively produce their own peer worlds and cultures" (p. 24). Childhood is the rock and the hard place that requires a constant negotiation between freedom and necessity. This is an important theoretical framework for the practice of theater for youth and educational drama practitioners, as well as literacy scholars and educators.

SHARED PERSPECTIVES IN THEATER STUDIES AND LITERACY EDUCATION

While there is some scholarly debate about the value of classifying (or expanding or contracting) particular terms, for the purposes of this essay, these terms—*critical pedagogy, literacy,* and *critical literacy*—are examined with regard to the meaningful intersections between theater studies and literacy studies. Building off of the work of Freire (1970) and Boal (1979), critical pedagogy is a dialogical philosophy of education rooted in the everyday experiences of the participants which simultaneously develops literacy skills and critical consciousness or the ability and willingness to question political, social, and cultural hegemonic practices. Freire and his later advocates, Giroux (1981, 1983) and McLaren (1998), promoted a practice that positions the teacher as colearner rather than depending on what Freire called the "banking" method of education, or the teacher as all knowing depositing information into a blank mind. A focus on critical pedagogy spotlights power relations, "making power a central category of . . . analysis" (Gore, 1993, p. 3). Feminist poststructuralists have further extended the exploration of power relationships into the term *critical* itself, exposing universalizing tendencies based on enlightenment patterns of stable knowledge domains and colonial practices (Ellsworth, 1989; Lather, 1992).

Proponents of critical literacy acknowledge that teaching and learning are not value neutral, but rather that schools and educational environments are ideological spaces framed by large-scale ideological discourses. Critical literacy builds on critical pedagogy to explore the power structures embedded in media texts. Critical literacy promotes analytical thinking habits exploring both the social contexts and subject matter of any text with an eye toward discovering deeper meanings. In addition, critical literacy should build skills in applying the insights gathered to one's own personal or social situation. It is not enough merely to acknowledge injustice or to recognize hegemonic practices. Building bridges, between and around communities, individuals, stories, texts, and performances, framing values, and acknowledging hidden power flow is the task of critical literacy. As Freire (1970) stated, critical pedagogy "makes oppression and its causes objects of reflection by the oppressed, and from that reflection will come their necessary engagement in the struggle for their liberation" (p. 33).

Literacy has been undergoing revision related to the exponential expansion of communication technologies (Luke & Elkins, 1998, p. 4). Literacy educators have called for an expansion of the theoretical conception of literacy to address and to incorporate the multiple communicative and electronic modalities people use on a day-to-day basis (Alverman, Moon, & Hagood, 1999; Hobbs, 1997). As a result, the concept of literacy has been not only expanded but also adopted (co-opted) by various fields concerned with how people construct meaning, interpret, critically analyze, and create texts of various kinds. Hobbs (1997) wrote,

> Scholars and educators are coming to recognize that literacy is not simply a matter of acquiring de-contextualized decoding, comprehension and production skills, but that the concept of literacy must be connected with the culture and the contexts in which reading and writing are used. (p. 7)

Some of the common expansions of "literacy" include visual literacy, media literacy, critical literacy, information literacy, and technology literacy. Other contributors to this volume examine the ways in which the concept of literacy has been applied to better understand the meaning-making process of symbolic forms including photographs, films, popular culture, and the Internet.

These diverse understandings of literacy—regardless of the media forms upon which they focus—share two analytic concepts:

1. Structuring systems anchored in reading, interpreting/evaluating, and sometimes creating texts
2. Structures concerned with the texts' intentional and unintentional relationships to representation and authenticity

For example, Pailliotet, Semali, Rodenberg, Giles, and Macaul (2000) posited an intermedial theory of literacy briefly surveying relevant research in order to explore similarities across media and build fluid tactics anchored in reading processes. "Whether reading a book, watching a TV program, or constructing a Web site, readers and viewers interact with levels of information to construct meanings through dynamic processes" (Pailliotet et al., 2000, p. 209). Other scholars focus on audience and audience reception (based on poststructuralist understandings of meaning as being constructed by the reader) and concepts of popular culture and its relationship to the everyday lives of students (Alvermann & Hagood, 2000). The tight relationship between readers, texts, and contexts creates what Paul (2000) called "cultural synchronization," or the alignment and power flow between school cultures, the learning cultures of particular individuals, and students' home or environmental cultures. She pointed out that when media literacy educators acknowledge and celebrate the real-life experiences of students, the learning experience can then build on students' cultural capital rather than teacher-structured positionality.

Similarly, theater and drama educators share a fascination with meaning making, context, the real and the authentic, and creating moments that activate rather than lull. This can be seen at all levels and in all general forms of theater and drama from actor training to aesthetic structures designed to dialogically engage reality with the hyperreality of the stage, such as Brecht. The structuring systems of theater and performance are however based not on the conceptual organization of *reading* with all that implies, but rather on *performance.*

PERFORMANCE AS CULTURAL ACTIVITY

The concept of performance has enormous value to literacy educators who are seeking to understand the relationship between childhood, culture, literacy, drama, and education. The term has been almost unilaterally co-opted to describe metaphorically nontheatrical manifestations of social interaction. Carlson (1996) described performance and performativity as "ubiquitous tropes" which "owe allegiance to no particular field or discipline" (p. 193). Theater and performance studies are indebted however to the many diverse disciplines, which developed performance as both metaphor and analytic tool—in particular, cultural studies which theoretically decentered as objects "text," "identity," "play," and "performer" and reconceptualized them as complex products and processes of cultural interplay. Culture, here, can be considered a type of code necessary to the understanding of practically everything else. Consider Goldbard's (2005) poetic definition of *culture:*

> Culture is the sum-total of human creativity and invention: Language, signs and symbols, systems of belief, customs, clothes, cooking, tools, toys and adornments, everything we build and everything we use to fill it up—and by the way, art.

It is important, however, to differentiate between understandings of culture as textual—or clusters of phenomena to be read or interpreted—and understandings of culture as something that are performed, created, and by extension, consumed. "Only middle-class academics could blithely assume that all the world is a text because texts and reading are central to their life-world, and occupational security" (Conquergood, as cited in Taylor, D., 2003, p. 27).

A primary difference in these two interpretations concerns agency. Only the second conceptualization of culture positions people as active cultural agents *situated communally.* Even reader-response theories and poststructuralist conceptualizations of subject-positionality construct first with language positing that meaning is made internally by a reader in context. Reading is generally described in ways that generally position texts as static and readers as fundamentally separate from those texts. Writing in the *Complexity of Connection*, Jordan and Walker (2004) pointed out that the metaphor of a singular, autonomous self grounds many core Western beliefs including social, psychological, and economic systems. "Our Western psychologies focus on individual personality traits, movement toward autonomy, independence, success accomplished through competitive achievement" (Jordan & Walker, 2004, p. 2). Western educative and assessment systems too often highlight competency defined by competitiveness, winning, or being the best. Writing about constructivist developmental psychology, Corsaro (1997) articulated, "Even when others (parents, peers, and teachers) are taken into account, the focus remains on the effects of various interpersonal experiences on individual development" (p. 17).

As a structuring frame, reading also posits a fundamentally disembodied perceiver building on Enlightenment patterns of rationalist thought. A related difference can be found in how one understands the "real." In a textual interpretation of culture, one starts first with discourse which can be peeled away to reveal deep layers of fundamental core "truth." But culture understood broadly as performance places "truth" squarely in public acts negotiated and embodied. Goffman (1959), for example, noted, "A 'performance' may be defined as all the activity of a given participant on a given occasion which serves to influence in any way any of the other participants" (p. 15). This broad definition opens out modernistic understandings of behavior as outward manifestations of inward realities and turns behavior onto its head. "The theater of performances is not in people's heads, it is in their public acts. People encounter each other's minds only by interacting, the quality and character of these interactions comes to constitute the consequential reality of everyday life" (Brissett & Edgley, 1990, p. 37).

Performance can be understood on multiple and sometimes competing planes. Diamond (1996) succinctly pointed out, "Performance is always a doing and a thing done" (p. 1). In other words, performance exists both at the point of the act (present in time, framed, located in specific space, and observed) and in the complete event (finished, ephemeral, located in memory). Bauman (1989) wrote that performance exists in the execution of an action in dialogic tension with a mental ideal, potentiality, or memory of that action. In both understandings, performance locates a type of doubled consciousness in which there exists both the awareness of the phenomena and the "memory" of an ideal toward which the action points. Performance, unlike text, appears and disappears to be replaced by memory and drawn from memory. And since, individuals construct reality differently, performance highlights the slippages between the real and the perceived.

CONSTRUCTIONS OF CHILDHOOD IN PERFORMANCE

An example will illustrate how childhood is constructed and performed within one of the most omnipresent children's theater (and television) events, *Annie.* Based on the 1920s comic strip, the musical *Little Orphan Annie* (Meehan, 1977) opened on Broadway in April 1977 and played for well over 2,300 performances. *Annie* can be considered a ubiquitous representation of American childhood with over 400 different productions around the United States each year. The success of *Annie* also inspired a recent and somewhat unsuccessful Broadway revival (and associated tour), a beautifully illustrated children's book, the 1982 movie produced by Columbia, and the rather lackluster 1999 Disney version shown on television (to 26 million viewers) and then marketed straight to video, as well as ongoing attempt to mount *Annie 2* on Broadway. Frankly, the only things missing from this list are campy, plastic, redheaded, "Tomorrow" singing dolls and a Saturday morning cartoon. There are however, Annie lunch boxes, Halloween costumes, jewelry, and china all available for purchase on eBay. Annie the character, *Annie* the performance circulates between both the material goods associated with her presentation, the songs, and lyrics of the play, and the live/virtual performances themselves.

In fact, *Annie* cannot be considered a "text" as such but rather a fluid, performative event deeply representative of U.S. nostalgia for idyllic childhoods and visions of uncomplicated goodness. Performance theorist Taylor (2003) noted, "Instead of focusing on patterns of cultural expression in terms of texts and narratives, we might think about them as scenarios that do not reduce gestures and embodied practices to narrative descriptions" (p. 16). Annie functions as a scenario of childhood—what Taylor spoke of as belonging to a cultural repertoire.

The irony embedded in this representation of childhood is that it is not about children, but rather *Annie* is about adults. One of the first questions that undergraduates explore in learning to analyze drama is, to whom does the play belong? The traditional, tried and true answer to this question is that the play belongs to the character who struggles to overcome some obstacle or conflict and who changes from the beginning of the play to the end. While she does struggle to overcome, Annie does not change. From the beginning of the play, she is portrayed as virtuous and loving, incorruptible in horrific circumstances—this is important. Like the title character from Charles Dicken's *Oliver Twist* and in the style of Horatio Alger's *Raggedy Dick*, Annie's power is to transform the adults around her through her innate virtue, ultimately even rescuing the nation. Like a pint-sized messiah, Annie functions to save the soul of Oliver Warbucks. The play rightfully belongs to him. Warbucks embodies power, money, and the "American dream." A billionaire, Warbucks essentially represents the self-made man under a liberal, Enlightenment framework. The man lives for his job and the market economy spending his time in the public/civic sector even when he is "at home." Although he has plenty of money, he has no one to share it with and he belongs to no one. Although Annie is the obvious orphan, Warbucks is also orphaned and disconnected from the greater community of belonging. His individual fate is mirrored at the national level as the United States suffers through the Great Depression disconnected and tormented. The play features an entire scene and song set in a shantytown—a Hooverville—that highlights the uncertainty of everyday life during the Depression. Played out against a background of hunger and homelessness, Annie's transformative innocence focuses on the power of hope. Annie's song "Tomorrow," reprised twice, makes her innocent and incorruptible virtue clear. And it is this virtue which ultimately transforms Warbucks and the nation. In the play, she sings "Tomorrow" for a discouraged and depressed Franklin D. Roosevelt and his entire cabinet, inspiring them to institute the New Deal. In the movie version, the cabinet is replaced by Eleanor Roosevelt and a private dinner, moving the scene from the civic to the domestic, but the outcome remains the same. As Roosevelt said in the play, "No, thank *you,* Annie. You're the kind of person a President should have around him" (Act II, Scene 3, p. 17).

Why does Annie's innocence have so much power? The question of how or why Annie remains a virtuous person never arises since she is not really a complex character, but rather the embodiment of an ideal. Annie's goodness stems from earlier scenarios of childhood building on Romantic constructions of children as closer to nature, to God, and to the ideal. Under Romanticism, children held within themselves the seeds of virtue that needed only to be nurtured. Adults, however, were corrupt and had forgotten the most important elements of living. Adults must return to the state of childhood to relearn and reinvigorate communion with the natural, unspoiled world. Literary expression of this ideal is common among 19th-century authors, for example in the works of American essayist, Ralph Waldo Emerson (1803–1882) and British poet, William Wordsworth (1770–1850). For example, Wordsworth's 1807 poem, "My Heart Leaps Up" connects wonder and joy in nature and natural phenomena to childhood:

> My heart leaps up when I behold
>   A rainbow in the sky:
> So was it when my life began;
> So is it now I am a man;
> So be it when I shall grow old,
>   Or let me die!
> The Child is father of the Man;
> And I could wish my days to be
> Bound each to each by natural piety.

The belief that children are, by their very nature, moral creatures with "natural piety" answers liberalist predicaments stated clearly by George Will when he claimed that statecraft is inevitably soul craft, or Solzhenitsyn's critique of Western society, in which he pointed out that we cannot ignore the relationship between political and moral virtue because a state is ultimately judged by the kind of people it produces. Annie relieves that anxiety. Not only does she exhibit "natural piety," but through her example, her innocence, and her representation of family, she "saves" Warbucks. Oliver Warbucks sees everything as a commodity (he hangs the Mona Lisa in his bathroom) and understands all human relationships using a model of exchange with a single purpose, the pursuit of possessions. But Annie transforms Oliver Warbucks into *Daddy* Warbucks, repositioning him as situated in community, in family, in morality. Daddy Warbucks is not simply the sum of his desires then, as is Oliver Warbucks. Annie, then, answers the hyper-capitalist, postmodern condition by providing roots and a reemphasis on tradition. *Annie* comes down strongly on the side of love and sociability predicated on the performance repertoire of childhood as morally incorruptible—innocent—and intrinsically pious. But Annie is not a complex character, she is an adult fantasy relieving adult anxieties.

This performed scenario also reveals complex nostalgia circulating at multiple levels of personal and social memory. As Blau (1987) pointed out, "The bottomless source of the future is the inexhaustible past . . . [and] the only real paradise is the paradise that is lost" (p. 140). Psychologists have long known that individuals reconstruct memory in such a way as to feel better about themselves. One's childhood is no exception.

My personal experience bears witness to this: I never really thought—clearly and viscerally—of my own childhood until I had a child myself. Whether those memories were brought to the surface because the experiences vibrated in tune with my daughters' or because "all beginnings contain an element of recollection" (Connerton, 1989, p. 6) remains unimportant. My stories frame and practice control over my children's stories. And so we come back to silences and stories, stories we tell ourselves about ourselves—stories we perform for and into our children.

Performance is not only an interpretive grid or theoretical framework. Performance is also an embodied, collaborative way of knowing. From Plato and Aristotle on, Western philosophers have acknowledged theater's innate capacity to teach but even beyond that, performance exists as epistemology. Performance as a paradigm operates on multiple levels everyday in every individual's life experiences, from the primarily physical to mental and psychological patterns of memory and imagination. As Taylor (2003) stated, "Cultural memory is, among other things, a practice, an act of imagination and interconnection" (p. 82). To conceptualize *Annie* as performance—rather than text—is to understand that Annie the character exists as a master scenario both reflecting and constituting (reenacting) the lived experience of young people, particularly of young girls. Performance fundamentally is the mode through which we are incorporated into social, familial, and cultural life as well as being the mode through which we resist that inculcation. The performing arts construct polymodal experiences in which participants can struggle with the contradictions and ambiguities of life. Bodies, relationships, space, shape, force, time, light, shadow, symbol, color, contiguity, rhythm, narrative, are all modes through which performance communicates embodied practice. The performance of childhood locates children in multiple and often conflicting social and political spaces. Performed childhood, particularly in the US, is full of contradictions and paradoxical representations of children: Children are emotionally priceless, yet economically worthless; children locate both potential and peril; children are seductive, yet innocent; children must be protected from the market economy, yet they are marketable goods. Children are our angels; children are our demons.

REFERENCES

Alvermann, D. E., Moon, J. S., & Hagood, M. C. (1999). *Popular culture in the classroom: Teaching and researching critical media literacy.* Newark, DE: International Reading Association.

Alvermann, D. E., & Hagood, M. C. (2000). Critical media literacy: research, theory, and practice in new times. *Journal of Educational Research, 93*(3), 193–205.

Bauman, R. (1989). Performance. In E. Barnouw (Ed.), *International encyclopedia of communications.* Oxford, U.K.: Oxford University Press.

Blau, H. (1987). *The eye of the prey: Subversions of the postmodern.* Bloomington, IN: Indiana University Press.

Boal, A. (1979). *Theater of the oppressed.* New York: Theater Communications Group.

Brissett, D., & Edgley, C. (1990). The dramaturgical perspective. In D. Brissett, & C. Edgley (Eds.), *Life as theater, a dramaturgical sourcebook* (2nd ed., pp. 329–343). New York: Aldine de Gruyter.

Carlson, M. (1996). *Performance: A critical introduction.* New York: Routledge.

Connerton, P. (1989). *How societies remember.* New York: Cambridge University Press.

Corsaro, W. A. (1997). *The sociology of childhood.* Thousand Oaks, CA: Pine Forge Press.

Diamond, E. (1996). Introduction. In E. Diamond (Ed.), *Performance and cultural politics* (pp. 1–14). New York: Routledge.

Ellsworth, E. (1989). Why doesn't this feel empowering? Working through the repressive myths of critical pedagogy. *Harvard Educational Review, 59,* 297–324.

Emerson, R. W. (1983). *Essays and lectures: Nature.* New York: Penguin Classics. (Original work published in 1836)

Fleischacker, S. (1994). *The ethics of culture.* Ithaca, NY: Cornell University Press.

Freire, P. (1970). *Pedagogy of the oppressed.* New York: Continuum.

Giroux, H. (1981). *Ideology, Culture, and the Process of Schooling.* Philadelphia, Pa. : Temple University Press.

———. (1983). *Theory and resistance in education.* South Hadley, MA: Bergin & Garvey.

Goffman, E. (1959). *The presentation of self in everyday life.* New York: Doubleday.

Goldbard, A. (2005). The story revolution: How telling our stories transforms the world. *Community Arts Network.* Retrieved January 10, 2005, from http://www.communityarts.net/readingroom/archivefiles/2005/01/the_story_revol.php

Gore, J. (1993). *The struggle over pedagogies: Critical and feminist discourses as regimes of truth.* New York: Routledge.

Grady, S. (2003). Accidental Marxists?: The challenge of critical and feminist pedagogies for the practice of applied drama. *Youth Theater Journal, 17,* 65–81.

Hobbs, R. (1997). Literacy for the information age. In J. Flood, S. B. Heath, & D. Lapp (Eds.), *Handbook of research on teaching literacy through the communicative and visual arts* (pp. 7–14). New York: Simon & Schuster-Macmillan.

James, A., & Prout, A. (Eds.). (1990). *Constructing and reconstructing childhood: Contemporary issues in the sociological study of childhood.* London: Falmer Press.

Jenks, C. (1996). *Childhood.* New York: Routledge.

Jordan, J. V., & Walker, M. (2004). Introduction. In J. Jordan, M. Walker, & L. Hartling (Eds.), *The complexity of connection: Writings from the Stone Center's Jean Baker Miller training institute* (pp. 1–8). New York: The Guilford Press.

Lather, P. (1992). Post-critical pedagogies: A feminist reading. In K. Weiler (Ed.), *Feminist engagements: Reading, resisting, and revisioning male theories in education and cultural studies* (pp. 120–1370). New York: Routledge.

Luke, A., & Elkins, J. (1998). Reinventing literacy in new times. *Journal of Adolescent and Adult Literacy, 42,* 4–7.

McLaren, P. (1998). Revolutionary pedagogy in post-revolutionary times: Rethinking the political economy of critical education. *Educational Theory, 48*(4), 431–462.

Meehan, T. (1977). *Annie.* New York: Music Theater International.

Pailliotet, A., Semali, L., Rodenberg, R. K., Giles, J. K., & Macaul, S. L. (2000). Intermediality: Bridge to critical media literacy. *The Reading Teacher, 54,* 208–219.

Paul, D. G. (2000). Rap and orality: Critical media literacy, pedagogy, and cultural synchronization. *Journal of Adolescent and Adult Literacy, 44,* 246–251.

Reinier, J. S. (1996). *From virtue to character: American childhood, 1775–1850.* New York: Twayne-Macmillan.

Stone, L. (1977). *The family, sex and marriage in England 1500–1800.* New York: Weidenfeld & Nicolson.

Solzhenitsyn, A. I. (1976). *Warning to the West.* New York: Farrar, Straus and Giroux.

Taylor, D. (2003). *The archive and the repertoire: Performing cultural memory in the Americas.* Durham, NC: Duke University Press.

Will, G. F. (1983). *Statecraft as soulcraft : What government does.* New York: Simon and Schuster.

6

THE DEVELOPMENT OF MEDIA EDUCATION IN ENGLAND: A PERSONAL VIEW

Cary Bazalgette

RESEARCHER AND CONSULTANT ON MEDIA LITERACY

Many media educators (including myself) have made brave assertions about the cultural and social significance of nonprint media, claiming that they should be valued as highly as books. Nevertheless, histories of media education can primarily be found in books constructed through references to other books. Paper-based print retains its preeminence as the trusted medium of historical record, not so much because it offers some mysterious guarantee of truth, but because the systems of access and cross-reference that have been developed for print are still far more sophisticated, and more widely understood, than anything yet devised for moving image, audio, or online media. Books also carry the feature of being more permanent than electronic media forms.

So here you are with a book in your hands, expecting to find out about the development of media education in England. You are, I hope, familiar with the concept "that historical 'truth' is not unitary or one-dimensional, and that we must settle for, at best, honest representations, and for most of the time, simple representations which will need to be interpreted in relation to the interests of their sources" (Masterman, 1985, p. 257). The way that media education has developed as a subject has already been covered by others (Alvarado, Gutch, & Wollen, 1987; Alvarado & Boyd-Barrett, 1992; Buckingham, 2003), but the story I have to tell comes from my personal experience of interventions, encounters, and constant struggles. I am not an academic, and much of what I say is unverifiable, but it is, I hope, as honest as I can make it.

As someone who has worked for 26 years in one cultural institution, I can be guaranteed to represent a particular perspective; whose "interests" I may be said to represent may be a little more complicated. The British Film Institute (BFI) was founded in 1933 and has been funded by the British taxpayer through various government departments as a "nondepartmental public body"—that is, at arms' length from the government, largely responsible for its own policies, and, of course, nonprofit. The first BFI Education Officer was appointed in 1950, and the status, number, and location of its education staff have always fluctuated through sometimes-dramatic crises. For at least the first 15 years of my time at the BFI, no one at senior level seemed to care very much what we did, but the education department had already established a particular ethos that continues to survive.

Like most of our colleagues, BFI education staff is conscious of their public service responsibilities. The BFI holds one of the world's great national collections of moving image material and related artifacts such as books, stills, posters, designs, and private papers, and it showcases international moving image culture in the National Film Theatre in London. We talk unselfconsciously about "serving the nation" and are frequently, perhaps inevitably, castigated as a smug, patronizing, metropolitan elite. But the particular ethos of the education staff stems from the fact that most of us have been teachers, and as a result, we maintain a learner-centered perspective.

In common with education staff in many cultural institutions, this ethos can often be at odds with the management view that education is simply there to "interpret the collection"—that is, to be content-driven rather than learner-centered. From the learner perspective, we can see that the skills of interpreting moving image media are not as simple or easily acquired as one might think. In addition, because we engage with them every day, we know how little the wider worlds of education and public policy care for learners' rights to acquire such skills. Our mission, therefore, has been—and still is—to make them care. The BFI's education staff appropriated this mission for themselves; it was never handed down by senior management nor imposed by government. Over the years, the BFI has played a key and sometimes leading role in the development of media education in the United Kingdom, engaging with a huge range of external institutions and individuals, and evolving its strategy in response to external threats and opportunities.

The whole of my professional life—37 years, first as a teacher, then at the BFI—has given me an extensive, and inevitably biased, view of the development of media education in the United Kingdom. In this chapter, I will describe the crucial interventions, key moments, and significant people and agencies, arranged in a more or less chronological order. I shall focus on formal education in schools, despite the huge range of important work in higher, continuing, and informal education. Also, although I have worked with colleagues in the other three U.K. nations (Scotland, Wales, and Northern Ireland), I shall concentrate mainly on England.

A SNAPSHOT FROM THE '70S

In 1971, eight years before I joined the BFI, I was one of a group of London teachers summoned to help devise a film-study course aimed at sixth formers (16- to 18-year-olds, staying on voluntarily in full time education, many of them to take courses leading to university entrance). In these digital days, it may be necessary to remind you that before the late '70s, the only possible way of seeing and studying film in a classroom context was to hire a 16mm print and show it yourself on a projector. Direct study of television was impossible except through live school broadcasts. Although there was a thriving film study sector in schools, it was very small because of the lack of training, resources, and infrastructure.

Like my colleagues on the course team, I had begun to show films in school out of personal interest and enthusiasm. I was enabled to do so because the Inner London Education Authority (ILEA) was already collaborating with the BFI to provide free loan of 16mm films to schools, and the BFI had begun in the 1960s to distribute not only short films for classroom use, but also clips from the major classics of world cinema. The proposed new course, set up jointly by the BFI and ILEA, took a significant step by establishing film study on a much larger scale. Through the autumn and spring terms, 550 students from 38 schools attended the National Film Theatre on alternate weeks to watch feature films. These films ranged from Don Siegel's remake of *The Killers* (1964) and Elia Kazan's *Wild River* (1960) to Wajda's *Ashes and Diamonds* (1958), but included film culture standards such as *Citizen Kane* (1941), *Battleship Potemkin* (1925), and *Wild Strawberries* (1957). The radical interventions came in the intervening weeks, when the students stayed in school and worked from materials, devised by the course team, that took them through concepts such as the film industry, montage, symbolism, and technical developments in cinema.

The course started in 1972 and ran for over 10 years, evolving over time, despite resistance from some teachers who found the disciplined and systematic approach to film study hard to take. It had enormous influence, establishing an approach to the study of moving image media as texts that can still be discerned in course specifications today (institutions, language, audience, representation), including recent mainstream titles in media study, and pushing at the boundaries of resource provisions to schools.

"MICKEY MOUSE" SUBJECTS

A few months ago, I asked a well-traveled and respected American colleague to guess the percentage of British high school students taking examination courses in media studies. "Eighty percent?" he ventured. The correct answer, I explained after I had finished laughing, is about 6%. The reason for his misunderstanding is that for over 20 years, the principal preoccupation of those leading the development of media education in Britain was to get it established as an examination course. Bear in mind that the United Kingdom is so called because it consists of four nations. Scotland has always had its own education system and administers its own system of public examinations through a state institution. Until recently, England, Wales, and Northern Ireland shared the same system, but are now starting to diverge in the wake of political devolution. In England, schoolchildren currently follow a National Curriculum from the beginning of school (usually before age five) until the age of 16, when they can legally leave; however, at age 14, they can opt for a range of courses, which culminate in General Certificate of Secondary Education (GCSE) examinations at age 16. Although the courses they choose must include the "core" National Curriculum subjects of English, math, and science, students can also choose from range of other subjects. After GCSE, students who stay on full time can take further courses culminating in more exams at ages 17 and 18. At this level, there is a wide range of qualifications, some with a clear vocational emphasis, but the most widely known qualification is Advanced Level General Certificate of Education ("A" Level) which is taken in two stages—(a) AS Level at age 17 and (b) A2 at age 18—and is the basis for admission to university courses.

Schools can pick and choose subject areas because the examination system is not administered by the state, but by a number of private (nonprofit) "awarding bodies" who effectively compete to provide schools with examination specifications and to administer and mark the examinations. Three of the awarding bodies offer Media Studies at GCSE.

The whole system is regulated by the government's Qualifications and Curriculum Authority (QCA), who assert that each awarding body meets the same rigorously monitored standards and that everything is transparent and fair. Each awarding body is nevertheless open to approaches from external groups wishing to set up new examinations. If an awarding body thinks that the QCA will approve the proposed examination specification, and if their marketing department advises them that there will be a demand for it, they are likely to take it on.

It was on this basis that the first formal examined courses in film study were established in the 1970s. The system was more open (and probably less rigorous) then, with a two-tier examination system at age 16, more awarding bodies, and the option for schools to develop and administer their own examinations, with external moderators to maintain standards. Through this route, many of those who later became subject leaders were able to design specifications and courses that were appropriate and challenging for their students. Although assessment always had to include a written and timed examination, many specifications allowed students to present portfolios of coursework for substantial parts of the assessment.

The importance of these courses for the long-term development of media education was that they took the subject beyond the province of isolated enthusiasts and into the realm of established, visible practice. Schools offering Media Studies had to employ staff to teach the courses, and to allocate budgets for resources and equipment. Although there were schools—and still are a few—whose institutional support for media teaching was incredibly mean, the existence of public examinations conferred status and sustainability.

The real expansion came in the mid-1980s, when the examination system was revised and GCSE was established, and again at the end of the '80s, when A Levels were reformed and specifications for media and for film studies were set up at that level. Candidate numbers grew rapidly, which attracted media attention. In Thatcher's Britain, where attacking education was a favorite pastime of a large section of the press, media studies rapidly became known as a "Mickey Mouse" subject—it was seen as teachers who were hopelessly in thrall to "relevance" and pandering to fashion. The same prejudice extends to higher education, where the range of media-related courses and student numbers has also expanded.

Of course, candidate numbers for GCSE and A Level Media and Film courses have grown, but not as dramatically or as steadily as people tend to think. From 2001 to 2005, there was a renewed and steady increase in GCSE media studies, culminating in nearly 46,000 candidates or 7.6% of the age group, an increase of 14.5% on the previous year's entry. More 17-year-olds take one of these subjects, with 41,534 sitting the examinations in 2005 as against only 28,340 18-year-olds sitting the A2. Both figures represent less than 5% of the total entries for all subjects, and an average 6% increase in numbers on the previous year. The total number of people in each age cohort or year group in the United Kingdom is about 600,000.

If there is anything alarming about the growth of media studies, it is that there is still hardly any initial formal training for media studies teachers, and schools are often reluctant to pay the teachers' course fees or to release them from school to attend in-service training. There has been a perception at the government level that media studies is pretty similar to English and that therefore any English graduate could teach it (despite the efforts of the QCA to ensure that all subject offers are distinct). A large segment of our activity at the BFI is dedicated to the production of resources and the provision of teacher training for this sector, but as candidate numbers increase, more teachers are required, and too many start with little or no knowledge about how to teach the subject. The worrying fact that the percentage of "A" grades for media studies is consistently low (currently 13.6% at A2, compared to 20.7% for English, 24.3% for art, and 34.3% for French) and students find the courses extremely challenging.

Media studies makes a huge demand on students, both in terms of the breadth of *content* (e.g., an A Level student could expect to cover topics such as the Hollywood studio system, the history of public service broadcasting in the United Kingdom, marketing in the music industry, gender in teenage magazines, and the technical and creative demands of a group production) and of *concepts* (media institutions, languages, audiences, and representation). It must also address theories of mass media and film such as uses and gratifications or Todorov on narrative structures.

In 2005, the government announced yet another round of reforms to the examination system, providing a new opportunity to consider the range of options available to young people in the field of media education (Department for Education and Skills, 2005). As new technologies expand the range of media in use, it becomes increasingly difficult to justify the argument that Media Studies has to cover all media. Masterman's (1985) argument for "the importance of thinking of the media systematically, and of clarifying their common functions and practices, as well as their important differences" (p. 19) can be addressed through the comparison of two or three media, and must be for those students who want to study a few media in depth rather than many at a superficial level.

This is not an argument for narrowing or recuperating what has been achieved in the development of media studies courses, but for recognizing the maturity of the field and the space for a wider range of options. It was on this basis that I worked with Ian Wall of Film Education on a new specification, which we persuaded the Council for the Curriculum Examinations and Assessment (CCEA) in Northern Ireland to take on. Moving Image Arts, which enables students to take courses with a higher proportion of practical production work and to study all kinds of moving image media, has proved successful at its pilot stage in Northern Ireland and is piloting in three schools in England in 2005–06. We hope it will lead to an increasing breadth of course offerings for young people.

This long-established sector of formal media courses for the 14–19 age group does make the United Kingdom's experience of media education distinctive and significant. My account of it may illustrate why U.K. teachers distinguish between *media studies* (the name given to accredited courses) and *media education* (the whole range of media teaching and learning, which is much wider). We have a core sector of teachers with substantial, long-term media studies and/or film studies teaching experience who work to keep up with developments in the media and to help students understand challenging concepts. We also have an accumulating evidence base about student achievement, measured against more or less constant standards, which provides an important source of knowledge about what media teaching and learning actually achieves in practice. Nevertheless, the numbers on these courses represent a relatively small sector in a total school population of over nine million. What about the rest?

SPECIALIST COURSES ARE NOT ENOUGH

In 1982, word got around that the schools' inspectorate were examining media education. Paranoid fantasies flourished: could this be a plot to shut it all down? The truth was rather more remarkable. Sir Keith Joseph, the then Secretary of State for Education, had a chauffeur who kept him in touch with the preoccupations of ordinary folk. One day this chauffeur complained to Sir Keith about a nasty influence corrupting the nation's youth: a tea-time BBC drama serial called *Grange Hill*, set in a comprehensive (high school) and portraying all sorts of shocking subjects such as drugs, bullying, and impertinence to teachers. Sir Keith commanded a special screening of an episode from this (actually excellent) series, to which he invited a number of senior civil servants and schools inspectors. Of course, the BBC supplied the most innocuous episode of *Grange Hill* that it could find, but in any case, most of the assembled mandarins were (unlike politicians) reasonably au fait with the conventions of British realist TV drama and found little to complain about.

Wanting to repair his reputation for responsible and decisive action, Sir Keith ordered the establishment of a working group to look at the question of popular television and schoolchildren. A group of teachers convened under the leadership of James Learmonth, a school inspector who had studied at the Centre for the Study of Mass Communications in Leicester and had written a thesis on media education. The group's report was modest and rather bland, to the disappointment of media education activists, who had been hoping for a decree in favor of media education for all. Learmonth knew the psychology of government departments better than that: the report was cunningly worded to keep the jury out on media education, and he was allowed to set up ten regional conferences across the country to debate the topic further. Each event brought together educators and media professionals in an uneasy dialogue, but some of the conferences grew into established groups through which a new agenda for media education emerged.

A key, widely quoted sentence in the group's report was, "Specialist courses in media studies are not enough: all teachers should be involved in examining and discussing television programmes with young people" (Department of Education and Science, 1983, p. 27). It was to be another five years before the announcement of the first National Curriculum for England and Wales, but the "great debate" on education that prime minister James Callaghan had called for in a speech at Ruskin College, Oxford in 1976 had begun the process towards what many considered unthinkable: a bascurriculum with universal standards. Key to this concept was the principle of entitlement: the need to think about education in terms of what all children should have the right to expect, not in terms of imposing restrictive and utilitarian requirements.

I had started working at the BFI when my own children were very young and was keen to develop media education for primary school children, but was discouraged by my colleagues, who felt that it was hard enough trying to get media education courses established in secondary schools; however, the Popular Television and Schoolchildren initiative fired my imagination. I was designated as the BFI link to the initiative, and traveled with James Learmonth to many of the conferences. He became my mentor and remained a good friend until his untimely death in 2003. It was from him that I began to see the possibility of more ambitious aspirations for media education: why shouldn't it be the entitlement of every child? But I also learned how educational change can happen.

The fact that Her Majesty's Inspectorate and the Department of Education endorsed the regional conferences made a surprising difference to who attended. Media education began to be an acceptable issue for local education authorities to address, and many began to appoint advisers for media education. In 1986, I decided to convene a working group for primary media education, bringing teachers and academics together to discuss and try out ways of teaching about the media with children. We met for residential weekends three times a year for three years, finally hammering out a curriculum statement (British Film Institute & Department of Education and Science Working Group, 1989) which went to the working group preparing the definition of English for the new National Curriculum (Department of Education and Science, 1989) and ensured a reference to media as an entitlement for all.

HARD LESSONS

A curriculum statement, however, is like a marriage in soap opera: it is the start of new intrigues, rather than a happy ending, and destined not to last. The hasty introduction of the National Curriculum in England and Wales in 1990 was fraught with controversy and compromise. Media education was relegated to the tail end of the English curriculum in the mysterious category of "nonliterary texts," which tended to mean what it had always meant in English: writing text in columns and calling it a newspaper; looking at magazine advertisements and spotting the stereotypes. Studying moving image media remained too much hassle for most, apart from the occasional screening of a filmed Shakespeare play. As the lead agency arguing for media education to be written into English in the National Curriculum, the BFI was criticized for failing to go to battle for media education as a separate subject. I saw that idea as on a par with overthrowing capitalism or ending world poverty: obviously desirable, but not likely in my lifetime, and certainly not obtainable from a right-wing Conservative government. Their return for a fourth term in office in 1992 signaled grim times ahead for everyone in the public sector. We'd had bluff approval from Secretary of State Kenneth Baker in 1988 who is reported to have quipped, "I'm all for media education. It'll show children how left-wing the BBC is!" Media education had become an emblem of teacher laziness and incompetence; in April 1993 proposals for the revision of English were published, removing all requirements to study media texts in their own right.

The BFI tried to counter these proposals by setting up a two-day event at the National Film Theatre in November 1993, cheekily entitled "A Commission of Inquiry into English: Balancing Literature, Language and Media in the National Curriculum" ("cheeky" because commissions of inquiry are usually set up by government). Here, a panel of distinguished and impeccably middle-of-the-road figures, chaired by Baroness Mary Warnock, listened to evidence for and against media education from 20 "witnesses" and delivered their verdict some months later at the front of a published transcript of the whole event. "It appears from the evidence," they said,

> that the idea of learning about the media as a general entitlement is now a widely accepted principle, which we would endorse. . . . We recommend that flexible and gradual ways be found to ensure that the curriculum begins to incorporate both critical and creative work with media, starting from modest beginnings, and subject to careful monitoring. (Bazalgette, 1994, p. 16)

While that sort of thing was never going to set the world on fire, it probably helped to save media education from being thrown into the incinerator. It would have been easy for the government to reject shrill demands from media education activists; it was much harder for them to ignore reasonable, modest proposals from respectable folk. The National Curriculum's minimal, ambiguous references to media education remained.

NEW LABOUR, NEW MEDIA EDUCATION

The years 1990 to 1996 saw bitter struggle to hold on to some of what had been won in the 1980s and engage with the enormous changes happening in digital technologies, which were clearly going to transform the ways people would engage with—and learn about—the media. In May 1997, with the election of Tony Blair's "New Labour" government, we entered a new era.

Labour's election campaign had been supported by sections of the media, particularly the film industry, which had been poorly treated by the Tory regime. One of the new government's early decisions was to set up a Film Policy Review Group, whose report, *A Bigger Picture*, was produced in 1998 by the Department for Culture, Media and Sport (DCMS). Like all reports on the British film industry, it had to acknowledge the fact that U.K. film exhibition and TV broadcasting of film are both massively dominated by Hollywood product. No one in U.K. government or industry, given the United Kingdom's dependence on U.S. investment in our talent and facilities, was going to even think of the words "cultural imperialism," but the review group had to come up with something to bolster the ever-failing fortunes of British film. It proposed setting up a Film Council that would pull together all the state-funded U.K. film institutions and would become the BFI's funding body.

A Bigger Picture also hypothesized that the reason British audiences did not attend British films as much as they should was because they lacked the "cine-literacy" to appreciate them. The group therefore proposed setting up a Film Education Working Group that would make proposals about the ways in which people could learn about film. The BFI was asked to convene this group. I was its secretary, with the responsibility of drafting the report.

The group included a number of key figures in British media education, but the dilemma was that none of us wanted to single out "film" in this one chance we might have for a serious influence on government policy. For this reason, the report uses the term "moving image media" rather than "film" wherever it can, and the introduction clearly stakes the claim for television as part of moving image culture (Film Education Working Group, 1999).

The report's 22 recommendations set out an agenda that, if they had all been followed, would have substantially transformed media education in the United Kingdom. One small but key triumph, agreed to before the report was published, was to specify "moving image media" in the National Curriculum's references to media education, thus preventing teachers from confining all their media work to print forms. Responses to the report, however, showed the political will was not there. John Woodward, the BFI director who had secured the BFI's role as the working group convener, had moved on to become the director of the new U.K. Film Council and had other things on his mind, while the BFI was struggling to define its new role as subordinate to an industry-led body. Nevertheless, beginning in 1999, the BFI worked with some success to realize the six recommendations that related to formal education. These recommendations are

1. To include well-annotated moving image extracts.
2. To include advice to teachers about learning outcomes and progression.
3. To identify pedagogic strategies.
4. To provide interest and challenge appropriate to the level of learning progression.
5. To provide material suitable for the target age group
6. To make appropriate use of genuinely interactive digital technology whenever possible. (Film Education Working Group, 1999)

We also used the model of learning progression that shows learning outcomes of moving image media to be applied to mandatory education courses (Film Education Working Group, 1999, pp. 73–79) as the basis of two general guides for teachers (see British Film Institute, 2000, 2003).

NEW LITERACY EXAMINES RELATIONSHIPS BETWEEN PRINT AND MOVING IMAGE TEXTS

In the education sector, consternation arose as people realized that the Labour Government was determined to continue issuing central directives to maintain a target-driven culture. An early intervention was the National Literacy Strategy, a vast project aimed at ensuring that by 2002, 80% of 11-year-olds should have reached a basic level of reading competence (National Literacy Trust, 2006). A National Literacy Framework was devised, a network of advisers was set up, and—more controversially—a Literacy Hour was enacted, to be followed in all primary schools every day, a concept originally proposed by the Conservative government in 1996.

Soon after it was created, the National Literacy Strategy management approached the BFI and asked us to run a seminar for them and their regional directors to look at the relationship between print and moving image media. By the end, we had agreed that the study of moving image media could make a significant contribution to "text level" learning, especially if this were done through the study of complete short films rather than clips.

This began a fascinating and important phase of work. The National Literacy Framework proposes three levels of literacy learning: (a) *word level*, which deals with vocabulary and spelling; (b) *sentence level*, which deals with grammar; and (c) *text level*, which deals with whole-text concepts such as narrative, character, and genre. It was this last level that teachers found difficult. We argued that text-level concepts are not medium-specific: they are concepts that very young children are learning through their television and video viewing (Van den Broek, 2001). We became excited at the prospect of developing teaching resources that would broaden the concept of literacy to include critical skills and wider viewing of moving image texts. They would enhance and extend traditional literacy learning without compromising what we would want children to learn for media literacy.

Since that date, the BFI has developed three such resources—(a) *Starting Stories* for ages 3–7, (b) *Story Shorts* for ages 7–11, and (c) *Screening Shorts* for ages 11–14)—with five more in the pipeline. These resources were piloted with a wide range of schools and are now sold to schools, with over 6,000 copies purchased far (British Film Institute, 2006a).

On this basis we calculate that the resources reach over a million children annually; there are 6.6 million 3- to 14-year-olds in the United Kingdom, so we have some way to go. The Strategy has supported this initiative by inviting us to locally train their regional directors and groups of advisers and consultants, so all primary-school classes can include three weeks of moving-image-related activity in every term.

The BFI's latest development in this initiative has been to offer advanced training to nominated individuals from local education authorities, who will become Lead Practitioners for what we are calling "moving image media literacy." Local authorities buying into this scheme have to produce a plan for using the Lead Practitioners to roll out this approach to their schools. So far, we have 40 local authorities committed to the scheme and another 33 showing interest. There are 147 local authorities in England; we hope to cover them all by 2007. We are supporting similar schemes in Northern Ireland and Scotland.

Each of the resources we have produced contains a compilation of material selected through an exhaustive process of research to find—and clear rights on—films that are short enough, appropriate for the age group, and above all, rich enough to reward repeated viewing and analysis. They were not necessarily made originally for children; some are nonnarrative; several are challengingly different from mainstream film. It is the powerful impact of these films on both teachers and children that has been key to the success of this initiative.

Looking back, there are lessons to be learned here that may be valuable for educational practitioners and policy leaders around the world. First, educational change is never achieved just through curricular directives or classroom resources. It has to be supported by training and advocacy. Secondly, we have found that no educational initiative can succeed unless it is premised on the idea of offering a positive and desirable new experience for learners. However fascinating and important it has been for all of us to learn that the media are dominated by global corporations dedicated to profit, that fact on its own is not enough to open up a space in the core curriculum. Media education solely based on protecting children from exploitation and ideological manipulation is destined to occupy the same kinds of marginal curricular space—and the same status in learners' eyes—as health and drugs education. What media education has to offer to learners, if it is to occupy the central curricular role that it deserves, are high expectations of what the media can achieve. That then offers the necessary motivation, context, and rationale for an approach to media education that can and must include learning about media institutions, bias, and stereotyping.

ENTER THE MEDIA INDUSTRY REGULATOR

New Labour had other plans for U.K. media besides the Film Policy Working Group. The government decided to rationalize the plethora of institutions set up to regulate media industries by creating a new authority, the Office of Communications (Ofcom), initially established in 2002, with responsibility over all broadcast and electronic media (except the BBC, which continues to be regulated by its Board of Governors, or the press, advertising, or film industries, which maintain their own watchdogs). Despite this comparatively limited brief and regulatory role, the Communications Act of 2003 gave Ofcom responsibility for "media literacy." This was the first time that any statutory body had been given explicit powers for anything to do with media education.

All national regulatory bodies for media in the 21st century know that their powers are limited in a digital age. Most of them make some sort of nod towards education as a means towards citizens regulating their own media consumption: keeping their kids away from Internet pedophiles, knowing how to complain about offensive content, and so forth. Does it matter, therefore, that media literacy is "given" to a regulatory body? Ofcom has a duty to work *with others* to promote media literacy; the definition given in the Act is so broad that hardly anyone would want to disagree with it (Office of Communication, 2003, December 29). Staff at Ofcom have been clear from the outset that they have no desire to colonize the concept or extend their media literacy remit beyond what a regulator would be expected to cover: protecting vulnerable consumers, especially children, and ensuring that citizens have the skills and knowledge necessary to access electronic media content.

Is this, therefore, an acceptable approach? Yes and no. It is good that media literacy has a higher public profile, but bad that, whatever efforts Ofcom makes, media literacy is bound to become more closely associated with their remit than with the kinds of activity established over the years in the education sector. Anticipating this, the U.K. Film Council collaborated with the BFI and with two major terrestrial broadcasters, the BBC and Channel Four, to set up an event in January 2004 called "Inform and Empower," designed to win a consensus from both industry and education stakeholders around a definition of media literacy that was wider than Ofcom's definition. The event was dominated by industry rather than education, and was successful in the sense that a wide range of media institutions did get a sense of U.K. media education as a diverse and active field in which a great deal of excellent work is taking place.

In the wake of that event, the same quartet of agencies convened a Media Literacy Task Force to take forward the ideas aired during "Inform and Empower." Again, the problems inherent in giving the media literacy remit to a regulatory body surfaced in the Task Force. Broadcasters are required to win Ofcom's approval for their media literacy activities; they do not have to win education sector approval. The Department for Education and Skills can now regard media literacy as primarily the responsibility of their sister department, the DCMS, not as something that they need to add to their list of problems.

The Media Literacy Task Force therefore devised another solution: to establish, exemplify and strengthen the fragile consensus won at "Inform and Empower" by creating a Charter for Media Literacy, to be signed by industry and education bodies alike, intended to establish the more liberal version of media literacy in the public sphere (Euro Media Literacy, 2006). The Charter lists seven key competences that a media literate person should have, and identifies three essential elements of media education:

- **Cultural**: Learners broaden their experience of different kinds of media form and content.
- **Critical**: Learners develop skills in analyzing and assessing media.
- **Creative**: Learners develop skills in using media for expression, communication, and participation in public debate.

These "three Cs" will seem pretty general and simplistic to anyone who has been centrally involved in media education over the years, but I have found them essential in talking to people who want magic bullets and one-stop solutions, if only to keep my foot in the door and hold on to the principle that quick fixes and education do not mix.

FUTURE POSSIBILITIES FOR MEDIA EDUCATION

Reading many of the extant accounts of media education in the United Kingdom, you could be forgiven for thinking that it has somehow just evolved through some kind of natural process of growth. Changes in practice and attitudes are described but not accounted for; apparently they just happen. Although there is grass roots practice, and it is, after all, the most important aspect of media education as far as learners are concerned, the most salient fact about it as far as any attempts at a comprehensive account are concerned is that *no one actually knows what is going on*. We can all describe the comparatively small amounts of practice that we actually see and have read about, from an extensive collection of evidence about a certain kind of media learning at certain levels, in our Media and Film Studies examination system in the United Kingdom. But to map the whole field of media education in a national context is extremely expensive and difficult, precisely because there is a lot going on in a very wide range of settings. The BFI has attempted it four times (Barrett, 1998; Dickson, 1994; Kirwan, Learmonth, Sayer, & Williams, 2003; Learmonth & Sayer, 1996). Of these, *Mapping Media Literacy* was the most expensive of the four studies, costing its cofunders £30,000. It took five months, only addressed the 11–16 age group, and produced sketchy and unsurprising results. For example,

> Overall, the levels of media literacy are low, although there is some contribution being made to media literacy, mainly through English in schools, for young people aged 11–16. This is because in media education, policy-making, planning and provision are fragmentary and this is not seen as a priority area for education. (Office of Communication, 2003, March 7)

The corollary of never being able to know what is happening is that no one can know who or what has really affected what is happening. As the employee of a public service institution with a responsibility of developing media education in the United Kingdom, I find myself in the interesting position of being attacked both for being completely ineffectual (Hart, 2001) and for having sinisterly far-reaching powers (Masterman, 2002). Of course, neither is true, but I would not be doing the job that I do if I felt that the BFI wasn't achieving anything through its events, resources, training, research, and advocacy—most of which is done by my fantastic team of colleagues (see British Film Institute, 2006b). In this chapter, I have staked a claim for the BFI's role in the development of U.K. media education; however, I leave others to judge what our real impact may have been. Furthermore, there have been many other key individuals and agencies over the years who have made significant contributions to media education in the United Kingdom; therefore, the question is: how will this field develop in the future?

One danger facing media education at the moment is that it will become dominated by "creativity" at the expense of the other two C's: (a) the cultural and (b) the critical. The ease of access now afforded by digital technologies makes this temptingly easy, but anyone who knows anything about teaching creative subjects knows that learning in this area needs to be underpinned by cultural breadth and critical skills: a point effectively made in a recent BFI-led study of a large digital video project in England (Reid, Burn, & Parker, 2002). The perception also persists that "creativity" with moving image media means film making, and that the creative "moment" of filmmaking is using the camera. In fact, the creative centre of filmmaking is editing, as anyone who has edited moving images will know. In addition, if we consider what is actually feasible for large numbers of learners, we must recognize that their likeliest point of access to creative activity with any time-based media (is moving image or audio) is likely to be at a computer, working with "found" or freely accessed material to create their own meanings. The important concept of "creative commons" (see Creative Archive License Group, 2006) means that learners' access to material previously restricted by copyright is likely to change, and with it our notion of what "counts" as creativity. I predict that this will be the next focus of debate for media education, not only in the United Kingdom, but in many other countries as well.

REFERENCES

Alvarado, M., & Boyd-Barrett, O. (Eds.). (1992). *Media education: An instruction*. London: British Film Institute.

Alvarado, M, Gutch, R., & Wollen, T. (1987). *Learning the media*. London: Macmillan Education.

Barrett, A. J. B. (1998). *Audit of media in English*. London: British Film Institute.

Bazalgette, C. (Ed.). (1994). *Report of the commission of inquiry into English: Balancing literature, language and media in the national curriculum*. London: British Film Institute.

British Film Institute. (2000). *Moving images in the classroom*. Retrieved May 15, 2006, from http://www.bfi.org.uk/education/teaching/miic/

British Film Institute. (2003). *Look again! A teaching guide to using film and television with three- to eleven-year-olds*. Retrieved May 15, 2006, from http://www.bfi.org.uk/education/teaching/lookagain/

British Film Institute. (2006a). *Teaching resources*. Retrieved May 15, 2006, from http://www.bfi.org.uk/education/teaching/

British Film Institute. (2006b). *Who's who in education*. Retrieved May 15, 2006, from http://www.bfi.org.uk/education/about/whoswho.html

British Film Institute and Department of Education and Science Working Group. (1989). *Primary media education: A curriculum statement*. London: British Film Institute.

Buckingham, D. (2003). *Media education: Literacy, learning and contemporary culture*. Cambridge: Polity Press.

Creative Archive License Group. (2006). *Homepage of the Creative Archive License Group*. Retrieved May 15, 2006, from http://creativearchive.bbc.co.uk/index.html

Department of Education and Science. (1983). *Popular TV & schoolchildren: The report of a group of teachers*. London: Department of Education and Science.

Department of Education and Science. (1989). English for ages 5–16 (Report of the National Curriculum Working Group on English, also called Cox Report). London: Department of Education and Science.

Department for Education and Skills. (2005, February 23). 14–19 Education and Skills—White Paper. Retrieved May 15, 2006, from http://www.dfes.gov.uk/publications/14-19educationandskills/

Dickson, P. (1994). *A survey of media education in schools and colleges*. London: British Film Institute.

Euro Media Literacy. (2006). *European charter for media literacy*. Retrieved May 15, 2006, from http://www.euromedialiteracy.eu/index.php?Pg=charter

Film Education Working Group. (1999). *Making movies matter: Report of the film education working group*. London: British Film Institute. Retrieved May 15, 2006, from http://www.bfi.org.uk/education/research/advocacy/mmm/pdf/fewg.pdf

Hart, A. (2001, February). Researching media education in schools in the United Kingdom. [Electronic version]. *Studies in Media & Information Literacy Education*, 1, n.p. Retrieved May 15, 2006, from http://www.utpjournals.com/jour.ihtml?lp=simile/issue1/hartfulltext.html

Kirwan, T., Learmonth, J., Sayer, M., & Williams, R. (2003, March). *Mapping media literacy*. London: British Film Institute, Broadcast Standards Commision, and Independent Television Commission.

Learmonth, J., & Sayer, M. (1996). *A review of good practice in media education*. London: British Film Institute.

Masterman, L. (1985). *Teaching the media*. London: Comedia.

Masterman, L. (2002). *Down Cemetery Road*. [Booklet]. Self-published. Available from L. Masterman, Upper Health Cottage, 90 Downham Road South, Heswall, Wirral, CH60 5SQ.

National Literacy Trust. (2006). *The national literacy strategy* (England). Retrieved May 15, 2006, from http://www.literacytrust.org.uk/Update/strat.html#Background

Office of Communication. (2003, March 7). *News Release 14A/03: Review of Media Literacy Skills amongst the UK population reveals that there is a clear demand for increased learning*. Retrieved May 15, 2006, from http://www.ofcom.org.uk/static/archive/itc/latest_news/press_releases/release.asp-release_id=679.html

Office of Communication. (2003, December 29). *Media Literacy*. Annex B, supporting document: Section 11 Communications Act (2003). Retrieved May 15, 2006, from http://www.ofcom.org.uk/consult/condocs/strategymedialit/ml_statement/annexb/?a=87101

Reid, M., Burn, A., & Parker, D. (2002, October). *Evaluation report for the BECTA digital video pilot project.* London: British Film Institute. Retreived May 15, 2006, from http://www.becta.org.uk/page_documents/research/dvreport_241002.pdf

Van den Broek, P. (2001). *The role of television viewing in the development of reading comprehension.* University of Minnesota. Retrieved May 15, 2006, from http://www.ciera.org/library/archive/2001-02/200102pv.pdf

7

USING A MULTIMODAL THEORETICAL LENS TO EXPLORE STUDIES PERTAINING TO ENGLISH LEARNERS IN THE VISUAL AND COMMUNICATIVE ARTS

Cynthia Brock, Rod Case, and Julie Pennington
THE UNIVERSITY OF NEVADA, RENO

Guofang Li
MICHIGAN STATE UNIVERSITY

Rachel Salas
UNIVERSITY OF NORTH CAROLINA AT GREENSBORO

Large and growing numbers of children who do not speak English as their first language inhabit U.S. classrooms (Nieto, 2002; Garcia, 2000). For example, Thomas and Collier (2004) estimate that by the year 2040, children who speak a first language other than English will comprise almost 40% of the population of school-aged children in America. Already, English is not a first language for over half of the public school students in California (Garcia, 2000). While approximately half of the children who immigrated to the United States in the 1990s came from Latin American countries, the remaining immigrants came from countries all over the world speaking a vast array of different first languages (Malone, Baluja, Constanzo, & Davis, 2003).

Many prominent scholars (e.g., August & Hakuta, 1997; Nieto, 2002) argue that we, as an educational community, have not been successful in our efforts to provide a quality education for children in our schools who are learning English as an additional language. Our failure is evidenced in many ways, such as (a) lower test scores for English learners on standardized tests of reading and writing, (b) higher school drop-out rates for English learners, and (c) overrepresentation of English learners in remedial programs and lower academic tracks in school systems (Fitzgerald, 1995; Rose, 1989; Trueba, 1989; and Walker-Moffat, 1995). Clearly, providing a quality education for English learners is a crucial issue that must be addressed by educators at all levels.

One way to proceed in our efforts to improve our work with English learners is to examine what we, as a field, currently know and understand about learning and instruction for English learners. Our current knowledge base can then serve as a foundation for future plans and directions regarding the education of English learners. Consequently, in this literature review, we explore how current research in the visual and communicative arts informs our thinking and understanding about the literacy learning of English learners.

We use the following definition of the visual and communicative arts put forth by Flood, Heath, and Lapp (2005): "Visual arts encompass everything from dramatic performances to comic books, television, and video arcade games. The communicative arts, such as reading, writing, and speaking exist both independently and as integral elements of the visual arts" (p. xvi).

Four sections follow this introduction. In the next section, we articulate the theoretical lens that we used to inform our work. Then we describe the process we undertook to select studies to review for this work, and we explain how we analyzed the studies. After discussing the results of these studies, we then step back and discuss the ramifications of this body of work for English learners, teachers, and researchers.

BACKGROUND

In this subsection, we articulate the theoretical lens we used in our work. Text reading is a complex theoretical endeavor; this is true whether one is referring to visual texts, oral texts, written texts, or texts within other semiotic domains such as mathematical texts (Mailloux, 1990). Mailloux referred to two ways we proceed when we read, or interpret, texts: "*toward* a text to be interpreted and *for* an audience in need of the interpretation. That is, the interpreter mediates between the translated text and its new rendering and between the translated text and the audience desiring the interpretation" (p. 121, emphasis in original). It is the process of *mediation* between the new rendering of the translated text and the audience desiring the interpretation that we elucidate in our work as we interpret studies pertaining to English learners in this manuscript. We draw on the work of Kress and Van Leeuwen (2001) to point us in a useful conceptual direction regarding this process of semiotic mediation.

Kress and Van Leeuwen (2001) theorized a process by which textual interpretations are mediated. This process involves exploring the practices surrounding interrelationships between many different modes of communication; modes of communication include—but are not limited to—language, image, music, sound, gesture, and so forth. Kress and Van Leeuwen referred to practices surrounding the juxtaposition of many different modes of communication as multimodality, and they refer to their theory as a multimodal theory of communication. In short, in their theoretical work, Kress and Van Leeuwen sought to explore how "people use a variety of semiotic resources to make [and interpret] signs in concrete social contexts" (p. vii).

Kress and Van Leeuwen (2001) posited that four domains of practice merit attention in their multimodal theory of communication. These domains of practice include (a)discourse, (b) design, (c) production, and (d) distribution. Discourse, for Kress and Van Leeuwen, referred to socially situated forms of knowledge about aspects of reality. Artists (and researchers, of course) function within discursive communities of practice that enact, create, and recreate ways of using symbols to communicate in and through their work. Thus, individuals immersed in particular discursive practices—whether communities of artists or communities of scholars—produce particular kinds of texts in particular ways and interpret particular kinds of texts—for themselves and others—in particular ways. How do these notions of discourse relate to our work in this review of literature? We are studying the discourses of studies pertaining to the literacy learning of English learners as they relate to visual literacy and the communicative arts. We see one aspect of our work as rendering visible the oftentimes-invisible discourses in which we operate as researchers and scholars.

Design is the second domain of practice that Kress and Van Leeuwen (2001) highlighted in their theory of multimodal communication:

> Design stands midway between content and expression. It is the conceptual side of expression, and the expression side of conception. Designs are (uses of) semiotic resources, in all semiotic modes and combinations of semiotic modes. Designs are means to realize discourses in the content of a given communication situation. But designs also add something new: they realize the communication situation which changes socially constructed knowledge into social (inter-)action. (p. 5)

In a sense, designs are the blueprints created by architects that guide the actual construction of a building or the lesson plans created by teachers to guide the enactment of a lesson. Design and production are inextricably intertwined.

Production is the third domain of practice. "Production refers to the organization of the expression, to the actual material articulation of the semiotic event or the actual material production of the semiotic artifact" (Kress & Van Leeuwen, 2001, p. 6). For visual artists, this refers to the making of a work of art. In education, the actual execution of a lesson plan is the production of the lesson. In some instances, the production leaves traces—such as the painting presented in this manuscript or the words and paragraphs in this manuscript. In other cases, the result of the production is ephemeral. The sounds created during a speech or music production dissipate, for example. The music score or the written speech (e.g., the design) may remain, but even with a blueprint to follow, the actual production of a speech, a music production, or a lesson plan varies as it is enacted from one rendition to another. In the case of our work, we attended to two levels of analysis in the write-up (or production) of our review of literature. First, we strove to look closely at the meanings of the original studies we reviewed. Then, as we looked across the studies using the theoretical lens we employed in our work, we rendered unique interpretations of the studies we analyzed.

Kress and Van Leeuwen (2001) cautioned their readers that relationships between design and production merit our careful attention because they can be, or become, limiting. In education, teachers,

> . . . May either design their own lessons or merely 'execute' a detailed syllabus designed by expert educators. In other words, when design and production separate, design becomes a means for controlling the actions of others, the potential for a unity between discourse, design and production diminishes, and there is no longer room for the 'producers' to make the design 'their own,' to add their own accent (p. 7).

Thus, if teachers enact lesson designs handed to them by others not familiar with their unique contexts, or if researchers implement research designs without adjusting them based on unique and specific research contexts, or if painters merely paint-by-numbers using the designs, materials, and colors suggested by others, the impact of the lesson, the research, or the artwork, may be diminished.

Dissemination is the fourth, and final, domain of practice. Dissemination, as the term implies, refers to presenting a product to a broader audience. So, in the case of music, for example, musicians can create CDs that are then distributed to audiences. Of course, the broader the dissemination, the more the musicians' work is out in the general public so that the musicians become known and earn revenue. Artists typically disseminate their work by featuring it in art shows or different art galleries. In the field of education, textbooks can serve as dissemination venues for lesson plans, and journals—electronic and paper—can serve as dissemination venues for the studies conducted by researchers. For Kress and Van Leeuwen (2001), dissemination is semiotic; it adds meaning or meaning potential to symbols and symbol systems. With respect to our review of literature, the studies we reviewed were already disseminated in the broader research community. We are well aware, however, that our rereading of these studies, using the theoretical lens we employ and presenting our findings in the venue of this handbook, will afford opportunities for new renderings of the original work.

In summary, Kress and Van Leeuwen (2001) purported that deep, rich, conceptual understandings of semiotic mediation require attention to the process of meaning construction and the practices involved in mediation with sign systems. They argue that four domains of practice—which they call *strata*—serve as useful tools for exploring the process of semiotic mediation. These include discourse, design, production, and distribution. Discourses, research designs, and the processes of producing and disseminating research outcomes are subject to particular discursive practices in particular communities of practice. In the introduction of this review of literature, we presented research and scholarship that suggests that we, as an educational community, have much to learn about effectively educating English learners. We explained that one of our central goals in this work is to examine what we, as a field, know and have learned about the literacy instruction and learning of English learners. We believe that employing a unique lens in looking at ourselves and our work through Kress and Van Leeuwen's theory of multimodal communication may afford unique insights into what we already know about the literacy instruction and learning of English learners, as well as what we have yet to learn.

METHODS: SELECTING AND ANALYZING THE STUDIES

We began searching for studies using large data-based search engines such as ERIC and Psych Abstracts. We used keyword such as the following in our searches: Second language learners, English learners, English as a second language (ESL), English language learners, literacy instruction and learning, communicative arts, visual arts, drama, graphics, illustrations, reading, writing, speaking, listening, viewing, and so forth. In addition to these large, data-based searches, we worked together to craft a list of possible journals that we thought might contain studies relevant to our work. We reviewed the abstracts from 1996 through 2006 for a list of the 31 journals we identified as well as the abstracts of studies from our data-based searches. (See Table 7.1 for a list of the journals we reviewed.) While there was some overlap in the list from our data-based searches and our list of journals, we used this approach because we sought to be thorough in our search for studies.

Our criteria for selecting studies for this review of literature included the following. First, the studies had to focus on the literacy learning and/or instruction of English learners. Second, we examined studies between 1996 and 2006. Third, we selected studies that focused on literacy instruction and learning as it relates to classrooms. While we didn't seek to omit studies that involved many different kinds of literacy, all of the studies we reviewed related to school-based literacy in some way. In particular, for example, we omitted studies solely related to aspects of second language acquisition that didn't also relate, in some way, to literacy learning. Finally, we only selected studies that involved K through 12 students in U.S. classrooms or classrooms abroad. Our extensive search yielded a set of 69 studies that we analyzed for this work.

TABLE 7.1. List of Journals We Reviewed for Literature Review

	Journal Titles
1.	*American Educational Research Journal*
2.	*Anthropology and Education*
3.	*Applied Linguistics*
4.	*Applied Psycholinguistics*
5.	*Art Education*
6.	*Bilingual Research Journal*
7.	*The Canadian Modern Language Review*
8.	*Child Language Teaching and Therapy*
9.	*Computer Assisted Language Learning: An International Journal*
10.	*Contemporary Educational Psychology*
11.	*Discourse Processes*
12.	*Education and Urban Society*
13.	*Elementary School Journal*
14.	*English for Specific Purposes*
15.	*English Today*
16.	*English World-Wide*
17.	*Journal of Literacy Research*
18.	*Journal of Second Language Writing*
19.	*Language Arts*
20.	*Linguistics and Education*
21.	*National Reading Conference Yearbooks*
22.	*Reading and Writing Quarterly*
23.	*Reading Research and Instruction*
24.	*Reading Research Quarterly*
25.	*Research in the Teaching of English*
26.	*Review of Educational Research*
27.	*Review of Research in Education*
28.	*Studies in Second Language Acquisition*
29.	*Teaching and Teacher Education*
30.	*TESOL Quarterly*
31.	*Written Communication*

Analysis Procedures

Once we collected the 69 studies that related to our parameters for this literature review, we began the process of analyzing the studies. We engaged in a three-step analysis process. First, we read through all of the studies and wrote a brief summary of each. This summary included the study purpose and research questions, the theoretical framework that informed the work (if a theoretical framework was identified), and an overview of the methods, results, and conclusions of each study.

As we met and talked through the studies we were reading, we began to craft our second level of analysis. We noticed that, in general, the studies we reviewed coalesced around three general categories: studies that foregrounded (a) teachers and/or students (e.g., a focus on the individuals in the study contexts), (b) language and literacy (e.g., a focus on content), or (c) literacy instruction (e.g., a focus on instruction). First, studies that foregrounded teachers and/or students were often case studies of English learners and/or English learners and teachers engaged literacy teaching and learning. Some studies in this category focused on characteristics of large groups of students such as ethnicities of students who spoke English at varying levels of proficiency, or numbers of students of particular ethnicities. Thus, the overarching reason for categorizing studies in this section was that they focused primarily on some aspect of characteristics of English learners and/or English learners and their teachers. Studies in the second category foregrounded language and/or literacy. For example, some studies emphasized vocabulary or comprehension development as outcome variables. Other studies emphasized levels of English language proficiency in relation to some aspect of literacy learning. Consequently, if studies foregrounded some aspect of language and/or literacy, we classified them in this category. Finally, if scholars emphasized programs, methods, or instructional interventions in their work, we placed them in the category labeled "instruction." We wish to emphasize that these three categories were not treated in a discrete manner in the studies we reviewed; rather, we grouped the studies based on the conceptual focus the scholars emphasized in their work.

Once we grouped studies in the three general categories listed above, we employed a multimodal theoretical lens to further categorize the studies based on the extent to which the scholars employed different modes of communication in their research. We drew on the work of Kress and Van Leeuwen (2001), as well as the work of Flood and colleagues (2005), to define modes of research in our work. Here's how. Kress and Van Leeuwen (2001) suggested that modes consist of language, image, music, sound, gesture, and so forth. Flood and colleagues (2005) crafted this handbook to focus on both the visual and communicative arts. Combining the notions of all of these scholars in our own work, we define modes as reading, writing, speaking, listening, and all manner of the visual arts including, but not limited to, drama, plays, poetry, comic books, music, graffiti, and so forth.

Consequently, after grouping our studies based on a focus on individuals (e.g., teachers or students), content (language or literacy), or instruction, we further attended to the extent to which the researchers who designed and conducted the studies attended to multimodality in their work. Thus, we categorized studies on a tripartite continuum from monomodal to mixed-modal, to multimodal. Studies categorized as monomodal typically dealt with only one aspect of the communicative arts—such as reading or speaking. Moreover, studies in this category tended to omit a discussion of the context in which the studies were conducted. The second category, mixed-modality, focused on a combination of the communicative arts. Thus, studies classified as mixed-modal tended to focus on several aspects of the communicative arts such as reading and writing, or writing and speaking and listening. Additionally, researchers in this category tended to provide a more explicit discussion of the communicative contexts in which the studies were embedded. Finally, studies classified as multimodal dealt with one or more aspects of the communicative arts and one or more aspects of the visual arts. In general, researchers whose work we classified in this category spend a great deal of time discussing the communicative context in which their studies were embedded.

Overall, then, we classified the 69 studies we reviewed using a 3 × 3 grid. (See Table 7.2, following.) The three vertical categories are labeled "teachers/English learners," "language/literacy," and "instruction." The three horizontal categories are labeled "monomodal," "mixed mono-" and "multimodal."

RESULTS

We structure the results of our work into the following three major sections: (a) studies classified as monomodal, (b) studies classified as mixed mono- and multimodal, and (c) studies classified as multimodal. Within each of these three major sections, we further categorize studies as either focusing on (a) teachers and/or English learners, (b) language and/or literacy, or (c) instruction. Clearly, Table 7.2 serves as a heuristic for the organizational structure of our results section. Depending on the nature and quantity of studies within the categories we have just specified, some of the subsections may be further divided into additional subcategories.

Studies Classified as Monomodal

Monomodal Studies That Focus on Teachers and/or English Learners. We classified two studies as monomodal focusing primarily on teachers and/or English learners. Here's why: monomodal, as we define it, deals primarily with one aspect of the visual or communicative arts and tends to do so in a decontextualized manner—that is, studies we labeled as monomodal tend to be large scale, more general, and tend not to focus on English learners in specific, richly articulated communicative contexts. For example, one of the two studies in this section (e.g., Helman, 2005) focused on one component of a large-scale assessment (Phonological Awareness Literacy Screening) that was given to students in 52 schools in Nevada. For this study, Helman (2005) analyzed anonymous student written responses from two of the 52 schools in her broader study seeking to explore, in more depth, why children responded as they did to the large-scale assessment. Overall, 18,000 students were assessed in Helman's large-scale study. One hundred and five were closely analyzed in terms of the nature of the students' writing on the assessments for this work. Results revealed that the English learners were, overall, at least one year behind their English-speaking counterparts. In the researcher's own

TABLE 7.2. Classification of Studies for Review

Category	Monomodal	Mixed Mono- and Multimodal	Multimodal
Teachers and/or English Learners	2 studies	10 studies	3 studies
Language and/or Literacy	14 studies	6 studies	2 studies
Instruction	3 studies	26 studies	3 studies

words, these data illustrate that "there is a crisis in meeting state and national literacy levels" for English learners (Helman, 2005, p. 220).

A second study in this subsection sought to ascertain students' perspectives or insights regarding their understanding of their reading. The researcher, Avalos (2003), asked 22 fourth-grade English learners to do written recalls of their reading. The researcher then analyzed the written recalls to ascertain the students' comprehension of their reading, as well as the errors in their writing. Avalos found that the creation of meaning for her subjects tended to be based on the students' backgrounds and cultural knowledge, as well as their knowledge of English vocabulary and syntax and the nature of the texts they read. Thus, the researcher suggested that teachers must attend to both text-based features and reader-based features when designing literacy instruction for English learners.

Several important issues surface regarding this subcategory. First, one benefit of studies in this category is that larger monomodal studies such as the ones we discuss here point readers to trends regarding specific aspects of the literacy learning of English learners. Helman's (2005) study, for example, illustrates that many English learners are performing significantly below their English-speaking peers on assessments of writing. Another benefit of studies in this subcategory is that they focus on English learners rather than instruction or language or literacy-related processes. In the case of the work of Avalos (2003), the researcher strove to understand the perceptions of the students, themselves, with respect to their understanding of texts. Scholars (e.g., Erickson & Shultz, 1982; Pearson, 1997) have long asserted that we, as an educational community, should attend to the voices and perceptions of students in our efforts to ascertain what students need to be successful literacy learners. While studies in this category do point out problematic trends in the education of English learners, they do not give readers specific insights about the nature of instruction that can "work" for specific English learners. Moreover, studies in this subsection do not capture the nuanced complexity surrounding the education of English learners in specific school and community contexts.

Monomodal Studies That Focus on Language and/or Literacy. Fourteen of the studies we reviewed were monomodal and foregrounded language and/or literacy. We classified studies in this section if they focused on discrete aspects of language and/or literacy—that is, studies in this group tended to focus on language and/or literacy as a disembodied code. We divided these studies into three additional sub-categories: (a) seven studies involved different language and/or literacy related skills in a child's first and second language, (b) three studies looked at the transfer of skills across languages, and (c) four studies examined the development of a skill or skills in a second language.

The studies exploring different literacy-related skills in a child's first and second language included a focus on (a) phonological awareness (four studies), (b) causality or clausal markers in writing (two studies), and (c) relationships between Spanish orthography and English spelling (one study). In general, researchers that focused on phonological awareness in both the first and second language found that phonological skills in both the first and second language are related to a child's ability to read in her first and second language (Dufva & Voeten, 1999; LaFrance & Gottardo, 2005). Even if a child has developed phonological skills in both her first and second languages, however, the nature of the first or second language matters in terms of using phonological skills to read (Loizou & Stuart, 2003). For example, Loizou & Stuart found that children whose first language was English and whose second language was Greek outperformed students whose first language was Greek and second language was English. The researchers postulate that English to Greek students outperformed Greek to English students because Greek is more orthographically regular than English, and it is easier to move from a language that is less structured to one that is more structured than the other way around. Other scholars (D'Angiulli & Siegel, 2001) compared phonological skills with syntactic skills to see which skills had the greatest impact on reading comprehension, finding that phonological skills had the greatest impact on reading comprehension.

The remaining three studies in this group—all focusing on discrete aspects of language and literacy—looked at causality in writing across L1 and L2 (Reynolds, 2002; Silliman, Bahr, Brea, Hnath-Chisolm, & Mahecha, 2002) and relationships between Spanish orthography and English spelling. All three of these studies offer evidence that while unique patterns of development can exist for English learners in both spelling and writing—depending on such factors as a child's native language, level of literacy and language proficiency in L1 and L2, and so forth—the overall process of acquiring spelling and writing skills in both a first and second language is related.

Three studies explored the issue of transfer of language and literacy-related skills across languages. Wang and Geva (2003) explored the transfer of literacy-related skills in children who spoke Cantonese as their first language. Their work illustrates that the orthography of a language impacts transfer of language and literacy-related skills and the manner in which instruction is presented matters. The Chinese children in their study, for example, were especially adept at spelling tasks that involved visually presented materials. The researchers hypothesized that this is because Chinese is a logographic language rather than an alphabetic language such as English.

Jimenez, Garcia, and Pearson (1996) examined the strategies that successful English learners use, as well as whether or not these transfer. They found that successful English learners focused more on vocabulary, monitored their comprehension better than less successful English learners, and actively and successfully transferred information across languages.

Perez and Flores (2002) examined children's achievement in Spanish and English in a two-way immersion program. The researchers used standardized tests to measure achievement. In particular, they sought to understand if children who learned to read in Spanish first would be able to transfer to English reading on grade level in the third grade. The researchers found that "children's mastery of Spanish reading was a stronger predictor of their performance in English reading than was their initial English oral language skill" (p. 125).

The work of all of these scholars who have studied transfer illustrates that literacy-related skills do transfer across languages. Consequently, literacy skills in a first language are beneficial to English learners. The relationships between the nature of the first and second languages, however, matters in the transfer process—that is, when languages are alphabetic (such as Spanish and English), transfer may more readily occur than when children move from logocentric languages (such as Chinese) to alphabetic languages (such as English).

Four studies examined the development and or assessment of a skill(s) in a second language. These studies ranged from the work of MacCoubrey, Wade-Woolley, Klinger, and Kirby (2004), which examined a method of early identification of at-risk readers in French immersion classrooms; a study by Aarts and Verhoeven (1999), which examined levels of literacy attainment of Turkish students in the Netherlands at the end of primary school; a study by Nuwash (1999), which explored relationships between listening skills and reading in English learners; to a study by Carlisle, Beeman, Davis, and Spharim (1999), which examined relationships between second language development and metalinguistic development. Two common findings cut across all of these studies. First, the more we know about the language and literacy proficiency of children in their native languages, the more we can predict their success in acquiring language and literacy-related skills in a second language. Second, ascertaining children's native language and literacy proficiency can be a complex undertaking, since schools and districts may not have the wherewithal to assess students across a wide array of first languages.

Monomodal Studies That Focus on Literacy Instruction. We classified two studies in this subsection because each of these studies focuses primarily on instruction, but each study also focuses on one discrete aspect of literacy, so we classify these studies as monomodal. Carrier (2003) set up a treatment and control group to explore the impact of instruction through a listening strategy on the learning of high school English learners. Working with 109 high-school Dutch students, Snellings, Van Gelderen, and De Glopper (2004) set up a treatment and control group to explore the impact of computerized training for fluency of lexical retrieval on second language writing. The researchers in both of these studies found positive outcomes regarding the instructional interventions they were testing.

While the positive outcomes for each of these studies are encouraging, it is unlikely that the results of these studies may significantly impact classroom instruction. First, the researchers tested only discrete aspects of literacy/language in each of their instructional interventions. Second, the work reported—especially the work by Snellings and colleagues (2004)—is highly technical. Questions arise. For example, how might these discrete aspects of language and literacy relate to the complex and interconnected array of skills and strategies that classroom teachers must teach daily in complex settings to students from vastly different cultural and linguistic backgrounds? How might the findings of such studies be made available and applicable to classroom teachers?

Studies Classified as Mixed Mono- and Multimodal

The category titled, "mixed mono- and multimodal" is more than a catchall for the studies that could not easily be defined as mono- or multimodal. Rather, as the largest of the three categories, it represents the norm of research into literacy instruction for English language learners for the past ten years. Consistent with a socially situated view of identity and discourse (Gee, 1990), learning—as described in the studies in this category—was most often placed within a sociocultural framework (e.g., Barton & Ivanic, 1991; Camitta, 1993; Cook-Gumperz & Keller-Cohen, 1993; Street, 1993; Weinstein-Shr, 1993). In opposition to a skills-based view of literacy, sociocultural theorists argue that becoming literate is a social act, and understanding how students derive meaning from a text must be tied to a larger discussion of group norms, beliefs, values, and social practices. According to Schiefflein and Cochran-Smith (1984),

> To understand the observed behaviors of any social group, we have to know what literacy means to the group. We have to understand which genres are seen as appropriate to master at different points in time. . . . Without serious consideration of what literacy means and does not mean for those people who are introduced to it, it will be impossible to make sense of the ways literacy organizes and is organized by different social groups. (pp. 20–22)

Research in this category involved various ethnographies and quantitative investigations into the group-defined practices of African American (Heath, 1983), Hispanic (Delgado-Gaitan & Trueba, 1997), Native American (Philips, 1983) and Hawaiian (Au & Mason, 1981) children. Success for the students in these studies depended upon finding a match between the literacy practices of their homes and those of the schools. Of the 40 studies reviewed in this subsection, only Kamberlis and Luna (1996) and Volk (1997) described a match between home and school literacy environments. The remaining studies explored discontinuities.

Of the 40 studies we categorized for review within the mixed mono- and multimodal column, 10 focused on teachers and English language learners (Athanases, 1998; Brock, McVee, Shojgreen-Downer, & Dueñas, 1998; Butler & Gutiérrez, 2003; Li, 2004; McCarthy, 2001; Weber & Longhi-Chirlin, 2001; Reese, Garnier, Gallimore, & Goldenberg, 2000; Wilkinson, 1998; Xu, 1996); six more focused primarily on language and/or literacy (Bauer & Montero, 2001; Carlisle, Beeman, Davis, & Spharim, 1999; Francis, 1999; Garcia, 2002; Gutiérrez-Clellen, 2002); and the remaining 24 focused primarily on instruction.

Mixed Mono- and Multimodal Studies That Focus on Teachers and/or English Learners. The primary question asked within the English language learners' subsection was, "How does the researcher draw on theory, data and research design to represent the literacy learning experiences of English language learners?" In the mixed perspective, researchers drew from the sociocultural framework described above and positioned the lives of students within a discussion of the larger social, cultural, and gendered forces that drive how literacy is taught and learned. In contrast to the monomodal category, the struggles that English language learners experience in learning to read and write were clearly explored in many of these studies. Students who found continuity between their language and literacy learning practices gleaned from their own cultural and linguistic backgrounds and the literacy practices of the school succeeded. Those who entered classrooms that did not value the literacy practices of different groups and did not provide scaffolding through various visual media missed out on opportunities to learn and often struggled. We address each of these trends in the following two subsections.

Climate as discontinuity. In subsection one, researchers provided highly descriptive ethnographic accounts of the school and home settings of English language learners. We included six qualitative studies (Athanases, 1998; Brock et al., 1998; Li, 2004; McCarthy, 2001; Weber & Longhi-Chirlin, 2001; Xu, 1996) within this section. Researchers identified discontinuities in the literacy learning experiences of Hispanic students (McCarthy, 2001; Weber & Longhi-Chirlin, 2001), Filipino students (Xu, 1996), Chinese students (Li, 2004) and mixed language groups (Athanases, 1998) within school settings.

Li (2004) explored the mismatch between home and school literacy practices of Chinese Canadian children. By placing her findings within an ethnographic research tradition and a sociocultural framework, Li moved away from the ways that English learners were represented in the monomodal category as anonymous and undefined. Li's work illustrates that the question of how the literacy experiences of English language learners are represented commands a complex and context-specific answer. Li framed the specific literacy practices of Billy and Jake within a discussion of their larger cultural, linguistic, and historical backgrounds as Chinese Canadians. Li found that Chinese students struggle with unfamiliar instructional methods which emphasize more contextualized interpretation of text versus a heavy emphasis on word-by-word decoding and comprehension, different explanations for why students fail, different expectations around homework, and poor communication between the home and the school.

McCarthy's (2001) study extended the discussion on how to represent the literacy experiences of English language learners. Like Li (2004), McCarthy placed the experiences of her focal students within their specific linguistic and ethnic backgrounds, but extended the findings by exploring the connections between identity formation and literacy learning. Her attention to identity formation and literacy development allowed for a dialogue between individual students' experiences and struggles with literacy and the larger forces playing out in their schools. The connections that she made are many. Findings showed the ways in which advanced students identify more closely with reading than struggling readers, the influence of different settings on identity formation, and the importance of subidentities (Mishler,1999) in forming connections with reading.

Climate as a constellation of factors. In three studies (Butler & Gutierrez, 2003; Reese et al., 2000; Wilkinson, 1998), researchers identified features of the home and school which predicted whether or not whether English language learners would be successful readers. Work presented within this subsection shares a focus with research by Athanases (1998), Brock and colleagues, (1998), Li (2004), McCarthy (2001), Weber and Longhi-Chirlin (2001), and Xu (1996). Butler and Gutierrez (2003), Reese and colleagues, (2000), and Wilkinson (1998), however, cast a broader net—that is, their work does not focus exclusively on home/school relationships, nor are findings organized within in a sociocutural framework. Research methods for Butler and Gutierrez, for example, were qualitative, used a limited number of participants, and focused deeply on a few variables. Reese and colleagues and Wilkinson framed their work from a quantitative perspective, measured a number of variables, and included more than 3,000 participants in their respective studies.

When the research design variables mentioned above are considered in light of the question, "How does the researcher draw on theory, data and research design to represent the literacy learning experiences of English language learners?", the reader is left with a very different perspective on who English language learners are. Butler and Gutierrez (2003), for instance, interviewed 61 fourth graders in the San Francisco Bay Area on questions concerning native English speakers and English language learners' perceptions of bilingualism. The findings indicated that strong English language learner readers had more positive perceptions of their "(a) their own language-mixing activities, (b) their own L1 literacy skills, (c) their fathers' level of English proficiency; and (d) the influence of their L1 on their English reading" (p. 185).

These findings are not striking. Most researchers or experienced teachers of English language learners would guess that English language learners who struggle with reading would have a more positive perception of their bilingual skills than English language learners who are proficient readers in English. After reading the study, the reader is not left with the feeling that English language learners are somehow powerless or victims of a larger educational machine. Consider the responses below to the question, "How do you think other people, who only speak English, feel about you being able to speak two languages?"

ELL+: I think they [native English speakers] think it's cool, because you can learn more and you can understand other people.

ELL+: They think I am lucky.

Consistent with the purpose of their research, Butler and Gutierrez (2003) interpreted these responses as two advanced students who hold positive perceptions of their bilingual skills. Outside of these interpretations, the reader also hears the voices of young English language learners who use upbeat words such as *cool* and *lucky.* They also have mastered English and made some friends with native English speakers without sacrificing their own bilingual abilities. While the study was limited in size and data collection, it is reasonable to conclude that these students have begun to bridge the gap between home and school that Athanases (1998), Brock and colleagues, (1998), Li (2004), McCarthy (2001), Weber and Longhi-Chirlin (2001) and Xu (1996) explored.

Wilkinson (1998) was also interested in identifying the contextual factors that contribute to success in reading among English language learners, but the methods and presentation of the data leave the reader with a very different answer to the question of how the literacy learning experiences of English language learners are represented. Over 3,000 students from 176 primary schools were studied. The large sample necessitates a quantitative design in which the findings are reported in complex charts and graphs. Like the work by Butler and Gutierrez (2003), Wilkinson (1998) explored the many factors within the school climate that facilitate or hinder literacy development.

Wilkinson's (1998) work is complex, thoughtful, thorough, and detailed. It is highly useful to researchers or school administrators who would like to be able to interpret larger trends within the literacy achievement of English language learners. What it does not do is include the voices of the students. Rather, it describes the English language learners as members of large ethnic groups and members of testing communities; however, unlike the work of Athanases (1998), Brock and colleagues (1998), Li (2004), McCarthy (2001), Weber and Longhi-Chirlin (2001), and Xu (1996), it does not offer individual accounts of the students. The interviews that drove the Butler and Gutierrez (2003) study are absent. English language learners are identified at a group level, as part of a larger movement. They are defined not by their words, but the numbers of on a large-scale assessment.

Mixed Mono- and Multimodal Studies That Focus on Language and/or Literacy. The primary question asked within the English language learners' subsection was, "How does the researcher draw on theory, data, and research design to define second language and literacy use among English language learners?" A review of six studies (Bauer & Montero, 2001; Davis et al., 1999; Francis, 1999; Gunderson & Clarke, 1998; Gutiérrez-Clellen, 2002; Haritos, 2003) revealed two themes concerning second language and literacy use and proficiency. First, the benchmark of second language proficiency is no longer the monolingual speaker. According to Haritos (2003), a number of researchers (Grosjean, 1985, 1998) have argued that a "monolingual bias" exists within bilingual research. For many years, monolingual language use and proficiency has represented the benchmark and led many researchers to argue that second language proficiency is, at best, an approximation of the monolingual's ability.

Research within the mixed category (Davis et al., 1999; Haritos, 2003), however, departs from this position and creates a separate category for second language proficiency in which bilingualism was explored as an asset—not a deficit. This was seen in the literature review and purpose within the Haritos study. The purpose of the Haritos' study was to study the organization of memory structures of bilingual children in relationship to the languages they speak. While Haritos conceded that there is no single agreed upon definition of bilingualism, Haritos did draw on research by Marian and Neisser (2000), Otoya (1987), Aragno and Schlachet (1996), and Perez-Foster (1998) to illustrate the complexities of bilingual proficiency and memory.

In the second theme, literacy proficiency is described within a larger social framework and is consistent with the sociocultural perspective. Researchers whose work falls within this theme emphasized the socially situated nature of literacy and the ties between first and second literacy skills. Of interest to researchers was the argument put forward by Cummins (1979) on the interdependence between first and second language literacy development. Cummins argued that gaining literacy skills in one language will assist learners in a second language. Cummins described this as a common underlying proficiency (CUP), and it is the basis of bilingual research.

Six of the studies (Bauer & Montero, 2001; Davis et al., 1999; Francis, 1999; Garcia, 2002) within the mixed category drew on (Cummins, 1979; Cummins & Swain, 1986) work. At the broadest level, Gunder and Clarke (1998) attempted to validate the CUP concept. Gunderson and Clarke conducted a survey of 24,987 school-age English language learners on 135 different variables related to language and literacy development and background. Interviews were conducted as well on students' views of their achievement. Findings confirmed (Cummins, 1979; Cummins & Swain, 1986) model of CUP.

Cummins and Swain (1986) elaborated on the CUP concept and showed how "common cross-lingual proficiencies underlie the obviously different surface manifestations of each language" (p. 82). As such, other researchers (Bauer & Montero, 2001; Davis et al., 1999; Francis, 1999; Garcia, 2002) also identified specific cross-lingual proficiencies and the extent to which they will transfer. Davis and colleagues (1999), for instance, asked three questions: "1) Are significant differences between children's English and Spanish writing proficiency apparent at the first-, second-, and third-grade levels? 2) Is performance on English and Spanish writing measures significantly related? 3) Are listening and reading comprehension significantly related to written language performance in each language?" (p. 241). The setting was an elementary parochial school in Chicago, populated almost exclusively by Hispanic students. Participants included 19 first graders (10 girls), 17 second graders (7 girls), and 15 third graders (9 girls). Spanish was the language of instruction 20% of the time, and all of the students could read and write in Spanish.

In response to the first question, findings revealed that students made significant progress in their writing proficiency between second and third grade, supporting the argument for a common underlying proficiency. Second, performance on English and Spanish writing measures was related, but the ability to spell and write long words in English was not significantly related to Spanish productivity. Finally, English listening comprehension was "related to English productivity, spelling, long words, and discourse, but not to linguistic complexity" (Davis et al., 1999, p. 245).

Mixed Mono- and Multimodal Studies That Focus on Instruction. Looking back to Table 7.2 in the Methods section of this manuscript, it is apparent that we classified the majority of the studies reviewed in this category; in fact, 26 of the 70 studies we reviewed fit in this category. After reading and analyzing the studies in this subsection, we noticed that instruction-related studies coalesced around two themes. Seventeen of the studies focused in instructional interventions pertaining to different aspects of literacy such as comprehension, vocabulary, oral language, phonological awareness, literature-based instruction, or writing. The remaining nine studies provided thick, rich, multifaceted descriptions of the discursive practices and/or activities in classroom contexts whereby the focus of instruction was literacy. We discuss each of these two major themes following.

Literacy-related instructional interventions. Five of the studies in this category examined instructional interventions related to comprehension alone or combined several literacy-related skills with comprehension (Denton, Anthony, Parker, & Hasbrouck, 2004; Droop & Verhoeven, 1998; Jimenez, 2000; Linan-Thompson, Vaughn, Hickman-Davis, & Kouzekanani, 2003; Van den Branden, 2000). Droop and Verhoeven (1998) and Jimenez (2000) found that when texts were culturally familiar to readers, their comprehension improved. Van den Branden (2000) found that different levels of language proficiency impacted English learners reading comprehension—that is, students with higher levels of language proficiency comprehended better. Within the context of her study, Van den Branden (2000) also sought to explore the effects of peer negotiation as compared to teacher negotiation during reading. Van den Branden (2000) found that English learners demonstrated superior comprehension when negotiating the meaning of a text with their teacher. The findings across these studies, while important, are not surprising.

Three of studies in this group of studies relate to comprehension, but look also at other literacy-related skills (Denton, Anthony, Parker, & Hasbrouck, 2004; Droop & Verhoeven, 1998; Jimenez, 2000; Linan-Thompson, et al., 2003). Thus, these three studies all looked at more complex interrelated conceptions of literacy and found that the literacy skills targeted in the interventions, for the most part, positively impacted the aspects of reading that were targeted in the interventions for the English learners. For example, Denton and colleagues (2004) looked at two literacy-related tutoring methods. One intervention (called Read Well) focused on combined systematic phonics with practice in decodable text. Another intervention (called Read Naturally) looked at repeated reading with contextualized vocabulary and comprehension instruction. Students receiving the "Read Well" tutoring made higher gains in decoding and vocabulary than students receiving instruction in the "Read Naturally" approach. What is interesting here, however, is that neither approach appeared to produce significant gains in comprehension, and the "Read Well" intervention primarily related to context-free word reading—which was the focus of the intervention.

This raises the question of the value of interventions that do not appear to improve students' comprehension when reading meaningful texts.

Another subgroup of four studies looked at phonology, vocabulary, oral language, or a combination of these areas (Carlo, August, McLaughlin, Snow, Dressler, Lippman, Lively, & White, 2004; Giambo & McKinney, 2004; Nag-Arulmani, Reddy, & Buckley, 2003; and White & Turner, 2005). Like the studies that looked at comprehension instructional interventions or instructional interventions that combined comprehension and other literacy-related skills, these researchers found that the instructional interventions they employed tended to produce significant outcomes relative to student learning. Several findings are worth noting here. For example, Carlo and colleagues (2004) designed a vocabulary intervention for English learners and sought to explore the impact of the intervention on English only students as well as English learners. They also explored relationships between improvement in vocabulary and improvement in reading comprehension. They found that improvement in vocabulary did, in fact, improve students' reading comprehension. Moreover, the intervention effects were as large for English learners as they were for English-only students. Their findings are especially important because of the persistent gap that exists between the English literacy development of English learners and English only students. Their work, in particular, seems to point the educational community in a useful direction for narrowing that gap.

Two studies (Morrow, Pressley, Smith, & Smith, 1997; Saunders & Goldenberg, 1999) explored various aspects of using literature-based instruction with English learners. Saunders and Goldenberg (1997), for example looked at the impact of using literature logs only, instructional conversations only, or a combination of literature logs and instructional conversations with English learners. Interestingly, they found that the combined literature log and instructional conversation group scored higher than the control group and the literature log only group, but not the instructional conversation group only. Their work illustrates that instructional decisions for English learners are nuanced and complex. For example, the combined use of instructional conversations and literature logs improved the factual and interpretive story comprehension for all students in their study; however, the extent of the combined effects depended on the language proficiency of the English learners—that is, limited English proficient students appeared to benefit more from the combined use of literature logs and instructional conversations than students at other levels of English proficiency.

Six of the studies in this subsection explored writing interventions (Fazio, 2001; R. Gomez, Parker, Lara-Alecio, & L. Gomez, 1996; Hernández, 2001; Huang, 2000; Kuball & Peck, 2006; Kucer & Silva, 1999). These studies raise several common issues and tensions in writing instruction for English learners. For example, most of these researchers looked at the tenuous balance in writing instruction between providing holistic and meaningful opportunities for children to write while still providing enough structured guidance to teach children writing strategies and skills. Either extreme end of this continuum (e.g., just letting students write without providing guidance and instruction vs. focusing instruction primarily on isolated skills related to writing) appears to be problematic for the writing development of English learners. For example, Kuball and Peck's (2006) work makes clear that Spanish-speaking English learners should not be placed in lower level skills-based programs in order for their writing to improve. Hernández (2001) found that too much attention to mechanics in instruction can impede English learners' abilities to learn to attend to audience, ideas, and organization in their writing. On the other hand, R. Gomez and colleagues (1996) found that English learners do need systematic guidance in their writing instruction for their writing to improve.

Thick, rich descriptions of literacy instruction for English learners. Nine studies comprise this subcategory (Barone, 2003; Fitzgerald, & Noblit, 1999; Jimenez, 2000; Kamberelis & de la Luna, 1996; Manyak, 2000, 2001; McCarthy, 1997; Truscott & Watts-Taffe, 1998; Volk, 1997). While all of the instruction-related studies in this mixed mono- and multimodal group that we have been discussing to this point are different from the instruction-related studies in the monomodal group, this particular group of nine studies stands in stark contrast to the corollary group of instruction-related studies in the monomodal category because the researchers in this group of studies have not only attended to multiple modes of literacy in the communicative arts in their work, they provide extensive discussions of the complex contexts and/or interactions within those contexts in classrooms; however, there were different foci across these rich descriptions of classroom instruction. For example, some of the studies (e.g., McCarthy, 1997; Volk, 1997) tended to place more emphasis on the discursive practices within and beyond classrooms. Other studies, (e.g., Barone) tended to focus more on the nature of classroom activities. While all of the studies in this subsection merit careful attention because of the insights they have to offer regarding literacy instruction for English learners; it is beyond the purview of this chapter to provide an extensive discussion of each of these complex studies. Consequently, we highlight one study here that serves as an example of the complex studies in this subcategory.

Manyak (2000) engaged in a yearlong ethnography of a primary grade immersion classroom in California. In his work, he sought to explore the literacy practices available to the children in this classroom, the children's participation in those literacy practices, and the children's development of language and literacy skills as a result of their engagement in classroom literacy practices. The classroom was comprised of 20 native Spanish-speaking Latino children. Ms. Page, the classroom teacher, spoke English and Spanish fluently. Manyak conducted his work in the wake of Proposition 227 in California, emphasizing practices such as the following: immersion classes were to focus on "promoting oral language development rather than reading" (p. 98), and immersion classes were to emphasize the use of English. Manyak's work documented the ways in which Ms. Page made explicit decisions, and engaged in specific instructional practices, to teach her children to read and write in the ways that she deemed most beneficial to them based on her education and experience. In his work, Manyak (2000) explicated how, despite the Proposition 227 mandate, Ms. Page designed a classroom literacy curriculum that was rich and complex and promoted the literacy learning of her children.

Studies Classified as Multimodal

Overall, the studies in this category reflected significant attention to one or more of the communicative arts and one or more of the visual arts. While each study was situated in a unique context and possessed a unique inquiry focus, the work involved was multimodal.

In addition to the predominate focus on multimodal views of literacy in various contexts, the studies reviewed here reflected similar views of language acquisition its relationship to identity. Most of the studies in this section were based on strong theoretical foundations and the researchers articulated how they drew on theory in the overall design, implementation, and interpretation of the findings. Theories used ranged from Vygotskian and Neo-Vygotskian perspectives of language to Gee's (1996) notion of discourse. The use of these theories of language demonstrated these researchers' preferences for viewing language as socially constructed. Thus, studies in this section clearly denoted the social and contextual nature of first and second language acquisition. Viewing language through these complex theoretical perspectives opened the door to recognizing multiple modes already in use in these various settings and encouraged investigation of their relevance for the literacy learning of English learners.

Multimodal Studies With a Focus on Teachers and/or English Learners. We classified the following studies as multimodal with a focus on teachers and/or English learners: Rubinstein-Avila (2003) and Moje, Ciechanowski, Kramer, Ellis, Carrillo, and Collazo, (2004). Both studies explored students' use of language in social interactions with an eye toward collecting and analyzing data that reflected the contextualized and purposeful use of language in the contexts studied. Rubinstein-Avila (2003) observed second graders reading in pairs and found the students switching roles between tutor and tutee while they made use of codeswitching, and metalinguistic scaffolds to read books together. The use of both texts and oral language skills in readings activities demonstrated the study's attention to the nuances of student behaviors within the complex classroom setting.

Moje et al. (2004) examined language use across naturalistic contexts. Their focus on home, community, and schooling environments for middle-school students included exploring students' use of discourse in family, community, and school relationships. In addition to noting the school and home factors, the authors described the activities and materials the adolescence students engaged with such as the Internet, print magazines, news, media such as television, and movies. Moje and colleagues' (2004) study represented an acknowledgement of many modes of language used by children across contexts. The authors' use of ethnographic methods over the course of five years provided a window into how the English language learners' in their study were utilizing language sources and resources across a wide array of contexts.

Multimodal Studies With a Focus on Language and/or Literacy. Multimodal work with a particular focus on aspects of language and literacy was illustrated by Sarroub (2002) and Parks, Hout, Hamers, and Lemonnier (2005). Sarroub (2002) and Parks et al. (2005) both viewed the enactment of language activities and practices across many modes of expression including texts and technology. These studies focused on how the different modes of discourse used by informants in the studies affected the uses to which the discourses were put and the myriad ways that the discourses functioned in the lives of the informants in the studies. Sarroub's (2002) analysis of religious texts used by Yemeni high-school girls included not only their textual environment in English and Arabic, but also their larger cultural and social worlds. This expanded textual milieu illustrated what Sarroub (2002) described as the hidden texts of high school, weddings, parties, and illustrated how her informants' identities modified their interpretations of texts as they vacillated between American and Yemeni personas.

Parks and colleagues (2005) investigated the use of technology within a "History of Theater" Web site project focused on writing. The modes of technology and writing were studied for a four-year period with secondary English language learners in Quebec. The researchers found that the students' appropriation of the use of technology during their writing increased along with the personal investment experienced by students. Integrating technology as a mode of language use in the study led the researchers to recommend multi-authored texts and expansion of the production of texts to include forms such as Web sites.

Multimodal Studies With a Focus on Instruction. A focus on instruction as it related to English learners was evident in these three studies. Ulanoff and Pucci (1999), Sun and Dong, (2004), and Chapman, (2000) attended to pedagogical tools to aid in second language literacy acquisition. Ulanoff and Pucci (1999) examined three modes of read-aloud presentation to third grade students. One group listened to a story in L2 as compared to another group that received concurrent translation into L1 for the same story, and the last group who received prereading L1 translation of key vocabulary and concepts. Their findings indicated that the previewing of the vocabulary and concepts prior to reading made a significant difference, emphasizing the importance of attending to students' background knowledge in vocabulary achievement. Sun and Dong (2004) also looked at vocabulary instruction using the mode of multimedia. In their work with Chinese speaking seven year olds, Sun and Dong (2004) found the use of animation to facilitate vocabulary development when it coincided with specific learning support.

Chapman (2000) viewed modes of oral communication and nonverbal gestures that first grade English language learners and English language speakers use as they begin to read in their second language. Chapman's (2000) study of English language learners in the context of peer interactions demonstrated the ways in which children constructed modes of communicating about text that worked in their specific contexts. The first graders used pointing, demonstration, and elaborate gestures to accompany their oral language interactions. Finally, Pardue (2004) studied the use of hip-hop, street dance, and graffiti ethnographically in Brazilian state institutions. Observing the ways in which the under-eighteen males participated in and used the language of these various modes represented the strength of exploring language use in multiple forms as determined by the users contexts and knowledge.

Note that the studies we placed in this category illustrated multimodal discourse in research because they attended to multiple modes in the visual and communicative arts. We now turn to a discussion of the broader themes of literacy as they relate to the theory of multimodal discourse proposed by Kress and Van Leeuwen (2001).

Discussion. This study involved an in-depth analysis of 69 articles on the topic of literacy and English language learners. Studies were placed on a 3 × 3 grid, which allowed for an analysis that was consistent with Kress and Van Leeuwen's (2001) theory of multimodal discourse (See Table 7.2). Within the teacher/learner category, we asked, "How does the researcher draw on theory, data and research design to represent the literacy learning experiences of English language learners?" This question allowed for an examination of the intersection between research design, theory, and data collection as a means to discern larger trends in how literacy learning experiences were represented. While the studies ranged just 15 years apart, each category—monomodal, mixed, and multimodal—offered a unique answer to that question. We use Kress and Van Leeuwen's (2001) framework to discern themes across the categories of teachers and/or English learners as well as language and/or literacy and instruction. To analyze the teachers and/or English learners and language and/or literacy categories, we used concept of discourse. The concept of production informed our analysis within the instruction category.

The concept of discourse, as described by Kress and Van Leeuwen (2001), refers to the ways in which we make sense of or interpret what we know about our surroundings. The premise underlying this statement is key: It is that two people may have vastly different interpretations of the same event, the same text, or the same conversation. The source of these differences can be driven by gender, social class, or—in the case of English language learners—language and culture. Groups of individuals who occupy one these categories will share a set of communicative or interpretive practices that allow them to communicate without misunderstandings and hesitations. Often, these groups are referred to as discourse communities. Research mentioned above on Hispanic students (McCarthy, 2001; Weber & Longhi-Chirlin, 2001), Filipino students (Xu, 1996), Chinese students (Li, 2004) and mixed language groups (Athanases, 1998) within school settings taps communicative practices of these communities. When discourse is used to understand literacy research, we can begin to understand how discourse and discourse communities separate representations of English language learners and teachers across the categories of monomodal, mixed, and multimodal.

We begin with a discussion of the discourse community within the monomodal category of English language learners and/or teachers. Two studies were within this category. Both represented excellent examples of sophisticated, large-scale studies, and both gave strong insights of the specific skills that English language learners lack. As such, the discourse was one of teachers and students who are members of large groups whose discourse communities are in opposition to the majority and thus represent a problem. In both studies, data on the failure rate of English language learners is presented; the beliefs of students about literacy are identified; the search for the nature of the specific problem is undertaken; and recommendations for how to solve the problem are presented. While both the Helman (2005) and the Avalos (2003) studies are strong contributions to literacy research, they leave the reader with a picture of English language learners and teachers as opaque and undefined.

In the monomodal language and/or literacy category, we placed 14 studies divided into three additional subcategories. The question asked within this category was, "How does the researcher draw on theory, data, and research design to define second language and literacy use among English language learners?" Researchers in this category relied heavily on quantitative and mixed methods that allowed them to identify and evoke a discourse in which the act of acquiring a second language and becoming literate involves cracking a code. To that end, researchers were interested in identifying specific linguistic skills of English language learners. Topics include phonological awareness (e.g., Dufva & Voeten, 1999; LaFrance & Gottardo, 2005), writing and spelling (e.g., Reynolds, 2002; Silliman et al., 2002), the transfer of metalinguistic skills (e.g., Jimenez et al., 1996; Perez & Flores, 2002; Wang & Geva, 2003), and the development of assessment skills (e.g., Aarts & Verhoeven, 1999; Carlisle et al., 1999; Nuwash, 1999; MacCoubrey et al., 2004).

The mixed category of English language learners and/or teachers presses the reader to make sense of the different ways in which particular English language learners and teachers interpret their surroundings. Within the teachers and/or English learners category, the search is for defining the specific features of language and culture that separate the majority group (often, white female middle-class teachers) from the minority group (often, Spanish speaking students). Consistent with research from the sociocultural perspective, a discourse around difference was often evoked. Frequently, the focus was on simply describing the various ways in which discourse communities are different, but the researchers stopped short of placing the blame on the teachers, the schools, the students or the parents. Instead, suggestions were made such as in the Li (2004) article, which called on teachers and school personnel to recognize these differences and develop clearer lines of communication.

In the language and/or literacy mixed category, researchers extend the sociocultural framework within the above descriptions of English language learners and teachers by forwarding the discourse of difference about the competency of English language learners. As in the descriptions of English language learners and teachers, a new space is established to describe the competency of English language learners where the monolingual English speaker is no longer the benchmark for competency in a second language. Researchers argue that the ways that English language learners use language are different and not a problem. The specific features of language are often described (e.g., Bauer & Montero, 2001; Davis et al., 1999; Francis, 1999; Garcia, 2002), and the use of these specific features is often referenced to specific discourse communities.

Within the multimodal category, discourse is developed around exploring the unknown and uncovering what is invisible. These studies, however, are not simply a rehash of the mixed categories. Rather, they ask readers to invent new categories for their students that capture them as individuals who are involved in literacy learning and teaching in nontraditional ways. In the category of English language learners and/or teachers, for instance, Rubinstein-Avila (2003) showed how code-switching and metalinguistic scaffolds form a new category to describe the literacy activities of students. Moje, and colleagues (2004) described English language learners as members of discourse communities that involve the Internet, print magazines, news, media such as television, and movies. In such studies, researchers move between the individual and the larger group or discourse community to explain literacy. The outcome is a powerful one. Readers see a larger scale study in which the practices of discourse communities are identified without losing the nuances of individual's lives and literacy practices.

Researchers within the language and/or literacy multimodal category develop a broad but complementary definition of language. Researchers examine the interplay between discourse communities and such disparate texts as religious documents (Sarroub, 2002) and computer Web sites (Parks et al., 2005). Pardue's (2004) study, while not placed within the language and/or literacy multimodal category, is still informative. It broadened a definition of language and literacy use to include hip-hop dancing, graffiti, and rapping, and it showed how such forms of literacy are connected to a larger class-based social movement in Brazil.

The remaining category is instruction. While there are clearly opportunities to discuss the discourses that run through the category of instruction, they would be limited. Instruction is a topic of research that is tied inextricably to a performance, and the concepts of production and design are more appropriate points of analysis. Production, according to Kress and Van Leeuwen (2001), refers to the "organization of the expression . . . or the actual material production of the semiotic artifact" (p. 6), while design is the "conceptualization" of various semiotic events. Thus, a designer of a lesson or unit of study is the one who arranges and organizes various activities, or events, based upon a theory of what might enhance student learning. In contrast, a producer of a lesson is the individual who actually conducts the lesson.

There are instances in which the producer and designer of instruction are separate. Scripted curricular approaches are an example of designers focusing heavily on the conceptualization of a unit or method of instruction in the absence of production. When teachers are enlisted to carry out such approaches, they act as producers who may be able to add their own individual accent, but ultimately have little or no input into the design. Below, we classify the findings into three categories: (a) isolated producers of literacy instruction, (b) limited producer/designer, and (c) designers of literacy instruction and producers of literacy instruction.

The isolated producer of literacy instruction is one who works from a technical basis of research. In order for teachers to play a role in design, they must interpret fairly sophisticated research on discreet aspects of language. Language functions as a code and is the object of instruction. The research design is often quantitative and captures a large participant base. As a result, students occupy an anonymous role. Just two studies fit within this category: (a) Carrier's (2003) study of listening strategies among high students and (b) Snellings and colleagues' (2004) study of lexical retrieval among second language learners. Both are highly technical studies of language and provide design suggestions in the absence of data on how instruction is produced.

The second category, limited producer/designer, draws on broad research from the sociocultural framework in which a differences model is forwarded. Researchers, acting in the design role, may offer broad concepts or principles on which to base instruction, but then also encourage teachers to add their own personal touches to the instruction. This movement from a highly technical base of instruction seen in the monomodal category to a base that is accessible to teachers nudges teachers closer to the mixed designer/producer role. Topics of research in this category appropriately addressed such familiar problems as how to balance skills and holistic instruction in writing (e.g., Fazio, 2001; R. Gomez et al., 1996; Hernández, 2001; Huang, 2000; Kuball & Peck, 2006; Kucer & Silva, 1999), the nature of discursive practice inside and outside the classroom (Barone, 2003; Fitzgerald & Noblit, 1999; Jimenez, 2000; Kamberelis & de la Luna, 1996; Manyak, 2000, 2001; McCarthy, 1997; Truscott & Watts-Taffe, 1998; Volk, 1997), and a host of intervention topics. These studies are relevant to a discussion of multimodal discourse because they allow teachers to interpret the findings on their own, add their own touches, and proceed with instruction in their own classrooms.

The final category is titled designers of literacy instruction and producers of literacy instruction. It is separated from the limited producer/designer because it often asks the teacher to take full responsibility for design and production of the lesson. The findings are broad, relying on definitions of literacy that include the production of graffiti and hip-hop dancing. Again, Pardue's (2004) study is relevant, as it called for instruction that recognizes and helps students to make connections between literacy and their social lives. Teachers and students work as agents of change within schools and their political lives.

While drawing definitive conclusions about the state of literacy is at best difficult, we do have some final observations. First, while we are disheartened by the limited amount of research into English language learners as it relates to visual literacy, we are encouraged by the quality and direction of research. When we began, we believed that most of literacy research on English language learners is devoted to scripted programs. Nothing could be further from the truth. The largest body of research was organized around a sociocultural model.

Second, we also would argue that the road ahead is not yet agreed upon by researchers. Each of the categories makes a valuable contribution and sets a different path. A monomodal perspective wants to set a path for teachers, but it is a narrow one—perhaps too narrow for all but the most scientifically minded. The mixed mono- and multimodal calls on teachers to learn more, to explore alternate possibilities and search out new roads. That search, however, is never-ending. The new multimodal perspective asks teachers and researchers to rewrite the map, abandon the old map and compass, and find new directions. Few have taken this path, but it is powerful because it calls on researchers and teachers to ask who we have left behind on the educational journey.

REFERENCES

Aarts, R., & Verhoeven, L. (1999). Literacy attainment in a second language submersion context. *Applied Psycholinguistics, 20*, 377–393.

Athanases, S. Z. (1998). Diverse learners, diverse texts: Exploring identity and difference through literacy encounters. *Journal of Literacy Research, 30*(2), 273–96.

Au, K. H., & Mason, J. M. (1981). Social organizational factors in learning to read. *Reading Research Quarterly, 17*, 115–152.

August, D. & Hakuta, K. (1997). *Improving schooling for language-minority children: A research agenda.* Washington, D. C.: National Academy Press.

Avalos, M. A. (2003). Effective second-language reading transition: From learner-specific to generic instructional models. *Bilingual Research Journal, 27*(2), 171–206.

Barton, D., & Ivanic, R. (Eds.). (1991). *Writing in the community.* London: Sage.

Bauer, E. B. & Montero, M. K. (2001). Reading versus translation: A preschool bilingual's interpretation of text. *National Reading Conference Yearbook, 50*, 115–126. Chicago: National Reading Conference.

Brock, C. H., McVee, M. B., Shojgreen-Downer, A. M., & Dueñas, L. F. (1998). No habla Inglés: Exploring a bilingual child's literacy learning opportunities in a predominantly English-speaking classroom. *Bilingual Research Journal, 22*(2–4), 103–128.

Butler, Y. G., & Gutiérrez, M. B. (2003). Learning climates for English language learners: A case of fourth-grade students in California. *Bilingual Research Journal, 27*(2), 207–224.

Camitta, M. (1993). Vernacular writing: Varieties of literacy among Philadelphia high school students. In B. Street (Ed.), *Cross-cultural approaches to literacy* (pp. 228–246). Cambridge, England: Cambridge University Press.

Carlisle, J. F., Beeman, M., Davis, L. H., & Spharim, G. (1999). Relationship of metalinguistic capabilities and reading achievement for children who are becoming bilingual. *Applied Psycholinguistics, 20*, 459–478.

Carlo, M. S., August, D., Mclaughlin, B., Snow, C. D., Dressler, D., Lippman, D. N., Lively, T. J., & White, C. E. (2004). Closing the gap: Addressing the vocabulary needs of English-language learners in bilingual and mainstream classrooms. *Reading Research Quarterly, 39*(2), 188–215.

Carrier, K. A. (2003). Improving high school English language learners' second language listening through strategy instruction. *Bilingual Research Journal, 27*(3), 383–408.

Cook-Gumperz, J., & Keller-Cohen, D. (Eds.). (1993). Alternative literacies: in school and beyond [Theme issue]. *Anthropology & Education Quarterly, 24*(4).

Cummins, J. (1979). Linguistic interdependence and the educational development of bilingual children. *Review of Educational Research, 49*, 222–251.

Cummins, J., & Swain, M. (1986). *Bilingualism in education*. New York: Longman.

D'Angiulli, A., & Siegel, L. S. (2001). The development of reading in English and Italian in bilingual children. *Applied Psycholinguistics, 22*, 479–507.

Delgado-Gaitan, C., & Trueba, H. (1997). *Crossing cultural borders: Education for immigrant families in America*. New York: Falmer.

Denton, C. A., Anthony, J. L., Parker, R., & Hasbrouck, J. E. (2004). Effects of two tutoring programs on the English reading development of Spanish-English bilingual students. *The Elementary School Journal, 104*(4), 289–305.

Droop, D. & Verhoeven, L. (1998). *Linguistic and cultural diversity and reading comprehension development*. Netherlands: University of Nijmegen Press.

Dufva, M., & Voeten, M. J. M. (1999). Native language literacy and phonological memory as prerequisites for learning English as a foreign language. *Applied Psycholinguistics, 20*, 329–348.

Erickson, F., & Shultz, J. (1982). When is a context? Some issues and methods in the analysis of social competence. In J. L. Green & C. Wallet (Eds.), *Ethnography and language in educational settings*, (pp. 147–160). Norwood, NJ: Ablex.

Fazio, L. L. (2001). The effect of corrections and commentaries on the journal writing accuracy of minority- and majority-language students. *Journal of Second Language Writing, 10*, 235–249.

Fitzgerald, J. (1995). English-as-a-second-language learners' cognitive reading processes: A review of research in the United States. *Review of Educational Research, 65*(2), 145–190.

Flood, J., Heath S. B., & Lapp, D. (2005). Handbook of research on teaching literacy through the communicative and visual arts. Mahwah, NJ, US: Lawrence Erlbaum Associates Publishers, 2005.

Francis, N. (1999). Bilingualism, writing, and metalinguistic awareness: Oral literate interactions between first and second languages. *Applied Psycholinguistics, 20*, 533–561.

Garcia, E. (2000). *Student cultural diversity: Understanding and meeting the challenge*. New York: Houghton Mifflin Company.

Garcia, G. E. (2002). Mexican-American Bilingual Students' Metacognitive Reading Strategies: What's transferred, Unique, Problematic? *National Reading Conference, 47*, 253–263.

Gee, J. P. (1990). *Social linguistics and literacies: Ideologies in discourses*. New York: Falmer.

Giambo, D. A., & McKinney, J. D. (2004). The effects of phonological awareness intervention on the oral English proficiency of Spanish-speaking kindergarten children. *TESOL Quarterly, 38*(1), 95–117.

Gomez, R., Jr., Parker, R., Lara-Alecio, R., & Gomez, L. (1996). Process versus product writing with limited English proficient students. *The Bilingual Research Journal, 20*(2), 209–233.

Grosjean, F. (1985). The bilingual as a competent but specific speaker-hearer. *Journal of Multilingual and Multicultural Development, 6*(6), 467–477.

Grosjean, F. (1998). Studying bilinguals: Methodological and conceptual issues. *Bilingualism: Language and Cognition, 1*(2), 131–149.

Gunderson, L. & Clark, D. K. (1998). An exploration of the relationship between ESL students' backgrounds and their English and academic achievement, *National Reading Conference Yearbook, 47*, 264–273.

Gutiérrez-Clellen, V. F. (2002). Narratives in two languages: Assessing performance of bilingual children. *Linguistics and Education, 13*(2), 175–197.

Haneda, M. (2005). Some functions of triadic dialogue in the classroom: Examples from L2 research. *The Canadian Modern Language Review, 62*(2), 313–333.

Haritos, C. (2003). Listening, remembering, and speaking in two languages: How did you do that? *Bilingual Research Journal, 27*(1), 73–99.

Heath, S. B. (1983). *Ways with words: Language, life and work in communities and classrooms*. Cambridge, MA: Cambridge University Press.

Helman, L. A. (2005). *Spanish speakers learning to read in English: What a large-scale assessment suggests about their progress*. University of Minnesota Press.

Hernández, A. C. (2001). The expected and unexpected literacy outcomes of bilingual students. *Bilingual Research Journal, 25*(3), 301–326.

Jimenez, R. T. (2000). Literacy and the identity development of Latina/o students. *American Educational Research Journal, 37*(3), 971–1000.

Jimenez, R. T., Garcia, G. E., & Pearson, P. D. (1996). The reading strategies of bilingual Latina/o students who are successful English readers: opportunities and obstacles. *Reading Research Quarterly*, International Reading Association, *31*, 90–112.

Kamberlis, G. & Luna, L. C. (1996). *Constructing multiculturally relevant pedagogy: Signifying on the basal*. University of Illinois Press.

Kress, G. & Van Leeuwen, T. (2001). *Multimodal discourse: The modes and media of contemporary communication*. New York: Oxford University Press.

Kuball, Y. E., & Peck, S. (1997). The effect of whole language instruction on the writing development of Spanish-speaking and English-speaking kindergartners. *Bilingual Research Journal, 21*(2–3), 213–231.

Kucer, S. B., & Silva, C. (1999). The English literacy development of bilingual students within a transition whole-language curriculum. *Bilingual Research Journal, 23*(4), 345–371.

LaFrance, A., & Gottardo, A. (2005). A longitudinal study of phonological processing skills and reading in bilingual children. *Applied Psycholinguistics, 26*, 559–578.

Linan-Thompson, S., Vaughn, S., Hickman-Davis, P., & Kouzekanani, K. (2003). Effectiveness of supplemental reading instruction for second-grade English language learners with reading difficulties. *The Elementary School Journal, 103*(3), 221–238.

Li, G. (2004). Perspectives on struggling English language learners: Case studies of two Chinese-Canadian children. *Journal of Literacy Research, 36*(1), 31–72.

Loizou, M., & Stuart, M. (2003). Phonological awareness in monolingual and bilingual English and Greek five-year-olds. *Journal of Research in Reading, 26*(1), 3–18.

MacCoubrey, S. J., Wade-Woolley, L., Klinger, D., & Kirby, J. R. (2004). Early identification of at-risk L2 readers. *The Canadian Modern Language Review, 61*(1), 11–28.

Mailloux, S. (1990). *Critical terms for literary study*. Chicago and London. The University of Chicago Press.

Malone, N., Baluja, K. F., Costanzo, J., & Davis, C. J. (2003). *The foreign-born population: 2000*. Retrieved November 8, 2005, from http://www.census.gov/population/www/cen2000/briefs.html

Marian, V., & Neisser, U. (2000). Language-dependent recall of autobiographical memories. *Journal of Literacy Research, 36*(1), 31–72.

McCarthy, S. J. (2001). Connecting home and school literacy practices in classrooms with diverse populations. *Journal of Literacy Research, 29*(2), 145–182.

Nag-Arulmani, S., Reddy, V., & Buckley, S.(2003). Targeting phonological representations can help in the early stages of reading in a non-dominant language. *Journal of Research in Reading, 26*(1), 49–68.

Nieto, S. (2002). *Language, culture, and teaching: Critical perspectives for a new century*. Mahwah, NJ: Lawrence Erlbaum.

Nuwash, C. F. (1999). *Reading and listening in English as a second language*. University of Texas Press.

Otoya, M. (1987). A study of personal memories of bilinguals: The role of culture and language in memory and encoding and recall. *Unpublished doctoral dissertation*, Harvard University, Cambridge, MA.

Pardue, D. (2004). "Writing in the margins": Brazilian hip-hop as an educational project. *Anthropology and Education Quarterly, 35*(4), 411–432.

Parks, S., Hout, D., Hamers, J., & Lemonnier, F. H. (2005). "History of theatre" web sites: A brief history of the writing process in a high school ESL language arts class. *Journal of Second Language Writing, 14*, 233–258.

Perez, B., & Flores, B. B. (2002). *Biliteracy development in two-way immersion classrooms: Analysis of third grade Spanish and English reading.* University of Texas Press.

Perez-Foster, R. (1998). *The power of language in the clinical process: Assessing and treating the bilingual person.* North Bergen, NJ: Jason Aronson.

Philips, S. U. (1983). *The invisible culture.* New York: Longman.

Reese, L., Garnier, H., Gallimore, R., & Goldenberg, C. (2000). Longitudinal analysis of the antecedents of emergent Spanish literacy and middle-school English reading achievement of Spanish-speaking students. *American Educational Research Journal, 37*(3), 633–662.

Reynolds, D. W. (2002). Learning to make things happen in different ways: Causality in the writing of middle-grade English language learners. *Journal of Second Language Writing, 11*, 311–328.

Rose, M. (1989). *Lives on the boundary: A moving account of the struggles and achievements of America's educational underclass.* New York: Penguin Books.

Saunders, W. M., & Goldenberg, C. (1999). Effects of instructional conversations and literature logs on limited- and fluent-English-proficient students' story comprehension and thematic understanding. *The Elementary School Journal, 99*(4), 277–301.

Schiefflein, B. B., & Cochran-Smith, M. (1984). Learning to read culturally; Literacy before schooling. In H. Goelman, A. A. Oberg, & F. Smith (Eds.), *Awakening to literacy* (pp. 3–23). Portsmouth, NH: Heinemann.

Silliman, E. R., Bahr, R. H., Hnath-Chisolm, T., & Mahecha, N. R. (2002). Spanish and English proficiency in the linguistic encoding of mental states in narrative retellings. *Linguistics and Education, 13*(2), 199–234.

Snellings, P., Van Gelderen, A., & De Glopper, K. (2004). The effect of enhanced lexical retrieval on second language writing: A classroom experiment. *Applied Psycholinguistics, 25*, 175–200.

Street, B. V. (Ed.). (1993). *Cross-cultural approaches to literacy.* Cambridge, England: Cambridge University Press.

Sun, Y., & Dong, Q. (2004). An experiment on supporting children's English vocabulary learning in multimedia context. *Computer Assisted Language Learning, 17*(2), 131–147.

Thomas, W. P., & Collier, V. P. (2004). A national study of school effectiveness for language minority students' long-term academic achievement. *Center for Research on Education, Diversity & Excellence (CREDE).*

Trueba, H. T. (1989). *Raising silent voices: Educating the linguistic minorities for the 21st century.* Boston, MA: Heinle & Heinle Publishers.

Ulanoff, S. H., & Pucci, S. L. (1999). Learning words from books: The effects of Read Aloud on second language vocabulary acquisition. *Bilingual Research Journal, 23*(4), 409–422.

Volk, D. (1997). Questions in lessons: Activity settings in the homes and school of two Puerto Rican kindergartners. *Anthropology & Education Quarterly, 28*(1), 22–49.

Walker-Moffat, W. (1995). *The other side of the Asian American success story.* San Francisco, CA: Jossey-Bass Publishers.

Wang, M., & Geva, E. (2003). Spelling performance of Chinese children using English as a second language: Lexical and visual-orthographic processes. *Applied Psycholinguistics, 24*, 1–25.

Weber, R., & Longhi-Chirlin, T. (2001). Beginning in English: The growth of linguistic and literate abilities in Spanish-speaking first graders. *Reading Research and Instruction, 41*(1), 19–50.

Weinstein-Shr, G. (1993). Literacy and social process: A community in transition. In B. Street (Ed.), *Cross-cultural approaches to literacy* (pp. 272–293). Cambridge, England: Cambridge University Press.

White, J. L., & Turner, C. E. (2005). Comparing children's oral ability in two ESL programs. *The Canadian Modern Language Review, 61*(4), 491–517.

Wilkinson, I. A. (1998). Dealing with diversity: Achievement gaps in reading literacy among New Zealand students. *Reading Research Quarterly, 33*(2), 144–167.

Xu, Y., Gelfer, J., & Perkins, P. (2005). Using peer tutoring to increase social interactions in early schooling. *TESOL Quarterly, 39*(1), 83–106.

8

CENSORSHIP AND CENSORSHIP POLICY: THE IMPACT ON TEACHING LITERACY THROUGH THE VISUAL ARTS

Nancy Frey
SAN DIEGO STATE UNIVERSITY

Consider the following disciplinary actions related to the use of instructional materials:

- An elementary music teacher in Bennett, Colorado is placed on administrative leave after showing excerpts of an educational video of the opera *Faust* to her students. A group of parents file a complaint about the opera's references to the devil (Fong, 2006).
- A Fort Pierce, Florida high-school English teacher is suspended for three days for showing a 20-minute excerpt of the R-rated movie *Dracula*. He did not show any parts of the movie containing nudity or other scenes that would prompt the movie rating (CBS News, 2003).
- A 37-year veteran teacher is given the choice of either retiring or being fired after showing the R-rated movie *Elizabeth* to his English literature class at South Gwinnett (Georgia) High School (Sugiura, 2005).
- Three Albuquerque Public Schools high-school employees win a civil rights lawsuit because of their suspension for posting antiwar literature in their classrooms and, in the case of one, their counseling office (American Civil Liberties Union, 2003).
- A third-grade teacher in Brooklyn is transferred after coming under fire for reading the picture book *Nappy Hair* (Herron, 1997) and photocopying illustrated pages of the book for her students. Critics assert that the illustrations are racist. She cites threats against her life as reason for the move (Leyden, 1998).
- In El Cajon, California, two Grossmont High School District teachers are suspended after one plays an audiotape and the other allows students to download the video of the beheading in Iraq of American captive Nicolas Berg (Sanchez, 2004).

Depending on your personal viewpoints and experiences, you mayagree or disagree with the outcomes of each of these incidences. In some cases, you may have felt the resulting actions did not fit the offense. There may be one or more incidences with which you are in complete agreement or disagreement. Regardless of the range of reactions these incidents elicit, one factor seems apparent: the policies used to make these decisions vary widely.

Censorship policies in schools, districts, and state education agencies are inexorably bound in the landscape of the broader culture. The hot-button issues of the day often result in the crafting of a new set of policies meant to protect students from violent, sexually explicit, or offensive materials, yet those same policies are confounded by the personal definitions of those crafting the policy. What is too violent? What is the difference between explicit and informative? Who is offended? In this chapter, I will discuss the history of censorship and the influence of society, popular culture, and current events on censorship policies. The remaining section of the chapter will address censorship and visual literacy, especially images, film, and public displays of information.

HISTORY OF CENSORSHIP

The idea that children needed to be protected from ideas, language, and images can be traced back to the Greek philosopher Plato, who argued that children should first learn morally and ethically honorable ideas because they were incapable of discerning the difference between truth and fiction (Plato, Grube, & Reeve, 1992). In the 4th century BCE, this was a rather radical notion, as children were not seen as needing to be shielded from the adult world (Heins, 2001). Human development was defined by an infancy that lasted until about the age of seven, followed by growth into a physical adulthood defined by one's ability to procreate and make war (Postman, 1994). Indeed, ancient mythology is filled with stories of young people (who we would now probably describe as "children"), involved in violent or sexual encounters that would seem unthinkable today. Postman described three factors to explain the absence of childhood: "The absence of literacy, the absence of the idea of education, the absence of the idea of shame—these are the reasons why the idea of childhood did not exist" (p. 17).

Ironically, the emergence of a more literate society led to the invention of childhood as a construct of human development (Postman, 1994). As literacy grew with the invention of moveable type in the 15th century, a notion of adulthood and childhood emerged over the next centuries. In this new model, adulthood was marked by literate ways, with a childhood devoted to becoming literate (Postman, 1994). The growth of schooling contributed to further delineation of a formalized time in human development between infancy and adulthood. This age span, typically occupying the years between 5 and 17, has come to be regarded as childhood. As such, society took on a role in the preservation and protection of childhood. The growth of Postman's three factors—(a) literacy, (b) education, and (c) shame—has become a primary influence on the policy of protection, and of censorship.

Censorship and Shame

Foucault (1984) traced censorship to the repressive practices of sexuality that began to emerge in the 17th century. His definition of censorship as "imposed silence" stands in juxtaposition to the preoccupation with sex, and especially its suppression in children, that marked the era (p. 301). Much has been written elsewhere about the role of Christianity, sexual repression, and the development of American culture (see Kessler, 1992, and Smith-Rosenberg, 1982, for thorough discussions). Carroll (1981) argued that the rise of guilt (closely related to shame) was spurred in part by the shift from small, agriculturally based communities of medieval times to the growth of cities and increased mobility during the 17th and 18th centuries. As communities became at once more loosely organized and more densely populated, guilt and shame became tools for controlling and suppressing deviant behavior.

As Puritanical beliefs of a punishing God gave way to the more "civilized guilt" of the 19th century, pornography and prostitution were increasingly tolerated by the upper classes (Carroll, 1981, p. 479). At the same time, public schools were being opened, promoted by the work of religious and educational leaders who viewed schooling as a way to ensure that children were being inculcated to the beliefs of the Christian church and the democratic principles of the young nation (Pulliam & Van Patten, 2003).

The availability of pornography, in particular, fueled the need for censorship laws to protect children from exposure to material deemed as too provocative. Thus, pornography, both literary and visual, became the primary focus of new local, state, and federal laws. One of the first cases occurred in 1815 in Pennsylvania, when a state court found a defendant guilty of displaying an obscene painting on loan from an Italian museum (Heins, 2001). In the 1840s, the first federal U.S. Customs law was passed regarding importation of indecent materials. In 1865, the reach of the federal government was extended to the U.S. Postal Service due to complaints about pornography being mailed to Civil War soldiers (Heins, 2001). The Federal Anti-Obscenity Act was passed in 1873, ostensibly to limit information on contraception. Thus, the precedent of government involvement in censorship was firmly established.

Censorship and the First Amendment

From the start, the challenge to the laws that were being created to restrict access to certain materials revolved around First Amendment rights. This portion of the Bill of Rights reads

> Congress shall make no law respecting an establishment of religion or prohibiting the free exercise thereof; or abridging the freedom of speech, or of the press, or of the right of people peaceably to assemble, or to petition the government for a redress of grievances. (US Constitution Amendment 1)

This amendment has been cited countless times in censorship trials by litigators on both sides of the issue. Perhaps the most well known case over the last century involved Joyce's (1990) *Ulysses*, which was seized by U.S. Customs in 1922 due to language and sexual content and subsequently burned. However, censorship was not limited to books, or to obscene content alone. In 1919, the U.S. Supreme Court found Charles Schenck guilty under the Espionage Act of "attempting to cause insubordination" for distributing leaflets through the mail encouraging peaceful resistance to the draft laws (*Schenck v. United States*, p. 49). The ruling, delivered by Oliver Wendell Holmes, Jr., contained the much-quoted "shouting fire in a theatre and causing a panic" rationale (*Schenck v. United States*, p. 51).

Materials deemed to contribute to the moral and ethical corruption of minors and adults were banned or restricted through legislative and judicial proceeding. The emerging film industry would soon follow as a target for censorship through the development of the Hays Code, which governed what could and could not be shown in movies. Local municipalities could apply even more stringent censorship codes. (Indeed, "Banned in Boston" would soon become a successful marketing tool for books and films.) What is notable is the inclusion of children, who were not the intended audience, as part of the rationale for banning these materials altogether. This set up a powerful precedent for the exclusion of materials created for children. And again, visual and literary forms led the way.

Censorship and Comic Books

The postwar era of the 1950s brought sweeping sociocultural changes to the American landscape. The baby boom, development of the suburbs, and newfound prosperity brought children and the importance of childhood into the spotlight as never before. The decade also had its dark side. The House Un-American Activities Committee hearings, led by Wisconsin Congressman Eugene McCarthy, cast a pall over the nation. The new medium of television brought the hearings into homes, and growing suspicions were fostered against writers, filmmakers, and other well-known persons. At the same time, the Cold War was escalating and the Soviet block was an increasingly ominous presence in the lives of Americans.

A book entitled *Seduction of the Innocent* (Wertham, 1954) was published, and its impact altered the comic book industry for decades. The author, a psychiatrist, interviewed jailed juvenile offenders and asked them what they read. "Comic books," came the reply, and in short order, comic books were demonized as a corrupting influence on the moral development of youth. The study itself was deeply flawed, if for no other reason than Wertham had failed to create a comparison group (Heins, 2001). If he had, he would have found that the majority of American youngsters read comic books. Indeed, a study of readership among seventh graders found that 75% of boys and 78% of girls read comic books on a regular basis (Blakely, 1958). Wertham's thesis was that the sexual, violent, and criminal activities portrayed in comic books fueled a lawless attitude and reckless behavior.

In short order Congress created the Comics Code Authority to pass judgment on the contents of comic books (Callahan, 2004). Several belief systems related to censorship in schools were now firmly in place:

- Children needed to be protected from materials that could prove detrimental to their moral and ethical development.
- Those materials included both the printed word and visual images.
- Content of a sexual or violent nature was of special concern.
- The preferred way to make censorship decisions was by specially appointed committees using codes that dictated what could and could not be seen or read.

CENSORSHIP AND THE USE OF VISUAL IMAGES

The Language of Censorship

The issue of censorship can become mired in the language used to describe such events in which materials are challenged. The Office for Intellectual Freedom (OIF), the American Library Association's division devoted to censorship issues, tracks books that have been challenged in schools and libraries. They categorize concerns into a hierarchy reflective of the intensity of the debate surrounding a book (OIF, n.d.). The Cooperative Children's Book Center has taken these categories and offers recommendations to educators in how to respond, as "[e]ach level advances the debate toward a more formal, and eventually, legal, case" (Pavonetti, 2002, p. 10).

Expression of concern. A teacher or librarian is questioned about a book or other material. The inquiry is not at the level of complaint, and the questioner is seeking information about material that has sparked a concern. The CCBC recommends that teachers and librarians furnish information to clarify educate.

Oral complaint. This may occur during a conversation, or in a note from a parent. There is a complaint about the appropriateness or suitability of material. The recommended response is to maintain an open dialogue with the complainant, listening to concerns and providing information. The CCBC notes that open conversations frequently reveal that the complainant has not read or viewed the material in its entirety, and may have focused on isolated portions only (Pavonetti, 2002).

Written complaint. This is a formal challenge following the prescribed procedures governing the local education agency. The CCBC observes that a common response among educators is to cease to communicate with the complainant. They advise attempting to maintain positive communication, and caution educators to familiarize themselves with the policy of the agency.

Public attack. Like the world of *Fahrenheit 451* (Bradbury, 1953), the public attack is meant to intimidate. By definition, it is conducted in a public forum, such as a meeting or in the broadcast media. The rise of Internet Web sites and blogging has made public attacks more common in the last decade. These are more difficult to respond to in a constructive way, particularly because they do not always accompany a written complaint (Pavonetti, 2002).

Censorship. This involves the removal or restriction of material from a library or classroom. The term "banned" can be used accurately only in these cases.

Why Do We Censor?

The Office for Intellectual Freedom, reports that parents are the frequent initiators of complaints against materials (1,526 of the 2,614 documented challenges between 2000–2004). Of these, the most common reasons were

- Offensive language (728 complaints)
- Sexually explicit (606 complaints)
- Unsuited to the age group (454 complaints)
- Violence (378 complaints) (OIF, n.d.)

Censoring Visual Images in Picture Books

Because picture books and graphic novels (Frey & Fisher, 2004) by definition rely upon illustrations to tell a story, they have been the targets of challenges due to their visual content. Often, the illustration is challenged on the grounds that it is unsuitable for the age group, a difficult construct to define. Other times, it is because of the content itself, due to representations of controversial behavior, nudity, or violence.

Controversial behavior. The picture book *Lucy Brown and Mr. Grimes* (Ardizzone, 1971) was withdrawn and reworked in 1937 after librarians in the United States objected to an illustration (Glover, 2000). The story concerns an older man who is portrayed as unattractive and somewhat frightening. He attempts to speak to children on a playground, most of who run away from him. He is drawn to one young girl in particular, and it is this illustration that raised objections because his facial expression was interpreted by critics as evidence of Mr. Grimes's sexual interest in Lucy (Alderson, 2003). The book was revised, but some have questioned whether it is a better version (Martin, 2000).

Some challenged books can serve as a lens for viewing the controversies of the time, especially at the local level. In 1959, librarians in

Montgomery, Alabama, moved the book *The Rabbits' Wedding* (Williams, 1958) to a restricted area because of its pictures. Written and illustrated by Garth Williams, creator of *Charlotte's Web*, the picture book depicted a black male rabbit and a white female rabbit in love. Although hard to imagine now, it is impossible to understand the incident without considering the location and its history. At a time when a community found itself at the center of the civil rights movement, librarians were moving a picture book for 2- to 5-year-olds off the shelves of the children's section (Sollors, 1997).

Nudity. As with text, challenged visual images in picture books often revolve around nudity. Maurice Sendak's (1970) *In the Night Kitchen* was famously challenged in public and school libraries because of illustrations of toddler Mickey's frontal nudity. Called "a masturbatory fantasy" by one reviewer (Braun, 1970, cited in White, 1974, p. 2), it was widely reported that some teachers and libraries drew shorts on Mickey (White, 1974). Three decades after its publication, *In the Night Kitchen* remains controversial. The American Library Association reported that it was number 25 on the list of the 100 most frequently challenged books from 1990–2000 (ALA, n.d.).

Censorship can occur before publication as well. Illustrator Werner Zimmermann (1989) reported his experience in the development of *Henny Penny.* The book had been previously published in Canada, but the American publisher balked at an illustration of a cow with anatomically correct udders. His revised illustration features four horses with their backsides to the reader (Jenkinson, 1993).

Violence. Objections to visual images can vary from region to region. For instance, the preschool book *Lizzy's Lion* (Lee & Gay, 1984) received more public complaints than any other in the early 1990s in Canada due to an illustration of a lion eating a burglar. The illustrator, Mary-Louise Gay, later explained her decision about how to portray the portion of the story when a criminal breaks into a child's room that is guarded by a lion:

> What I did was to dress the robber up in very distinctive clothes and the lion would rip them off. You could tell the lion was doing something, but we didn't have to see the blood. In the last fight image, the lion is holding the robber by the leg and the robber's head is cut off by the page. Now, who knows? Maybe the head had been bitten off, but it's left to the imagination. Two pages later, you have Lizzy looking at the room, and there are shredded clothes scattered all over the place and the robber's glove is hanging out of the lion's mouth. It is clear that the lion has devoured the robber, but the violence has never been graphically detailed. (Gay, n.d., ¶ 1)

Most complaints for the illustrations in *Lizzy's Lion* focused on the graphic and violent nature, yet the same book received almost no complaints in the U.S. (Blair, 1996). Ironically, Gay received several Canadian literature awards for *Lizzy's Lion*.

Policies influencing visual images. These and other challenges to visual images in books are influenced by the larger society and its concerns of the time. These concerns are confounded by the difficulty in ascertaining what, if any, effect visual images may have on children. The policies that governed the decisions made for each of these books—banning, refusing to publish, or limiting access—are a tangled combination of official actions and local standards. In 1968, the Supreme Court ruled that minors (those under the age of 18) possessed restricted First Amendment rights as they related to access to images and texts (*Ginsberg v. New York*). This was further codified in *Miller v. California* in 1973 when the language of "contemporary community standards" was introduced as a tool for making local decisions about restricting access to children and adolescents.

Censoring Film and Video Broadcasts in Schools

Film has long been acknowledged as a useful medium for teaching concepts and content. As early as the 1940s, the American Library Association worked with major film studios to produce information for classroom teachers (Goldstein, 1948). Yet schools have also had to deal with perception and beliefs about film since its inception. Jane Addams' 1912 criticism of film as a "filthy and poisonous" to young minds, and celebrity scandals in Hollywood, invited early and vigorous criticism of the new medium (Vaughn, 1990).

The nation's conflicted relationship with cinema is evidenced in the popularity of films chronicling the delinquency of youth. In postwar America, films such as *Blackboard Jungle* (1955) offered cautionary tales of wayward youth and their threat to society. Simultaneously, more salacious offerings such as *Reform School Girl* and *Dragstrip Riot* (1955) were blamed for contributing to, not tempering, teenage misbehavior (Cohen, 1997). Researchers have debated the question of whether film serves as a mirror of conditions or a catalyst for behavior. A host of studies, led by Bandura's (1968) work on the effects of violent television shows on children's behavior, suggest that some young viewers are vulnerable (Bandura, 1968; Hansen, C. & Hansen, R. 1990; National Institute of Mental Health, 1982). Although few would argue that a one-time viewing of a violent film or television program causes antisocial behavior, there does seem to be agreement that repeated exposure has a desensitizing effect on some children (Molitor & Hirsch, 1994; see also Pumpian & Fisher, this volume).

Nonetheless, film and video images are embedded in our society and in the popular culture of youth, and their exposure is increasing with the development of new technology. The availability of readily available moving images produced by professionals and amateurs has soaked into every corner of daily experience. The popularity of Web sites such as YouTube ("Broadcast Yourself"), where an estimated 50,000,000 videos are viewed daily, has made videos immediately available. The site promises that "[p]eople can see first-hand accounts of current events, find videos about their hobbies and interests, and discover the quirky and unusual. As more people capture special moments on video, YouTube is empowering them to become the broadcasters of tomorrow." (YouTube, n.d., ¶ 2)

As these advanced technologies become available to the general public, the need for society to rely on a small group of professionals to produce its own story diminishes. Now more than ever, children and adolescents are able to exercise control over what they view and when they view it.

It is into this swirl of visual information that teachers and administrators cautiously tread. Increasing availability of film and video, as well as the means to broadcast them, has made the use of such media more common than ever. Educators are faced with dilemmas about how to use professionally produced films and videos as enhancements to the curriculum. In addition, the use of video broadcasts of current events has raised censorship issues of other kinds.

Film in the classroom. The appeal of film in the classroom lies in its value as a literacy event. Baines (1997) argued, "Knowledge of how and why we create meaning through viewing a film is the kind of literacy that is transferable to the real world, a world inundated with visual and aural stimuli" (p. 552). The language of film, with its framing, editing, and mise-en-scéne, lends itself well to discussions of the literary elements of point of view, narrative arc, and the mood and tone of the piece (Golden, 2001). Others use film as a method for comparing and contrasting written texts and their filmed versions (e.g. Felter, 1993; Moore, 1998). Finally, film and video is useful for portraying critical sociological, psychological, and political events (Burton, 1988).

Policies influencing film use. Local policies governing the use of films vary widely. Some are vague with directives to use "segments [that] have been carefully previewed and screened for potentially offensive or controversial material" (Nathanson, 1992, p. 89). However, it is more common for districts to have specific policies on film. A review of district policies finds that many are similar to the following for Springfield Township Public Schools (STPS) in Pennsylvania:

> Teachers are responsible for assessing the maturity of their students relating to their readiness for the viewing experience, the value of the film to their curricular program, and understanding the culture of their immediate community. Prior to showing any video in the classroom, teachers should offer sufficient introductory preparation, which includes explanation of the educational purpose of the experience. Following, or during the course of the film viewing, teachers should present appropriate discussion and follow-up learning activities. (STPS, n.d., ¶ 2)

The policy also explains that films not already in the school library's collection must be "submitted to the Academic Standards Committee for approval and backing" and a letter of permission must be signed by a parent or guardian (STPS, n.d., ¶ 6).

Some districts use the Motion Picture Association of America (MPAA) ratings as a further guideline for use of film in the classroom. Unlike print media, films come with a rating of the content and images. These ratings provide a common language for discussing specific categories of film and its relationship to the age of the students. For example, the Davis (UT) School District has the following policy:

> 5.7 Upon receiving approval from the school-level review process, teachers may show a movie or video in a classroom according to the following audience guidelines:
> 5.7.1 A movie or video with a G, TV-Y, or TV-G rating may be shown to any grade (K–12) with teacher discretion.
> 5.7.2 A movie or video with a TV-Y-7 rating may only be shown in grades 2–12 with school approval and parent notification as outlined in this policy. (see section 7)
> 5.7.3 A movie or video with a PG or TV-PG rating may be shown in grades K–12 with school approval and parent notification as outlined in this policy (see section 7).
> 5.7.4 A movie or video with a PG-13 or TV-14 rating may only be shown to students in grades 9–12 with school approval and parent notification as outlined in this policy (see section 7).
> 5.7.5 R, NC-17, TV-M movies and videos are prohibited in Davis County Schools. (Davis School District, 2000, ¶ 5).

The apparent simplicity of the MPAA rating system masks a more complex issue around censorship. Can a portion of an R-rated film be shown in the classroom, if the segment does not contain material that earned the movie the rating? According to the news report in the opening of this chapter, the answer in Fort Pierce, Florida is no. But many other policies are not as clear, and teachers in those districts take risks when they show a film or film clip in the classroom. Others choose not to show films at all, figuring that it is not worth the trouble that a controversial film may invite. It is likely that this is the most insidious kind of censorship, because unlike written complaints, public attacks, and banned material, it cannot be easily tracked (Noll, 1994).

Video broadcasts in the classroom. While most district policies have relatively detailed policies regarding the use of films, there is less guidance on broadcast media. While some districts use the system developed by the TV Parental Guidelines Monitoring Board (such as the Utah district discussed earlier), few address the live broadcast of news events. Parents in Ashland, New Hampshire objected to teachers' decisions to watch the live broadcast of the 9-11 terrorist attacks in New York City, Washington, DC, and Pennsylvania (e.g., eSchool News, 2002). In response to this criticism, the school district created a new policy on the use of live television broadcasts of breaking news:

> In cases when the teacher is covering current events, the use of the media, particularly live coverage, may not be a part of the preplanned lesson. Permission slips are not feasible in these cases as the event may be unfolding as the students are watching, or in the same day. In these cases, the teacher must very carefully exercise his/her discretion in what is appropriate viewing for the classroom. While covering a current event it is the teacher's responsibility to put the incident(s) into the proper educational context. Such an event cannot be viewed and then not discussed, but rather should be a part of the overall lesson. It is the teacher's responsibility to follow-up [sic] the viewing so that the students understand the event and why they were watching. (Ashland Public Schools, 2004, p. 6176).

Other schools and districts made different choices on September 11, 2001. The principal of Anniston (AL) High School said, "There was no reason not to let the students be witnesses" (Douthitt, quoted in Ginsberg & Sieckmann, 2002, ¶ 14).

Controversy increases with the use of prerecorded broadcasts of news events. The news reports at the beginning of the chapter described the suspension of two California teachers for allowing students to view or listen to Internet-based broadcasts of the Nicolas Berg beheading on classroom computers. Critics of the decision have noted that students would have had access to the broadcasts themselves. Defenders of the decision have cited board policy that states, "The Board expects teachers to exercise caution and discretion when deciding whether or not a particular issue is suitable for study or discussion in any particular class. Teachers should not spend class time on any topic which they feel is not suitable for the class or related to the established course of study" (Grossmont Union High School District, 1993, p. 6144). One of the suspended teachers taught a photography class while the other taught a social studies course (Sanchez, 2004).

Policies such as the ones in Ashland Public Schools and the Grossmont Union High School District still leave room for teacher judgment. Depending on their age, many adults recall receiving news of the assassination of President John F. Kennedy, or witnessing the explosion of the space shuttle Challenger. In the case of the Kennedy assassination, some teachers turned their classroom televisions on to watch the news unfold. The Challenger disaster differed in that televisions were already on to witness Christa MacAuliffe fulfill her mission as the first teacher in space. In both cases, educators had to make minute-by-minute decisions about their teaching and whether they would continue the broadcast.

Decisions to watch prerecorded news events, however, are held to a higher level of scrutiny used for making decisions about sanctioned films. Because these broadcasts do not receive an MPAA or TV Parental Guidelines rating, weighing the value of the information as a current event against the violent content becomes murkier. Here, the Supreme Court's ruling on "contemporary community standards" is used to make decisions about the censorship of materials (*Miller v. California*, 1973).

Censoring Public Displays of Information in Schools

While far less common that the censoring of illustrations, films, and videos, the public display of information in classrooms and schools is worthy of discussion because of its implications for the free speech of teachers. Unlike most of the challenges discussed previously, these censorship claims revolve around distinctions between curricular speech and the First Amendment rights of citizens who are also teachers.

Curricular speech. In 1991, high school drama teacher Margaret Boring staged a controversial play called *Independence* (Blessing, 1998) with her advanced acting class. After reading a script of the play, the principal required that certain scenes be excised before the students could perform it at a competition. Boring later charged she was the subject of punitive actions by administration that led to her transfer to a middle school, and the district countercharged that she had failed to follow the district's policy for obtaining permission for using controversial materials. Boring argued that dramatic performances did not constitute part of the curriculum. An appeals court found that the performance was a part of the curriculum, and that Boring's First Amendment rights did not extend to curricular speech (*Boring v. Buncombe County Board of Education*, 1998). Ironically, the judges quoted Plato in their decision to support the district's decision to transfer her to another teaching assignment (Heins, 2001). This case has been used as precedent for the first part of decisions about educators' free speech rights.

Matters of public concern. A second determinant for ascertaining free speech rights of teachers relates to matters of public concern. This is decided using the *Pickering-Connick* standard, established through two Supreme Court cases regarding First Amendment rights of public employees in protection from retaliation by their employers. The first test is whether the challenged speech is delivered as a private citizen, rather than as an employee, and addresses a matter of public concern (Brooks, 2006). The second test is whether "the employee's interest in the speech outweighs the employer's interest in controlling the conduct of its employees in the operation of the venture" (Brooks, 2006, p. 61). Failure to prove both means that the speech is not protected.

Displays of information. Visual display of information in classrooms and school offices frequented by students have resulted in court challenges brought be teachers and districts. The three Albuquerque teachers mentioned at the beginning of the chapter had antiwar materials posted in their classrooms, including a poster in a window facing out that said "No War in Iraq" and student-made signs both in favor of and against the war. The counselor had posted a speech made by Senator Robert Byrd of West Virginia and an antiwar leaflet in his office. The anonymous complaints resulted in several days of suspension, and one teacher was transferred to another school. The school district charged that the educators violated the controversial issues policy which states, "the teacher will serve as an impartial moderator and will not attempt, directly or indirectly, to limit or control the opinions of pupils on controversial issues" (American Civil Liberties Union, 2003, ¶ 9). A settlement was reached and the educators were reinstated (Rethinking Schools, 2003). The incident did not constitute curricular speech, and it met the criteria needed regarding matters of public concern.

Another case serves as an example of the *Boring* test limiting a teacher's free speech when it is deemed to be curricular. In *Lee v. New York County School Division*, a high school teacher brought suit against the district after religious materials from his bulletin board were removed while he was on leave (Brooks, 2006). The materials included a poster for the National Day of Prayer. The court found that the materials were curricular "because he used them as part of his methodology of instruction and sought to instruct students on curricular matters through the postings" (National School Board Association, 2006). The court further found that even if it had passed the *Boring* test, it would not meet the criteria for the first part of the *Pickering-Connick* standard "because they did not raise matters of public concern and were not expressions made by the teacher in his capacity as a private citizen" (Brooks, 2006, p. 62).

Conclusion

The practice of censorship is bound in the now centuries-old tradition of shielding children from visual and print media that contain material deemed to be obscene, offensive, or violent. However, the factors for determining *what* is obscene, offensive, or violent are shaped by the broader context of the social landscape. Differences vary by region and time period. In some cases, visual material considered to be offensive in an earlier age would not be questioned today. Supreme Court rulings have further shaped decisions about the illustrations, film, and broadcasts. The First Amendment rights continue to be challenged in regard to the right of educators to express views that are controversial and are not strictly contained within the curriculum.

Many questions remain unanswered in the debates about censorship. As digital sources become more sophisticated and available, the line between library and classroom will blur. Will classroom educators be protected at the same levels as media specialists and librarians (Simmons & Dresang, 2001)? How does the filtering software installed on most school computers impact censorship issues? How does the Patriot Act impact censorship issues? Can students become critically literate if what they have access to is limited? Are the policies of censorship too subject to the political context of the moment? Should they be?

Barlow calls censorship of materials "the Holden Caulfield reflex" (1999, p. 39). The irony should not be lost that he has evoked the name of the protagonist of one of the most challenged books of the last half-century, *Catcher in the Rye* (Salinger, 1951). Barlow explains that society's urge to censor materials is analogous to Holden's deep desire to keep everything as it was. He is able to exercise a deluded sense of control in reminiscing about his own childhood (Barlow, 1999). Of course, Holden cannot prevent bad things from occurring, anymore than sanitizing or removing materials will preserve childhood.

Was Plato right? Do we need to expose young minds only to the most honorable stories? Was Foucault right: society talks most about that which troubles it most? It would seem that the answers to these and other questions could be found only through the free exploration of contradictory ideas.

REFERENCES

Alderson, B. (2003). *Edward Ardizzone: A bibliographic commentary.* New Castle, DE: Oak Knoll.

American Library Association. (n.d.). *The 100 most frequently challenged books of 1990–2000.* Retrieved December 18, 2005, from http://www.ala.org/ala/oif/bannedbooksweek/bbwlinks/100mostfrequently.htm

American Civil Liberties Union. (2003, November 11). *ACLU wins settlement for New Mexico teachers punished for posting anti-war materials.* Retrieved December 11, 2005, from http://www.aclu.org/freespeech/gen/11202prs20031114.html

Ardizzone, E. (1971). *Lucy Brown and Mr. Grimes.* New York: H. Z. Walck.

Ashland Public Schools. (2004). Use of media in the classroom: Instruction bulletin 6176. In *Ashland school district policy manual.* Retrieved June 10, 2006, from http://www.sau2.k12.nh.us/Ashlandweb/Policies/Series%206000%20-%20Instruction.pdf

Baines, L. (1997). Film, video, and books: Some considerations for learning and teaching. In J. Flood, S. B. Heath, & D. Lapp (Eds.), *Research on teaching literacy through the visual and communicative arts* (p. 545–557). Newark, DE: International Reading Association.

Bandura, A. (1968). What TV violence can do to your child. In O. Larsen (Ed.), *Violence and the mass media.* New York: Harper & Row.

Barlow, D. (1999). The Holden Caulfield reflex. *The Education Digest, 64*(9), 39–42.

Blair, L. (1996). Strategies for dealing with censorship. *Art Education, 49*(5), 57–61.

Blakely, W. P. (1958). Reading of comic books by seventh grade children. *The Elementary School Journal, 58,* 326–330.

Blessing, L. (1998). *Independence.* New York: Dramatist Play Service.

Boring v. Buncombe County Board of Education. 136 F.3d 364, 370 (4th Cir. 1998).

Bradbury, R. (1953). *Fahrenheit 451.* New York: Ballantine.

Brooks, M. (2006). Cases in point: The First Amendment and teachers. *Principal Leadership, 6*(9), 61–62.

Burton, C. E. (1988). Sociology and the feature film. *Teaching Sociology, 16,* 263–271.

Callahan, B. (2004). *The new Smithsonian book of comic-book stories from Crumb to Clowes.* Washington, DC: Smithsonian.

Carroll, J. (1981). The role of guilt in the formation of modern society: England 1350–1800. *The British Journal of Sociology, 32,* 459–503.

CBS News. (2003, April 24). Teacher suspended. Retrieved December 11, 2005, from http://cbsnews.com/stories/2003/04/25/national/main551149.shtml

Cohen, R. D. (1997). The delinquents: Censorship and youth culture in recent US history. *History of Education Quarterly, 37,* 251–270.

Davis School District. (2000, May 2). Movies and videos. In *Davis School District policy manual.* Retrieved June 7, 2006, from http://www.davis.k12.ut.us/policy/manual/Webdoc28.htm

Frey, N., & Fisher, D. (2004). Using graphic novels, anime, and the Internet in an urban high school. *The English Journal, 93*(3), 19–25.

eSchool News. (2002, January 1). *Parents want gag on TV news in classroom after 9-11.* Retrieved June 10, 2006, from http://www.eschoolnews.com/news/showstory.cfm?ArticleID=3391

Felter, D. P. (1993). Exploring Shakespeare through the cinematic image: Seeing "Hamlet." *English Journal, 82,* 61–64.

Fong, T. (2006, February 22). Teacher who showed "Faust" video awaits fate. *Rocky Mountain News.* Retrieved April 18, 2006, from http://www.rockymountainnews.com/drmn/local/article/0,1299,DRMN_15_4486164,00.html

Foucault, M. (1984). The repressive hypothesis. In P. Rabinow (Ed.), *The Foucault reader* (pp. 301–329). New York: Pantheon.

Gay, M. L. (n.d.) Cartoon art: Mary-Louise Gay. Retrieved May 15, 2006, from http://www.collectionscanada.ca/3/10/t10-301-e.html

Ginsberg, J., & Sieckmann, A. (2002, September 11). Students remember the day that changed their lives. *Anniston Star.* Retrieved June 10, 2006, from http://www.annistonstar.com/news/as-news-anniston.htm

Ginsberg v. New York, 390 U.S. 629 (1968).

Glover, M. (February 15, 2000). Visual arts: Crickey, they got into some scrapes! *The London Independent.* Retrieved February 18, 2006, from http://www.findarticles.com/p/articles/mi_qn4158/is_20000215/ai_n14289968

Golden, J. (2001). *Reading in the dark: Using film as a tool in the English classroom.* Urbana, IL: National Council of Teachers of English.

Goldstein, R. M. (1948). This is where we came in: A bibliography for the teacher of film evaluation. *The English Journal, 37*(9), 467–470.

Grossmont Union High School District. (1993). Board policy 6144: Controversial issues. In *Grossmont Union High School District policy manual.* Retrieved June 10, 2006, from http://www.gamutonline.net/indexframes40.html

Hansen, C., & Hansen, R. (1990). Rock music videos and antisocial behavior. *Basic and Applied Sociology, 11,* 357–370.

Heins, M. (2001). *Not in front of the children: "Indecency," censorship, and the innocence of youth.* New York: Hill and Wang.

Herron, C. (1997). *Nappy hair.* New York: Dragonfly.

Jenkinson, D. (1993). Good libraries don't: The censorship of Canadian picture books. *Canadian Children's Literature, 71,* 42–56.

Joyce, J. (1990). *Ulysses.* New York: Vintage.

Kessler, S. (1992). Toqueville's Puritans: Christianity and the American founding. *The Journal of Politics, 54,* 776–792.

Lee, D., & Gay, M. L. (1984). *Lizzy's lion.* Toronto: Stoddart.

Leyden, L. (1998, December 3). N.Y. teacher runs into racial divide. *The Washington Post,* p. A3.

Martin, R. (200). Edward Ardizzone revisited: Lucy Brown and the moral editing of art. *Children's Literature in Education, 31,* 241–257.

Miller v. California, 413 U.S. 15 (1973).

Molitor, F., & Hirsch, K. W. (1994). Children's toleration of real-life aggression after exposure to media violence: A replication of the Drabman and Thomas studies. *Child Study Journal, 24*(3), 191–207.

Moore, J. N. (1998). Street signs: Semiotics, "Romeo and Juliet," and young adult literature. *Theory into Practice, 37,* 211–219.

Nathanson, S. (1992). Guidelines for using videotape: A checklist for educators. *The English Journal, 81,* 88–89.

National School Board Association. (2006, March). *Lee v. York County School Division, No. 05-125* (E.D. Va. Feb. 23, 2006). Retrieved June 10, 2006, from http://nsba.org/site/doc_cosa.asp?TRACKID=&VID=50&CID=438&DID=38042

National Institute of Mental Health (1982). *Television and behavior: Ten years of scientific progress and implications for the eighties* (Vol. 1). Rockville, MD: U.S. Department of Health and Human Services.

Noll, E. (1994). The ripple effect of censorship: Silencing in the classroom. *English Journal, 83*(8), 59–64.

Office for Intellectual Freedom. (n.d.). *Support for dealing with or reporting challenges to library materials.* Retrieved May 8, 2006, from http://www.ala.org/ala/oif/challengesupport/challengesupport.htm

Pavonetti, L. (2002). It seems important that we should have the right to read . . . *Journal of Children's Literature, 28*(1), 9–15.

Plato, Grube, G. M. A., & Reeve, C. D. C. (1992). *Plato: Republic.* Indianapolis, IN: Hackett.

Postman, N. (1994). *The disappearance of childhood.* New York: Vintage.

Pulliam, J. D., & Van Patten, J. J. (2003). *History of education in America*. Upper Saddle River, NJ: Merrill Prentice Hall.

Rethinking Schools. (2003). Free speech win [Electronic version]. *Rethinking Schools Online, 18*(2). Retrieved December 11, 2005 from http://rethinkingschools.org/archive/18_02/shor182.shtml

Salinger, J. D. (1951). *Catcher in the rye*. New York: Little, Brown.

Sanchez, L. (2004, May 15). Teachers faulted over Berg video, audio. *San Diego Union-Tribune*. Retrieved December 11, 2005 from http://www.signonsandiego.com/news/metro/20040515-1999-1m15elcap.html

Schenck v. United States, 249 US 47 (1919).

Sendak, M. (1970). *In the night kitchen*. New York: HarperCollins.

Simmons, J. S., & Dresang, E. T. (2001). *School censorship in the 21st century: A guide for teachers and school library media specialists*. Newark, DE: International Reading Association.

Smith-Rosenberg, C. (1982). Davey Crockett as trickster: Pornography, liminality, and symbolic inversion in Victorian America. *Journal of Contemporary History, 17*, 325–350.

Sollors, W. (1997). *Neither Black nor White yet both: Explorations of interracial literature*. Oxford, England: Oxford University.

Springfield Township Public Schools. (n.d.). Springfield Township High School policy for using R-rated films in the classroom. Retrieved June 7, 2006, from http://mciu.org/~spjvweb/rratedpolicy.html

Sugiura, K. (November 15, 2005). R-rated movie costly for teacher: Educator resigns after showing 'Elizabeth' in class. *Atlanta Journal-Constitution*. Retrieved December 11, 2005, from http://www.ajc.com/metro/content/metro/gwinnett/1105/15south.html

Vaughn, S. (1990). Morality and entertainment: The origins of the Motion Picture Code. *The Journal of American History, 77*(1), 39–65.

Wertham, F. (1954). *Seduction of the innocent*. New York: Rinehart.

White, M. L. (1974). Censorship threat over children's books. *The Elementary School Journal, 75*(1), 2–10.

Williams, G. (1958). *The rabbits' wedding*. New York: Harper & Row.

YouTube. (n.d.). *What is YouTube*? Retrieved May 18, 2006, from http://www.youtube.com/t/about

Zimmermann, W. (1989). *Henny Penny*. Richmond Hill, Canada: North Winds.

9

HOW INTERNATIONAL ASSESSMENTS CONTRIBUTE TO LITERACY POLICY

Renate Valtin
HUMBOLDT UNIVERSITY

Cathy Roller
INTERNATIONAL READING ASSOCIATION

John Else
ACTION OUTCOMES

During the last decade, literacy issues have become a major focus of public policy. The results have been mixed. On the one hand, having public policy focus on literacy has increased public awareness and attention to literacy issues and increased the resources available to local schools. On the other hand, it has brought a variety of mandates that are sometimes not well informed by research.

These mixed results have caused some to ask whether it is wise for public policy to address the changing conceptualizations of literacy. Given the importance of literacy to navigating the world in an information age, however, it is unrealistic and indeed unadvisable to suggest that policy makers ignore literacy. Literacy is—and should be—a major focus of public policy throughout the world.

In this chapter, we describe two international assessment programs—(a) the Programme for International Student Assessment (PISA) and (b) the Progress in International Reading Literacy Study (PIRLS)—and discuss how they can contribute to the analysis of literacy issues and the public policies that could improve literacy. These two international assessment programs measure reading achievement and collect background information from students, parents, teachers, and principals across the globe. Because the assessments identify differing achievement patterns across countries, they provide comparative data that highlights important policy questions. While the assessments do not provide definitive answers about effective policy, they can help us identify and analyze important questions related to literacy policy.

INTERNATIONAL ASSESSMENTS

Briefly, PISA and PIRLS are international testing programs. We will refer to the PISA and PIRLS jointly as "the Assessments," but begin with separate descriptions (see http://www.reading.org/resources/issues/reports/pisa.html).

PIRLS assesses the range of reading comprehension strategies 9- and 10-year-old students use for literary and informational reading purposes. PIRLS is coordinated by the International Association for the Evaluation of Educational Achievement. PIRLS, which operates on a five-year cycle, was last administered in 2001, when 35 countries participated. The 2006 PIRLS will add seven more countries for a total of 42.

PISA assesses the extent to which 15-year-olds have acquired some of the knowledge and skills essential for full participation in society, particularly in the domains of reading, mathematics, and science. PISA is coordinated by the Organization for Economic Cooperation and Development (OECD), an intergovernmental organization of 30 industrialized countries. PISA 2000 focused on reading literacy, with 43 countries participating. PISA 2003 focused on mathematics literacy and problem-solving, with 41 participating countries. In 2006, PISA will focus on science literacy, with at least 58 countries participating.

DATA LIMITATIONS

Before we begin the discussion in this chapter, we want to make sure that readers do not overestimate the strength of the data produced by PISA and PIRLS. Both of the Assessments have several significant shortcomings. First, a different set of countries participated in PISA and PIRLS, with only 13 countries participating in both studies (with United Kingdom in PISA, and England and Scotland in PIRLS). Second, PISA & PIRLS have different data sources: in PISA, students and school principals completed a questionnaire, whereas in PIRLS, students, parents, teachers, and principals participated.

Third, it is difficult to compare the results from PISA and PIRLS. In PIRLS, the student is always the unit of analysis and the figures presented in the International Report (Mullis, Martin, Gonzalez, & Kennedy, 2003) are the percentages of students to which a certain characteristic applies. In PISA, results are reported in three different forms—(a) as percentages (sometimes embedded in graphic information and difficult to translate into numbers), (b) as scale values, and sometimes (c) as index values (with the average of zero and a standard deviation of one across OECD countries.)

Another caution is necessary. The background data for both surveys are based on self-reports rather than external observation, and there may be biases in the answers. Teachers, parents, and principals may answer according to the social desirability of certain responses. Responses may also be influenced by cross-cultural differences in response behaviour (such as modesty), and there may be cultural differences in the meanings connected to certain items. As long as the data are used to develop hypotheses and fuel careful analysis of each country's situation, however, the data provide information that is valuable and not otherwise available.

HOW ASSESSMENT RESULTS CAN SHAPE PUBLIC POLICY

One example of how results of the Assessments can influence policy comes from England, which has used the PISA and PIRLS results to shape literacy policy. In *Literacy Today*, Foster (2003) provided a summary of England's student performance on both tests. On PISA tests, the United Kingdom ranked seventh behind Finland, Canada, New Zealand, Australia, Ireland, and Korea. Foster quoted the PISA report, however, which states that 15-year-old students "who are highly engaged readers and whose parents have the lowest socioeconomic status achieve significantly higher than those whose parents have the highest occupational status but are poorly engaged in reading" (Foster, 2003, p. 1). In other words, being more enthusiastic about reading and being frequent readers was more of an advantage on its own than having well-educated parents in good jobs. The PISA report concluded that finding ways to engage students in reading may be one of the most effective ways to leverage social change. Given this finding, Foster (as well as many others) found it troubling that although England's 10-year-olds "are among the best readers internationally," they "have poorer attitudes toward reading and read less often for fun than pupils in other countries" (Foster 2003, p. 1).

In response to these data, the U.K. National Literacy Trust (2006) launched the National Reading Campaign (see http://www.literacytrust.org.uk/campaign/index.html). The Campaign's goal is "to ensure that as many people as possible enjoy the pleasures and benefits that reading can bring." The Campaign promotes reading for pleasure throughout the whole community to demonstrate the varied ways in which reading can inspire and sustain people to develop their skills, with a focus on those most in need. It "provides a network to bring the reading community together and maximize support for reading events, provides a one-stop shop for information about reading to spread the word about effective ways of promoting reading," and "encourages individuals and organisations to make reading part of their agendas (Foster, 2003, p. 1). It will be interesting to see if the Campaign has improved reading engagement among 9-year-olds in the 2006 administration of PIRLS.

U.S. READING PERFORMANCE

Perhaps the most important result from the data is that the United States had a significant drop in reading performance from elementary to secondary school level, whereas most other countries maintained their performance levels. The average score on both tests was 500. The U.S. performance on the PIRLS assessment (9- and 10-year olds) was 542, well above average, with the scores of only three countries (Finland, Canada, and New Zealand) significantly better. The scores for 15-year-olds (PISA 2000) in the United States, however, dropped to about average (504), with the same three countries significantly better (but 14 countries had better scores). The United States' PISA 2003 scores dropped further, to 495, with nine countries significantly better.

The data on the performance gap was equally revealing. While a high percentage of U.S. secondary students reached the highest level of competence (5) as measured by PISA, the United States also had a relatively high proportion of students scoring below the 1 level.

STRENGTHS AND WEAKNESSES IN THE UNITED STATES

Valtin (2006) conducted an analysis of the PISA and PIRLS results from 2000–2003 with a special focus on what they say about literacy education in the United States. She found that the Assessments highlighted both strengths and weaknesses that should inform the deliberations of U.S. policy makers as they develop literacy policies and initiatives. She structured her analysis of PISA and PIRLS data around variables related to the International Reading Association's *Children's Literacy Rights* (International Reading Association [IRA], 2000), which are presented below:

1. Children have a right to appropriate early reading instruction based on their individual needs.
2. Children have a right to reading instruction that builds both the skill and the desire to read increasingly complex materials.

3. Children have a right to well-prepared teachers who keep their skills up to date through effective professional development.
4. Children have a right to access a wide variety of books and other reading material in classroom, school, and community libraries.
5. Children have the right to reading assessment that identifies their strengths as well as their needs and involves them in making decisions about their own learning.
6. Children who are struggling with reading have a right to receive intensive instruction from professionals specifically prepared to teach reading.
7. Children have a right to reading instruction that involves parents and communities in their academic lives.
8. Children have a right to reading instruction that makes skilled use of their first language skills.
9. Children have the right to equal access to the technology used for the improvement of reading instruction.
10. Children have a right to classrooms that optimize learning opportunities.

Valtin (2006) identified the major strength of the United States as the resources that contribute to the development of literacy and that correlate with literacy achievement across the PISA and PIRLS countries. Compared with other countries, the contexts for learning in home and school are quite good. Valtin identified two U.S. problem areas highlighted by the data—namely, (a) the motivation to read/reading engagement and (b) the inequality of achievement between different socioeconomic groups.

Strength: Resources

The PIRLS assessment created an Index of Home Educational Resources. A high level indicates more than 100 books in the home, including more than 25 children's books, the presence of three or four educational aids in the home (e.g., computer, study desk for own use, books of their own, access to daily newspaper), and at least one parent who completed university (Mullis et al., 2003, p. 105). Students from homes with extensive educational resources had higher achievement in reading. Homes with many children's books (more than 100) had higher reading achievement than homes with fewer than 10 children's books. The United States was the country with the largest percentage of students in the highest Index of Home Resources at 37%. Norway was second with 33% and England was third with 27%. The international average was 13%.

Results from PIRLS and PISA concerning favourable educational resources in school suggest indicate that the United States is well-resourced. U.S. students are among the top three our four nations in several categories: (a) tied for first (with New Zealand, at 86%) in using a class or school library every day; (b) first in using a computer at school at least once a week (70%); and (c) fourth on the index of principals' views on the availability of school resources (77%). On the PISA index for the quality of schools' educational resources, the United States scored .40, well above the OECD average of .00, but not among the top nations, who scored .50 and .51.

These findings are consistent with other data. For example, in 2000, the United States ranked highest among the six "Group of 8" (or G8) countries for which data were available (U.S. Department of State, 2005) in dollars spent on education per child. The G8 consists of eight industrialized countries: (a) Canada, (b) France, (c) Germany, (d) Italy, (e) Japan, (f) the Russian Federation, (g) the United Kingdom, and (h) the United States. Outside the G8, expenditure per student in the United States is comparable only in Denmark, Switzerland, Austria, Norway, and Sweden.

Both the PISA and the PIRLS data indicate that the United States commits substantially more resources to K–12 reading instruction than most of the industrialized nations despite the fact that the United States is not a leader with respect to reading achievement.

Weakness: Attitude and Engagement

Valtin (2006) found that student attitudes toward reading were generally positive. Internationally, 51% of the students had a high PIRLS index of Students' Attitudes Toward Reading. On this index, the United States was near the bottom of the list of countries, with only two (Czech Republic and Belize) having less favorable results. The PISA results were similar, with the U.S. score of –.13 and an OECD average of 0.00.

Valtin (2006) examined the scores on three PIRLS indicators: (a) self-concepts in reading, (b) reading for pleasure outside school, and (c) self-efficacy, the belief in one's own ability to overcome difficulties and to handle learning situations effectively.[1]

U.S. students had positive self-concepts. While they are not among the top three nations on this indicator, they are above the average—PIRLS 46% (highest was 56%, international average 40%) and PISA 3.08 (highest 3.18, average 2.92). Both PIRLS and PISA scores suggest that U.S. students have strong reading self-concepts.

The results for reading for pleasure are less encouraging. Asked how often they read for fun outside of school, in PIRLS, only 35% of U.S. 9- and 10-year-old students said they read every day or almost every day, compared with the international average of 40 % of the students. Similarly, PISA scores for the United States are not favorable. Only 12% of U.S. 15-year-olds reported that they read for enjoyment outside school daily at least for one hour, as compared with the international average of 14.1% and Finland with 22.3%. The difference in percentages in PIRLS (40%) and PISA (18%) is consistent with international differences and consistent with other data suggesting that motivation to read declines as students move through school.

With regard to self-efficacy, the degree to which students believe they can deal with difficult learning challenges, PISA scores are highest in Brazil (2.78) and Mexico (2.76), with the score for the United States (2.56) equal to the OECD average.

Weakness: Achievement Gap

In all countries, socioeconomic background has an impact on student performance, though it does not determine performance. Some countries are more successful than others in softening the impact of socioeconomic background. These countries have both a relatively high student performance and relatively high equity between socioeconomic groups.

[1] As noted earlier, these scores are dependent on self-reports, and it is possible that students react to these questions differently because of varying cultural norms concerning modesty, skepticism or self-assertion. The PISA team sees these difficulties but suggests that the strength of the student attributes referring to self-concept in reading and self-efficacy can still be directly compared across cultures.

The data indicate that Canada, Finland, Japan, Korea, and Sweden have been relatively successful in moderating the relationship between social background and learning outcomes. The United States belongs to those countries whose student performance is average and who have wide differences between social groups (OECD, 2001, p. 191). The United States, France, and Switzerland are among the five countries whose students scored close to the OECD average, but showed greater than average inequality between different socioeconomic groups.

The PIRLS data have similar findings. Internationally, the average scores of schools with lower numbers of students from disadvantaged homes were considerably higher that those of schools with the majority of students from disadvantaged homes. The average difference in reading scores between low- and high-numbers of students from disadvantaged homes was 40 scale-score points. The difference in the United States was 73 points. (Two other countries with high difference were New Zealand and Israel.)

THE QUESTION OF CULTURAL ARTIFACTS

Another interesting set of data addresses the "cultural artifacts" and discussion of those artifacts in the home. Cultural artifacts include the traditional national literature, drama, and the arts. The PISA assessment has three indices correlated with reading performance: (a) Index of possessions in the family related to "classical culture," (b) Index of activities related to "classical culture" and (c) Index of communication with parents related to aspects of culture. The scores on these indices have an average of 0 and a standard deviation of 1. In the area of possessions related to classical culture, the United States score (–.12) was below the OECD average of .00, and well below Iceland's .67 and Latvia's .55. The U.S. score of .20 on participation in cultural activities and .22 for communication on aspects of culture were above the OECD average of .00, but well below Italy's .41 and Hungary .33.

The National Endowment for the Arts (2003) recently surveyed 17,000 U.S. adults. The survey investigated whether reading in the United States is declining, and asked if during the previous 12 months, they had read any novels, short stories, poetry, or plays in their leisure time, that were not required for work or school. The results indicated that there has been a sharp drop in literary reading from 1988 and 1992. The U.S. scores on the three PISA cultural indices raise questions about the role of literature in reading achievement in the United States. Why are there so few cultural artifacts in American homes? Have we ceased to have national traditions in the arts including literature, drama, and poetry? Is the lack of such a tradition related to lower reading achievement in the upper grades? Two of the highest scoring nations on these indices, Latvia and Hungary, are former Soviet states and may be experiencing a surge of nationalism. Iceland is a small modern state with a clear identity, and Italy has a long tradition in the arts and is often seen as a center of "traditional western culture." What is the role of multicultural literature and popular culture in enhancing reading achievement?

POLICY ISSUES AND QUESTIONS FOR THE U.S.

The above discussion demonstrates how U.S. educational policy might benefit from international comparative Assessments. It identified and highlighted one area (resources) where the U.S. scores on Assessment instruments are high—a dimension that is likely to have a favorable impact on student achievement. It also identified two important areas—(a) attitudes/engagement and (b) achievement gaps—where the U.S. scores are low and the opportunity may exist to learn from other countries. In addition, it identified another area: the role of cultural artifacts in reading achievement that raises many questions about the role of traditional national cultures in fostering reading achievement.

In short, we are encouraging policy researchers and policy makers to use the Assessments to identify areas for in-depth analysis that could produce guidance for policy makers. This will require policy researchers to examine the differences among the scores of countries on a wide range of variables and to examine and seek to understand the reasons for those differences.

One issue, of course, is how similar or different the conditions are in the various countries. For example, the relative homogeneity of Scandinavian countries may make comparisons with the U.S. difficult—though, even then, the potential for learning should not be dismissed. Another area for examination is the policies of countries that score higher on variables of importance to the United States and whether the potential exists for positive impacts of adopting similar policies in the U.S. context. Can we learn from Latvia and Hungary about the role cultural artifacts might play in raising reading achievement among 15-year-olds? Are there other countries to study closely for possible policy options and interventions? U.S. policy makers are surely concerned about the disparity in our rankings related to resources and achievement. Why do students in the U.S., with such a wealth of resources, have declining achievement scores from elementary to secondary school?

U.S. policy makers are clearly concerned about the achievement gaps in its schools. What explains the fact that, at the fourth-grade level, the United States has the third largest achievement gap of all participating countries—and what can we learn from other countries that might help the United States reduce this achievement gap? The answers may come if we (a) identify the countries with low achievement gaps (e.g., Canada, Finland, Japan, Korea, and Sweden) and analyze the impact of similarities and differences of those countries in comparison with the United States on variables such as cultural homogeneity, income disparity, school organizational structure, uniformity of curriculum, and resource distribution across school poverty levels; (b) identify countries with similar achievement patterns and analyze their similarities and differences with the United States and with the countries having a smaller achievement gap; and (c) develop policy alternatives and engage in public policy debates to determine what particular policy strategies will lead to desired outcomes.

An analysis of international Assessment data has the potential of providing many insights and hypothesis about how education in the United States can be improved. The challenge is to "listen to the data" and to learn from the experiences and policies of other nations.

REFERENCES

Foster, A. (2003). Making international comparisons. *Literacy Today, 26.* Retrieved May 31, 2006, from http://www.nationalliteracytrust.org.uk/Pubs/foster.html

International Reading Association (2000). *Making a difference means making it different.* Newark, DE: author.

Mullis, I. V. S., Martin, M. O., Gonzalez, E. J., & Kennedy, A. M. (Eds.). (2003). *PIRLS 2001 international report: IEA's study of reading literacy achievement in primary schools in 35 countries.* Chestnut Hill, MA: Boston College.

National Endowment for the Arts. (2003). Reading at risk: A survey of literary reading in America. Washington, DC: Author.

National Literacy Trust (2006).National Literacy Campaign Retrieved May 31, 2006, from http://www.literacytrust.org.uk/campaign/index.html

U.S. Department of State. (2005). The U.S. commitment to education. Retrieved May 31, 2006, from http://usinfo.state.gov/eur/Archive/2005/Aug/17-974400.html

Valtin, R. (2006, April). What PISA/PIRLS tells us about children's rights to high quality education. Paper presented at the Reading Research Conference, Chicago, IL.

I
VOICES FROM THE FIELD

MASTERING THE MEDIA

Alan Michel and Kim Slack
HOME, INC.

Schools are seeing the effects of the increasing influence of media upon students. Recent studies show that the average student spends as much time watching television as he or she does in the classroom (Kaiser Family Foundation, 2005). Whether it is TV or some other form of media, there is little doubt that media is shaping how young people view their world. Strong evidence exists as proof that media violence contributes to aggressive behavior in youth. A large proportion of media exposure includes acts of violence that are witnessed or "virtually perpetrated" (in the form of video games, violent films, and even the news) by young people. It has been estimated that by age 18, the average young person will have viewed 200,000 acts of violence on television alone (Levine, 1996).

As a result of increased concerns about media influence on youth and the rise in visibility of media literacy practices among practitioners in K–12 education curriculum standards for media literacy were developed in Massachusetts in the mid-1990s (Hobbs, 1998). As articulated in state standards for English Language Arts, the Media Strand consists of two components: (a) media analysis and (b) media production. Standard 28 says, "Students will identify, analyze, and apply knowledge of the conventions, elements, and techniques of film, radio, video, television, multimedia productions, the Internet, and emerging technologies, and provide evidence from the works to support their understanding." Standard 29 states, "Students will design and create coherent media productions (audio, video, television, multimedia, Internet, emerging technologies) with a clear controlling idea, adequate detail, and appropriate consideration of audience, purpose, and medium" (Massachusetts Department of Education, 2001).

Not surprisingly, many educators in Massachusetts are unaware of the presence of language arts standards articulating media literacy as a component of K–12 language arts. When we approached school administrators to explore a possible collaboration, few were aware of any previous efforts to introduce media literacy within the curriculum. With funding from the U.S. Department of Education and the National Endowment for the Arts, our nonprofit organization, Home Inc., worked with teams of four to six teachers from five schools in Boston (three high schools, two middle schools) over a three-year period from 2001 to 2004. Each team received ten hours of training in media literacy. Each teacher agreed to teach one part of a 15-hour project-based curriculum in media literacy that his or her team would develop themselves. Each school agreed to complete a project where students would explore how the media impacted one of three health issues: (a) substance abuse, (b) disrespect, and (c) violence. The project culminated in a public service announcement (PSA) video created by students for students at their school. To get to that point, each class would learn about three aspects of the media: (a) how to analyze and interpret the meaning from media messages; (b) how to best understand an audience in order to craft a message; and (c) how to produce a video message that has an impact. In order to best capture classroom learning experiences, we videotaped many of the activities to document the process and study the results.

MEDIA ANALYSIS: "WHAT'S THE REAL MESSAGE HERE?"

Teachers used media analysis and media production activities to strengthen critical thinking and communication skills. They first worked with students to analyze the messages they see and hear every day in the media, such as commercials, music videos, and films. Then students worked together to develop a media message of their own. For example, in learning to analyze media, Ms. Jones showed the opening shot of a PSA many times before students could accurately describe what they saw and heard. It showed a man squinting and frowning, but many students saw tough gang members. She experimented with turning the volume down and then had students close their eyes, in order to focus students' attention on the music, which was a somber, funeral-like melody. They worked to accurately "read" it, by looking at different elements such as tone, characterization, and visual composition.

When a student brought a gun to one high school and the event was reported on the local television news, a teachable moment occurred. Students had the opportunity to compare and contrast how the breaking news media coverage matched with their actual in-school experience of the event. After discussing the TV report with the principal, one teacher decided to discuss the media message with her class. Students were very animated about how the TV reporters covered the story about their school. "They shouldn't have shown the suspect the way they did—it makes all students look bad," one student commented. "The news reporters would do better by talking to students about the positive things that happen at our school to provide more context," another student suggested. "What about playing up the teacher who caught the student?" another wondered. Students also discussed how news stories present protagonists and antagonists to add drama to the story. As students actively discussed the event and the ensuing media story, they understood how reporters shaped stories about their community and made suggestions for how reporters could cover similar events. The teacher noticed that "the kids also had a lot to say about how the school responded to increase security and to prevent violence."

One key element of success was top-level support from school administrators. At Lewis Middle School, principal Brenda Jones believed media literacy was an important component in her school, and she was particularly concerned about violence, the ability to separate reality from fantasy, and the ability to evaluate the quality of information sources. Said Jones, "Our biggest task is to have children communicate and function in the real world. To do that they need to be able to look at media, judge what they see, and make good decisions. They need to know that everything they see or read should not be taken as 100% gospel truth."

Does the news media present biased perceptions about urban communities? Students at Lewis Middle School tested this hypothesis. Using the Internet, students went to different local news media Web sites and searched on "Roxbury," the neighborhood where the school was located. They recorded their findings according to the kind of story and whether it was TV or print media. They found that nearly 90% of the stories about their community shown on TV were negative—mostly about crime. As students discussed their findings, it became clear that the news media did impact their lives. "I don't want to tell anyone I live in Roxbury," was one student's response. The students found that print media coverage of their community was more balanced than TV news, with a greater proportion of positive stories. They discussed how TV news often would use a "if it bleeds, it leads" ethic, which inadvertently presented biased and disrespectful representations of urban neighborhoods.

In another class, boys and girls got separate lessons about disrespect and violence. Ms. Squires taught a lesson for girls about how the fashion industry used the media to promote certain "looks." She displayed different images of models taken from teen fashion magazines. "Why do you think one look is 'cooler' than another?" she asked. "I was surprised by how often girls said they wanted to have different physical characteristics, such as lighter colored eyes. Most of them believed changing their appearance would make them more attractive to boys," Ms. Squires observed. She pointed out to the students how each image was carefully constructed by explaining how most fashion models were much thinner than average, and how many photographs of models have been altered.

The boys in the same class worked with another teacher, Mr. Roland, examining how the media portrayed a "macho" image through visuals and lyrics in contemporary music. While looking at music videos, they discussed positive and negative images of men in the media. Mr. Roland mentioned that most music videos portray African American men as violent and with disregard for others. Gradually, the boys opened up about how they felt it was cool to act tough, and that the media reinforced this image. After the class, both teachers felt that it was important to separate genders in order to have more personal and authentic discussions with students.

As part of their training, teachers screened and discussed a 1997 episode of the PBS show *Frontline*, entitled "Merchants of Cool." Many teachers showed this documentary to students in order to illustrate how advertisers use youth culture to create "cool" product identities to sell their products to teens. One teacher from Brighton High School asked students to list all the elements of cool in contemporary culture; the teacher and her students were all surprised when they generated so much information that they ran out of room on the blackboard. Students began to see that advertisers were often more concerned with making money than with the values being represented in their ads. This documentary helped students to see the people behind the scenes developing their product's image by appealing to youth.

By analyzing different forms of media, students identified many common techniques used by advertisers, news, and media producers to target their audience and to create messages that glorify violence, disrespect, and substance abuse. By thinking critically, they saw how many messages were focused by the way the subjects were portrayed and presented. As a result, students also realized that they could use some of these same techniques for producing positive messages to reach other students and countering the stereotypes, violence, and hype they see representing teenagers in the media. Once students understood some basic techniques used in the media to influence opinions, they were challenged to develop their own message to reach their classmates using the same techniques. By producing media, students would learn firsthand about the many decisions needed to craft an effective message.

AUDIENCE RESEARCH: DISCOVERING THE IMPORTANT ISSUES

For the students to compose an effective PSA on a particular health topic, they realized they needed to do the same things advertisers did—listen to their audience to find out what health concerns were important. We developed a standardized opinion survey to ask students about violence, substance abuse, and disrespect in their school, since these were the overall health themes of this project. We put the survey on the Internet to facilitate the collection of data. Students in all the schools took the survey and had the results instantaneously and anonymously. Students analyzed the survey results from data supplied by their peers. They studied graphs, asked questions, and tested their hypotheses. In one school, participating students reported that the greatest threat to their health was violence within the school.

Many students analyzing the survey believed that the themes of conflict and violence were greater in their school because of the many ethnic groups represented. Students tested this hypothesis by seeing if other schools that took the survey had a similar ethnic makeup and similar concerns. As it turned out, other schools had similar percentages of Latinos, African Americans, Asians, and students of other ethnicities, but had concerns other than violence in the school. Animated discussion continued as students voiced their opinions—many ideas were immediately tested by analyzing the survey data. Students learned how to interpret surveys, calculate the margin of error, and appreciate how phrasing of questions could change the results. They also began to think deeply about the complex and multiple causes of violence and how it could be prevented.

At all of the schools, most students identified violence as the primary threat to their health. What emerged from their discussion and analysis of the audience survey was how most students were concerned about violence, how violence often started, and some ideas about what kinds of media messages might help to prevent youth violence. The next step was to develop ideas about a message and to create a storyboard for a 60-second public-service message that would make an impact on their audience.

CHALLENGES OF MANAGING YOUTH MEDIA PRODUCTION

When students from the Boston Public Schools first had the chance to use video production equipment in the classroom, the cameras and gear instantly triggered excitement, prompting choruses of "Can I shoot first?" Consequentially, some teachers struggled with channeling the students' energy toward the necessary planning steps. Instead of storyboarding or scripting their ideas, many students wanted to see what story they could develop by just playing around and shooting footage first. Finding the balance between planning and play proved to be one of the more challenging aspects of the project.

Project management was an important aspect to the media production part of the curriculum. This involved devising a realistic schedule, monitoring progress, offering support, and holding students accountable for performance and sticking to the schedule. For the many teachers involved in our project who had little prior experience with the use of projects in their curriculum, this role seemed daunting. In some schools, we tried to act as ad hoc project managers. This was complicated, since we were not at each school on a regular schedule and it required cooperation and communication around issues that had never been on the radar screen, such as how to recruit students to play different production roles.

Thinking about different ways to communicate the message through storyboarding—scripting the PSA with images—was often fun for students. They played with possibilities: "What if we use the sound of a heartbeat that goes to a flat line for the audio track?" and "He should say, 'Some cats in the villa out to get me!'" But for some students, it was difficult to move from the abstract—"We need to show people that there are consequences for their actions!"—to the concrete—"How can we shoot a scene that looks like it's in a hospital?"

To facilitate this, we provided teachers with examples of public service announcements that were either teen produced (Listen Up!, 2006) or on a topic of special interest to them. Where possible, we also provided storyboards for the PSAs so they could see how the filmmakers planned their shots. The teachers and students enjoyed these examples and studied them over and over. Another successful approach was using an art teacher to help kids conceptualize and draw their storyboards.

"Lights, Camera, Action!" Students loved these words! One of the first lessons teachers taught was how many people it takes to produce a good video, from actors to camera operators to writers. Many teachers used a short survey that was used in many schools to gauge student's interest in taking on various roles. When the student directors began their shoot, teachers started to act more as facilitators: answering questions, making sure many students were involved, and getting excited themselves.

Once students had gathered the raw footage for their productions, editing began. Few students or teachers were technically proficient at the use of video editing software. As a result, we first provided a number of hands-on demonstrations and tutorials to teachers and students. One lesson showed how altering the sound and image could change the entire meaning of a scene. Because of the time-intensive aspect of video editing, however, the staff of Home Inc. took responsibility for the majority of the editing, leaving a few scenes incomplete in order to solicit student input. We screened partially edited work with students, asking: "Should we add sound effects here? What kind and when should it start and stop? What would this action look like in slow motion? Does that help the viewer understand the serious nature of violence, or does it detract?" Students then had the opportunity to make these simple changes using video-editing software themselves, guided by more experienced editors.

Even though the production aspect of the project took the most time, students found it to be the most fun and gave them a visceral feel for how messages were created using certain effects. They also realized how acting and staging scenes were a kind of simulated reality, constructed solely to communicate their message. Students began to watch media to notice how camera angles were chosen and how images were edited. Media analysis and production went hand in hand reinforcing and deepening students' understanding of media.

Students at each school were genuinely proud to have helped produce a positive message and to achieve some mastery of media after challenging themselves to solve many production issues. One school even made movie posters to advertise their work and posted them around the school. Finally, there were celebrations for a finished project. Some teachers arranged for pizza parties where other students and school administrators could see the student's work. Others had students develop presentations on media literacy to other classes.

LESSONS LEARNED

Media literacy was well received in all the schools we worked within—teachers and administrators recognized that using media was an effective way of getting students to strengthen communication skills, critical and creative thinking, and better health. An administrator felt that there was definitely a connection between the violence students at his school see on television and the increased number of suspensions for aggressive behavior at his school over the past few years. Here are just a few lessons that we learned from our experience:

1. **Use media that kids watch.** When teachers chose popular music videos and youth oriented advertisements to show their class, the students were more interested than when teachers showed material that was more adult-focused.
2. **Communicate clear timeframes and expectations.** Teachers did best when they kept to a weekly schedule, communicated

about deadlines, and enlisted students in managing the tasks of the project.

3. **Have fun.** Teachers who had fun with the project got the most creative results from their students. Relishing the small surprises that occur with project-based learning went a long way to smoothing over inevitable conflicts among team members.
4. **Be a facilitator, not a video production expert.** Teachers who were comfortable with their role as facilitator and not as experts were able to get students to manage more of the project themselves.

Creative production activities were effective with this group of students, but this meant that teachers needed substantial levels of skill as project managers—the ability to create and communicate clear goals and timeframes as well as the ability to get everyone involved. Overall, we found that teachers needed more experience with project management themselves and more training in how to manage project-based learning.

CONCLUSION

Kids consume hours of media without fully understanding the meanings of the messages they receive. Often these messages glorify violence, disrespect, and substance abuse, and encourage youth to make poor health choices. Media literacy helps teachers reach their students by using the media students watch and by getting students to think more critically about what they see and hear. When the classes are well structured and examine the points of view and strategies behind the messages, students and teachers can engage in deep and meaningful questions. As a consequence, classrooms come to life and students have fun while they learn just what is being presented to them in the media every day. The students and teachers understand that the media is a vehicle for ongoing examination of issues from multiple points of view.

REFERENCES

Kaiser Family Foundation (2005). *Generation M: Media in the lives of 8 to 18 year olds.* Washington, DC: Author.

Hobbs, R. (1998). Media literacy in Massachusetts. In A. Hart (Ed.), *Teaching the media: International perspectives* (pp. 127–144). Mahwah, NJ: Erlbaum Associates.

Levine, M. (1996). *Viewing violence.* New York: Doubleday.

Listen Up (2006). *For educators.* Retrieved June 12, 2006, from http://www.listenup.org/community/educators.php

Massachusetts Department of Education (2001, June). *Curriculum frameworks for English language arts.* Retrieved June 12, 2006, from http://www.doe.mass.edu/frameworks/ela/0601.doc

UNEXPECTED OUTCOMES OF MEDIA ARTS EDUCATION

Elana Yonah Rosen and Erica Deiparine-Sugars
JUST THINK

Digital media's escalating presence and use in the United States and abroad has brought with it increased attention to the role and relationship between childhood and media literacy education. Scholars and other observers suggest that children are at the epicenter of the information revolution, a product of the evident shift from a post-industrial era to a new information age. To address this shift, much has been written about the effects of media on children, both from a "protectionist" stance which views media as having a predominantly negative influence (Masterman, 1985) and sees the viewer as relatively passive, as well as with a more exploratory view where audiences or receivers of media negotiate meaning and have power to determine media's influence (Hobbs, 2004; Potter, 2004).

Theories of active viewership where viewers are able to individually construct meaning (Fiske, 1987), as well as student-centered learning models have demonstrated some success in counteracting the charge that readers/viewers are in effect empty vessels open to receiving and accepting potentially damaging ideologies or other media influences. Despite these efforts, longitudinal studies in the United States have yet to adequately address the reality presented by the Kaiser Foundation's research results: the average 8–18 year old in the United States consumes an average of 8½ hours of media a day and engaging in media multitasking (often use more than one medium at a time). As the report advocated, "Anything that occupies this much of our children's time deserves our undivided attention" (Kaiser Family Foundation, 2005).

This essay draws on our experience with varied media literacy education programs, evaluated by peers and professionals locally and globally. By looking at a range of settings—(a) the first youth media education program in Bhutan, (b) a cross-cultural educational exchange program in Zimbabwe, (c) an inner-city after-school production memorializing the deaths of local youth, and (d) a United States Department of Education sponsored media arts program to develop a model curricula for middle school students—we offer our own contributions to the notion of incidental or supplementary learning in media literacy education. Unexpected learning outcomes can often be the most powerful life experiences for young people who learn to develop communication and critical-thinking skills using media tools and technologies.

Over a decade ago practitioners, policymakers, program officers, and scholars convened to address the fledgling vision of what constitutes media literacy. Put forth were the definitions, curricular, and policy implications associated with the increasing visibility of media education (Aufderheide & Aspen Institute Program on Communications and Society, 1993). While advances have been made toward a media literacy movement (Kubey & Baker, 1999), still little is known about the ways in which children and youth develop critical-thinking skills or acquire "critical discourses about the media" (Buckingham, 1993).

As teachers, youth workers, and media professionals search for creative and effective ways to support and respond to youth's creation, interaction, and perceptions of media, researchers are searching for meaningful ways to understand it as a theoretical construct. While exploratory studies offer preliminary evidence suggesting that media education and media literacy curricula can improve print literacy development (Hobbs & Frost, 2003), the field still contains few empirically based studies that systematically examine how youth voice in media creation and other activities influence schools, communities, and the youth involved.

Just Think (www.justthink.org), a Bay Area based nonprofit organization, delivers in-school and after-school programs that teach core principles and key concepts of media literacy and media art skills to youth. Our premise is that ensuring that the use of digital media is always accompanied by critical thinking will help children develop their own criteria and reflections on the media they view, and offer unprecedented knowledge acquisition. After observing two decades of digital media program delivery to K–12 students, Just Think has allowed for myriad practices resulting in unpredictable developments worthy of close examination. More than anything, pairing digital media with the use of inquiry results in measurable unexpected learning experiences; these have been consistently the most interesting discoveries we have made over the past decade.

MEDIA EDUCATION, ARTS AND LITERACY (MEAL)

The Media Education, Arts and Literacy (MEAL) program was made possible by a grant from the U.S. Department of Education's Arts in Education Model Development and Dissemination Program. The multiyear project was designed to demonstrate the effectiveness of integrating media literacy and media production skills into core middle-school curriculum. The project activities were rooted in widely recognized key media literacy core principles and included a comprehensive teacher training with hands-on digital media production. Access to media and media tools, and the facility with which youth assimilate these tools, have resulted in a merging of theory and practice, as students were given the opportunity to immediately produce art, music, films, and Web sites using the concepts they had learned just moments before.

One student video project entitled "Our Culture" highlighted the multicultural makeup of students in the classroom. Students learned how to write, rewrite, and ask interview questions about another student's culture and country of origin. Students gathered information and images from primary (family members) and secondary sources. They practiced their interviews on camera and critiqued them in class many times before shooting the final video. "The program enhanced my curriculum in so many ways—from building self-esteem, honing the students' visual and oral presentation skills, critical thinking, sequencing, and listening skills were all involved in the projects," wrote Beverly Mann, a teacher at Marina Middle School in California. She commented, "Sometimes I forget that this is a speech and language-impaired class. No one would ever know that from their digital presentations and interviews—first they're learning about each other, then learning about their cultures, and then realizing they are communicating like students who are not speech or language impaired."

An unexpected outcome was noted in Jennifer Brilhart's classroom, a special education teacher at a school located in an urban neighborhood noted for prevalent violence. Her class was an exceptionally challenging one, with many of the students having had behavioral assessments. A positive breakthrough for her class occurred as the result of a teachable moment which happened during the local and national media frenzy over the Stanley "Tookie" Williams clemency case. Students became highly interested in the opinions generated by different newspapers and television news programs. The teacher began reading one of Williams' books to the class, had the students track the media coverage of the case, and had them write their own opinion pieces. Over the course of a month, students wrote about the death penalty, peace, and William's life—all contents for a book they would create in honor of "Tookie." Students who had never contributed in class wanted to talk about what they had heard or seen about the case. Some shared personal stories concerning their own family members in San Quentin or those who had been victims of violence. "This forum allows students to connect their personal lives to a current event and critically view the ways in which Tookie's life in prison was portrayed in the media," Ms. Brilhart wrote in her Web log when documenting the learning experience. She later wrote, "It exposes the students to something they may like, love or cause them to be engaged, interested and excited."

SAFE HAVEN AFTER-SCHOOL PROGRAM

A group of girls in Bay View/Hunters Point in San Francisco gathered for a media education project at Bay View Safe Haven after-school program. This community, with a statistically high level of crime, engaged in a semester-long, after-school program to learn the critical-thinking skills and hands-on media production tools to produce a film on the health issues facing young African American girls. The participants were pursuing the subject of media effects on body image, when four young men (peers, brothers, and cousins) were murdered by other young men in the community. The community was devastated and this group of young girls shifted their focus of subject matter in an effort to process the violence in their lives by memorializing their peers through the production of a digital film. Because of our strong beliefs in student-centered, student-directed approach, we supported the students' need to rework the subject matter of the proposed curriculum.

As the students engaged in their own research on the murders, the process of producing the work became a centerpiece for gathering and healing among members of the community. The students learned that neither the adult community members nor local police were able to arrest the gang members responsible for the murders. Our staff had noted that none of the girls who made the film had expressed themselves emotionally during the process of filmmaking. Then their film was selected to screen at the Gen-Y Studio of the Sundance Film Festival. This precipitated interviews on the nightly news, acknowledging the girls for their work throughout the San Francisco Bay Area. When a global community viewed their film at Park City, Utah, an unexpected outcome arose. Youth exposed to regular violence are often inured to the emotion pain or find it difficult to express it. But at this event, these young women opened up, and when their work screened for an outside audience, one student began to wail with sorrow, and the audience shared this pain as well.

We observed that at the culmination of their production—from learning key concepts to the differences between a close-up and a long shot—a purging of the deep sadness and loss over the deaths in the community was finally released. The students were empowered with the skills to produce their film *and* they were able to express their grief for the first time. They were able to publicly address the injustices that they live with on a daily basis.

ZIMBABWE EDUCATIONAL EXCHANGE PROGRAM

By connecting inner-city American and Zimbabwe students in a cross-cultural exchange program, students at Carlmont High School in Northern California from families that had not graduated from high school and/or had not been to college engaged in a media literacy education program for one semester. Students learned key media literacy concepts, developed basic critical-thinking skills, and produced their first media messages while Just Think program staff worked closely with social-studies teachers during school hours. Following the work in the classroom, students were offered an opportunity to spend five weeks in a cultural exchange program cohosted by teachers in both countries. Students from the United States shadowed Chitungwuiza students in Zimbabwe, integrating into their respective families for half of the trip before traveling to Victoria Falls, touring the country for the remainder of the time.

Just Think provided cameras and computers for the students, which allowed them to connect beyond their first "in person" meetings. The U.S. students were able to teach their Chitungwuiza colleagues the basic technology skills to stay connected in an ongoing dialog via digital technology. Through joint use of these tools, both groups dispelled preconceived ideas created by mass media while integrated into a completely different physical environment with substantive economic similarities to their home and ultimately reveled in their self-discovery.

The students from the U.S. left computers with the Chitungwuiza students, corresponded for six months following the peer-teaching in Chitungwuiza, and then reciprocated the students' hospitality by hosting the Zimbabwe students six months later. The media literacy training allowed all of the students to apply their critical-thinking skills to the new environments, stay connected to their new relationships, and then produce media messages for their peers upon return from their exchange programs. Furthermore, this led to scholarship opportunities, and continued peer-teaching opportunities. One of the students from the United States is currently finishing his degree from San Francisco State University in Computer Science and Film, the result of a scholarship he was awarded through Just Think because of his work teaching media literacy education. He is working on a film about the diamond war in Sierra Leone, and the unconscious link between his country of origin and the hip-hop community in the United States. In his video, Dominic asks, "How could anyone who knew how many children and their families died acquiring these diamonds flaunt their *bling*?" His acquisition of critical-thinking skills, media-production skills, and confidence have integrated seamlessly enabling this young man to participate actively and powerfully as a member of society.

OUR BHUTAN

In 1999, the Minister of Education of the country of Bhutan responded to the introduction of television and the country's first Internet connection by allowing members of our organization to work with teachers, students and the Bhutanese Broadcast System (BBS, which was previously a radio-only station). In three two-week intensive sessions over one year, Just Think worked with educators and the head of Youth Programming (after-school activities) to select a group of students to produce a series of 12 short films for broadcast on the BBS (one per month). Transporting a modest digital editing studio from the United States to Bhutan, along with a small media archive for critical viewing, Just Think trained students, teachers, and members of the station with the creative and technical skills to utilize the newly integrated medium to effectively voice their ideas and observations.

The objective of the program was to assist Bhutanese students in the mastery of basic critical-thinking skills and media production methodologies. The underpinning purpose of these productions was to provide young people in Bhutan with the ability to understand new media information and think for themselves. The first session focused on selecting schools, students, and supporting adults, as well as orchestrating logistics in a country where electric power to the capital city, Thimpu, was sometimes intermittent and its students often live miles from schools without any transportation. The second session included a comprehensive training in key media literacy concepts, critical viewing and discussion, brainstorming of ideas and presentations of story ideas to the group. An anonymous vote was conducted to determine which two story ideas would advance first into story boards and then into preproduction. By the end of session two, the group self-selected into two teams to work on the productions, and completed story boards for the two films. They began experimenting with shooting styles, and then had three months before the next intensive session to develop their shooting skills. The third session focused on full-fledged production of the films. Logging, editing, viewing rough cuts for critique, additional shooting, music selection, and more editing concluded with a screening for the head of Youth Programming for the country of Bhutan, students, and family members.

In an effort to demonstrate this model program, Just Think met with the former vice president of the Sundance Film Festival and showed her a rough cut of the students' work. This resulted in a sponsored trip to the film festival in which four students presented their two finished works: (a) "Our Bhutan" a documentary about the cities and culture in Bhutan, and (b) "Parents We Miss You" a sentimental film about the emotion experiences of students at boarding school when separated from their parents. The screening included a meeting with Robert Redford in which the Bhutanese youth expressed their gratitude for having the opportunity to present their work, and Redford explained that the reason he started the festival was so voices like theirs could be heard. On the final evening of their trip, the students approached Just Think staff with an unexpected request: "If our parents donate land for the first Royal Media Institute of Bhutan, will you help us get the continued education we need to create it?" Although this was not in our projections for the outcomes of the project, Just Think has supported two Bhutanese students through community college in the United States and a third is following his master's degree in Education in Bhutan to become an instructor. We continue to seek funding in an effort to support their potential enlivenment of a media institute of their own.

CONCLUSION

In each of these programs, some fascinating unexpected outcomes resulted. In one case, students lowered their self-consciousness about their communication disabilities. The powerful use of the teachable moment, generated by a news event perceived as relevant to students and the community, provided an opportunity for increasing student engagement. In another case, young people reconnected with deeply felt but deeply buried feelings of grief when seeing unfamiliar audiences view their documentary film. One student discovered his mission as a filmmaker through a cross-cultural learning opportunity that reshaped the social meaning of the status objects of Western culture. Another group of students developed their creative voices and used their proficiency with media tools to advocate for the development of media literacy education in their home country. The exploration of language, social interaction, and self-directed education with media can now be used to support learning in high- and low-achieving communities alike. As a result of creative opportunities to develop media literacy skills, students learn, exercise judgment, and think systemically. Ultimately, they begin to actively understand themselves and the society in which they live.

REFERENCES

Aufderheide, P. A., & Aspen Institute Program on Communications and Society. (1993). *Media literacy: A report of the national leadership conference on media literacy.* Washington, DC: Communications and Society Program, The Aspen Institute.

Buckingham, D. (1993). *Reading audiences: Young people and the media.* New York: Manchester University Press.

Fiske, J. (1987). *Television culture.* New York: Methuen.

Hobbs, R. (2004). A review of school-based initiatives in media literacy. *American Behavioral Scientist, 48*(1), 48–59.

Hobbs, R., & Frost, R. (2003). Measuring the acquisition of media-literacy skills. *Reading Research Quarterly, 38*(3), 330–355.

Kaiser Family Foundation. (2005). *Generation M: Media in the lives of 8 to 18 year olds.* Washington, DC: Author.

Kubey, R., & Baker, F. (1999). Has media literacy found a curricular foothold? *Education Week, 19*(9), 17.

Masterman, L. (1985). *Teaching the media.* London: Comedia.

Potter, W. J. (2004). *Theory of media literacy: A cognitive approach.* Thousand Oaks, CA: Sage Publications.

Part II

METHODS OF INQUIRY IN THE COMMUNICATIVE, VISUAL, AND PERFORMING ARTS

Donna E. Alvermann
UNIVERSITY OF GEORGIA

Margaret C. Hagood
COLLEGE OF CHARLESTON

Leslie S. Rush
UNIVERSITY OF WYOMING

In the decade that has passed since the publication of the first *Handbook of Research on Teaching Literacy Through the Visual and Communicative Arts*, several milestones have occurred. Most notable, perhaps, has been the research community's embrace of a broadened definition of literacy—one that speaks, in plurals, of multiliteracies and multimodal research designs. A less heralded but equally influential milestone has been the literacy field's gradual turn toward greater interdisciplinary awareness. Currently, it is not an exception to find scholars from various disciplines collaborating on a single research project, though we do acknowledge that such collaboration is still more likely to occur within the social sciences than across the humanities at large. That said, this new volume in which we situate our section on methodology is filled with examples of how the visual, communicative, and performative arts permeate the thinking of researchers in the social sciences, and particularly in education.

Not only has communication across disciplines and literacies changed, but also timing has changed, with advancements in technologies that leave not a nanosecond unused and most nanoseconds used in multifaceted spaces by users' multiple identities. The authors in this section explore media as a symbol system to represent, investigate, and engage multiple trajectories of literacies. The chapters present an array of methodologies and illustrate the cacophony of voices unavoidably and richly apparent in research that examines users' literacies across time and space. Beginning with Kress' discussion of symbol systems and Tierney's examination of multimodal forms, chapters in this section exemplify techniques, perspectives, and issues at the forefront of research on the complexities and mutations of literacies that abound within and across contexts and for various constituents across the globe.

10

"LITERACY" IN A MULTIMODAL ENVIRONMENT OF COMMUNICATION

Gunther Kress
UNIVERSITY OF LONDON

SOME FRAMING REMARKS

What if we assumed seriously that meaning—in the fullest sense—is made in modes other than speech and writing? Of course, it will be said immediately: "But we all do, we have always taken that into consideration." We know the work done in psychology on nonverbal communication, whether in its focus on gesture, on gaze, or in its studies of the differential effects of the use of word rather than image on comprehension or recall for instance (Argyle, 1990; Paivio, 1971). We know that art historians (Gombrich, 1960; Arnheim, 1972, 1974) have always dealt with the meaning of images, and we know that there are whole subdisciplines devoted to image, whether as visual culture or as the sociology of the image (van Leeuwen & Jewitt, 2001; Rose, 2001; Becker, 1981; Chaplin,1994). Even in mainstream linguistics the nonverbal, the extralinguistic or paralinguistic are acknowledged, even if in passing.

Yet speech and writing remain at the center of cultural attention as far as public, communicable, rational forms of meaning (making) are concerned. Art—painting, music, sculpture—are somewhere else, over there in the domain of the aesthetic. Art can move us and can touch our lives, but its meanings are felt to be of a different kind to those we make in speech and writing; *emotion* and *affect* are words used in relation to them. And, while the sociology of image can provide useful contextualization of meanings otherwise established, it cannot, so it is assumed, provide us with the core meanings, which word, syntax, and text give us (Wulf, 2005), or so at least another part of that story goes.

There are uncomfortable challenges to the mainstream position. Representational systems such as numbers, geometry, chemical formulae, and musical notation all clearly have the capacity for representation as speech or writing do, differently, yet as precisely or more so, and in some of the same areas as language does. And, there is the semiotically unsettling challenge to conceptions of the centrality of speech and writing provided by sign language's highly developed resources for making meaning in which gesture—the faculties of parts of the body, such as arms, hands, and fingers, in movement against the spatial frame of the upper part of the human torso—, of gaze, and of facial expression—has been developed into a full resource for the representation of human meaning and social needs, even if very differently so than in either speech or writing. Here, over the last three or four decades, work of enormous significance has been done (Bellugi & Klima, 1983; Emmorey & Lane, 2000), which is equally important in its social, cultural, and political impact as in theoretical, semiotic terms; and more profoundly still, in demonstrating a nuanced, fully articulated semiotic resource for human representing and communicating which draws on entirely different potentials of the body than of the voice and speech organs.

In this chapter, I sketch an approach that acts on the assumption that image or gesture, music or writing, sound track or dance, and action or the body's positioning in (a framed) space can all be used to make meaning, so much so that it would be as sensible to refer to writing as "paravisual" or to refer to speech as "extragestural" as it would be to call image or gesture "extralingusitic" or "paralinguistic." The multimodal approach to representation outlined here is framed in a social semiotic theory. Multimodality (Kress, 2003; Jewitt & Kress, 2003a) declares what the field for enquiry is, namely all the modes available and used in making meaning, in representation and in communication. It does away with both the need and the reasons for the paras and extras because in redrawing the boundary it brings all the modes into a single frame. The previous insistence on the autonomy of semiotic resources such as language, music, gesture, and image is replaced by the insistence that the relevant domain of inquiry, theory, and application is that of making meanings and of the resources culturally available in that. In that integrated domain, none of the resources has, in principle, greater priority, is more central, or carries greater weight than any of the others. Social semiotics (Hodge & Kress, 1988; van Leeuwen, 2005) provides a coherent theoretical approach in which the many modes that are in use can be and are integrated; it provides descriptive and analytical tools to deal with the variety of resources, which appear in multimodal ensembles in the same theoretical framework.

In other words, the decisive shift from the previous position—"We have always attended to this"—lies in the integration of previously disparate fields of inquiry into the now single integrated domain of multimodality. Where before there were separate fields, each with questions arising out of its own disciplinary approach, now there is a coherent, integrated, single domain. Multimodality indicates what is to be attended to, namely all the modes that appear in multimodal ensembles; social semiotics provides the theoretical, descriptive and analytical tools for dealing with the range of questions which now appear—as well as those which were present before: focusing on the specificity of the differing potentials of modes for making meanings, describing and analyzing the interrelations among the modes which are present in multimodal ensembles, the orchestration of modes, describing what meaning each brings and deals with, and describing the meanings formed in their interrelations. A constant question concerns the distinctiveness *and* the complementarities of modes in always complex designs, the affordances of modes and their aptness in representation.

Many consequences follow from an approach, substantive as well as methodological, and I will focus on just some of these: for theories of meaning and therefore for learning; for theories of representation and therefore for literacy; and for what needs to be attended to and how.

THE ISSUE: "TO TEACH LITERACY USING ONE OR MORE OF THE COMMUNICATIVE AND VISUAL ARTS"

Consider the two texts below. They were produced by two 13-year-old students in an inner London school's science classroom. After four lessons on cells, their teacher asked the class, working in groups of four, to prepare a slide from a piece of the epidermis of an onion and, still working together in the same group of four, to look at the slide through the microscope. They were then told, "Draw what you saw, and write what you did." The teacher gave two further instructions: "Don't use colored pencils" and "put your writing first, at the top of the page."

An interest in meaning leads me to look at the distinctly different ways in which the two had responded to the instructions. In some ways, each carried out the instructions given, and in some ways, each did not. One placed the drawing at the top; the other used color pencils. Above all, the two produced entirely different drawings and the written text elements they produced differ markedly in terms of genre. The written part of Text 1 we might call a "recount"—that genre which records relevant events in the chronological sequence in which they happened; the written part of Text 2 we might call "procedure"—that genre which acts as an instruction to someone to perform specified actions in the sequence indicated.

By now, my interest in literacy is foregrounded. While the recount is an appropriate response to the teacher's request "write what you did"—it does set out what actually went on—,the procedure is not—it does not tell us what the girls did; rather it indicates what ought to happen.

Here are the written parts of the texts.

Text 1

Looking at cells

What I did

At first, Amanda and I collected all the equipment. Amanda peeled the skin off the onion, while I got the microscope. Amanda put the onionskin on the slide, then I put a drop of iodine on the onion then we put a cover slip on top of it. We then sorted the microscope out then we put the slide underneath on the stage.
We then looked in the eyepiece. It was interesting to look at and draw.

Text 2

Looking at Cells

Step 1
Peel off a bit of onionskin and put a drop of Iodine on it.

Step 2
Place the onionskin on to a microscope slide and put a cover slip on top.

Step 3
Put the slide on the microscope and get it into focus. Search for a pattern like a honeycomb.

An interest in teaching literacy might lead me to ask further questions. For instance, I might focus on the relative imprecision of the teacher's instructions—"Write what you did"—and explore the effects of that imprecision. I might question what resources the teacher himself had available explicitly to make his request more precise, had he wanted to do so. I might ask, what outcome did he have in mind by his request for a response in drawing and in writing? I could focus on the teacher's brief written comments on each of the two pieces, which suggest that he had not really focused on these differences, that he had not been aware of what they might lead to, and that he had not really worried about them. It might lead me to ask the teacher—and myself of course—whether the difference between the recount and the procedure is one that actually matters in the biology curriculum and its aims.

And it would be important to ask the young writers (and their two friends) about their reasons for responding to the instructions in the way they had done and maybe to ask them about their senses of meaning differences produced in layout, in drawing, and in writing. I might explore what consequences would follow from a discussion with the teacher for his future pedagogic actions or what consequences this example ought to have for the teaching either of literacy or of science, in the science classroom or much more generally. A look through the lens of multimodality opens questions and possibilities in many directions.

However the task in this chapter is to reflect on methodological issues (Jewitt & Kress, 2003a) relevant to "teaching literacy using one or more of the communicative and visual arts," and so I attend to the fact that these texts consist of a written element and of a drawing—in accordance with the teacher's instruction. The further task is to consider the meaning of the writing and the drawing separately but also of the meaning made in the interrelation of drawing and writing, if there is such a relation; and then to reflect on the meaning of the texts overall and on their effects. Behind this stands the twin question "what is literacy and how shall we define it?" I will return to this at the end of the chapter.

In his written comments on the two texts, the teacher engaged neither with the meanings of the drawings, with the information they contain, nor with the meaning of the written texts for that matter. His comments focused on specific technical aspects—for instance the degree of magnification used, on forms of labeling—or else they have to do with marginal pedagogic, procedural aspects: copying up missed work, and so forth. Implicitly the comments pose the central question of a multimodal approach to representation: Do we need to pay (equal) attention to all the modes present in the text overall—here, to both writing and drawing? Or do we see them as differently significant? Do we continue to treat the written part of the text as central and regard the other elements as more or less marginal? The latter has been the approach for a century or more and implicitly it is reflected in the teacher's comments.

In principle, a multimodal approach privileges neither speech nor writing above other modes used; here it gives equal attention to the drawing and to the written elements in each text. From a pedagogic perspective, what is most in need of explanation is the difference between the two drawings and the two written genres. From a methodological (and pedagogical) perspective, the urgent question is how do we account for that difference? How do we assess that difference? Do we, with our present focus on linguistic modes, have the means for assessing meanings made in other modes? From a social semiotic perspective, a quite different set of questions pose themselves—challenging questions around agency and authority: What forms of assessment are adequate to and necessary for an assessment of that difference, forms which would do justice to the students' semiotic and intellectual work (Kress, Jewitt, Ogborn, & Tsatsarelis, 2001; Jewitt, 2003; Johnson & Kress, 2003)?

Text 1 (brick wall) has the drawing at the top; it is done using soft, black pencil. Between the drawing and the written part of the text there is a clear space; the written text has a heading. The drawing is of a structure of four rows of squarish "entities"—the cells—relatively uniform in size and shape. At each end, the structure is left unfinished or open—the implication being that what we have here is simply a section of a larger structure. Within the structure, there are some bubble-like, round forms (actually air bubbles formed under the cover slip of the slide), quite unlike the square shapes which constitute the majority of the structure. Over the course of the preceding four lessons, the students received a handout sheet that described, in image and word, how to conduct this experiment; it contained a sentence: "you will see a structure a bit like a brick wall; each brick is a cell."

In Text 2, the image is at the bottom, drawn using colored pencils. Visually, in layout, it is partially integrated into the written text. It does not have a separate heading. It shows a carefully drawn circle to indicate the eyepiece of the microscope. Within the circle, wavy lines delineate irregularly shaped entities, by and large ovoid or trapezoid in shape; there are also the larger, round, bubble-like shapes of the drawing of the first text. While the four young women had worked around the microscope, one of them said that she thought she saw something much more like a "wavy weave" than a brick-wall-like structure.

Clearly, the handout's written reference to the brick wall appears in the first text's drawing. The meaning/content has been drawn across from writing to image. My sense of this drawing is that this young woman had said to herself something to the effect of "theory tells me what I am supposed to see. It brings order to an otherwise messy world. I will represent what theory tells me is the case." She draws the bubble-like shape, which was there on the slide, even though the theory they had been given (on the handout) had nothing to say about either air bubbles or the resulting shapes (part of the messiness of the world); the scientific demand of accurate recording requires that it be represented. The drawing of Text 2 suggests to me that this young woman had said, "to be scientific is to be as accurate as we can be in the visual/graphic recording of the world." What is crucial is to be true to reality; if the resulting representation does not conform to theory, then it is nevertheless true to reality and demanded by practices of being scientific "to be precise and accurate (and honest) in our recording."

Each drawing records a distinctly different stance on what "being scientific" means. If we compare each drawing with the meaning of the written genre of the same text, we see an interesting disjunction. The brick wall drawing shows what ought to be, the priority of and accountability to theory. It is accompanied by the recount, which describes what is; the recount gives priority to empirical accuracy, to the truth of how things are—"everything that happened is recorded here: it is empirically accurate." For this young woman "being scientific" consists in the conjunction of these complex, internally contradictory, and seemingly opposed meanings: how things ought to be is represented by the drawing, how things are is represented by the writing. The eyepiece drawing, by contrast, shows what is: truth and accountability to the empirical world. It is accompanied by the procedure, which states what ought to be and specifies actions in an explicitly given sequence, which are to be followed in that order. For this young woman "being scientific" also consists in the conjunction of two complex seemingly opposed, contradictory meanings: the truth of how things are is represented by the drawing, and the truth of how things ought to be represented by the writing.

The complex and contradictory meaning of "being scientific" in the two texts can be shown in this way:

	What ought to be/accountability	*How things are/accuracy/truth*
Fig. 10.1	drawing (brick wall)	writing (recount)
Fig. 10.2	writing (procedure)	drawing (eyepiece)

If the teacher wanted to understand what his students saw as the meaning of "being scientific," he would need to attend to both writing and image, fully and with equal attention and care.

One effect—a rhetorical benefit maybe—of multimodal representation is that it allows contradictory meanings to be expressed in the one text without it appearing openly paradoxical. When contradictory meanings are represented in different modes, the contradiction is less apparent. Each text shows the two young women attempting to solve the same real problem, namely how to reconcile two versions of "being scientific," which I assume coexisted in this classroom: truth to what is and accountability to theory. Had both meanings been expressed in writing, the contradiction would have been apparent. Multimodal representation presents the students with the means for a solution to this uncomfortable situation. Expressed in the distinct modes of writing and image, the contradiction is not immediately visible or at the very least, tolerable. Given the teacher's seeming lack of awareness of what meanings are expressed here, an opportunity is lost for focusing on this central issue in this subject and for bringing it into the open for discussion and reflection.

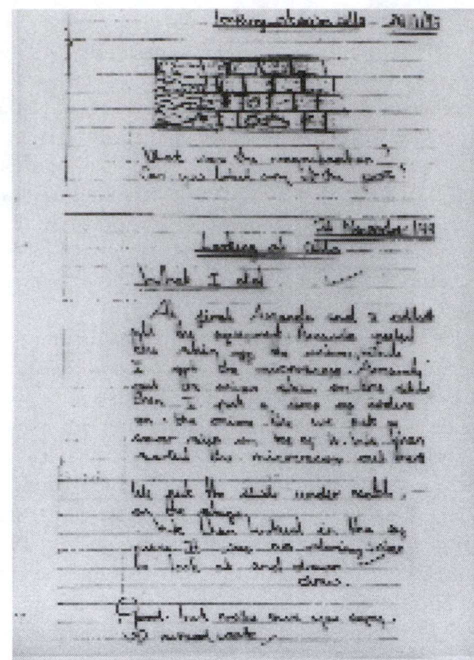

FIGURE 10.1 Brick wall.

"MODE" AND MULTIMODE: AFFORDANCES AND LOGICS

In these examples, the students used writing and image to represent distinct scientific views and different epistemological positions. They show that each mode is capable of representing distinct epistemological positions, even if differently. It is not the case that only writing or speech is capable of expressing such meanings and that image is not. However, the students also used writing and image differentially in relation to the content they wanted to represent. Both used writing to "tell" actions and events; and both used image to "depict" what they had seen or what they felt they ought to have seen in the world. In other words, here writing is used for telling actions and events, and image is used for showing what is in the world.

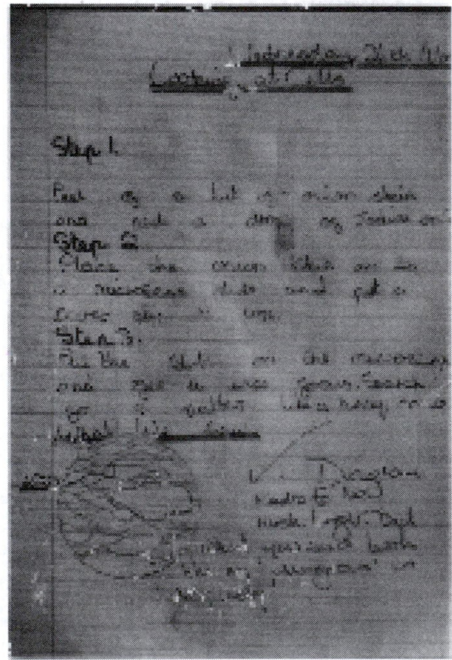

FIGURE 10.2 Eyepiece.

This raises the question whether each mode offers distinct and different potentials, or affordances, for representation; these need to be understood. In the two texts here, writing is used to represent actions and events, and image is used to represent states of affairs in the visible world. It is of course possible to use writing to describe what cells look like—as I have attempted to do above—or to use images in sequence to represent actions. However, what happens when I do that, when I represent an account produced in one mode in a different mode, or when I move from image to writing? I will use my description from above to illustrate.

> The drawing is of a structure of four rows of squarish "entities"—the cells—relatively uniform in size and shape. At each end, the structure is left unfinished or open, the implication being that what we have here is simply a section of a larger structure. Within the structure there are some bubble-like, round forms (actually air bubbles formed under the cover slip of the slide), quite unlike the square shapes which form the majority of the structure.

For a start, this is a description of a representation, not the representation itself: it does not show a structure, it talks about it. I am telling you what I see because maybe you cannot see it yourself or maybe I want to influence how you will see. To do this, I have to name parts of the image. I have to use words for what I see, such as *squarish "entities"*—where my quotes around entities indicates unease about this naming. I might have used other words, such as *blocks, squares, bricks, or rectangles*, but each of these noun names would have committed me to adopt a more definite position to which I do not really want to be committed. These things are not really blocks, squares, or rectangles, they simply are what they are in the drawing: Words do not provide a comfortable fit for them. The insecurity of my commitment is represented through the adjective *squarish* and modified further by the adverb *relatively*. I have proceeded similarly with "relatively uniform in size and shape," "some bubble-like forms," and so forth. In my written description, I suggested, "The implication being that it continues in that fashion more or less ad infinitum;" the drawing actually does not suggest anything, but it simply depicts what is.

Similarly with my other attempt

> The drawing is done in colored pencils. It is of a sharply and carefully drawn circle to indicate the eyepiece of the microscope. Within the circle, wavy lines delineate irregularly shaped entities, by and large maybe ovoid or trapezoid in shape—if anything. Within the circle and within the shapes there are also the larger, round, bubble-like shapes of the drawing of the first text.

It too talks about a representation; it is not the representation itself. Again, it names things that are depicted in the drawing; the phrases "wavy lines" and "irregularly shaped entities" are even less satisfactory than "square entities." Here too I have to name relations between depicted entities; these relations exist only if I give them names in my writing, such as the verb *delineate* for instance. In the drawing itself, these lines do not delineate anything: They are quite simply what is there.

Writing and speech require that I use words such as *drawings* and *eyepiece* and that I use syntactic categories such as nouns and verbs. Verbs relate nouns to nouns such as "lines *delineate* entities" and "a circle *indicates* the eyepiece." In main clauses, grammar dictates that verbs have tense to indicate whether the action is in the past, in the present, or in the future.

Image has none of these. That does not mean that such meanings are impossible but that they are differently expressed; certainly, they are not obligatory. Where image has depictions, writing has names; where image has spatial relations of entities, writing has syntax. In a written text, the elements are in a certain order and the text is read in that way. The order of reading of the relation between entities in an image tends to be much more open, it is much more under the reader's control.

Writing and image each force me into an epistemological commitment on representing that is specific to the mode. If in writing, I say, "When I looked through the eyepiece, I could see the cells very clearly," then I make no commitment at all about the shape of the cells. In drawing however, I simply cannot avoid giving these "entities" a shape, no matter what it might be. A viewer of the drawing is entitled to infer that the shape that he or she sees is the shape that was actually there and visible in the eyepiece. As my contrast of the two representations shows clearly (and, just to repeat, of the same slide, viewed through the same lens of the one microscope), that is anything but a straightforward assumption to make or to accept. In using any mode, I enter into specific epistemological commitments that I simply cannot avoid; they come with the use of the mode, a hidden freight that I cannot shed.

MEANING, "LITERACY," AND TEXT

Here are two further examples. Both concern early stages in children's engagement with script systems; hence, both are about literacy, though in a way that foregrounds the take and the effect of a multimodal approach and requires a further theoretical extension.

Most of us who live in cultures that use alphabetic scripts will be familiar with examples just like this (Bissex, 1980; Kress, 2003). It is important how we name such things, as the name provides a potent orientation for understanding. If we call this a "scribble," we have assigned it to a different category than if we call it "early writing;" in the former, the maker of these marks is not accorded the status of someone who makes meaning and who acts with deliberation, with reason, or with principle; in the latter, we attribute intent to the maker, at the very least. If we call it a "drawing," we have moved away from the domain of writing—or literacy—into the more general area of mark making. As Fig. 10.4 shows, this might not be a bad move.

In my view, there are clear affinities between this drawing and the marks in Fig. 10.3; that is, we are entitled to think that in each case the three-and-a-half-year-old girl engaged seriously with a part of the world that had caught her attention and interest and that the resulting marks were an attempt to represent the salient and relevant features—from her perspective—of that world as accurately as she could. That would hold for the drawing of early writing as much as for the drawing of the model of the dinosaur.

The question in the framework is, "Is this meaningful?" and if so, "How is it meaningful?" In my discussion of the cell examples, I attempted to show that meanings are made in modes other than the two linguistic modes of speech and writing. We know that speech and writing are meaningful; after all, there are words, words have meaning, and they occur in a particular order, which gives a meaning that arises from the sequence. Some readers may have remained doubtful whether the children's onion-cell drawings are actually about the meaning in a similar enough way. But how are the marks in Fig. 10.3 meaningful?

An approach through language and linguistics can give no answer, even though this is about early literacy. These marks lie outside what linguistics would describe. My approach is via (a multimodal) social semiotics, in which signs are the basic units. Signs are made in very many different resources; that is the multimodal aspect. The social semiotic aspect comes for me from the underlying premise that human social action, or work, produces change and meaning. This change affects the tools with which the work is done, it affects that which is worked on, and it affects the "worker." Two major forms of semiotic work are transformation and transduction. The former is orderly change within one mode; the latter is the drawing across of content material from one mode to another. Both transformation and transduction produce changes in meaning—transduction more profoundly so than transformation. In Fig. 10.3—which I regard as an instance of transformation—, what has been worked on is the script system; the tools

FIGURE 10.3 Alphabetic writing.

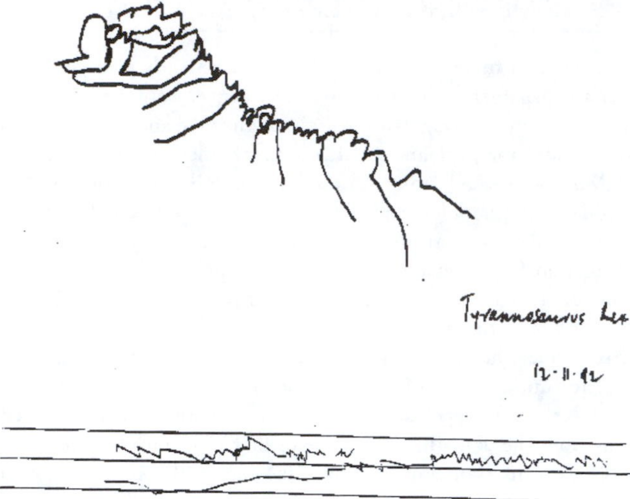

FIGURE 10.4 Tyrannosaurus Rex.

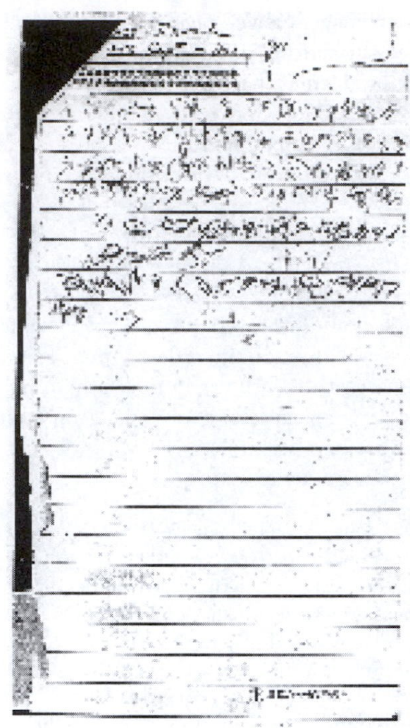

FIGURE 10.5 Ideographic writing.

that have been used are the principles brought to bear by the child in her engagement with the script system; and the change to the child herself is the result of the change to the tools—her principles/resources—that she had used. As the result of her work, she now has different resources/tools; she herself is changed by the semiotic work she has done.

However, this does not yet answer how these marks are meaningful: it poses the question and sets a frame for dealing with it. A comparison of Fig. 10.3 with Fig. 10.5 might help to get further. Fig. 10.5 shows the attempt by a three-and-a-half-year old in Taiwan to represent the result of her engagement with the script system of her culture.

If either attempt was simply scribble, then we ought not to be able to recognize the difference between the two nor to be able to assign each to a particular script system. Yet in my frequent use of the two examples, I have not come across any instance where confusion occurred. Both mark makers captured criterial aspects of the two script systems. In the first case, the child has established for herself several principles: The elements of the script are relatively simple, are at times repeated, are of regular size, are connected, appear in sequence, and are in a linear arrangement. In the second case, the child has also established several principles: The elements of the script are complex, each one differs from the others, they are of regular size, are not connected, appear in sequence, and are in a linear arrangement. In both cases, the child also observed a right to left writing direction.

The examples show that the engagement with the world in the frame happens on the basis of principles, and these representations are the record of this principled engagement. That is, the meaning that is made here is not meaning in the usual (linguistic) sense nor is it accessible through linguistic means. It is however deeply significant. The constant, ongoing change in the tools and in the resources is readily observable if we track the results of such semiotic work over any length of time, as many people have done of course (e.g., Bissex, 1980; see my own tracking and comments in Kress, 2003).

Methodologically, I might note that these meanings are not accessible with hitherto available linguistic means; for after all, the marks do not belong within language. In a multimodal approach however, this issue does not arise: They are graphic marks, they are drawings, and they belong to the mode of image. They are visual representations of an aspect of the cultural world. In this example, we can see both how a multimodal approach reveals something quite profound about script systems, which in this instance is what has become the focus of interest of the two children; and we can see that the theory and its methodology are essential for understanding what may be the meaning of the representation.

This bears directly on the question of literacy and its definition: Do we think that such meanings are significant, should they be recognizable and recognized, and if so, how do we rethink the notion of literacy? It raises what is for me a more than mildly interesting point: From one perspective, we are in the domain of literacy, yet none of the linguistic (nor, I would say, psychological) tools of literacy studies will give us ways of making sensible inroads here. Outside a social semiotic multimodal approach, there is not all that much to say; within it, there is no particular need, at a first step, to worry with labels such as "early literacy." Rather, what we are dealing with is sign making in which, from the children's perspective, there may not be a distinction (yet) to be made between writing and drawing. And, it is the reason why the drawing (or writing) of the Tyrannosaurus Rex belongs unproblematically to this set of examples: the mode distinction of image and writing is not (yet) one that shapes the children's engagement with the world. For them, the issue seems to be to document their senses of what the world is like.

In my discussion of the onion-cell examples, I had raised the question of the text in a multimodal approach. What is the multimodal text? We might ask here too, did the two children produce texts? The three representations in Fig. 10.3, Fig. 10.4, and Fig. 10.5 are the result of principled engagement with the world and record the result of that engagement. All three are meaningful, all three are complete, and all three are internally coherent. All three were, at the time of their making, coherent with the environment in which and for which they were produced. That meets my definition of text.

AFFORDANCES, LOGICS, TRANSFORMATION, AND TRANSDUCTION

When I represented the content of the onion-cell drawings in writing, the question of mode and affordance of mode presented itself. Put one way, too simply and too directly, it is this: Can any mode do what can be done with any other mode? Can speech do what writing does? Can image do what speech does? Can writing do what image does? A somewhat more nuanced version might be, can I as easily achieve with writing what I can readily achieve with image, or with image what I can with writing? These new questions require a theory that transcends one mode; they require a methodology with tools that open these questions up to the possibility of description and analysis.

Writing and speech have words, grammatical categories, and syntactic categories, such as noun, verb, subject, sentence, phrase, and clause. The visual mode does not have words, sentences, and subjects. Both modes have textual forms, genres, though very differently realized (see Kress, 2003). Despite many attempts to find equivalences in descriptive/analytical categories across different modes or to impose equivalences onto modes, that has not proved a productive route to take (e.g., Metz, 1974). The affordances of modes (Gibson, 1986) derive from the interaction of the material of which they are constituted (sound, movement, graphic marks, etc.) and the shaping work which a culture performs on that material for what are often—by human standards—very long periods of time. When we move meaning material from one mode to another that entails the representation, the reconfiguring of meaning expressed through the categories of one mode through the usually entirely different categories of another. This is a more far-reaching change than that of transformation; it is more than translation, it is a reconfiguration, a deep and thoroughgoing reconceptualization.

The material of the mode of speech is sound, that is, variation of pressure in air, received and interpreted by human (and nonhuman) ears, produced by the vibrations of the vocal chords, modulated/shaped by the so-called speech organs—the oral and nasal cavities, the tongue, lips, teeth, and so on. These variations happen in time; one speech sound—but also one word, one clause, one sentence, and one paragraph—follows another. Consequently, the organizing logic of speech is time, and sequence in time is a major semiotic resource available for making meaning. The material of the mode of image is that of graphic marks on a surface, visible to and interpreted by human (and of course nonhuman) eyes. Graphic display is spatial and the elements of a graphic display are simultaneously present to a viewer. The organizing logic of the visual mode is space, and the spatial relations of simultaneously present elements in a (usually) framed space are a semiotic resource available for making meaning.

The two logics of time and space, and the consequent facts of sequence or of simultaneous presence of elements, provide a fundamental semiotic resource for meaning making in a culture. The opposition of sequence and simultaneity has far-reaching consequences. The former means, for instance, that the receiver of a spoken message (or of a message in any temporally organized mode) has to wait until all the elements (or most of them at any rate) are delivered before a full interpretation can be made. In the case of the receiver of the visual message (of a still image), all of the elements are simultaneously present. That gives very different powers to the maker and to the receiver of the two kinds of representation/message: With speech, as receiver, I must attend to the unfolding order of the elements before attempting my interpretation. The author's ordering is paramount and difficult for me to counter. In the case of the image, all of the elements are simultaneously present to me when I engage with it: Usually, I am quite free to produce the order in which I wish to engage with the image and its elements.

Inevitably, cultures use both the resource of sequence in time and of simultaneity in space to make meaning. What is first can be used for different meanings, differently of course in different cultures. In English, *first* might be that which is most salient to me or to my interlocutor (Sally is the one who won); it might be the actor in an action (Henrietta married Jeremy); or it might be topically salient (This year, winter just will not let up). In many languages, what is first often has the meaning of "causally prior." Take two clauses: "The mists dissolved" and "The sun rose." If one makes a conjoined sentence from them, then depending on their sequential ordering, sentences with quite different meanings result.

The mists dissolved and the sun rose.
The sun rose and the mists dissolved.

Temporal (though also linear) sequence is an available means for making meaning; how cultures use that resource is a matter of the needs and characteristics of a culture. In languages with few or no inflectional markers (in English, only the possessive 's remains, e.g., John's wallet), word order is relatively fixed, because it has to do grammatical work (e.g., marking the subject of a sentence). In languages with strong (case) inflection, the semantic-grammatical relation between nouns in a clause is indicated by case-markers, so that word order is freed to carry other meanings. In the example above, "being first" has—among others—the meaning "being causally prior."

My next two examples, Fig. 10.6a and Fig. 10.6b, are organized by the spatial logic of image; causality is not an issue. Here the

FIGURE 10.6A Georgia central.

FIGURE 10.6B Georgia marginal.

spatial relation of elements in the framed space is—among other means such as height and color—a major resource for making meaning.

The child drawer uses placement—a resource of spatial relation—to make meaning. In Fig. 10.6a, the small figure—depicting Georgia—is placed between that of her mother and her father. If we had to turn the meaning of this image into speech or writing it would have a number of readings—"being in the middle of," "being surrounded by," "being enveloped by," "being between," and so forth. However, it is only when we attempt to move, in transduction, from image to words, that the need emerges to make the meaning specific and to name and fix one of these meanings. As an image, the meaning is perfectly satisfactory; it is quite simply what is there, with no sense of ambiguity, ambivalence, or vagueness. In Fig. 10.6b, the small figure is next to her mother (a change made by me). The meaning has changed. Examples of other forms of meaning making here through the logic and the affordances of space are the height of the child relative to her parents; the relative similarity in height of mother and father (when in fact the mother was a much taller and bigger person than the father). However, the major difference in meaning between Fig. 10.6a and Fig. 10.6b derives from the placement of the figure of Georgia relative to her parents.

The logic of space and the logic of time each afford means for making meaning—each differently so. Some modes combine both logics: for instance, dance, moving image, and particularly significant from the perspective of human communication, the mode of gesture. In its elaboration into so-called sign languages, this mode combines the logics and affordances of space and time, with the potentials of both available in the one mode. Alphabetic writing leans on the temporal logic of speech (writing in the guise of a transliteration of speech) as well as offering some of the potentials of the logic of space, and so affords aspects of both.

In the change from Fig. 10.6a to Fig. 10.6b, I have stayed within the same mode; what I did was to alter the order of the entities. A different meaning resulted. This is an example of transformation. Transformations allow the user to make meanings differently and newly and to remake meanings in response to the specific needs of the environment, while staying in the same mode. The difference between the genre of procedure and that of recount can be described in terms of transformation: A teacher aware of this potential can ask students to transform a recount into a procedure or vice versa, and then ask them to reflect on the difference in meaning. I have already discussed examples of transduction: my written account of the images of the onion cells, the relation between the written handout comment "what you will see are bricks, each cell is brick in a brick wall," and the visual representation of the brick wall in the drawing of one of the students.

In school, there are constant demands—different in different subjects—that involve both transformation and transduction, usually without overt recognition of what is at issue in the tasks; the semiotic processes and principles involved are yet largely unexplored and unknown. What we take to be (curricular) knowledge changes profoundly in transduction: for instance, the requirement to represent the curricular knowledge of blood circulation, once as a story of the journey of a red blood cell around the body and then in the form of a concept map. These demands and practices will increase exponentially given the affordances of digital media, which make the use of multimodal representation easy and relatively cost free.

Transduction is a process of profound difficulty. At times, I have attempted to produce a written or spoken equivalence of Georgia's image—not a description, that is, not "in this image I see a house, conventionally drawn, with three figures," but an attempt to produce, in writing and in an appropriate genre, the content substance of Georgia's drawing—maybe something like "I live in my house with my mum and dad. I love them very much. My mum is very beautiful." What becomes of real interest is to see what selections are made from the original, what *is* present and what *is not* present in the transduction, how modal affordance demands a fundamental reconfiguration of what is presented. Some things have to appear in the transduction, given the issue of affordances: What was depicted before now has to be named, the names have to be allocated to grammatical categories such as noun and verb; names as nouns have to be related to other names as nouns through verbs in actions—"I live in my house," "I love them very much," where in the image time did not figure, now it has to be introduced as tense, and so on. And, there is the (seemingly) utterly banal fact that a written or spoken text has to have a beginning; Georgia's drawing does not.

It is at such points that methodological questions arise, in sharp form. What is needed here are categories that function at a level above the specificity of particular modes, yet retain the precision needed to make useful descriptions and comparisons. Tense, for instance, is not a category of the image, though time might be; syntactic sequence of sentence is not applicable to the image, though ordered relations is and will allow us to compare ordering in both a written and a visual representation. Salience (here as centrality) is a feature of the image, and in a quite different way is a feature of written or spoken texts also—as theme or topic for instance.

RHETORIC, DESIGN, AND INNOVATION

The possibilities provided by multimodal representation put the issue of how to achieve what I want to achieve in communication much more into the foreground than it had been in the (seemingly) monomodal representational world of yore. On the one hand, technology makes modally varied choice relatively easy, while on the other hand, in the increasingly unframed and unstable social world, my relation to my audience is also much more unstable and now requires much closer attention to aptness of choice and specificity of address—the equivalent of choice in the niche markets of contemporary consumer society. There are new relations of author and reader with a redistribution of power between them, and arising out of that as well as out of technological change, distinctively different practices and forms of reading (Kress, 2003). In that larger level social change, the linked questions of rhetoric and of design of the message have become central. The reemergence of a widespread interest in rhetoric over the last 25 years or so can be read as a response to a new constellation of insecurity, fluidity, dynamism in environments of communication, accompanied by far-reaching changes in power. In social environments where previously existent norms and frames have frayed or disappeared, each situation of interaction/communication demands an assessment each time of what the communicational environment is and what the social relations are, including an assessment of distributions of power, what expectations are held by the actual or potential participants, and so on. In other words, each communicational situation presents itself as potentially new, and consequently, in each instance, a rhetorical stance fit for this situation has to be established.

In this context, design becomes a crucial component of representational and communicational practices. Where in periods of stability competence in the use of resources was sufficient or where for a period there seemed a need for critique, now the requirement for effective communicational participation is that of the sharp social and political awareness of the rhetor, and the equally astute semiotic sensibility of the designer. Rhetorical assessment provides an outline of the requirements of the social environment in which communication happens; design provides the means for translating the needs of the rhetor and his or her interests into projections for implementation, with full awareness of the characteristics of the audience, the requirements of the subject matter, the interests of the rhetor and the available representational and medial resources.

This marks a deep shift away from a requirement of competence in one mode, to a situation where a rhetor, each time acting in a potentially new communicational situation, assesses the salient features of the communicational environment. On the basis of this, a new message design is articulated. Each design is specific to the requirements of this environment at this moment; and in that respect, it is always new. The processes of transduction and transformation are involved at all points, in all parts of the process and that too contributes to the novelty of each message. Design, as a response to rhetorical demands leads to configurations of modal resources that correspond to the rhetor's conception of what is required, here, now, in this environment. The resources that are used have been culturally produced and are made socially available; yet in these designs, they are always newly assembled in new communicational configurations. This practice, characteristic of every instance of communication, constitutes the entirely unremarkable and constant core of creativity and innovation, in thought as in representation.

"LITERACY"

Meaning is made in many modes and made differently in each of the modes used. Each affords its users the benefit of representing specific things aptly, whether actions and events or the look of things. The meanings made by a receiver of a multimodal text are the result of meanings made in engagement with the parts to which the reader attends. In a multimodal text, each modal component carries a part only of the overall meaning of the text. This partiality of modes is a factor that hitherto has not been acknowledged overtly and explicitly. To be forced to think of language as partial can be an uncomfortably challenging notion, one with far reaching implications. Most importantly, it undercuts the idea that language is a full means of representation; in all multimodal texts—and in my view, all texts are—, attending to the linguistically carried meanings does not give access to the total meaning of the text.

Do we then treat all the modes that contribute to the meaning of a graphically displayed text as a part of the resource of literacy? Is literacy that resource, phenomenon, ability, or skill that describes all of the means, all of the resources, and all of the practices through which meanings are represented? Or, do we wish to retain the possibility of greater differentiation of terminology and with it the possibility of precise naming? Over the next decades, the task will be to describe these modal differences and their implications. For that to happen, precise tools will be essential, in name, theoretically as much as in actual or potential applications.

I have been dealing with the use of image and writing in various representational tasks. Analytically, one benefit of the multimodal approach is that it allows us to stand outside of speech or writing (or of any mode) and get a new view, as if from a satellite. On the one hand, that allows us to see writing as one of many resources available in making meaning, and on the other hand, it reveals its affordances, in its potentials and limitations. That is an advance on the assumption that language is capable of fulfilling all communicational needs. Understanding both the potentials and the limitations of speech or writing takes us an enormous step to a new awareness in the use of representational resources. A multimodal semiotic approach requires many descriptive, analytical, and theoretical tasks to be undertaken; one of these is to establish a new sense of writing as just one resource among others, with its specific potentials for representing but also with its limitations. There remains the large task of understanding the affordances of all modes involved in the making of texts in at least the same detail as those of writing or speech.

We will need to decide how we want to use the label "literacy." Do we see it as covering all of the modes that are involved in the making of graphically instantiated texts, or do we attempt to describe, analyze, and understand each mode in its own distinct terms? For academic work, my preference is for precision in naming: Each mode has its distinct affordance and needs to be understood in its own potentials and if possible named accordingly. Seeing the mode of writing—for me, literacy—in the whole environment of the resources available for making meaning, newly reveals the affordances of literacy in its potentials as well as its limitations, shows us what writing does easily, what it does well, what it might not do as easily as other modes, or what maybe it does not do at all. That makes the teaching of literacy into quite a new task.

ACKNOWLEDGMENTS

I wish to thank Jeff Bezemer for his insightful comments on a draft of this chapter.

REFERENCES

Argyle, M. (1990). *Bodily communication.* London: International Press.

Arnheim, R. (1972). *Toward a psychology of art.* Berkeley, CA: University of California Press.

Arnheim, R. (1974). *Visual thinking.* Berkeley, CA: University of California Press.

Becker, H. S. (1981). *Exploring society photographically.* Evanston, IL: Northwestern University.

Bissex, G. (1980). *Gnys at wrk: A child learns to write and read.* Cambridge, MA: Harvard University Press.

Bellugi, U., & Klima, E. S. (1983). From gesture to sign: Deixis in a visual-gestural language. *Journal of Visual/Verbal Languaging, 3*(2), 45–54.

Chaplin, E. (1994). *Sociology and visual representation.* New York: Routledge.

Emmorey, K., & Lane, H. L. (2000). *The signs of language revisited: An anthology in honour of Ursula Bellugi and Edward Klima.* New York: Laurence Earlbaum Associates.

Gibson, J. J. (1986). *The ecological approach to visual perception.* Hillsdale, NJ: Lawrence Erlbaum Associates.

Goodman, S., Lillis, T., Maybin, J., & Mercer, N. (Eds.). (2003). *Language, literacy and education: A reader.* Stoke on Trent, U.K.: Trentham Books.

Gombrich, E. H. (1960). *Art and Illusion: A study in the psychology of pictorial representation.* New York: Parthenon.

Jewitt, C. (2003). Rethinking assessment: multimodality, literacy and computer mediated learning. *Assessment in Education, 10*(1), 82–102.

Jewitt, C., & Kress, G. R. (Eds.). (2003a). *Multimodal literacy.* New York: Peter Lang.

Jewitt, C., & Kress, G. R. (2003b). A multimodal approach to research in education. In S. Goodman et al. (Eds.), *Language, literacy and education: A reader* (pp. 277–292). Stoke on Trent, U.K.: Trentham Books.

Johnson, D., & Kress, G. (2003). Editorial. *Assessment in Education, 10*(1), 82–102.

Hodge, R. I. V., & Kress, G. R. (1988). *Social semiotics.* Cambridge, U.K.: Polity Press.

Kendon, A. (1983). Gesture. *Journal of Visual/Verbal Languaging, 3*(1), 21–36.

Kress, G. R. (2000). *Early spelling: Between convention and creativity.* London: Routledge.

Kress, G. R. (2003). *Literacy in the new media age.* London: Routledge.

Kress, G. R., Jewitt, C., Ogborn, J., & Tsatsarelis, C. (2001). *Multimodal teaching and learning.* London: Continuum.

Kress, G. R., & van Leeuwen, T. (1996/2006). *Reading images: The grammar of graphic design.* London: Routledge.

Messaris, P. (1994). *Visual "literacy": Image, mind & reality.* Boulder, CO: Westview Press.

Metz, C. (1974). *Film language.* New York: Oxford University Press.

Mitchell, W. J. (1992). *The reconfigured eye: Visual truth in the post-photographic era.* Cambridge, MA: MIT Press.

Paivio, A. (1971). Imagery ability and visual perception of verbal and non-verbal stimuli. *Perception and Psychophysics, 10,* 429–432.

Rose, G. (2001). *Visual methodologies: An introduction to the interpretation of visual materials.* London: Sage.

van Leeuwen, T. (2005). *Introducing social semiotics.* London: Routledge.

van Leeuwen, T., & Jewitt, C. (Eds.). (2001). *The handbook of visual analysis.* London: Sage.

•11•

LEARNING WITH MULTIPLE LITERACIES: OBSERVATIONS OF LIVES EXPLORING MEANINGS, IDENTITIES, POSSIBILITIES, AND WORLDS

Robert J. Tierney
UNIVERSITY OF BRITISH COLUMBIA

> . . . Paintings continue to help Kunwinjku to understand the fundamental connection between individuals, and the social and ancestral order. Kunwinjku experience the worth of the knowledge revealed in paintings because it helps to structure so many aspects of their experience of the world in a way that makes such experience intelligible . . . the experience of understanding the artistic system takes the revelations of the truth of knowledge relating to the Ancestral Beings. Paintings help to create the meaningful texture of their religious understanding. (Taylor, 1987, pp. 336–338)

> Today's kids see the screen as an environment to be explored, inhabited, shared, and shaped. They're blogging. They're building their My Space Pages. They're constructing elaborate fan sites for their favorite artists or TV shows. They're playing immensely complicated games, like Civilization IV—one of the most popular computer games in the world last autumn—in which players re-create the entire course of human economic and technological history. . . . The skills that they are developing are not trivial. They're learning to analyze complex systems with many interacting variables, to master new interfaces, to find and validate information in vast data bases, to build and maintain extensive social networks cross both virtual and real-world environments, to adapt existing technologies to new uses. . . . (*Time Magazine,* March 27, 2006 p. 42)

Through the ages peoples have appropriated symbol systems as metaphorical vehicles with generative syntax, and these symbol systems have afforded new possibilities for engagement with self, others, and this world. Our various means of representation serve to open us to new possibilities, including achieving new insights and ways of transacting with others, ourselves, and ideas and problems. Descriptions of indigenous artists, preschools in Italy and the United States, and the emerging generation of digital users portray similar phenomena when they are given the opportunity to use different media or symbol systems to explore their world or problem solve. They use cutting and pasting, drawing, talking, playing, audio tracks, video interfaces, and other media to achieve different perspectives on their world, explore identities, solve problems, make plans, and communicate with others. With advances in technology, the same is apparent with electronic media. Projects are apt to involve a mix of transactions including talk, faxes, word processing, or blogs; video as different media are accessed separately and together for purposes of composing communications and pursuing problem solving, and as a means of exploring ideas, taking perspective, and deepening or acquiring new understandings. Such circumstances share many things, especially the power of the symbol systems to engage students in deep and complex explorations of issues as well as constructive discussion and debate. Paradoxically, schools may struggle with transitioning these new literacies into school settings in ways consistent with their potential, including the possible shifts in power dynamics that might occur.

As I stated in the earlier rendition of this chapter, I believe that multimedia environments (involving the use of more than one medium, regardless of whether it is the electronic environment or everyday media such as paper, string, glue, and tape) can serve as the basis for the social construction of self and others, making multiple probes about issues or concepts and problem solving, and empowering students in a host of ways. The presence of multiple symbol systems allows for constructing oneself and for achieving different "takes" on an issue or problem with one "take" supporting (complementing, extending, or challenging) another—that is, different ways of knowing and being known.

There are several key concepts that help capture the view that I am espousing. They are (a) multisymbolic, (b) representational, (c) indeterminate, (d) ongoing, (e) perspectival, (f) identity forming, (g) communal, (h) generative, (i) developmental, (j) systemic, (k) learner centered, and (l) empowering.[1] *Multisymbolic* (as contrasted with unisymbolic or reliance upon a limited range of media) highlights the pursuit of media in various combinations. *Representational* suggests that these media afford new ways to represent ideas, especially in combination with other ideas.[2] *Indeterminate* and *ongoing* refer to the constant shifts that incurred with meanings associated with such representation such that meaning should never be viewed as fixed.[3] Media used together or in concert serve as ways of crisscrossing explorations en route to achieve multiple perspectives or be *perspectival.* Sometimes these perspectives are achieved by individuals working in collaboration with themselves; at other times they are achieved in collaborations with others. *Identity forming* focuses upon the relationship between self or the hybrids of self within and across the spaces spurred as learners engage with one another in different circumstances including created worlds. *Communal* suggests the various senses of community that media afford, including the multiple roles in the context of ongoing conversations/collaborations with oneself and others. I have chosen the word *generative* as a way of pursuing a view of multimedia that involves new and open-ended uses rather than canned and receptive uses of knowledge. The word *developmental* reflects a concern with how media use shifts over time. As educators, we need to develop an environment whereby we are sensitive to the students' emerging uses of media, developing expertise, growing understandings with media and expanding possibilities for media. *Systemic* reflects concerns with how media are woven into the social fabrics of individual and group experiences and relationships within different institutions such as schools.[4] *Learner centered* highlights the preeminent position of the student. I envision that our goal is not to have the media or an activity displace the student, but to have the students achieve ownership of the media, so they can use the media in various ways including developing representations of their own meaning. Finally, *empowering* suggests that the study of multimedia also has to do with empowering individuals within different institutions. In other words, as individuals do or do not gain access and expertise, they may gain or lose access to certain opportunities that may carry with them an increase or decrease in power or the opportunity to participate in certain decision making.[5]

To illustrate the integration of multimedia literacies in teaching and learning and the conditions necessary for media to act as a meaning-making tool, I have extended the observations of learners engaged in multimedia engagements offered in the original chapter. The first extends my observations of my own son's recent involvement with boogie boarding. The second is taken from one of the many projects pursued at one of the preschools within the Reggio Emilia project in Italy and some observations of a similar project undertaken in a U.S. preschool. The third derives from my involvement with the Apple Classroom of Tomorrow, specifically, from my observations of the multiple literacies of students at West High School in Columbus, Ohio (Tierney, Kieffer, Stowell, & Desai, 1992) and subsequent follow up (Tierney, Bond, & Bresler, 2006). The observations of their multiple literacies are informed by various perspectives akin to the aforementioned concepts: (a) learner centered, (b) identity forming, (c) multisymbolic, (d) perspectival, (e) communal, (f) generative, (g) developmental, (h) systemic, (i) representational, (j) indeterminate, (k) ongoing, and (l) empowering. They are addressed by descriptions of practices through the lens of a range of perspectives including sociosemiotic (e.g., Siegel, 1995; Kress & Van Leeuwen, 1996, and Lemke, 1998), Marxist (e.g., Habermas, 1983), critical and sociocultural (e.g. Street, 2003: Stuart & Hall, 1996), and cognitive (e.g., Bransford, Brown, & Cocking, 2000; Spiro, 2004). Overall, these observations suggest that these multimedia literacies embedded within cultural practices can serve to signal and spur values as well as transform, challenge, and shape self and others socially, politically, personally, and culturally.[6]

[1] Hall, (1996) drawing upon Derrida (1981), Foucault (1970), Freud (1921/1991) and others, suggested that "identity are never unified and, in late modern times, increasingly fragmented and fractured; never singular but multiply constructed across different, often intersecting and antagonistic, discourses, practices, and positions. They are subject to radical historization, and are constantly in the process of change and transformation" (p. 4). The notion of hybridization draws from my own experience as a cross-national and the intertextual, Bakhtinian dialogical and the cultural sensitivities, histories, and perhaps acumen that one experiences as one moves across borders as a subaltern, cosmopolitan, interloper, or resident alien. They include the positions, licenses, or roles afforded or chosen by one's selves as these selves do or do not "follow the grain" of these changing spaces or the learner's recreations of them.

[2] The Cognition and Technology Group at Vanderbilt University used the term representational literacy to refer to the flexible use of multimedia for communications and learning.

[3] Bloome (1993) provided a detailed discussion of the indeterminate nature of meaning in reading and writing that can be extended to other forms of representation and argues for the "refractive" versus "reflective" nature of ongoing meaning making.

[4] Green, Weade and Graham (1988) discussed schooling as "learning to student" rather than learning as may otherwise be defined. Street (1984) discussed the differences that may exist between literacy practices as defined within the institution of schools versus other cultural settings. The former tended to treat text as autonomous and the acquiring of psychological competence of a series of skills versus acquiring literacy practices.

[5] Critical theorists, sociolinguists, and various systemic linguists have underlined the extent to which various forms of literacy can serve to exclude or empower individuals or groups. (see Fairclough, 1992; Lemke, 1990; Luke, 1988: Wignell, Martin, & Eggins, 1982). There have been a number of discussions to the extent to which technology may exclude certain groups from being afforded access. For example, with the advent of e-mail, certain groups have the potential to shift all communications to e-mail, thus excluding those who do not have or choose not to use this technology.

[6] Gee (1998) has described discourse as "a socially accepted association among ways of using language, of thinking, believing, valuing, and acting that can be used to identify oneself as a member of a socially meaningful group of 'social network' or to signal (that one is playing) a socially meaningful 'role'" (p. 143)

BOOGIE BOARDING

When my son Shaun was nine years old, he became interested in boogie boarding during an extended trip to Australia. While his introduction to the sport had begun on the East Coast of the United States, his sustained and in-depth engagement occurred in Australia when his cousins loaned him a boogie board and discussed various aspects of about boogie boarding, including cutting, doing spinners, and going for the better waves. With little encouragement and without much of the paraphernalia (flippers, wet suits, gloves etc.), my son set out on his first trip to the beach with his cousins—a kind of initiation for which my son needed little prodding. At the beach, he watched other boogie boarders and, alongside his cousins, made his way through the breakers close to the shore where he caught his first wave. In the ocean, he watched his cousins who were full of expert advice and whom he hoped would watch his successes. Once on shore again, the conversations represented a mixture of expletives about the great waves that were caught, some stunning wipeouts, and analyses of how to better "read" the waves. Away from the shore, the discussion continued—the advantages of wet suits, flippers, and the kind of boogie board needed to maximize possibilities. Then they reviewed and analyzed videos, magazines, and posters of surfing. Then they returned to the beach to try boogie boarding repeatedly—each time under somewhat different wave conditions. Before long, boogie-board posters surrounded my son's bedroom walls and he was negotiating with us how to purchase his own "manta" board, flippers, and so on. He began reading the newspaper for information about tides and weather forecasts as well as anything that might pertain to surfing conditions. Conversations addressed the sand bars, the uniqueness of each wave, each wave set, the dangers of rips, kinds of conditions, as well as issues of balance, weight distribution, and the relationship of body position to direction and speed. And, sharks, stingers, and seaweed were discussed.

It was not until I wrote this piece on boogie boarding that I truly realized what boogie boarding entailed. Consider, if you will, what my son learned: First, he learned a very sophisticated skill in becoming "a boogie-board rider." Such experience, while seemingly frivolous, should not be slighted; it entails knowledge of the ocean, especially waves, currents, tides, the dangers of rips, different kinds of breaks, and sea life. It also entails an understanding of flotation, momentum, water temperature, body temperature, sunlight (especially ultraviolet light), the effects of salt water, pollution, and the characteristics of various materials (rubber, foam, salt water, fiberglass) and their effects on one another.

Also consider the media that were used. My son enlisted conversations, photos, magazines, videos, first-hand experience, observations, self and peer analysis, and advice across a range of situations. At the same time, he sent letters and e-mail messages back to the United States to friends about surfing and used his expertise to have conversations with grandparents, uncles, and his little brother. The media were rarely separate and discrete for these interactions; indeed, the media were embedded within and a part of the social situations. The media were a vehicle for learning (prompting questions, arousing interests, affording comparisons and connections, analysis, evaluations, and goal setting).

To be a boogie-board rider entailed walking, talking, watching, and analyzing boogie boarding. It was a space where a variety of identities found play. Increasingly, cultural theorists are exploring how identities surface, including the interplay between physical space as well as biology and culture. Using concepts such as performativity, cultural theorists such as Omrod (1995) and Damarin (1995) explored how practices such as boogie boarding entail performances involving gender, race, class, and age. As they suggested, my son's engagement with boogie boarding and now his surf-board riding involves an array of performances around his gender and age as well as other features of his past and my own. Further, they also discussed the notion of transparency—that is, when there is a sense of harmony between themselves, nature, and the technology or when riders might consider they have engaged in a perfect wave.

A great deal more could be said. However, suffice it to say, my son's experience represents a real-world learning experience involving self in relationship to identity formation via various media in a complex and dynamic fashion that is inseparable from the learning experience itself. The media were used in combination with one another as boogie boarding was explored, problems were solved, new perspectives were achieved, expertise was developed, knowledge was advanced, and identities were explored.

Learning experiences such as this parallel some of the descriptions of learning in classrooms that afford possibilities with media. The projects that are pursued in conjunction with the Reggio Emilia preschools represent such situations, as do some of the projects described in conjunction with the Apple Classroom of Tomorrow.[7]

SELECTED REGGIO EMILIA PROJECTS

A large number of projects have been described in conjunction with the now world-famous Reggio Emilia Preschool initiatives, originally in Italy and now in several locations in the world. My interest in describing the projects relates to the richness and emphasis on representation—that is, an approach to learning that builds upon the use and study of multiple literacies to engage students in the exploration of their world. As Forman (1995) suggested, ". . . there is a belief that all children learn best when they can use multiple symbol systems to understand complex relations, particularly when these complex relations are part of a real-world project that gives these relationships a holistic gestalt" (p. 188).

The Long Jump Project involved the development of an athletic event by a subgroup of Reggio Emilia students who volunteered to plan the event with some input from the class. Some of the activities emerged; others were planned with teacher and classmate input. The teachers identified the long-jump event as viable and believed it had potential for measurement, research, representation, and student involvement. The initial project goal was for the class to holding a long-jump event. Later goals included having the students investi-

[7] Unfortunately, a detailed description to the Reggio Emilia's educational approach is beyond the scope of this paper, since it would require an extensive discussion of a range of features: the involvement with parents and the community, the integrative nature of projects, the practical nature of these projects, the discussions among teachers regarding the development of projects, the use of children's ideas, and multiple representation. I will focus on the use of media as a symbol system to represent, explore, and engage with new ideas. George Forman (1998) and a number of others have used the Long Jump Project as a way of illustrating some of the elements of the Reggio Emilia approach.

gate possibilities, such as researching the long jump in conjunction with exploring the event at the Olympics and discussing videos of athletes jumping and then jumping themselves. For the exploration, the students discussed what they might do, especially in the context of an event in which all of the students would be involved. This entailed thinking about issues such as space for running and jumping as well as spots for spectators and judges. To this end, the students developed plans and then a model with replicas, and problem solved how they would compare the length of jumps with strings. Sometimes in conversations, peers advised one another, compared observations, discussed simulations, pursued replays, etc., en route to making decisions as to how they would carry out the event and its planning for participants, judges, and spectators with different needs and interests. The list of issues that were discussed, planned, and reviewed ranged from rules for runners (starting, run up, foot placement, clothing) to rules for judging, measurement, disqualification, and etiquette as well as advertising, announcements, applications to participate, awards, etc. Forman (1993) provided a chronological listing of activities involved in the project:

> Looking at and acting out photographs of Olympic long jumpers
> Verbal outpouring of initial knowledge of long jump making an initial sketch of the track, the jumpers, and how to score
> Drawing the track layout
> Experimenting with running speed × jumping distance
> Laying out the track in the courtyard wit white chalk
> Debating about handicap for girls using small replica objects
> Designing six posters for rules to the long j
> Place to start
> Three false starts allowed
> Speed and place of run-up
> The touch of the foot
> Measurement of the footprint
> Presenting the rules to the whole class
> Designing training, clothes, diet
> Making posters calling for registration of each participant
> Making posters for designating ability flights
> Making posters for calendar of competition by ability flights
> Writing a letter of invitation to all children of the school
> Designing posters of citywide advertising
> Writing the rules for prizes
> Writing the closing speech for the competition
> Making a poster of rules for measuring three jumps per person
> Learning to measure distance-six phases
> Using string to record the distance jumped
> Trying to use the tape measure
> Correcting the tape measure
> Transcribing tape measure symbols to paper
> Comparing the tape measure to carpenter's rule.
> Reinventing convention place value notation
> Preparing insignia for each jumper to wear at meet
> Writing rules for the referee and assistants
> Implementing the plans: the day and the final competition
> The run and the long jump measuring each jump with string
> Posting the strings on the wall
> Using the tape to measure the longest strings
> Awarding the trophies
> The kisses from the misses and misters (Forman, 1993, pp. 173–174)

During the exploration, teachers supported the students and prompted comparisons, speculations, and planning, and especially ways to represent using various symbol systems as a means of exploring a range of issues, maintaining records, engaging in simulations, and communicating. As Forman stated, sometimes the discussion focused on the worth of different symbolizations and created "the type of constructive conflict we deem to be the power of this multi-symbolic approach to education" (p. 187). Further, he stated:

> As these children sought to gain a more coherent understanding of time, distance, and rules of equity, they externalized their nascent theories as icons, gestures, speech, text, pictograms, diagrams and notations. These symbols were embedded in the coherence of the real-world event, which in turn helped convert a random list of symbols into a symbol system. This holism assures that the symbol system will ultimately converge to deepen knowledge rather than increase facts (p. 188).

A range of other projects were described in various Reggio Emilia sites, especially as preschools in the United States and elsewhere have emulated the practices. Tierney and Damarin (1998) described the Creature City project at the Sophie Rogers preschool at the Ohio State University where their teachers had adopted a project orientation based upon the Reggio Emilia tenets.

The Creature City projects emerged from discussion between the teacher and the children who decided to build the city, including buildings, schools, parks, sports stadiums, a zoo, etc. The project took months as the children went on excursions around their community to study and contemplate their own city, photograph buildings and streets en route to sketching, and gather all sorts of material. It also involved working together on the different city constructions using each other's emerging expertise about the city, including construction elements such how to represent grass on the baseball stadium, relative heights and distances etc., their plans for showing people or developing games, and other activities to go along with their city as well as refining the city by the addition of signage, photographs, etc.. Throughout the project, they used parents and friends as advisors as well as participants in activities involving the city. Finally, they mapped out the city on plywood boards and everyone was invited for a finale-type celebration of their city.

With the long-jump project, students created an experience with a basis in reality; with Creature City, they developed a city informed by observations of a city, but based upon their imagination. During the act of creating a city or pursuing the long-jump project, the media became both the basis for sharing and a means of sharing. As the students worked together, they acted as a community and in so doing adopted different roles and achieved different status within that community. Across both projects, their participation was multi-faceted—constructor, consultant, researcher, user, critic, and mentor or host to others. In this way, the projects are similar. In other ways, however, they are different.

In a host of ways, the Reggio Emilia approach resembles the kind of learning with media used by my son when he learned to boogie board or the projects described later in the Apple Classroom of Tomorrow. Just as my son engaged with integrated technology, self, and nature, so do these preschoolers enlist a range of overlapping media. The preschoolers and the high-school students which are described next, enlisted a variety of media integrated with the world that they are observing, creating, and engaging. The extended projects in the preschool and high school involved a host of planned and unplanned learning, materials, the world around us, working with others, problem solving, and the use of media. Also, the use of media and the projects themselves were socially constituted; that is, it is impossible to separate them from the other social negotiations and events that were occurring/developing. Just as these explorations are inseparable from the social fabric of the learning situation, the media serve as vehicles for learning and become part of what is being learned. In other words, the conversations, observations, and use of other tools have a symbiotic relationship with the events themselves and assume an opportunity for exploring roles, having agencies, and engaging with self and others in ways that are identity forming.

DIGITAL LITERACIES SITE

The third set of observations focuses upon the multiple literacies I observed in conjunction with a six-year study and a later follow-up study of high-school students and later graduates in a learning environment (an "Apple Classroom of Tomorrow" site) that provided students as much access to multimedia-based digital literacies as students in regular classrooms have to books, pens, and paper. The Apple Classroom of Tomorrow represented an attempt to provide students with state-of-the-art technology in a constructive learning environment wherein they could enlist media to explore topics, solve problems, and pursue their own projects. Students were able to interact with a community of learners in various subject areas within a context that allowed them to explore and learn with a range of multimedia software, databases, and word-processing software. For example, in their science or history class, they could pull together projects using PageMaker, HyperCard, and SuperCard using a mix of scanned images, video, and multilevel stacks of ideas. They also had access to computers at home where they could pursue class work or projects that they might decide to initiate themselves.

The site involved careful planning similar to that carried out by the teachers at the Reggio Emilia school. Projects and units were selected, planned, and implemented with student problem solving and issues in mind. Throughout the projects, the Apple Classroom of Tomorrow teachers considered ways to facilitate student engagement with issues, concepts, and problems as they used media as adjuncts to their learning and simultaneously studied the value of the media for so doing. The students themselves offered each other help in various forms including expertise, if needed, as well as ongoing critical feedback.

The projects with which the students were engaged represented a range of problems, topics, and issues. Students developed and launched their own rockets, developed video portfolios about themselves, construct a scaled-down version of the city of Columbus, developed leaflets for community agencies using desktop publishing, and pursued projects tied to different topics and themes. Often projects involved an extended exploration of a topic, such as their exploration of the China Project. This project was one of many projects in which students were encouraged to explore topics using a range of media as vehicles for such explorations and to culminate their explorations in the presentation of an exhibit or demonstrations for others (classmates, teachers, students in other classes, and interested public). The China Project coincided with a rare exhibition of Chinese artifacts dating back to the earliest emperors in China. The students were encouraged to explore various facets of life in China during early imperial dynasties and, to these ends, were given access to the exhibit and other resources including experts of that period, video, and laser discs. The students grouped themselves in terms of their interests and, in the context of conversations with collaborators, began gathering resources such as books, pamphlets, photographs, videos, etc. With the digitally based technologies and other media, each project became a composite of media involving the development and capture of conversations, observations, scanned images, and video clips, or firsthand experience of the food of the times, different ways of dressing, sporting activities, and so forth. The explorations of their specific topic involved a mix of conversations tied to readings, viewing films, examining actual artifacts at the exhibit, the aforementioned firsthand experiences, and interviews with experts. Each student's explorations took a variety of different turns as he or she explored his or her topic with these media.

The media served as vehicles for developing understanding as well as a kind of portfolio from which students could keep track of their explorations and a palate from which they could pursue their own expressions or customized presentations. The students discussed what they wanted to do as they directed one another's attention to material that they had located in books and other reference materials, portions of video that they had discovered, and scanned images and text that they had generated. As they examined the stacks of material, the explorations of the topic and their projects moved forward. Sometimes the discussions centered on the scope of the topic (what was relevant, what was irrelevant, how ideas were related); at other times the discussion focused on how the different media could complement one another or which medium was more effective. As they explored different topics, students generated video screens that combined text, images, and sound, and these screens connected with one another sequentially and hierarchically. With the electronic media they were using, students could insert graphical buttons which, if clicked on, accessed other layers of information (perhaps a map depicting the Great Wall, additional information on related events, a graphic display of the sequence of events, a video clip, etc.). The technology appeared to increase the likelihood of being able to pursue multiple lines of thought, as well as entertain different perspectives. Ideas were no longer treated as unidimensional and sequential; the technology allowed students to embed ideas within other ideas, as well as other forms of multilayering and interconnecting between ideas. The students spent a great deal of time considering how ideas were laid out—that is, how the issues that they were exploring might be presented across an array of still pictures, video segments, text segments, and sound clips. It was apparent that the students had begun exploring images, sound tracks, and text interconnected in very complex ways (i.e. multifaceted, multilayered ways) using a smorgasbord of image, sound, and print. The presentations themselves included the computer-based presentation of a mix of multilayered visual information together with text on various facets of a topic. Supplementing the technology-based presentations were food tasting, posters, verbal presentations, and demonstrations of sports.

The multisymbolic or multimedia texts that they created were, as the students stated, "more inviting, dynamic, and open than regular text." Students realized the possibility of developing texts that were more pictorial and concrete at the same time as they allowed for making connections between concepts that were more complex, multi-layered, and immediately accessible. In conjunction with being able to explore the integrated use of various graphics (animation, video segments, scanned images or various ways to graphically depict data), they began to utilize various media as a way of achieving different perspectives on issues they were exploring in physics, history, and other subjects. Just as an author might look for the right word or twist in their text, these students were exploring ways to integrate images with written text to achieve different takes and twists. They found themselves free to develop texts that were nonlinear and multilayered.

If outsiders come to these learning situations with traditional views of media and learning, they may not realize what is occurring. Some might view these learning situations as different forms of project learning; others might see them as ways to make learning more concrete. However, educators attuned to the role of the media in transforming ways of knowing are likely to recognize that these situations represent environments where students are exploring their world with media that afford the enlistment of multiple symbol systems. Moreover, they are apt to see some confirmation of Olson's (1974) contention that symbol systems create new possibilities for ways of knowing, including deepening and shifting understanding as well as transacting with others. These situations represent learning conditions that reflect an orientation to learners, learning, and the role of less-traditional media—especially in terms of the nature of knowledge, the pursuit of knowledge, and the role multiple media assumes.

With the technology, they were able to do things they might not have otherwise done and were astutely aware of the potential utility of these tools for their own advancement and, in turn, their families. Across their high-school engagements with these literacies, their commitment and sense of possibilities had expanded, become more refined, and shifted. They had goals arising from their abilities with these new literacies that transcended the classroom. All of the students viewed the expertise as affording them advantages in the workplace or college and a way to help family members with projects. The acquisition and appropriation of these literacies were socially transforming.

The students' involvements with the new multimodal literacies were seen as integral to whom they could become and what they might imagine. It seemed as if the students were afforded access to "genres of power": new texts, new ways of negotiating meaning, and ways of knowing. Furthermore, these literacies appeared to be transformative in terms of lives. The observed experience of these students befits notions of "culture capital" (Bourdieu, 1986) similar to the value that Brandt discussed in her analysis of the literate lives of Americans born between 1895 and 1985 (Brandt, 2001). As Brandt stated,

> Workers these days produce wealth not only by processing raw materials but by supplying those raw materials themselves in the form of knowledge and skills, including communication skills. (p. 6)

A follow-up study of some 20 students five years after their graduation from ACOT and high school reinforced this claim. Based upon our observations and student interviews, these acquired literacies provided access to further education and also were great assets in the transition from school to work. It seems as if their engagement and expertise with these new literacies had contributed somewhat to a shift from cautious optimism about themselves to what might be viewed as respect for their own capabilities. They developed a sense of their own expertise, a recognition of various functions that these literacies could serve, and an appreciation of the skills they needed, including the ability to work with others. In many ways, we came to see these new literacies as having served to provide a lifeline for students. Many noted that without the program they would not have had these opportunities. Several had even experienced homelessness during high school; others lived in foster homes during high school and credited their engagement with these new literacies and their learning environment with affording them opportunities which otherwise would have been out of reach. The follow-up study suggested that students availed themselves of the skills and strategies that they had acquired and integrated them into a repertoire that contributes to who they were as students or what they did or were able to do in the workplace. Interestingly, many of the students noted that their university instructors were not receptive to having them enlist these multimedia technologies in their submission of the equivalent of term papers. Traditional image-free and linear text was still the standard. In contrast, for some students, these new literacies afforded them an advantage that made them preferred candidates for employment with the colleges that they attended. Within department and research offices, these digital literacies afforded them advantage and essential skills. Subsequent to college, it often directly influenced their profession. For example, one of the students now oversees the layout of several newspapers, and another works with the computer systems at Chemical Abstracts. Others are pursuing doctorates in lesser-related areas such as "women's studies" and "social work."

The digital literacies engagements of these students should not be viewed as unique. Indeed, a large number of today's students have grown up with a variety of multimodal literacies, including new genres of texts which are multilayered and image rich, as well as various forms of text messaging, conversations, video games, multimedia downloads, and Web environments for purposes of research, documentation, analysis, and presentations. Their ability to navigate across, among, and within the complex array of past and emerging literacies has become a reality rather than a hope and for many has become core rather than supplemental

DISCUSSION

Many educators have struggled with or been uncertain what to do with notions of multiple literacies, especially the ascendancy of new digital literacies. Some of the uncertainty may stem from their own knowledge of and use of digital literacies that may pale against those of the students; some of the uncertainty may arise from the failure to have understandings or guidelines on the interface between these new literacies and curriculum; some of the uncertainty may stem from problems of access to the hardware, software, and support systems needed to ensure a seamless engagement with the tools. In some situations, these digital literacies may involve the purview of a separate subject area and be restricted to laboratories rather then distributed across classrooms. Oftentimes, these new literacies are framed as discrete skills such as programming, Internet access, or presentation skills rather than as learning tools with complex palates of possibilities for students to access in a myriad of ways. It is as if learning with technology is being perceived as "learning the technology" rather than using a range of multimodal literacy tools (supported by these technologies) in the pursuit of learning.

Further contributing to the uncertainty are unanswered questions: Some have questioned whether learning technologies enhances learning. Indeed, some have claimed that technologies might actually be perpetuating rote learning or learning that is more gloss than substance, more product driven than process oriented, and more isolating than collaborative. In some circumstances where there is an increased emphasis upon accountability, teachers may retreat to teaching what is testable. And, what is testable seems tied to traditional teaching objectives rather than these new literacies and multimodal and media-based learning technologies. To engage students with these new literacies may not be considered core, but "bells and whistles." Further, for some, digital technologies may be seen as contributing to a myriad of problems (e.g., inequities in education access, uncontrolled access to questionable material, or even an imperialistic form of globalization and subjugation). Added to the uncertainty is the lack of sustained study of these literacies from the perspective of social practice.

As stated by Cynthia Lewis and Bettina Fabos (2005) in *Instant messaging, literacies, and social identities:*

> If we mourn the loss of print literacy as we think we once knew it, then we may find ourselves schooling young people in literacy practices that disregard the vitality of their literate lives and the needs they will have for their literate and social futures at home, at work, and in their communities. (p. 498)

Or, as Selfe and Hawisher (2004) argued,

> If literacy educators continue to define literacy in terms of alphabetic practices only, in ways that ignore, exclude, or devalue new-media texts, they not only abdicate a professional responsibility to describe the ways in which humans are now communicating and making meaning, but they also run the risk of their curriculum no longer holding relevance for students who are communicating in increasingly expansive networked environments. (p. 233).

I am both optimistic and pessimistic about the advancement of multimodal literacies in schools. After over 10 years of studying learning technologies for the advancement of these new and emerging literacies in schools, I am convinced that these new literacies and their multimodal possibilities contribute to learning opportunities in ways that support complex and collaborative engagement with problems and issues, projects and topics, process and product, and inquiry and discussion. It is consistent with the assertion by Kozma (1991) that,

> . . . capabilities of a particular medium, in conjunction with methods that take advantage of these capabilities, interact with and influence the ways learners represent and process information and may result in more and different learning (p. 179).

Overall, my explorations of the students' lives confirmed the emergence of a repertoire of rich literacies in a fashion that was empowering in both the short- and long-term learning. The newly developing literacies enhanced ways of knowing and had an impact extending to the sociopolitical fabric of their lives. As Siegel suggested, these multimedia explorations have "a generative power that comes from juxtaposing different ways of knowing . . . as a way of positioning students as knowledge makers and reflective inquirers" (p. 473). Examined sociopolitically, these engagements with these new literacies interface with emerging identities and serve as a bridge between school and the students' lives, and do so in ways that print may not support as dynamically—especially for disengaged learners (Hull & Zacher, 2004; Rogers & Schofield, 2005).

SUMMARY AND REMARKS

Increasingly, our worlds involve being able to engage with and enlist multimodal literacies involving image rich and multilayered texts, various forms of digitally based interactions, audio and multimedia downloads, Web environments for purposes of research, documentation, analysis, and presentations. In turn, these developments have given rise to calls for educators to realize the notions of multiliteracies. Among the most overt pronouncements of this need emanated from the work of a team of leading literacy scholars who called themselves the "The New London Group" and their call for a "Pedagogy of Multiliteracies" (New London Group, 1996). As they argued,

> . . . literacy pedagogy must account for the burgeoning variety of text forms associated with information and multimedia technologies. This includes understanding and competent control of representational forms that are increasingly significant in overall communications environment, such as visual images and their relationships to the written word

This call is consistent with some more avante garde curriculum developments. For example, New Basics, which represents a cutting edge new curriculum for schools developed by the Queensland Department of Education (2000a), suggested that literacy should be defined as ". . . the flexible and sustainable mastery of a repertoire of practices with the texts of traditional and new communication technologies via spoken, print and multimedia" (p. 9).

This definition of literacy suggests a reorientation away from just print media or reading to a range of engagements with intersecting and multilayered texts. It is consistent with orienting technologies to their use as tools for learning versus the learning of tools as ends unto themselves. As the International Society for Technology in Education has stated, digital technologies "enable students to become capable information technology users; information seekers, analyzers and evaluators; problem solvers and decision makers; creative and effective users of production tools; communicators, collaborators, publishers, and producers; and, informed, responsible, and contributing citizens . . ." (International Society for Technology in Education, 2002).

These new literacies represent new spaces to negotiate and create new selves and relationships with others. These spaces have the potential to be transformative in terms of learning befitting notions of "culture capital" (Bourdieu, 1986), similar to the productive value that Brandt (2001), Leu (2006), Selfe and Lewis (2005), and Selfe and Hawisher (2004) argued is essential preparation which schools should be providing for today's changed world.

These multimedia environments are spaces that Rogers (2006) has argued afford students the possibility of having their literacy practices travel across spaces, in and out of schools, blurring traditional boundaries and forms of literate practices. These spaces also allow students to "juxtapose and transform genre practices for critical purposes, engage in the playful instability of genres, selves, and messages, and renarrate their stories and identities in the process" (Rogers, 2006, p. 29).

REFERENCES

Barton, D., & Hamilton, M. (1998). *Local literacies: Reading and writing in one community.* London: Routledge.

Blanchard, J. S. (1996). Issues in technology and literacy education. In R. D. Robinson, M. C. McKenna & J. M. Wedmar (Eds.), *Issues and trends in literacy education* (pp. 316–326). Boston: Allyn & Bacon.

Boirrdieu, P. (1986). The forms of capital. In J. G. Richardson (Ed.), *Handbook of theory and research for the sociology of education* (pp. 241–258). New York: Greenwood.

Brandt, D. (2001). *Literacy in American lives.* Cambridge, England: Cambridge University Press.

Bruner, J. (1986). *Actual minds, possible worlds*. Cambridge, MA: Harvard University Press.

Costanzo, W. (1994). Reading, writing and thinking in an age of electronic literacy. In C. L. Selfe & S. Hilligosi (Eds.), *Literacy and computer: The complications of teaching and learning with technology* (pp. 195–219). New York: MLA.

Damarin, S. (1995). Technologies of the individual: women and subjectivities in the age of information. *Research on Technology and Philosophy, 13*, 185–200.

Derrida, J. (1981). *Positions*, Chicago: University of Chicago Press.

Education Queensland (2000a). *Literate futures: Report of the literacy review for Queensland State Schools*. Brisbane, Australia: Education Queensland.

Education Queensland (2000b). *New basics—Curriculum organizers*. Brisbane, Australia: Education Queensland.

Edwards, C., Gandini, L., & Forman, G. (Eds.). (1998). *The hundred languages of children: The Reggio Emilia approach to early childhood education*. Norwood, NJ: Ablex.

Forman, G. (1998). Multiple symbolization in the Long Jump Project. In C. Edwards, L. Gandini, & G. Forman (Eds.), *The hundred languages of children: The Reggio Emilia approach—Advanced reflections* (2nd ed., pp. 171–188). Greenwich, CT: Ablex.

Foucault, M. (1970). *The order of things*. London: Tavistock.

Freud, S. (1991). Group psychology and the analysis of ego. In *Civilization, society and religion* (Vol 12 Selected Works). Harmondsworth, England: Penguin. (Original work published 1921)

Gee, J. (1996). *Social linguistics and literacies: Ideology in discourses* (2nd ed.). London: Taylor and Francis.

Green, J. L., Weade, R., & Graham, K. (1988). Lesson construction and student participation: A sociolinguistic analysis. In J. L. Green & J. O. Parker (Eds.), *Multiple perspectives analyses of classroom discourse* (pp. 11–47). Norwood, NJ: Ablex Publishing.

Hall, S. (1996). Introduction: Who needs identity? In S. Hall and P. du Gay (Eds.), *Questions of cultural identity* (pp. 1–17). London: Sage.

Hall S., & du Gay, P. (1996). *Questions of cultural identity*. London: Sage.

Hull, G., & Zacher, J. (2004). What is after-school worth? Developing literacy and identity out of school. *Adolescent Literacy VUE Number 3, Winter/Spring 2004*. www.annenberginstitute.org/VUE/spring04/Hull.html

International Reading Association. (2001). International reading association position statement on integrating literacy and technology in the curriculum. Adopted September, 2001.

International Society for Technology in Education. (2002). *National educational technology standards for teachers preparing teachers to use technology*. Eugene, OR: International Society for Technology in Education.

Johnson, S. (2006). Don't fear the digital. *Time*, March 27, 2006.

Johnson-Eilola, J. (1994). Reading and writing in hypertext: Vertigo and euphoria. In C. L. Selfe & S. Hilligosi (Eds.), *Literacy and computer: The complications of teaching and learning with technology*. New York: MLA.

Kinzer, C., & Leu, D. (1997). The challenge of change: Exploring literacy and learning in electronic environments. *Language Arts*, Vol. 74.

Kress, G., & Van Leeuwen, T. (1996). *Reading images: The grammar of visual design*. London: Routledge.

Landow, G. P. (1992). *Hypertext: The convergence of contemporary critical theory and technology* (pp. 2–3). Baltimore: Johns Hopkins University Press.

Lemke, J. L. (1998). Metamedia literacy: Transforming meanings and media. In D. Reinking, M. McKenna, L. Labbo, & R. Kieffer (Ed.), *Handbook of literacy and technology: Transformations in a post typographic world* (pp. 283–301). Hillsdale, N.J.: Lawrence Erlbaum.

Leu, D. J. (2005). New literacies, reading research, and the challenges of change: A deictic perspective of our research worlds. Presidential address presented at the National Reading Conference, Miami, FL.

Leu, D. J. Jr., & Kinzer, C. K. (2000). The convergence of literacy instruction with networked technologies for information and communication. *Reading Research Quarterly*, 35, 108–127.

Lewis, C., & Fabos, B. (2005). Instant messaging, literacies, and social identities. *Reading Research Quarterly*, 40(4), 470–501.

Luke, A. (2004). Teaching after the market: From commodity to cosmopolitan. *Teachers College Record 106*(7), 1422–1443.

Luke, A. (2005) Foreword. In K. Pahl, & J. Rowsell (Ed.), *Understanding literacy education: Using new literacy studies in the elementary classroom*. Thousand Oaks, CA: Sage.

New London Group. (1996). A pedagogy of multiliteracies: Designing social futures. *Harvard Educational Review, 66*(1), 60–92.

Ormrod, S. (1995). Leaky black boxes in gender/technology relations. In K. Grint and R. Gill (Eds.), *The gender-technology relation: Contemporary theory and research* (pp. 31–47). London: Taylor and Francis.

Pahl, K., & Rowsell, J. (2005). *Understanding literacy education: Using new literacy studies in the elementary classroom*. Thousand Oaks, CA: Sage.

Reinking, D. (1997). Me and my hypertext: A multiple digression analysis of technology and literacy (sic). *The Reading Teacher, 50*(8).

Rogers, T., & Schofield, A. (in press). Things thicker than words. Portraits of multiple literacies in an alternative secondary program. In J. Anderson, M. Kendrick, T. Rogers, & S. Smythe (Eds.), *Portraits of literacy across families, communities and schools*. Lawrence Erlbaum Publishers. Routledge.

Selfe, C., & Hawisher, G. E. (2004). *Literacy lives in the informational age: Narratives of literacy from the United States*. Mahwah, N.J.: Erlbaum.

Siegel, M. (1995). More than words: The generative power of transmediation for learning. *Canadian Journal of Education, 20*(4), 455–475.

Spiro, R. J. (2004). Principled pluralism for adaptive flexibility in teaching and learning. In R. B. Ruddell & N. Unrau (Eds.), *Theoretical models and processes of reading*, (5th ed., pp. 654–659). Newark, DE: International Reading Association.

Street, B. (1984). *Literacy in theory and practice*. Cambridge, England: Cambridge University Press.

Street, B. (2003). What's "new" in New Literacy Studies? Critical approaches to literacy in theory and practice. *Current Issues in Comparative Education, 5*(2), 1–14.

Tierney, R. J. (1987). The engagement of thinking processes: A preliminary study of selected Apple Classroom of Tomorrow students. Report prepared for Apple Computer, Inc.

Tierney, R. J. (1988). The engagement of thinking processes: A two year study of selected Apple Classroom of Tomorrow students. Report prepared for Apple Computer, Inc.

Tierney, R. J. (1996). Redefining computer appropriation: a five year longitudinal study of ACOT students. In C. Fisher (Ed.), *Education and technology: Reflections on a decade of experience in classrooms*. San Francisco: Jossey-Bass.

Tierney, R. J. (2006). Global/cultural teachers creating possibilities: Reading worlds, reading selves and learning to teach. *Pedagogies, 1*, 77–87.

Tierney, R. J., Bond, E., & Bresler, J. (2006). Examining literate lives as students engage with multiple literacies: The thread, the needle and the fabric. In *Theory into Practice*, *45*(4), [Special Issue].

Tierney, R. J., & Damarin, S. (1998). Technology as enfranchisement, cultural transformation and learning practices. In D. Reinking, M. McKenna, L. Labbo, & R. Kieffer (Ed.), *Handbook of literacy and technology: Transformations in a post typographic world* (pp. 253–268). Hillsdale, N.J.: Lawrence Erlbaum.

Tierney, R. J., Kieffer, R. D., Whalin, K., Desai, L. E., & Moss, A. G. (1992). Computer acquisition: A longitudinal study of the influence of high computer access on students' thinking, learning, and interactions. ACOT Report #16, Apple Computer, Inc.

Tierney, R. J., & Rogers, T. (2004). Process/content/design/critique: Generative and dynamic evaluation in a digital world. *The Reading Teacher, 58*(2), 218–221.

·12·

CHILDREN OUT OF BOUNDS: THE POWER OF CASE STUDIES IN EXPANDING VISIONS OF LITERACY DEVELOPMENT

Anne Haas Dyson
UNIVERSITY OF ILLINOIS AT URBANA-CHAMPAIGN

"You're not supposed to leave the underworld," screams Liliana (alias Venus) at Sammy (alias Pluto). The third graders are playing Greek gods. They have named the boundaries of the relevant worlds, and Sammy is clearly out of bounds. He is supposed to be on the sand by the climbing structure, not on the grass by the fence. "But I'm good now," he pleads, trying to redefine himself. He is tired of the lonely and hot underworld and longing for the more sociable and tree-shaded space guarded by the firm Liliana.

Out on the playground, children claim and define spaces, whether their game is Greek gods or kickball, cops-'n-robbers or hopscotch. And, of course, who's "in" and who's "out" is often a matter of contention. In many ways, this same task of establishing and maintaining boundaries faces adults who construct case studies, that is, studies of "bounded" human experience (Stake, 1988, p. 256). The case might be a community, group, activity, or, of particular interest herein, individual. Whatever the unit, however, the "case" has a way of going out of bounds.

Consider, for example, another scene involving 8-year-old Sammy, a "case" in a qualitative study (Dyson, 1997); the bounded experience being studied was that of learning to write.

> Sammy is sitting on the classroom rug, head bowed. He had looked forward all morning to Author's Theater, when his classmates would act out his story. But all had not gone well, especially with Michael. Sammy had written the death of a superhero—an untenable text, according to Michael. Unable to ignore Sammy's misery, I tell him that just because Michael didn't like his story doesn't mean Michael doesn't like him. But Sammy is not buying this—and neither is his peer Makeda sitting beside him.
>
> Makeda: But a story is kinda like *your* life. It's like it's kinda like it's what you're doing and they're doing. . . . [to Sammy] Just say, "Oh yeah, I'm gonna get you. I'm not gonna be your friend no more. If you don't like my story, I don't like your story either." . . . Like Lettrice say, "I don't like your story." I say, "I don't like your story either. And I'm not your friend any more.". . . So she never did mess with me. (Pause) She saw my big brother. . . . So that's what happened.
>
> And Sammy and Makeda go to lunch.

I had begun by observing one child's writing but, soon, was enmeshed in a complex social drama featuring many children. Moreover, I was attending to symbols other than the written marks on the page; as Sammy's story was enacted, discussed, argued about, and literally cried over, its personal and public meaning was mediated through many symbolic forms—spoken words and written ones, dramatic movement and expressive gestures. Thus, to understand Sammy's writing development, the conceptual boundaries—the definitions—of writing and of development needed to be drawn in ways that could accommodate his complex experience. And that experience forced me as an observer to attend to children other than Sammy, to symbols other than written ones.

In this chapter, I explore the way in which the intense study of individual experience can destabilize, not physical playground boundaries, but *conceptual* ones and thereby allow new perspectives. To this end, I offer the case of three cases written over a 15-year period; collectively, these cases illustrate the methodological dynamics of case studies, the ways in which they may force an observer both to articulate conceptual boundaries and to go beyond them, to go out of bounds, as it were. The specific cases highlighted herein are all young children making sense of and through written language.

Over the years, startling statistics have proclaimed the challenges schools face in supporting children's literacy, especially in schools like Sammy's, schools serving poor children in urban and rural settings. In its annual yearbooks, The Children's Defense Fund (e.g., 2005) presented the shameful statistics: the number of children living in poverty, labeled as "unready" for school, as "academically behind," and, eventually, as "dropouts." Of what importance, then, are the experiences of one child? Of what worth are the hours, months, and, indeed, years that may be spent constructing a small number of cases? These, ultimately, are the questions addressed through the case of the three cases. First, however, I elaborate on the process of constructing a case in the *interpretive* tradition (Dyson & Genishi, 2005; Erickson, 1986; Ortner, 1999).

CONSTRUCTING A CASE: THE WORK OF DEFINITIONS AND DETAILS

Insight into the nature and the value of case construction comes, interestingly, from a biologist, Barbara McClintock. She was, wrote Stephen Gould (1987), committed to "following the peculiarities of individuals, not the mass properties of millions," (p. 167) and to tracing their complex interactions with each other and their environment, a commitment all the more intriguing because McClintock followed stalks of corn. In her own words, spoken to her biographer Evelyn Keller, one must understand,

> how it [each plant] grows, understand its parts, understand when something is going wrong with it. [An organism] isn't just a piece of plastic, it's something that is constantly being affected by the environment, constantly showing attributes or disabilities in its growth. . . . So I know every plant in the field. I know them intimately and I find it a great pleasure to know them. (as cited in Gould, 1987, pp. 167–168)

McClintock followed the narrative thread of an individual intent on understanding a phenomenon—the workings of biological inheritance and development. Her work disputed the notion of a simplistic, one-way flow of information, from genome, to RNA, to DNA; and it revealed a fluid and mobile process in which information could enter the genome from the outside environment (as it does in AIDS) (Gould, 1987, p. 159). A single organism reverberates in an environment and, in the process, reveals the complexity within and without and highlights potentially critical points of contact (of, to stretch a word, negotiation) with that environment.

McClintock, then, spoke about respect for bounded complexity, about attention to its unfolding story, and, thus, about cases. Some unit of integrity (a person, an activity, a group) is both outlined and contained by a researcher, who is studying, not the case itself, but a case of *something,* some phenomenon (e.g., not maize, but biological inheritance). Thus, the researcher is constantly making decisions about what is, or is not, within the constructed bounds, meaning what is, or is not, relevant to such a case.

Negotiating Conceptual Boundaries

Inherent in the process of bounding is a critical challenge—and strength—of case-study analysis: the need, in the midst of the flow of unbounded experience, to make decisions about basic definitions of what exactly is being bound, that is, about the phenomenon of interest. Writing of anthropological cases of communities, Geertz (1973) grappled with this strength and challenge:

> The locus of study is not the object of study. . . . You can study different things in different places. . . . It is with the kind of material produced by . . . almost obsessively fine-comb field study . . . that the mega-concepts with which contemporary social science is afflicted—legitimacy, modernization, integration, conflict . . . meaning-can be given the sort of sensible actuality that makes it possible to think not only realistically and concretely *about* them, but, what is more important, creatively and imaginatively *with* them. (p. 23)

In interpretive research, one aims to understand some aspect of human experience and, given its complexity and, indeed, its abstractness, one needs to situate that experience within people's actions and reactions to the materiality, the local specificity, of their everyday worlds.

This link between probing phenomenon and bounding them in particular locales has been problematized in these times of global media and transnational migration. It is no longer possible to imagine pristine units—individuals or groups—set in their geographic places and their traditional ways (Erickson, 2002; Gupta & Ferguson, 1997). Still, we as human beings realize ourselves in material time and space, even as our experienced worlds are interwoven into the historical, political, and cultural dynamics of larger social structures (Ortner, 1999). Indeed, case studies of experienced-but-situated worlds can themselves probe and articulate a version of the fluidity and complexity of contemporary life and, thereby, problematize too-neat categorizations of written language and of children learning, the phenomena of interest herein (e.g., Vasquez, Pease-Alverez, & Shannon, 1994; Guerra, 1998).

Detailing Lived Experience

Implicit in the textual construction of a human actor is a second strength and challenge, one that highlights intentional *mind,* not genetic matter—the need to enter into, and try to understand, another's consciousness, another's world. This strength contains within it a potential weakness, the possibility of looking, not to understand, but to confirm what is "known," research reduced to illustrative anecdote of truths already held. Researchers, after all, are not ventriloquists (Geertz, 1988). They do not speak for others. They are writers who construct others' lives. Researchers' own life experiences and social positioning—their age, gender, ethnicity, indeed, their very status as outsider, "both enable and inhibit particular kinds of insight" (Rosaldo, 1989, p. 19).

However, as writers, researchers *can* work to make another's life world more perceptible, more accessible, by respecting the details of that world, the recurring themes and rhythms of the other's life scenes. Such respect entails time and presence—and painstaking reliving, as scrawled field notes are typed out, voice-packed audiotapes transcribed, and crumpled child papers are smoothed over again and again. And it also entails depicting the other's actions in descriptive words, rather than glossing them with abstractions like "competent," or not, "cooperative," or not, "motivated," or not; observers attend to the contextual specifics—the who's, what's, where's, and when's—of others' actions, attempting to grasp *their* value judgments, their interpretations (Bogdan & Biklen, 2003).

Observers do, of course, have their own feelings about and reactions to the observed. The need to acknowledge but interrogate—literally bracket in one's notes—such responses accounts, at least in part, for the self-knowledge that may accompany attempts to understand others (Emerson, Fretz, & Shaw, 1995). For example, one might ask, Who do I (and other participants in the scene) assume is competent or not? On the basis of what kinds of actions in what settings, using language to accomplish what purposes in what ways? What does this concept, *competence,* mean here? This potential for seeing new dimensions of experience connects this second challenge with the first, the potential to go beyond old assumptions and conceptual boundaries, through, in McClintock's words, "the pleasure of know[ing] another."

STUDYING YOUNG WRITERS: BOUNDING "LITERACY" AND "GROWTH"

In studying literacy development, researchers face very basic definitional questions. Most important, perhaps, is, What is "it" that develops? What is reading, writing, or literacy? Where does one look for "it"? What boundaries should be drawn around "it"?

In the opening anecdote about Sammy, for example, is his writing in the *graphics*, in the symbols he formed on the page? Or is it in the *orthographics*, in the linking of graphic signifier with signified in systematic ways? Or, maybe it is in Sammy's *process*, his planning of a message and his monitoring and revising of its objectified form. Yet another possibility: writing could be his *discourse* or *genre form*, his story—or, maybe, it's a *functional tool* at work in a particular *cultural event*, one involving the specifics of who, to whom, with what message and form, in what place and time, and, of course, for what reason. Or maybe writing is in the ideology of the society as a whole, its *societal discourse*; Sammy and Michael have different expectations about what can and cannot be written in the context of a superhero story—and Makeda has clear notions about what can or cannot be said about another's story (or at least about the stories of authors with big brothers).

In other words, should an observer attend primarily to the writing on the paper? The behavioral evidence of individual mind at work? The enactment of writing as social happening and cultural activity? Or, perhaps, the textual constituents of ideological beliefs about what can or cannot be said by whom? Moreover, these questions can be asked from different perspectives. Sammy, Sammy's friends and family, his teacher, and his adult friend (the researcher) may all have different ways of defining what it means to write.

And as if these issues were not challenging enough, basic issues must be addressed about "development." Again, what and where is it? Moreover, what sort of developmental pathway should one prepare to follow? Is growth a linear unfolding? A zigzagging phenomenon? A moving away from social supports? A gradual integration into social life?

It is such definitional decisions that undergird researchers' ways of drawing boundaries around, and paying attention to, children. Conceptual definitions influence what is foregrounded and what is left in the background, what is carefully detailed and what is glossed over. Conversely, it is the details—the descriptions of daily life—that in turn may challenge the viewing frame itself. In writing cases, researchers must deal with the dangling threads—the child actions and reactions that cannot be understood, that suggest the need to refocus, to clarify and, sometimes, to redefine.

Indeed, one theoretical perspective portrays the act of writing itself as a struggle with given words (like "literacy" and "development"). Writing is dialogic, argued Bakhtin (1981, 1986); it not only mediates interactions between writers and their audiences, but also mediates between writers' minds and the collective mind of the discourse community that has given them their words. Thus, in constructing cases, writers negotiate with available words, stretching them, rethinking them, aiming to make them "fit" their data. Then, through publications like this *Handbook*, they participate in the process of figuring out what can legitimately be said about "writing" and "development" within the circle of people concerned about children and literacy.

UNRAVELING CASES

To illustrate the methodological dynamics of case-study construction, I present abbreviated forms of the cases of Rachel, Jake, and Tina. The children were from similar sociocultural backgrounds (e.g., urban children whose heritage was predominantly African American, and whose socioeconomic circumstance was primarily working class); they were all given to imaginative storytelling, all had complex relationships with peers—and all were singularly complex people. The children were of different ages: Rachel was just 5, Jake was 6, and Tina (a classmate of Sammy's) was 7. However, my aim herein is not to trace developmental patterns from child to child; rather, it is to examine the definitions, the viewing frame, that shaped each construction—and how that frame was complicated by the case itself. I chose these three from a larger set of 38, because they engendered clear and distinctive conceptual shifts.

For each case, I provide situational context, an edited sample of the case, details of analysis tools, and, finally, the conceptual understandings *and* puzzles yielded by the completed study. Collectively, the cases illustrate the boundary negotiation—and the theoretical reenvisioning—possible through sustained attention to the unfolding stories of children's lives.

Rachel: Writing as Symbol System

For the first case, that of Rachel, the viewing boundaries were tightly set: the single child in the viewing frame. Rachel was one of five focal children in a study of young children's writing (Dyson, 1983). There was no child writing in her classroom, which had been designated my site by the school district. So, I set up a classroom writing center and invited the children to come write, however and whatever they wanted.

The center was just another choice during "free" time; there were no classroom expectations guiding what was produced, nor were there any social forums through which ways of talking about writing might become routine. The center seemed mainly to provide children with a space to explore the written medium. Children would arrange and rearrange known letters and letter-like forms on their papers, asking me if they had quite done "it" yet (e.g., written anything that could be read); and they also spent quite a bit of time writing known (or guessed at) names of important people in their lives. Most significant, the writing children *talked* a great deal, to themselves, to me, and to each other. As a researcher, I was drawn to this talk and, thus, the specific question guiding the project became, What role does children's *oral* language play in their early *written* efforts?

Of all the regular child visitors to the center, Rachel stood out for her people-oriented personality; she was a mover and a shaker in the kindergarten scene. Relative to her peers, she was much more likely to use the writing center for the production of dramatic adventures. Now I would think of her as a performer in search of an audience (and I was convenient). Then I approached her primarily as a child writer; I asked what, how, and why she wrote and what role her talking—and Rachel was a talker—had in her efforts.

The Drama—and the Dramas of—Rachel

The following event is representative of how Rachel wrote a story and also of how I narrated her case:

> Rachel is composing an elaborate story about two feuding sisters, one in a series of stories about sisters who are always together but always at odds. Rachel's dominant composing media are pictures and dramatic dialogue and gesture. As her picture takes shape, she acts out a scene in which one sister has just locked the other out of the house.
>
> Rachel: "Sister, open up the door. [Rachel knocks twice on the table.] You dummy. Sister, you better come and open this door or else I'm gonna throw this pumpkin shell on your head—"
>
> Quite suddenly, Rachel has a plan:
>
> That's what it's gonna be saying!

Rachel now writes the "teeny tiny" print-like markings, all in a line, in the uppermost left-hand side of her paper (see Fig. 12.1). The writing, though small, stands for the loud orders and threats of the sister on the outs:

> It says, "Open the door, Sister. Open, open, open, else I'm gonna throw this pumpkin shell right on your head."

FIGURE 12.1 Rachel's feuding sisters.

Later, Rachel explains to me (her so-called observer but, in this event, her audience) that she wrote little "'cuz I wanted you to try to guess."

Rachel did not always use such unconventional writing. Sometimes, her intention involved the more limited writing of names (e.g., a "note" or "letter," containing a picture and the addressee's name). In her "notes," the letters were legible and the words quite readable. For elaborate stories, though, pictures, dramatic talk, and "teeny tiny" writing were the favored media.

Defining the viewing frame: Analytic tools. From much observing and taping of events like the story of the feuding sisters, file boxes began to fill with observational notes, transcripts, and child products. Using such diverse materials to construct a case requires a vocabulary or coding system, a way of describing the dimensions of the "bounded" experience (e.g., learning to write); in this project, it required a means for describing how the children went about writing and the role of talk in that writing.

The nature of such a vocabulary is dependent upon those basic questions asked earlier, including, What is writing? Where, in the mass of data, is it located? In the academic dialogue of the late 1970s, researchers emphasized the graphic and orthographic features of early writing (e.g., Clay, 1975; Read, 1975) and the decision-making processes through which children crafted information on paper (e.g., Graves, 1975). These definitions suggest that a researcher should focus on a child's ways of shaping (e.g., of planning, encoding, and monitoring) inner meanings in written forms.

Thus, I constructed Rachel's case—and those of four other children—by describing her actions during, and related to, her production of letters or letter-like shapes on paper. I developed an analytic vocabulary or category system that described the "components" of her process (e.g., *formulating a message, encoding it, forming the letters, and rereading*) and how those components varied. For example, in Rachel's feuding sister story, her message was *specific* (e.g., she did not simply say "This is gonna say something about my sister") but her encoding was not *systematic* (e.g., she did not use any evident orthographic system) nor were her forms *conventional*. However, in writing her notes (which involved people's names), Rachel's specific message was systematically encoded in conventional forms.

In addition to writing process components, the category system included descriptors of the "functions" served by talk during writing. For example, in Rachel's feuding sister story, talk served primarily to *represent* or narrate the story, although it also served to *evaluate* (e.g., to express Rachel's attitude toward the world, particularly the obnoxious behavior of sisters) and to *interact* (e.g., to ask me to attend to her story). It served minimally to help her *encode* (e.g., to help transfer oral symbols to written ones through "sounding out").

Uneasy answers: Rachel pushes the boundaries. Fine-grained analyses of the focal children's writing and talking led to tentative conclusions. Talk, it seemed, is initially something young children do *about* writing (e.g., "This is my mama's name"), rather than something young children encode *in* their writing. Over time, children's speech becomes both writing's raw material and its guiding tool—young children use speech to monitor and encode their ideas. Thus, their writing becomes more able to stand on its own, independent of any accompanying talk.

This suggested developmental pattern fit with the then dominant definition of development (e.g., development is an orderly transformation of child behavior, reflecting underlying changes in conceptual systems; Piaget & Inhelder, 1969). Moreover, it was also compatible with the dominant view of writing development. That development was a moving apart, a child learning to articulate and manipulate meaning without support from the immediate material and social context (Olson, 1977). The sense of such a portrayal was dependent upon the viewing frame, upon those tight boundaries drawn around individual children and their writing processes.

However, such narrow tight boundaries could not quite contain the lively Rachel. As composer, Rachel did much more than write—she also drew and dramatized. The roots of her eventual accomplishments as a storywriter could not be in that line of teeny tiny writing alone. Moreover, her composing processes were highly variable but related to her end goal. Her action on the page could not be understood separately from her intention in the world.

Finally, those narrowly drawn boundaries were also at odds with the project's methodology. Such boundaries implied a telescopic perspective on children, an attempt to make sense of their behavior from the faraway viewpoint of the adult world. However, *interpretive* methodology aims to situate child behavior within the meaningful webs of present aims and social connections. The next case, that of Jake, continued to fray the edges of the existent conceptual boundaries.

Jake: Writing as Mediational Tool

The project involving Jake aimed to examine one of the dangling threads from the study just described—the drawing, storytelling, and dramatic gestures that seemed to serve as the developmental roots of conventional writing, at least as much as if not more so than lines of child mock writing (Dyson, 1989). The project initially focused on eight focal children. Their use of multiple media when composing was studied along with how their use of media changed overtime. In this study, then, child writers became child symbol users, and that transformation opened up more viewing space.

Jake's school was very different from Rachel's. In this small, K–3 magnet school, writing was an integral part of classroom culture. That culture was enacted primarily through a daily journal time, which was guided by Margaret, the K–3 language arts teacher; journal time included a sharing time, in which Margaret led discussions about children's accomplishments as artists and composers. Thus, individual children's ways of writing were shaped by—and were shaping—the literacy life of the school as a whole; my own role as instigator and interactional partner during writing time was minimal; very quickly, most of the youngest children began to emulate the story writing of the oldest ones.

During the first year of this two-year project, Jake was a first grader—a talkative, outgoing one. Despite his own sense of being "slow" in learning to read and write, he was highly engaged during journal time. Like Rachel, he composed dramatic stories, primarily by drawing and talking. His stories, though, were not about relationships but about fast-paced adventures, often involving speedy vehicles and clashes between good guys and bad guys. Moreover, the stories were not used to gain the attention of an adult interested in children's writing; they were used to gain the attention of his peers, especially his "straight man," so to speak, the calm, quiet, and artistic Manuel.

The drama—and the dramas—of Jake. The following vignette illustrates Jake's propensity toward wild adventures, his playfulness, and, most especially, his delight in teasing his friend Manuel. The vignette centers on the drawing in Fig. 12.2.

> Jake has just drawn the ground and the sky and—
>
> Jake: Now I'm gonna make a mechanical man.

Manuel, sensible and calm, seeks some clarification:

> Manuel: A mechanical man? You mean a robot man?
>
> Jake: Yeah, I'm gonna make a robot man. You got it, Manuel.

Jake begins to elaborate in his talk and in his picture:

> Jake: Here's a bomb head. It's gonna explode. It hasn't even exploded yet. When it does—

Manuel's a bit concerned:

> Manuel: I hope it explodes in the next century.
>
> Jake: Here comes the bomb explosion! There is the fire, a little smoke. (makes quick back-and-forth motions with his marker) . . . It's gonna explode in the next few days.
>
> Manuel: I hope it happens on the weekend and then I won't be around.
>
> Jake: Not for long this school will be around . . . (adds another figure) I'm gonna make a flying earthling!

FIGURE 12.2 Jake's robot man and flying earthling.

Jake's dynamic narratives were woven with talk and drawing; but his writing was neither dynamic nor narrative. Jake struggled with encoding, and, for support, he "copied offa" his pictures, capturing only its static, flat surface. For his robot man story, he wrote,

> Once upon a time there were two men. One was flying up in to the clouds. The other man was staying on the ground. The and

Over the two years of the project, Jake's social nature and flair for the dramatic did not change—but his composing did. As a second grader, Jake's drawings often were sequenced to reveal key moments in his story; further, his playful interactions with peers could now occur *during* writing. The following vignette presents Jake in action one year after the "robot man" event.

As is his custom, Jake is sitting beside Manuel. While Manuel works on the story of a snowman that comes to life, Jake has other plans:

> Jake: (to Manuel) I'm deadly. I'm deadly. I'm gonna put your name in this story and . . . I'm gonna make sure you get blown to pieces. (laughs)
>
> Manuel: Blown to pieces. (softly and a bit awed)
>
> Jake: Yes sir. You won't be able to see your mommy ever again.
>
> Jake writes, *Once there was a boy that is named Manuel.*

Manuel playfully retaliates:

> Manuel: In my story, you're going to meet a magician who's going to turn *you* into a snowman.
>
> Jake: Well, actually, guess wha—
>
> Manuel: And melt you flat.

Jake seems to back down:

> Jake: Actually, um, I I'm, I—we're gonna, I'm writing about um us flying the fastest jet in the world. None of us—both of us are—isn't gonna get blown to pieces because it's the fastest jet—it can out run any bullet.
>
> Manuel: Oh wow! I like that.
>
> Jake: And it's as bullet-proof as it can get.

But later:

> Jake: Watch out Manuel! (writes *blow up)*
>
> Manuel: Just at the very end when they're just so happy, it's almost—they're just so happy and they read the entire story and they loved it, I get blown up.
>
> Jake: Yeah.
>
> Manuel: And they cry and cry and cry and cry—it's so dramatic.

Later, Jake reads his story to Manuel:

> Once there was a boy that is named Manuel. Manuel is going to fly the fastest jet and I am going to fly the jet too. But Manuel's headquarters is going to blow up But I am OK. But I don't know about Manuel but I am going to find Manuel. . . . But I think I see him. He is in the jet. Manuel are you OK? yes I am OK. you are being attacked. I will shoot the bad guys out of the universe. OK yet shoot them now. The end.

In this event, as in others in the second grade, Jake played with Manuel, not only around his writing, but through the writing itself.

Defining the viewing frame: analytic tools. The case record of Jake was filled with the taped voices, written records, and collected products of the many children whose school lives were interwoven with his own. To make sense of Jake's data set—and those of seven of his peers—I took from the literacy dialogue of the mid-1980s a definition of writing as a mediational tool used to participate in social events (Basso, 1974; Heath, 1983): Writers do not only use forms to represent meaning; they use those forms to mediate their relationships with others. This definition of writing—this conceptual boundary—would frame both child symbol maker and coparticipants in the observed event. Moreover, it would situate any particular event in a larger cultural world within which that event had some function and had gained some meaning.

Accompanying new views of literacy were new perspectives on development as well, most notably, sociocultural ones informed by Vygotsky. These definitions would also encircle children's interactional partners, for children would be seen as "grow[ing] *into* the intellectual life of those around them" (Vygotsky, 1978, p. 77; emphasis added). In Jake's case, however, the boundaries that "fit" the data were not those of child apprentices to adult-governed worlds (e.g., Ninio & Bruner, 1978). The data were gathered through close observation of children, not through close observation of adult/child encounters. Those children had attended mainly to each other; adults had faded in and out of the viewing frame.

Thus, in dialogue with both theory and data, I drew my analytic boundaries around children engaged with other children—children brought together and guided by adults in official worlds but children who organized their own life spaces in response to those worlds (Corsaro, 1985). The research question became, how did writing come to be a useful tool within the social lives and the symbolic repertoire of Jake and his peers?

To help answer the project question, I developed coding categories to describe how children used talk, pictures, and written texts to create and to enter into their own and others' composed worlds. As in the earlier project, one set of categories referred to the functions of the children's language. Another set examined the *meaning elements* represented in children's interwoven talk, drawing, and writing, including, for example, objects, actors, actions, placement in space and time (past, present, future) and sensorimotor qualities (direction, force, speed, volume). It was this vocabulary that revealed, for example, that, as a first grader, Jake's narrative talk during drawing moved through time, but his written language was stuck within the static space/time dimensions of his completed picture frame.

Jake pushes boundaries As the 2 years of the study passed, Jake and his peers both clarified and complicated the guiding definitions of writing and development. Like Rachel, Jake was a child who used stories to express his feelings about—his evaluations of—the world. However, this use was not seen simply as an attribute of Jake, nor was his composing seen as a direct reflection of placement along a linear evolution of writing behavior. Rather, Jake's composing was seen as shaped at the intersection of his symbolic resources and social intentions, which were themselves influenced by the social structure and interactional possibilities of his classroom and, more broadly, his school.

Initially, Jake and his peers used the familiar tools of drawing and talk to participate in journal time. However, gradually, functional shifts occurred: writing itself began to assume more of the social and intellectual work of composing. Thus, a second-grade Jake interacted with (teased) his good friend Manuel through writing as well as through talk. He manipulated the words on the page in order to manipulate Manuel. Moreover, he used evaluative techniques (Labov & Waletsky, 1967), like suspending narrative action at critical points (e.g., "I am OK but I don't know about Manuel"), to express his feelings about his world (especially his consistent theme of friends threatened but saved, by him of course).

However, Jake's talk did not become less important; for Jake and his peers, as for academics, texts became embedded in, and integral to, the ongoing social life. In fact, it was this embedding that fueled and guided Jake's writing. He *was not moving away from the social world;* he was learning new ways of engaging with it.

These new conceptual boundaries for viewing child writers began to fray even as they took form. One reason simply was time. It is different to spend 2 years with a child, rather than a few months, as with Rachel. Jake was not just a child composer; he was a complex character—a peer among children, a sometimes struggling student, and, he hoped, a "tough" and "slick" kid. His choices of topic, characters, and plot events, his way of interacting with others about his texts, all said something about Jake's relationship to his social and ideological worlds (e.g., to being a boy, a vulnerable child in what he regarded as the tough and "crazy part" of the city). And yet, specifics of content choices and issues of sociocultural identity were not highlighted in Jake's case. However, they came to the foreground in the case of Tina.

Tina: Writing as Social and Ideological Dialogue

In Geertz's (1973, p. 23) words, one can "study different things in different places"—and Tina's school was a place in which issues of identity became strikingly visible. Her urban K–3 school served primarily two neighborhoods, one an African American, low-income, and working-class community, where Tina lived, and the other, an integrated but primarily European-American more middle-class community. At the preceding school, Jake's close friends had included children from diverse ethnic backgrounds, most of whom lived in his integrated working-class neighborhood. Tina's close friends were also from her neighborhood, but it was not integrated. Tina, like most of her peers, interacted with those from across the economic divide primarily in official school activities. Thus, studying child literacy in the context of child social relationships brought into the viewing frame the interrelated issues of race, class, gender, and culture.

The project (Dyson, 1997) began with an informal visit to Tina's second-grade classroom during writing time, when I noticed the pervasiveness of superheroes, figures like teenage ninjas (both the human and the "mutant turtle" variety) and X-Men (a team of mutant humans, both women and men, with great powers). These superheroes were especially visible during an optional practice named "Author's Theater" by the children's teacher, Kristin; in this practice, the children chose classmates to act out their written stories.

Given that popular media stories appeal to children's desires as members of a gendered, classed, and racialized society (Kline, 1993), I wondered how such stories figured into their social and literacy life (e.g., who wrote such stories, to be enacted by whom, with what sort of changes over time in textual content and structure). Although superhero stories were written mainly by boys, some girls did evidence interest—all working class girls, among them, Tina.

A tiny child with large glasses, Tina was a complex character, one who voiced a strong sense of identity as an African American, as a caring person who "love[d] the world," and as a "tough" kid. The complexity of Tina—and her intense reaction to being excluded from anybody's story world—is evident in the summarized drama below.

The drama—and dramas—of Tina. For weeks, the boys in Tina's second-grade class had been writing stories for Author's Theater about ninjas, ninja turtles, and X-Men, and for weeks Tina and her friend Holly had been begging for a part to play, with no luck at all. The only boy who regularly included girls in superhero dramas was Sammy, and he, like other boys, picked only Melissa or Sarah, two slender, middle-class, and outgoing White girls—just as were the ninja's "foxy babes" in the popular media stories. Seldom did any girl become a tough superhero, despite the presence of strong women, including women of color, in the X-Men comics and cartoons.

Tina had had it. Usually, when she wrote in her journal (titled "The Peace Book"), she wrote brief texts expressing her love of family and friends. But on this day, Tina enticed Holly to write a superhero story with her. "And no boys," she said firmly, "'cause the boys doesn't let us play."

Sitting side by side, Tina and Holly began playfully planning an X-Men story. Initially, Tina was to be the X-Men character Rogue, who can fly through the air and absorb the powers of others with a single touch. But she quickly became "the toughest guy in the world. . . . We're all Blobs!" (Blobs are huge, fleshy mutant humans, virtually indestructible and very bad guys.) "'Cause if somebody threw a metal ball at me, the energy go right through me and I would never know. And we're sisters robbing the world. . . . And we'll never get sick. And we'll never die."

The sisters evolved, Tina becoming Uncle Blob and Holly becoming niece Blob. As the girls became more animated, they moved to the classroom rug, deep in play. In the drama, Uncle Blob Tina captured Rogue, cutting off her long hair. Uncle Blob drank that hair, absorbing its fiery power, giving just a small bit to his begging niece Holly Blob. "The only thing you can do," he tells the girl, "is just shoot out fire at them [the X-Men] and then just call me." (There are shades here of the ninja stories and of the girls who call for help.)

Class composing time ended before the children had put pencil to paper. The next day Tina was absent, and so each girl eventually authored her own X-Men story. However, given the intensity of peer pressure, each girl also found it impossible to write the planned drama. When Tina tried to write her Blob story, both girls and boys begged for powerful good-guy roles and expressed great unhappiness with the unapologetic bad guys Tina had in mind. This pressure resulted in a story without the Blob family but, also, a story without the usual good-guys-defeat-the-bad-guys encounter. Following is an edited excerpt from Tina's story:

> Once there were 4 X-Men [Storm, Rogue, Jean Gray, and Archangel]. And the X-Men fought others. One X-Men died. And the rest of them were sad. They cried.

This was an unusual superhero story for Tina's class: there was a predominance of women, enacted primarily by girls of color; there was also a death among the good guys; and, most strikingly, a good cry by the superheroes. During the peer enactment of her story, Tina reinforced the disruption of the usual gendered order:

> Tina: (reading) "One of the X-Men *died*. . . And the rest were very sad. They cried." Everybody [all of the child actors] cry now, even the *boys*.

As a third grader, Tina temporarily abandoned her interest in X-Men stories—"too boyish," she explained. Still, she continued to campaign for roles in boys' superhero stories, and, in February, egged on by the continued absence of female roles, she began once again writing about powerful women. She even complained during a class composing time discussion that "in every story the boys always have to win. And that's really not fair to the girls. . . . The boys are always doing things for the girls, and it seems like the girls are weak."

In the last month of school, Tina wrote a superhero story that included diverse female/male roles. Moreover, it included both superhero themes from the popular media and information from a class unit on the superheroes of ancient Greece. In that unit, Tina chose Venus, goddess of beauty, as her project topic, as did her friend Makeda. Sitting side by side, Tina and Makeda initially drew Venus as fair-haired and White. Lena, also at their table, drew her goddess Black but commented that she was sure it was "wrong," because "people from Greece are not Black."

"Yes, they can be," countered Tina. When Makeda reiterated that her Venus was White, Tina commented, "Well, maybe she's White to you, but not to me." And Tina (and later Makeda) drew a Black goddess as well. Moreover, Tina wrote the piece excerpted below, in which Venus, whose middle name is Tina, saves the world for both boys and girls:

> Once there was a boy and girl in the park and two men was walking by the park and the men saw the two kids. So the two men started to run after them. And the kids ran. . . . So when Venus Tina heard about this she was mad. So she came down . . . and picked the kids up on her magical flying horse named Makeda. It was a girl horse and she took the two kids . . . in the sky. . . . Then she took them home. They said what about those two mean men. Venus Tina made them nice. And on earth was fun again. She made parks safe for us kids of the world. By Tina. Love Tina.

Defining the viewing frame: Analytic tools. In Tina's case study, the child in the viewing frame was interacting with others in the local situation but, at the same time, that local interaction was substantiating—and, in some ways, challenging— interactions that took place beyond the classroom walls. Understanding such complexity required a perspective on literacy that made explicit provision for the ideological dimension of language use.

Thus, I appropriated the language of Bakhtin's dialogism (1981, 1986), a theoretical perspective gaining increased visibility in the literacy dialogue of the 1990s. From a Bakhtinian vantage point, the conceptual boundary around Tina would include her interactional partners in the immediate social scene, just as it had in Jake's case. However, the voices within that context would have ideological echoes. That is, from a dialogic perspective, writers not only use words in particular situations to interact with others; they also adopt or resist the expected words, the words available to them in those situations as women or men, as people of varied ages and heritages, of different roles, statuses, and dispositions.

Moreover, this vantage point also suggested new visions of development. In these visions, children were not unproblematically "growing into the intellectual life of those around them" (Vygotsky, 1978, p. 77). Rather, they were also growing into, or in some way against, the existent social order through which that life was enacted. Social identification and social conflict—not only internal psycholinguistic conflicts and interactional guidance—influence the direction of learning (Miller & Goodnow, 1995).

Thus, my research question became, what is the nature of the interplay between the changing interactional and ideological dynamics of children's participation in the classroom community and the changing nature of their writing processes and products? To construct Tina's case, then, I used ethnographic analysis of all class members' official and unofficial discussions of gender, race, and power (e.g., strength) *and* case-study analysis of the content and structure of Tina's writing and talking.

Just as in the cases of Rachel and Jake, many children in Tina's room initially made minimal use of actual print. Indeed, their written texts functioned primarily as props for (or, more accurately, as "tickets" to) the theater: their texts were largely invisible; they stood up and pretended to read texts that were not actually written. And, as in Jake's case, over time children's texts became more central to their social life in this classroom. In this project, however, I aimed to detail the children's social goals and the precise ways in which texts mediated those goals.

Thus, I constructed a category system to describe the children's social goals (e.g., affiliating with others, resisting them, or, more equitably, negotiating with them) and also the ways in which written texts served those goals. For example, their texts could serve as *representations of valued characters and actions,* as *reinforcers of their authority as authors,* their right to say how the world is, and as *dialogic mediators* between themselves and others, as ways of anticipating and responding to others' reactions to their stories.

Tina pushes boundaries. To construct the case of Rachel, a child's writing was set against the backdrop of a developmental scheme of child literacy. To construct the case of Jake, a child's writing was first situated within the interactional dynamics of his daily school life. To construct the case of Tina, that writing was also set within the *ideological* dynamics of her classroom community; and those dynamics sometimes fore grounded gender, race, or class.

In both the second and third grade, Tina's ways of developing her texts (e.g., the characters she included, the elaborations of basic descriptions and actions she added) were linked, in part, to ongoing class discussions about issues of gender, which were interrelated in complex ways with those of race. In Bakhtin's sense, Tina had something important to "say" in the ongoing class conversation. For example, in her Venus story, Tina notes that both the boy and the girl were subject to the same fate (e.g., being chased by the mean men), and she explicitly marks the flying horse as a girl horse, as Makeda.

Further, Tina was not only developing her own text. She was a key player in the classroom collective; she "talked back" (hooks, 1990), raising issues that reverberated in the class and caused others to rethink—not in grand moments of collective classroom revolution, but in small moments of shifting positions. For instance, urged on by the resistance of her tough friend Tina (and encouraged by her approving teacher Kristin), Makeda imagined a Black Venus, despite the classroom books filled exclusively with fair-haired, light-skinned goddesses.

Just as Tina stretched the meaning of "Venus" in the local culture of her classroom to include her, so too the construction of her case involved stretching definitions of literacy and of development to include the complexity of her experiences. Thus, like Rachel and Jake, Tina's case provided material to think with, particularly, material to consider the interrelated ideological and interpersonal dynamics of learning to write.

More case studies have followed on the heels of Tina, each informed both by the constantly changing intellectual and political conversations about childhood and literacy and by the day-to-day experiences of children in local public schools. For example, Marcel and his friends (the self-named "brothers and sisters") led me into the constitutive role of popular media in childhood cultures and popular literacies (Dyson, 2003); Tionna and her peers are allowing me access to children's grappling with a "basics" curriculum and, in the process, helping me reimagine those basics (Dyson, 2006). To use Geertz's (1973) words, each case has not moved from "already proven theorems to newly proven ones" but, rather, has "plunged" more deeply into the same thing, that is, into the experience of learning to write (p. 25).

SHIFTING CONTEXTS: THE ROLE OF CASES IN PROFESSIONAL DIALOGUE

What, then, is the role of case studies in the repertoire of scholarly ways of studying literacy? What professional contribution can be made through close observation of small numbers of children, given the thousands of children in our schools?

To answer that question, one might turn it on itself and ask, what *can* be done with thousands of children *but* count them? In mass, children, and the challenges they present, are faceless, nameless, and overwhelming. However, these massive numbers of children are not isolated individuals; they are social participants included, or so we hope, in particular classrooms and schools, in particular institutions and communities.

Through interpretive case studies, researchers offer no specific laws of causation, no precise predictions of the outcomes of one teaching strategy or another. However, they do offer a means for identifying and talking about the dimensions and dynamics of living and learning in classrooms and other educational settings. In Hymes' still-relevant words, studies of particular classrooms and communities "suggest new things to notice, reflect upon, and do . . . [But] in the last analysis, it is the understanding and insight of those in the concrete situation that will determine the outcome" (1972, p. xiv).

The illustrative cases in this chapter all focused on the dimensions and dynamics of learning to write. Rachel, Jake, and Tina highlighted the importance of children's symbolic resources and social partners, the nature of classroom public forums, and the possibilities and constraints constructed through those forums (e.g., the accepted—and rejected—topics, themes, and genres). Moreover, the cases may yield points of reflection unanticipated by me, points that occur to teachers and other professionals in diverse roles, who bring their own concerns and vantage points to the details of specific cases.

Differing vantage points on the particularities of classroom life could be remarkably productive for all concerned. Indeed, they might contribute to democratic participation in educational knowledge-creation. And yet, the very details that may contribute to dialogic encounters may also contribute to the rigidity of conceptual and professional boundaries. When articulating "implications for practice," researchers may separate details of behavior from the social and cultural circumstances that made those details locally sensible, and they may separate them as well from the conceptual issues that make those details nonlocally useful as material for reflection. Thus, made anemic, case studies may give rise to illegal prescriptions, to suspect normative guides.

For example, the "emergent literacy" behaviors of selected young children in particular settings have been represented as set behaviors to be expected from other children in other contexts, children with different resources and end goals, children who may follow different developmental paths (for critiques, see Dyson, 1999). Similarly, the actions of specific teachers in specific school settings may become suggested "methods," instructional scripts to be enacted in other settings with different human and material resources (cf. Willis, Garcia, Barrera, & Harris, 2003). Case studies may thus become ideological tools that help transform human variety into human deficiency.

Such a use of case-study details—with its accompanying dismissal of situational complexity and theoretical depth—is antithetical to the very nature of case studies. Indeed, it is precisely because such a use *is* inappropriate that case-study methodology has the potential to further true professional dialogue and, moreover, to widen our visions of children, their resources, and their literacy possibilities. Even in one school district teachers work in an amazing array of classroom situations, greeting children who bring to school diverse language and cultural resources, varied histories, and relationships with literacy and, moreover, with educational and societal institutions. Rigid curricula and rigid teaching based on narrow visions of children's lives will not help teachers in their work

In the introduction of this paper, Makeda said that a story was "kinda like *your* life," and, in a very fundamental sense, she was right. Stories, including those we tell about other people, are also about ourselves, written from our particular vantage points. In interaction, each speaker or writer infuses given words like *literacy* and *development* with new accents and new dimensions, because each is positioned differently in the social and ideological ground. Crossing conceptual boundaries is thus linked with crossing human ones: when we, with our diverse experiences and our common concerns, converse, we push each other out of bounds, we help each other attend to the world a bit differently.

In this chapter, I have suggested that one possible means for bringing adults out of their own distinctive professional boundaries and into common conversation is a mutual interest in, appreciation of, and pleasure in knowing the young. When studied in depth, individual children emerge from the shadows, as Sammy did from the underworld, potentially enriching the ongoing conversation about literacy, development, and schooling.

AUTHOR'S NOTE

Support for this work was provided by the Spencer Foundation and by the Educational Research and Development Center Program (grant number R117G10036 for the National Center for the Study of Writing) as administered by the Office of Educational Research and Improvement, U.S. Department of Education. The findings and opinions expressed in this report do not reflect the position or policies of the Spencer Foundation or the U.S. Dept. of Educ.

REFERENCES

Bakhtin, M. (1981). Discourse in the novel. In C. Emerson & M. Holquist (Eds.), *The dialogic imagination: Four essays by M. Bakhtin* (pp. 259–422). Austin: University of Texas Press.

Bakhtin, M. (1986). *Speech genres and other late essays.* Austin: University of Texas Press.

Basso, K. (1974). The ethnography of writing. In R. Bauman & J. Sherzer (Eds.), *Explorations in the ethnography of speaking* (pp. 425–432). Cambridge: Cambridge University Press.

Bogdan, R., & Biklen, S. (2003). *Qualitative research for education* (4th ed.). Needham Heights, MA: Allyn & Bacon.

Bruner, J., & Haste, H. (Eds.). (1987). *Making sense: The child's construction of the world.* New York: Methuen.

Children's Defense Fund. (2005). *The state of America's children.* Washington, DC: Author.

Clay, M. (1975). *What did I write?* Auckland: Heinemann.

Corsaro, W. (1985). *Friendship and peer culture in the early years.* Norwood, NJ: Ablex.

Dyson, A. H. (1989). *Multiple worlds of child writers: Friends learning to write.* New York: Teachers College Press.

Dyson, A. H. (1997). *Writing superheroes: Contemporary childhood, popular culture, and classroom literacy.* New York: Teachers College Press.

Dyson, A. H. (1999). Transforming transfer: Unruly children, contrary texts, and the persistence of the pedagogical order. In A. Iran-Nejad & P. D. Pearson (Eds.), *Review of research in education: Vol. 24* (pp. 141–172). Washington, DC: AERA.

Dyson, A. H. (2003). *The brothers and sisters learn to write: Popular literacies in childhood and school cultures.* New York: Teachers College Press.

Dyson, A. H. (2006). On saying it right (write): "Fix-its" in the foundations of learning to write. *Research in the Teaching of English, 41,* 8–42

Emerson, R., Fretz, R., & Shaw, L. (1995). *Writing ethnographic fieldnotes.* Chicago, IL: University of Chicago Press.

Erickson, F. (1986). Qualitative methods in research on teaching. In M. C. Wittrock (Ed.), *Handbook of research on teaching* (pp. 119–161). New York: Macmillan.

Erickson, F. (2002). Culture and human development. *Human Development, 45,* 299–306.

Geertz, C. (1973). *The interpretation of cultures.* New York: Basic Books.

Geertz, C. (1988). *Works and lives: The anthropologist as author.* Stanford, CA: Stanford University Press.

Gould, S. (1987). *An urchin in the storm: Essays about books and ideas.* New York: W. W. Norton.

Graves, D. H. (1975). An examination of the writing processes of seven-year-old children. *Research in the Teaching of English, 9,* 227–41.

Guerra, J. (1998). *Close to home: Oral and literate practices in a transnational Mexicano community.* New York: Teachers College Press.

Gupta, A., & Ferguson, J. (1997). Beyond "culture": Space, identity, and the politics of difference. In A. Gupta & J. Ferguson (Eds.), *Culture, power, place: Explorations in critical anthropology* (pp. 33–51). Durham, NC: Duke University Press.

Heath, S.B. (1983). *Ways with words: Language, life and work in communities and classrooms.* Cambridge: Cambridge University Press.

hooks, b. (1990). Talking back. In R. Ferguson, M. Gever, T. Minh-ha, & C. West (Eds.), *Out there: Marginalization and contemporary cultures* (pp. 331–340). New York: The New Museum of Contemporary Art; Cambridge, MA: MIT Press.

Hymes, D. (1972). Introduction. In C. Cazden, V. John, & D. Hymes (Eds.), *Functions of language in the classroom* (pp. xixvii). New York: Teachers College Press.

Kline, S. (1993). *Out of the garden: Toys, TV, and children's culture in the age of marketing.* London: Verso.

Labov, W., & Waletsky, J. (1967). Narrative analysis: Oral versions of personal experience. In *Essays on the verbal and visual arts: Proceedings of the* 1966 *spring meeting of the American Ethnological Society* (pp. 12–44). Seattle: University of Washington Press.

Miller, P., & Goodnow, J. J. (1995). Cultural practices: Toward an integration of culture and development. In J. J. Goodnow, P. J. Miller, & F. Kessel (Eds.), *Cultural practices as contexts for development* (pp. 5–16). San Francisco: Jossey-Bass.

Ninio, A., & Bruner, J. (1978). The achievement and antecedents of labeling. *Journal of Child Language, 5,* 1–15.

Olson, D. (1977). From utterance to text. *Harvard Educational Review, 47,* 247–279.

Ortner, S. (1999). Introduction. In S. Ortner (Ed.), *The fate of "culture": Geertz and beyond* (pp. 1–13). Berkeley: University of California Press.

Piaget, J., & Inhelder, B. (1969). *The psychology of the child.* New York: Basic Books.

Read, C. (1975). Pre-school children's knowledge of English phonology. *Harvard Educational Review, 41,* 1–34.

Rosaldo, R. (1989). *Culture and truth: The remaking of social analysis.* Boston: Beacon Press.

Stake, R. (1988). Case study methods in educational research: Seeking sweet water. In R. M. Jaeger (Ed.), *Complementary methods for research in education* (pp. 401–446). Washington, DC: AERA.

Vasquez, O., Pease-Alvarez, L., & Shannon, S. (1994). *Pushing boundaries: Language and culture in a Mexicano community.* New York: Cambridge University Press.

Vygotsky, L. (1978). *Mind in society.* Cambridge, MA: Harvard University Press.

Willis, A. I., Garcia, G. E., Barrera, R., & Harris, V. (2003). *Multicultural issues in literacy research and practice.* Mahwah, NJ: Erlbaum.

13

THEATRE AND THEORY PARTNERED THROUGH ETHNOGRAPHIC STUDY

Steven Z. Athanases
UNIVERSITY OF CALIFORNIA, DAVIS

Though the ancient Greeks depicted Apollo and Dionysus as distinct and contrasting, these gods embodied halves of a self. The Greeks believed Dionysus transforms us through wine and theatre, sense and emotion, and instinct and the erotic; through sacred trance that puts us in touch with the primordial elements. The Greeks believed Apollo, in contrast, represented purity and strength, clarity and the rational, the reasoned, and the deliberate. Dionysus, god of celebrations, ruled in the dark of winter; Apollo ruled in the summer when bright light exposed all. Apollo was linked to the static arts of sculpture and architecture and of distanced introspection and repose. Dionysus was god of dynamic arts such as drama, music, song, and dance; of art as life in process, shared in moments of ecstasy as a social experience; and of emotion and embodied expression. Apollo was god of theory, of clear and rational understanding. In a study of classical Greek literature, Nietzsche identified the Apollonian and the Dionysian as opposites existing together in the Greek culture and person—the rational and ordered life improved when invigorated by the sensual, dynamic, irrational, and socially shared experience (Mencken, 1908/2003). In this view, to be healthy and spirited requires the dance of Dionysus and deliberation of Apollo.

Schools typically strip from curricula the Dionysian elements: what is embodied, sensual, instinctual, erotic, and social. Schools favor what is countable, individual, easily named and categorized, dependent on the cognitive, amenable to memorization and testing. Theatre (including varied forms of classroom drama, improvisation, and performance) enables the Dionysian: the sensual and felt need of texts (Bacon, 1972); the use of body as a site of knowing (Conquergood, 1991); the kinesthetic dimensions of speech in the body (Forrest, 1969); the orality that restores a printed record to a dynamic event (Fine, 1990); and a socially shared experience. However, though theatre has held a place in schools in some countries at some times, in U.S. secondary schools these instances have been few overall, particularly in contrast to schools in the United Kingdom (Freedman, 1994; Squire & Applebee, 1968, 1969). Theatre remains primarily extracurricular in U.S. high schools. These performances of school plays and Broadway musicals engage relatively few participants and perpetuate mainstream U.S. culture, failing to reflect a multicultural society or the power of devised drama that can engage more youth, mirroring their diverse experiences and worldviews (Cousins, 2000).

Recently, we have seen more published accounts of drama and performance processes among youth in K–12 and other settings. However, we still have relatively few empirical studies of the processes and impact of performance in K–12 sites. Seldom are descriptions accompanied by an Apollonian meditation on processes and impact of theatre, on what in performance is sensed, felt, and discovered about language, emotion, literary interpretation, character, empathy, cross-cultural understanding, point of view, or perspective. Ethnography is one means of tapping Dionysian encounters with text and experience, situating study within processes that unfold over time, generating data that aid new discovery, and considering reflections and an Apollonian clarity that theorizes values and problems in uses of drama and performance. This chapter explores ethnography as a research method, highlighting new tools and technologies all well suited to study of classrooms and other sites where such acts of performance play a prominent role.

Theatre and theory derive from the same Greek word, *thea*, or view. Though they use different dimensions of the self, different media, tools, and forms of representation, both theatre and theory—the Dionysian and Apollonian dimensions—enable us to view and examine human experience and phenomena. Together they integrate dimensions of the self and of understanding. Engagements with theatre can, through effective research methods, generate theories of performance with youth, which in turn can shape new theatre experiences and generate and refine theory. Ethnography offers a means to uncover particular forms of understanding about the processes and impact of performance and to theorize more learning-rich opportunities.

EXPANDED USES OF PERFORMANCE AND DRAMA IN K–16 AND OUT-OF-SCHOOL SETTINGS

Elsewhere I mapped five forms of performance used in K–16 settings (Athanases, 1997). These included (a) storytelling; (b) spontaneous oral readings; (c) dramatic improvisations (e.g., Heathcote, 1981); (d) scripted group performance of literature, including readers theatre (e.g., Kleinau & McHughes, 1980; Long, Hudson, & Jeffrey, 1977) and chamber theatre (Breen, 1978); and (e) solo performance of literature (e.g., Lee & Gura, 2000). Many educators have advocated the learning potential of experiences that feature process over final performance product. In Wagner's (1990) conception, in story drama students enact scenes in and related to literature, while theme-oriented drama guides students through historical imagining and empathy work on various curricular topics. Although dramatizing at the center of texts may include improvisations, it features drama work with print text; dramatizing at the edges of texts features many forms of constructed texts that may begin with print and extend beyond (S. Wolf, Edmiston, & Enciso, 1997).

In my earlier review, I also surveyed performance genres explored in university settings that held potential for K–12. These included story making from oral histories, personal narratives, and scripted imaginary monologues of fictional characters; replication of life performances including conversational transcripts; and performance art that invites audience participation and explores intertextuality (Park-Fuller & Pelias, 1995). Other genres supported historical understanding, such as oral histories from taped interviews (Stucky, 1995); disruption of audience members to parallel disruptive historical events (Olsen, 1992); and invented debates of historical figures, performance of speeches and manifestoes, and imaginary journals written by social leaders (Fuoss & Hill, 1992). Recent developments in classroom and community uses of drama and performance provide new and compelling reasons to study these communicative art forms. What makes the projects new varies. In some cases, it is the context of the project, new social formations that support dramatic performance experience for youth; in other cases, it is about new foci, new theoretical explorations, or new possibilities (including new forms of data collection) to capture the unfolding learning and literacy affordances of performance projects.

Community-Based Engagements With Drama and Performance for Youth

Recent research on literacy learning in arts and other community-based organizations has documented ways programs engage youth in cycles of performance and production that often balance structure with creative release (Heath & McLaughlin, 1993). Youth theatre projects, acting companies, classrooms and youth groups have used drama to bring missing information to curricula, explore multiple points of view, engage in creative problem solving, and provide satisfaction of genuine achievement, as youth write, rehearse, and review "the performance of their own lives" (J. L. Wolf, 1997, p. 75). Community plays promote growth in youth if they share ownership of content (Horitz, 2001), and youth theatre can support transitions into adulthood (Hughes & Wilson, 2004). Poetry slams engage youth in writing and performing poetry, appealing to a democratic stance in who gets to write and perform and who judges excellence (Dillard, 2002; Glazner, 2000).

Digitally Mediated Performances

Young people increasingly explore many forms of performance enhanced by technology. Youth radio, for example, a nonprofit broadcast training program based in the San Francisco Bay Area, engages young people in shaping programs, interviewing, constructing radio scripts, and producing and performing audio (Chávez & Soep, 2005). Often rehearsed and taped before airing, these radio shows reach a mass audience though both radio and Web outlets. Video productions, podcasts of audio shows, Web casts of live performances, and digital storytelling represent other ways in which young people engage in scripting, rehearsal, and performance outside the context of live performance with a copresence of live bodies as audience. In such genres, the physical distance between performer and audience may be great. However, audiences can engage in multiple forms of response and interactivity with performers and other audience members (through online chats and other media). In this way, such digitally mediated performances (DMP) allow more intimate exchange with audience members than do live performances (Chvasta, 2005). While some argue that the presence of a performer's body with a live copresent audience is essential to performance, Chvasta argued that the essence of performance is virtual and not real, and that DMPs challenge us to rethink notions of performance and practice through multiple modes of engagement to understand what is gained and lost through technology. All of this invites study.

Many youth construct Web logs (blogs) that include role playing and dialogue; playing video games; writing fanfiction; and assume on-line roles they write and "perform" in emerging constructed dialogues. While they do not embody or speak for the characters, participants in these activities often consciously and creatively engage in underlying dramatic processes of role playing, character development, and negotiation of conflict. On one online site, for example, participants do an initial posting of what their invented character looks like and what he or she does when walking into a bar. At any time around the clock, the Web site includes a built-in logging of instant messaging between pairs of characters and individual characters' histories of interactions with others. Such activity invites the application to classroom contexts and study of participants' engagements. The medium is dynamic; of interest to educators might be the processes of learning to understand the trail of cause and effect and the cognitive strategy of speculating on what will happen next if one's character says or does this or that, given one's knowledge of the other characters present in the virtual space at the time. Activities such as these raise many questions about the nature of engagement and learning young people experience in such activity and how it relates to other forms of performance, literacy activity, and learning.

THE CASE FOR ETHNOGRAPHY IN STUDY OF YOUTH ENGAGEMENTS WITH PERFORMANCE AND DRAMA

For many reasons, ethnography proves a good fit for study of these many forms of drama and performance with youth in school and out-of-school settings.

Some Principles for Conducting Ethnography

The central goal of ethnography is the discovery of cultural patterns achieved through long-term fieldwork of participant observation. The researcher becomes immersed in the culture, using a relativistic view in which cultural norms are examined on their own terms, rather than through a deficit lens. Extensive complementary scholarly study helps frame emerging cultural patterns. Principles for conducting anthropological research can guide ethnographic language studies in classrooms and other sites (e.g., Atkinson & Hammersley, 1993; Ellen, 1984; Goetz & LeCompte, 1984; Heath, 1982; Sanjek, 1990; Saville-Troike, 1982; Sperber, 1982). Recent work also delineates how teachers and students can move from being participants in someone else's ethnography to actors shaping the ethnography and the unfolding understandings (Green & Bloome, 1997). We hear few students' voices about their own engagements in drama (Innes, Moss, & Smigiel, 2001); ethnography can provide this emic perspective.

The ethnographer situates the study of the culture firmly within contexts and intertwining social systems. To understand conditions that have shaped what occurs in the setting, the ethnographer collects data on the nested contexts within which the setting is situated (McLaughlin & Talbert, 2001). In addition, ongoing analysis through early review and coding of data enables the researcher to use emerging cultural patterns and insights to shape further survey and interview questions and to begin to track evidence for early claims and evidence that counter those claims. Validity and reliability, while contested concepts in ethnographic study, can enhance rigor of the study and credibility of claims (Athanases & Heath, 1995; Goetz & LeCompte, 1984).

Why Ethnography Is Well Suited for Studying Drama and Performance Among Youth

Ethnography holds potential for investigations of drama and performance for various reasons. First, ethnography's reliance on long-term participation and observation as a primary method of data collection can enable the investigator to track unfolding learning over time and during multiple phases of often rather long-term rehearsal periods or performance units. Ethnography can situate youth performances in the context of the sweep of a season or school year and is embedded in a full set of activities. Teachers who use classroom activities dealing with performance frequently plan them for various times over the course of the school year. Ethnography can capture how the things students learn in some domains get taken up in others.

Performances in out-of-school spaces and DMP contexts also evolve over time. Youth theatre events evolve through writing and rehearsals, and ethnography can capture the unfolding perspectives and learning, highlighting emic perspectives. In some DMP contexts, young people first engage in online spaces, such as fanfiction sites, as spectators. As they more fully engage in particular cultures of performance practice, young people develop ways of engaging texts, performances, and each other. Understanding such development benefits from the long-term fieldwork afforded by ethnography. Data collection can include drafts of online stories and forms of documentation of performance engagements and emerging reflections and learning, such as e-mail messages, blogs, interviews, and live or online discussions and chats.

Because it requires immersion into a culture, ethnography enables a researcher to examine performance learning in multiple classroom and out-of-class contexts and can prove particularly appropriate for investigating development of a "performance culture" in classrooms and other settings where performance holds a central role in curriculum or programming. A researcher can investigate cultural patterns related to learning: How do students learn in this environment to do what they learn to do? How does a class get socialized into acts of performance? What kinds of responses and learning occur when performance holds a key role? In out-of-school settings, for example, Soep (2006) studied how a culture of critique developed among youth in arts-based projects. Similarly, in youth media productions, long-term fieldwork enabled development of theory about how youth and adults engaged in four principal features of pedagogy of collegiality—(a) joint framing, (b) youth-led inquiry, (c) mediated intervention, and (d) distributed accountability (Chávez & Soep, 2005).

Ethnography also requires attention to contexts of school, home, and community, including the many sites where youth engage technological tools, games, and communication media that figure in new forms of drama and performance. How does performance figure in these varied settings and mediated sites where students spend time? This attention to context can help frame an understanding of cultural patterns that occur in engagements with drama and performance.

New Access to Studying Drama and Performance Activity

Not only do we see a richer array of drama and performance activity available to youth; we also have new access to studying these activities, due to two factors: (a) changes in instruction in classroom performance contexts and (b) development of new media tools.

Drama and performance embedded within literacy-rich activity. In school contexts, increasingly, educators and researchers articulate ways in which drama and performance activities are embedded within literacy-rich cycles of activity. Not merely add-on moments or events dropped down into a program or curriculum, these performance activities serve a range of purposes that map to larger literacy goals. In this way, educators often link drama meaningfully to English language arts (ELA) curricula and align performance events with standards-based ELA work. In writing about such activity, these teachers, artists, and researchers also provide more compelling and persuasive arguments for use of such work, particularly important in a time of standards-based reforms, increasingly scripted curricula, and high-stakes assessments. One final important merit arises from these efforts: These educators and researchers provide countless means of unlocking young people's perceptions of drama and performance activity, developing understandings, and new learning. Instructional artifacts, student work samples such as performance planning journals, ongoing written and group shared reflections, performance process notes, follow-up critical reflections on performance, and peer evaluations of performances represent just a sampling of ways in which the instructional process provides access to studying what occurs, what it means, and its impact.

For example, in Wagner's study (1990), children clustered characters' traits and mental associations, enacted imaginary conflicts of characters meeting, and then wrote diary reflections on the conflicts. Heathcote's students (Wagner) listed health-care problems and wrote detailed records of patients' development while enacting with health-care workers. A ninth-grade class interviewed in pairs from imaginary literary perspectives, conducted an inquiry, put a character on trial, and wrote in role following improvisations (Rogers & O'Neill, 1993). Students in S. Wolf's study of classroom theatre (1994) planned and wrote scripts and reflective responses to "what-if" questions. In a seventh-grade unit, students engaged *Othello* and its themes through readers' theatre, improvisation, writing and performing modern-day scenes, and writing before and after performance (Landay, 2005). Shosh's students (2005) recorded in an acting journal observed behavior in public places, discussed observations, and used these to write and perform character monologues. Production teams read self-selected plays, broke scripts into scenes, read and analyzed play reviews, researched the play's period, wrote memos to the principal for funds to support production, wrote performance programs, and engaged in critical self- and peer-evaluation of performances. In these ways, young people engage in literacy activity surrounding drama and performance, and leave written and spoken trails of ongoing planning, reflections, and developing understandings.

When these literacy activities are foregrounded and the learning made concrete and visible, we open a window into the world of learning through performance. Such an approach moves the focus from merely the culminating act of performance to encompass more broadly the cognitive, kinesthetic, aesthetic, and communicative processes students exercise during performance study. All of these processes invite study, and ethnography is well suited to this task. Using multiple data-collection tools, ethnography provides rich documentation of learning as it unfolds and varies over time, describing varied processes and products of student learning.

New media tools for studying drama and performance. New forms of media strengthen access to students' performance perceptions and learning. For example, while I once used written and audiotaped student reflections on rehearsals I studied, we now have other means of capturing students' in-the-moment understandings and post-rehearsal and post-performance reflections. New tools represent technologies in use at the point of this writing, and clearly, others will evolve and replace these. The point here is not to valorize these particular tools but to point out how the range of technologies enables increased access to capturing students' emic perspectives.

E-mail, for example, enables easy two-way or group exchange to track developing reflections. Online chat rooms enable many to talk at once, logging reflections in nearly real time. Students, teacher, and outside researcher gain instant access to fleeting thoughts of actors and viewers in transcripts of online chat. Instant messaging offers more individualized chat but also quick and easy access to transcribed interactions that develop and display ongoing reflections. Young people's use of mobile phone text messaging can be mined if they have access to and skill with the technology. Digital video offers young people a way to engage each other in conversation and critical reflection on performance activity.

More sophisticated online conversational spaces develop and display cognitively more complex turns at talk to support knowledge building. Knowledge Forum, for example, enables development of customizable scaffolds to support discourse of a particular community and its needs (Scardamalia, 2004). One version used a template for conversational moves such as offering a theory, building on another's remarks, disagreeing with another's theory, and synthesizing group conversation. All of these media provide records of conversational interaction that can be played back and, in many cases, read as online text for easier analysis. These forms of data serve any researcher, but also provide students with access to data for reflection on their own and their peers' developing understandings and experiences with drama and performance. In this way, students can "go meta" on the activities, reflecting on their own processes and how they and their peers are using the activity, how it does and does not serve their learning, and what it yields. Students as ethnographers can engage in study of their peer group in these ways. Powerpoint offers one way in which individuals and groups can display their developing understandings; these group results also can serve as data for cross-group reflection and analysis of emerging themes. Such Powerpoint presentations can include audio and video excerpts from performances to illustrate themes and provide images others can use for ongoing analysis. Vignettes from class data can serve as touchstones for ideas the class wants to explore more fully. Also, students can videotape skits that briefly develop counter arguments and counter themes.

RESEARCH QUESTIONS AND THEORIES IN ETHNOGRAPHIC STUDY OF PERFORMANCE AND DRAMA

Research Questions Worth Asking About Youth Experiences in Performance and Drama

The teacher or researcher interested in investigating the learning that any one of the many forms of performance yields might ask any number of questions. How, for example, might performing Chief Seattle's speech on the destruction of American land shape, alter, and deepen a student's understanding of and appreciation for the environmental history of the United States or American views of land? What impact does interviewing African American veterans of the Vietnam War and performing their oral histories for peers have on students' understanding of that war and of the ways racism figured into the armed forces in the 1960s? What kinds of cultural understanding and language opportunities do children receive from role playing children in other societies? What do youth learn about the language of poetry through speaking it, rehearsing it, and singing it? In classrooms and other sites where performance plays a central role, what kinds of things occur in young people's language use, behavior, attitudes, and values? In school-based studies, if classroom experiences with performance appear to have an impact on students, to what can we attribute this impact? What features of a performance-rich learning environment shape what kinds of student learning? In what ways? With which students? These are a sampling of the many questions that teachers and researchers might ask about the potential values of performance for young people.

However, it is not adequate to ask generic research questions that conflate varied purposes or to ask what drama and performance yield for youth. We need to ask far more specific and contextualized questions that investigate the particular forms, purposes, and contexts of the activities. For example, a too-generic question is this: What do drama and performance yield and how do its participants understand it? We need to instead ask, What do drama and performance yield and how do its participants understand it and experience it when it is in this/these form(s), in this context, using these structures, over this much time, for these purposes, supported by these particular activities that enable this kind of rehearsal, these explorations? What in a particular process of drama or drama-like activity proves particularly powerful for children's learning? In what ways? With which children? What specific theoretical lenses provide explanatory power for particular engagements with drama and performance the ethnographer encounters? These forms of specificity align with the situatedness that ethnography enables.

Aligning Theories and Methods

Good ethnography aligns theoretical perspectives with methods. What forms of data will shed light on particular theoretical concerns and how can these best be collected? For example, in a dialogic approach to drama, "Text's narrative is reshaped to make room for additional narrative pathways, perspectives, images, and positions" (Edmiston & Enciso, 2003, p. 870). An ethnographer interested in such a model would collect data sensitive to students' fits and starts of exploring new pathways. Studying how drama enables exploration of features of spoken language that increase social capital (Kempe, 2003) requires repeated language sampling and close linguistic analysis. Similarly, data and analyses may need to be tailored to other new theoretical perspectives: how dramatizing school subcultures enables youth to rethink social categories (Wright, 2000); how process drama can promote exploration of ethics and contradictory points of view (Cabral, 2001); how role playing can interrupt sexist stereotypes (Zumhagen, 2005).

ETHNOGRAPHIC TOOLS FOR THE STUDY OF CLASSROOM PERFORMANCE

A study examining performance in the context of a full literacy program might employ a range of data collection tools to capture learning in the assortment of classroom or out-of-school activities that occur. For example, I conducted a study in a 10th-grade English class in which the teacher and I taught a unit on the performance of poetry and investigated how students came to understand the performance concepts taught and how students worked on interpreting poetry through performance (reported partially in Athanases, 2005). For one portion of the unit, each student worked with a single poem over an 8-day period. The setting was an urban public school serving primarily children of middle- to low-income families. The class was heterogeneously grouped and ethnically diverse: more than one third of the students were African American, and the rest were Chinese American, Latino, Filipino, and European American. I refer to this study simply as the 10th-grade performance study.

Table 13.1 shows data collected during just the focal unit of the 10th-grade performance study. Other ethnographic data were collected during the school year, such as teacher interviews, observation field notes of class sessions, instructional artifacts, student work samples, and data on context. The following discussion highlights some of the tools of Table 13.1 and explores ways the ethnographer might investigate learning in the context of classroom performance. Some of these methods are most relevant to studies in which the

TABLE 13.1. Data From 10th-Grade Study of Solo Performance of Poetry

Focus	Data Collected
Students' initial understandings	Teacher reports: class community, student performance Observation field notes Audiotaped class sessions Survey: understandings, experiences with performance Written response to a single performed poem
Instruction on performance	Audiotaped whole-class instruction and discussions Observation field notes Instructional artifacts Interviews and debriefings with teachers, researcher Student interviews
Performance planning	Packets of written responses and planning notes
Rehearsals	Audiotaped small-group work sessions, discussions Student journal entries
Performances	Audiotaped performances in small groups Selected videotaped performances for full class Audiotaped assessment conferences: teacher and researcher Students' written reflections on their own and other students' performances
Reflections and impacts	Student interviews Post-write on same poem from beginning of unit Survey Class discussion

researcher is also the classroom teacher or, as in the case of the 10th-grade performance study, works collaboratively with a teacher to design tools both to foster and to reveal student thinking and learning through the performance process. Methods described address one very particular kind of performance (solo performance of individual poems). Principles and data collection tools are described, however, to provide ideas for ethnographers investigating many other forms of drama and performance in classrooms and beyond. References to other studies are provided to extend the discussion.

Documenting Instruction, Coaching, and Their Impact: Baseline Data and Beyond

Documenting instruction and coaching/directing in performance helps frame investigation into how students learn about performance and become socialized into environments that foster certain kinds of performance. For the 10th-grade performance study, I sampled students' initial understandings of literature and performance before documenting instruction on performance. As Table 13.1 shows, data for investigating these initial understandings were collected using some conventional tools of ethnography: field notes, surveys, interviews, and taping. Surveys were designed to capture students' varied perceptions of performance and its purposes, past experiences with performance, and notions of literary interpretation (an area that may well be affected by students' involvement in performance of literature). Student work samples and other data on student performance (including field notes and audiotapes of classroom interactions) provided profiles of students' practices in literary understanding before classroom initiation into performance experience. The final item in this first category of data, however, shows an attempt to gather baseline data on students' responses to a single published poem that featured a dramatic situation described in challenging language.

Once instruction began, data for this portion of the 10th-grade performance study included field notes supported by instructional artifacts and selected audiotapes or videotapes of teaching, which helped track the instruction students received. In addition, teacher and student post-class debriefings and longer interviews provided information on class participants' reflections on the instructional process and the content being taught. Similarly, in her study of elementary school students' experiences of 10 weeks of classroom theatre, S. Wolf (1994) collected baseline data on students' notions of drama, then tracked the instruction conducted by a guest drama director and interviewed students regarding their notions of classroom drama and the sources of that understanding. She was able to learn from these data sources how students moved from a sense of drama as uncontrolled action with no limits and imitative of action films to a deeper understanding of drama and its rules, roles, and resources. Students reported certain features of instruction and classroom practice that shaped these new understandings.

Situating instruction on performance within larger language arts curricula is aided by mapping the arc of focal activity within a full timeline of relevant work, using a part-whole approach (Green, Dixon, & Zaharlick, 2003). Also important is locating and precisely documenting key events or things with sustaining influence within the project or classroom (Green & Bloome, 1997). For example, students may report in interviews that certain instructional moments proved particularly useful in developing performance resources and knowledge. These events, then, warrant particularly careful documentation and analysis. Only through long-term participation in a community can the ethnographer (whether teacher, student, or outsider) develop such a situated approach to study of every day life (Green & Bloom, 1997), meaningfully embedding microlevel analysis within streams of activity. Also, to make cultural practices of drama activity visible for others, the ethnographer can catalogue taxonomies of terms, practices, and processes as perceived by community members (Green et al., 2003). A teacher's or director's notions of activities and the purposes they serve may or may not coincide with those of students, and so students' voices and views must be central in the ethnographic database.

Documenting Performance Planning and Learning

For group performances of various kinds, planning sessions can be observed and taped to track how students construct scripts and performances and how they learn about content goals. Field notes and tapes of planning sessions can be supported by copies of student planning notes to enable student, teacher, and researcher to understand the student's evolving interpretations. The packet of written responses and planning notes identified in Table 13.1 as data on performance planning drew on activities to cultivate the performer's resources (Long & HopKins, 1997) and foster application of performance understanding to multiple texts and performance experiences. In these activities, students engaged in a range of literacy events (reading, writing, imagining, researching, discussing, and speaking) as they planned for the rehearsal and performance process.

Documenting Learning From Rehearsals

For performances of whole or excerpted literary works, a valuable data source is students' evolving transactions with the work. As Rosenblatt (1978) demonstrated, a reader's perceptions of a work evolve over time and with new influences. Students can record first encounters or soundings of the work through written, taped, or online journal entries. With rehearsal as a key learning site, the performance journal (or even blog) becomes a place to record reflections in and out of class, during and after rehearsal, from in-class small-group "rough-draft performance" sessions with peer critiques to solo rehearsals in and out of class. Written, taped, or online journal prompts can be general or focused, depending on student needs and research focus. Journal entries such as these that explore new knowledge, new sense, and new problems within a work prove particularly valuable for tracking evolving interpretations and understandings.

Tracking Focal Students' Performance Experiences

The range of data ethnography uses enables the teacher or outside researcher to look closely at focal students' experiences with drama and performance. For example, in the 10th -grade study, I tracked focal students' engagements with poems they selected for study, rehearsal, and performance. Using writing samples, observation field notes, interviews, journal entries, and taped rehearsals, I analyzed the ways in which students engaged the poems, tracking their evolving transactions with the literary works. I studied the challenges students found in performing the speaker's drama and how students resolved performance problems. I used the case of Warren, an African American male, to illustrate responses to a single poem and how rehearsing it presented Warren with opportunities to reflect on his own values and personal history as they compared with those of the speaker in his chosen text (Athanases, 2005). Using a similar range of data, Medina (2004) studied fifth graders' drama engagements with a picture book. Her ethnographic perspective and rich database enabled Medina to trace responses and drama engagements of one boy as he enacted and spoke from various positions throughout the drama. Medina's close examination of George's engagements enabled her to use theatre to theorize ways drama affords interpretation of Latina feminist literature.

Documenting Performances

Table 13.1 shows that for the 10th-grade study taped records of performances served as key data. The last piece of data on performances, however, features students' reflections. For example, before students performed for peers, they wrote about the rehearsal process, responding to selected questions and suggestions such as these: What problem or challenge did you find in performing this work? Why did this problem arise? How have you attempted to resolve it? Discuss something you came to realize, understand, or feel about the literary work through rehearsing it or an excerpt from it. Discuss something you especially want to convey in your performance. How have you attempted to do that in rehearsal? Discuss any risky performance choice you have made and why. Other data sources for students' reflections on performance are discussions and workshops that invite students to explore how their literary interpretations compare with those other readers bring to the same works (for example, when listeners ask questions of the performer and make concrete suggestions so that the performer may revise the performance). This process of "checking out" a reading in relation to others provides data for investigation. For those working with the many other genres of performance, ongoing reflections likewise prove invaluable.

Retrospective Reflections and Impacts

In cases where students have engaged in multiple performance experiences over many months or a year, students will have collected a great deal of data from their performance process, from perhaps taped protocols of responses and written, taped, or online journal entries through various stages of the planning, rehearsal, and performance process. All of these data can serve as material for the student's investigation into his or her performance process, culminating in a short reflective journal entry or even a case study analyzing a theme emerging from the data—something that pulls together ongoing reflections from many stages and experiences of performance.

In tracking impacts of a 10-session classroom theatre project, S. Wolf (1998) noted how before, during, and after the project teacher and students made shifts in instruction, orchestration, and attitudes. The teacher moved from pure round-robin reading and focus on decoding to more story interpretation, and students began to see ways to move more deeply into stories rather than view texts as being boring and torturous. It was because she stayed in the class for the better part of a school year and collected multiple forms of data, particularly interviews that provided emic perspective and observations followed by questions and probes of participants, that Wolf was able to note these shifts. In a South African youth-theatre company, participants constructed a space-age drama involving peace negotiations between Earth and an alien empire as a way to explore respect and tolerance of others as a goal not yet realized in South Africa (van Vuuren, 2004). Journal entries enabled assessment of the degree to which participants engaged the drama, externalized their own values, and compared these to values held by characters they enacted. In the 10th-grade study, I had students revisit a poem they had written about before the performance unit began (Table 13.1). With understanding the poem's drama as goal, I compared pre- and post-unit writings. Nearly all students showed growth in this on-demand writing about the drama of an assigned poem, using and applying concepts we practiced, including the dramatic situation, dramatic speaker of the poem as distinct from poet, and subtext of a poem's language as dramatic action. As with the other projects, my immersion in the site as ethnographer enabled me to track not only impacts but also challenges and conflicts as students engaged performance experiences.

CONCLUSION

Uses of drama and performance in classrooms and other settings evidence new genres, purposes, ways of working, and underlying theories. Most projects share a basic premise that entering the world of another through drama and taking on other perspectives through performance is a medium for learning (Henry, 2000). However, despite the advocacy literature on performance, little research has provided thick descriptions and critical treatment of what occurs when students engage in performance processes. For the researcher interested in conducting investigations resulting in such descriptions and analyses, ethnography holds possibilities that this chapter has discussed. The ethnographer can investigate performance in the context of larger literacy curricula or program experiences and can document the complexities of students' planning, rehearsals, performances, and reflections as essential sites for learning.

An ethnography of drama and performance can draw on a wide array of data-collection tools, including many new technological ones, to capture the learning students do in such work. This chapter has outlined a variety of such tools. In addition, brief illustrations have been provided from a recent study conducted in a 10th-grade English class in order to make concrete the data collection tools described. Perhaps these research guidelines, data-collection tools, and illustrations can help serve the cause of good research and can help advance the knowledge base on the power of drama and performance for student learning in literature and other subject areas, in a range of out-of-school contexts and for the many new purposes recent authors have theorized.

As explored in the opening of this chapter, schools need an infusion of the Dionysian elements: dynamic arts, embodied experience, sense, and emotion. Theatre exemplifies these elements and can be enriched when recoupled with its Apollonian brother of theory. As the ancient Greeks knew, we learn by viewing human experience through both the drama of theatre and the deliberated exposition of theory. Coupled, these modes of learning and representation join sensual, dynamic elements that can engage youth, with careful inquiry into what such experiences afford and mean. Ethnography as a method can capture the rich dynamism of drama and performance and enable theorizing about what it yields.

AUTHOR NOTE

Thanks to Eugenia Berdali and Schooner Carper for their generous sharing of insights that shaped portions of this chapter.

REFERENCES

Athanases, S. Z. (1997). Ethnography for the study of performance in the classroom. In J. Flood, S. B. Heath, & D. Lapp (Eds.), *Handbook of research on teaching literacy through the communicative and visual arts* (pp. 97–109). New York: Simon and Schuster Macmillan.

Athanases, S. Z. (2005). Performing the drama of the poem: Workshop, rehearsal, and reflection. *English Journal, 95*(1), 88–96.

Athanases, S. Z., & Heath, S. B. (1995). Ethnography in the study of the teaching and learning of English. *Research in the Teaching of English, 29*(3), 263–287.

Atkinson, P., & Hammersley, M. (1993). Ethnography and participant observation. In N. K. Denzin & Y. S. Lincoln (Eds.), *Handbook of qualitative research,* (pp. 248–277). Thousand Oaks, CA: Sage Publications.

Bacon, W. A. (1972). The act of interpretation. *Oral English, 2,* 6.

Breen, R. S. (1978). *Chamber theatre.* Englewood Cliffs, NJ: Prentice-Hall.

Cabral, B. A. V. (2001). Ritual and ethics—Structuring participation in a theatrical mode. *Research in Drama Education, 6*(1), 55–67.

Chávez, V., & Soep, E. (2005). Youth radio and the pedagogy of collegiality. *Harvard Educational Review, 75*(4), 409–434.

Chvasta, M. (2005). Remembering praxis: Performance in the digital age. *Text and Performance Quarterly, 25*(2), 156–170.

Conquergood, D. (1991). Rethinking ethnography: Towards a critical cultural politics. *Communication Monographs, 58,* 179–194.

Cousins, H. (2000). Upholding mainstream culture: The tradition of the American high school play. *Research in Drama Education, 5*(1), 85–94.

Dillard, S. (2002). The art of performing poetry: Festivals, slams, and Americans' favorite poem project events. *Text and Performance Quarterly, 22*(3), 217–227.

Edmiston, B., & Enciso, P. E. (2003). Reflections and refractions of meaning: Dialogic approaches to classroom and reading. In J. Flood, D. Lapp, J. R. Squire, & J. M. Jensen (Eds.), *Handbook of research on teaching the English language arts* (pp. 868–880). Mahwah, NJ: Lawrence Erlbaum.

Ellen, R. F. (Ed.). (1984). *Ethnographic research: A guide to general conduct.* New York: Academic Press, Harcourt Brace Jovanovich.

Fine, E. C. (1990). Student performance of literature. In S. Hynds & D. L. Rubin (Eds.), *Perspectives on talk and learning* (pp. 179–194). Urbana, IL: National Council of Teachers of English.

Forrest, W. C. (1969, July). The poem as a summons to performance. *British Journal of Aesthetics, IX,* 298–305.

Freedman, S. W. (1994). *Exchanging writing, exchanging cultures: Lessons in school reform from the United States and Great Britain.* Cambridge, MA: Harvard University Press.

Fuoss, K. W., & Hill, R. T. (1992). A performance-centered approach for teaching a course in social movements. *Communication Education, 41*(1), 77–88.

Glazner, G. M. (Ed.). (2000). *Poetry slam: The competitive art of performance poetry.* San Francisco: Manic D Press.

Goetz, J. P., & LeCompte, M. D. (1984). *Ethnography and qualitative design in educational research.* New York: Academic Press, Harcourt Brace Jovanovich.

Green, J. L., Dixon, C. N., & Zaharlick, A. (2003). Ethnography as a logic of inquiry. In J. Flood, D. Lapp, J. R. Squire, & J. M. Jensen (Eds.), *Handbook of research on teaching the English language arts* (pp. 201–224). Mahwah, NJ: Lawrence Erlbaum.

Green, J., & Bloome, D. (1997). Ethnography and ethnographers of and in education: A situated perspective. In J. Flood, S. B. Heath, & D. Lapp (Eds.), *Handbook of research on teaching literacy through the communicative and visual arts* (pp. 181–202). New York: Simon and Shuster Macmillan.

Heath, S. B. (1982). Ethnography in education: Defining the essentials. In P. Gilmore & A. A. Glatthorn (Eds.), *Children in and out of school: Ethnography and education,* (pp. 32–55). Washington, DC: Center for Applied Linguistics.

Heath, S. B., & McLaughlin, M. (1993). *Identity and inner-city youth: Beyond ethnicity and gender.* New York: Teachers College Press.

Heathcote, D. (1981). Drama as education. In N. McCaslin (Ed.), *Children as drama* (2nd ed., pp. 78–90). New York: Longman.

Henry, M. (2000). Drama's ways of learning. *Research in Drama Education, 5*(1), 45–61.

Horitz, T. (2001). "B-O-U-R-N-E-M-O-U-T-H! Our town!" Effects on male teenagers of participation in a community play. *Research in Drama Education, 6*(1), 69–84.

Hughes, J., & Wilson, K. (2004). Playing a part: The impact of youth theatre on young people's personal and social development. *Research in Drama Education, 9*(1), 57–72.

Innes, M., Moss, T., & Smigiel, H. (2001). What do the children say? The importance of student voice. *Research in Drama Education, 6*(2), 207–221.

Kempe, A. (2003). The role of drama in the teaching of speaking and listening as the basics for social capital. *Research in Drama Education, 8*(1), 65–78.

Kleinau, M. L., & McHughes, J. L. (1980). *Theatres for literature.* Sherman Oaks, CA: Alfred Publishing Company, Inc.

Landay, E. (2005). Give me moor proof: Othello in seventh grade. *English Journal, 95*(1), 39–46.

Lee, C., & Gura, T. (2000). *Oral interpretation* (10th ed.). Boston: Houghton.

Long, B. W., & HopKins, M. F. (1997). *Performing literature: An introduction to oral interpretation* (2nd ed.). New York: Kendall Hunt.

Long, B. W., Hudson, L., & Jeffrey, P. R. (1977). *Group performance of literature.* Englewood Cliffs, NJ: Prentice-Hall.

McLaughlin, M. W., & Talbert, J. E. (2001). *Professional communities and the work of high school teaching.* Chicago: University of Chicago Press.

Medina, C. (2004). The construction of drama worlds as literary interpretation of Latina feminist literature. *Research in Drama Education, 9*(2), 145–160.

Mencken, H. L. (2003). *The philosophy of Friedrich Nietzsche.* Tucson, AZ: See Sharp Press. (Original work published 1908)

Olsen, D. (1992). Floods and church secretaries, Buffalo Creek and Northwestern: Struggling with the seams between. *Text and Performance Quarterly, 12*(4), 329–348.

Park-Fuller, L. M., & Pelias, R. (1995). Charting alternative performance and evaluative practices. *Communication Education, 44*(2), 126–139.

Rogers, T., & O'Neill, C. (1993). Creating multiple worlds: Drama, language, and literary response. In G. E. Newell & R. K. Durst (Eds.), *Exploring texts: The role of discussion and writing in the teaching and learning of literature* (pp. 69–90). Norwood, MA: Christopher-Gordon.

Rosenblatt, L. (1978). *The reader, the text, the poem.* Carbondale: Southern Illinois University Press.

Sanjek, R. (Ed.). (1990). *Fieldnotes: The makings of anthropology.* Ithaca: Cornell University Press.

Saville-Troike, M. (1982). *The ethnography of communication: An introduction.* New York: Basil Blackwell Ltd.

Scardamalia, M. (2004). CSILE/Knowledge Forum. In *Education and technology: An encyclopedia* (pp. 18–192). Santa Barbara: ABC-CLIO.

Shosh, J. M. (2005). Wrighting: Crafting critical literacy through drama. *English Journal, 95*(1), 69–74.

Soep, E. (2006). Critique: Assessment and the production of learning. *Teachers College Record, 108*(4), 748–777.

Sperber, D. (1982). *On anthropological knowledge.* Cambridge: Cambridge University Press.

Squire, J. R., & Applebee, R. K. (1968). *High school English instruction today.* New York: Appleton-Century-Crofts.

Squire, J. R., & Applebee, R. K. (1969). *Teaching English in the United Kingdom*. Urbana, IL: National Council of Teachers of English.

Stucky, N. (1995). Performing oral history: Storytelling and pedagogy. *Communication Education*, *44*(1), 1–14.

van Vuuren, P. J. (2004). Meeting the mentor: The role of the teacher-director in engineering a hero's journey for participants in an educational drama workshop. *Research in Drama Education*, *9*(2), 211–227.

Wagner, B. J. (1990). Dramatic improvisation in the classroom. In S. Hynds & D. L. Rubin (Eds.), *Perspectives on talk and learning* (pp. 195–212). Urbana, IL: National Council of Teachers of English.

Wolf, J. L. (1997). Balancing act: Using drama to even the exchange of information in the classroom. In J. Flood, S. B. Heath, & D. Lapp (Eds.), *Handbook of research on teaching literacy through the communicative and visual arts* (pp. 68–76). New York: Simon and Shuster Macmillan.

Wolf, S. (1994). Learning to act/acting to learn: Children as actors, critics, and characters in classroom theatre. *Research in the Teaching of English*, *28*(1), 7–44.

Wolf, S. A. (1998). The flight of reading: Shifts in instruction, orchestration, and attitudes through classroom theatre. *Reading Research Quarterly*, *33*(4), 382–415.

Wolf, S., Edmiston, B., & Enciso, P. (1997). Drama worlds: Places of the heart, head, voice and hand in dramatic interpretation. In J. Flood, S. B. Heath, D. Lapp (Eds.), *Handbook of research on teaching literacy through the communicative and visual arts* (pp. 492–505). New York: Simon and Shuster Macmillan.

Wright, D. (2000). Drama education: A "self-organising system" in pursuit of learning. *Research in Drama Education*, *5*(1), 23–31.

Zumhagen, P. (2005). Using improvisational workshop to explore gender issues in "The untold lie." *English Journal*, *95*(1), 82–87.

•14•

MAKING "COLLABORATION" PROBLEMATIC IN COLLABORATIVE SCHOOL-UNIVERSITY ACTION RESEARCH: STUDYING WITH URBAN TEACHER RESEARCHERS TO TRANSFORM LITERACY PRACTICES

Christine C. Pappas
UNIVERSITY OF ILLINOIS AT CHICAGO

Those who have been involved in school-university collaborations have frequently remarked that "collaboration is not always an easy process" (Oja & Smulyan, 1989, p. x) or have characterized it as a very messy, uncertain, and time consuming enterprise (e.g., Bickel & Hattrup, 1995; Miller, 1990; Ravid & Handler, 2001). Despite these difficulties, for several decades now, many have taken on the challenge to create communities that educate both those of the university and of the schools by expanding relationships and social networks with each other (Allen, 1999; Lieberman, 1986, 1992; Nespor & Barylske, 1991; Wells, 2001).

I argue that the messiness in these collaborations is largely due to new conceptualizations about power/participant structures and the nature of knowledge, which, in turn, have required changes in educational research methodologies. The major aim of this chapter is to insist that, because of these changes about power/knowledge, collaboration itself in collaborative arrangements has to be made constantly problematic—that is, it has to be an ongoing, integral facet of methodological concern. Moreover, integral to this thesis is an examination of the role of videotaping in the research process.

This chapter has been organized into three major sections. The first section outlines the characteristics of collaborative action research (CAR), which is the term frequently used to refer to the kind of research performed in many current school-university partnerships. In doing so, perspectives around knowledge and power, informed by qualitative research, especially from humanistic psychology and feministic approaches, are discussed. The second section describes two particular examples of CAR projects (in which I have been, and am presently, involved) that explore the efforts of urban teachers to enact socioconstructivist/sociocultural, dialogic practices. Also discussed is the role of videotaping as a methodological tool to examine together classroom interactions. Finally, the last section considers several methodological issues of CAR, including notions of validity and reliability and the role of university-based researchers' expertise in CAR.

CHANGING PERSPECTIVES REGARDING POWER AND KNOWLEDGE: THE DEVELOPMENT OF COLLABORATIVE ACTION RESEARCH

Changing Voices in Educational Research

Changes in power and knowledge exemplified in school-university collaborations are frequently expressed as finding, gaining, hearing, or creating voice (e.g., Gitlin & Russell, 1994; Miller, 1990; Richardson, 1994; Schratz, 1993). Bakhtin's (1981, 1986) conception of "voice" provides a useful initial frame to examine the kinds of relationships that are developed in these collaborative arrangements. "Voice" is Bakhtin's notion for the "speaking personality, the speaking consciousness" (Holquist & Emerson, 1981, p. 434). Indeed, for Bakhtin, utterance (his term for text or the real unit of speech communication, oral or written) exists only by being produced by a voice. Voice, here, is a point of view that always enacts particular social values by addressing—or being in dialogue with—other voices (Cazden, 1992; Nystrand, 1997; Wells, 1999; Wertsch, 1991). And, because language is fundamentally dialogic in that we use and create language by speaking with others, any new instance of use is entwined with other previous uses and voices. There is, then, conflict in this process. In Bakhtin's (1981) words, "[Language] is populated—overpopulated—with the intentions of others. Expropriating it, forcing it to submit to one's own intentions and accents, is a difficult and complicated process" (p. 294).

In such a view, because our language is already used and reflects previous and present speakers, the finding of our voice also involves hearing the echoes of others (Burbules, 1993). This may explain why the challenge of altering the traditional relationships regarding power/knowledge between educators in universities and schools has been so distinctive and so difficult in collaborative ventures. These enterprises represent new ways to conduct educational research that are marked by attempts to develop a climate of open participation by partners so that the dialogue between them is one of discovery and exploration, but one that is frequently marked with uncertainty. Thus, there is a commitment to see things through, and, despite the conflict the effort entails, a struggle to ensure that all voices are heard and valued. Moreover, as is argued later, a similar, parallel struggle exists for teachers as they orchestrate classroom routines so that both their and their students' voices are given prominence.

School-University Collaborations as CAR

A variety of school-university collaboration models have emerged over the years (Handler & Ravid, 2001), but the emphasis here is on those involved in action research—the inquiry around the classroom practices of teaching and learning (for examples of action research in a range of disciplines—e.g., medical clinical work, business, social work, nursing, and natural resource management, see Reason & Bradbury, 2001a).

A general aim of CAR is the modification and elaboration of theories of teaching and learning. This research can take different forms, depending on the purpose of particular projects and the ways in which teachers or other school personnel are involved. However, according to Oja and Smulyan (1989), there are four major characteristics that CAR projects have in common.

First, of course, CAR is collaborative in nature. That is, it permits mutual understanding among the participants through democratic decision making for some common action. There is an emphasis for both teachers and university researchers to work together to set common goals, plan the research, analyze data, and report results. Responsibilities and roles are determined together, which may shift during the course of a project, but teacher *and* university researchers contribute their own knowledge and insights to the process; both partners offer resources to be mobilized in the project (Gaventa & Cornwall, 2001). There is an assumption that participants communicate frequently and openly to prevent any possible conflicting perceptions stemming from their different social networks, values, expectations, and so forth, and to encourage and support teachers' ongoing practice and responsibilities.

Second, as indicated above, CAR projects focus on practice. Often CAR addresses the immediate problems or agendas of participating teachers. Sometimes, university researchers may have a particular issue or topic of interest for consideration and invite teachers to participate with them in investigating it. Or, teachers or a school may identify the problem and ask for university researchers' collaboration to help in examining and studying it. Nevertheless, within each framework, there is a teacher-as-researcher emphasis of some kind. Inquiry emanates from, or generates questions about, classroom events that involve analysis and reflection by teachers to make sense of their experiences. In doing so, CAR calls attention to "teachers as knowers and to the complex and distinctly nonlinear relationships of knowledge and teaching as they are embedded in the contexts and the relations of power that structure the daily work of teachers and learners in both the school and the university" (Cochran-Smith & Lytle, 1993, p. xi).

Third, CAR enhances teachers' professional development by supporting or providing the impetus to improve and change their classroom practice. Through CAR, they construct new knowledge to deal with their immediate difficulties, expand their professional knowledge, and acquire research skills for future teacher inquiry. In addition, because university-based researchers gain new understandings about the praxis created in these classroom and school contexts in their interactions with collaborating teachers, their own professional development is facilitated.

Finally, CAR stresses the need for a project structure that enables the above three elements to occur. This structure requires regular and open communication among participants; democratic project leadership; recurring cycles of planning, acting, observing, and reflecting; and positive relationships with the school or schools in which the project is conducted.

Thus, in CAR projects, traditional views of power/knowledge and theory/practice in educational research are challenged and interrupted. Such action research reflects feminist perspectives that problematize systematic relations of power in the social construction of knowledge (Borthwick, 2001; Gore, 1993; Maguire, 2001), arguing, "Knowledge is always provisional, open-ended and relational" (Luke & Gore, 1992, p. 7). Moreover, it avoids the dichotomized view of theory and practice. Because it incorporates the "inside-outside" stance of teacher research (Cochran-Smith & Lytle, 1993), "living forms of theory" are evoked within practice (McNiff, 2002, p. 8). There are ample opportunities to address the questions that teachers pose (Gitlin, 1990; Gitlin et al., 1992).

Emphasis on keeping true to the personal, original voices in educational contexts has led to more qualitative approaches that employ interpretive orientations that aim to be "empirical without being positivist; to be rigorous and systematic in investigating the slippery phenomenon of everyday [classroom and school] interaction and its connections, through the medium of subjective meaning, with the wider social world" (Erickson, 1986, p. 120). In addition, CAR reflects humanistic psychological views of research participants as persons (Heron, 1981a, 1981b, 1992; Reason, 1988; Reason & Bradbury, 2001b; Reason & Heron, 1986). For example, Heron (1981a) has argued,

> Persons, as autonomous beings, have a moral right to participate in decisions that claim to generate knowledge about them. Such a right . . . protects them . . . from being managed and manipulated. . . . The moral principle of respect for all persons is most fully honored when power is shared not only in the application . . . but also in the generation of knowledge. (p. 155)

Thus, such a view argues that since participants in educational research are authors of their own intentions, choices, and actions, methods must be used to respect such agency in the generation of knowledge. CAR represents "empowering research" in that it is research with subjects that seeks their active co-operation: It is always attempting to make research methods more open, interactive, and dialogic (Cameron, Frazer, Harvey, Rampton, & Richardson, 1992).

TWO EXAMPLES OF COLLABORATIVE ACTION RESEARCH IN URBAN ELEMENTARY CLASSROOMS

Both examples of CAR to be described reflect the four major characteristics listed before; however, the arrangements of university-based researchers with collaborating teacher researchers are different. The first involved 13 teachers, from two elementary schools, who studied ways in which they could take on collaborative styles of teaching in various literacy topics (Pappas & Zecker, 2001a, 2001b). In this CAR project, the teachers posed their own inquiries. The second CAR project, in which I am presently involved (with science educator, Maria Varelas), centers around studying how primary-grade children develop scientific and generic discourse understandings in two integrated science-literacy units. In this project, Maria and I, as university researchers, had a topic of interest in mind and invited six teachers (two each from first, second, and third grade) to participate with us in investigating it. Both projects reflect similar major theoretical frameworks; thus, the socioconstructivist/sociocultural views on teaching learning that underlie them are discussed first, followed by the role of videotaping as a tool in the two CAR projects. Subsequently, a vignette from each project is described to highlight the nature of collaborative inquiry.

Socioconstructivist/Sociocultural Perspectives

Socioconstructivist/sociocultural views reflect conceptualizations about how teachers and students might work together so that knowledge can be seen as their joint construction of meaning (Miller, 1992; Oyler, 1996; Pappas, Kiefer, & Levstik, 2006; Wells, 1999, 2001; Wells & Chang-Wells, 1992). This classroom collaboration between teachers and students represents a challenge to our long-lasting, transmission-oriented tradition in schooling. Based on Vygotskian's (1962, 1978) ideas that have been extended from others (Gonzalez, Moll, & Amani, 2005; Gutierrez, 1994; Lee & Smagorinsky, 2000; Moll, 1990; Newman, Griffin, & Cole, 1989; Wells, 1999; Wertsch, 1989, 1991), students are seen as active meaning makers and "knowers" so that learning is accomplished through collaborative interaction and transaction as teachers share their expertise to guide and assist learners to construct their own understandings. Such an approach—what Willinsky (1990) has called the "new literacy"—involves teachers' attempts to redefine literacy by studying their roles and instructional interactions to make reading and writing more connected and meaningful to the lives of their students.

Such classroom transactions are realized in a different type of classroom talk. Instead of the traditional teacher-controlled initiate-respond-evaluate (IRE) talk structure (Cazden, 2001; Edwards & Mercer, 1987; Mercer, 1995; Sinclair & Coulthard, 1975; Young, 1992), dialogic classroom discourse is enacted where both the voices of students and teachers are privileged (Nystrand, 1997; Pappas, et al., 2006; Wells, 1999). In such dialogic inquiry, teachers provide spaces for students' comments and questions, thereby providing opportunities for teachers to take up and contingently respond to students' ideas to sustain and extend them. There are no scripts for teachers to follow here. Instead, as Sawyer (2004) has argued, these constructivist, inquiry-based, and dialogic teaching methods are best termed as "teaching as improvisational performance," because in effective classroom practice, "the flow of the class is unpredictable and emerges from the actions of all participants, both teachers and students" (p. 13). Improvisational teaching is especially important to allow for urban students who come from diverse ethnolinguistic backgrounds, students who have their own "ways with words" (Heath, 1982, 1983), to contribute to classroom interactions. Such an approach provides opportunities for negotiation or consideration of these children's styles of interaction (Au & Jordan, 1981; Delpit, 1995; Foster, 1992; Heath, 1983; Lindfors, 1999; McCollum, 1991; Michaels, 1981; Nieto, 2000; Reyes, 1991, 1992).

Thus, in CAR projects, a parallel struggle to collaborate exists at two levels—among teachers and students and among school-university partners—to enact democratic discourse processes in which the voices and expertise of all participants are acknowledged and valued.

Using Videotape as a Tool in Collaborative Action Research

In both CAR projects to be illustrated, videotaping was a major tool of data collection in teachers' classrooms and documentation of our collaborative work. However, since around the 1990s, there has been a move to focus on the visual in particular and how it contributes to the "reflexive turn" in investigation (Knowles & Sweetman, 2004). That is, the recent emphasis on multimodal literacies—a consideration of linguistic modes *and* visual images, and other modes of communication (Cope & Kalantzis, 2000; Jewitt & Kress, 2003; Kress, 2000, 2003; Kress & van Leeuwen, 2001; Unsworth, 2001)—has led to exploring more specifically the methodology in the use of visual images as a representation of what researchers *see*.

In our projects, we produce transcriptions of videotapes, but we also watch together video clips of collaborating teachers' classroom (and these sessions are also videotaped). Thus, our reviewing of videotaping of classroom life incorporates consideration of both linguistic and visual images. Moreover, because "visual images are quite different in nature from words in their allusion to 'reality', and participants see themselves and can be seen by others" (Prosser, 2000, p. 117) and because what we see involves acts of interpretation just as much as our making sense of words (Knowles & Sweetman, 2004), videotaping raises new methodological issues in CAR projects and offers new contributions for understanding the relationships between images and words (Tucker-Raymond, Pappas, & Varelas, 2005).

Thus, using videotaping invites "new ways of working with people, words and images with an emphasis on *processes* of research and representation" (Pink, 2004). That is, focusing on visual images invites new stances on "reflexivity"—the self-consciousness of the cycles of interactions and perceptions that characterize the relationships with other human beings in research (Delamont, 1992; Glesne, 1999; Kamberelis & Dimitriadis, 2005). In our discussions around the videotapes, the images helped elicit verbal narratives (Hughes-Freeland, 2004) about what was seen and heard. Thus, the images of videotaping have a new important role for imagination or "seeing" new ideas to consider; they represent another means for exploration in CAR projects.

(It is important to note that other means of data collection are also used in CAR projects—e.g., school- and university-based researchers' fieldnotes, classroom and student artifacts, audiotaping and videotaping of project meetings, interviews, etc. Space restrictions do not allow for discussion of these other data sources; however, more information on them can be found in Pappas, 1997; Pappas & Zecker, 2001c).

Two Vignettes of CAR

Both CAR projects discussed below involved collaborating Chicago Public School teacher researchers. Each had a project structure that included regular meetings to consider the ongoing facets of the action research—see the final fourth characteristic of CAR projects previously discussed. Each vignette of the two projects consists of discussion of university- and school-based researchers discussing a video clip from a collaborating teacher's read-aloud. Mehan (1993) explained why he used videotape as an instrument in educational research: "Cognitive skills don't reside in the heads of people, including children in schools, they reside in social situations which are composed of people" (p. 94). This is a "situated cognition" perspective (Kirshner & Whitson, 1997; Lave, 1988; Rogoff & Wertsch, 1984) that emphasizes that student performance varies as a function of the situation in which they find themselves. Thus, videotape enables the researcher, Mehan argued, to listen and look at this social life in classrooms more closely than is otherwise possible. What I want to stress, here, is how the multimodal nature of the videotape permits teacher researchers to "hear" *and* "see" critical dimensions of their inquiries. It helps them—in collaboration with others—to "interrupt" the everyday routines to carefully examine the teaching learning they have chosen to investigate.

Exploring Dorothy's read-aloud of Darkness and the Butterfly *(Grifalconi, 1987).* This first CAR project (Pappas & Zecker, 2001a, 2001b) centered upon individual teacher researchers' posing their own inquiry questions. Dorothy's question focused on how she might orchestrate read-alouds to better understand her mostly Latina or Latino third graders' responses to a range of multicultural children's literature she had collected the previous summer. Because she had felt more comfortable in the past in dominating the discussions about books, to accomplish her present inquiry, she attempted to find ways to have more collaborative, dialogic read-alouds (for more details on her inquiry, see O'Malley, 2001; Pappas, Hart, Escobar, Jones, & O'Malley, 2001).

In this CAR project, two-member teams worked with the same teachers the whole year, one who operated the video camera, another who took fieldnotes. The duration of these videotaping sessions varied according to the length of the routine in which individual teachers had their inquiries—as short as 20 minutes or as long as over an hour. An edited video clip (decided upon from input from the teacher and the research assistants working with the teacher), which reflected both "good" and "vulnerable" parts, was shared in an author's chair fashion at a weekly meeting at each of the two schools/sites (seven teachers at one school and six at Dorothy's school). Also, we found it useful to provide a brief editing note, on which we listed short descriptors of the edited segments, for everyone at the meeting so that we could all better follow what would be shown.

Throughout the year, Dorothy had drastically changed her style of interaction by providing spaces for student initiation. In our meeting that day, we had already seen other segments of the videotape on Dorothy's reading of *Darkness and the Butterfly* (Grifalconi, 1987), which had occurred a few weeks earlier. We had gotten to the part that had to do with a boy's interruption of Dorothy's reading by asking, "Is that a poem?" I had been in the classroom that day, too, and I was recalling—before we had yet viewed this particular videotape segment—my impression of it. Here, we focus on two types of discourse in sequence: first, discourse from the meeting is provided, followed by classroom discourse from the videotape, and then more on our meeting discussion.

Present at the meeting that day were teacher researchers, Dorothy, Hawa, Sonia, and Sue, and university researchers, Chris, Diane, and Shannon. Table 14.1 presents the explanation of transcription conventions.

Chris: This was really great in lots of ways. Again there's the notion of intertextuality cause they were talking about things they did on poetry. But it doesn't get to // you didn't ask the kid, "well, why did you think. . . ?"

Dorothy: I see, I did ask [pointing to the video screen] // somebody said it was a story though, so I moved it, which kind of didn't make sense, but* . . .

Chris: Which is okay, too. We should listen to it. (Weekly Meeting, March 29, 1995)

Initially I brought up the idea of intertextuality as it occurred in the classroom discourse as I remembered it. *Intertextuality,* as we had been using it in our project, follows Bloome's (Bloome & Bailey, 1992; Bloome & Egan-Robertson, 1993) and Lemke's (1985) ideas on the topic. When teachers leave spaces for student initiation, children frequently make intertextual links in the classroom discourse; that is, they connect other books, songs, movies, prior curricular information they have studied, personal stories from their homes and communities, and so forth, with the topic being discussed. According to Bloome, for these student offerings to be considered as instances of intertextuality, they must be proposed, recognized, acknowledged, and have social significance for the participants. Thus, intertextual links that begin from student initiation are characteristic of collaborative talk, which was something that Dorothy and the other teachers in the project were attempting to promote.

As can be seen in the following excerpt, when the student asked about whether the book was a poem, the students, who had some earlier curricular experience regarding poems, brought in their own ideas about poetic characteristics, mostly to argue that the present book was not a poem, but a story.

TABLE 14.1. Conventions of Transcription for Discourse Examples

Unit:	Usually corresponds to an independent clause with all dependent clauses related to it (complex clause or T-unit). Sometimes includes another independent clause if there is no drop of tone and was added without any pausing. Units here are punctuated as sentences.
Turn:	Includes all of a speaker's utterances/units.
Key for Speakers:	First name is listed for teacher-researcher and children. C, C1, C2, and so forth are noted for individual children (with "m" or "f" to refer to the gender of a child): C is used if a child's voice cannot be identified; Cn is used to identify particular children (but not by name) in particular section of the transcript (so that C1 or C2, etc., is not necessarily the same child throughout the whole transcript). Cs represents many children speaking simultaneously.
//	Repetitions or false starts or abandoned language replaced by new language structures.
...	Small/short pause within unit.
... ...	Longer pause within unit.
*...	Breaking off of a speaker's turn due to the next speaker's turn.
===	A speaker's pause at the end of uncompleted utterance, seemingly to encourage another speaker to talk.
< >	Uncertain words.
(***)	One word that is inaudible or impossible to transcribe.
(*** ***)	Longer stretches of language that are inaudible and impossible to transcribe.
Underscore:	Emphasis.
# #	Overlapping language spoken by two or more speakers at a time.
CAPS	Actual reading of a book or someone's writing.
{ }	Teacher's miscue or modification of a text read.
[ ]	Identifies what is being referred to or gestured and other nonverbal contextual information.
....	Part of a transcript has been omitted.

[Dorothy read the part of the book where Osa, a girl who is afraid of the dark, is talking to the Wise Woman, who is trying to help Osa overcome her fear. A boy in the back of the room raised his hand. Dorothy acknowledged him and he asked a question.]

Dorothy: "BUT LOOK AT THAT LITTLE BUTTERFLY, OSA; SHE MUST THINK SHE IS THE SMALLEST OF THE SMALL. DARKNESS PURSUES HER TOO--YET SHE FLIES ON!" SLEEPILY, OSA THOUGHT ABOUT THAT. "MAYBE SHE HAS A SECRET?" {AND} THEN SHE SHOOK HER HEAD. "BUT I HAVE NO WINGS TO FLY." OSA HEARD THE WISE {WOMAN CALL FORTH}: "YOU WILL FIND YOUR OWN WAY. YOU WILL SEE." OSA NODDED, AND BEFORE SHE KNEW IT, SHE FELL INTO A DEEP SLEEP.
Cm1: That's a poem?
Dorothy: Pardon me?
Cm1: That's a poem. Or is that a poem or is it a story?
Dorothy: Is this a poem or is it a story? What do you think?
Cm1: #A story.#
Cs: #Story.#
Dorothy: Why do you think it's a // excuse me, why do you think it's a story? Who else thinks it's a story?
Cs: [About 9 kids raise their hands.]
Dorothy: Cm2, why do you think it's a story?
Cm2: It doesn't have <things> that rhyme.
Dorothy: It doesn't have very many rhyming words.
Cm2: It doesn't have stanzas.
Dorothy: It doesn't // it's not written in stanzas, good.
Cm3: It doesn't have four lines*...
Dorothy: Okay, do some stanzas have four lines? Do all stanzas have four lines in a poem?
Cs: No.
Dorothy: No, do all stanzas have rhyming words?
Cs: No.
Dorothy: Is it too long?
Some Cs: #Yes.#
Some Cs: #No.#
Dorothy: Well, we haven't read very long poems, I agree. But poems can be very, very long. They can be longer than a story. (***) Do you think this story could be made into a poem?
Cs: Yes.
Dorothy: Probably so, probably so.

(Edited videotape shared March 29, 1995 from classroom videotape, March 1, 1995)

Actually, although the author/illustrator of the book, Grifalconi (1987), wrote this book as a story, she also included poetic qualities in it, both in its format and in its lyrical phrasing. So, Cm1's question was probably a very reasonable one. And, the idea that there were not any stanzas in the book is not really accurate because the text was written in a stanza-like fashion, with each line beginning with a capital letter, for example. However, this was probably not very noticeable to the students since usually there was only one stanza per page and they would not have been able to see the punctuation from their seats.

Dorothy had subsequently looked at this book and the student's question about it quite differently since we examined it in our meeting, but here in the upcoming excerpt of the meeting discussion, her attention was on other facets of the interaction.

Diane: I thought that was a really good wrap up question, "Can this be made into a poem?" And all the kids answered, "Yeah, sure."
Dorothy: Well they did // they did kind of do a little bit of that when we kind of went in and out of poetry. I couldn't get them to come up with a poem. We had a theme to send to the..dental week or something and they just*. . .
Chris: [facing Dorothy] See, it's just that the kind of conversation would have been quite different if you had said, "Tell me why did you // what makes you <u>say</u> that, what makes you think that this might be a poem?"
Dorothy: Mmm, I'm getting too direct here [pointing to the video screen]. The question is becoming looking for an answer instead of just a comment and let them go in what direction they // and I can hear that now, where I could never hear that // I mean, I wouldn't // I thought that was good! [As Dorothy talks, she waves her hand in front of her face as if to wave off her own lack of hearing herself before now.]
Chris: Yeah, yeah.
Dorothy: I mean I'm beginning to see that because you cut them off you're looking for yes, or no, or the whole class responds.
Chris: Usually, yeah, usually there is a whole // yeah, there's a real clue when the whole class is going "yeaaah" or "noooo" [lowers her voice and makes it long, like a mechanical answer, and the whole group laughs]. You know that "whoops, I'm definitely asking a pseudo question here!" But you know there's some points where that might be appropriate because you're trying to make connections to other kinds of instruction, you know.
Hawa: Or sometimes you get them when they say "yeah" and you ask them "why?" and they say, "uh, well, uh . . ."
Sonia: That's because they expect this, they expect* . . .
Chris: Well, you know people call this procedural display and mock participation. In other words, kids know the routine but sometimes there's no // and lots of teachers accept that they've understood and it's really just surface procedures so people call it procedural display and mock participation. It's that IRE where the teacher does this, the kids say that, and teacher evaluates. It's the kind of thing that you guys are trying to challenge.
Sonia: It's hard.
Dorothy: It's hard, but it's neat though [pointing to the video screen]. It's hard too because // I think this is the first time that I've seen value in looking at my video. I can relate to things now and actually I heard that and it sounded awful. I mean just the kids says, "yesss" and before perhaps I would have thought, "Gee, isn't that good, they're all responding [sort of with an exaggerated smile as if to show how silly that was].
Shannon: And they all got the right answer.
Dorothy: And not even the right and wrong answer but just that they were . . .
Chris: Engaged.
Dorothy: [pointing to Chris] Yes, engaged. And somebody wasn't. Which isn't as good as* . . .
Chris: Yeah, a kid could be looking over there [Chris turns in her seat to look away from the group] and said "yeah."
Dorothy: Right.
Chris: Well, maybe you can hear it because you have gone beyond in your inquiry in some way.

The discussion then changed topic to see and consider the last segment of the video. (Weekly Meeting, March 29, 1995)

There are two important, interrelated points I want to emphasize about this discussion. The first is that Dorothy had come to a critical understanding about her interactions with students in her inquiry. That is, she decided that what had been comforting to her or evidence of engagement in the responses of "yes" or "no" from students in certain classroom interactions is now problematic and indicative of mostly mock participation and procedural display (which I put a label to, drawing again from some ideas in Bloome, 1994) instead of more substantive meanings being developed. Thus, besides teachers making the effort to provide opportunities for students' initiations around books in classroom discourse, they are learning how best to contingently respond to students' initiations to sustain and further extend them is an issue in developing collaborative talk.

The second point is Dorothy's belief that there was great value in viewing the videotape of her classroom interactions because it enabled her to "hear"—and also "see"—what she had not been able to hear and see before. Thus, she might have missed an important opportunity to respond to her student's question on this particular day in a way that might have contributed to her understanding of her students' interactions with this book, which was at the core of her inquiry. However, with the help of the videotape, she was given a chance to become more explicitly aware of what she has to do in the future to accomplish that goal in her inquiry.

Although it might seem to readers of this chapter that I was extremely fortunate to have Dorothy's overt testimony on the value of videotaping as an important tool in her teacher inquiry, many of the teachers have also commented on its utility. In fact, teachers suggested its use in the first place, since they are unable to observe each other in their classrooms.

Moreover, although we had not expressly asked for it, several of the teachers discussed the advantages of the use of videotape in their inquiries in our individual end-of-the-year interviews. For example, in the beginning of her conversation with us, Hawa, who taught second grade at the same school as Dorothy, listed what she saw as the pluses in her inquiry for the year, which also focused on her read-alouds. She specifically addressed how viewing videotapes in particular contributed: "Another one was seeing yourself after you had // did a read-aloud . . . seeing yourself on tape, saying 'ooh I did *that*,' or 'didn't do that,' or 'that was good,' or 'I liked that.' That's one of the positive things I liked about it, too."

Sarah, a colleague at the same school who taught a second grade bilingual class, also remarked on positive benefits of videotape. She felt that the sharing of videotapes promoted collaboration. She thought that it got the teachers in the group talking to each other at the meetings, of course, but also that it spilled over in that it fostered conversations about what they were doing among their group when they saw each other in the halls, at lunch, or other times in school. Videotape, she also said, gave her "'a third eye' . . . it gave me not only a resource but also an outlet . . . to what was going on and what carried on. . . . It makes everything self-conscious."

Exploring Ibett's read-aloud of What Is the World Made of? All about Solids, Liquids, and Gases *(Zoehfeld, 1998).* As already noted, this second, current CAR project focuses on teaching and learning in two integrated science-literacy units. In this case, when we (Maria Varelas and I) received funding (based on preliminary work with two teacher researchers over several years—for more information, see Pappas, Varelas, Barry, & Rife, 2003, 2004; Varelas & Pappas, in press a, in press b; Varelas, Pappas, & Rife, 2005), we invited six primary-grade teachers (two teachers per grade) who indicated an interest in the topic to join us to develop and study the integrated units. We are now in the second year (considered the collection year) of a three-year project. We also have weekly meetings with the teacher researchers at the university. In the summer, after the first pilot year, we created a range of video clips and worked together to rethink the various activities of the units (e.g., read-alouds, hands-on explorations, drama activities, small-group sharing of literature circle readings, ongoing teacher-led semantic mappings, and so forth) based on data collected over the previous year.

In this CAR project, teachers are also attempting to enact dialogic read-alouds—providing spaces for students' own ideas, comments, and questions, to which teachers can take up and respond. So, we reviewed video clips from each teacher's classroom to explore and analyze strategies that teachers had used and could use next year to make their read-alouds collaborative. An important factor in successful dialogic read-alouds of information books is the teacher's knowledge of the science content. That is, if teachers do not have the relevant science understanding, they may not recognize students' initiations of emergent ideas, or appreciate their use of life-world wordings (Gee, 2004) as they offer tentative explanations for scientific phenomenon, therefore making it difficult for them to adequately respond to these student efforts.

Below is the discourse from a video clip from Ibett's read-aloud of *What Is the World Made of? All about Solids, Liquids, and Gases* (Zoehfeld, 1998) to her bilingual, Latina and Latino second graders, followed by our discussion on it. This read-aloud was from the first unit that was implemented, states of matter, which we referred to as the "SOM unit." (Turns are numbered for better reference during the discussion.) Subsequently, our discussion around this classroom video clip is presented.

1 Ibett: HAVE YOU EVER PLAYED WITH A LEMONADE DOLL,
2 Cs: Nooo.
3 Ibett: OR PUT ON MILK FOR SOCKS?
4 Cs: Oh no.
5 Ibett: Have you ever tried that, (***)?
6 C: No.
7 Cs: (*** ***).
8 Ibett: Your socks aren't made out of milk?
9 Cs: Nooo.
10 C: (*** ***).
11 Ibett: Oh no, (*** ***).
12 Ibett: WALLS AND BLOCKS, DOLLS AND SOCKS. MILK AND LEMONADE. ROCKS AND TREES. ALL OF THESE THINGS ARE MADE OF MATTER. My little voice says it is a new word for me. What's "matter"? Good question. . . . THE AIR IN THE BREEZE THAT BLOWS THE LEAVES. WATER FLOWING IN THE CREEK. EVERYTHING ON EARTH IS MADE OF MATTER.
13 Celia: <Water>.
14 Ibett: Celia said water. I guess she remembered yesterday we had lots of water. But it is matter. LUCKY FOR US, IT'S EASY TO TELL THAT NOT ALL MATTER IS ALIKE.
15 Gena: <What's "matter"?>
16 Ibett: We're still getting questions. Gena is saying "what's 'matter'?" Well, let's go back and see. It says matter are [pointing to individual "matter" words] {WALLS, BLOCKS, DOLLS, SOCKS, MILK, LEMONADE, ROCKS, TREES.} {THAT'S MATTER.} Now let's go back here. It says {THE WIND THAT BLOWS THE LEAVES, THE WATER.} EVERYTHING ON EARTH IS MADE OF MATTER.
17 Cs: #(*** ***)#
18.Cm: #I got it now.#
19 Ibett: Marcella has raised her hand. Let's listen to her.
20 Marcella: All the thing they don't call their name. They are not like // here I think their name they are all matter. (*** ***).
21 Ibett: They're matter. Everything. Jon.
22 Jon: I think // what do you call . . . umm like cement? When // when it is not made // that's a // when you pour like that // the..// that sand you pour to make cement. I think that's matter. That made // she said ah the walls are made of matter.
23 Ibett: Very good. Jon is telling us that you see // have you ever seen when you make cement? Before you make it into a watery thing? It's like sand so you pour it. He is saying that is matter. Okay. LUCKY FOR US, IT'S EASY TO TELL THAT NOT ALL MATTER IS ALIKE.
24 Marcella: Teacher.
25 Ibett: Yes.
26 Marcella: Matter is another word like . . . // matter is like . . . "it doesn't matter if she can." Or (*** ***) matter like* . . .
27 Ibett: #Okay umm.#
28 Cs: #Oooooo.#
29 Ibett: Marcella is confusing another // there are two meanings of "matter," okay? One is "oh it doesn't matter // it doesn't matter if you want to or not," okay? But the other thing is some thing. It's a thing. Matter is like "oh that is how you feel." But there is another matter where it's a thing. That's the thing we are talking about. Because we are talking about everything on earth is matter. So let's say "is it matter?" [points to an object in book illustration].
30 Cs: Yes.
31 Ibett: Yes. It is right on earth. Right. Is this matter? [points to another object in illustrations]
32 Cs: Yes.
33 Ibett: How about this? [points to another object in illustrations]
34 Cs: Yes.
35 Ibett: Ah, a rock? Is that matter?
36 Cs: #Yes.#

37 Cs: #No.#
38 Ibett: Everything on earth is a matter. How about a chair?
39 Cs: Yes.
40 C: Shoes.
41 Ibett: Your shoes. That's matter.
42 C: Our hair.
43 Ibett: Our hair.
. . . . *[Students bring up other things that are matter, and Ibett accepts them.]*
44 Ibett: What's your question?
44 Jon: What . . . // is matter hard or is liquid?
45 Ibett: That's a good question. Let's find out. . . .

{Classroom videotape, November 10, 2004}

The analysis of this classroom episode is considered below as part of meeting discussion. Unfortunately, the videotape of our discussion of it often skipped; thus, I have noted these occasions in the transcription below with "[SKIP]." Also, I have added reference units of the above classroom discourse ("[see CD unit . . .]") to better understand what was referred to in the meeting talk. In addition, because our camera was on a tripod in the back of the room, it did not catch all speakers, so *Part.* was used for those participants who could not be identified by sight or voice.

Not all of the discussion is included below, but several important topics were addressed: (a) Ibett's reactions to hearing and seeing herself just providing many evaluations of "yes," "right," and so forth to what students said; (b) her strategy of going back to rereading sections of text; (c) a discussion about a child's initiation about two meanings of the word *matter*; (d) comments on a child's reasoning about solids and liquids; (e) Ibett's strategy in dealing with a seemingly incorrect student remark; (f) the issue of student participation in read-alouds; and, (g) teachers' tensions as teacher versus researcher in our CAR project.

We all had a copy of the transcription of the classroom video clip, and to begin the discussion, I asked Ibett if she wanted to bring up anything first. (During at this part of the meeting only four of the six teachers, Ibett, Anne, Jennifer, and Neveen, were present, along with Maria and me and other university researchers, one of whom, Justine, contributed to the conversation.)

1 Ibett: I was just noticing what I was talking about, that sometimes I just say, "yeah," "right," "you're correct." I do that a lot. [See CD 31, and those units excerpted out of the transcription between units 43 and 44.]
2 Maria: You said, "very good." [See CD unit 23.]
3 Chris: Well, you know, don't get paranoid on this either, you know. I mean if you do that a lot, you know, it's going to be hard for you to change your whole life here.
4 Maria: What else? What are we noticing?
5 Jennifer: I like how you went back and said, "Oh, let's go back to the text and see," like when a kid had a question and kind of modeled that you can go back and reread something that you had already read [see CD units 15–16].
6 Maria: The text is a source of information #for#*...
7 Jennifer: #Right.#
8 Maria: For // for the // for all of us.
9 Jennifer: The kids will often just think of reading it once, and then they're done with it.
10 Maria: And // and // and still // I mean, they're not reading, but you're reading to them as a source of information. [SKIP] that is critical.
11 Justine: I thought it was interesting when the girl said, you know, she used the word, "what's the 'matter'?" and then differentiating those two kinds of ways of using the word "matter" from the scientific concept of matter to the ordinary um, "how-are-you-feeling?" sort of matter, kind of [see CD units 26–29].
12 Chris: And that's really the difference between like story language [SKIP]. We use (***) words and make it into a particular scientific term. Um so // um um so again [SKIP]. See, we wouldn't have this nice clarification if there wasn't an opportunity for the kid to ask that question.
13 Maria: I think in my mind um, Ibett, um made the space for these contributions by // even right at the beginning um, [SKIP] and you have (***) question to be asking me. Whether we pose it that way or not, right? You set up the // the // the stage for the kids to be asking [SKIP] to ask themselves this question, right? Whatever style they use to // to do that. "My little voice" works for you and for your kids. It's wonderful. It doesn't mean all of us have to do it that way. [SKIP] It's good. "I can ask this question," right? "My teacher kind of encouraged me to ask this question. She's asking this question in her mind," right? "What's matter?" And um contributions [SKIP] [see CD unit 12].
. . . .
14 Anne: I think this Jon <one> too is interesting. I think it's his // it's his understanding [SKIP]. And then you have cement, a solid again, you have the walls, and then, how the walls are made of matter. And you say "very good." Jon is telling us [SKIP]. He's really* . . . [see CD units 22–23].
15 Ibett: Trying to figure out* . . .
16 Anne: Really trying to figure out what it // it is all about. It's excellent.
17 Ibett: He's really trying to put his brain around it.
. . . .
18 Maria: So Jon is saying // he's using the reasoning that something is matter when it makes other matter, right? . . . Because the // the cement, right?, makes the walls. But that's a very interesting way of reasoning, right?, scientifically. And look again, we won't be able to analyze these kind of things unless we have Jon offer this contribution. And I think [SKIP]. So how do we value the kind of the meaning making that the kids are doing? It's // it's coming across to them, I think, without sitting them, like the first day of class, and say, "Kids, this year we're going to have meaning making." And they say what? But what we do // how we talk with them, how we // we model for them. how do I ask questions in my head, right? All this gives them the idea we are for real, you know?
19 Ibett: Now I see this, like, I could have developed it more to get more. But I'm // that was one of my questions is, like, when do I step in to get // to develop it more? I just repeated what he said. And I could have, like, maybe, asked a different question to get someone else involved in it.
. . . .

20 Chris: Well, well, yeah, I mean, well, but you're making these decisions in absolute time, you know. And this kid's bringing this, and this kid's bringing this, and you're bringing this, you know. So, when you // I mean, because we can look at these things and say, "Oh, you could of done this or you could of done that, and whatever." But, you know, you're // it's very hard to make these decisions as a teacher (***) making these things. That's why you want to be thinking about some major principles in your own head and some strategies that you can think about, but then you just have to hope that you can, you know, to implement them when // in the best ways that #you can#.

21 Ibett: #Yeah.#

22 Chris: You know what also was interesting is, too, what you do with Celia's. Instead of saying "matter" she said "water." And she said, "Celia says 'water.' I guess she remembered yesterday there was a lot of water" but // but it is water too // it is matter, I mean. So you um // you connected it to #(*** ***)#. [See CD units 13 and 14.]

23 Part. (*** ***)

24 Chris: I've seen Anne do this too. When kids come up with something, and it seems kind of weird or something, um she'll say, "Oh, I think you're saying that because da, da, da." In other words, you give value to the thinking that the kids might have had. Um so it might be out of the blue, or it's not a correct answer, but you know maybe where that might have come from. . . .

. . . .

25 Chris: I think what's interesting here too is that except for Jon all the other contributions are girls, and that's another issue too. Sometimes we have a tendency to pay attention to the boys' contributions and not the girls'.

26 Part: Or vice versa . . .

27 Chris: Ah, you know? Or vice versa, you know.

28 Ibett: This is (***) in the beginning of the year when a lot of them were limited [in English]. And that was before I started the code-switching [to Spanish].

. . . .

29 Chris: Yeah, but // I mean, but again these are // these are the things that you yourself as a teacher knows about your kids...that the RAs and // would <u>not</u> know. So // but those are the things that you // so // you have. You // you see Marcella. Marcella doesn't hardly ever say anything per se, whatever, and all of a sudden her little hand goes up [slaps hands], you're going to be // you're going to be <u>watching</u> and paying attention to her...you know? But // or thinking, okay, at the end of each (***) did // did // who really contributed? Who didn't? How can I encourage those other kids who were not really participating (***)? But // but on the other hand, we have a couple kids, right?, who bring up always very interesting things that // that // that spur the conversations in very meaningful, #fruitful# ways.

30 Anne: #Yeah.#

31. Chris: So we don't want to "gaggle" them, you know, either* . . .

32 Anne: You know that they're the focal child, and you know they're going to be, you know, really contributing greatly to // maybe adding on or, you know, making the conversation (*** ***). You're purposefully going to get to them.

. . . .

33 Maria: And that is the tension, I think again, now, some people talked last year about—um a more instructional stance versus a more researcher stance, right? Because if you put your hat as a researcher at a particular point, you make decisions on calling different kids sometimes than when you put your hat as a teacher, as an instructor. Because as a teacher you may really want to get to Marcella, who has never said anything before and you really want to get to understand her thinking and then help her develop these ideas. But as a researcher you may really want to call on a focal kid because you really know we're going to try to trace this kid's understandings over a period of time and see how they develop. These are very // these are really conflicting tendencies, right? And that's one of the things we've talked about before, and // and at this point I would say, you know, just do your best as a teacher. . . . These are instructional units. Yes, you are part of a larger team that is trying to do research, but we're not going to compromise the quality of the teaching that you want to do for all your kids in the classroom in order to satisfy research goals, right? We're going to try to kind of do our research around our <u>teaching</u> priorities. So um for any reason, you know, you want to go with this kid, and your little voice inside you is telling you, you know, as a teacher I would pick this one but I think, you know, I would have had more interesting contributions if I picked the more focal one, forget it, you know. Don't pick the more focal one because at this point your responsibility's also as a teacher to reach out and // these kids learn something out of these units. Not only that we do them and // and we, you know, satisfy our [funding's], you know, grant that we got. But it's really priority // um should be our teaching and that obviously us knowing how you make those instructional decisions. (*** ***) with your RA, having conversations, you know, after the end of that lesson or periodically so we get the feel for, you know, you sensing this tension, you know, "I really don't have a lot of kids contributing this session. I don't know why. Maybe these are difficult ideas for them. So, I make these instructional decisions for them." That's fine for us to know, so we can // as we look at the data we put this context around them, and we understand them better. . . . (Summer Meeting, June 20, 2005)

In unit 1, Ibett seemed to be bringing up the kinds of concerns that Dorothy had been grappling with. Towards the end of the classroom excerpt, Ibett was utilizing more of a IRE structure, evaluating students comment with a "yes" or "right" or later, just repeating student ideas (some of which were not included in the transcript but were in the video clip). She was thinking that perhaps she should have developed students' ideas more (see also CD unit 19), rather than having the kinds of exchange she had had. Since many of us felt that there were many occasions of dialogic conversation, I tried, in unit 3, to support the overall style she had used in the read-aloud (more about this issue is examined later).

As we began to notice other facets of the read-aloud, Jennifer (a third grade teacher) commented how she appreciated Ibett's strategy to use a student-initiated question to go back to the book to read sections, and Maria remarked how the rereading gives children the idea of rereading the book as a source for their questions. Then, Justine (an RA) brought up Marcella's question about the "it doesn't matter if she can" sense of the word *matter* (CD unit 26), which led to Ibett's explicit differentiation of the everyday, life world use of the word versus the scientific sense being used in the information book. I, then, commented how that the clarification that was made in the classroom discourse arose because Ibett provided spaces for her students to bring up such ideas. Maria followed up by pointing out on Ibett's early strategy of modeling how to think of ideas and words that are unfamiliar in reading. By letting her students know how she asks questions "in my little voice," she is also suggesting—or setting the stage—that her students could do the same thing.

Subsequently, in unit 14, Anne (a first grade teacher, who was also a teacher researcher in the other CAR project, and who worked with Maria and me in earlier research on integrated-science units before we received our current funding) pointed out Jon's thinking about the states of matter of liquid and solid as he tried to make sense of pouring cement that might become walls (CD unit 22). Maria noted (in unit 18) how Jon's reasoning reflected the idea of matter (pouring of cement) making another kind of matter, which again brought out the idea that if there were not these dialogic spaces we would not know of Jon's contribution to analyze. She emphasized that students realize that such initiations in meaning making are possible and encouraged not by explicitly telling students this, but by the ways in which the read-alouds are orchestrated by Ibett and the other teachers. Once again, as Ibett (unit 19) brought up that she might have developed the classroom conversation more, I reiterated how it is difficult to make such decisions "in absolute time," but that underlying principles and strategies could guide the moment-by-moment implementation.

Then, in unit 22, I focused on Ibett's response to Celia's seemingly incorrect "water" answer that provided Celia a rationale for her answer—that "I guess she remembered yesterday we had lots of water." Because I have observed Anne use a similar strategy, which is another type of intertextual link to previous curriculum or discourse, I remarked that such an approach gave value to students' ideas even when they may not seem relevant or correct.

In unit 24, I also brought up the lack of boys speaking in the read-aloud video clip. Ibett explained that she thought that girls spoke more because, in the beginning of the year, the boys in her bilingual classroom were limited in English, but that had changed later when she began to code switch to Spanish. Pursuing the participation issue in general, I talked about the importance to be on the lookout for those students, who did not talk as much, to encourage their contributions. Anne, then, brought up the question of how to involve focal students or not. As part of the research, 10 focal students in each classroom are identified, so we can have in-depth profiles of students' development during the two units. In the last unit, Maria addressed the tensions—the stance as a teacher versus the stance as researcher—that teachers experience in a CAR project as ours. She stressed that if they are conflicted about which stance should be adopted, they should consider teaching priorities over research ones and that we would document their decisions regarding them in the context of the research.

Thus, critical points were examined in our meeting discussion of Ibett's read-aloud. Moreover, the last concern that was addressed raises differences between the two CAR projects. Although both rely on the same principles, in the first CAR project, the teacher researchers' role reflected more agency because their own inquiries were center stage, which were facilitated and documented by the project as a whole. In the second project, all teachers implemented the same activities in the same order in the two units (because we want to explore within and across grade differences), although they had flexibility in doing them. And, in this second CAR project, as previously indicated, we had focal students we were tracking in these classroom experiences, as well as others we had only with them (e.g., pre- and postinterviews about the content of the two units and their views of being scientists). Thus, the role of the teacher researchers in this second project was different and the tensions they felt as teachers versus researchers were more prominent and explicit for them—and the university-based researchers.

Lincoln and Guba (1985) commented on how videotape recordings can provide the means to "capture and hold" episodes in the classroom that can later be examined and compared with other data, thereby furnishing referential adequacy for interpretations in studies. Certainly, videotape once again is serving this function for all of us in the research process in this second collaborative project. But importantly, its utility from the teacher researchers' perspective is that the videotape enables them to relive "being there," making it possible for them—actually, all of us together—to document and understand the teaching and learning in urban classrooms around integrated science-literacy curriculum.

In summary, both vignettes represent two different versions of the CAR principles discussed earlier in the chapter. They reflected efforts to enact dialogic discourse in the classroom and in our project meetings, thereby illustrating the kinds of struggles that occur when attempts are made to incorporate and value the voices of all participants. To this end, videotaping afforded a multimodal means to make sense of what we saw and heard as classroom practice unfolds. It evoked issues of the power/knowledge concerns realized at both the classroom and the project level as we participated in the reflexivity required to conduct collaborative action research.

ONGOING ISSUES AND CHALLENGES FOR COLLABORATIVE ACTION RESEARCH

There are many ongoing issues and challenges in present and future collaborative action research. Here, I have concentrated on two interrelated ones that have been especially relevant in our project, and are likely to be pertinent in other collaborative school-university arrangements.

Issues of Validity and Reliability

Because collaborative action research involves an expanding notion of legitimate knowledge, teachers who have historically been silenced now have opportunities to develop their voice. And, in telling their educational stories, they have the right to debate and challenge the authority of others—university researchers certainly, as well as business people and parents, and district and state policy makers. Thus, when the central purpose of the educational research process is to empower voice, concepts of validity and reliability have to be reconceptualized. For example, as Gitlin et al. (1992) argued, old views of validity have to be altered:

> The validity or "truthfulness" of the data can be understood no longer as something extracted by [a university researcher] armed with a set of research procedures, but rather as a mutual process pursued by [university and teacher researchers] . . . that recognizes the value of practical knowledge, theoretical inquiry, and systematic examinations. The [university] researchers' knowledge is not assumed to be more legitimate than the [teacher researchers'], nor is their role one of helping the needy other. Rather, the researcher and [teacher researcher] attempt to come to a mutual understanding based on their own strongly articulated positions. (p. 27)

Thus, validity cannot be ignored, as Lather (1994) argued, because "[it] is . . . one that repeatedly resurfaces, one that can neither be avoided nor resolved, a fertile obsession given its intractability" (p. 37), but it has to be viewed differently from established renditions of it. In collaborative inquiry, all those involved are both co-researchers—everyone is involved in the thinking and decisions that generate ideas, manage the project, and come to conclusions about the whole research experience—and co-subjects—everyone participates in the inquiry enterprise that has been researched (Reason, 1994). In such a reciprocity, validity has more to do with validating and developing insights among university and teacher researchers; it involves a dialogue on how to interpret data by considering alternative perspectives (Altrichter, 1993), or as Lather (1986) suggests, it is "catalytic validity," which is the capacity of the research process to foster participants' knowing of their reality and urge them towards self-determined action.

According to Reason and Bradbury (2001b), there are five major questions about validity that can be posed in this "living process that is action research" (p. 11). At the core are *questions about emergence and enduring consequences* because of the emergent, evolutionary nature of action research. Due to the focus on teaching learning, *questions of outcome and practice are prominent*, which also concerns the validity of how different forms of knowledge themselves contributed by CAR projects, leading to *questions about plural ways of knowing*. Our relationships realized in our interactions that sustain the research evoke *questions of relational practice*. Finally, the major purposes of CAR projects—whether the topics of inquiry are worthwhile to pursue—involve *questions about significance*. Thus, accomplishing a new rigor to promote a "validity of knowledge in process" (Reason & Rowan, 1981) is quite complex and is an ongoing challenge in collaborative action research.

Reliability has been seen in a new light as well. Naturally occurring situations, such as those found in classrooms, are changeable. Moreover, the aim of collaborative action research is to disrupt the status quo by developing and putting into practice certain action strategies in the hope of changing and improving it. Consequently, the traditional idea of reliability as a kind of "repeating the research," that is, the ability of different independent researchers being able to come up with the same conclusions by using the same procedures, is clearly problematic in collaborative research (Altrichter, Posch, & Simekh, 1993; Gitlin et al., 1992). When voice is the goal of research, it is not expected (indeed, nor even desirable) that team members of university and teacher researchers would initially come up with the same conclusions. Procedures have to be developed in particular projects, even when CAR projects reflect different arrangements, as the two vignettes illustrated. As Gitlin et al. (1992) argued, "Reliability . . . cannot be based on duplicating procedures, but rather must center on attempts to satisfy the underlying principle of voice and its relation to a particular type of school change" (p. 28). Thus, because particular procedures cannot be applied unchanged from context to context, each collaborative project has its own challenge in developing its specific "reliability of voice."

Claiming Expertise Without an Authoritarian Voice

Closely related to the teachers' struggles to co-construct knowledge and share power with their students in dialogic instruction and discussion in the classroom is the issue of university researchers' struggles to shed their authoritarian voices in collaborative arrangements. In the efforts to develop and leave spaces for the voices of teachers who have been historically silenced, there has been a tendency on the part of university researchers to draw back so as not to impose these outsiders' views too much. Yet, a true collaboration has to have both university and teacher researchers claiming their respective expertise in the research process (Oyler & Pappas, 1992). This is because in such a partnership there is an assumption that neither is more "needy" of the other, or that neither contributes knowledge to the collaborative process that is more legitimate (Gitlin et al., 1992; Lewis & Ketter, 2004; Treleaven, 1994). Too frequently, teachers sharing authority with their students have been conceived of as merely teachers moving away from the "hard place" of authoritarianism to the other side of the dichotomy, namely the "soft place" of abdicated authority (Oyler, 1996; Oyler & Becker, 1997). Such a view does not regard this sharing of authority as the coconstruction of knowledge by both teachers and students. Thus, so as not to make the same mistake, university participants have to overcome their reluctance not to share their ideas or interpretations in collaborative inquiry.

That does not mean that in so doing, there would not be times when university researchers might go beyond their claiming expertise in their interactions with teacher researchers. For example, in the weekly meeting discourse provided in the previous section, there were places where I, in the first CAR vignette, and Maria and I, in the second vignette, shared our expertise. For example, in the first vignette, I asked Dorothy to reexamine her responses to the boy's question about whether the book was a poem, since I thought it was so relevant to her inquiry, and then later I brought up the terms *mock participation* and *procedural display* to put a name on the phenomenon that Dorothy and the other teachers were recognizing and questioning in their practice. However, as I have reflected on my responses in this discourse with Dorothy, I felt that I might have cut her off a couple of times, and although I believe that my role was to ask questions for the teacher researchers to consider, I have also wondered if I might have been too pushy—that is, gone over some collaborative boundary, so to speak. In the second vignette, while Ibett and two other teachers (of the four teachers present during the meeting at that time) contributed to our conversation, Maria and I certainly talked the most. Thus, although I think we were supportive of Ibett's efforts in enacting dialogic read-alouds and raised important issues for her and all teachers to consider, some of which were specific and important to the particular arrangement of this second CAR project, I have deliberated if we should have found ways to encourage Ibett to respond more on her analysis of the read-aloud, or invited Neveen, the fourth teacher present, to bring up what she noticed about the classroom interactions and talk.

Thus, I am now publicly vulnerable in these exchanges in terms of collaboration. However, as I have read and reviewed the many writings on collaborative action research, I have noticed that it is rare to find quotes of the discourse used by university researchers in this work; there seems to be resistance to express the details of their part of the dialogue that they have with teacher researchers. Thus, besides making problematic the representation and the voice of teacher researchers in our writing, we have to think long and hard about why university researchers have been unable to represent themselves—warts and all—in academic discourse. Consequently, this is another ongoing challenge in developing new genres to report on collaborative action research.

Summary and Making "Collaboration" Problematic to "Keep Voices Alive and Well"

Throughout this chapter, I have stressed the importance and difficulty of making collaboration ever present in the methodologies in collaborative action research. Because of the dominant perspectives in educational research, only by being vigilant in the entire collaborative research process will there be any chance to "keep authentic voices alive and well" (Schratz, 1993). To return to the Bakhtin (1981, 1986) framework offered in the first section of the chapter, as attempts are made to include the point of view and "speaking consciousness" of both university and teacher researchers in the dialogue of collaboration, there will be an ongoing conflict in this process because of this history.

Moreover, as it challenges the traditional hierarchical differences between university researchers and teacher researchers within the educational community, CAR projects represent a new activism to become practically critical as to promote democratic schooling (Gitlin, 1994; Noffke & Stevenson, 1995; Reason & Bradbury, 2001b). Creating dialogic classroom discourse in urban classrooms so that children from diverse ethnolinguistic backgrounds are not viewed as being "deficient" but instead are viewed as "knowers" who are able to contribute greatly to the understandings coconstructed with their teachers is a political enterprise (Pappas, 1999). That is, such CAR projects also struggle to incorporate a "political view of validity" (Gitlin et al., 1992). Thus, as in jazz, new improvisations will need to be woven into the methods of this research (Oldfather & West, 1994) to achieve these good intentions of inclusion and emancipation, and, as been argued here, videotaping in CAR projects has a new role in these efforts.

ACKNOWLEDGMENTS

The research reported in this chapter has been supported by two grants: a Spencer Foundation grant to Christine C. Pappas; and a National Science Foundation ROLE grant (REC-0411593) to Maria Varelas and Christine C. Pappas. The data presented, statements made, and views expressed in this chapter are solely the responsibilities of the author.

REFERENCES

Allen, J. (Ed.). (1999). *Class actions: Teaching for social justice in elementary and middle school.* New York: Teachers College Press.

Altrichter, H. (1993). The concept of quality in action research: Giving practitioners a voice in educational research. In M. Schratz (Ed.), *Qualitative voices in educational research* (pp. 40–55). London: Falmer Press.

Altrichter, H., Posch, O., & Somekh, B. (1993). *Teachers investigate their work: An introduction to the methods of action research.* London: Routledge.

Au, K. H., & Jordan, C. (1981). Teaching reading to Hawaiian children: Analysis of a culturally appropriate instructional event. *Anthropology and Education Quarterly, 11,* 91–115.

Bakhtin, M. M. (1981). *The dialogic imagination: Four essays by M. M. Bakhtin.* M. Holquist (Ed.) (M. Holquist & C. Emerson, Trans.). Austin, TX: University of Texas Press.

Bakhtin, M. M. (1986). *Speech genres and other late essays.* C. Emerson & M. Holquist (Eds.) (V. W. McGee, Trans.). Austin, TX: University of Texas Press.

Bickel, W. E., & Hattrup, R. A. (1995). Teachers and researchers in collaboration: Reflections on the process. *American Educational Research Journal, 32,* 35–62.

Bloome, D. (1994). Reading as a social process in a middle school classroom. In D. Graddol, J. Maybin, & B. Stierer (Eds.), *Researching language and literacy in social context* (pp. 100–129). Bristol, PA: Multilingual Matters.

Bloome, D., & Bailey, F. (1992). Studying language and literacy through events, particularity, and intertextuality. In R. Beach, J. L. Green, M. L. Kamil, & T. Shanahan (Eds.), *Multidisciplinary perspectives on literacy research* (pp. 181–210). Urbana, IL: National Conference on Research in English.

Bloome, D., & Egan-Robertson, A. (1993). The social construction of intertextuality in classroom reading and writing lessons. *Reading Research Quarterly, 28,* 305–333.

Borthwick, A. C. (2001). Dancing in the dark? Learning more about what makes partnerships work. In R. Ravid & M. G. Handler (Eds.), *The many faces of school-university collaboration: Characteristics of successful partnerships* (pp. 23–41). Englewood, CO: Teacher Ideas Press.

Burbules, N. C. (1993). *Dialogue in teaching: Theory and practice.* New York: Teachers College Press.

Cameron, D., Frazer, E., Harvey, P., Rampton, M. B. H., & Richardson, R. (1992). *Researching language: Issues of power and method.* London: Routledge.

Cazden, C. B. (1992). *Whole language plus: Essays on literacy in the United States and New Zealand.* New York: Teachers College Press.

Cazden, C. B. (2001). *Classroom discourse: The language of teaching and learning.* Portsmouth, NH: Heinemann.

Cochran-Smith, M., & Lytle, S. L. (1993). *Inside/Outside: Teacher research and knowledge.* New York: Teachers College Press.

Cope, B., & Kalantzis, M. (Eds.). *Multiliteracies: Literacy learning and the design of social futures.* London: Routledge.

Delamont, S. (1992). *Fieldwork in educational settings: Methods, pitfalls and perspectives.* London: Falmer Press.

Delpit, L. (1995). *Other people's children: Cultural conflict in the classroom.* New York: The New Press.

Edwards, D., & Mercer, N. (1987). *Common knowledge: The development of understanding in the classroom.* London: Routledge.

Erickson, F. (1986). Qualitative methods in research on teaching. In M. C. Wittrock (Ed.), *Handbook of research on teaching* (3rd ed.) (pp. 119–161). New York: Macmillan.

Foster, M. (1992). Sociolinguistics and the African-American community: Implications for literacy. *Theory into Practice, 32,* 303–311.

Gaventa, J., & Cornwall, A. (2001). Power and knowledge. In P. Reason & H. Bradbury (Eds.), *Handbook of action research: Participatory inquiry and practice* (pp. 70–80). London: Sage.

Gee, J. P. (2004). Language in the science classroom: Academic social languages as the heart of school-based literacy. In E. W. Saul (Ed.), *Crossing borders in literacy and science instruction: Perspectives on theory and practice* (pp. 13–32). Newark, DE: International Reading Association.

Glesne, C. (1999). *Becoming qualitative researchers: An introduction*. New York: Longman.

Gonzalez, N., Moll, L. C., & Amanti, C. (Eds.). (2005). *Funds of knowledge, theorizing practices in households, communities, and classrooms*. Mahwah, NJ: Lawrence Erlbaum Associates.

Gitlin, A. (1994). The shifting terrain of methodological debates. In A. Gitlin (Ed.), *Power and method: Political activism and educational research* (pp. 1–7). New York: Routledge.

Gitlin, A., Bringhurst, K., Burns, M., Cooley, V., Myers, B., Price, K., et al. (1992). *Teachers' voices for school change: An introduction to educative research*. New York: Teachers College Press.

Gitlin, A., & Russell, R. (1994). Alternative methodologies and the research context. In A. Gitlin (Ed.), *Power and method: Political activism and educational research* (pp. 181–202). New York: Routledge.

Gitlin, A. D. (1990). Educative research, voice and school change. *Harvard Educational Review, 60*, 443–466.

Gore, J. M. (1993). *The struggle for pedagogies: Critical and feminist discourses as regimes of truth*. New York: Routledge.

Grifalconi, A. (1987). *Darkness and the butterfly*. Boston, MA: Little Brown.

Gutierrez, K. D. (1994). How talk, context, and script shape contexts for learning: A cross-case comparison of journal sharing. *Linguistics and Education, 5*, 335–365.

Handler, M. G., & Ravid, R. (2001). Models of school-university collaboration. In R. Ravid & M. G. Handler (Eds.), *The many faces of school-university collaboration: Characteristics of successful partnerships* (pp. 3–10). Englewood, CO: Teacher Ideas Press.

Heath, B. (1982). What no bedtime story means: Narrative skills at home and school. *Language in Society, 11*, 49–76.

Heath, S. B. (1983). *Ways with words*. Cambridge, U.K.: Cambridge University Press.

Heron, J. (1981a). Philosophical basis for a new paradigm. In P. Reason & J. Rowan (Eds.), Human inquiry: A sourcebook of new paradigm research (pp. 19–35). NewYork: John Wiley & Sons:

Heron, J. (1981b). Experiential research methodology. In P. Reason & J. Rowan (Eds.), *Human inquiry: A sourcebook of new paradigm research* (pp. 153–166). New York: John Wiley & Sons.

Heron, J. (1992). *Feeling and personhood: Psychology in another key*. London: Sage.

Holquist, M., & Emerson, C. (1981). Glossary (M. Holquist & C. Emerson, Trans.). In M. Holquist (Ed.), *The dialogic imagination: Four essays by M. M. Bakhtin* (pp. 423–434). Austin, TX: University of Texas Press.

Hughes-Freeland, F. (2004). *Working images: Epilogue. In S. Pink, L. Kurti, & A. I. Afonso (Eds.), Working images: Visual research and representation in ethnography* (pp. 204–218). London: Routledge.

Jewitt, C., & Kress, G. (Eds.). (2003). *Multimodal literacy*. New York: Peter Lang.

Kamberelis, G., & Dimitriadis, G. (2005). *Qualitative inquiry: Approaches to language and literacy research*. New York: Teachers College Press.

Kirshner, D, & Whitson, J. A. (Eds.). (1997). *Situated cognition: Social, semiotic, and psychological perspectives*. Mahwah, NJ: Lawrence Erlbaum Associates.

Knowles, C., & Sweetman, P. (2004). Introduction. In C. Knowles & P. Sweetman (Eds.), *Picturing the social landscape: Visual methods and the sociological imagination* (pp. 1–17). London: Routledge.

Kress, G. (2000). Design and transformation. In B. Cope & M. Kalantzis (Eds.), *Multiliteracies: Literacy learning and the design of social futures* (pp. 153–161). London: Routledge.

Kress, G. (2003). *Literacy in the new media age*. London: Routledge.

Kress, G., & van Leeuwen, T. (2001). *Multimodal discourse: The modes and media of contemporary communication*. London: Arnold.

Lather, P. (1986). Research as praxis. *Harvard Educational Review, 56*, 257–277.

Lather, P. (1994). Fertile obsession: Validity after post-structuralism. In A. Gitlin (Ed.), *Power and method: Political activism and educational research* (pp. 36–60). New York: Routledge.

Lave, J. (1988). *Cognition in practice*. New York: Cambridge University Press.

Lee, C. D., & Smagorinsky, P. (Eds.). (2000). *Vygotskian perspectives on literacy research: Constructing meaning through collaborative inquiry*. Cambridge, U.K.: Cambridge University Press.

Lemke, J. L. (1985). Ideology, intertextuality, and the notion of register. In J. D. Benson & W. S. Greaves (Eds.), *Systemic perspectives on discourse: Selected theoretical papers from the 9th international systemic workshop, Vol. I* (pp. 275–294). Norwood, NJ: Ablex.

Lewis, C., & Ketter, J. (2004). Learning as social action: Interdiscursity in a teacher and research study group. In R. Rogers (Ed.), *An introduction to critical discourse analysis in education* (pp. 117–146). Mahwah, NJ: Lawrence Erlbaum Associates.

Lieberman, A. (1986). Collaborative research: Working with, not working on. *Educational Leadership, 43*, 28–33.

Lieberman, A. (1992). The meaning of scholarly activity and the building of community. *Educational Researcher, 21*, 5–12.

Lincoln, Y., & Guba, E. (1985). *Naturalistic inquiry*. Beverly Hills, CA: Sage.

Lindfors, J. W. (1999). Children's inquiry: Using language to make sense of the world. New York: Teachers College Press.

Luke, C., & Gore, J. (1992). Introduction. In C. Luke & J. Gore (Eds.), *Feminisms and critical pedagogy* (pp. 1–14). New York: Routledge.

Maguire, P. (2001). Uneven ground: Feminisms and action research. In P. Reason & H. Bradbury (Eds.), *Handbook of action research: Participative inquiry and practice* (pp. 59–69). London: Sage.

McCollum, P. (1991). Cross-cultural perspectives on classroom discourse and literacy. In E. H. Heibert (Ed.), *Literacy for a diverse society: Perspectives, practices and policies* (pp. 108–121). New York: Teachers College Press.

McNiff, J., with Whitehead, J. (2002). *Action research: Principles and practice*. London: Routledge/Falmer.

Mehan, H. (1993). Why I like to look: On the use of videotape as an instrument in educational research. In M. Schratz (Ed.), *Qualitative voices in educational research* (pp. 93–105). London: Falmer Press.

Mercer, N. (1995). *The guided construction of knowledge: Talk amongst teachers and learners*. Clevedon, U.K.: Multilingual Matters.

Michaels, S. (1981). "Sharing time": Children's narrative styles and differential access to literacy. *Language in Society, 10*, 423–442.

Miller, J. L. (1990). Creating spaces and finding voices: Teachers collaborating for empowerment. Albany, NY: State University of New York Press.

Miller, J. L. (1992). Exploring power and authority issues in a collaborative research project. *Theory into Practice, 31*, 165–172.

Moll, L. C. (Ed.). (1990). *Vygotsky and education: Instructional implications and applications of sociohistorical psychology*. Cambridge, U.K.: Cambridge University Press.

Nespor, J., & Barylske, J. (1991). Narrative discourse and teacher knowledge. *American Educational Research Journal, 28*, 805–823.

Newman, D. P., Griffin, P., & Cole, M. (1989). *The construction zone: Working for cognitive change in school*. Cambridge, U.K.: Cambridge University Press.

Nieto, S. (2000). *Affirming diversity: The sociopolitical context of multicultural education*. New York: Longman.

Noffke, S. E., & Stevenson, R. B. (Ed.). (1995). *Educational action research: Becoming practically critical*. New York: Teachers College Press.

Nystrand, M. (1997). *Opening dialogue: Understanding the dynamics of language and learning in the English classroom*. New York: Teachers College Press.

Oja, S. N., & Smulyan, L. (1989). *Collaborative action research: A developmental approach*. London: Falmer Press.

Oldfather, P., & West, J. (1994). Qualitative research as jazz. *Educational Researcher, 23*, 22–26.

O'Malley, D. A. (2001). It is never too late to change! Rethinking read-alouds for third graders. In C. C. Pappas & L. B. Zecker (Eds.), *Teacher inquiries in literacy teaching-learning: Learning to collaborate in elementary urban classrooms* (pp. 143–155). Mahwah, NJ: Lawrence Erlbaum Associates.

Oyler, C. J. (1996). *Making room for students: Sharing authority in Room 104*. New York: Teachers College Press.

Oyler, C. J., & Becker, J. (1997). Teaching beyond the traditional-progressive dichotomy: Sharing authority and sharing vulnerability. *Curriculum Inquiry, 27,* 453–467.

Oyler, C. J., & Pappas, C. C. (1992, October). *Claiming and sharing our authority in collaboration.* Paper presented at the Bergamo Conference, Dayton, OH.

Pappas, C. C. (1997). Making 'collaboration' problematic in collaborative school-university research: Studying with urban teacher researchers to transform literacy curriculum genres. In J. Flood, S. B. Heath, & D. Lapp (Eds.), A *handbook of research on teaching through the communicative and visual arts* (pp. 215–231). New York: Simon Schuster Macmillan.

Pappas, C. C. (1999). Becoming literate in the borderlands. In A. Goncu (Ed.), *Children's engagement in the world: Sociocultural perspectives* (pp. 228–260). Cambridge, U.K.: Cambridge University Press.

Pappas, C. C., Hart, S., Escobar, D, Jones, H., & O'Malley, D. A. (2001). Two teachers' efforts to transform the reading-aloud curriculum genre for collaboration: Examining shifts of process and content dimensions of sharing authority. In C. C. Pappas & L. B. Zecker (Eds.), *Transforming literacy curriculum genres: Working with teacher researchers in urban classrooms* (pp. 127–156). Mahwah, NJ: Lawrence Erlbaum Associates.

Pappas, C. C., Kiefer, B. Z., & Levstik, L. S. (2006). *An integrated language perspective in the elementary school: An action approach.* Boston, MA: Pearson Education.

Pappas, C. C., Varelas, M., Barry, A., & Rife, A. (2003). Dialogic inquiry around information texts: The role of intertextuality in constructing scientific understandings in urban primary classrooms. *Linguistics and Education, 13(4),* 435–482.

Pappas, C. C., Varelas, M., Barry, A., & Rife, A. (2004). Promoting dialogic inquiry in information book read-alouds: Young urban children's ways of making sense in science. In E. W. Saul (Ed.), *Crossing borders in literacy and science instruction: Perspectives on theory and practice* (pp. 161–189). Newark, NJ: International Reading Association.

Pappas, C. C., & Zecker, L. B. (Eds.). (2001a). *Transforming literacy curriculum genres: Working with teacher researchers in urban classrooms.* Mahwah, NJ: Lawrence Erlbaum Associates.

Pappas, C. C., & Zecker, L. B. (Eds.). (2001b). *Teacher inquiries in literacy teaching-learning: Learning to collaborate in elementary urban classrooms.* Mahwah, NJ: Lawrence Erlbaum Associates.

Pappas, C. C., & Zecker, L. B. (2001c). Urban teacher researchers' struggles in sharing power with their students: Exploring changes in literacy curriculum genres. In C. C. Pappas, & L. B. Zecker (Eds.), *Transforming literacy curriculum genres: Working with teacher researchers in urban classrooms* (pp. 1–31). Mahwah, NJ: Lawrence Erlbaum Associates.

Pink, S. (2004). Introduction: Situating visual research. In S. Pink, L. Kurti, & A. I. Afonso (Eds.), *Working images: Visual research and representation in ethnography* (pp. 1–12). London: Routledge.

Prosser, J. (2000). The moral maze of image ethics. In H. Simons & R. Usher (Eds.), *Situated ethics in educational research* (pp. 116–132). London: Routledge/Falmer.

Ravid, R., & Handler, M. G. (Eds.). (2001). *The many faces of school-university collaboration: Characteristics of successful partnerships.* Englewood, CO: Teacher Ideas Press.

Reason, P. (Ed.). (1988). *Human inquiry in action.* London: Sage.

Reason, P. (1994). Human inquiry as discipline and practice. In P. Reason (Ed.), *Participation in human inquiry* (pp. 40–56). London: Sage.

Reason, P., & Bradbury, H. (Eds.). (2001a). *Handbook of action research: Participative inquiry and practice.* London: Sage.

Reason, P., & Bradbury, H. (2001b). Introduction: Inquiry and participation in search of a world worthy of human aspiration. In P. Reason & H. Bradbury (Eds.), *Handbook of action research: Participative inquiry and practice* (pp. 1–26). London: Sage.

Reason, P., & Heron, J. (1986). Research with people: The paradigm of co-operative experiential inquiry. *Person Centered Review, 1,* 456–475.

Reason, P., & Rowan, J. (1981). Issues of validity in new paradigm research. In P. Reason & J. Rowan (Eds.), *Human inquiry: A sourcebook of new paradigm research* (pp. 239–262). NewYork: John Wiley & Sons.

Reyes, M. de la Luz. (1991). A process approach to literacy instruction for Spanish-speaking students: In search of a best fit. In E. F. Heibert (Ed.), *Literacy for a diverse society: Perspectives, practices, and policies* (pp. 157–171). New York: Teachers College Press.

Reyes, M. de la Luz. (1992). Challenging venerable assumptions: Literacy instruction for linguistically different students. *Harvard Educational Review, 62,* 427–446.

Richardson, V. (1994). Conducting research on practice. *Educational Researcher, 23,* 5–10.

Rogoff, B., & Wertsch, J. V. (1984). *Children's learning in the zone of proximal development.* San Francisco: Jossey-Bass.

Sawyer, R. K. (2004). Creative teaching: Collaborative discussion as disciplined improvisation. *Educational Researcher, 33,* 12–20.

Schratz, M. (1993). Voices in educational research: An introduction. In M. Schratz (Ed.), *Qualitative voices in educational research* (pp. 1–6). London: Falmer Press.

Sinclair, J. M., & Coulthard, R. M. (1975). *Toward an analysis of discourse.* London: Oxford University Press.

Treleaven, L. (1994). Making a space: A collaborative inquiry with women as staff development. In P. Reason (Ed.), *Participation in human inquiry.* London: Sage.

Tucker-Raymond, E., Pappas, C. C., & Varelas, M. (2005, November). *That's a lot to digest: Exploring methodological issues in multimodal analysis of competent communication in an elementary school classroom.* Paper presented at the National Reading Conference, Miami, FL.

Unsworth, L. (2001). *Teaching multiliteracies across the curriculum: Changing contexts of text and image in classroom practice.* Buckingham, U.K.: Open University Press.

Varelas, M., & Pappas, C. C. (in press a). Intertextuality in read-alouds of integrated science-literacy units in primary classrooms: Opportunities for the development of thought and language. *Cognition and Instruction.*

Varelas, M., & Pappas, C. C., with Rife, A. (in press b). Exploring the role of intertextuality in concept construction: Urban second-graders make sense of evaporation, boiling, and condensation. *Journal of Research in Science Teaching.*

Varelas, M., Pappas, C. C., & Rife, A. (2005). Dialogic inquiry in an urban 2nd grade classroom: How intertextuality shapes and is shaped by social interactions and scientific understandings. In M.-W. Roth & R. Yerrick (Eds.), *Establishing scientific classroom discourse communities: Multiple voices of research on teaching and learning* (pp. 139–168). Mahwah, NJ: Lawrence Erlbaum Associates.

Vygotsky, L. S. (1962). *Thought and language.* Cambridge, MA: MIT Press.

Vygotsky, L. S. (1978). *Mind in society: The development of higher psychological processes.* Cambridge, U.K.: Cambridge University Press.

Wells, G. (1999). *Dialogic inquiry: Toward a sociocultural practice and theory of education.* Cambridge, U.K.: Cambridge University Press.

Wells, G. (Ed.). (2001). *Action, talk, and text: Learning and teaching through inquiry.* New York: Teachers College Press.

Wells, G., & Chang-Wells, G. L. (1992). *Constructing knowledge together: Classrooms as centers of inquiry and literacy.* Portsmouth, NH: Heinemann.

Wertsch, J. V. (1989). A sociocultural approach to mind. In W. Damon (Ed.), *Child development today and tomorrow* (pp. 14–33). San Francisco: Jossey-Bass.

Wertsch, J. V. (1991). *Voices of the mind: A sociocultural approach to mediated action.* Cambridge, MA: Harvard University Press.

Wlllinsky, J. (1990). *The New Literacy: Redefining reading and writing in the schools.* New York: Routledge.

Young, R. (1992). *Critical theory and classroom talk.* Clevedon, U.K.: Multilingual Matters.

Zoehfeld, K. W. (1998). *What is the world made of: All about solids, liquids, and gases.* New York: HarperCollins.

•15•

REMAKING SENSE, RESHAPING INQUIRY: REIMAGINING METAPHORS FOR A LITERACY OF THE POSSIBLE

Lorri Neilsen
MOUNT SAINT VINCENT UNIVERSITY

> Unable to see her, I speak in a kind of blindness, not knowing what dance is being made of me, what puns of the thumb, tough similes of the fingers, how I translate into bone. (Atwood, 1995)

Our responsibility as literacy educators and researchers is to bring literacy to life. We see inquiry into literacy as a process of changing an abstract concept into a transformative verb. Coming to an understanding of the cultures of the home, the school, and the academy as sites of struggle and hope, encoded and inscribed with politically charged values, expectations, and assumptions, we begin to see inquiry and research in literacy as partial, limited, shifting, and actively constructed. We see literacy as not merely an intellectual activity, but a way we are in the world. (Neilsen, 1989)

And, the way we are in the world is embodied. Our literacies and our inquiries are not limited to our head; they are also of the heart and of the body. We are beings who make sense, in all the many meanings of that term. As Abram (1996) suggested, the flesh of language and experience are mutually constitutive; the ground of our human and material lives shapes us as our language shapes us, and the process is unending. Inquiry is a stance to the world that knows interpretation to be an ecological process, a project of integrating and furthering sustainable growth. We are connected, and we are responsible—please keep response-able . . . it's an intentional play on the word, it's not a misspelling .

As an educator, researcher, and poet, I am intrigued by the way the metaphors we use can shape how we do what we do. What are the metaphors that have guided our inquiry into literacy? How might we work against metaphors that constrain, and how might we imagine otherwise?

IMPOSSIBLE METAPHORS

Traditional notions of literacy and literacy research have been guided by impossible metaphors that have limited our notions of literacy. Like carefully dressed, clipboard-carrying assistants trailing theory down its many well-defined hallways only to discover darkness, dead ends, or a painted movie set, these metaphors have succeeded in shaping methods of inquiry, often in less than helpful ways. They have not always achieved what we hoped they would achieve: robust and generative understandings of what literacy is, does, and can be; ways of supporting and sustaining growth in literacy for children of all cultures, between and within our national and global communities; and creating the groundwork for educational reform, including schooling practices that invite students and teachers into—rather than alienate them from—themselves, their communities, and a sense of all that is possible.

Even our pluralizing the concept of literacy—computer, media, visual, among others—has not reduced our tendencies to define, and hence confine; to describe, only to prescribe; and to teach, which too quickly can turn to test.

Three pervasive metaphors for literacy—the industrial model, the medical model, and the training model—have roots in educational research, but the growth still creeps among the public and policymakers, covering more ground than we have any hope of reclaiming. Each of these models is informed by a verbocentric ideology; each tends to separate reading and writing from other ways of knowing.

The industrial or mechanistic model (Neilsen, A., 1989) characterizes literacy in terms of parts and components within a well-functioning machine. Learning literacy involves learning perfectible subskills; teaching literacy involves sequencing the instruction of these skills in such a manner as to result in a well-functioning machine. In society, this industrial metaphor plays itself out in functional notions of literacy as a measurable competence. It is also largely pan-contextual and inert.

The medical metaphor characterizes our literacy in terms of wellness or pathology. Terms such as *deficiency, diagnosis,* and *treatment* mark this perspective. Diseased parts and aberrant behavior can, with the correct treatment, be replaced or eradicated. "Healthy," literate behavior is normal, standardized behavior: School reading and writing become the primary indicators of literacy and the sites for evaluation and assessment. Compliance becomes a marker for health.

The training center, however, is perhaps the most popular metaphor for literacy and literacy education. Behaviorist in its underpinning, this metaphor suggests that a diet of rewards—stickers to smiley faces to gold stars to scholarships—will foster literacy. Those who do not perform as required receive frowns, Fs, threats of being held back, or continual reminders of their statuses in the academic basement. My youngest son's teacher devised a sticker system to encourage his sitting still to do his worksheets. His refusal both shocked and puzzled her: She sincerely believed he would work for stickers. Certainly, some children will do this in some circumstances; other children will not, regardless of the reward.

What do these metaphors reveal about our sense of what literacy is and does? Each tends to externalize the learning and teaching of literacy, perpetuating the myth that literacy is something we think about and do, rather than something we live inside. Each of these metaphors spawns research activity that reinforces the metaphor, closing off possibilities for new forms of inquiry.

But, more germane to this discussion is that these metaphors for literacy learning and research are verbocentric, patriarchal, and paternalistic: They reinforce the text's power to create us in an image whose values include preservation of the hierarchy, of competition, and of accountability, and whose means of naming the world have limited imaginings of text and textuality.

Countless feminist researchers and educators have written about instituions' tendencies to appropriate text into their discursive practices in ways that alienate, silence, and violate the majority of the world's population striving for a literacy of the possible (Neilsen, L., 1998). As a researcher and teacher educator, I must work on my own practice. I must seek integrity between my pedagogy and my inquiry so that these practices continually find each other out.

The questions, then, are not about course syllabi but about daily work in the relations among people and ideas. What do I do in my own classroom to perpetuate silence and disembodied knowing about literacies? And, by promoting principles of feminist and critical inquiry that have evolved in my practices as a researcher, how do I avoid creating another regime which silences and alienates teachers from themselves and their inquiry? How do I engage in my own inquiry to nudge myself toward a more responsible way of living? SEE earlier note: Please keep response-able (meaning: ability to respond).

LIVING INQUIRY

The nights are cooler now that summer is passing; they seem darker, full of unplayed drama. An early morning walk reveals the goldenrods, now as tall as my child, and the velvet white stalks of pearly everlasting along the path. The air is heavy, even sweet, and the woods are so silent that, when I step on the spongy moss, I cannot hear my steps. It is only the tensing, and then breaking, of filament against my skin, a spiderweb spun across trees in the night, which reminds me that I am both myself and Other here. Here? Where is here? In these woods, in this part of the country, this season, this world of worlds.

Just as in late summer, I come to embody August; I have found over the years that I have come to embody inquiry and writing. Words have shaped, guided, informed, constrained, and told my life across many texts and many years.

My love affair with words, like any love affair, is fraught with tension and passion. To begin writing, I do a dance I have since found is common: I read, I tidy the house, I ponder, flirt with an approach and then abandon it with a shrug, pore over books and papers and leave them open on the floor, the desk, the bed. I embrace the rhythm of certain ideas (right now, I am waltzing with both Franck's, 1993, notion of the reflex arc and Zwicky's, 2003, perspectives on metaphor and domestic understanding). I will move across many floors of understanding until the gestures, the nuances of these ideas become part of me, part of how my mind moves into words and the life they carry.

I will create a working environment, for a week or a month, that looks to others as though the room has been tossed by the Mafia. My mind will buzz with words, with continuities and discontinuities, and I will argue with myself until I reach clarity, insouciance, arrogance, humility, or boredom; any of these states will be fine. It is the processing, the induction, after all, the reaching for a state in medias res, hearing the hum in the center of silence. To write, I must wade into a textual ocean and disappear in order to appear. I come to embody words.

This state has nothing to do with finding the Muse or being a prose prima donna. Insight (or perception, or creativity, whatever one wants to call the state) has more to do with how attuned we are to the world around us. When I draw, I must become so saturated with my seeing that my fusion with the so-called object transcends conventional physical borders. Franck (1993) called this a state of seeing/drawing, meditative activity that requires us not to "look at" (for that is what separates us from objects, creating Other) but see: fully perceiving, the body, the eye, the hand becoming acutely sensitive antennae.

And that is where writing and inquiry begin, I believe. At a place as individuals where we are so attuned to the process we are connected to the world. This space is where literacy lives and breathes, where struggles and connection shift and strain. It is not an easy place to be, but it is alive, a kind of lyric presence that keeps us open (Neilsen, L., 2006). Name a human experience that calls on us as fully human and multidimensional and we all can list examples of that state of being: singing in a choir, weeding a garden, tinkering at the piano late on a winter's night. Each of these experiences opens up our perceptual pores, awakens in us responsiveness to the world in all its pain and beauty. Typically, though we let the stirring giant go back to sleep again, promising ourselves to allow life in more often.

Berman (1989) is not, I think, hyperbolic in his assertion that when we lose awareness of our bodies, our sense of ourselves as a tiny cell in a larger living planet, we look for -isms, and "from there it is a short step to seeing other -isms as life-threatening, and to seeing the Other as an enemy" (p. 343). The despair of mothers of sons across enemy lines is silent testimony to our failure as a species to cherish life more than the contest of ideologies. The alarming rate of extinction of species on this planet reminds us, on that rare occasion when we stop to think about it, how we have made an Other of the organism which feeds us. Creating an Other allows us to avoid response, and hence, responsibility. Keep response-ability—Do not correct, as it is not a misspelling—it's intentional

WHEN WE DEAD AWAKEN

> The flesh of my body is also the flesh of the earth, the flesh of experience. To know your own flesh, to know both the pain and joy it contains, is to come to know something much larger. (Berman, 1989, p. 344)

Once that awareness is reawakened, once we begin to hear, see, know, feel, and touch again, our alienation from others—from colleagues, from ideas, from the many Others we create to simplify our thinking and to dull our feeling—seems to diminish. As researchers, we are better equipped to communicate our experience when we see the inquiry process as a relationship, not only among people or participants, but also with our unarticulated selves and the earth which bears us. Greene (1988), writing about passivity and disinterest that can infect schooling, urged us to focus on "the range of human intelligences, the multiple languages and symbol systems available for ordering experience and making sense of the lived world" (p. 125). Reawakening our own and our students' understanding also reawakens our connections to others.

As adults, we are often alienated from the thinking and feeling of our body selves (John-Steiner, 1985). Children, especially preschool children, are not. They use all of their senses and abilities passionately to create knowledge and to embrace the world. In order to help children maintain the freshness of their perspectives throughout their schooling, we must nurture those same possibilities—the uses of a myriad of symbol systems and ways of knowing—in ourselves. What can we do, as educators, to awaken in ourselves the responsiveness necessary to hone, promote, and celebrate our own multiple ways of knowing the world, of making sense? What can we doing to resist institutional practices that stifle our growth as professionals? How can we foster our lyric understanding and appreciation of the world?

The metaphors we have used for literacy shape the educators as well as the learners. If we seek metaphors of embodiment and sense making, metaphors often used in feminist thought, we may find our perspectives on literacy and learning change, and so do we. In seminars on qualitative and feminist inquiry, I have attempted to promote new perspectives on our many human literacies in the hopes that educators will take these perspectives into their lives and their classrooms and, as a result, teach with more confidence, autonomy, humility, and joy.

CREATING A PATH BY WALKING

It will be hot in the city today but, here, on the rocks of Peggy's Cove, the early morning air is cold. The sun will burn off the fog by ten, but for now, we have sweaters as we walk among the whale-sized rocks whose lines dip toward the Atlantic. As teachers, we are careful to wear our sensible shoes; the notice posted near the lighthouse reminds visitors that the sea here is merciless; waves can, and do, reach up over the rocks and pull us in. I walk among the rocks and around the cove, stopping to admire the brightly colored homes. What must the residents think when visitors arrive, as we have, at 7:00 A.M.?

Agnes is on the wharf, talking to the fishermen who are loading their lobster traps. John is behind the lighthouse, at the edge of the water, using a tape recorder to capture the sound of the waves crashing against the boulders. Linda is perched next to a pool, a microcosm of aqua life nestled in the boulders, observing the movements of insects and suckers. Patricia is sketching, using an HB pencil to show the play of shadow and line in the rocks as the sun breaks through the fog. At the peak of the largest boulder, I can see Allison, prone on the grey expanse, a notebook in her hand. Near the shore, Carole aims her camera at a gull poised like a weathervane against the sky.

We are here before the busloads of tourists because the stunning beauty of Peggy's Cove is guaranteed to pull us out of words and texts and ideas into the physical power of the so-called natural world. It is guaranteed to bring us to our senses, and it does. This event, which I often include when I am teaching a summer course reminds us how bound we are to rooms and desks and constructions of words in various formats and guises; the alphabet for all its power can take us away from the unmediated experience of being in the landscape. When we return to text, it is with revised, sense-charged notions. Typically, a day such as this produces poetry, which always surprises the writer: he or she will return to class the next day, poem in hand, full of wonder and renewed inspiration. I felt alive again on those rocks, and I wrote this: Is this real research, she will ask?

Other opportunities have arisen over the years: creating a mural, performance poetry, working as a collective to create an art gallery installation, using dance or sound or paint or movement or music as forms of inquiry—engaging in the artistic practice for the sake of the practice—in ways that cause us to see inquiry (and thus, research) as integral to how we live and work in the world.

And, it is here, then, that we can begin. What is research? Who does it? What counts as knowing, and whose knowing is valued? Is there a line between research and inquiry, and if so, what is it? From the outset, I make my agenda explicit. As a researcher and as a teacher educator, my aims include the following:

- To demystify and to reclaim research and the inquiry process
- To encourage the use of multiple sign systems—many ways of knowing—particularly as they reawaken body understanding and aesthetic sensibilities, in order to open up the inquiry process, and in so doing, to revitalize professional commitment
- To promote an understanding of our multiple selves in relation to the cultures of the home, the school, and the academy and in so doing, promote our responsibility to those around us
- To encourage resistance of practices in the educational and institutional hierarchy that devalue situated inquiry and multiple ways of knowing; and to be open to understand how I am co-opted by those practices, and how I perpetuate them
- To demystify and to reclaim research and the inquiry process

> As people mature, they cease to believe in sides or Headmasters or highly ornamental pots. At any rate . . . it is notoriously difficult to fix labels of merit in such a way that they do not come off. (Woolf, 1929, p. 101)

Woven in the story of who I am and what I do as a researcher are, of course, the stories that form my history as a student, a teacher, a graduate student, an academic, and a poet. My struggle, which was much less painful than most, reminds me of my responsibility to other students, particularly women, who have felt outside themselves, silenced, and trivialized in education as a whole, and in the research process in particular. After all, research has created "a place where none of us lives and works—an 'objective' place wherein we are contrasted, compared, designed, and interpreted" (Chandler, 1992, p. 130). The study of research perspectives is often characterized by curricula which present research as hygienic, "out there" (Neilsen, L., 1998), and like a headmaster, authoritative in a way that does not promote resistance or critique.

The language of theory making and knowledge construction generalizes more than it particularizes; its coin is the testable assertion. Even though we know that theories are merely stories we tell ourselves about how the world works, we often give the assertions of theory much more credibility than our own experience. Teachers especially have been expected to be professionals: to silence or mask their preferences, their cultural biases, their ethnicities, and their politics to uphold a discourse of neutrality and objectivity.

The task of demystifying and reclaiming research and the inquiry process begs the question, "What counts as research?" Discussions around the seminar table with teachers invariably reveal how deeply encoded are the conventional notions of research. Men and women alike, even those who have conducted their own classroom research, continue to believe that real research searches for an objective truth, is synonymous with science, is conducted in institutions elsewhere by funded academics, and has little practical relevance to their home or their working lives. Research is logical, value free, tidy, and replicable. It claims merit and authority merely by its mention. Academic practices around research, which so often go unchallenged, reify text as the sole purveyor of research knowledge, elevate scientists and science, and perpetuate verbocentric practices in inquiry at all levels.

As the seminar facilitator, my task becomes showing the many ways by which we can take apart existing research products, to look behind them to see how they are constructed within political and personal exigencies and constraints and to recognize their fleeting and mutable nature. For example, teachers who want to explore classroom talk and who see that other researchers have published studies in that area must first be convinced that classroom talk is not closed as a topic, has not "been done," or has not been "covered already." They must then work to understand that their perspective on a subject will be unique. (Much of the work I do, I realize, is enmeshed in the problems created by our lack of professional esteem, how we are schooled to defer.) I remind people that everybody comes from somewhere, including a researcher. Using my own inquiry works well: The text they read, then, is connected to a face, a voice, and a history, none of which are "objective" or unflawed. The published text can then be seen as partial, provisional, exploratory, and tentative.

What works best to dismantle notions of "research" and "researcher," however, has been to invite teachers to engage in inquiry that arises from their own experiences, not as individuals, but as situated, relational beings. This "kitchen table" inquiry, as I called it (Neilsen, L., 1998), aims to create a space in the academy to make our daily micropolitical acts, the many circumstances and challenges of the ordinary, legitimate areas for study. Such inquiry both reveals experience and makes it problematic, and, as a result, forces new syntheses, different identity relations. Like Tai Chi, the movements are not static; the body moves fluidly from one position to another, poised momentarily, each movement leading to the next in order to maintain balance. Stylized moving with awareness, in tune with the world, makes inquiry come alive.

- To encourage the use of multiple sign systems, particularly as they reawaken body understanding and aesthetic sensibilities, in order to open up the inquiry process, and in so doing, to revitalize professional commitment

> The governing of our kind of society is done in concepts and symbols. (Smith, 1987, p. 87)

The work of C.S. Peirce provides a basis for an understanding of sense making or meaning making as a semiotic activity. A sign, he claimed, is "something that stands to somebody for something in some respect or capacity" (Peirce, quoted in Neilsen, L., 1998, p. 79) We make sense through a process of semiosis, in which our responding to a sign creates a "thirdness"—our meaning or apprehension of and for the sign. Only in the last decade have we begun to recognize the power of alternative sign systems in learning, in classrooms, and in research. However, what counts as research and inquiry largely continues to be documented and written in conventional text (as is, of course, this chapter).

The courses I have taught in inquiry (whether a general course in qualitative inquiry, or more specifically, feminist inquiry), have invited teachers to use many sign systems—from music to the visual arts to performance art, among others—to communicate their learning using those systems, and to consider their classroom teaching in light of these multiple sense-making literacies. What are they doing about stretching themselves as fully sense-making humans, and what kind of environment do they then create for their own students?

With such permission (or perhaps, requirement) to explore sign systems other than conventional written text, teachers exchange insights using video, pencil and charcoal drawings, watercolor and oil paintings, dramatic performances, scripted plays, musical compositions, photographic essays, computer graphics, children's books, fabric arts, dance, and comic routines. Typically, they relish the freedom that such expression affords, but they are also somewhat reticent to declare their enthusiasm to colleagues; such learning seems too much like play.

Teachers who conduct their own inquiry into making meaning in diverse ways renew their professional enthusiasm. Bridging various sign systems, playing with their intereducative potentials, reminds teacher researchers that they are whole beings, aesthetically and somatically real and alive. Their confidence in having risked and thrived, the connections among the learning that ensues, and the liberation from the word as the only signifier all combine to shift ground, to propel them forward to a fertile awareness of themselves and their own students.

On at least five occasions in as many years, teachers I have worked with in a graduate literacy program have undertaken an end-of-term multimedia installation or event that includes performance art, music, poetry, photographic displays, sound collages, visual art, playwriting, sculpture, dance, to name just a few of their arts-based projects. Each person has taken on a topic or issue of importance to her, and each has documented not only the inquiry process, but produced an artifact or an event to demonstrate the results of their journey. Last year, Kristen wrote poetry about teaching that was stunning in its originality and, in doing so, offered others a glimpse into her own teaching practice and into writing in general; Frank learned stomp, taught his students, and then taught our seminar group a few moves. They both claimed that the inquiry not only energized their teachings, but also energized their colleagues: What they considered initially to be brave inquiry turned out, instead, to be the kind of inspiration that renewed their commitment as professionals and increased their feelings of collegiality.

Sign systems, however well we explore them and however well we integrate them, are neither neutral nor sapped of ideology. They are politically charged, encoded in our social practices in ways that can build empires and assign value. At a pragmatic level, disciplines and activities in schools are marked, encoded with political, economic, and social importance or irrelevance. When teachers realize their responsibility in these cultures for assigning and assuming value to certain sign systems, it can open understanding about the everyday, and create opportunities to challenge the values that form a backdrop to everything they do. Suddenly, teacher researchers will see schools in a different light, their inquiries work both as belonging to a culture of its own creation and responsible for its critique and renewal.

- To promote an understanding of our multiple selves in relation to the cultures of the home, the school, and the academy and in so doing, promote our responsibility in those cultures

> So, I think . . . "our" problem, is how to have simultaneously an account of radical historical contingency for all knowledge claims and knowing subjects, a critical practice for which recognizing our own "semiotic technologies" for making meanings, and a no-nonsense commitment to faithful accounts of a "real" world, one that can be partially shared and that is friendly to earthwide projects of finite freedom, adequate material abundance, modest meaning in suffering, and limited happiness. (Haraway, 1991, p. 187)

While we engage in ongoing debates about the nature and existence of truth, looking askance at those claims that no truth exists as being equally problematic, we still have to live and work, teach children, feed the dog, and pay for groceries. We continue to struggle with daily racism and sexism and the quotidian inequities around us. This is not mere information; these are the "stones in our shoe" (Neilsen, L., 1994). Whether we are eldest in a large family from rural Canada, the child of an alcoholic, an immigrant, or the sister of a man who has just died of AIDS, we are unique in our combinations of stories and perspectives. Each of us comes from somewhere, but that "somewhere" casts a different shadow in each of our encounters with others.

The recognition that each of us is a constellation of differing positions according to the culture or context in which we find ourselves—and that these "multiple selves" negotiate and monitor ever-changing positions in a complex web of relations in the world—can be liberating. We are reminded that the "self" is provisional, growing, and elusive and that we are what we do.

When I work with teachers in inquiry seminars, they work with the situations or issues in their own homes, work, or communities, which trouble, chafe, or intrigue them in some way. Research closer to home is less likely to be turned into an object, an Other, and the participants in the inquiry are more likely to have a face and a voice. These are situations from which the researcher cannot stand outside but in which he or she participates, and often, through the process, inspires or effects change. Thus, this kitchen table inquiry has a particularly striking effect on peoples' assumptions about researcher stance. Questions about research ethics rise to the forefront.

In a recent discussion, an art teacher described her colleague's recent practice of using a repetitive, cut and paste task with paper in her first grade classroom. Although the teacher had observed the class only one day, she judged her colleague as having "taught art badly," of having stifled the children's creativity. But, someone in the seminar group asked, could there other explanations? What are the assumptions here about inquiry and about teaching art? Another offered an alternative perspective on the activity: Was this teacher, perhaps, aiming to provide young children with an opportunity to practice motor skills and task completion, and not seeing this activity as related at all to art? How do we frame what we do? How do we frame what we see? Ought we to judge? How does the observed see him- or herself and his or her intentions? How does the researcher see the teacher? Whose perspective is closer to "true"? Are our observations different when we see ourselves as colleagues, not researchers? What is a research stance? Who benefits from it? Who decides?

It becomes more difficult, as we engage in inquiry closer to the communities in which we live, to take on the role of researcher like a glove, and to speak words outside of ourselves. It becomes more difficult, as we sit in a circle around the kitchen table, the seminar table, or the staff room table, to point a finger in the circle at others who do not meet our standards or see from our perspectives. Judging our colleagues is an unsavory practice at the best of times; inquiry that recognizes our multiple selves (and our many ways of knowing) provides us an opportunity to see from all sides and to avoid shutting out others or rejecting them out of hand. As Chodron (2000) wrote,

> Rather than own our own pain or learn about ourselves from what we reject, we find ways to justify our actions. . . . Whether it's ourselves, our lovers, our bosses, the local Scrooge, it's more daring and real not to shut anyone out. If we begin to live like this, we'll find we can't make things right or wrong anymore because things are a lot more slippery and playful than that. Everything is ambiguous; everything is always shifting and changing, and there are as many takes on any given situation as there are people involved. (p. 127)

- To encourage resistance of practices in the educational and institutional hierarchy which devalue situated inquiry and multiple ways of knowing; and to be open to understand how I am co-opted by those practices, and how I perpetuate them

My doctoral studies were filled with what might be called a feast of semiotic and artistic experiences. I particularly recall a writing seminar held by Donald Murray in which we engaged in one creative process, such as playing the piano or drawing, and used another process, writing, to explore how the processes informed one another. A more common practice nowadays, this was revolutionary 20 years ago. I also recall other seminars in which writing as an art form was valued, encouraged, and expected; discursive, highly bibliographic academic writing played a part, but not the major part, in my studies. Now, as a professor, I am fortunate to teach in an education department that has long held a reputation for holistic teaching perspectives and practices, albeit varying interpretations of those, and for responsi AGAIN—response-ableble, flexible, constructivist pedagogy.

Still, as fortunate as I have been as a graduate student studying inquiry and a faculty member both teaching and engaging in it, tensions remain. The symbolic order of the educational research marks doctoral institutions such as the one I attended as being from a "soft" research perspective, not "rigorous," or a place where "real" research is funded or pursued. Currently, the reflexive research practices associated with institutions such as these—practices that advocate for narrative, poetic, or visual inquiry—are often labeled unscientific, merely anecdotal. The rise in interest and practice of arts-based research in all its forms (Neilsen, L., Cole, & Knowles, 2001) has changed attitudes about what research is considered legitimate, but only to an extent. Calls for inclusiveness in education have reached the public school classroom; calls for inclusiveness in research approach and legitimacy, however, have not fully achieved their aim. Some argue that the arts in social science research are merely tolerated rather than welcomed; others, including me, wonder about the gendered understandings that may prevent us from embracing the arts in inquiry (Neilsen, L., 1998).

Writing, as we know, remains gender coded: public writing is usually associated with male discourse and private writing with female. Genres such as the narrative, expressive, and poetic tend to be coded female; propositional and argumentative discourse tend to be male. The resulting discrepancy in either respect or attention to these different genres remains, even in the 21st century. In postsecondary institutions, and in scholarly work, the expository and transactional modes of discourse prevail; women (who now comprise the largest percentage of the postsecondary population) find that the genres or forms they might prefer to use (journals, narrative, anecdotal writing, and poetry) are seldom used to evaluate their knowledge (Neilsen, L., 2006). Further, their lyric inquiries (Neilsen, L., 2006), writing in forms that express and extend the aesthetic, are rarely acknowledged as legitimate.

Outside the places where I am able to live and work I realize, to use Woolf's (1929) terms, I must identify my headmaster. While our program's students speak in passionate tones of the dramatic changes in their perspectives—indeed in their lives and their relationships with colleagues, family, and friends—as a result of studies in which they can explore alternative notions of literacy and inquiry, the universities which maintain the status quo, the patriarchal symbolic order, are nevertheless considered to be "real" or legitimate universities, the "scholarly" institutions.

In the meantime, I continue to celebrate and support, theoretically and empirically, work that, by redefining literacy and inquiry, seems to be want to redefine scholarship as we know it. In a time of decaying institutions and irrelevant structures it is necessary that we engage in inquiry that calls on an understanding of our whole signifying beings and in so doing has the potential to rewrite our institutional practices.

So, the circle turns, and this time the view is different. I consider it a step toward achieving Haraway's (1991) "earthwide projects" and Berman's (1989) "gaia politik" to resist the institutional practices that continue to define and, hence, constrain research that grows out of a particular context by attempting to name it, and to compare it to others' in different classrooms, other inquiry collectives. Whose ends does it serve for us to agree on a definition of qualitative, feminist, or science—to put fences around our -isms and marshal our forces—if children and adults continue to wander the earth deadened to its promise and its pain?

Woolf (1929) reminds me that we cease believing in sides as we mature, and the labels we use will come off anyway. Experience tells me, also, that even when I refuse a label, others will affix it on the work to quiet their own uncertainty. Over the last two decades, my work with teachers has changed dramatically. Variously, I have encouraged a focus on observation, reflection, reflexivity, and resistance, sometimes, or usually, all at once. The ways of inquiring and telling have included most aesthetic and technological media available. The sites for inquiry have ranged from a girls' soccer season to an immigrants' social club to the local newspaper, an individual's experience of racism in school, the experience of motherhood, to the conversational dynamic of our graduate seminar. In all cases, the researcher—with his or her perspectives, dilemmas, insights, and activities—is the sphere from which the inquiry begins, the axis on which the related and relational worlds spin.

Throughout these explorations, I have encouraged the body awareness and attunement that rejuvenates teacher researchers too long buried under dry and bloodless words. Together, we try to adopt beginner's mind, using our senses to reach beyond our inherited labels and structures of the world to new, sharp, and awakened experiences of the extraordinary in the ordinary. I have argued for the validity of inquiry that arises out of uncertainty, and indeed, invites more troubling of experience; this is the surest path I know to critical thinking, and thus, to critical inquiry. And, I have worked to support as many strategies for seeing, hearing, documenting, and codifying—a triangulation of methods, if you will, especially of methods that invite many forms of representing how we know. The academy thrives on categories, however: Such embodied and sense-making inquiry has been characterized as creative, arts based, and arts informed (Neilsen, L. et al., 2001), and as I see it, an integral dimension of feminist inquiry (Neilsen, L., 1998). Working to see the world through new perspectives, resisting prescribed and colonizing structures of thought, and opening ourselves to attunement—to each other, to phenomena—is an essential process in contributing well to the lives of others.

A classroom is still a classroom, however, and my own practices with people are open to question and to critique. My pedagogy can be a breath of fresh air for some, a terrifying open space with no guideposts for others. I must learn to adapt practices that recognize such differences. I must also recognize my own complicity in maintaining the symbolic order that excludes underrepresented and silenced groups, and places students at the bottom of a hierarchy. Grades and other such markers are still there, in spite of our work to take evaluation out of institutional practice. We can support growth through critique and conversation, create all the communities of inquiry we wish, but the grade sheets continue to appear on our desks.

It is instructive to continue to ask the impossible: How can educational institutions, and the practices of pedagogy themselves (however "empowering"), avoid becoming sites that silence or oppress in their own way? The ideal classroom does not exist. Classrooms are still situated within academic institutions that promote competition, and that find ways, through policies and everyday discourse, to exclude many people and their lived realities, all in the name of standards and rigor.

REIMAGINING METAPHORS

The philosopher Simone Weil claimed that the fixed point of view is the root of injustice (Zwicky, 2003). And Zwicky (2003) claimed that metaphors, unlike other structures of thought can be generative. Zwicky wrote, "Non-metaphorical ways of speaking conduct meaning, in insulated carriers, to certain ends and purposes. Metaphors shave off the insulation and meaning arcs across the gap" (p. 68).

Historically, voice—and its companion notions of ventriloquism, silence, and mutedness—has been a productive metaphor for women's experiences teaching and learning in the world. But, is voice the foundational sound of our "true" selves, or do we produce many tones in many ways over many years? Equally compelling and useful has been the metaphor of the body, the corporeal being, whether we articulate it in terms of invisibility, embodied knowing/disembodied knowing, skin as a cover, role playing or masks (Neilsen, L., 1998). Too often, however, we use the metaphor of body as an entity distinct from the mind, which only retains and perpetuates our long-held Cartesian perspectives on how we know and how we learn.

Shakespeare's sister, the 16th-century fictional young woman born with a gift of poetry, is the ghost in our collective consciousness, reminding us all of the blunted possibilities of women's imaginings. Woolf (1929), describing how the downward spiral to the young woman's death might have occurred, imagines her facing the impossible: Woolf wrote,

> All the conditions of her life, all her own instincts, were hostile" to the development of her talent. Between her and the incandescence of mind needed to write poetry, were attitudes, social practices, and assumptions which were insurmountable, even in her own mind. Her mind must have been strained by the need of opposing this, of disproving that. (p. 53)

Little has changed where issues of knowledge and inquiry for women and underrepresented groups are concerned. Even with the advent of aesthetic forms and representations in inquiry (Neilsen, L. et al., 2001), issues about validity, reliability, and credibility continue to plague those who engage in such inquiry (and interestingly, many of those who choose such inquiry are women and underrepresented groups; Neilsen, L., 2006). Considering a kitchen table metaphor for inquiry has a decidedly homespun, anti-intellectual flavor, challenging received notions of formal academic propriety; yet, I will continue to invite my colleagues to the conversation there.

As Nicholson (1994) wrote, "As one moves from the elementary to graduate and particularly professional schools, one finds an institution less and less 'homelike' and increasingly dominated by characteristics associated with the public world and masculinity" (p. 80). A living inquiry, as comfortable in the kitchen as the seminar room, attempts to bring research home, to be named and recognized in the same way we continue to lobby for recognition of unpaid labor, for the value of story beside statistic. Imagining inquiry as home like, or as a process around a kitchen table, enables us to drop defenses and posturing, speak the stories, and become fully aware of the intimacy of inquiry. Inquiry is work of the heart, the hands, our sense-making body, our many toned voices.

The issues are ones on which the world can tilt: learning about the world as though the body is inseparable from the mind; creating the discursive world from the axis of experiences of the silenced, the unnamed, and the disregarded; and exposing and composing our lives as researchers by including and examining who we are and what we do in the name of inquiry. Such issues are issues of legitimacy and of value. What and who and how do we value when we set out on the inquiry path?

But, like the histories of midwifery or herbal medicine—from necessary practice to a position outside the realm of "acceptable medical practice" to a growing, if qualified return to "legitimacy"—the history of inquiry, at least its history within the last 20 years, has been a battle of "regimes of truth" (Gore, 1993). But, who is right is not nearly as interesting or productive as the ongoing questions: Who benefits? What is the legacy of our work? Who and what are we not hearing, seeing, and knowing?

My intention, working with teachers in inquiry, is provide opportunities to reawaken aspects of themselves and their professional lives, to live the inquiry, and to be confident in its own particular truth. These practices of feminist inquiry, while they are satisfying and challenging, are part of the diversity and richness that marks the inquiry process as a whole, part of a mix of perspectives and methods we need to spark learning and force change. Such diversity, to the extent that the practices are not oppressive or irresponsible, is to be embraced in the same way our multimodal literacies ought to be embraced. Such feminist praxis ought to claim a space in the house we are constructing, not to replace the dwelling itself.

Metaphors become our lenses, our seat on the Ferris wheel, and our foot on the rocky bottom of the ocean. They shape how we respond and even who we are. No single metaphor can be selected here to speak for a feminist method of inquiry or inquiry as an enterprise: to propose one would be antithetical to what I am addressing here. But I am aware that metaphors that make sense—shape sense—for me in my teaching and inquiry practices are metaphors that call on the "body resonant." Living inquiry means that as relational beings, living in overlapping worlds, we touch and respond to those around us as we pursue the work we deem important. This perspective is a lyric perspective, and, as I have written elsewhere, lyric inquiry is a resonant process. As we engage in inquiry, we are changed. More than speaking a single voice, our presence resounds and reverberates; our senses take in all that surrounds us, and we in turn, give back. Our bodies live in the world like a cell lives within a larger being; literacies of the body resonant are living literacies.

No gods' (or goddess') eye view is enough; we are richer when we are close to the ground. Meanwhile, a Kurdish child, new to Canada, enters a school in Nova Scotia speaking no English. She feels the cold in the outside air and in the classroom climate. She aches with knowledge she cannot tell, and she sits near the window, her pencil poised at a paper with words to copy. Disembodied words do not touch any experience she knows. Elsewhere, the mother of two children enters a literacy program after 30 years of illiteracy and confesses she no longer feels like nobody. Literacy will make her somebody, she believes.

"Nobody," "somebody," and "disembodied"—our metaphors for literacy have created a world of schooled people outside their bodies, outside themselves, unable to connect their life to their words. New ways of imagining our literacies and our possibilities might help us all read, write, sing, touch, hear, and, in richer ways, resonate with the lives and the struggles of those we have missed on the paths. We are passionate, resonant bodies seeking connection and survival; we must aspire to a compassionate literacy.

REFERENCES

Abram, D. (1996). *The spell of the sensuous.* New York: Vintage Books.

Atwood, M. (1995). *Morning in the burned house.* Toronto, Canada: McClelland and Stewart, Inc.

Berman, M. (1989). *Coming to our senses.* New York: Bantam Books.

Chandler, S. (1992). Displaying our lives: An argument against displaying our theories. *Theory into practice, 31,* 126–131.

Chodron, P. (2000). *When things fall apart.* Boston, MA: Shambhala.

Franck, F. (1993). *Zen seeing, zen drawing.* New York: Bantam Books.

Gore, J. (1993). *The struggle for pedagogies: Critical and feminist discourses as regimes of truth.* New York: Routledge.

Greene, M. (1988). *The dialectic of freedom.* New York: Teachers College Press.

Haraway, D. (1991). *Simians, cyborgs, and women: The reinvention of nature.* New York: Routledge.

John-Steiner, V. (1985). *Notebooks of the mind: Explorations of thinking.* Albuquerque, NM: University of New Mexico Press.

Neilsen, A. (1989). *Critical thinking and reading: Empowering learners to think and act.* Urbana, IL: National Council of Teachers of English and ERIC.

Neilsen, L. (1989). *Literacy and living: The literate lives of three adults.* Portsmouth, NH: Heinemann Educational Books.

Neilsen, L. (1994). *A stone in my shoe: Teaching literacy in times of change.* Winnipeg, Canada: Peguis Publishers.

Neilsen, L. (1998). *Knowing her place: Research literacies and feminist occasions.* San Francisco, CA: Caddo Gap Press.

Neilsen, L. (2006). *Lyric inquiry: Notes on language, inquiry and poetry.* Unpublished manuscript.

Neilsen, L., Cole, A., & Knowles, J.G. (Eds.). (2001). *The art of writing inquiry.* Great Tancook, Canada: Backalong Books.

Nicholson, L. J. (1994). Women and schooling. In L. Stone (Ed.), *The education feminism reader* (p. 80). New York: Routledge.

Smith, D. (1987). *The everyday world as problematic: A feminist sociology.* Boston: Northeastern University Press.

Woolf, V. (1929). *A room of one's own.* London: The Hogarth Press Ltd.

Zwicky, J. (2003). *Wisdom and metaphor.* Kentville, Nova Scotia: Gaspereau Press.

• 16 •

REENVISIONING PRESERVICE TEACHER IDENTITY: MATRIXING METHODOLOGY

Stacy J. Miller
INDIANA UNIVERSITY OF PENNSYLVANIA

INTRODUCTION TO SPACETIME METHODOLOGY

As we try to reenvision or reimagine something in teacher education that has yet to come fully into existence, reconsidering methodological approaches that authenticate this kind of research presents new challenges.[1] As new methodologies emerge, we are challenged to imagine new ways of reconceptualizing and reconsidering findings and their efficacy in other fields. Specifically, methodologies in the visual and communicative arts are often nonbinary and spacetime theory enables us to reconceptualize how to make meaning of findings. This research directs us toward newfangled reconceptions of preservice teacher identity as illuminated by an imaginative methodology viewed through a spacetime lens.

Specifically, this research turns us toward the intersections of preservice English teacher identity and thirdspace as a methodology that is rooted and framed by illuminating the matrix that is coconstructing a preservice teacher identity during any space and time. This "methodological turn"[2] is illuminated by drawing from research that enters into a new space of nonbinary making meaning of preservice teacher identity through visual and communicative spatialities by reconceptualizing research devoid of spatial conceptualization. I reflect on the vulnerabilities of preservice teachers' identities, as they are coconstructed and co-reconstructed by a rapidly changing sociopolitical landscape of networked relationships that is affected by the space and time during which a preservice teaching identity is coming to be. By mining the matrix in which a teacher identity is coming to be, the matrix as methodology helps to illuminate current and future landscapes in which a preservice teacher is coconstructed during any space and time.

Reenvisioning Spacetime in Teacher Education

For teacher preparation to have power and to benefit from current and future democracies, it must stay true to a course in teaching for social change and social justice. Cochran-Smith (2004) responded by suggesting that for teacher education to move toward a social justice agenda it must be conceptualized as both "a learning problem and a political problem" (p. 2). This indicates that we must look outside of the educational axis at how teacher preparation is influenced by other fields and their methodologies, so that we might better understand how to appropriate, by expanding prior research, tools that can best prepare us to meet the demands of competing political agendas. Innovating visual and communicative methodologies prepares us with an efficacy that can have far-reaching implications that attends to a social justice agenda. Cochran-Smith's suggestion is a vital springboard to enacting innovative methodologies.

Terminology

The words *landscape* and *geography* will be used interchangeably and used in different contexts and references a large, ethereal, real area.

[1] The use of the prefix *re-* means to do again and thus honors the trailblazing work of researchers who have paved the way for others to build upon.

[2] Soja (2004) coined the idea "a spatial turn" to reference a new direction in spacetime studies. From this, I innovate the idea "methodological turn" that navigates us toward new ways of inventing methodologies within spacetime.

The landscape contains all of the "actants," or participators (Brandt & Clinton, 2002), and policies that are coimpacting the identity of the teacher during various spaces and times, and its mutability is consistent. Since there is never one particular actant coconstructing the identity of the preservice teacher, the preservice teacher is involved in the corelational dynamic of the very process of being coconstructed both within and by the landscape.[3] Through the preservice teacher's place within the landscape, the teacher is a coparticipant in the process capable of appropriating from, negotiating toward or against, or identifying with others his or her own preservice teacher identity. By asking participants what their teacher identities mean to them, we gain insight into the landscape which contains all of the actants that are participating in their coconstructions. Such a subjective act challenges and disrupts the recurrence of dominant binary paradigms and an often quiet subservient status quo in research methodologies that disables participants' voices, and instead, elevates the voices of the participants to a status of a coactant thus giving them agency and empowerment within research and possibly society at large. For this research, preservice teachers were not viewed as objects but rather as ontological subjects that could enhance a transdisciplinary conceptualization or that which "cuts across all perspectives and modes of thought" (Soja, E. W., 1996, p. 3). A transdisciplinary reconceptualization further challenges the notion that the past is spatially and temporally fragmented and can help us reenvision how teacher identities were being coconstructed both spatially and temporally.

The landscape that contains all of the elements that inform and construct preservice identities is bound by a specific space and time, or spacetime (Nespor, 1997, p. xi). By spacetime I reference the spatial (space), a place that "brings [specified factors constructing identity] all together and substitutes itself for each factor separating and enveloping it" (Soja, E. W., 1996, p. 45). Space also references the physical layout of the factors (social groups, communities that apprentice a teacher, institutions, media, policy, and research) and the places in which an identity comes to mean. By temporal (time), I reference the literal time in which the identity is being formed. The spacetime relationship is based on the premise that time and space are fluid and, therefore, are constantly changing. Most theorists have written the actual word *spacetime* by using a hyphen (-), so it appears as *space-time*; I however eliminate the hyphen to show that the terms are corelational. The boundedness of teacher identity by the relationality of spacetime suggests that preservice teacher identity then is fluid and constantly shifting. Consequently, preservice teacher identities are subject to stabilization and destabilization during any spacetime. *Stabilize* and *destabilize* are terms appropriated from Leander's (2002) study, *Locating Latanya*, in which he looked at how a student's identity was stabilized and destabilized by a banner placed in a classroom space and through the use of student and teacher discourse. Stabilization means that a preservice identity is steadied by some factor of the landscape that is coconstructing it, such as a space or a person, while destabilization means that a preservice identity is invalidated or unsteadied by some element that is coconstructing the teacher, like by a person or changes in policies in a particular space.

[3] By moving from the parenthetical prefix *co-* and then attaching the antecedent to a given word such as *corelational*, this represents a graduation in the writing style that symbolizes the corelational dimensions of the matrix as it illuminates the relationships coconstructing a participant's teacher identity.

This research enters into a new space of making meaning of identity through new spatialities by reconceptualizing spatialized methodologies. It exposes the polemic struggle between binary thinking in Soja's (1996) discussion of firstspace (real or actual space)—"concrete materiality of spatial forms, on things that can be empirically mapped" (p. 10)—and secondspace (imagined space)—"conceived in ideas about space, in thoughtful re-presentations of human spatiality in mental and cognitive forms" (p. 10)—, as they intersect with concepts of thirdspace—the amalgam of both the "real-and-imagined" journeys or the "thirding" of spatial awareness and imagination (p. 11). Examples of firstspace include, but are not limited to, such physical and real life texts and contexts as a grid, a map, or a rhizome. Examples of secondspace include, but are not limited to, such abstract or imagined concepts through contextual discourses as a discussion of life in outer space, speaking gibberish, or projecting oneself into the future. Both firstspace and secondspace thinking and research narrows and limits our understanding about identity and reinforces a binary recognition of preservice teacher identity because it delimits our lenses to what is readily visible to the researcher. For instance, firstspace and secondspace research might focus on what corporeal events in the classroom or in a school context and may even invite in some thinking about how to create change in the classroom. Thirdspace, on the other hand, is the "creation of another mode of thinking about space that draws upon the material and mental spaces of the traditional dualism but extends beyond them in scope, substance and meaning" (Soja, 1996, p. 11). When we view identity through thirdspace, we open up the possibilities that teacher identity is influenced by factors that are both invisible and visible, tangible and intangible, real and unreal, and present and future. It opens up the window to see that preservice teacher identity is vast and that it cannot be readily understood. Thirdspace gives us room to imagine and generate possibility for how we are seen and for how others see us. It allows us to reinvent ourselves. This research encourages and begets a spatial methodology that aligns with nonbinary meaning making.

This article will be divided into four parts. In part one, I contextualize and make a case for research on preservice teacher identity in the visual arts. I then review spatial and temporal terms that respectively ground the research design. In part two, I review the literature on spacetime theory and reenvision a spacetime theoretical framework for reconceptualizing preservice teacher identity. I also describe how the methodology and data analysis for this research contributes to furthering our conception of the visual arts. In part three, I draw upon one case study (Miller, 2005) to elucidate how methodology illustrates how secondary preservice English teacher identity is geographically "meaned." In the final part, I offer implications for the continued significance about conducting transdisciplinary research through visual, spatial, and imaginative ways and how that can disrupts dominant paradigms that have reinforced hegemony.

REENVISIONING A SPACETIME THEORETICAL FRAMEWORK

In order to understand preservice teacher identity and the significance of burgeoning methodologies in the visual and communicative arts, we must first reconceptualize identity in spacetime. Though there are competing theoretical studies on identity development,

I focus on the studies of identity through a poststructural lens of sociocultural theory and anthropological studies (Au, 1998; Heath, 1983; McCarthey & Moje, 2002; Ochs, 1988; Perez, 1998), which have paved the way for concepts of identity through spatiality and hybridity theories (Anzaldúa, 1987: Bhabha, 1994; Hagood, 2002; Hall, 1996; Gutierrez, Baquedano-Lopez, & Tejeda, 1999; Foucault, 1986; Leander, 2002; Luke, C., & Luke, A., 1999; Miller, 2005; Moje, 2002; Soja, E. W., 1996). Combined, these theories suggest that identities are changing, constantly in flux, stabilizing and destabilizing, as they transact and negotiate through activity and oppressive structures (Bakhtin, 1986; Gee, 1996; Freire & Macedo, 1987; hooks, 1989, 1994; Minh-Ha, 1989, 1991; Solorzano & Villalpando, 1998) with the world around them (through using discourse, identifying with artifacts, or being in different spaces). Identity is something that is coconstructed through competing forces and that our position in a space is "offered, accepted, rejected, and otherwise continuously negotiated" (Leander & Sheehy, 2004, p. 116) as individuals engage in social spaces. Within these spaces, identities are "produced, negotiated and hybridized within the flow of dialogue" (Leander, 2001, p. 637). Such an understanding of identity through a spacetime lens paves the way to making meaning of preservice teacher identity in spacetime.

Preservice teacher identity construction as a whole has been insufficiently researched. To a large degree, the preservice teacher identity is predetermined because of institutional and social expectations. I approached the literature with a transdisciplinary focus that pushed the boundaries of binary constructions and understandings of preservice teacher identity by relocating and forwarding its placement within various intersections of research fields outside of teacher education. I primarily focused on preservice teacher identity construction from spatiality/hybridity theories, critical literacy, and feminist studies. These fields share dialogical and dialectical perspectives on how identities come to be formed and how identities come to mean through transacting (Rosenblatt, 1994) with and within, various social spaces and through marginalization from various social spaces (Leander, 2002; Lefebvre 1991).

The related research to this guiding topic is limited in its scope of the social construction of preservice student teacher identities (Britzman, 1991; Danielewicz, 2001; Vinz, 1996). Research on preservice teacher identity construction in the schooling process is also quite underdeveloped in its breadth and depth of identity analysis (Britzman, 1991; Danielewicz, 2001; Vinz, 1996). Although some studies have been conducted regarding how student identities are constructed (Apple, 2002; Levinson, Foley, Holland, et al., 1996; Hagood, 2002; Leander, 2002; McCarthey & Moje, 2002; McLaren, 1986; Moje 2002), how teacher identities are constructed (Britzman, 1991; Danielewicz, 2001; Grossman, 1990; Vinz, 1996), and how preservice student teacher identities are constructed (Britzman, 1991; Danielewicz, 2001; Vinz, 1996), these studies tend to be nondisciplinary in focus. Few studies, if any, have looked at the spatiality and temporality of preservice student teacher identities (Britzman, 1991; Nespor, 1997). Appropriating postmodern concepts, while reviewing the literature on preservice teacher identity construction and viewing the data through both spacetime and feminist lenses, can help us reenvision preservice teacher identity altogether.

Postmodernism underscores that identities and ideas are not black and white but, rather, provides a kaleidoscopic lens that allows us to view concepts from a space outside of the object being viewed. Therefore, meaning can be found in relation to, rather than within, an object. For this research then, preservice teachers negotiated their identities and came to make meaning of what their preservice teacher identities meant to them both toward and against others, theories, pedagogies, policies, and the like. Rose (1993), Leander (2002), Moje (2002), and Hagood, (2002) suggested that identities can be shaped in response to oppressive structures and that "identity built on the opening of new spaces" (Soja, 1996, p. 111) relocates us to a place where counterhegemonic principles can lead to a liberal democracy. When individuals negotiate and contest their identity development by dominant culture, they may develop identities that may be marginalized by social groups that retain power. Rather than negotiating toward identities, these researchers suggest negotiating against identities. Their studies provide a framework for further research in this theoretical field (Bakhtin, 1986; Freire & Macedo, 1987; hooks, 1989, 1994; Minh-Ha, 1989, 1991; Solorzano & Villalpando, 1998). McCarthey and Moje (2002) looked at identity in relation to literacy and how individuals are "constructed and practiced within relationships of race, gender, class and space" (p. 228). They claimed that an identity is an "aspect of how humans make sense of the world . . . including their experiences with texts" (p. 228). Spatiality and hybridity theories illuminate how different identities might be interrogated in future literacy practices as they simultaneously challenge dominant notions of identity construction (McCarthey & Moje, 2002, pp. 234–235) and where cultural hybridities can "give rise to something different, something new and unrecognizable, a new area of negotiation of meaning and representation" (Bhabha as in Soja, 1996, p. 14).

Similar to spatiality and hybridity perspectives of identity, critical literacy perspectives of subjectivity suggest formations of self are "multiple, shifting and contradictory" and the "decentered self . . . pushes back on those identities, continuously shifting and changing, never fully locating oneself as for all in a particular identity" (Hagood, 2002, p. 255). Critical literacy as a theoretical field challenges dominant and oppressive structures and seeks to situate its theoretical research in such a way that space and time are inherently part of its theoretical lens. This study appropriates from critical literacy as it builds on the work of Hagood (2002).

Hagood's (2002) seminal study illustrated how both postmodernism and identity can be coconstructed as she repositioned and destabilized the readers' gaze so that we might better understand the experience of the actant. Timony, a young man, had been marginalized by his teachers and considered at risk for a variety of reasons, but specifically for wearing angst-ridden clothing, for carrying a Kurt Cobain (the lead singer, of the band Nirvana, who committed suicide) guitar pick which was perceived as a potential weapon, and for reading texts about Kurt Cobain. From a structuralist view, the teachers assumed the stance that identity is associated with and situated within what we read, and because of that stance, Timony's identity and feelings of self-worth went unrealized by them. However, Timony's discourse at school illustrated that he was, to the contrary, a critic of teen angst and against Cobain's suicide. If his teachers had truly listened to him, they would have known and recognized that Timony's identity was negotiated outside of his reading of Cobain and that he transacted the construction of himself against the text, not through the text itself. Had teachers understood a poststructuralist perspective or understood how meaning and identity can be reconstructed, perhaps Timony would not have been labeled as "at risk." Sadly, though, Timony's discourse was misinterpreted by those in school and, subsequently, he was positioned as an at-risk youth. Hagood's research admonishes us to reconsider the hazards of understanding situations or conducting research through myopic lenses.

REENVISIONING SPACETIME METHODS AND DATA ANALYSIS

> Analyzing the configuration of social practices and the shifts across time and context can help educators describe, interpret, and explain the ways of interacting, representing, and being that accompanies learning. Such configurations of practice often rub up against one another and are not mutually exclusive. (Rogers, 2004, p. 66)

Methodology/Data Collection

The "methodological turn" for this study continues as we reenvision spatial and temporal research methods and data analysis. Data was collected over four and a half months, during which preservice teachers were observed and interviewed in two different contexts: in secondary English university classes and in their teaching placements. While data collection varied, identity artifacts revealed unique findings that had key implications. Identity artifacts are how interactants mediate (Holland, Lachiotte, Skinner, & Cain, 1998) and stabilize a particular identity at a given point in time through an "instrument (material, tool, embodied space, text, discourse, etc.) that mediates identity-shaping activity" (Leander, 2002, p. 201). Participants were informed about the concept of an identity artifact, and they self-selected their own.

Appropriating analyses from critical discourse analysis (CDA; Bakhtin 1981,1986; Foucault, 1986; Rogers, 2004) and conversational analysis (CA; Wetherell, Taylor, &Yates, 2001) and viewing the findings through feminist and spacetime lenses, I reflected on the data that showed the experiences of the participants both in their university classrooms settings and in their field placements as they answered a series of questions about their experiences as learners and as teachers. Both CDA and CA align with feminism and spacetime because they are critical of how the epistemologies that are grounded in hegemony play out in schools and are concerned with understanding how power is involved in language and social relations in order to facilitate research for change and the emancipation of individual social relations in contemporary social life. What emerged from within the lenses of data analysis was a key methodological finding that helped to conceptualize all data: the matrix.

Matrixing the Data

The matrix. Janesick (1998), in her manuscript on considering the artful choreography of qualitative research design that she likens to a dance, urged researchers to push boundaries of methodology so that it becomes a meaningful and useful tool for future research designs. She reminded us that research alone should not mimic other studies for it is the design itself that can lead into new spaces for meaning and representation. Janesick influenced the development of the matrix. The matrix is an imaginary, yet real, space that emerged as a way to conceptualize the networked atomistic relationships that impacted teacher identity coconstruction. Although imaginary, it provides a way to frame and show how in spacetime and over spacetime intricate relationships network. Depending on the time in which an individual is teaching, he or she will be embodied by a different network of relationships. The matrix in 2004–2005 differed from the matrices in 2006, 2016, and 2096. Inside of Fig. 16.1 is a generic spatial map that illustrates several of the atomistic relationships that might be coconstructing identity at any given point and time. The inside of the matrix shows a dotted line, or the rhizome, which cannot be separated from the matrix as it is its lining, so to speak. The two are intimately connected and together they form a networked space where relationships intersect, are concentric, do not intersect, and can be parallel, nonparallel, perpendicular, obtuse, fragmented, and even marginalized. As a theoretical concept the matrix, it is both an invisible and visible space, which embodies all of the forces coconstructing identity.

Critical discourse analysis. By placing data in the matrix, I applied CDA to interrogate what identity artifacts meant or symbolized to the participants' preservice secondary language arts teacher identities and how they interacted with various texts: including curricular, political, and material artifacts. I borrowed Bakhtin's (1986) definition of *texts*, which includes *all* written or visual material, that are created with specific audiences in mind and are produced in anticipation of particular responses so they are, therefore, interactive. Texts for this study evoked semiotic responses between the reader and the text (e.g., television shows, conversations, films, billboards, syllabi, mission statements, etc.). By *semiotic,* I mean the "meaning-making through language, body language, visual images or any other way of signifying" an interaction with and through texts (Wetherell et al., 2001, p. 229).

As part of CDA, I focused on interactional analysis and interdiscursive analysis. While interactional analysis seeks to describe how texts are seen relationally as semiotic activity, interdiscursive analysis works from the assumption that texts mix genres and discourses and that some texts and discourses are hybrids (Wetherell et al., 2001, p. 241). The "heteroglossic" nature of texts has the potential to produce

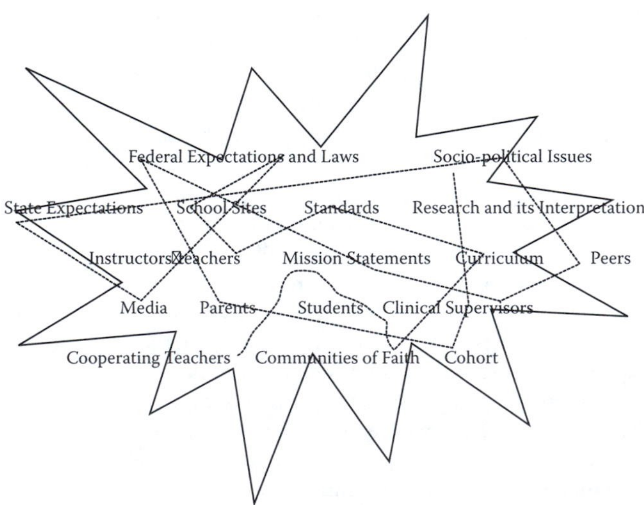

FIGURE 16.1 The matrix—an example of a generic matrix and the atomistic relationships coconstructing a preservice teacher identity.

hybridized identities. An aim of CDA is to position the self within the project, to become part of the social world in which the research is conducted, and to use some self-description and relation to the topic in the data (Wetherell et al., 2001). It was my intent then to understand preservice teacher identity and the semiotic experiences for both identity and material artifacts in the context of life and understand what significance they have for participants about their teaching identities through interview protocols. The matrix illuminated the rhizomatic intersections and on-intersections of data.

Conversational analysis. CA furthered the "methodological turn" because it allowed me to analyze transcriptions from interviews and observations of students in their teaching placements and in their coursework. I looked at how the naturally occurring discourse among participants' in-group interviews in their teaching placements and in their coursework showed the landscape in which they have come to interpret what their preservice teaching identities meant to them. In developing the matrix even more, I scrutinized the data for examples that illustrated how participants interpreted their teaching identities as they interacted in their coursework with peers and instructors, in their teaching placements with colleagues, co-operating teachers, and clinical supervisors, and in their cohorts. Since CA attempts to identify and describe language as it naturally occurs, it was not my intent to reveal underlying issues or beliefs for why their teaching identities mean what they appeared to mean; rather, it was my intent to investigate and share by identifying and describing their naturally occurring languages and their interpretations of what their teaching identities meant to each of the participants.

Feminist lens. A feminist analysis of data, like CDA and CA, is guided by some basic ethical principles, most of which are relational and based in reciprocity. Feminist research seeks to look for ways that authenticate the human experience and validate the differences that each person has. In my analyses of participants' responses, I was sensitive to the ways that masculinity has been reproduced through discourse and how that inevitably affects male responses. It was my intent to describe all participants' stories as authentically as possible through a combination of portraiture and narrative (Lawrence-Lightfoot & Hoffman Davis, 1997; Ritchie & Wilson, 2000) and to discuss at length any portion of content that I did not fully understand with my male participants. Not to do so perpetuated a female authoritative stance on male insights, which only further creates hierarchies of power. By employing feminist analysis, some of the power differential was eradicated (Blakeslee, Cole, & Conefrey, 1996; Rich, 1977).

Spacetime findings and their representations. Findings congealed along two metataxonomies: constructed through critique and constructed through "windowing." "Constructed through critique" references the notion that teachers largely saw themselves being constructed through their own critique of the teacher practices or beliefs of co-operating teachers, veteran teachers, or administrators. It was embedded within their critique that I unpacked their dissatisfaction with some element of how they were being constructed by those in positions of power.

"Constructed through windowing" draws from the physicality of a window as something we can see through that sometimes reflects back our image if sunlight has hit it at a certain point in the day, or it is something we can see through, which projects images outside of our periphery. Student teachers when constructed through windowing saw either aspects in others that they appropriated into their teacher identities or aspects of what they hoped to eventually emulate but which were beyond their present reaches. When we apply the idea of a window to the context of this study, we see that it acts as a reflection when participants saw in others aspects of ideals they wanted to instantly embody because they were capable of such an act during a spacetime, such as admiring one's ability to engage students or possessing the ability to deflect an argument. When participants knew that they hoped eventually to embody something, but because of their fledgling status did not embody it during this spacetime, such as a depth and breadth of knowledge on a text or understanding the interplay of literary allusions from text to text that acts as a future projection. Hence, this projection manifests in thirdspace as the "creation of another mode of thinking about space that draws upon the material and mental spaces of the traditional dualism but extends beyond them in scope, substance, and meaning" (Soja, 1996, p. 11).

REENVISIONING PRESERVICE TEACHER IDENTITY THROUGH JACOB

The findings that illuminated how preservice secondary language arts student teacher identities came to mean fell within larger metataxonomies, including five thematic areas: meaning (what something means to the participant such as teaching, learning, or observing), the value systems of the participant, expectations about the profession, communities of learning that apprentice the teacher, and policy, research, its interpretation, and its impact on communities of learning. I use Jacob's data to illustrate methodologically how his identity was coconstructed. The theme of meaning is used to contextualize his case study and is juxtaposed through the larger taxonomies of constructed through critique and constructed through windowing.

Jacob

Jacob, a 32-year-old, Chinese/Eurasian, working-class male, grew up in an upper-middle-class Buddhist household in the Pacific Northwest with loving and nurturing parents. Initially a self-identified "gifted bad kid" who devalued education, he now feels committed to helping young people create social change by giving them the tools to think critically about literature and through written expression. He strives to expose his students to ideas outside of their indigenous lives so that they can make informed choices about their futures and recognizes that for him the battle is in motivating students to want to learn when they already have a long history of resistance already instilled. I initially met him when he was a student in a class on teaching pedagogy that I taught prior to the year he dropped out of the secondary English education program. His sojourn away and his return frame his story.

Jacob was an outspoken and inquisitive member of the Secondary Language Arts Cohort (SLAC) who was eager to grow and learn. Unique to his personality was that he did not like to follow the pack. He demonstrated this through counterdialogue, assignment completion, and his outside hobbies. During the same year, I worked with him he dropped out of the program because of poor relationships with his clinical supervisor and his co-operating teacher, who thought that he was ill suited for teaching because of their perceptions of his performance in a classroom for remedial readers and his struggle to make necessary accommodations for them. His experience countered his supervisors' for he felt that his students enjoyed his sense of humor, attended his classes, and were doing their school work and that he was reaching them. His faith in his ability to teach however was unshaken although his teacher identity destabilized because teaching a class he was ill prepared to teach was a setup for failure. He admitted that he knew he had much to offer students and that he knew others' perceptions were a mismatch from his own. He said the system was at fault for not training him to work with these special needs students and he decided to dropout.

Upon reentry to the program the next fall he rededicated himself to making his teaching placement successful and in completing the program by the end of the fall semester. During the time of the study, I supervised Jacob when he was assigned to teach 10th grade at Carlos Martinez High School, rurally situated in the southwest with a predominantly Native American and Hispanic student population comprised of students from the nearby reservations. Many of his students came from a lower socioeconomic bracket, and they were exposed to excessive substance abuse and poverty; however, most students were meeting the expected skills for grade level. His school had not faced probation from the Public Education Office and was making AYP under NCLB. Based on conversations with his students, Jacob confirmed that most of his students were likely return to their nearby reservations after graduation from high school in order to support their families.

Meaning Constructed Through Critique

The meaning of Jacob's teacher identity came in part through his negotiation against others in his communities of learning. Meaning began through his own apprenticeships in the communities in which he engaged and then through how such meanings were either expanded or shifted within and by the communities of learning that were apprenticing his teacher identity. Although several communities impacted meaning for him, I focus on his experiences in the school space. Embodied by a culture or community are the values and practices it embraces and where meaning is birthed. The spacetime that the original meanings of his teacher identity came to be differed from the spacetime that his teacher identity fortified. The spaces he inhabited and the time inhabited by him in that space made his inchoate teaching identity vulnerable to destabilization. The critiques he shared with other participants helped to illuminate what his teacher identity meant to him and revealed similarities between participants' meanings.

While many factors helped Jacob understand his teacher identity, the meaning of his self-selected identity artifact most strongly illustrates this as it intersected with the expectations placed on him and from other teachers. Jacob's teacher identity was grounded in the artifact of a photo of his parents that he stated reflected their unconditional love of him. The photo represented their support over the years and for giving him the freedom to make choices about his goals and belief systems. Although he was a "gifted bad kid," his love of art and literature in high school took on new meaning in his adulthood. Such reminders took on meaning within the context of his school. He determined that the best way to support his students was to firmly embed himself within their experience because recognition of his students' communities could help him be a more effective educator for them. As a result, he felt he would be better prepared to support his students' values and their educational and sociocultural needs. His co-operating teacher affirmed his teaching and his efforts to know the families of his students. He met with families and Elders in order to assess what students needed in the classroom. He felt it was his responsibility as an educator to do whatever it took to know the students in the school space where he taught. As a nonnative, Jacob believed that it was his responsibility not to assimilate them to the system of the oppressor rather to build a bridge between the two, which meant to honor both state and school expectations and standards. His critique of the state standards was that they did not adequately reflect the sociocultural needs and values of his Native American students. He believed that when one connects personal meaning such as individual oppression, prejudice, or even love, to events, texts, and other areas of learning it increases one's ability to think for oneself. As he sees it, when one is taught to think critically about material and the world around them, it can lead to the possibility of agency, self empowerment, and then toward creating both personal and systemic social change.

What we see has happened to Jacob's teacher identity is a restabilization. Conversations between his peers, clinical supervisor, co-operating teacher, and university instructors assured him that this time around, he had every right to determine the kind of teacher he wanted to be in negotiation against or toward his co-operating teacher and clinical supervisor. Nonetheless, he protected himself this time because of prior experience by erecting a temporal border, a time-based border, around his teacher identity to help him restabilize until he had his own classroom. Although he spent a semester with a new co-operating teacher, who he admired for her ability to describe literary allusions from text to text and for her knowledge sustained by 30 years of teaching English, he observed her teach in a way that was dissonant from his own beliefs about teaching. He found her style to be "old school and dull," while he observed her unable to connect to her students' lives. He consciously negotiated his teaching identity against that aspect of her teaching. As he studied and participated in other communities such as the university and his cohort, and was validated in his beliefs, his teacher identity stabilized. Although he still struggled at times to connect material to students' lives and to teach content, it is important to keep in mind that his teacher identity remained intact because his values aligned with those in power outside of the classroom space. Perhaps had his network maligned with his values, he might have dropped out of the program a second time as he had during the first year when he lacked support and validation.

The networked matrix of relationships in Jacob's teaching life may not be obvious yet they included his students, their families and their sociocultural values, his university instructors, his clinical supervisor, his co-operating teacher, his family, his cohort, his prior teachers, school curriculum, and state and school standards. Each of these aspects of the matrix intersected and each was simultaneously coconstructing his teacher identity.[4] For Jacob, meaning of his teacher identity was generated by the contexts through which he learned and he was socialized. How he came to make meaning of his teacher identity largely impacted how he saw his role as an English teacher.

[4] There were other pieces of this networked matrix participating in his teacher identity coconstruction but they are beyond the scope of this piece.

Meaning Constructed Through Windowing

Many relationships were less obviously impacting the meaning of Jacob's teacher identity in thirdspace. These relationships cannot be separated because each one affects the other, and his participation in various relationships created links to others. Regardless of the nature of his relationships, they impacted how he participated and how he was affected by other relationships within the network. Since the overall network is coconstructing his teacher identity, no one particular relationship is singled out. Where one relationship might be poor or cause destabilization, another might help restabilize the teacher identity.

The matrix actualizes the concept of "windowing" as we also consider that Jacob was a nontraditional learner and teacher. His story provides a glimpse into his ultimate success as a preservice teacher. Recall that he dropped out of the SLAC the year prior because he did not feel supported in his teaching practices, which destabilized his teacher identity. He was also heavily criticized by those in power over him for his unorthodox and nonbinary methods of teaching. Jacob did not want to be a mainstream teacher. He wanted to follow a path all his own that spoke to his inner sense of self. Jacob, unlike many of his peers, could connect with any student, any time, and anywhere. His offbeat sense of humor and his ability to both understand and connect with students who have been marginalized by dominant society made him all the more effective in the classroom. His own background as a "gifted bad kid" sensitized him toward students who were not part of mainstream society. As part of the expectations for the program, he was required to observe veteran English teachers in his school. He noted that some teachers were "ghetto and boring" while others were "innovative and engaging." He respected his co-operating teacher's knowledge of texts and literary allusions and hoped someday to emulate it. Through the process of observations, he picked up teaching ideas and negotiated his teacher identity both toward and against the teachers whom he had observed.

While Jacob struggled for acceptance the first year in the program, he did not struggle during his second year because the network of relationships that were coconstructing his identity shifted. This networked matrix, which formed a heterotopia for him—a "real" place where there is a "sort of mixed, joint experience" or a "countersite," occupied and created by those who contest the dominant sites (Foucault, 1986, p. 24), affirmed his teacher identity and helped to restabilize the kind of teacher he wanted to be, affirmed what his teacher identity meant to him, and reinscribed a place for him in the profession.

The matrix is a simulation for the real, and the hyperreal, a place that Baudrillard (2001) suggested is a space that is divested of the "antireal" and is more real than the real, and because of that must vanish into simulation. The matrix is a space that binds all of the factors that concomitantly coconstruct teacher identity and takes on its shape because of its fluidity and its ability to change and morph as changes occur politically, in the lives of teachers, or socially. As a signifier of the fluid nature of teaching, it is important to recall that Jacob, like Timony (Hagood, 2002), was at risk of being mislabeled, but as we reconceptualize Jacob's predicament in the classroom during year one through a different lens, such as the matrix, and in applying thirdspace, we see that Jacob wasn't the problem—it was the myopic view of some. There *are* indeed places and spaces for different types of teaching styles and pedagogies that need to be enacted and performed.

In conclusion, as we continue to mine the matrix we can begin to unpack how preservice teacher identities are being coconstructed and, from there, foster and cultivate teacher identity. Consequently, we offer student teachers tools to help them co-opt their own teacher identities and consider how to negotiate with the elements that are coconstructing their teacher identities. Jacob might have become a teacher dropout statistic but thanks to the overall networked matrix coconstructing his teacher identity, he remains in teaching. Although restabilized in his teacher identity, this change in the network that was coconstructing his teacher identity speaks then to the need to cultivate and nurture diverse teachers who can meet students during any spacetime.

REENVISIONING TRANSDISCIPLINARY RESEARCH: IMPLICATIONS FOR EMERGING METHODOLOGIES

Implications for this study emerged from the methodology not atomistically but rather relationally at their intersections and nonintersections within the frame of the matrix that collectively contributed to the identity of the teacher and which activates our thinking about future research in the visual and communicative arts. First, research can foreground the matrix as a methodological frame to study the environment for educators and as a space wherein participants are contextually situated. Such a frame can become part of the methodological framework for future conversations around spacetime and utilized as a tool for analysis on how to understand specific identities. Although imaginary and real, it provides a way to frame and show how in spacetime intricate relationships are networked so that the fluid nature of the matrix has efficacy in other research contexts and spacetimes. By looking at the matrix during different times and by examining the relationships within it and within different spaces, we can reflect on what is coconstructing a participant during any given spacetime.

Next, by applying the larger metataxonomies that emerged from this study, "constructed through critique" and "constructed through windowing" to other transdisciplinary studies, we can further our understandings about unpacking data through a matrixed approach about identity, and specifically teacher identity construction during a spacetime. Looking at the concept of "constructed through critique" within the matrix, we not only validate and honor the voices of our participants, we also open up to new possibilities of understanding some of the necessary tensions facing them and enter into new spaces of investigation that speak to the realities of our participants. Looking at the concept of "constructed through windowing" through the matrix, we position ourselves within hybridized frameworks that will continue to morph in different spaces and contexts. The intersection of windowing with hybridized frameworks expands awareness into imaginative spaces. By pairing critique and windowing, and since each are infused with nonbinary meaning making, together they have the potential to be lifted and applied to contexts that have far-reaching implications. Over time, such concepts can be traced and referenced as a technique for data analysis within a matrix or in some other capacity.

Third, if our intention is to further a research agenda that challenges dominant society, our research must lead to both symbolic and literal theoretical border crossings and nonbinary thinking which can lead to new possibilities of making meaning in the visual and communicative arts. From a postmodern lens, research that is transdisciplinary by its nature is meant to challenge dominant binary thinking. Such a framework reframes our understanding about how teachers are coconstructed and relocates us into different contexts altogether. Thirdspace can open up doors toward liberating methodologies from binary results. Such spaces can be all inclusive, multilayered, and multidimensional, where the "same" and the "other" come together. If we aspire to conduct studies that authenticate the actual experiences of all individuals, some of whom may think outside of firstspace and secondspace binary constructs, research must mirror such experiences. To negate findings from nonbinary perspectives reinforces the notion of exclusion and reinforces binary meaning making.

Lastly, we need forums to conduct transdisciplinary conversations about spatiality and temporality in research across theoretical fields. Such a space can serve as a venue for other critical disciplines to share ways of collecting and interpreting data that are informed by spatiality and hybridity theories. Such a space can serve as an outlet for the dissemination, critique, and problematization of spatial methodologies and human geographies. Conversations with other disciplines can expand our understanding of the conditions that are coconstructing research methodologies and perhaps help create shifts within our own disciplines.

PROLEPTIC SPACETIME CONSIDERATIONS

Research in the visual and communicative arts must be responsive to how it is coconstructing identities because it is a key participant in creating the actants who will participate in the democracy in which they exist. If we hope for education to help challenge oppressive paradigms and binary thinking, and if we hope for our society to grow more liberal, free, and toward social justice for all, then our research agendas must reflect those values we embody. We need to remain thoughtful about our methods of inquiry and be conscious about how types of inquiry can reproduce dominant concepts that entrap education in antiquated paradigms. If we are to expand our own thinking and the borders that create the boundaries for teacher education, we must continue to create interdisciplinary approaches through transdisciplinary ways of analysis. Danielewicz (2001) said that teacher education programs should foster teacher identity development to the highest degree possible. In helping student teachers recognize their own identity constructions they become more informed about their own subjectivities which can empower them to challenge being co-opted by hegemonic-based discourse and thinking. Recognizing that their own teacher identities are situated within a complex networked matrix of spacetime relationships, can help them negotiate their identity constructions through both critique and windowing and help them relocate to spaces that stabilize their teacher identities. Preservice teachers can be technological actants who participate in coconstructing the identities of their own students across time and space and can teach their own students how to co-opt their own identities so that they are subservient to hegemonic thinking and power structures. We have a social responsibility to both conduct and analyze research through innovative methodologies that can help sustain and restabilize potential participant casualties. Jacob's state of destabilization is the consummate actualization of Cochran-Smith's (2004) admonishment for teacher education to be conceptualized as both "a learning problem and a political problem" (p. 2). By reconceptualizing and reconsidering findings through the visual and communicative arts, methodology has the potential to contribute to systemic change.

Educational researchers can continue to transcend the local by reconceptualizing how they conduct and reconceptualize research as they reconsider its dichotomous nature. We must reconsider for what purposes we are conducting research if we intend to have far-reaching personal, social, and political implications for our works in the visual and communicative arts. Methodologies in the visual and communicative arts must continue to be understood through postmodernistic lenses that can be disseminated across time and space. If education is to move toward social justice for all and gain privilege, we cannot address the learning without also addressing the political. Empowering ourselves with innovative methodologies will help us connect education to globalization because global processes, cultures, and technologies will continue to regenerate like transformers that have far-reaching implications for global literacies.

ACKNOWLEDGMENTS

I thank three people who have greatly influenced this work, because without their works, this research would not exist: Margaret Hagood for her copious feedback, her detailed analysis, her understandings of postmodern identity, and her enormous spirit; Kevin Leander who, in locating Latanya, helped to locate and activate my spatial and temporal interests; and Jacob, whose story I hope will inspire.

REFERENCES

Anzaldúa, G. (1987). *Borderlands: The new mestiza = La frontera*. San Francisco, CA: Aunt Lute Books.

Apple, M. (2002). *Official knowledge*. New York: Routledge.

Au, K. H. (1998). Social constructivism and the school literacy learning of students of diverse backgrounds. *Journal of Literary Research, 30*(2), 297–319.

Bakhtin, M. M. (1981). *The dialogical imagination: Four essays by M. M. Bakhtin* (M. Holquist & C. Emerson, Trans.). Austin, TX: University of Texas Press.

Bakhtin, M. M. (1986). *Speech genres and other late essays* (V.W. McGee, Trans). In C. Emerson & M. Holquist (Eds.). Austin, TX: Texas University Press.

Baudrillard, J. (2001). *Impossible exchange* (C. Turner, Trans.). London: Verso.

Bhabha, H. A. (1994). *The location of culture*. New York: Routledge.

Blakeslee, A. M., Cole, C. M., & Conefrey, T. (1996). Constructing voices in writing research: Developing participatory approaches to situated inquiry. In P. Mortensen & G. E. Kirsch (Eds.), *Ethics & representation in qualitative studies of literacy* (pp. 134–154). Urbana, IL: NCTE.

Brandt, D., & Clinton, K. (2002). Limits of the local: Expanding perspectives on literacy as a social practice. *Journal of Literacy Research, 34*(3), 337–356.

Britzman, D. (1991). *Practice makes practice: A critical study of learning to teach* (2nd ed.). Albany, NY: State University of New York.

Butler, J. (1990). *Gender trouble: Feminism and the subversion of identity.* New York: Routledge.

Cochran-Smith, M. (2004). *Walking the road: Race, diversity and social justice in teacher education*. New York: Teachers College Press.

Danielewicz, J. (2001). *Teaching selves: Identity, pedagogy and teacher education*. Albany: State University of New York Press.

Foucault, M. (1986). Of other spaces. *Diacritics, 16*(1), 22–28.

Freire, P., & Macedo, D. (1987). *Literacy: Reading the word & the world.* Westport, CT: Bergin & Garvey.

Gee, J. P. (1996). *Social linguistics and literacies: Ideology in discourses* (2nd ed.). New York: Falmer Press.

Grossman, P. (1990). *The making of a teacher.* New York, NY: Teachers College Press.

Gutierrez, K., Baquedano-Lopez, P., & Tejeda, C. (1999). Rethinking diversity: Hybridity and hybrid language practices in the third space. *Mind, Culture, and Activity: An International Journal, 6*(4), 286–303.

Hagood, M. (2002). Critical literacy for whom? *Reading Research and Instruction, 41*, 247–266.

Hall, S. (1996), Who needs "identity?" In. S. Hall & P. Dugay (Eds.), *Questions of cultural identity* (pp. 1–17). London: Sage.

Heath, S. B. (1983). *Ways with words: Language, life and community in classrooms.* New York: Cambridge University Press.

Holland, D. C., Lachiotte, W. Jr., Skinner, D., & Cain, C. (1998*). Identity and agency in cultural worlds.* Cambridge, MA: Harvard University Press.

hooks, b. (1989). *Talking back; thinking feminist, thinking Black.* Boston, MA: South End Press.

hooks, b. (1994). *Teaching to transgress.* New York: Routledge.

Janesick, V. J. (1998). The choreography of qualitative research design: minuets, improvisations, and crystallization. In Y. S. Lincoln (Ed.), *Handbook of qualitative research* (pp. 379–399). Thousand Oaks, CA: Sage.

Lawrence-Lightfoot, S., & Hoffman Davis, J. (1997). *The art and science of portraiture.* Hoboken, NJ: Jossey-Bass.

Leander, K. (2001). This is our freedom bus going home right now: Producing and hybridizing space-time contexts in pedagogical discourse. *Journal of Literary Research, 33*(4), 637–679.

Leander, K. (2002). Locating Latanya: The situated production of identity artifacts in classroom interaction. *Research in the Teaching of English, 37*, 198–250.

Leander, K., & Sheehy, M (Eds.). (2004). *Spatializing literacy research and practice.* New York: Peter Lang.

Lefebvre, H. (1991). *The production of space.* Oxford: Blackwell.

Lefebvre, H. (1996). *Writings on cities* (E. Kofman, & E. Lebas, Trans.). San Francisco: Jossey-Bass.

Levinson, B. A., Foley, D. E., & Holland, D., (Eds.). (1996). *The cultural production of the educated person.* Albany, NY: State University of New York.

Luke, C., & Luke, A. (1999). Theorizing interracial families and hybrid identity: An Australian perspective. *Educational Theory, 49*, 223–250.

McCarthey, S., & Moje, E. (2002). Identity matters. *Reading Research Quarterly, 37*(2), 228–238.

McLaren, P. (1986). *Schooling as a ritual performance: Towards a political economy of educational symbols and gestures.* New York, NY: Routledge.

Merriam, S. B. (2001). *Qualitative research and case study applications in education.* San Francisco, CA: Jossey-Bass.

Miller, S. (2005). *Geographically 'meaned' pre-service secondary language arts student teacher identities.* Ann Arbor, MI: Umi Dissertation Publishing. Retrieved July 15, 2006, from http://www.lib.umi.com/dissertations/fullcit/3177097

Minh-Ha, T. (1989). *Woman native other: Writing postcoloniality and feminism.* Bloomington, IN: Indiana University Press.

Minh-Ha, T. (1991). *When the moon waxes red.* New York: Routledge.

Moje, E. (2002). Reframing adolescent literacy research for new times: Studying youth as a resource. *Reading Research and Instruction, 41*, 211–227.

Nespor, J. (1997). *Tangled up in school: Politics, space, bodies and signs in the educational process.* Mahwah, NJ: Lawrence Erlbaum Associates.

Ochs, E. (1988). *Culture and language development: Language acquisition and language socialization in a Samoan village,* Cambridge, U.K.: Cambridge University Press.

Perez, B. (1998). *Sociocultural contexts of language and literacy.* Mahwah, NJ: Lawrence Erlbaum Associates.

Rich, A. (1977). *On lies, secrets and silence.* New York, NY: W.W. Norton.

Ritchie, J. S., & Wilson, D. E. (2000). *Teacher narrative as critical inquiry.* New York: Teachers College Press.

Rogers, R. (Ed.). (2004). *An introduction to critical discourse analysis in education.* Mahwah, NJ: Lawrence Erlbaum Associates.

Rose, G. (1993). *Feminism and geography: The limits of geographical knowledge.* Cambridge, U.K.: Polity Press.

Rosenblatt, L. (1994). Transactional theory of reading and writing. In R. Ruddell & N. Unrau (Eds.), *Theoretical models and processes of reading* (pp. 1057–1092). Newark: International Reading Association.

Soja, E. W. (1996). *Thirdspace: Journeys to Los Angeles and other real-and-imagined places.* Malden, U.K.: Blackwell.

Soja, E. (2004). Preface. In K. Leander & M. Sheehy (Eds.), *Spatializing literacy research and practice* (pp. ix–xv). New York: Peter Lang.

Solorzano, D. G., & Villalpando, O. (1998). Critical race theory and the experience of students of color in higher education. In C. A. Torres & T. R. Mitchell (Eds.), *Sociology of education* (pp. 211–224). Albany, NY: State University Press.

Vinz, R. (1996). *Composing a teaching life.* Portsmouth: Heinemann.

Wetherell, M., Taylor, S., & Yates, S. (2001). *Discourse as data.* London: Open University.

•17•

ANALYTIC DILEMMAS IN REAL AND VIRTUAL CONTEXTS: A TURN TO SPATIAL SEMIOSIS

Julie Cheville
UNIVERSITY OF MAINE

With the availability of new technologies, computer users are increasingly able to integrate multiple communicative modes (language, images, music) for expression in multiple media. Multimodality and multimediality pose distinct analytic challenges for sociocultural researchers who investigate language-based practices. In the case of video gaming and streaming video, moving images appear in activity sequences that may involve little or no linguistic mediation. In such contexts, users' perceptual habits and cognitive operations orient to spatial signification, a communicative context constituted by syntactical units that are imagistic rather than linguistic. As Tchertov (2002) suggests, "Spatial semiosis allows syntactic structures to be built in an essentially other way than the successive ordered chains of discrete signs, known for linguistics" (p. 443). In particular, the visual processing of spatial signs in real and virtual contexts involves distinct features not associated with the sequencing of linguistic signs. In the interpretation of spatially situated signs, the eyes move in sudden, rapid motions across the visual field in jumps known as "saccades" (Jacobs, 1995, p. 260). Each saccade "is followed by a *fixation,* a period of relative stability during which an object can be viewed. Even during a fixation, an eye does not remain completely still, but engages in several types of small motion. It drifts slowly, then is corrected by a tiny saccade-like jump (a microsaccade), which corrects the effect of the drift" (p. 260). Print texts require linear processing with few of the jumps, acceleration, and deceleration characterizing saccadic shifts in spatial signification, a process that is notably nonlinear and reversible across a visual field.

I begin this chapter by suggesting how Vygotskian (1978, 1987) and neo-Vygotskian theoretic frames overlook the ways in which cognition is spatially situated. I consider research in the area of biosemiotics that indicates how spatially coded sign relations appear to guide the neuronal processes responsible for agency and intersubjective understanding (Favareau, 2002; Gallese, 2001; Jackson, Meltzoff, & Decety, 2005; Ruby & Decety, 2001). The importance of both conditions to learning and to cognitive development underscores the need for an analytic framework sensitive to spatially situated signs, particularly as emerging digital technologies increasingly rely on imagistic syntax to communicate meaning.

THE BODY AS AN IDEATIONAL ARTIFACT IN SPATIAL SEMIOSIS

Recently, select researchers of the social semiotic have urged greater interest in the relation of semiotic and material tools (Leander, 2001, 2002; Lemke, 1997; Whitson, 1997). Leander's (2002) fascinating study of activity in one high school classroom disclosed how students' social and spatial practices recombine to situate identities. In its function as an identity artifact, the human body is at once semiotic (or constitutive of meaning) and material (an object of signification). Important to his account are the ways that interactants mobilize their bodies to redirect social activity toward specific ideological ends. What Leander investigated was a communicative context in which bodily activity influences but does not entirely *recode* a verbal plane of expression. While Leander's study provided an innovative and thorough analysis of how spatial orientations influence social practice, his method did not reveal the body's full potential as a sign.

Certainly, the kinesic properties of social practice in and outside the classroom have received attention, but concern for the human body is generally limited to how its activity reinforces, impedes, or redirects language.[1] As I noted elsewhere (Cheville, 2006), language-based perspectives necessarily restrict the human body to materiality, a condition of "having mass or matter and occupying physical space" (Haas, 1996, p. 10). Indeed, in the *social* semiotic (Halliday & Hasan, 1989; Halliday & Matthiessen, 1999; Hodge & Kress, 1988), where language supports meaning making, the body's activity remains material because it does not alter a prevailing "audio-temporal" sign system (Tchertov, 2002). The risk of language-based analytic approaches, however, is that overattribution of materiality to the human body prevents us from recognizing its ideational function in the *spatial* semiotic, a communicative domain constituted by visual-spatial expression.[2]

Perceptual operations in spatial semiosis include visual, as well as proprioceptive, associations that emerge from patterns of habituated bodily activity (Cheville, 2001, 2005).[3] For the purposes of illustrating spatial signification in the context of real-world activity, I briefly report on a qualitative investigation of female basketball players' athletic learning. The study was informed by my interest in how, for these participants, recurring configurations of spatial activity resulted in embodied mental schemata (Johnson, 1987). Johnson (1987) insisted that bodily activity is responsible for an array of "image" schemata that extend from patterns of concrete activity to guide abstract, even metaphorical, understanding. These mental structures are distinct from the propositional structures that originate from social activity. According to Johnson, "We have bodies connected to the natural world, such that our consciousness and rationality are tied to our bodily orientations and interactions in and with our environment. Our embodiment is essential to who we are, to what meaning is, and to our ability to draw rational inferences and be creative" (1987, p. xxxviii).

Among the host of embodied mental structures that players used to interpret and enact spatial activity, the schemata for systemic balance most clearly represents the human body's function as a sign vehicle in meaning exchange. To document the body's function in a context of activity where it served as primary mediational means, I spent two years studying the athletic play of members of the University of Iowa's women's basketball team (Cheville, 2001, 2005).

To frame the following discussion of how athletes' bodies functioned as sign vehicles in spatial signification, I draw on the work of Peirce (1931), whose semiotic theory supports the interpretation of visual-spatial signs. Peirce's conception of the triadic sign involves the dynamic relation of three elements: object, sign (representamen), and meaning (interpretant). An important feature of Peirce's semiotics is the notion of the meaning as the *effect* of the sign-object relation. For Peirce, the interpretant, or the semantic activity arising from the transaction of object and sign, not only tended toward habit but did so in either verbal or extraverbal forms, including "matter, energy, or information" (Lemke, 1997; Whitson, 1997). Peirce's triadic sign challenged traditional linguistic models, like that of de Saussure (1966), that reduced the sign to an interiorized linguistic concept and informational processing models that reduce messaging to unidirectional transfer. Instead, meaning emerges from the transaction of objects and signs in a sequence of ongoing message exchange framed by contextual affordances and constraints.

On the basketball court, the trajectory of the ball, as object, precipitated each player to engage her body as a vehicle that by virtue of its spatial practices communicated meaning to teammates. In possession of the ball, a player assumed object status and precipitated the sign activity of teammates who responded to the meaning communicated by her movement with the ball. With each pass, the sequence of sign activity proceeded in ever-changing sign relations until possession was completed or lost. In defensive or offensive sets, players aspired to intersubjective understanding that Crossley (1996) described:

> Their actions interlock and engage, each motivated and coordinated by and through an orientation to the other, but without conscious positing and reflective awareness of either self or other. They do not think about their other. They respond to them and are absorbed in a common action. Each action by the one calls forth an action in the other, which calls forth an action from the first, and so on. (p. 32)

In the context of the spatial semiotic, interpretive problems for the female athletes were not a solitary predicament. The struggle of novice players had short and long-term implications for the entire team. Any misinterpretation or disruption of the visual-spatial code inevitably jeopardized systemic balance. In fact, to only know and enact one's positional knowledge was to know nothing at all.

During one practice, to underscore the importance of collective understanding, the head coach relocated players to foreign positions on the court in a drill designed to test their knowledge of alternate orientations. With the post player looming at the point guard position, the coach ordered the freshman reserve point guard to the center position near the hoop. Within seconds of the first offensive play, the freshman was confused. Later, the experienced post player spoke with me about the significance of the drill:

> In a sense, everybody has to know what everybody else does. That's why when Stacy [freshman point guard] and I were on the court, and Stacy was going through play in her head like she does before every game, and I said, 'Okay, what does the post do in this play?', she said, 'I don't know what the post player does!' Karen [starting point guard] and I were like, 'You're the point guard. You're supposed to know what everybody does.' I said, 'I know what the guards do when we do the plays, so you gotta know what the posts do.' She's like, 'Okay. Okay.' So I asked her, 'Where does the post go in such and such a play?' And she was like, 'I don't know!' She didn't even know. It was crazy.

Each player had to learn to read the visual-spatial code in a manner consistent with the interpretation of her teammates. As Jackson and Delehanty (1995) wrote, "Basketball is a sport that involves the subtle interweaving of players at full speed to the point where they

[1] The analysis of socially grounded contexts of multimodality include emphasis on gesture and speech (Kendon, 1997; McNeill, 1992; Streeck, 1993, 1994), speech and gaze; Kendon, 1990; Streeck, 1993), speech and body position (Kendon, 1985), and speech, gaze, gesture, and body position (Goodwin & Goodwin, 1992). Educational researchers have also suggested how the body shapes identity (Boldt, 1996; Gee, 1990; Hagood, 2005; Hicks, 2002 Payne, 2000) and spatial practice (Rush, 2006; Leander, 2001, 2002; Leander & Sheehy, 2004).

[2] The "material bias" (Cheville, 2006) characteristic of sociocultural research is most pronounced in studies that incorporate Foucaultian poststructuralism to examine how the human body exists as an object of cultural inscription. While sociocultural and poststructural conceptual frames have disclosed how the human body is a discursive entity shaped by sociopolitical inequities and how, in turn, it can be mobilized to resist discourses, they have not, as Habermas (1987) argued in the case of poststructuralism, acknowledged the human body's signifying, or semiotic, potential.

[3] Proprioception is defined here as "the integrated [neural] signal arising from cutaneous, muscular, and joint receptors" (Farrer, Franck, Paillard, & Jeannerod, 2003, p. 610).

are thinking and moving as one. To do that successfully, they need to trust each other on a deep level and know instinctively how their teammates will respond" (p. 17).

In this section, I have briefly reported on the spatial signification characteristic of gross motor activity in a real-world context for which language did not serve as chief mediational means. My intent has been to indicate how the human body as a sign vehicle participates in spatial signification as a primary mediational means. Tchertov's (2002) characterization of spatial semiosis, Peircean in its nature, aligns with Johnson's (1987) theory of embodied understanding to suggest how body signs engender a visual-spatial code that is central to embodied cognition. In the next section, I consider research in biosemiotics and social cognitive neuroscience that argues spatial signification cannot be divorced from the sensory signification that characterizes the communicative activity of internal subsystems of the human body. I draw upon emerging research in biosemiotics to suggest how the perception of spatially situated signs appears to trigger cellular processes central to intersubjective understanding. Emerging interest in Peircean semiotics as a unified framework for explaining the communicative activity not just of externally situated spatial signs but of intradermal communicative processes promises to enrich our understanding of the effects of causation as one semiotic domain influences the function of another.

SENSORY SIGNIFICATION AND THE CULTIVATION OF INTERSUBJECTIVE UNDERSTANDING

Favareau (2002) is one of an increasing number who have turned to semiotics as a framework for rethinking conventional interpretations of life systems. Interest in "biosemiotics" emerged in the Soviet Union and the province of Estonia during the second half of the 20th century as semioticians began to shift their attentions from a cultural semiotics to other "secondary modeling systems" that semiotic principles appeared to explain. While the term *biosemiotic* originated in 1962 in Rothschild's (Küll, 1999) work in the area of psychiatric medicine, the analytic framework that stimulated widespread interest rested with Lotman (1977, 1990). Drawing on his own understanding of the hermeneutic relation of text and context, as well as von Uexküll's (1992) concept of "Umwelt," Lotman (1977, 1990) began to consider the interaction of organism and environment on semiotic terms.

Lotman (1977, 1990) wrote of the "semiosphere" to explain a context of intersecting semiotic processes that mediate meaning exchange. The concept emphasized three features of signification: communication, memory, and creativity (Lotman, 2002). Whether meaning in activity exhibits habituated or mutant response is important to all semioticians and those in the human sciences are particularly interested in the capacity of semiotic theory to explain the mutant responses central to disease and genetic disorders. At the same time that Lotman began to consider communication across semiotic domains, American semiotician Sebeok (1991) was contemplating a framework for biosemiotics. Characterizing it later, he wrote, "The process of message exchanges, or semiosis, is an indispensable characteristic of all terrestrial life forms. It is this capacity for containing, replicating, and expressing messages, of extracting their signification, that, in fact, distinguishes them more from the nonliving" (Sebeok, 1991, p. 22). Hoffmeyer (1995) later emphasized the sign "rather than the molecule" (p. 369) as the unit of analysis common to all communicative domains (social, spatial, neuronal, and genetic) and thus the construct most likely to reconcile methods of inquiry in the natural and social sciences. While biosemiotics is an analytic framework that does not alter prevailing biological tenets, it does necessitate interest in the *relation* of external and internal signifying processes. In particular, biosemiotics urges concern for how spatially situated sign use triggers a network of intradermal signifying operations central to body function and consciousness.

I focus on Favareau's (2002) analysis of neuronal cells, specifically mirror neurons, given its relevance to intersubjectivity, a central feature of thought and agency. Favareau (2002) described neuronal functions responsive to particular forms of motor activity. According to Favareau, intersubjectivity arises not only in the social practices that Vygotsky (1978) described, but also in sensory signification that is highly responsive to nonlinguistic signs.[4]

Because the first report of mirror neurons is recent (Rizzolatti, Fadiga, Gallese, & Fogassi, 1996), researchers have yet to crack the various codes that characterize the integrated function of motoric, visual, and neuronal processes. Favareau (2002) suggested that mirror neurons are "selectively 'tuned' by evolutionary and ontogenetic experience (e.g., that they 'take habits' in the Peircean sense)" (p. 70) and thus respond in a highly selective manner to particular spatial signs. He highlighted work in feature recognition (Kobatake & Tanaka, 1994) that indicates how individual neurons become exclusively responsive to specific images. Increasing evidence suggests that the intersubjective relation of human beings is dependent not chiefly on the audio-temporal code characterizing linguistic signification, but on the perceptual processing of spatially situated signs. In short, the mirror neurons central to intersubjective understanding appear responsive only to *motion* activity that an agent finds meaningful and goal driven (Gallese, Fadiga, Fogassi, & Rizzolatti, 1996; Gallese & Keysers, 2001; Metzinger & Gallese, 2003; Rizzolatti et al., 1996; Ruby & Decety, 2003). Citing others, Favareau reported, "The simple presentation of objects, or their manipulation in 'meaningless' or non-goal directed ways by hand (whether witnessed or performed) will not evoke the [mirror] neuron to discharge" (pp. 74–75). Interestingly, mirror neurons are triggered not only in the midst of spatial activity but also in contexts of "mental locomotion" where the observer feels himself a part of the activity he witnesses. In other words, the execution and observation of action appear to share the same neural pathway, the same communicative neural codes, and the same cortical region (Metzinger & Gallese, 2003).

Favareau (2002) bemoaned the neural conduit model, for its mechanistic and reductive character, that has long been used to explain the message transfer as "flow[ing] through the circuitry of neurons in much the same way as electricity flows through a computer motherboard (e.g., in ways in which neither the signal nor the

[4] For decades, research on infant development has indicated how the joint, embodied activity of caregivers supports the intersubjective response of infants. Cowley, Moodley, and Fiori-Cowley (2004) argued that semiosis begins with intersubjective behavior around the age of three months when "an infant's role in utterance-activity enacts a 'particular sense'. Eventually this property is complemented by culturally-based meanings which . . . stabilized around the age of 4" (p. 129). Work on primary intersubjectivity in infants challenges language as a desomatized activity (Cowley et al., 2004, p. 111) to argue that infant response involves a kinetics that grounds language development.

vehicle of its transmission are understood to be themselves interactive participants in the creativity of semiosis)" (p. 68). As a result, he suggested that neuroscientists have grossly underestimated how the interpretant that is mirror neuron activity arises from the perception of spatial sign relations to situate cognitive and affective response. Favareau argued,

> The totality of this systemic and incessant sign activity . . . is an ongoing, dynamic process of sign-exchanging cells embedded in sign-exchanging brains embedded in sign-exchanging bodies embedded in sign-exchanging worlds, the eternal interplay of self-organization and symmetry-breaking that characterizes the moment-to-moment experience of this recursively interactive system that constitutes, in a very real sense, the very essences of 'knowing' and 'the mind.' . . . Properly seen, body, brain, mind and cell are but levels of the same one endlessly interacting complex system. (p. 67)

The promising link between spatial and sensory semiosis asks educational researchers to realize the limits of the Vygotskian and neo-Vygotskian preoccupation with language as primary mediational means. Because the probable relation of spatial and sensory signification appears to support emotional and psychological conditions central to learning and knowing, educational researchers, particularly those interested in the visual and proprioceptive modalities responsive to digital video technologies, must begin to consider analytic frameworks oriented to spatial signs. With the increasing application of Peircean semiotics in the human sciences, there seems an opportunity for educational researchers, as well as social and human scientists, to collaborate in their analysis of spatial sign activity. In the next section, I examine how emerging digital technologies available to adolescents constitute a vital realm for interdisciplinary investigations of learning in the spatial semiotic.

EMERGING COMPUTER TECHNOLOGIES AND THEIR IMPACT ON ADOLESCENTS' PERCEPTION

As delivery vehicles, computer hardware and software have made available new configurations of sound, print, and images. Some have argued that the multimodal demands of hypertext, multimedia writing, and video gaming constitute a transformational stage in cultural activity that will prove as profound as the shift from orality to literacy (Bolter, 1991; Poster, 1995). Not surprisingly, literacy researchers have grown increasingly interested in the semiotic resources that new media make available to adolescent users (Alvermann, 2005; Cope & Kalantzis, 2000; Gee, 2003; Lankshear, Snyder, & Green, 2000; Luke, 2000; New London Group, 1996). In this section, I discuss the divergent perceptual modalities demanded of computer-mediated technologies. In disclosing both the limited and far-ranging semiotic potential of computer mediation, I hope to suggest the relevance of a spatial semiotic approach. In particular, I will emphasize emerging research in "perspective taking" that suggests how simulation technologies might begin to integrate social and spatial signification in ways that support the learning of struggling readers.

I begin with an examination of Criterion, an Internet-based scoring program that ETS Technologies currently licenses to school districts seeking improved student performance on large-scale writing assessments. I consider how the pseudointeractive features of this tool's design do little to mask the authority of a scoring engine that obligates the writer to text correction. While the representation of text in real and virtual contexts does indeed spatialize language (Goody & Watt, 1968), I argue Vygotsky's (1978) assertion that this textualization of linguistic units does not alter their conceptual effect but only orients our perceptual processes to a second order representation. In both oral and written language, meaning is processed according to a temporal sequence of sounds and letters respectively. That Criterion's material design avoids the use of spatially situated images to facilitate writing development indicates a rejection of the options generally associated with hypertext design. As Joyce (1995) maintained, "A constructive hypertext should be a tool for inventing, discovering, viewing, and testing multiple, alternative organizational structures as well as a tool for comparing these structures of thought with more traditional ones and transforming one into the other" (pp. 42–43).

In most states, on-demand writing tests require students to produce narrative, expository, and/or persuasive texts in short intervals of time. The rhetorical demands associated with these tasks, generally considered dubious by the research community (Cheville, 2004; Conference on College Composition and Communication, 2004; Fitzgerald, 1996; Herrington & Moran, 2001), have spawned the development of instructional materials and software programs designed to enhance students' written products. Among these, ETS Technologies' Web-based scoring program is calibrated to data that its parent division, the Educational Testing Service, has collected in its large-scale assessments. Currently marketed to kindergarten through age 16 institutions, Criterion offers teachers access to an online library of 108 writing prompts spanning all grade levels in narrative, expository, and persuasive modes. This topic function allows teachers to use prompts already tested and scored by ETS. Because these prompts are already calibrated to test trialed four- and six-point rubrics and their representative benchmark essays, a scoring engine offers writers an immediate, or "real-time" (ETS Technologies, Inc., 2002, p. 3), response just seconds after they submit an essay online. The key feature of the program is its automatic scoring capability.

At present, computational linguists have oriented the program's diagnostic capabilities to the following domains:

- Grammar—fragments, garbled sentences, subject-verb agreement, verb-form errors, pronoun errors, possessive errors, wrong or missing words
- Usage—article errors, confused words, wrong form of word, faulty comparison, nonstandard verb or word
- Mechanics—spelling, missing capitalization of proper nouns, missing initial capital letter in a sentence, missing question mark, missing final punctuation, missing apostrophe, missing comma, missing hyphen, fused words, compound words, duplicate words
- Style—repetition of words, inappropriate words or phrases, sentences with passive voice, long sentences, short sentences, sentences beginning with coordinating conjunctions
- Organization and development—introductory material, thesis statement, main ideas, supporting ideas, conclusion, transitional words and phrases (ETS Technologies, Inc., 2002, pp. 3–4)

A writer receives both a holistic score and descriptive feedback for each submitted essay. Essays return with highlighted portions of text flagging particular errors and concerns. By clicking on these highlighted areas, students receive additional "diagnostic analysis." For instance, a short sentence within a paragraph consisting of several other short sentences might be flagged for potential stylistic flaws with the following advice: "This is a short sentence. If there are too many short sentences in your essay, your writing might sound choppy. You can improve your sentence structure by using sentence combining" (ETS Technologies, Inc., 2002, p. 4). In a meeting with ETS Technology administrators, I raised questions about the program's crude conception of style and was informed that computational linguists had not yet developed an analytic capability beyond parts of speech and simple phrases (Cheville, 2004). In effect, the scoring engine is not yet equipped to identify clausal structures central to stylistic maturity. Regarding organization and development, the diagnostic analysis was geared to the fixed arrangement of parts. For example, the flagged portion in an expository essay might read, "Is this your thesis?"

Based on this diagnostic feedback, students may revise and resubmit essays during the evaluation period that their teacher has identified. According to the brochure, "Heuristic-based diagnostic feedback helps writers focus on the errors and features of their writing as they revise" (ETS Technologies, Inc., 2002, p. 3). While teachers may disengage the scoring function and create their own topics, the automated scoring feature is highlighted in promotional materials (ETS Technologies, Inc., 2002). Criterion's "evidence-based design" offers information on which to base instruction to teachers. At the end of an evaluation period, teachers have access to not only students' individual holistic scores, errors, and diagnostic commentary but also to a "class error report," which indicates the frequency of errors committed across student samples. Teachers may also interject comments, either by inserting their own thoughts, questions, and concerns or by drawing from a bank of preexisting "instructor's notes." Comments may be inserted in the essay or posted on a student's portfolio message board, where feedback from all readers, including peers, can be configured to appear. As the brochure suggested, "Students can conduct online dialogue [asynchronous] with you about their scores, feedback, revisions, and overall writing performance and progress" (ETS Technologies, Inc., 2002, p. 2).

Joyce (1995) claimed that ineffective hypertexts "assuage the hunger for automaticity with the full-bellied inertia of tradition. We know the bulk of this stuff; we have chewed on it for years" (p. 43). To be sure, literacy researchers and practitioners are familiar with designer-driven interaction and nonadaptive diagnostic response, features long characteristic of skill and drill instruction in language and writing. In effect, ETS's Internet-based writing program has little to do with multimodal design options, writer-driven goals, mutually created activity, or "new definitions of what we consider writing" (Hocks, 2003, p. 630). The technology has everything to do with the reliable, generalizable, and expedient scoring of student writing.

In contrast to programs like Criterion that reiterate the primacy of linguistic signification, computer-mediated activity also makes available simulation opportunities that engage users in profoundly different and arguably richer experiences of problem solving and reciprocal interactions. Research in the area of social cognitive neuroscience has begun to document the effects of simulated activity on the capacity of individuals to assume the perspective of others. Existing work in the area of "perspective taking" orients not only to computer-mediated interactions but also to impairments of perspective taking associated with autism, personality disorders, and learning disabilities. What this research suggests, in contexts of simulated activity, is that users' manipulation of a joystick or keyboard can trigger neural processes characteristic of real action execution (Cochin, Barthelemy, Roux, & Martineau, 1999; Decety & Chaminade, 2003; Fadiga, Fogassi, Pavesi, & Rizzolatti, 1995). In the case of games in which the user embodies a first person perspective (creates and becomes a character), players' engagement is mediated by an activity sequence of spatially situated signs that include images of other characters, symbols, and landscapes. Not unlike the action execution of athletes who become acculturated to spatially situated body signs, gamers process visual-spatial syntactic units appearing on screen. To be sure, the perceptual process framing online gaming is multimodal, including sounds, music, and language. Nevertheless, one's successful performance rests predominantly on her interpretation of visual images. The interpretive process is guided by the capacity of the user to initiate and sustain what social cognitive neuroscientists term *motor imagery*, a state in which the gamer feels as if he or she is actually anticipating and initiating the action represented in real time on the computer screen (Decety, 1996; Decety & Jeannerod, 1996; Jeannerod, 1994; di Pellegrino, Fadiga, Fogassi, Gallese, & Rizzolatti, 1992). In his argument for the multimodal significance of video games, Gee (2003) wrote,

> Good video games involve the player in a compelling world of action and interaction, a world to which the learner has made an identity commitment, in the sense of engaging in the sort of play with identities. . . . Thanks to this fact, the player practices a myriad of skills, over and over again, relevant to playing the game, often without realizing that he or she is engaging in such extended practice sessions. (p. 68)

On discursive grounds, Gee (2003) maintained that meaningful online games present compelling problems that require the level of attention, rehearsal, collaboration, and immersion characteristic of the most efficacious learning tasks. Social practices aside, I would go further by suggesting that the spatial signification experienced by gamers appears to trigger a neurophysiological response that mirrors the actual execution of the activity being simulated. In other words, "the feeling that [one] can cause an action" (Farrer et al., 2003, p. 619) has a neurophysiological basis. I argue that computer users' engagement with spatially situated signs involve higher psychological processes that pass unexplained by sociocultural methodologies attuned to the language practices surrounding a users' engagement with media. It seems increasingly possible that the perspective taking opportunities available through simulation software are precisely those that can support the comprehension of struggling readers. With opportunities to shift between textual and imagistic syntax and to actually "become the book" (Wilhelm, 1997), readers can assume the perspectives of characters in simulated activity as a way of supporting the visualization strategies required of their engagement with print.

As the powerful links between spatial and sensory signification become clear, the dangers of Vygotsky's (1978, 1987) original ambiguity on the relation of culture and nature in ontogenetic development grow apparent. An emphasis on socially mediated activity does not position us to acknowledge the intersemiotic connections across domains of social, spatial, and sensory signification or to enter interdisciplinary investigations that recognize superordinate "semiotic ecology" (Lang, 1997). Intersemiotic questions encourage us to investigate the relation of cultural and natural planes of activity—for instance, noting how greater access to visual-spatial codes might support students' mastery of language practices. Already, social psychologists, neuroscientists, cognitive psychologists, anthropologists, and sociologists are forging interdisciplinary projects aimed at understanding semiotic processes through a range of methods that include brain-imaging techniques. That educational researchers are not yet represented in these projects is unfortunate. Nonetheless, biosemiotic studies and cultural semiotics represent converging analytic frameworks of interest to international researchers who by virtue of their shared interest in Peirce's theory of signs appear poised to converse in important ways.

REFERENCES

Alvermann, D. (Ed.). (2005). Adolescents and literacies in a digital world, Volume 7: *New literacies and digital epistemologies*. New York: Peter Lang.

Boldt, G. (1996). Sexist and heterosexist responses to gender bending in an elementary classroom. *Curriculum Inquiry, 26*, 113–131.

Bolter, J. (1991). *Writing space: The computer, hypertext, and the history of writing*. Hillsdale, NJ: Lawrence Erlbaum Associates.

Cheville, J. (2004). Automated scoring technologies and the rising influence of error. *English Journal, 93*(4), 47–52.

Cheville, J. (2005). Confronting the problem of embodiment. International *Journal of Qualitative Studies in Education, 18*(1), 85–107.

Cheville, J. (2006). The bias of materiality in sociocultural theory: Reconceiving embodiment. *Mind, Culture, and Activity, 13*, 25–37.

Cochin, S., Barthelemy, C., Roux, S., & Martineau, J. (1999). Observation and execution of movement: Similarities demonstrated by quantified electroencephalography. *European Journal of Neuroscience, 11*, 1839–1842.

Conference on College Composition and Communication. (2004). *Position statement on teaching, learning, and assessing writing in digital environments*. Retrieved April 22, 2005, from http://www.ncte.org/cccc/resources/positions/123773.htm?source=gs

Cope, B., & Kalantzis, M. (Eds.). (2000). *Multiliteracies: Literacy learning and the design of social futures*. London: Routledge.

Cowley, S., Moodley, S., & Fiori-Cowley, A. (2004). Grounding signs of culture: Primary intersubjectivity in social semiosis. *Mind, Culture and Activity, 11*, 109–132.

Crossley, N. (1996). Intersubjectivity: The fabric of social becoming. London: Sage. de Saussure, F. (1966). *Course in general linguistics* (W. Baskin, Trans.). New York: McGraw-Hill.

Decety, J. (1996). The neurophysiological basis of motor imagery. *Behavioural Brain Research, 77*, 45–52.

Decety, J., & Chaminade, T. (2003). When the self represents the other: A new cognitive neuroscience view of psychological identification. *Consciousness and Cognition, 12*, 577–596.

Decety, J., & Jeannerod, M. (1996). Mentally simulated movements in virtual reality: Does Fitts law hold in motor imagery. *Behavioural Brain Research, 72*, 127–134.

di Pellegrino, G., Fadiga, L., Fogassi, L., Gallese, V., & Rizzolatti, G. (1992). Understanding motor events: A neurophysiological study. *Experimental Brain Research, 91*, 176–180.

ETS Technologies, Inc. (2002). *Criterion: Online writing evaluation*. Princeton, NJ: Author.

Fadiga, L., Fogassi, L., Pavesi, G., & Rizzolatti, G. (1995). Motor facilitation during action observation: A magnetic stimulation study. *Journal of Neurophysiology, 73*, 2608–2611.

Favareau, D. (2002). Beyond self and other: On the neurosemiotic emergence of intersubjectivity. *Sign System Studies, 30*(1), 57–99.

Farrer, C., Franck, N., Paillard, J., & Jeannerod, M. (2003). The role of proprioception in action recognition. *Consciousness and Cognition, 12*, 609–619.

Fitzgerald, K. (1994). Computerized scoring? A question of theory and practice. *Journal of Basic Writing, 13*, 3–17.

Gallese, V. (2001). The "Shared Manifold" Hypothesis: From mirror neurons to empathy. *Journal of Consciousness Studies, 8*, 5–87.

Gallese, V., & Keysers, C. (2001). Mirror neurons: A sensorimotor representation system. *Behavioral Brain Sciences, 24*(5), 983–984.

Gallese, V., Fadiga, L., Fogassi, L., & Rizzolatti, G. (1996). Action recognition in the premotor cortext. *Brain, 119*, 593–609.

Gee, J. (1990). *Social linguistics and literacy: Ideology in discourse*. New York: Falmer Press.

Gee, J. (2003). *What video games have to teach us about learning and literacy*. New York: Palgrave Macmillan.

Goodwin, C., & Goodwin, M. (1992). Context, activity and participation. In P. Auer & A. di Luzio (Eds.), *The contextualization of language* (pp. 77–99). Amsterdam: Benjamins.

Goody, J., & Watt, I. (1968). *The consequences of literacy*. In J. Goody (Ed.), Literacy in Traditional Societies (pp. 27–68). New York: Cambridge University Press.

Haas, C. (1996). *Writing technology: Studies on the materiality of literacy*. Mahweh, NJ: Lawrence Erlbaum Associates.

Habermas, J. (1987). *An alternative way out of the philosophy of the subject* (F. Lawrence, Trans.). Cambridge, U.K.: Polity Press.

Hagood, M. (2005). Bodily pleasures and/as the text. *English Teaching, Practice, and Critique, 4*, 20–39.

Halliday, M., & Hasan, R. (1989). *Language, context, and text: A social semiotic perspective*. London: Oxford University Press.

Halliday, M., & Matthiessen, C. (1999). *Constructing experience through meaning: a Language-based approach to cognition*. London: Cassell.

Herrington, A., & Moran, C. (2001). What happens when machines read our students' writing? *College English, 63*, 480–499.

Hicks, D. (2002). *Reading lives: Working class children and literacy learning*. New York: Teachers College Press.

Hocks, M. (2003). Understanding visual rhetoric in digital writing environments. *College Composition and Communication, 54*(4), 629–656.

Hodge, R., & Kress, G. (1988). *Social semiotics*. Ithaca, NY: Cornell University Press.

Hoffmeyer, J. (1995). *The semiotic body-mind*. In N. Tasca (Ed.), *Essays in honor of Thomas A. Sebeok* (pp. 367–383). Porto, Portugal: Porto.

Jackson, P., & Delehanty, H. (1995). *Sacred hoops: Spiritual lessons of a hardwood warrior*. New York: Hyperion.

Jackson, P., Meltzoff, A., & Decety, J. (2005). How do we perceive the pain of others? A window into the neural processes involved in empathy. *NeuroImage, 24*, 771–779.

Jacobs, R. (1995). Eye tracking in advanced interface design. In W. Barfield & T. Furness, III (Eds.), *Virtual environments and advanced interface designs* (pp. 258–288). New York: Oxford University Press.

Jeannerod, M. (1994). The representing brain: Neural correlates of motor intention and imagery. *Behavioral and Brain Sciences, 17*, 187–245.

Johnson, M. (1987). *The body in the mind: The bodily basis of meaning, imagination, and reason*. Chicago: University of Chicago Press.

Joyce, R. (1995). Of *two minds: Hypertext pedagogy and poetics*. Ann Arbor, MI: University of Michigan Press.

Kobatake, E., & Tanaka, K. (1994). Neuronal selectivities to complex object features in the ventral visual pathway of the macaque cerebral cortex. *Journal of Neurophysiology, 71*, 856–867.

Küll, K. (1999). Biosemiotics in the twentieth century: A view from biology. *Semiotica, 127*, 385–414.

Lang, A. (1997). Non-Cartesian artifacts in dwelling activities: Steps toward a semiotic ecology. In M. Cole, Y. Engeström, & O. Vasquez (Eds.), *Mind, culture, and activity: Seminal papers from the laboratory of comparative human cognition* (pp. 185–204). Cambridge, U.K.: Cambridge University Press.

Lankshear, C., Snyder, I., & Green, B. (2000). *Teachers and technoliteracy*. Sydney, Australia: Allen and Unwin.

Leander, K. (2001). "This is our freedom bus going home right now": Producing and hybridizing space-time contexts in pedagogical discourse. *Journal of Literacy Research, 33*(4), 637–680.

Leander, K. (2002). Locating Latanya: The situated production of identity artifacts in classroom interaction. *Research in the Teaching of English, 37*, 198–250.

Leander, K., & Sheehy, M. (Eds.). (2004). *Spatializing literacy research and practice*. New York: Peter Lang.

Lemke, J. (1997). Cognition, context, and learning: A social semiotic perspective. In D. Kirshner & J. Whitson (Eds.), *Situated cognition: Social, semiotic, and psychological perspectives*. Mahwah, NJ: Lawrence Erlbaum Associates.

Lotman, J. (1977). Myth-name-culture. In D. Lucid (Ed.), *Soviet semiotics* (pp. 233–252). Baltimore, MD: Johns Hopkins University Press.

Lotman, J. (1990). *Universe of the mind: A semiotic theory of culture* (A. Shukman, Trans.). Bloomington, IN: Indiana University Press.

Lotman, M. (2002). Umwelt and semiosphere. *Sign System Studies, 30*(1), 33–40.

Luke, C. (2000). Cyber-schooling and technological change: Multiliteracies for new Times. In B. Cope & M. Kalantzis (Eds.), *Multiliteracies: Literacy learning and the design of social futures* (pp. 69–91). Melbourne, Australia: Macmillan.

McNeill, D. (1992). *Hand and mind: What gestures reveal about thought*. Chicago: University of Chicago Press.

Metzinger, T., & Gallese, V. (2003). The emergence of a shared action ontology: Building blocks for a theory. *Consciousness and Cognition, 12*, 549–571.

New London Group. (1996). A pedagogy of multiliteracies: Designing social futures. *Harvard Educational Review, 66*, 60–92.

Payne, M. (2000). *Bodily discourses: When students write about abuse and eating disorders*. Portsmouth, NH: Boynton/Cook Publishers.

Peirce, C. (1931). *Collected papers*. C. Hartshorne & P. Weiss (Eds.). Cambridge: Harvard University Press.

Poster, M. (1995). Postmodern virtualities. In M. Featherstone & R. Burrows (Eds.), *Cyberspace, cyberbodies, cyberpunk: Cultures of technological embodiment* (pp. 79–96). London: Sage Publications.

Rizzolatti, G., Fadiga, L., Gallese, V., & Fogassi, L. (1996). Premotor cortex and the recognition of actions. *Cognitive Brain Research, 3*, 131–141.

Ruby, P. & Decety, J. (2001). Effect of subjective perspective taking during simulation of action: A PET investigation of agency. *Nature Neuroscience, 4*, 546–550.

Ruby, P., & Decety, J. (2003). What do you believe versus what do you think they believe: A neuroimaging study of perspective-taking at the conceptual level. *European Journal of Neuroscience, 17*, 2475–2480.

Rush, L. (2006). *Taking a broad view of literacy: Lessons from the Appalachian Trail thru-hiking community*. Reading Online. Retrieved April 22, 2006, from http://www.readingonline.org/newliteracies/lit_index.asp?HREF=rush/index.html

Sebeok, T. (1991). *A sign is just a sign*. Bloomington, IN: Indiana University Press.

Streeck, J. (1993). Gesture as communication I: Its coordination with gaze and speech. *Communication Monographs, 60*, 275–299.

Streeck, J. (1994). Gesture as communication II: The audience as co-author. *Research on Language and Social Interaction, 27*, 239–267.

Tchertov, L. (2002). Spatial semiosis in culture. *Sign Systems Studies, 30*(2), 442–453.

Uexküll, J. von (1992). Introduction: The sign theory of Jakob von Uexküll. *Semiotica, 89*, 279–315.

Vygotsky, L. (1978). *Mind in society: The development of higher psychological processes*. Harvard, MA: Harvard University Press.

Vygotsky, L. (1987). Thinking and speech. In R. Rieber & A. Carton (Eds.), *The collected works of L. S. Vygotsky, Volume 1: Problems of general psychology*. New York: Plenum.

Whitson, J. (1997). Cognition as semiosic process: From situated mediation to critical Reflective transcendance. In D. Kirshner & J. Whitson (Eds.), *Situated Cognition: Social, Semiotic, and Psychological Perspectives* (pp. 97–150). Mahwah, NJ:Lawrence Erlbaum Associates.

Wilhelm, J. (1997). *You gotta BE the book: Teaching engaged and reflective reading with adolescents*. New York: Teachers College Press.

18

DISABILITY STUDIES MATTERS

Kit Tisdale
MARYVILLE, TENNESSEE

The stakes for recognizing, utilizing, and valuing alternative approaches to literacy are high for people considered disabled. What may be exciting, cutting-edge work in the field of literacy—incorporating layers of visual media and alternative communication with the intention of enhancing traditional meaning making—is *necessary* work for people in the disabled community who already utilize less traditional modalities of media and communication because they may not have the visual or cognitive ability to read print, the fine motor skills to write, accessible entry to buildings where media are sold or presented, or opportunities to represent themselves in various media. The urgent, political, and personal work that defines the field of disability studies has much to offer the field of literacy in a discussion of research in visual and communicative arts.

Even though the work in disability studies is personal (many disability studies scholars are considered disabled or have loved ones considered disabled), disability studies is not about studying people who are disabled. Rather, it is a framework for considering the social, cultural, political, and historical conditions that are disabling in our society. Therefore, this chapter is really not aimed at people who would become special education teachers (although disability studies scholars hope that special educators are part of our audiences, special education teachers may be frustrated by the seeming dearth of specific techniques for teaching or researching students in special education programs). Disability studies is a broad framework that is arguably useful for all social science researchers and education practitioners. In this chapter, I hope to convince the reader that the field of disability studies *matters* even for people who believe they have able-bodied interests.

I start this chapter with an introduction to the field of disability studies. The field of disability studies is buoyed by work from scholars in England, Australia, and the United States, and I use this work throughout the chapter. The reader will notice, however, that I use statistics and terminology and refer to laws specific to the United States, where I am located. After the introduction to disability studies, I then consider the implications of a disability studies perspective on research methodologies as they relate to visual and communicative arts.

INTRODUCTION TO DISABILITY STUDIES

I will start with what the term *disability* means in a conventional sense. Basically, disability is an inclusive category that groups bodily difference. Thomson (1997) gave a good sense of the scope of the category:

> Disability is an overarching and in some ways artificial category that encompasses congenital and acquired differences, mental illness and retardation, chronic and acute illnesses, fatal and progressive diseases, temporary and permanent injuries, and a wide range of bodily characteristics considered disfiguring, such as scars, birthmarks, unusual proportions, or obesity. (p. 13)

The overarching nature of the category of disability is evident in the U.S. census, which has used the following typology of disability: sensory, physical, mental, self-care, go- outside- home, and employment (American Community Survey, 2003). It is also evident in educational law in the United States in which the category of disability has been used to describe children with mental retardation, hearing impairments, speech or language impairments, visual impairments, orthopedic impairments, autism, traumatic brain injury, other health impairments, specific learning disabilities, and emotional disturbance (IDEA, 1997).

The overarching category of disability is significant in the lives of many people. This broad category is used to describe about 20% of the population of the United States (McNeil, 1997) and is used to describe at least one member of 30% of U.S. families (Wang, 2005). During the 2000–2001 school year, 11% of school-aged children were defined as disabled and were served by special education (24th Annual Report to Congress on the Implementation of the Individuals with Disabilities Education Act, 2002).

The implications for being regarded as disabled are considerable. It has only been in recent history that people considered disabled have been guaranteed civil rights and have had guaranteed access to education, public spaces, transportation, services, telecommunications and employment (PL 94-142: Education for all Handicapped Children Act, 1975; PL 101-336: Americans with Disabilities Act, 1990). Access matters on many levels—perhaps most strikingly in the relationship of poverty and disability. In 2004, over 28% of people with a work-related disability lived with their families in poverty (Houtneville, 2005). A National Health Interview survey showed that, in 1994–1995, while 79% of adults without disabilities were working, only 37% of those with disabilities were employed (Loprest & Maag, 2001). It is believed that the worldwide literacy rate for adults with disabilities is as low as 3% (Helander, 1998). There are certainly economic, political, and cultural difficulties that go hand in hand with being considered disabled.

For some people and some disciplines, the existence of disability seems self-evident and their approach to studying disability is, according to Barnes (2003), "Rooted in conventional wisdom; namely, that accredited impairment, whether physical, sensory or intellectual, is the primary cause of 'disability' and therefore the difficulties: economic, political and cultural, encountered by people labeled 'disabled'" (p. 4). But, in the 1970s, activists considered disabled worked to counter this conventional wisdom (Finkelstein, 1998). Central to their movement was a conceptual distinction between impairment and disability (impairment being the medical condition and disability being the isolating and excluding practices imposed upon people labeled 'disabled'). The resulting critical, social model of understanding disability became the focus of a new field of study—disability studies.

Disability studies is an interdisciplinary field in the social sciences that focuses on bringing a social analysis to what has traditionally been a medical model of disability. Viewing disability as a physiological state of the body (a body that has seemingly deviated from the normal state of being), the medical model of disability positions the disabled body as an object of study for medical schools and rehabilitation sciences. Use of the medical model has extended beyond medical schools and rehabilitation sciences as the dominant way of understanding disability and has been taken up in social science fields such as special education where students considered disabled by and large are approached as students who have deviated from the norm. Disability studies is a reaction to the "cure" and "care" modes of approaching disability that are used in medical schools, rehabilitation sciences, and special education (Finkelstein, 1998). In contrast to seeing disability as a condition to be cured or cared for, within disability studies disability is approached "as a way of thinking about bodies rather than as something that is wrong with bodies" (Ware, 2001, p. 110). Disability studies provides a framework for scholars interested in examining the social, cultural, political, and historical conditions that create "disabled" bodies.

DISABILITY STUDIES AND METHODOLOGY

The way a researcher thinks about bodily difference matters even when the topic at hand is not disability. Many researchers are already familiar with the questions of knowledge and knowing (ontology and epistemology) that impact the ways that we choose to do research. For example, a researcher who privileges an individual's in-depth knowledge of an experience will conduct a phenomenological study with interview methods over a statistical study that uses a rating scale instrument. Similarly, a researcher's way of thinking about bodily difference is evident in the methodology and methods used. This connection is where disability studies offers some thought-provoking ideas for researchers. First, I will connect a researcher's stance on bodily difference to research methodology and research aims. Then I will look at some specific and concrete relationships between bodily difference, research methods, and visual and communicative arts.

Lather (1991; drawing in part from Habermas, 1971) conceptualized a way of connecting social theory with methodologies in research. She delineated four categories of "human interest that underscore knowledge claims" (p. 6). They are prediction, understanding, emancipation, and deconstruction. She then connected those categories to common methodologies or approaches to "generating and legitimating knowledge" (p. 7). For example, positivism is an approach for prediction, phenomenology is an approach for understanding, action research is an approach for emancipation, and poststructural methodologies are approaches for deconstruction.

Work in disability studies has occurred in all of the postpositivism categories (understanding, emancipation, and deconstruction). Although the categories (like all categories) are not cut and dry (for example, researchers may work with both emancipatory and deconstructive interests or may use positivist research data for emancipatory aims), they are useful in understanding how different researchers will approach bodily difference differently and how one's understanding of bodily difference will affect one's approach to research. I will take each in turn.

The medical model of disability is an example of a positivist position on social science. The knowable, objective reality, according to this position, is that the disabled body has deviated from the normal, healthy body. Disability is seen as an individual problem (Oliver, 1992). Research is typically quantitative and seemingly apolitical as there is usually not a discussion of the social or political context of the data. Researchers working from this orientation may gather survey data that show the rates of literacy in disabled adults (Helander, 1998) or the outcomes of the use of augmentative communication in young children (see Romski & Sevcik, 2005).

As I stated earlier, disability studies has been a reaction to the positivist position on disability (which is not to say that disability studies scholars do not recognize the utility of "hard statistics" in policy discussions). For some disability studies scholars, articulating a social model of disability has been their work and their aim has been to show that disability (conceptually distinct from bodily impairment) has been socially constructed and is a social problem (Oliver, 1987, 1992). The aim of scholars working with a social model is to promote understanding of bodily difference—what it is like to live the life of a person considered disabled (e.g., Matysiak, 2001)—and to promote understanding of the constructions of (the meaning made of) bodily difference by those considered able-bodied and those considered disabled.

Emancipatory disability studies scholars build on a social, constructionist view of the socially produced category of disability but have a more overt political orientation. Drawing on Marxist work, they examine the material realities that the social construction of disability has created and conceive of disability as a political problem (Oliver, 1992). Emancipatory disability research has a "transformative aim: namely, barrier removal and the promotion of disabled people's individual and collective empowerment" (Barnes, 2003, p. 6). In other words, it is not enough from this perspective to understand simply how meaning is made of bodily difference because those meanings have created oppressive realities for people considered disabled, which are urgently in need of change. Almost all disability studies work has some element of emancipation because there is a deep appreciation for the shaky political, economic, and social ground on which people considered disabled exist (for interesting discussions of citizenship and disability, see Berubé, 2003; Erevelles, 2002).

A deconstructive-oriented disability studies scholar focuses less on the material influences on disability and more on how knowledge and culture of disability is produced through language and power relations. Deconstructive orientations draw from postmodern and poststructuralist philosophers. In disability studies, those with deconstructive aims react to the idea that "both the medical model and the social model seek to explain disability universally, and end up creating totalizing, meta-historical narratives that exclude important dimensions of disabled people's lives and of their knowledge" (Corker & Shakespeare, 2002, p. 15). The dimensions that disability studies scholars working through postmodern and poststructuralist philosophies consider include what resistance looks like in children who are considered disabled (and usually represented as passive and dependent; Davis & Watson, 2002), the production of disabled people through assumptions and ways of talking about disability (Goodley & Rapley, 2002), and the production of "normal" and "deviant" in genetic diagnostic testing and counseling (Waldschmidt, 2005).

As seen here, the aims of research in disability studies are various. So too, are the disciplines that disability studies takes to task. Traditionally humanities-based, disability studies has been taken up in more and more disciplines as interest in and knowledge of it is shared. Researchers who take up the work of disability studies will often turn with new eyes to the topics and methods of research typically used by their disciplines, asking, how has my discipline contributed to or participated in the production of disability? How have our methods been insensitive to bodily difference? How can our work been done differently in light of disability studies? With this in mind, I now turn to consider how disability studies can inform the work of those interested in the visual and communicative arts.

BODILY DIFFERENCE AND RESEARCH IN THE VISUAL AND COMMUNICATIVE ARTS

Researchers working within disability studies couple an understanding of disability as the social practices of isolating and excluding particular bodies with the research aim(s) of understanding the lives of those considered disabled, transforming the material realities of those considered disabled, and/or deconstructing the knowledge, language, and categorization of disability. Researchers take this framework into the subject areas that are of interest to them—including visual and communicative media. Before I show some of the ways that disability studies can impact research methodologies (regardless of whether the topic is obviously related to disability), I want to share some of the ways that disability studies has informed research in the visual and communicative arts that is obviously related to disability. These studies show the complexity and fruitfulness of bringing a disability studies perspective to visual and communicative arts.

Bringing the Topic of Disability to Visual and Communicative Arts

For those interested in the content of media or the meaning or impact of media messages, the disability "angle" is an interesting one. Media and cultural analysts have found much food for thought in representations of disability. Thompson (1997), for example, produced an analysis of physical disability in American freak shows and literature. She argued that representations of disability, rather then simply illustrating the reality of a disabled body, produce bodies on both sides of the abled/disabled divide. Her work provided a good theoretical base for analyzing bodily difference and is considered one of the "must reads" in disabilities studies.

As another example, Riley (2005) wrote an interesting book in which he explored how disability is represented in movies, television, print media, disability memoirs, advertisements, and multimedia. For example, he pointed out that, while there is a sort of genre of disability movies (*Ray*, *Forrest Gump*, *Radio*) that are often well received by audiences (and awards shows such as the Academy Awards), there are so few actors with disabilities that "it does not even register on the charts" (Riley, 2005, p. 75). Furthermore, the representations of disability by and large reinforce a message of overcoming the disability in one way or another. He wrote,

> Producers, directors, and writers package disability in such a way as to safely ensure that the audience feels nobly uplifted, even ethically superior, for 'supporting' what is in effect a blatantly oversweetened version of life with a disability as concocted by a community that cannot countenance physical imperfection except in certain sanctioned and saccharine forms. The effects are often surreal. The blind star drives a sports car, the autistic or retarded lead utters a Hallmark aphorism that takes on Socratic weight in the nation's op-ed pages for the next two weeks ("Stupid is as stupid does"), the "wheelchair-bound" returning veteran or former athlete finds true love, or at least comes off as a total stud. (Riley, 2005, p. 71)

It is a provocative and uncomfortable read. It may also have been uncomfortable for him to write since he discusses his role in the failure of a dot-com that converted a successful print magazine about disability into an inaccessible, and subsequently unsuccessful, online zine about disability. There are many layers of the relationship of media and disability, including self-representation, accessibility, message, and money, on which Riley touches, that would make further interesting studies (and interesting classroom discussions).

Haller and Ralph (2001) used mixed methods (quantitative and qualitative) to analyze media coverage of disability. They have looked at how the U.S. media cover issues of disability generally by using a quantitative analysis of the types of disabilities presented, the frequency and length of coverage of disability related content, the topics of stories related to disability, and the terminology used in the stories. Additionally they have studied through a qualitative, thematic analysis the specific coverage of a British athletic coach saying negative comments about disabled people. Through this mixed-method study, the authors have been able to analyze and discuss ways of representing and making sense of disability through news media.

A content area that has been receiving attention is new technologies, such as advanced telecommunications and computers, that are sometimes assumed to level the playing field for people considered disabled by eliminating or making up for the persons' "deficits." For example, online relationships that use disembodied text for building relationships are assumed to enhance the lives of people otherwise "handicapped" by a body that is considered deviant. The belief in the potential of technology to set a person free from his or her "low functioning" body or mind is one I see often in our society; Goggin and Newell (2003) pointed out that this belief "rests upon the model of disability that construes it as the static, biologically originating deficit of a given individual, as opposed to a contingent phenomenon that is constituted through social structures and discourses" (p. 263). Certainly, technologies can enhance abilities to communicate and work, but technology is not going to ameliorate "disability." The following example of the practice of disregarding bodily difference in the development of cell phones shows how technology is not the issue—it is the human practices that produce and reproduce disability.

Goggin and Newell (2003) showed how the development of advanced communications (done largely without input from people considered disabled) have produced a host of inaccessible communication forms that interfere with hearing aids, have displays difficult for those with vision impairments to decipher, and tiny key pads that require the user to have advanced fine motor skills. These anti-universal designed phones are, through regulations and use, becoming the norm for citizens in western countries who carry individual cell phones and are accessible by phone all of the time. Goggin and Newell approached these new technologies as not merely technology, but drawing from Foucault (1978), as a system of governmentality that governs and disciplines bodies. In this case, the development of particular technologies often serves to "reinforce" to people considered disabled that they are less than full citizens because they cannot participate in the always available, cell-phone-carrying culture.

Computer technologies have been an interesting area for study within the field of disability studies because, in some ways, computer and online access remove some of the physical barriers that isolate people with physical or sensory impairments within the built environment. This access would seem to support relationships, communication, and work otherwise inaccessible to people considered disabled. Seymour and Lupton (2004) explored online relationships and found that while the computers can facilitate the development of relationships for people considered disabled, the relationships themselves are mostly conventional. The main bonds in those relationships were disability and kinship. Even so, the authors concluded that "text-based, interactive, virtual performance provides the means for people with disabilities to actively engage in the task of breaching the divide [of ability/disability]" (Seymour & Lupton, 2004, p. 303).

Access to online communications has raised personal and political issues for people considered disabled. The reliance on text for most online communication makes certain impairments invisible and the issue of disclosure of disability has been contentious (see Bowker & Tuffin, 2002). For some, this is seen as a personal choice. For others, it has deep political ramifications of disability awareness and identity politics. In other words, it is a content area with much potential for research and discussion.

These previous examples show how a researcher can combine an interest in the topics of disability and visual and communicative arts. Using a disability studies perspective, the researcher can critically study how the category of disability is formed and reformed through movies, advertisements, news stories, and Web sites; the researcher can study the process by which new technology creates and/or reinforces disability; the researcher can research the personally and politically complicated world of (seemingly?) disembodied communication through the internet. These researchers show the complexity of understanding disability not as something medically wrong with a person but as a set of social practices that exclude and isolate certain bodies. To explore further the complexity of seeing disability as excluding and isolating practices, I would like to turn now to the idea of bringing the concepts of disability studies into research methodologies. While the previous discussion of disability and cell phones may have seemed tangential to some of the readers because their interests are not at the intersection of disability and visual and communicative arts, I hope to convince the reader through this next section, that the intersection of disability studies and research is relevant to all researchers.

Bringing a Disability Studies Perspective to Research Methodology

There are various ways that disability studies can inform research practices. For some researchers (such as the researchers in the previous examples), the research question is informed by disability studies—researchers interested in the workings of advertisements explore how disability is represented in print media campaigns; researchers interested in cell phone communications explore how the creation of the technology becomes a part of the excluding and isolating practices of disability. For other researchers, disability studies makes them aware of bodily difference—bodies move, communicate, and think in various ways (I know that this sounds commonsensical, but most of our research practices show that we really don't understand or at least do not respect this concept). Awareness of bodily difference helps researchers realize the need to post calls for participants by stairs and elevators, and it helps researchers become aware of whether their professional meeting sites (conference, hotel rooms, and restaurants) are truly accommodating to all the types of bodies that researchers inhabit. Still other researchers will take disability studies into the heart of their research, adapting their data collection, data analysis, member checks, and data representation to insure that their research does not become part of the excluding and isolating practices of disability. In this section, I want to show two things: (a) some of the straightforward ways that disability awareness can impact the practical decisions of research, and (b) some of the more complicated ways that method decisions can be informed by disability studies.

Disability awareness is an important way that disability studies can inform research. I stated earlier that almost all work in disability studies had elements of the emancipatory aims of research. The incorporation of the emancipatory or transformative aims of research in disability studies stems from the awareness of the political, economic, and cultural hardships that go hand in hand with being categorized as disabled. Many societies simply assume that all bodies (or the bodies that matter) easily move through space on foot, communicate with their mouths, and process information at a particular speed. Because of this assumption, many bodies are excluded from entering built environments, joining the voting process, and enjoying mainstream entertainment. These bodies are also often excluded from the research process. One way that disability studies can inform researchers is by making them aware of variation in the ways bodies live. While many researchers may claim to appreciate the idea that people communicate, move, and think in different ways, it is not at all clear to me that the appreciation (and respect) for bodily difference makes its way into research practices.

Basic awareness of bodily difference will impact some of the practical aspects of research whether or not the topic in question relates directly to disability. For instance, recruiting participants will necessarily be a different practice once a researcher is more aware of bodily difference. I know (now) that I have unintentionally excluded people who are considered disabled from my studies simply because of the ways that I recruited participants or planned to collect data. Posting a call for participants on a bulletin board near a so-called main entrance that is only accessible by stairs excludes people who do not use the stairs. Planning to conduct traditional verbal interviews with children about the meaning and use of Hello Kitty accessories, a researcher may exclude the biggest third-grade user of Hello Kitty products in a school who also happens to use assistive technology to communicate. Awareness of bodily difference has made some researchers realize that typical surveys exclude people who do not communicate over the phone or who do not answer their front doors (Parsons, Baum, Johnson, & Hendershot, 2001).

Just as we have historically privileged the reading and writing of print-based media as literacy, in social science research, we tend to rely on data in the form of written or verbal language. Certainly, for many people, this form of communication is not their primary form of communication. Sign language, communication boards, drawing, and other forms of augmented communication may be used for communication—and can be forms in which to collect data. As researchers work to think outside of traditional written and verbal sources of data collection, those researchers used to working with young children may offer some guidance because they are used to gathering data with people who are not particularly verbal (for a discussion of encouraging sign language narratives in young children with developmental delays, see Grove & Tucker, 2003). When a researcher decides to value the stories, experiences, ideas, and expressions of all bodies, the researcher will find ways to collect data that does not exclude bodies based on their mode of communication.

The method of photovoice has been proposed as a viable data collection method for sighted people who have learning difficulties (or developmental disabilities) and may not have verbal fluency. Photovoice involves participants taking photos to share aspects of their lives and researchers analyzing the content of the photos (Wang & Burris, 1997, as cited in Booth & Booth, 2003). Booth and Booth (2003) used photovoice with a group of mothers with learning difficulties who were part of a support group. In the research project, the mothers were given disposable cameras and asked to take photos of important people, places, and things in their lives. After the film was developed (with a copy for the participants to keep), the participants met with the researchers to explain the importance of the photos or to identify elements in the photos. The researchers used this feedback as well as their own content analysis of the photographs to understand the lives of these mothers who are often marginalized and seen as unable to represent themselves.

Appreciation for the different modes of understanding and communicating will help a researcher design studies that are sensitive to bodily difference from a practical standpoint. Recruitment of participants and data collection methods are what I think of as practical decisions about methods that can be informed by awareness of how bodies differ in their mobility, senses, and communication methods. Certainly, this is important and vital work of disability awareness and is relevant to research whether or not the topic is directly related to disability. For those researchers who take to heart some of the urgent, political, and personal aspects of disability studies beyond those raised by disability awareness, there are method decisions, which I discuss later, that address the political, emancipatory aim of disability studies. Again, these are relevant even when disability is not the focus of the research because they are about making research practices less disabling.

For a long time, people with disabilities have been the subjects of research over which they had no control—the research has been used to their benefits, such as to support legislation or early intervention services and it has used to their determent such as to promote prenatal testing, which has lead to the overwhelming abortion of babies because of their disabilities. To counter this (mis)use and "top-down" research style, there is a current movement from within some communities of people considered disabled that there should be "nothing about us without us" (Charlton, 1998). Even still, some people with disabilities are leery of participating in research because they feel that they are always under scrutiny (Booth & Booth, 2003). The government, social, and medical apparatus that forms around disability (social services, schools, physicians, and therapists) is, in many ways, overwhelming in its presence and constant evaluations. Being evaluated and analyzed in a research study is not always a welcome addition to an already scrutinized life.

In order to attempt to adhere to the "nothing about us without us" mantra, some researchers enter into (complicated) relationships with organizations of people considered disabled to do research needed by the organization (Barnes, 2003). A researcher might volunteer his or her expertise to conduct a study on internet accessibility for the ARC (formerly known as the Association for Retarded Citizens). Other researchers critique this aspect of emancipatory research that "suggests that social investigators need to place themselves in the service of disabled people's organizations, and conduct research according to political priorities" (Corker & Shakespeare, 2002, p. 14).

Other researchers, sensitive to the "nothing about us without us" idea, have found ways of involving people considered disabled as coinvestigators. Medlen and Peterson (2001) researched "healthy lifestyles in adults with Down syndrome" and wrote about their collaboration, unique in the pairing of a dietician and an adult with Down syndrome (Medlen, 2001; Peterson, 2001). Developing survey questions over e-mail, field-testing the survey with Peterson's friends with Down syndrome, gathering data, and cowriting articles over email are some of the details of the process that they explain. The research process that they describe has the familiar give and take of professional research relationships, and it was possible because of the stance of the researchers that it *mattered*, personally, intellectually, and politically, for them to explore new ways of doing research. This inspirational partnership comes from mutual respect of bodily difference on the part of the researchers.

Another way has been found to involve participants in the research process. Matysiak (2001) spent time considering how she could conduct member checks with adults who are considered developmentally disabled. She used a few techniques to put the data and the findings in accessible forms for her participants. First, she videotaped the focus groups that she conducted and later transcribed the data. For a member check, instead of presenting the traditional textual version of the focus group data, she showed the video to the participants and asked the participants "to make sure that what was said was accurate and reflected issues they wanted raised" (Matysiak,

2001, p. 197). Secondly, she used a poster to represent the findings visually and used it in a presentation to the participants (and then she left the poster with the participant-related self-advocacy group to use in its own presentations). Lastly, she put her final research report (written in academic language) into a "parallel text format" (drawing from Ward & Flynn, 1994). Parallel text makes use of two columns of text on a single page with a simplified summary in one column adjacent to the original text. Matysiak's thoughtful "accommodations" take to the heart of research the understanding that bodies make meaning through different modalities, and it is worth the time and effort to change traditional research methods to include more "bodies." While in this example, the entire participant group was considered developmentally disabled, the principle of appreciating and planning for the different modalities through which participants make meaning would be wholly appropriate for groups of participants who were not all (currently) considered disabled.

The most common way of doing research that does not exploit has been with primary investigators who are considered disabled. It has been because of the activist work to make buildings accessible and make discrimination on the basis of disability illegal that it is possible for people with disabilities to enter into university settings as students and professors and thereby to conduct research. Neville-Jan (2004) provided an example of an autoethnography in the form of a "quest narrative linked as a self-reflective text" to her research on children and adults with spina bifida. Her work detailed her quest for a child and the concurrent pain and sexual dysfunction she experienced as a woman with spina bifida. She wrote in an attempt to fill the gap of scholarly work that includes the voice of a person in pain and a discussion of disability and sexuality. She proposed that autoethnography is a method "to construct stories that connect the personal (body and impairment) with the social (oppressive forces with society)" (p. 124).

Several of the examples I have given have shown the use of innovative methods, but one last point I would like to make here is that, sometimes, traditional data collection may be used within a study that still breaks new ground methodologically. For example, Scior (2003), working in London, used a discourse analysis of interviews with women considered learning disabled (in the United States, the term more frequently used is *developmentally disabled*). The significance of her approach is that people considered developmentally disabled are rarely interviewed for research "on the basis of their below average ability and frequent associated difficulties in communication" (Scior, 2003, p. 781). In other words, people considered developmentally disabled are believed to be too difficult to communicate with and as having nothing important to say anyway. A common stereotype is that people considered developmentally disabled just agree with whatever anyone else is saying. Challenging this damaging stereotype of incompetence, Goodley and Rapley (2002) showed that the frequent assumption of acquiescence bias on the part of developmentally delayed adults during interviews or surveys can be recast as situational artifact—something created in the interview through the interviewer's technique. For example, they show that interviewers sometimes do not accept an answer (again, assuming incompetence) and continue to "badger" the interviewee until the interviewee changes his or her answer. What looks to some as a respondent who does not know what he or she thinks about anything looks to these researchers as an interviewer who needs better interviewing skills.

Scior (2003) offered another understanding of what some see as the "confused" talk of people considered developmentally disabled:

> The tendency of people with learning disabilities to utter contradictions and inconsistencies has frequently been used to argue that interview data, if used at all, should be treated with great caution. However, by adopting a discourse analytic approach—which holds that at any given moment there may be varying possibilities for self-construction and individuals can thus be expected to use contradictory accounts—it was possible in the present study to examine the sources and functions of contradictions and tensions that arose in interviewees' talk. (p. 793)

For example, when one of the women talked about her sterilization, she employed what Scior (2003) described as the guardianship discourse (her ex-boyfriend and father kept asking her to have the operation and she consented) and the feminist discourse (she became angry because it was her body and her decision). While some might read the transcript and see a confused woman who could not explain her life, Scior saw distinct discourses in meaningful tension.

Angrosino (1997), also conducting research with adults considered developmentally disabled, used another strategy for the often dismissed "confused" talk of his participants. In his study, he collected life histories without the traditional long interview. Instead, he collected narratives in ten-minute snippets over the course of months and years, letting his collaborators set the agenda but working with them to generate narratives that would come together as a "life history." His work provided compelling life history data previously considered unattainable because of the supposed deficits of adults with developmental disabilities. Consequently, Angrosino showed the deficits in traditional research methods and in conventional understandings of people with developmental disabilities.

In these ways, disability studies can inform the methods and practices of a researcher interested in visual and communicative arts. Simply becoming aware of bodily difference can impact some of the practical aspects of research. Further thinking about bodily difference can influence the topic and the methods of data collection, representation, and analysis. Bringing a disability studies perspective to research methodologies involves a deep understanding that research has the potential to be and often is a disabling force in our society. This disabling force is not just about the ways that data and conclusions are used to isolate and exclude certain bodies from school settings or from being born in the first place. This disabling force comes with even seemingly small decisions that all researchers make—how data will be collected, who will be the participants, how and where will the research findings be presented. When methodological decisions are made without consideration and respect for all bodies, then certain bodies are positioned as bodies that do not matter and bodies that are incompetent, and research continues to be one of the excluding and isolating practices that is imposed on people who are considered disabled.

Thoughtful researchers, however, can change the ways that research is conducted in their fields. When a researcher takes to heart the belief that all bodies are valuable and that meaning is made through various modalities, the content and methods of research can become respectful of the variations in human development and/or critical of the forces that categorize and oppress by way of those variations. Disability studies provides the theoretical framework for a researcher to explore these ideas. Being considered disabled or having a loved one considered disabled is not a prerequisite for reading in disability studies. To be sure, having one of those two connections to the disabled community often provided the impetus for those of us who now consider ourselves disability studies scholars to seek an understanding of the category of disability beyond or outside of the conventional and medicalized understanding. But, it is my belief that researchers who strive to do good research will appreciate the opportunity that disability studies offers for them to learn about ways to improve their studies. Disability studies matters to those who want to do good research.

WHY DISABILITY STUDIES MATTERS

Coming at the issue of disability in various ways and from various disciplines is important because, frankly, the problem of disability is too big and too urgent to approach in limited ways. Our beliefs and attitudes about bodily difference permeate our lives in the ways we build structures, the ways we educate, the words we use, the medical care we seek and receive, our relationships with others, the entertainment we enjoy, and particularly relevant to this handbook, the ways we define literacy.

The privileging of traditional literacy has had a disabling affect on many people. Reading and writing print-based text is not something that every *body* is designed to do. Continued emphasis on making meaning through print-based text keeps people like my daughter who communicates with manual signs and expressive eyes from being seen as smart; it keeps classrooms from being universally accessible; it keeps many people isolated and removed from the political process. With traditional and narrow definitions of literacy, the "literate norm" is yet another ruler up to which bodies considered disabled do not measure.

A desire to open up definitions of literacy to include media beyond printed texts and communication beyond the written and spoken word suggests an understanding or the potential for understanding that meaning is made by different bodies differently. Carrying that understanding into ones' research has been the idea behind this chapter. Making use of an understanding that meaning is made by different bodies differently may influence one's research topic, recruitment and selection of participants, choice of research methods, or one's overall stance towards the aims of one's research. Research that works in the intersections of disability studies and a broadened notion of literacy has urgent, political, and personal implications for people considered disabled but also for those of us who are (only) currently considered able-bodied and who do not wish to further participate in the disabling practices that have, in part, defined our disciplines and our research methodologies.

REFERENCES

American Community Survey. (2003). *Subject definitions* [U.S. Census document]. Retrieved September 20, 2005, from http://www.census.gov/acs/www/Downloads/2003/usedata/Subject_Definitions.pdf

Angrosino, M. V. (1997). The ethnography of mental retardation: An applied perspective. *Journal of Contemporary Ethnography, 26*(1), 98–109.

Barnes, C. (2003). What a difference a decade makes: Reflections on doing "emancipatory" disability research. *Disability & Society, 18*(1), 3–17.

Berubé, M. (2003, Spring). Citizenship and disability. *Dissent*, 52–57.

Booth, T., & Booth, W. (2003). In the frame: Photovoice and mothers with learning difficulties. *Disability & Society, 18*(4), 431–442.

Bowker, N. & Tuffin, K. (2002). Disability discourses for online identities. *Disability and Society, 17*(3), 327–344.

Charlton, J. I. (1998). *Nothing about us without us: Disability, oppression, and empowerment.* Berkeley, CA: University of California Press.

Corker, M., & Shakespeare, T. (2002). Mapping the terrain. In M. Corker & T. Shakespeare (Eds.), *Disability/Postmodernity: Embodying disability theory* (pp. 1–17). New York: Continuum.

Davis, J., & Watson, N. (2002). Countering stereotypes of disability: Disabled children and resistance. In M. Corker & T. Shakespeare (Eds.), *Disability/Postmodernity: Embodying disability theory* (pp. 159–174). New York: Continuum.

Erevelles, N. (2002). (Im)material citizens: Cognitive disability, race, and the politics of citizenship. *Disability, Culture, and Education, 1*(1), 5–25.

Finkelstein, V. (1998). Emancipating disability studies. In T. Shakespeare (Ed.), *The disability studies reader: Social science perspectives* (pp. 28–49). New York: Cassell.

Foucault, M. (1978). *History of sexuality: Volume 1: An introduction.* Translated by Robert Hurley. New York: Vintage Books.

Goggin, G., & Newell, C. (2005). Foucault on the phone: Disability and the mobility of government. In S. Tremain (Ed.), *Foucault and the government of disability* (pp. 261–277). Ann Arbor, MI: The University of Michigan Press.

Goodley, D., & Rapley, M. (2002) Changing the subject: Postmodernity and people with "learning difficulties." In M. Corker & T. Shakespeare (Eds.), *Disability/Postmodernity: Embodying disability theory* (pp. 127–142). New York: Continuum.

Grove, N., & Tucker, S. (2003). Narratives in manual sign by children with intellectual impairments. In S. von Tetzchner & N. Grove (Eds.), *Augmentative and alternative communication developmental issues* (pp. 229–255). Philadelphia, PA: Whurr Publishers.

Habermas, J. (1971). *Theory and practice.* Boston: Beacon Press.

Haller, B. A., & Ralph, S. M. (2001). Content analysis methodology for studying news and disability: Case studies from the United States and England. In S. N. Barnartt & B. M. Altman (Eds.), *Research in social science and disability, Volume 2: Exploring theories and expanding methodologies* (pp. 229–253). New York: JAI.

Helander, E. (1998). *Prejudice and dignity: An introduction to community-based rehabilitation* (2nd ed.). New York: UNDP. Retrieved October, 8,2005, from http://wbln0018.worldbank.org/HDNet/hddocs.nsf/0/4fb28f8537d87c2a85256f56005b8a4c?OpenDocument#section9

Houtenville, A. J. (2005). Disability statistics in the United States. Ithaca, NY: Cornell University Rehabilitation Research and Training Center on Disability Demographics and Statistics (StatsRRTC). Retrieved October 3, 2005, from http://www.disabilitystatistics.org

Individuals with Disabilities Education Act Amendments of 1997 (IDEA). (1997). 105th Congress, 1st session.

Lather, P. (1991). *Getting Smart: Feminist research and pedagogy with/in the postmodern.* New York: Routledge.

Loprest, P., & Maag, E. (2001). Barriers and supports for work among adults with disabilities: Results from the NHIS-D 1994–1995. Washington, DC: The Urban Institute.

Matysiak, B. (2001). Interpretive research and people with intellectual disabilities: Politics and practicalities. In S. N. Barnartt & B. M. Altman (Eds.), *Research in social science and disability, Volume 2: Exploring theories and expanding methodologies* (pp. 185–207). New York: JAI.

Medlen, J. E. G. (2001). Partnering: Lessons learned working with an adult with Down syndrome. *Disability Solutions, 4*(4), 10–12.

Medlen, J. E. G. & Peterson, M. (2001). Focus: Healthy lifestyles survey. *Disability Solutions, 4*(4), 1, 3-8.

McNeil, J. M. (1997). *Census brief: Disabilities affect one-fifth of all Americans: Proportion could increase in coming decades.* Washington, DC: U.S. Department of Commerce, Economics, and Statistics, and Bureau of the Census.

Neville-Jan, A. (2004). Selling your soul to the devil: An autoethnography of pain, pleasure and the quest for a child. *Disability & Society, 19*(2), 113–127.

Oliver, M. (1987). Re-defining disability: Some issues for research. *Research, Policy, and Planning, 5*, 9–13.

Oliver, M. (1992). Changing the social relations of research production? *Disability, Handicap, & Society, 7*(2), 101–113.

Parsons, J. A., Baum, S., Johnson, T. P., & Hendershot, G. (2001). Inclusion of disabled populations in interview surveys: Review and recommendations. In S. N. Barnartt & B. M. Altman (Eds.), *Research in social science and disability, Volume 2: Exploring theories and expanding methodologies* (pp. 167–184). New York: JAI.

Peterson, M. (2001). Partnering: Lessons learned conducting research. *Disability Solutions, 4*(4), 8–9.

PL 94-142: The Education for All Handicapped Children Act. (1975, November 29).

PL 101-336: Americans with Disabilities Act (ADA). (1990, July 26).

Riley, C. A. II (2005). *Disability and the media: Prescriptions for change.* Hanover, NH: University Press of New England.

Romski, M., & Sevcik, R. A. (2005). Augmentative communication and early intervention: Myths and realities. *Infants and Young Children, 18*(3), 174–185.

Scior, K. (2003). Using discourse analysis to study the experiences of women with learning disabilities. *Disability & Society, 18*(6), 779–795.

Seymour, W., & Lepton, D. (2004). Holding the line online: Exploring wired relationships for people with disabilities. *Disability & Society, 19*(4), 291–305

Thomson, R. G. (1997). *Extraordinary bodies: Figuring physical disability in American culture and literature.* New York: Columbia University Press.

24th Annual Report to Congress on the Implementation of the Individuals with Disabilities Education Act. (2000). APPENDIX A DATA TABLES: Table AA12 Percentage (Based on 2000 Census Population) of Children Ages 6–17 Served Under IDEA, Part B by Disability, During the 2000–2001 School Year. Retrieved September 20, 2005, from http://www.ed.gov/about/reports/annual/osep/2002/appendix-a-pt1.pdf

Waldschmidt, A. (2005). Who is normal? Who is deviant? "Normality" and "risk" in genetic diagnostics and counseling. In S. Tremain (Ed.), *Foucault and the government of disability* (pp. 191–207). Ann Arbor, MI: The University of Michigan Press.

Wang, C., & Burris, M. (1997) Photovoice: Concept, methodology, and use for participatory needs assessment. *Health Education and Behaviour, 24*(3), 369–387.

Wang, Q. (2005). *Disability and American families* [U.S. Census document]. Retrieved September 20, 2005, from http://www.census.gov/prod/2005pubs/censr-23.pdf

Ward, L., & Flynn, M. (1994). What matters most: Disability, research and empowerment. In M. H. Rioux & M. Bach (Eds.), *Disability is not measles: New research paradigms in disability* (pp. 29–48). Toronto, Canada: Roeher Institute.

Ware, L. (2001). Writing, identity, and the other: Dare we do disability studies? *Journal of Teacher Education, 52*, 107–123.

19

MUSEUM LITERACY, ART, AND SPACE STUDY

A. Jonathan Eakle
JOHNS HOPKINS UNIVERSITY

Museum Literacy, Art, and Space Study

Crossings of methodological research boundaries have transformed the nature of literacy, which for more than a decade has been defined to include diverse multimedia usage (Alvermann, 1997; Flood & Lapp, 1995). As well, crossings from in-school literacy research areas into out-of-school contexts are popular topics in academic circles, especially given the expanding uses of new technologies (Hagood, Leander, Luke, Mackey, & Nixon, 2003; Hull & Schultz, 2001). Aligned with these notions, a purpose of this chapter is to present information about one such out-of-school literacy setting: the museum. Museums are especially useful sites to study and practice literacy as it is now conceived because their longstanding multimodal exhibits and practices often reflect the uses of diverse blends of communication media found in everyday contemporary life.

Crossings of methodological territories, expanded literacy notions, and novel research contexts suggest movement within literacy practices, and movement itself can encompass varied notions. Movement involves bodies, objects, and geographies; is a source of philosophical, scientific, and aesthetic abstraction; and is a common metaphor for civil and political action. These are broad and diverse areas, but a general thread running through these dimensions is that where there is movement, there is space.

Because space often involves varied movements, it can be an elusive concept. In keeping with this elusiveness, sometimes space carries with it notions of the unknown and infinitely expansive. Spatial concepts can be difficult to pin down; nonetheless, a second purpose of this chapter is to show how spatial theory and methodology can be used in studying literacy in places such as museums. To this end, in the following pages, I first present a brief overview of recent education research in museums. Second, I offer a section about spatial theories and how these theories influenced the construction of methods used in a museum study (Eakle, 2005). I conclude the chapter with a discussion of possibilities of space study for literacy, the visual and communicative arts, education research, and practice.

RECENT MUSEUM RESEARCH PERSPECTIVES

Museum Object Research

Although space is all around us, education research and practice often center on objects rather than space. Classroom practices typically involve print objects, and progressive instruction frequently includes hands-on learning with objects (Guthrie & Wigfield, 2000; Wade & Moje, 2000). In museums, objects are principal pedagogical tools that can range from the unique to the mundane; yet, most museum objects are those that are valued by cultures (Kirsheblatt-Gimblett, 1998). In fact, museums can be traced to displays of treasures and curiosities that were prized by the powerful and taken from others through wars, techniques of force, and domination (Hooper-Greenhill, 2001).

In many instances, museum objects are accompanied by print texts that describe their characteristics and histories. Further, museum print texts can draw associations between exhibited objects and other objects, concepts, and cultural practices. For example, Clifford (1997) in his encounter with "Paradise," an exhibition of continuity and change in New Guinea, described museum texts that made connections between seemingly disparate objects and practices. Displayed in a galley were

> metal and wood shields decorated with impressive designs based on South Pacific Lager labels and slogans such as "Six to Six." Panels explain the history and recent revival of interclan warfare in the highlands. Homemade guns hang on the wall. "Six to Six," a common expression for a party that lasts from 6 P.M. to 6 A.M., here proclaims a clan's ability to fight from 6 P.M. to 6 A.M. The phrase is combined with skulls, a border from San Miguel beer packaging (reminiscent of traditional designs), and Pacific Lager birds of paradise. (p. 148)

Indeed, print texts in museums are sometimes presented on labels, on wall panels, and on exhibited objects. Further, museum texts can include subtexts, captions, diagrams, and illustrations. Accordingly, museum walls can take on the appearance of school textbooks

(Eakle & Chávez, 2003). Because of such conventional qualities, it is reasonable that literacy educators and researchers could use and investigate museum texts much like they would any other text.

In the end, museum literacy is a matter of perspective, as is all literacy practice; people transact with texts differently based on a host of proclivities (Eco, 1984; Street, 1995; Rosenblatt, 1978). Nonetheless, theories, concepts, and methods that frequently govern education in schools are often mirrored in museums. For instance, museum education and research regularly operate under constructivist theory. In research of content area learning, for example, Hapgood and Pallinscar (2002) suggested that object-centered literacy practices used in constructivist classrooms, such as "guided readings" could be used in museum education. Additionally, Falk and Dierking (1992) argued that museum instruction should build upon prior knowledge, consider context, and be engaging. Further, constructivist meaning-making exchanges are often placed at the forefront of museum pedagogy and investigation (Leinhardt, Crowley, & Knutson, 2002). Indeed, constructivism holds sway in much museum education practice, as it does in many other education settings.

Along with constructivism, other conventional territories of theory and practice can govern museum literacy. Zeidler and Surber (1999) formally examined how "visual and verbal objects" in museum displays can be organized and structured to provide visitors memorable experiences, which is also a concern of many museographers while designing exhibitions. In truth, frequently museum designers carefully configure exhibited objects in regard to visitor flow, readability, and aesthetics, sometimes by use of mathematical formula, statistical tables, and other quantitative methods (Miles, Alt, Gosling, Lewis, & Tout, 1984). Such museum object organization, structure, formulae, and design again indicate particular perspectives, and in these cases, museum literacy can embody museum exhibition pragmatics.

Further, such pragmatic perspectives are often in keeping with notions of archival conservation, not only of objects, but also of particular histories that are attached to museum objects. These histories can be used as a source of critical analyses, of which I turn in detail the following section of this chapter. Nonetheless, conserving object-centered perspectives supported by various forms of text encompass much of the literacy practices that occur in museums.

Critical Museum Literacy

In some cases, museum object organization and exhibition design has provided the basis for critical museum analyses, where researchers seek to investigate, for example, colonizing attitudes and practices of museum display. In this vein, there are ongoing debates about museum appropriation practices and displays of controversial objects, such as the corpses frequently found in archeology museums (Simpson, 1996). Further, critical museum research can focus on how particular voices are silenced in favor of dominant cultural perspectives. For instance, Prosise (1998) described how Japanese perspectives were removed from a U.S. museum show after a public debate about its atomic bombings exhibition. Similarly, Hilden and Huhndorf (1999) pointed out that, although a Native American dance ritual was glorified in a museum exhibition, aspects of the practice that were associated with the brutal treatment of Native Americans by White settlers were not presented in the museum show. In comparison, some museum curators believe that exhibitions can function like "safety valves" that help to curtail civil unrest by celebrating objects and practices of less powerful groups (Eakle & Chávez, 2003). Indeed, because many museums promote dominant cultural values and perspectives, museums can be prime locations for conducting critical literacy research.

As with other critical projects, critical museum literacy research purports to look at material aspects of museums, empower and educate audiences, and offer alternative perspectives of not only museums and their contents, but also wider social and political practices (Eakle & Chávez, 2003). Because it not only looks at objects but also space, especially situated space, critical museum literacy could be an example of the application of spatial theory, to which I now turn in detail.

SPACE

As in the many ways that texts are considered and presented in museums, there are multiple ways to see space. Space has been of explicit concern in various fields such as geometry, geography, and astronomy; and, arguably, space is part of every discipline. Because space is viewed from many perspectives, a detailed review of it is beyond the scope of a single chapter. Nonetheless, in the following pages, I briefly present three spatial views that influence literacy studies and the visual and communicative arts and that provide a backdrop for research I conducted in museums.

Lefebvre's Space

Lefebvre (1974/2001) was a pioneer of critical space—its design, production, and consumption. He developed a historical, transformational view of space, which centered on a tripartite categorized as perceived, conceived, and lived space. Perceived space involves the senses and situates the body in physical space, through, for example, distance, scale, and color. Conceived space, according to Lefebvre, involves abstract systems such as Euclidian mathematics; it is a space of calculation. Lived space comprises social practices and everyday life. Each domain of Lefebvre's tripartite overlaps the others, however, in the end, his writings return to spaces that involve the repetitions, differences, and rhythms of lived situations.

A few literacy researchers have incorporated some of Lefebvre's (1974/2001) ideas to launch space studies. For example, Leander (2004) reversed the relation typically laid out in education research by using social space in the forefront of a study rather than as a contextual backdrop. Using a focal interaction, he showed how school space was transformed, how a school space was taken up and used over time, and how space produced identities and discourse. Similarly, coming to Lefebvre by way of Soja (1996), Moje et al. (2004) laminated spatial notions and situational literacy theories to construct a "hybrid" investigation that, like Leander, explored discourse and identity issues while arguing for the production of in-between "third space" (p. 67).

These studies advance along parallel pathways in that they looked at discourse and identity production in and out of schooled space. Yet, as space is placed upfront in a study, as in the case of Leander's (2004) investigation, notions involving objective forms and stable subjects fade on a distant horizon and aspects of difference become salient. A formal, modern goal was to extract identity from such difference. During the past century, practical and theoretical frames in art and philosophy have pointed to problems of such extractions, a topic of the following sections of this chapter.

Visual Art and Phenomenological Spaces

The metaphor of the frame is common in everyday life and in social research studies. Such framing comprises what I have thus characterized in this chapter through constructivist, pragmatic, and critical museum practices. Frames are constructs used to bracket fields of focus, to create spatial order in the visual and communicative arts and are conceptual and methodological tools in philosophy and research projects that attempt to bracket sensations and experiences.

The archetypal frame is comprised of vertical and horizontal restraints. Since the Renaissance, methods of rendering phenomena in space have been based in measurement within frames. Pictorial devices that employ grids between artist and model illustrate this ordering (Gombrich, 1965; see Fig. 19.1). Such devices allow the artist to fix and work with a monocular vanishing point, a point on the horizon to which diagonal planes recede. This artistic method produces a space of illusion, a psychology of "guided projection;" viewers are led to project, for instance, landscapes into dabs of paint (Gombrich, 1965, p. 203).

However, spatial perception, and for that matter social phenomena, is usually not situated around singular, stationary focal points. Life and perception is multiplicity, and so too became the theory and practice of much visual art during the last century. For example, Cézanne set out to capture natural phenomena, to paint what he saw, by establishing multiple spatial points of view (Rewald, 1977). This resulted in paintings that seemingly contained distortions: unusual bends, tilted tabletops, and elongated figures, and unpainted and unresolved regions of canvas. Through multiplicity, at the dawn of last century Cézanne's sensations began to float across canvases, through space, providing possibilities that altered the course of art.

Masters of modern art sought freedom from objective, spatial singularity by using the methods laid out by Cézanne. This eventually led to reductions and abstractions, such as in Mondrian's spaces of vertical and horizontal intersection. On the other hand, a few artists persisted in Cézanne's elusive goal to capture sensation. For instance, Giacometti tried to precisely measure and represent models in space, not as Dürer had done, but with both eyes open and with late, modern sensibilities. Yet, in the end he concluded that capturing what is seen is impossible; his canvases, full of erasures and searching lines are testaments of how space devours forms, which resist fixed representation (see Fig. 19.2). This notion mirrors crises of representation in social research and purported impossibilities of representing "others" (Spivak, 1992).

Such thinking has brought some social theorists and researchers to impasses. If the "other" cannot be represented, then why try? Thus, some researchers might turn to abstraction, as did many late modernists. Or, a response of others to abyssal deadlocks might be

FIGURE 19.1. Dürer's drawing machine.

FIGURE 19.2. Alberto Giacometti (1953) Diego. Oil on canvas, 39½ × 31¾ inches. Solomon R. Guggenheim Museum.

to remain in or return to the past. For instance, as shown earlier in this chapter, much museum education research mirrors mainstream school pedagogies, which are often tied to conventional notions that have stood the so-called "test of time." These stances and concepts, like objects conserved in archives such as museums and libraries, denote efforts to safeguard notions of the past, to frame matters in a way that avoid the impossibilities, multiplicities, and movements of space convincingly laid out during the last century by artists, such as Giacometti and Cézanne, and theorists of everyday life rhythms, such as Lefebvre.

Spaces of Other Possibilities

Outside archives are possibilities that involve futures. Often, futures are conceived as developments of past concepts to add to knowledge. Moreover, there are philosophers, who, like Cézanne and Giacometti in the visual arts, have pointed researchers to drastic breaks with the past. Among these philosophers, Foucault, Deleuze, and Guattari were revolutionaries whose theories involve spatial concepts (Eakle, 2007). They conceptualized ways of seeing space through power, not as a negative force, but as a positivity: a means of producing things such as strategies, desires, and subjects.

Deleuze, Foucault, and Guattari were keenly interested in the arts, in part, because artists creatively tread outside conserving convention. For example, Foucault (1970/1971) opened one of his well-known books with Velázquez's novel attempt to render space, and he used Magritte's art to illustrate spatial barriers between the visual and the verbal (Foucault, 1968/1983). As well, Deleuze (1981/2002) used art to advance arguments involving spaces of sensation and desire, and Guattari (1989/2000) viewed artistic collectives as bearers of radical social change: new space. Indeed, artists, such as Giacometti and Cézanne, are involved with possibilities and space, and so too were Deleuze, Foucault, and Guattari.

Thus, it is not surprising that much of what is to be learned from Deleuze, Foucault, and Guattari is not only in the ideas they created, but also in the methods they used in creating and presenting concepts. For example, Deleuze and Guattari (1972/2003) developed concepts of the unconscious, which they argued is comprised of "desiring-machines" that are always coupled to other machines (p. 5). To them, machines move in entangling productive networks, connecting to another, only to be blocked by zero points of antiproduction. Their view of the unconscious is mirrored in the social world where boundless desire is mediated by collective apparatuses manifested in institutions, such as governments, museums, and schools, that generate conserving strategies and practices (Bogue, 1996/1989).

Later, Deleuze and Guattari (1980/2002) used their ideas of production and antiproduction to develop long series of connective visual musings about topics ranging from linguistics to geopolitics. Similarly, Foucault (1975/1977) used connective constructions to show how power manifests at particular historical moments. For example, he extracted "before and after pictures" (Rajchman, 1988, p. 90), such as those of 18th century public spectacles of torture (before) and connected this to the distancing of bodies and the elimination of pain found in modern disciplinary and punishment practices, such as schooling and incarceration (after). Indeed, Foucault, like Deleuze and Guattari, was a master, visual constructionist who practiced an "art of seeing" (Rajchman, p. 88).

In essence, Deleuze, Foucault, and Guattari attempted to work outside conventional concepts with their constructions. Further, they were not necessarily interested in uncovering deep structure, meaning, identity, and experience. For example, notions of the autonomous modern self are what Foucault (1969/1994) would like to see disappear into an "anonymity of a murmur" (p. 222), like Giacometti's models and the elided subject of Velasquez's *Las Meninas*. Nonetheless, their constructions of possibilities were dependent on longstanding institutions that seek to conserve such conventions. For example, Deleuze and Guattari (1972/2003) fed off of psychoanalytic notions (e.g., partial objects of fixation, Freud's view of the mother/breast/child/unconscious relationship) in order to advance and proliferate their ideas involving machine-like production modes in capitalist systems. Without a doubt, their concepts of expansion feed off archives of knowledge. These are key points I used in research of museums.

A MUSEUM SPACE STUDY

In broad strokes, the museum study I conducted involved three museums of Marthasville, a large metropolitan area in the Southeastern United States (pseudonyms were used). Participants in the study included adolescents and teachers of school classrooms, out-of-school groups, museum educators, artists, and other museum visitors. Data collection methods included (a) participant observation recorded in field notes, (b) interviews conducted in various settings around the museums and other spaces, (c) written documents, and (d) photographs and other images produced in and involving the researched spaces. For eight months, museum observations were conducted two to three times per week for two to six hours per observational session. The data presented later in this chapter constitutes a small subset of what I collected during the investigation.

Constructing and Deconstructing

Following Deleuze, Foucault, and Guattari's notions of power, construction, and deconstruction in my museum investigation, principal purposes were to examine how people strategically use museum space and the relations of these strategies to particular subjects, objects, and concepts. In a nutshell, I visualized the concepts and objects that I encountered as manifestations of archival knowledge, strata that involve visibilities and statements, the seen and the said. Strategies constituted relations of force—power. The archive and strategies feed off one another creating an entangling web of knowledge/power. This web of force, which can be visualized as an exterior planar surface that ripples and folds, hollows out subject points, such as academic disciplines, persons, and education institutions such as museums (for a detailed map of this system, see Deleuze, 1986/2000).

In the museum study, first, I assembled a structure using ethnographic data collection techniques, collections from the rhythms of everyday life, which was a move aligned with Lefebvrean notions. However, my intent was to deconstruct these data as I advanced. To do this, I used late modern art approaches. I placed data points within a frame that was continuously reframed; and, the points were incessantly erased and expanded based on my observations in the museums. This aspect of my methodological approach was very much in the spirit of Cézanne and Giacometti's artwork.

The observations, interview transcripts, field notes, and collected artifacts were openly organized to avoid premature closure. I did this through data walking (Chávez, 2004), which was conceived as movement through data that is like wandering in museum space or searching along the surface of a canvas, as does a Giacometti line. As I transcribed interview data, for example, I stopped at notable text sequences, wrote bracketed notes, and highlighted key words and passages in different colors. On the other hand, I examined material

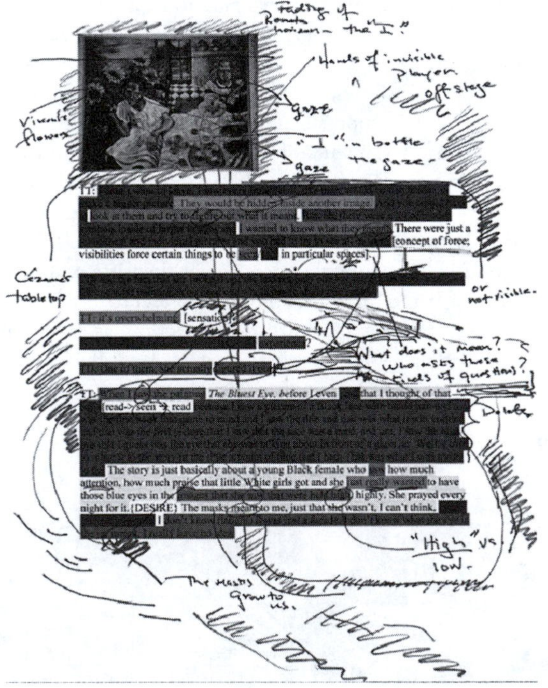

FIGURE 19.3 Traces of a data walk.

that held little interest to me and asked why, and cast these data into dark, recessive colors (see Fig. 19.2).

From these assembled data, I drafted auxiliary descriptive texts. This allowed me to sift further through the data from my data walks, and to begin to construct information that would provide future audiences contextual aspects of the investigation. Results of this process read much like ethnography, in these cases, more or less thickly described (Geertz, 1973), as shown in the following segment derived from field notes involving the Bedford Museum of Art, one of the museums I investigated that displays art of antiquity:

> Approaching the Bedford Museum of Art there is a sound of fabric gently tossing in the autumn breeze; large oblong multicolored banners announce the special events taking place at the museum: an African pottery show, lectures, and highlights from the permanent collection. The museum building is a three-story blend of old and new architectural traditions and stone artifices. The main entrance is ringed with polished granite and above it a large gray marble slab hangs. Chiseled in the stone with tall Romanesque letters is the museum's name.

As shown in this snippet, descriptions of designs of physical space can provide data to work from. The naming of museum buildings, for example, is a practice that denotes power of economics, patronage, and so forth. Moreover, these data formed what Deleuze and Guattari (1980/2002) characterized as tracings. Tracings are replete with description, interpretation, and are the conventional stuff of much qualitative research. Also, tracings often comprise collective, already said and already thought approaches to data and life, "everybody knows" ideas (Guattari, 1989/2000). Tracing suggests various degrees of strict framing. Pushing against this framing, on the constructed tracings I designed and laid out principal planes of analyses.

Research Maps

One plane of analysis involved making research maps that concentrated on power relations. First, I created literal, visual maps of the data traces I had assembled. These consisted of four principal place markers, mentioned earlier in this chapter, drawn from Foucault (1975/1977) and Deleuze (1986/2000): concepts, objects, strategies, and subjectification. I visualized this system as one of movement, force, and exchange, and thus, these markers or placeholders were not used in my study as categories, at least in the strict sense. That is to say, I shifted their positions on the visual grids and subjected them to transformations; the intent of these analyses was to examine the interchangeability of data tentatively placed within the four domains.

For example, according to its director an overarching mission of the Oppenheimer Museum (OM), another museum I studied that specializes in a blend of Eastern art and European realism, was to "bring high art to Marthasville." The director supported his statement with particular concepts and strategies:

> I mostly use the museum as a teaching device to try to teach culture to people who may not know about culture. High art has aesthetic values; it's kind of like essence, like the term Namaste in India, which means: "I worship the highest in you, that's the highest in me." Objects here [at OM] take on a prominent position and have presence. I think that high culture is different than pop culture; you don't get "wow, that's cool." I think people feel good about our objects and seem to be attracted to them, more subconsciously; the objects don't elicit verbal responses. (OM interview transcript)

Implied in the director's words are binary divisions of value: Opposed to high culture (essence), there is low, popular culture. This high/low division of value provided a backdrop for studying this museum and in creating an analytic visual grid. For instance, concepts of high art and culture, essence, and presence were manifested in the strategic designs of OM shows: Benign objects, flower arrangements, warm colors, and meditative music typically greeted museum visitors. Further, among other shows, one was based on flying mystics, whose curator regularly leads spiritual tours of the Himalayan Mountains. Indeed, high things and spaces were part and parcel of what took place at OM.

Responding to these purported "higher" aspects of culture, visitors reverently passed through the space, moving slowly and linearly from art piece to piece, speaking quietly, as if in a holy place. Signs reminding guests to be courteous, warnings that crossing certain marked, spatial barriers would sound alarms, and the watchful presence of museum personnel reinforced quiet order. This is an example of how concepts, objects, and strategies (power relations) smear to form ideal spaces (Foucault, 1986) and subjects, in this case, what Foucault (1975/1977) described as docile bodies. Such instances constituted the stuff of literal maps drawn during the study. In a nutshell, I would take salient topics, such as "high art," from my data and map how they functioned as object, strategy, and concept—as forces that form subjects.

Art, however, should never condone the status quo (Deleuze, 1981/2002: Laughlin, 1974). Art disrupts order, and so too should research mappings (Guattari, 1989/2000). Maps are not drawn with neat categories, interpretations, and conclusions; they are turbulent, like a Giacometti painting. Thus, on tracings I inserted transformations and resistance to the intended uses of museum space. As my museum study advanced, in the margins of the tracings I assembled writings that pushed the framed boundaries of the tracings. These amalgams led to further and concurrent analytic constructions through dramatization.

Dramatization

Another plane of analysis in my study involved drama as creative analytic practice (Richardson, 2000). As shown later in this chapter and in the spirit of Giacometti, Cézanne, Deleuze, Guattari, and Foucault, this constructive practice, nonetheless, involved deconstructive counterpoints alongside creative production. Drama also provided methods to display data on stage, in a "museum of human nature" (Foucault, 1975/1977, p. 202). The stage can become a plane where movements and intersections of concepts, strategies, objects, and forces that form particular subjects can be laid out and made visible. Further, because museums stage events in gallery spaces and theatrically display objects on pedestals, in glass cases, and in frames, casting museum research onto the stage seemed a reasonable way for me further to analyze and present data derived from museum space.

To be sure, people dramatize ad infinitum and thus, drama has provided methods and metaphors for a growing body of qualitative research. Spivak (1992) troubled notions of identity talk, "acting bits," and "the staging of culture" (p. 776), and terms such as *rehearsal, actor,* and *performance* glide through qualitative methods texts (Coffey & Atkinson, 1996). As well, drama has been used explicitly in qualitative research writings. Lather and Smithies (1997) laid out little stages to shift from one space to another, and St. Pierre (1997) used the aside, "a centuries old theatrical convention . . . to speak to the reader without the rest of the text hearing [her]" (p. 373).

The themes of the drama were chosen from salient and personally important aspects of the data that resulted from all planes of analyses. Certainly, the drama was one involving multiple perspectives, gathered together by an author. All is perspective and producing things always involves value (Richardson, 2000). In this vein, I am bound to certain conditions, points of view, just as is the reader/audience is restricted from complete views of the research/text/stage no matter how visible or confessional researchers wish conditions to be. However, my point is one of multiplicity, and dramatization allowed me to shift scenes and perspectives. In this respect, the drama I constructed was akin to montage.

Concerning these montages, I was an editor; I made selections, cut out areas of text, and juxtaposed scenes and sequences in before/after pictures that do not necessarily conform to conventional time. In other words, sometimes chunks of transactions were placed alongside portions that occurred at various times and even on different days; however, these transactions occurred in the same, yet differently experienced, physical spaces. Further, in the chunks of data displayed, I remained faithful to transcribed audio recordings; I did not alter participant words except in instances to make the drama more readable (e.g., tense changes, to reduce redundancy, etc.).

Further, I rendered scenes using specific theatrical devices. These were sometimes constructed from my imagination, such as stage sets I designed. However, even these devices were designed and intended to make certain concepts closer to the percepts and affects that were experienced in the real spaces of the museums. Sometimes, this was achieved through usual dramatic approaches such as lighting effects, changes in scene/space/time, and highlighting props.

Additionally, the drama was created with less conventional means in terms of social research. In this regard, I created in-between characters, adapting Deleuze's (1986/2000) indication of filling in, or coloring spaces, with conceptual personae (Deleuze & Guattari, 1991/1994). First, I assembled a chorus of goats from the concept of the early Greek cult of Dionysus that gave birth to tragic drama (*tragoedia* means goat song). The chorus danced in circles around the Dionysian altar and sang hymns to the god. I conceived my goat chorus as pointing toward empty centers and voicing commonplace, "everybody knows" perspectives (see Deleuze & Guattari, 1980/2003, p. 116). Goats are very present in everyday life. Although not directly taken from verbatim transcript data, their voices were assembled from impressions I collected from participants during the investigation and from "everybody knows" perspectives that tumble in and through culture.

In this respect, the goat concept is aligned with forces that dominate some current social practices and politics in the United States. The "everybody knows" perspectives voiced by the goats involve notions of "political correctness" and everyday articulations that are part and parcel of the forces associated with pastoral power relations (Foucault, 1982/1994). Domains of common goat expressions in U.S. culture are voiced through the drama as reactive comments to the real players I put to stage.

For instance, during the study when a schoolteacher was more interested in collecting resources in a museum than in looking at art, the goat chorus proclaimed, "Everybody knows that on Monday mornings there's work to be done in school. Everybody knows teachers on the front line *love* resources to get the work done!" In another case, a teacher of a Christian school used a museum experience to illustrate lessons of good and evil, and the goats joined in, paraphrasing Dante and the Bible:

> Everybody knows that blessed is the shepherd's flock. Everybody knows blessed are we goats. Blessed are all believers. Damned are the idolaters; set them on burning sand in a rain of fire. Damned are the blasphemers, cover them in boiling pitch. . . . Judge not or be judged. So say the Gospels. Amen.

As another voice to insert into dramatizations, I created Sam, a character who sees all and hears all within the drama and who is invisible to the other players but not the audience/reader. He also has a perspective: he is a trickster of sorts—a griot. More importantly, Sam was created to provide a reactive counterpoint to everyday values and the articulations of the goat chorus. In the drama, Sam wears many masks, but behind the mask, there is nothing; that is to say, he is a being of force and has no identity. Sam's words were taken from data traces and my readings (e.g., Nietzsche, 1878/1974). In the following section, a scene is presented that presents the various aspects of methods that I have laid out in this chapter and multiple players in Bedford Museum space.

A Scene from a Theatre of Values

Characters (in order of appearance)

Karen Beam, Bedford Museum of Art Education Director
Stephen D., a university researcher
Sam, invisible to and unheard by the players, a commentator
Maggie Hatcher, museum docent
Bishop, DiDi, Flo aka Mic, and Monisha, adolescent students on a school fieldtrip
The goat chorus, invisible to and unheard by the players, also commentators
Bart and Clifford, out-of-school adolescents

Into and out of Africa

[The scene opens with Maggie, a Bedford Museum docent, opening a door to "Africa," a narrow museum gallery set to stage left. It is bright space lined with a series of large African masks, a display case of tribal weapons, and several objects on pedestals and behind glass. Spotlighted at center stage stands a large colonial era object on a pedestal that contains a crucified Christ, his mother Mary, and a Nigerian goddess holding a snake. On the wall is a map of Africa and several lengthy print texts. At the far end of the gallery stands Karen Beam, the Museum Education Director, and Stephen D. standing before a large, highlighted, hunter's garment made of animal skin. It contains dozens of small mirrors that reflect rainbows of diffracted light back to the audience. Sam perches on a pedestal to the side in half-light wearing the mask of a prankster.]

Karen: I always bring up this hunter's coat when I'm here. It's one of the most *wonderful* things in this collection! It's from Mali, a Muslim country. [*Pointing to the object*] Wisdom texts from the Koran are in these many little pouches so the hunter can carry the wisdom with him. They are little written texts, the hunters put them in there, blow on them and close them up, never to open them up again!

Sam [jumping from the pedestal]: A wise move.

Karen: [Pointing to a claw hanging from the garment as Stephen D. contemplates the object] From a successful hunt he adds a trophy from the animal to the shirt and takes on the power of the animal. Kids love that. They just love it. And there's always speculation about all the mirrors, what does it mean?

Sam [in a speculative pose while gazing at the mirrored garment]: Yes, what does it mean? All these little mirrors that point to virtuality: I am there in that tiny looking glass, but I am not there. I am here, but not there, which way, which way? I position my gaze a bit to the side of one of the mirrors, and there is a distorted headdress and Jesus; I move a bit and a Nigerian goddess eclipses Him. And this sparkling mirror reflects other mirrors and displays an infinite regression of African warrior masks [turning and gesturing to the masks on the museum wall]. And there in the next little mirror is a refracted view of Maggie; she becomes larger, then smaller, she is there [looking at another little mirror] and she is there, [spinning around] and she is there.

Maggie [leading a serpentine line of field trip students at the other side of the gallery, passing the wall case with the display of weapons]: This is the African gallery and it's been redone and it's just sparkling! This is a shield and various weapons.

[The students linger at the weapons display as Maggie rapidly moves ahead through the sparkling space peppered with mirrored light from the hunter's garment.]

Maggie [advancing while pointing to a wall map]: And here, here's a map of Africa, which isn't a bad thing to have a look at to see all these different cultures that are represented in the gallery. From the Congo we have stuff, and from Cameroon . . .

Bishop [remaining at the weapons, whispering to Flo aka Mic]: What's that, a shield?

Flo aka Mic [whispering to Bishop]: That's neat. You could make a lot of bulletproof vests like this. And then a lot of people be living, cause it could block a billion bullets. [Pausing] It's like, it seems like these weapons are more real than they are today, 'cause when machines, uh, when you make stuff by hand you, uh . . .

Maggie [walking back to Flo aka Mic and interrupting]: Tell me. Have you been studying Africa in school? If there is anything that you would like to add or say to the group or if you have been studying a certain culture, or what have you, and you have something that you want to say?

[Flo aka Mic looks at Maggie and then lowers his head.]

Maggie: No? [*Turning to the side and with a sweep of her arm*] All right, now these masks were very important.

Chorus [chanting]: Blessed are the meek for they will inherit the Kingdom of Heaven. Blessed are the meek for they will inherit the Kingdom of Heaven.

Sam [gazing at the reflection of the visitors and weapons through the hunter's mirrors]: And blessed are those that smote with the sword, be it of steel or words. The slings and arrows of outrageous contradictions of education and other romances . . .

[Maggie heads the group rapidly past the masks and through the gallery, as Bart and Clifford walk in and over to the weapons display. Sam remains transfixed by the mirrors on the hunter's garment.]

Clifford [snickering]: Dude, these African sword like things, they look like they came out of a really bad movie. Like the shape of them and stuff, but it's interesting though, I like it. Weapons were a pretty big part of the time where all this stuff came from. They had to keep the civilizations going and the weapons had to win the wars. [Pausing] The materials that these weapons are made of could distinguish who won in certain time periods and places in the world.

Bart: Yeah, actually some of this stuff reminds me of video games I've played. Like I played one from like a bird's eye view where you build Roman cities. And with that one you can customize your powers and stuff, and a lot of these weapons look really familiar. But this is actually like very true instead of just a video game.

Clifford [contemplatively]: I wonder if any of these weapons actually killed people?

Chorus: Everybody knows of the snips and snails and puppy dog tails and trucks and guns and knives that little boys are made of!

Sam [appearing hypnotized by the hunter's mirrors]: This small bended mirror superimposes the reflections of the African warrior masks with the museum visitors behind me. [Moving his head and point of view] And with a slight movement of my gaze the masks devour them!

[Stephen D. and Karen pass Clifford and Bart and walk toward the weapons display.]

Karen: The African collection contains about a thousand pieces. [Pointing to the display] Aren't these just wonderful? The shield is amazing. It looks like it's metallic, but we learned in training that it's actually made of animal skin! These weapons are a favorite of boys; they are just really drawn to them. If you can really make it come back to the kids, to relate it to something they know, then they'll remember it. So, I'm really interested to see what kids are interested in. Boys have a lot to say about these weapons.

Stephen D.: What have they said?

Karen: Uh, I don't know, but the docents tell me that the boys are immediately drawn to weapons.

[Sam leaves the hunter's garment, approaches the audience and gestures to both sides of the African gallery set and recites]

In this monument aligns
A country's obsessive, ruinous lust
For violence, fear, and other signs
Of sinister training wielded by the just.
With tools of war, o' nadir dust.

[Sam retreats into the darkness at the edge of the stage as Maggie turns a circle and addresses the school group.]

Maggie [pointing to the wall of masks]: The masks in Africa were very important. These are various masks that you could use for various initiation ceremonies.

DiDi [whispering to Monisha]: I think this is cool. I've seen stuff like this in a book before, like in 7th grade when we were studying about the country that we used to have.

Maggie [turning and approaching DiDi]: Do you want to tell everybody what you are saying so we can all hear? No? [*Rapidly turning back to the display objects*] And here we have Camerooooooooon . . .

Flo aka Mic [to Bishop as they linger to look at the masks]: It's like, like they represent symbols in gladiator times. They used the masks to fight and protect their heads and stuff like that. And some symbols are meant to frighten you, to let you know who not to mess with and who to mess with. That's important. It's unique.

[Sam moves from the edge of darkness and into a glaring white spotlight in the center of the stage and recites]

A fear that bind the innocent
To clan relations, God, and State
A fear that now from mighty jets
Deliver gruesome mortal fate.
Behind masks of war is greed and hate.

[Sam moves out of the spotlight and back into the shadows.]

Maggie [Looking at her watch, passing the central colonial figure object, and glancing at the displayed hunter's garment]: Well, we've got to move on. On we go. We're going on to "Egypt." On we go.

DiDi [staying behind with Monisha and pointing to the colonial object containing multiple figures]: What's that?

Monisha [looking at a figure suspended on a crossbar]: That could be like

Monisha and DiDi [in unison]: Like Jesus! Like Jesus!

DiDi: And that could be Mary!

Monisha: Oh really? [Pointing at the Nigerian goddess figure holding a snake] And that must be his daddy or something.

DiDi: His daddy is God!

Monisha: I know but

DiDi: Naw.

[The girls turn move away from the object.]

DiDi: That woman docent must be from England, the way she talk.

Monisha: Yeah.

DiDi: I used to wanted to talk like that. I tried, but it never did work [*giggles*].

[The girls realize that Maggie and the group have left them behind and hurry around the corner, past a room where a stage performance is taking place; the stage lights fade.]

CLOSING THOUGHTS

Through this chapter I attempted to show various methods by which museum literacy research can be conducted. Particular perspectives guide these methods. Some methodological approaches are conserving, object centered, and aligned with traditional archives or traces of knowledge, while others involve expansive spaces that function in and through what Foucault, Deleuze, and Guattari indicated as cracks and ruptures of convention. The expansive methods of mapping and dramatization that I presented engage particular concepts of space and power; space and power that produces connected flows of strategies, concepts, objects, and subjects. These methods are dependent on, yet intended to disrupt, archival knowledge, such as that found in the descriptive data that I collected in and assembled from museums and subsequently traced.

The museum study that I conducted and in part presented in this chapter was an experiment in such methods of space. These methods very much involve the visual and other communicative arts, applied to what Lefebvre (1974/2001) laid out as the situations of everyday life. Methods of data walking, mapping, and dramatization are all about art and movement in and with collected data in space. These are not metaphors; space study is part of an art of seeing. Indeed, space is of great concern in the visual arts, yet, it has heretofore been mostly treated as a mere backdrop in literacy studies. In a time when visual communication is in many instances eclipsing verbal forms, as illustrated by image-filled pages of the Internet and tabloid presses, the education field needs to learn much from visual displays and spatial constructions, and museums can be prime sites for such learning.

Museums are also places where ideals are put on stage for pleasure as well as for the training of values, which is all about power. In the OM galleries, these values were explicitly stated through strategies of high/low division that created particular "high minded subjects". Further, the scene taken from the Bedford Museum showed how adult educators there carried forward similar strategies of value: with exclamations and observations about "wonderful" and "amazing" objects and "sparkling" galleries.

Yet, removed from the constructivist logic that pervades much museum education research and theory (e.g., Leinhardt et al., 2002; Hapgood & Palincsar, 2002), these educators were less observant of the interests of adolescents that moved through their museum space. There were occasions when students lingered and whispered among themselves about museum displays while Maggie, the Bedford Museum docent, went about her touring routine, swiftly moving through the African gallery and ignoring the very spaces that had captured the adolescents' attention. In fact, when Maggie noticed that the students were not giving her notice, she interceded using a disciplinary tactic: asking students to take the stage and, for instance, share what they had learned about Africa from the archive, in school. Indeed, alongside flows there are zero points, blocks to flow (Deleuze & Guattari, 1972/2003). These are forces that frame, display, and form compliant subjects who move through museum space with reverence toward the objects and the past or perhaps those who never venture to return.

In comparison, when unrestricted by adult educators, the tendency of young participants in the scene I presented was to treat strolls through museum space as a connective game involving notions and activities that were pleasurable to them. These connections covered wide, expansive territories from "bad movies" to video games to Jesus, Mary, and God-daddy. If engagement is a goal of education, perhaps educators could seize upon opportunities to capitalize on such connections rather than to tethers of institutionalized constructions of value, such as those found in "high culture." To be sure, future research of museum literacy could expand on these types of connections, and disconnections, between lines of the collective local and the ideals set up in and by museum space.

This chapter also involved other lines composed on planes of composition, space study, which can push against the status quo. The planes were principally constituted by use of the visual arts and performance arts, through insertions, erasures, drawings, and staging. In the spirit of Deleuze, Foucault, and Guattari, I have tried to show how smudges, smears, and research lines can be adventuresome, perhaps breakaway lines. Such adventures through the arts and space are especially important in times when education research is increasingly incorporated into conserving values and standards. Space study is research of affirmation, of possibilities, experimentation between points: a movement of light, words, and players on a stage—traces upon which other maps can be drawn.

REFERENCES

Alvermann, D. E. (1997). Introduction: Explorations in crossing boundaries. In J. Flood, S. B. Heath, & D. Lapp (Eds.), *Handbook of research on teaching literacy through the communicative and visual arts* (pp. 95–96). Newark, DE: International Reading Association.

Bogue, R. (1996). *Deleuze and Guattari*. London: Routledge. (Original work published 1989)

Chávez, R. A. (2004). *Integral evaluation of the creative personality: Clinical, genetic, and phenomenological features*. Unpublished doctoral dissertation, National Autonomous University of México, México City, México.

Clifford, J. (1997). *Routes: Travel and translation in the late twentieth century*. Cambridge, MA: Harvard University Press.

Coffey, A., & Atkinson, P. (1996). *Making sense of qualitative data*. Thousand Oaks, CA: Sage.

Deleuze, G. (2000). *Foucault*. In S. Hand (Ed. & Trans.). Minneapolis, MN: University of Minnesota Press. (Original work published 1986)

Deleuze, G. (2002). *Francis Bacon: The logic of sensation* (D. W. Smith, Trans.). New York: Portmanteau Press. (Original work published 1981)

Deleuze, G., & Guattari, F. (1994). *What is philosophy?* (H. Tomlinson & G. Burchell, Trans.). New York: Columbia University Press. (Original work published 1991)

Deleuze, G., & Guattari, F. (2002). *A thousand plateaus: Capitalism and schizophrenia* (B. Massumi, Trans.). Minneapolis, MN: University of Minneapolis Press. (Original work published 1980)

Deleuze, G., & Guattari, F. (2003). *Anti-Oedipus: Capitalism and schizophrenia* (R. Hurley, M. Seem, & H. R. Lane, Trans.). Minneapolis, MN: University of Minnesota Press. (Original work published 1972)

Eakle, A. J. (2007). Literacy spaces of a Christian faith-based school. *Reading Research Quarterly, 42*, 472–510.

Eakle, A. J. (2005). *Literacy in the art museum: A theatre of values*. Unpublished doctoral dissertation, University of Georgia, Athens.

Eakle, A. J., & Chávez, R. A. (2003). *Critical museum literacy in Mexico City*. Paper presented at annual meeting of the National Reading Conference, Scottsdale, Arizona.

Eco, U. (1984). *The role of the reader: Explorations in the semiotics of texts*. Bloomington, IN: Indiana University Press.

Falk, J. H., & Dierking, L. D. (1992). *The museum experience*. Washington, DC: Whalesback.

Flood, J., & Lapp, D. (1995). Broadening the lens: Toward an expanded conceptualization of literacy. In K. A. Hinchman, D. J. Leu, & C. K. Kinzer (Eds.), *Perspectives on literacy research and practice* (pp. 1–16). Chicago: National Reading Conference.

Foucault, M. (1971). *The order of things: An archeology of the human sciences*. London: Tavistock. (Original work published 1970)

Foucault, M. (1977). *Discipline and punish* (A. M. Sheridan Smith, Trans.). New York: Vintage Books. (Original work published 1975)

Foucault, M. (1983). *This is not a pipe. With illustrations and letters by René Magritte*. In J. Harkness (Ed. & Trans.). Berkley, CA: University of California Press. (Original work published 1968)

Foucault, M. (1986). Of other spaces. *Diacritics, 16*, 22–27.

Foucault, M. (1994). What is an author? In J. B. Faubion (Ed.); R. Hurley et al., (Trans.), *Aesthetics, method, and epistemology/Michel Foucault, 1954–1984* (pp. 205–222). New York: The New Press. (Original work published 1969)

Foucoult, M., (1994). The subject and power. In J. B. Faubion (Ed.); R. Hurley et al., (Trans.), *Power/Michel Foucault, 1954–1984* (pp. 326–348). New York: The New Press. (Original work published 1982)

Geertz, C. (1973). *The interpretation of cultures*. New York: Basic Books.

Gombrich, E. H. (1965). *Art and illusion: A study of the psychology of pictorial representation* (2nd ed.). New York: Pantheon.

Guattari, F. (2000). *The three ecologies*. New Brunswick, NJ: Athlone Press. (Original work published 1989)

Guthrie, J. T., & Wigfield, A. (2000). Engagement and motivation in reading. In M. L. Kamil, P. B. Mosenthal, P. D. Pearson, & R. Barr (Eds.), *Handbook of reading research* (Vol. 3, pp. 403–422). Mahwah, NJ: Lawrence Erlbaum Associates.

Hagood, M. C., Leander, K. M., Luke, C., Mackey, M., & Nixon, H. (2003). Media and online literacy studies. *Reading Research Quarterly, 38*, 386–413.

Hapgood, S. E., & Palincsar, A. S. (2002). Fostering an investigatory stance: Using text to mediate inquiry about museum objects. In S. G. Paris (Ed.), *Perspectives on object-centered learning in museums* (pp. 171–190). Mahwah, NJ: Lawrence Erlbaum Associates.

Hilden, P. P., & Huhndorf, S. M. (1999). Performing 'Indian' in the National Museum of the American Indian. *Social Identities, 5*, 161–183.

Hooper-Greenhill, E. (2001). *Museums and the interpretation of visual culture*. London: Routledge.

Hull, G., & Schultz, K. (2001). Literacy and learning out of school: A review of theory and research. *Review of Educational Research, 71*, 575–611.

Kirsheblatt-Gimblett, B. (1998). *Destination culture: Tourism, museums, and heritage*. Berkeley, CA: University Of California Press.

Lather. P., & Smithies, C. (1996). *Troubling the angels: Women living with HIV/AIDS*. Boulder, CO: Westview Press.

Laughlin, C. J. (1974). *The personal eye*. New York: Aperture.

Leander, K. M. (2004). Reading the spatial histories of positioning in a classroom literacy event. In K. Leander & M. Sheehy (Eds.), *Space matters: Assertions of space in literacy practice and research* (pp. 115–142). New York: Peter Lang.

Lefebvre, H. (2001). *The production of space* (D. Nicholson-Smith, Trans.). Oxford, U. K.: Blackwell. (Original work published 1974)

Leinhardt, G., Crowley, K., & Knutson, K. (Eds.). (2002). *Learning conversations in museums*. Mahwah, NJ: Lawrence Erlbaum Associates.

Miles, R. S., Alt, M. B., Gosling, D. C., Lewis, B. N., & Tout, A. F. (1984). *The design of educational exhibits*. London: Unwin Hyman.

Moje, E., Ciechanowski, K. M., Kramer, K., Ellis, L., Carrillo, R., & Collazo, T. (2004). Working toward a third space in content area literacy: An examination of everyday funds of knowledge and discourse. *Reading Research Quarterly, 39*, 38–70.

Nietzsche, F. (1974). *Human, all-too-human: A book for free spirits, part I* (H. Zimmern, Trans.). New York: Gordon Press. (Original work published 1878)

Prosise, T. O. (1998). The collective memory of the atomic bombings misrecognized as objective history: The case of the public opposition to the National Air and Space Museum's atom bomb exhibit. *Western Journal of Communication, 62*, 316–348.

Rajchman, J. (1988). Foucault's art of seeing. *October, 44*, 88–117.

Rewald, J. (1977). The last motifs at Aix. In W. Rubin (Ed.), *Cézanne: The late work*. (pp. 83–106). New York: The Museum of Modern Art.

Richardson, L. (2000). Writing: A method of inquiry. In N. K. Denzin, & Y. S. Lincoln (Eds.), *Handbook of qualitative research* (2nd ed., pp. 923–948). Thousand Oaks, CA: Sage.

Rosenblatt, L. M. (1978). *The reader, the text, the poem. The transactional theory of the literary work*. Carbondale, IL: Southern Illinois University Press.

Simpson, M. G. (1996). *Making representations: Museums in the post-colonial era*. London: Routledge.

Soja, E. W. (1996). *Third space: Journeys to Los Angeles and other real-and-imagined places*. Cambridge, MA: Blackwell.

Spivak, G. C. (1992). Acting bits/identity talk. *Critical Inquiry, 18*, 770–803.

St. Pierre, E. A. (1997). Methodology in the fold and the irruption of transgressive data. *International Journal of Qualitative Studies in Education, 10,* 175–189.

Street, B. V. (1995). *Social literacies: Critical approaches to literacy in development, ethnography, and education*. London: Longman.

Wade, S. E., & Moje, E. B. (2000). The role of text in classroom learning. In M. L. Kamil, P. B. Mosenthal, P. D. Pearson, & R. Barr (Eds.), *Handbook of reading research* (Vol. 3, pp. 609–627). Mahwah, NJ: Lawrence Erlbaum Associates.

Zeidler, A. L., & Surber, J. R. (1999). Understanding topic, structure, and importance of information in a visual and verbal display. *Journal of Experimental Education, 67,* 114–132.

20

"A PICTURE CAN DO THINGS WORDS CAN'T": TRANSFORMING REPRESENTATIONS IN LITERACY RESEARCH

Lalitha Vasudevan

TEACHERS COLLEGE, COLUMBIA UNIVERSITY

The stories that are currently being constructed and represented about adolescents' literacies are filled with tones of hopelessness and forewarn of an impending crisis. The decibels are especially high when shrieking in fear about the urban adolescent's literacy prospects. A recent report made to the Carnegie Corporation stated, "In urban centers . . . only an estimated 20 percent of students are reading at grade level and thus are prepared to master high-school level content" (Biancarosa & Snow, 2004, p. 8). As this and other reports (e.g., Ballator, Farnum, & Kaplan, 1999; Snow, Burns, & Griffin, 1998) demonstrate, literacy, to a large extent, continues to be measured, researched, and taken up in popular discourses within rigid definitions of reading, despite the rapidly changing landscape of reading, writing, and other communicative practices. Like Magritte's famous paradoxical painting, the representation of something is not, and can never be, the thing itself. Yet, for so long, test scores of many kinds have come to signify literacy, or more specifically an understanding of literacy, as "autonomous" (Street, 1995), and thereby a set of skills that is easily measurable (Irvine & Larson, 2001). While recognizing that representation is always necessarily partial, it is important, then, to strive for representations that better reflect the nuanced, multiple, socially situated, ideological, and layered nature of literacies. It is incumbent upon literacy researchers to extend the stories that are being told, shown, and demonstrated about literacies, particularly in the lives of youth living and growing up in urban centers. These stories characterize, and are characterized by, creativity, innovation, and texture in their representations, which chronicle both what has been learned through research and the story of the research itself.

In a study of African American boys' literacies, stories, and multimedia storytelling practices, I learned firsthand how significantly the context in which research occurs impacts how phenomena are explored as well as how they can be represented; context is not static, but rather, is dynamically constructed and lived space (Leander & Sheehy, 2004). This point was illuminated during an exchange between Cyrus, one of five boys who were part of the study and me. We had been talking about the different ways to convey stories when the subject of modalities and representation was broached. In particular, Cyrus and I discussed writing and the related editing process, something with which he was familiar from his school experiences and for which he had much disdain. I had suggested some possible ways for him to document his ongoing dissonance with a teacher at school—his latest storytelling topic of choice—and had named journaling and story writing and as two possible formats. But Cyrus shook his head; writing would not allow him to do what he felt he could accomplish with a more visual mode, such as photography. In the midst of this discussion, Cyrus remarked, "Ms. Lalitha, a picture can do things words can't. Pictures can make you *feel* things that words can't." Indeed, Cyrus's pictures—the ones he created, directed others to produce, and was the focus of—challenged "the picture of Black males that dominates popular media as well as the conceptualization that is generally advanced in the scholarly press [which] is a picture of pathology bordering on hopelessness" that Gordon (1999, p. ix) described, noting that these are images that are "sometimes found even among those whose motivations appear to be humane and sympathetic" (p. ix). Cyrus, along with the other participants in my study, produced, performed, and embodied images of urban, adolescent, African American males as artists, dreamers, readers, video game players, brothers, and more. These images call into question the persistent victim/perpetrator dichotomies that

FIGURE 20.1 Retrieved from http://www.west.asu.edu/koptiuch/ASB311_web/ASB311_images/surrealism/Magritte_pipe1.jpg

overwhelmingly define African American male youths' institutional experiences (Ferguson, 2000).

In that moment of Cyrus's declaration about the communicative power of images, the cacophony of my multiliteracies/multimodal theoretical rhetoric butting up against my unwittingly linguistic-oriented methodological and pedagogical practices resounded loudly. What would it mean, methodologically, to engage with Cyrus's observation? When would literacy research methods cease overprivileging linguistic modes of constructing and representing knowledge about literacy? What would it take to truly disrupt the overwhelmingly deficit narrative about African American boys' literacies that has been perpetuated across academic and popular discourses alike? In this chapter, I explore my responses to these questions as a guide for considering how the representation of literacy research, broadly, might be reconceptualized and transformed to reflect greater variation in and texture of literacies. I draw on the concept of counterstorytelling (Delgado, 1995) to engage this challenge, which advocates for stories that are often marginalized or told by individuals who are kept at the margins of social life (Ladson-Billings, 2000) to be placed at the center of inquiry. Such a practice privileges participants' experiential knowledge (Solorzano & Yosso, 2002) and allows for the study of literacy to live outside the predetermined bounds of test scores and reading levels. The methodological implications of this framework are discussed later in this article.

This proposal to transform literacy research representation impacts three key dimensions of the research process: the research space, roles and positionalities, and documentation and artifact collection. Collectively, these three dimensions of literacy research methodology shape how the stories of literacy research projects are interpreted and represented. Consequently, reimagining these dimensions can produce narratives that counterstory—both resist and offer new sites of inquiry about—existing literacy narratives in the lives of youth, generally, and in the lives of urban youth, in particular.

DIGITAL CULTURE AND THE EVOLVING LITERACY LANDSCAPE

In the last several years, the very essence of communication and representation has undergone significant changes. New media and technologies have gained prominence in daily social life as we increasingly rely on e-mail, blogs, podcasts, and Web spaces to acquire and disseminate information, connect with known and unknown others, and extend our "meatspace"[1] selves. We do so by drawing on a variety of communicative practices that are not solely linguistic or visual and that are not ones in which one mode simply complements the other. The concept of multimodality (Kress, 2003; Jewitt & Kress, 2003) gains heightened significance in this digital culture as people, and especially youth, orchestrate multiple modes for a variety of purposes in a given moment. Leander (2005) provided a rich example of this with a space-time analysis of a high school student's maneuvering between the physical space of her biology classroom and the digital spaces of a Word document, her blog, and an online reference Web site. He argued that in a given moment, the student is able to participate across spaces, leave an imprint in time, and inhabit various identities afforded through her use of the equally diverse modalities.

Other studies of literacies over the last several years present compelling evidence for rethinking what counts as literacy in different institutional contexts and social spaces (Barton & Hamilton, 1998; Knobel, 1999). Ongoing theorizing about literacy practices further suggests that what we see and understand about literacy is significantly shaped by the rapidly increasing availability of modes with which to communicate as well as the evolving landscape of spaces for making these literacy practices public (e.g., Gee, 2003; Jewitt & Kress, 2003; Lankshear & Knobel, 2002). Spaces such as instant messaging (e.g., Lewis & Fabos, 2005), online chat environments (Thomas, 2004), virtual worlds (Turkle, 1995), digital storytelling (Hull & Nelson, 2005), youth media production (Goodman, 2003), and others are both generative of and produced through multimodal and hybrid literacy practices that blur the lines between the visual and communicative arts. Harnessing the new affordances for multimodal composing that new technologies present, projects such as digital storytelling transgress the boundaries of print-based reading and writing and embody what Hull and Nelson (2005) proposed as the semiotic power of such texts. Digital storytelling,[2] for example, is more than the intentional convergence of visual and aural texts. In his 3 minute, 46 second story titled, "The Men's Day/Afternoon Out," TJ's orchestrated juxtaposition of a series of images, video clips, transition titles, a music track, and ending credits collectively conveys a strong statement about our storytelling project. Any one mode alone would only tell one piece of this story, and while any representation remains incomplete, the meaning conveyed by TJ's digitally multimodal creation is held in the design, story elements, and implicit assertions about the space that was generative of such production. As the aesthetic of literacy changes, so, too, do the purposes for communication, as in TJ's text and other digital stories that would not exist if not for the possibility of storytelling in this way.

In my work, a recognition of the hybrid and multimodal nature of meaning making meant that in a study of literacies in the lives of five

[1] *Meatspace,* a term made popular in cyberpunk fiction, refers to the physical world where our "meat" selves exist, as opposed to cyberspace where we can theoretically leave our "meat" behind. However, as Thomas (2004) suggested, "to think of cyberspace as only a playground for the mind is to forget that intimate connection between body and mind" (p. 364).

[2] The Center for Digital Storytelling uses the term *digital storytelling* to describe a wide variety of new media production practices that are usually highly personal, and bring together still images, a narrated script, and titles within a movie editing program such as iMovie (for more information, see http://www.storycenter.org/).

African American boys living and making their way in a northeastern city, I sought to understand literacies as not only manifested in textual products, but as embodied and performed (Blackburn, 2003) across a variety of modalities and locations (Vasudevan, 2004). This approach to literacies study follows an emerging tradition of scholars who understand the importance of recognizing the evolving and generative nature of literacy across contexts and diverse meaning making modes (e.g., Hull & Schultz, 2002; Hagood, 2004; Leander, 2005; Moje, 2000; Wissman, 2005, in press). Across these studies of literacy practices is a shared understanding of literacy as both social and multiple; a resistance to the overemphasis on schooled literacies by representing an increasingly rich range of youths' literate engagements beyond the school walls; and an implicit methodological commitment to imagining new sites and modes of inquiry in literacy studies.

METHODOLOGICAL CONSIDERATIONS

How do we research literacy? What methods do we use to explore literacy practices? And what are the ways in which we represent what we find? These questions are of significance to any research seeking to explore and make sense of how literacies are engaged and taken up across contexts; but they are of particular significance when pursued within the evolving digitally transformed literacy landscape. As noted above, these new terrains are the subjects of emerging and ongoing studies, yet the diverse field of literacy studies remains frighteningly singular in the matter of literacy research representation. By calling for literacy representations that are transformative, I mean the intentional researching and representing of literacy in ways that significantly alter the construction and representation of knowledge about literacy. This requires the reconceptualizing of three dimensions of the research process: the space of research—the practices and ways of interacting that come to signify when, how, and by whom the research is enacted; roles and positionalities—the ways that researcher and participants position themselves in relation to the research; and documentation and artifact collection—the ways that the roles assumed and the research space impact the type of data that is produced, collected and made available for subsequent representations.

These three dimensions were under constant revision in my research with Cyrus, Romeo, Jamal, TJ, and Shawn, who were between the ages of 11 and 13 for the duration of the study. What I had initially conceptualized as an ethnography of "naturally occurring" practices and stories of resistance quickly became reconceptualized as a collaborative, multisited, ethnographic coconstruction of a space for storytelling possibilities. In doing this work, I experienced what Weis and Fine (2000) term the "triple representational problem" (p. 53), which, in my work, involved the negotiation between representing myself in the research and as a researcher, the boys as storytellers, and the people and situations that were storied during the project. I contend, therefore, that in collaborative and participatory research, intentionally for working social change, we must move against and beyond "stock stories"[3]: *against* through the telling of different stories and *beyond* through telling stories differently.

[3] Guinier and Torres (2002) described "stock stories" as those narratives that have become sedimented in social life and legal discourse as "received wisdom" that often perpetuates predominantly held ideas as truths, as normal, or as the neutral position.

Research Space

My exploration of adolescents' literacies officially began on a jungle gym set atop a concrete play space within the fenced in property of a kindergarten through grade 8 school. All five of the boys who participated in the research attended this school and had just finished fifth grade when we began meeting together. As we took turns attempting the monkey bars and perching ourselves precariously on the steel structure, I proposed the idea of a summer project to the group; I had discussed the idea with a couple of the boys earlier in the year while I had spent time in their classroom working on another project with their teacher. As we hung out on the jungle gym, I told them that I needed their input to help shape the idea further. All of the boys seemed interested, and they were especially enthusiastic about the possibility of using cameras. Immediately they began sharing with me stories of trips they had taken with their respective families during which they had taken pictures. A couple of them had used "throw aways" (disposable cameras) and a couple had used "the kind you keep putting film in" (e.g., 35mm cameras that use film). Ideas for movies also quickly entered the conversation. Thus, from the beginning of the study, visual and audiovisual modalities were central in our space, and their importance in creating our space became cemented during our second meeting when we began brainstorming project ideas. Many of the initial ideas were about documenting familiar images including people the boys knew ("family" and "girls"), a daycare center ("people taking care of people"), "decent" cars, "decent" houses, and homeless people.

From those early meetings, our space as a group became characterized with dimensions of multiplicity: the multiple locations we traversed, the multiple modalities we engaged, and the multiple selves we authored. That is, since we were a group with no institutional home, the city streets, neighborhoods, eateries, and buildings became the canvas for our storytelling. I had access to, and regularly brought to meetings, a digital still camera, a digital video camera, digital voice recorders, disposable cameras, and a laptop, which we used to surf the Internet, use video-editing software, and to acquire and listen to music. The varied ways in which these modalities were engaged across locations, and in order to author different selves, was particularly salient to the construction of the research space; that is, the boys had and took advantage of the diverse ways to participate in, enact, and live this space.

Recently, scholars in the field of literacy studies have begun to apply theories of space, third space, and spatiality to the study of language, discourses, and literacies. Gutiérrez, Rymes, and Larson (1995) explored a third space that was created in a classroom situation when students and teachers engaged discourses that transgressed traditional school "scripts." In doing so, students and teacher together produced a glimpse at new and imaginative interactions. More recently, Moje et al. (2004) drew on the concept of "funds of knowledge" (Moll, Amanti, Neff, & Gonzalez, 1992) to suggest pedagogical practices that can create a third space in classrooms that would be reflective of a hybrid juncture of the "first space" of home funds and the "second space" of school funds. In both articles, third space is advocated for as an achievable pedagogical construction—a way of being that draws on the resources and discourses of all participants present.

The application of spatial theories to the study of literacies has been investigated in more depth in an edited volume by Leander and Sheehy (2004), who, in their introduction to the volume, considered the ways in which "context, in literacy research, has been over-determined in its meaning by a seemingly natural interpretation of material setting or place" (p. 3). They write that, "Space has been over-materialized" (p. 3). In addition to offering a way of understanding literacy, these studies of the spatial dimensions of literacy practices argue for a reconceptualization of how we conduct literacy research. If we take seriously their claim that any context in which research takes place is actually fluid and being intentionally "lived" (Soja, 1996), then we must concede that the lens of research cannot remain localized to one physical location or modal domain. Studies of literacies must consider how literacies are not only socially situated, but spatially situated, and attend to how literacy practices circulate and are transformed across spaces, time, and contexts (Schultz, 2006). Multisited ethnography (Marcus, 1995) offers one way to think about "[e]mpirically following the thread of cultural process" (p. 97), which in my research meandered across modes of communication, physical and virtual locations, and the many selves that were authored in the process. I found that in order to follow the threads of dialogue about race and institutional policies and practices, of the boys' engagement with technology, and of the relationships between literacies, technologies and our space, I had to think differently about what a research space entailed.

Ours became a third space of and for counterstorytelling—through the texts that were produced as well as the ways in which we communicated and interacted as a group about a variety of topics, including school and relationships between students and teachers. It was there that the research about literacies was lived. To say so is to recognize the layers of action, intentionality, and imagined possibilities that undergird any artifact produced in that space. In the next section, I explore the ways in which a research space can impact the dynamics of the selves we bring to the research.

Roles and Positionalities

Youth do not only exist in the ways they are portrayed in researchers' words, alliterations, and analyses; their lives existed before the research and continue on long after the final piece of data has been collected. The dynamic interactions that characterize the research space represent a moment of possibility to not only pursue research questions but also to inform what it means to *know*. My conversation with Cyrus, previously described, represented one such moment in which my response would shape the multiple roles I inhabited, including "adult," "researcher," and the person providing access to technologies. More specifically, the way I responded had implications for what kind of adult or researcher I would be known as in this group. This moment reveals how my meaning making power as a researcher was rewritten, as I was vulnerable to "being made" as a participant. To be found in this and other moments are rich instantiations of how subjectivities and discourses converge with epistemologies, moments that might not have occurred if I had maintained a more distanced stance or had been more rigid about the purpose of inquiry. I intentionally departed from a traditional ethnographic stance, as primarily observer, and instead resonated with the words of Ruth Behar (1996), who raised the quandary of vulnerability and noted that "[w]e ask for revelations of others, but we reveal little or nothing of ourselves; we make others vulnerable, but we ourselves remain invulnerable" (p. 273). Behar pushed us—those who engage in reflexive ethnographic research—further when she asked "who has the authority to speak for whom?" (p. 162) and "to whom do we speak?" (p. 166). My inclinations, as both a researcher and practitioner, echo Behar's perspective on the ethics, purposes, and responsibilities inherent when we engage in observation, documentation, and representation of people's lives.

Taking up the question of researcher vulnerability, Appleman (2003) revisited some of her past representations of youth to unearth what narratives lay hidden and unexamined in order to muse about the difference between recounting the "truth" and responsible research when the lives of young people are involved. She reflected on herself as a "White researcher describing and representing students of color" (p. 76) whose positionality is expressed in narratives steeped with "power relations of class and status" that belie her intentions as a researcher (p. 77). In this reflection, Appleman asked herself to look closely at how her intentions and unintended consequences were born out of her representations of youth and noted that narrative descriptions of youth run the risk of freezing identities in time. Of her work, then, I ask, "What would research representation look like if researcher and participant roles and positionalities were transgressed?"

Wissman's (2005) study of the photography and literacy practices of young women participating in a high school elective class entitled "Sistahs" implicitly engaged this question by the ways in which the young women in the study were engaged in the research. Positioned as a teacher researcher in this space, she explored the "pedagogical practices and relationships that can emerge when photography is viewed as a social practice within an in-school teaching and learning context" (Wissman, in press). Together with her students, she created a context that allowed all of them to explore photography and writing by women of color as coinvestigators. The young women who were a part of this elective class used the research space to enact hybrid roles as emergent photographers who were also storytellers, poets, authors, and social critics. In this space, photography was not a marginalized mode of meaning making, but rather one that afforded legitimate and valued participation in this space. Envisioning photography as a "medium of seeing" (Wissman, in press), Wissman described the ways in which the use of images honored the relationships in the young women's lives beyond the classroom walls. In doing so, the collective pedagogy of creating space for these relationships and their visual representations served to build new relationships within the classroom walls. Like Pink's (2001) work in visual ethnography, Wissman's work signaled the epistemological value of images for making sense of social and cultural realities, as well as for the new possibilities that emerge when participants assume the role of artifact producers. The positionalities of researcher and participants are impacted by the space that is constructed and consequently shape the ways in which the knowledge produced is documented and represented.

Consider my conversation with Cyrus (previously introduced), which took place on the block in front of his house. The group had finished meeting for the day, and as usual, I was walking east toward the university. Cyrus lived furthest east, and thus, he and I often had one-on-one conversations that spanned the duration of a few blocks. It was during one of these walks early in the study when Cyrus implicitly called into question my approach for engaging the boys' perspectives about literacies and their lives, in general. In commenting on what he felt was the communicative superiority of images over more linguistic modes of communication, Cyrus was both drawing on and calling into question the nature of our group space. In this moment, Cyrus was a participant in the study, as well as a coresearcher, and shaped the research space as he participated in it. Similarly, the space afforded him the opportunity to inhabit both of these roles at once and subsequently convey his point visually through a series of photographs about our group, activities in the park, filming, and outings. He rationalized that his in-school cacophony was in direct contrast to what happened during our group meetings, which he felt more moved to document. A few weeks later, while sitting in McDonald's, Cyrus noted that, unlike his school experiences, we did not have "attitude" in our group. "You know us, and we know you, Ms. Lalitha," Cyrus remarked, and he proceeded to talk about disconnect between teachers and students in school. In the same breath as he noted that his teachers did not bother to get to know him, he quickly added that he would not want them to know too much about him in the first place. I was aware of the power embedded in this decision and the agency that Cyrus exercised—as his words are constitutive of his action (Foucault, 1977) and as his images were his performative counterstory.

Thus, as I was aware of and intentionally responsive to how the research space was evolving, the boys also took on hybrid roles and new positionalities. As I discuss in the next section, our research space and the shifting roles and positionalities were generative of data and documentation that did not come with an instant analysis scheme or framework. Instead, when researcher and participants collectively produce the evidence that will be available subsequently to tell the stories of the research, the stories that are available to tell are altered and the representations of literacy research are transformed.

Documentation and Artifact Collection

Stories undergird the documentation of a study. The ways in which interviews, artifacts, documents, fieldnotes, and other data are collected are situated within larger narratives that govern our understandings of how knowledge is produced (Denzin, 2000). A storytelling methodology guided by lenses of counterstories and multimodality has implications for the way a research space is conceived (of and for stories that are constructed and performed), how participants are positioned (as storytellers who write themselves into the world in a variety of ways, and across modalities), and how the research is documented (what and from whom data is sought, and by whom it is produced). Multimodal counterstorytelling (Vasudevan 2004, 2006) was how I framed this approach of telling different stories differently, and the frame within which I situated discourses of visual methodologies, namely visual ethnography (Pink, 2001). The fields of anthropology and sociology have a history of using visual texts as research documentation; however, the researcher is often positioned as the primary collector or producer of these images. I propose that we deviate from the traditional research methods of photo elicitation or photographic interviewing used to ascertain a range of perspectives on a topic (Prosser & Schwartz, 1998) and instead engage the visual and other documents that are produced are markers that are indicative of the story of their creation. Just as visual texts are never exclusively visual (Duncum, 2004), so, too, are verbal, linguistic and other presumably monomodal texts in actuality multimodal and situated. That is, no artifact or piece of data, and particularly images and other visuals collected during research, is wholly unmediated. Of this, Pink (2001) noted,

> A reflexive approach to analysis should concentrate on how the content of visual images is the result of the specific context of their production and on the diversity of the way that video and photographs are interpreted . . . they are always representations of the subjective standpoints of the image producer and other viewers, including informants. (p. 114)

Thus, an understanding of literacy and related communicative arts as multiple and situated in social practices necessitates the collection of data about the social practices in which literacies are embedded. Ethnographic research provides "ways in" that reflect this emphasis on the sociocultural context; however, there is a potential danger of traditional ethnographic methods to render the researcher invisible and the representation of data to maintain a disembodied voice of authority. I addressed these concerns by situating traditional ethnographic methods within a methodological commitment to systematically construct ways to center the boys' counterstories, create a participatory research space with them, and engage a variety of modalities to collect and represent the stories that the boys and I coconstructed.

By situating a study of literacies in the context of digital storytelling, such as the DUSTY[4] project in Oakland, California, Hull and colleagues manifested the latent demands of an increasingly digital culture in which the practice and study of composing in these digital times are dynamically connected; thus, the lines between researcher and participants are similarly blurred. Qualitatively different from experimental evaluations of how *well* youth perform literacy, their studies of digital stories and the digital storytelling process takes seriously the act of "position[ing] . . . digital storytellers as authors, composers, and designers who are expert and powerful communicators, people with things to say that the community and the world should hear" (Hull & Nelson, 2005, p. 231). Arguing that multimodal texts such as digital stories are not merely the juxtaposition of images, sounds, text, and narration, Hull and Nelson (2005) noted that while "different semiotic modes may seem to encode the same content, they are nonetheless conveyors of qualitatively different kinds of messages" (p. 229). They offer an in-depth analysis of "Life-N-Rhyme," a digital story produced by Randy Young that offers a narrative about the life around him told from his vantage point. The multimodal composition presents numerous interpretive possibilities, and the authors' analysis of the text further reveals the semiotic power afforded by the artist's intentional orchestration and "copresentation" of multiple modes to convey a powerful, aesthetic, and evocative narrative. Hull and Nelson (2005) noted,

> As an irreducibly multimodal composition, "Lyfe-N-Rhyme" is not just a good poem whose meaning is enhanced because it has been illustrated and set to music; rather, we would argue that the meaning that a viewer or listener experiences is qualitatively different, transcending what is possible via each mode separately. (p. 251)

While their analysis focuses primarily on the text, there is another salient narrative embedded in this digital story; that is the one of how the story came to be. Emerging from Young's text are traces of what kind of space DUSTY is, the resources available, the roles assumed by participants and facilitators, and the kinds of relationships that existed in order for his and others' digital stories to come into being. I wonder, like the authors, "How many other poets and storytellers there are for whom multimodality would offer unexpectedly powerful affordances" (p. 253). Furthermore, the digital stories serve as compelling documentation of the intersection of the

[4] For more information on DUSTY or to view digital stories, go to http://oaklanddusty.org/

participants' lives, their multimodal communicative practices, and the new insights about the affordances of technologies in the production of new kinds of texts.

I return to Cyrus, whose simple words about images had a profound impact on how I reconceptualized the study I have been drawing on throughout this chapter. Cyrus was an adolescent who reveled in story, but was loathed to write despite his ability to do so. He relied heavily on nonlinguistic and nonprint modes of communication, such as bodily performance, photography, and other visual modalities, as spaces in which and from which to communicate. In doing so he extended his own, and the group's, palette of communicative practices. Cyrus was often seen in front of the camera as Romeo stood behind it, and Cyrus's spontaneous use of the video camera to initiate fake news by pretending to be an anchorman or, knowing the video camera was on, acting out a Sprite commercial, all contributed to one of the larger narratives about research and representation that emerged from this study: The ways in which participants are involved in the construction of the research space alters the representation of the research itself.

The following series of images (Figure 20.2) taken from the Sprite video, therefore, represents interconnected narratives that collectively represent our research space.

This sequence occurred while we were returning to the library, our usual meeting location, from a visit to Shawn's house. But these still images represent more than just the video clip from which they were taken. In these images is a glimpse of what comprised the literacy research space in which stories, literacies, and technology practices were explored. Our movement through the neighborhoods where the boys lived is the backdrop for the several other practices going on at the same time: Romeo is assuming his role as the video documenter; Cyrus is taking advantage of Romeo's skills and access to the camera to perform his own version of a popular text (the Sprite commercial); TJ and Jamal are walking ahead and discussing the dog we had just seen and run away from near Shawn's apartment building; and I am walking slightly behind Romeo with a digital voice recorder in my hand in an attempt to add to the audiovisual documentation that Romeo is gathering. This video was then viewed by all of us later that same afternoon as we ate water ice and huddled around Romeo who maintained control of the video camera and the small playback screen.

Thus, a multimodal, coconstructed space such as ours was generative of unscripted texts that drew on multimodal literacy performances and used digital spaces to disseminate these texts. At play were who and what was seen and unseen. Cyrus's commercial would not exist if not for Romeo's role as the cameraman. Romeo would not be the cameraman if there were not a camera to use. Had I been more rigid in my desire to control the images that were collected and produced, I might have had pages of transcripts but missed the play, humor, enthusiasm, and infectious curiosity that is reflected in so much of the video, digital voice recordings, and photographs that were produced over 15 months. Therefore, to look at the video clip of the performance of the Sprite commercial itself and see only the textual performance is to miss the stories of spaces, roles, and artifacts that the text holds. Multimodal documentation, therefore, stands as the third dimension of a framework for transforming literacy research representation. This practice invokes the other two dimensions of a research space signified by an ethos of collectivity, and research roles grounded in the practices of knowing.

FIGURE 20.2 Stills from Sprite Commercial.

THE CASE FOR TRANSFORMATIVE REPRESENTATIONS

Representations of literacies do not merely signify discrete moments or transactions, but are in fact necessarily partial depictions of what they aim to represent. In order to transform literacy representation, one must first believe that this is a viable endeavor and worth pursuing. Moje (2002) argued "that the lack of attention to youth is not a mere oversight and that it has consequences for how the literacy field thinks about literacy learning and teaching" (p. 99). In order to truly engage youth, then, literacy researchers must pay attention to the ways in which youths' literacies are situated in and draw on a variety of multimodal communicative practices. The five boys who participated in the research were central, in my work, to the creation of a space that evolved both organically and intentionally; a space that was welcoming and depended on their participation to exist; and, by its existence, actively sought to transform the entrenched notions of literacy learning, teaching, and research that too often limit the scope of participation by the individuals involved. It was not enough to make interview audio files accessible or include photographs as accompaniments to written text. Transformative representation must be situated in the belief that the written word allows us only limited and partial glimpses at the dynamic and fluid spaces of literacy practices (Leander & Sheehy, 2004).

Such a space was born on a spring day during course of the multimodal storytelling project, as Cyrus, TJ, Romeo and I were practicing hanging upside down on one of the steel structures spread throughout the local park. We were discussing ideas for upcoming photo essay projects after having spent the earlier part of the afternoon sitting in the pavilion in the center of the park and looking through the archive of photographs I had amassed on my laptop. I had distributed disposable cameras for each of them to take home following our meeting to document the images they wished to include. As we talked, Jamal commented that he was scared he would fall and leaned on the structure instead of hanging from it. Watching us, however, gave him an idea; he hurriedly unwrapped his camera from the plastic cover, ran about 15 feet away, and asked us to hang down at the same time. All of us were laughing and Romeo, Cyrus, TJ, and I obliged Jamal's request and hung upside down in unison when Jamal gave us the signal. That photo (Fig. 20.3) had rich and playful origins; however, its subsequent role in the story of the project resonates most loudly with the call for transforming the representation of literacy research.

One following afternoon, all six of us spent a couple of hours looking through photographs—physical ones that had been developed as well as digital images archived on my laptop. Instead of keeping their images together, the boys spontaneously began trading the photographs and suggesting category labels for them. I had asked

FIGURE 20.3 Upside down, A.K.A Activities in the park; Friends; A group that has fun; Play; Storytelling.

them what stories we could tell with the images we had collected, individually and as a group. Jamal's photograph was given several labels that afternoon, and several more over the course of the project including activities in the park, friends, a group that has fun, play, and storytelling.

According to Voithofer (2005), "When the language of description and representation changes, so does the object that is being described" (p. 11). This chapter engages the complex terrain of literacy research by not only exploring "the language of description and representation" but also the new identities, modalities, and spaces that are performed and created when the exploration of literacy is conceptualized as a multimodal endeavor. Thus, the proposal for transformative representations is not simply a call for audio and visual artifacts to accompany the written word. Rather, to seek transformation in our practices of literacy research means to extend the question "what counts as literacy" (Gallego & Hollingworth, 2000) and ask, what counts as literacy research and representation? Does it count, for example, when the researcher is not the sole data collector or producer? Or when tested research methods are compromised for the spirit of the research or new ways of exploration? Can we still claim to be researching literacy when there are no words involved?

Still largely absent from discussions about the study of literacies is a nuanced and comprehensive investigation of the range of communicative practices and multimodal orchestration involved in, and that are complicated when, conducting, performing, and representing literacy research in these new media saturated and digitized times. The salience of meaning making beyond the printed page (Vasudevan, Schultz, & Bateman, in press) is not being fully engaged in the methodological approaches to the study of these new communicative practices. Researchers continue to collect writing and reading artifacts, conduct interviews, and, for the most part, represent their findings within the bounded confines of the printed book or academic journal. A handful of emerging academic blogs and online academic journals offer new publication possibilities, but they remain both underrepresented and undervalued in academic discourses. Furthermore, and perhaps of greater significance for this chapter, the methods of data collection have not evolved with these changes in literacy and communicative practices. While there are a growing number of studies that explore new online spaces, they continue to rely on data collection formats and modes that are dominated by printed and verbal modes and texts (fieldnotes, interviews, written artifacts, etc.). Additionally, researchers maintain control of data collection and analysis and are still the primary producers and interpreters of research knowledge. A move toward rethinking literacy research and representation brings into question both the sources of information and interpretive practices that ultimately inform knowledge about literacy.

Understanding literacy in the new digital landscape as spatial, circulating, and multimodal provides the impetus for transforming how we research and ultimately represent knowledge and evidence of how literacies are engaged, particularly in the lives of youth. In this chapter, I have offered multimodal counterstorytelling as one approach by which these representations might be transformed in a process akin to the insidious ways in which racist practices continue to persist in American society. That is, everyday microaggressions (Solorzano, Ceja, & Yosso, 2000) subtly reinforce the inequity and racism that is embedded across our social institutions. In a similar manner, multimodal counterstorytelling proposes the intentional rethinking of multiple dimensions of the research process such that "empirical research *with* [italics added] young people provides an opportunity to increase our understanding of their lives" (Valentine, Skelton, & Chambers, 1998, p. 23) and their evolving engagement of literacies as well as visual and communicative arts. This is a proposal of microinterruptions that recognizes that research contributes to the social construction of youth (Valentine et al., 1998), and while no one photograph, video clip, or performance can fully represent or transform the nature of literacy research and practice, a collective movement of transformative representations might be able to do just that.

REFERENCES

Appleman, D. (2003). Are you makin' me famous or are you makin' me a fool: Responsibility and respect in representation. In D. Abt-Perkins, & S. Greene (Eds.), *Making race visible: Literacy research for cultural understanding* (pp. 71–88). New York: Teachers College Press.

Ballator, N., Farnum, M., & Kaplan, B. (1999). *NAEP 1996 trends in writing: Fluency and writing conventions* (NCES 1999-456).

Barton, D., & Hamilton, M. (1998). *Local literacies: Reading and writing in one community.* London: Routledge.

Behar, R. (1996). *The vulnerable observer: Anthropology that breaks your heart.* Boston: Beacon Press.

Biancarosa, G., & Snow, C. E. (2004). *Reading next—A vision for action and research in middle and high school literacy: A report to Carnegie Corporation of New York.* Washington, DC: Alliance for Excellent Education.

Blackburn, M. (2003). Disrupting the (hetero)normative: Exploring literacy performances and identity work with queer youth. *Journal of Adolescent and Adult Literacy, 46*(4), 312–324.

Delgado, R. (1995). *Critical race theory: The cutting edge.* Philadelphia, PA: Temple University Press.

Denzin, N. K. (2000). The practices and politics of interpretation. In N. K. Denzin, & Y. S. Lincoln (Eds.), *Handbook of qualitative research* (2nd ed., pp. 897–922). Thousand Oaks, CA: Sage Publications.

Duncum, P. (2004). Visual culture isn't just visual: Multiliteracy, multimodality, and meaning. *Studies in Art Education, 45*(3), 252–265.

Ferguson, A. A. (2000). *Bad boys: Public schools in the making of Black masculinity.* Ann Arbor, MI: University of Michigan Press.

Foucault, M. (1977). *Discipline and punish: The birth of the prison.* New York: Vintage Books.

Gallego, M., & Hollingsworth, S. (Eds.). (2000). *What counts as literacy: Challenging the school standard.* New York: Teachers College Press.

Gee, J. P. (2003). *What video games have to teach us about learning and literacy.* New York: Palgrave Macmillan.

Goodman, S. (2003). *Teaching youth media: A critical guide to literacy, video production, and social change.* New York: Teachers College Press.

Gordon, E. W. (1999) Foreword: the experiences of African American males in school and society. in V. C. Polite & J. E. Davis (Eds) *African American males in school and society: practices and policies for effective education.* pp. ix–xiii. New York: Teachers College Press.

Guinier, L., & Torres, G. (2002). *The miner's canary: Enlisting race, resisting power, transforming democracy.* Cambridge, MA: Harvard University Press.

Gutiérrez, K., Rymes, B., & Larson, J. (1995). Script, counterscript, and underlife in the classroom: James Brown versus *Brown v. Board of Education. Harvard Educational Review, 65*(3), 445–471.

Hagood, M. (2004). A rhizomatic cartography of adolescents, popular culture, and constructions of self. In K. Leander, & M. Sheehy (Eds.) *Spatializing literacy research and practice* (pp. 143–160). New York: Peter Lang.

Hull, G., & Nelson, M. (2005). Locating the semiotic power of multimodality. *Written Communication, 22*(2), 224–261.

Hull, G., & Schultz, K. (Eds.). (2002). *School's out! Bridging out-of-school literacies with classroom practice.* New York: Teachers College Press.

Irvine, P. D., & Larson, J. (2001). Literacy packages in practice: Constructing academic disadvantage. In J. Larson (Ed.), *Literacy as snake oil: Beyond the quick fix.* New York: Lang.

Jewitt, C., & Kress, G. (Eds.). (2003). *Multimodal literacy.* New York: Peter Lang.

Knobel, M. (1999). *Everyday literacies: Students, discourse, and social practice.* New York: Peter Lang.

Kress, G. (2003). *Literacy in the new media age.* London: Routledge.

Ladson-Billings, G. (2000). Racialized discourses and ethnic epistemologies. In N. K. Denzin, & Y. S. Lincoln (Eds.). *Handbook of qualitative research* (2nd ed., pp. 215–255). Thousand Oaks, CA: Sage.

Lankshear, C., & Knobel, M. (2002). Do we have your attention? New literacies, digital technologies and the education of adolescents. In D. Alvermann (Ed.), *Adolescents and literacies in a digital world.* New York: Peter Lang.

Leander, K. (2005). *Imagining and practicing internet space-times with/in school.* Paper presented at the National Council of Teachers of English Assembly for Research, Columbus, Ohio.

Leander, K., & Sheehy, M. (2004). Introduction. In K. Leander, & M. Sheehy (Eds.), *Spatializing literacy research and practice* (pp. 1–13). New York: Peter Lang.

Lewis, C., & Fabos, B. (2005). Instant messaging, literacies, and social identities. *Reading Research Quarterly, 40,* 470–501.

Marcus, G. (1995). Ethnography in/of the world system: The emergence of multi-sited ethnography. *Annual Review of Anthropology, 24,* 95–117.

Moje, E. B. (2000). "To be part of the story": The literacy practices of "gangsta" adolescents. *Teachers College Record, 102,* 652–690.

Moje, E. B. (2002). But where are the youth? Integrating youth culture into literacy theory. *Educational Theory, 52,* 97–120.

Moje, E. B., McIntosh Ciechanowski, K. M., Kramer, K., Ellis, L., Carrillo, R., & Collazo, T. (2004). Working toward third space in content area literacy: An examination of everyday funds of knowledge and discourse. *Reading Research Quarterly, 39*(1), 38–71.

Moll, L. C., Amanti, C., Neff, D., & Gonzalez, N. (1992). Funds of knowledge of teaching: Using a qualitative approach to connect homes and classrooms. *Theory Into Practice, 31*(2), 132–141.

Pink, S. (2001). *Doing visual ethnography: Images, media and representation in research.* London: Sage.

Prosser, J., & Schwartz, D. (1998). Photographs within the sociological research process. In J. Prosser (Ed.), *Image-based research: A sourcebook for qualitative researchers* (pp. 115–130). Bristol, PA: Taylor & Francis.

Schultz, K. (2006). Qualitative research on writing. In C. A. MacArthur, S. Graham, & J. Fitzgerald (Eds.), *Handbook of writing research.* New York: Guilford Press.

Snow, C., Burns, M. S., & Griffin, P. (Eds.). (1998). *Preventing reading difficulties in young children.* Washington, DC: National Academy Press.

Soja, E.W. (1996). *Thirdspace: Journeys to Los Angeles and other real-and-imagined places.* Oxford, England: Blackwell.

Solorzano, D., Ceja, M., & Yosso, T. (2000). Critical race theory, racial microaggressions and campus racial climate: The experiences of African American college students. *Journal of Negro Education, 69,* 60–73.

Solorzano, D., & Yosso, T. (2002). Critical race methodology: Counter-storytelling as an analytic framework for education research. *Qualitative Inquiry, 8*(1), 23–44.

Street, B. (1995) *Social literacies.* London: Longman.

Thomas, A. (2004). Digital literacies of cybergirl. *E-Learning, 1*(3), 358–382.

Turkle, S. (1995). *Life on the screen: Identity in the age of the Internet.* New York: Simon & Schuster.

Valentine, G., Skelton, T., & Chambers, D. (1998). Cool places: An introduction to youth and youth cultures. In T. Skelton, & G. Valentine (Eds.), *Cool places: Geographies of youth cultures* (pp. 1–34). London: Routledge.

Vasudevan, L. (2004). *Telling different stories differently: The possibilities of multimodal (counter)storytelling with African American adolescent boys.* Unpublished doctoral dissertation, University of Pennsylvania, Pennsylvania.

Vasudevan, L. (2006). Making known differently: Engaging visual modalities as spaces to author new selves. *E-Learning, 3*(2), 207–216.

Vasudevan, L., Schultz, K., & Bateman, J. (in preparation). *Beyond the printed page: multimodal storytelling with urban students.*

Voithofer, R. (2005). Designing new media education research: The materiality of data, representation, and dissemination. *Educational Researcher, 34*(9), 3–14.

Weis, L., & Fine, M. (2000). *Speed bumps: A student-friendly guide to qualitative research.* New York: Teachers College Press.

Wissman, K. (2005). *Can't let it all go unsaid: Self-definition, sisterhood, and social change in the literacy and artistic practices of young women of color.* Unpublished doctoral dissertation, University of Pennsylvania, Pennsylvania.

Wissman, K. (in press). This is what I see: (Re)envisioning photography as a social practice with young women of color. In M. L. Hill, & L. Vasudevan (Eds.), *Media, learning, and sites of possibility.* New York: Peter Lang.

•21•

LITERACY RESEARCH AND POLICY: ARE WE LEARNING ANYTHING?

Barbara Kapinus
NATIONAL EDUCATION ASSOCIATION

Cathy Roller
INTERNATIONAL READING ASSOCIATION

Like the world of politics itself, the world of literacy policy is constantly changing. In addition to the shifts that come with changes in administration at the national, state, and local levels, there are shifts in attention so that one day early reading is a target of concern and legislation and days or weeks later, due to a single incident, the prime concern is high-school safety. Shifts can occur because of international incidents, domestic disasters, and scandals. The world of politics is a world with a short attention span and shifting priorities. Consequently, it is sometimes difficult to discern patterns and trends. This chapter will examine two recent pieces of legislation that illustrate how policy can shift over a relatively short time and what activities were effective or ineffective in influencing policy. The legislation addresses reading education but the lessons may be applied to a range of literacy-related issues.

Communication and Visual Arts Aspects of Literacy

Currently, policy makers are not overly concerned with communication aspects of literacy or visual arts. Visual arts are not part of their definition of literacy. Indeed legislation mainly addresses only reading and not the larger concept of literacy. Many members of the literacy education community have raised concern that writing has not been included in literacy policy initiatives. They believe that writing instruction is an essential component of reading instruction, since learning how language works is integral to learning to read (Pressley, Dolezak. Roehrig, & Hilden, 2002). As policy makers grapple with improving adolescent literacy and high-school improvement, there is, however, growing acknowledgement that adolescents need more than just reading. For example, in *Reading to Achieve: A Governor's Guide to Adolescent Literacy*, the National Governors Association (NGA) included, among other components, the following in its "Elements of Effective Adolescent Literacy Programs": intensive writing, motivation and self-directed learning, text-based collaborative learning, and a technology component (2005, p. 9).

Current Literacy Legislation

The *No Child Left Behind Act* (PL 107–110), the 2001 Reauthorization of the Elementary and Secondary Education Act referred to as "NCLB," has resulted in at least two intervention programs focused on reading and literacy—Reading First (Title I, section B) and Striving Readers (authorized under Sec. 1502 Demonstrations of Innovative Practices). Reading First was an integral part of the reauthorization and was funded at the level of 5 billion dollars. Striving Readers was created as part of appropriations (HR 4818) and was funded at about 25 million dollars. These two programs illustrate both the shifting and constant characteristics of political use of educational data. The constants include a focus on the achievement gap; powerful statistics; accountability; funding for school-wide, classroom, and intensive interventions; an evaluation component; and an emphasis on scientific research.

The shifts include moving from a focus on learning to read in Reading First to reading to learn in Striving Readers; from little participation by the community of literacy professionals to broader participation; from tight prescriptive requirements to fewer prescriptive requirements; from general evaluation to experimental evaluation of intensive intervention for struggling readers.

WHAT POLICY FACTORS REMAIN CONSTANT ACROSS THE TWO LEGISLATED PROGRAMS?

Underlying both the Reading First and Striving Readers legislation is the drive to improve reading achievement as defined and promoted by NCLB. The two legislated programs recognize the need to provide schools, teachers, and students with resources targeted at reducing the achievement gap in reading. The National Assessment of Educational Progress statistic that 38% of fourth graders scored below basic on the 1998 NAEP in reading (U.S. Department of Education, November 1999) was constantly repeated in the rhetoric surrounding the passage of NCLB. The opening paragraph of the Striving Readers application also focused on NAEP data:

> According to recent data from the National Assessment of Educational Progress (NAEP), only about one-third of our nation's middle and high school students meet the standard of reading "proficiently" for their grade level. In a typical high poverty, urban school, approximately half of all in-coming ninth-grade students read at a sixth- or seventh-grade level and, on average, African American and Hispanic twelfth-grade students read at the same level as white eighth-grade students (U.S. Department of Education, November 14, 2005, p. 2).

In both pieces of legislation there was a focus on gaps in achievement between majority and minority children and a belief that the federal government can address the problem through specific programs. In both cases, funds were targeted for at-risk students in particular settings that are highly diverse or characterized by poverty. In the Striving Readers Program there is also a continuing focus on improving classroom instruction as a major objective along with attention to those students who need more intensive intervention beyond the classroom. In Reading First the focus on classrooms was mainly enacted through the requirement that schools receiving funds must have a "core reading program" and much of the professional development was focused on classroom teachers receiving training in how to use such a program. In addition, Reading First included attention to "intervention programs" or those that targeted students who needed more intensive instruction and the concept of diagnostic assessment to determine what instruction was needed. Similarly, in Striving Readers there were three required components:

- Enhance the overall level of reading achievement in middle and high schools through improvements to the quality of literacy instruction across the curriculum
- Improve the literacy skills of struggling adolescent readers
- Help build a strong scientific, research base around specific strategies that improve adolescent literacy skills (U.S. Department of Education, November 14, 2005, p. 3).

These components also emphasized interventions and improved achievement.

As in the Reading First legislation, the Striving Readers legislation focused on improving classroom instruction as well as providing interventions for students who are significantly behind their peers. The background material of the Striving Readers application included the following statement: "The basic skills adolescent readers need are those same foundational skills we expect younger students to master as they learn to read." This statement was followed by a brief explanation of the same five essential components of reading listed in the Reading First legislation: phonemic awareness, phonics, fluency, vocabulary, and comprehension. A closing sentence indicates, "Of particular concern with adolescent struggling readers are vocabulary, fluency and comprehension, as well as issues such as motivation and access to age appropriate reading materials." (U.S. Department of Education, November 14, 2005, p. 2)

Given the similarities in purpose, there was considerable potential for continuity between Reading First and Striving Readers programs. However, there were also some major differences.

WHAT CHANGES IN POLICY CONCERNS ARE DEMONSTRATED BY THE TWO PROGRAMS?

Despite the essential continuity in purpose between the two programs, there are some noticeable shifts in policy that occurred between the time of the Reading First legislation and the Striving Readers legislation, the most obvious being the move from a focus on K–3 students and learning to read to a concentration on the needs of middle- and high-school students and reading to learn across the curriculum. This shift indicates an acknowledgement that just having students reading on grade level according to a test in third grade does not ensure that those students will remain proficient through the next 9 years.

The second obvious difference is the magnitude of the two programs. Reading First was distributed to the states by a formula that targeted students most in need of reading help. Each of the 50 states, after completing an arduous application process, was awarded significant additional funding that was then distributed by the states through a competitive process. The grants were to last 6 years. The Striving Readers Program is a small grant program that was awarded on a competitive basis for project period of 5 years. The U.S. Department of Education made eight grant awards, ranging between $24 and $16 million dollars per year.

The Striving Readers Program was less prescriptive than the Reading First program, which assumed that we do have sufficient scientifically based knowledge upon which to build a program. The U.S. Department of Education Web site on Reading First offered this statement in 2002:

> Research has consistently identified the critical skills that young students need to become good readers. Teachers across different states and districts have demonstrated that sound, scientifically based reading instruction can and does work with all children. . . . Real, nationwide progress can be made when we bring together new federal resources to make sure that every child becomes a successful reader. (U.S. Department of Education, 2002a, p. 1)

In the background to the Striving Readers Program, the Department states that, "there is much less research and proven practice on the development of reading skills among adolescents and the identification, prevention, and remediation of reading difficulties in middle and high school students" (U. S. Department of Education, November 14, 2005, p. 2). Rather than insist on adoption of highly specified programs and interventions, the Striving Readers application provides a list of the types of activities that the Striving Readers funds must be used for. These include,

> . . . providing middle and high school age children reading at least two years behind below grade level with supplemental or replacement activities to improve basic skills, motivation, vocabulary, fluency and comprehension using research-based strategies. Such intervention may include extra time, "double-dosing," small group instruction, supplemental curricula for accelerated learning, a reading specialist or coach, access to reading materials that appeal to adolescent readers, administration of regular and ongoing, valid and reliable assessments, and professional development for teachers (U. S. Department of Education, November 14, 2005, p. 4).

Presumably the latitude in Striving Readers is necessary because less is known about what works. However, some news stories suggesting intrusiveness of the Reading First grant-making process might also have contributed to the loosening of the constraints evident in the Striving Readers legislation (Manzo, September 7, 2005; Manzo, November 9, 2005). There was enough evidence of staff from the U.S. Department of Education pressuring states to use certain programs and consultants that an investigation was initiated by the Government Accountability Office (GAO) and the U.S. Department of Education inspector general.

The differences in perception of the amount of research supporting what to do in the two legislative initiatives led to another key difference: the evaluation requirements for Striving Readers were much more precise and exacting than the evaluations of Reading First, which essentially required only that a state contract with an entity that was experienced in doing scientifically based research in order to assess program implementation. Striving Readers, in contrast, required an evaluation that would include a rigorous experimental research evaluation of the intensive targeted intervention for struggling readers. These evaluations must be conducted by an independent evaluator and include a randomized control trial. The school-level strategies also were required to have a rigorous evaluation by an independent evaluator that may, but need not, include a randomized control trial. (Remember, the legislation provided funding for both intensive intervention for groups of students and school-level programs or strategies.) This evaluation specification for Struggling Readers was partly because section 1502 of NCLB requires such evaluations, but it could also have been a reaction to the outcomes of the evaluations of Reading First, which in many cases were significantly less rigorous. The evaluation demands were also due to the perception that the Striving Readers funding should produce experimental evidence of the effectiveness of what was being implemented, since the research available at the time was not considered sufficient evidence on which to base interventions.

Another interesting difference in the two programs is the central place that motivation plays in Striving Readers. While motivation was included in the definitions of reading first enacted in the Reading Excellence Act and then incorporated in NCLB, there was a focus in Reading First on the "Five Essential Elements of Reading" which were the six elements of the definition of reading minus motivation. This probably occurred because the National Reading Panel evaluated the evidence of the five essential components but did not evaluate the evidence on motivation. Because of the lack of evidence surrounding middle- and high-school readers and the general recognition that as children grow older lack of motivation becomes more salient as contributing to reading difficulties, the Department of Education seemed more comfortable including motivation as a key area of focus for the striving readers' activities. This difference is also related to shifts in the definition of research, a topic addressed in the next section.

WHAT CHANGED BETWEEN THE LEGISLATING OF READING FIRST AND STRIVING READERS?

The comparison of the two reading programs indicates that many people have learned quite a bit about research and improving reading achievement over the period between the Reading Excellence Act in 1998 and the Striving Readers Program of 2005. On the part of the Department of Education, there seemed to be a willingness to acknowledge that the state of the research in adolescent literacy would not support a heavily prescriptive approach—hence the scaled-down program, the broader description of "types" of activities that will be funded, and the insistent call for rigorous evaluation.

Some have abandoned the idea that there are simple solutions and magic bullets that will solve the literacy problem. Early in the K–3 reading legislative efforts, there was a focus on "phonics" as the ultimate, reliable tool that would deliver us from all future reading problems. This was particularly obvious in the "Reading Deficit Elimination Act" that was briefly introduced in the aftermath of the release of the National Reading Panel Report. That act promoted materials from Grossen's *30 Years of Research on Reading: What We know About How Children Learn To Read— A Synthesis of the Research on Reading from the National Institute of Child Health and Development* (1997) that focused almost solely on phonics as the essential aspect of learning to read. The International Reading Association worked with panel members to convince the sponsors that their legislation was a misrepresentation of the National Reading Panel's findings and the legislation was withdrawn. From that point on there has been a growing recognition on the part of policy makers and political advisors of the magnitude and the complexity of learning to read. From the enactment of the Reading Excellence Act to that of the Striving Readers Act, there has been a gradual education of policy makers and education officials so that such simple solutions are not reified in legislation.

Much has been written about what the U.S. Department of Education and the National Reading Panel consider acceptable research; however, a brief review is warranted here, since this illustrates the evolution of the thinking about reading policy. The National Reading Panel and the U.S. Department of Education have considered scientific research, defined as experimental research that used random assignments of subjects to treatment and control groups, as the only really valid research upon which to base instructional recommendations. However, a report from the National Research Council (NRC) provided a broader concept of scientific research by acknowledging that what makes research scientific is not its methodology, but rather its acceptance by the research community of a specific field. The NRC further elaborated on the concept of scientific research by indicating that ". . . multiple methods, applied over time and tied to evidentiary standards, are essential to establishing a base of scientific knowledge" (2002, p. 2). At the time of the Reading First legislation, The National Reading Panel definition of scientific research was preeminent. After the National Academy of Sciences published its report, there was a gradual acceptance of a broader definition of scientific research.

Evidence also exists suggesting that the Department of Education has been more open to input from the field of reading including a wider range of researchers and practitioners. In fact, adolescent-literacy researchers have been actively promoting the need for intervention in middle and high schools relatively effectively since the publication of the *Adolescent Literacy Position Statement* (International Reading Association, 1999). That position paper was developed by the International Reading Association Commission on Adolescent Literacy. The Commission and many of its members have been active since that time, conducting briefings in Washington, DC, doing joint position statements with the Middle School Association, conducting forums, and in general keeping the focus on middle- and high-school students during a period when all of the policy focus was on K–3 reading. Therefore, when Congress was ready to consider the needs of adolescent literacy learners, there was a record of shared information and positions addressing the issue.

In addition to the change in the perceptions and attitudes of the U.S. Department of Education, there were several new players focused on creating legislation—including the Alliance for Excellent Education and the Carnegie Corporation of New York—who funded a set of new publications including, *Adolescents and Literacy: Reading for the 21st Century* (Kamil, 2003), *The Literacy Coach: A Key to Improving Teaching and Learning in Secondary Schools* (Sturtevant, 2003), and *Reading Next—A Vision for Action and Research in Middle and High School Literacy: A Report to the Carnegie Corporation of New York* (Biancarosa & Snow, 2004). In these publications, as well as in the earlier IRA adolescent-literacy position statement, a number of themes repeatedly appear in the Striving Readers application materials. For example, consider the seven principles for supporting adolescent-literacy growth from the 1999 position statement:

1. Adolescents deserve access to a wide variety of reading material that they can and want to read.
2. Adolescents deserve instruction that builds both the skill and the desire to read increasingly complex materials.
3. Adolescents deserve assessment that shows them their strengths and their needs and that guides their teachers to design instruction that will best help them grow as readers.
4. Adolescents deserve expert teachers who model and provide explicit instruction in reading comprehension and study strategies across the curriculum.
5. Adolescents deserve reading specialists who assist individual students having difficulties learning how to read.
6. Adolescents deserve teachers who understand the complexities of individual adolescent readers, respect their differences, and respond to their characteristics.
7. Adolescents deserve homes, communities, and a nation that will support their efforts to achieve advanced levels of literacy and provide the support necessary for them to succeed (Moore, Bean, Birdyshaw, & Rycik, 1999)

In the background material to the Striving Readers application (November 14, 2005, pp. 2–4) there are references to,

1. "Access to age appropriate and diverse reading materials"
2. "Master basic reading skills and comprehension," and "issues such as motivation" "self-selected reading at student's ability level to build motivation"
3. "On-going progress monitoring" "needs assessment," "includes the administration of student assessments"
4. "Direct, explicit instruction in reading comprehension" "improvements to the quality of reading instruction across the curriculum"
5. "Reading specialist or coach"
6. "Professional development for teachers"

In fact, these same themes permeated all the documents related to adolescent-literacy policy just listed. Some emphasized particular aspects, such as the importance of literacy coaches in schools for adolescents, and others both reinforced these themes and introduced other important themes, such as the 15 areas delineated in *Reading Next,* (Biancarosa & Snow, 2004) that also are represented in the Striving Readers application materials.

In the case of Striving Readers, the traditional literacy-education communities such as IRA were ahead of the curve, outlining the principles literally years before the policy community was ready to address them. In addition, there formed a coalition of advocates around activities funded by AEE, Carnegie, and the International Reading Association that kept reiterating the themes in policy meetings, hill visits, national forums, and meetings. They were successful in a small degree with the Striving Readers program. However, the scale of the activity is miniscule in comparison to the need, and we have miles to go before we sleep.

WHAT CAN WE LEARN FROM THE CHANGES IN POLICY REFLECTED IN READING FIRST AND STRIVING READERS?

Be Proactive

First, literacy experts and practitioners learned from the political activity surrounding state legislative initiatives, the Reading Excellence Act, and Reading First, that legislation can have a massive influence on what happens in classrooms and that as a field we cannot afford to be apolitical. This was a lesson the IRA Commission on Adolescent Literacy applied to its work very early. The commission marshaled its resources and produced a consensus statement highlighting the important aspects of adolescent-literacy instruction. Instead of responding to powerful legislation and producing materials after legislation had been shaped, it was ahead of the issue and created materials to help shape legislation.

Use Data

Second, we learned the importance of using statistics to define the issue. The early IRA position statement did not talk about a crisis or enumerate the magnitude of the problem. Each of the more recent documents used here as an example uses statistics to indicate a crisis. The documents are very clear about the percentage of adolescents who do not read well enough to be successful in college or at work.

Provide Information

Third, we learned the importance of reports in influencing legislation. The lesson of the National Reading Panel Report did not go unnoticed. Early on there were efforts to synthesize research and delineate the evidence related to adolescent literacy. *Reading Next* (Biancarosa & Snow, 2004) was quite successful in highlighting what is known about adolescent literacy. The attention it brought to the scarcity of the research base was instrumental in focusing research agendas by The National Institute for Child Health and Human Development (The Adolescent Literacy Research Initiative) and the Institute for Education Science (the reading comprehension program now called Reading and Writing).

Seek Consensus

Fourth, we learned the power of consensus. The recently formed National Adolescent Literacy Coalition (NALC) brought together individuals from over 60 organizations to address the issue of adolescent literacy. Clearly, the players in the adolescent literacy arena realize that a strong consensus increases legislative power. NALC has had to work diligently to gain recognition in policy circles for its efforts to promote effective policy and practice. Its influence is due to the power of its members working together.

Focus on Legislation With Broad Application

Fifth, reading experts and policy advocates from several organizations pushed for the Striving Readers legislation by working for the introduction of two Congressional acts, the PASS Act and the Graduation for All Act. While neither of these bills has had the necessary bipartisan support to move them, the activity around them did sustain discussion of the issues and keep them on the legislative agenda.Indeed, Striving Readers can be viewed as a means of addressing some of the concerns regarding secondary-school improvement within a more limited scope of activity and funding than that entailed in the two larger pieces of legislation. It seemed the best that could be accomplished at the time, a placeholder for broader efforts to improve adolescent achievement.

WHAT WASN'T EFFECTIVE IN MOVING POLICY?

For adolescent literacy there was an effective group of players united around a common cause. That same unity of purposed did not inform the work in early literacy and there were a number of activities occurring around early literacy that were relatively ineffective. Perhaps primary among them were impassioned exchanges over list serves and in professional meetings that decried the legislation of instruction and the imposition of legislative mandates on universities and schools. Although such exchanges were engaging and entertaining, they had literally no impact on early literacy or early literacy legislation. These groups simply talked to each other and did not frame their messages for critical audiences such as legislators and the public. Their time would have been better spent writing articles or letters to editors of popular magazines newspapers, and general education publications such as *Education Week* and *Educational Leadership*.

Books such as *The Manufactured Crisis* (Berliner & Biddle, 1996) and Elaine Garan's (2002) *Resisting Reading Mandates*, were widely read and praised by a segment of the literacy community, while policy makers and stakeholders beyond that group were either unaware of the existence of the books or ignored them. Denying that there was a real problem, complaining about the NRP report, and providing directions on how to undermine its use, simply didn't work. The public, congress, and state legislators viewed these educators as recalcitrant ideologues who refused to do anything but support the status quo. The efforts were nonstarters.

There were attempts to develop position and white papers that were written in such an academic style that they were very unlikely to be read by anyone outside of the research community. There were also impassioned debates in education journals and publications of research related to the issues. A dominant theme in this discourse was that "learning to read is very complex." Simple answers to reading problems were regarded with disdain. This type of assertion did not capture the attention of policy makers. The word "complexity" became a cue for policy makers' eyes to glaze over and for those making policy decisions to check out.

The result of this activity on the part of reading experts was largely negative and the fact that the recent long-term NAEP data showed that fourth-grade reading had improved over seven scale score points after 3 decades of being flat has made these efforts look even less effective. Reading advocates should provide simple clarification of what has happened. The message here is not that NCLB is improving reading. The message is that a policy focus on reading that has lasted more than a decade is improving early reading scores.

SO WHAT SHOULD WE DO?

The rest of the reading field must learn the strategies and lessons used by the adolescent literacy community and adopt them as effective ways to address any literacy issue. These are the lessons we must learn and implement:

1. Define the issues early.
2. Use statistics to get the attention of the policy community.
3. Provide a blueprint for action such as that provided in the principles outlined in the Adolescent Literacy Position Statement.
4. Build a consensus by,
   a. Carrying the message to policy makers at both national and state levels
   b. Investing as AEE and Carnegie did in producing effective policy documents
   c. Convening groups with similar objectives (NALC)
5. Engage in effective lobbying efforts, working with allies as much as possible.
6. Be ready to help our constituents take advantage of the legislation.
7. Check our attitudes and seek answers instead of blame.

While we are learning how to influence policy, there remains a need to conduct research that will clearly inform policy decisions. Some areas that are of high interest to policy makers and have little research to inform them include (a) what types of literacy coaching work best; (b) how educators can prepare to be effective literacy coaches; (c) determining common characteristics among successful students and intensive remediation for students who are not reading with any fluency; (d) determining how to motivate teachers to change their instruction and improve student learning? It is imperative that researchers begin to address these and other policy-related questions if the field is to influence legislation and funding for literacy development.

Research alone is not enough. We have examples of research that have been ignored, such as the effects of class size and high-stakes testing, and research that has been misrepresented, such as the importance of phonics in reading acquisition. It is important to put existing research such as the body of work around school-wide reading improvement (Taylor, Pearson, Peterson, & Rodriguez. 2005; Taylor, 2002; Lipsom, Mosenthal, Mekkelsen, & Russ, 2004) as well as emerging research in front of policymakers, so that they will attend to it. That means writing short pieces and working with the general press to get information to the public and those who supposedly represent them. For example, articles for such periodicals as *Woman's Day* or *Education Week* would reach those who influence policy makers. Currently, this does not help those seeking tenure, but schools of education should begin to recognize the impact of public opinion on education policy and encourage professors to write to inform the public as well as communities of scholars.

In closing, if we want to improve literacy learning through improved policy we have learned that we must produce the relevant research, make data known to policy makers, and work together with a focus on the needs of students.

REFERENCES

Berliner, D. C. & Biddle, B. J. (1996). *The manufactured crisis: Myths, fraud, and the attack on America's public schools.* White Plains, NY: Longman.

Biancarosa, G., & Snow, C. E. (2004). *Reading next—A vision for action and research in middle and high school literacy: A report to the Carnegie Corporation of New York.* Washington, DC: Alliance for Excellent Education.

Garan, E. (2002). *Resisting reading mandates: How to triumph with the truth.* Portsmouth, NH: Heinemann.

Grossen, B. (1997). *30 years of research on reading: What we know about how children learn to read—A synthesis of the research on reading from the National Institute of Child Health and Development.* Santa Cruz, CA: Center for the Future of Teaching and Learning.

Kamil, M. L. (2003). Adolescents and literacy: Reading for the 21st Century. Washington, DC: Alliance for Excellent Education.

Lipson, M. L., Mosenthal, J. H., Mekkelsen, J., & Russ, B. (2004). Building knowledege and fashioning success one school at a time. *The Reading Teacher, 57*(6) 534–542.

Manzo, K. K. (2005, September 7). States pressed to refashion reading grant designs. *Education Week on the Web.* Retrieved February 20, 2007 from http://www.edweek.org/ew/articles/2005/09/07/02read.h25.html?querystring=States%20Pressed%20to%20Refashion%20Reading%20First%20Grant%20Designs&levelId=1000

Manzo, K. K. (2005, November 9). Inspector general to conduct broad audits of Reading First. *Education Week on the Web.* Retrieved February 20, 2007 from http://www.edweek.org/ew/articles/2005/11/09/11read.h25.html?querystring=Inspector%20General%20to%20COnduct%20Broad%20Auits%20Reading%20First&levelId=1000

Moore, D., Bean, T. W., Birdyshaw, D., & Rycik, J. A. (1999). *Adolescent literacy: A position statement for the Commission on Adolescent Literacy of the International Reading Association.* Newark, DE: International Reading Association.

National Center for Education Statistics. (2004). *Long Term Trend.* Retrieved April 23, 2007, from http://nces.ed.gov/nationsreportcard/ltt/results2004/

National Governors Association Center for Best Practices. (2005). *Reading to achieve: A governor's guide to adolescent literacy.* Washington, DC: Author. Retrieved February 20, 2007 from http://www.nga.org

National Research Council. (2002). *Scientific research in education.* Committee on Scientific Principles for Education Research. In R. J. Shavelson & L. Towne (Eds.), Center for Education, Division of behavioral and Social Sciences. Washington, DC: National Academy Press.

No Child Left Behind Act. (2001). (P.L. 107-110). Retrieved April 23, 2007, from www.ed.gov/legislation/ESEA02

Pressley, M., Dolezak, S., Roehrig, A. D., & Hilden, K. (2002) Why the national Reading Panel's recommendations are not enough. In R. L. Allington (Ed.), *Big brother an the national reading curriculum* (pp. 75–85), Portsmouth, NH: Heinemann.

Sturtevant, E. G. (2003). *The literacy coach: A key to improving teaching and learning in secondary school.* Washington, DC: Alliance for Excellent Education.

Taylor, B. M. (2002, June). *Characteristics of schools that are effective in teaching all children to read.* Washington, DC: National Education Association.

Taylor, B. M., Pearson, P. D., Peterson, D. S., & Rodriguez, M. C. (2005). The CIERA School Change Framework: An evidenced-based approach to professional development and school reading improvement. *Reading Research Quarterly, 40*(1), 40–69.

United States Department of Education. (2002a, April). *Final guidance for the Reading First Program.* Retrieved February 20, 2007 from www.ed.gov/offices/OESE/readingfirst/grant.html

United States Department of Education. (2002b). *Inside Reading First, frequently asked questions.* Retrieved February 20, 2007 from http://www.ed.gov/offices/OESE/readingfirst/faq.html

United States Department of Education. (2002c). *Reading First Criteria for Review of State Applications.* Retrieved February 20, 2007 from www.ed.gov/offices/OESE/reading first/grant.html

United States Department of Education. (2005, November 14). Application for new grants for the Striving Readers Program, (Title I, Part E., Section 1502). Elementary and Secondary Education Act of 1965 as amended by the No Child Left Behind Act, 2001 Public Law 107-110. CFDA Number 84.371A. Retrieved February 20, 2007 from http://www.ed.gov/programs/strivingreaders/2005-371a.pdf

II

VOICES FROM THE FIELD

MUSIC IN A CHILD'S LIFE

Aliki Brandenberg
LONDON, ENGLAND

What would we be without music?

Music is part of life even before birth. It is in the pulse of a mother's heartbeat, the rhythm of a lullaby, the lilt of words, the muted sound of a Bach cantata.

Later a child will clap, bang on a pot, pound clay, skip, jump, hop, shake, dance to a melody—all in rhythm. And what a release of energy. Perhaps that is why children love poetry, or why Shakespeare wrote in verse—for his actors to better remember the words through their rhythmic patterns.

Music is everywhere. From early childhood onward, mine was saturated with all kinds. I painted to music. Years later, I still remembered the music I heard as if the melodies had been woven into the brush strokes. Many scientists, mathematicians, writers, actors, and others agree that music is an important part of their creative process.

I have no doubt that a child's early life and education are enriched by music. I was born into a musical environment with a pencil in my hand, but where would I have been, had it not been for the school I attended? I now know that our ordinary public school was extraordinary. It vibrated with music, art, and every opportunity for self-expression: band, orchestra, choir, chorus, musicals, concerts, plays, and all phases of the arts. What happens to a child with the seed of a talent, but without the opportunities to develop them? How else do we create a whole person?

I was lucky. I know I was lucky because I visit schools. I have seen all kinds. I can tell when I walk in the door if a school is "balanced" or "unbalanced." (We do have two sides of the brain to consider.) A "balanced" school has a beat. An enthusiasm. Writing and art projects flutter on the walls. Science projects clutter the halls. The sound of a band rehearsing comes from somewhere. There is a joyousness in such a school. A purpose. An "unbalanced" school lacks that excitement. Empty halls echo, and something is missing. I know tests are a way of life. But surely, much more is accomplished when music and art are present. They make learning fun, and gratify a young person's need for emotional and creative expression. My own pen gets stuck without music. Though I need quiet to concentrate and gather my thoughts, in most other situations—certainly drawing or painting my illustrations—music makes my hand flow.

Music is a language everyone can understand, whatever the age. On one school visit, I met a remarkable teacher with a love of opera. Her prekindergarten class of 4- and 5-year-olds had just studied *The Magic Flute*. With pride and delight, they shared with me all they knew—the plot, the arias, the characters' funny names, Mozart's life. On the wall were maps, visuals, and the children's paintings inspired by the opera. The teacher had done it using a few aids and her own passion and enthusiasm. What a lifelong gift she has given her students.

One is never too young for music. The earlier the better. After all, it was there even before the child was born.

Part III

FAMILY AND COMMUNITY CONTEXTS IN THE COMMUNICATIVE, VISUAL, AND PERFORMATIVE ARTS

Victoria Chou
UNIVERSITY OF ILLINOIS AT CHICAGO

Pamela J. Konkol
CONCORDIA UNIVERSITY

The chapters in Part III demonstrate how individuals create communities through an eye-opening array of communicative, visual, and performative literacies, primarily in out- of-school contexts. From swapping talk at the hair salon to analyzing the finer points of little known films, from instant messaging (IMing) to DJing, and from manga to zines to comic books, the 13 authors illustrate the power of literacies grounded in contexts that are personally significant and meaningful. Reminding us of Scribner and Cole's work with the Vai of Liberia, a people who achieved literacy outside of schooling, the learners described in these chapters have developed sophisticated higher order literacy skills primarily in family and community settings outside of schools. The authors invite us into these communities where learning is fueled by personal agency and authority.

Most of the participants portrayed in these descriptions of new literacy communities are relatively young, from middle-school students to high-school students and young adults. Yet these literacy communities are neither inscribed in standard kindergarten through grade 12 practices nor necessarily accepted as legitimate in traditional school sites. Until this scenario changes, we believe the disconnect between today's schools and today's students will grow. Bringing the full potential of the communicative, visual, and performative literacies into our nation's kindergarten through grade 12 classrooms will challenge educators' abilities to change, but we cannot afford to do otherwise if we want schools to play a significant role in students' literacy experiences. The authors of Part III demonstrate that such change is possible, at least in specific locales. Whether such remarkable innovations are possible at the level of entire school systems has yet to be demonstrated.

•22•

YOUTH CULTURES, LITERACIES, AND IDENTITIES IN AND OUT OF SCHOOL

Elizabeth Birr *Moje*
UNIVERSITY OF MICHIGAN

Why does youth literacy, culture, or identity matter to teaching the visual and communicative arts? More to the point, why does youth literacy—that is, the literacy practices and texts that young people engage in or with of their own volition—matter at all? The simple answer is that youth literacies should matter to researchers and teachers because they matter so much to youth. These literacy practices—and their accompanying texts—should matter in particular to visual and communicative arts teachers and researchers because, as researchers such as Cowan (2005), Ingalls (2005) and van Helden (2002) documented, youths' preferred texts are often multimodal. That is, youths' texts typically draw from and integrate print, images, spoken words, music, and even performances. But youth literacies should matter to all teachers, especially when the popular assumption is that youth do not read or write much in their out-of-school lives. Rather than lamenting the alleged crisis of youth aliteracy (i.e., "kids don't read anymore"), we should examine what young people do read and write. The emphasis in such work should be on understanding the kinds of texts and literacy practices that excite young people, with an eye toward both drawing from what youth know and love and expanding possibilities for youth to learn to use a wide variety of texts in their school, work, and play. Youth culture, literacy, and identity (YCLI) studies purports to do just that: to focus on what and why texts matter to youth and on how youth texts and literacy practices might inform academic literacy development.

And yet, two trends threaten the continued relevance of work that focuses on the literacy practices of youth. One trend revolves around the current focus on "struggling" adolescent readers. The focus on adolescents who struggle with academic literacies is, in and of itself, a long-awaited turn among adolescent literacy researchers. The focus on adolescent literacy is valuable and necessary. However, attempts to address the question of literacy *struggle* without defining what *struggle* is and how such struggle might be produced by school settings are worrisome. Left unattended is the question of why some youth who struggle with academic literacy enthusiastically tackle texts outside of school. Also left unattended is the question of how sophisticated and challenging these out-of-school texts are, and whether youths' practices out of school can be used to mediate their struggle with academic literacies demanded in school.

More important, however, is the fact that many current attempts to mediate adolescents' academic literacy struggles take the form of standardized programs of instruction driven by tightly defined conceptions of reading and writing (rooted in print), a move that diminishes or even rejects the value of youth literacy research. Such an approach predetermines student literacy learning goals, often with only school-like literacy tasks in mind, and begins with what we believe youth *should be able to do*, rather than beginning with what young people know, do, read, and write and *want to* know, do, read, and write despite their struggles with academic literacy. Furthermore, a prescribed, print only approach privileges assessment via standardized, school-like measures, rather than developing broad and deep profiles of adolescent literacy practice and proficiency in a host of contexts. Thus, such an approach has little need for research generated by youth literacy, culture, and identity scholars and research that focuses on the texts and literacy practices that youth engage in of their own volition and that shape youth identities and that forge different youth cultures.

A second—and equally worrisome—trend also threatens the continued relevance of this work, and that trend lies within the field of youth literacy research itself. It is the trend toward romanticizing youth literacy practices in a way that overlooks the social, political, and economic importance—indeed, necessity—of developing strong academic literacy skills and practices, particularly those focused on print. YCLI researchers often, in fact, argue strenuously for the turn to multimedia, and in doing so, we fail to acknowledge that simply introducing images, sounds, music, and other forms will not necessarily help young people navigate the print demands of classrooms and beyond (cf., Dressman, O'Brien, Rogers, et al., 2006). Dressman (personal communication, April 11, 2005) labeled this move the "New Literacies problem" and argued that we have ignored the real struggles of many young people to make sense of print as we have followed the interesting multimedia and digital literacy practices of highly proficient print readers.

We who study YCLI must take seriously these tensions, struggling to lift the field out of the cavernous dichotomy into which we have pushed ourselves. We must push the *so what* question of YCLI studies, moving it beyond answers such as, "Knowing this matters because these practices matter to youth." Such an answer is partial, and we may do a disservice to young people—particularly those who struggle or are marginalized in school—if we fail to recognize the consequences of this romanticization of new literacies. Youth literacy scholars—myself included—must resist the position of fascinated voyeur and do a better job of clarifying how such studies can inform and, indeed, deepen secondary school classroom practice. Doing so, however, will require some rigorous work on the part of youth literacy researchers to clarify and define the constructs under study and to illustrate how the findings of such research can inform and deepen academic literacy learning.

Consequently, I offer in this review some definitions of my own, with the acknowledgment that defining constructs can be both liberating and limiting. Nonetheless, I make a best effort at defining with discretion, because *lack of definition* can serve as an even more powerful limitation on the applicability of youth literacy research than some of the narrow definitions currently being offered. It is in a definitional void, after all, that narrow definitions can become firmly rooted and powerful, even determining, forces.

DEFINING CONSTRUCTS

Any number of terms might be used as starting point for defining construct related to adolescent/youth literacy. I, however, am choosing the following: texts and literacies, youth, cultures, and identities, using examples from my own work to exemplify the definitions. Following the definitional work, I present exemplar studies of youth literacies, cultures, and identities out of school and crossing the boundaries of in and out of school.

Texts and Literacies

Over the last three decades, definitions of *text* and *literacy* have expanded from purely cognitive foci on print and the processes involved in reading and writing print to perspectives that view texts as any communicative medium, and reading and writing as tools used for specific purposes in specific contexts (Gee, 1996; Scribner & Cole, 1981; Street, 1994). Sociocultural literacy theorists, in particular, understand text to be a social construction, a thing that is agreed upon by people acting and interacting in social settings. Texts, according to these perspectives, are generated and used for social purposes, but are not necessarily linguistic artifacts. In her work with the children and texts of three communities, Heath (1983), for example, illustrated how their different uses of texts—their "ways with words"—were both reflective of and reconstructive of particular cultural patterns: Texts, according to Heath, are more than sites of information or aesthetic expression; they are tools for establishing belongingness to cultural groups, identity enactments and subjectivities, and knowledge production patterns. Moreover, texts include the written, the spoken, the pictorial, and the performed; literacies include all of the social practices and forms of representation and communication (oral, visual, and performed) that revolve around making sense of written texts (see Heath & Smyth, 1999).

A number of perspectives have situated literacy and texts as deeply embedded in the building and maintenance of relationships, identities, and cultures that occur amidst deeply structured relations and systems of power. For example, sociocultural theorists argue that language and literacy are socially, culturally, and historically situated tools for exploring, claiming, or transforming thought and experience (Vygotsky, 1978). Who people are, or who they are allowed to be, is shaped in part by their literacy practices (Graff, 1987; Luke, 1996; Street, 1994; Volosinov, 1973). More recently, others argue that opportunities to learn are integrally tied to literate practices (Moje & Lewis, in press; Morrell, 2002; Purcell-Gates, in press). These critical sociocultural perspectives on literacy have also examined traditionally disenfranchised or marginalized groups' uses of literacy in a variety of contexts and as intimately tied to cultures, identities, and developmental periods.

Drawing from all of these stances, the definition of *literacy* that guides my work and this review is that literacy is the work that people do to make sense of symbol systems inscribed in some permanent way. Often, the symbol systems are print-based, but they may also involve numbers, musical notation, icons, or mathematical symbols. Moreover, the work that people do to make sense of these permanently inscribed symbol systems often involves other forms of representation, such as oral language, gestures, dress, facial cues, and images. Finally, literate practice is always part of other social, cultural, and political practices and is therefore never autonomous or decontextualized. Literacy, in sum, is not any and every act of communication or representation, but it does involve multiple modes of communication and representation, and it is a critical aspect of many social practices.

Youth/Adolescent

Given the focus on cultures, identities, and development (or age) in textual and literate practices, it seems wise to turn to the question of what counts as a youth or adolescent, as a way of establishing the ground for this review of youth literacies, cultures, and identities. Unfortunately, the terms *youth* and *adolescent* are broadly used and highly contested (see Lesko, 2001; Stevens, 2004). Current definitions focus on *age*, with the age range most commonly associated with youth being anywhere from 8 to 25 years (Lesko, 2001). Early theorists (Hall, 1904) labeled ages 8 to 12 as "youth" and 13 to 24 as "adolescence" (Stevens, 2004).

More recently, scholars have complicated the age-based definition by arguing that adolescence or youthfulness is defined as much by biology (e.g., onset of puberty), living conditions (e.g., independent living arrangements vs. living with parents), employment status, educational status, parenting status, and leisure habits, as it is by age (Arnett, 2002; Lesko, 2001; Stevens, 2004). Certainly, it is true that age alone cannot be used as a designate for youth: In some cases, 16-year-olds are parents, hold jobs, and live independently, whereas 28-year-olds may live at home, attend college, be childless, and have active, late-night social lives. Some of these differences in behavior are cultural, some are geographic, and some are individual. Thus, there is no easy definition of what counts as a youth or adolescent. Yet, I resist the stance that anyone and everyone can be counted in this group, primarily because people ages 12 to 18 have been overlooked in literacy education research and theory. Moreover, despite the controversy, among the scholars who claim to study adolescents, most focus on the range of 10 to 20 years. For those reasons alone, I subscribe to an age-based definition of youth or adolescent in this review, focusing on the age range that seems to feature prominently in popular cultural portraits, but virtually disappears (at least until recently) as subject of interest or possibility in literacy education research (Moje, 2002).

The decision to define the concept of *youth* at least in part by age is not without its problems, however—chief among them being the broad span of the age range that is typically used in such definitions. To consider the content and linguistic demands faced by a 10-year-old in reading the text of a content area equivalent to those faced by a 17-year-old in the same content area promises to lead to risks a glossing over on each end of that spectrum. More to the point of studying the relationship among youth literacies, cultures, and identities, the difference experienced by youth of different ages in access to information, relationships, and spaces is potentially enormous. Consider, for example, the differences observed among the youth I have studied for seven years in one Detroit community: In our early work (focused on the youth at age 12), we saw little evidence of book reading. When asked about their reading outside of school, the young women in the study produced magazines and music lyrics; the young men likewise talked about magazines, but never produced any artifacts of their reading, and they admitted reading at low frequencies. By contrast, the same young people five years later produce numerous books, articles, Web sites, and magazines as documentation of their reading. The female youths' reading continues to outstrip the males', but they are all talking about and evidencing reading with much greater frequency. Recently, for example, one young man introduced his reading of Nostradamus's predictions into a discussion about the selection of a new pope, admitting that he had stopped reading when the predictions hit too close to home.

Similarly, the young people's talk about sense of self and their concomitant identity enactments have shifted over time, especially with the introduction of work outside their communities, the ability to drive independently, and the girls' freedom to date after their quinceañeras (15th birthday rite of passage). Their talks about race, racism, and the city space in which they lived has changed dramatically as they have moved outside of their communities, with such movement enabled by the ability to work longer hours and to drive. Associated with these changed notions of self and community, these same youth have started to attend a local church youth group as a way, they claim, to deal with the challenges they are facing as residents of a violent and decaying urban setting. The following excerpt of a conversation among three of these youth underscores the importance of examining the role of age and development in these changes:

(E=Elizabeth; R=Ramiro; P=Pilar; Y=Yolanda)

E: You're all going to youth group? You, too, Ramiro?
R: Yeah.
P: It gives you ideas for how to deal with things in life.
Y: It's funny how for a while we were all reading, now we're all doing this.
--E: You're not reading anymore?
Y: We still read, but this we're doing together.
--P: I want this [youth group] to be more than a phase, though. I hope I keep doing this.

"More than a phase" stands out in this exchange as a recognition among the youth that their practices and identities have shifted with time, age, and development, all of which have provided them access to new and different practices, ways of thinking, and positive and negative experiences. Thus, references to youth literacies, cultures, and identities need to be regularly qualified with specific age designations in the interest of more rigorously specifying the phenomena of interest, as well as the instructional and policy implications that stem from findings of research with youth of different ages.

Youth Cultures

My review of the literature and my own work in this area suggests four definitional points in reference to the concept of *youth cultures*: (a) the plurality of youth cultures, (b) the simultaneous distinction between and overlap of youth cultures from popular cultures, (c) the simultaneous distinction between and overlap of youth and ethnic/racial cultures, and (d) the recognition of the influence of social class or socioeconomic status on the generation and maintenance of youth cultures.

Recognizing the many possible instantiations of youth culture. Perhaps the simplest definitional move to make in work on youth culture is to underscore the plurality of youth culture*s*. Too often, scholars and popular media alike refer to youth cultures as a singular construct, suggesting that all youth engage in the same practices, dress in the same ways, listen to the same music and watch the same television programs, and even, at some level, think the same thoughts.

This essential view of youth culture is somewhat ironic, given the dominant take on *culture* as a dynamic construct that prevails in most current studies of cultural groups (at least rhetorically, if not always analytically). It is worth noting that although youth cultures are not considered particularly stable, they are very often referred to in singular, essential ways, as if there is something that all can agree on as "youth culture." Yet, even a cursory flip through the literature or an abbreviated survey or ethnographic study of several different groups of young people would cast doubt on those assumptions. This essentializing of youth cultures has serious implications for classroom practice in the communicative and visual arts because it can lead well-intentioned researchers, teachers, and curriculum developers to design studies, choose materials, or plan lessons around idealized or essentialized images of young people, rather than around the particular youth cultural practices of actual young people in classrooms.

Youth cultures ≠ Popular cultures. The second point, focused on the elision of youth cultures with popular cultures, is particularly problematic. Certainly, youth cultures are informed by and often shaped by popular cultural texts and practices, but the reverse is also true. Youth cultures often construct, push, support, or challenge certain popular cultural texts and practices, as illustrated in this excerpt from an interview with two Latino youths in our ethnographic work:

(K=Kathryn/Interviewer; T=Tony; J=Juan)

T: I think that Black people and the Mexicans get along great, but I don't think that many White people get along with Mexicans.
K: Why is that?
J: 'Cause. You know how in movies the Black people and the Mexicans all look all . . . they're always like criminals and everything-
T: -Gangsters
J: Yeah, and they're always the criminals and everything. But not everybody's like that . . . not all the Mexicans and Black people are like that . . . a lot of Mexicans and Black people have good jobs and everything . . . but they . . . the people that do movies don't show us like that. (Moje & Ciechanowski, 2002)

The conflating of popular and youth cultures has been readily promoted and debated in mass media and in research literatures. Early research on popular cultures, sponsored by the Centre for Contemporary Cultural Studies (CCCS) in Birmingham, England, is in part responsible for the construal of youth cultures as constructs of popular cultural trends because of its emphasis on how youth cultures—which the CCCS termed *subcultures* and defined as resistant—were framed in response to the cultural practices in which they were embedded (Bennett, 2000).

However, later theorists began to question the unilateral framing of youth cultures as structures of resistance in response to larger cultural trends and posed perspectives that called for a more dialectical understanding of the relationship between youth cultures and popular cultures (Chaney, 1996). Many youth also use popular cultural texts for their own ends, outside the realm of the purposes imagined by the producers, as illustrated in this excerpt:

(K=Kathryn/Interview; J=Jovana)

K: What about how you talk? You said you talk like a White girl—
J: Cause I use words like "whatever" and "loser."
K: And, other people wouldn't use those words?
J: Yah, but *the way I say it*. Like "loser" with the "L" thing [she makes a hand sign].
K: So where did you learn how to do that?
J: TV. *I learn everything from there.*
K: You learn everything from TV, huh?
J: Even my hairstyles. Like at night I go through the channels to see which hair I like and if it's easy and (fashionable), I'll do it.
K: Where do you get the things you say . . . what do you watch to get those words?
J: Like Boy Meets World. (Moje & Ciechanowski, 2002)

The term *lifestyles,* however, is troubling because of its association with market research (Bennett, 2000), and even market *engineering* (Moje & van Helden, 2005), and in both cases, the terms suggest perhaps more choice and freedom than may be wise. Very few people, regardless of age, are free from the grip of popular cultural texts. Yet, popular cultural texts are rarely, if ever, taken up without question by youth or adults. And youth often use these texts in surprising ways. Recently, two young men described how the popular figurines and Web site associated with "Homies" (see http://www.homiestv.net) had influenced their thinking about staying in school, graduating, and changing what they considered negative stereotypes of Mexican people:

(I1=Interviewer 1, M=Mario, R=Ramiro, I2=Interviewer 2)

I1: What else do you read?
M: *Homies* . . . It's like a new way to express Mexican, Chicano, Hispanics.
I2: So what do they express about being Mexican? What do you think they express? Is there anything in particular that's part of the point?
M: The way Mexicans live. . . . Or things like sometimes these people become what they are because of problems they face. So yeah, that's what they explain why they are the way they describe them.
I2: So the thing that makes them all what they are is that they tell you something about—
M: —The background of the people.
I2: The background of the people. But they're supposed to be inspiring? They're supposed to be inspirational? Like people whose stories, they've overcome something difficult?
M: Yeah, because they have graduation or overcoming everything. They tell you to finish school, and stay cool and all that stuff. Stay out of drugs. Some of them try to take a message to the people.

Although these two young men interpreted and used these popular culture images and texts in a positive way, others—including members of our research team—read these texts and images in very different ways upon first encounters with them, underscoring the point that such texts are not uniformly interpreted or understood. Youth, in particular, have derived their own meanings particular to their affinity groups, lifestyles, and youth cultures. Thus, popular cultures and youth cultures depend on and give life to one another. Moreover, youth cultures can be vastly different from one space to another, from one ethnic or racial group to another, from one social class group to another, and from one gender to another.

Ethnic/youth/family cultures. The nod toward demographic differences (e.g., ethnicity, race, gender, social class, or socioeconomic status) introduces a third point of concern in studying youth cultures. Despite popular conceptions of youth resisting all input from family and community elders and living at the whim of popular cultures (e.g., Schultze et al., 1991), I have found that ethnic and racial cultures are often woven into both popular and youth cultures, as are family cultures. As illustrated in the previous example, ethnicity was an important aspect of the youth and popular cultures these young men built, maintained, or took up. In general, the youth in this community—a predominantly Latino/a identified community—made use of popular cultural texts and built youth cultures that derived from or allowed them to claim their ethnic cultural identities. Notebook stickers, for example, were a popular item collected by youth in the Detroit community. Common illustrations on the stickers included low-rider cars guarded by la Virgin de Guadalupe or women dressed in Mexican colors with the Mexican eagle (an eagle with a snake in his talons) prominent in the background. Some depicted Aztec leaders alongside Cesar Chavez. Many were adorned with the words, "Brown Pride," "Aztlan," or "Raza Unida [United in Race]." These stickers demonstrate how the youths used texts that both displayed and claimed ethnic identities to build youth cultures. Although no adults in the community would have ridiculed or outlawed the display of the stickers, nor were they buying them, decorating their walls or notebooks or other material goods with them. Such activities appeared to be a unique facet of the youth cultures observed in this community.

The valuing of ethnic culture among youth is illustrated in the musical choices among the youth I study in Detroit, with many of the youth preferring Mexican music—whether traditional or urban—over most other musical forms. Young women, in particular, routinely identified bands they like in terms of the band members' ethnicity, with two young women choosing the words Kumbia Kings (a Mexican musical group) and Chicano lovers as part of their e-mail addresses (see Moje & van Helden, 2005). In addition, the young men and women both routinely identify their relationship choices in terms of ethnicity, with young women talking most explicitly about their preferences for Mexican men and their lack of interest in men of other ethnic or racial backgrounds, as illustrated in this interview excerpt conducted at a local movie theatre:

(I=Interviewer; Y=Yolanda)

I: Isn't Tom Cruise beautiful [pointing to a large poster of the actor on a wall]?
Y *[shrugs] I guess.*
I: I love his eyes, don't you?
Y: Hmmm.
I: What about Brad Pitt? He's pretty cute, isn't he?
Y: I guess, if you like that.
I: Matt Damon? [This meets with another shrug.] . . . Who *do* you like?
Y: I don't know. . . I just don't like White boys, Miss.

Another important point to underscore in connecting ethnic cultural practices to youth cultural practices is that youth cultures—while recognizable as distinct from adult ethnic (or other) cultural practices—are never entirely separate from those elders' practices. As illustrated by the data exemplars from my own work, young people are drawing from intergenerational relationships in their construction of unique and dynamic youth cultures. Their youth cultural practices are distinct in part because they draw from many different practices, unlike adults who typically settle into more stable relationships as they settle into jobs, family responsibilities, and communities. But youth, who move across many different relationships and spaces (including popular cultural spaces made accessible through communication and information technologies), draw from a host of experiences to construct hybrid cultures and practices. J. Comaroff and J. L. Comaroff (2000) argued, "Youth tend everywhere to occupy the innovative, uncharted borderlands along which the global meets the local" (p. 308), and youth literacy studies increasingly provide evidence to support their claim.

Youth, thus, do not necessarily reject their parents' and other adults' values, experiences, and practices, but rather, they articulate the values and practices of adults to those of other spaces and relations in their daily lives, particularly as those practices represent ethnic cultural norms and values. These complex intersections among youth, ethnic, popular, and family cultures are often either overlooked, or acknowledged but not complicated in important ways, in research on youth literacies. More troubling, youth are regularly portrayed as resisting their parents' and other adults' values and attitudes. My research suggests the opposite—that, although young people may outwardly represent themselves as resistant to and resentful of their parents' and other elders' practices, they are consciously and unconsciously interweaving the practices of those role models into their own. Consider, for example, the talk of this young woman about one her recent text readings, taken from an informal lunch interview:

(Y=Yolanda; E=Elizabeth; I=Interviewer)

Y: My mom just bought me this book, it was soooo interesting, I read it in *two* days!
I: . . . The title is in Spanish, so are the characters Latino?
Y: yeah.
I: Do you know are they Mexican, are they Puerto Rican, are they Dominican? [Y shakes her head no.] You don't know. They don't identify that, you just know they're Latino. Where do they live? They don't tell that either? Like, they don't say this is in New York or Detroit or—?
Y: That's why it's so interesting. . . . because it doesn't give you, like, it's not going, "Aha!" they let you use your imagination. . . . And it has words in Spanish sooo big like, I go, "Mom, what is this? And she explains. Okay, that's cool.

Yolanda's comments clearly indicate the important role her mother, her ethnicity, and her preferred national language play in her motivation to read—and even to struggle through, or in Pat Alexander's words, to become an "effortful processor" of the text she describes. Equally important is the fact that the discovery of this book launched among a small group of young woman and type of book reading circle, in which the young woman exchanged and discussed the texts in this series. Thus, Yolanda's mother had a critical impact on not only her daughter's literacy practices but also the practices of a larger circle of youth.

Yolanda's experience is not isolated, but is, rather, representative of common reading practices among youth and their parents or elders. And in this excerpt from a formal interview, two young men describe affinity group relationships—which link to textual practices of reading *Lowrider Magazine*, with elder relatives (J=Juan, I=Interviewer, T=Tony):

J: Okay. Me and my uncle are in a car club. This car club is from like Los Angeles, but it's also here. . . . And like, so . . . he has a low rider and he's trying to . . . we're fixing it because it has to have a good sound system, has to . . . has to . . . have to . . . has to have a good hydraulic system, good paint job, has to be like good enough so we can show it. So right now we're like . . . with . . . they know us, but we're not with them because we still need to fix it up. So by like when the summer comes, we're like gonna finish.

Positioning youth cultures as resistant to "adult" cultures leads researchers, teachers, and other youth workers to miss important opportunities to observe how youth look to adult practices—including adult literacy practices, as illustrated by Yolanda's, Angela's, and Juan's and Tony's comments—for guidance and modeling.

Social class and youth cultures. Finally, one must consider the influence of social class and/or socioeconomic status on the generation and maintenance of youth cultures. The nature of any given youth culture and its particular processes of development and maintenance are heavily dependent on access to material and human resources. Moreover, how youth cultures are positioned relative to dominant society (e.g., as normalized or deviant, as service oriented or egoistic, as contributing to or detracting from academic literacy development) is related to the social and economic resources and networks that youth have at their disposal.

Access to material resources shapes the generation of youth cultures most obviously in terms of access to digital and other electronic technologies. Although it appears to be the case that some access issues are diminishing as costs of electronic hardware decrease, it remains that case that access to certain features, such as "instant" messaging, remain limited for youth who live in low-income or impoverished communities and homes. Approximately half of the youth with whom I work in Detroit now have cell phone access through which they can send text messages, but even that half finds it difficult to maintain enough "minutes" for reliable communication. Internet communication via e-mail, instant messaging (IMing), blogs, and chats is entirely dependent for most of these youth on school or public library access, and those access points restrict communications and access to certain sites with the use of firewalls. Thus, while youth with more disposable income increase their fluency with digital technologies as well as their access to information and global youth cultures, youth who live in low-income settings access a restricted range of information about other youth, ethnic, and popular cultures outside their own communities. Nevertheless, access to television and radio provide all youth with more information about youth in other spaces than ever before, thus expanding the reach of youth cultures across most socioeconomic strata. And, these youth cultures inform youth's textual choices, shape the development of subjectivities, and inform and produce identity enactments in different spaces, times, and relationships.

Youth Identities/Subjectivities

Typically, the questions that get the most treatment in current research on youth identities revolve around the stuff of identities, how identities develop or change, whether one should really use the term *identity* (mainly because it has the baggage of stability and individualism tied to it), and what the difference is between identity and subjectivity. A less often asked question is how do youth identities intersect with youth cultures, or even with cultures more generally conceived? Because education researchers have spent so much time debating the *what* of identity (or, perhaps more to the point, the lack of an identifiable, stable *what*), we have written and researched less about how identities are developed, constructed, or learned in cultural practices. Indeed, if identities are not inherent, stable, aspects of being that are reached, maintained, or threatened, then literacy education researchers interested in identities and their relationships to literacy should be asking questions about the relationships between the cultures in which youth are immersed, the texts and literacy practices to which youth are exposed, and the co-construction of identities with literacies and cultures.

Some perspectives on identity and culture. Social psychologists have dealt with the relationship between identity and culture by contrasting what they label "personal identity" with "social identities" (Tajfel, 1982), thus allowing for a stable personal or individual construct of identity that gets lived out in various forms depending on the social arrangements (one might read *cultures* here) in which one finds him- or herself. Roeser, Peck, and Nasir (2006) suggested that identities are (a) assigned by others—Gee (2001) would argue that they are "recognized" in addition to being assigned—, (b) afforded by particular resources and relationships, (c) encoded as bits of information in memory, (d) activated in particular contexts, and (d) enacted in certain ways dependent on the activation of encodings. These are not necessarily hierarchical or time-ordered aspects of identity; rather, identities are the product of all of these aspects.

The power of this argument is that it makes a case for how macrostructures, systems, and relations get integrated into and enacted by individuals in microprocesses and practices, as identity assignments, affordances, and recognitions are encoded into memories that constitute a "self." These encodings, I argue, develop through what Rogers (2002) called "histories of participation," a phrase that emphasizes the role of participation in spaces, relationships, and periods or histories in the production of knowledge structures or the encodings that shape identity enactments. As new encodings are integrated into the self-system, encodings of past participation may shift and change, linking to the new bits of information or being completely restructured. Encodings are activated through participation in new times, spaces, and relationships, sometimes leading to new and different encodings, or to particular enactments of identity.

Thus, identities can be conceptualized as enactments of self that are assigned, encoded, afforded, activated (Roeser et al., in press), and/or recognized in particular spaces, times, and relationships (Moje, 2004), always deriving from histories of participation (Rogers, 2002) and always are situated in relations of power. The power of a complex theory of identity that includes the biological, the cognitive, the social, the historical, and the political is that it makes a distinctive link between identities, times, spaces, and cultures, with an emphasis on the plural. Especially important to this review is the question of how individual youth identities are interwoven with the youth cultures they generate, become part of, or resist. Equally important is the role of texts (written, oral, and performed) and related literacy practices (whether texts are read in groups or individually, in or out of school, at work or at home, etc.) in constructing these cultures and identities

This theorization of identity and its relationship to culture, history, and context also addresses what many have viewed as the contradictory and fluid nature of identities in adolescence. Identities are not situated in stable cores that are somehow defined in and achieved at the end of adolescence, but encodings may remain relatively stable until new contexts are encountered that offer new assignments, affordances, and recognitions, or that activate already encoded bits of information in new ways, thus leading to new enactments of identity. Identities are, thus, not completely fluid either. They do derive from our histories of participation; they are based in constellations of encodings, and those encodings may produce coherent, if temporary, enactments. They may also produce seemingly contradictory identity enactments, however, in new and different contexts, or when recognized by those contexts in new and different ways.

And this is where texts and literacy practices play an important role. Texts can be chosen because they mesh with or reflect what youth know or believe about themselves, (as illustrated by a comment from one young woman in my Detroit research, who described her choice of a book series in the following terms:

> It [the book] could be about the gangs here. They talk about the 3 dot tattoo, which is Surenos Trese. She has a teardrop tattoo, one teardrop for each time she got out of the juvenile detention facility. . . . It was that she was Mexican, East LA, oh I want to read something about a gangsta, you don't read this every day. . . . I've been going to the library every single day for the past two weeks.

Texts can also be chosen because they push what youth know and believe about themselves, thus allowing them to enact different identities, as in the choice of another Detroit youth, Ramiro who read Elie Wiesel's, *Night*, for information about the Holocaust, or his friend, Mario's, use of an ROTC text to learn about Mexicans in the U.S. military. Texts support and serve youth developing identities that help them infiltrate or construct social networks and youth cultures, as illustrated by the tough cookies and social queens of Finders's (1997) study. The tough cookies and social queens carried certain books as identity markers, but read other books in the privacy of their own rooms. Even active resistance to mainstream literacy practices can serve as a type of identity enactment, according to a recent study of literacy practices among adolescent youth offenders (Finders, 2005).

In short, texts—and the different kinds of literacy practices that accompany them—can play an important role in developing youth cultures and in providing fodder for identity enactments, whether by serving as marker of identities that will be recognized in particular ways, or by providing the information necessary for youth to enact certain identities. This important role of texts and literacy practices in identity development has led a number of scholars to examine the role of youth literacies, in and out of school, as a way of understanding young people's meaning making with print and other forms of representation and, ultimately, of trying to enhance youth literacy and content learning in school.

BRINGING IT ALL TOGETHER: YCLI STUDIES

With these definitions as a frame, I now turn to studies that seek to explore the relationships among YCLI studies with a focus on how they can inform research on teaching in visual and communicative arts. In reviewing the field for this chapter, I noted three patterns in YCLI studies: These studies focus on youth perspectives on their own literacy practices, the studies reframe the so-called "struggling" school reader and writer, and they examine multiple media and forms of representation—including digital forms—in their documentation of literate practices. Each of these patterns has important implications for research on teaching the visual and communicative arts, as outlined in each section below.

YCLI From Youth Perspectives: More Than Deviant, Less Than Perfect

Several YCLI studies conducted have examined youths' literate practices, cultural experiences, and identity enactments from the perspective of youth, making spaces for youth to tell their own stories, rather than to report stories layered with adult, and often White and mainstream, assumptions about what it means to be a youth. Camitta's (1993) exploration of vernacular literacy practices among Philadelphia youth was one of the first YCLI studies to illustrate how urban adolescents use literacies in and out of school to take hold of their lives and to write themselves into a world that often refuses to acknowledge them. Shuman's (1986) study was similarly groundbreaking, although Shuman's work focused more on classroom writing practices than practices across multiple youth contacts. Nevertheless, both Camitta and Shuman paved the way for many other studies of youth literacy practices by refusing to see what Camitta called *vernacular* literacy practices as problematic, even when they might be considered risky or illicit (Blackburn, 2002; Alweis. Productions & Heath, 2000; Hunt, 1996; Moje, 2000; Smith, 1997; Weinstein, 2002).

Such work typically resists explaining youths' uses of literacy as resistant or deviant acts: My own work, for example (Moje, 2000), demonstrated that even young people most likely to be engaged in violent practices—gang-connected youth—were actively using texts and literacy practices to make sense of their everyday lives. In fact, their gang-connected literacies, often seen either as deviant (in that case usually not even considered *literacy*) or resistant, were more often than not simply ways of identifying with other youth, getting through the day, or finding a space to belong (cf., Weinstein, 2002; Smith, 1997).

Likewise, Cowan (2005) demonstrated that Latino youth's uses of visual symbols sometimes interpreted as gang connected are actually ways of bringing ethnic, community, and religious cultural symbols to bear on their written texts. Cowan, in particular, demonstrated the importance of visual imagery as incorporated into youth's literate practices by analyzing the subtle ethnic, social, and political meanings conveyed within youth cultural groups through their visual, as well as print, forms.

Heath's ArtShow film (Alweis. Productions & Heath, 2000) and resource guide (Heath & Smyth, 1999) drew from 10 years of ethnography that analyzed the literacy and other communicative practices of youth in after-school programs. Heath's work underscored the idea that youth not only learn or enhance literacy skill as they work across media, but they also extend their capacity for talking and expressing themselves across genres. In other words, communicative practices and skills are interdependent, and opportunities to work in multiple genre, media, and forms of representation can strengthen abilities in all of those genres, media, and forms.

Similarly, in his edited volume on youth's literacies in informal settings, Mahiri (2003) collected a series of studies that examine the various informal peer settings in which youth engage in literacy. Chapters in the Mahiri collection include studies of youth online fan fiction revolving around the X-Files television program of the 1990s (Trainor, 2003), young women reading romance novels as a way of practicing for their own romances (Stanley, 2003; strikingly akin to Radway's 1984, study of housewives' romance reading), and spoken-word performances among youth in a predominantly Black community (Sutton, 2003), among many other studies that trace youth's literate practices to popular and geographic or ethnic cultural contexts. The researchers in Mahiri's collection analyzed the different youth identities, activities, representations, and stories of the youth as each is situated in and mediated by particular literacy practices in particular social, political, economic, and historical contexts. These practices, Mahiri argued, shape youth identity enactments and produce unique youth cultures, which in turn shape their textual choices and literacy practices. Mahiri and colleagues asserted that the young people they studied engaged in activities and accompanying literacy practices that provided meaning and pleasure in life and that demonstrated a certain kind of literate proficiency not measured in standardized testing.

With one notable exception on how hip-hop could be used to teach canonical poetry (Morrell & Duncan-Andrade, 2003), these studies did not explicitly seek to examine what the practices mean for teaching academic literacy. What these studies did do, however, was challenge the notion that people simply respond to the conditions around them by resisting or accommodating experiences. From this stance, youth use popular cultural texts and experiences in unpredictable ways to make sense of and take power in their worlds. What is more important, in-depth, close studies of youth often show youth to be making productive use of literacy, to be sophisticated users of print and other forms, and even to be kind and generous people who are concerned about making a difference in the world.

At the same time, however, these studies try not to romanticize youth cultures and youth literacy practices. YCLI studies attempt to dig deeper into the practices of youth literacy, culture, and identity, analyzing both the potential and the problem in these practices. Several scholars, for example, argued that, although youth are fluent and adept readers and writers outside of school, many struggle to achieve success in mainstream, academic literacy practices (e.g., Alvermann, 2001; Mahiri, 2003 and call for greater attention to the intersection of such literacies (Hull & Schultz, 2002; Ingalls, 2005; Lee, 2001; Moje, 2002; Morrell & Duncan-Andrade, 2003), particularly for struggling adolescent readers and writers. YCLI studies, by and large, also examine how some youth engage in "unsanctioned" literacy practices as a way of claiming space and making texts in a world that marginalizes them, at times inadvertently participating in their own marginalization, even as they try to speak, write, or draw out against it (Moje, 2000). These studies thus have situated youth as more than deviant, but less than perfect, attempting—but not always succeeding—to avoid romanticizing youth literacies, cultures, and identities.

Challenging the Notion of "Struggling" Readers and Writers

The YCLI work of Alvermann (2001) is a classic example of work targeted specifically at questioning the notion of reading and writing "struggle." Alvermann illustrated the *Pokemon* proficiencies of one young man who was deemed a struggling reader. The young man combined print texts with other icons, images, numbers, and oral languages to construct sophisticated understandings of complex instructions for playing *Pokemon*; his teacher was amazed to learn that he could follow and teach the rules to others, an insight that changed the teacher's assumptions about his literacy potential (cf., Gee, 2003, on the sophistication of video game reading tasks; cf., Alvermann, Young, Green, & Wisenbaker, 1999).

O'Brien (1998) also rearticulated the "struggling" reader and writer through his analysis of high school students who were supported in dynamic reading and writing activities in a digital environment within a high school literacy lab for struggling readers. O'Brien demonstrated that the youth—many of whom were identified as "low literate" and "unmotivated"—came to life when engaged in constructing essays using digital forms that allowed them to integrate print, oral language, and, especially, musical forms into one presentation. O'Brien demonstrated the sophistication of these "struggling" students as they interacted with a digital environment that many print-literate, proficient adults in their midst found intimidating.

In these studies, the spaces or contexts in which youth read and wrote provided opportunities for guidance by and feedback from adults (or more knowledgeable others) as young people engaged in literacy, and yet, despite adult involvement, the participants in these venues suggested that they felt free to explore alternatives to conventional literacies. Relations of power in these informal institutions were shifted from the typical authority relations and standardization of formal schooling. Youth were allowed, even encouraged, to make use of many different forms of representation, such as visual images, oral language, and music, to make meaning in relation to the print texts they read and wrote. As important as specific teaching practices are to understanding youths' literacy practices, equally important is the notion that many settings can provide learners with some level of freedom to explore multiple forms and genres of text for expressing identity and representing understanding. In turn, this sense of freedom may engender the motivation necessary to push so-called struggling readers into "effortful processing" (Alexander, 2003) necessary to read and write print and other text forms with proficiency across the wide variety of academic domains of the secondary school.

Virtual Literacies: YCLI Studies in the Digital Sphere

One obvious and important focus in YCLI studies—particularly as YCLI relates to the visual and communicative arts—revolves around digital literacies and their impact on the development of new literacies that include multiple forms of texts, virtual youth cultures, and new spaces for identity enactments using texts. In *Adolescents and Literacies in a Digital World* (Alvermann, 2002), the authors examined a number of different digital and other literacy practices and learning outside the school, situated largely in young people's experiences reading and writing for themselves. Hagood, Stevens, and Reinking (2002), for example, provided data exemplars drawn from interviews of youths' experiences with using digital technologies. Lewis and Finders (2002) portrayed the "idealized youth" and "idealized teacher" using data drawn from two different studies of youth and teachers engaging with digital technologies. Most of the chapters focusing specifically on adolescents' uses of digital literacies, however, are largely theoretical, arguing why we need to examine youth literacies as digitalized (e.g., Bruce, 2002; O'Brien & King, 2002; Luke, C., 2002), rather than presenting data of actual youth using digital technologies for learning, work, or pleasure.

By contrast, using cases of European American, working- and middle-class youth, Lewis and Fabos (2005) illustrated that Internet technologies demand both sophisticated conventional literacies and innovative literacy skills unique to the Internet medium. The researchers illustrate that one young woman, Sam (a pseudonym), saw communication as her main goal for online literate activity and that she engaged in communication with many different audiences in many different ways. Sam's analysis of her audiences' social purposes and of the consequences of different kinds of language practices illustrated her sophistication with rhetorical strategies in writing and speech (with IMing, being as a close as one can get to "written talk"). Sam, for example, consciously used the language of her audience in her replies to establish community. She engaged with multiple audiences simultaneously, measuring her response time in terms of her relationship with her audience (e.g., one waits an appropriate time to respond to "popular" people in order to appear equally popular).

In an argument similar to the "safe space" argument of the informal institutional literacy settings (e.g., after-school programs), Lewis and Fabos (2005) argued that the Internet represented a safe space for Sam to experiment with various literate and rhetorical strategies, to develop relationships, to further social goals. Because Sam's physical body was not present in the interactions, she could hide her identity and play with other ways of being. Some would argue, then, that cyberspace—and its multiple venues, from chat rooms to IM networks to online fan fiction Web sites and multiple user domains (MUDS, and their derivatives, MOOs)—may represent the most liberating of out-of-school literacy settings, thus allowing for the greatest invention of new literacies, cultures, and identities (cf., Black, 2005; Dudfield, 1999).

Lewis and Fabos (2005) cautioned, however, that many of the same asymmetrical power relations apply to Internet settings, and that many of the same cognitive and linguistic skills are employed in engaging in online literacies. Experimentation on various Internet venues is not without consequence, but the possibilities for creativity are greater than in the constrained world of formal schooling when one type of literate practices and certain sets of texts are privileged (cf., Leander & Lovvorn, in press).

It is worth noting that it was challenging to find studies of youth actually engaged in digital literacies, particularly studies that moved beyond print-based forms (both Lewis & Fabos's, 2005, IM study and Dudfield's, 1999, MOOs study are print-focused). Knobel and Lankshear's (2002) examination of teen zines provided a starting place for studying how youth are using multiple forms of representation (e.g., oral, written, performed, pictorial, iconic, musical), but even Knobel & Lankshear's data represented many paper-and-pen-based forms. Eyman's (2005) study of college students using MOO (multiple user domains, object oriented) to "remediate" term papers in a college writing class provided a classroom-based example of uses of multiple forms of text, as did O'Brien's (1998) early work with struggling readers and writers in the "mediasphere" constructed via a high school literacy lab. Nevertheless, the list of studies that follow youth into digital worlds and the integration of multiple forms of representation outside of school is still developing.

To that end, Leander and McKim's (2003) call for a new ethnographic method that can more adequately and ethically (e.g., satisfy human subjects review boards) capture digital practices may pave the way for more work in this area. Such work is needed, many adolescent literacy scholars argue, because in the process of engaging with digital forms of texts, youth develop *new* literacies. That is, they develop literacy practices for gaining and maintaining the attention of others, for navigating across multiple texts quickly, and for critiquing the content and rhetorical strategies of the Web sites and their authors (Chandler-Olcott & Mahar, 2003; Coiro, 2003; Knobel & Lankshear, 2001; Lankshear & Knobel, 2002; Leu, 2005). It should be emphasized that these practices are necessary for paper texts as well, but are especially demanded in a global and technologized world where massive amounts of unedited information are available with the click of key. And it is these new literacies, cultures, and identities that potentially shape youth practices in classroom in school classrooms, and from which teachers of the visual and communicative arts may need to draw in order to capture the attention of youth who are busy capturing the attention of others in cyberspace (Lankshear & Knobel, 2002).

NEXT STEPS IN YCLI STUDIES

Removing literacy skill from the context of formal schooling—as has been accomplished in each of the studies mentioned—demonstrates that youth literacies are more than the qualities of individual cognition, more than static abilities to be learned, and more than basic comprehension of print alone. For many of the studies represented here, an examination of the relationship among youth literacies, cultures, and identities showed clearly that literacies could be considered to be tools used in everyday interactions to support and shape social practices, including the construction of youth cultures and related identities. Other studies similarly document the ideological and economic basis for engaging in particular literate practices, as well as the educational, economic, and political consequences of such engagements. Perhaps most important, these studies of literacy learning and use outside of school illustrated that individuals and groups often characterized as lacking in literacy abilities appeared to be fluent and capable readers and writers in contexts that valued their skills and allowed them to draw on other text forms to mediate their reading and writing with print. Finally, the youth cultural studies of literacy have illustrated that, when provided with freedom and opportunity, children, adolescents, and adults will experiment with new ways with words, and they will invent literate practices that meet the social demands and purposes of the setting. Such findings challenge literacy researchers and educators in the visual and communicative arts to find ways to adapt and study formal school settings to provide opportunities for invention, experimentation, and expanded literate possibilities and to link better to the worlds learners engage outside of school. At the same time, educators must tread lightly to avoid co-opting the pleasurable and "self-motivated" (Weinstein, 2002) practices of others for in-school gain. In addition, YCLI researchers must be wary of overgeneralizing the proficiencies of youth. In no cases that I could document, for example, have YCLI researchers, including me, assessed through some type of formal method the nature of reading or writing proficiency of youth reading out-of-school, everyday, peer, or popular-cultural texts. In addition, observations or assessments of proficiency with one group of youth do not translate to all groups of youth. Thus, YCLI researchers must be cautious about claims and seek ways to examine assumptions about the power and transfer of youth literacy skills and practices in and across multiple contexts and populations.

In sum, each of these studies, like many others in the growing body of peer group literacy practices, makes two critical points about literacy practices of youth in informal settings. First, what may seem on the surface to be deviant, resistant, or problematic practices can be tools for sense making, identity enactments, or formation of cultural practices and norms. These tools often require complex sets of sophisticated language and literacy skills that are not so cognitively different from—and certainly not less than—the literacies required in school settings (Mahiri, 2003; Moje, 2000). Second, the freedom afforded in informal settings to explore possibilities for interpreting and constructing all kinds of texts makes the literacies and accompanying texts potentially more motivating and more powerful than conventional, schooled literacies seem to be for youth, even though the practices share many of the same basic skill requirements. Thus, understanding the intersections among youth cultures, literacies, and identities can help the field better understand young people's motivations to read and write particular texts in particular ways. These studies thus have provided important insights into what youth care about, what they are invested in, and what they know. Such findings can be used to enhance youth learning and to multiply opportunities to learn. What those of us who study youth cultures, literacies, and identities have not done as well, however, is to link out-of-school—or youth cultural—literacies to those students are expected to learn in school (Hull & Schultz, 2002).

LINKING YCLI STUDIES WITH SCHOOL LITERACY/CULTURE/IDENTITY STUDIES

YCLI scholars have documented youth engaging in the skills that Guthrie and Metsala (1999) argued are necessary for high reading achievement on standardized measures: integrating information across multiple texts, relating textual meanings to personal experience, and composing complete messages in the form of stories and reports for actual audiences. Yet, the available standardized assessments of youths' literacy skills suggest that youth struggle with these skills in school. Why is there such a disparity in what we observe youth doing in ethnographic studies with literacy outside of school, as they engage with particular kinds of texts, and what we observe them doing in formal, standardized, constrained literacy activities? More important, how can we bridge that disparity with classroom practices designed to value youths' cultures, literacies, and identities, while also pushing them to develop new cultures, literacies, and identities?

Ingalls' (2005) study of youth's engagements in spoken-word performance out of school contrasted with their university and high school composition classes suggested some possible answers. First, Ingalls argued, we may need a different type of pedagogy in school, one that not only draws from what you know and do well outside of school, but one that explicitly attends to the differences in discursive practices and content knowledge demanded by the genres privileged in various textual activities and audiences. In short, YCLI researchers and theorists need to do more research on what it takes to explicitly navigate multiple genres and practices in attempts to construct "third spaces" in classrooms. Second, Ingalls borrowed from Bowden's (1993) metaphor of academic writing as *containment*, to argue that the writing classrooms are often seen by students as containing—and thus constraining—their writing practices. What makes Ingalls's research so interesting is that she demonstrated a similar containment in out-of-school spoken-word performances, but illustrates how spoken-word containment does not seem to constrain; rather, in many cases it provides an avenue for youth to express themselves, to take a voice, and to make change in their worlds (cf., Heath & Smyth, 1999; Alweis Productions & Heath, 2000). Ingalls's work thus underscored that the containment of language arts classrooms is a product as much from the discourses that shape activity and practice in classroom spaces as it is from the particular genres of writing themselves (cf., Leander & Lovvorn, 2006). Indeed, a number of researchers have documented that youth sanitize their experiences before introducing them to school classrooms (Fassio, 2000; Moje, Willes, D. J., & Fassio, 2002; Willis, A. I., 1995). The irony is that many YCLI researchers have worried about "co-opting" youth practices by bringing them into school; we might take a step back and realize that the danger of co-optation is minimal because the practices are so fundamentally changed as they enter classrooms spaces that youth fail to recognize or own the practices. Such findings suggest that YCLI researchers need to take steps to document and analyze how the structures of schooling mediate attempts to construct third spaces not only by drawing from what youth know, do, read, and write outside of school, but also by actively and explicitly teaching negotiation across different contexts and activities (Ingalls, 2005 Moje, Ciechanowski, Kramer, et al., 2004).

Although some scholars have made such connections in English language arts classes (e.g., Gallagher, 2007; Lee, 1993; 2001), there are fewer instances of sustained attempts to do so across the content areas (e.g., Moje, Ciechanowski, Kramer, et al., 2004; Morrell & Collatos, 2003). Gallagher's (2007) study makes the critical point that youths' experiences, and in some cases, texts, were taken up for academic purposes, neglecting to account for how purpose for engaging in a given literate practice shapes one's commitment to the practice and the texts associated with the practices. Moreover, in the few studies available, there is little information about the learning *outcomes* of those attempts. Lee's (1993) work was one of the few studies that measured student learning outcomes according to school-based, academic literacy measures.

What, then, should be the next steps of YCLI researchers? First, we need more studies in the tradition of Lee's (1993) work or Morrell and colleagues' research (Morrell, 2002; Morrell & Collatos, 2003; Morrell & Duncan-Andrade, 2003). Researchers should examine the skills that youth bring to their reading and writing of practices in and out of school (see Moje, Ciechanowski, Kramer, et al., 2004), and should document the effects on academic literacy learning of classroom initiatives to make connections across a variety of students' literacy practices. Even as they examine outcomes, however, researchers should be careful to publish descriptive and analytical accounts of the how teachers and students worked together, so that outcomes can be linked to particular practices. Finally, YCLI researchers should continue to theorize about the limits of building "third spaces" (Gutiérrez, Baquedano-López, Alvarez, & Chiu, 1999; Moje, Ciechanowski, Kramer, et al., 2004) by asking ourselves whether hybrids of popular cultural, community knowledge, and academic knowledge are always valuable or desirable? If not, then when are they most valuable? When are they desirable? What impact do they have on youths' school success? More research on innovative practices in this area is needed to advance youth literacy theory and youth literacy and content learning.

Adolescent literacy researchers have turned their attention to the cultural and literate practices of youth, but we risk descent into voyeurism if we do not move our research beyond an admiration for the exciting literacy practices in which youth engage. At the same time, the national attention to a certain conception of struggling adolescent readers threatens to turn attention solely to classrooms, with instruction framed by singular definitions of reading and writing. We thus risk an extreme bifurcation of the field, with some youth literacy researchers glorying in the sophistication of youths' out-of-school literacies and others lamenting the lack of strong academic literacy skills and developing programs of instruction designed to remediate the deficit. Both ends of this continuum deserve attention and integration or, as Peirce (1997) argued, we need to work toward "a third." If we hope to inform instruction and enhance learning opportunities for all youth, then youth literacy researchers need to find ways to merge the varied questions of adolescent and youth literacy into productive studies of the relationship among the literacies of youth cultural and identity groups and the literacies of secondary English language and visual arts classrooms.

REFERENCES

Alexander, P. (2003). Profiling the adolescent reader: The interplay of knowledge, interest, and strategic processing. In C. Fairbanks, J. Worthy, B. Maloch, J. V. Hoffman, & D. Schallert (Eds.), *52nd Yearbook of the National Reading Conference* (pp. 47–65). Oak Creek, WI: National Reading Conference.

Alvermann, D. E. (2001). Reading adolescents' reading identities: Looking back to see ahead. *Journal of Adolescent & Adult Literacy, 44*, 676–690.

Alvermann, D. E. (Ed.). (2002). *Adolescents and literacies in a digital world.* New York: Peter Lang.

Alvermann, D. E., Young, J. P., Green, C., & Wisenbaker, J. M. (1999). Adolescents' perceptions and negotiations of literacy practices in after-school read and talk clubs. *American Educational Research Journal, 36*, 221–264.

Alweis Productions (Producer), & Heath, S. B. (Director). (2000). *ArtShow: Youth and community development* [Motion picture]. Washington, DC: Partners for Livable Communities.

Arnett, J. J. (Ed.). (2002). *Adolescence and emerging adulthood* (1st ed.). Upper Saddle River, NJ: Prentice Hall.

Bennett, A. (2000). *Popular music and youth culture: Music, identity, and place.* Houndmills, U.K.: Palgrave.

Black, R. W. (2005, April). *(Tech)tual interaction: The dialogic nature of English language learners' activities in a fanfiction-based Website.* Paper presented at the American Educational Research Association, Montreál, Canada.

Blackburn, M. (2002). Disrupting the (hetero)normative: Exploring literacy performances and identity work with queer youth. *Journal of Adolescent & Adult Literacy, 46*, 312–325.

Bowden, D. (1993). The limits of containment: Text-as-container in composition studies. *College Composition and Communication, 44*, 364–379.

Bruce, B. C. (2002). Diversity and critical social engagement: How changing technologies enable new modes of literacy in changing circumstances. In D. E. Alvermann (Ed.), *Adolescents and literacies in a digital world* (pp. 1–18). New York: Peter Lang.

Camitta, M. (1993). Vernacular writing: Varieties of literacy among Philadelphia high school students. In B. V. Street (Ed.), *Cross-cultural approaches to literacy* (pp. 228–246). Cambridge, U.K.: Cambridge University Press.

Chandler-Olcott, K., & Mahar, D. (2003). "Tech-savviness" meets multiliteracies: Exploring adolescent girls' technology-mediated literacy practices. *Reading Research Quarterly, 38*, 356–385.

Chaney, D. (1996). *Lifestyles.* London: Routledge.

Coiro, J. (2003). Rethinking comprehension strategies to better prepare students for critically evaluating content on the internet. *The NERA Journal, 39*, 29–34.

Comaroff, J., & Comaroff, J. L. (2000). Millennial capitalism: First thoughts on a second coming. *Public Culture, 12*, 291–343.

Cowan, P. M. (2005). Putting it out there: Revealing Latino visual discourse in the Hispanic academic summer program for middle school students. In B. V. Street (Ed.), *Literacies across educational contexts: Mediating learning and teaching* (pp. 145–169). Philadelphia: Caslon Publishing.

Dressman, M., O'Brien, D. G., Rogers, T., Ivey, G., Wilder, P., Alvermann, D. E., et al. (2005). Problematizing adolescent literacies: Four instances, multiple perspectives. In J. V. Hoffman, D. L. Shallert, C. M. Fairbanks, J. Worthy & B. Maloch (Eds.), *55th yearbook of the National Reading Conference* (pp. 141–154). Oak Creek, Wisconsin: National Reading Conference.

Dudfield, A. (1999). Literacy and cyberculture. *Reading Online.* Retrieved date, from http://www.readingonline.org/articles/art_index.asp?HREF=dudfield/index.html

Eyman, D. (2005). Transformative remediation and multimodality in virtual environments. In V. Purcell-Gates (Ed.), *Cultural practices of literacy: Case studies of language, literacy, social practice, and power.* Mahwah, NJ: Lawrence Erlbaum Associates.

Fassio, K. J. (2000). *The politics of young students' lives and literacy practices.* Unpublished doctoral dissertation, University of Utah, Salt Lake City, Utah.

Finders, M. (2005). "Gotta be worse": Literacy, schooling, and adolescent youth offenders. In J. A. Vadeboncoeur & L. P. Stevens (Eds.), *Re/constructing "the adolescent": Sign, symbol, and body* (pp. 97–122). New York: Peter Lang.

Finders, M. J. (1997). *Just girls: Hidden literacies and life in junior high.* New York: Teachers College Press.

Gallagher, J. D. (2007). "You have to be bad or dumb to get in here": Reconsidering the in-school and out-of-school literacy practices of at-risk adolescents. In V. Purcell-Gates (Ed.), *Cultural practices of literacy: Case studies of language, literacy, social practice, and power* (pp. 155–168). Mahwah, NJ: Lawrence Erlbaum Associates.

Gee, J. P. (1996). *Social linguistics and literacies: Ideology in discourses* (2nd ed.). London: Falmer.

Gee, J. P. (2001). Identity as an analytic lens for research in education. In W. G. Secada (Ed.), *Review of research in education* (Vol. 25, pp. 99–126). Washington, DC: American Educational Research Association.

Gee, J. P. (2003). *What video games have to teach us about learning and literacy.* New York: Palgrave Macmillan.

Graff, H. (1987). *The legacies of literacy: Continuities and contradictions in western culture and society.* Bloomington, IN: University of Indiana Press.

Guthrie, J. T., & Metsala, J. L. (1999). Literacy in North America. In D. A. Wagner, R. L. Venezky, & B. V. Street (Eds.), *Literacy: An international handbook* (pp. 381–384). Boulder, CO: Westview Press.

Gutiérrez, K. D., Baquedano-López, P., Alvarez, H., & Chiu, M. M. (1999). Building a culture of collaboration through hybrid language practices. *Theory into Practice, 38*(2), 87–93.

Hagood, M. C., Stevens, L. P., & Reinking, D. (2002). What do *they* have to teach *us*? Talkin' 'cross generations! In D. E. Alvermann (Ed.), *Adolescents and literacies in a digital world* (pp. 68–83). New York: Peter Lang.

Hall, G. S. (1904). *Adolescence: Its psychology and its relations to psychology, anthropology, sociology, sex, crime, religion, and education.* New York: Appleton-Century-Crofts.

Heath, S. B. (1983). *Ways with words: Language, life, and work in communities and classrooms.* Cambridge, U.K.: Cambridge University Press.

Heath, S. B., & Smyth, L. (1999). *Artshow: A resource guide.* Washington, DC: Partners for Livable Communities.

Hull, G., & Schultz, K. (Eds.). (2002). *School's out! Bridging out-of-school literacies with classroom practice.* New York: Teachers College Press.

Hunt, M. (1996). *The sociolinguistics of tagging and Chicano gang graffiti.* Unpublished doctoral dissertation, University of Southern California, Los Angeles, California.

Ingalls, R. L. (2005). *Taking a page from their books: Negotiating containment and resuscitating rhetoric in writing across academic and spoken-word genres.* Unpublished doctoral dissertation, University of Michigan, Ann Arbor, Michigan.

Ivey, G. (2004, December). *Problematizing adolescent literacies.* Paper presented at the National Reading Conference, San Antonio, Texas.

Knobel, M., & Lankshear, C. (2002). Cut, paste, and publish: The production and consumption of 'zines. In D. E. Alvermann (Ed.), *Adolescents and literacies in a digital world* (pp. 164–185). New York: Peter Lang.

Lankshear, C., & Knobel, M. (2002). Do we have your attention? New literacies, digital technologies, and the education of adolescents. In D. E. Alvermann (Ed.), *Youth's multiliteracies in a digital world* (pp. 19–39). New York: Peter Lang.

Leander, K. M., & Lovvorn, J. (2007). Literacy networks: Following the circulation of texts, bodies, and objects in the schooling and online gaming of one youth. *Cognition & Instruction, 24*(3), 291–340.

Leander, K. M., & McKim, K. K. (2003). Tracing the everyday 'sittings' of adolescents on the Internet: A strategic adaptation of ethnography across online and offline spaces. *Education, Communication, & Information, 3*(2), 211–240.

Lee, C. D. (1993). *Signifying as a scaffold for literary interpretation: The pedagogical implications of an African American discourse genre* (NCTE Research Report, No 26). Urbana, IL: National Council of Teachers of English.

Lee, C. D. (2001). Is October Brown Chinese? A cultural modeling activity system for underachieving students. *American Educational Research Journal, 38*(1), 97–141.

Lesko, N. (2001). *Act your age! A cultural construction of adolescence.* New York: Routledge Falmer.

Leu, D. (2005, December). *New literacies, reading research, and the challenges of change: A deictic perspective of our research worlds.* Paper presented at the National Reading Conference, Miami, Florida.

Lewis, C., & Fabos, B. (2005). Instant messaging, literacies, and social identities. *Reading Research Quarterly, 40*, 470–501

Lewis, C., & Finders, M. (2002). Implied adolescents and implied teachers: A generation gap for new times. In D. E. Alvermann (Ed.), *Adolescents and literacies in a digital world* (pp. 101–113). New York: Peter Lang.

Luke, A. (1996). Text and discourse in education: An introduction to critical discourse analysis. In M. W. Apple (Ed.), *Review of research in education* (Vol. 21, pp. 3–48). Washington, DC: American Educational Research Association.

Luke, C. (2002). Re-crafting media and ict literacies. In D. E. Alvermann (Ed.), *Adolescents and literacies in a digital world* (pp. 132–146). New York: Peter Lang.

Mahiri, J. (Ed.). (2003). *What they don't learn in school: Literacy in the lives of urban youth.* New York: Peter Lang.

Moje, E. B. (2000). To be part of the story: The literacy practices of gangsta adolescents. *Teachers College Record, 102*, 652–690.

Moje, E. B. (2002). But where are the youth: Integrating youth culture into literacy theory. *Educational Theory, 52*, 97–120.

Moje, E. B. (2004). Powerful spaces: Tracing the out-of-school literacy spaces of Latino/a youth. In K. Leander & M. Sheehy (Eds.), *Space matters: Assertions of space in literacy practice and research* (pp. 15–38). New York: Peter Lang.

Moje, E. B., & Ciechanowski, K. M. (2002, April). *Literacy, language, and life in the millennial world: A study of Latino/a youth literacy in one urban community.* Paper presented at the American Educational Research Association, New Orleans, Louisiana.

Moje, E. B., Ciechanowski, K. M., Kramer, K. E., Ellis, L. M., Carrillo, R., & Collazo, T. (2004). Working toward third space in content area literacy: An examination of everyday funds of knowledge and discourse. *Reading Research Quarterly, 39*, 38–71.

Moje, E. B., & Lewis, C. (in press). Examining opportunities to learn literacy: The role of critical sociocultural literacy research. In C. Lewis, P. Enciso, & E. B. Moje (Eds.), *Identity, agency, and power: Reframing sociocultural research in literacy.* Mahwah, NJ: Lawrence Erlbaum Associates.

Moje, E. B., & van Helden, C. (2005). Doing popular culture: Troubling discourses about youth. In J. A. Vadeboncoeur, & L. P. Stevens (Eds.), *Re/constructing 'the adolescent': Sign, symbol and body* (pp. 211–248). New York: Peter Lang.

Moje, E. B., Willes, D. J., & Fassio, K. (2001). Constructing and negotiating literacy in the writer's workshop: Literacy teaching and learning in seventh grade. In E. B. Moje, & D. G. O'Brien (Eds.), *Constructions of literacy: Studies of teaching and learning literacy in and out of secondary classrooms* (pp. 193–212). Mahwah, NJ: Lawrence Erlbaum Associates.

Morrell, E. (2002). Toward a critical pedagogy of popular culture: Literacy development among urban youth. *Journal of Adolescent & Adult Literacy, 46*, 72–77.

Morrell, E., & Collatos, A. (2003, April). *Critical pedagogy in a college access program for students of color.* Paper presented at the American Educational Research Association, Chicago, Illinois.

Morrell, E., & Duncan-Andrade, J. (2003). What they do learn in school: Hip-hop as a bridge to canonical poetry. In J. Mahiri (Ed.), *What they don't learn in school: Literacy in the lives of urban youth* (pp. 247–268). New York: Peter Lang.

O'Brien, D. G. (1998). Multiple literacies in a high school program for "at-risk" adolescents. In D. E. Alvermann, K. A. Hinchman, D. W. Moore, S. Phelps, & D. Waff (Eds.), *Reconceptualizing the literacies in adolescents' lives* (pp. 27–49). Mahwah, NJ: Lawrence Erlbaum Associates.

O'Brien, D., & King, J. R. (2002). Adolescents' multiliteracies and their teachers' needs to know: Toward a digital detente. In D. E. Alvermann (Ed.), *Adolescents and literacies in a digital world* (pp. 40–50). New York: Peter Lang.

Peirce, C. S. (1997). *The collected papers of Charles Sanders Peirce* (Book 3). Cambridge, MA: InteLex Corp.

Purcell-Gates, V. (Ed.). (in press). *Cultural practices of literacy: Case studies of language, literacy, social practice, and power.* Mahwah, NJ: Lawrence Erlbaum Associates.

Radway, J. (1984). *Reading the romance: Women, patriarchy and popular literature.* Chapel Hill, NC: University of North Carolina Press.

Roeser, R. W., Peck, S. C., & Nasir, N. S. (2007). Self and identity processes in school motivation, learning and achievement. In P. Alexander, & P. H. Winne (Ed.), *Handbook of research on educational psychology* (2nd ed., pp. 391–424). Mahwah, NJ: Lawrence Erlbaum Associates.

Rogers, R. (2002). Between contexts: A critical analysis of family literacy, discursive practices, and literate subjectivities. *Reading Research Quarterly, 37*(3), 248–277.

Schultze, Q. J., Anker, R. M., Bratt, J. C., Romanowski, W. D., Worst, J. W., & Zuidervaart, L. (1991). *Dancing in the dark: Youth, popular culture, and the electronic media.* Grand Rapids, MI: William B. Eerdmans.

Scribner, S., & Cole, M. (1981). *The psychology of literacy.* Cambridge, MA: Harvard University Press.

Shuman, A. (1986). *Storytelling rights: The uses of oral and written texts by urban adolescents.* Cambridge, U.K.: Cambridge University Press.

Smith, D. (1997). Tagging: A way to make meaning. In D. Taylor, D. Coughlin, & J. Marasco (Eds.), *Teaching and advocacy* (pp. 125–142). York, ME: Stenhouse Publishers.

Stanley, J. (2003). Practicing for romance: Adolescent girls read the romance novel. In J. Mahiri (Ed.), *What they don't learn in school: Literacy in the lives of urban youth* (pp. 169–180). New York: Peter Lang.

Stevens, L. P. (2004, December). *What's so 'adolescent' about adolescent literacy?* Paper presented at the National Reading Conference, San Antonio, Texas.

Street, B. V. (1994). Cross cultural perspectives on literacy. In J. Maybin (Ed.), *Language and literacy in social practice* (pp. 139–150). Clevedon, U.K.: Open University.

Sutton, S. S. (2003). Spoken word: Performance poetry in the black community. In J. Mahiri (Ed.), *What they don't learn in school: Literacy in the lives of urban youth* (pp. 213–242). New York: Peter Lang.

Tajfel, H. (1982). *Social identity and intergroup relations.* New York: Cambridge University Press.

Trainor, J. S. (2003). Critical cyberliteracy: Reading and writing the X-files. In J. Mahiri (Ed.), *What they don't learn in school: Literacy in the lives of urban youth* (pp. 123–138). New York: Peter Lang.

van Helden, C. J. L. (2002). *Critical discourse studies of youth lifestyle media: Sexuality and polyvalent meaning.* Unpublished master's thesis, Amsterdam, The Netherlands: University of Amsterdam.

Volosinov, V. N. (1973). *Marxism and the philosophy of language* (I. R. Titunik, Trans.). New York: Seminar Press.

Vygotsky, L. S. (1978). *Mind in society.* In M. Cole, V. John-Steiner, S. Scribner, & U. E. Souberman (Eds.). Cambridge, MA: Harvard University Press.

Weinstein, S. (2002). The writing on the wall: Attending to self-motivated student literacies. *English Education, 35*(1), 21–45.

Willis, A. I. (1995). Reading the world of school literacy: Contextualizing the experience of a young African American male. *Harvard Educational Review, 65*, 30–49.

•23•

A WORLD OF EXPANDING LITERACIES: AUDIO VISUAL AND NONLINEAR DIGITAL FORMS IN EVERYDAY LIFE

JoEllen Fisherkeller
NEW YORK UNIVERSITY

ABSTRACT

The global predominance of multiple media cultures and systems that use audiovisual and nonlinear digital forms of communication challenge traditional schooling principles and practices, which are thoroughly based in print literacy. Today's students are aware tacitly, and sometimes explicitly, of the value (economically, socially, politically) of audiovisual and digital media—especially as they are part of an image making system that relies on celebrities, branding, and other means of giving symbols power in the contemporary world. In this chapter, I briefly review how schools have established print literacy development as the dominant purpose of schooling, as well as survey the presence and power of audiovisual and digital forms and systems of communication in the contemporary world. I locate adolescent understandings of commercial media as forms and systems within everyday social contexts and discuss the implications of their situated understandings. In closing, I call for educators and policy makers to teach students to create a new future for society by being critical media consumers and producers.

In the late 19th century in the United States, public schooling developed as mandatory for all youth in response to several social conditions of the time. The forces of industrialization drew families married to agrarian lifestyles into urban areas where factory and new industry work was promising. Economic and political situations in other lands prompted people to migrate to the United States in pursuit of careers and lifestyles not predetermined (or so it seemed) by feudal or class-based destinies. These migrations brought together culturally diverse groups that did not necessarily have the skills necessary to survive in the new industrial economy and might not speak the same languages. Likewise, members of these migratory groups were not well prepared as citizens and needed to know how to interpret and act on information and ideas pertinent to democratic governing systems.

Public schooling was conceived of and implemented as a means of providing all young people with the knowledge and skills that would enable them to be effective workers in the industrialized economy and knowledgeable and capable actors in a common public sphere (Graff, 1987). Since the dominant media of communication at this time were face-to-face talk, songs, and all manner of written and printed matter (books, letters, periodicals, newspapers, etc.), schooling emphasized the teaching of spoken and written language and literacy. Thus, ideally, if schools taught all young people how to speak and hear standard English effectively and to read and write standard English competently, all would have the means to become successful and participatory members of American society.

Today, economic and political situations once again prompt migrations that bring together culturally diverse groups whose members have to learn the knowledge and skills necessary to be effective workers and active citizens in new environments. However, the scope and nature of the industrial and governing systems people must negotiate today are quite different compared to those in the late 19th century, so that even nonmigrants are challenged as they prepare themselves for work and civic life. Technological advancements and globalization processes create a situation requiring all people in post-industrial countries to engage with workplaces and public spaces where networked information systems, utilizing multiple forms of communication and distribution, are ubiquitous. A sea of symbolic visuals and sounds generated and circulated via digital, electronic, and print-based media, permeate business, politics, and everyday life. Extrapolating on the rationale for teaching language and literacy when speech and writing forms were the dominant means of communication, young people today must be competent with all forms of communication that dominate the postindustrial marketplace and civic life (New London Group, 1996; Tyner, 1998). These include the following media/technologies:[1] an array of computer software and online environments; television, film, and a range of video and digital recorders and players; radio and a range of sound recorders and players; photographic imagery and cameras; video, handheld, and computer games; and cell-phone, pager, and palm-data devices.

Most youth encounter many of these media/technologies when away from school as consumers (if they can afford them, financially and time wise) or as audiences of messages and images that promote the need for owning and using these media/technologies. Students might use computers at school to play educational games, search Web sites and databases for information, and to do word processing. Students might be exposed to audiovisual media at school when their teachers use them to present subject matter relevant to the mandated curriculum. In these cases, digital and audiovisual media are often electronic substitutes for print-based texts that have historically, and officially, supported teaching and learning.

However, in schools in the United States, most youth do not learn about digital and audiovisual media as different forms and systems of communication, and they do not learn to use these media/technologies to express themselves (Kubey, 1997; Tyner, 1998). In this chapter, I frame, explain, and justify the following assertions about what young people need to know as they grow up in the contemporary multimediated environment. First, young people need to learn to think about digital and audiovisual media as symbolic objects, because these objects often convey messages, overtly and covertly, and images that are not representative of the full range of human experiences and global situations. Second, young people need to investigate the role that digital and audiovisual media play in their lives and society, because these media/technologies are an important part of economic, social, and political systems, all of which have very real consequences for their individual and collective possibilities. Third, young people should learn to create audiovisual and digital media, so that all can participate in the systems of production and distribution that are powerful forces in society, and exclude many diverse voices and images. Ideally, if young people learn to understand and use all media and communication technologies, they will be prepared for work and civic life as multiply literate human beings (Fisherkeller, 2000; New London Group, 1996; Tyner, 1998).

[1] My use of the term *media/technologies* is purposeful, as I intend to be all inclusive when referring to all of the audio, visual, and digital forms of communication that characterize the contemporary landscape. Typically, the term *media* is used to refer to mass communications, whereas the term *technology* is used to refer to computers and online communications. I am combining these terms to reference all forms, as I regard them all as media (e.g., means of communication) and as technologies (e.g., tools of communication). However, for convenience sake, I sometimes use the term *media* to refer only to all communication technologies.

WORLDS OF AUDIO VISUAL AND DIGITAL MEDIA

In postindustrial countries, it is hard to imagine life without media and communication technologies, whether considering the worlds of commerce, politics, leisure and recreation, or everyday practical functioning. Statistical analyses give a broad stroke indication of the position of media and technologies in the U.S. economy. Tables provided by the Bureau of Economic Analysis in the U.S. Department of Commerce show that in the year 2003, the media, information, and recreation industries—including publishing, motion pictures, broadcasting, information and data processing, computer/electronic products and systems design, and arts, entertainment, and recreation such as sports and theme parks—totaled $1784.4 billion in gross domestic product output.[2] The figures in this table do not include a category called "private goods and services" that has an output totaling more than $12,000 billion, a portion of which includes media, information, and recreation industries as well.[3] A report compiled by the International Intellectual Property Alliance showed that between 1977 and 2001, the U.S. copyright industries (including media and information producers of all kinds) grew more than twice as fast as the remainder of the U.S. economy. Within that same time, average annual employment in copyright industries grew more than three times as fast as the rest of the economy, and by 2001, foreign sales and exports in this sector were estimated at $88.97 billion, leading all major industry sectors, including chemicals and allied products, motor and aircraft vehicles and parts, and agriculture.[4]

What such statistics do not reveal is that the bulk of audiovisual and digital media that young people in the United States (and increasingly, around the world) encounter are created and sustained by commercial industries that are huge transnational enterprises. The majority of these mega-enterprises consist of companies that generate and circulate media in the form of computer program applications, Web sites, TV and radio programming, recorded music, movies, electronic games, newspapers, magazines, comics, and advertising. Media-making industries develop and distribute these media forms to compete in the corporate capitalist economic system, thus media makers intend to make a profit from their media wares (McChesney, 2004).

The profit-oriented sensibility of media-making industries affects the nature of media, in terms of the messages and images that media convey, as well as media styles and formats. Commercial media are supported by advertisers who target particular audiences in terms of how likely audiences are to purchase particular brands and styles of consumer goods, including media/technologies and nonmedia items such as soap, cars, and medicine. Advertisers seek to attract large target audiences in all age groups, but they are especially interested in grabbing the attention of masses of consumers with discretionary

[2] See U.S. Department of Commerce, Bureau of Economic Analysis Web site, Retrieved December 20, 2004, from http://www.bea.gov/bea/industry/gpotables/gpo_action.cfm?anon=15804&table_id=4133&format_type=0

[3] The total GDP output in 2003 was $19,732.8 billion; other categories include Agriculture, Mining, Manufacturing, Construction, Wholesale/Retail, Finance and Insurance, Transportation, Real Estate, Health, Professional, Educational, Scientific, and Government. See citation in footnote 2.

[4] See International Intellectual Property Alliance archives, Retrieved December 22, 2004, from http://www.iipa.com/pressreleases/2002_Apr22_SIWEK-rev.pdf_ Many thanks to Dr. Ted Madder for his help in locating these resources.

incomes who have decision-making options, providing them with a relatively wide array of choices (Miller, 1988). Commercial media thus target mass audiences in the middle and upper classes. This results in fare that generally appeals to these audiences' mainstream values and tastes, and also leads to the creation of content that is entertaining so as not to offend anyone with provocative points of view (Comstock, 1980), and that is stereotypical and formulaic, since such content is regarded as efficient in gaining mass-audience recognition (Gerbner, Gross, Morgan, & Signorielli, 1994; Lembo, 2000).

Sensational and spectacular styles and formats are also favored as a means of drawing audiences' attentions away from the sea of media that glut the symbolic environment. Rapid-fire deliveries, flashy movements, catchy sounds, famous celebrities, special effects, and glitzy, splashy adornments of all kinds characterize the look, feel, and sound of most commercial audiovisual and digital media forms. Programmers and advertisers target young audiences in particular via these strategies to secure young people's brand and product loyalties early on.

Many scholars and critics claim that the biased, formulaic, and sensational nature of commercial media have negative consequences for individuals and society. For example, some argue that commercial media erode our ability to learn about and reflect on issues vital to the public sphere (Postman, 1985). Furthermore, these media expose youngsters in particular to behaviors that are socially inappropriate (Meyrowitz, 1985) and reinforce the status quo of society, making it difficult if not impossible to accomplish necessary social change (Klapper, 1960). In addition, scores of media-content analyses reveal that entertainment media are loaded with stereotypes as well as lacking in representations of some social groups. This symbolically silences many of the voices that need and want to be heard, if principles of democratic equality and opportunity are to be upheld (Gerbner, et al. 1994; Means Coleman, 2000).

Others deplore how commercial media encourage needless consumerism, depleting the world's resources and diverting people's critical attention away from issues and problems in the civic and political realm (Clark, 1998; Kinder, 1999; Sefton-Greene, 1998; Steinberg & Kincheloe, 1997). Yet since the commercial media are seen to engage people so effectively as consumers, politicians and policymakers in the United States spend extraordinary sums of money to create and distribute media messages and images promoting their campaign and policy agendas (McIlwain & Caliendo, 2004). Globalization processes that introduce commercial media into local cultures that have norms, values, and ideas that may be strongly divergent from those represented by media systems, contents, and forms intensify these issues (Schiller, 1989).

Young people spend a great deal of time with media on a daily basis. Indeed, some claim that young people spend more time, over time, with media than they do at school, and since youth spend time with media both in and out of school, this might be the case. According to one report, young people ages 8 to 18 spend an average of 6.5 hours every day using media of some kind. Television is used the most, as young people watch approximately 4 hours per day. The next most used medium is music, listened to 2 hours per day. Young people use the computer for fun about 1 hour, play electronic games about 50 minutes every day, and read for pleasure about 45 minutes every day (Rideout, Roberts, & Foehr, 2005).

What these figures do not show is how often young people multitask, since many listen to music and/or have the television on at the same time as they do other activities, such as homework, chores, and eating, as well as use other media such as computers and online environments, magazines and comics, and/or talk on the phone (see Buckingham, 2000; Holloway & Valentine, 2003; Fisherkeller, 2002).

In sum, media systems, forms, and messages are ever more ubiquitous and pervasive as part and parcel of national and global political economies, and the everyday lives of young people. Given this reality, we need to consider how media play a role in the development of young people's sensibilities as workers in the contemporary environment, and as citizens in local and global societies. To do so, we must come to terms with how youth develop and learn, given established theories of development and learning, as well as current ideas about how young people themselves are coming to participate (or not) in the workplaces and public spheres that are permeated by the media.

AUDIO VISUAL AND DIGITAL MEDIA IN EVERYDAY CONTEXTS

In general, social constructivist perspectives argue that young people constantly make sense of their experiences based on their existing understandings about the world they live in and the world of media (Bryant & Anderson, 1983; Dorr, 1986; Kelly & Gardner, 1981; Wartella, 1979). These perspectives relate to cultural and media-studies approaches to children and adolescents that regard young people (and all people) as "active interpreters" of culture and of media/technologies rather than passive receivers of the messages and images conveyed by both cultural activity and media (Buckingham, 1993). All of these perspectives rely on a basic assumption about people as "agents" who come to terms with various social and cultural institutions, forms, and processes that structure human experience, but can be variously negotiated by particular individuals (Geertz, 1983; Goffman, 1959; Hall, 1980). Likewise, these perspectives all acknowledge the roles that different contexts play in people's interpretations of their experiences, and the subsequent learning that might occur (Eisenhart, 1995; Lave & Wenger, 1991; Wolcott, 1982).

Young people interact with countless forms of audiovisual and digital media when at home, while with their friends, and in various public spaces such as schools, neighborhoods, or shopping and recreation centers. All of these contexts, and the people who participate in them, give shape to the kinds of experiences young people have when they interact with media, and the learning that can ensue. That is, the material and social contexts of everyday life affect how young people use, value, and find meaning in media interactions (Buckingham, 1993, 2000; see also Lull, 1990).

Family systems and interactive styles affect how young people select and talk about media experienced at home (Alexander, Ryan, & Munoz, 1984; Messaris & Sarett, 1981; Reid & Frazer, 1980a, 1980b) and how youth "play with" and make sense of the content and forms of media (Bryce & Leichter, 1983; Palmer, 1986). Cultural and social norms about how parents should socialize their children, and about media materials in particular, inform how young people engage with media. Generally, it is assumed that families should control and screen their youngsters' media (Dorr, 1986; Singer, Singer, & Zuckerman, 1981). These studies suggested that families help youngsters incorporate media into their behavioral and belief systems.

Thus far, I have been writing in broad and general terms about young people, media/technologies, social and cultural contexts, and learning. In this section, I focus specifically (at times) on case study material from in-depth, ethnographic research I conducted with a small group of adolescents in New York City[5] to illustrate how particular young people negotiate and learn from their experiences with real people and media/technologies while located in particular everyday situations.

I argue that families provide young people with powerful frameworks for defining their personal goals and objectives, as well as their motivations for social and cultural achievements. These frameworks and motivations in turn influence how youth use and interpret media (Fisherkeller, 2002). For example, a 12-year-old New Yorker named Marina[6] came to the United States with her mother, who wanted a better life than what was possible in the Dominican Republic. Marina also wanted a better life for herself in the future, as her plan was to go to college, and "get a career that pays well" before marrying and having children. Marina wanted to escape the poor, working-class circumstances she lived with, a consequence of her mother's low-income job as a childcare worker with limited English skills and no degrees. Coming to this country, Marina saw "the good life" that she wanted on television. Indeed, she imagined living like the TV character Angela Bower who was one of the main figures in the situation comedy *Who's the Boss* (ABC, 1984–1992). Marina admired Angela Bower because she had a big house, nice clothes, and had "made something of herself" by running her own advertising agency. Advertising was even a career that Marina considered for herself because she thought it was amazing how some advertisers "(come) up with ideas for things" that could "really strike people," like an antidrug public service announcement she appreciated because it "gets their attention." Marina likewise admired Madonna, the highly successful pop-icon who is well known in part for challenging the social constraints of female sexuality and power. Marina admired Madonna because she was successful as a singer, dancer, and a media producer in charge of her own company (and thus her own image), and also because "she (Madonna) keeps going and going and going no matter what people say about her" provocative expressions. This aspect of Madonna's persona is important to Marina because Marina's personality and her family's Dominican heritage guide her to be proud of her mature female form and show it off via clothing, movement, and attitude (Pastor, McCormick & Fine, 1996).

Another specific example of family's influence on how young people use and interpret media is found in the case of a 12-year-old African American named Christopher. Like Marina, Christopher wanted a better life, having grown up in poor, working-class neighborhoods and housing situations, a consequence of his divorced parents' lower-income occupations. Christopher's father and other males in his large extended family motivated him to pursue a business career that would catapult him beyond the small apartment dwellings people of his color and class can afford. Christopher looked toward Bill Cosby as a role model, since Cosby was a successful Black male in a society dominated by White males. While Christopher did know personally any Blacks from his "real life" who had professional jobs such as lawyer or doctor—the positions held by Claire and Cliff Huxtable, the parent characters on *The Cosby Show*, (NBC, 1984–1992)—Christopher knew of actual parents who would "handle certain situations" in the way that the show's fictional parents did. That is, he knew of real people, like the Cosby characters, who would "raise their children right" when faced with similar everyday problems—a feature of the show that earned it praise as well as awards. Christopher's own father told him to "walk tall, walk straight up," taught him the "right thing to do," and gave him "confidence in (him)self." Thus, while Christopher strove to move up and away from his family's economic and occupational circumstances, his family's way of "handling situations" contributed to his interest in Bill Cosby's version of success.

Peers and social life at school also influence how youth use and interpret the media/technologies in their lives. Youth frequently watch and listen to programs and stations that are popular among their peers, coming together at school or during leisure times to exchange jokes, songs, dance moves, gestures, fashion styles, and other symbolic elements found in media (Buckingham, 1993, 2000; Dyson, 2003, 1997; Palmer, 1988; Willis, 1990).For example, Teniya Serita, an 11-year-old Latina, said she watches comedies on TV "'cause I like to laugh and stuff, I like to hear jokes , so I could tell my friends and stuff" (Fisherkeller, 2002). Youth often use popular media to express their identities in relation to, and perhaps as distinct from, others in their peer groups (Buckingham, 2000; Dyson, 2003, 1997; Fisherkeller, 2002; Steele & Brown, 1995). Many youth join fan clubs where they associate with other fans and sometimes make friends through mediated activity (Jenkins; 1992; Lewis, 1990). Sherry Turkle (1982; 1995) describes how some adolescents immerse themselves in video games and online simulations to explore aspects of their selves not readily expressed in their actual social worlds, as well as to share strategies of play with friends.

Experiences of the actual social world influence how young people use and interpret new digital media/technologies as well. If they have access, youth use instant messaging, e-mail, chat rooms, bulletin boards, and personal Web sites to communicate with each other one on one, one to many, and many to many about issues and aspects of everyday life that they share (Clark, 1998; Holloway & Valentine, 2003; Stern, 2002). For instance, Lynn Schofield Clark (1998) found that, when dating online, teenage girls and boys speak out in ways they cannot in face-to-face situations. The teens she interviewed claimed that their connections with others online were more authentic, since they could exchange thoughts and emotions that they could not "in real life," where they worry about biases against their physical appearances and offline social competencies. However, Clark noted that the apparent openness of teens' online dating rarely les to teens creating changes in their offline experience of bias against their appearances and competencies. At the same time, the faceless nature of online dating that allows for openness in communication seems to allow for a less-committed stance toward relationships overall.

In sum, family and peer contexts give a general shape to young people's uses and interpretations of media/technologies, while youth actively negotiate their particular experiences of actual and mediated worlds. What might young people learn about being success-

[5] This ethnographic research was conducted at an alternative public middle school over a period of 18 months in the early 1990s, with follow-up interviews taking place with the same case study individuals when they were in high school and then in college. In *Growing Up with Television: Everyday Learning Among Young Adolescents* (Fisherkeller, 2002), the Appendix on "Methodological Notes" describes more fully the approach, setting, participant profiles, and specific methods used to obtain the quotes and understandings I report on here.

[6] The participants in my research chose their own pseudonyms.

ful members of the contemporary workforce and participants in the public sphere, given the complex nature of their experiences with real people and media/technologies? What do young people learn about media/technologies as tools and systems that have power in the world? These questions are important, considering the role that education plays in helping all young people become literate in the dominant discourses of culture and society, and thus competent workers and active citizens.

LEARNING TO "MAKE IT" IN THE WORLD OF EXPANDED LITERACIES

Young people growing up today learn about how to be successful workers and how to be active participants in the public sphere through several contexts. Via local contexts, youth acquire information about the worlds of work through their parents, adult siblings, and extended family members, who might talk explicitly about the value and meaning of different kinds of work, and whose jobs and occupations give them implicit understandings about their position within structures of power. The individual youth discussed earlier, Marina and Christopher, knew that their parents' lines of work were not in the upper echelon of the social hierarchy, and in part this prompted both of them to aspire toward careers that would move them into the middle class, at least (Fisherkeller, 2002). Similarly, kids learn locally about work worlds through their teachers, the parents and family of their friends, and by coming into contact with workers in the establishments that they frequent, which vary depending on their social and material location. For example, youth in lower-income neighborhoods in New York City have regular contact with workers in the eateries, shops, and governmental and nonprofit organizations that service their communities. These local contacts provide youth with information about the actual requirements of these jobs and help them learn, tacitly, about the relative power and success of such positions.

Youth learn about participation in the public sphere in local contexts via adults in their communities who might be variously involved in local politics, whether official or not. When Christopher was 12, he observed his father facilitate meetings and engage in organizational planning activities that resulted in his apartment building being converted to a co-operational facility, which was owned and managed by its residents instead of being beholden to distant landlords (Fisherkeller, 2002). From this experience, I argue that Christopher acquired a sense of what it takes to participate in local governance and ground-level democratic decision making. Youth also learn about governance and democracy by participating in student and youth councils in their local contexts.

However, many youth acquire their sensibilities about the worlds of work and the public sphere through their experiences with commercial media. Depictions of the professions and positions that wield power in society dominate commercial media, especially television. Young people look to these depictions, and strive toward the success and power they represent, sometimes selecting future careers because of how glamorous they look in media. Yet even if they do not select a future career from among media depictions, youth are aware of the fame and fortune attached to certain professions and of the prestige given to public figures appearing in the media.

Young people today are also aware, at some level, that media makers, or the people who participate in the production and distribution of media (as producers, actors, writers, designers, technicians, etc.) are powerful and successful. Their awareness is implicit in their consumption of media, and suggested by their understandings about media systems of production and distribution. As consumers, young people know, whether consciously or not, that their worlds are permeated by media, informed by their own and other's consumption habits and by the amount of media available to them (Buckingham, 2000). They know that they can turn on the television and find hundreds of channels of programming available 24 hours a day, 7 days a week. They can turn on the radio and likewise scan for music programs across the dial, also available 24/7. They can walk into any number of video, music, and game stores, and go online, and be surrounded by scads of digitized discs and cassette tapes categorized according to the countless genres and subgenres that they know belong to these media forms. In these same stores or in bookstores, they can also find magazines tailored to all stripes of lifestyles and interests, as well as comics, popular fiction, and nonfiction informational texts that cover the gamut of everyday activities. Or, if they have access, they can go online and search thousands of Web sites, many of which are devoted to the distribution of media software (such as videos, music, games, books, and computer applications) as well as hardware. At the same time, through the Internet and increasingly, through cell phone, pager technologies, and digital cameras, young people who have access to these can communicate with others via text, visuals, and sounds that they can input, download, upload, and create from scratch.

As consumers, young people are also aware of some of the processes and strategies that contribute to the production and distribution of these media and technologies. Their awareness develops informally, through their hours and hours of engagement with the different commercial media in their everyday lives. Through their engagements with media every day, they perceive of patterns built into the system (Buckingham, 2000; Davies, 1996). In my own research (Fisherkeller, 2000), I found that young adolescents develop tacit understandings about television (in particular) as a system of communication with specific features and purposes in the Unites States. These adolescents' awareness of the system falls within three general categories. The first category includes their making judgments about what they prefer based on how different programs, stories, and characters are constructed. Young adolescents develop a sense of what makes a good story on television, or a sense about those elements of construction that make suspension of disbelief possible—a perception necessary for appreciating the ideas of any fictional construction. Like the viewers in Lembo's (2000) study of adults, adolescents know that television is not "real life" but they do evaluate programs based on how realistic programs seem to be, or on how well the emotional, moral, and aesthetic dimensions of programs represent plausible versions of reality. For example, 11-year-old Kelly, an Italian American, judged stories both in print and on TV based on how "believable" they were:

> (The stories I like) they're just written well. The situations are believable . . . (or) the characterization is really good. Like there was this trilogy that I started reading. And it had the most unbelievable situation, it had vampires and werewolves and curses and stuff. But the characters were just really believable. . . . (But on the cable TV comedy show) *Hey Dude* (Nickelodeon, 1989–1991) well, they're all too farfetched. . . . It's just that they're all 17-year-olds, and they do the most unbelievable things . . .

(The girl I really dislike is) too nice, well, she's just like, she's so nice she can't possibly exist. (Fisherkeller, 2000, p. 596)

And Teniya Serita, an 11-year-old Puerto-Rican American, saw how TV stories have typical kinds of characters that play off of each other, which is a familiar device of storytelling:

In almost all shows they have to (have someone) like, dumb, like, "duh," you know, doofy. (And) someone always has to be the oddball. (And someone always has to be conceited, or thinking she's the best . . . (And) one who, let's say, is teacher's pet, or someone who likes someone else [who doesn't like them in return]. (Fisherkeller, 2000, pp. 596–597)

In their qualitative studies, Buckingham (1996), Davies (1996), and Hodge and Tripp (1986) also found that children as young as six and adolescents make similar judgments about the constructed nature of television and film stories, using their own knowledge of "real" social and physical realms along with standards for crafting a story. Print-literacy educators might recognize how these evaluative processes embody basic concepts about the workings of genre, character, plot, thematic development, and authorship.

The second category of understanding about television as a system is associated with the nature and logic of TV programming and scheduling. Kelly lamented some of the decisions made by TV programmers:

They cancelled (a show I liked). I thought it was canceled a long time ago, but they were like showing it in the mornings, on Saturdays, but apparently, nobody was watching in. In the summer and the springtime they don't have any new shows on or anything, it's all the same stuff. They don't make any new episodes, it's just the same ones over and over again. (Fisherkeller, 2000, p. 597)

Kelly knows something about how programs make it, or not, based on viewership. Samantha, an 11-year-old Irish/Jewish American demonstrates explicit knowledge of the relationship between ratings and program strategies. She was a fan of talk shows, even though sometimes she was disgusted with their tactics:

Sometimes) I go, "oh god, I can't believe this is really true," like neo-Nazis and stuff like that. Like we all know people like that really exist, but we don't want to know, you know? And that's why they put them on these shows, "'Cause they do get the ratings, you know? They get the number one. (Fisherkeller, 2000, p. 601)

Both Kelly and Samantha, and others in this study, understand something about the relationship between audiences and the logic of programming, and see cyclical patterns of TV programming. Likewise, they know, implicitly, how TV targets particular audiences, such as people their age, or adults their parents' ages. They know this experiencing their own viewing patterns, especially changes in those patterns. That is, normally they find programming featuring youthful stars and youth-oriented themes during after-school hours, early evenings, and weekend nights and days. However, when young people have to stay home from school because they are sick, they find very different kinds of fare on television, as daytime TV normally targets women working at home, very young children not yet in school, and the homebound elderly. Also, older children are likely to be aware of the patterns associated with new movie and video game releases that are tied to holiday seasons and summer vacation schedules, when kids are out of school and thus more available as consumers of newly produced media.

In addition to seeing patterns in program scheduling, many young people are aware of patterns built into program formats. That is, besides seeing some of the regularities of characterization that Teniya Serita saw, and the placement of sensational persona for ratings that Samantha saw in talk shows, adolescents recognize and evaluate patterns particular to the construction of shows and genres. For example, 12-year-old Dezeray, a Dominican American, saw that the show *The Wonder Years* (ABC, 1988–1993) was

the same thing, always. His father misunderstands him, his mother doesn't understand him, his brother is stupid, and his sister is stupid, too, you understand? Then he likes this girl but she don't like him, and there's his friend Paul—it's like every episode is the same thing. The same thing could happen in *Roseanne* (ABC, 1988–1997), as like in another show. The shows are the same. (Fisherkeller, 2000, p. 602)

Kelly stopped watching a popular drama she liked because "now I think the writers are getting kind of desperate, they can't get such good ideas" (Fisherkeller, 2000, p. 602). Wolverine, a 12-year-old African American, also noticed racist and sexist patterns of representation. He said, "In every show almost, that has like Black people and White people in it, it's like, the White people always being on top." And he said, with women, "It's like the Black and White issue. It's always a woman looking up to a man. It's always like, damsel in distress, and a man comes to save her and all" (Fisherkeller, 2000, p. 602).

When these adolescents notice these patterns, they recognize commercial formulas, according to Lembo (2000), whose study of adult TV viewers revealed that they knew that series and genres had to maintain some predictable story lines so that people could follow a program. However, in addition, these viewers knew that the constraints of mass-media production encourage writers and producers to use story formulas that allow them to crank out programs like products in a factory, one after the other, all the same. It appears that some young adolescents are aware of the factory mentality of media production as well.

Indeed, in the third category of understandings about TV as a system, adolescents might perceive of television as a kind of factory, as they do know that it is an industry. Wolverine referred to this explicitly when he laid out a future business plan for himself:

I was watching how (cable TV) was making so much money, and I thought, like, maybe I can make my own movie cable channel. . . . I'm gonna have one movie that I play maybe every other week, not every day. I'm gonna try to get as many famous movies as I can. I'm gonna have so many movies that I won't have time to play another movie over again . . . (and) I'm gonna make my own movies and put 'em on there. (Fisherkeller, 2000, p. 597)

Wolverine and others in this study knew that people make money in the television industry as programmers and producers, as well as by acting, writing, directing, advertising, and being media technicians of all kinds. Many youth know that some people make hefty salaries working in this industry, information they gather through the medium's own entertainment magazines and talk shows that continuously discuss media projects and who is working on them, how much people are being paid, and what kinds of profits particular media ventures have garnered. Those who live in either Hollywood or New York, two media-making capitals, know of actual people who work as actors, models, writers, and technicians. What young people like these understand is that television and other media industries are actual entities that reward many people for participating in the making of media. These are real-world connections that young people make about the roles that commercial media systems play in people's lives and in society (see also Buckingham, 2000).

Young people's understandings about media as pervasive aspects of everyday life, patterned forms of representation and delivery, and real-life systems of production and distribution are acquired informally, through their daily contact with multiple media, and by casually talking and interacting with others about media. This informal kind of learning is similar to how children and adolescents develop understandings about language and print literacy, given their everyday encounters with "ways with words" (Heath, 1983). Informal language knowledge and competencies are considered a rich resource for further learning (Dyson, 1993, 1997, 2003; Heath, 1983; Kress, 1994).

Given the economic, social, and cultural value of audiovisual and digital media/technologies today, educators should build on young people's informally acquired awareness of the pervasive presence, systemic logic, and symbolic stature of multiple media forms and systems. Helping all youth in a formal manner to be analyzers and producers of all media will help them learn to "make it" in a world where multiple media forms and systems are a large part of contemporary discourses. Working with the best practices known to print-literacy educators (such as those in this volume) as well as media literacy educators (see for example Buckingham, Grahame, & Sefton Greene, 1995; Goodman, 2003; Tyner, 1998) we can teach young people how to deconstruct the codes and conventions of audiovisual and digital media forms, and how to construct their own messages and images using all of these forms. Helping all youth become media literate is a worthy endeavor in and of itself, but it also contributes to the development of print literacy, as media analysis and production requires engaging students in speaking, listening, reading, and writing activities about the media/technologies.

It is important to teach young people to analyze and produce multiple media not just so they can reproduce these media according to mainstream standards, but so that ultimately, they can create changes where necessary. Because in the long run we want young people to work toward their dreams, and also be pro-active citizens who effectively challenge the inequities and negative biases of society and culture. These are the goals of education writ large. To meet these goals, schools can include communication and audiovisual arts in teaching and learning activities not just as a means to enhance traditional literacy, but as objects, practices, and systems that students understand and use in a critical manner. Students would then be prepared as multiply literate workers and citizens to participate in a world saturated with media and communication technologies.

REFERENCES

Alexander, A., Ryan, M. S., & Munoz, P. (1984). Creating a learning context: investigations on the interaction of siblings during television viewing. *Critical Studies in Mass Communication, 1*(1), 345–364.

Bryant, J., & Anderson, D. R. (1983). *Children's understanding of television: Research on attention and comprehension*. New York: Academic Press.

Bryce, J., & Leichter, H. J. (1983). The family and television. *Journal of Family Issues, 4*(2), 309–328.

Buckingham, D. (1993). *Children talking television: The making of television literacy*. London: The Falmer Press.

Buckingham, D. (1996). *Moving images: Understanding children's emotional responses to television*. Manchester, UK: Manchester University Press.

Buckingham, D. (2000). *After the death of childhood: Growing up in the age of electronic media*. Cambridge, UK: Polity Press.

Buckingham, D., Grahame, J., & Sefton-Green, J. (1995). *Making media: Practical production in media education*. London: English and Media Centre.

Clark, L. S. (1998). Dating on the net: Teens and the rise of "pure" relationships. In S. Jones (Ed.), *Cybersociety 2.0: Revisiting computer mediated communication and community*. (pp. 159–183). Thousand Oaks, CA: Sage.

Comstock, G. (1980). *Television in America*. Beverly Hills, CA: Sage Publications.

Davies, M. M. (1997). *Fake, fact and fantasy: Children's interpretations of television reality*. Mahwah, NJ: Lawrence Erlbaum Associates.

Dorr, A. (1986). *Television and children. A special medium for a special audience*. Beverly Hills, CA: Sage Publications.

Dyson, A. H. (1997). *Writing superheroes: The social and ideological dynamics of child writing*. New York: Teacher's College Press.

Dyson, A. H. (2003). *The brothers and sisters learn to write: Popular literacies in childhood and school cultures*. New York: Teachers College Press.

Eisenhart, M. (1995). The fax, the jazz player, and the self-story teller: How do people organize culture? *Anthropology and Education Quarterly, 26*(1), 3–26.

Fisherkeller, J. (2000). "The writers are getting kind of desperate": Young adolescents, television, and literacy. *Journal of Adolescent and Adult Literacy, 43*(7), 596–606.

Fisherkeller, J. (2002). *Growing up with television: Everyday learning among young adolescents*. Philadelphia, PA: Temple University Press.

Geertz, C. (1983). *Local knowledge: Further essays in interpretive anthropology*. New York: Basic Books, Inc.

Gerbner, G., Gross, L., Morgan, M., & Signorielli, N. (1994). Growing up with television: The cultivation perspective. In J. Bryant & D. Zillman (Eds.), *Media effects: Advances in theory and research*. (pp. 17–42). Hillsdale, NJ: Lawrence Erlbaum.

Goffman, E. (1959). *The presentation of self in everyday life*. New York: Anchor.

Goodman, S. (2003). *Teaching youth media: A critical guide to literacy, video production, and social change*. New York: Teacher's College Press.

Graff, H. J. (1987). *The labyrinths of literacy: Reflections on literacy past and present*. Pittsburgh, PA: University of Pittsburgh Press.

Hall, S. (1992). The question of cultural identity. In S. Hall, D. Held, & T. McGrew (Eds.), *Modernity and its futures* (pp. 273–326). Cambridge, UK: Polity.

Heath, S. B. (1983). *Ways with words: Language, life and work in communities and classrooms*. Cambridge, MA: Cambridge University Press.

Hodge, B., & Tripp, D. (1986). *Children and television: A semiotic approach*. Stanford, CA: Stanford University Press.

Holloway, S. L., & Valentine, G. (2003). *Cyberkids*. London: Routledge.

Jenkins, H. (1992). *Textual poachers: Television fans and participatory cultures*. New York: Routledge.

Kelly, H., & Gardner, H. (Eds.). (1981). *Viewing children through television*. San Francisco, CA: Jossey-Bass, Inc.

Kinder, M. (Ed.). (1999). *Kids' media culture*. Durham, NC: Duke University Press.

Klapper, J. T. (1960). *The effects of mass communication*. New York: The Free Press.

Kress, G. (1994). *Learning to write*. London: Routledge

Kubey, R. (Ed.). (1997). *Media literacy in the information age: Current perspectives*. New Brunswick, NJ: Transaction Publishers.

Lave, J., & Wenger, E. (1991). *Situated learning: Legitimate and peripheral participation*. New York: Cambridge University Press.

Lembo, R. (2000). *Thinking through television: Viewing culture and the social limits to power*. Cambridge, UK: Cambridge University Press.

Lewis, L. (1990). *Gender politics and MTV: Voicing the difference*. Philadelphia, PA: Temple University Press.

Lull, J. (1990). *Inside family viewing: Ethnographic research on television's audiences*. London: Comedia/Routledge.

McChesney, R. (2004). *The problem of the media: U.S. communications politics in the 21st century*. New York: Monthly Review Press.

McIlwain, C. D., & Caliendo, S. M. (2004). Political issues in Black politics. M. K. Asante & A. Mazama (Eds.), *Encyclopedia of Black studies* (pp. 139–142). Thousand Oaks, CA: Sage.

Means Coleman, R. (2000). *African American viewers and the Black situation comedy: Situating racial humor*. New York: Garland.

Messaris, P., & Sarett, C. (1981). On the consequences of television-related parent-child interaction. *Human Communication Research, 7*, 226–244.

Meyrowitz, J. (1985). *No sense of place: The impact of electronic media on social behavior*. New York: Oxford University Press.

Miller, M. C. (1988). *Boxed in: The culture of TV*. Evanston, IL: Northwestern University Press.

The New London Group. (1996). A pedagogy of multiliteracies: Designing social futures. *Harvard Educational Review, 66*(1), 60–92.

Palmer, P. (1986). *The lively audience*. Sydney: Allen & Unwin.

Palmer, P. (1988). The social nature of children's television viewing. In P. Drummond & R. Paterson (Eds.), *Television and its audience: International research perspectives* (pp. 139–153). London: British Film Institute.

Pastor, J., McCormick, J., & Fine, M. (1996). Makin' homes: An urban girl thing. In B. Leadbetter & N. Way (Eds.), *Urban adolescent girls* (pp. 15–34). Philadelphia, PA: Temple University Press.

Postman, N. (1985). *Amusing ourselves to death: Public discourse in the age of show business*. New York: Penguin Books.

Reid, L. N., & Frazer, C. (1980a). Children's use of television commercials to initiate social interaction in family viewing situations. *Journal of Broadcasting, 24*, 149–157.

Reid, L. N., & Frazer, C. (1980b). Television at play. *Journal of Communication, 30*(4), 66–73.

Rideout, V., Roberts, D. F., & Foehr, U. G. (2005). *Generation M: Media in the lives of 8–18 year-olds*. Menlo Park, CA: Kaiser Family Foundation.

Schiller, H. I. (1989). *Culture, Inc.: The corporate takeover of public expression*. New York: Oxford University Press.

Sefton-Green, J. (Ed.). (1998). *Digital diversions: Youth culture in the age of multimedia*, London: UCL Press/Taylor and Francis Group.

Singer, D. G., Singer, J. L., & Zuckerman, D. M. (1981). *Teaching television*. New York: The Dial Press.

Steele, J. R., & Brown, J. D. (1995). Adolescent room culture: Studying media in the context of everyday life. *Journal of Youth and Adolescence, 24*(5), 551–576.

Steinberg, S. R., & Kincheloe, J. L. (1997). *Kinderculture: The corporate construction of childhood*. Boulder, CO: Westview Press.

Stern, S. (2002). Sexual selves on the world wide web: Adolescent girls' home pages as sites for sexual self expression. In J. D. Brown, J. R. Steele, & K. Walsh-Childers (Eds.), *Sexual teens, sexual media: Investigating media influence on adolescent sexuality* (pp. 265–285). Mahwah, NJ: Lawrence Erlbaum Associates.

Turkle, S. (1984). *The second self: Computers and the human spirit*. New York: Simon & Schuster, Inc.

Turkle, S. (1995). *Life on the screen: Identity in the age of the Internet*. New York: Simon and Schuster.

Tyner, K. (1998). *Literacy in a digital world: Teaching and learning in the age of information*. Mahwah, NJ: Lawrence Erlbaum Associates.

Wartella, E. (Ed.). (1979). *Children communicating: Media and development of thought, speech and understanding*. Beverly Hills, CA: Sage.

Willis, P. (1990). *Common culture: Symbolic work at play in the everyday cultures of the young*. Boulder, CO: Westview Press.

Wolcott, H. (1982). The anthropology of learning. *Anthropology and Education Quarterly, 13*(2), 83–108.

24

THE COMIC BOOK PROJECT: LITERACY OUTSIDE (AND INSIDE) THE BOX

Michael Bitz

TEACHERS COLLEGE, COLUMBIA UNIVERSITY

The idea of using comic books as an educational tool has been around for some time. Beginning in 1941, the Gilberton Company produced *Classic Comics*, a series of literature-based comic books designed to attract children to the likes of Shakespeare and Melville. The series lasted until 1971, but it never gained the same popularity as the Spider-man and Superman comics beloved by so many children, particularly boys. *Classic Comics* dwindled because the characters were staid, the writing was uninspiring, and the art was bulky. A student in the 1950s might have referred to them as "squaresville." Early efforts to bring comic books into the classroom were certainly not aided by Congressional hearings into the suspected relationship between comic books and juvenile delinquency (see U.S. Congress, 1955).

However, the premise behind *Classic Comics* has resonated for some educators: if children have something colorful and attractive in front of them, they just might read it. Over the decades, many have championed the use of comic books as a motivational pathway to reading (Anderson & Styles, 1999; Dorrell, 1987; Dorrell & Carroll, 1981; Eisner, 1974; Goldstein, 1986; Thomas, 1983; Wright, 1979). A handful of research-based studies have pointed toward the effectiveness of comic books as motivators for children to learn, or at least retain information (Goodwin & Igoe, 1982; Jenkins, 1994; Krashen & Ujiie, 1996). Research by Hayes and Ahrens (1988) indicated that the average comic book introduces children to twice as many words as the average children's book and five times as many words as the average child-adult conversation. Some even point to the expansive *International Comparative Studies in Education* (see Elley, 1992), ranking Finland as the nation with the highest student reading scores; Finland happens to have a high percentage of children who read comic books in their leisure time.

Unfortunately, those who focus on comic books as simple motivational bridges to reading are ignoring several decades of research in arts education. The compendium of studies in Deasy (2002) demonstrated that it is the active engagement in making art (or music, dance, and drama) that promotes the greatest learning and critical thinking in and out of the arts. Moreover, it is the sharing of the products resulting from the artistic process, and the confidence that goes along with presenting or performing, that are the most considerable motivators for children in and out of school (Catterall, 2002; Gardner, 1999).

Still reeling from misconstrued headlines about the Mozart Effect (see Rauscher, Shaw, & Ky, 1993, 1995), arts educators are wary of the term "direct transfer," which indicates that an experience in the arts can suddenly trigger outstanding performance on, say, a standardized math test. Those concerns are put into context by Oreck, Baum, and McCartney (1999), who highlighted the complex social, personal, educational, and economic issues that affect learning in and through the arts, particularly for urban youths. Nevertheless, there can be strong connectors between authentic arts experiences and academic learning provided that three criteria are met.

First, the arts content must be clearly and explicitly integrated with the academic content (Arts Education Partnership, 2002; Burnaford, Aprill, & Weiss, 2001). Regarding the integration of visual art and writing, nowhere else are the two so closely wedded than in a comic book. Therefore, children who create their own comic books have a unique opportunity to simultaneously advance artistic and literacy skills. The effectiveness of student-generated comic books in promoting literacy was highlighted by Wright and Sherman (1999) and Morrison, Bryan, and Chilcoat (2002).

The second criterion for successfully connecting arts and academic learning is that the educational context must be socially relevant. Dewey (1897) argued early on that "[the] only true education comes through the stimulation of the child's powers by the demands of the social situations in which he finds himself" (p. 77). Rarely do today's children find themselves in social situations surrounding Renaissance portraiture or Greek architecture. Rather, the visual art that speaks to most children and most frequently represents their identities is comic book and cartoon art, specifically the revolution of Japanese-style cartooning (*manga*) and animation (*anime*) that has captivated children around the world (Toku, 2002). Wilson (1988, 1997, 1999) has long demonstrated the social, artistic, and academic connections that children make through comic book art for the fact that it is *their* art. Dyson (1993, 1997, 2003) highlighted many of the same connections from a literacy perspective by exploring the potential of innercity children to write original stories about and reflections on comic book superheroes.

Finally, there must be an extraordinary amount of support from teachers, administrators, parents, students, and community partners for successful arts integration (Catterall & Waldorf, 1999; President's Committee on the Arts and the Humanities & Arts Education Partnership, 1999). Without these key support elements—and all of the challenges that accompany them, ranging from teacher turnover to standardized test performance—the integration of the arts into the academic curriculum is short term and often inadequate to advance learning in any meaningful way. In the South Bronx during the 1980s, a high-school remedial English teacher named Tim Rollins was one of the first to put the necessary pieces into place. His students, who dubbed themselves "Kids of Survival" or K.O.S., had failed academically year after year and were on the verge of dropping out of school. Rollins engaged the students in interpreting literature (including comic books) by creating original art. Not only were the students reported to learn to read and write, but also their artwork has been celebrated around the world (see Garrels, 1989).

From Research to Practice

Despite all the journal articles, books, research reports, roundtable discussions, and conference hearings, the arts remain marginalized in most school settings. Art teachers teach art; English teachers teach English. They might pass each other in the hallway, but that is typically the extent of their interaction. The Comic Book Project (CBP) launched in 2001 as a way of initiating wide-scale and sustainable change that meets the three criteria previously outlined. More than just a fun and motivational project for children, CBP began as a model for teachers, administrators, and students as to how the arts can exist—and, to be frank, survive—at the core of academic learning, specifically in the area of literacy.

A second and equally important goal that brought about CBP was to reach the at-risk children who too often fall through the gaping cracks of large urban school systems. This population is typically represented by students with limited English proficiency, from single-parent homes, with behavioral problems, with emotional problems, or from economically disadvantaged neighborhoods. CBP was meant to enable innercity youths to express and explore their identities. The aim was to get right at the heart of the educational crisis in urban America: children are neither engaged in nor empowered by the learning process. CBP put the creative control in children's hands, and then provided them with tangible evidence of their progress and achievements.

The concept was simple: children would plan, write, design, and produce original comic books on a socially relevant theme, and then publish and distribute their work for other children to use as learning and motivational tools. In partnership with Teachers College-Columbia University and Dark Horse Comics, CBP began with a single after-school program in New York City. The after-school community was the first to open its arms to CBP because of the paradox embodying most after-school programs: learning is mandatory but attendance is not. The project became a way to attract young people to after-school programs; to allow them to be creative in ways that rarely surfaced during the school day; and to reinforce their reading, writing, and communication skills in a nonthreatening manner.

That first after-school comic book class—led by the author and two college students—was focused on the theme of smoking prevention. The 24 fifth- and sixth-graders had been learning about the dangers of tobacco use for several weeks, and they had already immersed themselves in the theme by writing stories and creating animated public-service announcements. Now it was time to make comic books. The CBP process was born from the exploratory and rather improvised experience that follows.

The children first conceived their characters, then simultaneously wrote about and sketched those heroes and villains. Next, the students brainstormed plots, using their original characters to tell stories about smoking prevention. At that point, each child wrote a manuscript and outlined the pages of a comic book. The children wrote or planned the dialogue and captions in conjunction with sketches of how the characters would look and what might be in the background. Then the students in the class selected what they considered the top four stories, and they formed production teams to turn those manuscripts into comic books—each team had a writer, an artist, an editor/inker, and a color specialist. Figure 24.1 represents the manuscript plan for the first panel of a student comic book. Figure 24.2 shows how the panel appeared in the comic book itself.

When the comic books were complete, the children were extremely excited about what they had accomplished. They had created fully designed comic books that integrated intricate details ranging from a character's manner of speech to the color of a villain's shoelaces. Perhaps more significant, however, the students demonstrated that they had something important to say to their peers, parents, and teachers about the dangers of smoking. The stories were so captivating that a local comic book artist was commissioned to turn the students' work into a professional, digitized comic book. Figure 24.3 is a panel from a student comic book; Figure 24.4 is the professional artist's rendition.

The book—titled *Life Has a Limit with a Cigarette in It*—was printed and distributed to the students in the comic book class, as well as to hundreds of other students in the school district. The proud students had become stars to the point that their work was featured in a national youth publication (Davidson, 2003).

This comic book class taught everyone associated with CBP three important things. First, if children began with creative thinking—not necessarily paragraph writing or detailed drawing—then *all* of the children could be involved: the artists, the writers, the boys, the girls, the two who had immigrated to the United States just three

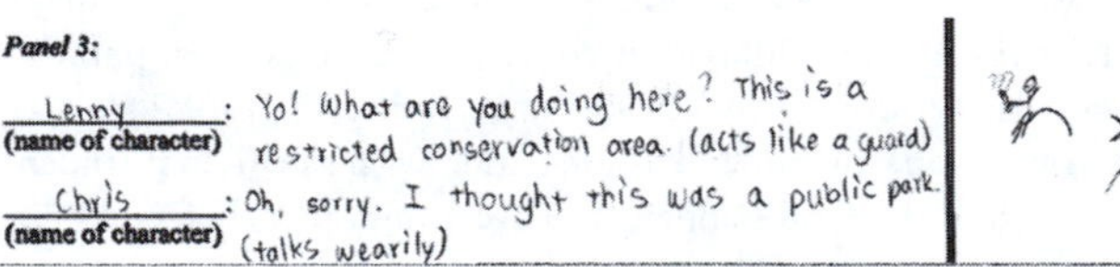

Panel 3:

Lenny (name of character): Yo! What are you doing here? This is a restricted conservation area. (acts like a guard)

Chris (name of character): Oh, sorry. I thought this was a public park. (talks wearily)

FIGURE 24.1 Example of student manuscript. Male, fifth grade, New York City.

FIGURE 24.2 Example of student comic book from manuscript sample.

weeks ago, the bored, the hearing impaired, and the one whom everyone had labeled as "the troublemaker in the corner." Second, children could learn an enormous amount from each other by reading, editing, and evaluating each other's stories. One group had each student take on the role of a character, and they acted out the story that had been written in the manuscript. It became quite clear to the entire class where the story needed revisions—long fight scenes soon transformed into quality plotlines and character developments. Finally, it seemed that the process of creating a comic book really could be a pathway to literacy, albeit an unconventional one, for students who struggle in school. This pathway was elucidated not only by the sheer volume of writing (and then reading) that children

FIGURE 24.3 Student panel (males and females, grades 5 and 6), New York City.

FIGURE 24.4 Artist's rendition of student panel.

had amassed during the project, but also by their excitement about the product they had created and the recognition they had received from it.

The Pilot Year

In 2002–2003 school year, CBP was officially piloted with 733 students (grades 4–8) in 33 after-school programs associated with The After-School Corporation, the Partnership for After-School Education, and the Fund for the City of New York. The theme of the pilot was rather open ended: children were to create comic books that represented their lives. Some of the driving questions were, What do you want to say about yourself, your neighborhood, your culture, your background? How will your story reflect who you are? What do you want your friends, families, teachers, and community members to learn from your comic book?

The results of the pilot, published in Bitz (2004a, 2004b), solidified the CBP model going forward, which consisted of the following steps:

Step 1. Teacher Training Instructors at the participating after-school programs attended a training workshop focused on the specifics of CBP, as well as the criteria for successful arts integration. Because these were the people who would actually work with the children on the project, it was integral that they not only understand the process, but also believe in the goals and adopt the project as their own. During the training session, the author and other workshop leaders introduced CBP, helped integrate the project into the after-school programs' curricula, explained the project components, designed an implementation schedule, discussed the background research, and distributed the project material. The after-school instructors also had the opportunity to create their own comic books, which highlighted the challenges that their students would almost surely encounter.

Step 2: Introductory Activities By the time children get to the third grade, they have already been identified as artistically talented or not. The older the "untalented" ones get, the more self-conscious they feel about making art. It was important that CBP include all children, not just those with artistic skills. Therefore, the emphasis from the very beginning was on creativity, which evened the playing field. In fact, some of the children with the best drawing skills demonstrated noticeable difficulty being creative. They were accustomed to drawing their favorite cartoon characters and had never developed original material.

Introductory activities were designed to help the general population of students embrace their creative energies and channel them toward literacy development. The activities focused on simple drawing techniques, story development, dialogue writing, and the creation of four-panel minicomics in which students created superheroes, formulated stories about their neighborhoods, and interpreted a current event.

Step 3: Writing the Comic Book Manuscript Children brainstormed, plotted, and drafted their comic books through the *Manuscript Starter.* This template encouraged children to sketch their comic book panels as they planned their stories. Doing so helped children conceptualize the final product, and it enabled visual learners, struggling writers, and English language learners to rely on the pictorial aspect of comic books and to make connections between what they wrote and what they drew.

Step 4: Creating the Comic Book The planning of the manuscript led to the *Comic Book Canvas.* This template provided children with blank panels to design their final comic books. Children drew the characters, wrote the dialogue, and colored the backgrounds to produce complete comic books. They also developed covers and provided representative titles for the comic books.

Step 5: Displaying the Work During the pilot, children displayed noticeable intrinsic motivation to create their comic books. They anxiously awaited the next comic book class, and many worked on their comic books at home. However, having learned the positive outcomes of exhibiting comic books from the original after-school program, the project staff promoted extrinsic motivation by displaying and celebrating the students' achievements. CBP began to foster extrinsic motivation in three specific ways: (a) a publication of select student comic books to be distributed across the city in which the project was implemented; (b) a community-based, public exhibit of the student comic books and accompanying awards ceremony for participating students; (c) Web-site galleries at www.comicbookproject.org, featuring the work of every student who completed a comic book.

The CBP pilot resulted in hundreds of comic books from children across New York City. Analysis of student work completed during the pilot highlighted many indicators demonstrating the ability of CBP to help children meet the New York State Learning Standards in English Language Arts. However, the comic books themselves, and the content within, were the truly intriguing results of the pilot. The students created comic books about growing up in the city, and their finished products turned out rather unlike the tradition of superheroes saving the world. Story after story focused on the harsh, occasionally hopeful but more often painful, realities of the urban experience. The children produced comic books about themselves, their peers, and their interactions with violence, drugs, and pregnancy. They put forth their identities as urban youths—who they are, what they see, and how they struggle with daily hardships. And, while adult comic books focus on fantasized worlds, the children's comic books were noticeably devoid of superheroes. When one fourth-grade student in the East New York neighborhood of Brooklyn was asked why his comic book lacked a superhero, the boy responded, "Superman don't come here."

New York City, 2003–2004

During the 2003–2004 school year, CBP impacted 10,000 elementary- and middle-school children in after-school programs across New York City. The theme was the environment, and the project was funded by the U.S. Environmental Protection Agency. Why focus on environmental issues? Urban youths often act on the mentality that the environment, being related to nature, is far removed from the inner city. Therefore, to simply tell urban youths about environmental problems such as pollution and energy waste is an approach bound for failure. The goal of this CBP implementation was to encourage children to think critically about the environment by incorporating the important issues into an illustrated story, that is, a comic book—one that would be experienced by thousands of other children and adults in the community.

In partnership with The After-School Corporation, a nonprofit organization dedicated to sustaining after-school programs in New York City, CBP began the school year by reaching out to perspective after-school programs. Interested after-school site directors completed an application in which they described how the project would fit into their club schedules, how they would staff the project at their sites, and what they would do in case of staff turnover—a common occurrence in after-school settings. Once selected, the site coordinators and line staff attended one of two training workshops focused on CBP and the theme of the environment. Then the project was in their hands.

Between October and April, the children delved into the process of researching and thinking about environmental issues in their neighborhoods, planning stories that embodied those issues, and designing comic books based on those stories. The author visited the after-school programs at least twice during the course of the project, once with a professional artist, to lend onsite support. At some sites children worked individually; at other sites they worked in groups. In April, comic books were collected and analyzed by an independent panel consisting of a literacy professor, an environmental expert, an art educator, and a professional comic book writer. The panel selected student comic books from each participating after-school program to appear in a publication titled *Save Our City, Save Our Planet*, which was distributed to children throughout New York City.

Created by a group of three fifth-grade boys, "The Radioactive Cockaroach" (sic) was one of the comic books included in the publication (see Fig. 24.5). The humorous and more than slightly sarcastic story highlights the boys' understanding of how altering an ecosystem can lead to catastrophic events.

As the story progresses, the cockroach attacks New York City and starts destroying buildings. A firefighter named Rust T. Gates eventually figures out how to shrink the bug down to size. The bug then falls into a sewer and flows out to Lake Erie. A fish eats the radioactive cockroach—the fish grows bigger and bigger and swims angrily toward New York City. The story ends with a classic "To Be Continued."

The wealth of creative art and writing produced in this implementation of CBP highlighted the abilities of students who in any other setting would have been labeled as "underachieving." Over half of those who participated were designated as English language learners, and only 26% were reading at their designated grade levels. Children who had been shuffled from bilingual programs to special-education classes to vocational tracks had blossomed into dedicated comic book artists and writers. Many students strove for perfection. They collaborated during recess to plan what would be the next event in the comic book story. They argued vociferously about how characters should look and act. They came to their teachers for help in spelling difficult words and putting the commas in the right places.

FIGURE 24.5 First page from "The Radioactive Cockaroach [sic]", Males, fifth grade, New York City.

The most logical explanation for these phenomena was that the children were doing these things because they wanted to. They had personal desires to tell their stories and have their voices heard. Not coincidentally, the process forged a sense of environmental activism that will remain with many of the children for years to come.

Cleveland, 2003–2004

One can imagine what it would entail for a school district to implement CBP during the school day. Art teachers would need to collaborate with English teachers on a regular basis, school and district administrators would need to support an art-based approach to literacy building, parents would need to understand how the process of making comic books could help their children learn, students would have to want to participate in that process, and community partners would have to assist the project by making the community at large aware of CBP's goals and progress. These extraordinary things occurred in Cleveland during the 2003–2004 school year.

Through a grant from the Cleveland Foundation, CBP impacted 10,000 children at Cleveland elementary and middle schools. The teachers selected the theme of conflict resolution in response to increasing violence in the Cleveland public schools. After a day-long training workshop, the teachers brought CBP into their classrooms, and the process was underway. Some teachers decided to have students write their manuscripts in English class and do the drawing in art class. In other schools, students worked on the entire project in art class and consulted with their English teachers on story development, writing style, and mechanics. Some schools worked on the project every day for a month; others implemented it once a week for the entire school year. A panel selected student comic books from each school to appear in a publication titled *Peace in Our Schools*, distributed across Cleveland. Included in the publication was "Mastermind," created by an eighth-grade boy. It is a story about a boy whose conscience comes to life and helps him make the right decisions (see Fig. 24.6).

Throughout the story, the conscience floats above and tries to encourage the boys to think about the consequences of their actions. It is a comic book rooted in reality; after all, one boy has already stolen a car—the conscience pleads for him to stop running from the police. In the end, nobody listens to the conscience figure. One character lands in prison, another gets arrested, and a third loses his life. The "mastermind" warns the reader that everyone *must* make a difference. If you do not listen to your conscience, you may find yourself in the same predicament as these characters. It is a clear message from one young person to another.

As in the parallel New York City project, the Cleveland implementation of CBP highlighted the ability of children to learn by way of making a comic book. The project evaluation consisted of three parts: (a) analysis of student writing, (b) student and teacher surveys, and (c) student and teacher interviews. Regarding the writing analysis, three scorers worked independently to analyze each participating student's writing in the *Manuscript Starter*. Using a scoring rubric adapted from the Ohio English Language Arts Academic Content Standards, the scorers rated the manuscript for each applicable standard. The scores were subject to statistical analysis, which indicated the effectiveness of CBP in relation to the children's ability to meet state performance standards. The analysis of student writing indicated that 74% of the children in the project met the Ohio English Language Arts Academic Content Standards.

FIGURE 24.6 First page from "Mastermind," Male, eighth grade, Cleveland.

The student and teacher surveys indicated that 92% of the students and teachers responded positively to CBP and hoped to continue the project in future years. The interviews confirmed the survey responses. A fifth-grade girl stated to a reporter at *The Washington Post,* "It's my favorite project ever. I love to read comic books . . . but I never thought I could do my own. I developed my artistic skills and learned where to put the [dialogue] bubbles. I learned how to write stories, too" (Strauss, 2004, p. A10). An art teacher of seventh-grade students revealed, "I've never seen my students so dedicated as they were during this project. I saw students in the hall talking about their story lines and running to class to get their ideas down. That is what school should be."

High-School Pilot, 2003–2004

Amidst all the activity in New York City and Cleveland, CBP launched its first high-school comic book club at Martin Luther King, Jr. High School in New York City. The group of 16 students met every Thursday and was instructed by the school art teacher, who volunteered his time after school. The class sketched their characters, wrote manuscripts, and designed comic books, very much like the younger children had done. However, the high-school students went far beyond: they inked their comic books with quality pens, scanned their pages into Photoshop, applied the colors digitally, and proceeded to produce a very professional publication. One of the stories, created by a ninth-grade boy, was about a man who contracts HIV from a prostitute and is forced to make difficult life decisions (see Fig. 24.7).

Once he learns the bad news, Joe goes to a bar and asks the bartender for a stiff drink . . . and the rest of the bottle. Determined to drown his sorrows, Joe marvels at his misfortune. He slurs, "That's it! I'm gonna go out and give some girl AIDS and see how she likes it!" It is Joe's father who eventually rescues him from his self-destructive misery. The father tells Joe that he is there for support and guidance no matter what happens. They agree to face Joe's problems together. The last panel shows Joe at the hospital where he takes his medicine and gets counseling. The young author also provides readers with Web sites where they can learn more about AIDS prevention. As a tribute to those who struggle with HIV and AIDS, the comic book ends with three simple yet powerful words: "NOT The End."

What About the Girls?

The words "comic book" and "adolescent male" seem to go hand in hand, and comic book publishers continue to enforce that association. In the majority of comic books, the heroes are males, the villains are males, and the stories cater to male tastes and sensibilities. Moreover, professional comic book writers, artists, designers, inkers, and editors have been and continue to be males, with very few exceptions. Yet creativity, original art, and storytelling have

FIGURE 24.7 First page from an AIDS prevention comic book, Male, ninth grade, New York City.

extraordinary powers to dispel social and sexual stereotypes—CBP has involved an equal ratio of male and female students. Both of the citywide publications from 2003–2004 featured comic books by girls, and their work demonstrated the ability of young females to use the genre as a means of identity exploration.

As one might expect, the heroes of the girls' comic books were usually female, although the villains were almost always male. The heroes rarely resorted to physical combat in solving problems; they usually developed alternative solutions and often worked together to confront conflicts. The contrast in problem-solving methods between male and female students was stark. For example, in the environmental comic books, it was not uncommon for the main characters to witness a group of people polluting a beach or park. The comic books created by boys often had the heroes beat up the polluters. In contrast, the girls would have the heroes confront the polluters verbally, or stage a rally or protest against pollution. The girls' comic books were not devoid of violence, but the fighting was insinuated more often than graphically displayed. A ninth-grade girl in New York City created a comic book about a female hero—part human, part wolf—who meets a shy kitten with a big appetite. The two combat evil by summoning special powers, but the comic book never displays actual fighting (see Fig. 24.8).

Literacy Outside the Box

A common phrase is often used to indicate simplicity: "Easy as riding a bike." However, consider all the incredibly complex skills and processes that encompass bicycle riding—the physics of gravitational forces, the subtle neuropsychological elements of steering, the simultaneous coordination between many body parts. Of course, one would never attempt to explain these complexities to a child before her first time getting on that special two-wheeler decorated with sparkles and tassels. She would never look at the thing again. Rather, children leave all the metacognitive and neuropsychological theory behind and—after a few scrapes and falls—simply ride. Why? Because in their hearts they know that the bike will give them freedom to explore and race and soar or simply to get to the corner bodega. In the end, they ride because they want to and need to.

In the effort to drill all the intricate skills and processes that embody reading and writing, many educators have forgotten to instill in children a sense of the power of communication, the freedom that accompanies the ability to express oneself. Many students look at a page of written paragraphs, or at the blank space in which they are to put their own paragraphs, and they hear echoes: "You can't speak the language." "You are below grade level." "You must pass this test, or you will be left behind." Moreover, socially irrelevant books that dominate the library shelves will never bridge the gap that "balanced" literacy claims they will. Without empowering children to tell their stories through their media for their communities, illiteracy will remain just another social quandary alongside gun violence and obesity.

Comic books are simply one genre of youth media through which children can communicate, and probably a relatively insignificant one at that. Children can build literacy skills by writing and recording rap songs, designing and programming video games, drafting and creating trading cards, or building and uploading Web sites. And, as outlets for youth communication change, so will the need for educators to respect those changes, adapt to them, and capitalize upon them in the classroom. Doing so should make the job of teaching easier, not harder. Yet doing so also mandates that teachers think outside the box of textbooks and workbooks, and that they give their students a voice. Moreover, educators must help students understand the value of making their voices heard.

Unfortunately, the systemic problems in urban education put insurmountable pressures on teachers—the notion of making comic books, or anything else outside the prescribed curriculum, would seem unthinkable to many. In innercity schools, the need to empower students is all the greater, but the resources are all the fewer. The least experienced teachers end up in the largest classrooms with students who have the most diverse needs. Classroom management overtakes classroom learning. Increased pressures from administrators to teach to the format and content of a standardized test subvert curricular standards and learning in general. The quality teachers who serve urban schools as a career clearly do so out of a charitable desire to help the children who need it most.

The realties of the situation became all too clear on April 27, 2004, a day the author will never forget. It was time to retrieve all the comic books from the teachers in Cleveland. They had a professional-development session scheduled and would bring the completed student comic books to the central location. The year-long process of brainstorming stories, writing manuscripts, and creating the comic books had finally come to a close. All the site observations and interviews indicated that the project had been a success. It was the comic books, however, that would truly vouch for what the students and teachers had accomplished.

FIGURE 24.8 Page from a comic book, Female, ninth grade, New York City.

However, as teachers entered the building, it was clear that something was very wrong. Most had dark bags under their eyes. Three sobbed together in a corner. Many embraced each other in consolation. As it turned out, the previous night the school district announced a 30% layoff of teachers. All professional development and after-school programs would be cut, and many of the initiatives that had made the arts so robust in the Cleveland schools would disappear.

The teachers formed a line to hand in their students' work. Lumps in their throats, many knew that these comic books would be the last testaments of all their efforts and hopes as teachers. They had demonstrated to the entire country how they could work together to successfully integrate the arts into the academic curriculum, help children think critically about important social issues, and provide an outlet for underserved youths to express themselves in a unique and powerful way. For some, the reward would be a pink slip.

Yet the comic books remain, and as with all art, they have meaning beyond the dialogue bubbles and color-pencil designs. They represent the labors of children and teachers to show that their voices are strong, and that their words, art, stories, and messages are important. Superman may not come to Cleveland, New York City, Philadelphia, Baltimore, or any of the other cities that struggle to give their children the educational resources that they so desperately need. However, children themselves become heroes when they understand the power of creativity and expression and use that power to do extraordinary things in school, after school, and in life.

REFERENCES

Anderson, H., & Styles, M. (1999). *Teaching through texts: Promoting literacy through popular and literary texts in the primary classroom.* New York: Routledge.

Arts Education Partnership. (2002, September). *Creating quality integrated and interdisciplinary arts programs.* Washington, DC: Author.

Bitz, M. (2004a). The comic book project: Forging alternative pathways to literacy. *Journal of Adolescent & Adult Literacy, 47*(7), 574–586.

Bitz, M. (2004b). The comic book project: The lives of urban youth. *Art Education, 57*(2), 33–39.

Burnaford, G. E., Aprill, A. & Weiss, C. (2001). *Renaissance in the classroom: Arts integration and meaningful learning.* Mahwah, NJ: Lawrence Erlbaum Associates.

Catterall, J. S. (2002). The arts and the transfer of learning. In R. J. Deasy (Ed.), *Critical links: Learning in the arts and student academic and social development* (pp. 151–157). Washington, DC: Arts Education Partnership.

Catterall, J. S., & Waldorf, L. (1999). Chicago arts partnerships: Summary evaluation. In E. Fiske (Ed.), *Champions for change: The impact of the arts on learning* (pp. 47–62). Washington, DC: Arts Education Partnership.

Davidson, B. (2003). The comic book project: Words and drawing against smoking. *Writing!, 26*(3), 4–8.

Deasy, R. J. (Ed.). (2002). *Critical links: Learning in the arts and student academic and social development.* Washington, DC: Arts Education Partnership.

Dewey, J. (1897). My pedagogic creed. *The School Journal, LIV*(3), 77–80.

Dorrell, L. D. (1987). Why comic books? *School Library Journal, 34*(3), 30–32.

Dorrell, L. D., & Carroll, C. E. (1981). Spider-Man at the library. *School Library Journal, 27*(10), 17–19.

Dyson, A. H. (1993). *Social worlds of children learning to write in an urban primary school.* New York: Teachers College Press.

Dyson, A. H. (1997). *Writing superheroes: Contemporary childhood, popular culture, and classroom literacy.* New York: Teachers College Press.

Dyson, A. H. (2003). *The brothers and sisters learn to write: Popular literacies in childhood and school cultures.* New York: Teachers College Press.

Eisner, W. (1974). Comic books in the library. *School Library Journal, 21*(2), 75–79.

Elley, W. B. (1992). *How in the world do students read: IEA study of reading literacy.* Hamburg, Germany: International Association for the Evaluation of Educational Achievement.

Gardner, H. (1999). The happy meeting of multiple intelligences and the arts. *Harvard Education Letter, 15*(6), 5.

Garrels, G. (Ed.). (1989). *Amerika: Tim Rollins + K.O.S.* New York: Dia Art Foundation.

Goldstein, B. S. (1986). Looking at cartoons and comics in a new way. *Journal of Reading, 29*(7), 657–661.

Goodwin, L. D., & Igoe, J. B. (1982). *An evaluation of the effectiveness of participatory health consumer materials for children* [Electronic version]. (ERIC Document Reproduction Service No. ED221483)

Hayes, D., & Ahrens, M. (1988). Vocabulary simplification for children: A special case of "motherese"? *Journal of Child language, 15*, 395–410.

Jenkins, L. (1994). *The reading-writing connection in the comic book genre: A case study of three young writers* [Electronic version]. (ERIC Document Reproduction Service No. ED369070)

Krashen, S. D., & Ujiie, J. (1996). Comic book reading, reading enjoyment, and pleasure reading among middle class and Chapter 1 middle school students. *Reading Improvement, 33*(1), 51–54.

Morrison, T., Bryan, G., & Chilcoat, G. (2002). Using student-generated comic books in the classroom. *Journal of Adolescent & Adult Literacy, 45*(8), 758–767.

Oreck, B., Baum, S., & McCartney, H. (1999). Artistic talent development for urban youth: The promise and the challenge. In E. Fiske (Ed.), *Champions for change: The impact of the arts on learning* (pp. 63–78). Washington, DC: Arts Education Partnership.

President's Committee on the Arts, & The Humanities & Arts Education Partnership (1999). *Gaining the arts advantage: Lessons from school districts that value arts education.* Washington, DC: Authors.

Rauscher, F. H., Shaw, G. L., & Ky, K. N. (1993). Music and spatial task performance. *Nature, 365*, 611.

Rauscher, F. H., Shaw, G. L., & Ky, K. N. (1995). Listening to Mozart enhances spatial-temporal reasoning: Towards a neurophysiological basis. *Neuroscience Letters, 185*, 44–47.

Strauss, V. (2004, June 15). *Thinking outside the box, inside the panel.* The Washington Post, p. A10.

Thomas, J. L. (1983). *Cartoons and comics in the classroom: A reference for teachers and librarians.* Littleton, CO: Libraries Unlimited.

Toku, M. (2001). What is manga?: The influence of pop culture in adolescent art. *Art Education, 54*(2), 11–17.

U.S. Congress. (1955). *Comic books and juvenile delinquency: Interim report pursuant to S. Res. 89, 83d Cong., 1st sess., and S. 190, 83d Cong., 2d sess., a part of the investigation of juvenile delinquency in the United States.* Washington, DC: U.S. Government Printing Office.

Wilson, B. (1988). The artistic tower of Babel: Inextricable links between culture and graphic development. In G. W. Hardman, & T. Zernich (Eds.), *Discerning art: Concepts and issues* (pp. 488–506). Champaign, IL: Stipes.

Wilson, B. (1997). Child art, multiple interpretations, and conflicts of interest. In A. M. Kindler (Ed.), *Child development in art* (pp. 81–94). Reston, VA: National Art Education Association.

Wilson, B. (1999). Becoming Japanese: Manga, children's drawings, and the construction of national character. *Visual Arts Research, 25*(2), 48–60.

Wright, G. (1979). The comic book: A forgotten medium in the classroom. *Reading Teacher, 33*(2), 158–161.

Wright, G., & Sherman, R. (1999). Let's create a comic strip. *Reading Improvement, 36*(2), 66–72.

25

INTERNET COMMUNICATION AMONG YOUTH: NEW PRACTICES AND EPISTEMOLOGIES

Cynthia Lewis
UNIVERSITY OF MINNESOTA

> Abby: It's like, 'Oh, It's 9 o'clock. I gotta get on the computer!' And it's like, if we can't, it's like . . . what am I going to do?!! . . . I don't know. It's just part of my night.
> Sam: Everybody does it. It's like I've grown up on it. It's like how you felt about stuff when you were growing up.

Sam and Abby were two 14-year-old girls who participated in a study on adolescents' uses of instant messaging (IMing; Lewis & Fabos, 2005). It seems apt to begin this chapter on out-of-school digital literacies with their voices because their words point to two important components of new media—immediacy and hypermediacy—as put forth by Bolter and Grusin (2000) in their book, *Remediation: Understanding New Media*. Immediacy occurs when the presence of the medium is so natural or immediate to the user that it no longer seems present or visible. Hypermediacy occurs when the medium is apparent (rather than transparent)—when it makes the user conscious of its presence.

We can see both of these strategies at work in Abby's and Sam's comments. On the one hand, they point to the invisibility and the naturalness of the act of IMing: "Everybody does it," "It's just part of my night." On the other hand, Abby, at least, is hyperaware of the medium: "I gotta get on the computer!" These two strategies, according to Bolter and Grusin (2000), are the means by which remediation, or the refashioning of prior media, occurs. The kind of refashioning central to their definition of remediation is evident in Sam's claim that the interviewer would have "stuff" in her life that she grew up with that seemed as natural to her as digital communication seemed to Sam. Here, Sam understands that the technology of IM, which often seems so complicated to middle-aged adults like me, is a refashioning of technologies with which those of my generation grew up. It could be said, for instance, that IM remediates the writing and passing of notes. Indeed, comparisons to note passing came up in several interviews as examples of an earlier "technology" with similar goals and pleasures.

The goals and pleasures of IM and the social identities afforded by its immediacy and its hypermediacy are central to the topic of this chapter, which focuses on synchronous Internet communication (IC), such as IMing and chat, among adolescents.[1] Having conducted an extensive study of Internet use among 9–19-year-olds in the United Kingdom, Livingstone and Bober (2004) found that young people prefer to use the Internet for communication rather than for information. Yet, the technology focus in schools has been geared toward the information rather than the communication component of information and communication technologies (Leander, 2004). Although several handbook overviews of Internet communication have been published (Baym, 2002; Beach & Lundell, 1998; Lewis, Alvermann, & Leander, 2004; Lewis & Fabos, 2005), none focused, as does this review, on its application to literacy practices in out-of-school contexts. In this chapter, I discuss fundamental theoretical claims about digital literacies and review key studies of young people's Internet communication (IMing and chat) with the goal of informing and extending our knowledge about out-of-school literacies and their implications for reconceptualizing the teaching of reading and language arts.

[1] In this chapter, I focus only on synchronous Internet communication, rather than electronic mail because large-scale studies (as well as my own case study research) have found that veteran Internet users prefer to communicate in real time, especially using Instant Messaging (Pew, 2001), and an increasing number of the general population of Internet users use Instant Messaging more often than email (2004). Participants in a study I conducted with Fabos (2005), used email only for specific purposes such as when buddies were not online or for messages requiring more time for reflection.

To begin, I discuss theoretical claims about digital literacies as put forth by scholars from literacy, new media, and communication studies. Next, I describe and illustrate three dimensions of practice related to digital literacy—performativity, hybrid textuality, and circulation (Lewis et al., 2004; Lewis & Fabos, 2005), using examples from published research on the uses of IMing and chat among young people. I argue that those of us involved in literacy education need to consider these new dimensions of practice as we rethink literacy education in digitally mediated times.

Digital Literacies: Key Claims

Literacy, as I am using it throughout this chapter, is seen as a social practice. This orientation to literacy, known as "New Literacy Studies" (Gee, 1990; Street, 1995), or "situated literacies" (Barton, Hamilton, & Ivanic, 2000), is concerned with the ways in which literacy practices are embedded in broader social goals, cultural practices, institutions, and power relations. From this standpoint, scholars of new media literacy, working from different disciplines, have produced a body of work that is expanding to keep up with new developments in uses of digital technology. I have organized my review of this scholarship around three key claims about digital literacies that are foundational to understanding young people's uses of Internet communication: digital literacies are (a) technologically and socially mediated, (b) multimodal, and (c) both local and global.

Digital Literacies Are Technologically and Socially Mediated

Examining the role of technology within a social literacies framework, Bruce (1997) pointed out that technology and literacy are often seen as autonomous rather than intersecting realms. Instead, he and others argued that technology and literacy are intertwined (Bruce, 1997; Leu, Kinzer, Coiro, & Cammack, 2004; Reinking, 1998). As such, technology shapes the evolution of what counts as a text just as the social practices of textuality change the material reality of technology. For example, technology has enabled youth to be hyperconnected through cell phones. The popularity of these fluid, portable, in the moment connections has fostered new technologies such as "smart mobs" (Rheingold, 2002), more advanced mobile technology that allows for short text messaging, e-mail, photo and video streaming, and so on. Thus, social practices related to cell phone technology played a role in changing its material and textual elements.

Lemke (1998) argued that literacy must always be defined "with respect to the sign systems deployed, the material technologies involved, and the social contexts of production, circulation, and use of the particular genre" (p. 284). Literacy has always involved technologies, be they pens or computers. It is not the computer or the Internet itself that is central to literacy, but the way that these tools of technology shape social relations and practices (Bigum, 2002; Bruce, 1997; Holloway & Valentine, 2003).

Those who have grown up immersed in digital culture have a lived understanding of how the Internet works and of the norms and social practices of particular digital communities. In a paper on how those who are "digitally at home" interact with digital texts, Lankshear and Knobel (2004a; 2004b) argued that the distance between text and reader, assumed in even the most interactive descriptions of book reading, breaks down in online reading/writing. By contrast, they view online literacy as highly interactive and practice oriented rather than text oriented. The role of readers/writers in this digital landscape is to carry out the "production, distribution, and exchange of texts" (p. 11). Although I would argue, following Fairclough (1992) and others, that production, distribution, and exchange are important components of readers'/writers' relationship to *any* text, I agree that these components are more visible and central to online practices, such as chat and IMing, for which reading and writing merge as users take in and produce rapid-fire messages, and creatively circulate these messages in ways I will describe in a later section of this chapter. Particular kinds of social practices tend to emerge in relation to the affordances of particular technologies.

Once the social practices around a particular technology become commonplace, people tend not to think of the technology as technological (Lankshear, Snyder, & Green, 2000). For instance, although using the Internet for communication purposes is the most preferred activity of young people (Livingstone, 2002), it no longer holds fascination as a novel technology. Instead they have come to naturalize IM and chat as a commonplace part of their lives (Herring, 2004). To underscore this point, the young participants in one ongoing study of digital literacy among adolescents did not include IM, e-mail, or chat in their responses to an interview question about the technologies they use (Townsend, S. & Van Scoy, S., personal communication, 2005). When asked directly about their use of these technologies, they explained that, of course, they used IM and e-mail on a daily basis, but did not consider these communication tools to be technological. E-mail and IM incorporate elements of phone conversations and note passing, but their status as a new technology is already evolving. For instance, teens make distinctions between the use of e-mail and IC, saving e-mail for communication with adults, including teachers, and IC for regular conversations with friends (Lenhart, Madden, & Hitlin, 2005). As is typical of digital literacies, such remediation involves a blending of modalities and genres (Luke, C., 2003).

It is notable that, in 2005, 87% of teens in the United States used the Internet, a 24% growth since 2001 (Lenhart et al., 2005). Although by 2005 the majority (68%) of Americans used the Internet (Pew Internet and American Life Project, 2005), this applied to only 49% of Americans with a household income of less that $30,000 and only 29% of those with less than a high school education. Nonetheless, the large and growing percentage of American teens that use the Internet would suggest that the divide might now be as much about age as it is about income or access. Young people who do not have access at home are getting online at schools, community centers, and libraries.

Among teens, the current digital divide may have more to do with access to speed and social space than it does to basic Internet access. In the general population, at least, those with dial-up rather than high-speed connections use the Internet less often and for a narrower range of activities (Lenhart et al., 2005) Moreover, a lesser known social divide may account for different Internet use in degree and kind. For instance, young people from middle-income families have been found to be more comfortable and confident about using home computers than those from low-income families. The larger number of computers in middle-income homes means that youth often have personal computers in their rooms. This results in less adult supervision and greater use of the Internet for recreational purposes. By contrast, lower income homes often have one centrally located computer, resulting in more adult supervision, more social interaction around the computer, and more Internet use for educational purposes (Ba, Tally, & Tsikalas, 2002). According to Buckingham (2002), differing "attitudes and orientations" (p. 79) toward technology result in different degrees of use. Nonetheless, the substantial growth in teen Internet use in recent years suggests a trend that should move those of us in the field of education to take seriously what we learned from the New London Group (1996) a decade ago: New literacies are about multimodal design. It is inevitable that young people will continue to increase the amount and range of their online activities, thus changing their writing practices and processes in ways that schools will increasingly need to address.

Digital Literacies Are Multimodal

New London Group (1996; 2000) captured the relationship between technology and literacy in their characterization of meaning making as multimodal design. These scholars argued for a reconceptualization of print literacy that relies on the metaphors of designing and redesigning social futures. The core concept here is that in order to make meaning, one must have access to available resources for designs (semiotic systems), ways to engage in design (semiotic processes), and the means to transform designs (a combination of received meanings and the agency to redesign them). The vision of social futures that this new notion of literacy infers relies on the assumption of multiple modalities and technologies. Although literacy has always been multimodal (relying at the very least on visual and aural cues), contemporary literacy practices rely on an increasingly complex range of modalities. The visual mode is particularly salient, with writing displayed alongside image (or with writing displayed graphically *as* image), demanding a new and sophisticated set of semiotic skills. Merchant (2001) gave the example of girls engaged in Internet chat who regularly send picture files and Web site URLs along with their written conversations. Social networking sites are attractive to users not only for their text messaging capabilities but because they allow users to create mutimodal online personalities. In 2006, 45% of active Web users signed on to social networking sites (with MySpace at the top) to connect with friends and represent themselves to others through photos, music, videos, and other graphics (Adegoke, 2006). As Kress (2003) argued, the linguistic elements of texts are becoming less complex (e.g., fewer embedded clauses) while the visual elements are becoming more so, shifting the focus from linguistic features to elements of design, a development that Kress and Jewitt (2003) believed will eventually change the nature of writing on the page as it has on the screen.

In fact, even now, movement from page to screen is not unidirectional. That is, the formats and concepts of screen reading and writing are often incorporated into the page as well. This is made clear by the plethora of children's and young adult literature that incorporate elements of screen formats used in online zines, e-mail, and chat (e.g., *Gossip Girl* series by Cecily von Ziegesar). In a study about seven- and eight-year-olds who drew upon popular culture for their school writing, one boy incorporated in his writing on the page not only the story line but the language used in his favorite multiplayer computer games (Ranker, 2004). Thus, typical screen language used when playing computer games, such as the term *death points,* was used in the written story, in effect creating a media mix or a remediation of the game world from the screen to the page.

This change in textual form and function has come with a change in literacy practices (Leu, 2000; Reinking, 1998; Reinking, Labbo, & McKenna, 2000). Readers and writers make meaning across modes, laterally. They sample the multimodal resources available to them (often on the screen), creating coherence from the panoply of surface features and the juxtapositions of texts and genres and modes (Luke, C., 2003). With the focus on design, the process of critical analysis centers on intertextual reading, not only across texts but across genres and modes as well (Buckingham & Sefton-Green, 1995; Leu, 2000; Myers, Hammett, & McKillop, 1998). In this move "from page to screen" (Snyder, 1998), the sort of reading that many readers of this chapter will find most comfortable—that is, deep analysis or reflection—can be viewed as *one* way of reading, rather than *the only* way to be a competent reader (Kress, 2003). As Lankshear and Knobel (2004a; 2004b) pointed out, reading online involves understanding the architecture of a Web page, in all of its multimodal complexity—from browser menus to hyperlinks and audio files. There is no evidence that online literacies have displaced more established forms of literacy, but certainly literacy practices have diversified and taken on new dimensions (Kellner, 2002; Livingstone, 2002).

Digital Literacies Are Both Global and Local

Karaidy's (1999) description of ICTs as "glocalized" aptly characterized the Internet as a space where the global and local intersect. As new technologies, such as IM, become integrated in young people's school days and daily lives, a space where young people enact and perform their identities, we need to consider what it means that they are owned and controlled by corporate interests, and have been since 1995 when the Internet became a fully privatized medium (Fabos, 2004). As such, young people's online experiences feed commercial interests. For example, in a study of an online community for adolescent females, Duncan and Leander (2000) found that while the commercially owned Web site may have provided a space for girls to display some sense of power and self-definition, its primary purpose was to produce consumer identities and serve commercial interests.

Many chat rooms and bulletin boards, in the guise of enabling young people to create content and speak their minds, are commercially sponsored Web sites where marketers monitor teens' postings to gather information about popular trends and products (Center for Media Education, 2001, p. 6). The separation of content from advertising erodes on the Web, targeting teens as a prime market, through chat spaces that serve as "branded communities" (Center for Media Education, 2001, p. 5) in which trendy brand-name companies create clubs with 'free membership" that include chat spaces, e-mail newsletters, fashion tips, and so on. Thus, online users become not only *subjects in*, but also the *objects of*, the new global capitalism.

The "glocalized" space of the Internet presents a particular set of research problems for those of us who approach our research using ethnographic tools. The "hypersociality" (Ito, 2005, p. 3) and everyday online practices of local peer groups shape and are shaped by "pervasive mass-media ecologies" (p. 2) that flow transnationally. The fact that AOL corners the market for IMing interfaces and that users must have AOL in order to chat with buddies whose families use AOL is one example of how transnational flows of capital shape local activity.

Moreover, as Ito (2005) suggested, "the real is being colonized by the virtual" (p. 3) in ways not directly connected to the political economy of the Internet. As I discuss more fully in the next section, young people's everyday interactions are shaped by their interactions online, and, in turn, reshape their online social worlds. This is true not only in terms of their online conversations, but also in terms of how they market their online personas across sites by carefully crafting profiles that become part of local and global flows. The challenge, then, for researchers who study cultural production in local contexts is to figure out how to study online activity from both a local and global perspective, how to study the activity up close using the usual ethnographic tools of participant observation, interview, video, and local artifacts and also trace this activity as it distributed across sites (Ito, 2004; Leander & McKim, 2003) and global flows (Luke, A., 2003).

Tracing the relationship between the local and the global is an important skill to develop in users as well as researchers. Several British researchers have found that U.K.-based chat users generally assume that other users are American (Livingstone, 2002; Merchant, 2001). The economic and linguistic dominance of the U.S. presence on the Internet makes such assumptions commonplace yet rarely interrogated by U.S. users. Building users' awareness of commercial interests and transnational flows is no easy matter. As a step in this direction, Burbules and Callister (2000) and Fabos (2004) argued for careful, critical readings of Internet sites and texts to uncover the politics of representation and commercial sponsorship, and A. Luke (2003) suggested that literacy education should provide "critical engagements with globalized flows of information, image, text, and discourse" (p. 20). Rather than viewing print as less important than graphical elements to this enterprise, Kellner (2002) believed that analytic reading of print online will remain important in order for people to thoughtfully examine, critique, and filter extensive amounts of information.

THE CHANGING DIMENSIONS OF LITERACY PRACTICES

The key claims of social mediation, multimodality, and "glocalization" are foundational to understanding practices more specific to Internet communication. I begin this section with a summary of the general findings from studies on electronic networks and follow with a discussion of three important changes in the dimensions of literacy practices that have implications for the teaching and learning of English/language arts in digitally mediated times. I will illustrate these changing dimensions of practice with examples from research on IC.

Findings Related to Internet Communication

IC has been found to hold potential for the development of new social and linguistic identities and relationships (Alvermann, 2002; Baym, 2002; Chandler-Olcott & Mahar, 2003; Kaplan & Farrell, 1994; Lewis & Fabos, 2005; Takayoshi, Huot, E., & Huot, M., 1999; Thiel, 2005; Thomas, 2005; Turkle, 1995). According to Danet, Ruedenberg-Wright, and Rosenbaum-Tamari (1998), the social and linguistic potential of electronic communication lies in its affinity to play as an activity that is "voluntary, intensely absorbing, done for its own sake, and . . . more or less rule-governed." Others, however, point to the potential for online communication to perpetuate, even exacerbate, inequitable social relations and limiting social roles (Gray, 1999; Herring, Johnson, & DiBenedetto, 1995; Silver, 1998; Thiel, 2005; Thomas, 2004; Warshauer, 2002). Along these lines, some studied have found that although girls often gain a sense of agency and control through IC, they also enact normative gendered discourses (Lewis & Fabos, 2005; Lewis & Finders, 2002). For example, one of our participants in the IM study posed on occasion as someone who was "blond-haired, blue-eyed" because she believed having these particular media markers of beauty would extend exchanges with boys she did not know. Given a social sphere that excludes the body, she inserted one that would work for her and gave her a sense of control. However, the fact that she resorted to traditional markers of white feminine beauty in the rare social sphere where it need not be central, shows that normative gender and race positions are not so easily erased even in a space that is sometimes hailed as a new form of social existence and multiple identities

Abbott (1998) claimed that chat pushes the envelope of literacy practices by offering young people "a highly sophisticated and complex means of speaking to their peers, to others interested in the same topics and to those they seek to influence" (p. 102). In a case study of a Chinese immigrant youth, Lam (2000) found that one youth was able to construct and reconstruct his social identity through his Internet communication with a group of transnational peers. Commenting on this study, Gee (2002) described this youth's social identity as one that develops around an affinity group rather than a cultural affiliation (see also Gee, 2001). Such affiliations, shaped by common practices, activities, and goals rather than through common identity markers such as race, ethnicity, age, or gender, have been found to flourish through Internet communication and other digital literacies (Alvermann, Hagood, & Williams, 2001; Thomas, 2005; Tobin, 2001).

In a large scale study conducted by researchers in the United Kingdom, Livingstone and Bober (2004) investigated uses of the Internet among young people (9–19) in order to find out how the Internet is shaping family life, peer cultures, and learning. Related to Internet communication, these researchers found that one third of the young people found chatting with friends online, more often than not local friends, to be at least as satisfying as talking face to face. Many of these youth used IC to engage in identity play involving some pretense about themselves (their ages, appearances, and so forth). Rather than thinking of offline and online spaces as separate social worlds, a number of studies have found that these spaces intersect and overlap. In fact, the maintenance of offline relationships is a documented feature of online communication (Holloway & Valentine, 2003; Leander & McKim, 2003; Lewis & Fabos, 2005; Valentine, Holloway, & Bingham, 2000), or many people writing online is used so often for the purpose of sustaining social relationships that its ordinariness is taken for granted as a part of the fabric of daily social life (Wellman, 2004).

These findings are consonant with findings from the study already mentioned of seven adolescents' uses of IMing and the social practices and identities afforded by the technology (Lewis & Fabos, 2005). We found that our participants demonstrated numerous skills as they engaged in IM. They were acutely aware of the various audiences they were addressing, adapting their subject matters and writing styles accordingly. They critically analyzed the language of IM in terms of the rhetorical context within which it was framed and in terms of what the texts could do for them. They demonstrated a degree of control (and pleasure) that emerged from their ability to make choices when using IM that gave them power in peer relationships. These conclusions, based on close analysis, were important in answering our research questions related to the functions and purposes of IM. However, when we turned to an analysis of literacy practices rather than literacy events (Barton & Hamilton, 1998; Street, 1995), turning our attention to what we could infer from the events that might have broader social and cultural meanings, we were able to understand more about the kinds of social identities that form around IM use and the potential consequences of these identity formations on students' lives in and out of school.

Performativity, Hybrid Textuality, and Circulation in Internet Communication

In her book, *Young People and New Media,* Livingstone (2002) asked a question pertinent to this section:

> "To the extent that we are indeed witnessing a transformation in the notion of the text, one must ask whether there are parallel changes in the user (or reader)? And if so, are such changes in young people's ways of knowing to be encouraged" (p. 229)?

Those of us interested in teaching and learning must focus our attention on the user (reader/writer) of digital texts, not so much because the texts themselves are not important—the earlier section on multimodality should make clear that the change in texts are, indeed, important—but because, as already mentioned, the distance between the text and the user is minimized when users engage in digital literacy practices. A prominent feature of IC is interactivity, with reader, writer, and text merging in a fast-paced exchange of words in print, words to be encoded, decoded, interpreted, invented, revised, inflected, and so on, moment to moment. Add to this drama the incorporation of graphical elements, such as photo and video streaming, emoticons, color, and font variations, and we can begin to imagine the active involvement of the user, and therefore the need for researchers to understand the user's role in the reading and writing practices online.

Lankshear and Knobel (2004a; 2004b) argued that classroom reading programs emphasize texts over practices, but that beyond the classroom, texts take a second seat to practices. That is, texts outside the classroom are most often used in the service of accomplishing particular practices and social interactions, thus increasing the central role of the reader in the reader/text transaction, and in shaping the nature of the text through interaction. Process, rather than product, plays a central role in forms of representation on the Internet (Livingstone, 2002). This change in the nature of literacy practices in new media and, especially, electronic networks, has implications for teaching and learning. As researchers and educators, we need to understand the changing nature of literacy—changing practices and epistemologies—in order to teach literacy effectively in 21st-century schools.

In this section, I discuss the literacy practices of our participants in the IM study. In discussing these practices—performativity, hybrid textualilty, and circulation[2]—I include some examples from this study as well as examples from three studies that focus entirely on adolescents' uses of chat or IM. These studies, by Merchant (2001), Thomas (2004), and Thiel (2005), reinforced the points I want to make about performativity, hybrid textuality, and circulation. Although the three practices intersect, for the purposes of clarity, I discuss them separately.

Performativity. In order to be a proficient IM user, one must "perform" a version of one's self, shifting voices moment to moment for many audiences at once. *Performativity* is the term I am using for the way that speakers and writers take up positions in relation to the expectations of others and the social codes and discourses available to them (Bauman & Briggs, 1990; Conquergood, 1989; Lewis, 2001). Individual and group identities are defined through repeated performances (ways of interacting, uses of writing and other semiotic systems) as participants "perform the self," which is always in relation to the group (Butler, 1990; Dyson, 1992; Enciso, 1998; Tobin, 2000). Writers in digital environments frequently address, and are addressed, by multiple audiences simultaneously, and consequently, discerning expectations and social codes can be complicated. To manage the task, users have to draw on the intertextual chains (New London Group, 1996, 2000) that exist through the textual history of each exchange and the larger textual network. One of the participants in our IM study, Abby, demonstrated her lived understanding of these intertextual chains in her ability to shift her performances almost instantaneously, performing "sympathetic conspirator" in response to one conversational buddy's hurt feelings about a girl who was ignored him, "casual acquaintance" with several other buddies, and "flirtatious friend" with a male buddy who wanted her to put him in her info box. "Only if I can be in yours," she replied. Although face-to-face interaction is also performative (e.g., Bauman & Briggs, 1990; Conquergood, 1989; Goffman, 1959), the need to fluidly shift performances from audience to audience is unique to the dyadic yet nearly simultaneous nature of IM.

Examining Abby's IM transcripts, we found out firsthand what scholars of digital literacies mean when they point to the skills needed to be a successful online reader and writer. Abby had to be able to scan across windows (often 10 at a time), spatially, to do the work of this kind of writing. She had to read and write quickly across surfaces, delving deeper only when a particular conversational thread kept surfacing, and thus demanding a more developed response. Thus, she quickly said "hey" to several friends, had a quick exchange about her day with another buddy, and dipped in and out of a more pressing exchange with another buddy. Making on-the-spot decisions about where to focus one's attention is critical to managing the flow across messages. This is an act most of us are not accustomed to performing in writing. It can be challenging to manage the continuing threads of conversations as they occur in time. When arranged spatially, however, with each buddy (and corresponding window) in its place in the stack, as Abby had them, she was able to manage the conversational flow with each of her buddies, and juggle the storylines that shaped her social world.

One reason that Abby is able to manage these performances of self is that she is situated *at once* within the techno-social space of the Internet and the social-embodied space offline. In their article on the past and future of Internet research, Leander and McKim (2003) destabilized the offline/online binary that underlies much of this research and argue for methodologies that trace techno-social-embodied networks across contexts and bounded notions of time and space. Merchant's (2001) study of girls' participation in Internet chat rooms made the further point that while buddies actually chat online, providing advice and support to offline friends, they often converse online about things that they would find difficult to take up in face-to-face conversation. He illustrated this point with a conversation between a boy and a girl in which the girl advised the boy that he was "crowding" the girl he fancied, something that would be difficult to say in person. Writers in the IM environment are constituted in voices, their own and others, that merge and overlap within and across contexts as the writing self is addressed by and answerable to others.

Identities online are enacted as temporary attachments, as Hall would have it, in order to be recognized as a particular kind of person

[2] These and other dimensions of practice related to digital literacy were developed in collaboration with Donna Alvermann and Kevin Leander (Lewis, Alvermann, & Leander, 2004).

(Gee, 2001) within particular histories of relationships and discursive formations. One of Thomas's (2004) participants reported making conscious linguistic choices in order to perform alternative identities online and playfully trick her friends. Instead of gender swapping in their role playing, however, most of her participants performed idealized versions of femininity through their choice of avatars (an image that represents each user) and their talk about appearance and the body. As mentioned earlier, one of the participants in our IM study chose to pose as blonde-haired and blue-eyed in keeping with her vision of what it means to be the idealized female. These are examples of participants enacting temporary attachments within particular historical and discursive formations of gender.

The enactment of these multiple identities calls into question what it means to have an "authentic" or "personal" voice as a writer. Envisioning voice as "authentic" or "personal" privileges stability across texts rather than the dynamic, fluid concept of voice exhibited by IM writers as they enact identities that depend upon a running analysis of complicated online and offline contexts. Users typically converse with buddies rapidly across multiple windows (no less than four windows at a time for any of the seven participants in our IM study). In Thiel's (2005) study of adolescent girls' uses of IM, she found that her participants presented themselves differently as they shifted from window to window, taking on different roles almost simultaneously. Such was the case in our IM study as well, and participants clearly articulated the shifts for us in interviews. They told us about using a "softer and sweeter" tone with a good friend and shifting to curt, one-word answers for those with whom they did not want to converse. Moreover, we witnessed these sometimes subtle and sometimes dramatic shifts as we watched each participant engage in an IM session. The technology (multiple windows, synchronicity, graphical possibilities) and hyper-sociality (Ito, 2005) of IC makes for a performative practice.

Circulation. Surveillance on IM is often achieved through the paths that messages travel as they are circulated. Leander and McKim (2003) suggested that examining how digital texts travel or circulate can lead to insights about the kinds of practices and relationships a particular technology affords.

One of the simplest methods of circulating participants' movements and messages online was through the commonly asked question, "Who else are you talking to?" resulting in IM buddies having indirect exchanges with a wider range of people through other buddies (e.g., "Tell her . . ."). This simple question allowed the question asker to have some degree of knowledge about and control over the movements and conversations of buddies outside of the immediate dyad. This way of monitoring the conversations of others is evident in the following conversation excerpt from Thiel's study (2005):

Caroline says: whos on for u?
Beth says: um . . . lemme check
Beth says: anne, bethany jack,carna,u,colleen,amy,mandy ,an my cuzs friend
Caroline says: sh except i have more (SH means "Same here")
Beth says: like who??
Caroline says: jeff, Dylan, chris, carrie and alotmorw
Caroline says: and jack
Beth says: how many peeps r on??
Caroline says: 10
Beth says: ic

In our study, conversations easily became part of other conversations within a given IM session. Participants routinely cut and pasted elements of one conversation and shared them with another buddy—often without disclosing their actions with the first buddy, who may have done the same with someone else. Several of the girls also tried surreptitiously to discover who was currently talking to whom and what they happened to be talking about by IMing inquiries to friends and asking them to report back. Abby, for instance, would report to her girlfriends to tell them about her conversations with boys, sometimes cutting and pasting the most important parts for her girlfriends' pleasure.

By circulating messages in this fashion, our participants cut and pasted, rearranged, and reconfigured elements of their lives to be offered up for scrutiny in the IM landscape. This kind of surveillance was expected, afforded through the technology and participants' relationships to the technology and to each other. IM produces identities that are accustomed to being both the agent and object of scrutiny and surveillance.

Being an agentic participant in these patterns of circulation requires quick in-process thinking. It required that users swiftly assess the nature of the circulating text, the purpose or agenda that led to its circulation, the audiences involved, the allegiances it may foster or damage, and so forth. Participants performed selves—enacted identities—in relation to these circulating texts. These patterns of circulation functioned to reinforce social connections, creating bonds between particular users, sometimes at the expense of others, adding the intrigue of surveillance to the IM experience, but also monitoring and reinforcing normative gender relations. For instance, some of our female participants manipulated their IM profiles to make themselves older and, they felt, more appealing to males in chat rooms.

In her book on young people's uses of new media, Livingstone (2002) pointed out that Internet spaces are more often "based on bricolage or juxtaposition." This representational style, Lankshear and Knobel (2003) and Leu (2000) suggested, is keyed to new epistemologies, new ways of being and thinking. I would argue that these new epistemologies are related to new practices of circulation, which depend on the cut and paste style of bricolage and juxtaposition for production and exchange.

Textuality. The hybrid nature of textuality in Internet communication also contributes to performative enactments of identity. The textuality of writing is used to perform the textual qualities of speech. This blending of spoken and written textuality results in hybrid language forms to represent the casual, insider exchanges of informal speech through written textual features.

To achieve a speech-like quality, electronic writers use syntax, vocabulary and usage more common in speech as well as abbreviations to make for quick speech-like exchanges and to communicate paralinguistic features of face-to-face communication contexts. Using examples from one of our participant's IM exchange, her speech-like syntax included, "I don't think they talk much tho," and her vocabulary included words with dropped endings—"just chattin'." Her abbreviations made for speedy responses, "Im" for (I am) and "u" for (you), as did her lack of punctuation. In other participants' IM exchanges, abbreviations such as LOL (laugh out loud) or POS (parents over shoulder) were used to communicate what interlocutors would have seen had they been communicating face to face. The textual shape that IM takes, then, is an innovative blending of speech and writing. As Merchant argued (2001) "traditional distinctions between speech as synchronous face-to-face communication in a shared location and writing as a means of communicating through time and space are challenged by new technology" (p. 299).

The textual shape of IC is significant as it relates to the kinds of social identities afforded through its use. Again, performativity is central to this discussion. As Thomas (2004) pointed out, "In the online context . . . to write is to exist . . . writing is an essential component for performing identity" (p. 366). One of the participants in Thomas's study explained in an interview the strategies she used to create interaction through textuality (e.g., exclamation points, references to actions, and facial expressions). Thomas made the link to identity performance:

> What is rarely reported is that the linguistic variations of cybertalk are directly related to identity performance. Violetta revealed that her words had to look just so, and that she would vary her style of speech according to the persona she was performing. (p. 366)

Our participants in the IM study enacted identities through language that had to sound—and look, semiotically—like speech, but be accomplished through writing. One of our participants, Sam, wrote her way into the textual worlds of a new group to which she wanted to belong, hearing the cadences of their inside jokes and trying to "sound" right in writing. She explicitly referred to her efforts to "talk like they do" when she posed as the friend of someone who accidentally got onto her buddy list. She copied the "voice" of this person in order to maintain the connection. "I'll use the same exclamations where she uses them and I'll try to talk like they do," Sam told us. In adapting the tone and content of the anonymous correspondent's message, Sam had to analyze how the girl's tone worked—how it accomplished its purposes. Besides adapting her tone, Sam was also careful to adjust her subject matter according to her particular audience.

In this way, IM writers produce the sound of speech. However, according to another of our participants, this virtual speech takes on a life of its own with adept IM writers using the disembodied textuality of writing to "sound smart and sophisticated" in ways that go beyond face to face. The virtual, it seems, may idealize the real, becoming the way that "real" speech ought to sound, thus further interrupting any facile distinctions between the virtual and the real, between speech and writing.

Enacting identities, then, involved performing multivocal textual repertoires with speed and flexibility, all within the boundaries of normative structures of gender and power. In spite of these boundaries, our participants were involved in the generative act of using texts in new ways, reconfiguring messages, cutting and pasting, parodying, creating textual forms to fit their social needs.

Digital Practices and Literacy in School

Internet communication draws on practices that shape users' relationships to knowledge and identities. These practices demand that users adopt habits of mind that are flexible, adapting across genres and modes, performing enactments of self (or identity) that relate to changing discursive and social spaces

Kress, Jewitt, and Tsatsarelis (2000) argued that the social politic outside of school—the global, fast-capital economy, the communicative webs, the multiple modes of representation—are all about multiplicity, performativity, flexibility, and adaptability, while the social politic in school remains centered on notions of stability, authenticity, and unity. Obviously, then, typical ways of being in school leave out the compelling lives many young people live outside of school. Kress et al. argued further that, for schools to meet the new demands of great economic and social change, educators need to begin to see learners as "remakers, constantly of the materials with which they engage" (p. 28).

Preparing for changing epistemologies, identities, and practices should not mean either appropriating young people's popular technologies for school use or disregarding the deep and deliberative reading and writing processes associated with analytic and critical understandings and interpretations. Although bringing IM or other forms of Internet communication into the classroom may be possible for particular projects and purposes, doing so should not be viewed as the lesson to learn from the body of IC research. In fact, such appropriation would change the objectives and motives of the activity, the roles of the young people engaging in the activity, and the group norms associated with the activity. One of the reasons that the youth we studied used IM literacy so productively is that they were very clear about these aspects of the activity. Their heightened knowledge of the objectives and motives, roles, and rules led to what is clearly a strategic and analytic use of literacy.

The question we need to ask is not how to actually use electronic communication in the classroom, but how to apply to school settings the literacy *practices* young people take up with a great deal of engagement. As we have tried to show throughout this chapter, the change in literacy practices is more significant than the change in literacy tools. The tools afford particular practices, but the practices themselves are producing new epistemologies. Because schools inevitably legitimize some epistemologies or others, it is important to introduce those epistemologies connected to literacies as they occur in a range of settings such as homes, libraries, work places, churches, and community centers (for ways to approach making these practices part of the classroom repertoire, see Lewis & Fabos, 2005). The dimensions of practice I have described in this chapter—performativity, hybrid textuality, and circulation—are expressed through other media as well. Many forms of popular culture and performance arts have at their core interactive and intertextual qualities that express literacy in combination with human voice, movement, color, music, and so forth. Drama, collage, comics, and videos are but a few of the media teachers can draw on to key into the dimensions of practice discussed in this chapter.

As a community of literacy educators and researchers, if we let our "generational anxiety over new forms of adolescent and childhood identity and life pathways" (Luke, A., & Luke, C., 2004, p. 105) get the best of us, and if we mourn the loss of print literacy as we think we once knew it, then we may find ourselves schooling young people in literacy practices that disregard the vitality of their literate lives and the needs they will have for their literate and social futures at home, at work, and in their communities. Now into the first decade of the 21st century, we have seen the publication of several satires on life in a digital age. One of these books (Johnson, 2005) included a brief satire on the inadequate educational benefits of books as compared to computer games from the perspective of adults in another universe where kids have been playing games forever but where books are the newest rage. Among those inadequacies: Books understimulate the senses, they are "tragically" isolating, and their fixed linear path limits the reader's imagination and interaction with the text. Although the author is purposely exaggerating the inadequacies of the book, the passage makes the important point that the commonplace perception of digital games as mindless has more to do with the practices and epistemologies we have normalized rather than those we might envision.

Finally, I'd like to return to Livingstone's (2002) words, quoted earlier:

> "To the extent that we are indeed witnessing a transformation in the notion of the text, one must ask whether there are parallel changes in the user (or reader)? And if so, are such changes in young people's ways of knowing to be encouraged"? (p. 229)

This chapter argues that there are, indeed, parallel changes in the user (or reader). I suspect it will not matter much if parents, educators, and other adults encourage the changes or not. Young people will continue to engage in Internet communication and other digital practices during their out-of-school hours. The question is whether we want to make school literacy more engaging for students and more meaningful to their present and future lives in a digitally mediated world. If so, then we need to understand the shifts in practices and epistemologies that have taken place and consider how these shifts should inform our teaching of reading and writing.

REFERENCES

Abbott, C. (1998). Making connections: Young people and the Internet. In J. Sefton-Green (Ed.), *Digital diversions* (pp. 84–105). London: Taylor & Francis.

Adegoke, Y. (2006, May 25). Why mainstream advertisers are launching into MySpace. *Marketing Weekly*, p. 30.

Alvermann, D. E. (2002). *Adolescents and literacies in a digital world.* New York: Peter Lang.

Alvermann, D. E., Hagood, M. C., & Williams, K. B. (2001). Image, language, and sound: Making meaning with popular culture texts. *Reading Online, 4.* Retrieved June 1, 2007 from http://www.readingonline.org/newliteracies/lit_index.asp?HREF=/newliteracies/action/alvermann/index.html

Ba, H., Tally, W., & Tsikalas, K. (2002). Investigating children's emerging digital literacies. *The Journal of Technology, Learning, and Assessment, 1.* Retrieved June 1, 2007, from http://www.jtla.org

Barton, D., & Hamilton, M. (1998). *Local literacies: Reading and writing in one community.* New York: Routledge.

Barton, D., Hamilton, M., & Ivanic, R. (Eds.). (2000). *Situated literacies: Reading and writing in context.* New York: Routledge Press.

Bauman, R., & Briggs, C. (1990). Poetics and performance as critical perspectives on language and social life. *Annual Review of Anthropology, 19,* 59–88.

Baym, N. (2002). Interpersonal life online. In L. A. Lievrouw, & S. Livingstone (Eds.), *Handbook of new media: Social shaping and consequences of ICTs* (pp. 62–76). Thousand Oaks, CA: Sage Publications.

Beach, R., & Lundell, D. (1998). Early adolescents' use of computer-mediated communication in writing and reading. In D. Reinking, M. McKenna, L. Labbo, & R. Kieffer (Eds.), *Handbook of literacy and technology* (pp. 93–112). Mahwah, NJ: Lawrence Erlbaum Associates.

Bigum, C. (2002). Design sensibilities, schools, and the new computing and communication technologies. In I. Snyder (Ed.), *Silicon literacies: Communication, innovation, and education in the electron age* (pp. 130–140). New York: Routledge.

Bolter, J., & Grusin, R. (2000). *Remediation: Understanding new media.* Cambridge, MA: MIT Press.

Bruce, B. (1997). Literacy technologies: What stance should we take. *Journal of Literacy Research, 29,* 289–309.

Buckingham, D. (2002). The electronic generation? Children and new media. In L. A. Lievrouw, & S. Livingstone (Eds.), *Handbook of new media: Social shaping and consequences of ICTs* (pp. 77–89). Thousand Oaks, CA: Sage Publications.

Buckingham, D., & Sefton-Green, J. (1995). *Cultural studies goes to school: Reading and teaching popular media.* Bristol, PA: Taylor & Francis.

Burbules, N. C., & Callister, T. A. (2000). *Watch it: The risks and promises of information technologies for education.* Boulder, CO: Westview Press.

Butler, J. (1990). Performative acts and gender constitution: An essay in phenomenology and feminist theory. In S. Case (Ed.), *Performing feminisms: Feminist critical theory and theater* (pp. 270–282). Baltimore, MD: John Hopkins University Press.

Center for Media Education. (2001). *TeenSites.com: A field guide to the new digital landscape.* Retrieved June 1, 2007, from http://www.cme.org

Chandler-Olcott, K., & Mahar, D. (2003). "Tech-savviness" meets multiliteracies: Exploring adolescent girls' technology-mediated literacy practices. *Reading Research Quarterly, 38,* 356–385.

Conquergood, D. (1989). Poetics, play, process, and power: The performative turn in anthropology. *Text and Performance Quarterly, 1,* 82–95.

Danet, B., Ruedenberg-Wright, L. & Rosenbaum-Tamari, Y. (1998). Hmmmm . . . where's that smoke coming from? Writing, play and performance on Internet Relay Chat [Electronic version]. *Journal of Computer-Mediated Communication, 2.* Retrieved June 1, 2007, from http://jcmc.indiana.edu/vol2/issue4/danet.html

Duncan B, & Leander, K. (2000, November). Girls just wanna have fun: Literacy, consumerism, and paradoxes of position on furl.com. *Reading Online, 4.* Retrieved June 1, 2007 from http://www.readingonline.org/electronic/elec_index.asp?HREF=/electronic/duncan/index.html Dyson, A. H. (1992). The case of the singing scientist: A performance perspective on the "stages" of school literacy. *Written Communication, 9,* 3–45.

Enciso, P. E. (1998). Good/bad girls read together: Pre-adolescent girls' co-authorship of feminine subject positions during a shared reading event. *English Education, 30,* 44–62.

Fabos, B. (2004). *Wrong turn! Education and commercialism on the information superhighway.* New York: Teachers College Press.

Fairclough, N. (1992). *Discourse and social change.* Cambridge, U.K.: Polity Press.

Gee, J. P. (1990). *Sociolinguistics and literacies: Ideology in discourses* (2nd ed.). New York: Falmer Press.

Gee, J. P. (2001). Identity as an analytic lens for research in education. *Review of Research in Education, 25,* 99–125.

Gee, J. P. (2002). Millennials and Bobos, Blue's Clues and Sesame Street: A story for our times. In D. E. Alvermann (Ed.), *Adolescents and literacies in a digital world* (pp. 51–67). New York: Peter Lang.

Goffman, E. (1959). *The presentation of self in everyday life.* New York: Doubleday.

Gray, J. H. (1999). *"Maybe . . . She was a down-low girl": How young adolescent students construct understanding of online peers.* Paper presented at the annual meeting of the American Educational Research Association, Montréal, Canada.

Herring, S. (2004). Slouching toward the ordinary. *New Media and Society, 6,* 26–36.

Herring, S., Johnson, D. A., & DiBenedetto, T. (1995). "This discussion is going too far!" Male resistance to female participation on the Internet. In K. Hall, & M. Bucholtz (Eds.), *Gender articulated: Language and the socially constructed self* (pp. 67–96). New York: Routledge.

Holloway, S. L., & Valentine, G. (2003). *Cyberkids: Children in the information age.* New York: Routledge.

Ito, M. (2004). *Technologies of the childhood imagination: Yugioh, media mixes, and Otaku.* Keynote address presented at the Digital generations: Children, Young People, and New Media conference, Centre for the Study of Children, Youth and Media, University of London. Retrieved June 1, 2007 from http://www.itofisher.com/mito/archives/000075.html

Ito, M. (2005). *Technologies of childhood imagination: Yugioh, media mixes, and everyday cultural production.* Retrieved June 1, 2007 from http://www.itofisher.com/mito/archives/000074.html

Johnson, S. (2005). *Everything bad is good for you: How today's popular culture is making us smarter.* New York: Riverhead Books.

Kaplan, N., & Farrell, E. (1994). Weavers of webs: A portrait of young women on the net. *The Arachnet Electronic Journal on Virtual Culture, 2.* Retrieved June 1, 2007, from http://www.monash.edu.au/journals/ejvc/kaplan.v2n3

Karaidy, M. M. (1999). The global, the local, and the hybrid: A native ethnography of glocalization. *Critical Studies in Mass Communication, 16,* 454–467.

Kellner, D. (2002). New media and new literacies: Reconstructing education for the new millennium. In L. A. Lievrouw, & S. Livingstone (Eds.), *Handbook of new media: Social shaping and consequences of ICTs* (pp. 90–104). Thousand Oaks, CA: Sage Publications.

Kress, G. (2003). *Literacy in the new media age.* New York: Routledge.

Kress, G., & Jewitt, C. (2003). Introduction. In C. Jewitt, & G. Kress (Eds.), *Multimodal literacy: New literacies and digital epistemologies* (Vol. 4, pp. 1–18). New York: Peter Lang.

Kress, G., Jewitt, C., & Tsatsarelis, C. (2000). Knowledge, identity, pedagogy, pedagogic discourse and the representational environments of education in late modernity. *Linguistics and Education, 11,* 7–30.

Lam, W. S. E. (2000). L2 literacy and the design of the self: A case study of a teenager writing on the Internet. *TESOL Quarterly, 34,* 457–482.

Lankshear, C., & Knobel, M. (2003). *New literacies: Changing knowledge and classroom learning.* Philadelphia: Open University Press.

Lankshear, C., & Knobel, M. (2004a). *From pencilvania to pixelandia: Mapping the terrain of 'new' literacies research.* Plenary address presented at the annual meeting of the National Reading Conference, San Antonio, Texas.

Lankshear, C., & Knobel, M. (2004b). *Text-related roles of the digitally 'at home.'* Paper presented at the annual meeting of the American Educational Research Association, San Diego, California.

Lankshear, C., Snyder, I., & Green, B. (2000). *Teachers and technoliteracy: Managing literacy, technology and learning in schools.* St. Leonards, Australia: Allen and Unwin.

Leander, K. M. (2004). *Home/schooling, everywhere: Digital literacies as practices of space-time.* Paper presented at the annual meeting of the American Educational Research Association, San Diego, California.

Leander, K. M., & McKim, K. (2003). Tracing the everyday "sitings" of adolescents on the Internet: A strategic adaptation of ethnography across online and offline spaces. *Education, Communication, & Information, 3,* 211–240.

Lemke, J. L. (1998). Metamedia literacy: Transforming meanings and media. In D. Reinking, M. C. McKenna, L. D. Labbo, & R. D. Kieffer (Eds.), *Literacy and technology: Transformations in a post-typographic world* (pp. 283–302). Mahwah, NJ: Lawrence Erlbaum Associates.

Lenhart, A., Madden, M., & Hitlin, P. (2005). *Teens and technology: Youth are leading the transition to a fully wired and mobile nation.* Retrieved June 1, 2007, from http://www.pewinternet.org/PPF/r/162/report_display.asp

Leu, D. J. (2000). Literacy and technology: Deictic consequences for literacy education in an information age. In M. Kamil, P. B. Mosenthal, P. D. Pearson, & R. Barr (Eds.), *Handbook of reading research* (Vol. III, pp. 743–770). Mahwah, NJ: Lawrence Erlbaum Associates.

Leu, D. J., Kinzer, C. K., Coiro, J. L., & Cammack, D. W. (2004). Toward a theory of new literacies emerging from the Internet and other information and communication technologies [Electronic version]. In R. B. Ruddell, & N. Unrau (Eds.), *Theoretical models and processes of reading* (5th ed.). Newark, DE: International Reading Association. Retrieved June 1, 2007, from http://www.readingonline.org/newliteracies/lit_index.asp?HREF=leu/

Lewis, C. (2001). *Literary practices as social acts: Power, status, and cultural norms in the classroom.* Mahwah, NJ: Lawrence Erlbaum Associates.

Lewis, C., Alvermann, D. E., & Leander, K. (2004, February). *Youth cultures, digital literacies, and intersecting methodologies.* Paper presented at the meeting of the National Council of Teachers of English Assembly for Research, Berkeley, California.

Lewis, C., & Fabos, B. (2005). Instant messaging, literacies, and social identities. *Reading Research Quarterly, 40*(4), 470–501.

Lewis, C., & Finders, M. (2002). Implied adolescents and implied teachers: A generation gap for new times. In D. E. Alvermann (Ed.), *New literacies and digital technologies: A focus on adolescent learners* (pp. 101–113). New York: Peter Lang.

Livingstone, S. (2002). *Young people and new media.* London: Sage.

Livingstone, S., & Bober, M. (2004). Taking up online opportunities? Children's uses of the Internet for education, communication, and participation. *E-Learning, 1,* 395–419.

Luke, A. (2003). Literacy education for a new ethics of global community. *Language Arts, 81,* 20–22.

Luke, A., & Luke, C. (2004). Adolescence lost/childhood regained: On early intervention and the emergence of the techno-subject. *Journal of Early Childhood Literacy, 1,* 91–120.

Luke, C. (2003). Pedagogy, connectivity, multimodalilty, and interdisciplinarity. *Reading Research Quarterly, 38,* 397–403.

Merchant, G. (2001). Teenagers in cyberspace: An investigation of language use and language change in internet chatrooms. *Journal of Reading Research, 24*(3), 293–306.

Myers, J., Hammett, R., & McKillop, A. M. (1998). Oppportunities for critical litereacy and pedagogy in student-authored hypermedia. In D. Reinking, M. C. McKenna, L. D. Labbo, & R. D. Kieffer (Eds.), *Handbook of literacy and technology: Transformations in a post-typographic world* (pp. 63–78). Mahwah, NJ: Lawrence Erlbaum Associates.

New London Group. (1996). A pedagogy of multiliteracies: Designing social futures. *Harvard Educational Review, 66,* 60–92.

New London Group. (2000). A pedagogy of multiliteracies: Designing social futures. In B. Cope, & M. Kalantzis (Eds.), *Multiliteracies: Literacy learning and the design of social futures* (pp. 9–37). New York: Routledge.

Pew Internet and American Life Project. (2005). *Digital divisions.* Retrieved June 1, 2007 from http://www.pewinternet.org/pdfs/PIP_Digital_Divisions_Oct_5_2005.pdf

Ranker, J. P. (2004). Responding to student-authored popular cultural fictions: Revaluing the literature studies-writing workshop formation. *Dissertation Abstracts International, Vol.*((UMI No. AAT 3129335). Retrieved June 1, 2007, from http://proquest.umi.com.proxy.cc.uic.edu/pqdweb?RQT=305&querySyntax=PQ&searchInterface=1&moreOptState=CLOSED&TS=1180732330&h_pubtitle=&h_pmid=&clientId=8224&JSEnabled=1&SQ=Ranker&DBId=G647&date=RANGE&onDate=&beforeDate=&afterDat=&fromDate=01%2F01%2F2004&toDate=12%2F31%2F2004&TITLE=&author=&SCH=&subject=&LA=any&MTYPE=all&sortby=REVERSE_CHRON.

Reinking, D. (1998). Introduction: Synthesizing technological transformations of literacy in a post-typographic world. In D. Reinking, M. C. McKenna, L. D. Labbo, & R. D. Kieffer (Eds.), *Handbook of literacy and technology: Transformations in a post-typographic world* (pp. xi–xxx). Mahwah, NJ: Lawrence Erlbaum Associates.

Reinking, D., Labbo, L., & McKenna, M. C. (2000). From assimilation to accommodation: A developmental framework for integrating digital technologies into literacy research and instruction. *Journal of Research in Reading, 23,* 110–122.

Rheingold, H. (2002). *Smart mobs: The next social revolution.* Cambridge, U.K.: Perseus

Silver, L. (1998). Same message, different medium. *WE (Women & Environment) International, 42/43,* 24–25.

Snyder, I. (1998). *Page to screen: Taking literacy into the electronic era.* New York: Routledge.

Street, B. V. (1995). *Social literacies: Critical approaches to literacy in development, ethnography and education.* London: Longman.

Takayoshi, P., Huot, E., & Huot, M. (1999). No boys allowed: The World Wide Web as a clubhouse for girls. *Computers and Composition, 16,* 89–106.

Thiel, S. (2005). 'IM Me': Identity construction and gender negotiation in the world of adolescent girls and instant messaging. In S. Mazzarella (Ed.), *Girl Wide Web: Girls, the Internet, and the negotiation of identity* (pp. 179–202). New York: Peter Lang.

Thomas, A. (2004). Digital literacies of the cybergirl. *E-Learning, 1,* 358–382.

Thomas, A. (2005). Children online: Learning in a virtual community of practice. *E-Learning, 2,* 27–38.

Tobin, J. (2000). *"Good guy's don't wear hats": Children's talk about the media.* New York: Teachers College Press.

Tobin, J. (2001). Save the geeks. *Journal of Adolescent & Adult Literacy, 44,* 504–508.

Turkle, S. (1995). *Life on the screen: Identity in the age of the Internet.* New York: Simon and Schuster.

Valentine, G., Holloway, S. L., & Bingham, N. (2000). Transforming cyberspace: Children's interventions in the new public sphere. In S. Holloway, & G. Valentine (Eds.), *Children's geographies: Playing, living, learning* (pp. 156–173). New York: Routledge.

Warshauer, M. (2002). Languages.com: The Internet and linguistic pluralism. In I. Snyder (Ed.), *Silicon literacies* (pp. 62–74). New York: Routledge.

Wellman, B. (2004). The three stages of Internet studies: Ten, five and zero years ago. *New Media and Society, 6,* 123–129.

26

ANIME AND MANGA FANDOM: YOUNG PEOPLE'S MULTILITERACIES MADE VISIBLE

Kelly Chandler-Olcott
SYRACUSE UNIVERSITY

In June of 2004, the following letter to the editor appeared in my local newspaper in response to a feature article the paper published about the Tokyo International Anime Fair. In the letter, high-school student Tatianna Smith (2004) expressed her keen interest in the Anime Fair, an annual convention sponsored by the city of Tokyo that draws tens of thousands of industry representatives and fans of animated films and television:

> I am writing in response to the article, "Suddenly, Japan is cool," in the May 12 edition of the *Post-Standard*. I am a big fan of all things Japanese, especially "J-pop," manga (comics), video games, and anime. So, of course I was drawn instantly to this article as soon as I heard about it from my friend. My first reaction was, "I hate whoever went there instead of me." My next reaction was that I thought it was cool that someone went to Japan and told the story of the Tokyo International Anime Fair. I must say that I enjoyed this article, even though it did not give me all the information that I would have liked. I would have enjoyed it if you would have given me a link to a Web site so that I could learn more about the Anime Fair.

In addition to being an encouraging indication that young people do see themselves as valued audience members for newspapers, Tatianna's letter demonstrates the important role played by *anime*, a term used to describe Japanese animation, in the lives of a growing number of young people in the West. Tatianna's description of her curiosity about what she calls "all things Japanese" points out the increasingly multimodal nature of fandom for many adolescents, whose passions for anime and its cousin, *manga* (Japanese comics), are closely tied to other interests in art, writing, music, and computer/video gaming. Tatianna's identification of the newspaper article's shortcoming—its lack of a link to an online source of further details—reminds us of the central place of digital communication technologies in providing young fans with up-to-date information about the objects of their fandom, as well as connecting them with each other. Each of these themes, among others, will be explored in more depth in the pages that follow.

The purpose of this chapter is to provide an introduction to anime and manga fandom for literacy teachers and researchers working with English-speaking youth in the West. In the first part of the chapter, I discuss the conceptions of fandom (Alvermann & Hagood, 2000; Jenkins, 1992; Storey, 1996; Trainor, 2004) and literacy (Cope & Kalantzis, 2000; New London Group, 1996) that inform the review. I include some definitions of anime and manga and some background about how these art forms are created, marketed, and understood in both Japan and the United States. Next, I share three patterns from the literature on anime and manga fandom, including my own recent work and that of my closest collaborator (Chandler-Olcott, 2004; Chandler-Olcott & Mahar, 2001, 2003a, 2003b; Mahar, 2003). I conclude by sharing some implications from these patterns that seem especially relevant for literacy research and practice.

CONCEPTUALIZING FANDOM AND LITERACY

In this section, I lay out two key concepts—(a) fandom and (b) multiliteracies—that ground the rest of the chapter. Like Brock, Boyd, and Moore (2003), I see it as important to make explicit the theories that "serv[e] as a framework for selecting and interpreting" (p. 446) the literature I review here; in this way, I hope to open up these ideas for others to consider, question, and debate in productive ways.

Fandom

A good deal of work on fandom has been grounded in the field of cultural studies, an interdisciplinary approach to understanding the meanings and practices of everyday life. One of the earliest and most influential studies in this tradition was Jenkins' (1992) *Textual Poachers*, an ethnography of fan subculture that followed devotees of popular media as they attended conventions; participated in computer-mediated discussions; and created artwork, songs, and fiction in response to those texts. Himself a long-time fan of the television show *Star Trek*, Jenkins argued that a number of dimensions of the subculture were important, including its "role in encouraging viewer activism," its function as an interpretive community setting particular standards for fans' work, and the social community it offered members (pp. 1–2). Drawing, in part, on Jenkins' (1992) work, Storey (1996) argued that a crucial aspect of fandom was not just consumption but also the production of texts such as fanfiction and fan art that responded to and borrowed elements from professionally produced media. More recently, contributors to an edited collection by Maira and Soep (2005) traced the connections between globalization and popular culture for young people living in a variety of countries, while Trainor (2004) argued that contribution of romance-themed fanfictions to the Gossamer Project, an online archive of material written by fans of the popular American television series *The X-Files*, allowed writers to construct different and more embodied "understandings of self" (p. 136) in a postmodern world that rarely privileges physical connection.

With teachers and researchers as their audience, Alvermann and Hagood (2000) articulated a conceptualization of fandom that made particular reference to adolescent literacy. Through two case studies, they demonstrated the often-sophisticated reading and writing practices associated with music fandom for two high school-aged students. The researchers' analysis led them to caution educators against stigmatizing youth's affinity for popular texts, arguing that a rigid distinction between high and low culture limits adults' opportunities to learn about young people's worlds. With this in mind, they argued that teachers take students' fandom seriously, making it a shared subject of inquiry in the classroom where possible:

> Exploring fandom with students may bring about insights into how students construct meaning from their personal interests and provide teachers with a window through which to view students' constructed identities. Along with this welcoming of fandom in the classroom would also come, we hope, an interest in critical media literacy instruction. An important premise in teaching critical media literacy is that teachers focus on respecting the pleasures adolescents experience as fans while simultaneously engaging them in a deeper understanding (through various reading, writing, speaking, and listening activities) of what it means to be a fan. (p. 437)

Multiliteracies

In addition to these cultural studies-influenced conceptions of fandom, this chapter is grounded in a conception of literacy best articulated by the members of the New London Group (1996; see also Cope & Kalantzis, 2000), a collective of literacy scholars from a variety of English-speaking countries who first met in New London, New Hampshire, in 1994. According to NLG members, existing theories of literacy teaching and learning were no longer adequate because they did not account for sociocultural shifts such as widening disparities in resources and opportunities between privileged and disadvantaged people or the increasing fragmentation of communities as they broke "into ever more diverse and subculturally defined groupings" (p. 61). The New London Group's framework was intended from the very beginning to acknowledge these trends and to develop a vigorous, powerful pedagogy that could contribute to a more just, equitable, and collaborative society. Indeed, "Literacy learning and the designing of social futures," the subtitle of the article that became the group's manifesto, made the activist nature of their work explicit.

Multiliteracies, the term the New London Group coined for the overall framework, was meant to reference two elements of their vision: (a) "the increasing salience of cultural and linguistic diversity" in contemporary society, and (b) "the multiplicity of text forms" associated with information and multimedia technologies (Cope & Kalantzis, 2000, p. 5). As their central metaphor, the NLG offered the concept of Design, an idea that for them,

> connect[ed] powerfully to the sort of creative intelligence the best practitioners need in order to be able continually to redesign their activities in the very act of practice. It connects as well to the idea that learning and productivity are the results of the designs (the structures) of complex systems of people, environments, technology, beliefs, and texts. (pp. 19–20)

Challenging an overreliance on traditional print as "anachronistic" (Cope & Kalantzis, 2000, p. 217), the New London Group argued that all semiotic activity uses "Available Designs," including not just linguistic, but also visual, audio, gestural, spatial, and multimodal resources for meaning-making, to create "The Redesigned," a new set of meanings. Unless school-based literacy pedagogy addressed these other modes, they warned, it stood no chance of addressing societal inequities and might, in fact, contribute to exacerbating them. Facility with multimodal thinking and multimedia composition was therefore a practical tool for life, not a frill or an add-on to traditional literacy skills and strategies.

Furthermore, in the New London Group's view, the process of Designing was not just about consuming or constructing texts, multimodal or otherwise. It was also about identity construction, as members argued that the outcome of Designing should always be seen as "a new meaning, something through which meaning-makers remake themselves" (New London Group, 1996, p. 86). They conceptualized the Design process as a complex interplay between "cultural resources," or "historically and culturally received patterns of meaning" (p. 86), and "uniquely positioned subjectivity," or the "unique product of human agency" (p. 86).

The combination of cultural studies and multiliteracies makes it possible to analyze the literature on anime and manga fandom in ways that would not be possible with only one framework. The cultural studies lens helps to place fans' transactions with anime and manga texts in sociocultural context, casting light on the influence of broad societal forces while simultaneously rejecting the stereotype of individual fans as media "dupes" (Buckingham & Sefton-Green, 2003; J. Tobin, 2004). The expanded definition of literacy associated with the multiliteracies framework helps enrich understanding of the multimodal and often technology-enhanced Designing embedded in fan-related practices. Both conceptions underscore the reshaping of cultural resources that is required by creation of fanfiction (the composition of new stories using characters, settings, and plot points from established media texts) and fan art (the creation of visual art borrowing from those same media texts). Without these theoretical perspectives, it would be far more difficult to identify patterns across the diverse types of literature presently available about anime and fandom. Before I move on to a more specific discussion of these patterns and their implications for literacy, however, let me provide some information about those sources and the processes I used to locate and evaluate them.

INFORMATION SOURCES FOR THIS CHAPTER

My analysis in this chapter focuses primarily on literature from the past decade, the period during which anime and manga have received the most attention by fans in the English-speaking world. Not surprisingly, the most recent five years of that range coincide with increased interest by teachers, library media specialists, and researchers in the West in the literacy-related implications of that fandom.

A combination of hand searches and database browsing yielded a pool of sources for review and analysis ranging from popular-media accounts of publishing trends to proceedings from a scholarly conference on the Pokémon phenomenon.[1] Some sources provided an introduction to notable texts, genres, and subgenres within one or the other form, while others sought to provide a more comprehensive historical perspective. Case studies of individual fans were the most common kinds of empirical research involving consumers of anime and/or manga. The only large-scale study in the pool was a survey of 297 Japanese college students' manga reading habits and preferences by English teachers Allen and Ingulsrud (2003). This tendency toward small-scale, intimate research is perhaps not surprising given that these media forms only recently appeared on many researchers' "radar screens."

Another interesting trend among available sources was the difference in frequency of attention to anime/manga between literacy-focused journals for practitioners and those aimed at a more scholarly audience. For example, during the four-year period of 2001–2004, five practitioner-focused journals sponsored by the National Council of Teachers of English and the International Reading Association published 13 articles devoted explicitly to some aspect of anime, manga, or graphic novels/comics. Over the same period of time, the three main research journals of those same two professional organizations published only one empirical study on any of those topics (Chandler-Olcott & Mahar, 2003a).

That considerably more attention has been given to these topics by teachers and teacher-researchers than by university-based scholars calls to mind an argument made by Leu (2000) about research trends related to technology-mediated literacy instruction. Leu framed a review of the literature on this topic in what he called a "deictic" perspective on literacy—one emphasizing the "continuously changing envisionments" that new technologies "initiate for information and communication" (p. 745). Because these changes are so rapid, he claimed, the possibilities of technology-mediated instruction have been demonstrated less by formal empirical research and more by the daily practices of exemplary and innovative teachers experimenting in the laboratories of their classrooms. In the case of anime and manga, a similar force may be at work: Because of their proximity to, and multiple interactions with, a wide range of young people, teachers and librarians may have a more immediate and possibly deeper sense of youth-culture trends related to reading and writing than most researchers taking an etic perspective. For this reason, practitioners' insights are well represented in a subsequent section on patterns from the empirical literature most relevant to the field of literacy. First, however, I will draw on information from a range of sources (including, but not limited to, traditional research) to provide some background and define some terms related to these two media forms.

WATCHING ANIME AND READING MANGA: DEFINITIONS AND BACKGROUND

The terms *anime* and *manga* are often used in combination with each other, as many fans enjoy both forms and move back and forth between them. As is indicated, however, by the title of *Watching Anime, Reading Manga* (Patten, 2004), a book collecting 25 years of writing on both subjects, they are not synonyms: One refers to a form meant to be viewed, the other read (though likely not in the way one would read a print-dominated text, as my discussion of patterns from the empirical literature will demonstrate later).

Manga, Japanese comics, are the older of the two forms, with some scholars tracing their origins as far back as Japanese temple scrolls of the 12th century (Schodt, 1996). The most popular reading material in Japan, manga are available in convenience stores, newsstands, and vending machines, as well as bookstores (Ito, 2002). The form is so ubiquitous and engrained in the country's reading culture that it is used for some technical manuals and educational materials published by government ministries (Poitras, 2004). Unlike their counterparts in the United States, Japanese comics are not read primarily by the young, are available in many genres, and only rarely feature traditional superheroes as central characters. They also tend to be different visually from American comics. According to Schodt (1996), manga have a "cinematic" style (p. 27) with less emphasis on print text and a greater use of multiple "frames and pages to depict an action or thought" (p. 26)—approaches that help manga artists to "develop their story lines and characters with more complexity and psychological and emotional depth" (p. 27) than is typically the case with American comics. Schodt pointed out that these culturally based differences are beginning to erode as American and Japanese artists mutually influence each other, but he maintains that it is likely fair to say that mainstream American comics "still resemble[e] illustrated narratives, while Japanese manga [are] a visual narrative with a few words thrown in for effect" (p. 26).

Manga and anime are related art forms, according to Napier (2000), because they share a style of "visual narration" relying "on the viewer's imagination," not dialogue, to move the story forward, and because "many, if not most, anime are based on stories that appeared first as manga" (p. 20). Although some people in the United States associate anime primarily with the science fiction and fantasy genres that are indeed well represented in the form, anime, like manga, encompasses many genres, including comedy, sports, romance, crime, and *hentai* (pornography for both heterosexual and homosexual audiences). Also like manga, anime is marketed in Japan to people from a wide range of age groups, including, but far from exclusive to, children. Although there has been some debate about how culturally specific anime and manga are in terms of their themes and content (Drazen, 2003; Iwabuchi, 2004), most would agree that characters in both media forms are often represented in ways—for example, with unusually large, round eyes—that tend not

[1] I would like to acknowledge the invaluable assistance in this process of my research assistant, Megan Cox Marx.

to look very Japanese. Some critics argue that these trends reflect the artists' internalization of Western ideals of beauty, while others take the market-driven position that a more internationalized portrayal is meant to make the products more appealing to a wider range of audiences (Schodt, 1996).

Both manga and anime have been important contributors to Japan's economy for many years.Manga sales represent nearly 40% of the total number of books and magazines sold in Japan, representing by some estimates a $5 billion industry (Schodt, 1996), and animated features account for about 50% of all movie ticket sales (Napier, 2000). In addition to the money associated with these commercially produced texts, an entire industry has developed surrounding *dojinshi*, a Japanese term loosely translated as "publications among friends" (Poitras, 2001, p. 67) used to describe 'zines created by manga fans for other fans. In Japan, conferences organized around dojinshi can draw as many as 300,000 people, with attendees receiving commercially published maps of the arena to help them find their favorite "non-professional" authors (Schodt, 1996). Anime and manga scholars point out that the circulation of these texts, which often take the form of parodies or narratives engaging characters from professionally produced manga and anime in unsanctioned romances, relies on a different ethos in Japan than in the United States regarding copyright and intellectual property. Schodt (1996) quoted an American manga fan living in Japan on this issue:

> In America we don't have a gray area in our copyright laws that allows this sort of fan art. It's not the way the copyright laws are written, but the way they're enforced. Copyright holders in the United States have to protect their trademark or it becomes public domain. That's not the case in Japan, so artists and publishers can afford to tolerate these homages. It doesn't mean they like it, but they don't want to do anything to alienate their customer base. The manga publishers benefit from happy fans, and some even send scouts to dojinshi markets to find aspiring artists. (p. 42)

According to anime creator and critic Okada Toshio, the relationship between professional Japanese animators and the fan communities produces a healthy and creative "system in which amateurs can influence professionals; the *otaku* [a Japanese term for passionate anime fans] form a kind of giant think tank" (Napier & Okada, 2003, n.p.).

Anime has been available in the West since the 1960s, when Japanese series such as *Astro Boy* and *Speed Racer* were broadcast on American television, although they were often edited of Japanese references and/or content considered to be too racy or profane for American audiences. In 1988, the film *Akira* earned number one status at the box office in Japan as well as a warm reception abroad: "Released in America and Europe the following year, it became both a critical and a cult hit and in many ways can be seen as the film that started the anime boom in the West" (Napier, 2000, p. 41). Another milestone took place six years later, when *Sailor Moon*, an anime series described by Drazen (2003) as "part magical fantasy, part romantic comedy, and part science fiction" (p. 11), began its run on American TV, attracting a new generation of young fans (especially females) to anime, as well as to manga. *Sailor Moon* was followed on American television, often on the Cartoon Network, by such popular anime as *Dragon Ball Z* (DBZ), a series of more than 500 episodes featuring Goku, a child with martial arts expertise and a golden sphere to summon the Dragon God; and *Pokémon*, the video-game-inspired hit series that launched intense sessions of game playing with intricately labeled playing cards for millions of American teens and preteens (J. Tobin, 2004).

As I write, anime and manga continue to increase their market penetration in Western countries. Insiders call manga one of the fastest growing segments of the American publishing industry, with sales estimated at about $110 million in 2003. Major publishing companies such as Del Ray Books are launching dedicated manga lines (Wheeler, 2004), while others—HarperCollins, for example—are entering into new partnerships with small companies such as TOKYOPOP that specialize in manga and anime (Wyatt, 2006). *Spirited Away*, an anime film by the acclaimed Japanese director Hayao Miyazaki that was distributed by Disney's Miramax division, won the 2003 Academy Award for best animated feature—the first time this honor was won by an anime submission. These trends suggest that anime and manga are becoming commercially viable commodities in the West, as they have been for many years in Japan.

As anime and manga become more common in the United States, young people pursue their fandom through membership in various communities. Some gather as members of informal, loosely structured groups of peers (Mahar, 2003; Vasquez, 2003), while others join extracurricular clubs with recognized status on high school or, more often, college campuses (Vidmar, 2004). Some attend conventions such as the Anime Expo, an annual event for fans of anime and manga that drew 25,000 people to Anaheim, California, in 2004 (Brand, 2004). Some contribute to electronic mailing lists or discussion boards, many of which are linked to Web sites with a fan audience (see, for example, the Anime Web Turnpike [www.anipike.com], an Internet clearinghouse with links to industry updates, electronic news groups, image galleries, fanfiction, and individual fans' anime-focused Web pages). Many fans belong to multiple communities, with their membership in one sparking membership in another—for example, a conversation at a face-to-face club meeting can lead to the recommendation of a URL address for an online community.

School and community libraries also serve as important spaces for young people to pursue their fandom (Halsall, 2004; MacDonald, 2004; Williams, 2003). Libraries across the United States report hosting manga- and anime-related events as a way to boost interest and circulation figures among young people. In one notable example, the New Orleans Public Library System hosted an anime film festival during the fall of 2003 as the centerpiece of a month-long initiative "targeting teens and reeling them back in" to library patronage (Williams, 2003, n.p.). That the festival's kick-off coincided with the library's launch of Teen Read Week, a national project sponsored by the Young Adult Library Services Association, was no accident. According to local media coverage of the festival, its organizers hoped to connect teenagers' interest in animated films with the reading of comic books and other print-based media available at the library. While many events such as this one involve film screenings, others in different locations have included author signings, "how-to" workshops, and club meetings (MacDonald, 2004). Often, they serve as catalysts for collaboration between library professionals and members of the community such as hobby-store owners and artists.

For all of these reasons, anime and manga can no longer be seen by literacy teachers and researchers as the province of a few hobbyists seeking to position themselves as "alternative" with their appreciation of Far Eastern culture. Instead, these media forms must be analyzed as legitimate forces in contemporary popular culture, especially for

American youth. As the texts become more readily available, more students in K–12 classrooms will likely identify themselves as fans. As they do, they will become apprenticed into literacy practices associated with that fandom that will influence, directly and indirectly, how they view and use literacy in other contexts, including school. Consequently, those of us who work with young readers and writers need to develop understandings of those literacy practices that will inform our classroom teaching and our conceptualization of future research.

PATTERNS OF ANIME AND MANGA FANDOM

This section discusses three patterns in the empirical literature on anime and manga fandom that are, from my perspective, of particular interest to those who teach, promote, and/or research literacy: (a) multimodal aspects, (b) the influence of the Internet, and (c) constructions of gender identity. Each of these themes is discussed next in turn.

Multimodal Aspects of Anime/Manga Fandom

Among the key aspects of the multiliteracies framework are its emphasis on the meaning-making potential of modes other than the linguistic and its reservation of special attention for texts that rely on a combination of modes for their meaning potential. According to New London Group member Gunther Kress, multimodality can be profitably seen as "the use of several semiotic modes in the design of an entire semiotic product or event, together with the particular way in which the modes are combined" (Kress & Van Leeuwen, 2001, p. 20; see also Kress, 2000). From such a perspective, semiotic activity in is about selecting which modes (e.g., spatial, visual, audio, gestural, and/or linguistic) need to be emphasized in a particular context to achieve a particular end. Composers of sophisticated and successful multimodal texts develop a clear sense of the constraints and affordances of each mode available to them in a given act of Designing.

The practices associated with anime and manga fandom offer rich opportunities to analyze multimodal meaning construction because young people's interests in these two forms are increasingly tied to their interests in other media forms such as music, video/computer games, Web sites, and art. Industry representatives have been keenly aware for some time that consumers' interests in anime and manga cross modal boundaries. According to Steve Kleckner, vice president for sales and distribution of TokyoPop, the leading manga publisher outside Japan, "Manga is the next generation for a reading public hooked to the Internet, PlayStation, and stories told through visuals and sound. There is a 92 percent crossover of CD, DVD, and manga buyers" (Wheeler, 2004, n.p.). Researchers in literacy and education have been slower than commercially motivated observers to recognize the connections between consumption of visually oriented media texts and print literacy, possibly because of concerns about the commercialized nature of popular culture (Tobin, 2000). Recently, however, a few educators who work closely with young people have begun to document the nature of anime and manga fans' multimodal meaning-making, usually in settings beyond the classroom (Chandler-Olcott & Mahar, 2003a, 2003b; Halsall, 2004; Lam, 2000; Mahar, 2003; Vasquez, 2003).

A notable example of this trend toward multimodality is Alvermann and Heron's (2001) portrait of Robert, a ninth-grade fan of the anime series *Dragon Ball Z* (DBZ) who participated in a library-based, after-school media club sponsored by the research team. Likely to be constructed as a struggling reader when viewed in light of his transactions with traditional print texts in school, Robert pursued an enormous amount of reading about DBZ on the Internet-connected computers in the library. His knowledge base about the series also depended on his meaning-making with texts relying on visual, spatial, audio, and gestural modes as much as, or more than, the linguistic mode; these included numerous movies, a television series shown on the Cartoon Network, and several video games. Because he could assemble a rich, coherent narrative from these seemingly disparate sources, he was positioned as a DBZ expert by students who gathered in the young adult section of the library. His case, therefore, provided an excellent example of the kind of expertise described by New London Group member Carmen Luke (2000): "Today, the expert is the one who sees and seeks the connection among related pieces of information, not the one who has the bare decontextualized facts" (p. 73).

The complexity of the multimodal literacy practices associated with anime fandom was also demonstrated by Vasquez's five-year study of her nephew's participation in a Pokémon club, an informal group of children committed to collecting and playing with trading cards associated with the popular anime show. Vasquez (2003) argued that membership in this community required a variety of sophisticated reading strategies, from identifying key words and phrases while flipping through a Pokémon magazine to situating oneself in space while "reading" a map in a strategy guide. She also suggested that drawing and recreating existing cards were important "participatory activities" associated with membership in the gaming community—a finding reminiscent of arguments made by Storey (1996) and Jenkins (1992) about the importance of fan production, not just consumption, of media-influenced texts. The Pokémon club's activities were also aggressively multimodal, as the children drew on visual, spatial, and, to a lesser degree, audio and gestural modes of meaning along with linguistic ones as they created new cards:

> The children often talked throughout their drawing, sharing details about how they were creating the various text and symbols. This talk involved a deconstruction of the cards—looking closely at the bits and pieces that made up a card to make sure that the new redesigns were recognizable to other gamers. Further, this talk usually was accompanied by sound effects and impromptu leaps into dramatizing Pokémon battle moves. At some level, Curtis and his friends were using drama as an editing tool to create their drawings. (p. 121)

The children's sessions thus provide a concrete example of how Designers can use multiple modes of representation such as talk, drawing, and drama in the creation of texts that are themselves multimodal (e.g., relying on a combination of words, symbols, and images to carry meaning). In this case, their texts integrated information gleaned from a range of what Vasquez calls "platforms"—the multimedia genres of television, film, games, and toys—that can easily be overlooked by researchers concerned primarily with print literacy.

In addition to creating new game cards, some fans of anime and manga create visual art that draws on favorite characters, settings, and even slogans from their preferred series. For example, when the local high school held a teen art show at the community library where she worked, young adult services librarian Jane Halsall (2004) was struck by how many students incorporated images and conventions from anime into their artwork. Her observations of this intertextuality led her to found a teen advisory board whose members collaborated with her in previewing and selecting updating the community library's collection. That she chose to recruit her teen advisory board members through local art teachers—not, for example, from those recommended as good readers and writers by the English teachers in those same schools—provides a vivid indication of how necessary it is to comprehend more modes than the linguistic when transacting with anime texts.

Anime- and manga-inspired artists were also among the primary informants for my own recent collaborative research on young adolescent girls' technology-mediated literacy practices (Chandler-Olcott, 2004; Chandler-Olcott & Mahar, 2001, 2003a, 2003b). Important multimodal aspects of fandom could be seen in the case of Eileen, a seventh grader who belonged to an electronic mailing list for anime and fantasy artists that she discovered while surfing the Web. Analysis of the postings related to critique of members' artwork (scanned images sent to others as electronic attachments) revealed several types of multimodality, ranging from the use of capitalization, emoticons, and other textual conventions to express physical gesture and tone of voice (e.g., *gasps* IT'S JAMES!!! *hugs it all to bits* ^_^) to primarily linguistic feedback in response to members' visual/spatial text attachments (e.g., The wispy hair is great; possibly a somewhat smoother fading would have made the highlight even better). The most striking examples of multimodality, however, came from responses to peers' work, like this one from Eileen, which combined verbal feedback in the body of the message with spatial and visual instruction and modeling in a piece of art that accompanied that print text:

> she is so cute. her dress is especially pretty. the only thi[ng] is her forearms—they are a little too thin. I attached an example of how they should look more like. I'm not perfect, but i hope I can help. ^-^

As she participated in online exchanges like this one, Eileen learned more about how other artists used visual and spatial modes of meaning to communicate with other anime fans as well as with a generalist audience. At the same time, her list membership gave her numerous opportunities to use linguistic modes to respond to other fans' work as well as to learn from their language-based response to hers. In many cases, the most effective communication was that which harnessed the power of multiple modes, rather than relying on one (Chandler-Olcott, 2004).

All of these studies point out that fandom for anime and manga enthusiasts was a multimodal phenomenon. As these young people constructed understandings of their favorite texts and shared their understandings and interpretations with other fans, they challenged the faulty assumption identified by Kress (2000): that language is a "communicational and representational medium which is fully adequate to the expression of anything that we might want to express" (p. 193). While they did not abandon language in their fan-related practices, the linguistic mode was rarely unaccompanied by visual and spatial modes in the form of images, symbols, and graphics. Often, the fans' multimodal Design process was facilitated by multimedia technologies, the influence of which will be discussed in this next section.

Importance of the Internet to Anime/Manga Fandom

The multiliteracies framework, unlike many conceptions of literacy, was grounded in awareness of and intended to account for the influences of information and communication technologies on contemporary literacy practices. In their original articulation of the framework, the New London Group (1996) made it clear that literacy pedagogy needed to help students develop,

> understanding and competent control of representational forms that are becoming increasingly significant in the overall communications environment, such as visual images and their relationship to the written word—for instance, visual design in desktop publishing or the interface of visual and linguistic meaning in multimedia. (p. 60)

Several years later, NLG member Carmen Luke (2000) explored these issues and their implications for schooling in more depth. She argued that the hypertext environments proliferating in homes, workplaces, and civic life demanded "a multimodal reading of laterally connected, multi-embedded and further hotlinked information resources variously coded in animation, symbols, print text, photos, movie clips, or three-dimensional and manouevrable graphics" (p. 73).

There is growing evidence (Alvermann & Heron, 2001; Chandler-Olcott & Mahar, 2003a; Lam, 2000; Vasquez, 2003) that anime and manga fans rely heavily on information and communication technologies, particularly the Internet, to access and share with other fans all of the meaning-making resources listed by Luke. Some fans even use the Internet to help them achieve among their peers the status of *otaku*, a term coined by the Japanese to describe, sometimes derisively, "young people with an obsessive interest in some aspect of popular culture" (Tobin, 1998, p. 109). While an otaku can specialize in almost any media form, the label is often associated with manga and anime fans, and it often applies, as Tobin (1998) pointed out, to "someone whose computer interest and acumen is in the service of their obsession" (p. 109). Consequently, technology use by and among fans is an important trend to consider.

Computer-mediated fan communication and its relationship to literacy and identity construction were central issues in Lam's (2000) study of Almon, a Chinese-speaking adolescent whose family immigrated to the United States from Hong Kong four years before the research began. After attending a high-school class on e-mail and Web browsing, Almon was inspired to construct a personal home page in English. Although the main subject of the page was a young Japanese pop singer whom Almon admired, he also included numerous references and links to anime (further evidence that these media forms are linked for many young people as was discussed in the previous section), and he chose to locate the page in a section of the commercial server's site described by its marketing materials as devoted to "Anime and all things Asian" (Lam, 2000, p. 469). Analysis of the site, as well as of Almon's e-mail and bulletin board communication with other fans of Japanese popular culture from Canada, Hong Kong, and the United States, led Lam to conclude that fan-related writing on the Internet helped Almon make a shift from the "sense of alienation from the English language" he experienced in traditional ESL classes to "a newfound sense of expressivity and solidarity when communicating in English with his Internet peers" (p. 468). While Lam acknowledged that the language skills Almon acquired via the Internet were representative of the global English of adolescent popular culture rather than the standard English of typical ESL instruction, she ultimately concluded that this was a healthy trend—one that allowed Almon to construct "an identity that [was] not available to him in the social environment and institutions of his adopted country" (p. 475). Via computer-mediated communication, he came to see himself, and positioned himself with others, as an expert on Japanese popular culture and as a valued member of the fan community.

Similarly, Vasquez (2003) found that technology-mediated reading and writing helped situate Curtis, a young Pokémon enthusiast who created his own gaming cards, as an expert within his fan community. In particular, Curtis used the Internet to learn more about the characteristics of various Pokémon characters. Not only did he cross-check his Web-derived data against the data he gathered from magazine sources, but he also printed the pages from especially helpful sites to share "his findings with his friends, who did the same with him" (p. 120). In this way, his use of digital technologies helped him to enter more deeply into what Vasquez called the "Pokediscourse," the "way of talking about gaming and using the cards" (p. 119) that helped cement relationships with his age peers and gave him more social status among older gamers. He also used the Internet to convert quantities related to his Pokémon's heights and weights from English measurements to the metric system used in his native Canada. In this way, his Pokémon-inspired and technology-mediated inquiries led him to find and manipulate scientific information privileged in school contexts, not just gaming.

My own research (Chandler-Olcott & Mahar, 2003a) revealed a reciprocal relationship between some seventh-grade girls' anime fandom and their use of technological tools. For instance, Rhiannon, one of our primary informants, initially connected with other young fans in an anime-focused chat room sponsored by her Internet service provider. As the fans shared likes and dislikes about characters, plotlines, and images, they also shared references to anime-focused sites. Intrigued by the Web design process as much as the content of those sites, Rhiannon began to construct her own multimodal fan pages using commercially available page-building templates and eventually the programming language HTML. She was aided in this process by help-site links and bits of source code sent to her via instant messages from her online friends. For these young people, Internet-based technologies served as "glue" to hold together a fan-related community of practice, but the community of practice also supported her in learning to use these technological tools (and others) in increasingly sophisticated ways.

Viewed from a multiliteracies perspective, this small but provocative body of research suggests that information and communication technologies, particularly the Internet, served two related but different functions for anime and manga fans. Initially, Internet-based technologies such as electronic mail, personal home pages, and electronic mailing lists were a source of Available Designs—a means for young people to learn a good deal of content about the anime and manga that interested them, as well as to see how other fans responded to those texts. For the fans in these studies, however, the process didn't stop there. The technologies also served as a means to produce and distribute their own texts (Kress, 2003) to a wider audience than would have been possible in their local communities. Drawing on some elements of the original sources combined with new material from the fans' personal experience or transactions with other texts (including some that were neither anime nor manga), these ReDesigned texts then became part of the Available Designs on which other fans drew. This recirculation of themes, language, and especially images helped fan communities to be fresh and innovative while at the same time keeping them from becoming fragmented and incoherent. It also helped fans to explore from different vantage points some important aspects of identity, including constructions of gender—the subject of the next section.

Gender Identity and Anime/Manga Fandom

As Willett (2004) pointed out in an analysis of three Pokémon fans' written narratives, "children use their positions as fans to establish their personal identities as well as to build social networks" (p. 226). Young fans' multimodal and often digitally mediated transactions with anime and manga texts offered them important resources or Available Designs (New London Group, 1996) for gender-related identity work. Some of this identity work replicated traditional stereotypes about gender, especially for females, but some of it problematized those rigid categories, creating space for young fans to question and talk back to conceptions of gender they encountered in the texts to which they responded and the communities to which they belonged.

At first glance, many anime and manga texts can appear to be gendered in ways that parallel contemporary life in Japan, where women continue to be disempowered relative to men (Ito, 2002; Napier, 2000). Both anime and manga include subcategories aimed specifically and dichotomously at one gender, with *shojo* (translated as "little female") comics for girls focused primarily on interpersonal relationships rather than the action, adventure, and humor characterizing texts for male consumers (Thorn, 2001). Similarly, Ito's (2002) content analysis of 184 examples of *redi komi* (manga marketed to Japanese women between the ages of 15 and 44) revealed that the stories emphasized stereotypically female concerns such as courtship, marriage, and caring for family members. From a visual perspective, female characters in popular anime series such as *The Slayers* and *Escaflowne* are often depicted stereotypically with large breasts and skimpy clothing. All of these examples might be read as disempowering to women and limiting to both sexes.

A closer look at both the texts and the textual practices that surround them, however, suggests that anime and manga also offer opportunities for young fans to play with and question rigid gender roles. Although Ito (2002) cautioned that *redi komi*, especially the sexually oriented texts, can be demeaning to women, she also proposed that the stories can make a positive impact on readers because they offer hints for how to deal with typical life problems; allow for stress relief with vicarious experiences; and perhaps most important, present their protagonists as "major and active players" rather than "bystanders and cheerleaders" (p. 84). The central theme of *Ranma 1/2,* a long-running manga that became a popular anime series, is related to shifting conceptions of gender, as the protagonist falls into a magic spring that causes him to turn into a girl when touched by cold water and into a boy when touched by warm water. According to Napier (2000), the series works on two different levels: "the issue of constructing gender identity at the individual level and the public level of society's expectations for gender norms," creating both its humor and its point by "a range of imaginative visual tropes and action sequences that consistently work to destabilize the 'normal'" (p. 50). Many popular-press accounts of manga fandom (Brand, 2004; Jones, 2004; Wheeler, 2004) include testimony from young women who were attracted to manga texts like these because they offered healthier, more active images of women than the superhero-dominated American comic market. As these examples demonstrate, anime and manga may provide youth with scripts for resisting narrow conceptions of gender just as easily as they do scripts for playing narrowly defined roles.

Emerging research data suggest that some young anime and manga fans are aware of the gender-related complexities in the texts they choose and that the texts contribute discourses about femininity, masculinity, and romantic relationships that they borrow from, reshape, and sometimes resist in a complex process of identity construction. A good example of this trend comes from the work of my longtime collaborator Donna Mahar (2003), an English teacher at a suburban middle school in New York. When Mahar opened her classroom to informal student gatherings about anime during lunch, she created space for an otherwise diverse group of young people to coalesce around their common interest while simultaneously assembling a group of mentors who could help her understand new forms of popular culture. One of her primary mentors was Madison, a seventh-grade girl whose family had emigrated to the United States from Montenegro. Madison wrote anime-inspired fanfictions and created fan art that was striking enough to be hung publicly in the school guidance office. She described herself to Mahar as "an anime fan, a manga artist, author, and anti-Barbie androgynous female" (p. 113), and her fandom clearly informed how she positioned herself in several discourse communities, including the lunch club and the larger school world. One of the fanfictions she gave Mahar to read was in response to *Princess Mononoke*, an anime feature that is among the highest grossing films of all time in Japan. Her explanation of the film's appeal to her revealed an awareness of the tensions surrounding female representation in many popular anime:

> I really like the female power in the shows like *Card Captor Sakura*, *Escaflowne*, and *Sailor Moon*. But these shows still have the women looking like Barbie with tight clothes and big breasts. Women have power if you really follow the story, but they have to look that way so that more people, especially guys, will watch. It's all about ratings. In *Princess Mononoke*, the women have power. Some still look all cutesy, but some are more androgynous, and that is how I like to look. (p. 114)

In her analysis of these comments, Mahar argued that Madison was able to consider *Princess Mononoke* in both a personal and cultural context because she had adapted school-based strategies such as text-to-text, text-to-self, and text-to-world connections (Keene & Zimmermann, 1997) to the unique demands of her personal literacy practices. Mahar concluded that data like this snippet and others from the study demonstrated that at least some of her students were "able to address aspects of popular culture," including complicated gender representations, "with a critical lens while at the same time retaining the pleasure they derive from the texts themselves" (p. 115). For Mahar, this flexibility of stance toward popular texts was crucial to the critical media literacy envisioned by Alvermann and Hagood (2000).

In my collaborative work with Mahar, gender also surfaced as a key issue (Chandler-Olcott & Mahar, 2003a, 2003b). We talked with girls who were able to identify stereotypical elements of anime and manga as they looked to those texts for guidance on how to represent themselves with their dress, talk, and media preferences in different discourse communities, particularly where romantic relationships were concerned. One of our primary informants, Rhiannon created a Web page related to her fandom with an image gallery of ***bishonen*** (a term borrowed from a manga subgenre that young anime fans use to describe males they find physically attractive) that included pictures of both her favorite anime characters and the young man she identified as her real-life boyfriend. While she was careful to position herself in all of these texts as heterosexual (she declared in an introductory page to a site devoted to the anime show *Gundam Wing* that it was "non-gay"), it was impossible to ignore that the "bishies" she included in her image gallery included characters represented in very androgynous ways (an issue that several of our other informants identified as well). Both Rhiannon and our other key informant wrote fanfictions with characters from favorite anime shows that included some stereotypically gendered elements (e.g., physical competition between two male characters over which would be a passive female character's romantic partner) and some that challenged these stereotypes (e.g., the heroine of one story being defended by a "knightess" rather than a male protector). As we have argued elsewhere, the hybrid nature of all of these fan texts may have allowed our informants "to do more identity work around female heterosexuality, particularly related to issues of power in relationships, than a more homogeneous text might have" (Chandler-Olcott & Mahar, 2003b, p. 563).

It is important to note, however, that girls are not the only ones whose anime and manga fandom may be implicated in their construction of gender identities. A case study of Jimmy, a fourth-grade Pokémon enthusiast attending the school in which Samuel Tobin (2004) served as computer teacher, demonstrated that fandom can also be related to boys' exploration—and in some cases, rejection—of dominant discourses about masculinity. Tobin argued that the early phase of the Pokémon phenomenon in the United States offered preadolescent boys "an attainable, coherent, socially recognizable way" to be masculine—an alternative to pursuits such as participating in athletics, following popular music, or playing video games. As Tobin saw it, collecting and trading the cards, game-playing, and mastering knowledge and facts about the media form were all fan-related practices that could be coded as sufficiently masculine to afford status to individual children. Because Jimmy's fandom was associated with more passive, and more feminized, practices such as reading a limited number of Pokémon stories and watching episodes of the television show, he was marginalized in his peer community. While Tobin acknowledged that this positioning was difficult for Jimmy personally, he also characterized Jimmy's failure to comply with the "norms and rules of acceptable behavior" in this context as "a sort of success" because it resisted "our culture's normalizing regimes of masculinity, heterosexuality, and maturity" (p. 252).

All three of these studies point out that fandom is connected to important, though not always easy, identity work for young people. In addition to the texts themselves, this work is influenced by a variety of discourses about gender, including those from classroom communities like Tobin's and from global corporations such as Nintendo, the creator, licensor, and distributor of Pokémon (Buckingham & Sefton-Green, 2003). Fans are influenced by these intersecting and contradictory messages, even when they are not consciously aware of them. The multimodal capacities of both anime and manga, however, can create more obvious tensions for fans to resolve when gender-related messages communicated in one mode (e.g., a female character visually represented as buxom or with a "baby doll" voice) conflict with messages communicated in another mode (e.g., the same character's decisive physical actions or intelligent dialogue). These tensions in anime and manga texts can be magnified as fans combine Available Designs from them with personal experiences and other intertextual references, creating ReDesigned art, fiction, and Web sites. When these new texts are shared, often electronically, with other members of their fan communities, they contribute additional Designs for others to take up and use in new ways in their identity work. These dynamic exchanges provide at least a partial explanation for why commercially produced popular culture resources that have the potential to reproduce existing inequities such as those associated with gender differences also have the potential to be "appropriated by young people for pleasure, identification, and a sense of personal power" (Mahiri, 2000/2001, p. 382).

IMPLICATIONS OF ANIME AND MANGA FANDOM FOR LITERACY RESEARCH AND PRACTICE

One of the most striking themes of my conversations with young anime and manga fans over the past few years has been the degree to which their fandom has been "invisible" in most school contexts. In some ways, this invisibility is surprising, as it was obvious to me that these students cared deeply about their fan-related fiction, artwork, and electronic communication. They talked at passionate length about their pride in being connected to global, rather than merely local, communities through their fandom; about their preference for what they viewed as anime and manga's nuanced characterizations and subtle themes as compared to Western cartoons and comics; and about their satisfaction in accessing information, often through technological means, that was difficult to obtain in the United States. Nonetheless, these young people reported sharing information about their fandom with only a few trusted adults (e.g., the art teacher who showed them a new computer program for manipulating images, the study-hall monitor who helped them obtain extra Internet access) and sometimes with no one at all. The teachers who were officially designated to support their literacy development usually knew very little about the Designing in which they invested so much time and energy. Sometimes this lack of communication was rooted in young people's desire to keep their pursuits private; in other contexts, it was tied to their beliefs that their teachers would misunderstand or even belittle their fandom.

While it is inevitable (and perhaps even quite healthy!) that young people reveal different facets of their identities in different contexts, I have come to believe that significant benefits can ensue when teachers know about their students' anime and manga fandom, particularly when this disclosure takes place in an open, supportive learning community where both parties can reflect on the literacy practices associated with that fandom. In this final section, I make some recommendations about classroom practices that can build on fandom-related knowledge and skills, and then talk about how an appreciation of fandom as a discourse community can contribute to a more complex vision of literacy teaching and learning for both teachers and researchers.

Connections Between Fandom Practices and Classroom Practice

Several teacher researchers have recommended using anime and manga texts in the classroom to increase student interest and achievement as well as promote strategic and critical thinking (Allen & Ingulsrud, 2003; Nagata, 1999). For example, Nagata (1999), a Japanese university professor, supplemented his biochemistry lectures with panels from the popular manga *Sailor Moon* that referenced scientific concepts such as protein metabolism and fermentation. When the 22 students in the class were surveyed about this approach, 17 of them reported that the manga had made it easier to remember the biochemical material, and all agreed that manga made biochemistry classes "more exciting" (p. 203). The possibilities of such a direct approach to integrating these texts into classroom practice seem limited, however, in the West, where the range of anime and manga related to concepts from traditional school disciplines is limited, and where the cultural contexts for interpreting those texts are very different from Japan. Moreover, concerns have been raised about the potential for co-opting youth's private pleasures by including them in formal curricula, especially if the popular media they appreciate stand to be critiqued in negative ways by peers or teachers (Alvermann, Moon, & Hagood, 1999).

More promising, in my view, are approaches to literacy instruction that are informed by, but not necessarily duplicative of, the textual practices associated with anime and manga fandom. For example, secondary English teacher Jim Burke (2002) learned a good deal about his students' strategic behavior when he observed them playing anime- and manga-influenced games such as Pokémon, Yu-Gi-Oh!, and Digimon during their lunch breaks. Upon taking a closer look at the cards themselves, Burke realized that they were "advanced learning tools," multifaceted texts using various modes of meaning such as color, symbols, images, print, and literary devices such as metaphor to create a "world of information" (p. 54) particularly enticing to boys, including some who struggled mightily with traditional reading and writing. To build on these new insights in his practice, Burke helped the students in his academic literacy class to design a new template for flash cards that harnessed some of the multimedia, interactive aspects of the game cards for school-based studying. Particularly central to the redesigned cards was a visual component that required students to devise, as many of their game cards did, "some symbol, icon, or image that represents the idea they are trying to master" (p. 55).

Students' fandom was similarly honored by Frey and Fisher (2004) as they designed an illustrated book project to be implemented in a ninth-grade English class. Having observed evidence of their students' engagement with anime and manga in "the margins of their writer's notebook pages, on the covers of assignment folders, and in the sheaves of drawings they squirreled away in their backpacks" (p. 19), the teachers hoped to channel this engagement into the improved school literacy achievement badly needed by many students in this high-poverty urban school. Frey and Fisher decided not to use students' preferred texts in the project directly, however, as they feared co-opting materials that "belonged" to the students, and they worried about the appropriateness for school use of texts with violent and/or sexual content. Instead, they planned lessons with selections from work by Will Eisner, an American graphic novelist whose urban subject matter was likely to appeal to students. Over the course of the unit, the teachers used extensive think-alouds and discussion to model for and explore with students the relationships between authors' print- and visual-text choices. They reported that the "visual vocabulary" provided by forms of popular culture like anime and manga helped to scaffold students, including English language learners and dysfluent writers, in their use of various literary techniques, especially those related to dialogue, tone, and mood. Although most students illustrated their texts with photographs they took with disposable cameras provided by the teachers, several included original anime-style art, thus bringing the multimodal project full circle with its inspiration.

Although both of these examples involved teachers making text choices for classes of students to capitalize on connections between literacy practices associated with fandom and those privileged in school contexts, it may also be fruitful to set up instructional scenarios that allow individual fans themselves to make decisions about which texts and textual practices, if any, they want to submit for a given learning community's consideration. For example, fanfiction inspired by anime and manga and written for out-of-school audiences might be among the range of texts that students are invited to submit for diagnostic purposes at the beginning of the year (Chandler-Olcott & Mahar, 2003b). Teachers reviewing these usually excluded texts as part of a larger set of texts are likely to get a wider view of students' interests, strengths, and needs than would be available from strictly "academic" writing. For a unit on genre study, students might be invited to nominate favorite Web sites related to their popular culture interests, including their anime and manga fandom, and to use the wide-ranging class list to develop a categorization scheme for comparing online genres with each other and with print genres (Chandler-Olcott & Mahar, 2001). Such student-centered and inquiry-based approaches would reposition anime and manga as worthy of consideration within a school discourse while simultaneously permitting students to set the parameters for what gets discussed and evaluated in that school context. Practitioners interested in initiating classroom activities like these could follow the lead of library media specialist Jane Halsall (2004) and recruit a small group of young fans for advice and recommendations about how to do so in respectful and engaging ways.

Making Multiliteracies Visible

While these suggestions can be helpful to teachers wanting to develop more responsive pedagogy, from my perspective there is a second—and potentially greater—benefit for literacy educators who develop understandings and appreciation of the literacy practices associated with anime and manga fandom: an opportunity to connect a generative theory with its implications for innovative, principled practice (see also Chandler-Olcott & Mahar, 2003b). Although there has been a good deal of scholarly interest in the multiliteracies framework since it was proposed nearly 10 years ago, only a few classroom-based research and curriculum initiatives have been grounded in it, especially in the United States. Conceptualizing literacy as Design and therefore expanding our sense of the resources for Designing to include nonlinguistic modes is not easy for people who came of age with different assumptions, even when those people (myself included) are generally sympathetic with the New London Group's (1996) arguments about changes in our work, personal, and civic lives necessitating new perspectives on literacy pedagogy. It can be hard even to envision what such a shift would look like—to think through in concrete ways how to design instruction that will foster these habits of mind or how to design research projects that would investigate the effects of that instruction. Lacking detailed classroom vignettes, detailed curriculum maps, and elaborated research findings, we must look elsewhere for guidance and insights.

I believe that examination of the literacy practices associated with anime and manga fandom specifically, and with communities devoted to aspects of popular culture more generally, is one of the ways to generate those insights. Anime and manga fans like newspaper letter-writer Tatianna Smith and the informants of the studies reviewed here show us in very concrete ways how the elements of the multiliteracies framework might play out in particular contexts. For instance, fans' platform-crossing practices (Vasquez, 2003) demonstrate that while English language arts instruction in many schools is still dominated by the linguistic mode in the form of traditional print, the Designing in which students are most engaged for their own purposes is decidedly more diverse. Not only do they regularly compose and construct meaning using various Designs in concert with each other, but they do so in communities that are often more culturally, ethnically, and linguistically diverse than their neighborhoods and classrooms. From these rich models of multimodal literacy in context, we might generate ideas about how to encourage multimedia composing in classrooms on a variety of topics, not just popular media, as well as how to research those pedagogical initiatives.

Similarly, the members of these fan communities offer examples of technology-mediated literacy behaviors—information seeking, solicitation of feedback, and so on—that have a lot in common with academic literacy practices typically valued and promoted in schools. Young people who have mastered these skills while pursuing personal literacies can be helped to transfer that knowledge to new contexts if their teachers honor those personal literacies and support students in building on them (Hinchman, Alvermann, Boyd, Brozo, & Vacca, 2003). Knowledge of the fan communities' practices may also point the way toward transforming how technology is employed in school, as fans' use of online tools appears to be much more democratic and inquiry-driven ways than is typical of technology integration in schools (Means, Penuel, & Padilla, 2001).

By analyzing the literacy processes that accompany fandom in terms of gender, we may be afforded new insights into the relationships between Designing and identity construction. We may also glean clues about other aspects of identity construction, including the influence of race, ethnicity, social class, language status, and (of particular interest given some of the studies reviewed here) peer status, all of which have important implications for literacy teaching and learning. Without a sophisticated understanding of how these identity markers intersect and interact with each other, it is unlikely that we will be able to design pedagogies that contribute to the New London Group's (1996) vision of just and equitable social futures for all literacy learners, including those identifying with groups that have traditionally been underserved by schools.

For all of these reasons, understanding youth's anime and manga fandom can help us to make the current potentials and future promise of a multiliteracies perspective on teaching and learning more visible than they have ever been before. Only when we look closely at, and take seriously, the literacy practices that engage young people in deep and satisfying ways will we stand a chance of creating classroom environments that will foster similar kinds of commitment to academic literacies. Only then will schools fulfill what Cope and Kalantzis (2000) call the "moral and practical civic mission" (p. 147) to create "new and productive interrelationships" from pluralism and diversity.

REFERENCES

Allen, K., & Ingulsrud, J. (2003). Manga literacy: Popular culture and the reading habits of Japanese college students. *Journal of Adolescent and Adult Literacy, 46*, 674–683.

Alvermann, D., & Hagood, M. (2000). Fandom and critical media literacy. *Journal of Adolescent and Adult Literacy, 43*, 436–446.

Alvermann, D., & Heron, C. (2001). Literacy identity work: Playing to learn with popular media. *Journal of Adolescent and Adult Literacy, 45*, 118–122.

Alvermann, D., Moon, J., & Hagood, M. (1999). *Popular culture in the classroom: Teaching and researching critical media literacy*. Newark, DE: International Reading Association/National Reading Conference.

Brand, M. (2004, July 7). Increasing popularity of anime in American culture. *National Public Radio*. Retrieved September 2, 2004, from LexisNexis Academic database.

Brock, C., Boyd, F., & Moore, J. (2003). Variation in language and the use of language across contexts. In J. Flood, D. Lapp, J. Squire, & J. Jensen (Eds.), *Handbook of research on teaching the English language arts* (pp. 446–458). Mahwah, NJ: Erlbaum.

Buckingham, D., & Sefton-Green, J. (2003). Gotta catch 'em all: Structure, agency, and pedagogy in children's media culture. *Media, Culture, and Society, 25*, 379–399.

Burke, J. (2002). It's all in the cards. *Voices from the Middle, 10*(1), 54–55.

Chandler-Olcott, K. (2004, April). *Exploring communities of practice that support multimedia design*. Paper presented at the meeting of the American Educational Research Association, San Diego, CA.

Chandler-Olcott, K., & Mahar, D. (2001). Considering genre in the digital literacy classroom. *Reading Online, 5*(4). Retrieved December 2, 2004, from http://www.readingonline.org/electronic/elec_index.asp?HREF=/electronic/chandler/index.html

Chandler-Olcott, K., & Mahar, D. (2003a). Tech-savviness meets Multiliteracies: An exploration of adolescent girls' technology-mediated literacy practices. *Reading Research Quarterly, 38*, 356–385.

Chandler-Olcott, K., & Mahar, D. (2003b). Adolescents' anime-inspired fanfictions: An exploration of multiliteracies. *Journal of Adolescent and Adult Literacy, 46*, 556–566.

Cope, B., & Kalantzis, M. (2000). Multiliteracies: Literacy learning and the design of social futures. New York: Routledge.

Drazen, P. (2003). *Anime explosion!: The what, why, and wow of Japanese animation*. Berkeley, CA: Stone Bridge Press.

Frey, N., & Fisher, D. (2004). Using graphic novels, anime, and the Internet in an urban high school. *English Journal, 93*(3), 19–26.

Halsall, J. (2004). The anime revelation. *School Library Journal, 50*(8), 6–12.

Hinchman, K., Alvermann, D., Boyd, F., Brozo, W., & Vacca, R. (2003). Supporting older students' in- and out-of-school literacies. *Journal of Adolescent & Adult Literacy, 47*, 304–310.

Jenkins, H. (1992). *Textual poachers: Television fans and participatory culture*. New York: Routledge.

Jones, V. (2004, July 28). Girl power: Young women are driving one of the hottest trends in pop culture. *Boston Globe*. Retrieved September 8, 2004, from ProQuest database.

Ito, K. (2002). The world of Japanese ladies' comics: From romantic fantasy to lustful perversion. *Journal of Popular Culture, 36* (1), 68–85.

Iwabuchi, K. (2004). How "Japanese" is Pokemon? In J. Tobin (Ed.), *Pikachu's global adventure: The rise and fall of Pokemon* (pp. 53–79). Durham, NC: Duke University Press.

Keene, E., & Zimmermann, S. (1997). *Mosaic of thought: Teaching comprehension in a reader's workshop*. Portsmouth, NH: Heinemann.

Kress, G. (2000). Multimodality. In B. Cope & M. Kalantzis (Eds.), *Multiliteracies: Literacy learning and the design of social futures* (pp. 182–202). New York: Routledge.

Kress, G. (2003). *Literacy in the new media age*. London: Routledge.

Kress, G., & Van Leeuwen, T. (2001). *Multimodal discourse: The modes and media of contemporary communication*. London: Arnold.

Lam, W. S. E. (2000). Literacy and the design of the self: A case study of a teenager writing on the Internet. *TESOL Quarterly, 34*(3), 457–482.

Leu, D. J. (2000). Literacy and technology: Deictic consequences for literacy education in an information age. In M. L. Kamil, P. B. Mosenthal, P. D. Pearson, & R. Barr (Eds.), *Handbook of reading research, Volume III* (pp. 743–770). Mahwah, NJ: Erlbaum.

Luke, C. (2000). Cyber-schooling and technological change. In B. Cope & M. Kalantzis (Eds.), *Multiliteracies: Literacy learning and the design of social futures* (pp. 69–91). London: Routledge.

MacDonald, H. (2004). Drawing a crowd: Graphic novel events are great ways to generate excitement. *School Library Journal, 50*(8), 20–22.

Mahar, D. (2003). Bringing the outside in: One teacher's ride on the anime highway. *Language Arts, 81*(2), 110–117.

Mahiri, J. (2000/2001). Pop culture pedagogy and the ends of school. *Journal of Adolescent and Adult Literacy, 44*, 382–385.

Maira, S., & Soep, E. (2005). *Youthscapes: The popular, the national, the global*. Philadelphia: University of Pennsylvania Press.

Means, B., Panuel, W., & Padilla, C. (2001). *The connected school: Technology and learning in high school*. San Francisco: Jossey-Bass.

Nagata, R. (1999). Learning biochemistry through manga: Helping students learn and remember, and making lectures more exciting. *Biochemical Education, 27*, 200–203.

Napier, S. (2000). *Anime from Akira to Princess Mononoke: Experiencing contemporary Japanese animation*. New York: Palgrave.

Napier, S., & Okada, T. (2003). Japanese anime and its American fans. *Japan Echo*. Retrieved September 8, 2004, from ProQuest database.

New London Group. (1996). A pedagogy of multiliteracies: Designing social futures. *Harvard Educational Review, 66*(1), 60–92.

Patten, F. (2004). *Watching anime, reading manga: 25 years of essays and reviews*. Berkeley, CA: Stone Bridge Press:

Poitras, G. (2001). *Anime essentials: Every thing a fan needs to know*. Berkeley, CA: Stone Bridge Press.

Poitras, G. (2004). *The librarian's guide to anime and manga*. Retrieved November 24, 2004, from http://www.koyagi.com/Libguide.html

Schodt, F. (1996). *Dreamland Japan: Writings on modern manga*. Berkeley, CA: Stone Bridge Press.

Smith, T. (2004, June 7). Student already knew that Japan is "cool" [Letter to the editor]. *Syracuse Post-Standard*, p. A7.

Storey, J. (1996). *Cultural studies and the study of popular culture: Theories and methods*. Athens, GA: University of Georgia Press.

Thorn, M. (2001). Shojo manga: Something for girls. *Japan Quarterly, 48*(3), 43–51.

Tobin, J. (1998). An American *otaku* (or, a boy's virtual life on the Net). In J. Sefton-Green (Ed.), *Digital diversions: Youth culture in the age of multimedia* (pp. 106–127). London: UCL.

Tobin, J. (2000). *"Good guys don't wear hats": Children's talk about the media*. New York: Teachers College Press.

Tobin, J. (2004). *Pikachu's global adventure: The rise and fall of Pokemon*. Durham, NC: Duke University Press.

Tobin, S. (2004). Masculinity, maturity, and the end of Pokemon. In J. Tobin (Ed.), *Pikachu's global adventure: The rise and fall of Pokemon* (pp. 241–256). Durham, NC: Duke University Press.

Trainor, J. S. (2004). Critical cyberliteracy: Reading and writing the X-Files. In J. Mahiri (Ed.), *What they don't learn in school: Literacy in the lives of urban youth* (pp. 123–138). New York: Peter Lang.

Vasquez, V. (2003). What Pokemon can teach us about learning and literacy. *Language Arts, 81* (2), 118–125.

Vidmar, J. (2004, February 24). Kent State anime club proves animation not just for kids. *Daily Kent Stater*. Retrieved October 18, 2004, from LexisNexis Academic database.

Wheeler, S. (2004, June 15). Manga mania: Japanese graphic novels finding booming fan base in US. *Denver Post*. Retrieved October 18, 2004, from LexisNexis Academic database.

Willett, R. (2004). The multiple identities of Pokemon fans. In J. Tobin (Ed.), *Pikachu's global adventure: The rise and fall of Pokemon* (pp. 226–240). Durham, NC: Duke University Press.

Williams, L. P. (2003, October 9). Library film fest aimed at teenagers; Japanese animation hopes to reel 'em in. *Times-Picayune*. Retrieved September 21, 2004, from ProQuest database.

Wyatt, Edward. (2006, March 28). Comic book publisher switches a deal to HarperCollins. *The New York Times*, p. c7. Retrieved May 24, 2006, from *New York State Newspapers* via Thomson Gale database.

27

READING, WRITING, AND WATCHING: THE INFORMAL EDUCATION OF FILM FANS

Kimberly Sheridan
GEORGE MASON UNIVERSITY

In 1967, seven-year-old Alan began fueling his film interest with *Famous Monsters of Filmland* magazine. He scoured the TV guide for chances to watch the old monster movies he read about. As he enjoyed the likes of *Godzilla, King Kong,* and *The Wolf Man*, he also learned about the genre's history and filmmakers. Watching and reading about these films inspired him to make his own short 8mm films (the first a 5-minute effort titled *Cry of the Werewolf*) and to write a monster movie magazine with his cousin.

At around age 10 or 11, a PBS series on silent films, an autobiography of director Frank Capra that came to his house as a "Book of the Month" bonus, and several "essential" guides to the movies (e.g., Joe Franklin's *Classics of the Silent Screen*, Bosley Crowther's *The Great Films*, and Parker Tyler's *Classics of the Foreign Film*) helped broaden Alan's film interests beyond monster movies. Starting with a late-night viewing of *Mr. Smith Goes to Washington*, he began his lifelong passion for classic films. (Over 30 years later, he still owns and uses these guides—now dog-eared and coverless—that he purchased when he was 11).

As a teen unpacking newspapers and magazines for his father's stationery shop, Alan discovered film criticism. Reading critics such as Sarris, Kael, and Agee introduced new ways of thinking about and analyzing films. He particularly embraced *The Village Voice* and its critic Andrew Sarris' philosophy of auteurism; he memorized large sections of Sarris' *The American Cinema*. In college, he attended screenings of classic films each weekend and enrolled in a film class.

In the years following college, Alan's film interests waned as demands of work and family increased. The purchase of a VCR in the mid 1980s, however, brought easy access to classic and foreign films and rekindled his interest. His passion for films returned to its childhood peak in the mid-1990s, when he joined an online classic-film discussion group. Inspired by this group to read, write, and watch more, he currently writes reviews of most of the four or five films he watches each week, regularly reads and consults film books, and spends several hours each week discussing films online with other fans.

Visual and written media are often thought of as in competition for our recreational attention, with written texts currently losing out for most of us. We would rather watch the movie than read the book; we would rather watch the news than read the paper. This would seem especially likely to be true for film fans. Alan and the other film fans in my study, however, illustrate a different, mutually reinforcing relationship between written and visual media. Alan's film fandom is as much a story of reading and writing about films as it is about watching them. Throughout his life, watching films has inspired him to read or write about them, and reading and writing about films has encouraged him to watch more. Reading *Famous Monsters of Filmland* magazine changed his early enjoyment of monster films into a more active and creative one. Watching a PBS series on silent films inspired him to buy a book on them. Reading and writing also deepen Alan's understanding of film. Reading film criticism as a teen helped him think theoretically about films. Writing reviews to the discussion group supports his interpretation and evaluation of films.

Alan and the other fans in my study are participants in a major online film-discussion site, where thousands of fans rate films and/or converse about films on message boards. I surveyed a random sample of adult (ages 18–70) participants of this site. These participants come from a variety of countries and educational backgrounds, but share a love and regular practice of watching and discussing films. Of the surveyed fans, I conducted in-depth e-mail interviews with 11 fans from different regions of the United States, who ranged in age from late teens to early 60s, and had completed education levels ranging from high-school to graduate study. Like Alan, each interviewed fan described a personalized routine of reading and writing about, and watching films. Since they are drawn from a group that reads and writes about films through online discussion, this relationship between visual and written literacy may not seem surprising. Given that researchers often view online conversations as a hybrid form of talking and writing communication (see Mann & Stewart, 2000, for review), however, we would not necessarily expect fans to engage in their wide range of literacy activities (e.g., reading and writing reviews, reading film books and magazines, analyzing films, and writing fiction inspired by films) just because they participate in online discussions.

In what follows, I construe their film fandom as an informal education. By education, I mean that the fans seek knowledge about film and engage in reflective practices that are meant to develop their understanding of films. It is a self-motivated and self-directed education that is highly interactive with a community of other film fans, and evolves with individual and community interests. I locate the activities and expertise of these film fans in relation to other research on hobbies, expertise, and other types of fans. Then, drawing on my survey and interview findings, I argue that most of the fans in my study see developing film knowledge as an important goal, and believe that their knowledge, skills, and habits can be characterized as a kind of expertise. I discuss how fans' routines, which evolve over time, illustrate a mutually reinforcing relationship among reading, writing, and watching, and also serve three broad, overlapping functions: (a) building *background knowledge* in film and aiding in the *selection* of films to see (e.g., reading journalistic reviews, film guides, criticism, history books, and other fans' reviews and recommendations), (b) helping fans *interpret and evaluate* films they have seen (e.g., rewatching films, writing reviews, reading reviews/criticism, and discussing films online), and (c) inspiring *imagination and creative works* (e.g., fantasizing, making movies, and writing stories inspired by films). In conclusion, I identify common features of fans' accounts that encourage them to sustain serious engagement with film and to link written and visual media. Although I do not claim that these fans' experiences in film generalize to other populations, I consider how their practices linking film and written text may give insight to educators seeking to help students make similar links.

BACKGROUND

Film fandom is a hobby, a pleasurable pursuit. Fans do not receive educational credit or salaries for their activities as fans (though for some fandom leads to formal education or careers in film). Yet, as Anna Freud (1965) noted, hobbies share many features of work. For children, hobbies are often a way to inculcate the work habits of adults (Freud, 1965). While many people enjoy watching films, some fans, such as the ones in this study, make it into a playful form of work. Their fandom can be characterized as "serious leisure," in that it is a leisure activity, but involves considerable time, effort, and commitment, and develops specialized knowledge or expertise (Stebbins, 2004; Stebbins, 2007). At this balance of work and play, people find strategies to challenge themselves and to maintain a sense of fun in their hobby; in Csikszentmihalyi's (2000) terms, they regulate the "flow" they experience.

Given this work aspect, film fandom can be characterized, in part, as an informal education in which fans develop expertise. Although not all consider themselves "students of film," the fans in my study show knowledge, skills, and habits central to film studies, and more broadly, to media studies (e.g., British Film Institute 2000; Monaco 2000; Tyner, 1998). Their film fandom is centered on developing understanding of films, not just being entertained. They engage in regular reflective practices aimed at developing this understanding. Fans do not acquire simply a mass of film trivia; they develop tacit skills of appreciation, the ability to notice and understand elements of films that they previously overlooked (Osborne, 1970). They develop rich conceptual networks that combine knowledge of film, skills of film analysis, standards of evaluation, and habits of critical reflection. These networks can be termed "appreciative systems," where preferences become intertwined with, and are shaped by, explicit and implicit knowledge and understanding (Gee, 2003; Schon, 1987). Organized conceptual networks such as these are characteristic of a wide range of other kinds of "experts"—from child dinosaur aficionados to adult physicists (e.g., Bedard & Chi, 1992; Chi, Feltovich, & Glaser, 1981).

The expertise of film fans may have a particular subjective bent. In their reading, writing, and watching routines, fans explore their own interests and develop their own standards of taste. In cultural and communication studies, studies of fans have played an important part in shifting the conception of audience from passive consumers of media to active coconstructors of its meaning. In their analysis of fans of *Star Trek*, *Twin Peaks*, cult media, and other cultural products, researchers have focused not only on the active, critical engagement of fans, but also on the ways fans' interpretations and evaluations reflect their own subjectivities, tastes, and interests. Fans rewrite stories, make idiosyncratic interpretations, and otherwise use cultural products to suit their own purposes (e.g., Abercrombie & Longhurst, 1998; Atkinson, 1998; Hills, 2002; Jenkins, 1992, 2000). This focus on audiences' responses rather than content analysis is informed by a long and broad history of subjective and reader-response criticism in literary analysis and education (e.g., Bleich, 1975; Iser, 1978; Rosenblatt, 1938).

Fans form their subjective interpretations and evaluations within a social context. Recent work theoretical accounts of cinephilia have emphasized the networked and social aspects of film fandom in recent decades (e.g., de Valck & Hagener, 2005; Rosenbaum & Martin, 2003). Participants in this study fit the profile of the "second generation" or "new" cinephile, for whom film fandom is centered on networked resources (Behlil, 2005; Elsaesser, 2005). All study participants identify themselves as film fans and regularly participate in international online discussions of films. Many research film databases, compile electronic reviews, submit reviews to online journals, or use networked resources to obtain hard-to-find films.

The context of the online discussion forum can be characterized as a kind of interpretive community (Jenkins, 2000). In varying degrees of firmness and explicitness, interpretive communities shape elements of acceptable interpretation and set intersubjectively valid standards of evaluation (Fish, 1980; Olson, 1994). This relationship between the subjective and intersubjective standards of validity has a long history in conceptions of the nature and formation of taste: Hume (1757/1965) and Kant (1790/1987) both stressed the relationship between subjective avowals and claims of universal or intersubjective validity in their discussions of taste judgments.

These aspects of film fandom—its intrinsic motivation, its playful approach to the work of studying films, the nature of its expertise, and its focus on subjective responses in the context of a social community—are relevant to current concerns in more formal education. Literacy educators, whether of traditional texts or of multimedia, also often teach at this nexus of work and play. They aim to develop students' expertise in analysis and habits of critical reflection, but also instill a love of texts. Educators want students to focus on their subjective responses and connect texts to their own lives, but also respond to the interpretations and standards of the broader academic and social community. They may gain insights that support these goals by looking at the experiences of these film fans, who have sustained a love of films for many years, regularly link written and visual texts, and have developed their knowledge of film and skills of film analysis through reflection and discussion with others.

SAMPLE AND METHOD

The fans' accounts are drawn from e-mail interviews (often spanning over several months) with 11 participants in a major Internet film-discussion site. In response to open-ended questions, fans gave detailed accounts of their history of interest in films and their current tastes and activities as a film fan. I selected these 11 fans to interview from my survey of a random sample of 101 active participants in the same site. (Active participants were defined as having been a participant for at least three months, and having posted to the site more than five times. Most respondents far exceeded these minimum criteria. The survey response rate was 60.5%.) In the survey, fans responded to questions about their activities and tastes in films, as well as their demographic information. While survey respondents were from a range of countries (with about half of respondents from the United States), the 11 interviewees are all from the United States. I selected interviewees to represent a balance of gender, a range of ages, and a diversity of perspectives on film (e.g., fans with narrow genre interests and fans with broader tastes, as well as people who had been film fans most of their lives and people who became fans at an older age). Although the bulk of my discussion draws on a cross-case analysis of interviews with fans, I also report relevant findings from the broader survey.

Film Fandom as Informal Education

For most of the fans in the study, being a film fan is not simply watching a lot of movies or liking them a lot; it also involves educating yourself in film. On average, the surveyed fans ranked "having more knowledge about films" as the most important distinction between fans and nonfans. Fans also ranked the two other statements related to expertise (e.g., paying closer attention and discussing and comparing films more) as more important in distinguishing film fans from nonfans than watching more movies or degree of emotional involvement in film. Paired t-tests comparing the means of each ranked statement show that the differences between these are statistically significant (See Table 27.1).

In addition, in response to an open-ended, short-answer survey question on why they participate in online film discussions, over one third of the people specifically mentioned the exchange of knowledge or information. For active participants of this discussion site, being knowledgeable is seen as central to being a film fan.

This focus on knowledge is also apparent in the activities fans perform to support their interest in film. Looking back to Alan, we see him reading about films, engaging with others in discussions of films, and writing about the films he watches. Similarly, fans' reported activities for the week prior to completing the survey shows the prevalence of researching and discussing films (see Fig. 27.1). Nearly 85% of survey participants reported reading a film review in the previous week, and slightly over half had read a film-related book or magazine. All participants had watched at least one film in the past week, and all discussed films with someone, usually both in person and online.

Fans' Routines of Reading, Writing, and Watching

My interviews with fans explore how these activities of reading, writing, and watching work together to form a personalized routine that supports developing expertise (see Table 27.2).

Each fan has developed a unique approach to film. Alan reads a lot of background history on a film; Celia prefers to focus on her own response before learning what others have said. The technical aspects of filmmaking intrigue Brian. He avidly watches the DVD "extras" on how a film was made and mentions technical details such as color, sound, and image quality in his reviews. Vicki, Celia, and Paul specifically mentioned lack of interest in such technical things. Alan sticks to classic films to avoid wasting time on marginal

TABLE 27.1 Survey Participants' Mean Rank of the Relative Importance of Each Statement in Distinguishing Film Fans From People Who Have a More Casual Interest in Movies (1=most important, 5=least important, n=101)

Ranked Statements (Ordered From Most Important to Least Important)	Mean Rank (SD)	Results (T) of Paired T-tests Between Mean Rank of Each Statement			
		St. 2	St. 3	St. 4	St. 5
1. Fans are more knowledgeable about films.	2.4 (1.14)	−1.21	−2.60*	−4.44***	−6.95***
2. Fans pay closer attention to details and aspects of how the film was made.	2.58 (1.14)		−1.47	−3.70***	−6.36***
3. Fans like to discuss and compare films.	2.86 (1.19)			−2.31*	−5.14***
4. Fans watch more films.	3.32 (1.32)				−2.64**
5. Fans get more emotionally involved in films.	3.84 (1.30)				

* = $p < .05$, ** = $p < .01$, *** = $p < .001$

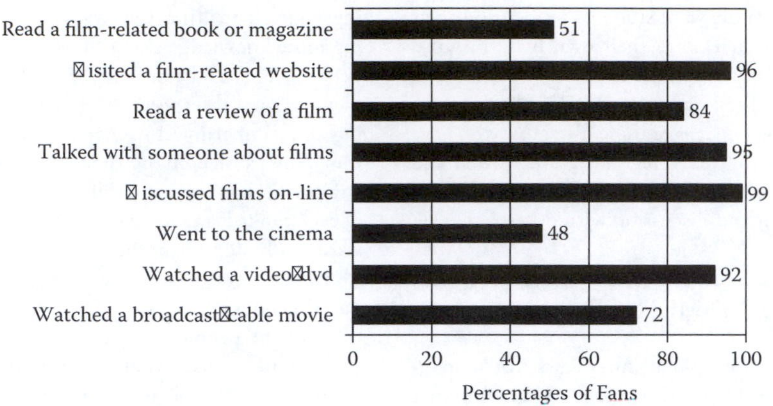

movies ("I don't have the time to follow the new releases, so I assume the great ones will eventually survive and I will catch up with them in twenty years."); Zach avoids classics because they take away the thrill of discovery ("The thing that keeps me at a distance is the fact that these are so universally revered that they lose the appeal of discovering them on your own."). Ian outlines key transitions in his taste development by which critic he was most influenced by at the time; Lily, Celia, and Zach try not to be influenced by critics. About eighty percent of the films Kira watches are ones she has seen before; Janet rarely rewatches a film.

Despite these differences, each fan watches, and reads and writes about, films in ways that develop his or her knowledge and understanding. These reading, writing, and watching routines serve three purposes: (a) building background knowledge and informing selection of films, (b) guiding interpretation and evaluation of films, and (c) inspiring imagination and creative works.

TABLE 27.2 Descriptions of Interviewed Fans' Routines of Reading and Writing About and Watching Films

Alias	Age	Educ.	Reading, Writing, and Watching Routines
Paul	Early 60s	Graduate study	Reads reviews and film books, researches film databases, discusses films online, and writes "thrice weekly essays" on films drawing on knowledge of politics and history.
Brian	Late 50s	Graduate Study	Reads reviews, writes an online review of nearly every film he watches, discusses films online, and regularly watches dvd extras of how films are made.
Alan	Mid 40s	B.A.	Reads reviews and film books, discusses films online, writes brief reviews of many of the films he watches, plays online film games. Watches 4–5 movies a week.
Vicki	Late 30s	High School	Reads film books on classic horror films, discusses films online. Likes rewatching favorite films.
Janet	Mid 30s	Some College	Reads reviews, discusses films online, focuses on paying close attention films. Watches one film each day, usually one not seen before.
Celia	Early 30s	Some college	Reads reviews (but only after seeing a movie), discusses films online. Writes fiction inspired by films. Likes to read books that films are based on.
Ian	Late 20s	B.A.	Reads reviews/film criticism, writes reviews and articles, discusses films online, plays online film-related games. Makes documentary films and screens them at festivals.
Zach	Mid 20s	Current part-time college student	Researches films through Web sites, read reviews after seeing films. Discusses films online. Rewatches films. Writes screenplays and is interested in filmmaking. Considering majoring in media studies.
Kira	Early 20s	High school	Reads reviews and film magazines, plays film related games, and discusses films online. Like rewatching films (about 80% of the films she watches are ones she has seen before). Likes to read books that films are based on.
Eric	Early 20s	Current full-time college student	Reads film books, reviews and other criticism, discusses films online. Likes rewatching particular scenes of movies. Sometimes writes reviews. Has made a few short films for school. Majoring in communications.
Lily	Late teens	Current full-time college student	Researches films with books and online databases. Reads reviews after seeing a film. Discusses films online. Watches a couple of movies a week. Interested in filmmaking. Considering a minor in film studies

Routines That Build Background Knowledge and Aid in the Selection of Films

For many casual moviegoers, choosing a film to see inspires some reading. We read back-of-the-box synopses as we peruse the video store; we glance over reviews to decide what to see in the theater. For most of the fans I interviewed, ideas for films to watch are just one byproduct of their ongoing research in film. As they read film books, magazines, and Web sites; participate in online discussions; or attend film classes, fans both build knowledge and generate possible film selections.

Some research is not aimed at finding films to watch: Alan reads on film history and filmmaking for pleasure and to fill gaps in his knowledge. Vicki enjoys reading about how her favorite classic horror films were made. Ian reads critics to learn from how they think about films, not for recommendations. Other research is directed at finding films: Zach frequents several Web sites to keep track of new and upcoming releases. Ian pays attention to festival listings and museum screenings. Lily consults the book *1000 Films to See Before You Die*. Through this research, fans develop long lists of films to see. The recent rise in availability of esoteric, foreign, or other previously hard-to-find films through DVDs, as well as easy access to films through online rental catalogs such as *Netflix*, have lengthened these lists considerably. Whereas as a child, Alan had to scour the TV guide for chances to watch films, fans can now easily find most films they want (though some fans still described elaborate processes for tracking down not yet widely available films).

Given this wealth of possibilities, at times, fans devise ways of organizing what they watch. For instance, Eric went through a period of watching mainly European films from the late 1950s and early 1960s, and Vicki explored horror films from other countries after years of watching mainly classic Hollywood horror films. The organization of viewing can be quite playful. Paul sees his "tracking down" of films as a kind of game:

> Because I have seen so many films, I very seldom make my choice on the genre vector. I tend to "track things down." I will get wind of something, and then pursue it. For example: I was led to *Days of Heaven* (1978) by a review of something. It was probably *Far And Away* (1992) but I'm not sure. Anyway, at *Heaven*, I met director Terrence Malick. So I tracked down *Badlands* (1978). I happened to see *Fear* (1996), which I compared to *Badlands*, especially the first half. This led someone to comment on Reese Witherspoon's *Best Laid Plans* (1999), which I had already seen, So I rejected that but turned to *Tape* (2001) which has some similar characteristics—of a plan laid down before the film begins and then carried out during the film.

He likes to follow a lead as far as it can go. In the above instance, he will likely search out further examples of films in which a plan is conceived before the film starts, taking pleasure in making unusual connections. Other fans organize viewing with more formal games. For instance, Alan plays a game where a group of fans agree to watch a set of films from a given year—say, 1957—and discuss their relative merits and reaward mock Oscars. In these cases, fans do not just watch whatever movie they are in the mood for; they select with purposeful criteria.

Fans' research of films affects how they watch them. For instance, when Eric selects a film because Martin Scorsese cites it as a key influence, his watching is shaped by that knowledge. The way viewing is organized also influences interpretation. When Paul watches *Tape* in relation to other films where a plan is laid down before the film starts, he will view it differently than if he were to watch it in a series of its director Linklater's work. When Alan and the other game players watch films in groups by different years, it sets up looking at films in a historical context. Vicki sets up a cross-cultural comparison when she broadens from classic Hollywood horror films to include horror films from Europe and Asia. When Kira watches a film after reading the book it was based on, she cannot help comparing them.

This research and organized viewing contributes to fans' expertise; knowledge about, responses to, and comparisons between films are more likely to cohere into organized and richly interrelated conceptual networks than when films are just chosen on a whim (e.g., Bedard & Chi, 1992); however, fans are careful not to let it become tedious. In addition to taking playful, game-like approaches to the work, fans also change courses if their fandom starts seeming too much like a chore. For instance, Alan cuts back on the reawarding Oscars game when he finds it dominates his viewing too much, or when he is not particularly interested in the year in question. Other fans avoid being "completist" as they explore the works of a given director, actor, or cinematographer. Zach described some "arty" films that have been lingering awhile on his to-see list: "While they sound enriching and rewarding, its not going to be a breath holding rollicking good time that you really want to rush out for . . . you have to be in the mood for some of these films." This can be a delicate balance for fans; several described instances where a film that was not initially appealing turned out to be a favorite. While the Epicurean mandate suggests that trading difficult pleasures for simple pleasures can bring more pleasure, it may be hard to know which "difficult" pleasures will have this effect.

In addition to keeping their fandom fun, fans also restrict research to protect their subjective response to films. About one third of the fans avoid reading reviews until after they have seen a film. Some, like Zach, avoid them because they give too many details about the film and ruin the effect of surprise. Others want to form their own view before reading others' opinions. As Lily explained,

> I do not read reviews ahead of time and now when I tell friends what movie I have selected to rent next, I ask them to please not give their own opinion of it, nor tell me what they think *I* will think of it. I'm trying my best to go into movies with an untainted view now, though of course that is probably impossible.

Routines That Support Interpreting and Evaluating Films

Fans support their interpretation and evaluation of films in ways beyond this background research and organized viewing. They watch (and rewatch) films, read critics' and other fans' perspectives on films, write reviews or other responses to films, and participate in online discussions and games. Through these activities, they not only gain insight into a particular film or films, they also clarify their criteria for evaluation and become aware of their particular method(s) of approaching films. As they watch, read, and write, fans described three important elements of interpreting and evaluating films: (a) paying close attention, (b) making comparisons between films, and (c) drawing upon other bodies of knowledge, personal experiences, and/or others' perspectives.

One way that fans pay close attention to films is by rewatching them. That a film sustained this rewatching well was a commonly cited reason for choosing it as a favorite. To use Goodman's (1976) terms, films are replete. A film's wealth of information is impossible to process as 24 frames speed by each second. To improve understanding, all of the fans cited sometimes rewatching films. For instance, Eric frequently rewatches key scenes to see how they relate to the film as a whole:

> To me, these scenes are not only enjoyable to watch, but they also embody the main themes of the film as a whole. . . . The first time I watch a movie, I pay close attention to plot and the sequence of events. I get a rough idea of what the director is trying to say, but I don't pretend to understand it fully. Once I have a few ideas of what might be going on, each additional time I watch the movie I look for things that either support or negate my hunches about what the director was getting at. Also, the more I understand about the ideas behind the plot, the more certain scenes will gain in meaning, and by extension emotional impact.

Several fans also described a mental rewatching of films; they "replay" scenes of films in their mind, thinking about their possible meanings. To be sure, fans do not only rewatch films for analysis—rewatching favorite films is comforting and entertaining—but every fan that discussed rewatching films also talked about the new insights it lent.

Beyond rewatching films, many fans stress paying close attention to films. Janet claimed a key aspect of her film fandom is that she pays close attention to every second of every film she watches, even ones she does not particularly like. Paul described how his attention has sharpened as he has become more of a film fan:

> I'll take *The Third Man* (1949), which I just saw for the third time, as a case in point. It's like I never saw it before. I feel like my senses are sharper, my appreciation of smaller things is greater. My questioning is stronger: Why do the sewers look like Escher's drawings? Accident or intent? Why are the streets deserted at night? Why take so long to introduce Harry Lime? Why does Harry have to meet Holly Martins under a Ferris Wheel? Why is the camera angle set to make the Ferris Wheel so surreal? Why can't Lime ask Holly to kill him? Why must it be done with a nod? How much is the novelist and playwright (Korda, and later Greene) warning us about Soviet intentions in Europe? Is Holly Martins a fool or an optimist? Is the film a warning to America not to project its templates onto a ravaged Europe?

As he watches, Paul notices details and asks himself questions about visuals, plot construction, and underlying political contexts and themes. He rarely did this before he became a film fan; he sees and understands more now while watching a film. He has developed skills and habits of appreciation (Osborne, 1970).

Fitting with Hume's second criteria for a "competent judge," many of the fans described how having seen more films improves their ability to evaluate them. For instance, after watching more movies, Zach realized some early favorites were just average examples of the same patterns played out over and over again. Seeing more films raised his standards for originality. Having seen more films also sets up comparative thinking. As Paul explained, "I think the matrix, the spider-web of comparing film to film is part of what makes each new viewing experience 'better.'" Sometimes comparisons are more targeted.

As Ian compared *The Thin Red Line* and *Saving Private Ryan*, two WWII films released in the same year, he realized that he values atmospheric and poetic films more than straight narratives.

> Watching *The Thin Red Line* made me feel that Spielberg, for all his taut, focused storytelling (something that Malick lacked) had basically pummeled me into a state of submission instead of elevating me to a higher state of understanding the world as Malick had done. I viewed these films as two completely opposite approaches to the same subject matter, and for a while they raged a war in my head as to their relative strengths and weaknesses . . . until finally Malick won out.

Watching Malick's *The Thin Red Line* in relation to Spielberg's *Saving Private Ryan* advanced Ian's understanding of both the films and his own aesthetic values. His discovery reflects the idea in aesthetics that comparative judgments can establish principles for taste judgments (e.g., Mothersill, 1991).

In addition to watching films closely and comparatively, many fans connect films with other interests and knowledge. For instance, Alan, Eric, and Paul share an interest in history. They use their historical knowledge to understand films, and look to films for insights into the historical context of when they were made. As Paul has become more experienced in film analysis, he draws on historical and political science knowledge that previously lay dormant (as he calls it, "dead stuff"):

> I think one of the things that has changed is that a whole boatload of history and political science that accumulated, not only from school and college, but also from post-formal education has come tumbling down on me. So that if I screen a film like *The Dancer Upstairs* (2002), the fascinating John Malkovich study of narcissistic revolution, it seems that more things are brought to bear on the viewing and interpreting than would have a decade ago—*even though I knew the same things a decade ago.* Dare I say this? Intense film viewing has augured larger holes in this reservoir of "dead stuff" and made it come alive for me.

Drawing on this body of knowledge not only sharpens his film analysis (refer back, for instance, to his political questions on *The Third Man),* but also enlivens his understanding of history and political science.

Other fans are less interested in historical or political contexts, and instead draw personal connections. While every fan makes some comparisons between films' narratives and his or her own experiences, about half the fans make this central in their interpretation and evaluation. Kira, Janet, Celia, Zach, and Ian's most valued films are ones that gave them insight into their own lives and experiences. Ian linked *Tokyo Story* to his experience as a student:

> I watched it in this tiny carrel in the library basement and by the end I was crying my eyes out, because it made me think of my family back home and how I'd come to this expensive college to become this writer/doctor I had envisioned, but it was falling apart because I couldn't keep up with the goals I had set and I felt incredibly inferior to the level of scholarship on display around me. I had really kind of hit bottom, but this movie in confirming my feelings in a sense offered a relief in ways I couldn't find elsewhere.

Janet also sought understanding through movies in difficult times in her life. When her mother committed suicide after years of mental illness, she turned to films as a "sort of counselor":

> I really think that I was looking for any explanation from a human perspective as to how people overcame devastation. Maybe even something that explained her state of mind or anything that allowed me to see that other people had similar feelings . . . I swear that part of the reason I made it through the three years following her suicide was in *huge* part due to the therapeutic sessions that film offered me.

In these cases, Ian and Janet focused on their subjective response, which were uniquely shaped by their current life situations—as a struggling student, as a mourning daughter. They did not aim to make distanced, critical evaluations of the films; they explicitly made sense of the films in terms of their immediate experiences.

Along with reflecting on their own responses, fans regularly seek out others' perspectives on films. Most of the fans described reading multiple reviews of the same film. They tend not to seek the "correct opinions" about a film, but rather, alternate ways of thinking. Fans often reflect how reviews reveal different standards of taste. As Brian noted in one of his reviews, "I dislike this film for all the reasons that critic Ebert gave it a favorable rating." But sometimes reviews lead fans to reconsider their opinions. For instance, Ian described reading critic Manny Farber and reconsidering his opinion on two of his favorite films:

> It was truly amazing because for once a critic didn't seem preoccupied with calling a movie "good" or "bad" but essentially describing it with words that seemed to perfectly capture the sensation of watching the film, and allowing us to evaluate those sensations on any number of levels: stylistic, symbolic, cultural, psychological, etc. He made me totally reconsider my position on two of my favorites, *The Third Man* and *Taxi Driver*.

Fans also learn from reading others' discussions. Two of the youngest fans, Lily and Eric, act as apprentices when they read the conversations of more knowledgeable fans as a way to learn new ways of thinking and writing to about films. As Eric explained, "I consider myself a relative novice and I love reading posts by users who know much more than I do. Their knowledge and enthusiasm is inspiring to me." Lily thought herself well versed in film until she came to the discussion site as a young teen:

> Most glaring was my limited knowledge of non-American movies and of older (e.g., pre-90s) movies . . . I also lacked any technical knowledge regarding direction style, lighting, sound, etc. Those were just not things I had I'd even thought to pay attention to. . . . Lastly, just reading users comments and posts, I realized that I was just not very eloquent in describing what made a movie "good." I knew if a film made me laugh or made me feel sad or scared, but other than my basic reaction I could make no other comment. . . . [Online discussions] taught me the basics of film analysis, which I had never thought to do before.

As she read these conversations, Lily recognized her comparative lack of knowledge and skill, and learned from these more experienced fans.

Alongside reading others' views, writing also plays an important role in fans' interpretation and evaluation of films. All of the fans write about films in online discussions, and about half write responses in more formal ways (e.g., reviews and essays). Brian, who has amassed an online database of over 800 film reviews, started to write reviews because he found himself often forgetting what he watched:

> I decided to write my own "user reviews" . . . because experience had shown me that not only did I often have difficulty remembering the essential story of a movie I had seen, I also sometimes didn't remember I had even seen the movie. That isn't so much a reflection of my memory powers, but it reflected the rather shallow manner in which I tended to watch movies. Writing reviews has made me a more active movie-watcher. I pay more attention to the plot and story line, and when I write my review it forces me to think more critically of what I have seen.

Writing about films not only solidified his memory, it changed how he watches films. He is now more attentive and analytical. Similarly, Paul writes "essays" on films about three times a week in response to various film discussion threads. He sees this "constant pressure to write" as what helped him learn to draw on historical and political knowledge in his film analyses.

While writing reviews or essays organizes thinking for many fans, online discussions often provide a more informal and collaborative way to interpret and evaluate films. Most fans claimed it is rare that a conversation will completely change their evaluation of a film. More often, good conversations lead them to see how someone might reasonably have a different opinion, show them something they failed to notice, or provide a different context of viewing. Lily described how her negative opinion of *Bite the Bullet* was moderated by discussion:

> In this movie, the main character is constantly shown doing acts of goodness, to other people, to horses, etc. etc. It was a bit much for me frankly, and I thought it seemed a bit self-righteous—it was a bit annoying to see someone portrayed as being *so* perfect. However, a discussion with another user made me soften this view a bit. We discussed the portrayal of friendship in the movie, and also the conditions of the Old West in which the movie took place, where the values portrayed may have been more necessary for living and getting along with other people. I will always think it was a bit much, but the other poster opened me up to the idea that the actions of the character were perhaps not as unrealistic as I thought.

While she still does not particularly like the film, she understands another's point of view and recognizes limitations to her own criticisms.

Online discussions that take the form of games are a key aspect of about one third of the fans' interpretive and evaluative routines. These games often involve drawing analytic comparisons among films and setting up criteria for evaluation. Players award Oscars, titles such as "greatest American director," or retroactive Nobel prizes in cinema. Ian described how these types of games broadened his thinking, and informed his standard of taste:

> This was an incredibly eye-opening and rewarding experience for me, because it cemented an ideal in my mind to be as cosmopolitan, as globally minded and as open-minded as possible to all kinds of cinema. I mean, when you've got people nominating Laurel and Hardy on one hand and Sergei Eisenstein on the other, or pitting a famous veteran Hollywood composer vs. an African director who according to the only person who knows him says is the most important African filmmaker of all time, you have to take all sides into consideration. This to me was an idyllic experience, this feeling of perpetual discoveries lying in wait with every week.

Games provide both structure and a sense of fun to the work of interpreting and evaluating films. The structure of the game forms a kind of interpretive community that allows each player to voice his or her own perspective on a common theme and to clarify through discussion their common and differing ideals (Fish, 1980).

Like Ian, other fans described how others' perspectives give them insight to their own "lens" on film. For instance, Alan found that he primarily takes a narrative approach to film (e.g., focusing on dialogue, character development, and plot construction), whereas many other fans he discusses films with approach it more visually (e.g., camera angles, ongoing visual themes, and style). Celia and Kira claimed that they focus on the emotive power of films and how the films relate to themselves personally. Celia contrasted her approach with that of a friend who attends more to technique:

> He will pick on things like the direction or lighting or composition. Many a time I don't care about these things. . . . Technical foibles in a film really don't bother me. I try not to see them anyway because it messes with the suspended disbelief. He analyzes the filmmaking process and technique whereas I will only rarely do that.

Through discussion, fans realize that films can be viewed in many ways, and they therefore gain a sense of the strengths and gaps of their own approach.

Imagination and Creative Works Inspired by Films

One of the powers of film is its ability to spark the imagination, and many fans described activities that draw on these imaginative influences. In childhood, this is mainly through fantasy play. About half of the fans recounted such play based on films. Janet imagined herself as each Disney heroine she saw; Alan stomped around the kindergarten playground as Godzilla. Zach reflected on how seeing *Indiana Jones* as a young child shaped his play and his ideals:

> When I got home I *was* Indiana Jones for the rest of the week, riding on a skateboard (on one knee) and using a rope or something for a whip. I remember all my feelings seemed intensified . . . it wasn't just that I was pretending—I learned what heroism looked and felt like from *Indiana Jones* and followed that model in my life . . . things [like rescuing my little brother from bullies] suddenly had a larger significance—it became part of a great adventure.

As adolescents and adults, this fantasy play merges into identification with characters, imagining themselves in their places and trying to see the world through their perspectives. Films create worlds they want to enter. Kira and Celia both read books that films are based on to extend the time they are in that imagined world.

Over one third of the fans harness the imagination sparked by films into their own creative works. Watching films inspired Alan to make his own monster movies as a child. In her obsession with film *The Goonies* at age 12, Celia rewrote the story of the film, adding herself as a "thinly disquised 8th Goonie." Films still inspire her to write stories, character sketches, and novels. A movie will spark a specific idea for a story, or just the imaginative process of watching a film "spurs her brain into action" for writing fiction. As a youngteen film fan, Zach became interested in writing screenplays (guided by books such as *Screenplay* and *The Screenwriter's Workbook*). After years of avidly watching films, Ian began making his own. Over the past four years, he has created a collection of documentary films, some of which he has screened at film festivals.

This creative process alters how they watch films. Celia sometimes analyzes how the story of a film is constructed. Zach credits his screenwriting (along with his reading of the books on the craft) with helping him develop a more critical view of films; for instance, writing helped him realized that characters needed to have motivations for their actions, something he saw lacking in some former favorite films. When Ian decided to become a director, he analyzed his favorite directors to figure out how they work and what makes them great. When fans write or make films themselves, they become sharply aware of the film as a created product and examine how it was made. Media literacy and films studies programs often include some element of creative production to promote this understanding (e.g., British Film Institute, 2000; Tyner, 1998).

DISCUSSION AND IMPLICATIONS FOR LITERACY EDUCATION

In these accounts of film fans, I have characterized their fandom as an informal education in film. I argue that their activities develop knowledge, skills, and habits central to film and media literacy (e.g., British Film Institute, 2000; Monaco, 2000; Tyner, 1998). All of the fans regularly participate in activities that build their knowledge in the domain, all exercise analytic and evaluative skills, and over one third of the fans also have explored elements of creative production in film. In addition, I argue that their film fandom reflects a mutually reinforcing relationship between written and visual media (e.g., reading about films inspires watching films, which inspires writing about films). Fans develop regular habits of reading and writing about films, as well as watching them.

Assuming that this case has been made, these fans' experiences can inform education that seeks to develop literacies in both written and visual media, and forge links between them. But there are, of course, caveats. First, the fans I interviewed are all adults. All have completed secondary school, most have some college education, and slightly over one third have earned a college or graduate degree. Their film fandom reflects the utilization and further development of already achieved, basic literacies. Second, fans' reading and writing activities are encouraged by their passion for films. Educators have long used content interests as a way to motivate reading and writing, and some have found this to be effective, even with students with dyslexia or other language-learning difficulties (e.g., Fink, 1998; Levine, 2002). While film may not, however, motivate reading and writing to the same degree for those not similarly passionate about it, the popularity of written materials about films (e.g., journalistic reviews, film magazines, and books about films) suggests there is a reasonably strong relationship between film and written texts. Third, as mentioned earlier, because I chose my sample from fans who regularly write on film-discussion boards, they may represent a subset of film fans particularly drawn to linking written and visual media. To be sure, there are many film fans who never write about films; however, the growing popularity of film-related discussion sites (my studied site alone has thousands of registered participants) indicates that these fans are not, in this respect, an anomaly. Finally, fandom does not involve formal educational goals. While fans' habits of reading, writing, and watching may develop expertise, I have not conducted any formal assessments of their learning. Caveats aside, I identify five factors across fans' accounts that may give insight to educators seeking to use films in their curriculum to develop both written and visual literacies, and to strengthen the connections between them: (a) personalized routine, (b) playful work, (c) diverse and accessible written materials on film, (d) beyond interpretation: comparison and evaluation, and (e) draw of the social community.

Personalized routine. Most of the fans have developed routines for researching, watching, and reflecting on films. Many of these routines began during middle childhood or adolescence, often spurred by a catalyst such as a film that provoked a strong reaction. The confusion Eric felt when he saw *2001: A Space Odyssey* spurred him to research the film; Celia loved *The Goonies* so much she extended the experience by writing her own version (with herself written into the story). Sometimes fans were inspired into a more sophisticated approach to film by a model of a critic or more experienced film fans. Reading Roger Ebert inspired Ian to write his own reviews; the more nuanced discussion of more experienced film fans led Lily to analyze her own experience of films more carefully. For many fans, the availability of new technologies such as online film databases, film review collections, film discussion boards, DVDs with documentaries, and other supplementary information about the film were also important in establishing their routines of researching films.

Fans' routines develop and reflect not just particular skills, but a broader disposition to approach films actively. A dispositional perspective stresses not only the importance of ability or skills, but also the *inclination* and the *alertness* to opportunities to use them

(Perkins, Jay, & Tishman, 1993). Each of these fans' experiences launched a more active approach to watching films that involved a routine of reading and writing about them. These routines are also *personalized.* Fans are drawn to different resources and approaches. Over the years, they develop routines that suit their different interests, tastes, and purposes.

Encouraging students to develop the disposition of approaching films reflectively and analytically may importantly involve supporting the development of this sort of personalized routine. Thus, teachers may (a) provide a wide range of resources to support film research, (b) supply students with models of different ways to analyze and reflect on films, and (c) give students space to establish a routine that reflects their interests and serves their aims. Students may already have nascent elements of a routine (e.g., checking reviews of films they watch, keeping lists of films they want to see, and looking up films online to see who played different parts) that can be built upon further. Though class assignments that carefully scaffold an analysis of a given film may help students produce more sophisticated work in the short term, helping students establish personalized routines may work more towards fostering a more ongoing disposition to develop an understanding of film that persists outside the classroom.

Playful work. While Anna Freud (1965) emphasized the work-like aspects of hobbies for children and adolescents, for adults, hobbies such as film fandom may serve as a way to retain a sense of playfulness in daily life. Whether through informal intellectual pleasures such as Paul's "track down process" or the more formalized group games discussed earlier, the fans in this study often found ways to make their routines of researching and analyzing films playful. Games often encourage fans to watch films they might not otherwise and think of them in new ways. For instance, in the game of reawarding Oscars, fans need to watch a series of films from a given year and make a case to others that one film, actor, or cinematographer deserves a particular award over another contender. The process of making arguments and responding to others' arguments makes explicit that many of the fans have different assumptions about how to judge merit in film.

Games are often used in education to increase student engagement, explore new ways of thinking, and harness the power of play for learning. Even games not intentionally designed to be educational are argued to have a lot of potential for learning (e.g., Gee, 2003). The repleteness of films and the extent of available film-related resources support many possible games to suit a variety of educational goals. For instance, if educators want students to think about what makes a film "good" and develop their skills of persuasive oral or written argumentation, games oriented to giving film awards may work well. The existence of elaborate and well-known award systems in film creates a ready structure for this sort of game. If educators are interested in broadening students' taste and inspiring them to think about films comparatively, they can design games that promote different types of comparisons. For instance, a game could be organized around challenges to find films that connect in some way, such as ones that use a similar narrative device such as showing the film's climactic event first, or revealing the plot through different characters' perspectives. Online databases and discussion forums on films make such research feasible. This type of game leads students to seek out films they may not otherwise know about, and compare films in new ways. The number, variety, and degree of sophistication of games that emerge spontaneously on film discussion boards also indicate that it would be fruitful to enlist students to design their own games.

Alongside designing formal games for education, the experiences of fans in this study underline the importance of retaining a sense of playfulness when approaching films in an educative way. Fans watch and read and write about films because they find it entertaining and because it enhances their enjoyment of films. Many fans enjoy searching for new films, finding unexpected pleasures, gaining new insights, and sharing their discoveries with others. It is important that efforts to make watching films more educational do not make them boring.

On the other hand, not all use of films is particularly educative. Most films are designed to be entertaining, and it is quite easy to watch them fairly passively or to focus on aspects that are difficult to justify as educational. Hills (2002) described and critiqued a recent trend in cultural studies towards valorizing fans as active and critical analysts of cultural products and neglecting their affective and consumerist impulses. In my focus on the educative aspects of film fandom, I am somewhat guilty of this valorization. Although the activities of the fans in my study support a view of their fandom as education, these activities are also sometimes just for fun. Fans also watch movies to escape, to unwind, out of habit, for nostalgia, because they find certain actors attractive, and to be entertained. Some may exert as much energy on buying products related to films as they do analyzing them or interpreting them. Educators seeking to use film in their curriculums must strike a balance to ensure that there is both an element of play to the work and work to the play.

Diverse and accessible written materials on film. A key asset for linking films and written text is the diversity of writing available on films and some natural motivations to read them. We read about films for pleasure, to avoid wasting time and money on "bad" ones, and to compare our responses with others. All of the fans read reviews, and many read multiple reviews and analyses of the same film by different critics, academics, and other fans. These diverse readings sensitize them to differences in authors' style and perspective, and differences in genre, as well as informing them about films. Several fans cited critics as key to their having become fans; the critics modeled a more active way of approaching films. Some did not even find films that interesting until they read how excited Pauline Kael, Roger Ebert, or Andrew Sarris were about them, and realized how much these critics were able to see in films. Ian described how he was inspired both by Roger Ebert's insights into films and his passion for them, and contrasted this with his other school subjects:

> When I was in college and bemoaning my inability to excel in my studies as well as others, I wondered why I didn't have an intuitive ability to appreciate subjects and I actually concluded that it was because I had never encountered a Roger Ebert of literature, a Leonard Maltin of biochemistry, when I was at an impressionable age. Someone who spoke about their passion in terms a 12 year old could understand and be captivated.

Fans' reading on films is not limited to reviews and criticism. Some read scripts, or books that inspired films. Some like reading more about the historical context of the film, or about the process involved in its creation.

There is no set relationship between watching films and reading film-related texts. Some fans are vehemently opposed to reading anything about a film before seeing it; others rarely will spend time watching anything they have not yet carefully researched. Some fans follow a critic and enjoy his or her way of thinking, even if they do not watch all of the films they review. Some fans appreciate the writing style of critics more than their accounts of films, and model their own writing after them. Others focus on which critics tend to make accurate predictions of which films they will like and dislike. Inspiration and understanding can flow in a variety of directions between film and written texts.

Educators should be remember the power that written texts on films can have for encouraging interest and deeper understanding. A first inclination may be to think that films enliven written texts for students, but the experiences of these fans show how many different sorts of texts can enliven and deepen their understanding of, and interest in, films. Educators should consider using the full range of written materials connected to films, and to encourage flexible and varied relationships between written and film texts. Written texts can be used in the classroom as guides to selecting films; as models for writing about films; as aids in analyzing, interpreting or evaluating films; as a way to encourage comparisons between writing genre (e.g., journalistic film criticism vs. academic film criticism); and as a way to put films into historical or cultural contexts.

Beyond interpretation: comparison and evaluation. The field of film studies has roots in literature departments, but film scholars debate on how it should differ from its literary predecessor. For instance, Bordwell (1989) critiqued film studies' overemphasis on "reading" films. He saw a near exclusive focus on explication and interpretation of films' meanings; a focus he claims grows out of literary analysis. Bordwell has suggested broader analyses of film's historical evolution, its visual style and composition, and its particular aesthetics. In precollegiate settings, there have been similar debates on how best use and study films (e.g., Baines, 1997).

The writings and discussions of fans in online communities, although they do not resolve such scholarly or curricular issues, suggest different approaches than just explicating and analyzing the meaning of individual films. For instance, making comparisons among films is a central part of film discussions. Since fans generally watch over 100 films each year, a single film is not always the best level of analysis. Discussions often center on comparisons: between different directors' bodies of work, between films in a genre or subgenre, and among films within a genre from different cultures. Likewise, film festivals are often organized to show a series of films that are related in some way.

Films offer a natural opportunity to work on the comparative thinking and writing that is an essential part of literacy. Whereas it may be unwieldy in a single class to focus on extensive comparisons among different books, several films can be watched and compared in a relatively short period of time. Guided by their curricular goals, educators can assign a series of films to encourage comparisons in a variety of ways.

A strong evaluative component also exists in film fans' discussions: fans assign and defend their ratings of films, play games that give mock awards, and argue about standards of evaluation. For several of the fans, this evaluative process was what first attracted their interest in films. For instance, Eric, who began writing reviews of films at age 13 after reading the film column in the local paper, said it was not so much anything specific about the critic that inspired him; rather, "there was definitely something about the ideas of 'grading' a film that appealed to me." At around the same age, Ian focused on cataloguing awards and "stars" given to various films. While there are arguments about whether this strong tendency towards evaluation is positive for understanding films and should be promoted in film studies courses (see, for instance, Bordwell & Thompson, 2001), many film fans place a lot of focus on this. Educators can use this natural appeal of "grading films" to help students move beyond simple assertions of preference in their evaluations to principled arguments, and to become aware of the disputes and tensions involved in evaluating films.

Draw of the social community. While an analysis of the effects of the online discussion forum on fans' activities is beyond the scope of this chapter, this social community is an important draw for many fans. The discussion boards gave many their first opportunity to connect with other passionate film fans and share their reactions to films.

Fans also cited ways the discussion boards shape their film fandom. For instance, Alan claimed he would never have thought of organizing his viewing by a game prior to joining the discussion group. For some, the audience of the discussion group provides motivation for writing. Although some fans wrote about films in private journals earlier in their film fandom, these tended to be sporadic and short-lived. Within the online community, fans are more likely to sustain the writing habit. In addition, with fans of all different ages and levels of film experience, the site supports apprenticeships. As in the cases of Lily and Eric, novice fans learn from the conversations of more expert fans that model more sophisticated forms of film analysis. This "apprenticeship" not only gives novices information, it shapes the way they think (Rogoff, 1990).

Educators also draw upon the social community aspect when they use a film as a basis for a class discussion; however, the communal aspect can be extended in many different ways, such as by providing shared forums for students' written reviews and analyses, creating group games related to films, collaborating on making a film, and hosting class "film festivals," during which students select films on a theme and write supporting materials. Students can be charged with envisioning and designing such communal activities around film. The community can be extended outside the classroom to the school and broader community, such as through film festivals, inviting students to submit their film reviews, criticisms or analyses to school publications or broader online film journals and discussion groups, hosting screenings of student films or film festivals.

Of course, the draw of the community can be used in the study of film in many ways. The point is that for the film fans studied here, the "interpretive community" of the discussion boards was a powerful force in helping fans stay engaged with films, learn from others, and developing new habits of watching and reading and writing about films.

These five elements do not work in isolation; they interact and, in combination, promote a more engaged interest in film. Through personalized, playful routines of watching and reading and writing about films, fans demonstrate an approach to films that pushes it beyond an enjoyable pastime into an informal education. As they discuss, compare, and evaluate films in the online discussion forums, they model ways of developing collaborative methods of interpretation and evaluation and communal standards of taste. While watching films is an enjoyable part of many of our lives, these fans reflect ways of approaching films that build knowledge and appreciation, and encourage habits of reflection and analysis. Their experiences demonstrate natural ties among watching and reading and writing about films. As educators seek to use film in the classroom and build connections between films and written texts, they can gain insights from these fans, who spend many hours, over the course of many years, developing their tastes and understandings in film.

REFERENCES

Abercrombie, N., & Longhurst, B. (1998). *Audiences: A sociological theory of performance and imagination.* London: Sage.

Atkinson, M. (1998). *The secret marriage of Sherlock Holmes and other eccentric readings.* Ann Arbor: University of Michigan Press.

Baines, L. (1997). Film, video and books: Some considerations for learning and teaching. In J. Flood, S. B. Heath, & D. Lapp (Eds.), *Handbook of research on teaching literacy through the communicative and visual arts* (pp. 545–556). New York: Macmillan Library Reference.

Bedard, J., & Chi, M. (1992). Expertise. *Current Directions in Psychological Science, 1*(4), 135–139.

Behlil, M. (2005). Ravenous cinephiles: Cinephilia, Internet, and online film communities. In M. de Valck & M. Hagener (Eds.), *Cinephilia: Movies, love and memory* (pp. 111–124). Amsterdam: Amsterdam University Press.

Bleich, D. (1975). *Readings and feelings: An introduction to subjective criticism.* Urbana, IL: National Council of Teachers of English.

Bordwell, D. (1989). *Making meaning: Inference and rhetoric in the interpretation of cinema.* Cambridge, MA: Harvard University Press.

Bordwell, D., & Thompson, K. (2001). *Film art: An introduction* (6th ed.). New York: McGraw Hill.

British Film Institute (2000). *Moving images in the classroom: A secondary teacher's guide to using film and television.* Retrieved May 31, 2006, from http://www.bfi.org.uk/education/teaching/miic/

Chi, M., Feltovich, P., & Glaser, R. (1981). Categorization and representation of physics problems by experts and novices. *Cognitive Science, 5,* 121–152.

Csikszentmihalyi, M. (2000). *Beyond boredom and anxiety: Experiencing flow in work and play* (25th anniversary ed.). San Francisco: Jossey-Bass.

de Valck, M., & Hagener, M. (Eds.). (2005). *Cinephilia: Movies, love and memory.* Amsterdam: Amsterdam University Press.

Elsaesser, T. (2005). Cinephilia or the uses of disenchantment. In M. de Valck & M. Hagener (Eds.), *Cinephilia: Movies, love and memory* (pp. 27–44). Amsterdam: Amsterdam University Press.

Fink, R. (1998). Literacy development in successful men and women with dyslexia. *Annals of Dyslexia, 48,* 311–346.

Fish, S. (1980). *Is there a text in this class? The authority of interpretive communities.* Cambridge, MA: Harvard University Press.

Freud, A. (1965). *Normality and pathology in childhood.* London: Hogarth Press and the Institute of Psycho-analysis, 1966, c1965.

Gee, J. (2003). *What video games have to teach us about learning and literacy.* New York: Palgrave Macmillan.

Goodman, N. (1976). *Languages of art.* Indianapolis, IN: Hackett Publishing Company.

Hills, M. (2002). *Fan cultures.* London: Routledge.

Hume, D. (1965). *'Of the standard of taste' and other essays.* New York: Bobbs-Merrill. (Original work published 1757)

Iser, W. (1978). *The act of reading: A theory of aesthetic response.* Baltimore: Johns Hopkins University Press.

Jenkins, H. (1992). *Textual poachers: Television fans and participatory culture.* New York: Routledge.

Jenkins, H. (2000). Reception theory and audience research: The mystery of the Vampire's Kiss. In C. Gledhill & L. Williams (Eds.), *Reinventing Film Studies* (pp. 165–182). New York: Oxford University Press.

Kant, I. (1987). *Critique of judgment.* Indianapolis, IN: Hackett Publishing Company. (Original work published 1790)

Levine, M. (2002). *A mind at a time.* New York: Simon & Schuster.

Mann, C., & Stewart, F. (2000). *Internet communication and qualitative research: A handbook for researching online.* London: Sage.

Monaco, J. (2000). *How to read a film: The world of movies, media, and multimedia: Language, history, theory* (3rd ed.). New York: Oxford University Press.

Mothersill, M. (1991). *Beauty restored.* New York: Adams Bannister Cox.

Olson, D. (1994). *The world on paper: The conceptual and cognitive implications of writing and reading.* New York: Cambridge University Press.

Osborne, H. (1970). *The art of appreciation.* London: Oxford University Press.

Perkins, D., Jay, E., & Tishman, S. (1993). Beyond abilities: A dispositional theory of thinking. *Merrill-Palmer Quarterly, 39*(1), 1–21.

Rogoff, B. (1990). *Apprenticeship in thinking: Cognitive development in social context.* New York: Oxford University Press.

Rosenbaum, J., & Martin, A. (2003). *Movie mutations: The changing face of world cinephilia.* London: British Film Institute.

Rosenblatt, L. (1938). *Literature as exploration.* New York: D. Appleton-Century.

Schon, D. (1987). *Educating the reflective practitioner.* San Francisco: Jossey-Bass.

Stebbins, R. (2004). *Between work and leisure: The common ground of two separate worlds.* New Brunswick, NJ: Transaction Publishers.

Stebbins, R. (2007). *Serious Leisure: A perspective for our time.* New Brunswick, NJ: Transaction Publishers.

Tyner, K. (1998). *Literacy in a digital world: Teaching and learning in the age of information.* Mahwah, NJ: L. Erlbaum Associates.

•28•

WORKING THE CROWD: YOUTH MEDIA INTERACTIVITY

Elisabeth Soep
YOUTH RADIO

ENGAGING INTERACTIVITY

Try finding a popular media product these days that does *not* contain "interactive" capabilities—prompts for consumers to click a choice, transmit a text message, or post a response, all mechanisms designed to include users in the production process. Blockbuster television franchises convert interactivity into stunning marketing profits and unprecedented consumer loyalty. New media authors, including bloggers and "citizen journalists," champion interactivity as well, touting its possibilities for democratizing coverage, developing peer-adjudicated editorial standards, and promoting fresh aesthetics. Interactivity is both a tool of mass-media expansion and an effort to undermine top-down regulation, manipulation, and consolidation of media content and style.

Media educators, too, highly value interactivity. Their main concern, of course, relates to student learning. Whether through video-game play, Internet research for homework assignments, Web-design projects, television fandom, or online social networking, young people expect their everyday media practices to contain interactive opportunities (Gee, 2003; Jenkins, 1992; Karaganis & Jeremijenko, in press). Educational uses of technology that build on these interactive capacities have the potential to invigorate student engagement and invite even reluctant learners into new literacy practices. The latest research suggests that students can develop "multimodal" literacies—the capacity to think and work across various semiotic systems, texts, and technologies—through sustained opportunities to produce and critique media (Goodman, 2003; Hull, 2003; Jewitt & Kress, 2003; Tyner, 1998). Hopeful findings are counterbalanced by the cautionary argument that students do not automatically learn anything of value through interactions with media, and that media literacy projects can inadvertently reproduce some of the same ideologies and inequalities they seek to critique (Buckingham, 2003; Fleetwood, 2005). These cautions notwithstanding, the media education literature clearly points to the potential for technological interactivity to promote new forms of student learning.

It seems important, against this enthusiastic backdrop, to consider the relationship between technological interactivity and the admittedly more old-fashioned phenomenon of social interactivity, particularly with respect to implications for new literacy studies. Brian Goldfarb (2002) made this important distinction in his analysis of "visual pedagogy" as a not-always-radical resource for nation building, globalization, identity formation, and youth-culture production. For Goldfarb, when media products allow consumers to make selections or otherwise respond to and shape content, they do not necessarily increase anybody's agency. Interactivity requires "an engagement of the user in the production of knowledge and meaning, and not simply in the mechanics of making 'choices'" (2002, p. 16). As examples of engaged interactivity, Goldfarb pointed to strategies various video makers have used to create meaningful opportunities for peer education and intimate dialogue through virtual—as well as face-to-face—encounters organized around screenings of their films.

Goldfarb (2002) highlighted possibilities for social interactivity as an after-the-fact outcome of media products. In this chapter, I focus on social interactivity as a before-the-fact property of media creation. This notion of interactivity requires some unpacking, especially the relationship between the two parts of the concept: (a) "inter-" and (b) "activity." If "inter-" means working between or among, and implies some degree of mutuality or reciprocity, then just what activities does this kind of work generate for young people? When media-making activities go beyond superficial "choices" among prefigured options, they have the potential to reorganize young people's virtual and face-to-face relationships, as well as their learning experiences, literacy practices, and the stories young producers go on to tell.

Interactivity marks the daily work of teen producers who publish newspapers, make movies, bust poems, and create radio stories through youth organizations across the United States. A basic form of interactivity might involve going online to fact-check a radio report, which is just what one teen reporter had to do at Youth Radio, a hybrid media-education program and independent production company in Oakland, CA. This reporter was working on a feature about sham military marriages. She had discovered that soldiers and civilians who barely knew each other were hooking up because the soldier, once married, gets a significant boost in pay, and the civilian gets world-class health benefits extended to military spouses. The reporter searched the Internet for statistics on the frequency of this phenomenon, precedent-setting court cases, and concrete salary comparisons between married and unmarried military personnel. She came up with nothing, so she picked up the phone and interviewed public-affairs officers in various branches of the military, in the process identifying additional characters and nuances for her story, new data, and better search terms that enabled more productive Internet research. Her initial clicks through various online choices transformed into challenging activities including interviews, analysis, and narrative production. Fact checking morphed into fact finding and sense making, which propelled her enterprise reporting on a story where the answers she needed were not yet available. She had to produce them herself.

Interactivity driven by and generative of further inquiry is not only a product of investigative journalism. Young producers working on intimate personal narratives often realize partway through their writing that there is something they do not know about their own lives. A young man writing about his mother's HIV-positive status showed his mom a draft of his piece, and that gesture led the two to discuss matters about her past that they had never before broached. The son understood the mother in new ways, rewriting their shared story—the one he told himself, and the one he shared with seven million listeners.

These forms of interactivity—through which inquiry drives technology use, media creation, and face-to-face communication—shed new light on what it means to be media literate. The analysis offered here rests on evidence that interactivity carried out through media production can bring about striking forms of engagement with real and imagined others. When young people collaboratively produce original media released to significant audiences, they immerse themselves repeatedly in a form of discourse I characterize as "crowded talk."[1] In crowded talk, participants communicate with their immediate interlocutors, as well as those who enter the "conversation" only indirectly, through quotations, invocations, and appropriations of other people's words. To be new media literate, young people need to be able to participate effectively in this form of heightened social interactivity embedded within the work of production.

YOUTH MEDIA METHODOLOGIES

The data reported here draw on my research, carried out independently and through participation in longitudinal national studies, on youth learning in community-based sites, including field work in more than 20 programs ranging from zine writing and poetry projects to video and radio collaboratives involving primarily low income and racialized youth (Chavez & Soep, 2005; Heath, 2001; Heath & Soep, 1998; Soep, 2002, 2003, 2005a, 2005b, 2006a, 2006b). These programs all contribute to an emerging youth media movement spreading across the United States and transnationally. Propelled in large part by community-based initiatives, but also working through school-based interventions, young media producers driving this movement use various technologies to generate and distribute original narratives across small and large audiences. The movement draws on journalistic, aesthetic, educational, and political traditions, espousing goals that range from improving students' academic achievement to enhancing self-expression to instilling critical thinking and promoting civic engagement (for reviews, see Buckingham, Burn, & Willett, 2005; Kirwan, Learmonth, Sayer, & Williams, 2003; Sefton-Green & Soep, 2007).

Research on community-based programs' effectiveness in reaching these and other goals yields mixed results, with considerable consensus around a call for more studies that theorize learning and go beyond advocacy-based accounts (Honig & McDonald, 2005). We still know relatively little about the moment-to-moment interactive features linked to youth learning through media production. Primary attention here centers on a single extended interaction based at one media organization, Youth Radio.[2] I have conducted participatory action research (Ginwright, Noguera, & Cammarota, 2006) at Youth Radio for more than five years, spending approximately 24 hours per week working with students, interns, and staff. I have occupied various positions within the organization, initially volunteering to teach writing a couple afternoons a week while completing my doctoral dissertation. Over time, I became the education desk editor and developed new research-based curriculum and assessment strategies, and I am currently (in 2006) a senior producer in the newsroom and the organization's education director.

Just as my official role within the organization has transformed, so too has my research methodology. Incorporating ethnographic techniques and discourse analysis, in my early work at other youth learning sites, I largely kept silent, observing and recording interactions among young people. My current research at Youth Radio builds on daily involvement with young people in the media-making process. With this emerging methodological orientation, I participate in editorial meetings where young people propose story ideas, accompany them on tape-gathering expeditions and interviews, and work with them on scripting, digital mixing, pitching, and editing with broadcast outlets. Alongside youth and adult colleagues, I participate in a "collegial pedagogy" through which professional and emerging media producers jointly create original work with high stakes attached, for significant audiences.

Throughout these media production phases, periodically I retreat from the immediacy of deadlines and facilitation responsibilities to

[1] Stuart Tannock's (1998) characterization of noisy, overlapping talk among young people as highly productive, if apparently chaotic, informs my conception of "crowded talk," as does Kris Gutierrez's study of the coexistence of various competing discourses within classroom conversations (Gutierrez, Rymes, & Larson, 1995).

[2] The extended discourse excerpt I have selected is representative of a consistent pattern across my ethnographic data, revealing a specific discourse quality, crowded talk, marking language young people use as they form, execute, and analyze their own stories and those of their peers. Crowded talk appears with particular potency during moments of judgment, drama, and tension. The confrontational conditions marking this interaction, while by no means universally in place when young people go out to cover stories, reveal how young people negotiate conflict as a property of media production.

interview my colleagues, generate my own field notes and solicit them from others, hold focus groups, and collect a wide range of evolving student texts. Analysis of these data reveals how collaborative media production organizes learning. Specific evidence I have tracked includes discourse patterns, cycles of interaction and inquiry, and features of media texts. Spontaneous conversations and planned feedback sessions with young people and adults inform my own emerging analyses of our shared work. It is an effort to ground data collection and analysis within the up-close vantage point of active participation. The process aims to produce scholarly knowledge from within a site that is typically considered an object and not an engine of original research (Soep, 2003).

YOUTH RADIO

Founded in 1992, Youth Radio is a nonprofit organization in which young people produce award-winning stories for local and national broadcasts on radio, television, and online outlets. Students are recruited primarily from local underresourced and heavily tracked public schools, and the majority are working class youth and young people of color. Participants enter the program through an 11-week series of introductory after-school classes. They arrive on a Wednesday, and by Friday of that same week, they go on air for a live two-hour local public radio show, *Youth in Control*. The show includes music segments the young people DJ, plus public service announcements, first-person commentaries, and news stories. Students rotate through workshops in each of these broadcast genres, while also producing video and Web-based elements, reflecting Youth Radio's focus on converged media and cross-platform storytelling. Every week, one young person is assigned the job of listening to the entire live show and offering a critique before everyone goes home after 9:00 P.M. that night. Students in the introductory class also meet with Youth Radio's resident academic coordinator, who works with each young person to devise an individualized educational plan supported by tutoring; college application, financial aid, and placement workshops (geared for entry to community colleges and four-year universities); and internship and employment placements.

After completing the introductory session, most students stay on for more advanced media and leadership training, with the opportunity eventually to take positions at Youth Radio as paid interns. At any given time, Youth Radio's payroll includes around 35 young people working as reporters, commentators, administrative assistants, engineers and music producers, event planners, fundraising and outreach assistants, and peer educators. This last role is among the most critical at Youth Radio, as peer educators are the ones actually teaching both the introductory and advanced classes, with guidance from adult mentors. Youth faculty develop skills in curriculum design, classroom management, and public speaking, as well as advanced technical capabilities in their fields of media specialty. Because of Youth Radio's dual mission, as both a youth-development organization and professional media-production company, young people with significant training are crucial for meeting broadcast commitments and "training up" newcomers to the program. That said, staff members periodically evaluate whether a young person who has been with the program for some time would be better served by moving on to a different educational or professional environment, despite the hole their absence would leave. Graduates of Youth Radio occupy key leadership positions as full-time senior staff members in every major department within the organization, including administration, production, and youth development.

In addition to on-site programs at Youth Radio's main location in downtown Oakland (recently relocated from Berkeley), the organization offers outreach classes in broadcast journalism and music production at local high schools, community agencies, and juvenile justice facilities, with additional bureaus in Atlanta, Los Angeles, and Washington, DC. Youth Radio's transnational desk has provided short-term media training and production opportunities in Mexico, Cuba, India, South Africa, and Afghanistan. Young people working across the organization produce digital music and talk segments that stream 24 hours a day, seven days a week on iTunes radio on the Web. Interns in the professional newsroom collaborate with adult producers on stories reaching the National Public Radio audience, currently estimated to serve more than 26 million listeners per week.

CROWDED TALK AND REPORTED SPEECH

Audiences for youth-created media comprise key players in the "crowds" that enter young people's discourse through every stage of production. In some cases, producers make decisions about story structure and content with a specific outlet in mind. In other cases, they refuse to do so, saying they care more about reaching other local young people with their stories than a distant audience of adults, no matter how huge it might be; and they know that an outlet might well "kill" their piece as a result. This level of editorial autonomy is facilitated by Youth Radio's broadcast relationships with multiple outlets, including several over which the organization has near complete control (there is always the Federal Communications Commission). Young people know that if one outlet turns down any given story, the newsroom has the option to "shop it around" elsewhere.

In addition to audiences, young people's peers, editors, and mentors, as well as community and family members, add to the mix of literal and figurative voices that enter media production discourse. This is what I mean by crowded talk: when young people strategically use language to align and distance themselves with respect to various real *and imagined* interlocutors, in the process working out issues of authority over the media being produced.

One discourse feature that holds particular relevance for crowded talk is something linguistic anthropologists, literary theorists, and other language scholars describe as "reported speech." Through reported speech, a speaker's utterances are "filled to overflowing" with other people's words, taking shape in quotes, indirect references and paraphrases, accents, and allusions (Bakhtin, 1934/1981; see also Baynham, 1996; Besnier, 1993; Buttny, 1997; Garber, 2001; Goodwin, 1990, 1998; Hill & Irvine, 1993; Hull & Katz, in press; Maclean, 1994; Myers, 1999; Oshima, 2006; Schiffrin, 1993, 1996; Tannen, 1989, 1995; Volosinov, 1930/1978). Amy Shuman (1986, 1993) traced the use of reported speech in adolescent fight stories, noting that apparent reports of past events were actually ways of renegotiating relationships among participants and matters of entitlement. Deborah Tannen (1989) argued that reported speech in the form of "constructed dialogues" intensified the drama and engagement of narratives in everyday conversation. In her critical ethnography of "schoolgirl speech" and "women's language" in Japan, Miyako Inoue (2006, p. 50) framed reported speech as a linguistic apparatus to "conquer alterity" by subsuming another's words within one's own, thus contributing to the consolidation of "the modern self." Richard

Buttny (1997) located reported speech in racial discourse, arguing that invoking or aligning oneself with respect to someone else's words is never simply an act of report: "It is also editorializing—making *evaluations* or *assessments*" (p. 501). Marjorie Harness Goodwin (1990) used the phrase "he-said-she-said" to describe a public dispute process among children who deploy reported speech to negotiate accusations of offense through "vernacular legal" arguments (p. 219).

Across this research, reported speech emerges as a property of heightened interactivity, surfacing often during moments of dramatization, judgment, tension, and negotiations of authority and entitlement. Reported speech is an inherent property of young people's media products. While planning and gathering tape for their stories, they decide what voices to include, who qualifies as an "expert," and what counts as a first-person account. Throughout the scripting process, producers determine how to present someone else's words—whether to name and paraphrase a source or use an actual clip of tape. Framing a clip as something a character "said," "reported," "claimed," or "admitted," for example, has serious consequences for how that character comes across in the story. Young people sometimes rail against journalistic conventions related to reported speech—for example, the standard tenet never to end a radio story with a voice other than your own, because the reporter should have the last word. At stake is how narrative authority is assigned and denied—a charged discussion among communities often ignored or distorted in mainstream media narratives.

One particularly intense case related to reported speech took place at Youth Radio, when two interns, on their way to an agency-wide retreat, were detained by the police at the subway station and erroneously accused of driving a stolen vehicle. It just so happened that a local TV team was on the scene and caught the incident on tape. When one of the Youth Radio interns decided to turn the experience into a radio feature about racial profiling as a rite of passage for Black males, he asked the TV team if he could use their tape, which captured his words. They said no. Apparently, they "owned" his speech, so he was left to paraphrase himself, rather than present the actual audio record of his experience.

Just as reported speech marks youth media products, it is also a property of the youth media process. Elsewhere, I have analyzed specific forms and functions of reported speech in the discourse youth media artists use as they prepare work for broadcast (Soep, 2006b). Young people invoke the words of peers, audience members, experts and professionals, imagined adversaries, and fictional characters to form arguments and assessments related to their own joint projects. Reported speech troubles the widespread tendency to frame youth media projects as hotbeds for "authentic" youth voice (Fleetwood, 2005). Individual young people use reported speech strategically to leverage, dramatize, and experiment with varied real and imagined voices, even in a single utterance.

Reported speech is both an empirical category and a lens through which to consider discourse more broadly, as a social practice. It is something to think *with*, and not just about; part of a linguistic ideology (Schieffelin, Woolard, & Kroskrity, 1998) that frames language as a process of situating oneself with respect to actual and imaginary others, even when no explicit quotations appear. Linguistic meanings, in this view, are always borrowed or recycled, as well as uncertain for both participant and analyst (Hendry & Watson, 2001). Interlocutors speak, directly or indirectly, "in the name of we," even when using the "I" (Goffman, 1983, p. 145). Speaking as a member of a crowd, or "in quotation marks," is a way of shoring up influence and authority, even in the absence of explicit citations (Garber, 2001).

"AUTHORITY"

In the following discourse excerpt from Youth Radio, authorization was not just a subtext of the conversation, but its pointed focus. In 2001, the newsroom began investigating the effects of standardized tests on students and teachers in public schools around the country. There was a great deal of interest at that time in students who were "opting out" of state standardized testing. Much of the public focus centered on young people from privileged school districts, whose parents claimed that testing was forcing teachers to relinquish valuable class time, sacrifice meaningful projects, and "dumb down" the curriculum in order to teach to the test. Parents in those districts were organizing to find ways for their children to opt out of the tests.

Meanwhile, community groups not drawing nearly as much attention were trying to expose test-related injustices and inform students in underresourced public schools about their rights not to take certain tests. One Youth Radio reporter took on the story of finding out what happens when students in high schools serving primarily poor and working-class families opt out of state tests. I worked closely with this young reporter on what turned out to be her first national investigative story, participating in a very concrete sense in the "we" in the name of which she spoke. The reporter knew she would need to talk to students who took the test as well as those who opted out. She arranged to gather classroom scene tape at a city public school on test day, and to talk with teachers, administrators, and a university-based national expert on measurement and school accountability.

Before the youth reporter headed to the school campus for her interviews, back in the newsroom, we did some research about legal protections and guidelines for reporters conducting interviews on school campuses. We learned that for news reports, a journalist was legally free to enter a school campus and record interviews with students if (a) minors knew and appreciated that they were talking to a journalist and that their comments could be broadcast, and (b) so long as the interview in no way disrupted the educational process.[3] We reviewed these guidelines carefully with the Youth Radio reporter and discussed the various "gray areas" she needed to think about as she prepared for the interview and considered both the ethics and effectiveness of her approach. For example, while Youth Radio was committed to producing hard-hitting education stories, the organization depended on goodwill from school teachers and leaders, as key decision-makers in recruitment sites, fellow educators, and story sources; it was critical to protect Youth Radio's reputation and respect within school circles.

The reporter was in the school library, recording her interview with a student, Paula,[4] who had obtained a waiver to opt out of the test, when the school principal entered the scene.

[3] James Ewert, California media law expert and legal counsel. Personal Communication.

[4] The names of this student and all other Youth Radio participants have been changed, with the exception of my own ("Lissa" in the transcript) and that of my colleague, Rebecca Martin, who has generously reviewed and offered feedback on this chapter.

Are you authorized to be here? Part 1

Principal: Who are you?
Reporter: [Reporter says her name] with Youth Radio . . .
Principal: Are you authorized to be here?
Reporter: Yeah.
Principal: By whom? . . .
Reporter: It's not against the law or anything. I talked to [name] and asked them, I set this up with Paula.
Principal: You set it up with Paula?
Reporter: She's not taking the test. I already talked to [name], a security guard just checked to make sure I was here—
Principal: But I'm the principal. The thing is, I want to know who you authorized this through.

The principal's first concern in this exchange was, quite understandably, a question of authorization. As the leader responsible for her students' safety and well-being on the school campus, she wanted to know who had allowed the reporter to initiate and record the conversation, regardless of its content. The reporter's initial response, "It's not against the law or anything," gestured towards her awareness of her legal rights as a journalist, but she immediately then named specific others known to the principal—a person on her staff, Paula, the security guard—making herself *not alone* in determining that the interview was appropriate and allowed to take place. She began to situate herself, in other words, among a crowd, strategically defined; however, it did not suffice to name individuals. The principal's question suggested not just a person, but a process of authorization, which she went on to elaborate.

Are you authorized to be here? Part 2

Reporter: Who I authorized this through?
Principal: Yeah, who did you ask for permission to come here?
Reporter: Oh, it's a public school. I didn't think that I needed—
Principal: You do, you need my permission.
Reporter: I asked my editors and everything, and they said by law—
Principal: Who's your editors?
Reporter: Lissa and Rebecca Martin. We can go talk to them right now—
Principal: Well we can't, because I'm in the middle of doing something else. But you have to understand that everything has to come through me, okay, with my permission, and so I'm going to stop this right now until we go through the right process.
Reporter: And what's that?
Principal: Well, you could contact our public information office, that's what I have all reporters do, and if they authorize you to come on here, they'll call me and say it's okay, and then we'll make it work.

The talk grew even more crowded at this point. The reporter contextualized her work in two ways—locating the interview in "a public school," which carried specific implications for access, and then situating her inquiry within a journalistic framework, naming her "editors" (me and a Youth Radio colleague) as having informed her of her legal rights. The principal extended the reporter's journalistic frame at that point, spelling out the proper bureaucratic process for school site interviews. Striking in this move on the principal's part was her affirmation of the reporter's positioning as a member of a journalistic collective: "that's what I have all reporters do. . . ." She used the reporter's own logic to insist upon a certain protocol. It seems worth noting here that the principal had an opportunity at this point to belittle the reporter's status by pointing to her age, but instead she accepted the reporter's membership in the journalistic profession.[5] That said, methods within that profession remained in dispute, as the reporter went on to elaborate.

Are you authorized to be here? Part 3

Reporter: Okay, because it was my understanding that it's okay for me to come here, because we're a youth program, and we're just trying to talk to young people and see—
Principal: But all the young people are taking the test. And Paula I know has a waiver so she's not taking the test, but so you're only getting Paula's side. So I want you to call—

Here was the first moment when the principal indicated her awareness of the content of the interview. But first, the reporter aligned herself with another social category, as a participant in a "youth program." Notably, she pluralized her own efforts—"We're just trying to talk to young people"—describing a scenario to which an educator such as the principal might have a hard time objecting (it's hard to find fault in kids just talking to other kids—about something substantive, no less). The principal, however, voiced some concerns, reinforcing the prior journalistic frame by raising questions about the reporter's objectivity; she described Paula as an exception, one side of the story—in this sense, not representing enough of a crowd.

Are you authorized to be here? Part 4

Reporter: Well, what happened is, we're getting both sides of the story, but this is the side we also need. We talked to an analyst from [Name] University and he gave us a very objective point of view about the testing and about taking the test.
Principal: Do you understand that you didn't go through the proper channels to be here?
Reporter: I'm not sure what the proper channels are, because it was my understanding that we could just come here and do the interview and just talk to students, but it's okay, I'll—Can I have your card?
Principal: I don't have a card. I can give you my name and you have the school phone number . . . [the principal says her name here]. . . . Now the thing is, you're just here to interview Paula?
Reporter: Yes, that's all—
Principal: You can finish your interview with Paula. And then the next time you want to come on—because I'm interested in youth, in Youth Radio—I want you to follow procedures.
Reporter: Okay.
Principal: Okay? Thank you.

[5] I make this observation knowing that it can be problematic, ethnographically speaking, to highlight what a person in any given context does not do, but the point seems worth making nevertheless, given the frequency with which adults, unlike this principal, dismiss young people's legitimate involvement with serious work. Not so this principal.

In this final stretch of talk, the reporter aligned herself with another source of authority. She was not talking only to other young people, after all. "We" were consulting experts from prestigious universities, and abiding by the same journalistic ideals of even-handed storytelling the principal had invoked. The reporter's response here seemed a turning point in the conversation. The principal shifted gears to focus on what the reporter understood, rather than what she was allowed to do. In an exchange so crowded with various others—school administrators and security officers and students and journalists and young people and university professors—next came a moment of compelled individualization. The reporter requested the principal's card, foregrounding her specific identity as the person shutting down the interview—and leaving open the possibility of further contact. In the end, after reinforcing the limits of what she was approving, the principal allowed the interview to carry on, so long as the reporter understood that next time, she would need to "follow procedures."

This encounter reveals a particularly intense moment of crowded talk in the context of youth media production, where a powerful adult contested a young person's authority and ultimately stood convinced. By aligning herself with other people's words and positions, the reporter maintained access. Two actual individuals populated this talk, alongside categories of practitioners, whose influence both speakers leveraged in their negotiations to determine whether the interview could continue, and on what terms.

THE AUDIENCE INTERACTS BACK

The episode between principal and reporter revealed a moment of social interactivity set before a story's completion, but the process does not end when a story airs. Audience members influence youth media as well. They intervene not only when producers invoke hypothetical listeners' reactions while preparing stories for broadcast; actual listeners can speak for themselves.

Youth Radio's mission and methods build on the belief that media has the capacity to promote social action. The specific manifestation of that action is something young producers quickly realize they cannot control. Radio in particular has, since its inception, depended on listeners' willingness to "complete" audio stories by projecting their own images and individual meanings, through a kind of "auditory voyeurism" (Douglas, 1999, p. 18). Public radio in particular aspires to extend civic life, free communication, and participatory democracy (Engelman, 1996). Media advocacy efforts by definition rest on the power of stories to motivate collective action and policy-making. Various on-air conventions, from live talk-show formats to weekly recitations of listener letters, give audiences airtime and bring them literally into the production process.

One Youth Radio commentator had a feeling her story would elicit a strong audience reaction when she first proposed her piece, "Young Moms' Club," focused on an informal group including herself and some friends who had had babies very young. To be good mothers, they found that it helped a lot to get out every now and then, to meet for a drink, or listen to music, so they could still feel young—like they hadn't completely given up their former lives; however, it wasn't easy to do so. At one point in the story, the commentator described a scene where she was headed out for a preplanned date with friends, when her grandmother brought her screaming baby to the door and yelled to the whole neighborhood, "What kind of mother are you?!" The young mom pulled her car back into the driveway and stayed home. You then hear the grandmother herself, lamenting the times when she is left at home with her great granddaughter late into the night. Still, "Even my psychotherapist says, 'You have to make time for yourself,'" the commentator said, "'or you might end up resenting your life and your child, and it might lead to depression.'"

Two days after this story was broadcast nationally, the show host read letters from listeners, saying the mailbox had been filled with responses to the Youth Radio story. While the commentator might be a good mother, many listeners seemed to feel that she was an "inconsiderate granddaughter," the host said. One listener wrote in to say that the young mother "feels that she's entitled to go out with friends and have some 'me' time and still be young. . . . Wrong. The only person who has the right to be free from childcare worries is her grandmother."

While Youth Radio has a track record of receiving many more positive listener responses than negative, an e-mail like this is never a huge surprise to young producers. Many are committed to reaching beyond like-minded thinkers with their stories. In this case, the commentator was thrilled that her story received such a strong response, that her perspective moved listeners to take the time to write, even if it was to criticize her account. "I never take it personal," the commentator said, "I take it that I helped them take a step towards framing the way they feel about the issue at hand." This producer, like other young artists and journalists, knows that relinquishing some measure of control over their own voices, lives, and experiences comes with the territory of youth media production. One of the most important lessons young people learn in the process is how to work across various audiences, when to allow listeners' projected responses to influence a particular story, and how to draw insight and further inspiration when audiences do talk back.

WORKING THE CROWD

As evident in the various examples offered here, crowded talk marks diverse media genres, including investigative reports (the military marriage piece and the feature on educational testing), first-person essays (by a young man whose mother is living with AIDS), and multivocal commentaries (the stories about racial profiling as rite of passage for young Black males and "Young Moms' Club"). In his account of multimodal literacy, Kress (2003) defined genre as "that textual/social category which realizes in text the social relations of the participants involved in the social interaction that gives rise to the text" (p. 174). To produce each of these genres, young people "realized" relationships to their own texts by situating themselves within imagined social worlds, in some cases explicitly recycling other people's words, and in other cases using indirect references and alignments. Crowded talk was an arena for social maneuvering through which young people worked out the specific principles and logics behind each media genre they developed.

Young people, like all producers, are continually called upon to negotiate their own textual authority as it relates to the influence and control exerted by others, real and imaginary, present and absent. Struggles over authority mark the media texts themselves, and the seemingly endless conversations that inform and shape their production. At this juncture in the media world, when the most established professionals face tough questions regarding credibility, integrity, and social relevance, young people are driving a youth media movement that is challenging longstanding formulas and expectations for what stories should be about, and how they should unfold. Youth media producers intentionally experiment with hybrid genres, such as first-person investigative reporting, and news features where spoken-word poets provide policy analysis. To make these innovations, young people constantly form complex judgments, negotiating familiar and unexpected sites of storytelling authority. In doing so, they are never alone. They throw themselves, linguistically speaking, into ever-shifting crowds—and then they put those crowds to work.

REFERENCES

Bakhtin, M. (1981). Discourse in the novel. In M. Holquist (Ed.), *The dialogic imagination: Four essays by M. M. Bakhtin* (pp. 259–422). Austin: University of Texas Press. (Original work published 1934)

Baynham, M. (1996). Direct speech: What's it doing in non-narrative discourse. *Journal of Pragmatics, 25*, 61–81.

Besnier, N. (1993). Reported speech and affect on Nukulaelae Atoll. In J. Hill & J. Irvine (Eds.), *Responsibility and evidence in oral discourse* (pp. 161–181). Cambridge: Cambridge University Press.

Buttny, R. (1997). Reported speech in talking race on campus. *Human Communication Research, 23*(4), 477–506.

Buckingham, D. (2003). *Media education: Literacy, learning and contemporary culture.* Cambridge: Polity Press.

Buckingham, D., Burn, A., & Willett, R. (2005). *The media literacy of children and young people.* London: Centre for the Study of Children, Youth and Media.

Chavez, V., & Soep, E. (2005). Youth Radio and the pedagogy of collegiality. *Harvard Educational Review, 75*(4), 409–434.

Douglas, S. (1999). *Listening in: Radio and the American imagination.* Minneapolis: University of Minnesota Press.

Engelman, R. (1996). *Public radio and television in America: A political history.* Thousand Oaks, CA: Sage.

Fleetwood, N. (2005). Authenticating practices: Producing realness, performing youth. In S. Maira & E. Soep (Eds.), *Youthscapes: The popular, the national, the global* (pp. 155–172). Philadelphia: University of Pennsylvania Press.

Garber, M. (2001). "" (quotation marks). In S. I. Salamendsky (Ed.), *Talk talk talk: The cultural life of everyday conversation* (pp. 121–146). New York: Routledge.

Gee, J. (2003). *What video games have to teach us about literacy and learning.* New York: Palgrave Macmillan.

Ginwright, S., Noguera, P., Cammarota, J. (Eds.). (2006). *Beyond resistance! Youth activism and community change: New Democratic Possibilities for practice and policy for America's youth.* New York: Routledge.

Goffman, E. (1983). *Forms of talk.* Philadelphia: University of Pennsylvania Press.

Goodman, S. (2003). *Teaching youth media: A critical guide to literacy, video production, and social change.* New York: Teachers College Press.

Goodwin, M. H. (1990). *He-said-she-said: Talk as social organization among Black children.* Bloomington: Indiana University Press.

Goodwin, M. H. (1998). Games of stance: Conflict and footing in hopscotch. In S. Hoyle & C. T. Adger (Eds.), *Kids talk: Strategic language use in later childhood* (pp. 23–46). New York: Oxford University Press.

Goldfarb, B. (2002). *Visual pedagogy: Media cultures in and beyond the classroom.* Durham: Duke University Press.

Gutierrez, K., Rymes, B., & Larson, J. (1995) Script, counterscript, and underlife in the classroom: James Brown versus Brown v. Board of Education. *Harvard Educational Review, 65*(3), 445–471.

Heath, S. B. (2001). Three's not a crowd: Plans, roles, and focus in the arts. *Educational Researcher, 30*(7), 10–17.

Heath, S. B., & Soep, E. (1998). Youth development and the arts in nonschool hours. *Grantmakers in the Arts, 9*(1), 9–16.

Hendry, J., & Watson, C. W. (Eds.). (2001). *An anthropology of indirect communication.* New York: Routledge.

Hill, J., & Irvine, J. (Eds.). (1993). *Responsibility and evidence in oral discourse.* Cambridge: Cambridge University Press.

Honig, M., & McDonald, M. (2005). From promise to participation: Understanding after-school programs as settings for learning. *Robert Bowne Foundation Occasional Paper Series, 5,* 1–26.

Hull, G. (2003). Youth culture and digital media: New literacies for new times. *Research in the Teaching of English, 38*(2), 229–233.

Hull, G., & Katz, M. (2006). Crafting an agentive self: Case studies on digital storytelling. *Research in the Teaching of English, 40*(1), 43–81.

Inoue, M. (2006). *Vicarious language: The political economy of gender and speech in Japan.* Berkeley: University of California Press.

Jenkins, H. (1992). *Textual poachers: Television fans and participatory culture.* New York: Routledge.

Jewitt, C., & Kress, G. (2003). *Multimodal literacy.* New York: Peter Lang.

Karaganis, J., & Jeremijenko, N. (Eds.). (in press). *Structures of participation in digital culture.* Durham, NC: Duke University Press.

Kirwan, T., Learmonth, J., Sayer, M., & Williams, R. (2003). *Mapping media literacy.* London: British Film Institute, Broadcasting Standards Commission, Independent Television Commission. Retrieved October 31, 2005, from http://www.ofcom.org.uk/static/archive/itc/uploads/Mapping_media_literacy1.pdf

Kress, G. (2003). Genres and the multimodal production of 'scientificness.' In C. Jewitt & G. Kress (Eds.), *Multimodal literacy* (pp. 173–186). New York: Peter Lang.

Maclean, R. (1994). Language education, thematic studies and classroom learning: A Bakhtinian view. *Language and Education, 8*(4), 231–250.

Myers, G. (1999). Functions of reported speech in group discussions. *Journal of Applied Linguistics, 20*(3), 376–401.

Oshima, D. (2006). *Perspectives in Reported Discourse.* Unpublished doctoral thesis, Stanford University, Palo Alto, CA.

Schieffelin, B., Woolard, K., & Kroskrity, P. (Eds.). (1998). *Language ideologies: Practice and theory.* Oxford: Oxford University Press.

Schiffrin, D. (1993). "Speaking for another" in sociolinguistic interviews. In D. Tannen (Ed.), *Framing in discourse* (pp. 231–263). New York: Oxford University Press.

Schiffrin, D. (1996). Narrative as self-portrait: Sociolinguistic constructions of identity. *Language in Society, 25*(2), 167–203.

Sefton-Green J., & Soep, E. (2007). Creative media cultures: Making and learning beyond school. In L. Bresler (Ed.), *International handbook of research on arts education* (pp. 835–854). Dordrecht, The Netherlands: Springer.

Shuman, A. (1986). *Storytelling rights: The uses of oral and written texts by urban adolescents.* Cambridge: Cambridge University Press.

Shuman, A. (1993). 'Get outa my face': Entitlement and authoritative discourse. In J. Hill & J. Irvine (Eds)., *Responsibility and evidence in oral discourse* (pp. 135–160). Cambridge: Cambridge University Press.

Soep, E. (2002). Art in the city beyond school. *Kappa Delta Pi Record, 39*(1), 12–16.

Soep, E. (2003). Learning about research from youth media artists. *Perspectives on Urban Education, 1*(2). Retrieved May 6, 2007 from http://www.urbanedjournal.org/archive/Issue3/commentaries/comment0004.html.

Soep, E. (2005a). Making hard-core masculinity: Teenage boys playing house. In S. Maira & E. Soep (Eds.), *Youthscapes: The popular, the national, the global* (pp. 173–191). Philadelphia: University of Pennsylvania Press.

Soep, E. (2005b). Critique: Where art meets assessment. *Phi Delta Kappan, 87,* 38–40, 58–63.

Soep, E. (2006a). Critique: Assessment and the production of learning. *Teachers College Record, 108*(4), 748–777.

Soep, E. (2006b). Beyond literacy and voice in youth media production. *McGill Journal of Education. 41*(3), 197-213.

Tannen, D. (1989). *Talking voices: Repetition, dialogue, and imagery in conversational discourse*. Cambridge: Cambridge University Press.

Tannen, D. (1995). Waiting for the mouse: Constructed dialogue in conversation. In D. Tedlock & B. Mannheim (Eds.), *Dialogic emergence of culture* (pp. 198–218). Urbana: University of Illinois Press.

Tannock, S. (1998). Noisy talk: Conversation and collaboration in a youth writing group. In S. Hoyle & C. T. Adger (Eds.), *Kids talk: Strategic language use in later childhood* (pp. 241–266). New York: Oxford University Press.

Volosinov, V. N. (1978). Reported speech. In L. Matejka & K. Pomorska (Eds.), *Readings in Russian poetics: Formalist and structuralist views*. Ann Arbor: Michigan Slavic Publications. (Original work published 1930).

Tyner, K. (1998). *Literacy in a digital world: Teaching and learning in the age of information*. Mahwah, NJ: Lawrence Erlbaum Associates.

29

BOTH SIDES OF THE MIC: COMMUNITY LITERACIES IN THE AGE OF HIP HOP

Jabari Mahiri, Malik Ali, Allison Lindsay Scott, Bolota Asmerom, and Rick Ayers

UNIVERSITY OF CALIFORNIA, BERKELEY

> To me, hip-hop says, "Come as you are." We are a family. It ain't about security. It ain't about bling-bling. It ain't about how much your gun can shoot. It ain't about $200 sneakers. It is not about me being better than you or you being better than me. It's about you and me, connecting one to one. That's why it has universal appeal. It has given young people a way to understand their world, whether they are from the suburbs or the city or wherever.—DJ Kool Herc (Chang, 2005, p. xi)

DJ Kool Herc, one of the originators of hip-hop (Chang, 2005; Rose, 1994), might seem overly optimistic about the meaning and potential of this phenomenon that has indelibly shaped the popular cultural landscape for the past 30 years. Despite the negative ways that hip-hop styles and activities are characterized in the public discourse of mainstream media (Koza, 1994), this cultural movement has many attributes that bring youth together in positive ways. Herc's claim that hip-hop "has given young people a way to understand [and we add, participate in] their world" (Chang, 2005, p. xi) is central to the focus of this chapter. These considerations framed our research on the local manifestations of hip-hop culture in the Bay Area of Northern California, a region long known as the home of major Black activists who used their poetry and performance to advance the civil rights movement. Moreover, this area holds a central place in the history of jazz and maintains strong patterns of apprenticeship by young aspirants to well-known figures. The region is also home to some of the earliest spokespersons for nation rap and to the resistance to commercialization of rap and hip-hop by Hollywood filmmakers and music companies. Critical also within the history of this geographic locale is the expectation that writing, slamming, rapping, and performing "the word" has strong potential for influence well beyond the region.

BOTH SIDES OF THE MIC

Hip-hop is considered the voice of contemporary youth, a voice that is electrified and now digitized, spoken through rappers' s, DJ music mixes, break-dancing and other dance styles, and graffiti. These four elements—(a) DJing (mixing and playing a variety of sound texts), (b) MCing (rapping, mastering ceremony), (c) B-Boying (break-dancing, and now various other dance styles), and (d) graffiti (spray painting colorful words and images, tags and murals, on public spaces)—are considered the pillars of hip-hop (George, 1998; Rose, 1994). Kitwana (2005) added a fifth pillar: "doing the knowledge" (p. xii); however, all of these authors acknowledged that hip-hop is much more. DJ Kool Herc (quoted in Chang, 2005, p. xi) noted that it is also "the way you walk, the way you talk, the way you look, the way you communicate." Essentially, Herc is invoking Gee's (1991) notion of a discourse: "an 'identity kit' which comes complete with the appropriate costume and instructions on how to act and talk so as to take on a particular role that others will recognize" (p. 3) inside a given discourse community.

The mic of the DJ or MC is a potent symbol at the intersection of power and pleasure on hand in this dynamic discourse community. The mic also marks the intersection and interaction of production and consumption of hip-hop texts and styles. Our research team was aware that this discourse community represented much more than DJing or MCing, yet we narrowed our focus to these two prominent aspects of hip-hop in order to look at specific ways that they fostered literacy as it is traditionally (and perhaps untraditionally) conceived. Local enactments of hip-hop are certainly influenced by ways in which it is promoted and perceived nationally and internationally, but there are important cultural distinctions between its community practices and its commercial productions. We wanted to understand how the practices of DJing and MCing were engaged in by local urban youth (rather than noted hip-hop celebrities) and how they were revealed in everyday ways of talking, walking, dressing, and other forms of communicating.

This chapter presents the results of an interview study carried out by the authors on four focal informants: Elias, a DJ; 5-Milli, an MC; Yared, a Black youth who considers himself to be one of the true hip-hop heads (or "headz": devotees); and Damien, a White youth who considers himself to be a hip-hop head.[1] Consequently, this study explored community literacies connected to both speaking in and listening to the voice of hip-hop through the practices and perspectives of urban informants on both sides of the mic.

THE AGE OF HIP-HOP

The cover story of the January 4th, 2005 issue of *The Village Voice* by Greg Tate was entitled "Hiphop turns 30: Whatcha celebrating for?" After noting the testimonials and tributes to this anniversary, Tate (2005) acknowledged that hip-hop was the face of Black America in the world today, but questioned what all the celebration was about when what we call hip-hop and the commercialization of hip-hop now seemed inseparable. He also noted that true hip-hop heads tend to get mad when one does not make that separation. Therefore, beyond recognition of the last 30 years as the "Age of Hip-Hop," Tate identified one of its major contradictions or tensions: the odd coupling of hip-hop culture and the commercial rap industry. Another major tension linked to the first is who should participate in, benefit from, and be represented by hip-hop. Chroniclers of hip-hop life and culture extensively debate these tensions, and they were also revealed in the lives and literacy practices of our informants.

In an important work that analyzed the influence of Black culture on the world in the post-segregation era, Kitwana (2002) claimed and used the term "hip-hop generation" interchangeably with the term "Black youth culture." He noted, "No other term better defines this generation of Black youth, as the entire spectrum of Black youth (including college students and young professionals, as well as the urban masses)" (p. xiii). He further noted that although many other racial/ethnic groups have been "influential in and touched by hip-hop culture," it is indisputably Black youth who dominate the numerous iterations of rap music and hip-hop culture both commercially and on the streets (p. 200).

Other chroniclers contested Kitwana's (2002) primal link between African American youth and hip-hop culture. Chang (2005) questioned, "How could one accept a definition of a Hip-Hop Generation . . . that excluded those who had come to claim and transform hip-hop culture, but were not Black or born in America" (p. 2)? Chang argued that the Hip-Hop Generation should include "Anyone who is down" (p. 2).

In another work, Kitwana (2005) addressed these considerations by examining the complex relationship between White youth, who are major consumers of rap music, and hip-hop culture, in which Blacks are the major creative force. He argued that five key factors made it possible for White youth to embrace hip-hop (pp. 17–51). In the 1980s, there was growing alienation by White youth from mainstream American culture brought on by shifts to a global economy. During this period hip-hop's antiestablishment culture appealed to many White youth. After a boom period, the dot-com bust at the end of the 1990s was also accompanied by intensified White alienation.

Kitwana (2005) further noted that over time the civil rights movement ideology of inclusion was becoming institutionalized in mainstream American folklore and national culture. Additionally, many Black rappers preached inclusion, in part to increase crossover music sales. Finally, there were the vibrant, off-the-radar local scenes of hip-hop joined with numerous information sources available about every imaginable hip-hop subtopic. He additionally suggested that it was hip-hop's emergence during a global information age that "vastly increased its capacity to reach beyond anything the world has ever seen" (p. xii) in contrast to other music genres.

Digital natives. In conjunction with the age of hip-hop, the past 30 years have also marked the rise of the digital age. Those who are under 30 years of age can be seen as digital natives of this age. Of interest to this research was the fact that there have always been provocative connections between hip-hop and technology. For example, rap artists were quickest to exploit digital samplers and sequencers when these and other technologies suited their cultural purposes (Miller, 2004). Rose (1994) noted that "hip hop transforms stray technological parts intended for cultural and industrial trash heaps into sources of pleasure and power. These transformations have become a basis of digital imagination all over the world" (p. 22). Now, contemporary youth in the United States and globally are utilizing technological resources to sample, cut and paste, and remix multimedia texts for replay in new configurations, just as hip hop DJs reconfigure images, words, and sounds to play anew.

Manovich (2001) argued that because computers translate all existing media into numerical data, earlier audio and visual media eventually converged with, or were consumed by, digital computer technologies. The result, according to Manovich, was a "new media" that incorporated sound, moving images, graphics, shapes, and other forms of texts into "computable" data. The very nature of digitalizing media allowed for greatly increased mobility, interchangeability, and accessibility of texts and signs while they magnified and simplified the processes for authorial assemblages such as remixes, collages, samples, and cut-and-pastes (Gibson, 2005; Manovich, 2001; Miller, 2004). Essentially, the emergence of new media *enabled* new literacies. These new forms of literacy tied to new technology offered additional possibilities for creating meaning and identity for contemporary youth (Gee, 2003; Hull, 2003; Johnson, 2005; Mahiri, 2004). For hip-hop these new media transformed both the production and consumption of a variety of cultural texts.

Sonic signification. Music is very central in the lives of many youth. Miller (2004) claimed, for example, "The selection of sound becomes

[1] Our lead researcher on Elias was Malik Ali; for 5-Milli, it was Allison Lindsay Scott; for Yared, it was Bolota Asmerom; and for Damien, it was Rick Ayers. Jabari Mahiri initiated, framed, and guided the research and drafted its write-up incorporating all of the contributions. Malik, Allison, and Bolota are from the Hip-Hop Generation, while Rick and Jabari are from the Baby-Boomer Generation. With the exception of the lead author, the order of the authors' names for this chapter reflects only the order in which each informant was discussed. Actual names of informants have not been used, but "5-Milli" is the MC pseudonym of that informant.

narrative" (p. 85). By this, he meant that the selection of music was expressive of life stories and themes that connect to ways that youth identify in their worlds. Our research explored how some of the core interests and themes in hip-hop culture were signified via musical texts and provided insights into additional schema that youth broker to produce and share meanings.

RESEARCH METHODS

To adequately assess the fluid literacy and representational practices of our informants that were often acquired in situated learning through participation (Lave & Wenger, 1991) in particular segments of the hip-hop discourse community, we incorporated an analytical framework of "literacy practices" as defined by Street (1993), but expanded to include what Gee (2003) called "semiotic domains." Street moved beyond Heath's (1982) notion of "literacy events" to a broader concept of literacy practices that included both behavior and conceptualizations related to the use of reading and writing (Street, 1993, p. 12). Gee's concept of semiotic domains was pitched broader still to include "any set of practices that recruits one or more modalities (e.g., oral or written language, images, equations, symbols, sounds, gestures, graphs, artifacts, etc.) to communicate distinctive types of meanings" (2003, p. 18). These frameworks from Street (1993) and Gee (2003), in conjunction with those from Lave and Wenger (1991), helped us to account for and illuminate the varied practices of literacy and representation taking place on both sides of the mic.

From January through March of 2006, our research team set out to understand and collect data on the literacy practices of local urban youth who were either DJing or MCing, or who considered themselves to be avid members of the hip-hop discourse community as reflected by their cultural practices and affiliations. This second category of youth would be potential audiences for people like the DJs and MCs in the first group.

Our research was conducted in urban sites in the San Francisco Bay Area of Northern California at a time when a local hip-hop phenomenon called the hyphy movement was just starting to gain national attention. The word *hyphy* is derived from *hyper*, and although definitions of the term vary widely, it is basically about releasing inhibitions and getting a little crazy. (Hartlaub, 2006) like "riding ghost on the curve," hanging a bit precariously out of a swerving car, or group dancing in a style called "going dumb." The essence of the movement, however, is about Black cultural pride and youth coming together for healthy music and dance competitions similar to the "crump" hip-hop phenomenon in Southern California that was colorfully depicted in the 2005 documentary film *Rize*.

In these Bay Area hip-hop discourse communities, we documented specific literacy practices and how they were manifested and linked to situated, sociocultural settings and semiotic domains. We identified focal informants to observe and interview. In addition to our research question of what were the specific literacy practices, we also wanted to find out what was the knowledge content, and how one became socialized into these local discourse communities. We (a) conducted one-on-one interviews with our informants, (b) examined samples of their writings or other literacy texts and artifacts, (c) took field notes on what we observed and discussed with them, and (d) developed individual written profiles of their literacy practices and semiotic domains.

THE HIP-HOP DJ

Our DJ informant, Elias, attended a Northern California high school where Malik gave a guest lecture on Black language in 2002. After the lecture, Elias introduced himself and initiated a friendly dialogue on music and culture that continued for several years. Clearly, Elias was a big hip-hop fan, but it was later learned that he had also been an amateur digital DJ throughout his high-school career. As he went on to college, he also made a transition from amateur to semiprofessional DJ.

Elias traced his interest in DJing back to "sometime in middle school," and estimated that it was fostered shortly after hearing rappers Puff Daddy and Mase perform the song "Can't Nobody Hold Me Down."[2] While Elias has never used this song in his own sets (it is outdated for his audiences), his interest was sparked by this primary text of the dance DJ—the song. DJs take numerous songs and sequence them throughout what can be seen as a key literacy practice, the "set," or "gig." Essentially, a DJ programs the music for a dance audience at a club or party.

Reading text. Elias identified in Puff Daddy and Mase's song what he considered to be the most important aspect that a DJ must "read" for: the "beat." He explained that he was initially drawn to this song because it had a "beat that I could move to." His reference is to the musical background of the song, as opposed to the lyrics, and he believes that all dance DJs must privilege the beat over the lyrics.

Elias's response to Puff Daddy's song also revealed an important means of discourse acquisition for DJs. Gee (1991) defined "acquisition" as "a process of acquiring something subconsciously by exposure to models and a process of trial and error" (p. 5). The dance DJ must have a "knack" for beats—that is, he or she must have an idea of the musical backgrounds of songs that will most likely inspire a large group of people to dance. To hone this literacy skill, Elias listens to music everyday at home and in his car imagining what beats will make people move rhythmically. Therefore, despite the song being a multimodal text, the DJ reads it primarily for one crucial aspect: the beat.

Practices of reading texts extended to Elias's manipulation of electronic equipment as an integral part of his DJ performance. His primary piece of equipment is the "mixer" (specifically, a CDJ mixer), that allows him to read two songs simultaneously on separate compact discs and evaluate (and occasionally manipulate) their compatibility in terms of volume, pitch, tempo, timbre, and so forth. This evaluation is done through an input channel to earphones specially designed to reduce outside noise. Simultaneously, the mixer also outputs music from one or both compact disc channels to the speaker system that itself is pivotal to the success of the gig.

Elias acquired his mixer literacy through apprenticeship (Lave & Wenger, 1991), or what he termed "watching a DJ in the moment." During high school, he apprenticed under a professional DJ with whom he connected via a mutual friend. He reported that the professional DJ was convinced of his worthiness as an apprentice by seeing his "passion for hip-hop and patience learning the equipment." They used a smaller, NuMark mixer, outputting the sounds into home stereo speakers. This audience of two, and smaller scale sound output were key aspects of his apprenticeship practices.

[2] The song was released on Puff Daddy and the Family's July 1997 release, *No way out* (allmusic.com).

Indeed, he introduces other friends (often fellow college students) to the world of DJing in the same manner. For even his smallest professional functions, however, Elias uses speakers at least three times as powerful as those he apprenticed on.

According to Elias, his apprenticeship was most valuable when he could actually watch and assist an established DJ during a professional gig. His first experience of this occurred at a community center dance in 2004. "It was important to see [the professional DJ] doing all of these things and seeing how people responded to it when they were out [on the dance floor], questions they would ask him, songs they would request."

Digital DJing may also be learned via computer DJ programs. Most of Elias's early practice was done on various computer programs available for purchase or download, and rehearsed at home. Occasionally, Elias would DJ publicly using a computer program; he sometimes performs low-stakes (usually smaller, private) events on his laptop computer through a DJ program called Visiosonic; however, Elias is emphatic that this DJ experience, while helpful, is far less enjoyable than using a disc mixer.

A "digital divide." Elias's evolving practices of DJing apprentices and socializes him into a particular discourse community: that of the digital dance DJ. This discourse community is uneasily intertwined with that of the vinyl dance DJ, who performs on music mixers that read and play from vinyl records (as opposed to the compact discs or digital data files of the digital DJ). While Elias has not yet "spun vinyl," he nonetheless offered insightful assessments of the relationship between the two discourse communities in terms of art on the one hand, and practicality on the other. He favored digital DJing as more practical and gave the following rationale:

> If you're trying to come up with the least amount of money, digital is the way you want to go. You're also moving along with the digital age, with digital technology and laser technology, so [digital DJing] just makes sense. Vinyl costs more money and [ultimately] a record is plastic. It wears through and you have to go replace that record. Who knows where you're gonna find that record. You search all around and then you end up paying twice for the same record. With digital music, that song will never wear. And you're also carrying less and lighter equipment around all the time.

He also framed a counterargument for vinyl, however, primarily in terms of traditional DJ aesthetics:

> As far as credibility goes, spinning vinyl is the old school way to go. The old school does bring a different sound, a more raw sound quality that goes back to the beginnings of the hip-hop sound. More traditional DJs are seeking out that sound. But in the ears of the regular person going to a club . . . it doesn't really make a difference. So people like me can get out here and do what we wanna do.

Despite Elias's partial dismissals of vinyl DJing as an anachronism, the traditional aesthetic of vinyl DJ performance still clearly weighs heavily upon his conception of DJing in general.

Literacies of the gig. Elias's favored term for the performance venue of DJing is the "gig." Instrumentalists and singers have used this term at least as far back as the early jazz and blues era. Elias's gigs are primarily high-school and college dances, parties thrown by organizations (such as fraternities and sororities), and private parties. One literacy practice at the gig beyond those already discussed was what Elias called the "sacrifice." He noted that there are additional terms for this practice, but the practice itself is an unspoken norm for DJs.

The sacrifice is a "banger" that is played early in the gig to establish communication between the DJ and the audience. Bangers are songs that excite the audience to dance energetically and/or stylishly. Usually, bangers are reserved for—and, according to Elias, make up about 60% of the music selection of—the second half of the gig. He plays one or two "bangers" early (in the first thirty minutes), however, to draw the audience to the dance floor. Then, the DJ's job becomes consistency and maintenance of the audience's full participation and communication. Or, as Elias put it, "from that point until the time you leave, I want it to feel like one song experience, a lot of twists and turns, but one consistent high."

Toward this end, the DJ must exhibit another form of literacy at the gig; he or she must read the cues of the dance audience. To do this, Elias divides the audience into two groups: (a) skilled and unskilled dancers, and (b) male and female dancers. He noted that the DJ attempts to achieve a level of communication with skilled dancers, and that they are the ones who are important to reach throughout the night. He discussed how the DJ must read the audience to identify the skilled dancers and how this can be accomplished by playing songs with intricate or unusual rhythms. In profiling skilled dancers, he noted, "I'm looking for the person that makes what they want of the beat while [maintaining relationship to] the beat, not trying to figure out what they're *supposed to do* with the beat. You can't improvise unless you've conquered the beat, or some beat like it. You have to have been there before."

Regarding the other group, Elias definitively asserted that the DJ must absolutely focus on the actions of the women in a dance crowd.

> The guys don't matter. As far as cues, the people you look for are all the girls. That's all that really matters because girls [often] dance together, and a guy will do anything as long as a girl is doing something. As long as a girl is attracting a crowd, as long as a song will attract a girl, I'll play that song. The only thing that means anything is how much fun everyone had overall, and that's dictated by the girls.

Elias offered compelling informant perspectives on the discourse community of digital dance DJs, a community with highly specific literacy demands and practices within the larger culture of hip-hop that he acquired in the main through participation and situated learning. As will be shown in the next section, these literacy of the digital DJ are intricately connected to those of the rap MC.

THE HIP-HOP MC

Numerous young rap artists in Northern California cities, suburbs, and towns aspire to create music that will be locally and globally embraced, and 5-Milli is one of them. Allison documented his experiences, perspectives, and practices of literacy as a rap MC. He creates and records rap music, produces his own music tracks, and contributes to the graphic design and promotion of his music through a record label that he jointly owns with a partner. His evolution as a rap MC began as a teenager. He began rapping and engaging in freestyle battles with his friends in high school. He described his early involvement as "almost like a pastime. Rapping and freestyling was like playing cards with friends. . . . Whenever I hung out with my friends, we always ended up rapping and battling each other."

5-Milli was further immersed in hip-hop music and culture when he went to live with his father and uncle in a midsized, Midwestern city. His uncle was deeply into the hip-hop scene of this city, and he would engage 5-Milli in extensive conversations about hip-hop artists, lyrics, and styles. His uncle took him to underground shows and recording studios, and 5-Milli recorded his first three-minute track at the age of 15.

By 2003, 5-Milli had spent time in the military, attended junior college, and eventually went on to study graphic design at another college. Throughout these experiences, he stayed connected to rap by intermittently writing and recording rap songs and through his own analyses and critiques of prominent rap artists and lyrics. To date, 5-Milli has made guest appearances on his business partner's first album and on a second mix-tape (that 5-Milli helped to produce). He is currently working on his first solo album.

As he became more involved in his career as a rap artist, he took on the pseudonym "5-Milli." This rite, enacted by many youth in the Hip-Hop Generation, of "dropping" birth names in favor of new names is actually a distinctive literacy practice that reflects their dynamically evolving identities. For example, the RZA, the mastermind of the Wu-Tang Clan who is lauded as the "Creator of one of the most influential sounds and styles in hip-hop history" (the RZA, 2005, p. 4), noted that these names are alter egos (different sides of the artist's personality, or different ways of representing oneself). They also reflect various changes that a person has gone through. The RZA is a prominent example of this practice. His birth name was Robert F. Diggs. His AKA includes the Abbot, Bobby Digital, Bobby Steels, Prince Rakeem, the RZA-recta, the Scientist, Prince Delight, Prince Dynamite, and Ruler Zig-Zag-Zig Allah.

Skill acquisition. 5-Milli believes that his immersion in hip-hop culture from a young age influenced both his desire and his ability to gain the knowledge and skills required to become a rap artist. His evolving mastery reflected Lave and Wenger's (1991) notion of the movement of newcomers toward full participation in the practices of a given community (p. 29). Importantly, these authors argued, the "learning through legitimate peripheral participation takes place no matter . . . whether there is any intentional education at all" (p. 40). These considerations were directly applicable in the case of 5-Milli. He noted, "It is difficult because there is no school for rappers; no one teaches us how to get in the game, how to hustle, manage finances, and do promotions." There are specific kinds of knowledge and skills required to participate in the discourse community of rap MCs, and 5-Milli provided insights into his acquired utility with verbal and written skills along with music critique skills needed to become successful as a rap MC and entrepreneur. Our use of the word "skills" in conjunction with these practices is consistent with the definition of literacy by Mahiri and Sablo (1996) as skills in the construction of meaning in texts in context. It calls for expanded consideration of the range of "skills," as well as the array of "texts," that are utilized to encode, decode, and represent situated "meanings."

Critique skills. 5-Milli described his musical influences as including Tupac, NWA, Ice Cube, Nas, Jay-Z, DMX, and numerous other rap and reggae artists. He recalled being drawn to the lyrical content of these artists' music. Additionally, his peers and family members often engaged in discussions about this music, comparing and critiquing its content, style of delivery, performance, and the innovation of musical beats. From these experiences, 5-Milli developed his own stance toward and critique of the music. For example, if an artist produced a song that had no "substance," or creativity, or diversity in lyrical content, 5-Milli would decide that the artist was not credible, and he would stop listening to his songs. He looks for substantive messages in the music beyond the artist talking about basic things such as selling drugs, buying cars, and so forth. He also looks for originality in the "beats," catchy "hooks," and fluid verbal styles.

In addition to critiquing lyrical content and style, 5-Milli analyzes contemporary rap music in terms of its presentation: its video style, CD packaging, and production quality. He has had to refine his listening (and comprehension) skills including the ability identify similarities and differences between various rap artists and their songs. This involves identifying particular uses of lyrical words and phrases, specific uses of rhythms and rhymes, and novel usages of language and vocabulary.

Writing skills. As a teenager, 5-Milli was more engaged in free styling and battling (rapping competitions) than in writing lyrics. He commented that he did not really learn all of the nuances associated with writing lyrics until meeting his current business partner and becoming serious about recording music. He noted that there are different repertoires of skills needed for each style of rapping. "In my experience," he explained, "rappers that can freestyle usually can't write as well, and rappers that can write well usually can't freestyle . . . it's like a trade-off to build up your skills in one of the areas." He acknowledged that freestyle rapping is essential in battling and in certain other arenas of rap music, but his interest in recording and producing music required him to develop specific writing skills. His business partner taught him about numbering bars (16) to fit within one verse, and then writing the chorus (8 bars) in a defined format. Although 5-Milli was able to write lyrics before learning this particular style, he stated that it became much easier for him to record written information within the format that he compared to the structure of an essay. He said "[it's] easier to write when you are given a format."

5-Milli stated that writing lyrics is a skill that can only be obtained through practice and trial and error. In addition to practicing and writing frequently, he said that he never throws away his lyrics; instead, he revises them until they feel right for his songs. When he was asked whether he writes for a certain beat or hears the beat and then writes lyrics, he stated that he preferred to hear the beat first, and was then able to keep the beat in his head while writing lyrics to it.

Once 5-Milli has the beat and begins to write, he stated that he writes in ways to understand his own thoughts. In other words, words are intentionally misspelled or shortened, and visual representations are often used. In this way, he is able to first communicate his thoughts on paper, and then read them back aloud while recording a track. Similarly, he purposefully uses nonstandard English in his songs. His critique of standard English within rap music was not centered on the comments of many who describe hip-hop and slang as an exclusionary mechanism or as a countercritique to mainstream language styles. Instead, he commented that by being immersed in Black English, he was able to more freely and comfortably convey his thoughts. He noted that if he had to write and perform his lyrics using Standard English, it would be much harder to convey his ideas, and, thus, it would stifle his creativity. 5-Milli viewed his use of language as a way to "set an example, be a voice to the listener about what I have done in my life, but I don't want to glorify it. I want to teach lessons and have a positive message at the end." Influences on 5-Milli's lyrical content include current events, life events, personal experiences, community-based stories, and the work of other rappers. For example, he often draws on his own life experiences that he feels are relevant to his listener's lives, and he tells of potential harm in these situations in order to dissuade them from making the same mistakes. The only written texts that he reads besides his own work are hip-hip magazines such as *The Source* and *XXL*. He reads interviews and stories about rappers that have become successful to increase his knowledge of the styles of rap music that is being embraced nationwide.

Verbal skills. Another essential literacy practice for 5-Milli was translating written lyrics into performative raps. Verbal literacy skills are crucial to rap artists because their performance is most visible to hip-hop audiences. 5-Milli felt that his verbal skills were acquired through his personal exploration, development, and practice of a unique oral performance style. He discussed the "personality" of the musician in terms of speed and style of delivery. Their unique personalities set them apart. He gave examples of the use of creative, made-up words delivered in a goofy manner by E-40, the amazing speed of Twista's lyrical skills, and the serious demeanor of Nas. He commented that a key mistake is trying to sound like another rapper because it is the originality and individualism of the oral performance of the rap that is valued by audiences and fellow rap artists.

Additionally, 5-Milli noted that the use of various "tones" provided characteristics in oral performances that could not be conveyed in written texts alone. For example, anger, sadness, seriousness, and elation are all emotions that 5-Milli conveys using different tones. He also consciously varies the delivery speed of his raps which adds to both the emotions conveyed (e.g., slow = somber, serious; fast = excited, elated, or angry) and the amount of information that is intentionally allowed to be extracted and understood from the lyrics.

Recording skills. The literacy skills that 5-Milli acquired and developed to analyze and critique music, create written lyrics, and transform written texts into oral performances are key to being a member of the discourse community of the rap MC. He also talked, however, about additional knowledge and skills that distinguished "real" rappers from those who just rap. He described several terms associated with the recording process that could reveal the incomplete knowledge and skill of a novice within this community. "If you put them in a recording studio," he said, "and they are unfamiliar with terms like 'punch-in' (to stop and breathe while recording, and then back the recording up to where you were when you took a breath), 'dubs' (recording the verse once and then putting another recording of the same verse on top of it), 'ad-libs' (adding words into the background of the lyrics), and '16s' (the number of bars in a verse), then they are just rappers and not rap recording artists." Acquiring this knowledge comes from experience and immersion in this community of practice, and 5-Milli traced the development of his knowledge back to his first recording of a track at age 15. This discussion of his critiquing, writing, performing, and producing of rap music since then provides a view of the extensiveness of his practices of literacy and reflects key aspects of varied and nuanced literacies that are practiced throughout local hip-hop communities.

THE BLACK HIP-HOP HEAD

The initial informant Bolota contacted to get an insider's perspective on the local experience of hip-hop culture in everyday life did not work out. He quickly became upset about what he considered to be current transfigurations of hip-hop. He was particularly frustrated when he began to explain what it meant to be a "hip-hop head" by referencing the kind of head that he was not: "the White boy with baggy pants wearing his hat to the side that you see on MTV." He expressed how "hip-hop was more than just the music, it was a way of being, a lifestyle. . . . One has to be knowledgeable in all types of music, not just rap because being a head is knowing as much as possible about what concerns Black people and Black culture." He then refused to discuss the subject further and said, "I'm out man, let's go."

Bolota's next informant, Yared, did work out. Like the first informant, Yared is a true believer in hip-hop in that his primary sense of identity is reflected through language, music, dress, and other styles of hip-hop culture. When he was younger, he was a break-dancer and a tagger (graffiti artist); now, in addition to being a rapper/hip-hopper, he is also a lecturer at a local university. Unlike the first informant, Yared was excited to talk about the culture and his participation in it.

"Doing the knowledge." Yared also believes there are two different types of hip-hop heads and two different hip-hop cultures: (a) "real" hip-hop and (b) "mainstream" hip-hop. Similar to the first informant, Yared explained his identity as a hip-hop head by describing what he was not, referring to "the White boy from the suburbs wearing baggy jeans, a backpack, and a hat to the side." He felt that this was a hip-hop head that the mainstream acknowledged, but it was not an authentic hip-hop head. Yared noted that a head's whole existence revolves around hip-hop culture in its original form. He also noted, "The elements that created the low socio-economic realities as well as oppression gave rise to hip-hop. . . . Thus, a hip-hop head has to also emerge from the same elements as well." Yared felt that he did not just "become" a head but inherited this way of being from his surroundings and his general reality as a Black man in America. His experiences gave him the "knowledge" that one needs in order to be a hip-hop head, but to maintain his legitimacy he felt he had to play an active role by "building on [this] knowledge," or in the terminology from Kitwana (2005), "doing the knowledge."

Yared's past experiences as a rapper, graffiti artist, and break-dancer provided a foundation for this "knowledge," but he also felt that extensive discussions with other heads as well as intensive study of African and African American history and culture made his identity and status as a head more "legit." He noted that mainstream hip-hop heads were devoid of these experiences, and, hence, were unable to attain or even comprehend the knowledge of the authentic hip-hop-head community.

Yared felt that his main role as a true head was "to build on the knowledge." The term "knowledge" refers to the collective consciousness of the hip-hop-head community and is connected to the goals of the Black Power movement. It is seen in related terms such as "knowledge reign supreme," "knowledge of self," or "know-the-ledge." Yared claimed that his whole being revolved around guiding others toward a positive and progressive path of consciousness. Consequently, he felt that he had to inject this understanding of hip-hop into every aspect of his teaching and general presence.

Importantly for Yared, this presence does not necessarily have to be rich in images, Black vernacular, or the body language that mainstream society generally perceives as associated with the hip-hop culture. For instance, Yared argued that James Brown is a hip-hop head in the same way that Dead Prez and Public Enemy are. He pointed out that all three represent integral aspects of Black culture and struggle, but each has an individual style and language through which they facilitate consciousness raising and resistance. He believes that there is not a specific language or attitude that a hip-hop head has to attain. Instead, he stressed the general need for individuality and originality as the core of hip-hop. According to Yared, "It is an ever evolving and changing form because it is a mode of resistance to the dominant culture."

Ultimately, Yared believed that "real hip-hop" was dying as a result of the proliferation of the mainstream variety. He noted that "hip-hop reached it's apex in '88. . . . Everyone looked different; everyone had their own claim and style. Now it's processed . . . it's like a McDonald's burger, packaged and sold." He further explained how all of the values that constituted a legitimate hip-hop artist were not essential ingredients any longer. The skills, knowledge, and intricacies of the true hip-hop artist and his or her work are now not essential for commercial success. This is how hip-hop has been transformed. Consequently, it has made Yared's existence as a hip-hop head much more difficult. Now, it's much harder, he claimed, "to keep it real."

A WHITE HIP-HOP HEAD

As a part of this research, Rick focused on a White male student in his class who affected hip-hop clothing and Black vernacular language and cultural styles in pervasive ways. As a White hip-hop head, Damien was a key informant, albeit with some initial reluctance that extended from how he chose to position and represent himself physically and culturally, as well as in the academic discourse of schooling. He often scowled at his teachers; he usually resisted the topics and flow of discussions in classes; and he generally resisted doing schoolwork. He also stood out because of his style of dress. Tall, but in a perpetual slouch, his blond hair was cut close to the scalp. He sported the latest hip-hop attire: super-baggy jeans, an oversized White T-shirt with an original painting on it, and Nike shoes with a large swoop. He argued that he had constructed his own from his experiences and discounted any influence from his parents. He reported, however, that his parents were definitely outside the mainstream of American culture, as his mother was an avant-garde artist and his father was an inventor.

Damien once announced to the class that this year, he just wanted to "keep it gully." Rick asked Damien what this phrase meant. Instead of explaining it, he just shrugged and laughed. He was not always ready to act as an informant, especially in front of the class. Later in the day, a young, Black, male teacher explained what he thought the phrase meant. "Keep it gully, you know, like keep it gangster." After further questioning, he elaborated. "Keep it gangster. Keep it real. Don't sell out. Stay with the game."

Clothing texts. At first glance, Damien might be construed an aberration, a White guy who affected African American dress and language styles. His construction of identity, however, was much more complicated and specific than that. Many White kids have baggy pants, and many use African American language in their speech; however, Damien is of a particular mold. He described his clothing style as "street wear, urban wear, artistic." It turned out that he has a small business with another young man making hip-hop art T-shirts. Pressed more, he said, "Yes, this kind of shirt is a fad, and I like it. It's comfortable. Preppy clothes are hella gay." It was of interest that he used hip-hop clothing styles in contrast to mainstream "preppy" styles to mark sexual identity, and this issue will be addressed later.

Damien explained that he adopted the hip-hop style "because of, one, my personality. I went to a school when I was young that had only one Black kid and when I got out here I went to . . . a kind of hippy school, and I had mostly Black friends. And, two, it is a style I picked up. I have played basketball since second grade and that was just the style, not like preppy." So, it became clearer that through peripheral participation in African American culture in basketball and at his elementary school, Damien acquired key aspects of hip-hop style.

Whiteness texts. Damien presented a style that is generally identified as African American; however, in discussion after discussion, he has ridiculed any time the conversation has gotten into issues of "White privilege." In fact, he was most likely to say, "That's just some White guilt trippin'!" or "Come on, just blame it on the White man, what an easy answer." In discussions of border issues, of the tensions that led to the 1992 riots in Los Angeles, of the ideas of affirmative action or reparations, Damien was most outspoken in opposing the idea that White people bear any blame.

One book read for class, *Angry Black White Boy* by Adam Mansbach (2005), presented Damien with a dilemma. The main character in this book is a White young man named Macon who fiercely identifies with African American hip-hop culture and hates White people, calls them devils. Macon is deeply concerned about White privilege and wants White people to apologize for White history and to pay reparations. Many students joked that Damien was our own angry Black White boy, but while he dressed like Macon might, he was not at all similar in his political views.

Surprisingly, many of the African American students in class, especially those who are most nationalist and most critical of White power, regard Damien positively. These students get angry in class discussions with the White liberals, those who express "support" for the Black struggle, but who seem blind to their own patronizing attitude. When Damien comes up in conversation, however, the nationalists indicate that they respect him. It turns out that Damien has extensive social contact and friendships with African American students in the school.

Hip-hop texts. One thing that Damien was enthusiastic about was his entrée into hip-hop music production. He "makes beats," and has teamed up with another White student to fix up the high school's radio studio and turn it into a sound studio for recording groups that come in to cut CDs. Damien finds that he identifies more with hip-hop music making than with school. He has decided to not go to school next year, but instead to get a job and try to expand his music business in engineering, writing, and making beats. He has dreams of making it big through hip-hop. Interestingly, while Damien rejected the dominant culture's formula for success, he still identified with the dominant cultural model of entrepreneurship and payoff for sacrifice.

Oral texts. To understand more about Damien's discourse community, he was asked if he spoke differently when looking for a job or with White people who might now understand his language style. He initially replied that he was always himself and that he did not change his style when talking to people in authority; however, he added that when he was working at a job, he did use language that the boss would understand, but he was not selling out. He then mentioned that he had an adopted brother who is African American. His brother told him he had to "proper himself" when looking for a job.

Damien strongly resisted any call to proper himself in school, and this was often reflected orally. For example, as noted earlier, he had strong feelings about sexuality and was quick to attack anything he regarded as "gay." He reacted with noises and body language when issues of homophobia were directly broached in his classes. Even though he argued that everyone had a right to his or her sexual orientation, he was still very negative about queer identity. He would readily use words such as "gay," "faggot," and "bitch," despite the fact that these words were forbidden in class. He would eventually refrain when called on it, but it was clear that he continued to use these terms away from school authority.

In contrast, Damien revealed a different sensibility regarding racial discourse. For example, when asked about the use of the "n-word," he replied, "I don't say n-----r, that's ignorant. It is just offensive and stupid. They can say it. I mean you hear comedians say it, and other Black people just say it to each other." As for White people's use of the term, he continued, "it's different if you hear White kids say [it]. . . . Since I lived out in the country, like 100 miles outside of Seattle, I would hear White kids talk like that all the time. . . . Just recently I was kickin' it with a bunch of White kids at [another high school] and one kid said [it]. Really, though, I don't care what people say. . . . It doesn't really matter. I'm about myself. So, if someone is ignorant, that's nothing to me."

Damien claims hip-hop language and cultural styles as a primary way of being. His ways of speaking are strictly circumscribed by his values and sense of identity. While he seemed disengaged, he read every discussion closely, weighed them by his value system and, thereby, either attacked or agreed with them. He had strong formal discourse boundaries (how he talked and how he would never talk), but he would code switch to engage people in other discourse communities and to communicate in ways that they could understand.

CONCLUSION: "LEGITIMATE" LITERACIES—CONTESTED CULTURE

Elias, 5-Milli, Yared, and Damien's varied positions and participation in local, Bay Area hip-hop culture revealed a wide array of literacy practices. The music DJ and the rap MC are at the core. This chapter has illustrated something of the nature and range of their practices of literacy. These practices included reading for the beat, and understanding that for the dance DJ, the beat must be privileged over the lyrics. Both the DJ and the MC needed to recognize and construct beats that would motivate people to dance. This goes to the original party purposes at the root of hip-hop culture. These parties or "gigs" required simultaneous skills in multiple literacies as they necessitated DJs and MCs effectively operating in semiotic domains that were inherently multimodal. DJs and MCs also had to successfully read their audiences, and for the DJ, this included developing an analytical scheme for recognizing who to focus on and primarily direct the music (especially the bangers) toward the females first and foremost, but also toward the most skilled dancers. Our focal DJ and MC additionally revealed considerable technical skills—operational knowledge and skills with various computer programs, digital mixers, compatible electronic equipment, and technical equipment and terms needed in the recording studio.

There were also numerous literacy practices on the other side of the mic. Hip-hop heads were "doing the knowledge": reading the world through the words of rap music as well as studying hip-hop culture, specifically, and African and African American culture, in general. They represented and made meaning in various oral, as well as visual, texts. The content of their knowledge, as well as the process for acquiring it, was usually directly linked to how they were socialized into these hip-hop discourse communities and revealed in their everyday ways of talking, walking, dressing, and other forms of communicating.

These socialized ways of representing were also the sites of dramatic tensions in hip-hop communities. Specific kinds of knowledge, skills, and styles were markers that distinguished the quality and kinds of DJs (digital versus vinyl) and MCs ("real" rappers versus those who just rap, or "real" versus commercial rappers). They were also used to distinguish between different individual and group levels of authenticity of participation in hip-hop highlighted by those who were "keeping it real," "keeping it gully," and "not selling out." These dynamic cultural practices complicate our notions of the kinds of knowledge, skills, and texts that members of the Hip-Hop Generation appropriate for personal power and pleasure, as well as for identification and communication. The legitimacy of these practices (and the legitimacy of those who practiced them), however, was often contested by forces and perceptions that operated both outside and inside of hip-hop and on both sides of the mic.

Considerations of legitimacy and authenticity go back to the roots of hip-hop in the United States, and they are a continuation of considerations that go further back to the African roots of Black performative practices. In her work on the significance and influences of West African praise singers on other national cultures, for example, Ebron (2002) also explored the challenges to notions of the legitimacy of distinctive performance practices from Africa and how they were romanticized and/or denigrated in mind and media of Western portrayals. Ways that youth in hip-hop culture also engaged concerns with legitimacy must ultimately be seen inside of this larger historical context.

Beyond the rich array of literacy practices, the contestation of hip-hop was a key consideration for our informants. Black hip-hop heads, along with a number of hip-hop chroniclers, felt that the essence of hip-hop was its Black roots and Black cultural manifestations—"the face of Black America in the world today" (Tate, 2005). In other words, hip-hop originated as (and should be kept) Black. The contradiction, however, is that as commercialization and globalization of hip-hop's wide appeal revealed many of its fundamental markers and practices, other heads have turned to participate in, represent through, benefit by, and *change* its language and literacy practices and styles.

REFERENCES

Chang, J. (2005). *Can't stop won't stop: A history of the hip-hop generation.* New York: St. Martin's Press.

Ebron, P. A. (2002). *Performing Africa*. Princeton, NJ: Princeton University Press.

George, N. (1998). *Hip hop America*. New York: Penguin Putnam.

Gee, J. P. (1991). What is literacy? In C. Mitchell & K. Weiler (Eds.), *Rewriting literacy: Culture and the discourse of the other* (pp. 3–12). New York: Bergin and Garvey.

Gee, J. P. (2003). *What video games have to teach us about learning and literacy*. New York: Palgrave Macmillian.

Gibson, W. (2005, July). *God's little toys: Confessions of a cut & paste artist. Wired, 13*(7), 118–119.

Heath, S. B. (1982). Protean shapes in literacy events: Ever-shifting oral and literate traditions. In D. Tannen, (Ed.), *Spoken and written language: Exploring orality and literacy* (pp. 91–117). Norwood, NJ: Ablex.

Hull, G. A. (2003). Youth culture and digital media: New literacies for new times. *Research in the Teaching of English, 38*(2), 237–241.

Johnson, S. (2005). *Everything bad is good for you: How today's popular culture is actually making us smarter*. New York: Riverside Books.

Kitwana, B. (2003). *The hip-hop generation: Young Blacks and the crisis in African American culture*. New York: Basic Civitas Books.

Koza, J. E. (1994). Rap music: The cultural politics of official representation. *Review of Education/Pedagogy/Cutural Studies, 16*, 171–193.

Lave, J. and Wenger, E. (1991). *Situated learning: Legitimate peripheral participation*. New York: Cambridge University Press.

Mahiri, J. (2004). *What they don't learn in school: Literacy in the lives of urban youth*. New York: Peter Lang.

Mahiri, J., & Sablo, S. (1996). Writing for their lives: Non-school literacy of urban, African American youth. *Journal of Negro Education, 65*(2), 164–180.

Manovich, L. (2001). *The language of new media*. Cambridge, MA: MIT Press.

Mansbach, A. (2005). *Angry black white boy or the miscegenation of Macon Detornay*. New York: Crown/Three Rivers Press.

Miller, P. (2004). Rhythm science. Cambridge, MA: The MIT Press.

Rose, T. (1994). *Black noise: Rap music and black culture in contemporary America*. Middletown, CT: Wesleyan University Press.

RZA. (2005). *The Wu-Tang manual*. New York: The Penguin Group.

Street, B. (Ed.). (1993). *Cross-cultural approaches to literacy*. New York: Cambridge University Press.

Tate, G. (2005, January 4). *The Village Voice*. New York: Village Voice Media, Inc.

•30•

NOVELNESS IN ACTION: THE ROLE OF SELF-GENERATED DRAMATIC ARTS ACTIVITIES IN THE LITERACY DEVELOPMENT OF ADOLESCENTS

Christopher Worthman
DEPAUL UNIVERSITY

In this chapter, I present data collected from two research sites: TeenStreet, an urban youth theater group, and Herrero School, an urban pre-K through eighth-grade school. Drawing on sociolinguistic definitions of literacy (Barton & Hamilton, 1998; Gee, 1996; Scribner, 1984; Scribner & Cole, 1981; Street, 1993) and M. M. Bakhtin's theory of knowledge (1990, 1993, 1994a, 1994b, 1998), including his concepts of *aesthetic contemplation*, *heteroglossia*, and *novelness*, I show how self-generated dramatic arts activities position adolescents in both out-of-school and in-school contexts to engage one another's stories and aesthetically make meaning of those stories and use them to make sense of their lives. The self-generated dramatic arts activities enhanced these adolescents' senses of agency by facilitating critical and creative perspective taking. The adolescents perceived and even experienced ways of being that are different from their lived realities. My focus is also on the writing generated by these adolescents, individually and in groups, in response to self-generated dramatic arts activities. The adolescents described in this chapter came to see the self-generated dramatic arts activities and writing as mediational means that could be used not only to make sense of their own lives but also to share that sense-making with others in an act of bringing forth multiple perspectives and aesthetically contemplating those perspectives. Bakhtin called this act "novelness" (1990, 1993, 1994a, 1994b, 1998). Within the context of self-generated dramatic arts activities, I call it "novelness in action."

SOCIOCULTURAL DEFINITIONS OF LITERACY

Sylvia Scribner (1984), writing after she and Michael Cole (Scribner & Cole, 1981) completed their groundbreaking literacy research with the Vai of West Africa, noted that "most efforts at definitional determinations [of literacy] are based on a conception of literacy as an attribute of individuals; they are to describe constituents of literacy in terms of individual abilities" (p. 7). She argued, however, that "the single most compelling fact about literacy is that it is a social achievement" (p. 7), and much research since has shown this to be true. What this research shows is that, although we cannot deny the importance of decoding and encoding skills to literacy development, more than skills mastery is involved in learning to read and write. And, as such, literacy involves more than only reading and writing. The context in which reading and writing take place is important and greatly influences how and why participants in that context are reading and writing. Literacy development is inherently tied to context or to the nature of interaction that takes place around that development.

James Gee (1996), like Scribner, believed the focus of literacy studies should be on social interactions, which again leads us away from only looking at reading and writing or even at language and "towards [looking at] social relationships and social practices" (p. 137). In emphasizing the importance of social interaction, Gee defined literacy as "mastery of a secondary Discourse" (p. 143). A Discourse is

> a socially accepted association among ways of using language, other symbolic expressions, and "artifacts," of thinking, feeling, believing, valuing, and acting that can be used to identify oneself as a member of a socially meaningful group or "social network," or to signal (that one is playing) a socially meaningful "role". (p. 131)

A secondary Discourse is a Discourse representative of institutions and contexts outside one's home environment or one's first or primary Discourse. In Gee's conceptualization, the TeenStreet adolescents and the Herrero School English language learners that I introduce later were being apprenticed into secondary Discourses, which include particular ways of interacting. Obviously, then, Discourses can and do vary in their "socially accepted association[s]" (p. 131). There are multiple Discourses and, thus, multiple literacies. In looking at TeenStreet and Herrero School, or any site of pedagogical practice, we need to ask what type of literacy is facilitated by the nature of the interaction or dialogue that takes place in that context and what the effect of that literacy on participants is.

For the purposes of this chapter, *literacy* refers to the mastery of a secondary Discourse, whereas *literacies* refers to the multiple literacies or the mastery of multiple secondary Discourses that a person achieves during her lifetime and can appropriate at different times and in different contexts. Through participating in the literacy of a secondary Discourse, that literacy, to varying degrees, becomes part of the participant's repertoire for engaging the world beyond the boundaries of that particular Discourse. In other words, participants take their literacies with them as they move among different secondary Discourse contexts. It is for this reason that understanding the social nature of literacies is important. Our literacies shape how we engage and make sense of the world, including how we use texts and to what purposes, even outside the contexts in which we mastered those literacies.

BUILDING A LITERACY CURRICULUM

My belief that literacy is significant to our lives because of its role in human interaction leads me to ask what theories or ideologies inform the interaction or literacy development at TeenStreet and Herrero School. And what exactly are the defining characteristics of that literacy? The TeenStreet instructors were guided by beliefs about creating theater and about what theater can do for people, but, essentially, what drove their practices was a belief about the power of self-generated dramatic arts activities to create new meaning and, thus, to create innovative and creative material for scripts (Worthman, 2002). I find affinity between what was happening at TeenStreet and Bakhtin's theory of knowledge, particularly Bakhtin's concept of dialogue and of novelness as a type of dialogue. At Herrero School, I adapted TeenStreet practices to facilitate the English language and literacy development of sixth and seventh graders who had been in the United States for two years or less. In the following sections, I show how Bakhtin's thought helps define what is happening at TeenStreet and Herrero School and why I see self-generated dramatic arts activities as an invaluable part of the literacy that is being developed at both sites.

Dialogism: Bakhtin's Theory of Knowledge

Theories of dialogism, or the role of human interaction in human development, arise in part from understanding Bakhtin's theory of knowledge. Michael Holquist (1991) wrote, "Conceiving being dialogically means that reality is always experienced, not just perceived, and further that it is experienced from a particular position. Bakhtin conceives that position in kinetic terms as a situation, an event, the event of being a self" (p. 21). All events, or experiences, help us position ourselves in the world in particular ways, depending on who we are, on the event, and on the nature of the interaction. Bakhtin saw all interactions falling somewhere on a continuum of dialogue because he saw human existence as contingent on dialogue or interaction (Bakhtin, 1993, 1994a). Thus, one's individual existence is defined in relation to others' existences. An individual experiences the world from a particular place and time and, because neither place nor time is static, experiences evolve and are transformed as events play out. As interactions play out somewhere on the continuum of dialogue, participants negotiate meaning in a process that only ends when we die. Existence is, thus, a series of interactions, or utterances that necessitate a response—hence, Bakhtin's claim that there is no alibi in existence (Bakhtin, 1990). As human beings, we must always respond. And as human beings, our understanding of the world is contingent on others' responses. Essential to our human agency, however, is the nature of the interaction taking place among participants in particular contexts. That is, where does the nature of interaction in which we each find ourselves involved fall on Bakhtin's continuum?

In the data I present in this chapter, all the activities positioned participants to respond to one another in particular ways to develop a particular secondary Discourse. The activities called for the use of multiple mediational means, even as they evolved back to efforts to explicate meaning using language. In this regard, the activities positioned adolescents so that they consciously responded, reflected on their responses, and were responded to. Although Bakhtin might have said that we, as humans, do this naturally with only the nature of the dialogue to be decided, seldom are we in contexts in which we are encouraged to do it in the way facilitated at these two sites of practice, a way Bakhtin (1990) referred to as "aesthetic contemplation."

Essential to Bakhtin's theory of knowledge is our ability to contemplate aesthetically others' ideas and experiences. Of the idea, he wrote,

> The idea *lives* not in one person's *isolated* individual consciousness—if it remains there only, it degenerates and dies. The idea begins to live, that is, to take shape, to develop, to find and renew its verbal expression, to give birth to new ideas, only when it enters into genuine dialogical relationships with other ideas, with the ideas of *others*. Human thought becomes genuine thought, that is, an idea, only under conditions of living in contact with another and alien thought, a thought embodied in someone else's voice, that is, in someone else's consciousness expressed in discourse. At that point of contact between voice-consciousnesses the idea is born and lives. (p. 87–88)

Although our understanding of our own and others' ideas and experiences is not contingent on aesthetic contemplation, it is through aesthetic contemplation that we are most focused on—most empathetic toward—others' ideas and experiences. Aesthetic contemplation fosters the transformation of ideas and experiences and, thus, knowledge.

Bakhtin (1990, 1993) wrote that aesthetic contemplation is the act of "empathizing into an individual object of seeing—seeing it from inside in its own essence" (1993, p. 14). In regards to our interactions with others, I interpret this as an individual's conscious effort to understand the ideas and experiences of others and to consider what they mean for her or his own ideas and experiences. Bakhtin wrote about aesthetic contemplation:

> I empathize *actively* into an individuality and, consequently, I do not lose myself completely, not my unique place outside it, even for a moment. It is not the object [what another person says or does] that unexpectedly takes possession of me as the passive one. It is *I* who empathize actively into the object: empathizing is *my* act, and only that continues it productiveness and newness. . . . Empathizing actualizes something that did not exist either in the object of empathizing or in myself prior to the act of empathizing, and through this actualized something Being-in-event [one's lived life] is enriched. (Bakhtin, 1993, p. 15)

It was this idea of aesthetic contemplation that I witnessed at TeenStreet and hoped to foster in my teaching at Herrero School.

In my research with the teen ensemble, voice activities that had teenagers "standing in the place" of others or anticipating what others may say fostered empathy because they positioned the teens to listen critically and creatively to others. Bakhtin wrote that the "first step in aesthetic activity [contemplating] is my projecting myself in him [or her] and experiencing his [or her] life from within him [or her]. I must experience—come to see and to know—what *he [or she]* experiences; I must put myself in his [or her] place and coincide with him [or her], as it were" (1990, p. 25). Yet, this contemplative act can never be fully empathetic because of the perspective from which I see. Because the other already occupies a particular place and time—that is, because he has his own unique perspective—and because my empathizing is grounded in my own place and time, in my own unique self or perspective, I never really "stand in another's place"—that is, I never can fully know another's experience. Yet, the act of consciously trying to understand, of trying to "stand in another's place," positions me to empathize critically and creatively. It also positions me, in my relations to others, to realize the limitations of my perspective and, thus, the need to engage others to inform and transform my ideas and experiences.

Self-Generated Dramatic Arts Activities on the Continuum of Dialogue

For Bakhtin, existing in dialogue did not mean that every event or activity required two or more individuals to be present for interaction to take place (Bakhtin, 1994a, 1994b). We live in dialogue even when we are alone. In this regard, Bakhtin saw inner speech—or what he called "inner language"—much as Vygotsky (1986) did: as a manifestation of the internalizing of social engagement, or social influence on thinking (Bakhtin, 1990; Clark & Holquist, 1984). For example, Bakhtin posited that literature is an utterance demanding a response—that is, it is an interaction we enter into when we read, with our inner voice engaging the voices of the text, both the author's and the characters'. This is a theory not without support in literary studies and literature pedagogy, as it finds theoretical and research support in the work of Rosenblatt (1983) and others (Tompkins, 1980; Wilhelm, 1997).

What literature—and, for Bakhtin, specifically the novel—can offer readers is a particular manifestation of dialogue or a specific place on the continuum of dialogue. This manifestation is an interaction between an individual and a text that sheds light on the human condition and facilitates the individual's discovery of the other. Literature, as such, provides opportunities for aesthetic contemplation. It does this by potentially providing an individual multiple voices on the world beyond what one can experience on his or her own. It also does this by suspending time and place and allowing the reader to perceive other times and places through the words and actions of others. Bakhtin called this capacity "novelness" based on his belief that the novel genre best fosters this type of dialogue (Bakhtin, 1990, 1993, 1994a, 1994b, 1998). The work of Dostoevsky, he believed, best represented novelness.

Holquist (1991) wrote that novelness allows us to "see the world by authoring it, by making sense of it through the activity of turning it into a text, by translating it into finalizing schemes that can order its potential chaos—but only by paying the price of reducing the world's variety and endlessness: novelness is the body of utterances that is least reductive of variety" (p. 84). As such, novelness offers us a chance to engage diverse voices in a contrived, closed-off event and negotiate meaning or understanding that can inform our existence in other events. Novelness provides us access to the greatest amount of ideas and positions us to contemplate aesthetically those ideas.

Holquist (1991), in summing up Bakhtin's thought about novelness and its relation to literature, wrote, "Literature is essentially a perceptual activity, a way to see the world that enriches the world's communicability" (p. 85). As a perceptual activity, in reading literature, place and time are suspended. Our experience is the act of reading. We aesthetically contemplate the text, which, although speaking of experiences, positions us in such a way that we are not really experiencing those experiences of which it speaks but perceiving them, or, as is often noted, vicariously experiencing them.

In the following sections, I show that self-generated dramatic arts activities work in similar ways as literature. However, unlike with literature, self-generated dramatic arts activities can position us not only as perceivers of others' ideas and experiences but also as actors in that we are positioned to engage those ideas and experiences in real time, in the here and now. With self-generated dramatic arts activities, our experience is not of a written, bounded text but of the event unfolding before us as participants. Whether we are participant actors or participant observers, our experience is playing out. Through self-generated dramatic arts activities, novelness becomes novelness in action, transforming what is the vicarious experience of reading, or novelness, into a real experience in real time and place, or novelness in action.

METHODS

TeenStreet

TeenStreet is part of a larger community-based theater organization in Chicago called Free Street. Free Street was founded over 35 years ago to "literally take theater" to the more than 97% of the American population who did not attend live drama performances (Worthman, 2002). TeenStreet, the year-round ensemble, is made up of teenagers from around the city. Most of them have no theater experience when they join the ensemble. Most are public-school students. I was a participant-observer of two ensemble productions from 1995 to 1997, or for two years.

Each ensemble included 15 teenagers, with some carryover from year one to year two. In total, 27 teenagers participated during my two years of participant-observation. Of them, 15 self-identified as African Americans, five as Hispanics, five as Whites, one as Cambodian, and one as Korean American. All but three teenagers self-identified as being from low socioeconomic homes.

The data presented here are part of a larger project (Worthman, 2002) that included over 500 hours of participant observation, the collection of program artifacts (including promotional materials, adolescent writing, and scripts in various stages of development), structured interviews with adolescent participants and program staff, and field notes from audience and cast postperformance discussions. I interviewed six of the 27 teenagers, as well as all four members of the staff.

The collection of data using multiple methods allowed for data triangulation (Denzin, 1970; Mathison, 1988) and the creation of rich descriptions of program activities (Geertz, 1973). I used the constant comparative method (Glaser & Strauss, 1967) to guide my continued data collection, including soliciting feedback from the adolescents and staff on my analysis of the data and of their interview transcripts. I analyzed data and developed categories, beginning with the broad category of literacy development, and using analytical induction, refined categories in an effort to capture the dynamic nature of the interactions taking place at TeenStreet.

Early on in my research, I learned that the workings of each ensemble are pretty much the same from year to year. The teenagers rehearse six hours per week, two hours on Thursdays after school and four on Saturdays. Movement, writing, music, voice, drama, and improvisation workshops fill the first five months (October to February) of the eight-month production process. For the purposes of this chapter, since all the activities were self-generated—meaning that the adolescents created their own texts, whether through movement, a piece of music, a written text, a dialogue, or a dramatic scene—I have classified them as self-generated dramatic arts activities. I have done this because of these activities' goals of, first, positioning the adolescents to interact creatively or aesthetically around their real and imagined experiences without the use of outside texts, and second, generating material from those interactions for an ensemble script.

An ensemble script made up entirely of the teenagers' writing and incorporating the movement, dance, drama, and music of the rehearsals was gleaned from the workshops. The workshops were in the tradition of experimental theater. Professor of Performance Theory Richard Schechner (1985) described the workshop method:

> In theater that comes from workshop, there is no preexistent script—or there are too many scripts ("material" or "sources"). The words do not determine everything else but are knitted into a performance text. . . . This kind of work borders on the "human potential movement," a movement that has taken a lot of its technique from theater, dance, and music. . . . When workshops and rehearsals are used together, they constitute a model of the ritual process. Workshops which deconstruct ordinary experience, are like rites of separation and transition while rehearsals, which build up, or construct, new cultural items, are like rites of transition and incorporation. (pp. 20–21)

Simply put, the TeenStreet creative process is one of deconstructing the ordinary lived experiences of the teenage participants and transforming those experiences into "new cultural items," or possible ways of looking at the world, a new secondary Discourse. The process is dialogical, capturing in essence the Bakhtinian concept of dialogism (Bakhtin, 1993, 1994a). For me, the outcome or script was secondary to the process, to the living out and recreating or reimagining of experiences in collaboration or across mediational means. This process of living out or recreating is premised on a particular type of human interaction. The interaction takes place in the reciprocity of self-generated dramatic arts and writing activities. I call this interaction, grounded as it is in aesthetic or creative contemplation, "imaginal interaction" (Worthman, 2002).

All the writing done at TeenStreet represented the concept of imaginal interaction, where as a mediational means, writing was woven with other mediational means such as oral language, movement, music, gestures, drama, and improvisation, with adolescents using multiple mediational means to imaginatively interact with one another. For example, they improvised then wrote, wrote then acted, moved and wrote, revised others' writing, first talked then wrote, and wrote then talked. The adolescents' participation in imaginal interaction did not come naturally at first, but over time it appeared to become second nature to them. It was similar in some ways to descriptions of the sociocultural aspects of emergent literacy development (Bruner, 1983; Dyson, 1995; Heath, 1983; Sulzby, 1985; Teale & Sulzby, 1986), with the TeenStreet adolescents being immersed into a context in which language and texts were used in particular ways and the adolescents coming to appropriate those ways as part of their own repertoires.

A number of researchers and educators have studied out-of-school and community-based dramatic arts settings (Heath & McLaughlin, 1993 Somers, 1996). Heath and McLaughlin found that these out-of-school contexts fostered meaningful and relevant engagement among adolescents who typically struggled in formal school settings. In *Drama and Theatre Education*, Somers (1996) presented drama activities and programs that have both educative and agency-development goals. Practices in these contexts usually positioned participants—both adolescent and adult—to appropriate discourses of critique and possibility to identify and begin addressing issues and concerns relevant to their lives. Such practices were the cornerstone of dramatic theorist Augusto Boal's (1985) work and have become associated with critical pedagogy. Heath and McLaughlin's, Somers', and Boal's work suggested that drama as a way to explore one's life is effective at helping people make sense of and communicate their experiences and understandings of what is being explored, whether that is their lives, communities, or some other content. Although I, too, was interested in the effectiveness of TeenStreet practices, in this chapter I theorize why the practices were effective—that is, how is it that the type of secondary Discourse promoted by TeenStreet positioned teenagers to interact, and to what end.

Herrero School

A central question of mine during this research was what might the use of self-generated dramatic arts activities, and the imaginal interaction that takes place around those activities, mean for and look like in a more formal education structure such as a classroom. The difference between school and out-of-school contexts is that the boundaries of what is possible in school often has to be negotiated through and around the curriculum, yet this in and of itself does not minimize the value of self-generated dramatic arts activities in classroom contexts. Mandell and Wolf (2003) described the social nature of dramatic activities within a classroom context and offered numerous activities to facilitate such original play development that incorporates existing curriculum. Like Mandell and Wolf and many other educators, I draw on the work of Dorothy Heathcote (Heathcote & Bolton, 1995) and Betty Jane Wagner (1999) to define what is possible within a classroom that incorporates the dramatic arts. Their work supports the adapting TeenStreet practice for classroom instruction as a way of making content relevant to students' lives and as a way of helping students take ownership not only of the curriculum but also of language and literacy practices.

A year or so after I finished my research at TeenStreet, I taught writing to 15 sixth- and seventh-grade English language learners (ELLs) two days per week for 90 minutes each day, in a large urban public school I will call "Herrero School." Many of the students in this classroom had been in the United States for two years or less, and all of them had begun their school lives in Mexico, Puerto Rico, or Ecuador. All the students spoke Spanish as their first language but had developed or were developing communicative competence in English (Cummins, 2001) and were beginning to develop conventional English reading and writing abilities. All of the students were from low-income, working-class families.

My work with the students at Herrero School was done in conjunction with and in support of the regular classroom teacher's language arts program. However, I developed my own curriculum and was responsible for the three hours per week we spent together. During this time, the classroom teacher assisted me. My goal was to help the adolescents improve their English language arts skills. I did this by modifying and implementing many of the self-generated dramatic arts activities that I learned at TeenStreet. Modification included incorporating the class's language arts goals and standards into activities, using classroom resources such as children's books and textbooks, and making prominent the use of talking, listening, reading, and writing during the activities.

Over the course of my year teaching writing to this group of adolescents, I wrote field notes after each class session, reflecting on the activities of that session, and subsequently I wrote narrative descriptions that I shared with the classroom teacher. I also collected students' writing and drawings, and often had conferences with students to discuss their work. The notes from those conferences are part of my dataset. Data were analyzed through the lens created by my understanding of sociocultural definitions of literacy and Bakhtin's theory of knowledge. This lens was tinted by my experience at TeenStreet. The relationship of these two experiences—my teaching writing to ELLs and my working with a teen theater ensemble—proved serendipitous to my evolving understanding of literacy development and the role of self-generated dramatic arts activities in that development.

SCENE ONE: NOVELNESS IN ACTION

The teenagers at TeenStreet had just finished a voice activity in which they stood face to face and tried to anticipate—to contemplate aesthetically—what one another said. David, the executive director and one of the instructors of the program, pulled all but one of four groups—the group of Anita, Jared, and Lisa—off the floor. He told the other teenagers to get notebooks. He asked two of the teenagers to try to write down everything that is said and done by Anita, Jared, and Lisa. He asked the others to write whatever they want, focusing either on what is being said or done, or what they, as writers, are thinking. David positioned Jared, Anita, and Lisa shoulder-to-shoulder and facing the other teenagers. He told them to start talking, focusing on, and responding to one another's words. By this, he meant that the three were to listen closely to what one another was saying and respond with whatever came to mind, a free flow of conversation analogous to freewriting activities. It was a process I came to identify as one of many self-generated dramatic arts activities that made up the secondary Discourse of TeenStreet.

As the three talked, one of them mentioned the color brown, and Anita started talking about brown milk and chocolate milk with white marshmallows.

Jared interrupted her. "What are you talking about?" he said. "Do you know what brown is?" He started talking about other colors—red, blue, green—finally saying that red dirt is really brown. Then he said his skin is brown. He held one of his arms straight out in front of him. "Brown skin," he said over and over, "like the soil, like the Earth." Jared continued, his words evolving into the assertion that African Americans are workers of the soil and of assembly lines. "We always worked. Still do," he continued.

As he talked, Lisa looked at Jared and then held her arm up to his. Hers was a lighter brown color than Jared's. Anita was still between them. Lisa's and Jared's arms aligned in front of her. "My skin is light brown," Lisa said.

Jared appeared not to hear what Lisa said, and continued with his own connections to the color brown: "We were promised 40 acres and a mule for slaving. . . . But we got nothin'. Nothin'," he repeated over and over.

Anita stared down at their arms, and then looked from Lisa's face to Jared's. She held up her arm next to their arms. Hers was a pale red color, not quite pink but not white either. "I'm a marshmallow," she said as she stared at the three arms.

Jared continued: "We still worked. We grew cotton . . . picked it . . . everything. That's our marshmallow. That's brown and white together. Our brown hands made it. . . . We came north to work in your factories."

"Chocolate with marshmallow middle," Lisa said, laughing. "Ooh, I like chocolate with marshmallow middles. They taste good."

Anita concurred and talked about the chocolate melting on her face and the gooey marshmallow getting stuck between her teeth.

Jared refused to let Lisa and Anita steer the conversation away from his concerns, even as it appeared they did not want to listen to him. He pulled his arm away from theirs and rolled his eyes at both of them. Lisa continued, her voice becoming more high-pitched as she spoke, as if she were becoming younger and younger. "Hmmm, hot chocolate with melted marshmallow all mixed together. Light brown, like me."

Anita quickly looked at Jared but continued to hold her arm next to Lisa's. She did not say anything. She looked at her arm and Lisa's arm and then at Jared's face, who only shook his head and said, "This is serious brown." It appeared as if Anita and Lisa did not hear Jared because they continued talking about chocolate and marshmallows. End Scene One.

Anita's and Lisa's failures to hear or take up Jared's story were alleviated by Jared's success at getting the other teenagers—the ones who were writing—to respond. Here was what three teenagers wrote in response to the interaction:

> A human being can explode by holding so much anger inside or just certain things that irritate, haunts, or bothers them. A human being can lose their self control, or temper, and explode by being ticked off a lot or

being hurt real badly emotionally. Some human beings can explode by being overwhelmed by things that they are not used to, hallucinating or just exaggerating things.

A human being can only take so much. But none y'all do not hear me though.

* * *

Radical Noise, Gospel, Jazz Rhythm and Blues, Rap
Black Music.
Illegal...........Distribute.
Illegal sale's distributed, sex, drugs.
Black Market.
Stock market crash.
Black!
The bad guys wear black. Objection your honor.
Evil mistress, black widow,
Followed by evil black shadow.
You think I don't know.
When disease wipes out millions of people. God is punishing us. God is black.
Santa is black.
You think I don't know. Self-conscience—psychology in reverse.
You think I don't know.
You think I do not know that everything you hear is black.
I am black and the world shall bow as I cross thy path for I am the one who
Brings bad luck.
Black Cat.
No one cares what you have to say—at least no one in your community cares, because you keep pushing it in my face trying to shove it down my throat that I am black, like I don't know that already.
Your cameras.
Your indifference.
Do you care or do you want people to think you do?
Why you keep on pushing me? A train going faster than my chaotic brain is all I see. Why? Okay! Who cares?
Are you deprived, underpriveleged? And yet those Jordans [designer basketball shoes] wouldn't suggest it. No goodwill tags on your floor.
A kiss up. Wanting to look bad in order to look good.

These responses demonstrate multivoicedness in the interpretation of the scene, complicating it by adding nuance and even contradiction. The responses appear empathetic, ironic, and skeptical, respectively, as they weave other voices into the mix of making sense of this scene. As such, the scene presented the interaction of multiple perspectives that interpreted differently what Jared, Lisa, and Anita were doing and saying. These perspectives represented the other teenagers' ability to critique and reflect creatively on and make sense of the words and actions that played out before them.

In Scene One, Jared was obviously dissatisfied with Anita's and Lisa's responses to his figurative interpretation of the color brown and the historical and social implications he made in this interpretation. His idea or understanding was ignored. As he saw it, the discussion should have been more serious ("This is serious brown.") than Anita and Lisa took it to be. They were obviously uncomfortable, however, with where Jared was trying to direct the interaction. They tried to redirect it—or respond—by redefining the imagery and intonation of the discussion. Their understanding of brown was different than Jared's, and was captured in the image of chocolates with marshmallow centers. Their intonation was not serious, and as Jared pressed the seriousness of his concerns, Anita and Lisa appeared to become childlike in their responses. The scene was a heteroglossia, a roiling mass of voices demanding to be responded to. And it was dialogical, even as it was not satisfying to all participants.

Part of the dialogue of Scene One was the adolescent writing. I presented only three of these voices. The first appeared sympathetic to Jared. Psychological in form, this piece empathized with Jared's struggles of not being heard, which gives additional representation to the historical and social concerns of which Jared spoke. The piece presented a perspective that was grounded in individual struggle and internal turmoil that was caused by the world. The second piece offered competing perspectives of race, a theme implicit in Jared's voice. The piece poetically played on the figurative meaning of *black* or *blackness*, presenting stereotypes (black as deficient, evil, and bad) and challenging our conceptions ("psychology in reverse"): "Santa is black." "God is black." Together, these contradictory notions problematized racial relationships, and implicitly brought into question taken-for-granted perspectives. The third piece, unlike the first two, responded directly to Jared, being the voice of the other and speaking to why Jared was not heard. It was a voice that was explicit in its interpretation of Jared's words, possibly in support of Lisa's and Anita's refusal to take up what he said. This piece was a challenge to Jared's perspective, a counter-perspective, asking, "Do you care or do you want people to think you do?"

In my making sense of what was happening in the scene and in the subsequent writing, I drew on the adolescents' voices, allowing them to inform my understanding in a process similar to what Bakhtin believed happens when we read literature. The texts, in the forms of the event playing out and of the subsequent writing, were created as the scene unfolded, as Anita, Jared, and Lisa interacted. Thus, unlike with my aesthetic contemplation of all that took place and was written, for the adolescents, through their participation in the self-generated dramatic arts activities, there was immediacy to their experience of the event and the writing. Unlike with literature, the self-generated dramatic arts activity positioned the adolescents to take up authorship and to move beyond being only perceivers. The adolescents experienced, perceived, and negotiated understanding of the event not only by positioning their voices in response to others but also by hearing others respond to their own utterances, something that occurred in the interaction between Jared, Anita, and Lisa and in the subsequent sharing of the writing among all the adolescents.

Having teenagers respond to each other's writing and movement was TeenStreet's way of facilitating aesthetic contemplation. Yet, TeenStreet took this interaction further than Bakhtin could possibly warrant in his description of a reader's engagement with a text. With self-generated dramatic arts activities, the participants' experiences are not of the distantly authored text and remote characters but of the events unfolding before them in their interactions with one another, including the close-by authors of written text. TeenStreet, in effect, positioned teenagers to take up aesthetic contemplation by creating a space and a means for them to take text, written or otherwise, in different directions descriptively and thematically, to literally conceptualize possibilities and allow them to play out on stage and in discussion.

Through self-generated dramatic arts activities, the teenagers experienced what played out on the stage before them. These experiences were bounded by a defined time and space, allowing the teenagers to act on those experiences in their totality. Yet, unlike with published literature, the experiences on stage were immediate and real, being lived out in present time. They were each teenager's real and imagined experiences being not only aesthetically contemplated but also aesthetically created and recreated by the teenagers through their interactions.

None of this is to suggest that the event or scene was a free-for-all, with all voices having equal authority or relevance, or even that the speaker was heard in ways that he or she wished, as Anita and Lisa showed in their refusal to engage Jared. Emerson (1997) wrote:

> Read Bakhtin carefully, and you will see that nowhere does he suggest that dialogue between real people necessarily brings truth, beauty, happiness, or honesty. It brings only concretization (and even that is temporary), and the possibility of change, of some forward movement. Under optimal conditions, dialogue provides options. But there can still be mutual deception, mountains of lies exchanged, pressing desires unanswered or unregistered, gratuitous cruelty administered on terrain to which only the intimate beloved has access. By having a real other respond to me, I am spared one thing only: the worst cumulative effects of my own echo chamber of words. (p. 152–153)

What novelness in action offers, and, in turn, what self-generated dramatic arts activities facilitate, is a way for people to move beyond their unique yet limited perspectives and experience other perspectives, including possibly more diverse perspectives than they could experience in everyday life. Novelness in action has the potential to help participants move beyond their own experiences and enter into genuine dialogical relationships with other ideas, with the ideas of others.

SCENE TWO: CREATING AND RECREATING OUR STORIES AT HERRERO SCHOOL

TeenStreet fostered a particular type of literacy, one premised on the importance of participants' interaction around one another's real and imagined stories. Ultimately, the value of this literacy is in what it adds to the repertoires of those who master it. Although I have no evidence to suggest that the secondary Discourse of TeenStreet improved participants' language, reading, and writing skills, the Scene One description does suggest that the adolescents readily engaged one another using both oral and written language and in doing so proffered possible interpretations for one another's real and imagined experiences. These possible interpretations demonstrated the adolescents' abilities to appropriate others' experiences and language use and not only make sense of them but also imbue them with new meaning. In this regard, they were participating in meaningful language use.

Based on Gee's conception of Discourses and Bakhtin's ideas about inner speech, I saw the ability of the adolescents to engage one another aesthetically at TeenStreet as a literacy that they will take with them as they move among other sites of practice. This literacy has the potential to help the adolescents engage and make sense of other perspectives and other sites of practice. Because the adolescents readily took up the TeenStreet secondary Discourse and mastered it, and through that mastery began to use language in ways they seldom had before—using it to engage one another aesthetically—I saw this type of literacy as potentially relevant to other contexts, such as school, in which one of the goals is to get students to use language to make sense of their experiences. In the case of school, these experiences are often of academic content and of learning ways to use language and text. The students at Herrero School were all English language learners who had to learn both a new language and new academic content. Ways of getting them to engage one another and the academic content were essential to their school success. Bringing the secondary Discourse of TeenStreet into the classroom was one way of doing this.

To get the adolescents I taught at Herrero School to experience telling their stories and to begin to apprentice them into the type of literacy I experienced at TeenStreet, during the first month of our time together I had each student stand in front of the class and act out and orally tell about a recent experience he or she had. I modeled this process by telling of an experience I had as a youth and role-playing different parts of the experience. Most students welcomed this type of activity after overcoming initial hesitations. A few students, however, refused to participate, but, through observing, came to demonstrate in their own writing the process of storytelling I was introducing.

In an effort to encourage the participation of all the students, we spent two classes in a whole-group format imaginatively describing our walks to school. At first, many students said they never saw anything on their way to school. This led us to create group stories on an overhead projector about seeing what we never would expect to see, such as Martians, two-headed people, talking animals, and an assortment of television superheroes. Our stories about walking to school were our first efforts at transforming stories or allowing multiple voices to enter into them—that is, to contemplate aesthetically others' stories.

The acting scenarios and oral retellings introduced students to the nature of interaction that I thought would foster the literacy I experienced at TeenStreet. I also thought it would help them build a repertoire of stories—theirs and others'—upon which to draw later. An example of this oral retelling and transformation of an experience is the following story told by Eduardo with the help of my prompts.

Eduardo: On Sunday, I went to a baby shower of my cousin. It was a surprise shower.
Chris: Oh yeah. Was she surprised?
Eduardo: Yes.
Chris: What did you do to surprise her?
Eduardo: She came in and we—we were hiding—and we jumped up. She came in and we jumped up and yelled "surprise."
Chris: That's good. What did she do?
Eduardo: She jumped. She—she had the baby [laughing] right then . . . and . . .
Chris: Really? That must have—
Eduardo: No (laughing). She just look like it.

Eduardo's first line was the retelling of an event. He set out a conflict: wanting to surprise his cousin without her finding out. With my prompting, an imaginary crisis arises, one that was humorously created by Eduardo but grounded in a real experience (including what his cousin looked like when she was surprised). The imaginary crisis of the cousin going into labor from the shock of the surprise arose from Eduardo aesthetically contemplating not only his experience but also his cousin's—that is, what it must have been like for her to be surprised and what possibly could have happened.

Over time, the whole-class storytelling activities demonstrated to me that my students understood what I meant when I asked them to tell of an experience and to envision other possibilities of that experience. After it was clear to me that they understood, I often put students in pairs where they would tell their partners about experiences from the past week. I walked around the room and listened to the talk, focusing on language use. Students then shared their partners' stories with the whole class with the prerequisite of needing to interpret from their own perspectives the experiences of their partners.

During one of these pairing-up sessions, instead of asking them to retell their partners' stories to the whole group, I asked the students to write a fictionalized account of their partners' stories, either reimagining the experiences or taking words, phrases, or incidents from the experiences that appealed to them and creating a story around those excerpted parts. Rachel told Alicia of her weekend dilemma of having to choose between the need to clean her room and the desire to go shopping for a winter coat. In her story, she cleaned her room instead of going shopping with her father, who could not wait for her because he had to go to work. Alicia took Rachel's story, interpreted it, and wrote this story:

> At morning, a girl named Jasmyn went to go to breakfast in her house. Her mother called Jasmyn to go and clean her room. After she clean her room, her father came from work and said do you want to go to the store to buy a jacket.

This was typical of Alicia's writing style and length. In this story, she aesthetically contemplated Rachel's story and tried to respond to her dilemma by reversing the order of events. Instead of going shopping and then to work, Jasmyn's father came from work and asked Jasmyn to go shopping, after she had already cleaned her room.

The next class period, with Rachel's and Alicia's permission, I wrote Alicia's story on the board. Two students took turns reading it aloud. After they read, I asked both students what stood out to them, what they wanted to know more about, and what they would have done in that situation. After that, the class talked about the story, ending this discussion with the sharing of ideas or brainstorming about what other things could have happened to Jasmyn in the morning. The students honed in on Jasmyn's breakfast experiences. Because of that, I asked students about their own breakfast experiences. We discussed these experiences, and then began to write a different version of Jasmyn's morning on the overhead projector, with a majority of the students contributing to the process.

> In the morning, Jasmyn went to breakfast. She didn't want to eat her mother's cooking anymore. I don't like your cooking mama. I want to cook my own food. Do it then, said Mama. I'm tired of cooking for you. Jasmyn was suddenly happy and started cooking. I'm going to make comote con leche. She got out all the stuff and started to make her breakfast. The mother was mad and she stood there staring at her daughter. Jasmyn told her mother that she was a better cook than her mother. No, you're not, I'm better. I don't care about that. Try this. Jasmyn tried to give her mother some of the camote con leche. Her mother said, Oooh, that's nasty. But later on when Jasmyn was eating her mother asked her if she liked it. Jasmyn said of course I like it. Do you want some? The mother said let me taste. She liked it. She said, Jasmyn, you cook better than me. But you said you never would eat my food but now you finished it, said Jasmyn.

The group story took on a different theme, moving away from Rachel's story and Alicia's account of it. Working as a class, students developed the group story in a matter of minutes, although each plot twist and the end were not known ahead of time. The students were living out the story as it was written. Each line or idea was fodder for others' ideas and thoughts.

Six of the 14 students present that day were active participants in the group storywriting process. They continually suggested story ideas and provided descriptions and sentence possibilities without being prompted. I copied students' sentences verbatim and asked if that is what they wanted to say. Five other students added to the story when asked what they thought. Throughout the process, I asked such questions as: "What do you think happened next?" and "What would you do if this were you?"

Because I was unsure of what *camote con leche* was, we spent 20 minutes during the middle of our composing time discussing how it is made and listing the ingredients and the cooking steps on the chalkboard. We had three different recipes, each offered by a different student. Sara and Miguel, two of the recipe providers, stood in front of the class and improvised making *camote con leche*, explaining as they went along what they were doing as if they each hosted a television cooking show. When we finished the story, three groups of mothers/fathers and daughters/sons acted out the story.

Scene Two, like Scene One, is an example of novelness in action. The adolescents aesthetically contemplated the text as it was revealed and recreated, authoring it by infusing it with multiple voices. They did this through talk and improvisation and by writing individual stories and then a group story. The evolution of Rachel's story to the group story was grounded in a growing perspectival complexity. First, Alicia transformed the events of Rachel's story to solve Rachel's dilemma. In it, she voiced another possibility: cleaning her room and then going shopping after her father returned from work. More significantly, however, Alicia created a mother figure in her story. In her oral telling, Rachel did not mention her mother. She also said that cleaning her room was something she did every Saturday morning without being told. Alicia introduced the mother—in this case, Jasmyn's mother—and had her take up the domestic responsibility of ensuring the home is in order. Thus, within this short new story, another voice (the mother's) was added. Whether purposely or not, Alicia added a complexity and tension to the story that was not explicit before.

The tension that is possible around domestic responsibilities was made even more explicit in the group story as a conflict is created around differences of perspective. In this story, the mother's domestic responsibility was broadened to include the role of cook. The students captured a tension that commonly arises around domestic events: adolescents asserting their independence by taking up perspectives and acting contrary to expectations. In other words, Jasmine challenged the role of her mother as cook by claiming to be a better cook. After first saying her food was nasty, the mother finally agreed that Jasmine was a better cook. The mother's perspective evolved as the event unfolded. In the mother's validating of Jasmyn's perspective, the tension was alleviated and there appeared to be new understanding between the mother and Jasmine, an understanding that broadened the mother's perspective and enhanced Jasmine's. The students arrived at this possible reality through aesthetically contemplating the event originally recalled from Rachel's perspective, interpreting the story from their own places and times, and thus creating a new story infused with their own understandings and, I suggest, their aspirations.

This new story and the self-generated dramatic arts activities that took place around it demonstrate evolving perspectives around the stereotypical role of the mother who is first presented in Alicia's story. By the time the students began role playing the making of *comote con leche* and the group story, a reversal of roles was taking place with boys in the class taking on those stereotypical roles. The self-generated dramatic arts activities facilitated these role reversals. The dramatization of the story presented alternative realities that individually the students had not considered. In the end, these realities appeared to be viable options, or viable ways of acting and speaking in the world. As Bakhtin might have noted, these students authored a possible world.

SELF-GENERATED DRAMATIC ARTS ACTIVITIES AND THE LITERACY THEY FACILITATE

Scenes One and Two demonstrate how self-generated dramatic arts activities mediate and communicate adolescents' understanding of the world. Here, I would also include the writing of the whole-class story as a dramatic arts activity because of the role-play it precipitated. I suggest that self-generated dramatic arts activities enhanced these adolescents' senses of agency by emboldening them to be critical and creative in their perspective-taking and to perceive and even experience ways of being that are different from their lived realities. This is the potential of novelness in action. I have four reasons for thinking all of this. These four reasons are characteristics of the literacy developed with the use of these activities.

First, the self-generated dramatic arts activities affirmed the adolescents' lived experiences, while allowing them to reveal only what they wanted to reveal of those experiences. The reciprocal use of self-generated dramatic arts activities and other mediational means, including writing, helped communicate experience in ways the adolescents chose. It also allowed others to contemplate aesthetically those experiences in ways that they wanted. Thus, the adolescents' perspectives of the world were given prominence in the activities and seen as viable interpretations of the world.

Second, and in relation to the first characteristic, self-generated dramatic arts activities can involve various combinations and uses of movement, dance, improvisation, drama, and writing, or what I have termed "imaginal interaction." The adolescents, however, used language, including written text, as a primary mediational means. It was a means that usually mediated other mediational means. However, with self-generated dramatic arts activities, the adolescents used language and experienced writing for the purpose of aesthetic contemplation. This purpose appeared to be more relevant and meaningful to the adolescents, giving writing a relevance it often did not have in other contexts and enhancing their abilities to make sense of the world using multiple mediational means (Worthman, 2002).

Third, the self-generated dramatic arts activities allowed adolescents to enter into dialogue with one another as manifested in the concept of novelness in action. They were introduced to multiple voices or perspectives and encouraged to contemplate aesthetically those voices in relation to their own. The adolescents had a chance to voice their understanding of their and others' real and imagined experiences, and to transform through language and other mediational means what these experiences looked like or might mean. As such, the adolescents' understanding of themselves and of the world was enriched by other perspectives, or, as Bakhtin might say, new ideas were born and lived.

And last, self-generated dramatic arts activities enhanced the adolescents' telling or discourse ability by providing practice in storytelling and by creating a reservoir of knowledge—one's own stories as well as others'—to draw on in future interactions. The activities allowed the adolescents to bring prior knowledge to the fore as a resource to draw on in language use, both oral and written, and to take away from these experiences other stories and, more importantly, new ways of interacting and using texts that can be appropriated in other contexts.

The activities apprenticed the adolescents into a new literacy, one that through active and conscious participation they were mastering. The adolescents were learning not only the skills associated with this literacy—the ways of decoding and encoding texts—but also the behaviors, or the ways of thinking, feeling, acting, and interacting, that define this literacy. This literacy is premised on the importance of human interaction and the sharing of real and imagined experiences. It is also premised on listening and responding to others as a conscious act, wherein listening and responding are part of an effort to aesthetically contemplate other possibilities, and other ways of making sense of the world. Bakhtin believed that novelness as a way of dialogue fostered this type of contemplation. Self-generated dramatic arts activities have the potential to do the same, but with more immediacy and, because participants' stories form the text of interactions, more relevance.

For those concerned about encoding and decoding texts, telling one's stories or experiences positions adolescents to use text in meaningful and relevant ways, ways precipitated on dialogue that offers up as many voices as participants present. And with self-generated dramatic arts activities, there are more mediational means, and there may be more voices as participants create and try out new perspectives. The written texts become objects of engagement, with writers having opportunities to hear how others make meaning of their texts and to learn of other possibilities, both in content and form. Ultimately, as Bakhtin believed, we can only expand our own understanding by learning of others' perspectives, and self-generated dramatic arts activities position us to do that.

REFERENCES

Bakhtin, M. M. (1990). *Art and answerability: Early philosophical essays* (V. Liapunov, Trans.). Austin, TX: University of Texas Press.

Bakhtin, M. M. (1993). *Toward a philosophy of the act* (V. Liapunov, Trans.). Austin, TX: University of Texas Press.

Bakhtin, M. M. (1994a). *Problems of Dostoevsky's poetics* (C. Emerson, Trans.). Minneapolis, MN: University of Minnesota Press.

Bakhtin, M. M. (1994b). *Speech genres & other late essays* (V. W. McGee, Trans.). Austin, TX: University of Texas Press.

Bakhtin, M. M. (1998). *The dialogic imagination* (C. Emerson & M. Holquist, Trans.). Austin, TX: University of Texas Press

Barton, D., & Hamilton, M. (1998). *Local literacies: Reading and writing in one community.* London: Routledge.

Boal, A. (1985). *Theater of the oppressed* (C. A. McBride & M.-O. McBride, Trans.). New York: Theater Communications Group.

Bruner, J. (1983). *Child's talk.* New York: Horton.

Clark, K., & Holquist, M. (1984). *Mikhail Bakhtin.* Cambridge, MA: Harvard University Press.

Cummins, J. (2001). *Negotiating identities: Education for empowerment in a diverse society* (2nd ed.). Los Angeles: California Association for Bilingual Education.

Denzin, N. K. (1970). *The research act: A theoretical introduction to sociological methods.* Chicago: Aldine.

Dyson, A. H. (1995). Writing children: Reinventing the development of childhood literacy. *Written Communication, 12*(1), 4–46.

Emerson, C. (1997). *The first hundred years of Mikhail Bakhtin.* Princeton, NJ: Princeton University Press.

Gee, J. (1996). *Social linguistics and literacies: Ideology in discourses* (2nd ed.). London: Falmer.

Geertz, C. (1973). Thick description: Toward an interpretive theory of culture. In C. Geertz (Ed.), *The interpretation of cultures* (pp. 3–30). New York: Basic Books.

Glaser, B., & Strauss, A. (1967). *The discovery of grounded theory.* Chicago: Aldine.

Heath, S. B. (1983). *Ways with words: Language, life, and work in communities and classrooms.* New York: Cambridge University Press.

Heath, S. B., & McLaughlin, M. W. (Eds.) (1993). *Identity and inner-city youth: Beyond ethnicity and gender.* New York: Teachers College Press.

Heathcote, D., & Bolton, G. (1995). *Drama for learning: Dorothy Heathcote's mantle of the expert approach to education.* Portsmouth, NH: Heinemann.

Holquist, M. (1991). *Dialogism: Bakhtin and his world.* London: Routledge.

Mandell, J., & Wolf, J. L. (2003). *Acting, learning, & change: Creating original plays with adolescents.* Portsmouth, NH: Heinemann.

Mathison, S. (1988). Why triangulate? *Educational Researcher, 17*(2), 13–17.

Rosenblatt, L. (1983). *Literature as exploration* (4th ed.). New York: Modern Language Association.

Schechner, R. (1985). *Between theater and anthropology.* Philadelphia, PA: University of Pennsylvania Press.

Scribner, S. (1984). Literacy in three metaphors. *American Journal of Education, 93*(1), 6–21.

Scribner, S., & Cole, M. (1981). *The psychology of literacy.* Cambridge, MA: Harvard University Press.

Somers, J. (Ed.). (1996). *Drama and theatre in education: Contemporary research.* North York, Ontario: Captus.

Street, B. V. (Ed.). (1993). *Cross-cultural approaches to literacy.* New York: Cambridge University Press.

Sulzby, E. (1985). Children's emergent reading of favorite storybooks: A developmental study. *Reading Research Quarterly, 20*(4), 458–481.

Teale, W. H., & Sulzby, E. (Eds.). (1986). *Emergent literacy: Writing and reading.* Norwood, NJ: Ablex.

Tompkins, J. P. (Ed.). (1980). *Reader-response criticism: From formalism to post-structuralism.* Baltimore, MD: Johns Hopkins University Press.

Vygotsky, L. S. (1986). *Thought and language* (A. Kozulin, Trans.). Cambridge, MA: The MIT Press.

Wagner, B. J. (Ed.). (1999). *Building moral communities through educational drama.* Stamford, CT: Ablex.

Wilhelm, J. D. (1997). *"You gotta be the book": Teaching engaged and reflective reading with adolescents.* New York: Teachers College Press.

Worthman, C. (2002). *Just playing the part: Engaging adolescents in drama and literacy.* New York: Teachers College Press.

•31•

"WE AS STYLIST ACTUALLY BECOME LIKE PSYCHIATRISTS": PROBLEM SOLVING IN PUBLIC PERFORMANCE

Yolanda J. Majors
UNIVERSITY OF ILLINOIS AT CHICAGO

My consideration of socially situated literacy practices begins by examining the process of social reading of oral narrative texts within an African American hair salon (Majors, 2004).[1] The rapid change of U.S. demographics is just one of several factors that have politicians, researchers, and educators clamoring to understand the relationship between particular social, cultural, and/or ethnic group membership and school performance (Gee 2000; Darling-Hammond, 2002). Many claims have been made suggesting that there is educational importance in the literate knowledge base that students, in particular minority students, construct through their social and linguistic practices (Barton & Hamilton, 1998; Cazden, 1988; Cole, 1996; Delpit, 1995; Gee, 1992; Heath, 1983; Hull & Schultz, 2002; Lee & Majors, 2003). Recent studies, for example, call attention to the "difference in the social and academic prestige of written" texts in the home and school lives of ESOL students (Skilton-Sylvester, 2003). It is important to be aware of such differences, in value and practice, of home and school literacy across contexts.

Bringing attention to the range in students' literacy practices across contexts, however, "does not translate into an intentional building of bridges" between them (Resnick, 2003). Neither does it translate into an acceptance of home and community practices, which shape and frame the literate skills the students bring into the classrooms or teachers' abilities to harness these in important and productive ways. Unfortunately, few empirical studies exist that investigate the socially and academically relevant literate skills cultivated within and across communities and culturally responsive classrooms (Ladson-Billings, 1994; Lee & Majors, 2003; Ball, 1992; Gay, 2000).

Further research is warranted examining the interplay of language and community in meaning-making practices that goes beyond acknowledging an existence of cultural funds. In recent years, researchers have contributed valuable empirical evidence as to how these funds are taken up in classrooms, in particular by those who are labeled "underachieving" (Gutierrez, Baquedano-Lopez, & Tejeda, 1999; Lee, 2004). This is important, particularly as our tendency is to posit overly generalized questions regarding the inequities in student achievement and performance, while our assumptions about the identities, values, skills, and reasoning abilities of students who academically underperform, the languages they speak, and the communities they come from seemingly embody the same deficit models, limiting our responses.

Specifically, this paper looks to examine the role of culturally situated discourse and nonlinguistic practices within a community hair salon. This work argues that an inquiry that investigates literacy practices through African American Vernacular English (AAVE) in particular is needed across multiple sites if educators and researchers are to respond to the discontinuities between cultural ways of knowing and school knowledge.

Researchers of language and learning have argued that success and failure in school is contingent upon one's ability to successfully navigate processes of meaning making through discourses (Cazden, 1988; Cole, 1996; Delpit, 1995; Gee, 1992; Heath, 1983; Lee & Majors, 2003). What role, then, do the processes and skills

[1] Portions of the research described here were funded by a Spencer Foundation Dissertation Fellowship Award to the author in 2000 and The National Council of Teachers of English Cultivating New Voices Among Scholars of Color Grants Program. The views expressed here are those of the author and do not reflect those of the Spencer Foundation or NCTE.

of reading linguistic and paralinguistic cues play in facilitating this navigation?

THE SKILL OF SOCIAL READING

Social reading is an active evaluation of some action in events by protagonists (texts), whose actions, thoughts, and feelings are collaboratively and publicly interpreted by local group members in light of local notions of what is right, wrong, and just. The skill of social reading involves both coherence and an appropriation of cultural norms for talk and tellership; temporal, logical, and referential continuity; inferencing as well as narrative composing; and telling skills as a way of fathoming the social and moral meanings of life and everyday events. In social reading, both collaborative sense making and performance are critical. Readers of narrative texts "may dialogically probe alternate, sometimes conflicting, versions of what (could have) transpired in an event and attempt to piece together moral perspectives on events" (Ochs & Capps, 2001). Readings of narrative texts call for openness to contingency, improvisation, and revision. In the context of everyday conversation (discourse), such narratives also require skillful collaboration with interlocutors "who may desire soothing coherence, but may yield to the quest for experiential complexities and alternative possibilities" (2001, p. 63).

The skill of reading the social relations and intentionality embedded within socially constructed oral narrative texts—instances of oral or written language in use within specific social (group) discourses—are rehearsed and developed within specific discourse communities like the African American hair salon. Arguably, cultural border-crossers—people who actively move across the socially constructed and imposed divides (borders) that help to distinguish cultural groups/discourse communities—one from another, develop the skills of social reading through their participation within such communities as well as through their movement across different kinds of communities (Majors & Orellana, 2006). In this paper I am asking how discourse frames social reading while also impacting meaning-making within one African American hair salon. Though the focus of this paper is the community context, my ultimate concern does not end there, but rather in the urban high-school classroom where I teach and where my students and I construct meanings with and through similar patterns of discourse.

Arguably all people (not just those who frequent hair salons) engage in reading social texts and performing roles. However, the skill of reading the social relations and roles embedded within these oral display texts may be heightened for many African American people who have simultaneously and historically been denied societal power, yet must navigate across institutions, and interface daily with groups who hold and exercise such power (Majors & Orellana, 2006). The skill of reading social relations within events that are socially reconstructed as oral narrative texts (Fairclough, 2003; Ochs & Capps, 2001) is one that can be harnessed and should be acknowledged and cultivated by teachers of linguistic and cultural minority students in general, African American and Latino students in particular. Why?

While members of these historically oppressed and marginalized groups may be skillful readers of social relations and sophisticated problem solvers in community-based contexts, too often they do not experience success at navigating the processes of problem solving in school. When their linguistic, social, and cultural toolkits are recognized, they are too often viewed as localized, impermeable, and harnessable only within contexts rather than across them. My current body of work challenges the tendency in research, which assumes that bringing attention to the range in students' literacy practices will generate success. It also challenges the current practice of ignoring how students' out-of-school skills can be incorporated into successful problem solving strategies.

Though this chapter focuses on my study of talk in urban hair salons, my work as a Secondary Language Arts Instructor in an urban high school has shown that students will take up similar discourse patterns that involve social reading while engaging in problem solving strategies. For example, during one day's writing unit discussion (framed around understanding structures of argumentation), my 10th to 12th graders engaged in a process of social reading while attempting to take up alternative perspectives in written texts. The written text was a downloaded news release from CNN.com, referring to William Bennett's statement that aborting "every black baby in this country" would reduce the crime rate was a sound argument (CNN.com, 2005). However, it seemed that before students could take up this written text, there was some heavy engagement in which the students spent a great deal of time representing their own perspectives across three contexts: their own lives, the broader social community, and the textual context in which Bennett's comments were made. In doing so, students were able to use discursive practices familiar to them to engage in strategies for determining what the text was, who was meant to be the reader, and how to best respond to a text that could be disempowering. These discursive practices involved both social-reading strategies and norms for talk that were similar to those found within the discourse in the salon (Majors, 2007).

THEORETICAL ORIENTATION

Elsewhere, I have considered how participants within the hair salon read the ways in which they and other members of the community are positioned within academic discourses and evaluated by others (Majors, 2003). Such readings are illuminated in this chapter, which focuses on the public performances of African American women jointly involved in Shoptalk in an African American, Midwestern hair salon (Majors, 2003, 2004). "Shoptalk" is my invented term for a specific genre of conversational discourse (Majors, 2003). The term focuses on not just the location of talk, but also (a) a discourse of shared technical and professional expertise; (b) an interactional and highly dynamic way of talk that includes both stylists and clients; and (c) a transformative medium through which both participants and nonparticipants can interrogate, contest, and make sense of the world. It is often through Shoptalk that the activities of the participants and their subsequent roles within many rural and urban, African American hair salons get directed.

In this chapter I direct my attention to one particular aspect of Shoptalk: participants' narrated readings of social texts as attempts to forge their own identities and problem solve in the context of cross-cultural interactions. Individuals' constructions and readings of social texts are constituted and narrated through talk in the hair salon, talk which reflects participants' racialized, gendered, and social-class positions. As indicated in the introduction of this chapter, the present work focuses on examining the role of culturally situated discourse and nonlinguistic practices within a community hair salon. Such practices may provide an alternative space that structures opportunities for students to work through the academic tasks they are expected to take up. In the following section, I provide a review of critical discourse analysis, and related constructs.

A CRITICAL CALL TO CONTEXT

For this focused look at readings of narrations of cross-cultural encounters, Goffman's (1969, 1974, 1981) construct of participation framework and critical discourse analysis (CDA) provided conceptual lenses through which I view the experiences of the adult women in the hair salon.[2] To think about African Americans as participants of an activity means to move beyond systems of language (prosody, lexicon, syntax, tense, and aspect) and to include in that inquiry the artifacts that participants' use and the fuller experience of what it means to be a participant of a speech community. CDA enables us to do just that by "focusing not only on texts, spoken or written, as objects of inquiry. A fully 'critical' account of discourse would thus require a theorization and description of both the social processes and structures within which individuals or groups as social historical subjects, create meanings in their interactions with texts" (Wodak & Meyer, 2001).

Discourses from this perspective are viewed as "ways of behaving, interacting, valuing, thinking, believing, speaking, writing and 'reading' that are accepted instantiations of particular roles by specific groups of people" (Hull & Schultz, 2002, p. x). A critical view of discourse enables us to consider the very complex roles, social identities, or social perspectives from which people are invited (summoned) to speak, listen, act, read, write, think, feel, and value in certain characteristic, historically recognizable ways in combination with their own individual style and creativity (Bourdieu, 1977; Foucault, 1980; Gee, Hull, & Lankshear, 1996). Methodologically, CDA provides a useful tool for considering the varied ways in which the use of African American English in activity acts as a mediational tool through which participants of classroom- and workplace-based activities communicate to achieve a particular goal (Wodak & Meyer, 2001).

Furthering my consideration of discourse, I draw on Goffman's (1969, 1974, 1981) construct of participation framework in order to understand the social phenomenon of practice, in particular the role of identities and power relations in the workplace learning contexts. Goffman's (1959, 1974, 1981) participation framework identified the roles that participants play in an act of communication. These roles include animator (one who gives voice to the message), author (one who crafts the words of the message), and principal (the source that provides authority to the message). The distribution of these roles across participants allows ideas to be put forth, amended, elaborated, extended, and contested (Lee & Majors, 2003). Furthermore, the distribution of these roles impacts relations of power within the group and invites dialogic relationships with other discourses, ideas, and persons who may not be present in the communicative act. These roles are constituted not only by the creative and idiosyncratic intentions of individuals, but also are socially constituted through the historical traditions of discourses. Thus, as people learn over time to participate in different discourse communities, they also learn to take on particular kinds of roles in talk (Lee & Majors, 2003).

CONTEXT OF THE INVESTIGATION

This article draws from an ethnographic study informing my understanding of the phenomenon of "Shoptalk." The corpus of data for the study of Shoptalk includes field notes based on participant observation. In addition, audiotaped and videotaped records of activity were collected in order to account for participant interactions, talk within these interactions, linguistic and nonlinguistic cues, physical activity including movement and the appropriation of space, participants' physical attributes, and participation structures. Data have been analyzed in a number of ways, including through activity setting analyses (Majors, 2002, 2003, 2007) and interactional sociolinguistic analyses (2003). The focus of these analyses is on interaction patterns; the role and structure of personal narratives, in particular those identified as cross-cultural narrations of experience; and other genres of talk drawn from the sociolinguistic literature on African American Vernacular English discourses (Foster, 1987; Jacobs-Huey, 1997; Morgan, 1998).

This article draws from my own data collection over a six-month period in an urban hair salon, P.A. Hair Salon.[3] Within this site I closely examined the processes involved in community discourse practices, specifically storytelling, hairdresser/client communication, and the appropriation and sharing of resources among shop employees. For this study of narrations of cross-cultural encounters within the context of the hair salon, I focus on one of the individual participants, "Darlene," through transcribed, semistructured informal interviews and audio records of interaction. She was selected for this particular focus on skills in reading cross-cultural interactions as she was one of the most self-reflective and colorful participants in this study. Among the often-told stories within the salon were those of participants' cross-cultural interactions with White Americans.

For this concentrated look at how one participant of Shoptalk reads cross-cultural interactions, I examined all video recorded and subsequently transcribed episodes of interaction and talk among study participants. I focus here on a single episode that provides a detailed narration of a cross-cultural encounter. I use this narrative to identify how the structure of that narrative contributes to a dialogic, group dynamic. Such a narrative structure and group dynamic provides insight into participants' readings of the social and cross-cultural relations that may not have been apparent in the actual encounter. I also focus on how Darlene reports on her role within the context of the salon, and how she positions herself in relation to the other participants across contexts by enacting multiple voices and identities, rather than taking up those imposed upon her. It is in the narration of experience that we can gain insight into some African American adult women's readings of social relations. It is also within this narration that we may view the problem solving potential embedded within such readings.

[2] Cultural Historical Activity Theory and Critical Race Theory also contribute to a broader consideration of the construction of knowledge through discourse in the larger corpus.

[3] All names in this paper are pseudonyms. See Majors (2001) for a more detailed description of this salon, its history, and the surrounding community.

FINDINGS

Participation Status Within the Discourse

The data for this analysis extend from one six-hour documented (field notes, audiotape) episode within one hair salon. However, a more detailed analysis, as representative of the fuller study, is reported in Majors (2001). The example of Shoptalk that will be illustrated here involves participants in the salon who each take on some form of participant status. The participants include Darlene, a self-described African American "hair technician," whose status within the participation framework are that of "animator," the one who renders the voice of the narrative (Duranti, 1997). In addition to this status, Darlene constructs several interrelated identities or roles for herself: stylist, medical expert, teacher, and analyst. These self-constructed roles speak to an appropriation of the stylist role in the salon as an artifact of the institutional organization of community practices in this particular salon. According to Darlene,

> "We as stylist actually become almost like psychiatrist because you work so closely with [clients] and because you are responsible for their outer image they reveal their inner selves to you. And for me, I manipulate the clients to get them to do that because I need to know who they are on the inside and therefore I can create a look for them on the outside. And that's the whole teaching experience. That's what I'm trying to get the girls to learn. . . . And when you're talkin' to your client, you don't need to tell them about your personal life. You don't need to be hearin' about Judy down the street. The only thing that you need to be talkin' to them about is them. And there has to be a way that you get focused into their life enough that you become very concerned about that person in that chair and that person only (Darlene 11/29/96).

In order to account for the role of the stylist in interaction with "clients," Darlene appropriates the expert medical term "psychiatrist." In doing so Darlene constructs an expert knowledge of not only the responsibility of stylists in general but the performative combination of roles and needs of all clients. Furthermore, Darlene unpacks this medical identity early on by suggesting that she "manipulates the clients." This revelation makes explicit not only the analogous relation between beauty expert and medical expert, but the transition from one to another. Furthermore, through her construction of this identity, Darlene enacts an epistemic stance (Jacobs-Huey, 1997) in order to construct her own expert knowledge by evoking "scripts" (Jacobs-Huey, 1997; Schank & Abelson, 1977; Gutierrez et al., 1999), the common everyday phenomena of what people, in this case doctors, do.

This expert knowledge leads Darlene to the construction of a second identity, that of teacher. Here Darlene appropriates the role of teacher, by asserting herself as "trying to teach the girls to learn." The term *girls* here represents the two additional hair stylists in the salon. This term also contributes to the construction a paradigm that asserts a community hierarchy of power and knowledge within the salon. Within this paradigm power and knowledge become tools that separate Darlene from not only the clients, who are unable to "treat" themselves, but the other stylists as well, who lack the knowledge required for such treatment. Furthermore this paradigm of power and knowledge contributes to the overlapping of identities, in which Darlene is expert "psychiatrist" and teacher, dominant to both client and "girls." Darlene unpacks this overlapping of identities by asserting an expertise of not only medical methodologies, but the use of these methods as a part of her instruction.

Finally, although hairstyling is the trademark tool in hair salons, in the aforementioned excerpt Darlene introduces the prescriptive role of Shoptalk. Shoptalk allows stylists to not only engage with their clients but to treat their clients' psychological, thus cognitive, needs. Furthermore, this treatment of hair through talkin' is the result of an analysis—one capable of being made by only the stylist, as a beauty/medical expert—of the client, as embodying something that is treatable. For Darlene, this complex construction of the stylist with the interrelated identities of beauty, medical, academic, and analytical expertise, is in her view to the benefit of the client.

In addition to Darlene, an audience of clients are "ratified participants" in the talk. Within Shoptalk ratified participants are entitled and expected to be a part of the communicative event. Furthermore, in addition to the nature of ratified participants in the hair salon, present at times also is one "unratified participant." Angela is a White female hair technician who, due to an ongoing lack of participation, is not expected to be a part of the speech event.

An analysis of discourse events between participants when Angela was present revealed a resistance to the notion of Shoptalk, on the part of Angela. For Darlene, Shoptalk serves as a prescriptive tool and mediational device between clients and stylists. Absent from Angela's professional stance as a hair stylist is a shared belief in the role of Shoptalk in situated activity in the hair salon. For example, when asked how she regards talk, Angela replies,

> *"I don't really talk much, and I don't know if people like that in me. . . . A lot of times they say your clients will come to you 'cause of your personality and not necessarily if you do their hair good or whatever. But I don't believe that. I think that people come to you to get their hair done, you know. And they want it done right. I do feel it slows me up to get in a conversation. . . . I don't like that at all."*

Angela's belief is that the role of the technician or stylist is to do hair. According to Angela, this is what the client wants. As indicated earlier, "people come to get their hair done. . . . And they want it done right." While Darlene constructs several interrelated identities for herself, Angela on the other hand, views her role in the salon as that of stylist, not as one in which she must engage in conversational discourse that functions as a prescriptive tool. I argue that this perspective is informed by a set of rules or standards, which do not include AAVE norms and are constructed and situated within a different cultural discourse, for the purpose of "doing hair" and not treating it, as Darlene puts it.

I would also argue that for various reasons (that include issues of time and efficiency) many individuals, both White and Black, share Angela's point of view concerning the relevancy of Shoptalk as a genre of discourse in the salon. However, Angela's expressed point of view might be characterized as embodying a "white perspective," according to Kochman (1981), in that it demonstrates "restraint set by standards for events in which expression is seen as having little or no functional role" (p. 114). This perspective deviates sharply from the mediating function of talk as a tool in the activity, an activity whose purposes are threaded in gendered speech events of the hair salon. Furthermore, because certain AAVE discourse norms, such as call and response, "are not in her cultural heritage," suggested Smitherman (1977), the White person "does not obviously engage in the response process, remaining relatively passive" (p. 118). According to Smitherman (1997),

> Judging from the white individual's seeming lack of involvement, the black communicator gets the feeling that the white isn't listening, and thus may repeatedly punctuate the call with questions, such as "are you listening to me?" . . . (p. 118).

Ideological Representations Through Hairsay

In addition to being a genre of conversational discourse, Shoptalk is distinct in that it is a publicly performed private conversation occurring within a hair salon. Furthermore, this genre of conversational discourse embodies varying degrees of what I have called "Hairsay" (Majors, 2001). Hairsay is defined as the dyadic/dependant relationship within speech events between public gendered and racialized speech, gendered roles within the broader cultural community, cultural definitions of such roles, the evaluation of presentation of style, and the AAVE norms and meanings that thread them together. These gendered and racialized attributes contribute to how participants make meanings of and within the multiple environments they navigate on a day-to-day basis. They also contribute to individuals' interpersonal decision-making processes, social representations within and across groups, self-perceptions, and understandings of the ways in which the world considers them racialized beings.

Hairsay is situated within Shoptalk, as a mediational and socializing tool. As a mediational tool, Hairsay's function is to shape the decision-making processes as an ideological value system that may or may not be shared between participants of Shoptalk. As a socializing tool, Hairsay is the displayed performance of a group member value system towards an adolescent, youth, or nongroup member for socializing them into the culture or group. Hairsay extends the definition of Shoptalk to inform socialization and intervention strategies inherent within the talk and make available to participants (and eavesdroppers, which often include youth and adolescents). These strategies consider the multiple meanings that the individual, the community, and the society at large will ascribe to African American behavior that is either appropriate or inappropriate, just or unjust, right or just plain wrong.

To that end, Shoptalk places Hairsay dead center in what it means to actively participate in the African American hair salon and to perceive of that space as a community of social practice. Within that talk such attributes are conveyed in actions, motions and gestures, and tone and pitch, but most importantly in the culturally shared and situated talk of its participants. Thus, the emergence of Hairsay through Shoptalk makes visible the links and dimensions of a broader and otherwise external African American speech community, through the voices of active participants, past and present, who engage in such talk. These gendered and racialized attributes are what define the African American hair salon as an AAVE speech community, created and recreated by those present.

"ANGELA'S HILLBILLIES"

In the following excerpt, for example, Darlene describes (before an audience that does not include Angela) public responses to Angela's presence as a stylist within the salon. Undergirding this narrative description, however, is Darlene's descriptive account of an interaction between Angela, Angela's client, and a group of onlookers. Within the salon this narrative description is situated within a discussion of the history of the salon, its vision for the future, and surrounding community perceptions of its role within the culture and community. With the exception of Angela, who is White, participants of this speech event share a common set of experiences and medational resources preparing them to participate in local Shoptalk, including commonly shared indexical referents. Their experiences over time within hair salons socialized them to the modes of AAVE discourse commonly appropriated within such contexts. Participants also share a common set of experiences as members of the African American speech community.

The following discussion is prompted when Darlene, the "animator," is asked about a public, cultural event that the salon was sponsoring within the community. This discussion brings the topic to the floor, which on the surface appears to be public perceptions of one stylist, but I would argue that the general message here is much more complex, involving culturally shared understandings with regards to the function of talk in the salon and the intrinsic relationship among speech, role, community, style, and race. Within this context Darlene retells of an event in which Angela was confronted by an African American female onlooker, to whom Darlene has previously referred as a "hillbilly."

1. **Darlene:** Cause at first I, I hadn't paid attention to what they were doin'. And, it
2. was like I just saw these kids standin' up there peekin' through these little
3. windows, and uh (2.0) Then I looked and I saw the grown-ups standin' in the
4. window too and I was like, 'this is cra:zy.'
5. **Client:** Standin' in the window?
6. **Darlene:** Yeah, standin' like in these little windows *right here* ((*she points to*
7. *the 2 cut out square openings directly above Angela's station and to her right.*))
8. **Client:** Oh. Are you se:ri:ous?
9. **Darlene:** *And they just lookin'. And this girl was sittin' there* with her head
10. down, you know, just gettin' her hair done. And so finally I hear this lady commin
11. around the corner and she goes (2.0), 'I wonna see this, I, I, now I'm gone see
12. this. Now this white woman gone do them wa:ves?' ((*Darlene speaks in the*
13. *woman's voice*))
14. **Client:** Are you serious?
15. **Darlene:** *And she got right, she walked intuh Angela's booth and she stood
16. right in front of her* *You know, hahaha* ((*Darlene laughs hard*)). And she
17. was like (.), she kept turnin' around lookin' at her family that was backin' her up
18. in the window you know and she's like, 'She doin' 'em, oh yeah uh-huh baby, she
19. doin' these waves'. ((*Darlene speaks in the woman's voice*))
20. **Client:** Uh-hum.
21. **Darlene:** Girl, I: laughed. I had never laughed so hard in all my life I had to
22. excuse myself. This woman was standin' there she was watchin' Angela do her
23. daughter, her granddaughter's waves, and she talkin' 'bout, "I can't believe it, if I
24. hadn't seen it, I wouldn't've believed it, but she, oh yea:h honey, she layin' them
25. waves." ((*Darlene speaks in the woman's voice, cracks-up*))
26. **Client:** O:h my goodness.

27. **Darlene:** So we, we=
28. **Client:** [Plus Angela has this demeanor that's like=
29. **Darlene:** =And Angela just kinda go 'humph.' But, but when she left we
30. laughed↑ <u>aw Go:d</u>. We laughed about that. Plus I tol' Angela I said the only
31. thing we missin' was Paw Kettle and the truck. Girl that woman, I said I could
32. just see her now tellin the story, 'Honey we walked up on in that shop. That little
33. ole' white girl came out there and got this girl, and she put her in that chair. Now
34. she, honey you see them waves? She <u>lai:d</u> them waves, baby *she put them waves
35. on* ' ((*Darlene speaks in the woman's voice, laughing at herself and slaps her*
36. *thigh*)) You know how, you know how they talk and all. And I can just see it,
37. slappin' her knee and crackin' up like, 'You couldn't tell me, if she had tole me
38. that and I hadn't seen it, I would've never believed it. But I'm tellin' you she <u>laid</u>
39. them waves, oh yea:h baby she laid 'em.'
40. **Client:** "Oh my goodness".

The Hair Salon as an AA Speech Community

This narrated event illustrates how people positioned on the borders between cultural groups/discourse communities may use cultural tools for reading social relations. It is in this daily activity of having one's hair done that participants take up an opportunity to read social relations both through their own positions within the discourse and through their shared experiences of being positioned in particular ways within society. While clearly many points can be made, I wish to focus on three key observations with regard to Darlene's narrative rendering of Angela's encounter and subsequent positioning: First, is how gendered and racialized attributes define the African American hair salon as an AAVE speech community.

For example, beginning with lines 8 and 14 ("Ohh, are you serious"), lines 20 and 26 ("O:h my goodness"), and ending at line 40 ("Oh, my goodness"), ratified participants employ *call and response* throughout the narrative. This feature of African American English (AAVE) is characterized as the spontaneous verbal and nonverbal interaction between speaker and listener in which all of the speaker's statements ("calls") are punctuated by expressions ("responses") from the listener (Smitherman, 1977, p. 104). This linguistic and paralingustic feature of AAVE establishes a rapport between speakers, as well as serves as an indicator of engagement, and serves as a back-channeling function in sustaining the talk across participants. Furthermore, such paralinguistic features conveyed in actions, motions, gestures like thigh slapping, and tone and pitch such as the uproar of laughter, make visible the links and dimensions of a broader and otherwise external African American speech community.

While Darlene's narrative rendering of real world events was prompted by the ordinary inquiry ("She was standin' in the window"), such an inquiry, during the course of the conversation, "can prompt a meandering away from the point, and into episodic journeys and over tributary rhetorical routes" (Smitherman, 1977, p. 148). As Smitherman (1977) has argued, in particular black discourse modes, "an ordinary inquiry is likely to elicit an extended narrative response where the abstract point or general message will be couched in concrete story form. Within this mode of discourse, the reporting of events is never simply objectively reported, but dramatically acted out and narrated out" (p. 148). As illustrated in lines 6, 12, 13, 16, 19, 25, and 35, Darlene invokes the use of "voice, body and movement as tools" to bring her narrative to life.

The narrative sequencing in this context of Shoptalk is jointly produced by active participants, who by virtue of their participation bring a shared knowledge of both Shoptalk as a genre of conversational discourse and the norms of AAVE to bear on its construction. Each participant contributes to the representation of Shoptalk and structure of the activity. First, they agree on the definition of the situation (Wertsch, 1985), which is to say Shoptalk, and second they implement a system of semiotic mediation (e.g., "black modes of discourse" (Smitherman, 2000)) as a sign of that agreement.

According to Smitherman (1977) the following features characterize AAVE discourse:

- Call and response
- Narrative sequencing
- Verbal inventiveness, including the use of exaggerated language, play on words, indirection, alliteration, repetition, and tonal semantics.

Call and response is a feature of AAVEV discourse typically associated with the African American Christian Church wherein the preacher talks and members of the audience reify and sustain the power of the preacher's words by responses that are intermittent, not necessarily at the end of a full turn in a conversational exchange. Call and response as a structure establishes a coconstructed rapport between speakers, serves as an indicator of engagement, and serves a back-channeling function in sustaining the talk across participants. Verbal inventiveness is central to AAVE discourse norms across speech genres and often serves as evidence of membership in this speech community. In certain speech events verbal inventiveness is expected and by virtue of such expectation invites engagement, as well as provides evidence of point of view. Narrative sequencing involves the interspersion of narratives inside expository or argument structures, in order to illustrate a point or provide grounding for claims warranted by folk theories of human action as analogies for some point to be made.

These are three characteristic features of AAVE discourse that may be viewed as separate from the common features of syntax that signal AAVE. That is to say, these discourse features may be observed by speakers of standard or vernacular varieties of African American English (Mufwene, 1993). Furthermore, and more fully explored elsewhere (Majors, 2007), such a narrative structure is unique in comparison to traditional models of narrative presented in most research with regard to discourse employed in both formal and informal learning contexts. This leads me to a second point, which is that within the salon, such attributes not only contribute to the discourse within that community, but to joint problem solving as well.

Working Through a Shared Cultural Past

Within the hair salon, Shoptalk provides a vehicle for participating members to engage in joint problem solving. In the instance of adults in the hair salon, however, Shoptalk, as a mediational device, embodies not only shared perceptions of the world surrounding each of its participants in speech events but also the jointly constructed labels used by these individuals in order to identify those mental perceptions, be it in words and/or gestures (e.g., calls and responses). For example, beginning in line 10, the identity and stance of Angela's onlooker within the salon is characterized and positioned by Darlene. This characterization is not only reflected through a representation of words but through voice, gesture, and tonal semantics as well. Tonal semantics refers to the use of voice rhythm and vocal inflection to convey a meta-meaning—that is, what words cannot covey—in black communication (Smitherman, 1977). When applied here, such semantics signal the presence of a meta-message within Darlene's narrative performance. I emphasize that I consider this cultural positioning, which includes the use of black modes of discourse as a public reading of the racialized subtext of the narrated event, a reading that Darlene shares with her audience. Darlene's reading of the event is structured by an African American narrative style in which she directs the speech encounter, with audience participating minimally.

As a social actor, Darlene has set up a reply of sarcastic disbelief from the client, whose status is that of recipient beginning in line 14, "Are you SER-I-OUS." Such a reply acts as an indicator of engagement and is spoken by way of intonational contouring. Spoken this way, the recipient's response makes visible a shared understanding of the underlying meta-message of what is being stated by Darlene, which is that Angela's observer has violated some implicit face-to-face rules and features of direct and indirect social interaction that constitute the African American speech community. Such features are situated within a complex system of adult conversational signifying,[4] the employment and maintenance of a cool social face[5] (Morgan, 1998), and indirectness.[6] These features combine to mark the African American speech community and are commonly a part of the social context in which African Americans interact.

Furthermore, the recipient's response of disbelief here is with regard to this meta-message, or what Smitherman (1977) called "deep structure" (p. 135) of Darlene's narrative account, and not the actual word. This deep structure is made visible to the audience through the tonal semantics employed by Darlene throughout the narrative. To both understand and "feel" tonal semantics, however, requires the listener to be of a cultural tradition that finds value and meaning in word sound (1977). In addition, the "response," beginning in line 14, to Darlene's call further indicates that the client has recognized that the sound of Darlene's performance is just as important as the sense. This sequencing of call and response and verbal inventiveness, locates both animator and recipient in the tradition of African American English discourse, thus giving greater psychological weight to their words.

[4] Signifying (Mitchell-Kernan, 1972, 1973; Smitherman, 1977) is characterized as the verbal art of insult in which a speaker humorously puts down, talks about, and needles—that is, signifies on—the listener.

[5] According the Morgan (1998), a cool face is the ability to act on symbolic incidents and subtle varieties of cultural practice with eloquence, skill, wit, patience, and precise timing .

[6] According to Morgan (1998), pointed indirectness requires local knowledge to understand what a speaker means and is seldom recognized by non-African Americans when it occurs.

Based on the shared responses of the audience, beginning in line 20 ("Uhm-hmm") Darlene's inventiveness is perhaps expected and reflects a shared point of view with regard to the rules for discourse within the salon. Furthermore, for each participant the world outside of the salon can be perceived not just through the eyes and the ears, which perceive the local, but also through the shared understanding of the presence of *tonal semantics* and *signifying.* Here the presentation of "black modes of discourse" employed by Darlene makes visible to the reader and her immediate audience as well, a culturally shared landscape, removed from the present but generated in the salon through community culture and style. While reading this racialized subtext Darlene appears to also be reading the responses of her audience and acknowledges their positions through that reading.

Certifying Knowledge Through Social Reading

In addition to embodying the jointly constructed labels symbolically ascribed to mental perceptions, AAVE discourse norms in Shoptalk enable participants to represent shared readings of the world. For example, beginning in line 11, Darlene's verbally performed representation of Angela's onlooker is an act of "signifying" in which she is humorously putting down the onlooker's failure to appropriate this culturally approved method of talking about someone through "verbal indirection." In so doing however, Darlene herself employs signifying through the usage of exaggerated language, humor and metaphorical-imagistic rooted in the everyday (e.g., line 21, "the only thang missin' was Pa Kettle[7] and the truck.")

What is especially important to note is that while signifying here appears to be lightly humorous on one level, on a meta level, such signifying is heavy in that it drives home a metacognitive message to the audience by suggesting that the onlooker's uncool response was not only culturally inappropriate, but socially unacceptable. Maintaining a cool social face, argues Gwaltney (1980), "is what African Americans respect the most in ourselves and look for in other people. That means being a person of sober, quiet judgment."

This heavy signifying at the meta level is geared toward making the audience, in this case Darlene's present audience, think about the implications of such behavior. As Darlene states later in the dialogue, "When I started to work with Angela, I told her what would happen is that there would be a lot of resistance. But because of the fact that I was the one introducing her into the shop, my clients would respect her."

While Darlene's official stance is made clearer here, it is set up during her narrative representation of the events through heavy signifying.

Furthermore, it is the shared understanding of this mode of Black discourse that allows Darlene to make her point, before the audience.

This process of collaborative meaning-making, or rather making sense of the world through Shoptalk, which includes signifying, tonal semantics, and call and response, is transformative. According to Wertsch, Del Rio and Alvarez (1995), "by being included in the activity," norms for talk "alter the entire flow and structure of mental

[7] A popular, male-patriarch character from 1940s–50s film comedy act, *Ma and Pa Kettle.*

functions" (p. 28). This is clearly the case for AAVE use within Shoptalk. Such inclusion determines the structure of a new instrumental act, just as a technical tool "alters the process of a natural adaptation by determining the form of labor operations" (p. 28). In other words, for the individual participant, AAVE changes how the problem, issue, and goal will be presented, solved, or accomplished. For example, rather than publicly lecture or preach her stance to Angela's onlooker as well as her audience, Darlene, in lines 11–36, chooses to employ signifying, an act unbeknown to Angela's onlooker but obvious to her audience in the salon. This choice places her in a position of power in that she has the ability to alter assumptions and drive home a cognitive message, thus hopefully altering behaviors.

By setting up this transformative dialogue, Darlene places herself in the interrelated expert position of psychiatrist, teacher, and analyst—and by virtue of her present activity of working on a client's hair while simultaneously rendering her narrative, stylist.

In terms of group interaction in joint activity, the transformatory capacity of language lies in the fact that not only does language serve to connect the individual, the community and the activity, but that "human action is mediated by language" (Wertsch, Del Rio and Alvarez, 1995), and for social purposes, it is a means of influencing and thus transforming others in the group.

Finally, as argued elsewhere, narratives that are produced within an African American discourse of Shoptalk provide a foundation from which to view the dialogicality of voice in the hair salon. According to Bahktin (1986), dialogicality precedes both utterance and voice. The utterance is filled with dialogic overtones (p. 54) including "[t]he dialogic orientation between the utterances of one person to the utterances of another." Here, within the hair salon, dialogic harmony is achieved and viewed throughout the rendering of the entire narrative through the responses of the audience to Darlene's calls. Furthermore, within the structure of this culturally shared and situated discourse, there is more than one narrator, as each member provides a support to the other in sense making. This presence of multiple narrators speaks to the participation framework of talk in the salon as it brings the shared understanding and acceptance of a culturally rooted past, for example the use of AAVE norms, into the present, making visible specific structures for meaning-making that move across boundaries of setting, space, and time.

Contributing to the Black American experience, argued Smitherman, is a folk tradition expressed by Black folks through utterance. These linguistic contributions, "folklore, folk utterances, songs and tales of folk expression," are comprised of "verbal strategies, rhetorical devices and folk expressive rituals which derive from a mutually understood notion of modes of discourse" (p. 103). These modes of discourse are in turn "part of the rich inheritance of the African background" (p. 103), and can be categorized into four broad categories: call-response, signification, tonal semantics, and narrative sequencing. Furthermore, according to Smitherman, with regard to each Black discourse mode, it is important and necessary to affirm that each discourse mode is manifested in Black American culture, and that,

> The traditional African world-view emphasizes the dualities to achieve balance and harmony in the universe and in the community of men and women. Thus, while the rituals of black discourse have an overall formuliac structure, individuals are challenged to do what they can within the traditional mold. Centuries-old group norms are balanced by individualized, improvisational emphasis. By virtue of unique contributions to the group approved communicative structure, the individual can actualize his or her sense of self within the confines of the group (pp. 103–104).

Although the experience of witnessing Angela's interaction with her onlooker was not shared, here within Shoptalk, the narrative is collaboratively produced through call and response and functions as a presentation of community within activity. Thus, from the perspective of guided participation, the function of Shoptalk can be viewed as a jointly constructed, mediational tool, bridging community and activity through language. Specifically, narrative in Shoptalk, as viewed through this lens, provides an account of the "processes and systems of involvement between people as they communicate and coordinate efforts while participating in culturally valued activity" (Rogoff, 1995, p. 142). Viewing this narrative from the perspective of guided participation, "each actor is responsible for her, as well as others' roles within the performance of the activity, and interdependently they must structure situations (whether by facilitating or limiting access) in which they observe and participate in cultural activity" (pp. 147–148).

CONCLUSION/IMPLICATIONS

As a cultural and linguistic site of labor-related activity, hair salons are traditionally places where coconstructed, community forms of talk—stories, personal narratives, jokes, folklore, and folktales—can be found. They are also sites in which these genres and AAVE interactional norms are used as resources for the construction of arguments. In considering the hair salon, my goal is to illustrate the potential of vernacular discourses to promote meaning-making. This perspective enables me to challenge distinctions between in-school and out-of-school settings that set up a false dichotomy. By foregrounding physical space (e.g., contexts outside the school door) or time (e.g., after-school programs), we may ignore important conceptual dimensions that more readily account for successful learning or its absence. We may fail to see the presence of school-like practice at home, or non-school-like activities in the classroom (Hull & Shultz, 2002). Therefore, my focus must not be localized agents, participants within the salon or classroom, but rather the conceptual dimensions employed by these agents and the culturally situated means that mediate them.

Lee (1992) made explicit the fact that speakers of African American Vernacular English (AAVE) use cultural toolkits when reasoning about complex oral and written texts. Within the hair salon the discourse norms and participation structures of narration invite readings of social texts. A view of the role of language and learning from this perspective takes into consideration culturally and socially situated activity systems, both inside and outside the classroom, which inform literacy and language practices, and mediate learning. A consideration of literate activity means to consider events, practices, activities, ideologies, discourses, and identities within systems of activity that contribute to learning, from multiple perspectives and across multiple contexts.

REFERENCES

Ball, A. F. (1992). Cultural preferences and the expository writing of African-American adolescents. *Written Communication, 9*(4), 5 01–532.

Bakhtin, M. M. (1986). *Speech genres and other late essays.* Austin: University of Texas Press.

Barton, D. & Hamilton, M. (1998). *Local literacies: Reading and writing in one classroom.* London: Routledge.

Bourdieu, P. (1977). *Language and symbolic power.* Cambridge, MA: Harvard University Press.

Bruner, J. (1959). Learning and thinking. *Harvard Educational Review, 29,* 184–192.

Cazden, C. (1988). *Classroom discourse: The language of teaching and learning.* Portsmouth, NH: Heinemann.

CNN.com (2005, September). "Bennett under fire for remarks on blacks, crime." Retrieved November 10, 2005 from http://www.cnn.com/2005/POLITICS/09/30/bennett.comments/

Cole, M. (1996). *Cultural psychology: A once and future discipline.* Cambridge, MA: The Belknap Press of Harvard University Press.

Darling-Hammond, L. (2002, January). *Redesigning schools for the 21st century.* Paper presented to faculty of Hillsdale High School, San Mateo, CA.

Delpit, L. (1995). *Other people's children: Cultural conflict in the classroom.* New York: The New Press.

Duranti, A. (1997). *Linguistic anthropology.* Cambridge: Cambridge University Press.

Fairclough, N. (2003). *Analyzing discourse: Textual analysis for social research.* London: Routledge Press.

Foucault, M. (1980). *Power/knowledge: Selected interviews and other writings.* Brighton, England: Harvester Press.

Gay, G. (2000). *Culturally Responsive Teaching: Theory, Research, and Practice.* New York: Teachers College Press.

Gee, J. P. (1992). *The social mind: Language, ideology, and social practice.* New York: Gergin & Garvey.

Gee, J. P. (2000). Discourse and sociocultural studies in reading. In M. Kamil, P. Mosenthal, P. D. Pearson, & R. Barr (Eds.), *Handbook of reading research* (pp. 195–208). Mahwah, NJ: Lawrence Erlbaum.

Gee, J. P., Hull, G., & Lankshear, C. (1996). *The new work order: Behind the language of the new capitalism.* Boulder, CO: Westview Press.

Goffman, E. (1969). *Strategic interaction.* Philadelphia: University of Pennsylvania Press.

Goffman, E. (1974). *Frame analysis.* New York: Harper and Row.

Goffman, E. (1981). *Forms of talk.* Philadelphia: University of Pennsylvania Press.

Gutierrez, K., Baquedano-Lopez, P., & Tejeda, C. (1999). Rethinking diversity: Hybridity and hybrid language practices in the third space. *Mind, Culture, & Activity, 6*(4), 286–303.

Gwaltney, J. L. (1980). *Drylongso: A self-portrait of Black America.* New York: Vintage.

Heath, S. B. (1983). *Ways with words: Language, life and work in communities and classrooms.* New York: Cambridge University Press.

Hull, G. & Schultz, K. (Eds.) (2002). *School's out: Bridging out-of-school literacies with classroom practice.* NY: Teacher College Press.

Jacobs-Huey, L. (1997). *We're just like doctors, we heal sick hair.*

Kochman, T. (1981). *Black and white styles in conflict.* Chicago: The University of Chicago Press.

Ladson-Billings, G. (1994). *The dreamkeepers.* San Francisco: Jossey-Bass.

Lee, C. D. (1992). Literacy, cultural diversity, and instruction. *Education & Urban Society, 24*(2), 279–291.

Lee, C. D. (2004). "Double voiced discourse: African American vernacular English as resource in cultural modeling classrooms." In A. F. Ball & S. W. Freedman (Eds.), *Bakhtinian perspectives on language, literacy, and learning.* New York: Cambridge.

Lee, C. D., & Majors, Y. (2003). "Heading up the street:" Localized opportunities for shared constructions of knowledge. *Pedagogy, Culture and Society, 11*(1), 49–67.

Majors, Y. (2001). Passing mirrors: Subjectivity in a mid-western hair salon. *Anthropology & Education Quarterly, 32,* 116–130.

Majors, Y. (2003). Shoptalk: Teaching and learning in an African American hair salon. *Mind, Culture and Activity, 10*(4), 289–310.

Majors, Y. (2004). "They thought I was scared of them, but they were scared of me:" Constructions of self/other in a Midwestern hair salon. *Anthropology and Education Quarterly, 35*(2).

Majors, Y. (2007). Narrations of cross-cultural encounters as interpretive frames for reading word and world. *Discourse and Society, 18*(4), 479–505.

Majors, Y., & Orellana, M. (In-review). Envisioning texts or reading the other. Manuscript submitted to *Linguistics & Education,* December, 2006.

Mitchell-Kernan, C. (1972). Signifying, loud-talking, and marking. In T. Kochman (Ed.), *Rakppin' and stylin' out: Communication in urban Black America* (pp. 315–335). Champaign, IL: University of Illinois Press.

Mitchell-Kernan, C. (1990). Signifying, in mother wit from the laughing barrel. In A. Dundes, (Ed.). *Mother wit from the laughing barrel: Readings in the interpretation of Afro-American folklore.* Jackson, MS: University Press of Mississippi.

Morgan, M. (1998). More than a mood or an attitude: discourse and verbal genres in African American culture. In S. S. Mufwene, J. R. Rickford, G. Bailey, & J. Baugh (Eds.), *African American English: Structure, history and use.* New York: Routledge.

Mufwene, S. (Ed.) (1993). *Africanisms in Afro-American language varieties.* Athens, GA: The University of Georgia Press.

Ochs, E., & Capps, L. (2001). *Living narrative: Creating lives in everyday storytelling.* Cambridge: Harvard University Press.

Resnick, M. (2003). Marci Resnick responds. In G. Hull & K. Schultz (Eds.), *School's out: Bridging out of school literacies with classroom practice.* New York: Teachers College Press.

Rogoff, B. (1995). Observing sociocultural activity and three planes: participatory appropriation, guided participation, and apprenticeship. In J. Wertsch, P. del Rio, & A. Alvarez (Eds.), *Sociocultural studies of mind* (pp. 139–164). New York: Cambridge University Press.

Schank, R., & Abelson, R. (1977). *Scripts, plans, goals, and understanding.* Hillsdale, NJ: Erlbaum.

Skilton-Sylvester, E. (2003). "Literate at Home but Not at School: A Cambodian Girl's Journey from Playwright to Struggling Writer." In G. Hull & K Schultz (Eds.), *School's out: Bridging out of school literacies with classroom practice.* New York: Teachers College Press.

Smitherman, G. (1977). *Talkin and testifyin: The language of Black America.* Boston: Houghton Mifflin.

Smitherman, G. (2000). *Talkin that talk: Language, culture and education in African America.* New York: Routledge.

Wertsch, J. (1985). *Vygotsky and the social formation of mind.* Cambridge, MA: Harvard University Press.

Wertsch, J., Del Rio, P., & Alvarez, A. (Eds.). (1995). *Sociocultural studies of mind.* New York: Cambridge University Press.

Wodak, R., & Meyer, M. (Eds.) (2001). *Methods of critical discourse analysis.* London: Sage Publications.

•32•

EXCHANGING LIFE NARRATIVES: THE POLITICS AND POETICS OF DO-IT-YOURSELF PRACTICES

Doreen M. Piano
UNIVERSITY OF NEW ORLEANS

> My hope is that women can read my zine & say to themselves, "Hey, I can go out & change my life & live better & be happier. I don't have to put up with this bullshit. I can fight back!" I'm not trying to start a revolution (yet). I guess I'm just trying to say, "This is where I came from & this is what I'm doing. You can do it too."
>
> —Ciara Xyerra, editor, *A Renegade's Guide to Love & Sabotage*

Through the use of do-it-yourself (DIY) practices—the act of taking cultural production into one's own hands, the early 1990s youth-oriented feminist movement known as Riot Grrrl constructed an ethical and political stance against male-dominance within North American punk culture primarily through the development of all-girl bands. Instrumental to the growth of this movement was the circulation of self-published magazines known as zines that provided a cheap and versatile method of communication among women involved in the movement. Used as an informal communication system among science-fiction fans in the 1950s, within British and U.S. punk cultures, zines not only relayed information among punks not covered by mainstream media, but also, though their makeshift appearance, conveyed an impression of "urgency and immediacy, of a paper produced in indecent haste, of memos from the front line" (Hebdige, 1979, p. 111).[1] By adapting the punk fanzine as a "safe space" for women to raise awareness about gender issues, Riot Grrrls were able to mobilize women who were estranged from the production of punk culture.[2] In discussing Riot Grrrl composing practices, Comstock (2001) notes that making and circulating zines fostered representational spaces for identity and community construction by embodying a multitude of social ills and pleasures at the site of the "traumatized girl body" (p. 387). In other words, what formerly had been a space for discussing myriad aspects of music production within punk culture became gendered spaces for both action and reflection.[3]

As the opening epigraph to this chapter illustrates, DIY as a cultural practice contains multiple possibilities as an engaged form of literacy for young women involved in feminism. First, DIY practices have the ability to exchange feminist discourse through informal communication networks, a practice described by Garrison (2000) as "oppositional technologics," a term she defined as "the political praxis of resistance being woven into low-tech, amateur, hybrid, alternative subcultural feminist networks that register below the mainstream" (p. 151). Second, they persuade others to join in the process of doing it yourself through the use of low-end technologies and skills. While

[1] The specific genre of zines that I analyze in this study are called "perzines." As opposed to fanzines, music zines, and political zines, perzines express the thoughts and experience of individuals (Duncombe, p. 24). Although the perzines that I study are concerned with identity politics, many are not. Thus, as a group, the perzines in my study were chosen for their particular emphasis on aspects of identity politics that include gender, race, sexual orientation, class, disability, and nationality.

[2] See Nguyen (2001b) for a discussion of how "safe space" within Riot Grrrl erased class and race differences. For a critical discussion of women-only spaces, see Emi Koyama's zine "A Handbook on Discussing the Michigan Womyn's Music Festival for Trans Activists and Allies," available at http://www.eminism.org.

[3] For articles that explore DIY subcultures, zines, and Riot Grrrl culture, see Comstock (2001), Garrison (2000), Gottlieb and Wald (1994), Harris (2003), Kearney (1997), Kearney (1998), Leonard (1997), Leonard (1998), Licona (2005), Nguyen (2001), Piano (2002), Piano (2003), Smith (1997), Soccio (1999), Sutton (1999). For a comprehensive analysis and history of zine culture in the United States, see Duncombe (1997). For a recent ethnographic study of North American women in punk cultures who do not identify as riot grrrls, see LeBlanc (1999).

the exchange of narratives among Riot Grrrls illustrated the power of reading and writing practices to cohere young women around issues central to their day-to-day lives, just as significant was the occupation of both textual and material spaces that signaled a shift of women's subordinate position from observers of culture to that of producers. Whether making zines, music, arts and crafts, or t-shirts or participating in the distribution of these products, Riot Grrrls were engaged in a struggle over not just symbolic meaning but also the means of production and distribution. Furthermore, while the public face of Riot Grrrl movement quickly morphed into a consumerist aberration of its former underground self, the DIY movement generated among women continues to attract newcomers, expanding its scope of production to include an array of arts and crafts such as buttons, soaps, clothing, candles, and alternative menstrual products.

In this chapter, I argue that DIY practitioners' participation in cultural production contains the possibility for rethinking the relationship between youth and subcultural activities as one invoking numerous literacy practices engaged in a collective struggle over representation and also distribution and consumption. While subcultural studies has always been invested in the politics of representation in everyday life, literacy studies has a tremendous amount to gain from viewing DIY as a collective literacy practice functioning outside of mainstream educational institutions. These practices have a number of ramifications for literacy studies, for feminism, and for composition studies. Foremost, when used as a collective and individual strategy of representation, DIY practices, especially exchanging zines, has the ability to disrupt dominant discourses through the use of visual and verbal forms of communication.

Furthermore, in light of current debates about the possibilities of electronic technologies for expanding our understanding of literacy, DIY practitioners display a complex use of high- and low-end technologies that reveal multivalenced subcultural forms of feminist knowledge making.[4] These cultural forms include the low-tech construction of texts such as zines and other women-oriented crafts and also high-tech systems of distribution. Lastly, pertinent to literacy scholars, education specialists, feminists, and writing practitioners, DIY practitioners traverse a number of discursive boundaries, being both public and private, visual and verbal, academic and popular, individual and collective, low and high tech, displaying through their cultural production, what Kress (2000) has defined as, "multimodal" learning, a process that involves selecting the means of representation and communication based on what media are made available within a particular culture (p. 194).

When viewed in this way, literacy can be defined as a rhetorical process (selecting and choosing available communication methods and forms), and one that is inherently political. Indeed, these practices have the ability to extend traditional definitions of literacy by taking into account how extra-textual activities of production and distribution are responses to living in an increasingly consumer-saturated, highly technological globalized world. A world, as anthropologist Appadurai (2001) attested, which is,

> . . . demonstrably creating increased inequalities within and across societies, spiraling processes of ecological degradation and crisis, and unviable relations between finance and manufacturing capital, as well as between goods and the wealth required to purchase them. (p. 17)

Within the highly mediated world of media communication, global capital, and information flows, DIY practitioners rely on electronic and reproductive technologies with the intent of "making culture" for themselves. In this regard, one cannot discuss DIY practices without examining their material aspects, particularly how the use and availability of print and electronic technologies has facilitated the growth and development of subcultural literacies that have also, so to speak, gone public. In doing so, I argue for a broader understanding of youth-related literacies occurring outside the classroom that function not only at the level of the text, (its visual, verbal, and tactile qualities), but also take into account the political uses of production and distribution.

The concept of literacy as being not "an autonomous, objectified artifact of education and refinement but also a fundamentally subjective tool, made meaningful within systems of belief" was aptly expressed by Royster (2000) whose definition bolsters my argument that DIY practices are significant to literacy studies because they grant young women "the ability to gain access to information and to use this information variously to articulate lives and experiences and also to identify, think through, refine, and solve problems, sometimes complex problems, over time" (Royster, p. 45). In other words, the young women practicing DIY employ rhetorical and pedagogical strategies to produce collaboratively shared spaces that enable them to exchange life narratives and engage in a form of critical consumerism within the larger rubric of Third Wave feminism.[5]

POPULAR PEDAGOGIES: SITUATING DIY PRACTICES WITHIN "COMPOSITION'S EXTRACURRICULUM"

> It becomes political whenever someone like me ever gets to speak, because for someone like me, not speaking is the norm. . . ."
>
> —Emi Koyama, gender queer activist and zine editor of *Transfeminism* and *The Whore Revolution*

Concurrent with the cultural turn in the humanities has emerged an increased interest in researching literacy sites outside the classroom that may not conform to or be dictated by conventional understandings of what it means to be literate.[6] As Daniell (2003) claimed, the significance of these studies, what she called, "little narratives of literacy," is that they can offer vital insights into learning that quantitative or theoretical literacy accounts cannot. In particular, she noted, ethnographic accounts of literacy reveal how power relations are deeply embedded in acts of reading and writing because,

> they are marked by a tension between Foucauldian determinism and human agency, showing the power of institutions to control people by controlling their literacy and the power of individuals and groups to use literacy to act in concert with or in opposition to this power. (p. 7)

[4] For studies that examine the relationship between subcultural feminists and electronic technologies, see Comstock (2001), Garrison (2000), Nguyen (2001b), Piano (2002), Rhodes (2005), and Wakeford (2000).

[5] For key texts on third-wave feminism, see Brooks (1997), Garrison (2000), Henry (2004), Heywood and Drake (1997), Purvis (2004), Siegel (1997), and Walker (1995).

[6] See Blot and Collins (2004), Gere (1987), Heath (1983), Royster (2000) for theories of literacy that unravel the illiterate/literate, oral/written binary that has informed dominant perceptions of what it means to be literate. For studies of community literacies, see Cushman (1998), Daniell (2003), Flannery (2005), Heath (1983), Matthieu (2003), Moss (1994), Trimbur (2001).

In fact, as Daniell suggested, literacy practices occur despite, and because of, tacit and overt constraints placed on certain populations to acquire formal education or to participate in civic activities. In *Literacy and Literacies: Texts, Power, and Identity*, literacy scholars Collins and Blot (2003) argued that coterminous with the 19th-century universalization of education and its promise of upward social mobility and personal growth was a marked predominance of the school as "a central institution through which the conditions of appropriate belonging were defined . . ." (p. 87). Additionally, Daniell (2003) pointed out that literacy should not be defined as a neutral set of skills to acquire but as a discursive formation "always already embedded in particular social structures, instantiating the values of particular groups and cultures, which are themselves organized in response to power" (p. 13). Thus, it is not surprising that state-sanctioned policies of exclusion, segregation, and marginalization were countered by the development of informal spaces of learning organized around aspects of race, class, and gender.

Defining these collaborative literacy practices as "composition's extracurriculum," a term encompassing writing practices extending "beyond the academy to encompass the multiple contexts in which persons seek to improve their own writing" (1994, p. 80), Gere (1987, 1994, 1997) has mapped out a rich topography of historical and contemporary sites of informal learning in North America. In doing so, she eloquently argued that extracurricular literacy practices contained a mixture of motives fuelled by personal desires, economic and social aspirations, and collective group interests (1994, p. 80). More than a history of auto-didactic practices, however, Gere's research illustrated how literacy practices are indeliby tied to collaborative learning, thus lending credibility to the assumption among many composition scholars that the best way to become literate is "to join with others" (Gere, 1987, p. 123). Similar to Royster's view of literacy as a socially engaged practice, Gere (1987) argued for an ideological definition, in which "literacy means joining a specific community through understanding the issues it considers important and developing the capacity to participate in conversations about those issues" (p. 120).

Gere's emphasis on literacy as a situated practice, one that does not simply facilitate individual learning and success but is invested in a group identity that transcends and sometimes resists traditional educational motives, has been central to expanding our understanding of the affective and social dimensions of textual production outside the academy. For example, in her analysis of literacy practices in African American churches, Moss (1994) confirmed Gere's definition of literacy by analyzing "literacy events" such as church sermons.[7] Through her analysis of three different churches, Moss claimed that the sermon has the ability "to create and maintain a sense of community. This feature sets this literacy event apart from the essay . . . because of the sermon's dependence on both participants—preacher and congregation—to be considered a successful text in the community" (p. 151). In Moss's view, the dialogic interaction between preacher and congregation thus determines the outcome and the formation of the text, one that is in direct contrast to the monologic process often imposed in academic settings.

Although Moss (1994) rightfully concluded that privileging the essayist mode of literacy excludes validating home and community literacies, one factor both she and Gere overlooked is how the spaces of literacy inform different kinds of learning. Therefore, while maintaining that literacies are organized by social relations having affective and political dimensions, I also expand Moss and Gere's purview by claiming that if we think of literacy as being more than the acquisition of a set of skills such as reading and writing, we need to articulate more clearly how other modes of communication contribute to the development of "composition's extracurriculum" within particular locations. In this regard, redefining "composition's extracurriculum" involves a discussion of how the spaces of literacy are determined by ideological and power relations.

For example, in his discussion of "hush harbors," Nunley (2004) soundly argued for the need to include spatial analyses as a method for reading sites of pedagogy for subaltern groups. Reading spatiality for its rhetorical dimensions in literary texts and nonofficial sites of learning such as barber shops, front porches, fraternity and sorority houses, Nunley (2004) observed that "hush harbor spaces are sites where certain African American counternarratives and narratives are acknowledged, privileged, and spoken and performed differently" (p. 229). Nunley's research highlighted how collective sites of group identification among subaltern groups are indelibly linked to survival, maintenance, and growth, thus implicitly illustrating how literacy acquistion is materially linked to asymetrical relations of power within the United States. By using the spatial as a category of analysis, Nunley is able to situate rhetorical practices as stemming from material and ideological conditions that influence certain kinds of literacy activities. Likewise, situating DIY as a literacy practice within composition's extracurriculum must take into account not only the production of texts and artifacts, but also the uses of subcultural spaces that produce pedagogical effects through the attainment of cultural and (as I will show later in this chapter) even economic power among its members. Acknowledging the spatial aspects of literacy can complicate our understanding of popular and subcultural literacies, which often involve complex uses of high- and low-end technologies and varied forms of nontraditional literacy practices.

Most often associated with punk culture's valorization of amateurism, the rallying cry of DIY, "If I can do it, so can you" engendered a subterranean communication network through its invitational nature. Acting as a powerful tool for predominantly young people to reject mass culture foisted upon them, DIY practices employed the use of low-end technologies to forge their own culture. As a response to the overly produced rock music of the 1970, the ethos of amateurism led to a particular aesthetic, what Hebdige (1979) described as its "spectacular style," positioning punk culture in opposition to the mainstream. This stance was conveyed not only aesthetically through punks' politics of form—the brash in-your-face confrontational stance conveyed in its music, lyrics, and attire—but also through its DIY philosophy that signified "a critique of the dominant mode of passive consumer culture and . . . the active creation of an alternative culture" (Duncombe, p. 117). Within this new social formation, punks utilized alternative spaces and low-end technologies to foster resistant practices such as the production of music and zines and the creation of a punk sartorial style.

As Duncombe (1997) noted, punk and hip-hop youth cultures signaled a resistance to the hegemonic culture industries of the baby-boomer generation that provided little oppositional or representational space for a new generation of youth (p. 120). Thus, these

[7] As defined by Shirley Brice Heath (1982) in "Protean Shapes in Literacy Events," literacy events are "any event in which a written document enacts participants' interaction and interpretation of the document" (350).

emerging subcultures reformulated alternative culture by reconnecting to underground music, inhabiting public spaces, and occupying often defunct and abandoned commercial spaces for street parties and nightclubs.[8] These semipublic places helped facilitate a generational fight over representational space that paralleled the social movements of the 1960s and 1970s and formed the basis of popular youth cultures that continues today.[9] In terms of spatial analysis, the Riot Grrrl movement gathered momentum through manipulating punk spaces that were both textual and material.[10] For example, in "Paper Planes: Travelling the New Grrrl Geographies," Leonard (1998) explained how Riot Grrrls' textual appropriation of zine making was inherently political. "By writing themselves into the text, through relating personal experiences and concerns, riot grrrls . . . expanded the discursive parameters of the fanzine" (p. 107). Additionally, Riot Grrrl musicians radically altered the way punk music was conventionally delivered in clubs where young women who were normally sidelined as spectators took to the stage as performers.[11] This positional change from consuming music to making music projected a different model of what it was to be a young woman in "the scene," in addition to promoting a particular style of feminism more attractive than conventional feminist thought. Nguyen's (2003) observation on her online journal *Slanderous* illustrated this point: ". . . who listens to teacher when the cute pink-haired girl next to you might argue the same thing, but with a guitar and a fanzine in hand?" Her comment reveals the powerful pedagogical effects that both zine and music making had on young women in the punk scene leading to a collective identity galvanized primarily around gender issues. In his introduction to *Popular Literacy: Studies in Cultural Practices and Poetics*, Trimbur (2001) has noted that these popular forms of literacy are focused more on "making" rather than "consuming" culture and that they are "modes of rhetorical action" that often have political ends (p. 5).

Interventions into predominantly White masculine space were not exclusive to Riot Grrrl feminism but had their roots in second wave feminism's emergence within 1960s liberation movements. In *Feminist Literacies: 1968–75*, Flannery (2005) analyzed similar literacy practices, having a broad pedagogical focus among second-wave feminists. With the onset of affordable printing technologies and the need to get the message out, second-wave feminists published a wide variety of independently produced publications for political purposes.[12] Through the production and distribution of print media, women "worked to educate themselves into feminism" (p. 14) with the intention of both attracting women to feminism and addressing concerns, issues, and divisions as the movement gathered momentum. Furthermore, Riot Grrrls' insistence on gender-specific spaces had connections not only to second-wave feminists' "consciousness-raising" groups but to radical lesbian communities in college towns and cities across the United States in the 1970s and 1980s, many of whom created an infrastructure of alternative spaces that included women-only bookstores, drop-in centers, exhibitions, and performances. (Kearney, 1997, p. 218).[13] Therefore, in understanding the multidimensional literacy activities that Riot Grrrls engaged in, it is important to see how gender-specific spaces created during the 1980s informed Riot Grrrls' own subcultural literacy locations.

As a form of cultural politics, DIY is not exclusively the domain of punk subcultures. For example, many disenfranchised communities existing within multiple public spheres use DIY practices to reinvest technologies as a mode of survival and a creative response to oppression. In discussing his documentary *Taxi-Vala* about the use of CB radios to create a low-tech communications network for South Asian taxi drivers in New York to counter growing anti-Asian racism and violence, Bald claimed,

> With limited resources and limited access, people have been using whatever technology they can get their hands on . . . and have been pushing it, stretching it, redefining it, and usually getting it to do much more than it was ever meant to do. (Nelson & Tu, 2001, p. 89)
>
> Using available technologies to engage in collective resistance can be seen as a kind of critical technological literacy in which people seek to gain cultural power by manipulating technology to suit their political concerns. R. Ohmann has argued "technology . . . is itself a social process, saturated with the power relations around it, continually reshaped according to some people's *intentions*" (1985, p. 681). Not surprisingly, most studies involved in analyzing the relationship between technology and literacy focus on computer literacy rather than low end technologies that DIY practices most often use, yet understanding how people manipulate available technologies for communicative purposes can lead us to more enriched and complicated studies of "composition's extracurriculum."

DIY FEMINISM: SUSTAINING DIALOGUE AND RESISTANCE OUTSIDE THE ACADEMY

> Zines serve a political function in their ability to suggest alternatives, to educate, and to provide readers with the kind of information that is important to critical thinking.
>
> —Celia Perez, i dreamed i was assertive #3

Despite the increase of studies of literacy practices outside formal education institutions and the enduring practice of DIY among young people since the 1970s, youth cultures have only recently been considered significant for research in women's studies, rhetoric and composition, and literacy studies. As an early proponent of studying subulctural composing practices, Comstock (2001) argued that zine editors largely

[8] For a more extended analysis of the material conditions that facilitated the emergence of punk and hip hop cultures, see Hebdige (1979) and Rose (1994).

[9] See Pough (2004) for a rhetorical study that addresses how hip-hop culture is part of a continuum of resistant practices enacted by Black women who have historically made use of different kinds of public and counterpublic spaces in the United States as forms of resistance, solidarity, and representation. Also see Flannery (2005), a rich cultural history of second-wave feminist literacy practices, particularly focused on the development of alternative media and a university without walls that bolstered and facilitated the women's liberation movement.

[10] For a comprehensive history of Riot Grrrl, replete with video interviews, articles, and chronologies, see Riot Grrrl Retro Retrospective at the Experience Music Project's website: http://www.emplive.com/explore/riot_grrrl/index.asp

[11] See Gottlieb and Wald (1994) for an excellent early analysis of how Riot Grrrl culture disrupted punk's White masculinity through a series of interventions, bodily, and textual.

[12] See M. L. Allen (1988) *The Development of Communication Networks Among Women, 1963–1983* Available at http://www.wifp.org/tableofcontents.html

[13] Interestingly, the post-Riot Grrrl subculture that I study has become less concerned with maintaining gender-specific spaces as many feminists attempt to become more inclusive of gender minorities such as transgender, transsexual, and intersex individuals.

have been ignored despite their ability to challenge "notions of feminism as primarily an adult political project" (p. 383). In part, this oversight may be due to the ephemeral aspects of youth subcultures in which music, writing, and craft making are often consumed in the moment rather than archived for future reference.[14] However, as some third-wave feminists have noted, divisive attitudes between 'the waves' may contribute to the lack of serious attention within the academy given to activities and practices that appear to be 'feminist light' or insignificant due to their subcultural status.[15] In understanding emerging literacy practices among second wave feminists, Flannery (2005) noted a primary concern of feminists was and continues to be what counts as knowledge.

> One must ask not only what was taught and learned, in what ways, by whom, and under what circumstances, but also how knowledge was conceptualized. (p. 15)

When applying this statement to zines and other popular and subcultural feminist production, we can see how feminism has been rendered invisible not only by mainstream media, which periodically declaims feminism as "dead," but also by institutionalized forms of feminism such as national organizations and women's studies programs, feminist journals, and conferences.[16]

Yet, in her ground-breaking article on subcultural feminism, Garrison (2000) pointed to new forms of feminist expression, some that barely register above ground, emerging in response to the feminist backlash and the impact of communication technologies on everyday life (p. 142). For third-wave scholars such as Garrison, feminist knowledge is not solely produced in the academy or within feminist institutions but covers a range of DIY activities including producing zines, arts and crafts, and music, and organizing annual conferences such as Ladyfest and Southern Grrrls Convention. In this section, I examine how DIY practices, particularly making zines, contribute to the development of a popular literacy that redefines feminism for a "younger" generation.[17] Specifically, I explore how DIY practitioners use narrative, invitational discourse, and popular cultural forms to facilitate a form of feminist pedagogy that holds "the potential for building learning conditions leading to full and equitable social participation" (The New London Group, 2000, p. 9).

The power of narrative as a pedagogical tool within this subculture lies in its focus on how "the everyday" is used for both action and reflection. In discussing the importance of narrative, Ciara Xyerra, editor of *A Renegade's Handbook to Love & Sabotage*, explained that, "Many zines seem to tell the story that gets lost in the shuffle of everyday life, because a lot of zines are chronicling things that are very ordinary & everyday, but that matter hugely to the people who experience them" (E-mail to Author (11/02/02). Ciara's comment suggests that a critical aspect of using narrative is its accessibility as a communicative form for both readers and writers. Commenting on the predominance of narrative as a third-wave feminist strategy, Jacob (2005) observed that personal narrative provides those who may not have access to more established publishing institutions with the ability "to document their lives and their histories" (p. 197).

Relying on their own experiences, zine editors are able to theorize a self deeply embedded in material and historical relations with others. As noted by McLaughlin (1996), zines enact a "vernacular cultural criticism," a subcultural discourse that cannot be inhabited by academic theory. "Zine theory has the advantage of operating within the culture it describes, with an intimacy and specificity not possible for the academic observer . . ." (p. 62); simultaneously, zine editors are able to use the tools of the academy to document "the theoretical work that goes on in everyday life" (McLaughlin, p. 62). The particular vantage point that zine editors occupy between popular and academic discourses allows zine editors to utilize popular cultural forms such as diary entries, comic strips, photo essays, maps, and popular iconic imagery to make theoretically sophisticated arguments.

While zines are deeply personal, often confessional, most zine editors integrate everyday aspects of their lives into their zines as a means of critique, self-reflection, and self-definition. As Celia Perez, editor of the zine *i dreamed i was assertive*, said, "I write mostly about the issues that affect my life and these are subjects like race, poverty, injustice . . . my writing is influenced by my experiences and supplemented by the things I read and . . . by the things I SEE" (E-mail to the Author, 1/21/02). Many zine editors consciously incorporate everyday experiences into their zines as a means of reflecting on how their politics have come to be defined by their own subject positions. For example, riding public transportation or grocery shopping grants Celia the opportunity to reflect on class and race politics. After describing the beauty of the produce at Whole Foods Market where there are "No straying brown lettuce leaves dangling over the edge. No squished grapes underfoot . . .," Celia (2002) compared the clientele to the Whole Foods workers:

> I noticed that while most of the employees at the store were African-American, Latino, or Asian, most of the shoppers were white. I started thinking about how many of the store's employees could even afford to shop there. (p. 7)

Later in the essay, she described the stores where her family used to shop in Miami—the bodegas and corner shops run mostly by immigrants—comparing the disparity of those experiences to what she has witnessed at a mega-grocery store like Whole Foods Market where relations between customers and employees are estranged. This excerpt also illustrates how the use of "the popular," what Trimbur

[14] In recent years, a growing number of academic and community libraries have begun zine collections, primarily at the insistence of feminist and queer librarians. Some of these collections are located at the Sallie Bingham Center at Duke University, Special Collections Library at San Diego State University, and Barnard College. Also, community-based zine libraries continue to spring up in many university towns and small cities. These spaces often act as a spatial nexus for alternative culture and feature DIY workshops, the distribution of zines, and political/community meetings.

[15] Debates concerning second- and third-wave feminism have generated numerous articles and books. See *Hypatia: Journal of Feminist Philosophy, The Journal of Social Philosophy 12.3* (1999), Signs: *A Journal of Women in Culture and Society* (1998), and NWSAJ (National Women's Studies Association Journal) (2004) for ongoing debates that reveal a variety of positions implied by the term 'third wave.'

[16] In a Bust interview with Kathleen Hanna and Gloria Steinem about feminism, Steinem admited to not covering the Riot Grrrl movement in *Ms.* magazine because "older feminists don't always recognize feminism when it comes in a different form" (54).

[17] I use the term "younger" not as an age differential but a marker that defines feminism differently from second-wave feminism. Often misrepresented as a rejection of feminism by young women or as an over-reliance on individual rather collective politics, third-wave feminism, as Garrison (2000) stated, is a term that must be viewed as an historical marker rather than a generational one. While acknowledging its affinities with prior feminist movements, Garrison (2000) claimed third-wave feminism has been influenced by "postmodern cultural conditions," that include "the media backlash, violence, and others kinds of historical remnants, products and monsters" (p. 149).

(2001) defined as "the ways in which ordinary people make the act of consumption—whether of texts, entertainment, or public places—into productions of cultural meaning" (p. 129), functions as a form of pedagogy. In other words, for readers an event as commonplace as a trip to the grocery store becomes an opportunity to critique how racial and class politics are woven into everyday life.

Researching public forms of writing taken up by Hmong immigrants in Wisconsin, Duffy (2004) defined "a rhetorical conception of literacy" as one in which the development of literacy skills is highly contextual, one in which "rhetorics of public and civic life influence how people learn, use, and value the possibilities of written language" (p. 226). Since their development in the early 1990s as a tool of feminist resistance, zines have moved beyond the borders of the hardcore punk movement in terms of audience. Acting as both private and public testaments to the power of theorizing the everyday, zines have the capability of "talking back" to dominant culture and among zine editors themselves. The political and emotional investments involved in producing this kind of cultural production facilitate a form of literacy that attempts to resist, if only symbolically, what Collins (2000) termed, the "matrix of domination," described as the "overall social organization within which intersecting oppressions originate, develop, and are contained" (p. 228). Many zine editors employ textual strategies that often begin by claiming one's identity markers as the epistemological basis in which to confront the world. Noemi Martinez, editor of *Hermana, Resist*, has described her desire to produce zines as being motivated by "reading other zines that did not entirely identify with my experience, didn't express the feelings of a chicana" (E-mail to Author 1/28/02). Often the motivation to make zines stems from a desire to be heard and represented not only within dominant culture but also within the subculture, and/or the feminist movement itself.

Questioning the inclusion of nondominant sexual, racial, and class identities is manifested through the production of collaborative texts that directly address exclusions, revealing that these subcultural sites are not utopian, conflict-free zones. In fact, in *Race Riot 2*, Nguyen stated in her intro that this compilation zine is geared toward disruption rather than harmony. "I don't want to make this comfortable, or comforting—*this is supposed to fuck with you*." Both in terms of pedagogical and political practices, compilation or comp zines such as *Race Riot* convey a range of experiences and critiques by subcultural members organized around specific identity markers or issues. Although limited in their distribution, these collaboratively produced and written texts reveal how hierarchical power structures are reproduced even within progressive communities.

Interestingly, both *Evolution of a Race Riot* edited by Nguyen and *How to Stage A Coup* edited by Helen Luu assumed an interventionist position within subcultural feminism, acting in a similar fashion to Anzaldua and Moraga's anthology (1981) *This Bridge Called My Back: Writings by Radical Women of Color* as a representational space for feminists of color. Reclaiming textual spaces by marginalized feminist identities disrupts the continuing representation that feminism is primarily for White, middle-class women. In addition, because of their handmade qualities, compilation zines, such as Nguyen and Lu's, contain richer possibilities for self-representational and collective practices in terms of design, editing, and layout of individual contributions. They insist on developing a collective voice, but rather than fusing identities through anonymous publications or collective editing as occurred in second-wave feminist publishing, the editors provide each contributor with the freedom to design her own contribution. In this way, comp zines display complex visual and verbal literacies that perform, so to speak, individual differences among the contributors. If, as Luke, suggested, feminist pedagogy is understood "as reversing women's silences, and as conducive to generating non-competitive dialogue among women about their shared and different experiences," (1998, p. 18), then the exchange of personal narrative in zines can provide one nontraditional learning space that is capable of generating awareness and respect for differences among women.

HIGH TECH/LOW TECH: CONSTRUCTING ETHICAL CONSUMER LITERACIES

> Making shit yourself is a fucking radical concept. Crafting is a political act in that it can enable one to opt out of a consumerist culture. . . . It's as much about aesthetics as it is about DIY, about proving that art is for everybody, and not some highbrow entity inaccessible to "regular folk" . . .
>
> —Lauren Martin, zine editor, *Quantify #5*

Analyzing the flexibility and expansiveness of the Internet as a communicative medium, Castells (2001) argued that it "lays the foundation for self-directed networking as a tool for organization, collective action, and the construction of meaning" (p. 55). Through the creation of electronic networks, emancipatory movements can connect with like-minded others on a more globally conscious scale. In this context, subcultural feminisms are deeply imbricated in global processes such as the redistribution of resources and capital, transitory flows of people, information, labor, and economies, the dominance of American military and cultural power, and the development of information technologies. In understanding contemporary feminism within a highly technologized world, Purvis (2004) observed that third-wave feminists use electronic technologies to foster "new spaces and methods for the dissemination of information and the implementation of feminist agendas, such as the maintenance of Web sites and the utilization of cyberspace for activism" (p. 105). While many DIY practitioners use electronic technologies for communicative and representational purposes, they also use these technologies for buying and selling zines, clothing, candles, soaps, alternative menstrual products, and a wide variety of other women-related items. In this section, I analyze how DIY practitioners imbue low- and high-end technologies with an ethical bent by utilizing various technologies for different ends. Thus, for example, while print zines and other crafts continue to be individually produced, electronic technologies are used for distribution and communication. DIY practitioners' nuanced approach to technology use may "fly in the face" of a predominant myth—that electronic texts will eventually make print-based culture anachronistic.

In *Technology and Literacy in the Twenty-First Century: The Importance of Paying Attention*, Selfe defined "technological literacy" as "a complex set of socially and culturally situated values, practices, and skill involved in operating linguistically within the context of electronic environments" (1999, p. 11). However, as Selfe later mentioned, how literacy is determined often depends on the official uses of certain kinds of technology such as using the Internet to do research rather than communicate with a friend online (p. 12). Within the context of zine production and distribution, definitions of technological literacy must also encompass making decisions about what medium to use in distributing knowledge.

Thus, while many zine editors engage in traditional literacy practices, they also participate in tactile literacies similar to those Gernes (2001) examined in "Recasting the Culture of Ephemera." Analyzing 18th- and 19th-century commonplace books and scrapbooks created by ordinary people, he noted how these popular artifacts become forms of identity construction crafted from "the material culture of ephemera" (p. 109). The innovative use of scraps and cutouts from discarded newspapers and magazines reveals how embracing popular discourses of everyday life contribute to literacy practices that move beyond functional skills to ones invested in personal, familial, and communal meaning.

Making zines also illustrates an ability to poach popular discourses, incorporating already made images and text in the construction of one's identity. For example, in her zine *Hermana, Resist*, Noemi Martinez included favorite Tejana recipes, popular Mexican iconography, and traditional *curandera* remedies to formulate a bicultural South Texas identity. This "cut-and-paste" tactile literacy cannot be reproduced in an electronic environment nor do many zine editors perceive electronic zines as the wave of the future. For example, Ciara Xyerra observed that, "There's just something more satisfying (to me) about having a zine to carry around with me, to read on the train or in the bathtub. Paper seems so much more intimate & personal." (E-mail to Author, 2/21/02). Additionally, ethical issues concerning accessibility surface in discussing electronic modes of zine production. Celia Perez pointed to the fact that "Online zines . . . contradict what zines are all about in that as much as we'd like to believe that computers and the Internet are connecting people across the world, these things are really only widely accessible to those who can afford to use them" (E-mail to Author, 1/28/02). Thus, when defining technological literacy within this DIY subculture, utilizing electronic modes of communication may have less to do with ability and more to do with how technology can be invested in values emphasizing accessibility, economics, and print aesthetics.

However, more and more, what one does see growing rapidly within this subculture are electronic subcultural distribution sites known as "distros." These sites convey a dual function: they sell and distribute handmade goods produced and consumed by women, and they act as congregating spaces for those who produce and consume these goods. As a method of distribution, distros do not necessarily supplant print catalogs that zine distributors have traditionally used to advertise and sell their zines, but they do provide faster and more convenient service as e-commerce sites do. Furthermore, distros also serve as meeting spaces for DIY practitioners, both experienced and inexperienced, to exchange information on message boards, write reviews, sign guest books, and access links to similar sites such as blogs, activist sites, and online journals. In this way, distros reclaim or decolonize already colonized or commercialized sites on the Web as well as facilitate a more dynamic and immediate "entrepreneurial infrastructure within youth cultures" (McRobbie, p. 135).

Subsequently, the circulation of feminist commodities challenges not only how feminist discourse is disseminated through academic and popular venues, but in what forms feminist discourse can arise. For example, while feminist discourse is typically delivered through forms such as scholarly publications, lectures, films, conferences, or women's studies classes, within DIY subcultures, zines and other women-oriented merchandise communicate information on issues concerning women's health and well being besides providing pleasure through the exchange of craft ideas, recipes, film, and book recommendations, etc. The distro itself, despite its virtual appearance, reclaims a more intimate relationship among distributors, producers, and consumers. And in many cases, these roles are interchangeable. Discussing this relationship in zines, Duncombe noted that, "Having readers become writers and writers become readers circumvents a fundamental tenet of the logic of consumer culture: the division between producers and consumers" (p. 124).

In *Consumerism Reconsidered: Buying and Power*, Nava argued for a critical consumerism intent on utilizing one's ability to choose what to buy. While her focus is mostly on organized boycotts and "selective buying," what she defined as "the buying of products which conform to certain criteria" (p. 59), an informal DIY economy also provides an alternative to buying mass-marketed goods by being "able to exercise control over production itself" (p. 59). Thus, for example, the rise of Internet distribution sites selling alternative menstrual products such as *Blood Sisters Project* and *Urban Armour: Kickass Alternative Menstrual Hardware* offer alternatives for many women dismayed by noxious chemicals such as dioxin that are used to produce menstrual products in addition to the expense and waste of disposable items. Reusable and handmade items such as these communicate values of sustainability and foreground women's health as a primary issue of concern.

In this way, critical consumerism becomes another form of literacy that DIY practitioners' engage in within this informal economy. Although women's roles as consumers in feminist studies have been, as Kearney (1998) noted, "over-privileged . . . as a form of political resistance" (p. 291), within this subculture, young women challenge the binary that equates adults as primarily producers and women/girls as consumers (p. 291). In choosing to make and buy individually produced products, DIY practitioners are able "to exercise some control over production itself, over what gets produced and the political conditions in which production takes place" (Nava, p. 59). While feminist discourse is communicated through print zines, the production of other products such as compilation tapes, patches, stickers, T-shirts, soaps, alternative menstrual products, and vegan items also contribute to valuing women-made products that use ingredients or methods of production that are ethical, safe, and ecologically sound. Including these feminist approaches to consumerism as forms of literacy extends Duffy's (2004) definition of rhetorical literacy to include not only written communication but other forms of discourse production that are critically geared toward attempting even at a microlevel to make our lives and the world better.[18]

Additionally, while distros assume market practices of buying and distributing products, they are nevertheless run as a service rather than for profit. For example, Jenn of the now defunct *Grrrl-style* distro, claimed on her mission page, "I started it because I am constantly inspired by the diy revolution, and . . . I wanted to help others, too." Establishing a reputation of goodwill and good service within the community is important in gaining trust and support for one's efforts. While it is problematic that women's work historically has been devalued and that the free labor that goes into maintaining

[18] Some online sites that are part of this diverse virtual landscape include *Blood Sisters Project* <http://bloodsisters.org/bloodsisters/index.html>, *Learning to Leave a Paper Trail*< http://www.papertrail.zinetastic.com>, *Craft Mafia* <http://craftmafia.com/>, *You Grow Girl* <http://www.yougrowgirl.com/index.php> and *Urban Armour: Kickass Alternative Menstrual Hardware* <http://urban-armor.org/urban-armor>.

such sites can be viewed as voluntary labor, at the same time, maintaining control over the choice of products one sells can also be seen as a form of activism.

Sociologist Giddens (2000) has described the spatial, cultural, and economic processes of globalization as forming "a runaway world." By this he contended that regardless of our privilege or lack of, we are all vulnerable to risks and uncertainties never faced before (pp. 20–21). While this prognosis of the world's social, environmental, and economic milieu may appear dire, in fact, as Giddens recognized, globalization's unpredictability simultaneously offers possibilities for political and collective practice by reinvesting global forms of communication and distribution with oppositional values and practices. Even more interesting, DIY practices of distribution and production of women-oriented crafts trouble the conventional methods in which feminist discourse is produced by invoking new forms of literacy that are socially and ethically invested in the use of low- and high-end technologies and their relation to global and local economies.

CONCLUSION

> "If multiculturalism and diversity are the future of the academy, then so is multiliteracy" (p. 177). —Beverly Moss

In order to recognize DIY practices as enacting various kinds of critical literacy, I look to Flannery's (1990) application of Foucault's concept of "subjugated knowledges" for a theoretical understanding of subcultural literacy practices. Through her consideration of the difficulties involved in institutionalizing nontraditional forms of knowledge, she suggested that we focus instead on recognizing their "multiplicity in its most radical form" (p. 213). In this respect, Flannery asserted that subjugated knowledges can reveal "a history of struggle" that can "provide tools for present use" (p. 211). As she explained it,

> The subjugated knowledges are opposed to systemizations, opposed to the sort of discourse that would posit a picture of the whole, opposed to canon and to unitary theories of anything, in order to honor productivity, difference, change. (Foucault "Two Lectures" 84, paraphrased in Flannery, p. 212)

In other words, literacy activities occurring within DIY subcultures may not and should not be wholly transferable to a classroom or curriculum; however, their study can lead us to recognize and accept variegated forms of knowledge making, particularly those that "work to make possible greater autonomy and self-determination" (Flannery, 1990, p. 213).

Exchanging information about feminist issues through nontraditional forms such as commodities or objects facilitates new ways of thinking about literacy and its relation to the global economy. Within this subculture, zine editors and distributors view production and consumption as a resistant and ethical act to global economic forces that have forged deep discrepancies between First and Third World, independent and dependent, and producer and consumer roles. In an attempt to circumvent contributing to these discrepancies, many DIY practitioners produce their own goods and services and in doing so they also challenge what it means to be a feminist through the complex uses of technology and popular forms of literacy.

REFERENCES

Allen, M. (1988). *The development of communication networks among women, 1963–1983.* Retrieved August 3, 2003, from the Women's Institute for Freedom of the Press Web site: http://www.wifp.org

Anzaldua, G., & Moraga, C. (Eds.). (1981). *This bridge called my back: Writings by radical women of color.* New York: Kitchen Table: Women of Color.

Appadurai, A. (2001). Grassroots globalization and the research imagination. In A. Apppadurai (Ed.), *Globalization* (pp. 1–21). Durham, NC: Duke University Press.

Bhavnani, K. K., Kent, K., F. W., & Twine. (Eds.). (1998). Special issue, feminisms and youth culture. *Signs: A Journal of Women in Culture and Society 26.1*

Castells, M. (2001). *The Internet galaxy: Reflections on the Internet, business, and society.* New York: Oxford University Press.

Collins, J., & Blot, R. (2003). *Literacy and literacies: Texts, power, and identity.* Cambridge, UK: Cambridge University Press.

Collins, P. H. (2000). *Black feminist thought: Knowledge, consciousness, and the politics of empowerment* (2nd ed.). New York: Routledge.

Comstock, M. (2001). Grrrl Zine Networks: Re-composing spaces of authority, gender, and culture. *Journal of Advanced Composition, 21,* 383–409.

Cushman, E. (1998). *The struggle and the tools: Oral and literate strategies in an inner city community.* Albany: SUNY Press.

Daniell, B. (2003). *A communion of friendship: Literacy, spiritual practice, and women in recovery.* Carbondale: Southern Illinois University Press.

Duffy, J. (2004). Letters from the Fair City: A rhetorical conception of literacy. *College Composition and Communication, 56,* 223–250.

Duncombe, S. (1997). *Notes from underground: Zines and the politics of alternative culture.* New York: Verso.

Flannery, K. T. (2005). *Feminist literacies, 1968–75.* Carbondale: University of Illinois Press.

Flannery, K. T. (1990). In praise of the local and transitory. In A. Lunsford, H. Moglen, & J. Slevin (Eds.), *The right to literacy* (pp. 208–214). New York: Modern Language Association Press.

Garrison, E. K. (2000). U.S. feminism—grrrl style! Youth (sub)cultures and the technologies of the third wave. *Feminist Studies, 1,* 141–170.

Gere, A. R. (1987). *Writing groups: History, theory, and implications.* Carbondale: Southern Illinois University Press.

Gere, A. R. (1994). Kitchen tables and rented rooms: The extracurriculum of composition. *College Composition and Communication, 45,* 75–92.

Gere, A. R. (1997). *Intimate practices: Literacy and cultural work in U.S. women's clubs, 1880–1920.* Urbana: University of Illinois Press.

Gernes, T. S. (2001). Recasting the culture of ephemera. In J. Trimbur (Ed.), *Popular literacy: Studies in cultural practices and poetics* (pp. 107–127). Pittsburgh, PA: University of Pittsburgh Press.

Giddens, A. (2000). *Runaway world: How globalization is shaping our lives.* New York: Routledge.

Gottlieb, J., & Wald, G. (1994). Smells like teen spirit: Riot grrrls, revolution and women in independent rock. In A. Ross & T. Rose (Eds.), *Microfiends: Youth music & youth culture* (pp. 250–272). New York: Routledge.

Harris, A. (2003). Jamming girl culture: Young women and consumer citizenship. In A. Harris (Ed.), *All about the girl: Culture, power, and identity* (pp. 163–172). New York: Routledge.

Heath, S. B. (1982). Protean shapes in literacy events: Ever-shifting oral and literate traditions. In D. Tannen. (Ed.), *Spoken and written language: Exploring orality and literacy* (pp. 348–370). Norwood, NJ: Ablex Publishing.

Heath, S. B. (1983). *Ways with words: Language, life, and work in communities and classrooms.* Cambridge, UK: Cambridge University Press.

Hebdige, D. (1979). *Subculture: The meaning of style.* New York: Routledge.

Henry, A. (2004). *Not my mother's sister: Generational conflict and third-wave feminism.* Bloomington: Indiana University Press.

Hex, C. (2000 Winter). Fierce, funny feminists. *Bust Magazine, 16,* 52–56.

Heywood, L., & Drake, J. (Eds.). (1997). *Third wave agenda: Being feminist, doing feminism.* Minneapolis: University of Minnesota Press.

Jacob, K., & Licona, A. C. (2005). Writing the waves: A dialogue on the tools, tactics, and tensions of feminisms and feminist practices over time and place. *National Women's Studies Association Journal, 17,* 197–205.

Kearney, M. C. (1997). The missing links: Riot grrrl—feminism—lesbian culture. In S. Whitely (Ed.), *Sexing the groove: Popular music and gender* (pp. 207–229). New York: Routledge.

Kearney, M. C. (1998). Producing girls: Rethinking the study of female youth culture. In S. Inness (Ed.), *Delinquents & debutantes: Twentieth century girls' culture* (pp. 285–310). New York: NYU Press.

Koyama, E. (Ed.). *Handbook on discussing the Michigan womyn's music festival for trans activists and allies.* No date. Self-published.

Kress, G. (2000). Multimodality. In B. Cope & M. Kalantzis (Eds.), *Multiliteracies: Literacy learning and the design of social futures* (pp. 182–202). New York: Routledge.

LeBlanc, L. (1999). *Pretty in punk: Girls' gender resistance in a boys' subculture.* New Brunswick, NJ: Rutgers University Press.

Leonard, M. (1998). Paper planes: Travelling the new grrrl geographies. In T. Skelton & G. Valentine (Eds.), *Cool places: Geographies of youth cultures* (pp. 101–118). New York: Routledge.

Licona, A. (2005). (B)orderlands' rhetorics and representations: The transformative potential of feminist third-space scholarship and zines. *National Women's Studies Association Journal, 17,* 104–129

Luke, C. (1998). Pedagogy and authority: Lessons from feminist and cultural studies, postmodernism and feminist pedagogy. In D. Buckingham (Ed.), *Teaching popular culture: Beyond radical pedagogy* (pp. 18–41). Bristol, PA: University College London Press.

Martin, L. (2003). I am making art. *Quantify, 5,* 22–29.

Matthieu, P. (2003). Not your mama's bus tour: A case for radically insufficient writing. In B. McComiskey & C. Ryan (Eds.), *City comp: Identities, spaces, practices* (pp. 71–84). New York: SUNY Press.

McLaughlin, T. (1996). *Street smarts and critical theory: Listening to the vernacular.* Madison: University of Wisconsin Press.

McRobbie, A. (1994). *Postmodernism and Popular Culture.* New York: Routledge.

Moss, B. J. (1994). Creating a community: Literacy events in African-American churches. In B. Moss (Ed.), *Literacy across communities* (pp. 147–177). Cresskill, NJ: Hampton.

Nava, M. (1999). Consumerism reconsidered: Buying and power. In M. Shiach (Ed.), *Feminism and cultural studies* (pp. 45–63). New York: Oxford University Press.

Nelson, A., & Tu, T. L. N. (2001). Appropriating technology: Interview with Vivek Bald. In A. Nelson & T. L. N. Tu (Eds.), *Technicolor: Race, technology, and everyday life* (pp. 88–99). New York: New York University Press.

New London Group. (2000). A pedagogy of multiliteracies: Designing social futures. In B. Cope & M. Kalantzis (Eds.), *Mulitliteracies: Literacy learning and the design of social futures* (9–37). New York: Routledge.

Nguyen, M. (Ed.). (1998). Introduction. In *Evolution of a Race Riot.* Self-published.

Nguyen, M. (Ed.). (2001a). Introduction. *Evolution of a Race Riot* 2. Self-published.

Nguyen, M. (2001b). Tales of an Asiatic geek girl: Slant from paper to pixels. In A. Nelson & T. L. N. Tu (Eds.), *Technicolor: Race, technology, and everyday life* (pp. 177–190). New York: New York University Press.

Nguyen, M. (2003). *Slanderous: An online journal.* Retrieved August 3, 2003, from http://www.worsethanqueer.com/slander

Nunley, V. L. (2004). From the harbor to da academic hood: Hush harbors and an African American rhetorical tradition. In E. B. Richardson & R. L. Jackson II (Eds.), *African American rhetoric(s): Interdisciplinary perspectives* (pp. 221–241). Carbondale: Southern Illinois University Press.

Ohmann, R. (1985). Literacy, technology, and monopoly capital. *College English, 47,* 675–689.

Perez, C. (2000). Zines in libraries. *i dreamed i was assertive #3.*

Perez, C. (2002). The politics of grocery stores. *i dreamed i was assertive #4.*

Piano, D. (2002). Congregating women: Reading third wave feminist practices in subcultural production. *Rhizomes: Cultural Studies in Emerging Knowledges, 4.* Retrieved May 5, 2006 from http://www.rhizomes.net/issue4/piano.html

Piano, D. (2003). Resisting subjects: DIY feminism and the politics of spectacular style in women's. In D. Muggleton & R. Weinzierl (Eds.), *The post-subcultures reader* (pp. 253–265). Oxford, UK: Berg Press.

Pough, G. D. (2004). *Check it while I wreck it: Black womanhood, hip-hop culture, and the oublic sphere.* Boston, MA: Northeastern Press.

Purvis, J. (2004). Grrrls and women together in the third wave: Embracing the challenged of intergenerational feminism(s). *National Women's Studies Association Journal, 16*(3), 93–123.

Rhodes, J. (2005). *Radical feminism, writing, and critical agency: From manifesto to modem.* Albany: SUNY Press.

Rose, T. (1994). *Black noise: Rap music and Black culture in contemporary America.* Hanover, CT: Wesleyan University Press.

Royster, J. J. (2000). *Traces of the stream: Literacy and social change among African American women.* Pittsburgh, PA: University of Pittsburgh Press.

Selfe, C. (1999). *Technology and literacy in the twenty-first century: The importance of paying attention.* Carbondale: Southern Illinois University Press.

Siegel, D. (1997). The legacy of the personal: Generating theory in feminism's third wave. *Hypatia: Journal of Feminist Philosophy, The Journal of Social Philosophy* 12.3, 46–75.

Smith, J. (1997). Doin' it for the ladies—youth feminism: Cultural productions/cultural activisms. In L. Heywood & J. Drake (Eds.), *Third wave agenda: Being feminist, doing feminism* (pp. 226–238). Minneapolis: University of Minnesota.

Springer, K. (2002) Third wave black feminism? *Signs: Journal of Women in Culture and Society, 27,* 1059–1082.

Sutton, L. (1999). All media are created equal: Do-it-yourself identity in alternative publishing. In M. Bucholz, A. C. Liang, & L. Sutton (Eds.), *Reinventing identities: The gendered self in discourse* (pp. 163–180). Boston: Oxford University Press.

Trimbur, J. (2001). *Popular literacy: Studies in cultural practices and poetics.* Pittsburgh, PA: University of Pittsburgh Press.

Wakeford, N. (2000). Networking women and grrrls with information/communication technology: Surfing tales of the World Wide Web. In D. Bell (Ed.), *The cybercultures reader* (pp. 350–359). New York: Routledge.

Xyerra, Ciara. Email to Author. February 2, 2002.

•33•

EXAMINING SHARED DOMAINS OF LITERACY IN THE CHURCH AND SCHOOL OF AFRICAN AMERICAN CHILDREN

Gwendolyn Michele Thompson McMillon
OAKLAND UNIVERSITY

Patricia A. Edwards
MICHIGAN STATE UNIVERSITY

For many years educational researchers have attempted to improve the literacy development of African American children; despite their efforts, "the enigma" remains. What can we do to increase the reading achievement of African American children, thereby decreasing the gap between African Americans and their White counterparts?

As African American researchers, our research agendas focus on developing ways to alleviate the reading underachievement of African American children. We believe a large portion of the problem must be solved "in house"—in our homes, communities, and institutions that service our families. Therefore, in this chapter we share vital information by closely examining literacy practices in the African American Church environment, and considering how those practices might connect with, reinforce, and support literacy practices within the school environment. By utilizing our collective knowledge of two of the most significant institutions in the life of African American children, we hope to move the field closer to identifying possible solutions to the enigma surrounding African American children's reading failure.

Several researchers have emphasized the importance of considering the literacy practices of outside institutions in order to understand the literacy crisis within the classroom (Edwards, Pleasants, & Franklin, 1999; Heath, 1983; Hull & Schultz, 2002; McMillon & Edwards, 2000; Purcell-Gates, 1995; Resnick, 1990). In her groundbreaking study comparing the literacy practices of mainstream and nonmainstream communities, Heath discussed the importance of studying all the environments within a community including, "ways of living, eating, sleeping, worshiping, using space, and filling time" (p. 3), in order to understand the entire process of literacy acquisition and development.

As lifelong participants in African American churches, we recognize that the church is a valuable resource that has been underutilized by educational institutions in the United States. Although the church is the most influential institution in the Black community (Franklin, 1997; Frazier, 1963; Lincoln & Mamiya, 1990), it has not been invited into the conversation concerning the best way to educate Black children (McMillon, 2001). We believe that it is critical for educators to become knowledgeable about their students' cultural values and beliefs in order to develop creative connections for their students that build upon knowledge acquired from valuable out-of-school literacy experiences.

THE AFRICAN AMERICAN CHURCH

The African American Church was created from a combination of beliefs, and was specifically designed to meet the multifaceted, complex needs of African Americans (Lincoln & Mamiya, 1990). It has historically been recognized as a very powerful institution in the

Black community (Proctor, 1995; Smitherman, 1977), and was the site of the first formal learning environment organized specifically for African Americans. Worship service was held in the church on Sunday, and the church building was utilized as a school during the week (Cornelius, 1991). At church, the importance of literacy skills has historically been emphasized, and continues to be a focus today (Lincoln & Mamiya, 1990).

The African American Church is a rich environment for literacy development. However, for the purposes of this chapter, we are focusing specifically on activities that are considered "literacy events," defined by Heath (1982) as "any action sequence, involving one or more persons, in which the production and/or comprehension of print plays a role" (p. 92). The African American sermon fits this definition of a literacy event, and is the major literacy event that most African Americans have been exposed to in their communities, including those African Americans who do not attend church (Moss, 1994). In addition to the sermon, during worship service, students are given authentic opportunities to practice literacy skills by participating in various activities, such as singing in the choir, welcoming visitors, reading the announcements, and sharing the "thought for the day" with the audience (McMillon, & McMillon, 2003). Similar to the affirmation received at school by many White children who share primary and secondary discourse patterns with their classroom teachers (Delpit, 1995; Gee, 1991; O'Connor & Michaels, 1996), African American children are affirmed in the African American Church where their primary and secondary discourse patterns are similar to many of their teachers and adult leaders (McMillon, 2001).

The African American Church community creates a trusting environment where literacy and cultural practices are learned and reinforced. In Sunday School, Children's Church, and weekly Bible classes, instruction is often based on unique African American learning styles (Hale-Benson, 1986), and behavioral problems are essentially nonexistent because of close-knit relationships that are established between teachers and students. The importance of relationships is a cultural value taught and perpetuated in this environment (Fordham, 1988), where teachers often enjoy intergenerational relationships with parents, and hold high expectations for student performance (Edelman, 1999). Based on a positive self-fulfilling prophecy, most of their students achieve (Edwards, Danridge, McMillon, & Pleasants, 2001).

CONCEPTUAL FRAMEWORK

More than two decades ago, Anderson and Stokes (1984) observed families from Anglo-American, Black American and Mexican American populations to determine the average frequency of literacy events per hour of observation. They identified nine "domains of literacy activity" including (a) religion, (b) daily living, (c) entertainment (source, instrumental, media), (d) school-related activity, (e) general information, (f) work, (g) literacy techniques and skills (adult-initiated, child-initiated), (h) interpersonal communication, and (i) storybook time. In contrast to the belief that many minority children do not begin school with rich literacy backgrounds, Anderson and Stokes found that minority children in their study had varied literacy experiences in several domains of literacy activity. They found that 26.5% of all literacy activity for the Black American population in their study fell into the category of religion, surpassed only by the entertainment category (30.2%).

In addition to learning the importance of religious-oriented literacy activities in the lives of some Black Americans, Anderson and Stokes discussed social institutional influences that religious-oriented activities had on literacy practices and beliefs. They found information contrary to the belief that Black and Mexican American families who practice religion are only engaged in "oral tradition." In fact, the churches that the families in their study attended, encouraged—and in some cases required—an active, assertive approach to print, similar to the churches in our personal research studies.

In this chapter we extend Anderson and Stokes' religion category, specifically identifying *shared domains of literacy* (a phrase coined by the authors), in the church and school of many African American children. We have intentionally chosen to illuminate similarities in literacy practices at church and school, rather than differences. Although teachers may agree that difference does not mean deficit, it remains difficult for some of them to connect with students from diverse cultures. By helping readers look at literacy practices in the African American church through lenses of similarities, we establish a "common ground" that we hope will provide points of connection for teachers of African American students to utilize to improve literacy teaching and learning in their classrooms at school.

Conducting research in the context of the African American Church can provide educators with information concerning the educative processes utilized in a learning environment where many African American students are considered successful (McMillon, 2001). This information can assist teachers of African American students by illuminating possible points of connection through which school teachers may find creative ways to help students negotiate the cultural boundaries of their various learning environments. Additionally, we want to promote the idea of investigating students' cultural environments outside of school in order to identify ways to connect with students inside the classroom.

SHARED DOMAINS OF LITERACY

Based on our review of the literature and personal investigations of the African American church, we have identified five *shared domains of literacy.* They include (a) culturally responsive teaching (b) concepts of print, (c) phonemic awareness, (d) storybook reading and responses (e) oral language development and oral retelling. Table 33.1 provides an explanation of each category and examples from both settings.

Culturally Relevant Teaching

According to Ladson-Billings (1994), culturally relevant teaching refers to the kind of teaching that provides successful learning opportunities for students and helps them recognize and celebrate value in their own cultures. This type of teaching empowers students to be critical examiners of the educational content and process in which they are exposed—continuously questioning its role in creating a democratic and multicultural society. Culturally relevant teachers possess three important characteristics: (a) culturally relevant conceptions of self/others in which they see themselves as part

TABLE 33.1 Examples of Similarities in the Shared Domains of Literacy at Church and School

Shared Domains of Literacy	African American Church	School Classroom
Culturally Relevant Teaching	Developing a trusting, positive, nurturing, all-inclusive environment where children know that teachers have high expectations for them. Structure, repetition, and memorization are a vital part of this learning environment.	Utilizing teaching techniques and assessments that consider students' learning styles. Providing opportunities for students to share and celebrate cultural values and beliefs.
Concepts of Print	Authentic opportunities to "experience print" occur when reading the Bible, songbooks, class materials, and weekly church bulletins.	"Print" is experienced when reading the Morning Message, Big Books, pocket charts, flip charts, overhead projectors, chalkboards, white boards, books, and other materials.
Phonemic Awareness	Learning and singing songs written in poetic form; "reading" and learning speeches for special occasions (i.e., Easter, Christmas, Black History programs); reading books.	Learning nursery rhymes and other poetry; participating in activities that focus on word families and written word/spoken word correspondence; reading pattern books.
Storybook Reading and Responses	Listening to and reading Bible stories and stories with biblical themes. Examples of responses include: biblically based dramatic skits, speeches, mimes, and choral selections, as well as predicting, questioning, and connecting and Sipe's dramatizing, talking back, critiquing/controlling, and inserting.	Listening to and reading storybooks. Examples of responses include: making predictions, asking clarifying questions, verbal and physical responses; making connections to their own lives and other texts; thinking of alternate endings and/or storylines.
Oral Language Development and Oral Retelling	Participating in worship service and classroom activities that require oratory skills such as reading scriptures, extemporaneous prayers and testimonies, welcoming the visitors, and class discussions. Oral retelling include memorizing scriptures, songs, and Bible stories; and utilizing poster boards, flannel boards, puppets, and other manipulatives as mnemonics to help remember story details.	Reading workshop, book club, literature circles, sharing time, circle time, buddy and partner reading, all types of group discussions, Reader's Theater, other dramatic play activities; centers that require interaction between students, language experience stories, Morning message, retelling stories and poems, presentations, singing, working with nursery rhymes, school programs, student read alouds.

of the community having a responsibility to help students make connections between themselves and their community; (b) culturally relevant classroom social relations in which teachers display a connectedness with students and encourage them to build a community of learners instead of basing success on competitive individualism; and (c) culturally relevant conceptions of knowledge, in which teachers establish standards of excellence to assess and evaluate students, that are sensitive to student diversity and individual differences.

Many teacher-education programs, school districts, and individual schools are attempting to implement culturally relevant teaching ideas and techniques. In the school environment, culturally responsive practice is implemented in numerous ways. Some teachers facilitate relationships between students by concentrating on their responsibility to their peers through cooperative learning, including group discussions and other group activities. Having concern for students outside of their classrooms is encouraged through buddy reading and cross-age tutoring. Programs such as peer mediation and safety patrol also reinforce the importance of being responsible for fellow students. One of the greatest opportunities for students to express concern for others in the community has been for them to organize activities to help the victims of tragedies such as, 911, Tsunami, and Hurricane Katrina. Teachers, parents, and students organized many activities to provide money and other needed items.

Many teachers foster concern for others rather than individual competition by implementing cooperative learning as a major focus in their class. Group projects that require everyone to be responsible for various tasks encourage teamwork. Students understand that group grades will be earned, and therefore each individual must contribute his or her portion of the work in order to get a good grade.

Also, many teachers reflectively take time to cater to their students' various learning styles. They utilize assessment tools to inform when teaching, recognizing that their foremost goal should be to effectively facilitate student learning. Culturally responsive teachers understand the importance of building on their students' knowledge. They make a conscientious effort to gather information about their students by implementing activities such as "Star of the Week," which requires each student to bring in pictures and artifacts from home. Parents often get involved in this activity because the student shares personal information about out-of-school experiences. Teachers are also making attempts to connect with parents by sponsoring curriculum night, offering parent conferences during the evening for working parents, and sending newsletters to parents to keep them informed.

Similar to the ongoing push for teachers to implement culturally relevant teaching in the school setting, church teachers, parents, and students also participate in united efforts to assist victims of tragedies. Our current research site sponsors an annual clothing give away and "Back to School Rally" for families in the community.

During class sessions, cooperative learning is commonly utilized in the church setting. Many groups create dramatic skits, songs, rap, poetry, and artistic drawings/sketches to show teachers that they understand Biblical concepts and/or stories discussed during classes.

In addition to implementing many team-building activities, culturally relevant teaching is implemented in many African American churches in terms of classroom structure and related teaching techniques.

Teachers in various churches often utilize similar instructional methods based on foundational cultural beliefs, supported by scripture, and perpetuated in the church environment. They have high expectations for students in this learning context, and students respond accordingly. To assist students in reaching these high expectations, teachers display a commitment to create a positive, nurturing, all-inclusive environment in their classrooms, which they accomplish through structure and repetition (McMillon & Edwards, 2000; McMillon, 2001).

In our studies, teachers provided a structured class environment, which followed a weekly pattern that was very familiar to the students. The pattern was (a) opening period, (b) Bible lesson, (c) learning activity, and (d) closing period. This pattern was followed in Sunday School, weekly Bible study, Children's Church, and Vacation Bible School.

We found similar structured approaches in our studies of the school environment. Most teachers follow a repetitive structure each day in their classrooms at school. They begin with some type of opening activity. In early elementary, the opening activity is often called morning message. In later elementary and middle school, teachers may begin their classes with a discussion of current events or reminders about important school events. Regardless of how the class begins, many teachers have an established, structured way of organizing class time.

For example, many elementary teachers begin their afternoon sessions after lunch with a read aloud or independent reading. Preschool and kindergarten teachers often have independent reading/play during the first few minutes of class, and circle time is usually conducted at the same time every day.

Establishing a repetitive structure for class time helps some students become more comfortable because they know what to expect each day.

Concepts of Print

Concepts of print include awareness that print carries a message, and that there is a one to one correspondence between words read and printed text; there are conventions of print such as directionality (left to right, top to bottom), differences between letters and words, distinctions between upper and lower case, punctuation; and books have some common characteristics such as author and title (Clay, 1991).

In their classrooms at school, students have many opportunities to learn concepts of print. Some of these skills are taught explicitly by the teacher when she or he specifically shows students how to read from left to right and make a return sweep to get to the next line. Schoolteachers also provide authentic opportunities for their students to practice these concepts when they read the Morning Message, Big Books, and other materials during class. The use of pocket charts, flip charts, overhead projectors, chalkboards, and white boards give students opportunities to develop and reinforce concepts of print.

Print awareness is developed at church when students have experiences with print in the Bible, songbooks, class materials, and weekly church bulletins. Students understand the importance of print in the cultural community of the African American Church. They see many adult role models utilizing these tools and are taught from a very young age to "read" their Bibles, and bring them to church to use while in class and during worship service. In class, students receive take-home literature each week. Sunday School teachers have been taught to use the literature as an evangelistic tool to encourage students to attend classes, remind them to apply their lessons during their everyday lives, and as a way to keep parents informed concerning what their children are learning in class.

Sunday-school literature often includes a lesson sheet to be utilized during class and taken home to read with parents. The lesson sheet for emergent readers includes a colorful picture that is related to the lesson with a Bible scripture (referred to by teachers as the "memory verse") printed beneath the picture. Students are expected to memorize the memory verse during class and "read" it to their parents at home. The scripture is often short, and students follow along with their fingers as the teacher reads it first. Concepts of print, such as directionality and spoken/written word correspondence, are reinforced during this activity.

Advanced skills are developed and practiced when students use hymnbooks at church. The following song is taken from a popular hymnbook utilized in many African American churches (see Fig. 33.1):

Children who attend church learn how to follow the complex order of a song beginning on the first line, reading left to right, making a return sweep, going to the next line of music, reading the words on the first line again, and repeating this process until the first verse is finished. They also learn how to repeat the chorus. Adults and/or teenagers standing next to children are often found pointing at the words as they read and sing along.

In addition to following along on lesson sheets and in hymnbooks, requiring students to memorize scripture passages from the Bible also helps them develop print awareness and concepts of book print (McMillon & Edwards, 2000). Students were aware that memory verses were excerpts from the Bible (which contained many verses), and they understood that letters were used to make the words in those verses (an important prereading skill). Teachers frequently included the scripture reference when teaching the memory verse, and often explained that the Bible is divided into books, chapters, and verses. In fact, when memory verses are quoted, children were taught to end the verse by stating the book, chapter, and verse. For example, during data collection one child quoted, "I can do all things through Christ who strengthens me, Philippians 4:13." The "4:13" means the quote is found in the fourth chapter and the thirteenth verse of the book of Philippians.

Of course, we do not want to neglect what we believe is still one of the most important ways to teach concepts of print—simply by reading books. Read alouds are presented in both the school and church learning environments.

FIGURE 33.1 Jesus Loves Me

Phonological and Phonemic Awareness

Phonemic awareness is the awareness of constituent sounds of words and the ability to detect and eventually manipulate auditory units that do not necessarily hold syntactic meaning (Snow, Burns, & Griffin, 1998). Phonological awareness encompasses emergent readers' abilities to detect progressively smaller units of sound within spoken words with three commonly identified levels: (a) syllables, (b) onset-rimes, and (c) phonemes. Thus, phonemic awareness is a subset of the broader construct of phonological awareness (Snow et al.) and involves conscious awareness of the smallest distinguishable auditory units in words (Harris & Hodges, 1995).

Phonological awareness is the understanding that oral language is made out of sounds or groups of sounds. The process of developing phonological awareness begins when a child is able to recognize that speech is composed of words. This understanding is then extended until a child is able to recognize that words are composed of sounds, or phonemes, and he or she is able to manipulate those phonemes to accomplish various tasks (Griffith & Olson, 1992). One of the early phonological awareness tasks is to learn to recognize and generate rhyming words.

Teachers often utilize familiar and unfamiliar rhymes to help children develop phonemic awareness while enjoying the sounds and messages in the rhymes.

Although it seems reasonable to assume that orally reading books with a lot of rhyme and alliteration is likely to help some children become aware of the form of language, it is clear that this is simply not enough for many young children. Research demonstrates that directly teaching phonological awareness to young children causes them to respond more rapidly to beginning reading instruction and results in improved reading development (Byrne & Fielding-Barnsley, 1993; National Reading Panel, 2000).

Although researchers agree that children must have phonological awareness skills to learn to read, concern has been voiced in literature about teaching phonics skills in a decontextualized way to young children (Bredekamp & Copple, 1997). Providing direct instruction of phonological awareness skills using the words found in familiar storybooks has at least two advantages. It may be important in helping students, particularly students who are low achieving, to understand how phonological awareness relates to print. Using storybooks will make the phonological awareness activities more meaningful and connect them more clearly to print. Also, it is likely that the relationship to familiar storybooks will be motivating to students and teachers, resulting in increased levels of practice.

Learning phonemic awareness through songs, rhymes, and storybooks are productive literacy activities utilized in both the church and school environments.

Music in the context of the African American church not only enhances children's' concepts of print, but also promotes phonological and phonemic awareness. Many children's songs are written in verse form with rhyming words, or in a patterned, repetitive format, such as "Jesus Loves Me" in Figure 33.1.

Children who participate in activities in the context of the African American church are exposed to many songs. They have numerous authentic opportunities to strengthen their phonological and phonemic awareness skills.

In addition to singing songs that help develop phonemic awareness skills, children who participate in the literacy practices in the context of the African American Church are given opportunities to memorize speeches for special occasions, such as Easter and Christmas. These speeches are usually written in a poetic format. Children are expected to memorize them and share them during church programs.

The speeches that children learn for special occasions at church are similar to the nursery rhymes that children are expected to learn in the school environment.

Storybook Reading and Responses

Storybook reading enhances literacy development in children (Sulzby & Teale, 1991), assists with the development of a sense of story structure and narration (Phillips & McNaughton, 1990), increases vocabulary development and listening comprehension (Dickenson & Smith, 1994) and decoding and reading comprehension (Rosenhouse, Feitelson, Kita, & Goldstein, 1997); enhances knowledge of the conventions of print (Clay, 1991); and according to Wells (1986), the number of stories children hear read to them is the single greatest predictor of later success in reading.

Sipe (2002) contended that there are alternative ways that children respond to stories that he labeled "expressive, performative engagement," which can be demonstrated with words and physical actions, as the listeners become "active participants in the story." Sipe claimed that expressive engagement has five parts: (a) dramatizing, (b) talking back, (c) critiquing/controlling, (d) inserting, and (e) taking over. These actions move along a continuum with dramatizing being closely guided by the text, and taking over being at the extreme opposite end, allowing students to "rewrite" the story by deleting text and adding text extemporaneously.

Expressive and performative responses are highly valued by the African American community, and in our studies, we found that many teachers are encouraging the various types of expressive, performative engagement in their classrooms at school (McMillon & McMillon, 2003; McMillon & Edwards, 2004). Teachers understand the importance of children connecting with storybooks. They encourage students to make predictions, ask clarifying questions, and respond verbally and physically during storybook reading, They allow them to make connections to their own personal lives and other texts, and some teachers encourage students to think of alternate endings and/or storylines.

At school, children become familiar with storybook reading by listening to others read and memorizing and retelling children's stories and poems (Edwards, 1995a, 1995b). Similarly, students who participate in classes at church become familiar with storybook reading in their classes by listening to Bible stories and narratives with Biblically related themes. Listening to stories in both the school and church learning environments increases expressive and receptive language development in the context of literature. Most children enjoy listening to stories read to them by their teachers and other adults, and they respond to stories in various ways.

Sipe's (2002) explanation for the response to storybook reading is especially helpful in understanding the responses seen in the context of the church-learning environment during our studies.

Dramatizing was frequently utilized in the church settings, especially on special occasions such as Easter, Christmas, Black History month, and Thanksgiving. Children and youth participated in dramatic skits and performed speeches, mimes, and choral selections related to Bible stories during these special programs. Additionally, in weekly Bible study sessions, drama was utilized to assist students with comprehension. Dramatization varied—it was not always a skit presented by the students; sometimes the teacher used puppets or flannel boards to dramatize the Bible stories.

Talking back is a somewhat *natural* response in the African American church setting because regular discourse in this learning environment includes the call—response form of dialogue, especially during the Sunday morning sermon (Moss, 1994). The audience responds to the melodic, rhythmic exposition of the minister by saying "Amen," "Thank you, Jesus," "That's right," "Yes Lord" and varied affirmative grunts. Similarly, while participating in storybook reading, some students may respond verbally or with facial expressions and/or hand gestures.

Inserting is the final type of response that we want to expound upon. Inserting has a long-standing history in the context of the African American Church. Historically, Blacks have inserted themselves into the Old Testament "Exodus story." For many years, Blacks have compared their plight with the Children of Israel. Blacks' involuntary migration to America, their long-term slavery, their resilience to survive, and their commitment to God and belief that He will rescue them has many striking similarities to the story of the Children of Israel in the Exodus story. Thus, having a history of *insertion,* many African American children oftentimes respond to stories in this way.

Oral Language Development

Children's oral communicative ability is vital to the development of their literacy skills and has been directly linked to their literacy development (Torrence & Olsen, 1984). Dickinson and Snow (1987) pointed to the need of more refined work in this area by asserting that the connection between language skills and reading was more often assumed than demonstrated. In response to this challenge, several researchers found that the individual sounds produced when speaking, called *phonemes*, have a compelling influence on literacy development (Ehri, Nunes, Willows, Schuster, Yaghoub, & Shanahan, 2001). Additionally, Cooper, Roth, Speece, and Schatschneider (2002) contended that there is a developmental relationship between oral language and phonological awareness skills, which directly supports reading. In their study of over 200 students in kindergarten through second grade, they found that "general language skill measured in kindergarten predicts a significant and meaningful proportion of unique variance in phonological awareness skills, from kindergarten to second grade, beyond the influence of letter and word knowledge (p. 411)."

The functionality of language is vast. Talking can help children make sense "out loud" as they attempt to understand new ideas. It is the bridge that helps them connect relationships between what they know and what they are coming to know. It is through speech that children learn to organize their thinking and focus their ideas (Lyle, 1993). Furthermore, children who are allowed to develop their oral language skills in a variety of settings do better on formalized literacy tests (Galda, Shockley, & Pellegrini, 1995). Throughout life, oral-language skills will remain essential for the communication of ideas and for engagement in intellectual dialogue and activities.

Across cultures, variations in the ways of speaking reflect important differences in beliefs, practices, values, and norms. These differences enter into the organization and systemic use of language at many levels in every community. It follows, then, that when children are acquiring their language, they are spoken to and are learning to talk to others according to ways of speaking that reflect the beliefs and values of their particular speech community. Much of the language children learn reflects the language and behavior of the adult models they interact with and listen to (Strickland & Morrow, 1989). Adults scaffold children's language learning by providing a model that is expressive, responsive, and enjoyable. At church, the sermon, with its expressive "call-and-response" pattern, provides an important language model for children (Moss, 1994).

At school, several classroom teaching methods and activities teach and reinforce oral language development. Sharing time (also called "show and tell") is a recurring classroom language activity, where children are called upon to give a formal description of an object or a narrative account of some important past event. (Michaels, 1981). Sharing time can be an important event in the oral preparation for literacy (Michaels). Other activities include reading workshop, book club, literature circles, sharing time, circle time, buddy and partner reading, all types of group discussions, reader's theater, other dramatic play activities, centers that require interaction between students, language experience stories, morning message, retelling stories and poems, presentations, singing, working with nursery rhymes, participation in school programs, student read alouds, and many other activities emphasizing oral language development in the context of school.

The oral tradition of the Black Church requires members to give extemporaneous prayers, testimonies, and speeches (Edwards, et al., 2001). Sunday School and other classes are a "training ground" to develop and refine oral language skills, and prepare students to participate in worship services with adults.

In addition to the weekly classes and monthly worship service opportunities to develop and practice oral skills, the African American church encourages language development by encouraging students to participate in programs for special holidays, such as Easter, Christmas, and Black History Month. To prepare for the programs, children are given speeches to memorize and share with an audience. Some students also get a chance to participate in dramatic skits or full-scale plays with stage props, costumes, etc. In our studies, the younger children were given speeches, and the older children participated in the dramatic presentations. These programs are festive occasions that children and adults prepare for with great anticipation. Children attend rehearsals to practice their speeches and dramatic presentations. They have to repeat their parts numerous times until the coordinator of the program is satisfied with their performance. During this time of preparation, children learn the importance of practice and are often told, "practice makes perfect." When the day of the program arrives, the children do not disappoint. They make their presentations to the awaiting church audience and receive immediate encouragement and gratification in the form of standing ovations, and verbal responses from the adults such as "amen," "good job," and "beautiful children—that's beautiful" (McMillon & McMillon, 2003).

Oral language development is emphasized in both the school and church learning environments. Teachers in both settings provide numerous opportunities and activities that help children acquire and develop oral language skills. One of the most prevalent areas of language development found in these settings was *oral retelling.*

Oral Retelling A number of researchers have explored children's understanding of the story genre through the use of retellings, a postreading recall during which children relate what they remember from reading or listening to a particular text (Gambrell, Pfeiffer, & Wilson, 1985). As Irwin and Mitchell (1983) noted, "Retelling reveals what a child comprehends . . . as well as how the child comprehends" (p. 392). Moreover, retellings afford children the opportunity to play an active role in reconstructing text. Such experiences have been shown to enhance the development of comprehension, oral language, and sense of story structure (Zimiles & Kuhns, 1976). Story retellings have also been used as assessment tools in the examination of developmental trends in story comprehension (Mandler & Johnson, 1977).

In school, some teachers use retelling to provide practice time for oral language development, while others use it as an authentic assessment tool for student comprehension. Retelling stories with the appropriate sequence of events, including issues related to character development, plot, themes, and setting inform teachers of student understanding of story structure and components of narrative texts. Retelling takes on many forms at school including skits, puppetry, art, and written form.

Storytelling and retelling require memorization, a skill that is well developed in the African American Church (McMillon & Edwards, 2000). Bible stories are frequently retold and students memorize the stories after hearing them repeatedly. The Sunday-School teacher in one of our studies also utilized story telling as a way to help students understand abstract concepts and assess student comprehension.

During data collection, students were asked to retell stories utilizing a poster board and heaven box as mnemonics to assist with details of the stories (McMillon & Edwards, 2000). Regular class members are expected to remember these stories and be prepared to share them with younger students and new students until they also learn them. Requiring students to memorize and retell stories helps develop oral language as a bridge to reading (Searfoss & Readence, 1985) and fosters the beginning of metacognitive strategies for reading comprehension (Mason, McCormick, & Bhavnagri, 1986). Students are able to ask questions that address specific issues about the story. Teachers provide clarification on these issues and help students think about ways to apply the story to personal circumstances. Oral retelling activities also build confidence by giving students opportunities to share their knowledge with others.

WHERE DO WE GO FROM HERE?

Although many researchers have attempted to address the problem of reading failure among African American children, the enigma still persists. Standardized test scores and other assessments reveal that Black children lag behind their counterparts. While there are many possible reasons for this problem, the purpose of this chapter was to explore possible solutions. By identifying shared domains of literacy between the church and school environments of African American students, we believe that we increase the possibility of alleviating the reading achievement gap.

When first considering this body of work, there may be a tendency to take a pessimistic stance. After all, in the United States there is a separation of church and state. However, a relatively recent paradigm shift in the field of education toward a sociocultural perspective challenges us to broaden our scope by becoming willing to admit that the culture of teachers and students influences classroom literacy teaching and learning. We know that many teachers are afraid to "trespass" into the unknown territory of their students' out-of-school lives. Some teachers believe that their focus should be what goes on inside their classroom at school. They think that whatever goes on outside of their classroom is not "their business."

On the contrary, we believe that it is imperative that teachers learn to draw on the rich resources of outside institutions, including the home and church. How can we get teachers to do this? The solution to the enigma begins with teachers' willingness to tap into their students' funds of knowledge (Moll, Amanti, Neff, & Gonzalez, 1992).

We know that children who are read to and talked to in certain ways easily transition into school, especially students who share primary discourse patterns with their teachers. Denny Taylor's *Family Literacy* (1983) is a classic example of how middle-class White children easily transition from home to school. Their home activities mirrored school literacy activities. However, Taylor's book with Dorsey-Gaines, *Growing Up Literate* (1988), provided examples of school and inner-city home literacies not being connected. It is clear when children's literacies are aligned with school, these literacies are recognized, accepted, and built upon. Others are ignored and dismantled.

The time has come for teachers to think more critically about the needs of their students. How do their out-of-school lives connect with what goes on in their classrooms? Perhaps the students are not just simply disinterested or incapable of learning. Instead of rushing to judgment, critical discussions about specific, practical ways that schools can incorporate multiple literacies within their curriculum need to take place. Why do we accept some students' literacies and reject others? As researchers, our challenge is to unveil the masks of disillusion and doubt and reveal realistic possibilities—practical solutions to the problem of reading failure among African American students. We can no longer ignore the environment where African Americans are succeeding, especially the African American Church where they have historically been successfully educated. We must make the school environment recognizable and inviting for children from multiple out-of-school literacy environments.

Drawing from the *shared domains of literacy* discussed in this chapter, we have several suggestions for teachers of African American students:

1. Develop a relationship with your students. Most students work harder for teachers with whom they connect. Remember, for some students the old cliché is operative: "You can't teach me until you reach me." Many African American students are relationship oriented and their teachers need to be culturally responsive to their need to bond with significant adults in their lives.

2. Develop a home-school connection. Parents are a child's first and most important teacher. They hold the key to unleashing your students' literacy learning potential and your literacy teaching potential. Let parents know that you value their input and need them on your team by asking them to share vital information about students' past and present out-of-school literacy experiences. Show parents that you genuinely care about their children through honesty, open-mindedness, and consistency.

3. Provide structured class time. African American students who participate in church classes may benefit from having school teachers who provide structured class time, because they are accustomed to this approach to classroom teaching and learning. If students know what to expect, they can focus on the tasks/activities, rather than spending time trying to figure out what happens next. We found that a higher level of comfort and increased participation resulted when teachers began to implement more structured class time.

4. Develop creative memorization and repetition activities based on class content. Two integral parts of "structure" in the African American Church setting are memorization and repetition. Many teachers in school do not understand the importance of these two concepts for students with certain styles of learning. Students who are musically oriented have great memories and understand the importance of repetition, because repeated practice is a major part of their development. In our studies, children learned scriptures by repeating them rhythmically. Kinesthetic learners love clapping their hands, marching, and dancing to the beat. At church, children are encouraged to enthusiastically move and groove while learning. Mathematical formulas, Standard English language rules, historical dates, important speeches, vocabulary definitions, and word wall words are examples of school-related topics that can be put to rhythm and or music, repeated, and memorized by creative students and teachers.

5. Provide all children with opportunities to develop their oral language skills. A child's language is one of the outward manifestations of personality and we have to do everything within our powers to make him or her feel that it is worthwhile, even though he or she may speak a different language and come from a home where respect for language is slight or nonexistent.

Teachers of African American children need to understand that they often utilize a "topic-associated" way of communicating, as opposed to the "topic-centered" method that is more frequently used by middle-class Whites (Michaels, 1981; McMillon & Edwards, 2000). Unintentionally, teachers can "deny access to key literacy-related experiences" (Michaels, 1981, p. 423) when they have differing communicative styles than their students. These miscommunications can lead to students becoming uncomfortable in class and may result in student frustration or resistance.

6. Teach students how *to interact in acceptable ways in various environments.* We fail children if we do not help them learn to use commonly accepted speech patterns. For example, students need to be explicitly taught that talking in dialect and speaking out of turn when talking with friends is perfectly acceptable. However, in the classroom, during certain activities, specific participation structures are often required by various teachers. Students who do not develop an ability to communicate "appropriately" based on the teacher's expectations may suffer academically and socially (McMillon & Edwards, 2000; McMillon, 2001).

7. Enhance students' comprehension skills by encouraging expressive, performative engagement of texts and oral retelling. Allow students to become personally engaged with texts by teaching Sipe's five alternate ways to respond to stories. Scaffold their attempts to dramatize, talk back, critique/control, insert, and take over in response to stories. Develop activities that reinforce these responses. Also, find ways to connect expressive, performative responses directly with oral retelling as a way of comparing author's intent, and audience perception.

THE PROPER RESPONSE TO "THE ENIGMA"

The African proverb, "It takes a village to raise a child" is true. Working together, researchers, schoolteachers, church teachers, and other significant members of the community can collaboratively provide the proper response to "the enigma". We believe African American students can and will become successful in America's classrooms when members of their literacy network systems, in and out of school, build bridges that connect the gaps between influential institutions in their lives. As African American researchers, we are facilitating this process by illuminating shared domains of literacy between their school and church learning environments. Our goal is to help African American students become "border-crossers"—successfully negotiating the cultural boundaries between their multiple literacy worlds.

ACKNOWLEDGMENTS

The authors gratefully acknowledge the support of research reported in this article from the Spencer Research Training Grant Fellowship Program at Michigan State University, the Spencer Dissertation Fellowship for Research Related to Education, and the Oakland University Faculty Research Fellowship.

REFERENCES

Anderson, A. B., & Stokes, S. J. (1984). Social and institutional influences on the development and practice of literacy. In H. Goelman, A. Oberg, & F. Smith (Eds.), *Awakening to literacy* (pp. 24–37). Exeter, NH: Heinemann.

Bredekamp, S., & Copple, C. (Eds.). (1997). *Developmentally appropriate practice for early childhood programs.* Washington, DC: National Association for the Education of Young Children.

Byrne, B., & Fielding-Barnsley, R. (1993). Evaluation of a program to teach phonemic awareness to young children: A 1-year follow-up. *Journal of Educational Psychology, 85,* 104–111.

Clay, M. M. (1991). *Becoming literate: The construction of inner control.* Portsmouth, NH: Heinemann.

Cooper, D. H., Roth, F. P., Speece, D. L., & Schatschneider, C. (2002). The contribution of oral language skills to the development of phonological awareness. *Applied Psycholinguistics, 23,* 399–416.

Cornelius, J. D. (1991). *When I can read my title clear: Literacy, slavery, and religion in the antebellum south.* Columbia: University of South Carolina Press.

Delpit, L. (1995). *Other people's children: Cultural conflict in the classroom.* New York: New Press.

Dickenson, K., & Smith, M. W. (1994). Long-term effects of preschool teachers' book readings on low-income children's vocabulary and story comprehension. *Reading Research Quarterly, 29,* 105–122.

Dickinson, D. K., & Snow, C. E. (1987). Interrelationships among prereading and oral language skills in kindergarteners from two social classes. *Early Childhood Quarterly, 2,* 1–25.

Edelman, M. W. (1999). *Lanterns.* Boston: Beacon Press.

Edwards, P. A. (1995a). Combining parents' and teachers' thoughts about storybook reading at home and school. In L. M. Morrow (Ed.), *Family literacy: Multiple perspectives to enhance literacy development* (pp. 54–60). Newark, DE: International Reading Association.

Edwards, P. A. (1995b). Connecting African-American parents and youth to the school's reading curriculum: Its meaning for school and community literacy. In V. L. Gadsden & D. Wagner (Eds.), *Literacy among African-American youth: Issues in learning teaching and schooling* (pp. 263–281). Creskill, NJ: Hampton Press.

Edwards, P. A., Danridge, J., McMillon, G. T., & Pleasants, H. M. (2001). Taking ownership of literacy: Who has the power? In P. R. Schmidt & P. B. Mosenthal (Eds.), *Reconceptualizing literacy in the new age of pluralism and multiculturalism:* Vol. 9. Advances in reading and language research (pp. 111–134). San Francisco: Jossey-Bass.

Edwards, P. A., Pleasants, H. M., & Franklin, S. H. (1999). *A path to follow: Learning to listen to parents.* Portsmouth, NH: Heinemann.

Ehri, L. C., Nunes, S. R., Willows, D. M., Schuster, B. V., Yaghoub, Z. Z., & Shanahan, T. (2001). Phonemic awareness instruction helps children learn to read: Evidence from the National Reading Panel's meta-analysis. *Reading Research Quarterly, 36*(3), 250–287.

Fordham, S. (1988). Racelessness as a factor in black students' school success: Pragmatic strategy or pyrrhic victory? *Harvard Educational Review, 58*(1), 54–84.

Franklin, R. M. (1997). *Another day's journey: Black churches confronting the American crisis.* Minneapolis, MN: Fortress Press.

Frazier, E. F. (1963). *The Negro church in America.* New York: Schocken Books.

Galda, L., Shockley, B., & Pellegrini, A. D. (1995). *Talking to read and write: Opportunities for literate talk in one primary classroom* (Research Rep. No. 12). Athens, GA: NRRC, Universities of Georgia and Maryland College Park. (ED377462)

Gambrell, L., Pfeiffer, W., & Wilson, R. (1985). The effects of retelling upon reading comprehension and recall of text information. *Journal of Education Research, 7,* 216–220.

Gee, J. (1991). What is literacy? In C. Mitchell & K. Weiler (Eds.), *Rewriting literacy: Culture and the discourse of the other* (pp. 3–12). New York: Greenwood Publishing Group.

Griffith, P. L., & Olson, M. W. (1992). Phonemic awareness helps beginning readers break the code. *Reading Teacher, 45*(7), 516–523.

Hadaway, N. L., Vardell, S. M., & Young, T. A. (2001). Scaffolding oral language development through poetry for students learning English. *Reading Teacher, 54*(8), 796–806.

Hale-Benson, J. E. (1986). *Black children—their roots, culture, and learning styles.* Baltimore: The John Hopkins University Press.

Harris, T. L., & Hodges, R. E. (1995). *The literacy dictionary: The vocabulary of reading and writing.* Newark, DE: International Reading Association.

Heath, S. B. (1982). Protean shapes in literacy events: Evershifting oral and literate traditions. In D. Tannen (Ed.), *Spoken and written language: Exploring orality and literacy* (pp. 91–117). Norwood, NJ: Ablex.

Heath, S. B. (1983). *Ways with words: Language, life, and work in communities and classrooms.* Cambridge, MA: Cambridge University Press.

Hull, G., & Schultz, K. (2002). *School's out! Bridging out-of-school literacies with classroom practice.* New York: Teachers College Press.

Irwin, P. I., & Mitchell, J. N. (1983). A procedure for assessing the richness of retelling. *Journal of Reading, 2*, 391–396.

Ladson-Billings, G. (1994). *The dreamkeepers: Successful teachers of African American children.* San Francisco: Jossey-Bass.

Lincoln, C. E., & Mamiya, L. H. (1990). *The Black church in the African American experience.* Durham, N.C.: Duke University Press.

Lyle, S. (1993). An investigation into ways in which children talk themselves into meaning. *Language and Education, 7*(3), 181–187.

Mandler, J. M., & Johnson, N. S. (1977). Remembrance of things parsed: Story structure and recall. *Cognitive Psychology, 9*, 111–151.

Mason, J. M., McCormick, C., & Bhavnagri, N. (1986). How are you going to help me learn? Lesson negotiations between a teacher and preschool children. In D. B. Yaden, Jr., & S. Templeton (Eds.), *Metalinguistic awareness and beginning literacy: Conceptualizing what it means to read and write* (pp. 159–172). Portsmouth, NH: Heinemann Educational Books, Inc.

McMillon, G. M. T. (2001). *A tale of two settings: African American students' literacy experiences at church and at school.* Unpublished doctoral dissertation. Michigan State University, East Lansing.

McMillon, G. M. T., & Edwards, P. A. (2000). Why does Joshua hate school? . . . but love Sunday school? *Language Arts, 78*(2), 111–120.

McMillon, G. M. T., & Edwards, P. A. (2004). The African American church: A beacon of light on the pathway to literacy for African American children. In E. Gregory, S. Long, & D. Volk (Eds.), *Many pathways to literacy* (pp. 182–194). London: Routledge Falmer.

McMillon, G. M. T., & McMillon, V. D. (2003). The empowering literacy practices of an African American church. In F. B. Boyd & C.H. Brock (Eds.), *Multicultural and multilingual literacy and language: Contexts and practices* (pp. 280–303). New York: Guilford Publications.

Michaels, S. (1981). Sharing time: Children's narrative styles and differential access to literacy. *Language in Society, 10*(3), 423–442.

Moll, L. C., Amanti, C., Neff, D., & Gonazalez, N. (1992). Funds of knowledge for teaching: Using a qualitative approach to connect home and classrooms. *Theory Into Practice, 31* (2), 132–141.

Moss, B. J. (1994). Creating a community: Literacy events in African-American churches. In B. J. Moss (Ed.), *Literacy across communities* (pp. 147–178). Cresskill, NJ: Hampton Press.

National Institute of Child Health and Human Development. (2000). *Teaching children to read —An evidence based assessment of the scientific research literature on reading and its implications for reading instruction* (report of the National Reading Panel; NIH Publication No. 00-4769). Washington, DC: U.S. Government Printing Office. Available http://www.nichd.nih.gov/publications/nrp/smallbook.htm

O'Connor, M. C., & Michaels, S. (1996). Shifting participant frameworks: Orchestrating thinking practices in group discussion. In D. Hicks (Ed.), *Discourse, learning and schooling.* New York: Cambridge University Press.

Phillips, G., & McNaughton, S. (1990). The practice of storybook reading to preschoolers in mainstream New Zealand families. *Reading Research Quarterly, 25*, 196–212.

Proctor, S. D. (1995). *The substance of things hoped for: A memoir of African American faith.* New York: G.P. Putnam's Sons.

Purcell-Gates, V. (1995). *Other people's words: The cycle of low literacy.* Cambridge, MA: Harvard University Press.

Resnick, L. B. (1990). Literacy in school and out. *Daedalus, 199*(2), 169–186.

Rosenhouse, J., Feitelson, D., Kita, B., & Goldstein, Z. (1997). Interactive reading aloud to Israeli first graders: Its contribution to literacy development. *Reading Research Quarterly, 32*, 168–183.

Searfoss, L. W., & Readence, J. E. (1985). *Helping children learn to read.* Englewood Cliffs, NJ: Prentice-Hall, Inc.

Sipe, L. R. (2002). Talking back and taking over: Young children's expressive engagement during storybook read-alouds. *The Reading Teacher, 55*(5), 476–483.

Smitherman, G. (1977). *Talkin' and testifyin'.* Boston: Houghton-Mifflin.

Snow, C. E., Burns, M. S., & Griffin, P. (1998). *Preventing reading difficulties in young children.* Washington, DC: National Academy Press.

Strickland, D. S. & Morrow, L. M. (1989). Oral language development: Children as storytellers. *The Reading Teacher, 44*(3), 260–261.

Sulzby, E., & Teale, W. (1991). Emergent literacy. In R. Barr, M. Kamil, P. Mosenthal, & P. D. Pearson (Eds.), *Handbook of reading research, II* (pp. 727–757). New York: Longman.

Taylor, D. (1983). *Family literacy: Young children learning to read and write.* Portsmouth, NH: Heinemann.

Taylor, D., & Dorsey-Gaines, C. (1988). *Growing up literate: Learning from inner-city families.* Portsmouth, NH: Heinemann.

Torrence, N., & Olson, D. (1984). Oral language competence and the acquisition of literacy. In A. D. Pelligrini & T. Yawkey (Eds.), *The development of oral and written language in social contexts* (pp. 167–181). Norwood, NJ: Ablex.

Wells, G. (1986). *The meaning makers: Children learning language and using language to learn.* Portsmouth, NH: Heinemann.

Zimile, H., & Kuhns, M. (1976). A developmental study in the retention of narrative material. Final report. New York: Bank Street College of Education. (ERIC Document Reproduction Service No. ED160978)

•34•

VIOLENCE AND THE VISUAL, PERFORMING, AND COMMUNICATIVE ARTS

Ian Pumpian and Douglas Fisher
SAN DIEGO STATE UNIVERSITY

For decades, parents and politicians alike have expressed concern about the role that media plays in violence. Does viewing violence on TV or at the theater, reading a violent graphic novel, or playing a video game that simulates violence or murder result in children and young adults who are more violent or aggressive than their peers who do not engage in such activities? Or do children and youth know the difference between media and simulated violence and real life? As one young man said, "I know the difference between a real man and a TV man" (Brozo, Walter, & Placker, 2002, p. 530), but is that the case for most children and youth? In this chapter, we hope to explore what is known, and what questions remain, about the role that the visual, communicative, and performing arts play in violence. While most of the evidence presented here—evidence used to make our general arguments—comes from the United States and Canada, the border is virtually nonexistent so far as transfer of the media are concerned. As such, this chapter has implications for the world.

CONCERNS ABOUT TV CONTENT WHEN MARCUS WELBY M.D. WAS THE TOP-RATED SHOW . . .

In the late 1960s, upon request of the U.S. Senate, the U.S. Surgeon General assembled a prestigious committee of behavioral scientists to study the effects of violent media content on children and youth. In 1972, the U.S. Surgeon General issued his committee's report and concluded that there was no doubt that televised violence had negative effects on certain individuals. At that time, 52% of Americans owned a TV and they relied on three major broadcast channels. Large bulky calculators that could add, subtract, multiply, and divide were available to a few very wealthy people while everyone else depended on slide-rules, adding machines, and pencils. A few FM radio stations were beginning to broadcast in stereo, color TV was just becoming the standard, Sony was just introducing Betamax, and Super8 home movie cameras did not yet have sound. UHF and portable cassettes and public TV were the buzz of the day. The 50-pound, $9,000, 16-kilobyte portable computer was three years in the future, although Wang had just produced a word processor. In that year, IBM Selectronic typewriters were the industry standard and Pong was introduced. Cell phones, VCRs (let alone DVDs), Internet, laptops, pixels, chips, and Sony Walkmans were not in the world's vocabulary. Cher's belly button was being censured from the airways. Most of the technology that was available was restricted to the wealthy or the military.

Even with this limited access, limited quality, and limited product, the Surgeon General and his committee recognized, and were concerned with, the impact of media violence on youth. But media technology, access, and content are profoundly different now than in 1972. As Dr. Michael Rich of the American Association of Pediatrics testified, "the problem has gone from worrisome to something that is truly a public health emergency."

TIMES ARE A-CHANGING . . .

Following a group of teenagers today reveals a very different level of access to technology as well as the content they use. The following is based on field notes, observations, and interviews:

> As most other mornings in the fall of 2006, Carlos and his friends meet at the corner at 7:00 a.m. and walk the next seven blocks to school together. They drop off Maria's little brother Sammy at the elementary school on the way. Carlos has 10,000 songs in his shirt pocket and scans through the list to find IceCube's *Better Off Dead*. He downloaded the entire album (*Ameirkkka's Most Wanted*) during lunch yesterday. He blasts the tune through his one-ounce, bass-boosted earphones, raps the lyrics, and still

listens to what Liz is saying about the "homiez" who live upstairs. Another in the group, Raquel, is using her cell phone to take and send digital pictures of James to her cousin in Guadalajara. Meanwhile, James receives an instant message on his blue tooth cell phone from a friend who writes him about a new game he can download free. James proceeds to do so.

He has the game, *Hit Man, Blood Money*, downloaded and nearly mastered before he arrives at the school gates where the security guard reminds him to "put that thing away." He complies but takes it out after he passes the guard and has enough time between the school's front gates and the classroom to get to the next level. He accomplishes that feat while continuing his conversation with the friends he is walking with and the "whad-dups" of the peers he passes by. Just before the teacher waiting to greet him at the door tells him again "to put away that thing or it's mine," he instant messages his buddy back telling him "the game was tight and will be wooky-sweet to play on Maria's 60inch [plasma TV] afterschool."

In the meantime, Raquel receives an instant message back from her cousin saying "pics were too cool, the guy is blaze." As Raquel types back "U no it, filthy girlfriend," she sees her teacher glaring from the doorway and she types "time 2 clip. Gotta bounce." The first bell rings and the students sit down ready for the education we have to offer them.

Meanwhile, James's mom has some talk show playing through the satellite radio system in the house she cleans. She is listening to some expert warning her to make sure she knows what her children are doing online in their bedroom. The expert makes her wonder just what is on James's computer and she will ask him about it tonight. The problem is, James seldom uses his antiquated desktop computer anymore. He and his friends carry more sophisticated equipment in their pockets and backpacks each day. Twenty-five percent of youth use Internet as their major source of information; 200,000 of them will join MySpace.com this year while well over 5 trillion instant messages will be sent and received.

It is little 10-year-old brother Sammy who heard his sister Maria's friends on his way to school mention the name of a free site for "downloading music and stuff." After school Sammy goes online to find a song he likes and accidentally stumbles across a downloaded video clip. Unknowingly he opens up a graphic, violent, and degrading pornographic clip depicting a sadomasochistic fantasy rape scene. He does not quite understand it or the fact that he is aroused. He knows he has done something very bad and files his secret and shame. Sammy's mother did not have the benefit of hearing the same radio show James's mother heard.

THE POTENTIAL IMPACT OF THE CHANGING TIMES

Technical advances in the area of media and communication between 1972 and now are significant and pronounced (Roberts & Foehr, 2004). These changes have brought a level of affordable, portable technology to the overwhelming majority of Americans that is more substantial than what was available to the military and the elite a mere three decades ago. Even under pre-1972 conditions of access and graphic-technical quality, there was enough compelling evidence existing for the U.S. Surgeon General to issue a report on the impact of televised violence and to conclude that there was no doubt that televised violence had negative effects on certain individuals. One wonders what that committee would have concluded if they had a crystal ball and understood today's media technology and the access children and youth have to that technology. Undoubtedly, there has been a significant increase in the number of media outlets in which violence is featured, the graphic-technical and viewing quality of those media outlets, and the access and exposure to those outlets. In their groundbreaking *Joint Statement On the Impact of Entertainment Violence on Children* (2000), the American Academy of Pediatrics, American Psychological Association, American Academy of Child and Adolescent Psychiatry, American Medical Association, American Academy of Family Physicians, and the American Psychiatric Association relied on over 1,000 studies to conclude that "viewing violence can lead to increases in aggressive attitudes, values and behavior, particularly in children. Its effects are measurable and long-lasting" (n.p.).

Given the technological advances and access that most children and youth have to technology, coupled with the research findings related to media violence, it is reasonable to hypothesize that,

1. more individuals susceptible to the negative impacts of media violence will view it and view it more often;
2. the range and nature of people susceptible to the negative impacts of media violence could expand; and
3. unless public policy and conscience do not significantly change such that access and exposure to media violence becomes more limited, more people will be at risk of that media having a negative impact on them in particular and society in general.

Extensive limiting of such access and exposure appears unlikely. It is more likely that that access and exposure will continue to expand with technological and production advances. In addition, policy changes regarding access, production, and usage controls are beyond the scope and immediate interests of the authors. Instead our present concerns are how responsible educators (and other adults) might mitigate the negative impact media violence is likely to have on growing numbers of children and youth.

Anderson and Bushman (and their colleagues) are among the most well respected media violence researchers in the United States. Their studies and testimony are cited throughout the literature, popular press, and congressional records in the United States and Canada. Readers interested in further research on this topic are encouraged to visit www.psychology.iastate.edu/faculty/caa/index.html for additional information.

Anderson and Bushman (2002b) conducted a meta-analysis of 284 studies on the effects of violent media content on youth. The analysis consisted of 49 longitudinal studies involving 4,975 participants; 86 cross-sectional samples involving 37,341 participants; 28 field-experiment samples involving 1,976 participants; and 124 laboratory experiment samples involving 7,305 participants. They concluded that regardless of the research method, there is a clear positive link between media violence and aggression. They further concluded that the link has proven to be both associative and causal. Their review of longitudinal studies revealed there are long-term effects of early media violence exposure in both children and youth, including incidence of later aggressive acts. They also cited evidence of increased immediate aggression with short-term exposure. Finally, their review suggested that media violence appears to affect a much larger group of people than what was proposed in the 1972 Surgeon General report. Anderson and Bushman frequently argued that the evidence supporting the link between media violence and aggression is more substantial than the evidence implicating the effects of second-hand smoking or lead exposure. In their words

> We recently demonstrated that even as the scientific evidence linking media violence to aggression has accumulated, news reports about the effects of media violence have shifted to weaker statements, implying that there is little evidence for such effects. This inaccurate reporting in the popular press may account for continuing controversy long after

the debate should have been over with, much as the cigarette smoking/cancer controversy persisted long after the scientific community knew that smoking causes cancer. (Anderson & Bushman, 2002b, p. 2,377)

VIRTUAL REALITY AND TECHNOLOGY ADVANCES MAKE THE DISCUSSION OF TV VIOLENCE SEEM PRIMITIVE

The majority of longitudinal studies conducted thus far have examined televised violence and videogames. Our expectation is that media violence researchers will engage in new studies involving televised violence viewed on 60-inch high-definition TVs supported by six-channel surround sound and violence-oriented videogames experienced through three-dimensional, total-sensory virtual reality equipment. We hypothesize that the behaviors and attitudes noted earlier will become more evident and pronounced as virtual reality becomes commonplace. Anderson and Dill (2000) suggested that the potential for interactive violent content to influence aggression is high since the participants actually engage in aggressive activity via fantasy.

The question of graphic novels, anime, manga, and other print-based visual information and its impact on violence is not yet understood. For example, Zellers (2005) noted that graphic novels are often accused of promoting violence and exploiting women. Her analysis of the content of 10% of the graphic novels contained in the library at the University of North Carolina confirmed that there is graphic violence and that women are regularly objectified. It is important to note that many graphic novels are successfully used in the classroom and that this genre is very popular with students (Frey & Fisher, 2004). What we do not yet know is how these print-based visual media impact children and youth in terms of violence.

However, the real Pandora's box will be access and exposure to violence via the Internet. The Internet provides immediate unfettered access to nearly every form of media. At the time of this writing, public policy, attention, and critique of Internet use seems to focus on the vulnerability of youth to sexual predators and on the ease of access to pornography. There is no doubt, however, that the Internet has already become the quickest, most accessible, and most difficult to monitor and regulate source through which youth can access content ranging from how to build a bomb or buy a weapon; sexual exploitation and violence; and studying, bragging, planning, organizing, and communicating about violent acts, games, interactions, events, or thoughts (Funk, Baldacci, Pasold, & Baumgardner, 2004; Roberts & Foehr, 2004; Ybarra & Mitchell, 2004).

It was difficult enough to monitor such activities when the mode of delivery was a computer workstation. Now, anytime, access is available through the phones and watches that even children living in poverty seem to have. These developments provide media violence researchers an endless source of issues to consider and study.

The nation is now in a declared "war on terrorism." Children and youth are bombarded daily with commentary and news reports on worldwide acts of violence and war via every conceivable media source they access. The impact of being a nation in a highly visible and extended war is of concern. The media portrays a world replete of violent agendas, acts, and intentions. Real-world violence regularly and graphically depicted throughout in the media increases concern with respect to effect on the emotions and behaviors of children and youth (Byrnes, 2001; Ladd & Cairns, 1996).

Youth communications via chat rooms, message boards, blogs, and text messaging are now being attributed as a major forum for engaging in various forms of bullying and intimidation (Paulson, 2003). This media-sponsored violence blurs the lines between interactive media and reality. It is an area gaining considerable research and policy attention (Keith & Martin, 2005). Issues concerning bullying are pervasive in the understanding of youth violence and, as argued later in this paper, responding to it must be a part of any comprehensive attempt to attenuate youth violence.

COMING TO A THEATER NEAR, AND NEARER, TO YOU

In 2004 the Canadian Ministry produced a comprehensive review of research, practice, and policy pertaining to media violence. This blueprint action agenda's findings and recommendations addressed a variety of media sources that include

1. Television. Statistics on TV-watching habits suggest that children will have spent more hours watching TV by the time they get to high school than hours in class (Anderson & Bushman, 2002b; Strasburger & Donnerstein, 1999). Johnson et al. (2002) concluded that there is a significant association between the amount of TV watched and the likelihood of engaging in subsequent violence. The negative impact of TV wrestling, for example, has proven to hold a positive association with dating violence and other high-risk behaviors (Spitzer, Browne, & Hamilton-Giachritsis, 2005). Donnerstein (1993a) reported that very healthy people exposed to 10 hours of very graphic forms of violence, especially against women, became sensitized to the point of being more sympathetic defense jurors in simulated rape cases.

2. Movies. Researchers and policy makers (Government of Ontario, 2004; Huesmann, Moise-Titus, Podolski, & Eron, 2003) are concerned with the effects of "slasher films." All-night gross-out teen parties where the main media feature is graphic and erotic scenes of female mutilation, rape, or murder were used by the Canadian Ministry to illustrate this point. If in 1989, 92% of males had seen *Playboy* by age 15 (Brown & Bryant, 1989), then one must presume a similar percentage of youth have seen exploitative films via DVD and Internet. Experts express concern about an entire generation of boys viewing films, and reinforcing a visual imagery, showing women mutilated during in an otherwise erotic context (Government of Ontario, 2004).

3. Video games. Exposure of children and youth to mature rated video games has been quantified and a source of concern (Thompson, Tepichin, & Haninger, 2006). Song and Anderson (2001) supported other contentions that video games are likely to have a larger impact on aggressive behavior than TV and movies because the games provide practice, repetition, reward, and reinforcement. They, and others (e.g., Anderson & Dill, 2000; Browne & Hamilton-Giachritsis, 2005; Gentile & Anderson, 2003), described the effects of participant modeling and suggested it to be a rather ideal learning environment. Similarly, Funk and Buchman (1996) noted that what may be learned via video games is that "violence is fun, obligatory, easily justified and essentially without negative consequences" (p. 12). The issues of learned aggression through media will be further discussed latter in this article. Provenzo (2000) testified that video games could be the equivalent of genetic engineering that "leaves us with a with a 2 lb. mouse." Of particular concern are games that involve first-person shooters and virtual reality. Retired West Point professor Lieutenant Colonel Dave Grossman spent his career researching the psychiatry of killing for the U.S. Army. He proposed that killing is not a natural human response; rather it is a learned one. The conditions, he states, are repeated exposure to violence and associating violent acts with pleasurable experiences. He believed that the first-person shooter games that are available to youth are of sufficient content and quality to train military and law enforcement personnel to shoot with accuracy, reflexively, emotion, and comfort. Even more alarming are the quickly advancing technologies involving virtual reality. The effective use of such devices for behavior modification and professional training (pilots, truck drivers, ship captains, tank operators, etc.) has researchers and policymakers particularly concerned with what effect these media may have on youth who may soon be able to spend hours fully engaged in a violent scenario.

4. Music. More recently studies that have examined the impact of song lyrics (Anderson, Carnagey, & Eubanks, 2003) have showed similar increases in aggressive thoughts and emotions. Strasburger and Donnerstein (1999) cited strong correlations in the prevalence of violence, gun use, sexual activity, and drug use in music lyrics (and other media) and subsequent aggressive behavior. Anderson, Carnagey, and Eubanks (1993) concluded that lyrics can increase violent thoughts in three different ways. Violent lyrics can increase aggressive word vocabulary, reading speed, and word completion. These findings should be familiar to literacy instruction practitioners and researchers who are familiar with the use of song lyric to facilitate literacy skills (Fisher, 2001; Fisher, McDonald, & Strickland, 2001).

We can deduce that (a) there is ample evidence to conclude that, at minimum, an association exists between media violence and aggression in youth; and (b) as media violence researchers examine the rapid and pronounced advances in media technology and access, concerns over the impact of media violence on youth is likely to also significantly increase.

LIKE BEES TO HONEY

Slater and his colleagues' research (Slater, 2003; Slater, Henry, Swaim, & Anderson, 2003; Slater, Henry, Swaim, & Cardador, 2004) further extended Anderson's findings. Much of the work done by Slater's team focused on selective exposure. That is, the decision certain individuals make to seek out and focus their attention on media that is specifically violent. They argued that the "relationships between certain risk taking orientations such as sensation seeking and media violence almost certainly represent selective exposure" (Slater, Henry, Swaim, & Anderson, 2003, p. 716). They suggested that it is likely that media violence effects aggressive behavior and that individuals may be attracted to violent media content because of their violent tendencies. Their study, which deployed a *downward spiral model*, further blurred this distinction by predicting a pattern of reciprocal relationships between aggressive behavior and selective violent media use. It almost becomes a chicken-and-egg argument. They suggested certain youth may be more vulnerable to the effects of violent media content than others are, much the way that some individuals are more likely to suffer the negative consequences of smoking or drinking than others do.

Slater, Henry, Swaim, and Cardador (2004) submitted two alternative sources that impact this vulnerability. The first, they suggested, is internal. That is, certain youth may have a greater personality predisposition to respond to media violence or to engage in aggressive behaviors. They cited other research and researchers who contended that such individuals are likely to seek out (e.g. select) violent media content (e.g., Krcmar & Greene, 2000; Slater, 2003; Swaim, Henry, & Baez, 2004).

Slater, Henry, Swaim, and Cardador (2004) identified the second source of vulnerability as social and developmental. They proposed this second source of vulnerability stems from environmental factors such as family dynamics, school failure, alienation, deviant peer associations, and substance abuse. This finding underlies a basic assumption we make in this chapter—namely, that growing up in poverty exacerbates this second source of vulnerability because poverty exacerbates these compromised and stressed social and developmental conditions. Slater and his colleagues argued that because of this social stress, youth are both more vulnerable to media influence and more likely to seek out (e.g. select) violent media content. On the other hand, youth who have either little personality predisposition for aggressive behavior and/or few extended or intense social stresses are far less likely to be influenced by violent media content whether they seek it out or not. The intervention challenge the authors address in this chapter is what can be done within a school and educational context to mitigate the impact of social and developmental stresses such that violent media content is both less sought out but more importantly less likely to result in further aggressive behavior.

Perhaps one of the most significant areas of review in the aforementioned 1972 U.S. Surgeon General's report was the consideration of evidence of common origin (third variable) interpretations. That is, whether some antecedent condition(s) could further explain or exacerbate the associations between media violence and aggressive behavior. Stated another way, the report contends, "The array of possible influences and concomitants [to youth aggressiveness] is vast. . . . Television [media] the specific focus of our inquiry, is only one" (p. 78). Certainly, the Slater et al. (2003) downward spiral model suggested a level of cyclical interplay between media use and behavior in the real world. The Surgeon General's report questioned the context of the real-world environment for these youth and whether that context is a contributing factor in the established association between media use and aggression. Can circumstances faced by particular youth increase the likelihood that media will have an impact on their aggressiveness?

Among the Surgeon General's major implications was a need to examine the issue of media influence in the context of the "totality" of environmental influences. Among the third variables reviewed in that report, issues of socioeconomic status, age, and gender received attention. Personality traits did as well; however, those factors appear less germane to the educational implications sought in the present analysis. Describing and advocating for quality mental-health services interfaced with school programs is unfortunately beyond the scope of this paper. A third variable area related to family issues (e.g., parental control over media use, parental interpretation of media content, parental affection, punishment, parental emphasis on aggression, parent-child communication) may provide insight into information to be communicated with families through school-parent centers, home contacts, and home-school partnership agendas. In addition, it may be that school programs and services may be designed to provide children and youth a broader range of experiences related to adult interpretation, affection, discipline, communication, and related emphases (Roberts & Foehr, 2004).

Slater et al. (2004) proposed that at times of greatest social conflict and stress, youth would be more likely be "vulnerable to the effects of violent media" (p. 643). Slater et al. (2004) cited previous studies to support their own findings that a major source of vulnerability to the effects of media violence is the social experiences of the developing adolescent. Their work extended previous youth-behavior-and-development findings to youth who are particularly stressed by, and therefore feel alienated at, home and school, and thus are "especially vulnerable to deviant behaviors such as substance abuse, aggression, and the antisocial influence of deviant peers" (p. 643). The general category of "alienation" would appear to be a major third variable to which educators must consider systemic and programmatic responses. If such feelings cause youth to be more vulnerable to the effects of media violence, we would hope that they might also be somewhat "vulnerable" to more educational uses of media.

The Slater et al. (2003) discussion of their downward spiral model study cited the fact that their sample was comprised of youth was drawn from 10 nonmetropolitan school districts. They suggest that this would actually produce a conservative bias. We agree. A sample that included urban schools with more socioeconomic, cultural, and language diversity would likely yield even greater support for their hypothesis. It is surprising that few studies actually addressed media influence on children and youth who grow up in conditions of abject poverty. Most studies try and control for SES (e.g., Anderson & Bushman, 2002a; Donnerstein, Slaby, & Eron, 1994) and the Surgeon General's report identifies SES as a likely third variable (Surgeon General's Scientific Advisory Committee on Television and Social Behavior, 1972). However, it would seem warranted that given the appreciation of environmental context in its totality on the effects of media violence and aggression, it would appear appropriate to design study specifically if and how growing up in poverty presents particular concerns regarding the media-aggression association.

We submit that special attention must be devoted to issues pertaining to aggression and violence among children who live in poverty. As a group, the fact is they are exposed to more violent events and conditions than their more affluent peers are. As a group, their responses to violent (or potentially violent) situations will tend to beget more violence and/or victimization. Payne (2001) wrote extensively about the culture of poverty and proposed that those that grow up in generational poverty are less likely to know, or use, middle-class solutions. She argues that many children and youth living in poverty have much more tolerant perspectives on prison, weapons, punishments, and fights than their middle-class peers do. Urban communities with large immigrant populations may also bring to their new communities a different set of norms regarding crime, punishment, and honor. Strausburger and Donnerstein (1999) was a more extensive review linking exposure to violence and its impact on violent thoughts and behaviors. They propose that media acts as a "super peer" influence. This influence can further teach youth that violence can be used to achieve goals and settle conflict and that youth that are regularly exposed to violence and there daily life may be most prone to the impact of this super peer influence.

Fisher, Obidah, Pelton, and Campana (2005) went so far to contend that growing up in poverty may in itself be a form of violence. It would therefore appear warranted to focus research of media violence on these youth. Clearly many of the conditions in the existing literature associated with vulnerability to the effects of media violence exist in this population. Slater, Henry, Swaim, and Anderson (2003) emphasized that "the downward spiral model, then, also suggests that the effects of media content that reinforces tendencies to antisocial attitudes and behavior should be most conspicuous among youth who are most vulnerable to those attitudes" (p. 731). As previously noted, they suggested that either personality or environmental experiences (social and developmental) increase vulnerability which can, by definition, increased can the likelihood of a more aggressive predisposition to future events. "Those youth with such a predisposition are likely to have predispositions reinforced [via media violence], and their preexisting aggressive tendencies magnified" (p. 733).

Young people's immediate environment and experiences help teach them strategies to live with and respond to violence. According to the Archives of Pediatric medicine (California Attorney General's Office, 2002), "children who have witnessed violence are more likely to miss school, get poor grades and exhibit emotional problems. Children with higher exposure to violence exhibit more depression and anxiety than children with low exposure" (p. 969). In concentrated areas of San Diego's urban communities the incidence of violent juvenile crimes are three times higher than the combined incidences in other San Diego areas. Some evidence suggests that every student in an urban school has experienced violence as either a victim, perpetrator, or witness by the time he or she reaches high school (Fisher, Obidah, Pelton, & Campana, 2005).

Consider, for example, the Youth Risk Behavior Survey (2003) which reported that 28.1% of Latino males carried a knife, gun, or club in the past 30 days; 10.2% carried that weapon in school; 9.4% of African-American and Latina girls report not wanting to go to school in the past 30 days because they felt unsafe traveling to and from it. Also, 52.1% of 9th-grade boys and 34.1% of 9th-grade girls reported one or more physical fights in last 12 months; 10.8% of girls report having been forced to have nonconsensual sexual intercourse and 31.1% of all high-school students (including 49% of Latinas) reported experiencing more than two weeks of feeling sad or hopeless such that they stopped doing many usual activities. Given those data it is alarming, but not surprising that 17.6% of Latinas actually attempted suicide during the previous 12 months. Given this context, researchers would predict the influence of media violence to function as a "super peer" to be greater (Strausburger & Donnerstein, 1999). Over 30 years ago, researchers were already finding that boys who were more highly exposed to violence were more likely than not to hold attitudes favorable to aggression (Dominick & Greenberg, 1972). It is reasonable to hypothesize then that youth growing up in poverty are more vulnerable, as a group, to the negative effects of witnessing violence in their lives.

Having said that, we warn against drawing any conclusions or presumptions that limit the resilience of the majority of individuals living in poverty. Individuals living in poverty do by and large show the resilience to withstand the negative impact of the violence that is a part of their lives; they draw from internal and external resources to make good decisions; and they live decent and moral lives (Fisher, 2006). Nor are we suggesting that more affluent individual youth are all protected from witnessing devastating violence in their lives or engaging in acts of aggression. The argument here is the conditions associated with poverty increase the numbers and percentages of youth exposed to everyday violence. Therefore our position considers the vulnerability of these youth as a group and our challenge is to examine educational responses that might attenuate this vulnerability and foster resilience.

CURIOUS MINDS WANT TO KNOW

As previously noted, Slater, Henry, Swaim, and Cardador (2004) identified that environmental factors (social and developmental) can increase vulnerability to get tangled in a downward spiral of increased selection of violent media content and increased aggressive emotions and behaviors. Issues facilitating vulnerability due to social factors are described in greater detail elsewhere in this paper with a particular focus on poverty and negative life experiences which poverty tends to exacerbate. Attention in this section will instead focus on the developmental factors. It is important to remind ourselves that children and youth are not simply big people in little people's bodies. Their capacity to learn and view the world around them is substantially different from adults. When we casually use the phrase "she is not ready for that" it is more than simply a paternal/maternal tendency to keep the ugliness of the real world from our children as long as we can. The substance of the phrase is rooted in brain research and learning theory. Dahl (2004) described adolescence as a time when feelings and rational thought become linked together. Contradicting earlier assumptions that the adolescent brain is largely complete, brain researchers believe that the adolescent brain goes through a period of organizational development as important as that which takes place in the first two years of life (p. 22). Restak (2001) believed that the teenage brain is a work in progress and that the choices adolescents make during their development influence the quality of the brain's development.

Brown and Hamilton-Giachritas (2005) reviewed the effects of TV watching on children and youth and noted that they are more vulnerable to the effects of media violence than adults. They believed that the media can be a means of facilitating rote learning during formative years. The brain has the capacity to learn as more activity or concept examples are received. The brain's organization of these examples involves shaping synaptic connections. This process is called "neuroplasticity" (Shaw & McEachern, 2001). There is ample evidence to suggest that there is a dramatic and continuing reduction in this plasticity with age. With regards to "impressionability, it would appear that children in elementary school are highly susceptible to this learning" (Kaiser Family Foundation, 2003, n.p.). The Huesmann, Moise-Titus, Podolski, and Eron (2003) longitudinal studies of children (e.g., 8 year olds) who watched many hours of TV violence suggested that these children were significantly more likely to become adult criminals. Even before the media boom, Bandura, Ross, and Ross (1961) reported aggressive imitative acts impact on 3–5-year-old TV viewers. This is alarming when considering the results of the Kaiser Family Foundation survey (2003) that estimated 66% of children under the age of six, including those as young as six months, spend an average of two hours per day in front of a TV, computer, or video. This critical period of development sets a foundation for behavior patterns and learning. As the developing brain organizes information and experiences, certain synaptic connections are made and strengthened and others are ignored and weakened.

In his testimony, Anderson (Government of Ontario, 2004) referred to these neuro-accomplishments as knowledge structures. He explained knowledge-structure development (and developing personality) using a slow-hardening clay metaphor. The clay gets shaped by our experiences. This shaping is consistent with the notion of vulnerability of violent media exposure due to social factors. To continue the metaphor, the changes are easy when the clay is soft, but as time passes the clay gets harder to mold. Of particular concern is Anderson's assertion that aggression-related structures formed in young children begin to harden at age eight and are easier to reinforce than change with age.

ALL THE WORLD IS A STAGE, AND ALL THE "CHILDREN" ARE MERELY PLAYERS . . .

The notion of knowledge structures provides significant insight into the constructs of human aggression and how media may influence it. Anderson and Bushman (2002a, 2002b) offered the General Aggression Model (GAM) to depict how these structures function. GAM is an integrated framework incorporating various learning theories including cognitive neo-association (Berkowitz, 1984), Social Learning Theory (Bandura, 1977) and Script Theory (Schank & Abelson, 1977), Excitation Transfer Theory (Zillman, 1983), and Social Interaction Theory (Tedeschi & Felson, 1994). GAM recognizes the interrelated concepts of each of these theories. Anderson and Bushman's model provides a perspective of processes in play when an individual experiences an episode (e.g. a human interaction). There are three foci in their model: *inputs* (the person and the situation), *rotes* (personal internal state of affect, cognition, and arousal), and *outcomes* (the assumptions and choices made). The resulting actions and responses further impact the situational input and the process are cyclical until the interaction ends. As time paces each episode (e.g., experience) significantly affects the inputs, routes, and outcomes we will use in the future. When our "clay is soft," certain types of repeated or pronounced experiences are likely to create and reinforce aggressive (or nonaggressive) knowledge structures that will influence future behavior. Figure 34.1 is reprinted from Anderson and Bushman (2002a). It depicts how repeated exposure to violent media can lead to changing both internal personality and social variables. This speaks to the aforementioned vulnerability of youth based on media experiences. It also reinforces increased vulnerability of youth exposed to continual real-life violence. Once again the downward spiral identified by Slater et al. is credible if youth are experiencing repeated exposure to violence in both the "media" and the "real world."

Current research in child and adolescent development suggests that humans learn how to "perceive, interpret, judge and respond in the physical and social environment" (Anderson, 2000, n.p.). As such, we learn a set of rules for how to interact with whom and how. We also learn behavioral scripts and use them to interpret events and actions of others and to guide our own actions.

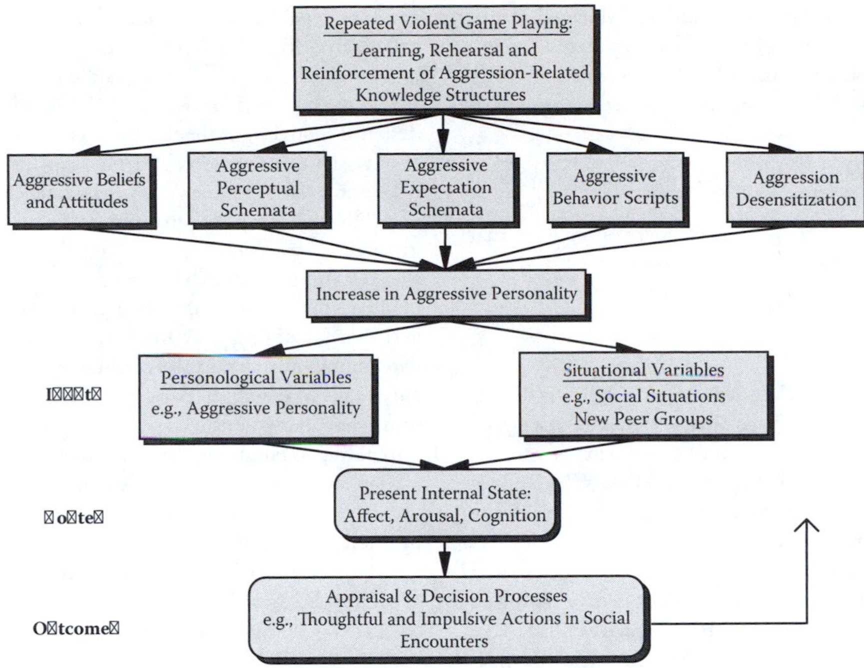

FIGURE 34.1. How repeated exposure to violent media can lead to changes in both internal personality and social variables.
Source: Anderson, C. A., & Bushman, B. J. (2002). Human aggression. *Annual Review of Psychology*, 53, 27–51.

SYSTEMS FOR CREATING AGGRESSIVE KNOWLEDGE AND BEHAVIOR

As a result of our literature review, we offer seven plausible mechanisms that can be factors in creating aggressive knowledge structures and behavioral scripts. The evidence collected thus far suggests that either individually or in combinations these factors work to create aggressive knowledge structures and behavioral scripts such that children and youth become violent.

1. Desensitization. Individuals get used to violence and what once might have seemed outside normal life experience becomes accepted as part of life experience (Huesmann & Eron, 1986; Slater, Henry, Swaim, & Cardador, 2004). We might presume that the first time a child sees another carrying, or using a gun; or injecting drugs; or beating a woman, the experience might be traumatic. At what point will such an occurrence become an accepted norm? The question is, to what extent does repeatedly viewing and participating in similar media-sponsored events add to that desensitization? Graphic novels can also provide opportunities for youth to be desensitized about violence as students process the visual images of fights, murder, rape, and such.

2. Personal identification. Youth look to others as a means of shaping and modeling their own behaviors and aspirations (Anderson & Bushman, 2001; Anderson & Bushman, 2002b; Government of Ontario, 2004; McLeod, Atkin, & Chaffee, 1972; Surgeon General's Scientific Advisory Committee on Television and Social Behavior, 1972). Payne (2001) portrayed a young boy who is following in the footsteps of his uncle. His uncle is the male role model in his life as his father was killed in a gang-related incident. His uncle makes his living selling drugs, plans to avenge his brother's death, and does not expect to live past 30. Although his uncle spends periods in jail and in exile in Mexico, this 6-year-old sees his uncle as a breadwinner and protector. The boy learns to expect and eventually assume violence, jail, and early death as a part of everyday life. What then is the added impact of a successful gangsta rapper singing about murder and rape? Anderson (2003) discussed the impact of video games in which identification with the aggressor leads to imitation of the aggressor. In many video games, players must become a violent character and winning the game is a function of using weapons effectively, e.g. killing people (Funk, Buchman, & Germann, 2000; van Schie & Wiegman, 1997).

3. Active participation and learning. Experience is among the best teachers. Repeated experience is an effective learning tool. In the case of violence, it is a means to acquire aggressive knowledge structures and behavioral scripts. In the case of video games, participants are rewarded for learning an aggressive storyline and in learning how to act aggressively and retaliate aggressively. Unlike TV watching, these game scenarios require participants to rehearse the entire story. The participant is required to make active choices and those choices impact the way the game ends. Anderson (2003) pointed out how much more passive TV is. Consider then, abusive exchanges between two or more youth in a chat room. With the immediate safeguard of physical challenge removed, this medium allows youth to hone their verbal attack skills—their nastiness, if you will. The impact of both the perceived aggressor and victims of these exchanges can be hypothesized using the RAM (Anderson

& Bushman 2002b). Anderson and Bushman's RAM model identified cognitive sources in their model for explaining aggression and violence. McLeod, Atkin, and Chaffee (1972) also studied the "cognitive effects" of learning and the role of media related to the participation and learning that occurred in at least three ways:

- Acquisition of knowledge about techniques (e.g., how to hit someone),
- Acquisition of knowledge of pertinent facts of life (e.g., that hitting someone is in fact one way of gaining ends), and
- Acquisition of values (e.g., that hitting someone is a preferred way of gaining needs).

4. Alienation and victimization. Issues pertaining to media depicting violence within sexual content have already been discussed elsewhere in this chapter. The sexual abuse and exploitation of youth is a major international concern and the impact on those victimized by it is both intuitive and documented (Thornburg & Lin, 2000). Murder and suicide also represent the most serious consequences and causes of further alienation and abuse (Fisher, 2005). Initiation into gangs by getting jumped is supposedly designed to show you are tough enough and worthy enough to be accepted (Hill, Lui, & Hawkins, 2001). What role does the media play in further desensitizing, suggesting, valuing, reinforcing, and communicating these violent abuses? Only recently has the professional and general public become more aware of the impact of being picked on and/or bullied (Slater, Henry, Swaim, & Cardador, 2004). This form of victimization, left unchallenged, appears to be a leading cause of every known behavior and emotion associated with aggressive knowledge structures. Is aggressive media content sought out when youth feel isolated or victimized? Does the nature of that content further aggressive behavior? Evidence would suggest "yes" to both questions, and that the downward spiral model would be in effect.

5. Fantasy and reality. McLeod, Atkin, and Chaffee (1972) studied the impact of media on aggressive behavior by focusing on whether the media violence appeared linked to real-life events. They found that linkage was a plausible mechanism along with identification and learning. Thus the vulnerability of youth to the effects of media violence may also be increased by the degree to which the lines between reality and fantasy are blurred. Generally speaking, younger children are less able to differentiate reality from fantasy than adults (Surgeon General's Scientific Advisory Committee on Television and Social Behavior, 1972). How does a teenager really know whether a gangsta rapper who is singing about raping women or shooting policemen is really engaged in or endorsing that behavior? How do youth using a video that has simulation effects that are so real that it can be used for police officer training, separate that experience from the need to carry a gun and be prepared to defend him- or herself? (Song & Anderson, 2001; Grossman & DeGaetano, 1999). With active participation, prolonged and repeated exposures, and high-quality real-life images and audio effects, it is reasonable to presume linkages are more possible than those McLeod, Atkin, and Chaffee (1972) confirmed in passive TV watching. One of the major responsibilities in childrearing is to help children learn and differentiate fantasy and reality. If, on the other hand, children and youth spend excessive time accessing highly graphic and realistic-appearing media, it is more likely that such distinctions will be overlooked. Finally, much of media violence children experience through TV and Internet are conveying real-life events. What effect does graphically conveyed reality have on the aggressive knowledge structures and behavioral scripts of young audiences? Growing numbers of TV shows are so-called "reality shows"; some (e.g., Jerry Springer) are designed to highlight the most perverted and distorted relationships that exist in our society, and physical fighting is rewarding with claps and encouragement from the audience along with other forms of public indecency. At what point do these shows change a child's knowledge structure? Consider the ability of youth to manipulate their way onto a site where live cams expose supposedly real people engaging in what has never before been publicly displayed or even imagined? It is easy to see how such material may exacerbate date abuse and rape and other high-risk behavior (Brown & Bryant, 1989; Marshall & Barrett, 1990). Youth have new avenues to somewhat anonymously engage in providing, viewing, reading, and responding to language, stories, and attacks that require no face-to-face contact. Finally, we have become painfully aware of adults who use media sources to sexually exploit children through fantasy and by arranging real-life encounters (Tarbox, 2000). If the fantasy-reality linkage is a contributing factor to increased vulnerability, there is no doubt that media is blurring the distinction and too many children are not being helped to establish that distinction.

6. Reinforcing stereotypes. Fisher et al. (2005) addressed the myths perpetuated about youth from traditionally underrepresented backgrounds. Those myths are reinforced through the media. It may be that youth who are the victims of that stereotyping may be most influenced by it. It is plausible for a student to think, "If violent media content resembles my community and the problems that exist in it, it may be that the Hollywood scripts for how to survive and live in my community might be influential in creating my behavioral script." Clark (1971) argued that the media could both be violent and convey violence, and cited media as a means to help learn about self-worth and that of others. They suggested that media portrayals can portray minority groups in ways that lower self-esteem. By the same token, TV can reinforce the culture of poverty and the rules for surviving in poverty (Payne, 2001). Payne argued that culture and those rules and norms are a barrier for supporting mobility into the middle class. The rules, appearance of reality, and the seductive identification with characters makes media an influence affecting how we grow, learn, behave, and treat each other. Most media is designed to entertain and to sell product; it appeals to arousal and vicarious thrill seeking and voyeurism. Entertainment media inevitably reflects the values, the points of view, and the expectation of the audience response held by the producers (Surgeon General's Scientific Advisory Committee on Television and Social Behavior, 1972). In this respect, media can very easily perpetuate, reinforce, or modify social stereotypes about groups.

7. Family patterns. Parenting strategies have a far greater impact on a child than their immediate effect on behavior. Parents teach the child by example, or lack thereof, how situations are to be handled, what behavior is normal and acceptable, and how others important in their lives treat and feel about them. Parenting behaviors model and teach attitudes and behaviors that will influence the child's immediate and long-term subsequent attitudes and behavior repertoires. How families deal with punishment, media use and monitoring, reading, responses to frustration, violence, crises, communicating, school expectations, nutrition, role modeling, and after-school supervision are just a beginning list of the unconscious and planned parental behaviors children witness. To the extent that overall parent behavior reinforces rather than attenuates media violence will impact the impact of the media (Anderson, Carnagey, & Eubanks, 2003; Huesmann & Eron, 1986).

YES ALL ARE MERELY PLAYERS, BUT EACH "CHILD" IN HIS TIME PLAYS MANY PARTS, HIS ACTS BEING SEVEN AGES . . .

Heretofore we have attempted to provide a realistic, daunting perspective regarding how vulnerable youth are to developing aggressive knowledge structures. Furthermore we have attempted to establish that at the very least media violence can be a significant contributor to that vulnerability. Finally, we know that certain youth live in families, and/or communities, in which violence is too much a part of their everyday lives and that media violence may be simply fuel on their personal fires. We chose to complete our modified Shakespearian quote from the previous section in the title of this section in order to suggest that all is not in vain. We argue there are interventions that can challenge the behavioral scripts a violent world may be writing for our children. What ways might educators introduce new lines, new characters, and new roles, which challenge the behavioral scripts our children are learning and rehearsing? Inherent in the answer to this question is to understand and exploit those factors that facilitate resiliency and thereby reduce vulnerability toward aggressive behavioral structures.

Many of the resiliency factors are mirror images to the negative third variables the Surgeon General proposed in their report. For example, The Search Institute's Healthy Communities toolkit (1998) delineated 40 developmental assets that are associated with youth who are more likely to demonstrate resiliency in the face of violence and adversity. These assets are organized into eight general categories including support, empowerment, boundaries/expectations, constructive use of time, commitment to learning, positive values, social competencies, and positive identity. The means to modify or create alternatives to the development of aggressive knowledge structures follows the same model (e.g., GAM) Anderson and Bushman (2002a) proposed to account for aggression.

We do not believe it is possible as a beginning step to change the impact of media with violent content on children and youth simply by expecting we can limit its use or censure its content. We are not arguing against improved efforts to monitor usage or limit access. We know that parental and adult guidance, and responsible media producers, can have an impact on reducing the content children and youth select and use. However, too many youth do not get this guidance and the ones who do are lucky indeed. However, we are too realistic to expect access will be reduced instead of increased. Therefore our most immediate response must be to teach students to be more critical and discerning consumers of the media and real-world violence they witness, and give them experiences and information that may create some cognitive dissonance between a violent act and a previously scripted behavioral response to it.

It is also possible to consider using the same eight plausible mechanisms that can be factors in developing aggressive knowledge structures and behavior scripts as a means to modify, change, and attenuate those structures and scripts. Thus, we have chosen to use those eight mechanisms as a means of considering some literature-specific intervention concepts and examples.

Future Research

Our review suggests future research needs in several areas. Of most concern to the authors are two related strands of research.

The first strand of future research needs to focus on the relationship between the impact of violent media content and poverty and its combined impact on children and youth. Violence researchers would make a significant and substantial impact to the field if this relationship was better understood. It would appear that many of the longitudinal, cross-sectional, field and laboratory studies and methodologies that have been used to establish a clear link between media violence and aggression in children and youth could be deployed to establish this research focus. In addition, violence researchers and theorists could use this new database to further refine, exemplify, and extend the constructs and models that currently exist for illustrating how aggressive thoughts and actions are created, challenged, reinforced, and/or increased. Social scientists who study resiliency should also benefit a great deal and contribute to this strand of research.

The second strand of future research that our review and concerns suggest is under the purview of educational researchers and practitioners. As we gain more insight and understanding on the relationship between violent media content, poverty, and children, research-based educational practices will be needed that mitigate negative media impact and/or enhance youth resiliency. The most practical and deployable practices are likely to be ones that can be integrated within the current standards-based curriculum as it is difficult to imagine adding more to an already over-packed instructional day. The authors plan to focus research on how aggression and the impact of media violence can be mitigated in a school's comprehensive literacy framework. Educational technology researchers should be particularly influenced and contribute to both aforementioned strands of research. Further, there is the need for those researchers to understand how the power of new and emerging technologies can be harnessed to promote resilient, tolerant, and healthy children and youth.

REFERENCES

American Academy of Pediatrics. (2000). *Joint statement on the impact of entertainment violence on children.* Congressional Public Health Summit. Monograph. Washington, DC.

Anderson, C. A. (2000, March). *Testimony before the U.S. Senate Commerce Committee hearing on the impact of interactive violence on children.* Washington, DC: U.S. Senate.

Anderson, C. A. (2003). Violent video games: Myths, facts, and unanswered questions. *Psychological Science Agenda, 16*(5). Retrieved May 27, 2006, from www.apa.org/science/psa/sb-anderson.html

Anderson, C. A., & Bushman, B. J. (2001). Effects of violent video games on aggressive behavior, aggressive cognition, aggressive affect, physiological arousal, and prosocial behavior: A meta-analytic review of the scientific literature. *Psychological Science, 12,* 353–359.

Anderson, C. A., & Bushman, B. J. (2002a). Human aggression. *Annual Review of Psychology, 53,* 27–51.

Anderson, C. A., & Bushman, B. J. (2002b). The effects of media violence on society. *Science, 295,* 2377–2378.

Anderson, C. A., Carnagey, N. L., & Eubanks, J. (2003). Exposure to violent media: The effects of songs with violent lyrics on aggressive thoughts and feelings. *Journal of Personality and Social Psychology, 84*, 960–971.

Anderson, C. A., & Dill, K. E. (2000). Veideo games and aggressive thoughts, feelings, and behavior in the laboratory and in life. *Journal of Personality and Social Psychology, 78*, 772–790.

Bandura, A. (1977). *Social learning theory*. New York: General Learning Press.

Bandura, A., Ross, D., & Ross, S. A. (1961). Transmission of aggression through imitation of aggressive models. *Journal of Abnormal and Social Psychology, 63*, 575–582.

Berkowitz, L. (1984). Some effects of thoughts on anti- and prosocial influences of media events: A cognitive-neoassociation analysis. *Psychological Bulletin, 95*(3), 410–427.

Brown, D., & Bryant, J. (1989). Uses of pornography. In D. Zillman & J. Bryant (Eds.), *Pornography: Research advances and policy considerations* (pp. 3–24). Hillsdale, NJ: Lawrence Erlbaum.

Browne, K. D., & Hamilton-Giachritsis, C. (2005). The influence of violent media on children and adolescents: A public-health approach. *Lancet, 365*, 702–710.

Brozo, W. G., Walter, P., & Placker, T. (2002). "I know the difference between a real man and a TV man": A critical exploration of violence and masculinity through literature in a junior high school in the "hood." *Journal of Adolescent & Adult Literacy, 45*, 530–538.

Byrnes, D. A. (2001). War and conflict: Educators advocating for the protection of children. *The Educational Forum, 65*, 227–232.

California Attorney General's Office (2002). *Reducing children's exposure to violence: Promising strategies and programs resource guide*. Sacramento, CA: Author.

Clark, C. (1971). Race, identification, and television violence. In G. A. Comstock, E. A. Rubinstein, & J. P. Murray (Eds.), *Television and social behavior* (5). Washington, DC: Government Printing Office.

Dahl, D. (2004). Adolescent development and the regulation of behavior and emotion. *Annals of the New York Academy of Science, 1021*, 294–295.

Dominick, J. P., & Greenberg, B. S. (1972). Attitudes towards violence: The interaction of television exposure, family attitudes and social class. In G. A. Comstock & E. A. Rubinstein (Eds.), *Television and adolescent aggressiveness* (pp. 314–335). Washington, DC: U.S. Government Printing Office.

Donnerstein, E. (1993). Mitigating the effects of mass media sexual violence. *Aggressive Behavior, 19*, 50.

Donnerstein, E., Slaby, R., & Eron, L. (1994). The mass media and youth aggression. In L. Eron, J. Gentry, & P. Schleagal (Eds.), *Reason to hope: A psychosocial perspective on violence and youth* (pp. 219–250). Washington, DC: American Psychological Association.

Fisher, D. (2001). Early language learning with and without music. *Reading Horizons, 42*(1), 39–50.

Fisher, D. (2005). The literacy educator's role in suicide prevention. *Journal of Adolescent and Adult Literacy, 48*, 364–373.

Fisher, D. (2006). When students disclose the violence in their lives, how should their teachers respond? *English Journal, 95*(6), 65–70.

Fisher, D., McDonald, N., & Strickland, J. (2001). Early literacy development in our musical classrooms: A sound practice! *General Music Today, 14*(3), 15–20.

Fisher, D., Obidah, J., Pelton, M. H., & Campana, J. (2005). Violence as a factor in the lives of urban youth. In J. Flood & P. Anders (Eds.), *The literacy development of students in urban schools: Research and policy* (pp. 68–96). Newark, DE: International Reading Association.

Frey, N., & Fisher, D. (2004). Using graphic novels, *anime*, teen magazines, and the Internet in an urban high school English class. *English Journal, 93*, 19–25.

Funk, J. B., Baldacci, H. B., Pasold, T., & Baumgardner, J. (2004). Violence exposure in real-life, video games, television, movies, and the Internet: Is there desensitization? *Journal of Adolescence, 27*, 23–39.

Funk, J. B., & Buchman, D.D. (1996). Video and computer games in the '90s: Children's time commitment and game preference. *Children Today, 24* (1), 12.

Funk, J. B., Buchman, D. D., & Germann, J. N. (2000). Preference for violent electronic games, self-concept, and gender differences in young children. *American Journal of Orthopsychiatry, 70*, 233–241.

Gentile, D. A. & Anderson, C. A. (2003). Violent video games: The newest media violence hazard. In D. A. Gentile (Ed.), *Media violence and children* (pp. 131–152). Westport, CT: Praeger Publishing.

Government of Ontario, CN. (2004). *Action agenda: A strategic blueprint for reducing exposure to media violence in Canada*. [Monograph]. Ontario, CN: Queen's Printer.

Grossman, D., & DeGaetano, G. (1999). *Stop teaching our kids to kill: A call to action against TV, movie and video game violence*. New York: Crown.

Hill, K. G., Lui, C., & Hawkins, J. D. (2001). *Early precursory gang membership: A study of Seattle youth*. [Monograph]. U.S. Department of Justice, Office of Justice Programs. Washington, D.C.

Huesmann, L. R., & Eron, L. D. (1986). *Television and the aggressive child: A cross-national comparison*. Hillsdale, NJ: Erlbaum.

Huesmann, L. R., Moise-Titus, J., Podolski, C. L., & Eron, L. D. (2003). Longitudinal relations between children's exposure to TV violence and their aggressive and violent behavior in young adulthood: 1977–1992. *Developmental Psychology, 39*, 201–221.

Johnson, J. G., Cohen, P., Smailes, E. M., Kasen, S., & Brook, J. S. (2002). Television viewing and aggressive behavior during adolescence and adulthood. *Science Magazine, 295*, 2468–2471.

Kaiser Family Foundation (2003). *TV violence key facts*. [Monograph]. Washington, DC.

Keith, S., & Martin, M. E. (2005). Cyber-bullying: Creating a culture of respect in a cyber world. *Reclaiming Children & Youth, 13*, 224–228.

Krcmar, M., & Greene, K. (2000). Connections between violent television exposure and adolescent risk-taking. *Media Psychology, 2*, 195–218.

Ladd, G. W., & Cairns, E. (1996). Introduction-children: Ethnic and political violence. *Child Development, 67*, 14–18.

Marshall, W. L., & Barrett, S. (1990). *Criminal neglect: Why sex offenders go free*. Toronto: Doubleday Canada.

McLeod, J. M., Atkin, C. K., & Chaffee, S. H. (1972). Adolescents, parents, and television use: Adolescent self-report measures from the Wisconsin sample. In G.A. Comstock & E.A. Rubinstein (Eds.), *Television and social behavior: Vol. 3. Television and adolescent aggressiveness* (pp. 173–238). Washington, D.C.: U.S. Government Printing Office.

Paulson, A. (2003). Internet bullying. *Christian Science Monitor, 96*(24), 11–12.

Payne, R. K. (2001). *A framework for understanding poverty* (revised edition). Highlands, TX: aha! Process, Inc.

Provenzo, E. F. (2000, March). *Testimony before the U.S. Senate Commerce Committee Hearing on the impact of interactive violence on children*. Washington, DC: U.S. Senate.

Restak, R. (2001). *The secret life of the brain*. Mississippi State, MS: Branton Berryhill Publisher.

Roberts, D. F., & Foehr, U. G. (2004). *Kids & media in America*. Cambridge, UK: Cambridge University Press.

Schank, R. C., & Abelson, R. (1977). *Scripts, plans, goals, and understanding*. Hillsdale, NJ: Erlbaum Associates.

Shaw, C. A., & McEachern, J. (2001). *Toward a theory of neuroplasticity*. Oxford: Taylor & Francis, Inc.

Slater, M. D. (2003). Alienation, aggression, and sensation-seeking as predictors of adolescent use of violent film, computer and website content. *Journal of Communication, 53*, 105–121.

Slater, M. D., Henry, K. L., Swaim, R. C., & Anderson, L. L. (2003). Violent media content and aggressiveness in adolescents: A downward spiral model. *Communication Research, 30*, 713–736.

Slater, M. D., Henry, K. L., Swaim, R. C., Cardador, J. M. (2004). Vulnerable teens, vulnerable times: How sensation seeking, alienation, and victimization moderate the violent media content-aggressiveness relation. *Communication Research, 31*, 642–668.

Song, E.H., & Anderson, J.E. (2001). How violent video games may violate children's health. *Contemporary Pediatrics, 18*(5), 102–119.

Spitzer, M., Browne, K., & Hamilton-Giachritsis, C. (2005). Influence of violent media on children and adolescents. *The Lancet, 365*(9468), 1387–1388.

Strasburger, V. C., & Donnerstein, E. (1999). Children, adolescents, and the media: Issues and solutions. *Pediatrics, 103*, 129–139.

Surgeon General's Scientific Advisory Committee on Television and Social Behavior. (1972). *Television and growing up: The impact of televised violence.* U.S. Government Printing Office, Washington, DC.

Swaim, R. C. Henry, K. L., & Baez, N. E. (2004). Risk-taking, attitudes toward violence, and violent behavior among rural middle school youth. *Violence and Victims, 19*, 157–170.

Tarbox, K. (2000). *Katie.com: My story*. New York: Dutton.

Tedeschi, J. T., & Felson, R. B. (1994). *Violence, aggression, and coercive actions.* Washington, DC: American Psychological Association.

The Search Institute. (1998). *Healthy communities, healthy tool kit.* Minneapolis, MN: Author.

Thompson, K. M., Tepichin, K., & Haninger, K. (2006). Content and ratings of mature-rated video games. *Archives of Pediatric Adolescent Medicine, 160*, 402–410.

Thornberg, D., & Lin, H. S. (Eds.). (2000). *Committee to study tools and strategies for protecting kids from pornography and their applicability to other inappropriate internet content.* Computer Science and Telecommunications Board, National Research Council (US). National Academy Press. Washington, DC.

van Schie, E. G. M., & Wiegman, O. (1997). Children and videogames: Leisure activities, aggression, social integration, and school performance. *Journal of Applied Social Psychology, 27*, 1175–1194.

Ybarra, M. L., & Mitchell, K. J. (2004). Youth engaging in online harassment: Associations with caregiver-child relationships, Internet use, and personal characteristics. *Journal of Adolescence, 27*, 319–336.

Youth Risk Behavior Survey. (2003). San Diego, CA: San Diego Unified School District.

Zellers, J. H. (2005). *Naked ladies and macho men: A feminist content analysis of a burgeoning graphic novels collection*. Unpublished master's thesis in library sciences, University of North Carolina.

Zillman, D. (1983). Transfer of excitation in emotional behavior. In B. L. Cacioppo & L. L. Petty (Eds.), *Social psychophysiology: A sourcebook* (pp. 215–240). New York: Guilford Press.

III

VOICES FROM THE FIELD

AWAKENING VOICE AND LOSING SLEEP: WHEN ADULT SOUTHERN LEARNERS BECOME WRITERS

S.D. *Collins*

TENNESSEE TECHNOLOGICAL UNIVERSITY

AWAKENING VOICE AND LOSING SLEEP: WHEN ADULT SOUTHERN LEARNERS BECOME WRITERS

Their days begin long before the sun starts its climb up the sloping mountains of East Tennessee. In cars dusted with weather and limestone, they curve their way through areas that bear descriptions for names: Hanging Limb, Crooked Creek, Bone Cave. Some traveling for more than an hour and a half, they leave behind hometowns where they commune with their neighbors through Sunday morning services and Friday night football. They are deep country; they are rural America—they are nontraditional university students studying to become elementary teachers.

As a professor of literacy studies, it is my privilege to be a part of a university initiative to serve the needs of students who are bound by the constraints of where they live or the time involved in receiving a university education. Officially known as the "2+2 Elementary Education Program," the southeast, mid-level university at which I teach has partnered with select area community colleges to offer onsite delivery of the third and fourth years of its elementary teacher licensure program. The students in the 2+2 Program are predominantly Caucasian females in their late 20s or early 30s; 10% of the students are Caucasian men of a slightly older average age. Both the men and women in the program live in rural areas where there are fewer jobs and educational opportunities. Most of the students in the 2+2 Program are first-generation postsecondary students. Though the university supplies these students with the same resources enjoyed by the students at the university's main campus (professors, texts, laptops, digital cameras, laser printers, technology support, etc.), balancing children, part-time jobs, long drives, and the cost of a university education is sometimes difficult; however, due to the hardworking ethic of their communities and heritages built on a mix of faith and determination, the program enjoys a high completion rate because the students are tenacious and dedicated.

For three semesters I have traveled to as many community college campuses that serve as sites for the 2+2 Program to teach a block of literacy classes. I launch the language arts course, in which writing serves as the primary focus, by asking students to complete a survey that begins, simply, "Are you a writer?" (adapted from Atwell, 1998). I also ask the students to think of three specific times in which they were engaged in a writing project and to briefly list those situations. From their list, I ask that they choose one of the situations and describe anything and everything that stands out to them about that writing experience.

From the 75 preservice teachers who have completed the survey to date, more than 70% responded that they were not writers. When describing their experiences with writing, they frequently used words such as "afraid," "nervous," "stressed," "worried," "anxious," "intimidated," and "inadequate." Deborah wrote, "I couldn't write anything without being haunted if what I was writing was what my teacher was looking for." Nancy expressed a similar frustration: "I would write my essay, read it, rip it up, and begin again—all the while wondering about the wrongs my teacher would say were there. Now I truly have a fear of writing and would prefer to do anything except write."

Even the few who identified themselves as writers did not described writing as an enjoyable act or as a process they felt confident doing. In fact, they used the same distressing descriptors used by the "nonwriters." Interestingly, there were two self-identified writers who wrote positively of their writing experiences—both merely described receiving good grades for their completed writing assignments.

When Writing Stopped Being Fun

By the time we are old enough to attend school, most of us have acquired many of the adult forms of grammar and know a handful of letters—this is enough to begin writing labels and calendars, letters and stories, poems and songs (Calkins, 1994; Sharples, 1999). Writing, at least early in our school careers, is fun. Yet, by the end of high school, most of us take a markedly different stance toward writing; many come to dislike writing, perhaps even fear it, and often avoid doing it when at all possible (Elbow, 1998).

Conceivably, the traditional manner in which we teach writing may have much to do with dramatic shifts in attitude. We assume that proficient writers know exactly what they will write before they begin writing, that the composing process is linear and that teaching students to write has more to do with teaching "editing skills" than any writing processes (Hairston, 1982). This approach to teaching writing assumes that students are merely vessels waiting to be filled with academic language through which one learns to sound like someone else and works against the inescapable presence of one's natural language (O'Donnell, 2002, p. 50). This can be especially troublesome for those of us whose cultural vernacular and dialect (in our case, Appalachia) is inconsistent with the language of the Academy. Paulo Freire (1970/2002) conceptualized this approach to education as "banking" whereby "students are depositories and the teacher is the depositor" (p. 72). Sophie, a 2+2 student, explained, "In my past writing experiences, I was programmed into believing that meaningful writing was only produced by a communistic approach in a controlled classroom." Similarly, Emily said, "Writing was something you had to do like you were told and was not meant to be enjoyed."

The effects of such teacher-centered, prescriptive approaches to teaching writing can be devastating to developing writers. Emily continued, "I never put much effort into those writings because I assumed that the red ink all over my paper meant my words did not matter." For Jami, it was in the sixth grade that she became a different writer. She had just completed writing and illustrating her own children's book and was excited about her work and looked forward to sharing it with children in the lower grades. However, Jami's final product didn't match with the expectations of her teacher; thus, she wasn't allowed to share her book. Jami wrote, "My teacher was highly critical of the creative aspects of my book. From that day on I became self-conscious about anything that I would write. I lost confidence in my writing abilities and myself. That's when writing stopped being fun."

Although most of us have experienced this type of education as students, possibly even unknowingly perpetuating the approach as teachers, the ramifications go far beyond turning people off to writing. According to poet Jeff Daniel Marion, one of the great values of humanity and one of the humane qualities of writing is how it connects, not separates. When we separate students from their learning—when we alienate them from their own decision-making—we transform them into objects (Freire, 1970/2002). Michael, who returned to school after a four-year stint with the Air Force, wrote, "Because I couldn't write like I was supposed to write [according to his teachers], I felt like I was dumb; after that I pretty much applied myself like I was dumb." Once students see themselves as incapable of writing, once they lose interest in writing, once they become instructional automatons, they lose that which makes them unique: their voice.

Awakening Voice

Simply defined, "voice" is what distinguishes one writer's work from another writer's work—"voice" is the distinctive words of an individual that speak to us from the page (Fletcher, 1993; Murray, 2004). For the majority of adults who successfully endure their educational sojourn, becoming disconnected from their learning and losing their voices is all a part of becoming educated. But for those of us who return to classrooms as teachers, especially those of us who have a role in teaching writing to children, we must reevaluate the purpose and role writing holds in our lives and strive to awaken our dormant writing voices (provided we want to move beyond teaching how we were taught).

Drawing from reports published by the National Association of Elementary School Principals and the National Commission on Teaching and America's Future, The National Writing Project and Nagan (2003) emphasized that teachers' knowledge and expertise of the subjects they teach is vital to student success—even more so than students' socioeconomic backgrounds (p. 59). To be effective teachers of writing, teachers must engage in their own writing. Graves (2004) wrote, "We simply can't teach writing if we haven't experienced the process as well as the joy of fashioning a text for our peers" (p. 89). But, keep in mind that over 70% of the adult learners surveyed in the three language arts classes did not think of themselves as writers; any writing in which they did engage was assigned by a professor. They largely wrote disconnected from their topics and detached from any audience; their writing was purposeless (except to secure a grade) and voiceless.

Fortunately, it takes little to turn a student, even an adult student, into a writer: "a human connection, teacher modeling, supportive conversations before writing begins, an appreciation of the student's efforts, sincere affirmation, real writing for a purpose, and reader that the student values" (Routman, 2005, p. 21). These elements can exist only within the context of a close-knit community. In order to establish this type of community and provide an opportunity for the rural adults to rediscover their writing voices, we began each writing workshop—which occurred at the beginning hour, four days a week—by reading aloud to each other.

What we read was not as important as the fact we were reading to each other. Perhaps there is no greater act of benevolence a teacher can offer students, regardless of their age, than to read to them. Provided they are comfortable enough, mature enough, and willing enough to read themselves, students reading to each other is just as powerful. In our situation, where everyone was from similar communities, we heard speaking voices that sounded like our own and were drawn to them. There exists a rhythm, an underlying music, in the Appalachian dialect. Certain words come curved and smooth, devoid of brash edges. With oral traditions playing a vital role in southern literacy, read-alouds became text performances. How we read a poem or a story or an essay helped us slip into the skin of the work to gain a fresh perspective of the piece's words and images (Heard, 1998). We shared memorable characters, stirring words and phrases, and intriguing new worlds; reading aloud to each other brought us together in a way incomparable to anything else we did as a class (Ray, 1999).

The more we listened to each other's outer voices, the more whisperings began stirring deep inside each of us. These were not our writing voices, not yet; they were our inner voices that drive our curiosity, which eventually feed our writing voices. Having lain dormant for so many years, students were often surprised by the memories that sprung from nowhere while listening to read-alouds. They remembered odd details from their childhoods, like the headline of Kennedy's assassination on a piece of newspaper used as wallpaper in a great-grandparent's house. Ghosts of past relationships were also resurrected by the inner voices. In order to cultivate more of the inner voice murmurings, we talked with each other about what we were experiencing; in order to corral the information, we jotted down the ruminations as best we could in our journals or in notebooks or on half-used napkins or whatever other writing surfaces availed themselves (Fletcher, 1993).

Gradually we moved from listening to others' words and tuning into our inner voices and began to commit to paper the words and ideas that surfaced most often. Melissa began a letter to her mentally disabled brother; Elise began drafting a poem about the long commute necessary to see her fiancé. Many were not expecting the words to be there at all, but like gardenias and jasmine that reveal their fragrant beauty only when the sun sleeps, the words appeared. And peculiar as those words were, especially because they were peculiar, we knew they were ours. By and by we shook loose the coils of doubt and insecurity and began writing about subjects we were drawn to, we began writing for people—real people—with whom we wanted to share our writing, and we experimented with genres that best fit our purposes. We shared our writing in peer-to-peer meetings as well as with the entire class. The cycle of speaking our words and listening to others grew our community and strengthened us as writers. We had awakened our writing voices.

The Effects of Awakening Voice

By the end of each short eight-week writing workshop, 100% of the students reported some change in how they viewed writing. Although not everyone experienced the same degree of passion or productivity in the writing workshop, each person did experience writing as an authentic task. They completed pieces of writing that stemmed from their own interests or life experiences; they selected their own genres—many choosing genres they had never experienced (at least experienced in a positive manner); they wrote anticipating that a daughter or a group of coworkers would read their work; and, regularly, they shared their writing with their classmates. Each reading was a performance—not to satisfy the writer's ego but to pay homage to the words themselves. In a letter in which I asked students to evaluate their experience in the writing workshop, Lauren wrote, "This class changed me. I was amazed the words came. I guess the moral is, if you give your students regular time to write, set high expectations, give them encouragement, help them discover their writing territories, and a steady dose of minilesson, they, too, will find their voices and amaze themselves."

But arousing the slumbering writing voice brings unexpected consequences. Students described how their eyes were opened to worlds they had long ignored or never knew existed in the first place. Some spoke of the natural world and how distracting driving a valley road became once they began seeing the rural landscape as a writer. For instance, Shelley noted in her journal how in a stand of oaks near her house the naked limbs weaved through each other and resembled the webbed nests of silkworms. Others meant their eyes were opened to the world of writing itself—how powerful of a tool writing can become once we discover our own purposes for putting pen to page or fingers to the keyboard. This generated an excitement about untapped possibilities for some. Others grieved the years they wasted hating writing; Tom became viscerally angry at the educational system responsible for his waste.

The most often mentioned consequence of when our inner voice conspires with our writing voice was the increased incidence of insomnia. Nancy admitted, "Developing my writing voice has not been easy; I have lost several hours sleep thinking about what to write. I lay awake planning how I can put to paper the bird or squirrel I found myself watching earlier that day." According to Lauren, "You will probably love this, but I was irritated that I would even wake up in the night puzzling over a piece of writing. I couldn't believe that writing had the power to control even my subconscious mind."

But, by far, the most positive effect of watching these Southern adult learners rouse their writing voices, transform themselves into writers, and speak their words to each other was the relationships forged between people who would have otherwise never spoken to each other in the course of a semester. More than half of the students mentioned these relationships in their evaluation letters. For example,

> We have learned so much about each other and ourselves through our writing and sharing. Hearing what my fellow classmates have written has made me realize that we're really not that different. Many of the fears and triumphs my classmates experienced, I, too, have experienced. Knowing they understood where I was coming from made me feel closer to all of them. (Janelle)
>
> I have been in classes with these same people for more than a year now, but I just now feel like I know them: I see them in a totally different light. As they shared, their feelings and emotions jumped from their paper to my ears and into my heart. We went from a competitive classroom to a close community—all within half a semester. (Charity)
>
> I genuinely enjoyed my classmates sharing their writings in class. I felt like it made the class closer as a group. (Sally)

To communicate, to make a connection with another human being, to perhaps learn something about one's self or the world in the process—these are the reasons we write. Historically, we teach writing in ways that convince children to fear or hate the process; little do they see in writing that belongs to them. Too often, little do we see in writing that belongs to us, the adults responsible for developing children's literacy. But, as long as we have others to connect with, to talk to, to listen to, to affirm and be affirmed by—to have opportunities to build communities that celebrate their members' lives and words—writing will have its opportunity to emerge. Our writing voices may drowse dormant for a time, but as sure as the sun will shine on Hanging Limb, there will come an awakening.

REFERENCES

Atwell, N. (1998). *In the middle: New understandings about writing, reading, and learning* (2nd ed.). Portsmouth, NH: Boynton/Cook Publishers—Heinemann.

Calkins, L. M. (1994). *The art of teaching writing.* Portsmouth, NH: Heinemann.

Elbow, P. (1998). *Writing without teachers* (2nd ed.). New York: Oxford University Press, Inc.

Fletcher, R. J. (1993). *What a writer needs.* Portsmouth, NH: Heinemann.

Freire, P. (2002). *Pedagogy of the oppressed* (30th anniversary ed.). (M. B. Ramos, Trans.). New York: The Continuum International Publishing Group, Inc.

Graves, D. (2004, November). What I've learned from teachers of writing. *Language Arts, 82*(2), 88–92.

Hairston, M. (1982). The winds of change: Thomas Kuhn and the revolution in the teaching of writing. *College Composition and Communication, 33*(1), 76–88.

Heard, G. (1999). *Awakening the heart: Exploring poetry in elementary and middle school.* Portsmouth, NH: Heinemann.

Murray, D. M. (2004). *A writer teaches writing* (Rev. 2nd ed.). Boston, MA: Heinle.

National Writing Project & Nagan, C. (2003). *Because writing matters: Improving student writing in our schools.* San Francisco: Jossey-Bass.

O'Donnell, T. G. (2002). Conventions and the teaching of writing. *Journal of Teaching Writing, 20*(1–2), 47–70.

Ray, K. W. (1999). *Wondrous words: Writers and writing in the elementary classroom.* Urbana, IL: National Council of Teachers of English.

Routman, R. (2005). *Writing essentials: Raising expectations and results while simplifying teaching.* Portsmouth, NH: Heinemann.

Sharples, M. (1999). *How we write: Writing as creative design.* New York: Routledge.

PICTURE BOOK BIOGRAPHIES TO PROMOTE INTERCULTURAL UNDERSTANDING

Colleen P. Gilrane
UNIVERSITY OF TENNESSEE

> Once upon a time, it may have made sense to imagine that we could be satisfied knowing only the history of our region or country, or that our literature was a complete and uncontaminated collection of all the texts we needed to know. In that time, we might also have believed that our religion, politics, social values, language, work, and daily practices could go on without concern for what others "far away" might do. But today, it is evident that everything we know and do is but a small thread in a larger social fabric that we cannot escape, even if we wished to do so (Bruce, 1997, pp. 878–879).

Chip Bruce's words from the first volume of this *Handbook* are, if anything, even more compelling to us today than they were then. As I write this in the fall of 2004, the United States is at war with Iraq. In the three years since the September 11, 2001 terrorist attacks, homeland security measures have made it increasingly more difficult for our international students and faculty to travel in and out of the United States. And in May of 2004, the International Reading Association annual convention was moved from Toronto, Canada, to Reno, Nevada, to accommodate restrictions on funding that prohibited traveling outside the country for many U.S. convention attendees. The need to develop intercultural understanding is clearly urgent. Prophetically, Diane Stanley's 11th picture book biography, *Saladin: Noble Prince of Islam* (2002), was in production in September 2001. Lamentably, it has to date sold less well than any of the others, despite the fact that she considers it the most important work she has done.

We can only imagine how differently our society might respond to persons and events from the Middle East if American schoolchildren grew up hearing about the Crusades from a non-Western perspective. What if they were as familiar with Stanley's description of the 1187 siege of Jerusalem

> The Muslims had never forgotten the shocking massacre that marked the Christian takeover of Jerusalem back in 1099. Yet Saladin did not seek revenge. He posted guards around the city to make sure his soldiers behaved in an orderly and respectful manner. Even the Christian chroniclers admit that none of their people was mistreated.

as they are with Robin Hood cartoons that portray Richard the Lionhearted as a hero? Perhaps they would be more likely—and more capable—of evaluating critically the attitudes, policies, and procedures that should always be under discussion in a democracy. Diane Stanley's meticulously researched, exquisitely painted picture book biographies hold enormous potential for supporting the growth of intercultural understanding in readers of all ages who are able to spend time experiencing them.

All of the historical persons Stanley chose as subjects for her biographies are from outside the United States, as she does not believe that American children get enough exposure to them in their school materials. She spends at least a year researching each book, and beginning with *Charles Dickens: The Man Who Had Great Expectations* (1993), this has included family research trips to the places where her subjects lived. The result is a series of books with high levels of authenticity in their artwork and their perspective-taking that promote a critical researcher stance in their readers.

CULTURAL AUTHENTICITY IN ARTWORK

The art in Diane Stanley's picture book biographies does much more than "illustrate" the text—it is at least as important as the text itself in supporting meaning making. It is so important to Stanley that she persisted until she talked her publisher into adding metallic gold during the production process of *Joan of Arc* (1998), to enhance the book's resemblance to medieval illuminated manuscripts. The faces in *Joan* are expressionless, as in a medieval book of hours, and the faces of saints and angels are surrounded by gilded haloes. Thus one can read about the Middle Ages from the text, but one can go so far as virtually to be a medieval reader by experiencing the artwork as well.

In several other books, Diane Stanley used styles of art that were authentic to the period or the artist about whom she was writing. In *Charles Dickens*, there are black and white vignettes on the text pages that are in the style of Victorian engravings. In *Leonardo da Vinci* (1996), Stanley used knotted page borders adapted from one of Leonardo's designs, and she made the back cover a mirror image of the front, in the spirit of Leonardo's notebooks written in reverse script. *Good Queen Bess: The Story of Elizabeth I of England* (1990) opens with an illuminated initial letter, such as might appear in a medieval prayer book or Bible that Elizabeth herself might have read.

Perhaps the most authentically represented art is that of the artists themselves in *Leonardo da Vinci* and in *Michelangelo* (2000). Stanley used photo prints of Leonardo's paintings that she collaged into her illustrations after researching and recreating the original settings, such as putting two pillars back into the Mona Lisa to have it appear in the book as it did originally. She also included drawings on the text pages that are copied from Leonardo's notebooks. By 2000, Stanley was doing more work digitally, and the images of Michelangelo's art that appear in the book are embedded in her illustrations via the use of Photoshop software.

Diane Stanley's respect for the culture about which she is writing is evident in all of the artwork. Page borders are important aspects of each book's design, and in an interview found in *Contemporary Authors Online* (Gale, 2003), Stanley said, "One of my favorite aspects of creating these books is choosing something in the art or culture of the subject's country and period to use as a design theme throughout the book—such as the Zulu bead work in *Shaka* and the mosaics in *Cleopatra*." Further authentic touches in Cleopatra (1994) came from Stanley's research to find out what Cleopatra—a Macedonian Greek—actually looked like, as all statues of her were torn down by her enemies after her death. Stanley found coins that remain from the era, and used them as her models for the images of Cleopatra that appear in the book.

NONDOMINANT CULTURAL PERSPECTIVE

In the "new kind of world in which we will all soon be living at the border" (Bruce, 1997, p. 878), it will be useful to be able to see ourselves as others see us, rather than to assume that our point of view is a universal one. Diane Stanley's research and sensitivity allow her to write about historical places and events in ways that might be different from—and sometimes challenging to—the perspectives students are usually exposed to in American schools. *Saladin* has already been mentioned; depending on their cultural and religious backgrounds, readers may be either affirmed or affronted by his story, his piety, and his mercy and trust toward those he defeated.

Other books also present perspectives that might differ from what students expect or with which they are familiar, such as the ruthless "Westernization" of Russia in *Peter the Great* (1986), and portrayal of *Shaka: King of the Zulus* (1988) as a gentle man and a military genius. The native Hawaiian point of view taken in *The Last Princess: The Story of Princess Ka'iulani of Hawai'i* (1991) presents the annexation of Hawaii by the United States as something to be mourned rather than celebrated and may encourage readers to take a critical look at colonialism. *Charles Dickens* is portrayed as being enormously disappointed when he visited America, a country he had long admired—he was appalled by slavery, by tobacco spitting, and by too much conversation about politics and money.

CRITICAL RESEARCHER STANCE

By encouraging her readers to do their own research, and by pointing out how incomplete historical information often is, Diane Stanley "comes clean" about her own filling-in of the gaps in the record, and may nudge students toward taking a more critical stance toward all texts they read. All of the picture book biographies have lists of reference works about their subjects and/or periods, and most of these lists highlight resources that would be particularly helpful to young readers. Other background information is included and explained in forewords and afterwords and by such features as a map of Africa in *Shaka*, a list of his own works consulted for the book in *Charles Dickens*, and a pronunciation guide to Hawaiian in *The Last Princess*.

In a few instances, Stanley is explicit about the incompleteness or bias of historical information and the interpretation that all writers do in deciding how to tell a story. In the authors' note in the front of *Bard of Avon: The Story of William Shakespeare* (1992), is written

> William Shakespeare is one of the most famous men who ever lived. Yet much of his life is a mystery to us. He did not keep a diary, and none of his personal letters has survived. We do not even know exactly when he was born—only the date on which his baptism was registered. We know a little about his parents, his wife, and his children. Besides his plays and poems, the only other documents we have are business transactions, court papers, and his will.
>
> . . . In writing this story, we have tried to show how historians investigate a life lived long ago. Like detectives, historians gather all the known facts together until a pattern begins to appear. And when that pattern reveals the life of one of the most exceptional writers of all time, what an exciting discovery that is!

Wording in the text itself is consistent with this message, such as the statement "We do not know what play they performed," when describing a performance in Stratford in 1569.

The situation is somewhat different for *Cleopatra* and for *Joan of Arc*—in their cases much is written, but its accuracy is suspect. Stanley includes a preface in *Cleopatra* pointing out such information as the fact that Cleopatra did not live in the time of the Pharaohs, and that she was not Egyptian herself but a Macedonian Greek, the last of the royal line of Ptolemies. The preface is followed by a "Note on Ancient Sources" cautioning readers that "everything we know about Cleopatra was written by her enemies" and that any accounts that might have been written by her supporters were destroyed. Stanley alerts readers that "all historians who have written about [Cleopatra] since have turned frequently to Plutarch—but with caution" as he lived 100 years after Cleopatra and was likely influenced by the sources written by her enemies. We can only hope that readers who take this to heart will bring a critical stance to any subsequent biography of Cleopatra that they read!

Bias tends in the other direction for Joan of Arc, who has been portrayed as saint, martyr, heroine, and legend. Diane Stanley made the brilliant decision to use the transcripts of Joan's heresy trial, as well as those of her Trial of Rehabilitation (requested by King Charles and ordered by Pope Calixtus III, following the end of the Hundred Years' War), as the sources of all of the quotes in the book. Stanley points out to readers that the existence of these transcripts means that there is more information available about Joan than about any other woman predating the modern era. I find it exciting to think of this book inspiring young researchers to consult primary sources themselves, particularly now that so many of them are available digitally via the Internet!

CONCLUSION

If indeed "literacy means control over discourses that use and communicate complex forms of knowledge" (Bruce, 1997, p. 875), it requires a great deal more than reading words. It requires at least reading images; expressions; actions; and social, political, and cultural practices. It requires finding, sifting through, and evaluating critically an ever-growing number of texts and images available in hard copy and in digital form—and then deciding what to do with them. Diane Stanley's picture book biographies are valuable as high-quality products of such processes, but they do not stop there. Because she has along the way deconstructed her own thinking and decision making in the crafting of these books, spending time with them affords readers an apprenticeship in these essential literacy processes themselves.

DIANE STANLEY'S PICTURE BOOK BIOGRAPHIES

Peter the Great. (1986)
Shaka: King of the Zulus. (1988)
Good Queen Bess: The Story of Elizabeth I of England. (1990)
The Last Princess: The Story of Princess Ka'iulani of Hawai'i. (1991)
Bard of Avon: The Story of William Shakespeare. (1992)
Charles Dickens: The Man Who Had Great Expectations. (1993)
Cleopatra. (1994)
Leonardo da Vinci. (1996)
Joan of Arc. (1998)
Michelangelo. (2000)
Saladin: Noble Prince of Islam. (2002)

REFERENCES

Bruce, B. C. (1997). Current issues and future directions. In J. Flood, S. B. Heath, & D. Lapp (Eds.). *Handbook of research on teaching literacy through the communicative and visual arts* (pp. 875–883). New York: Macmillan/International Reading Association.

Gale. (2003). Diane Stanley. In *Contemporary Authors Online.* Retrieved August 17, 2004 from http://galenet.galegroup.com.proxy.lib.utk.edu:90/servlet/LitRC?vrsn=3&OP=contains&locID=tel_a_utl&srchtp=athr&ca=1&c=1&ste=6&tab=1&tbst=arp&ai=U13017926&n=10&docNum=H1000094258&ST=Diane+Stanley&bConts=2191.

Part IV

INTO THE LANGUAGE ARTS CLASSROOM THROUGH THE VISUAL AND COMMUNICATIVE ARTS

Nancy Roser
UNIVERSITY OF TEXAS

Dorothy Strickland
RUTGERS UNIVERSITY

The researchers and teacher-researchers who write in Section IV of the *Handbook* share a commitment to the changes that will make classrooms places of deeper, richer literacy learning. The collected works also reflect an understanding of the changing world in which we live.

Whether the research derives from early childhood classrooms that stretch the contexts of dramatic play or from cross-grade considerations of literate discussions, all authors focus on the creation of more meaning-filled environments. Chapters address not just changing technologies (including digital storytelling, graphic novels, and multimodal texts)—but changes in the ways teachers and students are approaching meaning making in more familiar forms, from picture book to film. The authors share a commitment to careful consideration of media techniques and purposes—drawing on the classroom and from the popular culture. Together, the section expresses commitment to change in education that allows schools to stay attuned to students' present and future lives.

Overall, these chapters illustrate the many ways in which humans learn and in which young learners can create and direct aspects of their learning in the context of classrooms that value the performative, visual, as well as verbal arts.

Each chapter offers rich examples of how schools and teachers support multiple pathways for acquiring, using, and sharing knowledge. Each pathway is both unique and interdependent. For example, what is learned through reading and writing is used for listening and speaking. What is learned through visual and dramatic presentations and representations is both a stimulus for and a product of the other communication arts. Each domain has strong cognitive aspects and each allows students to take advantage of a variety of media to support learning in purposeful ways. Good teaching capitalizes on this. Classrooms in which students are encouraged and guided to learn in multiple ways are more apt to produce learners who are active, productive, and successful.

•35•

LITERACY CLASSROOMS: MAKING MINDS OUT OF MULTIMODAL MATERIAL

Randy Bomer
UNIVERSITY OF TEXAS AT AUSTIN

There is a new baby in our family—Kaleigh—my wife's niece, who will turn 1 year old as I write this. We bought her board books for her birthday, which were engineered for biting and mouthing, texts with a circulation that expects teeth marks to be added to the print and pictures. She also has books made of fabric, which have doors, pockets, and pop-outs. The one she likes best at the moment is about a kitten. It has pages of soft fur for petting and a sandpaper tongue that feels rough to the touch. She also has some of the usual kinds of books, with words and pictures, or sometimes just pictures, that stay flat on paper pages that turn in the customary manner. She will probably, when no one is looking, amend some of these books like commonplace books, making her marks alongside those of the authors and illustrators. She will arrive at school, as most children do, with some conception of literacy—that there are things with words in them, which people read and make.

She will arrive at school, as most children do, expecting that these objects with words in them are also more than words. They have the material reality of stories in them, the pictures of the animals, which she can see right there. When the books are opened, someone starts to speak or sing with exaggerated intonation and a variety of timbres to bring alive the diverse voices of the characters in the story. When the stories happen, when they come to take over her mind, she usually will have climbed up into someone's lap and gotten comfortable, though sometimes she also will have played the whole story out in the dining room while her parents made dinner. When she arrives at school, it will never have occurred to her that words could be stripped of the sensual nests in which they usually live—with varying admixtures of image, pretending, movement, and sound.

By the time she arrives at school, Kaleigh will have moved through a thick forest of symbols and texts of many kinds. She will have watched television, played on the computer with "talking books," and played both digital and cardboard games. She will have studied the paintings on the walls of homes and restaurants, seen familiar stories about her father enacted again and again, and come to expect specific scripted interactions around dinnertime. She will have made books and paintings and sculpted figures, and she will have played dramatically with small figures occupying various dioramas like dollhouses, castles, vehicles, and adventurescapes. Books will seem like just one instance in a collection of similar experiences, and there will seem to be little reason to segregate "reading" into a new kind of abstract skill learning.

When a child arrives at the schoolhouse door, he or she conceives of texts as situated in the moving, booming, material world—a world of pictures and movies, of games and songs and playing house, of buying groceries and crawling into laps. It involves the alphabet and printed words and literate language always situated among and within other kinds of symbols— images, video, music, movement, pretendings, and touchings. As researchers like Martens (1996) and Wolf and Heath (1992) have shown, learning for young children is embedded within multiple systems of meanings and signs, such as those of art, movement, play, and oral language. Looking at similar life histories from the other side of growing up, college composition teacher-researcher Diana George (2002) wrote,

> For students who have grown up in a technology-saturated and an image-rich culture, questions of communication and composition absolutely will include the visual, not as attendant to the verbal but as complex communication intricately related to the world around them. (p. 32)

If children enter school with a conception of text as multimodal, it is becoming increasingly apparent that people should also *depart* school, 13 or 17 or 20 years later, with a similar understanding—that print texts are not ethereal whispers of pure thought; they are material objects, things that are seen, heard, touched, and acted upon by people's real bodies. Forms of literacy, as they are being transformed in an era of rapid changes in information and communications technology, present readers and writers with multiple modes of thinking, understanding, knowing, and expressing. On the Internet, on television, in video, and in film, in business communication, and in higher education, communities of readers and writers are finding new value in multimodal texts—where print and image do the work of meaning together, where sound and music contribute to the perspectives readers are asked to take, where bodily performance works in tandem with the written word, where print itself is animated and choreographed. The forms of literacy needed in the workplace are rapidly changing, becoming increasingly multimodal (Hull, 1997; Rose, 2003; Witte & Haas, 2001). In fact, these dimensions of textuality are not at all new and are in fact enveloped in the histories of writing systems and technologies (Faigley, 1999), but developments in electronic, digital technology have placed in more people's hands the capacity to create and receive multimodal texts in far greater numbers than ever before, and this is increased even since a time as recent as the publication date of this handbook's last edition (Flood, Heath, & Lapp, 1997). More than ever before, makers and readers of texts have a wide range of choices about what their hands, eyes, and bodies will feel like as they transact meaning, the colors their eyes will see, and the degrees to which image and sound will combine.

So, it turns out that some of the understanding young children bring with them to school are close to the kind they need when they leave school. All that is asked of school, in that case, is to extend, organize, and direct children's understanding, which children have already begun to construct, and not to mess this up. It is likely, however, that many common instructional practices, as well as the ideologies of language and literacy that are most common in school, tend to militate against such a multimodal and materially situated view of literacy and to restrict the focus to the alphabet, print, and comprehension as a linear something that occurs gradually, incrementally, stepwise, and inside individuals' heads. This section of the *Handbook* is about some of the efforts to reform that tendency of schools and classrooms.

To introduce this section of the *Handbook*, this chapter will provide a practical rationale and theoretical basis for the use of visual and communicative arts in literacy classrooms. The chapters to come in this section range widely from play to the arts to media studies, and this brief overview will suggest some of the ideas that provide some coherence to such diversity. In what follows, I will sketch some of the diverse theoretical underpinnings for research in classrooms, from neo-Vygotskian activity theory, multiple intelligences, and aesthetic education. Then, I will name some of the policy realities that enable and constrain curricula and pedagogy that invite multiliteracies. After that, I will consider two modalities—(a) the making of pictures and (b) performing/enacting—and draw connections from early childhood through schooling to new literacies. I have stated that desirable outcomes for new forms of literacy are already present in young children's emergent and early literacy experience. I want to show how this is so with respect to visual composition and drama. I will then conclude with some questions about the interaction between the current policy environment and the development of the forms of literacy being valued here.

BODIES, TOOLS, AND SIGNS

Educators participating in the curricular reforms of which I am writing base their teaching and research in varied theoretical and disciplinary perspectives. All their work, however, subscribes to a conception of humans as bodies, and as coming to know the world through the senses and extending that knowledge through signs and representations that transact with the material world. Their ways of knowing, thinking, and intuiting, therefore, are rooted in their ways of sensing. As philosophers from Husserl (1999) to Marleau-Ponty (1964) to Greene (1995, 2001), to Sebeok (1994) to Johnson (1987) to Todes (2001) have argued, people think and know in images, in sounds, in tactile sensations, and in movement, because it is through seeing, hearing, touching, and moving that they experience their lives. As an extension of their immediate sensual perceptions of the world, people use tools to interact with their environment and to change it. Humans come to know nature as they transform it, and the work of doing so creates the shape and character of knowledge (Engels, 1883). The tools people use, inasmuch as they shape the nature of labor/activity, come to shape not just trees into walls but also the very character of thinking.

One of the most important kind of tools human beings have developed is signs (Volosinov, 1973; Vygotsky, 1971, 1986)—marks, sounds, or gestures that stand for something other than themselves (Eco, 1979). Signs include spoken words, pictures, written words, vocal tones and inflections, gestures and other movements, sculptures, and architectural forms and musical elements. They exist in systems of signs, in collections of instances in which a sign might appear: words exist in utterances; images exist among collections of pictures; a musical note exists in harmonic and melodic relation to other notes and within a particular musical idiom. All signs come to have their meanings socially, as people come to share in the attributing of sense (an inner, mental dimension) to a material symbol they can share (a concrete, social dimension; Hanks, 1996; Lemke, 1989; Peirce, 1991; Saussure, 1986; Witte, 1992). We know the world in the ways in which we represent it. Therefore, we employ a range of representation practices—material media in which we externalize our meaning making with signs (semiosis)—to learn and think.

One of the most influential concepts in Vygotsky's theory is the concept of mediation, which is the use of media or tools for thinking. Vygotsky made much of this notion that people use external devices to regulate their behavior and to make thinking possible, which would otherwise be difficult. For instance, in the "Forbidden Colors" test, Vygotsky (1978) and his coresearchers played a game with children during which the children were told that the rules dictated that they could not say certain color names or repeat any answers. They then asked a series of trick questions designed to get children to say just those colors and to repeat their answers, and most of the children could not respond without breaking the game's rules. However, when given cards with the colors on them, some of the older children (not the 5- and 6-year-olds) used the cards to remind themselves of what they couldn't say and what they had already said. One girl, for example, turned all the cards face up except for the forbidden colored cards. These she saved down. Then, whenever she said a color answer, she turned that card face down, too, to remind herself that it was not a good response anymore. The cards became a medium for remembering, a mediational means, a tool. Similarly, a knot in a handkerchief can serve as a reminder, remaking the process of remembering by placing it on an external object (Vygotsky, 1978). Remembering, an internal state of mind, is transformed into an external, visible, and tactile activity. The person uses an object outside her skin to organize her inner thoughts and states of mind. Of course, for this to work, she must have assigned a meaning to the knot so that the knot has come to stand for something else. She must have allowed the knot to become a sign, to signify. Though a knot is an unusually simple sign, other sign systems, such as language, pictures, and enactments are especially complex and open to nuanced uses. They also have the potential to change minds (Bomer, 2003).

When a person has engaged with a tool for a significant stretch of time, he or she appropriates ways of thinking that characterize the form of activity that tool affords (Vygotsky, 1978, 1986; Wertsch, 1985, 1991). When I use a saw to cut many pieces of wood, I internalize ways of thinking about wood, metal, cutting, and sharpness, ways of looking along the edge of a blade, and ways of taking care for fingers' safety. When I perform many dances, I appropriate the ways of flowing an emotion through a series of muscular impulses, of composing visually interesting lines with my body, of anticipating the way a body will sculpt space as it moves across time. Like tools, the signs and sign systems we use outside our skin become our ways of thinking. Mediation becomes mind.

CURRICULUM AND MIND

Gardner (1983, 1993, 1999) and his colleagues have argued that individuals are naturally (as in biologically, neurologically) disposed to particular forms of intelligence. Someone disposed to a kinesthetic intelligence, from this point of view, would learn best when they could mediate their thinking and demonstrate their understanding in the whole body and its movement. Forcing such a person to sit all day and learn from text or a disembodied voice deprives them of the primary means by which they could achieve an education. This theory of multiple intelligences implies that bringing the arts and other diverse forms of knowing and thinking into classrooms is in fact a matter of basic, democratic fairness. School's verbocentrism privileges those students who happen to be neurologically disposed to a verbal form of mediation and limits everyone else's access to quality learning. Gardner's theory has been sharply criticized of late (Kincheloe, 2004) for being individualistic, culturally elitist, and antidemocratic. Nevertheless, Gardner comes to mind for many educators when they think of the arts as means of learning, and his theory of intelligence serves as part of the framework for some research in this area.

Curriculum based upon Gardner's theory of multiple intelligences has much in common with a semiotic approach to curriculum, but the two are not identical. A semiotic or multimodal or multiliteracies approach may stipulate that individuals may be predisposed to learning with particular tools, but it does not stop there. Rather, a multiliteracies approach insists that all students, even those who are predispositionally "verbal," need to learn multiple mediational tools for thinking, expressing, and knowing. Mindful that forms of text are becoming increasingly multimodal, some literacy educators see an urgent need for all students to learn to read and compose in multiple media and modes, and therefore to exercise multiple intelligences. Though an individual may often lead with the use of a particular sign system, the literacy educator is obliged to diversify the semiotic resources available to an individual and valued by a community—in order to teach learners to communicate effectively with audiences possessed of diverse intelligences as well.

Intelligences—or minds—are ideals. They are intangible, abstract. The processes by which minds are developed, however, or intelligences are grown, are material, concrete. Mediation occurs when learners change their minds by messing with things outside their skin— by reading and writing, painting, sketching, making collage, sculpting, enacting, gesturing, and moving. Classrooms, then, are places where people, together, use material objects and processes in order to create and change minds: they are spaces for material processes toward ideal results.

Everything that occurs in a classroom is concrete, embodied, and multimodal—oral language (vibrating air and human membranes, along with gestures and proxemics) is as material as a torn paper collage or an improvised dance. Teachers teach by planning what bodies will do, what objects will be involved, and how bodies and objects will be transformed and moved through space and how learners will interact with one another, with concrete things, and with cultural history. The essential materiality of classroom learning is not contingent upon the particulars of teaching practice, either; a classroom limited to lecture and readings is no less material than one in which students construct visual, musical, and dramatic representations; the former is just narrowly limited. The notion of ideality forming materiality and vice-versa is essential to being able to see classroom practices as both the material practice they are and also as cultural values, privileged ways of acting, formed by powerful discourses that create and constrain the possible meanings of everyday activity.

Classrooms that use multiple modalities for thinking and expression are sometimes also characterized by inquiry, an approach to learning that views knowledge as unfinished, and the curriculum as always in process. This approach to *the known* (Dewey & Bentley, 1944/1991) allows learners to maintain a transaction—an approach to substance that requires their energy and involvement, because their interpretations, experiences, and perspectives are assumed to transform the content of instruction. Semiotic theory actually requires this inquiry approach because, as Peirce (1991) theorized, when a person interacts with a sign, he or she interprets it, and the interpretation, the new understanding, is itself a sign—and therefore is open to new interpretation. Knowing does not stand still or finish, but tumbles and transforms from sign to sign. Through a process of transduction (Kress, 2003) or transmediation (Semali, 2002; Siegel, 1995; Suhor, 1984), students move their thoughts from one sign system—talk, for instance—through drawing to drama and thence to writing. Of course, their thinking, even about the same topic, as they move through successive layers of mediation, is not a single thought simply being expressed in varied media; rather, this process of thinking can transform what they understand.

A curriculum, then, is built in the interest of students learning to draw upon semiotic resources, to develop and use their understandings of such questions as how images affect a viewer, how images relate to one another, how images relate to words, movements, music, or sound, drama, and other sign systems. The resources upon which most students can and must draw are usually those which they have appropriated in everyday life and those from mass media (Harste, Woodward, & Burke, 1984). A significant body of research has documented the extent to which students, even young children, draw upon popular culture as an intertext in negotiating their way through the literacy curriculum. One implication of this research is that, with popular media texts being so influential on students, it is important to teach them productive and emancipatory ways of thinking about those texts. Moreover, with visual, rhythmic, dramatic, and kinetic resources so dense in students' minds, these resources provide a strong foundation or framework for learning new materials, if teachers are skilled at making the necessary connections. When the focus of learning is on the ways in which texts and tools work to mediate thinking and social relations, rather than on the texts themselves, divisions between "high" culture and "low" or popular culture become unimportant. (Several chapters in this section focus on students' use of popular culture in school.)

One curricular perspective that draws upon multiple forms of mediation is aesthetic education. Educators who think of their work in this way may be likely to use a different vocabulary and pursue some different values than do people who view their work as based upon semiotics, multimodal composition, or new media. Aesthetic education goes beyond the use of so-called artistic media such as paint, dance, and poetry. Creation of and transaction with works of art are specific purposes, beyond the simple use of mediational forms other than print. Maxine Greene (2001) wrote that aesthetic education is

> a part of the human effort (so often forgotten today) to seek a coherence in the world. We see it as an effort to move individuals (working together, searching together) to seek a grounding for themselves, so that they may break through the 'cotton wool' of dailyness and passivity and boredom and come awake to the colored, sounding, problematic world. (p. 7)

She viewed education as a

> process of enabling persons to become different, to enter the multiple provinces of meaning that create perspectives on the [artistic] works. To enter these provinces . . . the learner must break with the taken-for-granted, what some call the 'natural attitude,' and look through the lenses of various ways of knowing, seeing, and feeling in a conscious endeavor to impose different orders on experience. (p. 5)

Aesthetic education, then, is more than just expressing and thinking in varied media. It involves a disruption, a breaking with the everyday and a reaching for a new way of seeing. Print literacy can achieve this, as literary art, as can other art forms, but it is not a simple matter of transmediation. Bloomberg television or any financial Web site is multimodal, but that does not mean that it provides anything like the disruption of the given or new forms of attention that are the essence of the aesthetic experience. In what follows, the research I discuss will be drawn from perspectives embracing aesthetic education, neo-Vygotskian theory, and/or the theory of multiple intelligences. These perspectives are not necessarily mutually exclusive, and in a world where the use of multiple modalities in literacy is still relatively rare, the distinction among them is perhaps not a crucial matter. I will now discuss two different forms of semiotic activity that mediate literacy learning: (a) picturing, and then (b) performing. In each case, I will trace the ways in which young children's early experience with textuality connects with certain special practices throughout K–16 schooling.

PICTURING—MAKING AND READING IMAGES

Young children, at ages as early as 3, can tell the difference between print and images, but they are eager to combine these resources in varying inventive ways in order to accomplish their communicative or intellectual purposes, as well as to use the sign system that is most appropriate for their meaning and intent (Harste et al., 1984; Rowe, 1994). In other words, children do not draw simply because they do not yet know how to write; they draw and write, for meaningful and strategic purposes (Kress, 1997).

Children's drawing, cutting-out, collage assembly, sculpting, and other visual representing are resources for the construction of meaning, just as is print (Matthews, 1999). Moreover, their drawing is not completely naïve but employs conventionalized semiotic resources, as they use elements of composition, rhythm, mass, shape, color, and layout in ways that are meaningful, because they are culturally appropriate (Gardner, 1980; Hubbard, 1989; Kress, 1997; Matthews, 1999). Their work at visual composition also begins to engage them in a sense of process—maintaining a focused intention long enough to exert their vision upon resistant materials. Children often learn to revise first when they fix things in their drawings (Karelitz, 1988; Newkirk, 1989). Many researchers of early writing have chosen almost to ignore the multimodal character of children's early texts, forcibly bracketing the print off from the rest of the page (e.g., Clay, 1979).

The field of reading perhaps tends to take too little notice of the fact that children's first reading experiences are multimodal. Young children experience literacy visually, aurally, and kinesthetically especially because there is a gap in time between their first engagement with text and their ability to read print. The experience of having picture books read aloud in the home (Wolf & Heath, 1992) or in childcare settings (Cochran-Smith, 1984) affords children the opportunity to learn how texts work as multimodal objects in which words and pictures interrelate meaningfully (see chapters by Sipe and Kiefer, this volume).

Some work in K–12 schooling has attempted to capitalize on children's familiarity with the picture-book form in the teaching of writing. Reasoning that young children's composing should be as close as possible to play or to making things, writing teachers have used the concept of making books in order to move children into their initial literate composing (Graves, 1982; Ray, 2004). The books are multimodal, and the students sometimes spend more time making the images than they do writing text, though Graves (1982) and Ray (2004) did not emphasize the visual elements of the compositions. More attention has been directed to the visual elements of children's composing of picture books, however, when teachers devote a unit of curriculum to the deliberate study of the genre (Calkins & Harwayne, 1991; Hindley, 1996). These inquiries are most deliberate when they are undertaken by writers mature enough to experience the picture book within the context of a reading and writing life that includes other kinds of text as well, so that they, in fact, perceive of the picture book as a genre with particular textual features. Hindley (1996), for example, reported explicitly teaching her third graders about page composition, foreground and background, overlaying, varied artistic media and techniques for images, and style of imagery. Picture books are very clearly a distinct genre compared, for example, to the difference between a story and an argument. Picture books, therefore, afford an opportunity for teachers to make clear the notion that a genre is a textual form or type of structure. Other chapters in this section will thoroughly review the reading of picture books in schools.

Researchers and theorists working within a perspective grounded in semiotic theory see art as a form of literacy, not only a means of teaching print-centric reading and writing (Albers & Murphy, 2000; Berghoff, Borgmann, & Parr, 2003; Leland & Harste, 1994; Rowe, 1994; Siegel, 1995; Suhor, 1984; Suhor & Little, 1988). Albers and Murphy (2000), for example, studied the work of students in a middle-school art class, interrogating the personal and social meanings signified in the students' work. Ernst pursues much the same theoretical agenda (Ernst, 1993, 1996), taking students' image making as a form of composition fundamentally similar to writing, drawing on the same compositional processes as well as similar habits of mind and activity.

In much literacy classroom research, the emphasis regarding visual representation has been on the use of picture making as a medium for responding to literary texts. Situated within reader response theory, especially the transactional theory of Rosenblatt (1938/1983, 1978), this approach views the action of reading as the creation of a world in the reader's mind (Bruner, 1986, 1990), a world that is, at least for sighted readers, envisioned (Langer, 1995). The physical making of pictures, then, is a way of using concrete tools such as paper, paint, markers, or modeling clay, as mediational means (Wertsch, 1991) for working with a visual form of thinking outside the skin, where an image can be manipulated and revised by the learner, negotiated and shared with other learners, and assessed and extended by a teacher. Whitin (1996a, 1996b, 2005) employed a strategy known as *sketch-to-stretch* (Harste, Short, & Burke, 1988) in order to observe fourth graders' meaning making through the use of visual tools and semiotic resources. The visual response strategy encouraged social negotiations of meaning, the assumption of multiple perspectives, and metaphorical thinking. These achievements permitted an extension of students' abstract, interpretive thinking about text and the world. Enciso (1992, 1996) employed a research procedure she called a "symbolic representation interview" to allow children she interviewed to mediate their rethinking about literary works using cut-outs or found objects to dramatize characters, ideas, feelings, or other dimensions of the work and to position themselves within the work. Wilhelm (1997) adapted this strategy in his secondary classroom teaching and research and then extended student visual work through a sequence of activities. He found that these visual response strategies permitted readers, who had been struggling, to enter the story world, relate to characters, remember what they read, weigh significance, and interpretively reflect on literary meanings. Smagorinsky (1991, 1997) and his coauthors (Smagorinsky & Coppock, 1994; Smagorinsky & O'Donnell-Allen, 1998a, 1998b, 2000), in a series of studies related to visual responses to literature, found that composing visual responses to text not only permitted students to extend their interpretive thinking, but also made visible a range of social processes, from the cultural mediation of individual thinking to conflict over status in groups. It is notable that this extensive work has been undertaken, not in the direct reading of visual/print texts, not in the composition of new texts, but in the mediation of the dialogue between reader and text. Ehrenworth (2003a, 2003b) explored the inverse process, taking students' response to works of visual art as points of departure for writing. These educators, then, have used visual picturing as a doorway toward print literacy, rather than visual composing as an end in itself.

In university composition classrooms as well, multimodal composition, sometimes referred to as *visual rhetoric* (George, 2002), is becoming more commonplace, sometimes in response to the multimedia character of composition in the wider world, especially in students' lives outside of school (Bernhardt, 1986; Shipka, 2005; WIDE Research Center Collective, 2005; Wysocki, Johnson-Eilola, Selfe, & Sirc, 2004; Yancey, 2004). This move to broaden the profession's understanding of literacy should not be understood simply as instrumental, a matter of preparation for the workplace, but rather as a principled reconception of the discipline's purpose: to engage students in forms of literacy that have the potential to matter to them outside their lives in school.

PERFORMANCE, DRAMA, AND INTERACTIVITY

Vygotsky (1978) wrote, "[A] child's greatest achievements are possible through play, achievements that tomorrow will become her basic level of real action and morality" (p. 100). In play, children enact roles, take on personae, and perform functions available in the culture but not yet available to them as individuals fully participating. Play, like drama and literary imagination, is an antidote to the limitations of living a single life. Role-playing mediates the taking on of perspectives different from our usual subjective ones and makes imagined scenes concrete, embodied, and three-dimensionally visual.

New literacies require that people be able to function at the crossroads of many perspectives and agendas. Digital networks place every reader and writer in the midst of many overlapping voices from all over the world. A globalized economy requires that individuals, corporations, and nations see themselves and their actions through the eyes of others with very different sets of experiences in order to anticipate the consequences of actions. And the ease of digital production of multimodal texts demands that authors imagine the interactivity possible in the worlds they create through words, images, and varied actions of the user's body. The assumption of varied perspectives is a dimension of literate thinking as well, and it is increasingly appropriate to new literary forms that employ the narrative strategies of gaming (Gee, 2003; Wardrip-Fruin & Harrington, 2004). School, therefore, needs to connect the embodied and visual interactivity of children's play to the embodied, visual interactivity of new forms of literacy—forms in which children already participate but which will change substantially several times during their years of schooling.

Ample research into early literacy has demonstrated that play forms an important foundation for early literacy learning (see Galda & Pellegrini, this volume). Literacy may be integrated into play, especially in the sorts of dramatic play in which children enact adult roles, such as playing office, house, or doctor. Daiute (1989, 1990) found that play, like writing, was a powerful means of mediating thought through symbolic transformations and was a helpful strategy for young children's composing, especially that of boys. Gallas (1994, 2003), too, emphasized the continuity between children's vocalic symbolic representations in play and their development of thinking, understanding, and ultimately, literacy. Dyson (1993, 1997, 2003), Rowe, Fitch, and Bass (2001), and Bomer and Laman (2004) found that play (or play-like) interactions occurring while children write in classrooms create important social contexts for developing writing identities, positions, and practices. Rowe, Fitch, and Bass (2003) invited children to play with small plastic toy people and animals in order to create stories that could give them ideas for writing, connecting literacy directly to play. Rowe (1998) has also researched curricular invitations that connect book reading to play. In each of these studies, play dramatizes relations among social actors that are part of every literate action between a reader and writer, among a writer and other writers, or among characters in a story. Furthermore, it is never obscure to children when they are playing that the world unfolds only as they construct it and act within it—a fact of literate experience and especially true of new interactive forms of narrative.

Both Gallas (2003) and Paley (1990, 1997, 2004) have shown the ways in which children's dramatic play can be extended into performance scripts. Sometimes (almost always, for Paley), this extension occurs through the child dictating a play script to the teacher and then the children acting it out in front of the rest of the class. In this way, imaginative enactments that were fleeting and almost immediately forgotten become fixed and entextualized, and dramatization becomes a bridge from play into literacy. The dramas also permit children to appropriate discourses, to reason through social relations, and to imagine possibilities.

In order to extend the virtues of play into formal educational settings, educators have developed methods for using improvisational drama both to respond to literature and to compose new stories and meanings. David Booth (1994, 2005), for example, used stories read aloud as the foundation for extended improvisations in which both teacher and students take on roles that permit them to explore the social and ideological tensions in the story, sometimes stopping in the midst of the improvisations in order to write in role (Booth, 1998). Often, the students are assigned roles of competing voices in a community, and the teacher takes on a role of some kind of judge, which forces the students to take a position within the boundaries of the story world. Of course, as soon as their positions start to settle into certainty, the teacher develops a new wrinkle in the given circumstances that requires substantial reorganization. The same spirit of inquiring, open-ended dialogic improvisation characterizes the work of Cecily O'Neill (Taylor, 1995), who begins her "process dramas" with a pretext, just a sentence or two that forms a point of departure for the construction of an elaborated world of interaction in which the teacher/drama leader functions sometimes in role but more often as a source of information about the world the students are composing. Situations center on a moment of change in which members of a community are under pressure, so that the drama is a process of using language and other signs in active, social problem-solving (O'Neill, 1995). Both Booth and O'Neil were influenced by the work of Dorothy Heathcote (Johnson & O'Neill, 1991).

Some research indicates that these forms of work in drama may help students develop habits of mind that might, under the usual circumstances of school, seem unteachable (Edmiston & Enciso, 2003; Wagner, 1998). Medina (2004a, 2004b) found that when students engaged with process drama and writing in role in response to Latino/a literature, they developed rich interpretations and tried on identities and positions that might otherwise have been unavailable to them. Laakso (2005) likewise found that, for preservice teachers, process drama developed broad and deep forms of learning, including transformations of meaning, constructive understanding, and interpretation, as well as group processes, empathy, and self-knowledge. Edmiston (2000) wrote that this kind of dramatic work can be seen as a form of moral education as well as education in the use of Bakhtinian dialogic language for emerging understanding. Bomer (1995) found that the use of improvisational drama exercises helped to develop community in middle-and high-school English classes, as well as to awaken adolescent writers to their immediate sense perceptions of the world and other forms of awareness they could then use in their writing. Heath and Wolf (2005), in a series of research reports for the Arts Council of England and Creative Partnerships, described work with drama that helped students develop empathy, moral reasoning, commitment and responsibility, mental agility with ideas and roles, and language as a medium for entertaining possibility and doubt. Such dispositions are part of literacy development—as essential for reading a novel or a piece of interactive fiction as they are for doing a play.

Another area of research on drama concerns the experience of translating print into artfully voiced language—reading aloud, hearing text with actual ears (Bomer, 2006). Some researchers and teachers have used forms of performance for motivating and giving purpose to repeated readings (Barton & Booth, 1990; Martinez, Roser, & Strecker, 1999; Moffett, 1990; Strecker, Roser, & Martinez, 1998; Worthy & Broaddus, 2002; Worthy & Prater, 2002). Repeated readings have been shown to support students' development of reading fluency (Dowhower, 1994; Hoffman & Isaacs, 1991), but when reading something aloud over and over again is rehearsal for a performance, the readers are doing something that readers outside of school do as well. The environment in that case affords not just the opportunity to "get better at reading," but also to get better at reading in order to please (and look good in front of) an audience (Martinez et al., 1999). Students, therefore, have the opportunity to internalize not just the habits of phrasing, intonation, stress, pitch, and volume, not just the embedded language structures of which the text is made, not just the interpretive practices that help one know how a sentence should sound, but also to internalize motives adults attach to such activity (Hakkarainen, 1999). Wolf (1998) found that third- and fourth-grade struggling readers, given an opportunity for repeated readings in which they had opportunities to express understanding through multiple semiotic systems, improved in decoding and comprehension, as well as in interpretation and in their self-concept as readers. Borrowing an identity as actors permitted them to appropriate an identity as readers as well (Wolf, 1995).

Performance is also interacting with literacy at the university level. From the days of Aristotle, one of the canons of rhetoric (the principle areas of attention of which rhetoric is made) has been "delivery." In Roman times, that meant expressly the oral delivery of one's argument. Today, rhetoricians have become concerned anew with this long-neglected aspect of rhetoric, as the materiality of linguistic transactions becomes increasingly within the immediate, deliberate control of a text's maker. Though new ideas about delivery are often concerned with digital composition and the World Wide Web (Welch, 1999), closest to the ancient meaning of this canon is the view of delivery as actual embodied performance.

As part of a longitudinal study on the breadth of college students' writing both in and out of school, Fishman, Lunsford, McGregor, & Otuteye (2005) reported that many of their participants described live enactment of their own writing as an important part of their literate lives. They wrote, "Grounded in the body, our focus on performance locates textual exchange in specific sites; it makes delivery interactive; and it turns the idea of audience into something concrete and participatory" (p. 228). Furthermore, they explicitly connected writing as performance to new forms of literacy, arguing, as I have throughout this article, that

> Today's eighteen- and nineteen-year-olds belong to a generation that learns to drive—if not to walk or crawl—on an information superhighway crowded with multiple media, and when these students arrive at school they take for granted the interplay between bodies, screens, and documents. Performance has a tremendous appeal for many of these students, and, during the early college years, we believe it helps them learn to work with different systems of signification in multiple modalities and to participate effectively as well as eloquently in a culture of secondary literacy. (p. 246)

POLICY: IS LITERACY EXPANDING OR CONTRACTING?

Though many teachers may be persuaded that the arts and varied media are valuable in the practice of literacy, mandated curricula militate against incorporating the arts or new literacies in classrooms. From 2001 to 2006, schools and districts in the United States, responding to financial pressures from federal and state governments, reduced an already hyperliterate, verbocentric approach to learning to a stripped down test preparation approach, with a nothing-but-phonics approach for the inexperienced or struggling. In an environment of high-stakes testing, the curriculum is reduced to accommodate the tests (Amrein & Berliner, 2002; McNeil, 2000). It is difficult for any teacher to spend ample time on composing soundscapes, video essays, and interactive fiction, when his or her students will be judged only with a multiple-choice reading and grammar test. These large-scale policy restrictions just add to the reluctance some researchers have found among teachers to engage their students with the arts (Oreck, 2004) or digital literacies (Kist, 2005). Some voices in teacher education continue to try to open spaces in educators' imaginations for the use of varied modalities and media (Albers, 2006; Whitin, 2006).

Despite a domineering policy environment that narrows literacy, there are agents within the policy sphere attempting to advance a multimodal view of literacy. The National Council of Teachers of English (NCTE) has led the way in this agenda, passing in 2003, for example, a resolution in favor of teaching students and future teachers to compose in nonprint media, and in 2005, a set of principles on education in multimodal literacies. NCTE worked, as well, with the Partnership for 21st Century Skills (2005) in composing an ICT Literacy Map for English. With governmental policymakers committed to a narrow, controlled, and particulate vision of literacy, it may fall to professional organizations, working in partnership with the computer industry as well as arts organizations, to be the policy voices calling for expanded, future-oriented visions of literacy. The situation is not hopeless, since many states, even some with restrictive testing policies, do have standards pertaining to viewing and listening (e.g., Texas, see http://www.tea.state.tx.us/rules/tac/chapter110/ch110c.html). Teachers' perceptions, however, follow the distortions often created by high-stakes testing, whereby only the tested areas of the curricula receive significant attention.

It is ironic, indeed, that in a time when literacy, as it is commonly employed in the world, is becoming increasingly multimodal, when young people outside school are creating new forms of literacy and combining these forms with other media and purposes, at that very time, the environment of schooling constricts the forms of literacy available to them in official learning environments. For many educators and students, it is, therefore, difficult to view a curriculum focused on those genres and skills easiest to test as a raise in standards. At a time when there is much reason for hope and excitement, because of advances in literacy, advances in theory and research, and advances in school-aged children's practices outside of school, there is also reason for serious concern.

REFERENCES

Albers, P. (2006). Imagining the possibilities in multimodal curriculum design. *English Education, 38*(2), 75–101.

Albers, P., & Murphy, S. (2000). *Telling pieces: Art as literacy in middle school classes*. Mahwah, NJ: Lawrence Erlbaum Associates.

Amrein, A. L., & Berliner, D. C. (2002). High-stakes testing, uncertainty, and student learning. *Education Policy Analysis Archives, 10*(18).

Barton, B., & Booth, D. (1990). *Stories in the classroom: Storytelling, reading aloud, and roleplaying with children*. Portsmouth, NH: Heinemann.

Berghoff, B., Borgmann, C. B., & Parr, C. (2003). Cycles of inquiry with the arts. *Language Arts, 80*(5), 353–362.

Bernhardt, S. (1986). Seeing the text. *College Composition and Communication, 37*, 66–78.

Bomer, R. (1995). *Time for meaning: Crafting literate lives in middle and high school*. Portsmouth, NH: Heinemann.

Bomer, R. (2003). Things that make kids smart: A Vygotskian perspective on concrete tool use in primary literacy classrooms. *Journal of Early Childhood Literacy, 3*(3), 223–247.

Bomer, R. (2006). Reading with the mind's ear: Listening to text as a mental action. *Journal of Adolescent and Adult Literacy, 49*(6), 2–13.

Bomer, R., & Laman, T. (2004). Positioning in a primary writing workshop: Joint action in the discursive production of writing subjects. *Research in the Teaching of English, 38*(4), 420–466.

Booth, D. (1994). *Storydrama: Reading, writing and roleplaying across the curriculum*. Markham, Ontario, Canada: Pembroke.

Booth, D. (1998). Language power through working in role. In B. J. Wagner (Ed.), *Educational drama and language arts: What research shows* (pp. 57–76). Portsmouth, NH: Heinemann.

Booth, D. (2005). *Story drama: Creating stories through role playing, improvising, and reading aloud*. Portland, ME: Stenhouse.

Bruner, J. S. (1986). *Actual minds, possible worlds*. Cambridge, MA: Harvard University Press.

Bruner, J. S. (1990). *Acts of meaning*. Cambridge, MA: Harvard University Press.

Calkins, L. M., & Harwayne, S. (1991). *Living between the lines*. Portsmouth, NH: Heinemann.

Clay, M. M. (1979). *What did I write?* Exeter, NH: Heinemann Educational Books.

Cochran-Smith, M. (1984). *The making of a reader*. Norwood, NJ: Ablex.

Daiute, C. (1989). Play as thought: Thinking strategies of young writers. *Harvard Educational Review, 59*(1), 1–23.

Daiute, C. (1990). The role of play in writing development. *Research in the Teaching of English, 24*(1), 4–47.

Dewey, J., & Bentley, A. (1991). Knowing and the known. In J. A. Boydston (Ed.), *The later works: 1925–1953* (Vol. 16, pp. 3–130). Carbondale: Southern Illinois University Press. (Original work published 1944)

Dowhower, S. L. (1994). Repeated reading revisited: Research into practice. *Reading and Writing Quarterly, 10*, 343–358.

Dyson, A. H. (1993). *Social worlds of children learning to write in an urban primary school*. New York: Teachers College Press.

Dyson, A. H. (1997). *Writing superheroes: Contemporary childhood, popular culture, and classroom literacy*. New York: Teachers College Press.

Dyson, A. H. (2003). *The brothers and sisters learn to write: Popular literacies in childhood and school cultures*. New York: Teachers College Press.

Eco, U. (1979). *A theory of semiotics*. Bloomington: Indiana University Press.

Edmiston, B. (2000). Drama as ethical education. *Research in Drama Education, 5*(1), 63–84.

Edmiston, B., & Enciso, P. E. (2003). Reflections and refractions of meaning: Dialogic approaches to classroom drama and reading. In J. Flood, D. Lapp, J. R. Squire, & J. M. Jensen (Eds.), *Handbook of research on teaching the English language arts* (pp. 868–880). Mahwah, NJ: Lawrence Erlbaum Associates.

Ehrenworth, M. (2003a). Literacy and the aesthetic experience: Engaging children with the visual arts in the teaching of writing. *Language Arts, 81*(1), 43–51.

Ehrenworth, M. (2003b). *Looking to write: Children writing through the visual arts*. Portsmouth, NH: Heinemann.

Enciso, P. (1992). Creating the story world: A case study of a young reader's engagement strategies and stances. In J. E. Many & C. Cox (Eds.), *Reader stance and literary understanding: Exploring the theories, research and practice* (pp. 75–102). Norwood, NJ: Ablex.

Enciso, P. (1996). Why engagement in reading matters to Molly. *Reading and Writing Quarterly, 12*, 171–194.

Engels, F. (1883). *Dialectics of nature*. Moscow, Russia: Progress Publishers.

Ernst, K. (1993). *Picturing learning: Artists and writers in the classroom*. Portsmouth, NH: Heinemann.

Ernst, K. (Ed.). (1996). *New entries: Learning by writing and drawing*. Portsmouth, NH: Heinemann.

Faigley, L. (1999). Material literacy and visual design. In J. Selzer & S. Crowley (Eds.), *Rhetorical bodies* (pp. 171–201). Madison: University of Wisconsin Press.

Fishman, J., Lunsford, A., McGregor, B., & Otuteye, M. (2005). Performing writing, performing literacy. *College Composition and Communication, 57*(2).

Flood, J., Heath, S. B., & Lapp, D. (Eds.). (1997). *Handbook of research on teaching literacy through the communicative and visual arts*. New York: Macmillan.

Gallas, K. (1994). *The languages of learning: How children talk, write, dance, draw, and sing their understanding of the world*. New York: Teachers College Press.

Gallas, K. (2003). *Imagination and literacy: A teacher's search for the heart of learning*. New York: Teachers College Press.

Gardner, H. (1980). *Artful scribbles: The significance of children's drawings*. New York: Basic Books.

Gardner, H. (1983). *Frames of mind: The theory of multiple intelligences*. New York: Basic Books.

Gardner, H. (Ed.). (1993). *Multiple intelligences: The theory in practice*. New York: Basic Books.

Gardner, H. (1999). *Intelligence reframed: Multiple intelligences for the 21st century*. New York: Basic Books.

Gee, J. P. (2003). *What video games have to teach us about learning and literacy*. New York: Palgrave Macmillan.

George, D. (2002). From analysis to design: Visual communication in the teaching of writing. *College Composition and Communication, 54*(1), 11–39.

Graves, D. (1982). *Writing: Teachers and children at work*. Portsmouth, NH: Heinemann.

Greene, M. (1995). *Releasing the imagination: Essays on education, the arts, and social change*. San Francisco: Jossey-Bass.

Greene, M. (2001). *Variations on a blue guitar: The Lincoln Center Institute lectures on aesthetic education*. New York: Teachers College Press.

Hakkarainen, P. (1999). Play and motivation. In Y. Engeström, R. Miettinen, & R.-L. Punamäki (Eds.), *Perspectives on activity theory* (pp. 231–249). Cambridge, U.K.: Cambridge University Press.

Hanks, W. F. (1996). *Language & communicative practices*. Boulder, CO: Westview Press.

Harste, J. C., Short, K. G., & Burke, C. L. (1988). *Creating classrooms for authors: The reading-writing connection*. Portsmouth, NH: Heinemann.

Harste, J. C., Woodward, V., & Burke, C. (1984). *Language stories and literacy lessons*. Portsmouth, NH: Heinemann.

Heath, S. B., & Wolf, S. A. (2005). *Dramatic learning in the primary school*. London: Creative Partnerships.

Hindley, J. (1996). *In the company of children*. York, ME: Stenhouse Publishers.

Hoffman, J. V., & Isaacs, M. E. (1991). Developing fluency through restructuring the task of guided oral reading. *Theory into Practice, 30*(3), 185–194.

Hubbard, R. (1989). *Authors of pictures, draughtsmen of words*. Portsmouth, NH: Heinemann.

Hull, G. (Ed.). (1997). *Changing work, changing workers: Critical perspectives on language, literacy, and skills*. Albany: State University of New York Press.

Husserl, E. (1999). *The essential Husserl: Basic writings in transcendental phenomenology*. Bloomington: Indiana University Press.

Johnson, M. (1987). *The body in the mind: The bodily basis of meaning, imagination, and reason*. Chicago: University of Chicago Press.

Johnson, L., & O'Neill, C. (Eds.). (1991). *Dorothy Heathcote: Collected writings on education and drama*. Evanston, IL: Northwestern University Press.

Karelitz, E. B. (1988). The rhythm of writing development. In T. Newkirk & N. Atwell (Eds.), *Understanding writing: Ways of observing, learning, and teaching K–8* (pp. 40–46). Portsmouth, NH: Heinemann.

Kincheloe, J. L. (Ed.). (2004). *Multiple intelligences reconsidered*. New York: Peter Lang.

Kist, W. (2005). *New literacies in action: Teaching and learning in multiple media*. New York: Teachers College Press.

Kress, G. (1997). *Before writing: Rethinking the paths to literacy*. London: Routledge.

Kress, G. (2003). *Literacy in the new media age*. London: Routledge.

Laakso, E. (2005). Encountering drama experiences: The learning potential of process drama in the light of student teachers' experiences. *Research in Drama Education, 10*(3), 355–356.

Langer, J. (1995). *Envisioning literature*. New York: Teachers College Press.

Leland, C. H., & Harste, J. C. (1994). Multiple ways of knowing: Curriculum in a new key. *Language Arts, 71*, 337–345.

Lemke, J. L. (1989). Social semiotics: A new model for literacy education. In D. Bloome (Ed.), *Classrooms and literacy* (pp. 289–309). Norwood, NJ: Ablex.

Marleau-Ponty, M. (1964). *The primacy of perception*. Evanston, IL: Northwestern University Press.

Martens, P. (1996). *I already know how to read: A child's view of literacy*. Portsmouth, NH: Heinemann.

Martinez, M., Roser, N., & Strecker, S. (1999). "I never thought I could be a star": A readers theatre ticket to fluency. *The Reading Teacher, 52*(4), 326–334.

Matthews, J. (1999). *The art of childhood and adolescence*. London: Falmer.

McNeil, L. M. (2000). *Contradictions of school reform: Educational costs of standardized testing*. New York: Routledge.

Medina, C. (2004a). The construction of drama worlds as literary interpretation of Latina feminist literature. *Research in Drama Education, 9*(2), 145–160.

Medina, C. (2004b). Drama wor(l)ds: Explorations of Latina/o realistic fiction through drama. *Language Arts, 81*(4), 272–282.

Moffett, J. (1990). Ways of teaching literature. In S. B. Straw & D. Bogdan (Eds.), *Beyond communication* (pp. 301–317). Portsmouth, NH: Boynton/Cook-Heinemann.

National Council of Teachers of English. (2003). *Resolution on composing with nonprint media*. Retrieved May 7, 2007, from http://www.ncte.org/about/over/positions/category/media/114919.htm

National Council of Teachers of English. (2005). *Multi-modal literacies*. Retrieved May 7, 2007, from http://www.ncte.org/about/over/positions/category/media/123213.htm

Newkirk, T. (1989). *More than stories: The range of children's writing*. Portsmouth, NH: Heinemann.

O'Neill, C. (1995). *Drama worlds: A framework for process drama*. Portsmouth, NH: Heinemann.

Oreck, B. (2004). The artistic and professional development of teachers: A study of teachers' attitudes toward and use of the arts in teaching. *Journal of Teacher Education, 55*(1), 55–69.

Paley, V. G. (1990). *The boy who would be a helicopter*. Cambridge, MA: Harvard University Press.

Paley, V. G. (1997). *The girl with the brown crayon: How children use stories to shape their lives*. Cambridge, MA: Harvard University Press.

Paley, V. G. (2004). *A child's work: The importance of fantasy play*. Chicago: University of Chicago Press.

Partnership for 21st Century Skills. (2005). *ICT Literacy Map—English*. Retrieved May 7, 2007, from http://www.21stcenturyskills.org/index.php?option=com_content&task=view&id=31&Itemid=33

Peirce, C. S. (1991). *Peirce on signs: Writings on semiotic*. Chapel Hill: University of North Carolina Press.

Ray, K. W. (2004). *About the authors: Writing workshop with our youngest writers*. Portsmouth, NH: Heinemann.

Rose, M. (2003). Words in action: Rethinking workplace literacy. *Research in the Teaching of English, 38*(1), 125–128.

Rosenblatt, L. M. (1983). *Literature as exploration*. New York: Modern Language Association. (Original work published 1938)

Rosenblatt, L. M. (1978). *The reader, the text, the poem: The transactional theory of the literary work*. Carbondale: Southern Illinois University Press.

Rowe, D. W. (1994). *Preschoolers as authors: Literacy learning in the social world of the classroom*. Cresskill, NJ: Hampton Press.

Rowe, D. W. (1998). The literate potentials of book-related dramatic play. *Reading Research Quarterly, 33*, 10–35.

Rowe, D. W., Fitch, J. D., & Bass, A. S. (2001). Power, identity, and instructional stance in writers' workshop. *Language Arts, 78*(5), 426–434.

Rowe, D. W., Fitch, J. D., & Bass, A. S. (2003). Toy stories as opportunities for imagination and reflection in writers' workshop. *Language Arts, 80*(5), 363–374.

Saussure, F. de. (1986). *Course in general linguistics*. Chicago: Open Court.

Sebeok, T. (1994). *An introduction to semiotics*. Toronto, Ontario, Canada: University of Toronto Press.

Semali, L. M. (Ed.). (2002). *Transmediation in the classroom: A semiotics-based media literacy framework*. New York: Peter Lang.

Shipka, J. (2005). A multimodal task-based framework for composing. *College Composition and Communication, 57*(2), 277–306.

Siegel, M. (1995). More than words: The generative power of transmediation for learning. *Canadian Journal of Education, 20*, 455–475.

Smagorinsky, P. (1991). *Expressions: Multiple intelligences in the English class*. Urbana, IL: National Council of Teachers of English.

Smagorinsky, P. (1997). Artistic composing as representational process. *Journal of Applied Developmental Psychology, 18*, 87–105.

Smagorinsky, P., & Coppock, J. (1994). Cultural tools in the classroom context: An exploration of an artistic response to literature. *Written Communication, 11*, 283–310.

Smagorinsky, P., & O'Donnell-Allen, C. (1998a). The depth and dynamics of context: Tracing the sources and channels of engagement and disengagement in students' response to literature. *Journal of Literacy Research, 30*, 515–559.

Smagorinsky, P., & O'Donnell-Allen, C. (1998b). Reading as mediated and mediating action: Composing meaning for literature through multimedia interpretive texts. *Reading Research Quarterly, 33*(2), 198–226.

Smagorinsky, P., & O'Donnell-Allen, C. (2000). Idiocultural diversity in small groups: The role of the relational framework in collaborative learning. In C. D. Lee & P. Smagorinsky (Eds.), *Vygotskian perspectives on literacy research: Constructing meaning through collaborative inquiry* (pp. 165–190). Cambridge, U.K.: Cambridge University Press.

Strecker, S., Roser, N., & Martinez, M. (1998). Toward understanding oral reading fluency. In T. Shanahan & F. Rodriguez-Brown (Eds.), *47th yearbook of the national reading conference*. Chicago: National Reading Conference.

Suhor, C. (1984). Towards a semiotics-based curriculum. *Journal of Curriculum Studies, 16*(3), 247–257.

Suhor, C., & Little, D. (1988). Visual literacy and print literacy—Theoretical consideration and points of contact. *Reading Psychology, 9*(4), 469–481.

Taylor, P. (Ed.). (1995). *Pre-text & storydrama: The artistry of Cecily O'Neill & David Booth*. Brisbane, Queensland, Australia: National Association for Drama in Education.

Todes, S. (2001). *Body and world*. Cambridge, MA: MIT Press.

Volosinov, V. N. (1973). *Marxism and the philosophy of language* (L. Mateijka & I. R. Titunik, Trans.). Cambridge, MA: Harvard University Press.

Vygotsky, L. S. (1971). *The psychology of art*. Cambridge, MA: M.I.T. Press.

Vygotsky, L. S. (1978). *Mind in society: The development of higher psychological processes*. Cambridge, MA: Harvard University Press.

Vygotsky, L. S. (1986). *Thought and language*. Cambridge, MA: MIT Press.

Wagner, B. J. (Ed.). (1998). *Educational drama and language arts: What research shows*. Portsmouth, NH: Heinemann.

Wardrip-Fruin, N., & Harrington, P. (Eds.). (2004). *First person: New media as story, performance, and game*. Cambridge, MA: MIT Press.

Welch, K. (1999). *Electric rhetoric: Classical rhetoric, oralism, and a new literacy*. Cambridge, MA: MIT Press.

Wertsch, J. V. (1985). *Vygotsky and the social formation of mind*. Cambridge, MA: Harvard University Press.

Wertsch, J. V. (1991). *Voices of the mind: A sociocultural approach to mediated action*. Cambridge, MA: Harvard University Press.

Whitin, P. (1996a). Exploring visual response to literature. *Research in the Teaching of English, 30*, 114–140.

Whitin, P. (1996b). *Sketching stories, stretching minds: Responding visually to literature*. Portsmouth, NH: Heinemann.

Whitin, P. (2005). The interplay of text, talk, and visual representation in expanding literary interpretation. *Research in the Teaching of English, 39*(4), 365–397.

Whitin, P. (2006). Forging pedagogical paths to multiple ways of knowing. *English Education, 38*(2), 123–145.

WIDE Research Center Collective. (2005). Why teach digital writing? *Kairos, 10.1*.

Wilhelm, J. D. (1997). *You gotta BE the book: Teaching engaged and reflective reading with adolescents*. New York: Teachers College Press.

Witte, S. P. (1992). Context, text, intertext: Toward a constructivist semiotic of writing. *Written Communication, 9*(2), 237–308.

Witte, S. P., & Haas, C. (2001). Writing as an embodied practice: The case of engineering standards. *Journal of Business and Technical Communication, 15*(4), 413–457.

Wolf, S. A. (1995). Learning to act/acting to learn: Children as actors, characters, and critics in classroom theatre. *Research in the Teaching of English, 28*(1), 7–44.

Wolf, S. A. (1998). The flight of reading: Shifts in instruction, orchestration, and attitudes through classroom theatre. *Reading Research Quarterly, 33*(4), 382–415.

Wolf, S. A., & Heath, S. B. (1992). *The braid of literature: Children's worlds of reading*. Cambridge, MA: Harvard University Press.

Worthy, J., & Broaddus, K. (2002). Fluency beyond the primary grades: From group performance to silent, independent reading. *The Reading Teacher, 55*, 334–343.

Worthy, J., & Prater, K. (2002). "I thought about it all night": Readers theatre for reading fluency and motivation. *The Reading Teacher, 56*(3), 294–297.

Wysocki, A. F., Johnson-Eilola, J., Selfe, C. L., & Sirc, G. (2004). *Writing new media: Theory and applications for expanding the teaching of composition*. Logan: University of Utah Press.

Yancey, K. B. (2004). Made not only in words: Composition in a new key. *College Composition and Communication, 56*(2), 297–328.

·36·

A CRITICAL REVIEW OF RESEARCH INTO CHILDREN'S RESPONSES TO MULTIMODAL TEXTS

Evelyn Arizpe
UNIVERSITY OF GLASGOW

Morag Styles
UNIVERSITY OF CAMBRIDGE

As the title suggests, in this chapter, we provide an overview of studies in the area of visual/multimodal texts that take into account the response of the child reader.[1] Our aim is to look at how this field has developed over the last few decades and learn from the findings that have been presented. "Multimodality," according to Kress and Van Leeuwen (2001), is "the use of several semiotic modes in the design of a semiotic product or event, together with the particular way in which these modes are combined" (p. 20). Most of the texts to which we refer in this chapter combine a limited variety of "modes" which make a significant contribution to meaning, such as print and visual elements (illustration, layout, typography, etc.), and we have chosen to concentrate on picture books as one of the primary literatures of early childhood. With the proliferation of "multimedia" texts, there is also, of course, a growing critical literature on children's responses to a wide range of interactive texts. While we mention a few examples, most are beyond the scope of this review. However, a) recent clarification of multimodal is a useful reminder here:

> The increasing number of texts which include words and images mean that there are difficulties about how to describe them. Many of these texts are produced using digital technologies, emphasizing the *medium* of communication, for example:
>
> - The computer
> - Paper-based texts—picture books, magazines, novels, information books
> - Sound and visual media—radio, television, videos, and DVDs
>
> Whatever the medium, texts are made up of different combinations of *modes:*
>
> - Writing or print, including typographical elements of font type, size and shape
> - Images—moving and still, diagrammatic, or representational
> - Sound: spoken words and music
> - Gesture and movement
>
> (Bearne, E., Ellis, S., Graham, L., Hulme, P., Meiner, J., and Wolstencroft, H. [2005, p. 6].)

We have also limited our review to those studies which report on the verbal, written, or visual responses of children to multimodal texts, whether at home or in a formal educational setting. Many critical studies look at literary, artistic, emotional, and other aspects of multimodal texts, and in particular picture books. Although they may be well informed about how children "read" texts, if they do not actually engage with children, we have not included them. At the other end of the spectrum, there are also many studies on how to use picture books and other multimodal texts in the classroom, but most of them are not based on systematic research. We have mentioned a few of the latter only when we considered that they provided new insights into how children respond to visual texts. We end this review by gathering together some of the main findings of scholars,

[1] Parts of this chapter are based on the literature review that appeared in the first two chapters of our book, *Children Reading Pictures: Interpreting Visual Texts* (Arizpe & Styles, 2003).

while also pointing out possible directions for future research. Inevitably, we have had to be selective in our decision about which texts to include in this brief round-up and our selection is no doubt biased by our fuller knowledge of British criticism in this area.

". . . THAT MOST DANGEROUS OF IDEAS"

Tucker (1974), the educational psychologist, reviewed the catalog of an exhibition on children's picture books written by Brian Alderson, a leading critic of children's literature. Among other things, he took issue with Alderson for not taking into account "the psychology of perception" of the young audience of these picture books, with particular reference to the illustrations of Dick Bruna. Alderson responded by writing, "The possible character of the child's response was given some consideration, but only within the larger compass of an allegiance to quality in illustration" (Alderson, as cited in Tucker, 1974, p. 51). He pointed out that, in terms of criteria to judge picture books, the "proven appeal to children . . . will lead to judgements that have nothing to do with illustrations as such," and he referred to Tucker's phrase "the child's eye view" as "that most dangerous of ideas" (Alderson, as cited in Tucker, 1974, p. 50). Without realizing it, both scholars were raising questions and setting up a debate that would be highly significant in the development of research in the field of children's responses to visual texts.

Two years later, H. Crago and M. Crago (1976) published an article in which they, in turn, took issue with Tucker's phrase "the untrained eye" to refer to young children's viewing of pictures. They reported on their three-year-old daughter 's response to the images in Felix Hoffman's *Rapunzel* and concluded,

> This 'eye' is sometimes the product of adult determination to restrict the child to what it can easily cope with. A diet of [Dick] Bruna may produce a child good at dealing with stylized figures surrounded by heavy black outlines but unsure of himself [sic] outside such a convention; our own experience with Anna shows that *her* early book experience produced a child easily able to deal with subtleties of line and color, but initially perplexed by Bruna's 'simplicity' (Crago, H. & Crago, M., 1976, p. 151).

They also noted the fact that "adult responses can be made explicit, whereas a child's may be implicit in an overall pattern of comment and questioning that is all too easy to dismiss without close analysis as naïve and purely pragmatic" (Crago, H. & Crago, M., 1976, p. 151). While the Crago's case study showed that children can indeed deal with complex images from a young age as well as the value of exploring this "child's eye view," it also raised many of the problems which plague research on children's responses to texts (visual or not). The subject of their study was their own daughter, which meant that although they possessed in-depth and intimate knowledge of her reading (albeit with the limitations of a three-year-old's ability to articulate her response to a picture book), the context is particular and controlled (see other classic studies of children's literacy conducted by parents, such as Bissex, 1980; Wolf & Heath, 1992). As the daughter of academics, Anna had been surrounded by a rich array of visual texts for all of her short life and had probably had some first class modeling of what to "look for" in an illustration. In other words, her eye had clearly been "trained."

The so-called "child's eye view" began to be taken into account in some of the initial critical approaches to picture books published in the 1980s, although these tended to focus more on the text than on the reader. In-depth analysis of this genre by critics such as Bader (1976), Doonan (1986; 1991; 1993; 1996; 1998; 2000), Graham (1990; 2004), Lewis (1990; 1992; 1996; 2001), Meek (1988), Nikolajeva and Scott (2000; 2001), Nodelman (1988; 1996), Sipe (1998; 2000a; 2000b), and J. H. Schwarcz (1982; Schwarcz, J. H. & Schwarcz, C., 1991), among others, have been invaluable in understanding how the visual and written features of a picture book interact, as well as how to appreciate them as aesthetic objects. Articles on picture books, which sometimes included reference to children's responses to them, became a regular feature of scholarly journals devoted to children's literature from the 1990s in North America, Australia, and the United Kingdom. In Britain, the children's literature journal *Signal* (and their associated Thimble Press), published articles and monographs by some of these scholars and played an important role in furthering studies on picture books and informing succeeding research on children's responses. More pedagogically oriented publications, such as Jill Bennett's (1982) *Learning to Read with Picture Books* and Liz Waterlands' (1985) *Read with Me*, helped to promote a more prominent role for picture books in the classroom generally and, more specifically, in the early stages of teaching reading. Meek's (1988) seminal *How Texts Teach What Readers Learn* is an outstanding account of how quality pictorial texts (such as *Rosie's Walk* by Pat Hutchins) teach young children sophisticated narrative lessons.

CHILDREN READING PICTURES

The 1990s saw the publication of more focused research on children's responses to picture books. These included books by Michaels and Walsh (1990) and Baddeley and Eddershaw (1994), as well as Kiefer's (1995) comprehensive *The Potential of Picture Books: From Visual Literacy to Aesthetic Understanding*. Lewis (1992), Watson and Styles (1996), Day (1996), Madura (1998), and Evans (1998a; 1998b) also approached this topic. Most of this research was motivated by the desire to understand how children make sense of picture books and to extend their knowledge and appreciation of this literature.

In *Up and Away*, Michaels and Walsh (1990) also discussed different types of picture books and reader response to visual texts and considered ways that they could be used in primary and secondary classrooms to teach aspects such as narrative, gender, and register. Baddeley and Eddershaw (1994) followed a similar line in *Not So Simple Picture Books*, where they reported on the sophisticated visual and intellectual knowledge children bring to the challenges offered by many visual texts. Both publications listed a wide range of interesting picture books to use with children and an array of possible activities for developing their interpretative skills.

Kiefer (1993; 1995) was participant observer in various American primary school classrooms. She also conducted single and paired interviews on different picture books by distinguished illustrators, including Maurice Sendak's *Outside Over There* and Lizbeth Zwerger's *Hansel and Gretel*. Kiefer constructed a descriptive framework for the children's responses based on Halliday's seminal work on the functions of spoken language. She focused on four categories employed by the children in verbal responses to picture books: (a) *informative,* where comments focused on the content of illustrations, the story line, and text to life observations and made comparisons with other books; (b) *heuristic,* where problem solving is involved, inferences are made, and hypothetical language is commonly used; (c) *imaginative,* where children enter into the life of the book, often using figurative language; and (d) *personal,* where children express feelings and opinions, relate to characters, and evaluate the illustrations.

Kiefer's (1993; 1995) study showed developmental differences in the way children approach picture books. Noticing details seems to come first and, so strong is the urge that children often see features adults miss. Kiefer (1993) found that the children "developed more critical thinking not only about cognitive factors but also about aesthetic factors and that this awareness was different depending on the age of the child" (p. 278). She also mentioned that awareness of artists and their intentions seemed to develop in parallel with age, though "all children seemed to be familiar with elements like lines, shapes, and colors, although they didn't always have the correct nomenclature" (Kiefer, 1995, p. 37). Kiefer (1995) concluded, "Studying children's responses to picture books in these classroom settings has convinced me that picture books can and do provide children with purposeful talk, increase their literacy, deepen their response to books, and open up their awareness of art and aesthetics" (p. 41).

Madura (1998) closely followed the progress of four learners in their first years of primary school as they responded to the work of two American picture book artists, Patricia Polacco and Gerald McDermott. As a teacher/researcher, she documented the reading and writing of these children in their natural setting, as well as working in one-to-one, paired, and small group sessions to explore their responses to visual texts. It should be noted that Madura approached her teaching with a commitment to integrated literature/literacy approaches and consciously taught children about art and aesthetics. Madura's findings were as follows: *Descriptive responses* to picture books involved retellings and plot summaries, though Madura did puzzlingly include within this category "comments on illustrations and how they were created." (It does seem to us that while the former were the most simple responses to be expected from young children, the latter were not necessarily so.) *Interpretive responses* included comments about the story, text to life, and personal experiences; *thematic trends* showed the children appreciative of the artist/authors' themes, styles, and techniques. Madura (1998) concluded that these response patterns were a result of the classroom approach to books in which "discussion concentrated exclusively on the unified exchange between text and illustration that each author/illustrator presented" (p. 375).

In his article on John Burningham's *Where's Julius?,* Lewis (1992) compared his own reading of this picture book with that of his two children, aged five and eight. He described the book in detail and the way in which his understanding of it changed through hearing the children's difficulties with retelling this story. He then discussed the way in which the conventional relationship between word and image is subverted and how a game was played by the readers in order to make sense of a metafictive and open-ended picture book such as this one. He argued that this type of text forced the child (and the adult) reader to use critical skills that teach us about the actual nature of reading pictures. Although he stresses the importance of taking both children's and adult's responses into account, his more recent, *Reading Contemporary Picturebooks* (Lewis, 2001) focused more on the nature of this literary form than on children's understandings of it. However, he did occasionally draw on his conversations with primary school children about some of the books under discussion.

In Canada, Day (1996) read picture books with 60 elementary schoolchildren and then listened to small groups rereading and discussing the books. She also read three Canadian picture books (Ian Wallace's *Hansel and Gretel,* Rafe Martin's *The Rough-Face Girl,* and Jim McGugan and Murray Kimber's *Josepha*) to older pupils and analyzed their conversations about the books. She sorted out the responses based on Doonan's (1993) categories of "denotation" and "exemplification" and added three others: references to artistic techniques, allusions to other literature, and creation of dialogue (Day, 1996, p. 155). As the children made connections, she noted their emotional reactions and how they built on each other's knowledge, although she also found they had difficulties with unfamiliar artistic styles. Day ended by suggesting that teachers need to help children build the schemata for negotiating a variety of styles and understanding the interplay between word and image.

The articles in *Talking Pictures* (Watson & Styles, 1996), which discuss the responses of children in England to picture books and comics, open up several possibilities for further research. For example, Styles (1996) reported on the responses of five- and six-year olds, as she read "postmodern" picture books with them. Steve Johnson and Jon Scieszka's *The Frog Prince Continued* was a typical example. She showed how children are drawn to the humor and games of postmodernism and have few difficulties in comprehending these complex texts. Rosen (1996) wrote about his six-year-old son as an "expert" reader of *The Beano,* analyzing his understanding of genre, structure, and ideology, among other aspects, of this weekly comic. He concluded that this experience gave his son confidence to "read" both literary and graphic forms, enabling him to move on to more varied and complex texts. Bromley (1996b) followed the progress of a six-year-old child of Pakistani heritage adapting to literature in a foreign classroom. She showed how this child "read" emotions in a picture book and how important her responses became to the rest of her class. Finally, two articles by Watson (1996a; 1996b) were based on his reading with two little girls over two years when they were aged between four and six. He showed how sophisticated texts, like Anthony Browne's *The Tunnel* and Burningham's *Granpa,* turned the children into "postmodernist readers" (see also Watson, 1993). He also revealed the extent to which they noticed details, and wove them into a "narrative web" of meaning (Watson, 1996b, p. 151).

Even though the findings from these case studies cannot be generalized, they provide fascinating insights into the nature of reader response. The same is true of some of the articles in *What's in the Picture?* (Evans, 1998b). For example, Graham (1998) listened to the retellings of wordless picture books, such as Quentin Blake's *Clown,* by children between ages 5 and 12 and pointed out the difficulties this involved. Evans (1998a) looked at how eight- to nine-year-old children responded to a picture book that presented an unconventional view of a traditional fairytale, *The Paper Bag Princess,* by Robert Munsch and Michael Martchenko. Responses, both oral and visual, revealed a resistance to the subverted gender roles and unexpected story line. Laycock (1998) briefly reported on the responses by two children who are new to English to another wordless picture book, John Prater's *The Gift.* She found their experience served "to reinforce the pleasures of reading, as well as allowing them to draw on existing skills of storytelling in their community language" (Laycock, 1998, p. 82). These studies pointed to the possibilities of exploring response with particular kinds of genres to highlight issues such as gender and cultural diversity.

Children's responses to picture books were considered by a wide range of commentators in edited volumes by Styles, Bearne, and Watson (1992; 1994; 1996), which came out of children's literature conferences held at Homerton College, Cambridge, in the 1990s. For example, in chapters that deal with their artistic intentions in creating picture books, Jan Ormerod (1992) and Anthony Browne (1994) mentioned young readers' reactions to their works while talking to them in classrooms. Barbara Jordan (1992) analyzed children's responses to humor in picture books, Geoff Fox (1996) considered how to help young teachers develop children's understanding of multimodal texts, and Anne Rowe (1996) drew on her knowledge of children's responses to wordless picture books. Although Satoshi Kitamura (in Watson 1996c) said he did not think of children as a distinctive audience for his books, he did suggest that they were "ideal readers" in their receptiveness to the integrity of his work (p. 241).

Further texts from the same stable followed in 2000 by a wider range of editors. For example, in *Teaching Through Texts* (Anderson & Styles, 2000), Mary Purdon (2000) showed the sophisticated responses of five- and six–year-olds, both through oracy and drawing, to Browne's picture books; Helen Bromley (2000) examined the visual challenges of *The Beano* through her young daughter's eyes; and Kate Rabey (2000) explored the complex demands made on young readers by some metafictive picture books. Jane Doonan (2000) and Tina Hanlon (2000) concentrated more on the artistry of picture books than children's responses in *Tales, Tellers and Texts* (Cliff Hodges, Styles, & Drummond, 2000), while Frances Sword (2002) showed the huge potential of working with children in art galleries by emphasizing their intelligent responses to paintings and artifacts. Several chapters in Styles and Bearne's (2003) *Art, Narrative and Childhood* focused on children: Colin Grigg (2003) looked at literacy through art by describing a project at the Tate Gallery with artists and children; Margaret Mackey (2003a) drew attention to physical and performative aspects of collaborative reading of visual texts as she reported on older pupils' responses to David Macaulay's *Shortcut*; Eve Bearne (1995; 2003a, 2005) drew on classroom research about how children produce and receive multimodal texts to develop an "integrated theory of text;" while the authors of this chapter focused on children's metalinguistic capacity to understand multimodal texts.

RESEARCH TRENDS IN THE 21ST CENTURY

Thinking about literacy has changed substantially in recent years, Bearne (2003b) wrote,

> Children now have available to them many forms of text which include sound, voice, intonation, stance, gesture, movement, as well as print and image. These texts have changed the ways in which young readers expect to read, the ways they think and the ways they construct meaning. Necessarily, children bring to their reading and writing a wide and varied array of resources and experience through which they interpret any unfamiliar texts that they meet. However, it isn't just a matter of investing texts with the voices, sounds and gestures, which are part of children's reading (and viewing) experience, but that their reception of text assumes different organization—one which is spatially cohesive and which uses a different kind of orchestration of elements which make up any act of reading. (p. 128)

Mackey (2002; 2003a; 2003b) pointed out how literacy is changing in a multimedia world and how these shifts require a better comprehension of "how developing readers transfer interpretive capacities across media" (2003b). Shirley Brice Heath (2002) observed, "Current work in neurobiology and physics brings new understanding of just how important engaging with the visual arts can be for broadening neural circuitry involvement of the brain" (p. 121).

Eliza Dresang (1999) identified the "radical change" categories in children's books (similar to those characteristics of modern picture books discussed by children's literature specialists, e.g., Anstey, 2002; Anstey & Bull, 2000; Bull, 2002; Bradford, 1993; Styles, 1996 and Watson, 1993) which reflect aspects of the digital age and allow the "Net generation" to engage with them in nontraditional ways. Clare Bradford (1993) noted the postmodern "tensions" in picture books, while Michèle Anstey and Geoff Bull (2000; Anstey, 2002 and Bull, 2002) considered the place of picture books in a multiliterate world. Recent research on reader response has taken on board the idea of multimodality, including the work of many scholars involved in the Harvard Graduate School of Education's Project Zero (http://www.pz.harvard.edu). Studies published in the new millennium include a variety of visual texts, including analysis of children's own artistic creations—either on paper or on the Internet. We cannot discuss all these studies here, but we shall touch on some of those that, in our opinion, take research on response to multimodal texts a step further.

Working with a clear example of a postmodern picture book (David Macaulay's fragmented and ambiguous *Black and White*), Jill McClay (2000) conducted a study with 20 children ages 7 to 12. Interestingly the research also included 25 adults, mainly teachers and librarians, who read and discussed the text. During unguided discussions, subjects negotiated reading strategies together as well as the construction of meaning. The adult readers in particular found that traditional reading strategies were not sufficient to understand what was going on in the picture book and that knowledge of other media was essential in constructing meaning from this complex narrative. Several rereadings, flexibility, and a tolerance for ambiguity were also found to be necessary.

Sipe (e.g., 1997; 2000a) published extensively on children's literary understanding of the verbal and the visual in picture books and traditional stories. In one of his articles, he described the intertextual connections made by primary age children as they read versions of the traditional tale *The Gingerbread Boy*. Although his research did not focus exclusively on the visual, the children based many of their responses on the pictures as well as on the language and made intertextual connections through both, thereby allowing children to develop their literary understanding for both hermeneutic and aesthetic purposes (Sipe, 2000b, p. 77). Sipe (2000b) formulated a key question for further research: "How do children use the connections to other visual texts to understand the composition, media, and semiotic significance of illustrations" (p. 87)?

The study that involved the largest cohort of children responding to picture books was co-ordinated by Arizpe and Styles (2003) together with a team of researchers. The principal aim of the research was to investigate how visual texts were read by children using the picture books of Anthony Browne (*Zoo* and *The Tunnel*) and Satoshi Kitamura (*Lily takes a Walk*). It involved ethnographic, qualitative methodology based on theories from various disciplines, from psychology to aesthetics, language theory, and visual literacy. In-depth, semistructured interviews were conducted with a selection of the pupils from seven schools, ranging from multiethnic and economically deprived settings in north London to suburban schools outside the capital. In total, 84 individual children were interviewed, 21 of whom were followed up in a second interview. The class teacher's estimate of the reading ability of each child was obtained, providing a useful point of comparison when assessing children's abilities to read pictures (although researchers had no knowledge of these "reading abilities" until after the interviews had taken place). Many of the interviewed children were bilingual and a few had learning difficulties. The children were also set an open-ended task, inviting them to draw a picture in response to the text, which had been the focus of the interview. The purpose of this was to access some of their knowledge, which may not have been articulated during the interviews. Among other things, pupils were questioned about the themes of the books; actions, expressions, and feelings of the characters; intratextual and intertextual elements; and what the artist needed to know in order to draw and the way in which he used color, body language, and perspective. After the individual interviews, 147 children participated in a group discussion.

Overall, findings suggested that complex, multilayered picture books provoked deep, intelligent responses in young readers and the more experienced they were with visual texts, the better they were at constructing meaning—whether or not they were considered "good" readers by their teachers. There were few marked differences between children for whom English was an additional language and native English speakers in terms of their appreciation and interpretation of visual texts. It was also found that gender differences were more apparent in inexperienced readers who were less confident not only about their abilities to understand but also to express their thoughts in front of others. The findings pointed to many different areas for potential research such as analyzing linguistic and cultural elements, furthering readers understanding of word/picture interaction or "reading" the children's own drawings.[2]

In the last few years, Sylvia Pantaleo (e.g., 2002; 2004a; 2005a; 2005b) published several articles on a study which explored the responses of children to picture books with metafictive devices, such as Macaulay's *Shortcut,* Browne's *Voices in the Park,* and David Weisner's *The Three Pigs,* among others. She worked in Canadian elementary schools with first grade children to whom she first read the books. The children then participated in both small group and whole class interactive read-aloud sessions. Afterwards, they were asked to "visually represent their responses." Pantaleo discussed her findings based on different aspects of the children's response, such as their reaction to the metafictive devices or the relationship between the pupils' verbal and visual texts with respect to storytelling and the way in which adults "read" children's pictures. Pantaleo reported on the many "reading lessons" which the reader viewers experienced by "reading" metafiction, such as lessons about narrative framing devices, indeterminacy, multiple narrators, and parodic appropriations, among many others. She argued that these books allowed them more agency as readers and required them to be more involved in creating meaning. She suggested that this metafictive awareness would help children grow as readers as they encounter other multimodal texts, particularly those with Dresang's (1999) "radical change characteristics" (Pantaleo, 2004b).

Other examples of recent research on response reveal different approaches to visual texts. In Greece, Angela Yannicopoulou (2004) tested 356 preschool children on visual conventions commonly found in comics and other multimodal texts. Her quantitative analysis revealed that preschoolers were familiar with these conventions, for example, speech bubbles and the meaning of letter sizes, even though they could not yet read. In Britain, Kate Pahl's (2005) research focused on ephemera and artifacts made by children in the crossover between home and school; her findings implied that these sort of creations can also be considered as forms of response to texts, such as, for example, drawings of the character Super Mario.

Visual Learning in the Community School (Heath & Wolf, 2004) is a series of booklets that came out of a Creative Partnerships Project based at Hythe Community School in Kent, where an artist and architectural designer worked on visual literacy with young children for a year. The outcomes are five well-designed and appealing texts that consider different aspects of visual learning for teachers. The most relevant booklets for the purposes of this review are *Art Is All About Looking: Drawing and Detail* and *It Looks to Me as if: Talking About Picturebooks.* The former takes as its starting point the fact that children's artistic endeavors involve cognitive work; it begins with a quote from the poet William Carlos Williams: "A youngster drawing in a youngster thinking" (Williams, as cited in Heath & Wolf, 2004a, p. 5). The latter shows how "illustrations support and extend the meaning of printed material" (Heath & Wolf, 2004b, p. 9).

Finally, we also have the presentation of strategies helping students develop their critical responses to picture books and multimodal texts.[3] For example, in a useful follow-up to *Pictures on the Page,* Graham (2004), in *Cracking Good Picture Books,* described, analyzed, and offered activities for the classroom related to 30 well-chosen picture books. She believed that picture books should be at the heart of literacy teaching for young children. A particularly clear framework that provided scaffold instruction for the understanding of picture books was presented by Tina Sharpe (2005). Through questions about visual and verbal "framing," based on Kress and van Leeuwen's (2001) visual grammar, she gave an example of how Sendak's *Where the Wild Things Are* could be approached. Although intended for older children, this approach is useful for teachers and could be also be adapted for younger children. Another example of how response can be integrated with classroom practice is that of Nicole Strangman's (2003) multimodal project on *Alice in Wonderland.* Strangman, a fourth-grade teacher, read this book to her class and encouraged them to respond to both the written text and Tenniel's illustrations. As well as making their own illustrations—which they posted on their website—they made a toy theater production of this classic of children's literature. Janet Evans' (2005) edited volume also offered an impressive range of projects set in classrooms dealing with popular culture, new technologies, and critical literacy.

[2] Useful books for analysing children's drawings are, among others, Lewis and Greene's (1983) *Your Children's Drawings—Their Hidden Meanings,* Cox's (1992) *Children's Drawings,* and Anning and Ring's (2004) *Making Sense of Children's Drawings.*

[3] Picture books have also been used to teach concepts of literary theory to older students, as in *From Picturebook to Literary Theory* (Stephens & Watson, 1994).

MULTICULTURAL PERSPECTIVES

By the 1990s, scholars had begun to look more closely at the response of culturally diverse pupils to picture books. For example, in *Multicultural Picturebooks: Art for Understanding Others* and its sequel, *Multicultural Picturebooks: Art for Illuminating our World*, K. Marantz and S. Marantz (1997; 2005) considered the picture book's potential for teaching children about other cultures by reviewing examples from many parts of the world. Their criteria highlighted the authentic characterization of specific cultures, as well as more conventional features, such as content, design, layout, and style of artwork. More research-focused publications include Eve Gregory's (1994) work, which intended mainly to show how bilingual children construct and negotiate meaning in a new language and how the picture book genre invited interaction with text. For example, Gregory reported on a five-year-old Bengali speaker's progress during his first 18 months at school, pointing out the "reading lessons" that one child acquired as he and his teacher shared picture books.

Coulthard (2003) built on this and Gregory's other extensive research on emergent bilinguals by analyzing the interpretive steps and emotional engagement of second language learners in two of the schools that participated in this study. Working with pupils from a variety of nationalities, she found that Browne's picture books stimulated them to profound meaning making, despite alternative cultural traditions. She showed how bilingual children rose to the intellectual challenge and were able to overcome their hesitation of using of a new language in order to communicate this meaning to others. Based on the study's questioning techniques, Coulthard went on to design a series of lessons (mainly for use with the curriculum for England and Wales but which can be adapted to any classroom), which incorporate activities around the visual and the dramatic to further the literacy skills of any child (see Coulthard, Arizpe & Styles, 2003). Other researchers, such as Bromley (1996b) and Laycock (1998), previously mentioned, also followed Gregory's work, but there is still more to be done on the response of culturally diverse children to multimodal texts.[4]

Heather Mines (2000) completed her doctoral study on research with Anthony Browne's *The Tunnel* and three groups of five- and six-year-olds with distinct cultural backgrounds—Bangladeshi newcomers, second generation Bangladeshi immigrants, and English children from rural Sussex. As well as detailing her own analysis of the picture book, Mines studied the transcripts with codes based mainly on Barthes' semiotics, which links the text to the real world and builds on readers' social and intertextual knowledge. This is particularly relevant to a text like *The Tunnel* where the limits of the real world are blurred and knowledge of other texts is required to make sense of the story. Mines contended that the reader approaches the text as a cultural being, bringing to the transaction with the text their own experiences of life and the world in order to make the new culture less strange. Thus, for example, the recent immigrants to Britain saw snakes and dragons in the forest, while the Sussex children recognized the references to familiar fairy stories. Mines found cultural differences in each group's reading, particularly with respect to their response to (a) the everyday objects in the book, (b) intertextual references, (c) the ideology of the text, and (d) the secondary world within the text.

In a study conducted in Australia, Walsh (2000; 2003) read two picture books (*I Went Walking* by Sue Machin and Julie Vivas and *Felix and Alexander* by Terry Denton) with primary children in the first two years of school. Some of these pupils were second language learners; others were English background speakers. The research involved reading sessions with individual children after books had been studied in their classrooms. Walsh found the books activated emergent reading behavior through a range of cognitive and affective processes as well as cultural understandings. There were few differences between the ranges of comments made by the two groups. She also noticed that most pupils were able to label, observe detail, and create links to their own experience.

A final example of research with children from culturally diverse backgrounds is that conducted by Marion Colledge (2005). Over one year, she looked at the response to a selection of classic picture books used in English schools, such as Jill Murphy's *Peace at Last* and Trish Cooke and Helen Oxenbury's *So Much*. She built up case studies of six emergent bilingual Bengali speaking children, ages five to six, in their first year of schooling. She found there were cultural gaps where these children did not grasp intertextual allusions as well as their British or European peers did. However, "The books formed a bridge between the known and the culturally unfamiliar, giving children access to an understanding of scenes from types of homes other than their own" (Colledge, 2005, p. 24).

MULTIMEDIA AND RESPONSE— SOME EXAMPLES

Recent research has also looked at the response of pupils of different ages to particular kinds of multimedia. In the articles brought together by Jackie Marsh's (2005) *Popular Culture, New Media and Digital Literacy in Early Childhood*, the responses of children to new (and not so new) technologies were analyzed, from under two-year-olds and an episode of *The Teletubbies* (Roberts & Howard, 2005) and toddlers and CD-ROM games (Smith, 2005), to six- and seven-year-olds and console games (Pahl, 2005). Since the early 1990s, David Buckingham (1993; 1996; 2000; Buckingham & Bragg, 2004) led research on television and the "electronic generation." He explored televisual literacy and the emotional response of children and young people to different genres, in particular horror, violence, and sex. On the subject of media literacy, he argued, "Children will only develop the competence to produce meaningful statements in the media, or to make their views known, if they are given sustained and well-supported opportunities to do so" (Buckingham, 2000, p. 205).

Len Unsworth (e.g., 2001; Unsworth, Thomas, Simpson & Asha, 2005) wrote extensively on new electronic formats and literary texts for children. In their book on children's literature and computer-based teaching, Unsworth, Thomas, Simpson, et al. (2005) looked at the "opportunities for children to produce online responses to literary texts" (and respond to other children's posted comments), as well as "their collaborative online production of multimodal narratives" (p. 43). Their reports on classroom practices showed that, as

[4] At the time of writing, the Scottish Executive Education Department is providing a research grant for Evelyn Arizpe and Jim McGonigal (University of Glasgow) to undertake one such project: *Learning to read a new culture: How immigrant and asylum seeking children experience Scottish identity through children's books.*

participants in role-playing virtual communities, children needed to use sophisticated literacy skills, both oral and written as well as learning how to handle the technology involved.

Jon Callow's (e.g., 2003; 2006; Callow & Zammit, 2002) work on the visual aspect of multiliteracies included children's understandings of their own multimedia productions. He not only explored the theoretical implications of new literacies, but also included examples of research and classroom practice using multimodal texts. In one study, he focused on the language 11-year-olds used to describe and explain their presentations on science and technology topics, such as food production. Callow (2003) stressed the importance of encouraging his pupils to learn a metalanguage for their discussions about how they chose and created PowerPoint presentations, mentioning color, size, fonts, layout, and design. In another study, he looked at the role of images in political advertising. Pupils began by responding to particular pictures in Browne's picture book, *Zoo*, noting representational, interactive, and compositional elements. They then created their own political pamphlets and discussed the images they included (Callow, 2006). Callow's findings from his first study echo those of other researchers on "technoliteracies."

> The key findings from this study show that when working with visual and multimodal texts, particularly in the electronic medium, students need to understand not only technical skills in manipulating text, image, and color but how these elements work to create meaning. . . . The students in this study showed that they certainly had a strong, if mainly intuitive, visual literacy knowledge in these areas. The question is how to scaffold this initial knowledge. (Callow, 2003)

As this brief section illustrated, with new technologies constantly developing, there is a huge potential for research on texts that involve modes from different types of media. Mackey (2003b) set out some of the challenges for this research, for example,

> Researchers must also find ways to accommodate interpretive phenomena such as the unique text (e.g., a singular reading of a hypertext, an individual instantiation of a computer game) and the collective text (e.g., a chatroom discussion of the details of a movie or television program). Such examples offer challenges concerning both how to record and how to assess interpreters' experiences of text in such situations.

Yet, even as new forms of technology are explored, Mackey (2003b) reminded us that "an emphasis on context or on particulars of decoding also must not overwhelm the intensely private and interior meaning making that is at the heart of reading."

DRAWING CONCLUSIONS

What is most striking about research on response to visual and multimodal texts in the past couple of decades is the wide range of texts studied and how researchers are struggling to keep up with new technologies and to adapt methodologies when considering these developments. The multimodal aspects of new texts, the multiliterate experiences children bring to their reading and writing (as well as to drawing and other creative responses) and the diverse cultural backgrounds of many children in English speaking countries today means that most research on response involves qualitative methods, although Yannicopoulou's (2004) study was an example of how a quantitative survey can be useful as an initial step.

Populations involved in these studies are usually either individuals or small groups of children and the setting is usually the classroom, although exploration of some new media, such as computer games, is also taking place at home. The multimodal texts involved in the research are usually contemporary picture books or new media texts from popular culture. Research is conducted by either a teacher or a participant observer who initially shares the children's reading. Data is gathered through semistructured interviews, group discussions, retellings, dramatic reenactments, or visual art. Categories used to analyze the data usually arise from the data itself and are based on a variety of theories, from linguistics to literary criticism and aesthetics.

Interestingly, despite the differences in terms of the texts, the population and the methodologies involved in these studies, there are many similarities in the findings and conclusions. First and foremost are the observations on the strength of the engagement, satisfaction, and pleasure of the reader-viewers with most of the texts they are confronted with. This occurs especially once the children found a "way" into the text, either through empathy, particular visual details, or a sudden realization about meaning. Studies show how many children forged emotional bonds with the texts as they connected with experiences from their own lives. The underlying excitement comes across through the transcripts of their engaged discussion, video, and field notes of their gestures and other physical reactions and a realization of the potential of children's own multimodal creations in response to these texts.

Other findings, common to many of the reviewed studies, can be listed as follows, from seemingly obvious points (but often not taken into account in the classroom) to more crucial factors:

- Researchers stress the need for enough time for both teachers and students, to look closely at the texts in question, to reread, to go back and forth between images (rereading should not be seen as a failure in understanding, but as a necessary activity for the confirming of hunches).
- Studies show that responses to the visual aspects of texts sometimes go unnoticed as teachers tend to focus on the verbal aspects of texts.
- The text knowledge which children bring from outside school should be taken into account in order to make the interaction with classroom knowledge possible.
- Children from culturally diverse backgrounds bring their own experiences to the texts and may have difficulties with intertextual references or culturally specific features; however, their comments can be just as insightful as any of their peers.
- Inexperienced readers of print can become successfully engaged through visual aspects of texts which in turn can help them develop reading skills.
- Talk and discussion becomes a scaffolding activity, whether it occurs between children and their peers, teachers, or the researchers; it is recognized as a major factor in encouraging and helping participants to make more connections and arrive at better understandings of the texts in question.
- Providing or expanding the terms or metalanguage to discuss visual aspects is crucial to developing better understanding of the texts (this means teachers also need to be familiar with such language).
- An understanding of the interaction between word and image (and any other modes that appear in the texts) gives the reader insights into the creation of picture books and other works of visual art.

- Visual responses, in the form of drawings or virtual creations, are an important source of information for the researcher and should be taken into account together with oral and written responses.
- Multimodal texts allow for more collaborative meaning making; the reader/viewer is often put in the position of a "coauthor" and forced to engage more fully with the texts; they also encourage the reader/viewers to adopt a questioning stance, to keep an open mind, to tolerate ambiguity, to make intertextual connections, to predict and revise hypothesis, and to use other interpretive strategies, all of which leads to critical thinking and meaningful learning.

MULTIPLE PATHWAYS: WHERE DO WE GO FROM HERE?

Bringing together studies on response shows the sheer range, diversity, and possibilities of research in this field, as well as what can be achieved in the classroom. Although the overall results from the studies mentioned above are encouraging in terms of the way in which participants were motivated to engage with a range of texts and the way in which most of them developed deeper understandings of them, this overview also throws up questions about certain problematic research issues which need to be addressed. In the first place, the term *reader response* has its detractors within the field of literary criticism from which it originally sprung. Wolfgang Iser's (1978) theory of textual "gaps" that need to be filled in by readers active in the assembling of the text's meaning is now almost taken as a "given" when discussing interaction between readers and texts.

Feminist, poststructuralist, and other critics have pointed out the problems with reader-response theory, such as the fact that it mostly ignores social, cultural, and ideological issues (e.g., Gilbert, 1987). From a more pedagogical stance, both Louise Rosenblatt (1990) and Meek (1990) took issue with Iser (1978) because they saw him as talking about the experience of a privileged, critical reader rather than the experience of a developing, emotionally engaged reader. Another problem related to this point is that when trying to find out more about readers' responses to multimodal texts, researchers obtain only a fragment of what goes on during the reading process which, in turn, is subject to the ability of the readers to express their thoughts and feelings.[5]

It is worth noting that within this tradition, "reader response" is taken to refer exclusively to the printed word. Response to the visual elements requires, as many have suggested, not only a different language but also a different approach to the printed word given the complex relationship between these two aspects. Perhaps we now need a different term that incorporates viewing, reading, and responding to other multimodal aspects of the new texts for children.

Another aspect of this type of research that needs a closer look is the way data has been classified and analyzed. Many studies are not clear enough about how this was done, and in some cases, little account seems to be taken of other researchers' attempts to categorize response. Many of the categories suggested by researchers are similar and these could be built on to enhance the metalanguage necessary to discuss visual and multimodal texts. Finally, it is important to include categories that emerge from the discussion of issues such as marketing and ideology.

With respect to classroom practice, it is clear that in order to carry out activities with multimodal texts, teachers need to be familiar with a wide range of them and have some knowledge of how they work and how they can be used with students. It has often been pointed out that teachers do not generally have enough time to invest in small group discussions or individual sessions. In countries like England, they are constrained by a National Curriculum and Primary National Strategy, which, until recently, took little account of the visual or the multimodal. Media studies and ICT may be taught separately with little or no connection to language and literature. However, the tide began to change at the end of the 1990s with the publication of *All Our Futures: Creativity, Culture and Education* (Department for Education and Employment, 1999), which promoted visual literacy and encouraged teachers to foster children's creativity through the arts. This was followed by *More Than Words 1 & 2* (QCA/UKLA, 2004; 2005) in a similar vein. Such publications offered teachers some guidance and inspiration for probing children's responses to multimodal texts in the classroom. It is to be hoped that lessons on visual literacy will not become part of another checklist or set of skills to be acquired, but rather remain questioning, open and subject to change.

Assessment of visual literacy is another problematic issue because children's responses cannot often be easily quantified in order to provide a "grade." Unsworth, Thomas, and Bush (2004) reported on a study that analyzed literacy tests in New South Wales involving questions about the comprehension of images. They concluded that "while recent syllabus documents require the teaching of 'viewing' or the reading of images, there is a paucity of research-based theoretical frameworks to guide the teaching and assessment of students' understanding of how images contribute to the interpretive possibilities of texts" (Unsworth, Thomas & Bush, 2004). They suggested developing models of image/text relationships and generating "questions that will indicate how young readers are accessing the range of image/text relationships entailed in such a model in their comprehension of different types of reading materials." As the importance of reading images in the curriculum is more widely recognized, more research on the subject of how this skill is assessed would be valuable.

Meek (1990) felt there was a need to "problematize" reading by asking questions like "What counts as response?" and "What part does my response to their responses play in their understanding of what they are doing *when* they read?" (p. 2). She said teachers and researchers should be aware that

> Response, then, can never be singular; it is always multiple, layered, combining understanding and affect, involving mental images and gestures for which the surface feature of words always seems inadequate. For me, and for the children I know, responses are other *versions*, rediscoveries, sets of possibilities, hazards, risks, a change of consciousness, a social interaction. (Meek, 1990, p. 10)

Awareness of all of these difficulties in researching children's responses to multimodal texts might encourage a more careful interpretation of the data obtained. The possibilities for further studies on

[5] For these reasons Michael Benton (2004) described reader response as the "Loch Ness Monster of literary studies;" however, he concluded that "reader-response criticism accommodates both the reader and the text; there is no area of literary activity where this is more necessary than in the literature that defines itself by reference to its young readership" (p. 124).

multimodal texts are endless, for academic researchers, teachers, and students. It remains one of the best ways of engaging and developing in all of us that skill sought after by artists, teachers, and researchers alike—"the child's eye-view."

REFERENCES

Anderson, H., & Styles, M. (Eds.). (2000). *Teaching through texts: Promoting literacy through popular and literary texts in the primary classroom*. London: Routledge.

Anning, A., & Ring, K. (2004). *Making sense of children's drawings*. Maidenhead, U.K.: Open University Press.

Anstey, M. (2002). More than cracking the code: Postmodern picture books and new literacies. In M. Anstey & G. Bull (Eds.), *Crossing the boundaries* (pp. 87–105). Frenchs Forest, Australia: Pearson Education.

Anstey, M., & Bull, G. (2000). *Reading the visual: Written and illustrated children's literature*. Sydney, Australia: Harcourt.

Arizpe, E., & Styles, M. (2003). *Children reading pictures: Interpreting visual texts*. London: Routledge Falmer.

Baddeley, P., & Eddershaw, C. (1994). *Not so simple picture books: Developing responses to literature with 4–12 year olds*. Stoke-on-Trent, U.K.: Trentham Books.

Bader, B. (1976). *American picture books: From Noah's ark to the beast within*. New York: Macmillan.

Bearne, E. (Ed.). (1995). *Greater expectations: Children reading writing*. London: Cassell.

Bearne, E. (2003a). Ways of knowing; ways of showing—towards an integrated theory of text. In M. Styles & E. Bearne (Eds.), *Art, narrative and childhood* (pp. ix–xxvi). Stoke-on-Trent, U.K.: Trentham Books.

Bearne, E. (2003b). Playing with possibilities: Children's multidimensional texts. In E. Bearne, H. Dombey & T. Grainger (Eds.), *Interactions in language, literacy and the classroom* (pp. 129–143). Milton Keynes, U.K.: Open University Press.

Bearne, E. (2005). Multimodal texts: What they are and how children use them. In J. Evans (Ed.), *Literacy moves on: Popular culture, new technologies and critical literacy in the elementary classroom* (pp. 16–30). London: Heinemann.

Bearne, E., Ellis, S., Graham, L., Hulme, P., Meiner, J., & Wolstencroft, H. (2005). *More than words: Multimodal texts in the classroom*. London: Qualifications and Curriculum Authority/United Kingdom Literacy Association.

Bennett, J. (1982). *Learning to read with picture books*. Stroud, U.K.: Thimble Press.

Benton, M. (2004). Reader-response criticism. In P. Hunt (Ed.), *International companion encyclopedia of children's literature* (2nd ed., Vol. I, pp. 112–128). London: Routledge.

Bissex, G. L. (1980). *Gnys at work: A child learns to read and write*. Cambridge, MA: Harvard University Press.

Bradford, C. (1993). The picture book: Some postmodern tensions. *Papers: Explorations in Children's Literature, 4*, 10–14.

Bromley, H. (1996a). Spying on picture books: Exploring intertextuality with young children. In V. Watson & M. Styles (Eds.), *Talking pictures* (pp. 101–111). London: Hodder and Stoughton.

Bromley, H. (1996b). 'Madam! Read the scary book, Madam'—the emergent bilingual reader. In V. Watson & M. Styles (Eds.), *Talking pictures* (pp. 136–144). London: Hodder and Stoughton.

Bromley, H. (2000). 'Never be without a Beano!': Comics, children and literacy. In H. Anderson & M. Styles (Eds.), *Teaching through texts: Promoting literacy through popular and literary texts in the primary classroom* (pp. 29–42). London: Routledge.

Browne, A. (1994). Making picture books. In M. Styles, E. Bearne, & V. Watson (Eds.), *The prose and the passion* (pp. 176–198). London: Cassell.

Buckingham, D. (1993) *Children talking television: The making of television literacy*. London: Falmer Press.

Buckingham, D. (1996). *Moving images: Understanding children's emotional responses to television*. Manchester, U.K.: Manchester Univesity Press.

Buckingham, D. (2000). *After the death of childhood*. Cambridge, U.K.: Polity Press.

Buckingham, D., & Bragg, S. (2004). *Young people, sex, and the media: The facts of life?* Basingstoke, U.K.: Palgrave Macmillan.

Bull, G. (2002). The postmodern picture book: its place in post-literate pedagogy. In M. Anstey & G. Bull (Eds.), *Crossing the boundaries* (pp. 49–64). Frenchs Forest, Australia: Pearson Education.

Callow, J. (2003). Talking about visual texts with students. *Reading Online*, 6. Retrieved September 27, 2005, from http://www.readingonline.org/articles/art_index.asp?HREF=callow/index.html

Callow, J. (2006). Images, politics and multiliteracies: Using a visual metalanguage. *Australian Journal of Language and Literacy, 29*.

Callow, J., & Zammit, K. (2002). Visual literacy: From picture books to electronic texts. In M. Monteith (Ed.), *Teaching primary literacy with ICT* (pp. 188–201). Buckingham, U.K.: Open University Press.

Cliff Hodges, G., Styles, M., & Drummond, M. J. (Eds.). (2000). *Tales, tellers and texts*. London: Cassell.

Colledge, M. (2005). Baby Bear or Mrs. Bear? Young English Bengali-speaking children's responses to narrative picture books at school. *Literacy, 39*, 24–30.

Coulthard, K. (2003). *Image conscious: Bilingual learners responding to visual texts*. London: LcaS.

Coulthard, K., Arizpe, E., & Styles, M. (2003). 'Getting inside Anthony Browne's head': Pupils and teachers asking questions and reading pictures. In E. Bearne, H. Dombey, & T. Grainger (Eds.), *Interactions in language, literacy and the classroom* (pp. 77–89). Milton Keynes, U.K.: Open University Press.

Cox, M. (1992). *Children's drawings*. Harmondsworth, U.K.: Penguin.

Crago, H., & Crago, M. (1976). The untrained eye? A preschool child explores Felix Hoffmann's Rapunzel. *Children's Literature in Education, 22*, 135–151.

Day, K. S. (1996). The challenge of style in reading picture books. *Children's Literature in Education, 27*, 153–166.

Department for Education and Employment. (1999). *All our futures: Creativity, culture and education*. Sudbury, U.K.: Author.

Doonan, J. (1986). The object lesson: picturebooks of Anthony Browne. *Word and Image, 2*, 159–172.

Doonan, J. (1991). 'Satoshi Kitamura: Aesthetic dimensions'. *Children's Literature, 19*, 107–137.

Doonan, J. (1993). *Looking at pictures in picture books*. Exeter, U.K.: Thimble Press.

Doonan, J. (1996). The modern picture book. In P. Hunt (Ed.), *International companion encyclopedia of children's literature* (1st ed., pp. 231–241). London: Routledge.

Doonan, J. (1998). Drawing out ideas: A second decade of Anthony Browne. *The Lion and the Unicorn, 23*, 30–56.

Doonan, J. (2000). 'Beware beware': Image, word and apprehension. In G. Cliff Hodges, M. Styles & M. J. Drummond (Eds.), *Tales, tellers and texts* (pp. 102–116). London: Cassell.

Dresang, E. (1999). *Radical change: Books for youth in a digital age*. New York: Wilson.

Evans, J. (1998a). 'Real boys don't go to dance classes': Challenging gender stereotypes. In J. Evans (Ed.), *What's in the picture? Responding to illustrations in picture books* (pp. 96–114). London: Paul Chapman.

Evans, J. (Ed.). (1998b). *What's in the picture? Responding to illustrations in picture books*. London: Paul Chapman.

Evans, J. (Ed.). (2005). *Literacy moves on: Popular culture, new technologies and critical literacy in the elementary classroom*. London: Heinemann.

Fox, G. (1996). Reading picture books . . . how to? In M. Styles, E. Bearne, & V. Watson (Eds.), *Voices off: Texts, contexts and readers* (pp. 157–176). London: Cassell.

Gilbert, P. (1987). Post reader-response: The deconstructive critique. In B. Corcoran & E. Evans (Eds.), *Readers, texts, teachers* (pp. 234–250). Milton Keynes, U.K.: Open University Press.

Graham, J. (1990). *Pictures on the page*. Sheffield, U.K.: NATE.

Graham, J. (1998). Turning the visual into the verbal: Children reading wordless picture books. In J. Evans (Ed.), *What's in the picture? Responding to illustrations in picture books* (pp. 25–43). London: Paul Chapman.

Graham, J. (2004). *Cracking good picture books*. Sheffield, U.K.: NATE.

Gregory, E. (1994). Negotiation as a criterial factor in learning to read in a second language. In D. Graddol, J. Maybin & B. Stierer (Eds.), *Researching language and literacy in social context* (pp. 49–61). Cleveden, U.K.: Open University Press and Multilingual Matters.

Grigg, C. (2003). The painted word: Literacy through art. In M. Styles & E. Bearne (Eds.), *Art, narrative and childhood* (pp. 127–136). Stoke-on-Trent, U.K.: Trentham Books.

Hanlon, T. (2000). The art and the dragon: Intertextuality in the pictorial narratives of Dragon Feathers. In G. Cliff Hodges, M. Styles & M. J. Drummond (Eds.), *Tales, tellers and texts* (pp. 79–94). London: Cassell.

Heath, S. B. (2002). Seeing our way into learning. *Cambridge Journal of Education, 30*, 121–132.

Heath, S. B., & Wolf, S. A. (2004a). *Visual learning in the community school: Art is all about looking: drawing and detail*. London: Creative Partnerships.

Heath, S. B., & Wolf, S. A. (2004b). *Visual learning in the community school: It looks to me as if: talking about picturebooks*. London: Creative Partnerships.

Iser, W. (1978). *The act of reading*. London: Routledge and Kegan Paul.

Jordan, B. (1992). 'Good for any age'—Picture books and the experienced reader. In M. Styles, E. Bearne & V. Watson (Eds.), *After Alice: Exploring children's literature* (pp. 113–125). London: Cassell.

Kiefer, B. (1993). Children's responses to picture books: A developmental perspective. In K. Holland (Ed.), *Journeying: Children responding to literature* (pp. 267–283). London: Heineman.

Kiefer, B. (1995). *The potential of picture books: From visual literacy to aesthetic understanding*. Englewood Cliff, NJ: Merrill.

Kress, G., & Van Leeuwen, T. (2001). *Multimodal discourse*. London: Arnold.

Laycock, L. (1998). A way into a new language and culture. In J. Evans (Ed.), *What's in the picture? Responding to illustrations in picture books* (pp. 79–95). London: Paul Chapman.

Lewis, D. (1990). The constructedness of picture books: picture books and the metafictive. *Signal, 62*, 131–146.

Lewis, D. (1992). Looking for Julius: Two children and a picture book. In K. Kimberley, M. Meek & J. Miller (Eds.), *New readings* (pp. 50–63). London: A & C Black.

Lewis, D. (1996). Going along with Mr. Gumpy: Polysystemy and play in the modern picture book, *Signal, 80*, 105–119.

Lewis, D. (2001). *Reading contemporary picturebooks*. London: Routledge Falmer.

Lewis, D., & Greene, J. (1983). *Your children's drawings—Their hidden meanings*. London: Hutchinson.

Mackey, M. (2002). *Literacies across media: Playing the text*. London: Routledge Falmer.

Mackey, M. (2003a). 'The most thinking book': Attention, performance and the picturebook. In M. Styles & E. Bearne (Eds.), *Art, narrative and childhood* (pp. 101–114). Stoke-on-Trent, U.K.: Trentham Books.

Mackey, M. (2003b, July–September). *Researching new forms of literacy. Reading Research Quarterly*. Retrieved September 27, 2005, from http://reading.org/Library/Retrieve.cfm?D=10.1598/RRQ.38.3.4&F=RRQ-38-3-Hagood-supp_5.html

McClay, J. K. (2000). 'Wait a second . . .': Negotiating complex narratives in Black and White. *Children's Literature in Education, 31*, 91–106.

Madura, S. (1998). An artistic element: Four transitional readers and writers respond to the picture books of Patricia Polacco and Gerald McDermott. *National Reading Conference Yearbook, 47*, 366–376.

Marantz, K., & Marantz, S. (1997). *Multicultural picturebooks: Art for understanding others*. Worthington, OH: Linworth.

Marantz, K., & Marantz, S. (2005). *Multicultural picturebooks: Art for illuminating our world* (2nd ed.). Lanham, MD: Scarecrow Press.

Marsh, J. (Ed.). (2005). *Popular culture, new media and digital literacy in early childhood*. London: Routledge Falmer.

Meek, M. (1988). *How texts teach what readers learn*. Stroud, U.K.: Thimble Press.

Meek, M. (1990). Why response? In M. Hayhoe & S. Parker (Eds.), *Reading and response* (pp. 1–12). Milton Keynes, U.K.: Open University Press.

Michaels, W., & Walsh, M. (1990). *Up and away*. Melbourne, Australia: Oxford University Press.

Mines, H. (2000). *The relationship between children's cultural literacies and their readings of literary texts*. Unpublished doctoral dissertation, University of Brighton, Brighton, U.K.

Nikolajeva, M., & Scott, C. (2000). The dynamics of picturebook communication. *Children's Literature in Education, 31*, 225–239.

Nikolajeva, M., & Scott, C. (2001). *How picturebooks work*. London: Garland.

Nodelman, P. (1988). *Words about pictures: The narrative art of children's picture books*. London: The University of Georgia Press.

Nodelman, P. (1996). Illustration and picture books. In P. Hunt (Ed.), *International companion encyclopedia of children's literature* (1st ed., pp. 113–124). London: Routledge.

Ormerod, J. (1992). The inevitability of transformation: designing picture books for children and adults. In M. Styles, E. Bearne & V. Watson (Eds.), *After Alice: Exploring children's literature* (pp. 42–55) London: Cassell.

Pahl, K. (2005). Narrative spaces and multiple identities: Children's textual explorations of console games in home settings. In J. Marsh (Ed.), *Popular culture, new media and digital literacy in early childhood* (pp. 126–145) London: Routledge Falmer.

Pantaleo, S. (2002). Grade 1 students meet David Wiesner's The Three Pigs. *Journal of Children's Literature, 28*, 72–84.

Pantaleo, S. (2004a). The long, long way: Young children explore the fabula and syuzhet of Shortcut. *Children's Literature in Education, 35*, 1–20.

Pantaleo, S. (2004b). Young children and radical change characteristics in picture books. *The Reading Teacher, 58*, 178–187.

Pantaleo, S. (2005a). Young children engage with the metafictive in picture books [Electronic version]. *Australian Journal of Language and Literacy, 28*, 19–28.

Pantaleo, S. (2005b, Spring). *'Reading' young children's visual texts*. Early Childhood Research & Practice. Retrieved September 27, 2005, from http://ecrp.uiuc.edu/v7n1/pantaleo.html

Purdon, M. (2000). Drawing lessons from Anthony Browne. In H. Anderson & M. Styles (Eds.), *Teaching through texts: Promoting literacy through popular and literary texts in the primary classroom* (pp. 82–93). London: Routledge.

QCA/UKLA. (2004). *More than words: Multimodal texts in the classroom*. London: Author.

QCA/UKLA. (2005). *More than words 2: Creating stories on page and screen*. London: Author.

Rabey, K. (2000). Beyond the text: Metafictive picture-books and sophisticated readers. In H. Anderson & M. Styles (Eds.), *Teaching through texts: Promoting literacy through popular and literary texts in the primary classroom* (pp. 94–102). London: Routledge.

Rosen, M. (1996). Reading The Beano: A young boy's experience. In V. Watson & M. Styles (Eds.), *Talking pictures* (pp. 123–135). London: Hodder & Stoughton.

Rosenblatt, L. (1990). Retrospect. In E. J. Farrell & J. R. Squire (Eds.), *Transactions with literature: A fifty year perspective* (pp. 97–107). Urbana, IL: National Council of Teachers of English.

Roberts, S., & Howard, S. (2005). Watching Teletubbies: Television and its very young audience. In J. Marsh (Ed.), *Popular culture, new media and digital literacy in early childhood* (pp. 91–107). London: Routledge Falmer.

Rowe, A. (1996). Voices off: Reading wordless picture books. In M. Styles, E. Bearne & V. Watson (Eds.), *Voices off: Texts, contexts and readers* (pp. 219–234). London: Cassell.

Schwarcz, J. H. (1982). *Ways of the illustrator: Visual communication in children's literature.* Chicago: American Library Association.

Schwarcz, J. H., & Schwarcz, C. (1991). *The picture book comes of age.* Chicago: American Library Association.

Sharpe, T. (2005). Scaffolding student's responses to picture books. *Literacy Learning: The Middle Years, 13*, i–xii.

Sipe, L. R. (1997). Children's literature, literacy and literary understanding. *Journal of Children's Literature, 23*, 6–19.

Sipe, L. R. (1998). How picture books work: A semiotically framed theory of text-picture relationships. *Children's Literature in Education, 29*, 97–108.

Sipe, L. R. (2000a). The construction of literary understanding by first and second graders in oral response to picture storybook read-alouds. *Reading Research Quarterly, 35*, 252–275.

Sipe, L. R. (2000b). 'Those 2 gingerbread boys could be brothers': How children use intertextual connections during storybook read-alouds. *Children's Literature in Education, 31*, 73–88.

Smith, C. R. (2005). The CD-ROM game: A toddler engaged in computer-based dramatic play. In J. Marsh (Ed.), *Popular culture, new media and digital literacy in early childhood* (pp. 108–125). London: Routledge Falmer.

Stephens, J., & Watson, K. (Eds.). (1994). *From picturebook to literary theory.* Rozelle, Australia: St. Clair Press.

Strangman, N. (2003). *Literary and visual literacy for all: A fourth-grade study of Alice in Wonderland.* Reading Online, 6. Retrieved September 27, 2005, from http://www.readingonline.org/articles/art_index.asp?HREF=voices/edinger/index.html

Styles, M. (1996). 'Inside the tunnel': A radical kind of reading—picture books, pupils and post-modernism. In V. Watson & M. Styles (Eds.), *Talking pictures* (pp. 23–47). London: Hodder & Stoughton.

Styles, M., & Bearne, E. (Eds.). (2003). *Art, narrative and childhood.* Stoke-on-Trent, U.K.: Trentham Books.

Styles, M., Bearne, E., & Watson, V. (Eds.). (1992). *After Alice: Exploring children's literature.* London: Cassell.

Styles, M., Bearne, E., & Watson, V. (Eds.). (1994). *The prose and the passion: Children and their reading.* London: Cassell.

Styles, M., Bearne, E., & Watson, V. (Eds.). (1996). *Voices off: Texts, contexts and readers.* London: Cassell.

Sword, F. (2002). Tell me a picture: Stories in museums. In G. Cliff Hodges, M. Styles & M. J. Drummond (Eds.), *Tales, tellers and texts.* London: Cassell.

Tucker, N. (1974). 'Looking at pictures'. *Children's Literature in Education, 14*, 37–51.

Unsworth, L. (2001). *Teaching multiliteracies across the curriculum.* Buckingham, U.K.: Open University Press.

Unsworth, L., Thomas, A., & Bush, R. (2004). *The role of images and image-text relations in group "Basic Skills Tests" of literacy for children in the primary school years.* Australian Journal of Language and Literacy, 27. Retrieved September 27, 2005, from http://infotrac.galegroup.com/itw/infomark/407/934/74640851w5/purl=rc1_EAIM_0_A136339001&dyn=5!xrn_5_0_A136339001?sw_aep=glasuni

Unsworth, L., Thomas, A., Simpson, A., & Asha, J. (2005). *Children's literature and computer based teaching.* Maidenhead, U.K.: Open University Press.

Walsh, M. (2000). Text-related variables in narrative picture books: Children's responses to visual and verbal texts. *The Australian Journal of Language and Literacy, 23*, 139–156.

Walsh, M. (2003). 'Reading' pictures: what do they reveal? Young children's reading of visual texts. *Reading, 37*, 123–130.

Waterland, L. (1985). *Read with me.* Stroud, U.K.: Thimble Press.

Watson, V. (1993). Multi-layered texts and multi-layered readers. *Cambridge Journal of Education, 23*, 15–24.

Watson, V. (1996a). Her family's voices: One young reader tuning into reading. In V. Watson & M. Styles (Eds.), *Talking pictures* (pp. 112–122). London: Hodder & Stoughton.

Watson, V. (1996b). The left-handed reader: linear sentences and unmapped pictures. In V. Watson & M. Styles (Eds.), *Talking pictures* (pp. 145–163). London: Hodder & Stoughton.

Watson, V. (1996c). Small portable galleries: The picture books of Satoshi Kitamura. In M. Styles, E. Bearne & V. Watson (Eds.), *Voices off: Texts, contexts and readers* (pp. 235–247). London: Cassell.

Watson, V., & Styles, M. (Eds.). (1996). *Talking pictures.* London: Hodder & Stoughton.

Wolf, S. A., & Heath, S. B. (1992). *The braid of literature: Children's worlds of reading.* London: Harvard University Press.

Yannicopoulou, A. (2004). Visual aspects of written texts: Preschoolers view comics [Electronic version]. *Educational Studies in Language and Literature, 4*, 169–181.

•37•

READING THE ART OF THE PICTUREBOOK

Barbara Kiefer
THE OHIO STATE UNIVERSITY

Experiences with picturebooks play a major role in the daily lives of many young children. The child, sitting on an adult's lap and held in a warm embrace, is likely to be engaged socially, intellectually and emotionally as the pages of the book are turned and as the book is returned to again and again. We know that early book-reading experiences positively influence language and concept acquisition (Bruner, J. & Senechal, M., 1997). In addition to the impact of book reading on language and cognition, we must also consider the emotional power of picturebook reading experiences. Children don't just learn from books; they learn to love books. (Butler, 1980) The interplay of intellect and emotion, of sign reading and picture appreciation, all enter into the experience that we call picturebook reading.

"Seeing" a picturebook, even for a child, will involve equally complex meanings that are compounded by the fact the picturebooks consist of consecutive images bound between covers, endpapers, and front and back matter.

The title of this chapter, "Reading the Art of the Picturebook" implies complex questions that have to do with seeing. Is seeing different from reading? Is reading the same as experiencing? Are picture storybooks read or experienced differently than picturebook nonfiction? Researchers in the fields of semiotics, aesthetics, and children's response to literature may help to provide answers to (or at least clarify) some of these questions. In this chapter, I will discuss theories and research that may shape the way we "read" the art of the picturebook.

DILEMMAS IN READING AND ART

John Berger (1977) discussed the complexities of the visual in his book, *Ways of Seeing:* "Seeing comes before words. The child recognizes before it can speak" (p. 7). However, even this act is not a simple one. Berger elaborated, "All our lives, seeing establishes our place in the surrounding world. . . . The relationship between what we see and what we know is never settled" (p. 7).

To Berger, if we view a painting, we view it not just as what it says to us but "what it is" (p. 21). Berger used DaVinci's "Virgin of the Rocks" as an example. If we view the painting hanging in the National Gallery in London, we may see it as a painting of a mother and children, or we may see it as a spiritual or religious experience. We may see it as one of very few paintings created by a master artist, or we may see it from the perspective of history of the Renaissance. We may also see it as the original work of a reproduction we have seen in countless books, or as an object worth millions of dollars. Even the idea that we are seeing an "original" work of art is not assured as the Louvre Museum also claims the National Gallery has a copy of its own original "Virgin of the Rocks."

WHAT IS A PICTUREBOOK?

When we speak of today's picturebooks, we generally assume that the book is a combination of image and idea, that the implied "reader" is a child, and that the child's experience with the book will be influenced by both the words and the images within. In her introduction to *American Picturebooks: From Noah's Ark to the Beast Within* (1976), Bader defined a picturebook as,

> text, illustrations, total design; an item of manufacture and a commercial product; a social, cultural, historical document; and foremost an experience for a child. As an art form it hinges on the interdependence of pictures and words, on the simultaneous display of two facing pages, and on the drama of the turning page. (p. 1)

Any book with such a format can be included under the umbrella term picturebook. A picturebook might be an alphabet book, a counting book, a concept book, a picture storybook, or a nonfiction book. A picturebook can also be wordless. In most cases, a child's reading of a picturebook involves written (or spoken) language and pictorial images. Our understanding of children's reading of and their responses to picturebooks is complicated by the dual nature of the two systems and their interaction over the sequence of turning pages that Bader described. Theorists from the fields of linguistics (de Saussure, Peirce, Barthes), anthropology, (Lévi-Strauss), aesthetics (Langer), art history (Gombrich), and psychology (Arnheim) have contributed to current understandings of "reading" picturebooks. Their work has influenced current thinking in the fields of semiotics, transmediation, systemic functional grammar, and aesthetics that enhance our awareness of the potential for meaning making, which occurs in a child's experience with a picturebook.

PERSPECTIVES FROM SEMIOTIC THEORY

Semiology (Saussure, 1916) sought to define the ways in which signs mean. Barthes (1967) stated that "semiology aims to take in any system of signs, whatever their substance and limits; images, gestures, musical sounds, objects and the complex associations of all of these, which form the content of ritual, convention and public entertainment; these constitute if not languages at least systems of signification" (p. 9). The field of semiotics, then, has influenced systems of analysis that can inform our understanding how children might read the art of the picturebook.

Walter Moebius (1986) was one of the first to apply semiotic theory to a system of categories for understanding the meanings of images in picturebooks. These include "codes of position, size and diminishing return"; "codes of perspective"; "codes of the frame, the right and the round"; "codes of line and capillarity"; and "the code of colour." According to Moebius, codes of position revolve around the size of a subject and its position on the page. Codes of perspective include the presence or absence of a horizon and the contrast between two-dimensional or three-dimensional depiction. Framing, boxing, or otherwise enclosing an image, accounts for a third way of reading the illustrations. The use of lines—curving or jagged, parallel, or at angles—can also be decoded, as can the presence or absence of crosshatching (short overlapping pen strokes). Finally, Moebius reminded us of the psychological meanings we attribute to color hue and intensity. Using *Where the Wild Things Are* by Maurice Sendak (1963) as an example, Moebius showed that according to the "code of position," characters on the left-hand side of the page are in a more secure position. In *Where The Wild Things Are*, Max is shown on the right-hand side as he makes mischief and is punished. It is not until he arrives at the island of Wild Things that he moves to the left-hand side of the double-page spread. The codes of the frame, and of the "right and the round" help us to understand that at the beginning of the book, Max's' universe expands from the small framed picture of himself in a room to the unframed double spread of himself in the place where the Wild Things live" (p. 141). Using the "codes of line and capillarity," Moebius demonstrated how the intense crosshatched lines (capillarity) indicate the nervous energy of Max's psychological state in the book's early pages. As Max gains control of the Wild Things, these lines give way to larger areas of pure painted washes.

In *Words About Pictures* (Nodelman, 1988) and *The Pleasures of Children's Literature* (Nodelman & Reimer, 2003), Nodelman provided a thoroughly developed scheme for how pictures provide information about stories. He included the categories of "Format and first impressions"—how the cover image, the size of the book, the endpapers, and so on, provide information. A second category titled "Mood and Atmosphere" described how elements of art such as the use of color, shape, line, and the choice of original artistic media affects our understanding of the story. The "style" of the illustrations—Surrealistic, Impressionistic, national styles, and individual artists' styles—comprise a third category of meaning, and "the meanings of visual objects" such as symbols, and cultural codes, gestures, and postures of characters comprise a fourth category. Like Moebius (1986), Nodelman (1988, 2003) discussed two- and three-dimensional pictorial codes but provided a more detailed analysis of the possible dimensions of each. Under the category of "two-dimensional effects," Nodelman included the use of shapes, size, and location of objects in the composition, the relationships of figure and ground, the placement of characters on the left or right, top or bottom of the page, and the use of color to draw attention to objects. "Three-dimensional effects" include the use of techniques of perspective, point of view, focus, overlap, light sources, and shadow blocking to create meanings for objects in pictures. Finally, Nodelman showed how a single picture can convey "movement and time" by the use of incomplete actions, linear continuance, distortion, left to right movement, the ongoing continuous narrative of the book, the context in a single picture, and the context of other pictures in relation to that picture. Nodelman also suggested that the relationship between pictures and text is always an ironic one; that is, "the words tell us what the pictures do not show, and the pictures show us what the words do not tell us" (1988, p.222). He argued, for example, that,

> When words and pictures combine, irony emerges from the way in which the incompleteness of each is revealed by the differing incompleteness of the other. The theoretically "fierce bad rabbit" in Beatrix Potter's book of that name looks soft and cuddly, anything but the evil creature that the text refers to. (p. 223)

Nodelman's reading of *Where the Wild Things Are* meshed with Moebius's, although his categories may be structured differently. Nodelman showed how changes in the pattern and color of Max's bedspread from first picture to the last is indicative of Max's changing mood. Nodelman showed how the category of size is put to use to highlight Max's figure among the Wild Things. Although he is small, Max is the only human among the many Wild Things. He also argued that Sendak uses color to imply "a connection between the moon and Max's wild dance . . . by making the moon and Max the only white objects in the pictures" (Nodelman, 1988, p. 291).

More recently, researchers (Kress, 2000; Kress & van Leeuwen, 1996; Lemkie, 1998) have begun to think of 21st-century literacy in "multimodal" terms. Today's children do not "read" only printed words in books but multiplicities of images and words in forms and formats that go far beyond the book. Working out of M.A.K. Halliday's (1985) system of functional grammar as a resource for making meaning, these researchers have developed a grammar that can be applied to images. This grammar is comprised of three main branches: (a) representational/ideational structures, (b) interactive/interpersonal structures, and (c) compositional/textual means. Although their work has focused as much on visual material in nonfiction (textbooks, advertising, Web pages), it can also be applied to the reading of images in picturebooks (Lewis, 2001; Unsworth, 2001). Unsworth described in detail the types of images within each of the three main branches of meaning making. Under the category of "Representational Structures," Unsworth included images that show events; visual representations of concrete, mental and verbal events; images that classify; images that show part-whole relationships; concrete and abstract representation in images; timelines; and symbolic images. Within the category of "Interaction," Unsworth included visual demands and offers; social distance (close ups, medium, and long shots); attitude (perspective and involvement or detachment); power (high-angle, low-angle and eye-level views); realism, (color, context, detail, depth, and light); objective images (cutaways, cross-sections, and explosions); and coding orientation (what counts as real?). A third category of "Composition" focused on the actual layout or composition of a double-page spread and included the information value of left and right, top and bottom, the use of center or margin layouts, the framing of the image, and the salience of the image. These last two categories corresponded most closely to previous schemes suggested by Nodelman and Moebius. For example, Unsworth suggested that, in Sendak's *Where the Wild Things Are*, the notion of power is shown by the changing angle or direction of view. We feel superior to Max when he is punished and sent to his bedroom, because our angle of view is downward. When he sails out of his room, our angle of view is suddenly forced upward, indicating that Max is now in charge of his situation. Moreover, this is the only scene in the book where Max makes a visual demand on the viewer by looking straight out of the picture page. By the end of the book, Max is once more viewed at a downward angle, indicating a return to normalcy.

Although the semiotic schemes just described can be useful in analyzing the content of illustrations, they do not go very far in showing how pictures and words work together within a picturebook. Several researchers have posited structures that allow us to look more closely at this interaction that some call the "iconotext." (Hallberg, cited in Nikaolajeva, & Scott, 2001). Golden (1990) suggested that there are five basic types of interaction that exist between picture and words in picture storybooks. These included (a) books where the text and pictures are symmetrical; (b) books in which the text depends on pictures for clarification; (c) books in which the illustrations enhance and elaborate the text; (d) books in which the text carries the primary narrative and illustrations are selective; and (e) books in which the illustrations carry the primary narrative and the text is selective.

Nikaolajeva and Scott (2001) provided a scheme for examining book types that exist along a continuum from word to image. Within this continuum, they identify five categories that are similar to Golden's (1990). These include (a) a "symmetrical" picturebook that has two mutually redundant narratives; (b) a "complementary" picturebook that has words and pictures that fill each other's gaps; and (c) an "expanding" or "enhancing" picturebook that has a visual narrative supporting the verbal narrative and, in turn, a verbal narrative that depends on the visual narrative; (d) a "counterpointing" picturebook has two mutually dependent narratives; and (e) a "sylleptic" picturebook has two or more narratives independent of each other. Nikaolajeva and Scott also asked, "Whose book is it ?" and argued that the context is affected by whether a book is authored and illustrated by different people or whether a book is authored and illustrated by the same person. They then proceed to an analysis of how pictures and text work together to create setting; characterization; narrative perspective; time and movement; mimesis and modality (literal and symbolic representation); figurative language, metafiction, and intertext (ways that picturebooks play with expectations about images and words); and picturebook paratexts (covers, endpapers etc.). Nikaolajeva and Scott demonstrated how the time and movement is developed in Sendak's *Where the Wild Things Are*. Max's two voyages, from left to right, and home again from right to left "are based on the way we perceive certain visual patterns as harmonious or disharmonious" (p. 155). Nikaolajeva and Scott also showed how words and pictures set up competing interpretations of mimesis, whether the story is literal or metaphorical. Is Max's journey one of a few minutes of time out in imagination (his supper is still hot at the end of the book)? Or does Max's journey really take place (the moon changes from a sliver to full over the course of the book)?

Sipe (1998) described the relationship between text and pictures as "synergistic" and proceeded to apply the concept of transmediation (Suhor, 1984; Siegel, 1995). Sipe provided a think-aloud reading of the words and pictures in one double-page spread of Maurice Sendak's *Where The Wild Things Are* to demonstrate the interplay that occurs between pictures and words and to show how that transaction becomes more complex as we read through the book: "Each new page opening presents us with a new set of words and new illustrations to factor into our construction of meaning" (p. 106). Sipe (1998) also argued that "visual texts are on an equal footing with verbal texts" (p. 107) in this process.

AESTHETIC READINGS OF PICTUREBOOKS

Although semiotic understandings of verbal/pictorial relationships might help us to "decode" a particular picturebook, such schemes do not account fully for a reader's aesthetic response, nor can they account for the excellence of one book over another in eliciting a deep response. The content of pictures that function almost as captions in a book may be no less effective in evoking a rich intellectual and emotional response than a book in which the pictures are absolutely necessary to understand the written text.

In most of the semiotic theories just discussed, the picturebook theorists do seem to agree that the picturebook should be defined as an aesthetic rather than a utilitarian object (perhaps with the exception of the work of Kress and van Leeuwen). The term "aesthetics" refers to the branch of philosophy that is concerned with the study of beauty. Kaelin (1989) argued that aesthetics proper "may be thought of as the discipline concerning itself with artistic communication—with the description of creativity of works of art, of artistic appreciation" (p. 71). Because the idea of an aesthetic reading of literature has been critical in the development of reader response theory (Rosenblatt, 1978), this leads us to work on reading the art of the picturebook that has been grounded in aesthetic rather than semiotic theory.

According to Langer (1953),

> Art is the creation of forms symbolic of human feeling. Something emerges from the arrangement of tones or colors which was not there before, and this, rather than the arranged material is the symbol of sentience. The making of this expressive form is the creative process that enlists mans' utmost technical skill in the service of his utmost conceptual power, imagination" (p. 40).

Marantz (1977) insisted that a picturebook is "a unique expressive form that gains its strength from the totality of its making including its paper stock, typography, binding and design" (p. 153). To read a picturebook, then, we must consider not only the content of the message but also how meaning is expressed and understood within that form. It may be useful then to consider the author's and the illustrator's choices as they create meaning in an art object that is a picturebook. To do that, we must consider how written language and visual art are both alike and different.

When considering how meaning is expressed, verbal and visual art have much in common. Both the author and artist have elements that convey that meaning. The author uses sounds and words, the phonetic and morphemic systems of language. The artist uses line, shape, color, value, and texture, the elements of art. Although language may engage the intellect in more precise meanings, it is also place specific. It can only be understood by speakers (and readers) of that language. Art may more readily evoke our emotions, and its elements and symbols are more readily understood across cultures and places. "In addition, both language and art have syntactic and semantic properties. Hellman (1977), for example, explained that we recognize the syntactic properties of art, such as the organization of lines and color, as well as the semantic properties, in which lines and colors evoke metaphors such as quiet, warm or angry. In addition, both authors and artists have principles of organization that they call composition. Aspects of composition like balance, rhythm, and pattern are common to both." (Kiefer, 1995 p. 117)

On the other hand, although both language and visual art have a meaning-expressing potential, the two are not identical and cannot be matched at a word or sentence level. Furthermore, the result of the readers' engagement with visual and verbal texts may be very different. Gombrich (1982) argued that although both language and visual images can express, arouse, and describe, the visual image is most effective in evoking emotions. However, it is unable to match "the statement function of language" (p. 138). These strands of communication—expression, arousal, and description—as they are interwoven with words and pictures in a picturebook account for the richness of the tapestry that is reader response.

Several theorists have suggested schemes for appraising the aesthetic values in a picturebook. Doonan (1993) argued that, in order to take an aesthetic stance toward picturebooks, readers need what she called "close looking," an active rather than passive reading of picturebooks. This echoes Rosenblatt's idea of the transaction between reader and text that is necessary with a literary work. Doonan organized such aesthetic reading into three main categories: (a) how the line, shapes, and colors have been set down and organized; (b) the choice of medium and its effect; and (c) what is being shown both literally and expressively. Doonan demonstrated such a reading using two picturebooks, *When Sheep Cannot Sleep* (Kitamura, 1986) and *Cloudy* (King, 1989) and finished with a brief analysis of the final page of *Where the Wild Things Are* (Sendak, 1963), describing Sendak's use of color and line to create tone, movement, texture, and perspective. Doonan showed how the use of muted colors sustains the dreamlike quality of the story. She pointed out Sendak's use of crosshatching lines and their effect of lowering the intensity of the color and creating illusion of depth.

Kiefer (1995) proposed that by defining the style of picturebooks as "a manner of expressing," we could approach a "reading" of picturebooks by looking at stylistic choices of both the author and illustrator. We need to consider the author's word choices, the theme of the book, the motifs and moods, the characters, and the setting and events depicted. We also need to consider the artist's choices of artistic elements, principles, and conventions to convey those meanings visually and how those artistic or stylistic choices have contributed to the overall aesthetic experience of the book. Finally, we need to consider the technical elements or format of book production that can also contribute to our reading of the picturebook. Kiefer proposed three major categories for looking at artistic choices of the illustrator. These were (a) "Design Choices," (b) "Choices of Historical or Cultural Conventions," and (c) "Technical Choices."

Under the category of "Design Choices," Kiefer included the elements of design (line, shape, color value, and texture) and how they convey meaning (Ocvirk, Bone, Stinson, & Wigg, 2005). For example, lines and shapes can convey action or rhythm; they can be strong and solid or diminutive and quick. Colors can convey mood and emotions. The choice of value (the amount of light or dark in a picture) can create highly dramatic meanings if they sharply contrast, or they can convey soothing effects when light in contrast. The artist's choices of these elements can also set up spatial tensions and patterns and depth that affect meaning. The principles of design or composition (balance, rhythm, repetition, variety in unity, eye movement) are also important to the meaning conveyed in the picturebook. We should consider how the artist has chosen to tie individual pages into a complete whole that reinforces the overall meaning of the book by the layout and size of pictures, the ways in which the illustrations carry the eye from page to page, and the way in which page design creates a rhythm in keeping with the meaning of the book.

In a second category, Kiefer also suggested that meaning could be conveyed by the artist's use of pictorial conventions borrowed from styles of art we associate with historical periods or by conventions borrowed from particular cultural groups' history to enhance and extend the meaning of the story or concept. Finally, Kiefer identified the category of technical choices associated with book production such as the artist's choice of original media, end papers, paper stock, typography, the cover and the size of the book, all of which can all affect the readers' aesthetic understanding of the picturebook. Kiefer then went on to show how particular choices from within these three major categories are exemplified in particular picturebooks.

Using Kiefer's framework, a reader might interpret *Where the Wild Things Are* by looking at Sendak's artistic choices. The shape of the book is horizontal rather than vertical and implies movement over a broad landscape. The cover picture, for example, shows an intriguing and gigantic creature, asleep beside an empty boat. The child reader is immediately invited to coconstruct this story by asking such questions as, "Who was in the boat? Is this monster scary?" The bold black letters of the title and author's name seem to offer stability and a reassuring answer. In addition, the monster is captured within the lines of type and by the white space of the borders. This monster is not likely to enter the child's world, just his imagination. The end papers, full of lush leaves seen through a screen of crosshatching lines, burst with energy and invite entry into the book. These forms are not the vegetation of the everyday world, however; they evoke an unfamiliar world and imply that something magical may be at work. Kiefer would agree with Doonan that Sendak's use of soft, muted watercolor washes over line drawings evokes a sense of unreality or mystery throughout the book. The crosshatched lines set up emotional tensions that ebb and flow across the pages. Sendak used curving shapes to create movement within each picture and to move our eye across each page. Also significant here is the layout of each double-page spread and the rhythm that is created as we proceed through the book. The small size of the early single-page pictures reflects the disciplinary reins placed on Max by his mother. As he sets off on his imaginary journey, those pictures break out of their rectangular white borders and grow out to the edges of the single page. They then begin to grow across the double-page spread until Max arrives upon his island. When the wild rumpus starts, there is no longer a need for white space or words at all. The three double-page spreads create the visual equivalent of three booming drumbeats, and the pictures fill the space just as sounds of the wild rumpus must fill the air. We know the book has reached a climax of excitement here because on the next double-page spread the picture begins to shrink, and white space and words reappear. Max returns home to his room on the last page, but he is not the same child. Sendak removed the white border and sharp edge that began Max's adventure and leaves him on the right-hand page in a full bleed (the picture extends to the edge of the page). Finally, Sendak borrowed painterly conventions from the work of French painter Henri Rousseau whose stylistic landscapes also evoke a magical, other-worldly air. It is unlikely that a young child would make that connection in early reading. However, it is quite possible that years in the future that child may encounter a painting of Henri Rousseau and bring the memory of *Where The Wild Things Are* to that viewing, a synergy (Sipe, 1998) of the most delightful kind.

POTENTIALS IN READING THE ART OF THE PICTUREBOOK

In this chapter, I have tried to present an overview of approaches to reading pictures and understanding the meanings in picturebooks. Although they are constructed from different theoretical bases, for the most part, these theories compliment each other, leading us to an appreciation of the complexity of the art of the picturebook. Among the two major approaches to analysis of illustrations, there are several areas of divergence. Semiotic readers seem to agree that the left-hand side of the page represents a more secure position. How does this notion conflict with or support the artist's need to move the eye to the right to turn the pages and proceed through the book? How then do we interpret picturebooks where the written text is always on the left and the picture on the right, as in Chris Van Allsburg's *Jumanji* (1981)? Semiotic readings also suggest that looking up an object from a worm's-eye view places the viewer in a submissive position while looking down on a scene from above puts the reader in a position of power (Unsworth, 2001). How does this notion fit with Van Allsburg's changing points of view in *Jumanji*? Is the artist's desire to create visual rhythm in the composition in the book supported or contradicted by semiotic explanations? Questions such as these open up interesting additional questions for future research.

Furthermore, an understanding of the various approaches to picturebook reading can help teachers understand the rich complexity of an art object that many might think of as simplistic or just for children. Appreciating the possibilities for meaning making in both text and pictures, teachers can give children the time and space to look, listen and read. They can also consider how they might open up these responses through active discussion and authentic artistic responses.

Marantz (1977) believed that "art objects are important because they have the potential for producing a transcendental experience, a state of mind where new and personal meanings can take shape" (p. 151). This, I believe, is the essence of the aesthetic experience possible as a result of a good picturebook.

REFERENCES

Barthes, R. (1967). *Elements of semiology* (A. Lavers, & C. Smith Trans.). London: Jonathon Cape.

Berger, J. (1977). *Ways of seeing*. London: Penguin.

Bruner, J., & Senechal, M. (1997). The differential effect of storybook reading on preschoolers' acquisition of expressive and receptive vocabulary. *Journal of Child Language, 24*, 123–138.

Butler, D. (1980). *Cushla and her books*. Boston: The Horn Book.

de Saussure, F. (1974). *Course in general linguistics* (W. Baskin Trans.). London: Fontana Collins. (Original work published 1916)

Doonan, J. (1993). *Looking at pictures in picture books*. London: Thimble Press.

Golden, J. M. (1990). *The narrative symbol in children's literature: Exploration in the construction of text*. Berlin, Germany: Mouton, 93–119.

Gombrich, E. H. (1982). *The image and the eye: Further studies in the psychology of pictorial representation*. Ithaca, NY: Cornell University Press.

Halliday. M. A. K. (1985). *An introduction to functional grammar*. London: Edward Arnold.

Hellman, G. (1977). Symbol systems and artistic styles. *Journal of Aesthetics and Art Criticism*, 35.

Kaelin, E. F. (1989). *An aesthetics for art educators*. New York: Teachers College Press

Kiefer, B. (1995). *The potential of picturebooks: From visual literacy to aesthetic understanding*. Englewood Cliffs, NJ: Merrill/Prentice Hall.

King, D. (1989). *Cloudy*. London: Hutchinson.

Kitamura, S. (1986). *When sheep cannot sleep*. London: A. & C. Black.

Kress, G. (2000). Multimodality. In B. Cope, & M. Kalantzis (Eds.), *Multiliteracies: Literacy learning and the design of social futures*. Melbourne, Australia: Macmillan.

Kress, G., & van Leeuwen, T. (1996). *A grammar of visual design*. London: Routledge.

Lacan, J. (1977). *Écrits* (A. Sheridan Trans.). London: Routledge.

Langer, S. K. (1953). *Feeling and form*. New York: Charles Scribner & Sons.

Langer, S. K. (1942). *Philosophy in a new key*. Cambridge, MA.: Harvard University Press.

Lemkie, J. (1998). Multiplying meaning: Visual and verbal semiotics in scientific text. In J. R. Martin, & R. Veel (Eds.), *Reading science: Critical and functional perspectives on discourses of science*. London: Routledge.

Lévi-Strauss, C. (1972). *Structural anthropology* (C. Jacobsen, & B. G. Schoepf Trans.). Harmondsworth, U.K.: Penguin.

Lewis. D. (2001). *Reading contemporary picturebooks*. New York: Routledge.

Marantz, K. (1977). The picturebook as art object: A call for balanced reviewing. *The Wilson Library Bulletin*, 148–151.

Moebius, W. (1986). Introduction to picture book codes. *Word and Image, 2*, 141–151.

Nikaolajeva, M., & Scott C. (2001). *How picturebooks work*. New York: Garland.

Nodelman, P. (1988). *Words about pictures: The narrative art of children's picture books*. Athens, GA: University of Georgia Press.

Nodelman, P., & Reimer, M. (2003). *The pleasures of children's literature*. Boston: Allyn and Bacon.

Ocvirk, O. C., Bone, R. O., Stinson, R. E, & Wigg, P. R. (2005). *Art fundamentals: Theory and practice* (10th ed.). New York: McGraw-Hill.

Rosenblatt, L. (1978). *The reader, the text and the poem: The transactional theory of the literary work*. Carbondale, IL. Southern Illinois University Press.

Sendak, M. (1963). *Where the wild things are*. New York: HarperCollins.

Siegel, M. (1995). More than words: The generative power of transmediation for learning. *Canadian Journal of Education, 10*, 455–475.

Sipe, L. R. (1998). How picturebooks work: A semiotically framed theory of text-picture relationships. *Children's Literature in Education, 29*, 97–108.

Suhor, C. (1984). Towards a semiotics-based curriculum. *Journal of Curriculum Studies. 16*, 247–257.

Unsworth, L. (2001). *Teaching multi-literacies across the curriculum: Changing contexts of text and image in classroom practice*. Philadelphia: Open University Press.

Van Allsburg, C. (1981). *Jumanji*. Boston: Houghton Mifflin.

•38•

YOUNG CHILDREN'S VISUAL MEANING MAKING IN RESPONSE TO PICTUREBOOKS

Lawrence R. Sipe
UNIVERSITY OF PENNSYLVANIA

This chapter focuses on theory and research related to how young children (of preschool age through third grade, approximately ages 4 to 8) make sense of, interpret and use visual information in picture storybooks. I also place particular emphasis on children's responses in classroom situations, rather than family settings or other out-of-school research. The chapter deals mainly with children's *talk,* though there is some treatment of children's drawing/painting in response to picturebooks. Almost all of the research studies cited in this chapter are qualitative, descriptive, and interpretive, occurring in naturalistic settings.

The chapter begins with a working definition of picturebooks, reviewing briefly the large amount of theoretical work on picturebooks and sketching some of the theories of text-picture relationships. The chapter continues with a substantial section devoted to research on young children's response to and interpretation of picturebooks, followed by a discussion of teachers' roles in this process. In the last section of the chapter, I address some of the many issues, problems, and questions that necessitate more research in this area.

What is a picturebook? The use of the term "picturebook" as a compound word emphasizes the integral unity of text and illustrations in such books, as well as highlighting that they are cohesive aesthetic wholes. This usage follows such researchers and theorists as Kiefer (1995), Lewis (2001), Nikolajeva and Scott (2001), and Arizpe and Styles (2003). Although there are various types of picturebooks (see Nikolajeva, 2003), the *sine qua non* of a picturebook is the way in which the words of the story give us information that the illustrations omit, while the illustrations convey information that is not in the verbal text of the story. In other words, a picturebook should be distinguished from an illustrated book because, in a picturebook, the pictures are critical in telling the story, and share equally with the words in this task, or may be even more important than the words. In an illustrated book, the pictures certainly add to our enjoyment and pleasure, but are not necessary: we can imagine *The Adventures of Tom Sawyer* without any illustrations (and Mark Twain wrote it as such), but *Where the Wild Things Are* would simply not exist without its visual components. Therefore, the relationship of words and pictures in a picturebook is central and will be outlined in the following section.

LITERARY CRITICISM AND THEORETICAL ANALYSES OF PICTUREBOOKS

Flood and Lapp have observed that "although educators have regularly recognized the importance of picture books in children's language and literacy development, the relationships between the pictures and the words (the language arts and the visual arts) have not yet been fully explored" (1995, p. 9). Theory and research specifically devoted to picturebooks and the ways in which children construct meaning from them have expanded considerably since Flood and Lapp's observation and the publication of the first volume of the *Handbook of Research on Teaching Literacy through the Communicative and Visual Arts* (Flood, Heath, & Lapp, 1997). It seems significant that, in the 1997 *Handbook,* although there were a number of articles devoted to picturebooks, they were all quite brief and placed in the last section, "Voices from the Field," and not intended to be reviews of research or theory. By contrast, in this current volume (published little more than a decade later), in addition to the article you are now reading, there are at least two substantive articles (by Kiefer and by Arizpe and Styles) about picturebooks, demonstrating the growing interest in viewing them as visual aesthetic objects that can teach visual meaning making as well as verbal literacy, and that can help children integrate the knowledge from visual and verbal sign systems into meaningful wholes.

W. J. T. Mitchell (1994) has observed that both academia and popular culture seem to have taken a "pictorial turn" (p. 11) and that, although we still tend to privilege words above visual images, nevertheless the onset of various technologies, including television, cinema, and the Internet and associated digital technologies has at least partially dislodged this complete dominance of the verbal (Kress & van Leeuwen, 1996). The rise of interest in picturebooks—where visual elements are at least as important as words in conveying meaning—can be taken as one small part of this general movement. One indication of this rise in interest by scholars and practitioners is that the number of book-length treatments of picturebooks has burgeoned in the last few decades. Earlier discussions of picturebooks, such as Alderson (1973) and Bader (1976) contained sensitive and insightful readings of individual picturebooks from historical perspectives; and analyses of individual acclaimed picturebooks, such as Lacy's (1986) and Marantz's (1992) close visual readings of the art and design in winners of the Caldecott Medal and other distinguished picturebooks demonstrated a commitment to bringing the traditional principles of visual design (such as line, color, shading, shape, texture, and representation of space) to bear on picturebooks, treating them as sophisticated aesthetic objects. Numerous collections of essays and interviews focus on the work of noteworthy picturebook illustrators (Martin, 1989; Marantz, 1992; Marantz & Marantz, 1992; Stanton, 2005), and critical works on especially prominent illustrators of picturebooks such as Maurice Sendak (Cech, 1995; Kushner, 2003; Lanes, 1980; Sonheim, 1991) highlight their oeuvres by examining their artistic styles, use of visual media, and common themes. This text-focused analysis of picturebooks continues in discussions of collaborations between authors and illustrators (Marcus, 2001). Resources intended for artists who want to illustrate children's books, such as Salisbury (2004), also contain examinations of the relationships of words and visual images and visual design. Moebius (1986) analyzed commonly occurring clusters of conventions in picturebooks, which he calls "codes," for example the code of color: the conventional association of dark colors with sadness, depression, or fear, and bright colors with joy, confidence, or light-heartedness. In a similar way, illustrator Molly Bang's (2000) *Picture This: How Pictures Work* presented the principles of visual design in a way that is accessible to teachers without formal art training. All of these books and articles are useful for educational practitioners and researchers who want to develop their own understanding of the "potential of picturebooks" (Kiefer, 1995).

The first books to focus on theoretical approaches to picturebooks (for example, the complexity of text-picture relationships) were by picturebook illustrators themselves, most notably Schwarcz (1982), Shulevitz (1985), and Schwarcz and Schwarcz (1991). Schwarcz (1982) introduced such terms as "continuous narration," to describe a sequence of pictures on the same page that depicts a series of chronologically related movements or actions. Schwarcz also introduced one of the first descriptions of the types of ways verbal texts may relate to the pictures, for example "congruency" (a harmonious relationship between text and pictures) and "deviation" (where the illustrations "veer away" (p. 15) from the text by opposing it in some way. Nodelman's (1988) *Words About Pictures: The Narrative Art of Children's Picture Books* was one of the first scholarly books to concentrate specifically on picturebook theory. Notable in his discussion of text-picture relationships is the notion of "irony"—that the text and pictures never tell exactly the same story, and are frequently in an ironic relationship with one another (Kümmerling-Meibauer, 1999). Nodelman's work was followed by Graham (1990), Doonan (1993), Kiefer (1995), Stewig (1995), Spitz (1999), Anstey and Bull (2000), Nikolajeva and Scott (2001), Lewis (2001), and Arizpe and Styles (2003). These books, while drawing, like Nodelman, on visual aesthetic theory, theories of visual literacy, and theories of graphic design, are a significant advance in that they not only focus specifically on picturebooks, but also, in most cases, draw on considerable experience with children's responses in educational contexts (Graham, Doonan, Stewig, Anstey, & Bull, and Lewis), or most powerfully, base their discussions on empirical classroom research on children's responses to picturebooks (Kiefer and Arizpe and Styles) to produce grounded theories of children's visual meaning making.

Theorists use various metaphors and concepts to envision the relationship of text and illustrations in picturebooks. Various metaphors are drawn from music; words and pictures are described as being similar to "counterpoint" (Pullman, 1989) and as comprising a duet (Cech, 1983–84), or as having an antiphonal fugue effect (Moss, 1990) on each other. Textile metaphors ("the interweaving of text and pictures") (Moss, 1990, p. 21) are also employed, as well as images from physics and wave theory, using the idea of "interference" in describing how two wave patterns may combine to form a new and more complex pattern (Miller, 1992). Continuing the scientific metaphors, Moebius (1986) referred to the "plate tectonics" of text and illustrations. Lewis used at least two terms, "polysystemy" ("the piecing together of text out of different kinds of signifying systems," (Lewis, 1996, p. 105) and "interanimation" (Lewis, 2001), referring to Margaret Meek's (1992) comment that the pictures and words on a page interanimate each other. Lewis (2001) also proposed that we think of the "ecology" of picturebooks, in terms of the interdependence of text and pictures, as well as the flexibility of the relationships, which can change from page to page. Lewis argued that an ecological view of picturebooks also implies that neither verbal texts nor illustrations are univocal, and that there is a great deal of complexity and almost endless diversity, just as there is in a biological ecosystem. In other words, we are not just talking about text and pictures, but perhaps about a number of different texts and a number of different kinds of pictures, all in a complicated relationship with each other in the same book. Moreover, verbal texts have visual features, such as the size and characteristics of the typeface or illuminated letters, while illustrations may have speech balloons or other incorporated words; thus, the distinction between words and pictures is not completely sharp. As well, some contemporary picturebooks incorporate more than words and pictures, adding movement (in "pop-up" books such as those by Robert Sabuda [2004]); a kinesthetic experience (touching the raised lines of the spider's web in Eric Carle's [1984] *The Very Busy Spider*); sound (Carle, 1999); and twinkling lights (Carle, 1995; Sabuda, 2005). All of these elements convey meaning and function in a complex ecological system of interdependence along with the words and pictures.

Sipe (1998a) argued that "synergy" is a good descriptor of text-picture relationships, because, together the text and pictures produce an effect that is greater than the effect that either would produce alone; he suggested that, in semiotic terms, Suhor's (1984) concept of "transmediation," "the translation of content from one sign system into another" (p. 250) may be key in understanding picturebooks, because readers "must oscillate it were, from the sign system of the verbal text to the sign system of the illustrations; and also in the opposite direction from the illustration sign system to the verbal sign system" (Sipe, 1998a, p. 102): we interpret the pictures in terms of the words, and the words in terms of the pictures, in a dynamic "relaying" (Barthes, 1978) process. A related idea of Nodelman's (1988) was that words and pictures "limit" each other: the words limit the pictures by telling us what is important to notice, out of the many visual details, and the pictures limit the words by providing specificity (for example, in *Snow White* [Grimm & Grimm, 1972] the sentence "At a window with a frame of ebony a queen sat and sewed" is limited by the accompanying illustration, which shows us exactly what that queen looks like). Doonan (1993) suggested that the verbal text drives us to read on in a linear way, whereas the illustrations seduce us into stopping to linger, so there is a recursive and reflexive process in our reading of picturebooks; therefore, they seem to demand rereading and re-viewing.

Theorists also advance various taxonomies of text-picture relationships (Agosto, 1999; Golden, 1990; Lewis, 2001; Nikolajeva & Scott, 2001). Nikolajeva and Scott's (2001) is perhaps one of the most comprehensive and highly articulated. They suggested that there are five different ways in which text and pictures may relate in a picturebook, on a continuum ranging from virtual equivalence of words and pictures (which they term "symmetry") to an absolute "contradiction" between the words and visual images. There are three intermediate steps between these two extremes of the continuum: (a) "complementarity" (words and pictures each contribute independently to one narrative); (b) "enhancement" (words and pictures extend each other's meaning) and (c) "counterpoint" (words and pictures tell different stories, which may be in an ironic relationship to one another). Additional complexity is provided by conceiving these five relationships as functioning "independently on the different levels of the picturebook narrative, such as plot, setting, characterization, perspective, and so on" (Nikolajeva, 2003, p. 238), thus giving us a rather dizzying number of possibilities. For researchers, an important implication of all this theoretical work is that, since readers are continuously shifting back and forth between words and pictures, children's visual meaning making may be frequently in tandem or integrated with their interpretation of the verbal text. Thus, it may be difficult to ascertain whether any particular comment or response is the result of their interpretation of the words or the pictures, since even quite young children have been shown to be capable of engaging in the dynamic process of "translating" from one sign system to the other.

CHILDREN'S INTERPRETATIVE WORK WITH VARIOUS TYPES AND GROUPINGS OF PICTUREBOOKS

In this section, research dealing with children's interpretive responses to various types of picturebooks is reviewed: wordless books or books with scant text; studies of children's responses to groups or sets of related books; research that focuses on particular components of picturebooks; research on postmodern picturebooks, which seem to have particular affordances for children's developing visual meaning making; and the use of visual information for specific purposes. The section ends with an overview of the various typologies of children's responses that have been developed.

Wordless Picturebooks

A small-but-growing subset of picturebooks has very few words or no words at all, and if there are words, they often are an integral part of the illustrations; thus, the burden rests almost completely on the illustrations to tell the story (Dowhower, 1997). Children's meaning making from wordless books is thus, by definition, virtually *all* visual meaning making. Numerous practitioners and researchers have investigated the potential of wordless picturebooks to support emergent literacy in young readers (Jalongo, 2002) through creating cooperative group stories (Lindauer, 1988), writing activities (Reese, 1996), and to teach disabled readers and linguistically and culturally nonmainstream students (Flatley & Rutland, 1986; Gitelman, 1990; Perry, 1997). Wordless picturebooks have also been used in assessment tasks (Paris & Paris, 2003; Van Kraayenoord & Paris, 1996), and it is argued that pictorial narratives place similar cognitive demands on the reader as text-based stories, "such as integration of information, inferential skills, knowledge about main story elements, and understanding of temporal and causal sequences" (Paris & Paris, 2003, p. 38). Some researchers have addressed the particular challenges brought about by interpreting the sequence of pictures in a picturebook, noting that this is a task more complex than interpreting a single isolated picture (Bornens, 1990). Crawford and Hade (2000) examined how three children of different ages (eight, five, and four) navigated wordless books and interpreted the visual clues they contained. Crawford and Hade identified five sense-making processes used by the children: (a) "applying their prior knowledge and experiences to the reading; (b) bringing many different texts to bear on the reading transaction; (c) assuming multiple perspectives in the telling of the stories; (d) incorporating story language and story rituals in each reading; and (e) including active, play-like responses as part of the reading event" (p. 72). They concluded that wordless picturebooks provide opportunities to see children's sense making at work.

Children's Visual Meaning Making Across Multiple Texts

Researchers have examined the ways in which children create meaning using several related books. Shine and Roser (1999), for example, studied preschool children's differential responses to four genres of picturebooks (fantasy, realistic fiction, informational books, and poetry). The children displayed different characteristic stances, according to the genre; in other words, their responses were demonstrably different for each genre. The researchers developed two principal categories for analysis: Focus of Talk and Type of Talk. Focus of Talk was further divided into Text as Experience (response to the story as a lived-through experience) (Rosenblatt, 1978) and Text as Object, which reflected children's interest in the craft of the book, both in the verbal text and illustrations. In the first category, Text as Experience, among the seven subcategories was "text-illustration links," though children clearly used their integration of meaning from both words and pictures in all the categories. The second principal category for analysis was Type of Talk, which included the subcategories of "identify," "describe," "infer," "connect," "predict," "explore," and "narrate," all of which included children's use of illustrations along with verbal text. That children so young should have "developed a rich repertoire of expectations, tacit knowledge, and types of response to four kinds of texts" (Shine & Roser, 1999, p. 244) suggests that preschoolers, in addition to developing the ability to use the "elements of visual grammar" (Kress & van Leeuwen, 1996), have the ability to apply this visual interpretive knowledge to different types of texts.

In another grouping of picturebooks, Sipe (2001a), in examining the intertextual connections made by first and second graders to five variants of the Rapunzel story, found that children made an increasing number of connections among the texts as they were read. Of the total conversational turns for all the stories, about 20% were these text-to-text connections. Of these connections, about 32% were connections between the language of the story ("in the last story the plant was called rapunzel, but in this story, it's called rampion"); 53% were connections between plot details and characters of one story and those of another; and 15% were connections of illustrations between variants ("when it shows the picture of the kids, Rapunzel has the [grownup] kids; in the other stories, they were wrapped up in blankets and they were babies").

In *Children Reading Pictures: Interpreting Visual Texts*, Arizpe and Styles (2003) reported on a 2-year study in seven schools with children ages 4 through 11 and diverse cultural and linguistic backgrounds. The researchers used two picturebooks by Anthony Browne, *The Tunnel* (1989) and *Zoo* (1994) and one picturebook by Satoshi Kitamura (*Lily Takes a Walk*, 1997). The data for this extensive study included interviews with the children (with reinterviews about the same books), group discussions, children's drawing in response to the illustrations in the books, and questionnaires about children's reading habits. The researchers' typologies of the children's visual responses are described in the following section dealing with categories of response. One important feature of the Arizpe and Styles study was their analysis of the drawing made by children in response to the picturebooks. The categories of analysis for the drawings were, (a) literal understanding (drawing events or people "to communicate story and content;" (b) the overall effect of the drawings, including "the aesthetics of the images and the colour, tone, form, and line" used by the children; (c) and the internal structure of the drawings, in terms of the "balance and the relationship between objects or characters and their relative scale" (p. 118). Also of note in this large study are comments of young children that display "what can only be described as intellectual excitement with the ideas raised by the book [in this case, *Zoo*] and aesthetic pleasure in the images" (Arizpe & Styles, 2003, p. 80). Children explored the perplexing and ambiguous features of the illustrations, discussed the way the illustrations made them feel, as well as the moral/ethical implications of the visual images (the animals' loneliness and the barrenness of their surroundings in the zoo). The children also analyzed the visual imagery, interpreting a close-up illustration of a gorilla with vertical and horizontal bars of the cage in front of him as "like Jesus's cross" and compared the gorilla's eyes to a "grandpa's eyes," showing their awareness of the ways in which the illustrator humanizes the animals. These types of comments also revealed the children's empathy for the animals' situation. All of these responses were based almost solely on the children's visual meaning making, which the researchers found deepened upon revisiting the story. Belfatti (2005), working with first and second graders, confirmed this impact of multiple exposures to *Zoo*, observing that "while at first students' responses centered on making predictions and personal connections with the text, later responses evidenced critical analysis of how perspective switches in *Zoo* blur the boundaries between human/beast and freedom/entrapment" (p. 1).

Focus on Special Features of Picturebooks

Picturebooks do not consist merely of the words of the story and the accompanying illustrations; the format of the picturebook also includes the dustjacket, front and back covers, front and back endpapers, title and dedication pages, and other elements that are all designed to be experienced as an aesthetic whole, along with the verbal text and pictures. These additional elements, commonly referred to as the "peritext," after the work of Gerard Genette (1997) and applied by Higonnet (1990) to picturebooks, afford rich opportunities for visual meaning making. To date, only a few studies have concentrated on children's interpretive work with peritextual features. Pantaleo (2003) studied the ways in which a class of first-grade children discussed the peritextual features of nine picturebooks. The children learned peritextual terminology (such as "endpapers" and "dustjacket"), and used peritextual elements to predict and to confirm their interpretations about characters, plot, setting, and tone of the books. Their talk about peritextual features was found to contribute significantly to their "aesthetic appreciation and cognitive and literary understandings of the books" (p. 74). Sipe and McGuire (2006) examined kindergarten, first-, and second-graders' interpretations of just one peritextual element—the picturebook endpapers—in picture storybook readaloud discussions. They found that children were highly engaged in using the front endpapers for predictive purposes, and often assumed that the endpapers in some way were a prelude or preparation for the story. For picturebooks in which the front and back endpapers were different, children thought critically about why the designer or illustrator made this choice, and what semiotic significance the differences indicated. Children recognized that, in some cases, the endpapers actually begin and end the story narrative, as in Steven Kellogg's (1991) version of *Jack and the Beanstalk*. Even for plain-colored endpapers, children wanted to speculate on why the color was chosen, attempting to connect the color to the book's design, content, or general tone.

Postmodern Picturebooks

The label "postmodern" means a great many things to different people, but perhaps the most central assumption of postmodern literature is that the purpose of literature is not to seduce the reader into the illusion of having entered another world (Lewis, 2001), but rather to highlight the fact that the text is an artificial construction. In other words, the text calls attention to itself *as a text* rather than functioning as a transparent window into an imagined "secondary world" (Benton, 1992). In addition to describing these *metafictive/self-referential* elements (Waugh, 1984, Stevenson, 1991), Sipe (2004), synthesizing theoretical work on postmodern picturebooks (Goldstone, 1999; Kümmerling-Meibauer, 1999; Lewis, 1990, 1992, 2001; Nikola-Lisa, 1994; Paley, 1992, Trites, 1994) identified five further common qualities of postmodern picturebooks: (a) *playfulness* (the text as a playground for readers); (b) *multiplicity of meanings* (multiple pathways through the text-world because of nonlinearity of plot and a high degree of indeterminacy, nonresolution, and ambiguity); (c) *intertextuality* (multiple types of texts and the juxtaposition of references to many other texts); (d) *subversion* (mocking of literary conventions and a general tone of irony, parody, or sarcasm); and (e) *blurring distinctions* between high and popular culture, between authors and readers, and distinctions among traditional literary genres. These elements are noticeable in increasing numbers of picturebooks, most spectacularly and fully in Jon Scieszka's (1992) bizarre sendup of traditional fairy tales, *The Stinky Cheese Man and Other Fairly Stupid Tales*. What has attracted the attention of researchers is that, in addition to their frequently creative manipulations of the traditional picturebook format, these books seem to offer great promise for eliciting new and sophisticated types of responses from young children.

Pantaleo's (2002, 2003, 2004a, 2004b, 2005) extensive research about primary grade children's responses to postmodern picturebooks with multiple plots, multiple narrators, and metafictive devices provided strong evidence for the potential ability of young children to negotiate the layered complexities of these texts. The children in Pantaleo's studies constructed semiotic significance from visual details such as different font sizes; used illustrations to make connections among the multiple narratives; understood how the illustrations represented, complemented, extended, and sometimes contradicted the text; and used visual peritextual features of the books to predict the plot and to interpret the relationships among storybook characters. Pantaleo (2004a) noted that the skills necessary to interpret postmodern picturebooks are similar to those required for "Web literacy": "attentiveness to information conveyed in the nontextual features, acquisition of multiple sources of information, analysis of information, and associative processing" (p. 17).

With slightly older children (in grades three through five), Serafini (2005), found that discussions of Anthony Browne's (1998) *Voices in the Park*, a nonlinear, multivocal text, challenged readers to "tolerate the disruptions to the linear structures and traditional forms of narratives . . . [and] to learn to recognize and understand the meta-fictive elements that are used, and enjoy the challenges reading these texts may present" (p. 60). He also found that "those readers with a higher level of tolerance of ambiguity and uncertainty were more capable of making sense of meta-fictive elements than their peers" (p. 60) and concluded that the greater challenges presented by postmodern picturebooks can assist children in becoming more active sense makers and critical readers. In a similar way, McClay's (2000) research with 20 children (ages 7, 10, and 12) and 25 adults reading Macaulay's (1990) *Black and White* demonstrated that the children could explore "multiple pathways through the text-world" (Lemke, 1993) of this challenging and ambiguous picturebook, which tells four seemingly separate stories, each with strikingly different illustration styles, which may or may not be related in a unified narrative. McClay found that the children's solutions to the problem of how to read such a text were, in general, more creative and flexible than the adults' attempts, and that, moreover, the children seemed to relish the challenges, whereas a number of the adults (mostly elementary teachers) seemed to resist the idea that the verbal texts in this book are subordinate to the illustrations in constructing interpretations.

Using Visual Information for Specific Purposes

The specific uses children may make of visual information have been explored by several researchers. Walsh (2003), in analyzing the oral responses of kindergarten and Year One children to two picture storybooks, found that their responses to the pictures (which constituted almost all of their total comments) could be categorized as "labeling" (identifying objects or situations); "observation" (providing more detail and information) and "[personal] comments" such as "My Mum doesn't let me climb trees," showing children relating the illustration to their own lives. Extending such work, Sipe and Brightman (2005) studied how first-grade children, during read-alouds of four fairytale variants, used "visual talk" (comprising a little less than half of their total responses) to describe details of the setting and background of illustrations; to interpret story characters' appearance, actions, relationships, feelings, intentions, and motivations; and to predict and confirm the plot. The children also worked to integrate the meanings gleaned from various components of the picturebook into more complex and holistic significance. They made comparisons between illustrations within the same book and also compared and contrasted visual features across the four stories. Finally, they took on the challenge of a postmodern version of *The Three Pigs* (Wiesner, 2001) by grappling with the idea of story boundaries, relying almost exclusively on the illustrations to understand how the three pigs moved from one story to another within this complicated picturebook. With a more narrow focus on one use of visual information, Sipe and Ghiso (2005) examined how children used illustrations in picturebooks to interpret and expand their understanding of the element of character. In their analysis of transcripts of picture storybook readaloud discussions, they found that kindergarten, first and second graders used illustrations to interpret story characters' physical appearance to draw inferences about the characters' inner states of mind and feelings. Children also were sensitive to the qualities of line (a fine line suggests delicacy, whereas thick, heavy lines suggest energy or force). Characters' rounded shapes were interpreted as comfortable and secure, whereas characters with angular shapes were seen as threatening. Children also paid attention to the size and proportion of characters, noticing when they broke the boundaries of the illustration frame, as well as interpreting the semiotic significance of colors to indicate emotions (for example, blue or green for calm and peace). Finally, children interpreted the illustrational groupings of characters. For example, one image in *The Tale of Peter Rabbit* (Potter, 1902) depicts Mother Rabbit and her three daughters clustered together in a solid mass, whereas Peter stands apart, facing away. A first grader commented, "Peter's turning away; he's already thinking about getting into trouble."

Typologies of Young Children's Responses to Picturebooks

A number of researchers have generated typologies of children's responses to picturebooks, built by grounded theory techniques (Strauss & Corbin, 1998) that assign conceptual labels to children's talk and then group these conceptual labels into a manageable number of categories. Kiefer's (1982) classroom research studied the responses of first and second graders to picturebook illustrations, adapting Halliday's (1975) categories of the functions of language, and described four types of response: (a) informative, (b) imaginative, (c) heuristic, and (d) personal. In *informative* response, children described the contents of the picture or compared and contrasted the picture to the real world. In *heuristic* response, children speculated and made inferences about the events depicted in the illustrations and how illustrations were made and predicted outcomes or events. In *imaginative* response, children entered the story world or created figurative images to describe it. In *personal* response, children made connections between their own life experiences and the book or evaluated the story. Drawing on both Kiefer's typology and on the work of Flinders and Eisner (1994) on the stages of the development of visual art criticism, Madura (1995, 1998) explored four patterns used by young children in talking about illustrations in picturebooks: (a) description, (b) interpretation, (c) evaluation, and (d) thematic issues.

In a study of what constituted literary understanding in a combined first- and second-grade classroom, Sipe (2000) found five types of responses to picturebooks. The first, *analytical* response, was a large category subdivided into five subcategories: (a) discussion of the book as an cultural aesthetic artifact, including talk about the author and illustrator as the makers of the book, publishing information, and the mechanics of publishing and editing; (b) discussion of the language of the story, and the meanings of words or phrases; (c) analysis of illustrations; (d) making narrative meaning from the text and pictures by describing, evaluating, predicting, or inferring about the plot, setting, and characters of the story; and (e) discussion of the relationships between fiction and reality. In the second type of response, *intertextual* response, children linked the picturebook being read to other books, television shows, videos, or other visual or verbal texts. The third type of response was *personal,* where the children connected the story to their own lives or stated what they would do if they were a storybook character. *Transparent* response, the fourth type, involved comments by the children that indicated that, for the moment, the world of the story and the children's world were merged, for example by "talking back" directly to the storybook characters. In *performative* response, the fifth type, children used the pictures or text of the book as a springboard for their own creative, playful subversion. Of note in these five responses is that analysis of illustrations (the third subcategory of the analytical) constituted 23% of the children's total conversational turns. Children discussed the artistic media that may have been used to produce illustrations; described the arrangement of the illustration or the illustration sequence by referring to double-page spreads, borders, or commented on the physical arrangement of the words and pictures on the page openings. They constructed semiotic significance for various illustration codes, such as the conventions for portraying movement or shadows, and the portrayal of three-dimensional space through perspective and point of view. They also made comparisons across illustrations and described the details or general background of illustrations. Although this subcategory was specifically concerned with illustration analysis, the children were using both the words *and* the illustrations to make meaning in all five main categories of response. A follow-up study by Sipe and Bauer (2001) found that these categories could be used to analyze the responses of a class of urban kindergarten children, and that the associated percentages for each of the categories were quite similar to the study with first and second graders. In both studies, there was evidence that children were "more attuned to the illustrator's rather than the author's craft" and were more likely to evaluate illustrations than text (Martinez, Roser, & Dooley, 2003, p. 224).

For child-initiated responses during readalouds in a second-grade class of working class and lower-income children from diverse ethnic backgrounds, Maloch and Duncan (2006) found six types of spontaneous student responses: (a) connecting (to personal experience, other texts, the world, future experiences, and shared experiences); (b) predicting; (c) clarifying information that was unclear or confusing; (d) making observations about both text and illustrations; (e) "entering the story world" by acting as if they were in the story or making suggestions about what they would change if they were the author; and (f) offering suggestions about how the teacher should read the book or arrange the activity. This typology has significant similarities to the studies cited above, and seems to add an element of agency to the children's active participation, by describing children's ways of controlling the readaloud with the teacher.

Arizpe and Styles (2003), in the study described previously, found that children in a wide age span from 4 to 11 displayed responses on nine increasingly sophisticated levels of interpretation, for example ranging from "no explanation given," "mis-readings (wrong)," and "literal explanation" to "engaged description," "interrogation: superficial/engaged/anticipation" and "imaginative deduction" (p. 258). Arizpe and Styles also identified 15 "categories of perception" to classify children's responses, for example describing the relationship between text and picture; speculating about the artist's intentions, appreciation of visual features of the illustrator's craft such as color and pattern; and interpretations of story characters' motives, relationships, expectation, and inner motives. Because of the wide age range on which they are based, it is unclear how these categories and levels of interpretation may apply to smaller age ranges within this span.

One difficulty with all these typologies, as Martinez and Roser (2003) wisely observed, is that "the many separate systems for categorizing responses make it difficult to compare across studies" (p. 810). In other words, the very strength of grounded theory (letting categories emerge from the data) also has drawbacks in terms of the applicability of the typologies to other studies and other situations. While it is true that qualitative interpretive research attempts to present description that is complete and nuanced enough for the readers of the research to make their own connections with other situations and contexts, the true challenge is to go beyond the "epistemology of the particular" (Stake, 1994, p. 240) into a generalizability that is nevertheless wary of the dangers of master narratives of any behavior, including children's literary and visual meaning making. Martinez and Roser (2003) suggested that researchers "try more replications of their own systems across studies" (p. 810) as one way of remedying this problem.

TEACHERS AS ENABLERS OF CHILDREN'S MEANING MAKING FROM PICTUREBOOKS

Most researchers who study young children's responses to picturebooks adopt a social constructivist (Berk & Winsler, 1995) approach, assuming that, together, children can help each other in refining and extending their individual interpretations through talking with each other. Another key component in the construction of meaning is the adult or "expert other" who assists children in various ways before, during, and after story reading (Martinez & Roser, 2003; Martinez, Roser, & Dooley, 2003). Though there is no lack of anecdotal reporting about the role of adults in the process of meaning making, surprisingly little empirical research has concentrated on the ways in which classroom teachers help children construct meaning from picturebooks. In general, as Golden and Gerber (1990) pointed out in their study of teacher-student-text interaction with *Where the Wild Things Are* (Sendak, 1963) in a second-grade class of Native American children, teachers perform or enact the picturebook by interpreting it through their reading of it. They may, for example, emphasize certain words, give dramatic voice to storybook characters, and provide other "instructional cues" (p. 217) such as pointing out important details of illustrations. Thus, the teacher facilitates the "potential text" of the book to become a "realized text" by the children through the teacher's and children's engaged involvement.

In mediating the experience of the picturebook in this way, teachers seem to perform a number of different roles. Roser and Martinez's (1985) research identified three roles (co-responder; informer; and director) for adults in talking about stories with preschoolers. Extending this work, McGee, Courtney, and Lomax (1994) found that, when reading picture storybooks to first graders, teachers played several roles, including that of *facilitator* (by managing turn taking, for example); *helper/nudger* (by summarizing, restating, or asking for clarification); *responder* (by introducing, expanding, or elaborating of topics); *literary curator* (by extending literary understandings during brief teachable moments [Eeds & Wells, 1989]); and *reader* (by reading the story). Sipe's (2001c) research with first and second graders found that the adults who facilitated picture storybook readalouds played quite similar roles as those in McGee's work: as *readers* (reading the text and also acting as tour guides or docents, by pointing out certain features like the endpapers or the dedication page); *managers/encouragers* (for example, by asking children to respond to the comments of their classmates and praising them); *clarifiers/probers* (linking children's remarks to each other, asking for more information or explanation, and questioning); *fellow wonderers/speculators* (wondering and questioning along with the children, situating themselves as fellow seekers and interpreters); and *extenders/refiners* of the children's responses, by identifying threads of conversation that could lead to teachable moments or summarizing groups of responses to achieve closure.

Further differentiating teachers' pedagogical techniques, Maloch and Duncan (2006), in the study described previously, analyzed a second-grade teacher's responses to child-initiated, spontaneous contributions during readalouds. They found that the teacher responded to the children's initiations by modeling an inquiry stance; acknowledging/affirming; restating and inviting students to restate; encouraging children to explain their ideas; clarifying students' strategies; directing students' attention to text and visual features and directing students back to the text and pictures; turning a student's question back to the other students; reminding students of textual and visual information and connecting this information with other parts of the story; clarifying student conclusions; setting up a frame for thinking through questions; managing the conversational turn taking; and encouraging intertextual connections to related books.

Sipe and Brightman (2006) found that, over a series of discussions of four picturebook variants of a traditional tale, read in increasing order of difficulty and ever-increasing departures from the more familiar version, the teacher's scaffolding roles changed subtly. For example, the teacher asked fewer direct questions for the last two picturebooks, playing more the role of a fellow wonderer and speculator. Across the four readalouds, the teacher spent about 25% of each discussion in exploring the (heavily visual) front and back covers, the endpages, title page, and dedication pages with the children *before* beginning to read the words of the story in order to help them predict what was going to happen and to begin to develop their schema for the story, which is an important scaffolding function. The teacher repeated or restated children's comments; clarified or extended a child's idea; connected children's ideas with one another; and positively reinforced children's ideas. The teacher's approach was neither laissez-faire nor rigidly controlling; she became more directive at crucial points, in order to extend the children's story schema. Clearly, the teacher's style of reading aloud is a factor in children's interpretation of picturebooks (Martinez & Teale, 1993; Dickinson & Smith, 1994). For example, Sipe and Daley (2005) found that one kindergarten teacher's "storytelling style" of reading aloud seemed to encourage rich spontaneous comments by African American children about the visual features of picturebooks.

FUTURE RESEARCH

Despite the growing amount of research devoted to children's visual meaning making from picturebooks, it would seem that practitioners and researchers have far to go before they fully exploit the theoretical advances (sketched in the first part of this chapter) in understanding picturebooks that have developed over the last two decades. For example, Kress and van Leeuwen's (1996) highly developed "grammar of visual design" has been applied theoretically to picturebooks by Lewis (2001), Unsworth (2001), and Williams (1998), but researchers are just beginning to take up this work in their empirical studies of children's visual meaning making. In general, we need more studies combining careful and theoretically informed examinations of the visual features and text-picture relationships in specific picturebooks *along with* analyses of children's interpretations of those same picturebooks.

Clearly, almost all of the research reported in this chapter concerns children's *talk* about picturebooks. Few studies have systematically examined the ways in which children may construct meaning from visual features of picturebooks using painting/drawing (Arizpe & Styles, 2003; Pantaleo, 2005b), drama (Adomat, 2005; Kornfeld & Leyden, 2005), sociodramatic play (Rowe, 1998) and other modes of response such as music, dance/movement, and combinations of these modes. As Gardner (1973) commented some time ago, nonverbal means of measuring children's competence in interpreting visual art may be preferable to verbal means. Important research with these types of nonverbal responses conducted with somewhat older children (Short, Kauffman, & Kahn, 2000; Whitin, 2002; Whitelaw & Wolf, 2001) suggested that investigations of young children's nonverbal meaning making in response to picturebooks would likewise be rewarding. As well, we know little about how children's visual meaning making from picturebooks may relate to their understanding of other combinations of visual and verbal formats such as the various types of fine art, comics, graphic novels, video, and digital Web-based texts that have a high degree of visual content. In other words, ways of integrating children's developing visual interpretive skills across many different types of texts need more examination.

The complex array of children's characteristics—their race, ethnicity, gender, cultural backgrounds and individual personalities—need to be taken into consideration when investigating their visual meaning making from picturebooks. To date, few studies have done this. An exception is the work of Arizpe and Styles (2003), who speculated that the kinds of questions they asked (open-ended and inferential) may have been unexpected and unfamiliar to some of the immigrant children in their study. Arizpe and Styles also found that some children's cultural backgrounds seem to have resulted in different interpretations of illustrations (for example, not every culture has the same ideologies and assumptions about confining animals in cages, which could partly explain the range of responses to Anthony Browne's [1994] *Zoo*). However, much more work is necessary before we have a nuanced understanding of the ways in which characteristics of readers shape, enable, and constrain their responses to the visual aspects of picturebooks. Certainly, visual images are very powerful in picturebooks that attempt to represent gender, race, and various cultures authentically, and must be rendered with as much care as the words of the story (Pace & Lowery, 2001; Chang, 2005; Thompson, 2001). Highlighting children's visual meaning making would add new dimensions to the fascinating and insightful analyses that have been done of the literary discussion (and critical inquiry) about picturebooks evidenced by children from various cultural and ethnic groups (Martínez-Roldán, 2003, 2005; Martínez-Roldán & Malavé, 2004; Martínez-Roldán & López-Robertson, 1999). Carger (2004), for example, integrated art making and art appreciation with picturebook readalouds, and found that the second- and third-grade bilingual children with whom she worked developed significant aesthetic response to the illustrations in (a) picturebooks, (b) classic works of art such as paintings by Van Gogh, and (c) their own artistic efforts; moreover, the children forged intriguing connections among these three resources.

We have some evidence that children may have differing individual response styles to picturebooks (Brightman & Sipe, 2006; Lopez-Robertson, 2005; Wolf & Heath, 1992). For example, Sipe (1996, 1998b) observed that one of the first graders in his set of case studies had a special interest in the layout and design of picturebooks, and was especially attuned to the ways in which peritextual features could be interpreted to contribute to the total effect of the picturebook. Another child was particularly fascinated with the artistic styles and media that illustrators had used, and frequently inquired about the process of illustration and the ways she could achieve similar effects in her own art. We know little about how children develop such particular interests and abilities, and how these interests may result in the development of greater capacities for visual meaning making, both for them and for their peers.

In addition to postmodern picturebooks, previously mentioned, other types of picturebooks may evoke different responses from children. Informational picturebooks, a growing subset of the picturebook format, have been the object of some study (Duke & Kays, 1998; Palmer & Stewart, 2003, 2005; Pappas, 1993, 2006; Smolkin & Donovan, 2004; Wolfenbarger & Sipe, 2007), but more work is needed, especially as researchers and practitioners have decried the scant amount of attention paid to informational texts in the early years of schooling (Duke, 2000). As well, an increasing number of picturebooks include references to the history of art, in the form of representations (or parodies) of specific artwork by well-known artists or references to historical styles of visual art (Sipe, 2001b). The ways in which children respond to these types of heavily "intervisual" texts is only beginning to be explored.

A significant number of educational practitioners may feel that they have an inadequate background in the principles of art and design, and may therefore be uncomfortable discussing the visual features of picturebooks in their classrooms. Research is needed that investigates the ways that teachers learn the language of picturebooks and take on the challenge of visual analysis and interpretation with children in both appreciative and critical (Leland, Harste, & Huber, 2005; Vasquez, 2004) ways that highlight and develop children's awareness of social issues through interpretation of illustrations as well as verbal texts.

Finally, longitudinal studies of children's visual interpretive abilities (with attention to multiple exposures to books) would illuminate the development and integration of these abilities over time; as Hickman (1981) and Kiefer (1988) observed, rich response grows slowly and organically and may best be described through a long-range lens. Although these types of studies are time consuming and methodologically and practically difficult, they could yield very rich and useful implications for pedagogy that exploits the tremendous potential of picturebooks.

REFERENCES

Adomat, D. (2005, December). *Outside, inside, and all around the story: Struggling first-grade readers construct literary understanding through dramatic response to literature.* Paper presented at the National Reading Conference, Miami, Florida.

Agosto, D. E. (1999). One and inseparable: Interdependent storytelling in picture storybooks. *Children's Literature in Education, 30,* 267–280.

Alderson, B. (1973). *Looking at picture books.* London: The National Book League and Bocardo Press.

Anstey, M., & Bull, G. (2000). *Reading the visual: Written and illustrated children's literature.* Sydney, Australia: Harcourt.

Arizpe, E., & Styles, M. (2003). *Children reading pictures: Interpreting visual texts.* New York: RoutledgeFalmer.

Bader, B. (1976). *American picture books: From Noah's ark to the beast within.* New York: MacMillan.

Bang, M. (2000). *Picture this: How pictures work.* San Francisco: SeaStar Books.

Barthes, R. (1978). *Image-Music-Text* (S. Heath, Trans.). New York: Hill and Wang.

Belfatti, M. A. (2005). *Revisiting Anthony Browne's* Zoo: *Young children's response to literature with repeated read-alouds.* Manuscript submitted for publication.

Benton, M. (1992). *Secondary worlds: Literature teaching and the visual arts.* Buckingham, U.K.: Open University Press.

Berk, L. E., & Winsler, A. (1995). *Scaffolding children's learning: Vygotsky and early childhood education.* Washington, DC: National Association for the Education of Young Children.

Bornens, M. (1990). Problems brought about by "reading" a sequence of pictures. *Journal of Experimental Psychology, 49,* 189–226.

Brightman, A. E., & Sipe, L. R. (2006, December). *First-graders' individual literary response styles during picturebook readalouds.* Paper presented at the National Reading Conference, Los Angeles, California.

Browne, A. (1989). *The tunnel.* New York: Knopf.

Browne, A. (1994). *Zoo.* New York: Knopf.

Browne, A. (1998). *Voices in the park.* New York: DK Publishing.

Carger, C. L. (2004). Art and literacy with bilingual children. *Language Arts, 81,* 283–292

Carle, E. (1984). *The very busy spider.* New York: Philomel.

Carle, E. (1995). *The very lonely firefly.* New York: Philomel.

Carle, E. (1999). *The very clumsy click beetle.* New York: Philomel.

Cech, J. (1983–1984). Remembering Caldecott: 'The Three Jovial Huntsmen' and the art of the picturebook. *The Lion and the Unicorn, 7/8,* 110–119.

Cech, J. (1995). *Angels and wild things: The archetypal poetics of Maurice Sendak.* University Park, PA: The Pennsylvania State University Press.

Chang, M. (2005). Daydreams of Cathay: Images of China in modern American children's books. In D. Henderson, & J. P. May (Eds.), *Exploring culturally diverse literature for children and adolescents: Learning to listen in new ways* (pp. 54–64). Boston: Pearson.

Crawford, P. A., & Hade, D. D. (2000). Inside the picture, outside the frame: Semiotics and the reading of wordless picture books. *Journal of Research in Childhood Education, 15,* 66–80.

Dickinson, D., & Smith, M. (1994). Long-term effects of preschool teachers' book readings on low-income children's vocabulary and story comprehension. *Reading Research Quarterly, 29,* 105–122.

Doonan, J. (1993). *Looking at pictures in picturebooks.* Exeter, U.K.: Thimble Press.

Dowhower, S. (1997). Wordless books: Promise and possibilities, a genre comes of age. In K. Camperell, B. L. Hayes, & R. Telfter (Eds.), *Yearbook of the American Reading Forum, 17*, 57–79.

Duke, N. K. (2000). 3.6 minutes per day: The scarcity of informational texts in first grade. *Reading Research Quarterly, 35*, 202–224.

Duke, N. K., & Kays, J. (1998). "Can I say 'Once upon a time'?": Kindergarten children developing knowledge of information book language. *Early Childhood Research Quarterly, 13*, 295–318.

Eeds, M., & Wells, D. (1989). Grand conversations: An exploration of meaning construction in literature study groups. *Research in the Teaching of English, 23*, 4–29.

Flatley, J. K., & Rutland, A. D. (1986). Using wordless picture books to teach linguistically/culturally different students. *The Reading Teacher, 40*, 276–281.

Flinders, D. J., & Eisner, E. W. (1994). Educational criticism as a form of qualitative inquiry. *Research in the Teaching of English, 28*, 341–357.

Flood , J., Heath, S. B., & Lapp, D. (1997). *Handbook of research on teaching literacy through the communicative and visual arts*. New York: Simon & Schuster Macmillan.

Flood, J., & Lapp, D. (1995). Broadening the lens: Toward an expanded conceptualization of literacy. In K. Hinchman, D. J. Leu, & C. K. Kinzer (Eds.), *Perspectives on literacy research and practice* (pp. 1–16). Chicago: National Reading Conference.

Gardner, H. (1973). *The arts and human development*. New York: John Wiley & Sons.

Genette, G. (1997). *Paratexts: Thresholds of interpretation* (J. E. Lewin, Trans.). Cambridge, U.K.: Cambridge University Press.

Gitelman, H. F. (1990). Using wordless picture books with disabled readers. *The Reading Teacher, 43*, 525.

Golden, J. (1990). *The narrative symbol in childhood literature: Explorations of the construction of text*. New York: Mouton de Gruyter

Golden J. M., & Gerber, A. (1990). A semiotic perspective of text: The picture story book event. *Journal of Reading Behavior, 22*, 203–219.

Goldstone, B. (1999). Brave new worlds: The changing image of the picture books. *The New Advocate, 12*, 331–344.

Graham, J. (1990). *Pictures on the page*. Sheffield, U.K.: National Association for the Teaching of English.

Grimm, J., & Grimm, W. (1972). *Snow-White and the seven dwarfs* (R. Jarrell Trans.). New York: Farrar, Straus, and Giroux.

Halliday, M. (1975). *Learning how to mean: Explorations in the development of language*. London: Longman.

Hickman, J. (1981). A new perspective on response to literature: Research in an elementary school setting. *Research in the Teaching of English, 15*, 343–354.

Higonnet, M. R. (1990). The playground of the peritext. *Children's Literature Association Quarterly, 15*, 47–49.

Jalongo, M. R., with Dragich, D., Conrad, N. K., & Zhang, A. (2002). Using wordless picture books to support emergent literacy. *Early Childhood Education Journal, 29*, 167–177.

Kellogg, S. (1991). *Jack and the beanstalk*. New York: Morrow.

Kiefer, B. (1982). *The response of primary children to picture books*. Unpublished doctoral dissertation, The Ohio State University.

Kiefer, B. (1988). Picture books as contexts for literary, aesthetic, and real world understandings. *Language Arts, 65*, 260–271.

Kiefer, B. (1995). *The potential of picturebooks: From visual literacy to aesthetic understanding*. Englewood Cliffs, NJ: Merrill.

Kornfeld, J., & Leyden, G. (2005). Acting out: Literature, drama, and connecting with history. *The Reading Teacher, 59*, 230–238

Kress, G., & van Leeuwen, T. (1996). *Reading images: The grammar of visual design*. London: Routledge.

Kümmerling-Meibauer, B. (1999). Metalinguistic awareness and the child's developing concept of irony: The relationship between pictures and text in ironic picturebooks. *The Lion and the Unicorn, 23*, 157–183.

Kushner, T. (2003). *The art of Maurice Sendak: 1980 to the present*. New York: Harry N. Abrams, Inc.

Kitamura, S. (1997). *Lily takes a walk*. London: Happy Cat Books.

Lacy, L. E. (1986). *Art and design in children's picture books*. Chicago: American Library Association.

Lanes, S. (1980). *The art of Maurice Sendak*. New York: Harry N. Abrams.

Leland, C. H., Harste, J. C., & Huber, K. R. (2005). Out of the box: Critical literacy in a first-grade classroom. *Language Arts, 82*, 257–268.

Lemke, J. (1993, December). *Multiplying meaning: Literacy in a multimedia world*. Paper presented at the National Reading Conference, Charleston, South Carolina.

Lewis, D. (1990). The constructedness of picturebooks: Picturebooks and the metafictive. *Signal, 62*, 131–146.

Lewis, D. (1992). Looking for Julius: Two children and a picturebook. In K. Kimberly et al. (Eds.), *New Readings*. London: A & C Black.

Lewis, D. (1996). Going along with Mr. Gumpy: Polysystemy and play in the modern picturebook. *Signal, 80*, 105–119.

Lewis, D. (2001). *Reading contemporary picturebooks: Picturing text*. London: RoutledgeFalmer.

Lindauer, S. L. K. (1988). Wordless books: An approach to visual literacy. *Children's Literature in Education, 19*, 136–142.

Lopez-Robertson, J. (2005, December). *Young Latinas' response styles during literature discussions: Personal life stories as meaning-making devices*. Paper presented at the National Reading Conference, Miami, Florida.

Macaulay, D. (1990). *Black and white*. Boston: Houghton Mifflin.

Madura, S. (1995). The line and texture of aesthetic response: Primary children study authors and illustrators. *The Reading Teacher, 49*, 110–118.

Madura, S. (1998). An artistic element: Four transitional readers and writers respond to the picture books of Patricia Polacco and Gerald McDermott. In T. Shanahan, & F. V. Rodriguez-Brown (Eds.), *National Reading Conference Yearbook, 47*, 366–376.

Maloch, B., & Duncan, D. (2006, December). *"Big loud voice. You have important things to say": The nature of student initiations during one teacher's interactive read-alouds*. Paper presented at the National Reading Conference, Miami, Florida.

Marantz, S. S. (1992). *Picture books for looking and learning: Awakening visual perceptions through the art of children's books*. Phoenix, AZ: Oryx Press.

Marantz, S. S., & Marantz, K. (1992). *Artists of the page: Interviews with children's book illustrators*. Jefferson, NC: McFarland.

Marcus, L. S. (2001). *Side by side: Five picture-book teams go to work*. New York: Walker & Co.

Martin, D. (1989). *The telling line: Essays on fifteen contemporary book illustrators*. London: Julia MacRae Books.

Martinez, M., & Roser, N. L. (2003). Children's responses to literature. In J. Flood, D. Lapp, J. R. Squire, & J. M. Jensen (Eds.), *Handbook of research on teaching the English language arts* (2nd ed., pp. 799–813). Mahwah, NJ: Lawrence Erlbaum Associates.

Martinez, M., Roser, N., & Dooley, C. (2003). Young children's literary meaning making. In N. Hall, J. Larson, & J. Marsh (Eds.), *Handbook of early childhood literacy* (pp. 222–234). London: Sage.

Martinez, M., & Teale, W. (1993). Teacher storybook reading style: A comparison of six teachers. *Research in the Teaching of English, 27*, 175–199.

Martínez-Roldán, C. (2003). Building worlds and identities: A case study of the role of narratives in bilingual literature discussions. *Research in the Teaching of English, 37*, 491–526.

Martínez-Roldán, C. M. (2005). The inquiry acts of bilingual children in literature discussions. *Language Arts, 83*, 22–32.

Martínez-Roldán, C., & López-Robertson, J. (1999). Initiating literature circles in a first-grade bilingual classroom. *The Reading Teacher, 53*, 2–14.

Martínez-Roldán, C., & Malavé, G. (2004). Language ideologies mediating literacy and identity in bilingual contexts. *Journal of Early Childhood Literacy, 4*, 155–180.

McClay, J. (2000). "Wait a second . . .": Negotiating complex narratives in Black and White. *Children's Literature in Education, 31*, 91–106.

McGee, L., Courtney, L., & Lomax, R. (1994). Teachers' roles in first graders' grand conversations. In C. K. Kinzer, & D. J. Leu (Eds.), *Multidimensional aspects of literacy research, theory, and practice* (pp. 517–526). Chicago: National Reading Conference.

Meek, M. (1992). Children reading—now. In M. Styles, E. Bearne, & V. Watson (Eds.), *After Alice: Exploring children's literature*. London: Cassell.

Miller, J. H. (1992). *Illustration*. Cambridge, MA: Harvard University Press.

Mitchell, W. J. T. (1994). *Picture theory: Essays on verbal and visual representation*. Chicago: University of Chicago Press.

Moebius, W. (1986). Introduction to picturebook codes. *Word and Image, 2*, 141–158.

Moss, E. (1990). A certain particularity: An interview with Janet and Allen Ahlberg. *Signal*, 61.

Nikolajeva, M. (2003). Visual and verbal literacy: The role of picturebooks in the reading experience of young children. In N. Hall, J. Larson, & J. Marsh (Eds.), *Handbook of early childhood literacy* (pp. 235–248). London: Sage.

Nikolajeva, M., & Scott, C. (2001). *How picturebooks work*. New York: Garland.

Nikola-Lisa, W. (1994). Play, panache, pastiche: Postmodern impulses in contemporary picture books. *Children's Literature Association Quarterly, 19*, 35–40.

Nodelman, P. (1988). *Words about pictures: The narrative art of children's picture books*. Athens: University of Georgia Press.

Pace, B., & Lowery, R. (2001). Power, gender scripts, and boy codes: Possibilities and limitations in picture books. *New Advocate, 14*, 33–41.

Paley, N. (1992). Postmodernist impulses and the contemporary picture book: Are there stories to these meanings? *Journal of Youth Services in Libraries, 5*, 151–162.

Palmer, R. G., & Stewart, R. A. (2003). Nonfiction trade book use in primary grades. *The Reading Teacher, 57*, 38–48.

Palmer, R. G., & Stewart, R. A. (2005). Models for using nonfiction in the primary grades. *The Reading Teacher, 58*, 426–433.

Pantaleo, S. (2002). Grade 1 students meet David Wiesner's three pigs. *Journal of Children's Literature, 28*, 72–84.

Pantaleo, S. (2003). "Godzilla lives in New York": Grade 1 students and the peritextual features of picture books. *Journal of Children's Literature, 29*, 66–77.

Pantaleo, S. (2004a). The long, long way: Young children explore the fibula and syuzhet of Shortcut. *Children's Literature in Education, 35*, 1–20.

Pantaleo, S. (2004b). Young children interpret the metafictive in Anthony Browne's Voices in the Park. *Journal of Early Childhood Literacy, 4*, 211–233.

Pantaleo, S. (2005). Young children engage with the metafictive in picture books. *Australian Journal of Language and Literacy, 28*, 19–37.

Pappas, C. (1993). Is narrative primary? Some insights from kindergartners' pretend readings of stories and information books. *Journal of Reading Behavior, 25*, 97–129.

Pappas, C. (2006). The information book genre: Its role in integrated science literacy research and practice. *Reading Research Quarterly, 41*, 226–250.

Paris, A. H., & Paris S. G. (2003). Assessing narrative comprehension in young children. *Reading Research Quarterly, 38*, 36–76.

Perry, L. A. (1997). Using wordless picture books with beginning readers (of any age). *Teaching Exceptional Children, 29*, 68–69.

Potter, B. (1902). *The tale of Peter Rabbit*. London: Penguin Books.

Pullman, P. (1989). Invisible pictures. *Signal, 60*, 160–186.

Reese, C. (1996). Story development using wordless picture books. *The Reading Teacher, 50*, 172–173.

Rosenblatt, L. (1978). *The reader, the text, the poem: The transactional theory of the literary work*. Carbondale, IL: Southern Illinois University Press.

Roser, N., & Martinez, M. (1985). Roles adults play in preschoolers' responses to literature. *Language Arts, 62*, 485–490.

Rowe, D. W. (1998). The literate potentials of book-related dramatic play. *Reading Research Quarterly, 33*, 10–35.

Sabuda, R. (2004). *America the beautiful*. New York: Little Simon.

Sabuda, R. (2005). *Winter's tale*. New York: Little Simon.

Salisbury, M. (2004). *Illustrating children's books: Creating pictures for publication*. New York: Barron's Educational Series, Inc.

Schwarcz, J. H. (1982). *Ways of the illustrator: Visual communication in children's literature*. Chicago: American Library Association.

Schwarcz, J. H., & Schwarcz, C. (1991). *The picture book comes of age*. Chicago: American Library Association.

Scieszka, J. (1992). *The stinky cheese man and other fairly stupid tales*. New York: Viking.

Sendak, M. (1963). *Where the wild things are*. New York: HarperCollins.

Serafini, F. (2005). Voices in the park, voices in the classroom: Readers responding to postmodern picture books. *Reading Research and Instruction, 44*, 47–65.

Shine, S., & Roser, N. L. (1999). The role of genre in preschoolers' response to picture books. *Research in the Teaching of English, 34*, 197–254.

Short, K. G., Kauffman, G., & Kahn, L. H. (2000). "I just need to draw": Responding to literature across multiple sign systems. *The Reading Teacher, 54*, 160–171.

Shulevitz, U. (1985). *Writing with pictures: How to write and illustrate children's books*. New York: Watson-Guptill.

Sipe, L. R. (1996). *The construction of literary understanding by first and second graders in response to picture storybook readalouds*. Unpublished doctoral dissertation, The Ohio State University.

Sipe, L. R. (1998a). How picture books work: A semiotically framed theory of text-picture relationships. *Children's Literature in Education, 29*, 97–108.

Sipe, L. R. (1998b). Individual literary responses styles of first and second graders. In T. Shanahan & F. V. Rodriguez-Brown (Eds.), *47th Yearbook of the National Reading Conference* (pp. 76–89). Chicago: National Reading Conference.

Sipe, L. R. (2000). The construction of literary understanding by first and second graders in oral response to picture storybook readalouds. *Reading Research Quarterly, 35*, 252–275.

Sipe, L. R. (2001a). A palimpsest of stories: Young children's construction of intertextual links among fairytale variants. *Reading Research and Instruction, 40*, 333–352.

Sipe, L. R. (2001b). Using picture storybooks to teach art history. *Studies in Art Education, 42*, 197–213.

Sipe, L. R. (2001c). Scaffolding first- and second-graders' developing literary understanding during storybook readalouds. *The California Reader, 34*, 9–18.

Sipe, L. R., & Bauer, J. (2001). Urban kindergartners' literary understanding of picture storybooks. *New Advocate, 14*, 329–342.

Sipe, L. R. (2004, December). *What is "postmodern" about postmodern children's picturebooks?* Paper presented at the National Reading Conference, San Antonio, TX.

Sipe, L. R., & Brightman, A. E. (2005). Young children's visual meaning-making during readalouds of picture storybooks. *National Reading Conference Yearbook, 54*, 349-361..

Sipe, L. R., & Brightman, A. E. (2006). Teacher scaffolding of first-graders' literary understanding during readalouds of fairytale variants. *National Reading Conference Yearbook, 55*, 276–292.

Sipe, L. R., & Daley, P. A. (2005). Story-reading, story making, and story telling: Urban African American kindergartners respond to culturally relevant picture books. In D. Henderson & J. P. May (Eds.), *Exploring culturally diverse literature for children and adolescents: Learning to listen in new ways* (pp. 229–242). Boston: Pearson.

Sipe, L. R., & Ghiso, M. P. (2005). Looking closely at characters: How illustrations support children's understandings of character through picturebook illustrations. In N. Roser & M. Martinez (Eds.), *What a character!: Character study as a guide to literary meaning making in grades K–8* (pp. 134-153). Newark, DE: International Reading Association.

Sipe, L. R., & McGuire, C. E. (2006). Picturebook endpapers: Resources for literary and aesthetic interpretation. *Children's Literature in Education, 37,* 291–304.

Smolkin, L. B., & Donovan, C. A. (2004). Developing a conscious understanding of genre: The relationship between implicit and explicit knowledge during the five-to-seven shift. In C.M. Fairbanks et al. (Eds.), *53rd Yearbook of the National Reading Conference.* Chicago: National Reading Conference.

Sonheim, A. (1991). *Maurice Sendak.* New York: Twayne Publishers.

Spitz, E. H. (1999). *Inside picture books.* New Haven, CT: Yale University Press

Stake, R. (1994). Case studies. In N. K. Denzin & Y. S. Lincoln (Eds.), *Handbook of qualitative research* (pp. 236–247). Thousand Oaks, CA: Sage.

Stanton, J. (2005). *The important books: Children's picture books as art and literature.* Lanham, MD: Scarecrow Press.

Stevenson, D. (1991). "If you read the last sentence, it won't tell you anything": Postmodernism, self-referentiality, and The Stinky Cheese Man. *Children's Literature Association Quarterly, 19,* 32–34.

Stewig, J. W. (1995). *Looking at picture books.* Fort Atkinson, WI: Highsmith.

Strauss, A., & Corbin, J. (1998). *Basics of qualitative research: Techniques and procedures for developing grounded theory* (2nd ed.). Thousand Oaks, CA: Sage.

Suhor, C. (1984). Towards a semiotics-based curriculum. *Journal of Curriculum Studies, 16,* 247–257.

Thompson, A. (2001). Harriet Tubman in pictures: Cultural consciousness and the art of picture books. *The Lion and the Unicorn, 25,* 81–114.

Trites, R. (1994). Manifold narratives: Metafiction and ideology in picture books. *Children's Literature in Education, 25,* 225–242.

Unsworth, L. (2001). *Teaching multiliteracies across the curriculum: Changing contexts of text and image in classroom practice.* Philadelphia: Open University Press.

Van Kraayenoord, C. E., & Paris, S. G. (1996). Story construction from a picture book: An assessment activity for young learners. *Early Childhood Research Quarterly, 11,* 41–61.

Vasquez, V. M. (2004). Negotiating critical literacies with young children. Mahwah, NJ: Lawrence Erlbaum Associates.

Walsh, M. (2003). 'Reading' pictures: what do they reveal?: Young children's reading of visual texts. *Reading: Literacy and Language, 37,* 123–130.

Waugh, P. (1984). *Metafiction: The theory and practice of self-conscious fiction.* New York: Routledge.

Whitelaw, J., & Wolf, S. A. (2001). Learning to "See Beyond": Sixth-grade students' artistic perceptions of The Giver. *The New Advocate, 14,* 57–67.

Whitin, P. (2002). Leading into literature circles through the sketch-to-stretch strategy. *The Reading Teacher, 55,* 444–450.

Wiesner, D. (2001). *The three pigs.* New York: Clarion.

Williams, G. (1998). Children entering literate worlds: Perspectives from the study of textual practices. In F. Christie & R. Misson (Eds.), *Literacy and schooling.* New York: Routledge.

Wolf, S., & Heath, S. B. (1992). *The braid of literature: Children's worlds of reading.* Cambridge, MA: Harvard University Press.

Wolfenbarger, C. D., & Sipe, L. R. (2007). A unique visual and literary art form: Research about picturebooks. *Language Arts, 84,* 273–280.

39

GETTING THE PICTURE: VISUAL DIMENSIONS OF INFORMATIONAL TEXTS

Barbara Moss
SAN DIEGO STATE UNIVERSITY

The ability to read informational text is a critical skill both in the workplace and in the classroom. The literacy needs of adults center primarily on obtaining information from nonfiction texts (Venezky, 2000), and the literacy demands of today's technological society require that students be able to read and write in the digital world as well as in the world of print (Schmar-Dobler, 2003). Success in navigating the digital world, for example, requires the ability to read the text found on Internet Web sites, which is primarily expository (Kamil & Lane, 1997), and to evaluate and synthesize information from multiple online sources (Schmar-Dobler).

According to Kamil (2004), for example, "Nothing is more important to a student's success in school than the ability to read and write expository text." By sixth grade, more than 75% of school reading demands involve non-narrative materials (Venezky, 2000). Furthermore, 50–80% of reading passages on standardized tests are informational (Calkins, Montgomery, Santman, & Falk, 1998; Daniels, 2002); to do well on such tests requires student familiarity with exposition and facility in reading this text type.

Standardized test data reveal that informational text continues to pose challenges for today's students. The "fourth-grade slump," first observed by Chall and Jacobs (1983), is one manifestation of this problem. These researchers noted that many low-income third graders reading on grade level experienced a sudden drop in reading scores in the fourth grade. Experts suggested that the shift in emphasis on standardized tests from decoding to the reading of expository text may help to explain this phenomenon (Snow, Burns, & Griffin, 1998).

Furthermore, results of the Progress in International Reading Study (PIRLS) also indicated the difficulty American children have with informational text. American 9-year-olds, for example, scored significantly higher on the Literacy Subscale than on the Information Subscale (Mullis, Martin, Gonzalez, & Kennedy, 2003). Results of the Program for International Student Assessment (PISA), an international comparison of 15-year-olds' performance in reading literacy and other areas, indicate that U.S. students ranked seventh internationally, while students in New Zealand and Finland ranked first and second, respectively (Organisation for Economic Co-Operation and Development, 2000). One explanation for the excellent performance of Finnish students may be their early school exposure to informational text (Gambrell, 2005).

In American primary classrooms, however, story continues to be the predominant genre of choice (Hoffman, Roser, & Battle, 1993; Pressley, Rankin, & Yokoi, 1996; Venezky, 2000). Duke (2000) for example, found very little informational text in the first-grade classrooms she studied, whether displayed on walls or in classroom libraries. Most importantly, she found that students spent on average only 3.6 minutes with information text per day.

Experts now recommend that students be provided with exposure to informational text early on and that they be provided with direct instruction in reading this text type (Palincsar & Duke, 2004; Saul & Dieckman, 2005). As Palincsar and Duke pointed out, there is no research to justify a delay or to suggest that children must learn to read before they begin to interact with informational text. This early interaction with informational text develops domain knowledge, or deep knowledge about a particular topic. By developing children's domain knowledge at the elementary level, we help to ensure later success with the increasingly demanding texts found in content at the upper-grade levels (Hirsch, 2006).

Furthermore, reading informational text allows children to develop critical information processing skills, referred to as "the forgotten component of the elementary and secondary language arts program" (Venezky, 1994, p. 10). Students who learn to use the organization and structure of informational texts are better able to comprehend and retain the information found in them (Goldman & Rakestraw, 2000; Pearson & Duke, 2002; Venezky, 1982).

A critical component of the development of domain knowledge and information processing skills involves the ability to process visual texts. Today's informational texts, which include trade books, textbooks, and magazines, are rife with an array of visuals of numerous types and varying complexity. Understanding these visuals is crucial to children's comprehension of particular content-area topics. With the advent of computer-generated graphics, these visuals have become more prevalent, more sophisticated, and more important than ever before.

Evidence of the increased interest in informational text and the visuals that accompany it is reflected in the recent redesign of the National Assessment of Educational Progress (NAEP). The newly developed 2009 edition of the NAEP (American Institutes for Research, 2005) will contain 50% informational text at the 4th-grade level, 55% at the 8th-grade level, and 70% at the 12th-grade level, approximating the increasing amount of expository text students are likely to encounter as they progress through the grades (Salinger, Kamil, Kapinus, & Afflerbach, 2005). Furthermore, the new NAEP will emphasize visual texts, in recognition of their increasing importance to our lives. They provide the following rationale for inclusion of these texts:

> Research indicates that adults spend considerably more time reading documents (i.e., information in matrix or graphical form) than they do reading prose materials. Documents and procedural texts are indeed common in our society; for example, we interpret bus schedules, assemble simple devices, order goods from a catalog, or follow directions to set the VCR clock. Such texts are used frequently in elementary and secondary schools, where students encounter textbooks that are replete with graphs, tables, and illustrations to accompany and expand traditional continuous text. (American Institutes for Research, 2005, p. 30)

THE NATURE OF VISUAL INFORMATIONAL TEXTS

The first illustrated children's book appeared in 1657, when Johannes Comenius published *Orbis Sensualium Pictus*, or *Visible World*. Interestingly, this was an informational text, one that provided an encyclopedic array of facts on biology, zoology, religion, and many other topics. The entries were accompanied by illustrative woodcuts explicating the text. Clearly, this early pairing of pictures and text demonstrated the value and importance of visuals to children's understanding of factual material.

Informational texts, like most other texts, have in the past been predictable in format. Today, however, because of the influences of electronic media and the production capabilities of computers, informational texts have changed. Visuals now assume a more prominent place and are an integral part of page layouts that are nonlinear in nature. Today's book designers, whether creators of magazines, newspapers, electronic texts, textbooks or information trade books, are creating informational texts that reflect the features, formats, and structures of digital texts.

These digitally designed texts are characterized by a variety of visuals including photographs, maps, charts, graphs, timelines, sidebars and so on. These visuals range from extremely representational and concrete, such as photographs, to extremely abstract, multilayered texts. Informational texts for younger children contain more representational visuals, including photos and artwork, while books for older children contain a much broader range of visuals at far greater levels of abstraction (Kerper, 1995). Theses visuals take on a dizzying array of forms and formats whether they appear in textbooks, children's magazines, trade books, or electronic texts.

These graphic texts are visually noteworthy also in terms of design and placement of words on the page. Text and graphics are no longer arranged in linear forms. Text in today's books is often organized in freestanding blocks, referred to as lexias. These lexia have been likened to the frames found in graphic novels and are often found in the ubiquitous and enormously popular Dorling Kindersley books. According to Dresang (1999b), in digitally designed books, words become pictures and pictures become words; they merge to create a particular meaning. These graphic informational texts can take many different forms. They can be completely wordless, like Tom Feelings' (1995) *The Middle Passage: White Ships/Black Cargo,* conveying information and creating emotional impact in the absence of language. Other graphic texts like *Maus: A Survivor's Tale* (Spiegelman, 1986), described serious subjects like the Holocaust through cartoon-like formats.

Another critical characteristic of these texts is their nonlinearity. Unlike linear texts, which must be read top to bottom and left to right, nonlinear texts can be read in any order. Headings and subheadings may appear random, and texts and multiple illustrations appear to be scattered around the page. Text often appears in chunks, rather than in the more traditional line-by-line format. Perhaps most significantly, these texts require reader independence. The author may do little to guide readers through the text; readers must make their way through the text on their own (Alvermann, Swafford, & Montero, 2004)

The Radical Change Phenomenon

According to Dresang (1999b), computers have created a radical change in books, a transformation that she viewed as both inevitable and natural in view of the evolution of our digital society. This has resulted in books that reflect the connectivity, immediacy, and interactivity of both images and texts. Furthermore, these books often contain texts and visuals that work synergistically in ways not found in books from the past.

Dresang identified several types of changes that characterize this shift in the nature of books for youth, including changing forms, formats, and perspectives. She argued that these changing forms and formats extend the traditional boundaries associated with graphical format and presentation. They are characterized by synergistic uses of words and pictures, nonlinear and nonsequential arrangements of information, multiple layers of meaning, and interactive formats reminiscent of hypertext formats. For example, the extraordinary *i see the rhythm* (Igus, 1998) demonstrates many of the unique characteristics of these texts. This book pushes the envelope in terms of form and format, both in terms of text and visuals. It combines the perspective of an artist, Michele Wood, on the history of African American music with that of the author. It integrates history, poetry, and paintings. In creating the book, Wood read historical accounts of early musicians and created illustrations based upon what she imagined life to be during that time. Toyomi Igus, the author, listened to the music of the period after seeing each of Wood's illustrations, and created poems and an accurate historical timeline reflective of each scene. The book is arranged in chronological order, but could not be described as truly linear. Each two-page spread contains a title, a painting depicting a period in African American music, a caption describing the people, places, and time period reflected in the painting, a timeline, and a poem. The poem is reflective of information provided by the painting, the captions, and the timeline, and uses multiple font types and colors for emphasis and interest. The interplay between the text, the visuals, and the music creates a unique synergy, and the perspectives of both the artist and author are united into a seamless whole.

This synergistic relationship between words and texts involves young readers in approaching these texts in new and different ways. Dresang (1999a) maintained that "books in the digital world use visual information in place of words and vice versa." (p. 81). Books employ visual clues that readers must attend to if they are to construct meaning from the text. Sometimes this relationship is made even more interesting through layering; whereby content is visually embedded in other content, adding yet another level of complexity to the text. Sometimes, for example, placement of text on a page cues the reader to its importance. In other instances, words appear *in* the illustrations, rather than alongside of them. Even white space performs an important function. In the popular Dorling Kindersley books, she argued that frequent use of white space provides "thinking space" or time for reflection about the book's content.

In these "digitally designed" texts, information is organized differently from that found in traditional texts. The headings, typeface, and type size sometimes provide cues to reader about the importance of content, as does the positioning of text one the page. In *The Magic School Bus on the Ocean Floor* (Cole, 1994), for example, illustrator Bruce Degins explained that he placed the children's reports, which provide an introduction for the topic of each page, in the upper left-hand corner, thereby simulating the pull-down file menus found in computer applications (Dresang, 1999a). This example points out the need for careful design of such books; illustrators who carefully design visual elements can effectively guide young readers through these texts by positioning information in clear, consistent ways.

These books, too, reflect multiple perspectives within a single book. Often these are the perspectives of individuals and groups who have, in the past, been denied a voice. The visual content of these books provides a meaningful, and sometimes dramatic, way to illustrate these multiple perspectives. *We Were There, Too!: Young People in US History* (Hoose, 2001) uses primary sources including diaries, letters, and photographs, to tell the stories of children of the past whose stories have, in many cases, never been told before. The book incorporates photographs, sidebars, quotations, and short, accessible thumbnail sketches to tell the stories of a diverse cast of children and young adults between 1492 and today who in some way made a difference in their world. We not only hear their voices through the descriptions and primary source documents, but we see their faces peering out at us from the past. The use of these photographs connects us to these children's lives in a way that mere words cannot.

THE ROLE OF VISUAL TEXTS

In the past, informational texts were characterized by extended amounts of text and a few visuals. The function of visuals was ancillary to text, or as an adjunct or extension to textual information. The traditional view of the role of visuals has been that the place of illustration is secondary to that of text.

Some experts, however, argue that a revolution has taken place and that the role of visuals has become at least as important as the text itself. In other words, these experts hold the view that making meaning from text derives not just making meaning from print, but from visuals. Moline (1995) for example, regarded visual texts as complementary to verbal texts. He characterized them as "integrated texts" where paragraphs, headings, visual elements and so on contain parts that support, explain, or provide context for one another (p. 14).

Still others, however, take a different view. Kress and van Leeuwen (1996), for example, argued that graphics hold more meaning in today's texts than words. In their research, Kress, Ogborn, and Martins (1998) found that today's science textbooks no longer contain visuals that support text explanations, but rather contain texts that support visual explanations. The view that informational visuals take precedence over traditional texts is an increasingly popular one, and not necessarily a new one. According to Roland Barthes (1977), "Formerly the image illustrated the text (made it clearer); today the text loads the image, burdening it with a culture, a moral, an imagination. Formerly, there was reduction from text to image; today there is amplification from one to the other" (p. 26). Traditionally, reading experts have focused on the concept of considerate text, or text that contain coherence and hierarchically arranged concepts that are easily discerned. According to La Spina (1998), through careful placement of visuals, the concept of considerate text is redefined; rather than representing clearly linked propositional units and lessons, structural principles may be adhered to pictorially rather than verbally.

PROCESSING DIGITALLY DESIGNED TEXTS

Children today seemingly not only prefer, but expect digitally designed texts. According to Marc Prensky (2001), today's students are Digital Natives, that is, they have lived their entire lives in a world where technology has provided immediate access to information. Here is how he characterized this generation: "Digital Natives are used to receiving information really fast. They like to parallel process and multi-task. They prefer their graphics *before* their text rather than the opposite. They prefer random access (like hypertext). They function best when networked. They thrive on instant gratification and frequent rewards." (p. 1).

His views are consistent with at least a few small studies from the field of educational technology. In these studies, children almost universally preferred limited amounts of text when selecting Web sites (Large, 2004) and preferred sites with high visual content and short, simple texts. These students reported that they liked to see animation and interactivity on the Internet (Bilal, 2004).

A small study by Dresang (2005) examined two sixth graders' responses to two Dorling Kindersley books. Students were videotaped and thought aloud as they read on two separate occasions. Both agreed that the format of texts was crucial for them. One student stated, "I am so accustomed to making choices in the information I access and in the visual guides along with words, and with words that are not all buried in huge blocks of text, that I would not have pursued the information in another more traditional format" (p. 3).

Today's informational texts depend as never before on the dual processing of both texts and visuals. Informational texts require that readers process two different sign systems: words and pictures. Research from the past provides information about the reading of such texts; however, until recently this research did not focus on digitally driven texts, but on more traditional couplings of texts and visuals. Clearly, there is a need for research related to the processing of these digitally designed texts.

Reading the complex digitally driven texts requires readers not only to understand text and images, but also to explore the relationships between the two. Readers must move back and forth from the linear presentation of verbal text to the two-dimensional visual text that can take a variety of forms including diagrams or icons. Today's informational texts, then, depend not just upon a reader, but a viewer-reader. This viewer-reader may encounter sidebars, boxed information, headings, steps in a process, charts, or cross-sections on a single two-page spread (Kerper, 1995). Kress (2003) explained the difference between reading a traditional page and a new page in the following way:

> The former coded a clear path, which had to be followed. The task of reading lay in interpretation and transformation of that which was clearly there and clearly organized. The new task is that of applying principles of relevance to a page that is open in its organization, and consequently offers a range of possible reading paths, perhaps infinitely many (p. 162).

In reading these texts, children point and click with their eyes, thereby simulating the computer experience in nonelectronic books. In these books, children organize information and make connections in a nonlinear, self-determined order. Children can start reading on any page and any text section might link to another, as is true with hypertext (Dresang, 1997). Meek (1995) described this phenomenon in another way; she argued that children engage in "radial" reading of these texts; the information can be thought of as a wheel with many spokes, and reading can begin at any spoke on the wheel.

Prensky (2006) maintained that, in previous generations, graphics were generally illustrations, accompanying the text and providing some kind of elucidation. For today's young people, the relationship is almost completely reversed; the role of text is to elucidate something that was first experienced as an image. Since childhood, the younger generation has been continuously exposed to television, videos, and computer games that put high-quality, highly expressive graphics in front of them with little or no accompanying text. The result of this experience has been to considerably sharpen their visual sensitivity. They find it much more natural than their predecessors to begin with visuals, and to mix text and graphics in a richly meaningful way. This shift toward graphic primacy in the younger generation raises some extremely thorny issues, particularly with regard to textual literacy and depth of information (p. 1). Obviously, one of the thorniest issues relates to the question of how children actually process these texts as well as the challenges that these texts might present. Studies dating from the 1970s have examined children's understanding of and response to visual texts. According to Kerper (1995), the ability to make meaning from visuals in informational texts requires that children not just detect the image, but understand its significance. This pictorial literacy is usually acquired by children at the age of 8 or 9 (Goldsmith, 1987). However, studies by Amen (1941), for example, indicated that younger children are more likely to focus on pictorial details, rather than the whole. Clearly, this will impact the meaning the child constructs. In addition, construction of meaning is culturally dependent and dependent upon experience (Fussell & Halland, 1978). For example, young children or children from particular cultures may not be familiar with symbols such as the circle/cross commonly used to denote "not."

Clearly, the dual processing requirements of texts and illustrations make comprehension more complex than would otherwise be the case. In studies of more traditional content involving science texts and accompanying visuals, readers were required to alternate between reading a text and inspecting a visual, which is often the case with digitally designed texts. In their study of older students' reading of science textbook content that included scientific diagrams, researchers found that students did not necessarily understand such visual texts instantly. Readers often found it necessary to inspect diagrams repeatedly and in detail, in order to obtain the information necessary to understanding (Hegarty, Carpenter, & Just, 1996).

Still other more recent studies have examined how children read images in picturebook texts (Arizpe & Styles, 2003). These authors concluded that children were sophisticated readers of visual texts, and often noted features that adults ignored. In his study of children's reading processes as related to information trade books and accompanying visuals, Kerper (2003) found that students read informational books in a process he described as linear with embedded recursion. He described their behaviors in this way:

> Young readers may begin at the front of a book, perusing the illustrations and reading the print as needed. They may skip over what does not make sense and progress toward the final page. However, as the visual experience expands their knowledge, the memory of anomalous material may cause children to flip back and forth through the pages as they construct new meanings. At other times, children may want to investigate an aspect of a topic in greater detail. This leads to close reading of the material (p. 42).

Questions still remain about the efficacy of these texts for instruction and how effectively students are able to navigate and comprehend these texts. With the recent adoption of textbooks rife with graphics, some critics make the case that text content has been subordinated to visual content—that visual elements have overtaken text in ways that have diluted the potency of the verbal message. Sewall (1992) expressed this concern in relationship to social studies textbooks: "The expository nature of the social studies textbook has atrophied. In the place of a strongly written text, textbooks have substituted a nervous, fragmented; kaleidoscopic, multivalent learning took that seems designed, really, for nonreaders. The gray, non-nonsense history primer of the past is long gone . . ." (p. 28).

Accounts by some teachers indicated that, at least for some children, these new texts are overwhelming. One teacher's study of how children actually react to these texts, for example, found that students were often simply confused by the panoply of images and text. Some children encountered difficulty in navigating these nonlinear texts and tried to read through a whole page from top to bottom as if it were a "traditional" text. Other students became confused by the sudden jumps into sidebar material and captions and looked at the picture captions but never read the text. Others read the text but never read the lesson titles (Budiansky, 2001).

Furthermore, little attention seems to be given to those children who are unfamiliar with digitally designed texts because of limited access to technology. Clearly, a digital divide continues to exist in our society; only about one fourth of Black and Hispanic households, for example, have access to technology. Levels of family education and income are important determinants of Internet use among school-age children. However, the mere presence of a computer in the home is not enough to ensure Internet use; children need access to technical support, expertise, and training in the home (Cleary, Pierce, & Trauth, 2006). These findings do not bode well for children of poverty. Many of these children lack access to the Internet, and do not have parents who can help them use the computer to locate information. Their parents may lack skills in English, and because they work in low-paying jobs, often in the service industries, their work experiences with computers may be minimal. For these children in particular, digitally designed texts may pose significant challenges.

Clearly, these children, and probably many others, need teachers who can help them find meaningful ways to process these texts. As Meek (1995) noted, the creators of visual texts often assume that children can read and understand their texts, but this may not necessarily be the case. She suggested that little real instruction related to visual texts typically occurs in schools. Today's children need teachers who can help them mediate these digitally designed texts and show them ways in which they can use text features to determine important ideas, interpret charts, diagrams, and graphs, and recognize the complex interplay between words and texts. As children increase their familiarity with the features and challenges of these texts, they can begin to create their own texts. In this way, they will deepen their understanding of the ways in which digitally designed texts convey information synergistically through words and pictures.

Without question, digitally designed informational texts are here to stay. There is little doubt that if children are to survive in the 21st century, they need to develop the visual and verbal literacy skills necessary to effectively construct meaning from these texts. Children need to learn to be flexible, strategic readers of these new text types, and they need to develop the analytical skills requisite for understanding complex visual content, verbal content, and the relationship between the two. Most importantly, children need teachers who understand the nature and quality of these new texts and who can support their efforts to effectively and meaningfully obtain information from these texts.

REFERENCES

Alvermann, D., Swafford, J., & Montero, M. K. (2004). *Content area literacy instruction for the elementary grades.* Boston: Allyn & Bacon.

Amen, E. W. (1941). Individual differences in a perceptive reaction: A study of the response of preschool children to pictures. *Genetic Psychology Monographs, 23,* 319–385.

American Institutes for Research. (2005). *Reading fram work for the 2009 National Assessment of Educational Progress pre-publication edition.* Retrieved November 1, 2005, from http://www.nagb.org/pubs/reading_fw_06_05_prepub_edition.doc

Arizpe, E., & Styles, M. (2003). *Children reading pictures. Interpreting visual texts.* London: Routledge Falmer.

Barthes, R. (1977). Rhetoric of the image. In S. Heath (ed). *Images, music, text* (pp. 32–51). New York: Hill and Wang.

Bilal, D. (2004). Children's information seeking on the Web. In M. K. Chelton & C. Cool (Eds.), *Youth information-seeking behavior* (pp. 271–291). Lanham, MD: Scarecrow Press.

Budiansky, S. (2001). *The trouble with textbooks.* Retrieved June 2, 2006, from http://www.project2061.org/publications/articles/articles/asee.htm

Calkins, L. J., Montgomery, K., Santman, D., & Falk, B. (1998). *A teacher's guide to standardized reading tests: Knowledge is power.* Portsmouth, NJ: Heinemann.

Chall, J. S., & Jacobs, V. A. (1983). Writing and reading in the elementary grades: Developmental trends among low-SES children. *Language Arts, 60,* 617–626.

Cleary, P. F., Pierce, G., & Trauth, E. M. (2006). Closing the digital divide: Understanding racial, ethnic, social class, gender and geographic disparities in Internet use among school age children in the United States. *Universal Access in the Information Society, 4,* 354–373.

Cole, J. (1994). *The magic school bus on the ocean floor.* New York: Scholastic.

Daniels, H. (2002). Expository text in literature circles. *Voices from the Middle, 9,* 7–14.

Dresang, E. (1997). Influence of the digital environment on literature for youth: Radical change in the handheld book. *Library Trends, 45*(4), 639–664.

Dresang, E. (1999a). *Radical change: Books for youth in a digital age.* New York: H. W. Wilson Company.

Dresang, E. (1999b). Radical change: Digital age literature and learning. *Theory into Practice, 38*(3), 160–168.

Dresang, E. (2005). The information-seeking behavior of youth in the digital environment. *Library Trends, 54,* 178–197.

Duke, N. K. (2000). 3.6 minutes per day: The scarcity of informational texts in first grade. *Reading Research Quarterly, 35,* 202–224.

Feelings, T. (1995). *The middle passage: White ships, black cargo.* New York: Dial.

Fussell, D., & Halland, A. (1978). Communicating with pictures in Nepal: Results of practical study used in visual education. *Educational Broadcasting International, 11,* 25–31.

Gambrell, L. B. (2005). Reading literature, reading text, reading the Internet: The times they are a'changing. *Reading Teacher, 58,* 588–591.

Goldman, S. R., & Rakestraw, J. A. (2000). Structural aspects of constructing meaning from text. In M. Kamil, P. B. Mosenthal, P. D. Pearson & R. Barr (Eds.), *Handbook of reading research* (Vol. 3; pp. 311–336). Mahwah, NJ: Lawrence Erlbaum.

Goldsmith, E. (1987). The analysis of illustration in theory and practice. In H. A. Houghton & D. M. Willows (Eds.), *The psychology of illustration: Volume 2. Instructional issues* (pp. 53–85). New York: Springer-Verlag.

Hegarty, M., Carpenter, P. A., & Just, M. A. (1996). Diagrams in the comprehension of scientific text. In R. Barr, M. Kamil, P. Mosenthal & P. D. Pearson (Eds.), *Handbook of reading research* (Vol. 2; pp. 641–668). Mahwah, NJ: Erlbaum.

Hirsch, E. D. (2006). *The case for bringing content into the language arts block and for a knowledge-rich curriculum core for all children.* Retrieved April 4, 2006, from http://www.aft.org/pubs-reports/american_educator/issues/spring06/hirsch.htm

Hoffman, J. V., Roser, N. L., & Battle, J. (1993). Reading aloud in classrooms: From the modal to a "model." *Reading Teacher, 46*(6), 496–503.

Hoose, P. M. (2001). *We were there, too! Young people in U.S. history.* New York: Farrar Straus Giroux.

Igus, T. (1998). *i see the rhythm.* San Francisco: Children's Book Press.

Kamil, M. (2004, August 4). *Reading to learn 2004.* Paper presented at the Reading to Learn Summer Institute, Escondido, CA.

Kamil, M., & Lane, D. (1997). *Using information text for first grade reading instruction: Theory and practice.* Paper presented at the National Reading Conference, Scottsdale, AZ.

Kerper, R. (1995). *Three children viewing and reading: Transactions with illustrations and print in informational books.* Unpublished doctoral dissertation, the Ohio State University, Columbus.

Kerper, R. (2003). Choosing quality nonfiction literature: Examining aspects of accuracy and organization. In R. A. Bamford & J. V. Kristo (Eds.), *Making facts come alive: Choosing and using quality nonfiction literature K-8* (pp. 41–64). Norwood, MA: Christopher-Gordon.

Kress, G. (2003). *Literacy in the new media age.* London: Routledge.

Kress, G., Ogborn, J., & Martins, I. (1998). A satellite view of language: Some lessons from science classrooms. *Language Awareness, 7,* 69–89.

Kress, G., & van Leeuwen, T. (1996). *Reading images: The grammar of visual design.* New York: Routledge.

Large, A. (2004). Information seeking on the Web by elementary school students. In M. K. Chelton & C. Cool (Eds.), *Youth information seeking behavior: Theories, models, issues* (pp. 293–319). Lanham, MD: Scarecrow Press.

LaSpina, J. A. (1998). *The visual turn and the transformation of the textbook*. Mahwah, NJ: Laurence Erlbaum.

Meek, M. (1995). *Information and book learning*. London: Thimble Press.

Moline, S. (1995). *I see what you mean*. York, ME: Stenhouse.

Mullis, I. V. S., Martin, M. O., Gonzalez, E. J., & Kennedy, A. M. (2003). *PIRLS 2001 international report: IEA's study of reading literacy achievement in primary schools*. Chestnut Hill, MA: Boston College.

Organization for Economic Co-Operation and Development. (2000). *Measuring student knowledge and skill: The PISA 2000 assessment of reading, mathematical and scientific literacy*. Paris: Author.

Palincsar, A., & Duke, N. K. (2004). The role of text and text-reader interactions in young children's reading development and achievement. *The Elementary School Journal, 105*(2), 183–197.

Pearson, P. D., & Duke, N. K. (2002). Comprehension instruction in the primary grades. In C. C. Block & M. Pressley (Eds.), *Comprehension instruction: Research-based best practice* (pp. 247–258). New York: Guilford.

Prensky, M. (2001). Digital natives, digital immigrants. *On the Horizon, 9*, 1-6.

Prensky, M. (2006). *Reaching younger workers who think differently*. Retrieved June 1, 2006, from http://www.marcprensky.com/writing/Prensky%20-%20Twitch%20

Pressley, M., Rankin, J., & Yokoi, L. (1996). A survey of instructional practices of primary teachers nominated as effective in promoting literacy. *The Elementary School Journal, 96*, 363–384.

Salinger, T., Kamil, M., Kapinus, B., & Afflerbach, P. (2005). *Development of a new framework for the NAEP reading assessment*, San Antonio, TX.

Saul, E. W., & Dieckman, D. (2005). Choosing and using information trade books. *Reading Research Quarterly, 40*(4), 502–513.

Schmar-Dobler, E. (2003). Reading on the Internet: The link between literacy and technology. *Journal of Adolescent and Adult Literacy, 47*, 80–85.

Sewall, G. T. (1992). Textbook organization and writing: Today and tomorrow. In J. G. Herlihy (Ed.), *The textbook controversy: Issues, aspects and perspectives*. Norwood, NJ: Ablex.

Snow, C., Burns, M. S., & Griffin, P. (Eds.). (1998). *Preventing reading difficulties in young children*. Washington, DC: National Academy Press.

Spiegelman, A. (1986). *Maus: A survivor's tale*. New York: Pantheon.

Venezky, R. L. (1982). The origins of the present-day chasm between adult literacy needs and school literacy instruction. *Visible Language, 16*, 113–136.

Venezky, R. L. (1994). Literacy and the textbook of the future. In N. J. Ellsworth, C. N. Hedley & A. N. Barratta (Eds.), *Literacy: A Redefinition* (pp. 39–54). Hillsdale, NJ: Lawrence Erlbaum.

Venezky, R. L. (2000). The origins of the present-day chasm between adult literacy needs and school literacy instruction. *Scientific Studies of Reading, 4*, 19–39.

40

DRAWING TO LEARN: VISUAL SUPPORT FOR DEVELOPING READING, WRITING, AND CONCEPTS FOR CHILDREN AT RISK

Anne McGill-Franzen
UNIVERSITY OF TENNESSEE

Jacqueline Love Zeig
UNIVERSITY OF FLORIDA

Early reading intervention has garnered much attention and effort in recent years. As a result, schools have implemented, or are implementing, instructional interventions to reduce early reading failures. Intervening early, typically with a focus on developing phonological skills and decoding proficiencies, is an essential element in ensuring that all children become readers. However, while the early intervention efforts have proven their worth, too many children struggle with reading comprehension in first, second, third, and fourth grades and beyond.

In a recent summer school intervention, we developed elementary grade teachers' expertise in the broad areas of reading—fluency, vocabulary, comprehension of narrative and informational text, and reading stamina. The National Reading Panel (NRP) report (available online at http://www.nationalreadingpanel.org) identified fluency, vocabulary, and reading comprehension as critical components of skilled reading. We believe that reading stamina, or persistence while reading texts of increasing challenge, is also critical and related to fluency, vocabulary, and comprehension. Recent analyses of student test performances (Guthrie, 2002) have noted that too many children seem unable to sustain independent reading for more than a brief period, and few children can sustain a theme or hold the details of longer texts (5–10 pages) often found in both school assignments and reading assessments. We call this reading stamina. Additionally, the National Assessment of Educational Progress (NAEP) data show that the longer the passage, the lower the proportion of children who are able to respond correctly, even when passage difficulty is constant. Similarly, the Progress in International Literacy Study (PIRLS), an international comparison of reading performances of nine-year-olds (fourth graders in the United States), dramatically illustrated the weaknesses American students have in reading informational texts compared with their peers internationally (available online at http://www.pirls.org). Although American children performed well above the international average in reading narrative texts, their performance in reading informational text fell well below. The available data indicated a need for interventions targeted to improving reading instruction beyond the early decoding skills, and especially an increased emphasis on reading informational texts, commonly referred to as "reading to learn." Finally, motivation—the desire to read—has received increased emphasis on the part of reading researchers. Without motivation to read, it is unlikely that students will develop the stamina and strategic reading behaviors that lead to increased performance on state and national standards. Motivation, in fact, has been called the "missing pillar" in the NRP report (Allington, 2005). Although essential for sustained engagement with reading (Guthrie, 2004), motivation was not listed as a critical component of reading instruction. In a recent meta-analysis of experimental and quasi-experimental studies, Guthrie and Humenick (2004) identified four kinds of classroom practices that were highly associated with motivation—(a) setting knowledge goals,

(b) providing students choices about what to read and with whom, (c) providing interesting texts, and (d) enabling peer collaboration while reading. Thus, the general framework for our intervention was determined both by current knowledge in the field of reading education, in particular, research that addressed the use of drawing and visual supports for students who struggle with reading and writing, and the present direction of policy toward a focus on the components of the NRP report.

For several summers, we conducted what we called "summer reading clubs" in high-poverty Florida schools, typically those that have not made adequate yearly progress as required by *No Child Left Behind Act* (NCLB; available online at http://www.ed.gov/nclb/landing.jhtml). Summer school in Florida, and increasingly in other states, is available only to children who fail high stakes assessments and are in danger of being retained. The majority of the retained children in our summer reading clubs were minority and poor with spotty attendance and high rates of mobility during the school year.

The purpose of the chapter is to locate drawings and other pictorial representations of content as a source of motivation and learning within a framework of access to books, choice, collaboration, and discussion in a summer intervention for at-risk children. In the first section, we provide background on the summer interventions—called "summer reading clubs"—and present data on the efficacy of these interventions to sustain or improve the achievement of at-risk children over the summer months; we briefly review the research that establishes the viability of our pedagogical tools and, in particular, the role of drawing or visual support in learning theory. In the second section, we more fully specify the instructional context within which we used drawing and pictorial representation to develop conceptual models of narration and classification and build peer collaboration and individual engagement.

SUMMER READING CLUBS

The research reported here represents the observations by the authors in collaborative curriculum development studies that involved several teachers across two summers in two different districts. We describe first a summer reading club, grades K–3 students (N = 89 treatment students; N = 39 controls), all of whom were retained in grade, in a large urban district (Grades K–3 Summer Reading Club). The second summer reading club involved only students in grade 3 in a much smaller district (N = 77 treatment students; N = 47 controls). These students failed the state mandated test and were scheduled to repeat grade 3 (Grade 3 Reading Club). For participating teachers in both summer reading clubs, we provided 25–30 contact hours including workshops, practica, and classroom coaching experiences. For participating students we provided access to engaging and appropriate books and intensive pedagogy designed to support readers who struggle. The purpose of the collaboration was to explore pedagogy that was both instructive in the essential components of literacy development and motivating for elementary students who failed or were at risk of failure in their respective grades. The interventions were extremely short in both summer reading clubs—approximately four to five weeks in both districts. Fewer students in control teachers' classrooms returned permission forms, thus unbalancing both projects.

Group sizes varied from school to school, as did the provision of extra supports, such as tutoring. The amount of time available for the intervention during the school day varied as well. In some cases, teachers were able to spend an hour each day; at the other extreme, teachers spent less than a half of an hour each day. The summer reading clubs were designed to fit into whatever time allocations or structures were already established by the school or district. In the large urban district (Grades K–3 Summer Reading Club), virtually all the students qualified for free or reduced lunch; only one school was less than 99% minority. The percent of free or reduced lunch participants varied in the small district (Grade 3 Summer Reading Club) from a low of 36% to a high of 92%. The majority of the students in the small district were also minority.

Grades K–3 Summer Reading Club

Our first summer intervention took place in a large, northeastern Florida urban district of over 126,000 students. Summer school was not held in every school. Instead, children residing within particular cachement areas attended designated summer schools, which may or may not have been the enrolling school for children during the school year. A convenience sample of volunteering teachers served as treatment or control teachers. Teachers were selected to participate in the project based on the proximity of their schools to the researchers and research assistants. Volunteer teachers who were not selected became the control teachers. Students were selected for inclusion in the project based on parent permission. Those children in treatment teachers classes who returned permission forms became the treatment students; those in control teachers classrooms who returned forms became the control students. Ultimately, 89 treatment students and 39 control students participated, the majority being first and second graders (46 first graders, 30 second graders, 13 third graders, and a small number of kindergarten students who were not assessed on our measures). All students were marked for retention in their respective grades based on district assessments (SAT-9) and teachers' recommendations. With the exception of one school, the majority of students in the summer reading club was African American and was eligible for free and reduced lunches.

Grade 3 Summer Reading Club

Our second intervention was conducted in a small Florida district of 29,422 students. We selected a convenience sample of all possible participants in the summer of 2003. Schools in which principals agreed to participate were included in the study as either a treatment school or a control school. All volunteer teachers within each school were selected to participate. In each school, we selected students based on parental permission. A total of 77 students in the treatment group and 47 students in the control group ultimately participated—all third graders. As in the previous study, fewer students in the control schools returned permission forms, creating a sample size discrepancy between treatment and control groups.

Outcome Measures

Proficiency reading trade books—both accuracy and fluency—was the major criterion for evaluating the effectiveness of the summer reading clubs. We selected a purposive sample of Scholastic Guided Reading Books (Levels A–Z) to ascertain students' instructional reading level and the number of words read correctly per minute on instructional level text (see Table 40.1 for a list of the trade books

TABLE 40.1. Scholastic Trade Books by Title & Guided Reading Levels

Title	Author	Genre	GR Level
What Do Insects Do?	Susan Canizares & Pamela Chanko	Non-Fiction	A
Hats Around the World	Liza Chalesworth	Non-Fiction	B
In the City	Susana Pasternac	Narrative	C
The Haircut	Susan Hartley & Shane Armstrong	Narrative	D
Just Like Me	Barbara J. Neasi	Narrative	E
Pizza Party	Grace Maccarone	Narrative	F
Who Stole the Cookies	Judith Moffatt	Narrative	G
Danny and the Dinosaur Go to Camp	Syd Hoff	Narrative	H
Too Many Puppies	Patience Brewster	Narrative	I
Fox and His Friends	Edward Marshall	Narrative	J
Shipwreck Saturday	Bill Cosby	Narrative	K
Cam Jansen & the Mystery of the Babe Ruth Baseball	David A Adler	Narrative	L
The Popcorn Book	Tomie de Paola	Non-Fiction	M
Dolphin's First Day	Kathleen Weidner Zoehfeld	Non-Fiction	N
The Spray Paint Mystery	Angela Shelf Medearis	Narrative	O
The Berenstain Bear Scouts Ghost versus Ghost	Stan & Jan Berenstain	Narrative	P
There's a Hamster in My Lunchbox	Susan Clymer	Narrative	Q
Pirates Don't Wear Pink Sunglasses	Debbie Dadey & Marcia Thornton Jones	Narrative	R
Catwings	Ursula K. Le Guin	Narrative	S
Animorphs	K.A. Applegate	Narrative	T
Bridge to Terabithia	Katherine Paterson	Narrative	U
Harry Potter and the Chamber of Secrets	J.K. Rowling	Narrative	V
Through My Eyes	Ruby Bridges	Non-Fiction	W
M.C. Higgins The Great	Virginia Hamilton	Narrative	X
My Brother Sam is Dead	James Lincoln Collier & Christopher Collier	Narrative	Y
Black Beauty	Anna Sewell	Narrative	Z

used for each gradient of text difficulty). Students also selected a text from the classroom library, and using the same guidelines for instructional level and words correct per minute, we ascertained students' abilities to self-select books that were appropriate to their reading levels. Using criteria established by Marie Clay (1993), we identified the three levels of difficulty as follows: an easy text (95–100% correct), an instructional text (90–94% correct), a hard text (80–89% correct). We subtracted the number of errors from the number of words read correctly out of 100 and then divided by 100 (total words read correctly/100 = % accurate) and coded the percentage correct as *easy*, *instructional*, or *hard*. During a second reading of the instructional level text, we determined the words correct per minute and followed the same procedure for the self-selected text. The purpose of these assessments was to determine how fluently students read at their instructional level and how fluently students were able to read a book they selected for independent reading. To assure interrater reliability all assessment sessions were tape recorded and dual scored. Because an important component of the intervention was providing students with access to interesting, appropriate trade books, the oral reading assessments were an ecologically sound measure of students' use of these books, the contribution of the intervention to the students' ability to read books of increasing difficulty, and to self-select books they were able to read independently.

Findings in Context

Like other summer reading interventions, the Grades K–3 Summer Reading Club and the Grade 3 Summer Reading Club mitigated summer reading loss. Over the summer, children from low-income schools typically lose two months of reading achievement (as measured on standardized tests and reported in grade equivalents) over the summer, while children from middle-income schools gain a month each summer. Looked at cumulatively over an elementary school career, summer reading loss can account for approximately two years of the achievement gap reported in the research literature (Entwisle, Alexander, & Olson, 1997; 2001). A high-quality summer school program, extended over at least three summers, not only stems summer loss, but also may contribute to achievement gains during the summer months (Cooper, Charleton, Valentine, & Muhlenbruck, 2000).

In the case of the summer reading clubs, both treatment and control groups not only maintained achievement, but most students were able to read trade books at increasing levels of difficulty. Students who participated in the K–3rd Grade Summer Reading Club increased the text level at which they could read with support: 58% of students at first grade increased instructional text levels, 50% at second grade, and 69% at third grade. Control students also demonstrated growth on this measure: 27% of students increased the level of instructional text at first grade and 66% increased instructional text levels at second grade (there were no third graders who participated in the control schools).

Students who participated in the Grade 3 Summer Reading Club, in addition, significantly improved in accuracy over the control group and modestly increased the instructional level of text that they were able to read with teacher support—from less than one level by control students to over one level by treatment students (see Fig. 40.1 for comparison of instructional text level growth between treatment and control groups). A Repeated Measures MANCOVA (covariates: class size & SES) determined significant differences between the treatment and control groups on instructional level text favoring the students who participated in the Summer Reading Club (p = .029) with an effect size of .41. Factor analysis reduced the variables of multiple assessment instruments (for example, passages from the Qualitative Reading Inventory-3; Leslie & Caldwell, 2001, a validated informal reading inventory, district level assessments, and the instructional text levels and words correct per minute, WCPM, on instructional and self-selected text) and identified the principle components of accuracy, fluency, and comprehension. Further analysis revealed an advantage in accuracy that accrued to Summer Reading Club participants. Treatment students scored approximately one third of a standard deviation higher than nonparticipants on multiple measures of accuracy.

Teacher Collaboration on Themed Unit

In addition to the summer collaborations, the second author collaborated with a teacher of low-achieving fifth-grade students in a homogeneously grouped class on a themed unit of study. The purpose of the collaboration was to extend the instruction offered in the core-reading program on the genre of biography. Because core programs often lack curricular depth and coherence and struggling learners typically need more intensive and explicit instruction, rather than less, we compiled a classroom library of biographies on prominent African American figures, both current and past. Students selected a subject, read multiple biographies, and constructed time lines to help them understand and remember salient events and turning points in the lives of the subject. In order to construct time lines, for example, students had to reread and revisit texts, determine important information, synthesize information, and make judgments about which events to incorporate. Not only did students learn the content, but also the need to select important information created an authentic context for rereading, thus developing fluency and strategic comprehension.

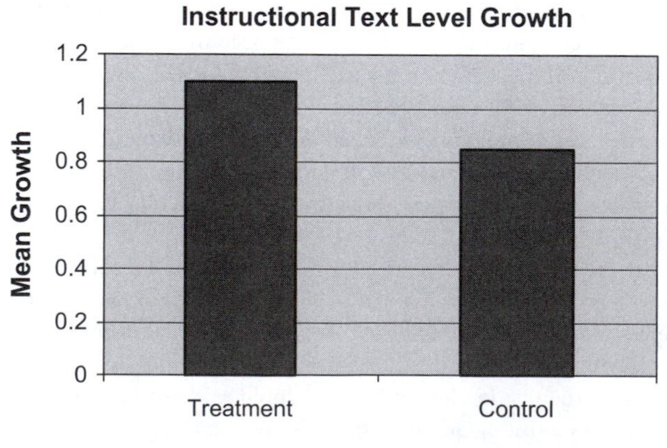

Instructional Text Level Growth

	Mean Growth
Treatment	~1.1
Control	~0.85

FIGURE 40.1 Treatment & control comparison of text level growth for Grade 3 Summer Reading Club.

As an outcome measure, we compared the performance of the students on the core program's benchmark assessments from theme 1 (prior to the intervention) to theme 2 (after the intervention). Although this comparison was not a prepost test design, we needed to demonstrate that engagement in more intensive study of a particular genre did not impede students' progress in the basal program. With one exception, every student scored at benchmark on theme 2, and the overall scores represented an improvement in performance (see Fig. 40.2).

Our intention in both the summer and themed unit collaboration was to support the development of fluency and comprehension of text while maintaining engagement and full participation by students representing a range of reading levels and writing abilities. After a review of relevant literature on factors that mediate understanding and sustain motivation, we turned to drawing as a way for all students to express learning and interpretations of text, facilitate discussion, and thereby sustain motivation.

Research-Based Pedagogical Tools

The major instructional goals of the intervention was to help teachers provide students with access to the strategic reading required in a "reading to learn" curriculum of the elementary grades and to enhance students' engagement and motivation to read. As we discussed earlier, students need to be able to process increasingly challenging texts, including informational texts as well as narratives, in order to succeed in the middle grades and beyond. Often students with excellent decoding skills fall by the wayside in the middle grades, phenomena referred to in the research literature as "the fourth grade slump" (Chall, 1983), because they lack vocabulary and comprehension strategies. The major pedagogy provided in this intervention—instructional read alouds, cognitive think alouds, and discussion—are the tools by which teachers helped students gain access to strategic reading. To enable discussion and the sharing of ideas, we turned to drawing as a vehicle of expression for struggling students, many with writing skills far below their abilities to talk about and understand complex concepts.

Although teachers typically read to children in the early grades, the instructional power of read alouds in the middle grades has been severely underestimated. Elley (1989) found, for example, that reading aloud to middle grade students significantly increased vocabulary test scores even without explicit instruction in those words. Likewise, reading aloud to students helps them to attend for long periods, motivates them to buy and read books on their own, and develops recall and inferential comprehension (Rosenhouse, Feitelson, Kita, & Goldstein, 1997). It seems that reading aloud by mediating adults helps students understand the structures and language of written texts, and these understandings transfer to other experiences reading both narrative and expository texts. Indeed, students take on the language of literary and expository texts and use these new vocabulary and syntactic structures on their own. Cognitive think alouds, in which the teacher makes visible his or her thinking as he or she works through a text, helps students understand not only the content of the text being read, but also helps them to under-

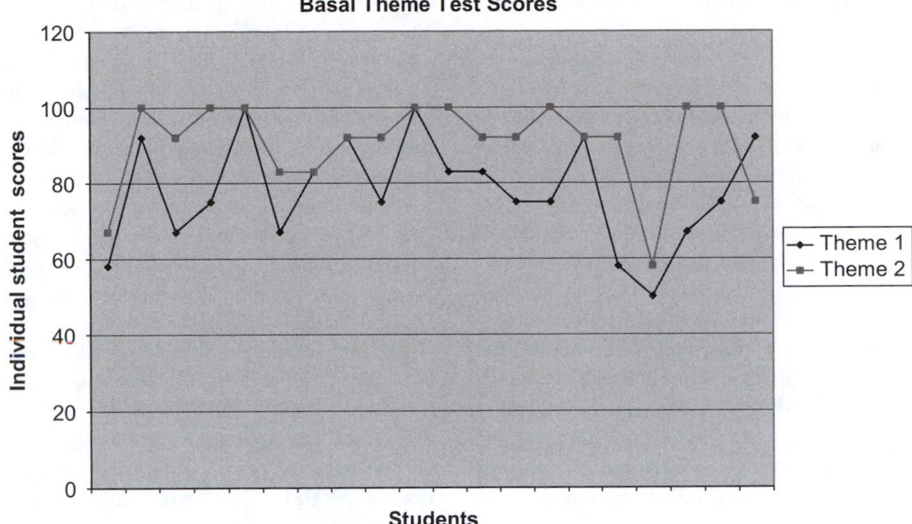

FIGURE 40.2 Fifth graders performance on theme 1 and theme 2 benchmark tests.

stand the process by which the text is understood (Kucan & Beck, 1997). Not only teachers, but other students as well, can model and talk about the thinking that helped them develop inferences and interpretations of particular texts. Collaborative discourse enables students to notice what others notice, to extrapolate patterns within and across books, to notice similarities and differences, and, most important, to build learning communities where reading and readers are valued and engaged. A recent hierarchical linear modeling analysis of classroom instruction found a strong effect for discussion on students' reading achievement (Applebee, Langer, Nystrand, & Gamoran, 2003).

Two other important elements addressed in the professional development were those of self-selected reading and access to texts that are written at a range of difficulty levels. Opportunity for voluntary, self-selected reading was a critical component of the project. Of all the variables that have been associated with improved reading achievement, the most potent correlate is time spent actually reading. By providing choice and access to books on a variety of topics and genres and varying levels of difficulty, teachers are likely to reach the whole range of learners and increase the possibility of sustained, out-of-school reading.

Thus, by learning how to engage the learner through choice, conversation, and accessible texts, we believed teachers would be able to improve fluency, develop vocabulary, enhance comprehension, and build stamina. Teachers learned to use instructional read alouds to develop familiarity with different text structures, background, and content knowledge in various content domains and in vocabulary that represents these domains. Moreover, teachers learned to model strategic reading explicitly through think alouds with expository and narrative texts. For example, teachers demonstrated how to build intratextual inferences by relating information presented later in the text to that which preceded it and how to develop interpretations by connecting evidence from the text with prior knowledge and experience. Teachers demonstrated to students how to talk about their learning, and to use discussion to mediate understandings. Teachers learned to match texts to readers' instructional and independent reading abilities and interests and to provide opportunities for self-selection and sustained reading. We believed opportunities for extended, uninterrupted periods to read self-selected books that were appropriately matched to the students' individual reading levels and interests would support the reading of longer and more complex texts, thereby building stamina, engagement, and ultimately, proficiency. We also introduced the concept of text sets, which are collections of trade books, both narrative and expository, written at a wide range of reading levels, and organized around specific topics and genres.

Visual Support for Discussion and Learning

Illustrations have a profound influence on children's understanding of texts, even among very young children, as Tower (2002) noted in her study of the responses of a small number of preschoolers to features of information books. Tower's study demonstrated the power of illustrations to shape children's interpretation of the text, even when text is read aloud to them. When the illustration did not match the text or when children misidentified the objects in the illustration, they struggled to understand the text, often letting misinterpretation of the illustration override the text information. Similarly, Oyler (1996) demonstrated that the most powerful influence on first graders' understanding of text read aloud is the content of the illustrations. Among older children, those who may be considered "reading to learn," versus "learning to read," Levin, Anglin, and Carney (1987) identified several functions that illustrations might play in "prose learning:" Illustrations can simply decorate, represent the objects or events of the text, organize the text information, assist interpretation, or transform the understanding of the reader. Just as illustrations support understanding of text read or listened to, the readers' drawings or illustrations of the content can support understanding and memory.

In an early summative assessment of the contribution of imagery to children's memory and comprehension of text, Pressley, Johnson, Symons, McGoldrick, and Kurita (1989) noted that training in using graphic metaphors (Baumann, 1984) and generating graphic maps, summaries (Armbruster, Anderson, & Ostertag, 1987; Berkowitz, 1986; Taylor & Beach, 1984), and representational imagery (Gambrell & Bales, 1986; Idol, 1987) improved recall of stories and informational text. Pressley et al. identified imagery as a strategy that children could be taught to use independently, but such instruction needed to be explicit: Teachers first described the strategy, modeled the use of the strategy, typically with think alouds; they described why the strategy was important and when it should be used; next, teachers provided guided practice and corrective feedback. Poor readers appeared to benefit the most from instruction in using imagery (Pressley et al., 1989, p. 25). Pressley et al. speculated that training in such strategy use "probably changes naturalistic reading" (p. 8), with gains predicated upon several conditions. One finding identified by the researchers was that students must generate their own graphic metaphors and summaries in order to reap the most benefit; prepared summaries, maps, or other graphics did not lead to great improvement in children's recall of information.

Several theories of learning and reading comprehension have emerged to help explain possible relationships between imagery and text comprehension. Researchers who espouse the "dual-coding" theory of cognition hypothesized two independent but interconnected mental systems of processing—the verbal and nonverbal subsystems (Pavio, 1990; Sadoski & Pavio, 2001). As interpreted by Gambrell and Jawitz (1993) in their research on children's use of illustrations and images to understand text, these dual-coding subsystems may work in tandem, with language evoking images and images evoking language (p. 28). The nonverbal subsystem consists of "nested sets of information" or images that operate without the logical constraints imposed on the verbal system. These nested images may serve as "conceptual pegs" for holding related information. In explaining the enhanced recall by children instructed to attend to story illustrations and make mental images of their own, Gambrell and Jawitz invoked the conceptual peg hypothesis, "which asserts that key images serve as mental 'pegs' to which associated information is hooked for storage and retrieval" (p. 28). Likewise, they viewed Rosenblatt's (1978) transactional theory of literary response as supporting the role of imagery, and images, in text comprehension by enabling the reader to more easily experience or "live through" the text world. More recently, the work of Langer (1990) called up a similar relationship between understanding literature and constructing images. In fact, her theory of reading comprehension was called "envisionment," and it requires the reader to step into and move through the story world, all the while building or envisioning possible scenarios for denouement.

Another related theory of cognition, somewhat different from the dual-coding model of information processing, is that of generative teaching. Wittrock (1991) differentiated information processing theories from that of generative teaching by saying that information processing models of cognition illustrate the role of memory, or stored knowledge, in comprehension, but do not describe how the learner (or teacher) establishes rapport between ideas in a subject area or within a text, and between that information and his or her own experiences, prior knowledge, and beliefs. Generative teaching supports the learner's knowledge construction by emphasizing self-monitoring and control of learning, sustained attention, and transformation of subject content into the learner's own words or images. In one study (Linden & Wittrock, 1981), upper elementary students were able to improve their comprehension by 50–80% when they were taught to talk with each other about their own interpretations and describe the images they used to relate sentences within a story and understand the story as a whole (Wittrock, 1991, p. 179). Student-generated drawings, illustrations, graphs, tables, and diagrams functioned like student-generated written summaries in the studies by Wittrock and colleagues (see also Osborne & Wittrock, 1983). In their own words, the generative teaching model proponents identified the "important principle [being to get] students to generate associations and relations that elaborate that text structure, make it more precise, and extend it, always using their own words or images to show how text concepts are related to one another" (Wittrock, 1991, p. 182).

Further, although drawing and other representational imagery have not received equal billing with reading and writing in school, Vygotsky (1978) believed that drawing was an essential conceptual tool for children. Studies by Edens and Potter (2003) and Van Meter (2001) support that contention.

USING DRAWING TO LEARN, REMEMBER, REFERENCE, AND RESPOND

Drawing is a way into discussion for emergent and early readers and writers and struggling readers of any age. If students are asked to draw, and write all around the drawing, for example, every child has a chance to contribute to small group or partner discussion, no matter what his writing may look like. Drawing as a springboard for discussion is similar to writing as a springboard—response, expression of learning, and interpretation. Drawing enables all students to initiate topics, generate questions, facilitate conversation, and position themselves as authority.

In our summer reading clubs, we asked teachers to have students draw a picture of "something they thought of" (Daniels, 2001) and write all around the picture, using sound spelling for words they were unsure of. Students met daily with partners or small group to share something from the book they were reading. Similar to a "talking stick," students joined the discussion, using their drawings to help focus their talks. They asked questions, compared books in a series, made predictions, and identified the best parts.

Besides providing impetus for talk about narratives and the elements of narratives, such as characters, drawing provided impetus for talk about particular concepts or topics, such as insects. Although most teachers were familiar with the concept of "literature circles" (Daniels, 2001) as a forum for peer-led talk, few actually implemented small group discussion in their classrooms prior to our work with them, and especially not with early readers or struggling readers at any grade level. Less well known to our participating teachers was the concept of "idea circles," defined by Guthrie and McCann (1996) as "a peer-led, small group discussion of concepts fueled by multiple text sources" (p. 88). Rather than all students in a group reading the same text, as is common in literature circles, each student read or listened to a different text, on the same topic, a related topic, or a different part of the same topic. Because each student located a variety of information on the same or related topic, each brought unique knowledge to the discussion. Students recorded this unique knowledge in different ways. For students in the summer reading clubs who struggled with both reading and writing, visual representation of their ideas by drawing, illustrating, constructing charts with Post-its, and creating diagrams opened up new possibilities for learning and remembering content knowledge.

Building on the Known

Because summer reading clubs met for such a short period of time, typically less than an hour a day for four weeks, few topics could be studied in depth. The topic of "bugs" transcended ages, grade levels, and geography. All students were interested in bugs, albeit in different bugs. If teachers had time for a single nonfiction topic, they chose bugs. All students had some background knowledge about bugs—no elaborate experiments were required. Similarly, students in coastal schools had deep interest in and background knowledge about ocean life—sharks, whales, and dolphins, in particular. In the wetlands of north-central Florida, students had at least passing experience with amphibians, especially frogs and alligators, and reptiles, like lizards, of all kinds. By providing access to interesting, appropriate texts through read alouds, partner, or shared reading, and instructional level texts supported by guided reading, teachers helped students across grade levels to elaborate the conceptual domains around these topics, specify technical vocabulary to represent these concepts, and revise, as necessary, students' everyday knowledge about these topics.

In order to develop narrative comprehension, we took a page from the work of Feitelson and her colleagues (Rosenhouse et al., 1997) who discovered the power of multibook series written by the same author to engage students, develop complexity in oral language expression, and improve comprehension achievement. The instructional use of series books "initiates a process which stimulates young readers to reread these books" (Rosenhouse et al., 1997, p. 169). Again, building on what children already know, we tapped into the everyday culture of TV cartoons, other media, and movies to motivate students to read, discuss, draw, and write about favorite characters and familiar settings.

From Self-Selected Small Groups to Jigsaws

In keeping with the evidence of research about motivation, students joined other students of their choice to research a topic, or to read books by the same author or in the same series. For example, one third-grade teacher selected "bugs" as a study topic during summer reading club. She made available over 50 trade books at different reading levels on the topic of bugs—including several field guides, which she referenced and read aloud, and several informational series books such as *DK Eyeopeners, Pebble Books,* and *Rookie-Reader Read-About-Science* series. All those interested in bees, for example, formed their own group (see Fig. 40.3 for a photo of the "bee group"), those interested in spiders formed their group, and so on, until all students had selected a species of bug to research and identified partners with whom to locate and discuss information. Upon completing fact sheets, drawings, diagrams, or some other visual support to help remember specific information on a particular subset of insects or arachnids, students recombined with different students—a jigsaw arrangement—and shared information gathered in the previous group. In that way, all students became experts, a repository of unique knowledge. Newly formed jigsaw groups compared bugs across species, looking for common elements and telling differences, and using their drawings to start to build theories about bugs.

FIGURE 40.3 Bee group.

Noticing, Referencing, and Responding

Teachers in the summer reading clubs practiced thinking aloud, making visible to inexperienced readers what skilled readers notice while reading narratives and informational books. Teachers modeled for students how to identify and record important information that provides keys to interpreting illustrations in field guides. One teacher in the Grade 3 Summer Reading Club used the book *Bugs* (Parker & Wright, 1988) as a mentor text, identifying through think alouds the text features that she noticed for each entry. When students recorded information on the particular bugs they had researched, they incorporated several of these features into their own illustrations, mimicking the format of a field guide (see Fig. 40.4). The example we provide here noted the gender and size of the spider, but also labeled the parts of the spider with annotations and provided a fact box with information about habitat.

As other examples, teachers modeled the construction of a time line to keep straight the important dates in the life of a historical figure; they demonstrated the drawing of cutaway diagrams to show the insides of houses, cars, mammals, and insects. They publicly displayed and referenced the graphic organizers they constructed to show relationships across species or to classify information according to domain categories. Again, students in the Grade 3 Summer Reading Club followed the lead of their teacher and posted a picture glossary on the wall for easy reference while compiling information about the insects and arachnids they had elected to study (see Fig. 40.5).

In narratives, the language used by characters is distinctive and often significant. In summer reading clubs, teachers shared with students what they noticed about characters and modeled for them ways to reference special attributes of fictional characters. Teachers modeled, for example, collecting quotes from characters across several books in a series to demonstrate what kind of a person that character is. A third grade student translated Scooby Doo's expres-

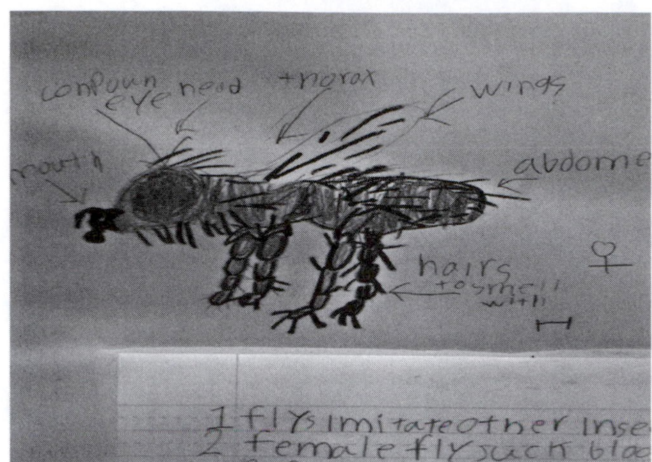

FIGURE 40.4 Field guide.

sions into conventional English and posted them in the classroom (see Fig. 40.6); he noticed the pattern that Scooby begins each word with an *r*—for example, "Rook!" means "Look!" and "Rah-chooy!" means "Ah-choo!"

In the section that follows, we present several additional examples of drawings by students from kindergarten to fifth grade. We provide the instructional context for these drawings, explaining the students' purposes in creating them, and our analysis of the concepts that each drawing represents.

Maddy. Maddy entered kindergarten with much enthusiasm for reading and writing but little knowledge of how reading and writing works. She identified only the upper case *M,* the first letter of her name. She could rhyme and match beginning sounds but thought the illustration carried the complete meaning in little books. After a full two months of instruction, Maddy automatically recognized a small number of highly frequent words at sight and used them as anchors to read very predictable little books with two-word sentences supported by explicit illustrations. Then, her teacher introduced the book log, a vehicle for kindergartners to discuss books they are reading, words they noticed, and a favorite part. Clearly, an emergent reader like Maddy would not have the writing vocabulary to express her ideas, but by drawing a picture of a cat with the caption "climb," Maddy was able to remember the "good part" to tell her friend during partner reading. Moreover, with each experience sharing her book log, she again experienced words in context. With repeated experiences, it is likely that she will remember not only "like" but also "climb" (see Fig. 40.7).

Marcus. At the end of his kindergarten year Marcus wrote a three-part story (see Fig. 40.8) with Clifford as the central character. Marcus drew three illustrations—one page for each part of the story. The first illustration introduced Clifford and the setting of the story; the second set up the problem, and the third drawing showed Clifford resolving the problem. Using his drawings as a guide, Marcus wrote three sentences—in effect, a caption for each illustration. Marcus wrote, "Clifford is going to New York. He wrote on an important paper. He erased his mistake." The illustrations provided strong support for this emergent reader to read and remember the words that he wrote—an example of drawing in service of reading and writing.

Sepket. Third grader Sepket lived near the ocean. He chose to research sharks and was surprised to discover that not all sharks were giants. In order to represent this new information, he decided to compare the size of the smallest shark with something familiar—his little brother—thereby making explicit the scale of the cookie cutter shark (see Fig. 40.9).

Haley. Dog enthusiast Haley was repeating first grade. She listened to, partner read, and independently read field guides on dogs. She particularly liked guides to pet care. After a read aloud by her teacher, Haley drew a comparison (see Fig. 40.10) of a dog's night

FIGURE 40.5 Bug glossary.

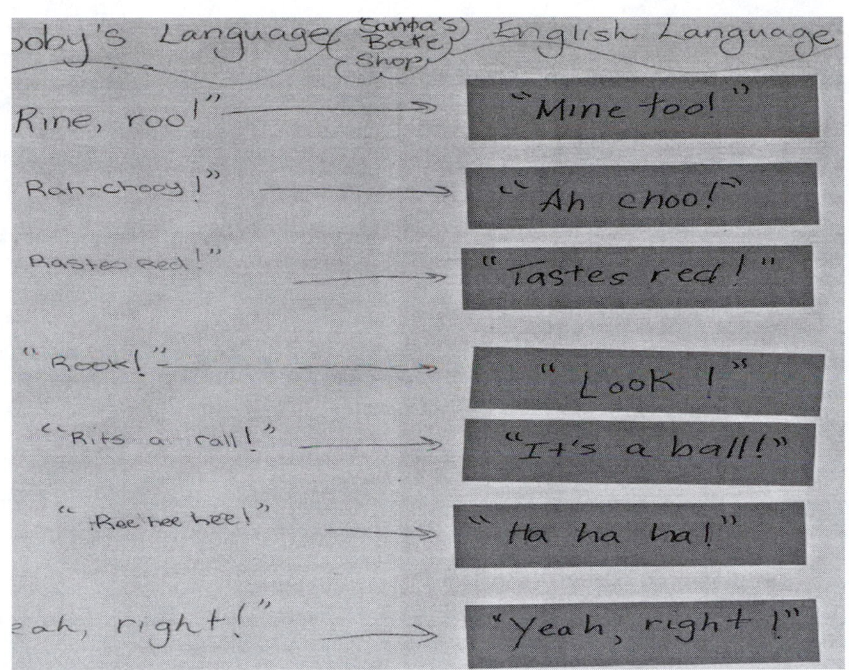

FIGURE 40.6 Scooby language.

FIGURE 40.7 Maddy's book log.

FIGURE 40.8 Marcus' Clifford story: "Clifford is going to New York."

FIGURE 40.9 Scale drawing of a cookie cutter shark: "A cookie cutter shark is as small as my little brother."

vision versus a person's night vision. Before becoming immersed in field guides about dogs, Haley believed that people had better vision than dogs. She revised her everyday knowledge to accommodate new information and expressed these ideas in the drawing. As part of a nonfiction unit on animals through idea circles and jigsaws, her teacher constructed a four-part chart to help first graders classify animals they were researching into mammals, fish, amphibians, and reptiles. Haley struggled with the ideas that dogs and humans were both mammals and, in this bit of talk we eavesdropped on, she wondered what that meant for raising a pet dog:

> It [Evans (2001)] said if your dog is bad, spank him a little hard, then a little easy, then put him in the cage. And I like this part. I like this part the most 'cuz it told you how to do a lot of things with your puppies. So it got me thinking about this. It got me to, like, write about my dog. So I think some people just let their dogs or their puppies do what they want to . . . but, I think if I was them, I wouldn't do that. The dog or the puppies . . . are like that. Are, like, are rude. . . . So our parents don't spank us. They just tell us to go to our rooms. . . kinda like humans. Dogs are kinda like humans. So, I think these dogs and these puppies or human beings and dogs and puppies are kinda in the same group.

Shawn. Third grader Shawn constructed a three-part pamphlet on his dog. He studied the descriptions of various breeds of dogs in the field guides and decided that his was a mongrel. He drew a dog, adapting an illustration from Gail Gibbons' (1997) *Dogs* to fit his own pet, and in doing so, demonstrated his knowledge of the word *mongrel* and the concept represented by it. "Some dogs like this one right here. Some dogs are pure breed. If they're not pure breed, they could look like this or this or this—a *mongrel*" (see Fig. 40.11).

Jered. Like Shawn's illustration, Jered's cutaway (see Fig. 40.12) of the inside of the shark bears the scientific labels of a field guide, including vocabulary such as *vertebra, dorsal fin, pectoral fin,* and *cartilage.* Although Jered copied elements of the diagram and the labels exactly from a field guide, researchers in science education have found that pictorial representations, even copying, supports students with little prior knowledge in building mental models of scientific concepts (Edens & Potter, 2003; Gobert & Clement, 1999).

Miguel. Third-grader Miguel was learning English as a second language. Although he made much progress, Miguel struggled to express his ideas in English, particularly in writing, and when at loss for an appropriate English word or expression, he substituted Spanish in oral discussion. Retelling in English was a particularly onerous task for Miguel; not only must he understand the narrative he listened to, but he must find the English to demonstrate that he did indeed comprehend. By sketching with stick figures each story event as it unfolds, then numbering in sequence each small sketch, Miguel held the narrative in time and space. The pictorial representation of the narrative enabled Miguel to focus on language use,

FIGURE 40.10 Haley's comparison drawing of a dog and a person: "Dogs can see better than a person."

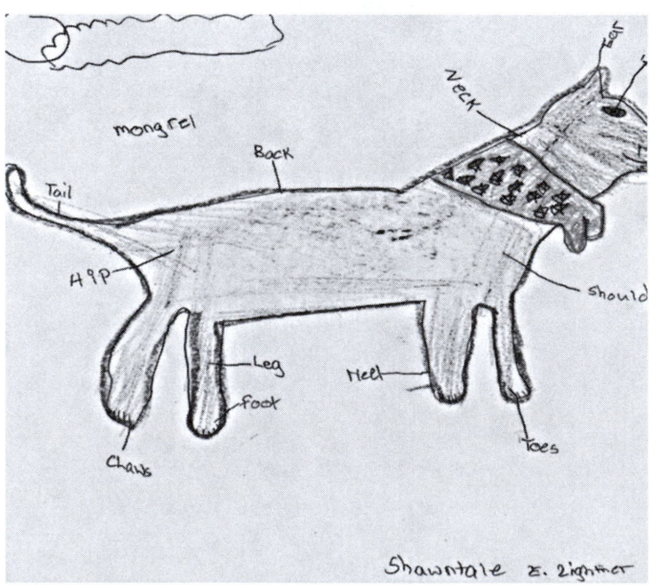

FIGURE 40.11. Annotated illustration of a mongrel.

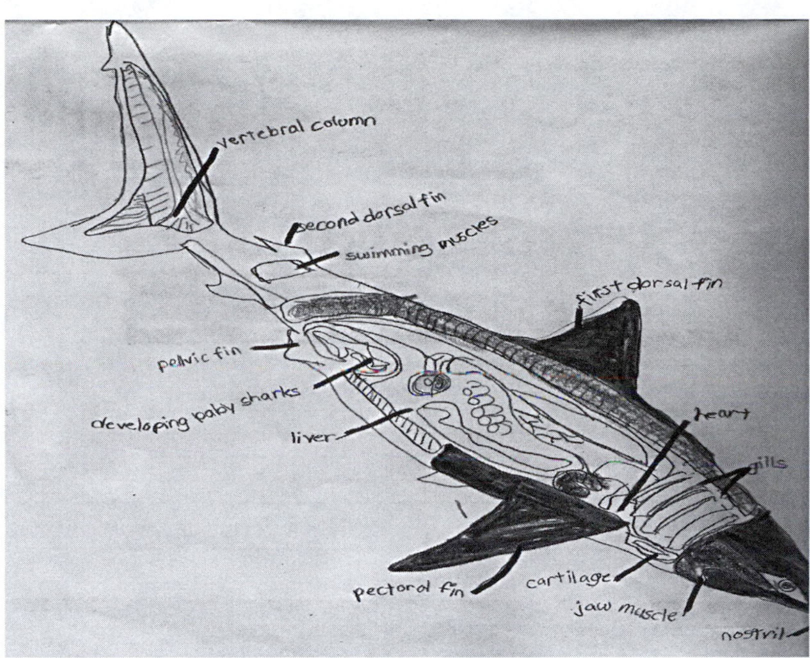

FIGURE 40.12 Annotated cutaway diagram of a shark.

FIGURE 40.13 Numbered pictorial sequence of the story events in *The Three Little Javelinas* (Lowell, 1992).

simplifying the retelling task, and anchoring his talk in a visual chronology (see Fig. 40.13).

Matt. Matt's time line was similar to Miguel's numbered sketches arranged in a particular sequence. As a fifth grader, Matt was responsible for particular genre knowledge, including characteristics of biography, that was to be assessed by benchmark tests within the core-reading program. His teacher, in collaboration with the second author, immersed his class in biographies, often reading them aloud. As she read the biographies, she guided students through think alouds to notice text language that represented significant events in the lives of prominent African Americans. She modeled the construction of a time line as visual support for remembering the events, in sequence, and as support for writing a biography that captured salient events or turning points in the lives of historical figures. Matt's time line not only identified Tubman's birth, escape from slavery, and death, but also identified critical knowledge that Tubman gained early in life from her parents: "Father taught her to hunt, swim, and imitate bird calls, and survive in the woods. . . . Mother taught her nursing and how to use herbs for medicine," teachings that enabled her escape to freedom and to help

Timelines – Sequence of Events

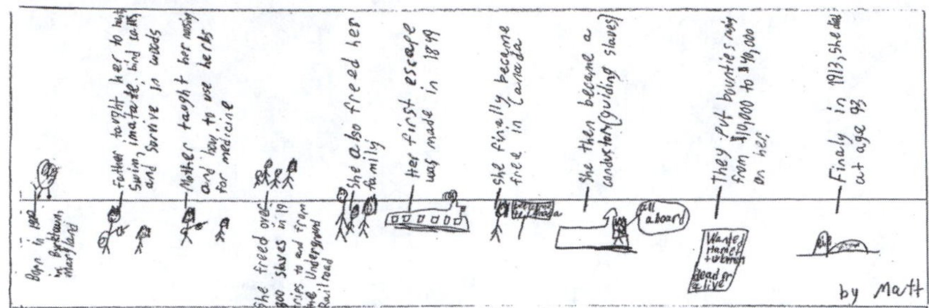

FIGURE 40.14 Timeline of Harriet Tubman's life.

others do so in the Underground Railroad. Matt sketched with stick figures and line drawings to support his memory for detail and dates and to use as a reference as he wrote (see Fig. 40.14).

Discussion

Our experience with drawing and other pictorial representations of content gives added weight to the converging research on the role of images in learning, and in particular, the support that visual tools provide learners who have more limited prior knowledge and academic success. We suggest two reasons for our view. First, generative drawings, and even copying, influence students' understanding of content, especially scientific concepts. As researchers in science education recently demonstrated, "Drawing tasks and annotated illustrations support the processes of selection, organization, and integration, which underpin the cognitive processes necessary for meaningful learning" (Edens & Potter, 2003, p. 140). Visual tools not only promote comprehension but they also support memory and serve as cognitive placeholders for children to call up and organize their oral and written language to express their understandings. Second, students who struggle with literacy may find particular motivation in drawing as a way to represent and share their ideas, and as seen from our examples of students' work, drawings need not be elaborate to convey understandings and unique expertise or to serve as a springboard for discussion and collaborative knowledge building with peers. Certainly, our achievement data from the Summer Reading Clubs demonstrated that even short-term interventions can engage struggling students and advance their instructional reading levels. We recommend that teachers consider drawings or "illustrations that instruct" (Mayer, 1993) as teaching and learning tools that together with other motivating classroom practices—access to appropriate and interesting texts, choice, collaboration, and opportunity to discuss—enable at-risk children to participate fully in a literate community.

REFERENCES

Allington, R. (2005). What counts as evidence in evidence-based education? *Reading Today, 3,* 16.

Applebee, A. N., Langer, J. A., Nystrand, M., & Gamoran, A. (2003). Discussion-based approaches to developing understanding: Classroom instruction and student performance in middle and high school English. *American Educational Research Journal, 40*(3), 685–730.

Armbruster, B., Anderson, T., & Ostertag, J. (1987). Does text structure/summarization instruction facilitate learning from expository text? *Reading Research Quarterly, 22,* 331–346.

Baumann, J. (1984). The effectiveness of a direct instruction paradigm for teaching main idea comprehension. *Reading Research Quarterly, 20,* 93–115.

Berkowitz, S. (1986). Effects of instruction in text organization on sixth-grade students' memory for expository reading. *Reading Research Quarterly, 21,* 161–178.

Chall, J. S. (1983). *Stages of reading development.* New York: McGraw-Hill.

Clay, M. (1993). *An observation survey.* Portsmouth, NH: Heinemann.

Cooper, H., Charleton, K., Valentine, J., & Muhlenbruck, L. (2000). Making the most of summer school: A meta-analytic and narrative review. *Society for Research in Child Development, 65*(1, Serial No. 260).

Daniels, H. (2001). Literature circles: Voice and choice in book clubs and reading groups. New York: Stenhouse.

Edens, K., & Potter, E. (2003). Using descriptive drawings as a conceptual change strategy in elementary science. *School Science and Math Journal, 103*(3), 135–144.

Elley, W. B. (1989). Vocabulary acquisition from listening to stories. *Reading Research Quarterly, 24,* 174–187.

Entwisle, D., Alexander, K., & Olson, L. (1997). *Children, schools, and inequality.* Boulder, CO: Westview.

Entwisle, D., Alexander, K., & Olson, L. (2001). Keep the faucet flowing: Summer learning and home environment. *American Education, 25*(3), 11–15, 47.

Evans, M. (2001). *Puppy: ASPCA pet care guidelines.* New York: Dorling Kindersley.

Gambrell, L., & Bales, R. (1986). Mental imagery and the comprehension-monitoring performance of fourth- and fifth-grade poor readers. *Reading Research Quarterly, 21,* 454–464.

Gambrell, L., & Jawitz, P. B. (1993). Mental imagery, text illustrations, and children's story comprehension and recall. *Reading Research Quarterly, 28*(3), 264–276.

Gibbons, G. (1997). *Dogs.* New York: Scholastic.

Gobert, J. D., & Clement, J. J. (1999). Effects of student-generated diagrams versus student-generated summaries on conceptual understanding of causal and dynamic knowledge in plate tectonics. *Journal of Research in Science Teaching, 36*(1), 39–53.

Guthrie, J. (2002). Preparing students for high-stakes test taking in reading. In A. Farstrup, & S. J. Samuels (Eds.), *What research has to say about reading instruction* (pp. 370–391). Newark, DE: International Reading Association.

Guthrie, J. (2004). Teaching for literacy engagement. *Journal of Literacy Research, 36*(1), 1–28.

Guthrie, J., & Humenick, N. M. (2004). Motivating students to read: Evidence for classroom practices that increase motivation and achievement. In P. McCardle, & V. Chhabra (Eds.), *The voice of evidence in reading research* (pp. 329–354). Baltimore, MD: Brookes.

Guthrie, J., & McCann, A. (1996). Idea circles: Peer collaborations for conceptual learning. In L. Gambrell, & J. Almasi (Eds.), *Lively Discussions!* (pp. 87–105). Newark, DE: International Reading Association.

Idol, L. (1987). Group story mapping: A comprehension strategy for both skilled and unskilled readers. *Journal of Learning Disabilities, 20,* 196–205.

Kucan, L., & Beck, I. (1997). Thinking aloud and reading comprehension research: Inquiry, instruction, and social interaction. *Review of Educational Research, 67*(3), 271–299.

Langer, J. A. (1990). The nature of understanding: Reading for literary and informational purposes. *Research in the Teaching of English, 24*(3), 229–260.

Leslie, L., & Caldwell, J. (2001). *Qualitative Reading Inventory-3 (QRI-3).* Boston: Allyn & Bacon/Longman.

Levin, J., Anglin, G, & Carney, R. (1987). On empirically validating functions of pictures in prose. In D. Willows, & H. Houghton (Eds.), *The psychology of illustration* (Vol. 1, pp. 51–86) New York: Springer-Verlag.

Linden, M., & Wittrock, M. (1981). The teaching of reading comprehension according to the model of generative learning. *Reading Research Quarterly, 18*, 44–57.

Lowell, S. (1992). *The three little javelinas*. Flagstaff, AZ: Rising Moon.

Mayer, R. (1993). Illustrations that instruct. In R. Glaser (Ed.), *Advances in instructional psychology* (Vol. 4, pp. 253–284). Hillsdale, NJ: Erlbaum.

Osborne, R. J., & Wittrock, M. C. (1983). Learning science: A generative process. *Science Education, 67*(4), 489–509.

Oyler, C. (1996). Sharing authority: Student initiations during teacher-led read-alouds of information books. *Teaching and Teacher Education, 12*, 149–160.

Parker, N., & Wright, J. (1988). *Bugs*. New York: Scholastic.

Pavio, A. (1990). *Mental representations: A dual coding approach* (2nd ed.). New York: Oxford University Press.

Pressley, M., Johnson, C., Symons, S., McGoldrick, J., & Kurita, J. (1989). Strategies that improve children's memory and comprehension of text. *The Elementary School Journal, 90*(1), 3–32.

Rosenblatt, L. (1978). *The reader, the text, the poem: Transactional theory of the literary work.* Carbondale, IL: Southern Illinois University Press.

Rosenhouse, J., Feitelson, D., Kita, B., & Goldstein, Z. (1997). Interactive reading aloud to Israeli first graders: Its contribution to literacy development. *Reading Research Quarterly, 32*(2), 168–183.

Sadoski, M., & Pavio, A. (2001). *Imagery and text: A dual coding theory of reading and writing.* Mahwah, NJ: Lawrence Erlbaum Associates.

Taylor, B., & Beach, R. (1984). The effects of text structure instruction on middle-grade students' comprehension and production of expository text. *Reading Research Quarterly, 19,* 134–146.

Tower, C. (2002). "It's a snake, you guys!": The power of text characteristics on children's responses to information books. *Research in the Teaching of English, 37*(1), 55–88.

Van Meter, P. (2001). Drawing construction as a strategy for learning from text. *Journal of Educational Psychology, 93*(1), 129–140.

Vygotsky, L. S. (1978). *Mind in society: The development of higher psychological processes*. New York: Academic Press.

Wittrock, M. (1991). Generative teaching of comprehension. *The Elementary School Journal, 92*(2), 169–184.

41

THE ROLE VISUALIZATION STRATEGIES PLAY IN STRUGGLING READERS' ENGAGEMENT, COMPREHENSION, AND RESPONSE TO TEXT OR "WAIT. YOU MEAN IT'S SUPPOSED TO MAKE SENSE EVERY TIME YOU READ?"

Mary Massie
NORTHEASTERN ILLINOIS UNIVERSITY

Karen Boran
NORTHEASTERN ILLINOIS UNIVERSITY

Jeffrey D. Wilhelm
BOISE STATE UNIVERSITY

Seeing people, scenes, and ideas in our mind's eye is a phenomenon that everyone experiences, with or without conscious control. If you misplace your keys, you may deliberately instruct your mind to visually play back your steps from the last time you had them in your hand. Conversely, you may find it difficult to block out a painful visual memory that keeps appearing unbidden on your mental screen. These are examples of visualization as we commonly know it.

In the context of teaching literacy, *visualization* is the process by which a reader forms mental images to build understanding while reading or listening to a text. It is one of a set of comprehension processes that readers initiate at specific points in a text to understand, apply, and appreciate authors' writings (Block & Pressley, 2003; Long, Winograd & Bridge, 1989). And for some of our students, it can be the critical missing step in the meaning-making process. Block and Pressley (2003) further noted that many more teachers provide instruction in these comprehension processes than had been observed in the mid-1990s.

This is certainly true in Chicago, where Karen Boran and Mary Massie have worked for many years as professional developers (starting in the mid-1990s as part of the Goals 2000 grant; for background on the Goals 2000 content area literacy initiative in Chicago, see Boran, 1999; Ogle & Hunter, 2000) and where Jeffrey Wilhelm has been a frequent and influential consultant. We are encouraged by the changes we see in reading instruction in Chicago and in Wisconsin, Maine, and Idaho, where Jeffrey Wilhelm has worked for many years. We believe an area that has tremendous potential for helping struggling readers is the explicit teaching of visualization strategies. As classroom teachers, we have witnessed that special "light bulb" moment of connection and power when a student enters what F. Smith (1988) called "the literacy club." Karen Boran glimpsed such a moment when Duarte, a 16-year-old Chicago high school student in a 10th grade environmental science class, turned to her in class and said, "Wait. You mean it's supposed to make sense *every time* you read?" For Duarte, and other struggling readers who have been given the opportunity to connect reading with a "picture" in their minds, this can be a moment of transformation.

Visualization is not as well understood by teachers as other reading processes, such as accessing prior knowledge, prediction, making connections, questioning, inferring, summarizing, and synthesizing. It *is* intertwined with each of the other processes, and it may well be the missing link for many students. For some of our students, visualizing as a means of constructing meaning during reading is unfamiliar and very difficult. Without explicit instruction in visualization, many struggling readers create significantly fewer mental representations than their more able peers do (Gambrell & Koskinen, 2002; Sadoski & Paivio, 2001). Wilhelm (1995; 1997) found visualization necessary for his students' comprehension and a prerequisite for a meaningful response to reading.

From inner-city Chicago schools to those in rural Maine and Wisconsin, we have seen particular visualization strategies open possibilities for middle and high school students who had nearly—or completely—given up on ever making sense of the reading process. These strategies are powerful devices that assist readers to engage, comprehend, and respond to text.

Today's students can learn to put their multimedia comprehension skills to work in the service of creating their own visualizations to enliven and inform the world of print that seems boring without a visual element (Leu, Kinzer, Coiro, & Cammack, 2004). We contend that visualization is a reading process deserving much more attention than it currently commands in published curricula, not only at the elementary level but also throughout middle and secondary education. In the teaching of visualization strategies, there is untapped potential to help students use all the strategies of proficient readers in concert, generating engagement, comprehension, and meaningful responses. We will review here the research regarding visualization's importance, and research on particular instructional techniques using and promoting visualization.

In addition, we propose that further investigations of visualization processes and their roles in reading instruction should draw upon legitimate findings from research of multiple methodologies and perspectives, particularly descriptive teacher research and action research involving promising instructional interventions and designs. As we do so, we will share some "tales from the front" from our own experiences and from teachers we have introduced to visualization strategies that promote reader engagement, comprehension, and response to reading.

IMPORTANT CONCEPT AND DEFINITIONS

Legitimate findings, as we use the term here, can be understood by applying Shanahan's (2002) taxonomy of terms to better differentiate among instructional designs and curricula that are said to be research based. In Shanahan's explanation, the term *research related* refers to ideas and curricula based on descriptive and correlational studies; the term *research based* refers to instructional strategies that are similar to but not the same as specific instructional interventions that have experimental evidence of effectiveness. Shanahan suggested that the term *research proven* should be applied only to specific programs or procedures that have been tested successfully in experimental research. The strategies we advocate in this chapter are research related or research based; as practitioners, we have not replicated or described research proven procedures precisely enough to make claims for our versions of them. However, we can state confidently that our strategies are classroom proven under a wide variety of challenging circumstances in public schools and that experimental studies have proven that similar instructional procedures result in improved student performance in reading. We are advocating that rigorous experimental studies be conducted to gather more definitive evidence of their effectiveness, but we also argue for the importance of classroom based teacher research that can inform future practice for oneself and others in ways that can be consider research related.

Struggling readers, as defined by the Department of Education's "Striving Readers" grant RFP, are those students, grades 6–12, who fall two or more years behind grade level in reading, who may also speak a language other than English in the home, and who may have an IEP for a learning difficulty in reading (U.S Department of Education, 2007). There are over six million United States students in grades 8–12 who are struggling readers (Joftus, 2002), with one in four adolescents unable to read well enough to identify the main idea in a passage or to understand informational text (Kamil, 2003). In 2003, the National Assessment of Educational Progress (Donahue, Daane, & Jin, 2003) showed that fewer than 6% of graduating high school seniors could identify evidence in support of main ideas or make inferential connections, and the 2005 scores show no significant improvement (NAEP, 2005).

Reading engagement is a state of being that can be experienced along a continuum of intensity (Smith & Wilhelm, 2004; Smith & Wilhelm, 2002). According to Guthrie and Ozgungor (2002), "Engaged readers are motivated and strategic in their processes of constructing new knowledge from text" (p. 275). In his work on adolescent reading expertise, Wilhelm (1995, 1997) argued that engagement includes a high expectation of print, motivation to read, and all the attendant strategies that readers use to construct meaning. He found that visualization was a necessary condition of engagement. Enciso (1990) described engagement in reading as "our entry into the world of the story and the intense involvement we feel as we imagine and interpret the characters, setting, events and thematic possibilities of literacy texts. It includes a complex interplay of imaginative and intellectual processes that are typically private and elusive, yet critical to comprehension and pleasure in reading" (p. 1).

Comprehension processes are "a set of meaning-making skills, strategies, and thought processes that readers initiate at specific points in a text to understand, apply, and appreciate authors' writings" (Trabasso & Bouchard, 2002, p. 178). Trabasso and Bouchard (2002) further noted that the teacher's goal must be to develop readers who actively use a repertoire of comprehension processes (e.g., prediction, questioning, *imagery*, relating to prior knowledge, monitoring and seeking clarification, and summarization). The National Reading Panel's (2000) report stated that "text comprehension is enhanced when readers actively relate the ideas represented in print to their own knowledge and experiences and *construct mental representation* [italics added] in memory" (p. 14).

Responses to reading are the outcomes of engagement and comprehension when reading processes are working and may take many forms. Rosenblatt's (1978) reader-response theory clearly applies here, as well as to the concept of reader engagement. When the reading transaction is kept private and internal, only the reader knows what responses occur. In social or instructional contexts, readers may share their responses by describing them directly in conversation or writing or by creating representational and symbolic artifacts using art forms or other means of communicating.

Key visualization strategies are interventions that we have found valuable in helping the struggling reader to develop the ability to make mental images before, during, and after reading so as to engage interest, deepen comprehension, and stimulate meaningful response.

The Case for Visualization's Importance to Engagement, Comprehension, and Meaningful Response in Reading

Studies by Wilhelm (1995; 1997) and others have found that struggling readers *do not employ imagery* and *do not know how* to do so. Simply prompting them will not suffice because these struggling readers need specific instructions in visualization strategies to activate their latent abilities. Wilhelm found that the salient difference between expert readers and inexpert readers was the ability to visualize. Student reading can be strengthened though strategically planned visualization instruction to deepen engagement and comprehension, and to increase the ability to respond, share, learn, and use new concepts (see Gambrell & Koskinen, 2002; Block, 2004; Wilhelm, 1995, 1997, 2004; Zeigler & Johns, 2005).

The report of the RAND Reading Study Group (2002) stated that, beyond the handful of strategies the National Reading Panel found to be research proven by experimental studies, "Additional strategies investigated in non-experimental studies that may also prove beneficial to students include mental imagery, knowledge activation, mnemonics, and expository pattern identification" (p. 32). The *Reports of the Subgroups* of the National Reading Panel (2000) included *mental imagery (visualization)* as one of those research proven categories of instruction, based in part on experimental studies.

Block and Pressley (2003) stated that all the new data they have reviewed regarding skilled comprehension confirm the concepts of active reading that were widely reported in the mid-1990s—for example, the practices of good readers reported in Pressley and Afflerbach (1995) and Pearson (1992). Block and Pressley emphasized imagery as one of the important practices of good readers (p. 115). Pressley (1976) presented compelling research on the value of imagery for comprehension decades ago and followed it with additional research that confirmed and extended his findings.

The Case for Visualization's Role in Reading Engagement

A substantial body of research indicates that when teachers establish the classroom conditions that allow readers to be engaged in text in a way that is both extensive and satisfying, students' reading comprehension and their measurable achievement increase (Guthrie, Wigfield, & Von Secker, 2000). In other words, students' growth in reading comprehension is strongly influenced by the breadth and depth of their reading engagement (Alvermann, 2001), and knowing how to visualize has been shown to increase engagement, comprehension, and response (Langer, 1995; Wilhelm, 1995; 1997).

Ninth grade reading classes in Chicago's neighborhood public high schools are filled with young men and women who doubt themselves as readers. Unmotivated by years of nonsuccess, these struggling readers no longer take risks with reading; they run their eyes uncomprehendingly over the words, waiting for the meaning to immediately appear; in practice, they equate good reading with fast reading. One of our favorite teachers, Susan Garr, started every year in her ninth-grade English class by brainstorming lists of what good readers do:

> As a class, we developed lists of what good readers do and what a 'not-so-good' reader does. They loved hearing my stories of being that not-so-good reader in high school. What surprised me was that the students seemed to always know what a good reader was supposed to do—ask questions, think, re-read, make connections—but if my students know what to do while reading, why don't they do it? Saying you know what a strategy is, or when to use it, is one thing; doing it—knowing when and how to use a reading strategy—is another.

Motivating struggling adolescent readers. Wilhelm (1997) noted that his more enthusiastic middle-school readers reported using what he eventually mapped out as an impressive collection of reading strategies, prominently involving imaginative visualization, whereas his weaker readers reported little or no mental imaging. Many of his struggling students responded with exasperation to even modestly inferential questions, protesting, "It doesn't SAY!" Over time, as their concerned teacher and as a researcher studying their cases, Wilhelm discovered that these students needed some tangible engagement and connection with the story world before they could find their way toward building the mental representations that reading requires and the visualizations that proficient readers make unconsciously. The gap between the haves and the have-nots of reading comprehension can be very wide indeed (Stanovich, 1986); the ability to visualize can largely explain this gap (Wilhelm, 1995; 1997).

The students who have the farthest to travel to become active readers often are not even aware that reading calls for any actions beyond the decoding of words; they expect to receive meaning, passively, from the text—what M. W. Smith (1992) called "submission." It began to dawn on Wilhelm (1997) that these students did not "see" anything when they read and that therefore they could not experience and think about what they had read. They had no ownership of the process of reading, they did not interact with texts, and they had no sense that doing so could work for them in personally meaningful ways. When they were assisted to visualize, they were able to overcome these issues.

We focus here on three of the many strategies that appear to have great promise in motivating struggling readers to engage, for example, to set purposes for reading, ask relevant questions, and encourage them to be full participants in the story world: (a) the use of art to stimulate thought before reading, (b) symbolic representation interview (SRI) and its variations, and (c) drama in education.

Art as a stimulus to thought before reading. Broudy (1987) told us that a rich bank of mental imagery is necessary to create complex mental images of sophisticated concepts. Activating students' prior knowledge prepares them to be ready to engage in reading. The use of imagery has been shown to be an effective means of activating readers' prior knowledge (Barry, 1997; Barry & Villeneuve, 1998; Wilhelm, 1995, 2004).

Barry (1997) and her colleagues used selected art works at a museum for their interdisciplinary preteaching students to review and respond to prior to their reading of core texts—in Barry's case, Shakespeare's *Julius Caesar*. After viewing the art, consulting with curators, and studying the relevant materials on the art, students responded in writing to the degree of knowledge activated and built by viewing three works of art before reading with overwhelmingly positive responses. Many felt they would implement these kinds of activities in their future classrooms, particularly as icebreakers.

Piro (2002) used artwork to help students in a third grade classroom create an advanced organizer of their study of Amsterdam. As the class continued to read and study about Amsterdam, they continued to view art (by Rembrandt and others) and continued to modify a class graphic organizer that visually represented what they had been learning. In addition, students drew images of vocabulary words (steeple, etching, or windmill). "When students in the Rembrandt lessons not only wrote but drew their newly acquired spelling words, they were using linguistic and nonlinguistic strategies to encode information in their memory as well as assist in its effective recall" (Paivio, 1990, as cited by Piro, 2002, p. 128).

Wilhelm (2004) described "floor-storming," a technique for frontloading students with visual images they can use in their reading (e.g., tossing photographs related to a reading on the floor and having students refer to their images as they read). "Frontloading lays the foundation of prior experience. New meanings are built on [frontloading], and all future learning of increasingly complex versions of the concept depends on creating a firm foundation" (Wilhelm, 2004, p. 75).

Symbolic Representation Interview (SRI). From its beginning as a data collection method (Enciso, 1990), Wilhelm (2004) used SRI as a means to motivate students to engage with a reading and continue to read, as a way to become metacognitively aware of what they do and could do as readers, and to provide a natural bridge between visualization and dramatic reenactment as a way of building engagement, comprehension and response. He asked students to create cutouts or find objects that would represent important characters, forces, events—anything—that the students felt played a role in their reading of the text. The students then used these objects—symbolic representations—to act out the content of the text and how they read it (Wilhelm, 1997). Wilhelm's interview with the students about their symbolic performances of their readings helped him understand how the students entered the story world and what they understood about how that world functioned. But beyond being a powerful teacher research technique, Wilhelm found that SRI served as a prosthetic device that helped students enter into the story worlds and to operationalize various reading strategies such as visualization and especially metacognition. Because they had a means of support, students were more motivated to read, and willing to be engaged in text longer.

Baer (2005) interviewed seventh graders using SRI to make reading visible and available to students and to find out what went on in the minds of adolescent readers. She found that the students she interviewed, by creating personal "snapshots" of the text—and placing themselves within the scene as they did so—not only brought the text to life, but they were able to bring their own experiences into the story world while being actively engaged in the meaning-making process.

A closely related technique is *Save the Last Word for the Artist* (Short, Harste, & Burke, 1996), which can be a powerful prereading activity fostering engagement. Although most commonly used after reading, this sketch-to-stretch variant (see Short et al., 1996) is a simple strategy that asks students to represent as an image on the paper of what they know, feel, or associate with a particular event, person, character, or idea. Students then show their picture to their colleagues, who interpret it as the student artist remains silent and listens to their interpretations. Then the student, as the artist, explains what the image (or symbol) *really* means. In Karen Boran's (1999) work with Chicago high school teachers, she found that this visualization activity is one teachers embrace easily, because of its broad range of application and the ease of implementation.

> It gets the kids using the language of the text before they read, which increases comprehension, fluency, and word recognition. For the teachers, it gives them a means of dipping their toes into the world of visualization without taking too many risks. *Save the Last Word for the Artist* is an excellent place to start if you're working with teachers who are nervous about using visualization in the classroom. (Boran, 1999)

Drama in education. If, as Wells and Chang-Wells (1992) said, "Knowledge is collaboratively constructed, validated, and modified in the purposeful activities in which [people] engage with others" (p. 28), then drama can become a powerful conduit for motivating passive learners. Why? Because cognitive growth is based on interactive play, children imagine themselves acting in worlds that are beyond their previously demonstrated ability (Wagner, 1998). We can move beyond our limitations because we have created new and possible worlds in our minds' eye. How does this happen? Bruner (1966) said that children develop from motor or sensory representation (enactive) to concrete representations (iconic) and then to abstract representations (symbolic). Dramatic play is an act of symbolic meaning making because students move from concrete action to abstract principle, thus scaffolding the child's learning through their zone of proximal development (Vygotsky, 1978). As children collaborate with their peers to enact the story world of text, they are obligated to use language and behaviors in previously untried ways. Bruner (1986) claimed that the creation of this story world is also the creation of meaning which makes use of visual and verbal representation. It is also another way of representing the intensely social nature of literacy.

Drama in education (called enactment or action strategies in Wilhelm, 2002) allows students new ways to find points of entry into the text. Many of these strategies require movement of students' bodies, but all require movement of students' minds (see Rose, Parks, Androes, & McMahon, 2000). Used as a prereading strategy, drama in education strategies can be used to support students as they prepare to successfully accomplish the numerous tasks good readers do before reading: activate prior knowledge, establish a purpose for reading, build background knowledge, and prepare emotionally and intellectually for the reading experience.

Wilhelm (1997, 2002) found that most drama in education strategies can be used throughout a reading or lesson to build comprehension or to support students' extended response to the text, of course, but he found some particularly effective before reading to increase student motivation and engagement. While working with teachers in Chicago, Wilhelm asked them to "vote with their feet," on certain critical issues that would be explored in a reading, requiring them to make a physical commitment to a space in the room identifying their position. Before reading a text that has a great deal of symbolism, he told his students they were going a journey and could take only one thing. This "precious object" (O'Neill & Lambert, 1982) helped the students to notice significant objects in the text through key detail, symbolism, and characterization (Wilhelm, 2002).

Mary Massie has found tableaux vivants to be an energizing and effective way to stimulate new understandings in a variety of content areas. *Tableaux vivants (living scenes)* is a French term often used for a drama technique that asks students to strike and hold poses to represent anything from a scene to a vocabulary word or a scientific concept. This can be used as a frontloading technique to stimulate students' thoughts about a topic before the actual reading of a text begins (Tortello, 2004). Before the class read *Journey to the Bottom of the World* by Jennifer Armstrong (2000), Massie gave each of her students a role sheet with a picture of, and several quotes about, a particular character. She then asked her students to represent their characters visually through tableaux vivants. As the rest of the class viewed each other's poses, they responded to these images, thus increasing their understanding of, and motivation to read, the text (Katz, Boran, Braun, Massie, & Kuby, 2003).

Karen Boran serves as curriculum support for the Chicago Shakespeare Theatre's "Hard Core, Bard Core" program, in which Chicago English teachers meet to develop standards based, arts integrated English curricula to engage their students in Shakespeare, as well as the reading of other difficult texts. *"Family portraits"* (O'Neill, 1995), a tableaux vivants variant that acts as a group snapshot of characters at the start of a play or scene, helps the students understand the characters and their relationships at the beginning of the play based only on their prior knowledge and what can be gleaned from stage directions, the *dramatis personae,* and any photos accompanying the text. The urban teachers with whom we work, those who spend their days in classrooms with struggling readers in neighborhood Chicago high schools, have also embraced other drama strategies: (a) stage directions (because Shakespeare wrote so few stage directions, Hard Core Bard Core teachers ask students to provide their own), (b) choral montage (students take short pieces of text that they emotionally connect to, and create a collaborative poem that includes each phrase), (c) sense webs (teachers lead a discussion of students' sensory responses to specific parts of text while creating a graphic organizer that represents the group's response), (d) machines (students, in character, create a moving collage of actions that represents their characters' response to a specific part of the text), and (e) disembodied lines (students explore their response to lines before reading by moving through space, saying the lines in different tones with a variety of accompanying actions).

We believe in drama in the classroom, not only because research literature supports its power to strengthen students' motivation, meaning making, and application of knowledge to new situations, but also because we have seen drama transform teaching and learning in the classrooms filled with struggling readers (Wilhelm, 1997; 2002; Wilhelm & Edmiston, 1998; Katz et al., 2003).

The Case for Visualization to Aid Struggling Readers' Comprehension of Text

Reading in the content areas is receiving more attention as teachers and researchers make explicit what a reader needs to know and be able to do to make meaning from discipline-specific texts (e.g., Katz et al., 2003; Lenihan, 2003). Specific strategies for helping students read and comprehend textbooks fill an increasing number of professional books for teachers (e.g., Beers, 2003; Buehl, 2001; Moline, 1995; Tovani, 2000). Better comprehension can be taught, and teenagers can learn from text when the conditions are right. However, secondary teachers must take responsibility for creating those conditions; and they must take responsibility for teaching their students *how* to read the texts of their discipline.

Traditional teaching methods are not effective for many adolescent readers who struggle to comprehend and may have given up trying to construct meaning from the texts they see in school. Regular classroom teachers need more effective and teacher friendly strategies for reaching these students, because the problems with reading comprehension are so prevalent today. We focus here on three research-based strategies: (a) induced imagery, (b) drawing as a response to text, and (c) visualizing and verbalizing.

Historical role of visualization in comprehension. Sadoski and Paivio (2001) provided a fascinating history of imagery's connection to cognition through the ages, beginning with Aristotle's (384–322 B.C.) contention that all knowledge comes about from sensory impressions and that thought never occurs without a mental image (p. 15). Their account continued through the medieval uses of imagery by scholars, the centrality of imagination in the worldview of Renaissance educators, the denouncing of imagery by behaviorists in the 20th century, and the constant connection of imagery to creative functions throughout history (pp. 11–41). Sadoski and Paivio noted that Miller (1984, as cited in Sadoski & Paivio, 2001) "showed how the entire progress of 20th century physics was a creative interplay between mental imagery and language" (p. 65), including Albert Einstein's extensive use of visualizing and sketching to formulate his theories.

Imagery and comprehension. Gambrell and Koskinen (2002) provided an excellent review of the reading research literature in their chapter on imagery as a strategy for enhancing both listening and reading comprehension in *Comprehension Instruction: Research-Based Best Practices* (Block & Pressley, 2002). Sadoski (1983; 1985) found that when third-, fourth-, and fifth-grade students created spontaneous imagery of a key story event (such as a climax), recall and deeper levels of comprehension improved. Glenberg, Gutierrez, Levin, Japuntich, and Kaschak, (2004) noted that actual and imagined manipulation of concrete objects found in preschool texts, when used to simulate the actions of the text, resulted in markedly better memory and comprehension of the material in very young children. Pressley (1976) taught third-grade students a mental imagery strategy to help them remember what they had read, and he gave them practice constructing images for longer passages. The imagery group outperformed the control group on measures of comprehension. McCallum and Moore (1999) found that students' comprehension was improved when imagery was constrained by the instruction to create images that matched the text. Imagery, they found, was effective as a means of improving comprehension, but only when supported by the text. Unconstrained imagery was a detriment to comprehension (see Bell, 1991).

Drawing as a means to increase comprehension. Sketch-to-stretch (Short et al., 1996) is a teacher-friendly strategy that asks students to create a visual image of what they have read. Whitin (2002; 2005) found that the sketch-to-stretch, when used with literature circles, encouraged students to embrace diverse perspectives in response to text, created a classroom climate open to discussion of differing ideas, and encouraged students to make personal connections to texts. Hibbing and Rankin-Erickson (2003) conducted a meta-analysis of the impact of visualization on comprehension, and found that teachers' and students' drawing in response to text aided comprehension.

Visualizing and verbalizing. Bell (1991) argued that an essential part of reading is the ability to create a "Gestalt," or a visual sense of a whole scene, idea, or plot progression. Her findings are supported by those of Wilhelm (1995; 1997) and Sadoski (2005; Sadoski & Paivio, 2001): Highly engaged, successful readers see details, ideas, and scenes; they are able to blend these together into an organic and dynamic whole.

In Bell's (1991) scheme (Visualizing and Verbalizing™, V/V), students are helped to visualize the meaning represented by written words. They are assisted, usually one on one, in moving from "word imaging" to "single sentence imaging" to "sentence by sentence imaging" with oral and then written language. Eventually, students progress to negotiating multiple-sentence imaging, whole-paragraph imaging, and paragraph-by-paragraph imaging. Throughout the V/V program, students are questioned and guided to make sure their imagery matches the given text to such an extent that they are able to answer accurately both literal recall and higher-order-thinking (HOTS) questions. The pacing for this progression of instruction is determined by the student's needs and development, but Bell has recommended an intensive approach of daily reinforcement for best results.

Tales from the front: V/V in practice. Skilled instructors of V/V have been able to help their students achieve significant growth in reading comprehension as measured by standardized tests. Based on a class Mary Massie taught one summer through Goals 2000 that included material on Bell's (1991) V/V system, ninth-grade Chicago teacher Susan Garr adapted Bell's program so that it became a small-group activity for classrooms after initial modeling and scaffolding by the instructor. Susan taught her class the simple basics of visualizing and verbalizing in the first two weeks of school. In her system, one student is the reader of a text, a second is the visualizer, and a third is the observer and questioner. The three jobs rotate as students move through three rounds of short readings. The teacher makes the reading selection assignments with students working at their individual independent reading levels so that they can focus their minds on visualizing and constructing meaning. Part of the long-range preparation for the activity includes teaching the students to construct their own recall and HOTS questions. The teacher circulates to assist the small groups as needed or sits in with one group at a time.

Mary Massie and Susan Garr worked together at the Chicago Teachers' Center of Northeastern Illinois University, and they continued to include visualizing and verbalizing in professional development whenever appropriate. Teachers who have adopted this approach, or their own customized variations, report significant improvements in comprehension, particularly among their English Language Learners and learning disabled or struggling readers. The principal of Otis School in Chicago in 2003, James Cosme, credited his teachers' adoption of the visualizing strategies Mary Massie introduced there with contributing to a jump in comprehension scores. In 1998, only 33.2% of eighth-grade students at Otis read at or above national norms as measured by the Iowa Test of Basic Skills; in 2000, 2 years later, that score had jumped to 50.0% at or above national norms.

The Case for Visualization to Promote Response

Visualization is an essential part of creative and original thinking, and as such, it is a prerequisite for meaningful responses to reading. Not all responses, however, are created equal (McCallum & Moore, 1999). We have found that students are much more likely to invest themselves in creating a learning artifact in response to a reading or at the end of a unit of study if they understand the purpose of the response as a meaning-constructive activity and know that they will have a real audience with whom to share and discuss their work (Leu, Kinzer, Coiro & Cammack, 2004). Will peers really examine what each person has created? Will the response artifacts contribute to ongoing discussions around issues of importance? If so, the energy devoted to creating an original response to the unit increases exponentially. It is immensely valuable to have students create a visual product to share with others to support their explanation of their ideas and new learning. Here, we focus on two key research based visualization strategies for promoting response that extends student thinking about reading: (a) mind mapping and (b) sketch-to-stretch and its variants.

Mind mapping. In *Mapping Inner Space: Learning and Teaching Visual Mapping*, Margulies and Mall (2002) explained and cleverly illustrated a collection of ways to use mind mapping for purposes including note taking, detailed planning, prewriting for written responses or exploration of reading, and displaying information for presentations (see Buzan & Buzan, 1996). Mind mapping is a particular style of graphically organizing almost anything on paper, using symbols as well as words. It can be thought of as a much more design-oriented form of clustering or visual outlining. Mind mapping is often more accessible to teachers and students than going directly to imagery through the "mental screen" or "mind's eye" to create mental images. Many students more readily understand the utility of sketching out visual symbols to explore, demonstrate relationships, and reconfigure (transmediate) ideas than using only mental imagery. Mind mapping can be an excellent way to introduce learners to the principles of visualization, and it can be equally helpful as a tool for exploration and as a response to reading.

One of the beauties of mind mapping is that it provides a simple structure, which is a main idea symbolized in word and picture at the center of a page, with curving lines radiating from the center, and additional subordinate lines coming from the primary lines as needed. On each of those lines is a concept represented in a few simple words and pictures. This format is vastly more user friendly and conducive to creative expression than a traditional outline or set of notes. Eventually, students will have such complex webs of ideas and symbols that they may move into creating what Margulies (1995) called "mindscapes." The inviting formats of mind mapping and mindscaping help students become comfortable with exploring ideas that are just emerging and following their creative impulses. Block (2004) suggested that images cannot readily emerge in response to reading, unless (a) readers know they are free to reach deep into their creative thinking, (b) blocks to students' literal decoding are removed through instruction, and (c) teachers are available when a difficulty with imagery occurs (p. 121). We think that there may be more reciprocity between imagery and creative thinking than Block implied because mind mapping a visual representation of emerging understandings stimulates further mental imagery, and vice versa. Mary Massie and Susan Garr have found that mind mapping is one of the most valuable tools they can teach teachers and students because the format can be adapted to so many purposes before, during, and after reading.

Tales from the front: Using imagery to prompt student response. Susan Garr vividly recalled her first year of using the visualizing and mind mapping strategies she learned in a summer course Mary Massie taught for in-service teachers through the Goals 2000 program. The climate of Susan's linguistically and culturally diverse high school classroom became much more thoughtful as the students began to realize that different individuals "saw" and interpreted things differently as they read and that many different visions were possible, while staying within the parameters of the text. Students felt much more comfortable answering the question, "What did this section make you picture?" rather than the boring old question, "What was this section about?"

As their comfort levels increased, so did the ability to produce and explain their mental imagery. It was clear that the students had more thoughts inside to express than they had shown previously. When Susan had her class mind map their way through the reading of *Romeo and Juliet*, they began producing remarkably insightful drawings. Even Felix, a transfer student who had missed out on the class's fall training in visualization and mind mapping, eventually caught the spirit. As Susan explained,

> By mid-quarter, Felix was failing the class. I had nothing turned in from him, and I really couldn't tell you what he knew or didn't know. He wouldn't write his "after reading" paragraphs and only minimally filled out his reading logs. Then we started *Romeo and Juliet*, using a video to help us create our own mental pictures of the scenes. As we finished each act, students were assigned to create a mind map to represent the most important parts of the act, with symbolism and lines from the play. Felix started doing his work. He kept a reading log. He shared his response paragraphs. He had each mind map done brilliantly—really beautifully detailed "mindscapes" packed with insight. He was clearly getting Shakespeare and the story. When he actually began to *speak* in class, I was in shock! By the end of the quarter, Felix was earning a B. He was a student who needed visualizing guidance and practice to express himself and show what he was learning. The visualizing scaffolded his thinking and speaking. When he got that, he became a pleasure to have in class, really making contributions. Felix—and the rest of the class—did really well on the unit exam, too.

Sketch-to-stretch. Another visual form of response to reading that is easy to launch in a classroom is "sketch-to-stretch," a strategy usually attributed to Short et al. (1996). In sketch-to-stretch, the students are instructed to think about drawing the *meaning* of the story, not about trying to represent a specific scene in a realistic fashion. This simple strategy of sketching a symbolic representation of a personal meaning can lead to rich discussion of students' responses to text during the sharing of the sketches. The discussion primes the pump for writing that is much more substantive and original than otherwise would occur (see Ogle & Blachowicz, 2001; Beers, 2003; Harvey & Goudvis, 2000).

Simple during reading responses. Wilhelm (2001, 2004) used visual protocols, prompting students to sketch anything they see, think, or feel as they read, as part of their think-aloud of a text. He typed an excerpt of text on the left side of a sheet and had students draw their responses on the right side, next to the textual cues that stimulated these responses. Drawings can be of scenes, ideas, elaborations, or even pictures of oneself reading. A variation is to provide students with sheets of paper and ask them to sketch their visualizations at particular points in the story and have them do a back-to-back description in which they identify the visual cues and structure words that inspired their drawings. They list these cues on the back of their pictures, so the relationship between verbal stimuli and visual response can be seen (Wilhelm, 2001, 2004).

Bustle (2004) used the term *visual representation* to include a wide range of visual meaning-making devices and symbols and argued that much more should be done to examine their possible roles in the assessment and evaluation of learning across the curriculum. She cited the following example of using a particular artistic medium in order to give the students some constraints that would guide their creative process. The teacher wanted students to better understand the relational aspects between characters in a play and to write more descriptively about them. She assigned each student the task of finger painting a portrait of a character, choosing that nonliteral medium so that her students would be forced to work "like abstract expressionists, capturing their character in art elements such as line, color, texture, and shape." The students wrote a short paragraph describing their work. The teacher discovered that the visual process helped her students tap into words that they might otherwise never find, providing scaffolding to increase motivation and interest, improve comprehension, and foster higher level, abstract, and critical thinking (Bustle, 2004, p. 3).

Tales from the front: Mind mapping and ninth-grade readers. Sharon teaches ninth-grade reading in a neighborhood Chicago Public High School. She first encountered mind mapping in one of Mary Massie's courses and embraced it right away to help her students organize information before writing, as she describes here.

> While reading of *A Jury of Her Peers* by Susan Glaspell, my students discovered the theme of isolation through mind mapping. Instead of journaling about their response after reading the short story, I asked them for homework to make mind maps. These were struggling readers, all below grade level, yet the symbols used on their maps showed a powerful response to the theme of isolation—birds in cages, I remember. During our debriefing the next day, they were able to make personal connections between the theme of isolation and other plot elements in the story.

Once Sharon's students became more experienced mind mappers, even the arrows connecting the central image to the secondary images began to take on symbolism.

> When we were reading *Their Eyes Were Watching God* by Zora Neale Hurston, I saw my students begin to sharpen their mind mapping skills. The arrows that emanated from the middle were used to convey information about the story. They drew a visual connection with the object by echoing that object. The arrow might be paved with dollar bills, if the object was about greed, or broken hearts, if we're talking about lost love.

Sharon found that mind maps are a much richer source of preparation for writing for her ninth-grade students than the traditional outline.

> Mind mapping pushes my students to be unsatisfied with their initial responses to the text. It helps them move beyond the words on the page, the literal level. ACT test results show that Chicago's 11th grade students do well with "right there" or literal level questions. But when they are asked to think deeply, to go beyond the lines to the reasons behind the words to the inferential level—that's where my students need the most help.

Visualization strategies, such as mind mapping and sketch to stretch, that involve creating symbolic images provide valuable scaffolding for students as they seek to gather their thoughts together and shape them into a form that that will allow their voices to be heard and understood.

CONCLUSION: WHAT'S NEXT FOR VISUALIZATION?

> Teaching children which thinking strategies are used by proficient readers and helping them use those strategies independently creates the core of teaching reading. If proficient readers routinely use certain thinking strategies, those are the strategies children must be taught. For the kindergarten-through-twelfth-grade-reading curriculum to focus primarily on those strategies, we need a new instructional paradigm: Our daily work with children must look dramatically different from the approaches in wide use in our schools today. (Keene & Zimmerman, 1997, pp. 53–54)

Agreeing with Keene and Zimmerman (1997) in their assertion that American public schools need reading instruction that is radically different from what usually occurs today, we urge reading educators to examine visualization as a powerful tool to open new paths in teaching and learning.

We have found that reading *is* seeing, and research is a way of "reseeing" that helps us to realize what is possible in our classrooms and that helps others to realize what is possible in theirs. We believe that Shanahan's (2002) taxonomy of research terms is a valid and viable device for thinking about the kinds of research that can help the community of reading teachers and students—and that teacher action research is an area that deserves further support and consideration from all parties, including university partners when working with classroom teachers.

We have found that a compelling body of research proven—as well as research related and research based—professional literature supports the explicit teaching of certain visualization strategies to improve engagement, comprehension, and response in struggling readers.

We have found evidence to support the use of key visualization strategies to improve students' engagement, comprehension and response—drama in education, SRI, mind mapping, Visualizing and Verbalizing™, drawing in response to imagery, as well as others—and that these interventions deserve further research in a variety of methods (Hibbing & Rankin-Erickson, 2003).

We believe that the explicit teaching of visualization strategies is critically important. We must go far beyond the "drive-by" practice of suggesting that students visualize and instead, provide students with clear, step-by-step instruction that teaches not only the why and what of visualization, but also the when and how (Wilhelm, Baker & Dube, 2001). When visualizing becomes part of the daily conversation of learning, such positive classroom side effects as a greater respect for differing perspectives, more sincerely curious student questions, and higher quality discussions will occur.

Finally, we contend that our struggling adolescent readers, whether rural, suburban, or urban, deserve to be invited into the "literacy club" (Smith, F., 1988), a club in which every person's individual vision matters. We can ensure that our students experience rapt engagement, deep comprehension, and meaningful responses as they read by teaching visualization in explicit, varied, and differentiated ways over time. This is a path by which students can discover their inner vision and power of imagination, so that they astonish us with their creativity and understanding. After all, reading *is* seeing, researching involves seeing anew, and learning is perceiving and understanding the new. And to achieve these, teachers and students alike need the assistance visualization techniques can provide.

REFERENCES

Alvermann, D. (2001). *Effective literacy instruction for adolescents.* Paper presented at the National Reading Conference, Chicago, Illinois.

Armstrong, J. (2000). *Journey to the bottom of the world: The extraordinary and true story of Shackleton and the Endurance.* New York: Crown Books for Young Readers.

Baer, A. L. (2005). Do you hear voices? A study of the symbolic story reading inventory. *Journal of Adult and Adolescent Literacy, 49*(3), 214–225.

Barry, A. L. (1997). Visual art enhances the learning of Shakespeare. *Education, 117,* 632–639.

Barry, A. L., & Villaneuve, P. (1998). Veni, vidi, vici: Interdisciplinary learning in the art museum. *Art Education, 51*(1), 16–24.

Beers, K. (2003). *When kids can't read, what teachers can do: A guide for teachers 6–12.* Portsmouth, NH: Heinemann.

Bell, N. (1991). Gestalt imagery: A critical factor in language comprehension. *Annals of Dyslexia, 41,* 246–260.

Block, C. (2004). *Teaching comprehension: The comprehension process approach.* Boston, MA: Pearson.

Block, C., & Pressley, M. (2003). Best practices in comprehension instruction. In L. M. Morrow, L. B. Gambrell, & M. Pressley (Eds.), *Best practices in literacy instruction* (pp. 111–126). New York: Guilford Press.

Boran, K. (1999). Rising from the ashes: A dramaturgical analysis of teacher change in a Chicago Public High School after probation. Unpublished doctoral dissertation, National-Louis University, Evanston, Illinois.

Broudy, H. S. (1987). *The role of imagery in learning.* Los Angeles: The Getty Center for Education in the Arts.

Bruner, J. S. (1966). *Toward a theory of instruction.* Cambridge, MA: Harvard University Press.

Bruner, J. S. (1986). *Actual minds, possible worlds.* Cambridge, MA: Harvard University Press.

Buehl, D. (2001). *Classroom strategies for interactive learning* (2nd ed.). Newark, DE: International Reading Association.

Bustle, L. S. (2004). The role of visual representation in the assessment of learning. *Journal of Adolescent & Adult Literacy, 47,* 416–423.

Buzan, T., & Buzan, B. (1996). *The mind map book: How to use radiant thinking to maximize your brain's untapped potential.* New York: Plume.

Donahue, P. L., Daane, M. C., & Grigg, W. S. (2003). *The nation's report card: Reading highlights 2003.* Washington, D.C: U.S. Department of Education: Institute for Educational Services. Available 12/15/06 at nces.ed.gov/nationsreportcard/pubs/main2003/2004452.asp

Enciso, P. E. (1990). *The nature of engagement in reading: Profiles of three fifth graders' engagement strategies and stances* (Order No. 9111696). Unpublished doctoral dissertation, Ohio State University, Columbus, Ohio.

Gambrell, L. B., & Koskinen, P. S. (2002). Imagery: A strategy for enhancing comprehension. In C. C. Block, & M. Pressley (Eds.), *Comprehension instruction: Research-based best practices* (pp. 305–318). New York: The Guilford Press.

Glenberg, A. M., Gutierrez, T., Levin, J., Japuntich, S., & Kaschak, M. (2004). Activity and imagined activity can enhance young children's reading comprehension. *Journal of Educational Psychology, 96*(3), 424–436.

Guthrie, J. T., & Ozgungor, S. (2002). Instructional contexts for reading engagement. In C. C. Block, & M. Pressley (Eds.), *Comprehension instruction: Research-based best practices* (pp. 275–288). New York: The Guilford Press.

Guthrie, J. T., Wigfield, A., & Von Secker, C. (2000). Effects of integrated instruction on motivation and strategy use in reading. *Journal of Educational Psychology, 92*(2), 331–341.

Harvey, S., & Goudvis, A. (2000). *Strategies that work: Teaching comprehension to enhance understanding.* Portsmouth, ME: Stenhouse.

Hibbing, A. N., & Rankin-Erickson, J. L. (2003). A picture is worth a thousand words: Using visual images to improve comprehension for middle school struggling readers. *The Reading Teacher, 56*(8), 758–770.

Joftus, S. (2002). *Every child a graduate: A framework for an excellent education for all middle and high school students.* Washington, DC: Alliance for Excellent Education.

Kamil M. L. (2003). *Adolescents and literacy: Reading for the 21st century* [Electronic version]. Washington, DC: Alliance for Excellent Education. Retrieved 12/05/06, from http://www.all4ed.orf/publications/AdolescentsAndLiteracy.pdf

Katz, C. A., Boran, K., Braun, T. J., Massie, M. J., & Kuby, S. A. (2003). The importance of being with Sir Ernest Shackleton at the bottom of the world. *Journal of Adolescent & Adult Literacy, 47*, 38–49.

Keene, E., & Zimmerman, S. (1997). *Mosaic of thought: Teaching comprehension in a reader's workshop.* Portsmouth, NH: Heinemann.

Langer, J. A. (1995). *Envisioning literature: Literary understanding and literature instruction.* New York: Teachers College Press.

Lenihan, G. (2003). Reading with adolescents: Constructing meaning together. *Journal of Adolescent & Adult Literacy, 47*, 8–12.

Leu, D. J., Jr., Kinzer, C. K., Coiro, J., & Cammack, D. (2004, March/April). Toward a theory of new literacies emerging from the Internet and other information and communication technologies [Electronic version]. *Reading Online, 7*(5). Retrieved 12/15/06 from http://www.readingonline.org/newliteracies/lit_index.asp?HREF=/newliteracies/leu

Long, S. A., Winograd, P. A., & Bridge, C. A. (1989). The effects of reader and text characteristics on reports of imagery during and after reading. *Reading Research Quarterly, 24*, 353–372.

Margulies, N. (1995). *Map it!: Tools for charting the vast territories of your mind.* Tucson, AZ: Zephyr Press.

Margulies, N., & Mall, N. (2002). *Mapping inner space: Learning and teaching visual mapping* (2nd ed.). Tucson, AZ: Zephyr Press.

McCallum, R. D., & Moore, S. (1999). Not all imagery is created equal: The role of imagery in the comprehension of main ideas in exposition. *Journal of Reading Psychology, 20*, 21–60.

Moline, S. (1995). *I see what you mean: Children at work with visual information.* York, ME: Stenhouse Publishers.

National Assessment of Educational Progress. (2005). *The nation's report card: Reading 2005* (Publication No. ERN3889P). Jessup, MD: U.S. Department of Education.

National Reading Panel. (2000). *Teaching children to read: An evidence-based assessment of the scientific research literature on reading and its implications for reading instruction* (Publication No. 00-4769). Washington, DC: National Institute of Child Health and Human Development.

Ogle, D., & Blachowicz, C. M. Z. (2001). *Reading comprehension.* New York: Guilford Press.

Ogle, D. M., & Hunter, K. (2000). Developing leadership in literacy at Amundsen High School. In M. Bizar, & R. Barr (Eds.), *Leadership in times of urban reform* (pp. 47–68). Mahwah, NJ: Lawrence Erlbaum Associates.

O'Neill, C. (1995). *Drama worlds.* Portsmouth, NH: Heinemann.

O'Neill, C., & Lambert, A. (1982). *Drama structures: A practical handbook for teachers.* Portsmouth, NH: Heinemann.

Pearson, P. D. (1992). RT remembrance: The second 20 years. *The Reading Teacher, 45*, 378–385.

Piro, J. M. (2002). The picture of reading: Deriving meaning in literacy through image. *The Reading Teacher, 56*(2), 126–134.

Pressley, G. M. (1976). Mental imagery helps eight-year-olds remember what they read. *Journal of Educational Psychology, 68*(3), 355–359.

Pressley, M., & Afflerbach, P. (1995). *Verbal protocols of reading: the nature of constructively responsive reading.* Hillsdale, NJ: Lawrence Erlbaum Associates.

RAND Reading Study Group (2002). *Reading for understanding: Toward an R&D program in reading comprehension.* Arlington, VA: Science & Technology Policy Institute.

Rose, D. S., Parks, M., Androes, K., & McMahon, S. D. (2000). Imagery-based learning: Improving elementary students' reading comprehension with drama techniques. *The Journal of Educational Research, 94*(1), 55–63.

Rosenblatt, L. M. (1978). *The reader, the text and the poem: The transactional theory of the literary work.* Carbondale: Southern Illinois University Press.

Sadoski, M. (2005). A dual coding view of vocabulary learning. *Reading & Writing Quarterly, 21*, 221–238.

Sadoski, M. (1985). The natural use of imagery in story comprehension and recall: Replication and extension. *Reading Research Quarterly, 20*, 658–677.

Sadoski, M. (1983). An exploratory study of the relationships between reported imagery and the comprehension and recall of a story. *Reading Research Quarterly, 19*, 110–123.

Sadoski, M., & Paivio, A. (2001). *Imagery and text: A dual coding theory of reading and writing.* Mahwah, NJ: Lawrence Erlbaum Associates.

Shanahan, T. (2002). What reading research says: The promise and limitations of applying research to reading education. In A. E. Farnstrup, & S. J. Samuels (Eds.), *What research has to say about reading instruction* (pp. 8–24). Newark, DE: International Reading Association.

Short, K., Harste, J., & Burke, C. (1996). *Creating classrooms for authors and inquirers.* Portsmouth, NH: Heinemann.

Smith, F. (1988). *Joining the literacy club.* Portsmouth, NH: Heinemann.

Smith, M. W. (1992). Submission versus control in literary transactions. In J. Many, & C. Cox (Eds.), *Reader stance and literary understanding: Exploring the theories, research and practice.* Norwood, NJ: Ablex.

Smith, M. W., & Wilhelm, J. D. (2002). *"Reading don't fix no Chevys": Literacy in the lives of young men.* Portsmouth, NH: Heinemann.

Smith, M. W., & Wilhelm, J. D. (2004). "I just like being good at it": The importance of competence in the literate lives of young men. *Journal of Adult and Adolescent Literacy, 47*(6), 454–461.

Stanovich, K. E. (1986). Matthew effects in reading: Some consequences of individual differences in the acquisition of literacy. *Reading Research Quarterly, 21*(4), 360–407.

Tortello, R. (2004). Tableaux vivants in the literature classroom. *The Reading Teacher, 58*(2), 206–208.

Tovani, C. (2000). *I read it, but I don't get it: Comprehension strategies for adolescent readers.* Portland, ME: Stenhouse.

Trabasso, T., & Bouchard, E. (2002). Teaching readers how to comprehend text strategically. In C. C. Block, & M. Pressley (Eds.), *Comprehension instruction: Research-based best practices* (pp. 176–200). New York: Guilford.

U.S. Department of Education (2005). *Fiscal Year 2005 Application for New Grants for the Striving Readers Program*, p. 9. Washington, D.C.

U.S. Department of Education (2007). *Helping readers achieve and succeed.* Washington, D.C: Institute for Educational Services. Available on 4/26/07 at www.ed.gov/nclb/methods/reading/strivingreaders.html

Vygotsky, L. (1978). *Mind in society: The development of higher psychological processes.* Eds., M. Cole, V. John-Steiner, S. Scribner, & E. Souberman. Cambridge, U.K.: Cambridge University Press.

Wagner, B. J. (1998). *Educational drama and language arts: What research shows.* Portsmouth, NH: Heinemann.

Wells, G., & Chang-Wells, G. L. (1992). *Constructing knowledge together.* Portsmouth, NH: Heinemann.

Whitin, P. (2002). Leading into literature circles through the sketch-to-stretch strategy: Sketching can help students deepen their understanding of story elements and nurture a collaborative classroom atmosphere. *The Reading Teacher, 55*(5), 444–451.

Whitin, P. (2005). The interplay of text, talk, and visual representation in expanding literary interpretation. *Research in the Teaching of English, 39,* 365–397.

Wilhelm, J. D. (1995). Reading IS seeing. *Journal of Reading Behavior, 27*(4), 467–503.

Wilhelm, J. D. (1997). *"You gotta BE the book": Teaching engaged and reflective reading with adolescents.* New York: Teachers College Press.

Wilhelm, J. D. (2001). *Improving comprehension with think-aloud strategies: Modeling what good readers do.* New York: Scholastic Professional Books.

Wilhelm, J. D. (2002). *Action strategies for deepening comprehension.* New York: Scholastic Professional Books.

Wilhelm, J. D. (2004). *Reading is seeing: Learning to visualize scenes, characters, ideas and text worlds to improve comprehension and reflective reading.* New York: Scholastic Professional Books.

Wilhelm, J. D., & Edmiston, B. (1998). *Imaging to learn: Inquiry, ethics, and integration through drama.* Portsmouth, NH: Heinemann.

Wilhelm, J. D., Baker, T. N., & Dube, J. (2001). *Strategic reading: Guiding students to lifelong literacy 6–12.* Portsmouth, NH: Boynton/Cook Publishers.

Zeigler, L. L., & Johns, J. L. (2005). *Visualization: Using mental images to strengthen comprehension.* Dubuque, IA: Kendall/Hunt Publishing Company.

42

FROM DRAWING TO DIGITAL CREATIONS: GRAPHIC ORGANIZERS IN THE CLASSROOM

Karen Bromley
BINGHAMTON UNIVERSITY, SUNY

"Drawing is the most immediate and natural tool for generating and expressing ideas" (Anderson, 2003, p. 17). As young children scribble and draw pictures, these graphic symbols often support the telling of stories that go far beyond the graphics they create. As older students create graphic representations, these visual displays can reflect what they know and support the generation of new knowledge. Graphic representations allow students to create and interpret ideas that are linked to these symbols, but are not limited by them. In classrooms where teachers connect the visual and verbal modes of expression by promoting the creation of graphic representations, literacy and learning thrive.

This chapter examines the development of a specific kind of graphic representation, the *graphic organizer,* reviews related theory and research, and discusses the use of graphic organizers to facilitate literacy and learning in elementary and middle school classrooms.

GRAPHIC ORGANIZERS: VISUAL REPRESENTATIONS

A graphic organizer is a visual representation of knowledge that structures information by arranging important aspects of a concept or topic into a pattern using labels (Bromley, Irwin-DeVitis, & Modlo, 1995). The graphic organizer has an interesting history that spans the last half century (Merkley & Jeffries, 2001). It developed from the notion of the *advance organizer* (Ausubel, 1968) an overview paragraph introduced before reading to connect a reader's existing knowledge to new knowledge contained in a selection to be read. From this, the *structured overview,* or outline format, was developed to enhance prereading, during reading, and postreading comprehension (Barron, 1969). This term was replaced eventually by the term *graphic organizer,* which is well known and used today (Dunston, 1992).

Often, graphic organizers go by other names, including (a)concept map, (b) semantic map, (c) semantic organizer, (d) web, (e) Venn diagram, (f) Vee map, (g) thinking map, (h) bubble map, (i) story map, and so forth. Regardless of the term used, graphic organizers are visual tools for constructing knowledge (Heimlich & Pittelman, 1986; Hyerle, 1996; Marzano, Pickering, & Pollock, 2001). The creation of graphic organizers requires engaging with information and grappling with what is known and unknown. Graphic organizers promote active learning by requiring the use of language as one reads, talks, listens, thinks, draws, writes, and creates. Coconstruction of graphic organizers permits group work between students and teachers and among collaborative peers, thus making graphic organizers devices for developing learning through social interaction.

Graphic organizers make visually explicit the organizational patterns of text. They can facilitate prereading, postreading, writing, revising, discussing, presenting, and reasoning. They can represent students' background knowledge and provide a framework for what is about to be learned, or they can be used to organize and reflect on newly acquired knowledge. When teachers and students create graphic organizers together, they learn from each other as they extend their understandings of concepts. Through this collaborative activity, students at all grade levels learn how to organize knowledge, and eventually use graphic organizers independently as a learning strategy. Because graphic organizers involve both visual and verbal information, they are beneficial for students with a wide variety of learning styles and ranges of ability.

GRAPHIC ORGANIZERS: UNDERLYING THEORY

Several important ideas from learning theory form a foundation for the use of graphic organizers as meaning-making devices. First, as information is stored in memory, it is "dual-coded" in two forms: (a) *linguistic* and (b) *imagery* (Paivio, 1990). Information is processed in linguistic form (e.g., print and meaning) and imagery or nonlinguistic form (e.g., visual and sensory images). Linguistic elements (e.g., graphemes, phonemes, and morphemes) are basic units for storing information in memory. Learning a word's linguistic elements is enhanced by storing a nonlinguistic form or sensory image (e.g., a picture, an emotion or feeling, a smell, a sound, and/or a taste) along with the linguistic image. Graphic organizers, as visual representations of ideas and information, contain both linguistic and nonlinguistic images and thus aid memory and learning.

Second, when important information is identified and isolated, as in a graphic organizer, one can see clearly how concepts are connected, thus making the relationships and information more easily understood (Novak & Gowin, 1984; Robinson & Molina, 2002). By omitting extraneous information and presenting only what is essential, a well-constructed graphic organizer with appropriate symbols, either pictures or text words, can simplify the learning task.

Third, the mind arranges and stores information in an orderly fashion (Ausubel, 1968). New information about a concept is thought to be filed into an existing framework of categories, networks, or *schema* that contains specific information about that concept (Rumelhart, 1980). Therefore, when prior knowledge is retrieved, this schema provides a framework into which new knowledge is integrated or attached. This is consistent with notions of assimilation and accommodation in learning (Piaget, 1974). Graphic organizers are visual depictions that represent networks and allow the addition or modification of background knowledge as new knowledge is processed.

Fourth, learning is expedited when a *semiotic mediator* is introduced (Vygotsky, 1962). A semiotic mediator is a mental tool that supports and facilitates memory and learning. Graphic organizers serve as mental tools because they contain only key ideas and important related information that is easier to remember than long, extended narrative or expository text. In addition, the information in a graphic organizer is visual as well as verbal, and as such, it acts as a mediator or mental tool to help the learner remember.

Last, constructivist theories of learning propose that learning is a social endeavor and meaning is coconstructed through interactions with other knowledgeable learners (Vygotsky, 1962). In creating a graphic organizer with others, the interplay between spoken language and visual representation results in *transmediation,* or forming meanings in one communication system and reframing them in another communication system, which reinforces meaningful learning (Bustle, 2003, 2004; Leland & Harste, 1994). When visual representations and spoken language are used together, learners are actively engaged in listening, speaking, reading, writing, viewing, and visually representing. As learners construct graphic organizers together, they engage in discussion and negotiation about what is important and related and/or unimportant and unrelated, as well as how or how not to represent it, which improves comprehension and learning.

RATIONALE FOR USING GRAPHIC ORGANIZERS

Graphic organizers are used routinely in business, industry, print, the Internet, and other electronic media. In schools, many basal readers, textbooks, computer programs, commercial publishers' assessments, and mandated state assessments include graphic organizers. The ability to examine, create, interpret, and critique these visual displays is a part of visual literacy now considered basic to a student's education (Cairney, 1997; Moline, 1995).

The International Reading Association (IRA) and the National Council of Teachers of English (NCTE; 1996) proposed two additional language arts: (a) *viewing* and (b) *visually representing.*. They join the original four—(a) listening, (b) speaking, (c) reading, and (d) writing—and reflect the growing importance of images and visual literacy in our culture (Tompkins, 2002). *Viewing* involves visually examining and comprehending media such as film, video, print advertisements, photos, illustrations, the Internet, and CD-ROM. *Visually representing* involves creating meaning in a visual text using multiple sign systems. Examples of visual texts are video productions, computer software creations, dramatic productions, illustrations, charts, and posters. The creation and use of graphic organizers as meaning-making instructional devices is in line with the IRA and NCTE standards.

Visual learners respond well to graphic organizers because they relate easily to a viewable image. If the graphic images are pictures, whether black-and-white or color, young beginning readers and struggling older readers can more easily respond to them and even create their own. When organizers are computer-generated with the addition of sound, auditory learners are reinforced as well. Students who are not linear and logical in their approach to learning however, may not respond to graphic organizers in the same way as students who have a preference for concreteness and linearity.

KNOWLEDGE ORGANIZATION AND GRAPHIC ORGANIZERS

In the past, graphic organizers were used by content area teachers to represent patterns of text organization (Vacca & Vacca, 2005). Typically, these organizers show the structure of information in material from a science or social studies text; however, virtually all sources of knowledge—not just print—contain meaning that can be represented in a graphic organizer. For example, information and ideas presented through film, lecture, video, the Internet, and discussion can be organized and depicted graphically. Today, graphic organizers are routinely found in elementary and secondary classrooms as teachers use them in curriculum planning, instruction, and assessment. Four basic patterns of knowledge organization—(a) hierarchical, (b) conceptual, (c) sequential, and (d) cyclical, as well as combinations and variations of these—can be represented with graphic organizers (Bromley, Irwin-DeVitis, & Modlo, 1995).

Hierarchical. This pattern includes a main concept and the ranks, or levels, of subconcepts under it. Generalizations and classifications are examples of this type of linear organizer. For example, "natural disasters" is a general idea or classification, and subcategories might be "earthquakes," "hurricanes," "typhoons," and "floods." Also, "government" is a general idea, and "legislative," "judicial," and "executive" are functions subsumed under it.

Conceptual. This pattern includes a central idea, category, or class with supporting facts such as characteristics or examples. Description, collection, problem-solution, and comparison-contrast are examples of this type of organizer. "Money" might be a central idea, with supporting facts such as "coins and paper," "buys us things," "every country has different kinds," "we earn it," "credit cards," and "banks." Another conceptual organizer, the Venn diagram, consists of two overlapping circles that represent a comparison of information. "New York" and "California" might be compared, with similarities noted in the overlapping section and differences in the open part of each circle.

Sequential. This pattern arranges events in chronological order. These organizers are useful in sequencing events that have a specific beginning and end into cause/effect, chronology, process/product, or problem/solution. Sequential patterns are usually linear, and timelines or flowcharts are classic examples of this pattern. Another example of a sequential pattern is a problem-solution organization. When "river pollution" represents the problem and "clean river" is the solution, the events leading up to the solution might be "people notice," changes suggested," "laws passed," "factories reduce dumping," and "sewers get fixed."

Cyclical. This pattern includes a series of events within a process in a circular formation. Events have no beginning or end; they occur in a continuous sequence. This type of organizer depicts information in a series, succession, or cycle, such as "the life cycle" or "the water cycle," for example. In the latter, examples of evaporation such as "sun heating the ocean," "steam from cooking or engines," and "condensation, rain, snow, and sleet" might appear in appropriate places within the circular pattern.

Variations. One or more of the four types of graphic organizers are often combined to represent different displays. For example, in the hierarchical organizer, where "government" is a general idea, conceptual organizers containing characteristics of "legislative," "judicial," and "executive" can be created. Variations of the conceptual organizer are the matrix and data chart, which can represent information about a single concept that stands alone or is subsumed under a larger concept. The number and kind of different arrangements of information in one graphic organizer is limited only by the ingenuity of the teacher and/or student(s) creating it (Irwin-DeVitis, Bromley, & Modlo, 1999; Junion-Metz, 2003).

While the content and organization of information usually determines the type of organizer to be created, the cognitive style of the person creating or using the organizer is also important (Irwin-DeVitis, Bromley, & Modlo, 1999). Individuals often prefer one type of organizer over another. For example, holistic, creative thinkers may prefer the nonlinear and open-ended characteristic of the conceptual organizer. The superordinate and subordinate structure of the hierarchical organizer and chronological structure of the sequential organizer appeal to linear and logical thinkers. Experience with a variety of organizers, however, allows teachers and students to explore different options and choose the type most appropriate for their purpose and content.

RESEARCH AND PROFESSIONAL EVIDENCE

Reviews of research report mixed findings for graphic organizer use to aid comprehension of content material. Robinson (1998) discussed the unsystematic use of graphic organizers and identifies the variability in their construction and use as a limitation that is responsible for mixed findings. Rice (1994) cited the unsystematic approach to analyzing graphic organizer research, which results in a lack of explanations for their effectiveness or lack of it. Dunston (1992) found the evidence inconclusive for improved reading comprehension related to the type of organizer used, when organizers should be introduced, and the type of students that benefit most from them. Moore and Readance (1984) completed an earlier review with similar results. Overall, variability in the creation, use, comparison groups, content areas, length of time, and results of these studies makes the evidence of their effectiveness ambiguous.

On the other hand, theoretical and professional literature presents graphic organizers as viable meaning-making devices and instructional tools. Although other uses are discussed in recent literature, by far the most popular use is as a classroom teaching tool. While we have long known that graphic organizers aid reading comprehension (Flood & Lapp, 1988; Heimlich & Pittelman, 1986), recent literature suggests that graphic organizers are used more broadly than this. The following discussion briefly addresses some of the recent literature related to the use of graphic organizers in elementary and middle school classrooms.

Curriculum and assessment. Teachers at various grade levels use graphic organizers for planning and developing all areas of the curriculum (Bromley, Irwin-DeVitis, & Modlo, 1995). Although they are a viable classroom assessment tool (Irwin-DeVitis & Pease, 1995), and they are found in mandated state tests, we have just begun to consider graphic organizers in the assessment of student learning (Bustle, 2004).

Reading. Graphic organizers are practical tools for facilitating comprehension during basal reading instruction (Kirylo & Millet, 2000). They stimulate prior knowledge, active participation, and understanding relationships among concepts. Specific understandings such as characterization can be developed with graphic organizers (Hobbs, 2001). In addition, some evidence suggests content area vocabulary (Allen, 2002), math vocabulary (Monroe, 1998), and reading vocabulary (Ainslie, 2001) improve with graphic organizer use.

Writing. More recently, research and professional articles focus on graphic organizers as aids to writing. In one study, low-achieving fourth graders using graphic organizers during writing workshop made more progress in their writing than high achieving students (James, Abbott, & Greenwood, 2001). In another study, middle-school students with learning disabilities who used graphic organizers provided significantly more related statements than the group without graphic organizers (DiCecco & Gleason, 2002). Accounts of classroom practice also report favorable results. Struggling middle-school writers gain confidence when they complete graphic organizers as part of the writing process (Mathena, 2000). Students with learning disabilities take better notes when they use graphic organizers because they learn to link and remember information (Dye, 2000).

Content areas. Accounts of classroom practice report the success of graphic organizers in math, science, and social studies. For students with learning disabilities, graphic organizers facilitate problem-solving skills in mathematics (Jitendra, 2002), and fifth-grade students of all ability levels learn to comprehend mathematics materials and problem solve with graphic organizers (Braselton & Decker, 1994). Fourth graders using the *graphic organizer notebook* in science produce better writing and higher test scores (Fisher, 2001). In social studies, a *discussion web* graphic organizer stimulates thinking and scaffolds discussion when students examine both sides of an argument after content area reading (Alvermann, 1991). Other organizers, as well as discussion guides, used during and after reading can improve learning in social studies (Wilson, 2002).

Special populations. In the past, graphic organizers have been used effectively both with gifted students and those with learning disabilities (Cassidy, 1991; Lehman, 1992). More recently, practical evidence (some of it previously mentioned) continues to report the benefits of graphic aids for learners who have difficulty organizing information (Baxendell, 2003). As well, more recent work suggests the benefits of graphic organizers with students who are deaf or hearing-impaired (Luckner, Bowen, & Carter, 2001), and some literature points to the use of web-based organizers for these students (Lang & Steely, 2003).

TEACHER-CREATED AND STUDENT-CREATED ORGANIZERS

Merkley and Jefferies (2001) provided guidelines for implementing graphic organizers, stressing that teacher planning should ". . . extend beyond construction of the visual to the deliberate consideration of the teacher's strategies to elicit prereading dialogue to accompany the visual" (p. 356). They believe this teacher-directed prereading dialogue stimulates students' prior knowledge, anticipation of what will be read, and the active reading of it. Many studies have reported the use of teacher-created organizers as prereading tools to aid comprehension and recall, but when elementary students construct graphic organizers after reading, their recall improves (Dunston, 1992; Griffin, Malone, & Kameenui, 1995). Jones, Pierce, and Hunter (1988) wrote that "When students construct graphic representations of text they read, they better understand which ideas in the text are important, how they relate, and what points are unclear" (p. 20), and they made suggestions for moving from teacher-created to student-created organizers. They proposed that teachers (a) present one type of organizer at a time, (b) share examples, (c) model an organizer's construction, (d) model their own thinking processes, (e) coach students, (f) provide opportunities to practice, and (h) accept individual differences along with gradually shifting responsibility to students.

DRAWN AND DIGITALLY CREATED GRAPHIC ORGANIZERS

Graphic organizers can be constructed on paper, the chalkboard, an overhead projector, or a computer screen. The chalkboard is easily accessible and erased, while the overheard projector allows teacher and/or student(s) to face the class while creating an organizer. Organizers made on paper or overhead transparencies can be photocopied for the class, and those on chart paper can be posted for future reference. Creating organizers using computer software with graphic capabilities adds another dimension. A projection unit lets students watch as an organizer is created, or view a teacher-made or commercial organizer for which paper copies can also be made for student use.

Software programs can be used to create graphic organizers (Alvermann & Phelps, 2002). *Inspiration 6.0* (Inspiration Software, 2000) lets students and teachers create webs, maps, diagrams, and outlines in which Clipart and pictures downloaded from the Internet can be imbedded (Ainslie, 2001). *TimeLiner 4.0* (Tom Snyder Productions, n.d.) allows for the creation of timelines of sequential events in both Spanish and English, which makes it especially effective for Spanish-speaking English language learners. The basic shapes, connector lines, text boxes, arrows, and Clipart accompanying most word processors permit graphic organizer creation as well. The addition of hypermedia, including print, images, and sound, to computer-constructed graphic organizers opens the door to a new age of literacy and new techniques for representing information graphically (Reinking, McKenna, Labbo, & Kieffer, 1998).

Some recent research with computer-created organizers as aids to writing is promising. Fifth- and sixth-grade students' reasoning and writing improved when they used web-based concept mapping linked to writing (Riley & Ahlberg, 2004). When eighth-grade students with learning disabilities created both hand-drawn maps and computer maps, they wrote more words and t-units, and received better holistic writing scores, while their attitudes were most positive after computer-mapping (Sturm & Rankin-Erickson, 2002).

Despite the advantages of using computer software to create graphic organizers, including student motivation, ease of accessibility, and the professional appearance of the finished product, computer-created organizers are not without problems (Anderson-Inman & Horney, 1997). When the size of an organizer or concept map becomes larger than the computer screen, all its parts cannot be viewed at once, which can be a frustration. In addition, it may be difficult to evaluate student learning or give feedback on a map's accuracy because of the variety of symbols and ways of showing relationships that may only make sense with the addition of a verbal explanation to accompany the organizer (Bromley, Irwin-DeVitis, & Modlo, 1995).

BENEFITS OF GRAPHIC ORGANIZERS

While graphic organizers aid learning for many students, they seem especially appropriate for those with language differences and processing difficulties. Graphic organizers highlight key vocabulary, provide an organized, visual display of knowledge, and facilitate discussion and sharing of ideas and information. They require the integration of language and thinking as students with different learning styles or rates of learning distill information into more easily digestible pieces. Graphic organizers are used for many reasons and in a variety of ways (Bromley, Irwin-DeVitis, & Modlo, 1995) because they perform the following functions discussed below.

Focus attention on key elements. To create a graphic organizer, both teachers and students pay close attention to important concepts and ideas. Students must distinguish among super-ordinate ideas, subordinate ideas, and supporting details.

Help integrate prior knowledge with new knowledge. Graphic organizers can represent students' background knowledge and provide a framework for the addition of new knowledge. When new information connects to what is already known, learning the new information makes sense and becomes easier.

Enhance concept development. Graphic organizers represent key ideas using appropriate vocabulary and thus help students see the important attributes of a concept. They aid comprehension and learning because they use vocabulary that explains, clarifies, and illustrates the informational structure of the concept.

Enrich reading, writing, thinking, and presenting. Students extend their language and literacy as they view, interpret, and create graphic organizers. When students design and discuss a visual representation of information, they read, reread, talk, reason, and see relationships that may not have been obvious before.

Support planning and revising. Graphic organizers—especially the conceptual organizer, since it is nonlinear and recursive—are effective ways to brainstorm, plan, and organize for speaking or writing. Ideas can be added to an organizer as they occur and then given a sequential order to be followed in a talk or report. Graphic organizers support revision as well since the writer can refer to them to learn what s/he may have inadvertently omitted.

Promote focused discussion. As students create graphic organizers, they negotiate with one another to construct shared meanings. They use language in authentic ways to (a) interpret, (b) analyze, (c) problem solve, (d) predict, (e) agree, (f) disagree, (g)cooperate, (h) validate, (i) connect, and (j)extend their learning about a specific topic or concept.

Provide assessment information. Students can create graphic organizers using pictures and key words to represent information and show relationships about what they have learned. Since graphic organizers do not require an extended narrative and are often quick and easy to construct, they are a viable assessment tool if students have had practice creating them and are given opportunities to explain them.

Assist instructional planning. Teachers who use graphic organizers in planning for instruction find them helpful. Graphic organizers provide a skeletal structure for exploration of a theme, topic, or piece of literature before teaching and a way to add information and ideas as a lesson or unit is taught to improve future instruction.

Some caveats related to the use of graphic organizers as instructional tools are worth considering (Bromley, Irwin-DeVitis, & Modlo, 1995):

- There are many ways to represent the same information and relationships in a graphic organizer, but no one correct way. The process of creating, discussing, sharing, and evaluating a graphic organizer is more important for learning than the organizer itself.
- Students learn from the active investigation and negotiation that accompanies the use of a graphic organizer. The discussion that accompanies the creation and interpretation of a graphic organizer is crucial to the learning process. Working with others helps students gain the ability to understand and apply learning independently.
- A gradual transition from teacher-created and directed graphic organizer activities to student-created, independent use of graphic organizers is best. Ultimately, the goal of instruction is to support students as they gradually become independent. Some students, however, will find graphic organizers more beneficial than others.

CONCLUSION

If visual language is "the hidden medium of communication" as Bonnici (1999) indicates in the title of his book, learning to deconstruct and design visual displays is a vital requirement in today's multiliteracy world. Whether teachers and students create and/or interpret a graphic organizer made with pictures, pencils, and markers or a web-based digital program, the visual display is an important meaning-making device. In its simplified form, the graphic organizer can represent rich and complex information and communicate ideas and emotions nonverbally as well verbally.

There is still much to be discerned from examining how and what students learn as they engage with graphic organizers. There is evidence that graphic organizers facilitate reading comprehension, and more recent research points to their support for discussion, reasoning, and writing in the content areas as well, especially for students with special needs. The social interactional learning that accompanies the coconstruction and cointerpretation of graphic organizers deserves the attention of future researchers and practitioners. Continued exploration of graphic organizers, both drawn and digitally created, should provide better understandings of them as individual and group meaning-making devices, specifically in the areas of vocabulary and concept development and the assessment of learning.

REFERENCES

Ainslie, D. (2001). Word detectives. *The Reading Teacher, 54*(4), 360–362.

Allen, J. (2002). "I am Thorgood, king of the orgies!" The reading challenge of content vocabulary. *Voices from the Middle, 9*(4), 22–27.

Alvermann, D. E. (1991). The discussion web: A graphic aid for learning across the curriculum. *The Reading Teacher, 45*(2), 92–99.

Alvermann, D. E., & Phelps, S. F. (2002). *Content reading and literacy: Succeeding in today's diverse classrooms* (3rd ed.). Boston: Allyn & Bacon.

Anderson, E. (2003). Design drawing: A means toward visual literacy and the exploration of ideas in the classroom. *The Technology Teacher,* 63(2), 15–17.

Anderson-Inman, L., & Horney, M. (2004). Computer-based concept mapping: Enhancing literacy with tools for visual thinking. *Journal of Adolescent and Adult Literacy, 40*(4), 302–307.

Ausubel, D. P. (1968). *Educational psychology: A cognitive view.* New York: Holt.

Barron, R. F. (1969). The use of vocabulary as an advance organizer. In H. L. Herber & P. L. Sanders (Eds.), *Research in reading in the content areas: First year report* (pp. 29–39). Syracuse, NY: Syracuse University Reading and Language Arts Center.

Baxendell, B. W. (2003). Consistent, coherent, creative: The 3 c's of graphic organizers. *Teaching Exceptional Children, 35*(3), 46–53.

Bonnici, P. (1999). *Visual language: The hidden medium of communication.* London: RotoVison.

Braselton, S., & Decker, B. C. (1994). Using graphic organizers to improve reading of mathematics. *Reading Teacher, 48*(3), 276–281.

Bromley, K., Irwin-DeVitis, L., & Modlo, M. (1995). *Graphic organizers: Visual strategies for active learning.* New York: Scholastic.

Bustle, L. S. (Ed.). (2003). *Image, inquiry, and transformative practice: Engaging learners in creative and critical inquiry through visual representation.* New York: Peter Lang.

Bustle, L. S. (2004). The role of visual representation in the assessment of learning. *Journal of Adolescent and Adult Literacy, 47*(5), 416–423.

Cairney, T. H. (1997). New avenues to literacy. *Educational Leadership, 54*(6), 76–77.

Cassidy, J. (1991). Using graphic organizers to develop critical thinking. *Gifted Child Today, 12*(6), 34–36.

DiCecco, V. M., & Gleason, M. M. (2002). Using graphic organizers to attain relational knowledge from expository text. *Journal of Learning Disabilities, 35*(4), 306–320.

Dunston, P. J. (1992). A critique of graphic organizer research. *Reading Research and Instruction, 31*(2), 57–65.

Dye, G. A. (2000). Graphic organizers to the rescue! Helping students link—and remember—information. *Teaching Exceptional Children, 32*(3), 72–76.

Fisher, A. L. (2001). Implementing graphic organizer notebooks: The art and science of teaching content. *The Reading Teacher, 55*(2), 116–120.

Flood, J., & Lapp, D. (1998). Conceptual mapping strategies for understanding information texts. *The Reading Teacher, 41*(8), 780–783.

Griffin, C. C., Malone, L. D., & Kameenui, E. J. (1995). Effects of graphic organizer instruction on fifth-grade students. *The Journal of Educational Research, 89*(2), 98–108.

Heimlich, J. E., & Pittelman, S. D. (1986). *Semantic mapping: Classroom applications.* Newark, DE: International Reading Association.

Hobbs, R. (2001). Improving reading comprehension by using media literacy activities. *Voices from the Middle, 8*(4), 44–50.

Hyerle, D. (1996). *Visual tools for constructing knowledge.* Alexandria, VA: Association for Supervision and Curriculum Development.

Inspiration Software. (2000). *Inspiration 6.0* [Computer software]. Portland, OR: Author.

International Reading Association & National Council of Teachers of English. (1996). *Standards for the English language arts.* Newark, DE: International Reading Association.

Irwin-DeVitis, L., Bromley, K., & Modlo, M. (1999). *50 graphic organizers for reading, writing, and more.* New York: Scholastic.

Irwin-DeVitis, L., & Pease, D. (1999). Using graphic organizers for learning and assessment in middle level classrooms. *Middle School Journal, 26*(5), 57–64.

James, L. H., Abbott, M., & Greenwood, C. R. (2001). How Adam became a writer: Winning writing strategies for low-achieving students. *Teaching Exceptional Children, 33*(3), 30–37.

Jitendra, A. (2002). Teaching students math problem-solving through graphic representations. *Teaching Exceptional Children, 34*(4), 34–38.

Jones, B. F., Pierce, J., & Hunter, B. (1988). Teaching students to construct graphic representations. *Educational Leadership, 46*(4), 20–25.

Junion-Metz, G. (2003). Graphic organizers. *School Library Journal, 49*(11), 32.

Kirylo, J. D., & Millet, C. P. (2000). Graphic organizers: An integral component to facilitate comprehension during basal reading instruction. *Reading Improvement, 37*(4), 179–186.

Lang, H. G., & Steely, D. (2003). Web-based science instruction for deaf students: What research says to the teacher. *Instructional Science, 31*(4/5) 277–298.

Lehman, H. (1992). Graphic organizers benefit slow learners. *Clearinghouse, 66*(1), 53–55.

Leland, H., & Harste, J. (1994). Multiple ways of knowing: Curriculum in a new key. *Language Arts, 71*, 337–345.

Luckner, J., Bowen, S., & Carter, K. (2001). Visual teaching strategies for students who are deaf or hard of hearing. *Teaching Exceptional Children, 33*(3), 38–44.

Marzano, R. J., Pickering, D. J., & Pollock, J. E. (2001). *Classroom instruction that works: Research-based strategies for increasing student achievement.* Alexandria, VA: Association for Supervision and Curriculum Development.

Mathena, T. J. (2000). Prompting kids to write. *American Educator, 24*(3), 16–21.

Merkley, D. M., & Jeffries, D. (2001). Guidelines for implementing a graphic organizer. *The Reading Teacher, 54*(4), 350–357.

Moline, S. (1995). *I see what you mean: Children at work with visual information.* York, ME: Stenhouse.

Monroe, E. (1998). Using graphic organizers to teach vocabulary: does available research inform mathematics instruction? *Education, 118*(4), 538–540.

Moore, D. W., & Readance, J. E. (1984). A quantitative and qualitative review of graphic organizer research. *Journal of Educational Research, 78*, 11–17.

Novak, J. D., & Gowin, D. B. (1984). *Learning how to learn.* New York: Cambridge University Press.

Paivio, A. (1990). *Mental representations: A dual coding approach.* New York: Oxford University Press.

Piaget, J. (1974). *Thought and language of the child* (M. Gabain, Trans.). New York: New American Library.

Reinking, D., McKenna, M. C., Labbo, L. D., & Kieffer, R. D. (1998). (Eds.) *The handbook of literacy and technology: Transformations in a post-typographic world.* Mahwah, NJ: Lawrence Erlbaum.

Rice, G. E. (1994). Need for explanations in graphic organizer research. *Reading Psychology, 15*(1), 39–67.

Riley, N. R., & Ahlberg, M. (2004). Investigating the use of ICT-based concept mapping techniques on creativity in literacy tasks. *Journal of Computer-Assisted Learning, 20*(4), 244–256.

Robinson, D. H., & Molina, E. (2002). The relative involvement of visual and auditory working memory when studying adjunct displays. *Contemporary Educational Psychology, 27*(1). 118–131.

Robinson, D. H. (1998). Graphic organizers as aids to text learning. *Reading Research and Instruction, 37*(2), 85–105.

Rumelhart, D. E. (1980). Schemata: The building blocks of cognition. In R. J. Spiro, B. C. Bruce, & W. F. Brewer (Eds.), *Theoretical issues in reading comprehension* (pp. 33–58). Hillsdale, NJ: Erlbaum.

Sturm, J. M., & Rankin-Erickson, J. L. (2002). Effects of hand-drawn and computer-generated concept mapping on the expository writing of middle school students with learning disabilities. *Learning Disabilities: Research and Practice, 17*(2), 124–139.

Tom Snyder Productions. (n.d.). *TimeLiner 4.0* [Computer software]. Watertown, MA: Author.

Tompkins, G. (2002). *Content and teaching strategies* (5th ed.). Columbus, OH: Merrill.

Vacca, J. L., & Vacca, R. T. (2005). *Content area learning: Literacy and learning across the curriculum.* New York: Pearson.

Vygotsky, L. S. (1962). *Thought and language.* Cambridge, MA: MIT Press.

Wilson, E. (2002). Literature and literacy in the social studies classroom: Strategies to enhance social studies instruction. *Southern Social Studies Journal, 28*(1), 45–57.

43

THE EFFECTIVE USES OF DIGITAL STORYTELLING AS A TEACHING AND LEARNING TOOL

Bernard R. Robin
UNIVERSITY OF HOUSTON

WHAT IS DIGITAL STORYTELLING AND WHAT ARE SOME OF THE MOST COMMON ELEMENTS OF DIGITAL STORIES?

Digital storytelling at its most basic core is the practice of using computer-based tools to tell stories. There are a wealth of other terms used to describe this practice, such as digital documentaries, computer-based narratives, digital essays, electronic memoirs, interactive storytelling, etc.; but in general, they all revolve around the idea of combining the art of telling stories with a variety of multimedia, including graphics, audio, video, and Web publishing. As with traditional storytelling, most digital stories focus on a specific topic and contain a particular point of view. However, as the name implies, digital stories usually contain some mixture of computer-based images, text, recorded audio narration, video clips, and/or music. Digital stories can vary in length, but most of the stories used in education typically last between 2 and 10 minutes. The topics used in digital storytelling range from personal tales to the recounting of historical events, from exploring life in one's own community to the search for life in other corners of the universe, and literally, everything in between.

Despite its emphasis on computer technology, digital storytelling is not a new practice. One of the field's most noted pioneers is Joe Lambert, the cofounder of the Center for Digital Storytelling (CDS), a nonprofit, community arts organization in Berkeley, California. The CDS has been assisting young people and adults in the creation and sharing of personal narratives through the combination of thoughtful writing and digital media tools since the early 1990s (CDS, 2005). The CDS is also recognized for developing the Seven Elements of Digital Storytelling, as described below.

Linda Hicks and Rachel Woodburn (2004), educators who teach digital storytelling at Scottsdale Community College in Arizona, called digital storytelling a "process of connection." They work with their students to help them harness the power of voice and imagery to connect people to their community by using technology "that's relevant to the way they live today." Woodburn stated,

> Storytelling has always been a vital part of every community. It is how we understand who we are in relationship to others. Through story we are taught all the important lessons in life. Story preserves our history, our language, and our culture. Story is how we connect generations within community. Without story we are lost; we are without connection. Digital is just a tool that we can use to cross those bridges and reconnect community.

British photographer, author, and educator Daniel Meadows (2005) had a more idyllic definition of digital stories as "short, personal multimedia tales told from the heart." The beauty of this form of digital expression, he maintained, is that these stories can be created by people everywhere, on any subject, and shared electronically all over the world. Meadows added that digital stories are "multimedia sonnets from the people" in which "photographs discover the talkies, and the stories told assemble in the ether as pieces of a jigsaw puzzle, a gaggle of invisible histories which, when viewed together, tell the bigger story of our time, the story that defines who we are."

Researcher and digital culture consultant, John Seely Brown (2003) described digital storytelling this way:

> I'm particularly interested in Digital Storytelling, in new ways to use multiple media to tell stories and in the ability of kids, who are now growing up in a digital world, to figure out new ways to tell stories. They have the ability to build interpretive movies very simply and to lay sound tracks around the content. They condition or "sculpture" the context around the content. The serious interplay between context and content is key to what film—and rich media in general—are about.

TABLE 43.1 The Seven Elements of Digital Storytelling

1. **Point of View**—what is the purpose of the story and the perspective of the author?
2. **A Dramatic Question**—a question that is posed and will be answered by the end of the story.
3. **Emotional Content**—serious issues that speak to us in personal and powerful ways.
4. **The Gift of your Voice**—a way to personalize the story to help the audience understand the context.
5. **The Power of the Soundtrack**—music or other sounds that support the storyline.
6. **Economy**—simply put, using just enough content and detail to tell the story without overloading the viewer with too much information.
7. **Pacing**—related to economy, but specifically deals with how slowly or quickly the story progresses and should fit with the theme and goal of the story.

Brown went on to say,

> Stories talk to the gut, while information talks to the mind. You can't talk a person through a change in religion or a change in a basic mental model. There has to be an emotional component in what you are doing . . . But if you can get to them emotionally, either through rhetoric or dramatic means, then you can create some scaffolding that effectively allows them to construct a new model for themselves.

As Brown noted, many practitioners of digital storytelling use video in their work to create minimovies. However, digital stories may also be created by just using a series of still images. Many powerful digital stories have been created by incorporating what has come to be known as the "Ken Burns Effect." This process, popularized by documentary filmmaker Ken Burns and now available in many current multimedia software applications, allows users to convert still images into moving images by creatively panning and zooming over photographs that have either been taken with a camera, or found in a book, on the Internet, or in a family album. Today's computer hardware and software capabilities are spawning a new generation of filmmakers who are using the Ken Burns Effect along with numerous other multimedia techniques to create high-quality digital stories that captivate the imagination and motivate students of all ages.

At the University of Houston, a Web site has been developed that is devoted to the educational uses of digital storytelling. This site features examples of digital stories created by students and educators as well as helpful information for those interested in learning how to create their own digital stories. The "Educational Uses of Digital Storytelling" Web site is online at, http://www.coe.uh.edu/digital storytelling/ and resources from the site are described throughout this chapter.

TYPES OF DIGITAL STORIES

As we begin our exploration of digital storytelling, it makes sense to try to sort these stories into a set of major topic areas or categories. One possible and subjective organizational structure might include (a) personal narratives—stories that contain accounts of significant events in one's life; (b) historical documentaries—stories that examine dramatic occurrences that help us understand the past; and (c) stories designed to inform or instruct the viewer on a particular concept or practice.

Digital Stories as Personal Narratives

One of the most popular reasons for producing digital stories is to create a personal narrative. High-school students at the Urban School of San Francisco participated in a large-scale oral history project that contains filmed interviews with Holocaust survivors. The "Telling Their Stories" project was conceived by Howard Levin, director of technology at the school and a former history teacher, who described the project this way:

> While expanding students' depth of understanding of the Holocaust, the project provides a public service through the publication of their interviews. It directly addresses part of the Urban School's mission of extending our reach to the community by meaningful engagement with the world outside the classroom . . . Our students' work provides valuable primary source material for students and researchers throughout the world. They are crossing the boundary of "learner" to "contributor." Their work has real meaning beyond the classroom, a concept I've dubbed authentic doing. (Levin, 2003, p. 23)

A good example of a digital story that uses a personal narrative is *Almost Paradise* (http://www.coe.uh.edu/digitalstorytelling/almost-paradise.htm). This story provides an account of a mother bringing her children to the United States from South Korea in search of a better life. It outlines the difficulties in coming to a different country, as well as the clashes between a daughter and her mother as they each have different feelings about life and their heritage. This type of story has multiple benefits in an educational setting. First, students who view the story learn about people from diverse backgrounds other than their own, and they can gain an appreciation of the types of hardships that are faced by some of their fellow classmates whose families have come from another country. A story such as this one can be used to facilitate discussions in class about such issues as race, multiculturalism, and the globalization that is taking place in the world. In addition, a student who creates such a story can benefit from sharing it with others. This type of information can be used to eliminate some of the distance that foreign-born students feel between themselves and their peers. A personal narrative such as this can also be a positive means for dealing with the some of the emotional family issues that were described in the story.

The CDS, whose major emphasis is on personal stories (Lambert, 2003), described the following types of digital stories:

- **Character Stories**—explore how we love, who we are inspired by, and the importance of finding meaning in our relationships.
- **Memorial Stories**—deal with memories of people who are no longer with us. These stories are often difficult but are emotionally powerful and can help with the grieving process.
- **Stories About Events in Our Lives**
  - *Adventure Stories*—revolve around places we visit and adventures we have in our travels.
  - *Accomplishment Stories*—deal with achieving goals and understanding defining moments in our lives.
- **Stories About Places in Our Lives**—examine the important places in our lives: our homes, our towns, and the experiences that connect us to our communities.
- **Stories About What We Do**—allow us to talk about our jobs, professions, and careers in terms of how we value and find meaning in the work we do.
- Other Personal Stories
  - *Recovery Stories*—deal with how we overcome great obstacles and challenges in our lives.
  - *Love Stories*—provide us with an opportunity to share some of the most meaningful parts of our lives with the people we most cherish.
  - *Discovery Stories*—let us reflect on what we have learned and illustrate our journeys of discovery.

In recent years, the Texas Association Against Sexual Assault's award-winning "Speak up. Speak out." public-awareness campaign, in collaboration with the CDS, provides training in digital storytelling to survivors of sexual assault in Texas. The highly personal stories produced by survivors, although often difficult to watch, are a powerful example of how digital storytelling can help us learn to overcome great challenges in our lives and teach others about trauma and the process of recovery. These courageous stories are available for viewing at, http://www.taasa.org/latest_news/article02012006.php

Digital Stories That Examine Historical Events

Although many personal narratives may include historical information to establish the context of the story, a different kind of digital story can be created from historical material that students might explore in a classroom. An audio recording of *Abraham Lincoln's Gettysburg Address* is used as the basis for a digital story based on what is arguably the most recognized speech in American history. The digital story is online at http://www.coe.uh.edu/digitalstorytelling/gettysburg.htm and was created using early photographs taken during the American Civil War in the 1960s as well as paintings and other materials found on the Internet.

Stories That Inform or Instruct

While it can be argued that all digital stories inform (and perhaps instruct), the distinction here is that there is room to create a separate category for stories that reflect instructional material in content areas such as math, science, health education, and instructional technology. *Aging Well*, located online at, http://www.coe.uh.edu/digitalstorytelling/agingwell.htm is an example of a digital story that was created to inform people about the aging process and some of the things they can do to improve their health as they grow older.

And of course, stories can be created using combinations of these three methods such as an autobiographical story using historical material as the backdrop for a personal narrative.

HOW CAN DIGITAL STORYTELLING BE USED AS AN EFFECTIVE INSTRUCTIONAL TOOL BY TEACHERS?

One of the first decisions that a teacher needs to make when considering the use of digital storytelling is whether he or she will create the digital stories or the students will do it. Some educators may decide to create their own stories and show them to their students as a way to present new material. An engaging, multimedia-rich digital story can serve as an anticipatory set or "hook" to capture the attention of students and increase their interest in exploring new ideas. A number of researchers support the use of anticipatory sets at the beginning of a lesson to help engage students in the learning process (Burmark, 2004; Ormrod, 2004) and to serve as a bridge between existing knowledge and new material (Ausubel, 1978). The Gettysburg Address is a good example of a digital story that can be used to engage students in an exploration of historical material. Although many students may be familiar with the words, the use of photographs and paintings of the soldiers in combat to illustrate scenes from the American Civil War serve to contextualize the words of Abraham Lincoln's famous speech and, in essence, bring the past to life.

Teacher-created digital stories may also be used to enhance current lessons within a larger unit, as a way to facilitate discussion about the topics presented in a story and as a way to make abstract or conceptual content more understandable. While many educators still lack a cohesive plan for integrating multimedia into their instruction, a growing number are interested in exploring ways to engage their students by including images, audio, and video elements in their instruction. Researchers such as Hibbing and Rankin-Erikson (2003) and Boster, Meyer, Roberto, Lindsey, Smith, Inge, and Strom (2007) have shown that the use of multimedia in teaching helps students retain new information and aids in the comprehension of difficult material. Digital storytelling can provide educators with a powerful tool to use in their classrooms.

HOW CAN DIGITAL STORYTELLING BE USED AS AN EFFECTIVE LEARNING TOOL FOR STUDENTS?

Digital storytelling can also be a potent tool for students who are taught to create their own stories. After viewing sample digital stories created by their teachers or other story developers, students may be given assignments in which they are first asked to research a topic and then choose a particular point of view and, as described in the Seven Elements of Digital Storytelling, a dramatic question. This type of activity can generate interest, attention, and motivation for the "digital-generation" students in today's classrooms. The process can capitalize on the creative talents of students as they begin to research and tell stories of their own while learning to use the library and the Internet to research rich, deep content while analyzing and synthesizing a wide range of content. In addition, students who participate in the creation of digital stories may develop enhanced communication skills by learning to organize their ideas, ask questions, express opinions, and construct narratives. Digital storytelling also can help students as they learn to create stories for an audience and present their ideas and knowledge in an individual and meaningful way.

In addition, when digital stories are published on the Web, students have the opportunity to share their work with their peers and gain valuable experience in critiquing their own and others' work, which increases emotional intelligence and fosters social learning. Digital storytelling appeals to students with diverse learning styles and also foster collaboration when students are able to work in groups and provides value in enhancing the student experience through personal ownership and accomplishment.

Increasing Student Literacy

When digital storytelling is used by students, it provides a strong foundation in many different types of literacy, including information literacy, visual literacy, technological literacy, and media literacy. Summarizing the work of several researchers in this field, Brown, Bryan and Brown (2005) labeled these multiple skills that are aligned with technology as "Twenty-First Century Literacy," which they described as the combination of

- **Digital Literacy**—the ability to communicate with an ever-expanding community to discuss issues, gather information, and seek help;
- **Global Literacy**—the capacity to read, interpret, respond, and contextualize messages from a global perspective;
- **Visual Literacy**—the ability to understand, produce, and communicate through visual images;
- **Technology Literacy**—the ability to use computers and other technology to improve learning, productivity, and performance;
- **Information Literacy**—the ability to find, evaluate and synthesize information.

Filmmaker and educator Nikos Theodosakis (2001) believed that we must ask ourselves how to best prepare children to live, work, and communicate in a visual world: "If we expect them to be fluent in this new visual language, where do we begin teaching the visual grammar and visual vocabulary skills that will help them both understand and present concepts and ideas that use images as well as or instead of text?" (p. 26).

Brown, Bryan and Brown (2005) discussed the need for technology literacy this way:

> In response to the new demands of the information age, teachers now integrate technology across the curriculum. Traditional literacy instruction involved the use of textbooks, skills lessons, ability groups, numerous worksheets and workbook pages, as well as writing that only the teacher read. In contrast, literacy in the 21st century requires that children not only communicate with classroom peers, but also read e-books, receive and send e-mail, locate and evaluate online information, prepare reports with presentation software, establish dialogue with learned individuals in other regions, and write for both a local and global community (Brown, Bryan & Brown, 2005).

In addition, other educators speak of "Representational Literacy" as the ability to understand the need for information, find this information, evaluate and effectively use it (American Library Association Presidential Committee on Information Literacy, 1989), and understand how meaning is created through information analysis (Rafferty, 1999).

However, there are also dissenting opinions that we should keep in mind. Our view of information literacy in the information age should not automatically include the assumption that students will become better consumers of information because they have access to the Internet, the greatest information source ever developed. Librarian Stanley Wilder (2005) argued that students for whom the Internet is their only source of scholarly information are not only drowning in too much information, but worse, are also unquestioningly accepting what they find without first learning how to critically analyze the material to determine its worth. The vast storehouse of material on the World Wide Web is a dramatic and powerful achievement, especially for students and educators; but it is not, nor should it be, a replacement for journals, books, and libraries. Knowing how to use all available resources is the true meaning of information literacy.

There is no denying that today's students need to improve their computer skills. The debate that is taking place in homes, schools, businesses, and governments is about how best to accomplish this. Theodosakis (2001) reflected the opinion of many of his fellow educators when he said that having students learn technology as just another skill set is not enough. He advocated teaching technology so that it may be used to solve problems, answer questions, present ideas, and communicate.

Riesland (2005) went even further and observed that even as the definition of the term "Visual Literacy" is being hotly debated by researchers and educators, there is no dispute that computer technology is at the heart of the debate. She challenged the educational community to reconsider what it means to be literate in the age of technology and argued that teachers must equip their students with skills that will enable them to understand and communicate through visual modes and "thrive in increasingly media-varied environments." Riesland went on to call for a new definition of visual literacy education, one that will allow students to successfully navigate and communicate through new forms of multimedia, and further stated that students must take on the role of information producer rather than information consumer. "Opportunities for web and hypermedia story design are passed over in the classroom every day in favor of traditional reading and writing exercises" . . . and as "countless other students are finding their way through new media, they leave their peers in the dust. Yet, our modern technology-driven society demands a level of communication that remains largely unaddressed in the classroom."

Proponents of digital storytelling believe that students involved in creating their own digital stories gain proficiency in many areas. By using software that combines a variety of multimedia tools including working with text, still images, audio, video, and oftentimes, Web publishing, they become active investigators, seeking new information, rather than simply passive recipients of that information. In the area of technological literacy, digital storytelling can provide a meaningful reason for students to learn to digitize media content using scanners, digital still cameras, and video cameras. In addition, as students create the narration and soundtrack for a digital story, they gain skills in using microphones, digitizing audio, and working with music and sound effects.

In summary, when students are able to participate in the multiple steps of designing, creating, and presenting their own digital stories, they increase a full complement of literacy skills, including,

- **Research Skills**—documenting the story, finding and analyzing pertinent information;

- **Writing Skills**—formulating a point of view and developing a script;
- **Organization Skills**—managing the scope of the project, the materials used, and the time it takes to complete the task;
- **Technology Skills**—learning to use a variety of tools, such as digital cameras, scanners, microphones, and multimedia authoring software;
- **Presentation Skills**—deciding how to best present the story to an audience;
- **Interview Skills**—finding sources to get interview and determining what questions to ask;
- **Interpersonal Skills**—working within a group and determining individual roles for group members;
- **Problem-Solving Skills**—learning to make decisions and overcome obstacles at all stages of the project, from inception to completing;
- **Assessment Skills**—gaining expertise critiquing their own work and the work of others.

Stephanie Barish, educator, multimedia developer and former creative director for the Institute for Multimedia Literacy at the University of Southern California, and Elizabeth Daley, dean of the University of Southern California's School of Cinema-Television and director of the Annenberg Center for Communication at USC (2005), have written about the use of multimedia as academic inquiry in higher education, a subject that holds the same promise for students using digital storytelling well before they begin attending colleges or universities. Their premise is that multimedia scholarship can no longer limit educators and students to just understanding the relationship between combinations of media types, but that to be literate must also include becoming competent in the ability to create new materials that facilitate new avenues of thought and analysis. The benefit of multimedia authoring, they maintain, is that it puts the power in the individual by allowing for the mixing of elements, issues, and perspectives, which ultimately lead to new constructions, new meanings, and greater comprehension.

WHAT ARE SOME CHALLENGES TO STUDENTS CREATING THEIR OWN DIGITAL STORIES?

Digital storytelling does present some challenges for students and educators. First, it can be argued that bad storytelling using digital media will simply lead to bad digital stories, and this often happens with students when they are first asked to create their own digital stories. It is almost predictable that students who have watched countless music videos think that a digital story can be created by simply adding a popular song to a series of digital images. It takes students (and educators, too) time to understand that developing a meaningful digital story requires planning, effort, and assessment, and each of these steps in the process takes time and thoughtfulness. When Hollywood film director Vincent Sherman was asked what words of advice he would give to young people interested in becoming filmmakers, he replied,

> I think the ability to tell a story is of vital importance. I think the guy who can sit in a room and tell a story to people, grab their interest and hold their interest—that's the first step. To know what makes a story hold, too. How to set up a problem, how to set up a situation, how to set up conflict, how to create interest in a character. (Sherman, 2005)

Many students have trouble learning to formulate an educationally sound argument, and just providing students with a library of digital images and computer-based authoring software will not be beneficial to students or educators. There are many resources that may guide students as they construct their own stories. The Visual Portrait of a Story, as shown in Figure 43.1 (Ohler & Dillingham, 2004) presents a description of story elements that students and educators may find helpful. A Questioning Toolkit (http://www.fno.org/nov97/toolkit.html) from the online journal From Now On (http://www.fno.org/index.html) is a resource that can be used to introduce students to effective questioning techniques that may help them in their attempts to formulate the dramatic questions that will form the basis of their own stories.

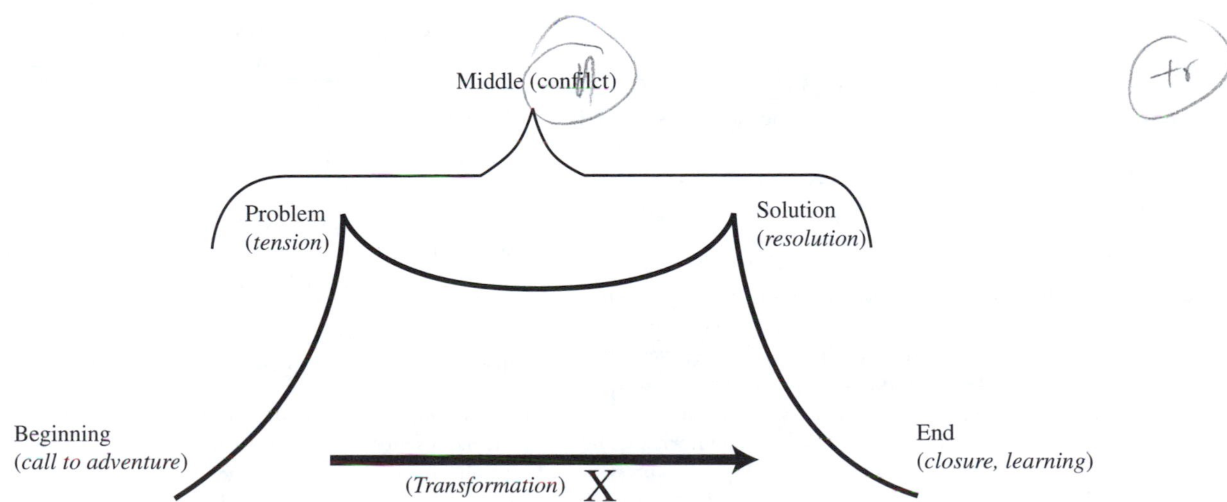

FIGURE 43.1 The visual portrait of a story.

Marco Torres, a nationally recognized social studies teacher and technology director at San Fernando High School in California, encourages his students to use multimedia projects to tell stories about their community and its history (Edutopia, 2002). Torres teaches his students to write scripts, develop storyboards, and construct timelines during a planning stage that is just the first part of the design-and-development process. The production stage is next. During production, students use technology such as computers, digital cameras, and microphones to collect or create the images, narration, and music and text that will be used in their projects. Torres also has his students present their projects and assess their work to examine what it means to have created a good project. His students construct rubrics to assess their projects in terms of the appropriateness of the elements they used. Such rubrics for evaluating student-created digital stories have been created by many educators, and many use the Center for Digital Storytelling's Seven Elements as a starting point, but add additional material that is more applicable for the classroom. One such rubric, based on earlier work of educators in this area, and described by Helen Barrett, a leading researcher on student learning and motivation, is shown in Table 43.2 (Barrett, 2005).

However, simply having a set of targets for students to try to attain does not insure success when students first attempt to create their own digital stories. K–12 teacher, Tom Banaszewski (2005) completed a master's thesis in which he investigated the use of digital storytelling in grades 4 through 12 by examining the storytelling process, the motivation of teachers, and the possible alignment of digital storytelling with curricular goals and school district or statewide education standards. In his study, Banaszewski echoed the opinion of many by pointing out that when the focus is solely on the technology of creating digital stories and other literacy skills are ignored, a number of troubling issues arise:

- Students cannot explain what digital storytelling is and why it is different from a computerized slideshow;
- Students do not recognize the power of their own voices;
- Students concentrate on using the computer before a story's script has been completed;
- Students waste time on unnecessary transitions and special effects.

Banaszewski proposed that the solution to these issues is for students (and teachers) to concentrate on developing narrative skills and focus on what makes a good nondigital story, the same established practices found in traditional writing and composition classes. In his own classroom, he noted that the technology was always secondary to the storytelling, a view that cannot be overemphasized.

As has been discussed, a major thrust of digital storytelling revolves around the telling of a personal story or narrative. When students are given the freedom to use digital storytelling to tell their own stories, it seems almost inevitable that some students will include material, ideas and/or points of view that either their teacher, other students in their classroom, or nonrelated viewers will find unsuitable. Care must be taken to inform students about what is and is not acceptable in a digital story; while this medium of expression facilitates exploration and new modes of expression, students must understand that there are rules of conduct and etiquette that come with this freedom of expression.

WHAT SUBJECT AREAS ARE MOST APPROPRIATE FOR CLASSROOM USE OF DIGITAL STORYTELLING?

The most commonly mentioned content areas for digital storytelling in education are those in the humanities, including English, language arts, history, and the social sciences. However, there are good examples of digital stories in just about every area including math, science, business, art, and music, and one of the most important aspects of digital storytelling is that it can be used with almost any subject area that educators and their students select. In addition, students at all levels, from young elementary-age children to adults enrolled in graduate-school programs, will find that digital storytelling can be an effective way to construct new learning and communicate knowledge and understanding.

WHAT SPECIFIC TECHNOLOGIES ARE REQUIRED TO BEGIN USING DIGITAL STORYTELLING?

Computer Equipment

A computer is a basic requirement for creating digital stories. Both PCs running the Windows operating system and Apple computers running the Macintosh operating system can be used for digital storytelling. The best advice for those who are just learning to create digital stories is to use the computer system with which they have experience and are already comfortable. A connection to the Internet and access to Web search engines such as Google and Yahoo are helpful tools that allow students to find useful written information and images that may be used in the construction of many digital stories.

Software Programs

Simple technologies such as Microsoft Word and PowerPoint can be used to create Digital Stories. Microsoft's free Photo Story 3 for Windows XP is a very powerful digital storytelling authoring program, while Apple Computer's iMovie can be a good choice for Macintosh computer users. In order to disseminate digital stories on the Web, an Internet server with the ability to stream content (QuickTime, Real, Windows Media) may be used although, some educators burn copies of their students' digital stories onto CD or DVD media for playback on a computer or a DVD player connected to a television set.

Other Technology Devices

An ever-growing variety of digital cameras, video camcorders, and scanners are available to help educators and their students create still images and video clips that can be included in their stories. Many of these devices are inexpensive, easy to use and with a little practice, and can produce very high-quality results.

Computer Microphones for Use With a Desktop Computer

Just about every computer that's been manufactured in the last several years has a sound card built in, and this card almost always has the capability to plug in a microphone so that the computer can be used to record audio. Most stores that sell computers or computer accessories will have a selection of inexpensive microphones. A microphone and headset combination may be a better option for use in a computer

TABLE 43.2 A Rubric for Evaluating Digital Stories Created by Students

Category	4 Points	3 Points	2 Points	1 Point
1. Purpose of the Digital Story	Establishes a purpose early on and maintains a clear focus throughout.	Establishes a purpose early on and maintains focus for most of the presentation.	There are a few lapses in focus, but the purpose is fairly clear.	It is difficult to figure out the purpose of the presentation.
2. Point of View	The point of view is well developed and contributes to the overall meaning of the story.	The point of view is stated but does not connect with each part of the story, although an attempt is made to connect it to the overall meaning of the story.	The point of view is stated but no attempt is made to connect it to the overall meaning of the story.	The point of view is only hinted at, or is difficult to discern.
3. Dramatic Question	A meaningful dramatic question is asked and answered within the context of the story.	A dramatic question is asked but not clearly answered within the context of the story.	A dramatic question is hinted at but not clearly established within the context of the story.	Little or no attempt is made to pose a dramatic question or answer it.
4. Choice of Content	Contents create a distinct atmosphere or tone that matches different parts of the story. The images may communicate symbolism and/or metaphors.	Contents create an atmosphere or tone that matches some parts of the story. The images may communicate symbolism and/or metaphors.	An attempt was made to use contents to create an atmosphere/tone but it needed more work. Image choice is logical.	Little or no attempt to use contents to create an appropriate atmosphere/tone.
5. Clarity of Voice	Voice quality is clear and consistently audible throughout the presentation.	Voice quality is clear and consistently audible throughout the majority (85–95%) of the presentation.	Voice quality is clear and consistently audible through some (70–84%)of the presentation.	Voice quality needs more attention.
6. Pacing of the Narrative	The pace (rhythm and voice punctuation) fits the story line and helps the audience really "get into" the story.	Occasionally speaks too fast or too slowly for the story line. The pacing (rhythm and voice punctuation) is relatively engaging for the audience.	Tries to use pacing (rhythm and voice punctuation), but it is often noticeable that the pacing does not fit the story line. Audience is not consistently engaged.	No attempt to match the pace of the storytelling to the story line or the audience.
7. Meaningful Use of an Audio Soundtrack	Music stirs a rich emotional response that matches the story line well. Images coordinated with the music.	Music stirs a rich emotional response that somewhat matches the story line. Images mostly coordinated with the music.	Music is ok, and not distracting, but it does not add much to the story. Not coordinated with images.	Music is distracting, inappropriate, OR was not used.
8. Quality of Images	Images create a distinct atmosphere or tone that matches different parts of the story. The images may communicate symbolism. and/or metaphors.	Images create an atmosphere or tone that matches some parts of the story. The images may communicate symbolism and/or metaphors.	An attempt was made to use images to create an atmosphere/tone but it needed more work. Image choice is logical.	Little or no attempt to use images to create an appropriate atmosphere/tone.
9. Economy of Story Detail	The story is told with exactly the right amount of detail throughout. It does not seem too short nor too long	The story composition is typically good, though it seems to drag somewhat OR needs slightly more detail in one or two sections.	The story seems to need more editing. It is noticeably too long or too short in more than one section.	The story needs extensive editing. It is too long or too short to be interesting.
10. Grammar and Language Usage	Grammar and usage were correct (for the dialect chosen) and contributed to clarity, style, and character development.	Grammar and usage were typically correct (for the dialect chosen) and errors did not detract from the story.	Grammar and usage were typically correct but errors detracted from story.	Repeated errors in grammar and usage distracted greatly from the story.

lab where multiple computers are being used simultaneously or in situations where computers do not have speakers attached. Use of the microphone-headset combination will allow students to hear their own recordings without disturbing others in the same location.

Regardless of which type of microphone is being used, practically all users of Microsoft's Windows operating system will be able to record audio on their computer. On the Windows operating system going back to Windows 95, the operating system itself comes with a software utility program called Sound Recorder. It's a small, basic sound recording and editing program that allows user to plug a microphone into the sound card and record short digital audio files that can be used in digital stories.

The options available with Sound Recorder are limited, and the major one is that no more than 60 seconds of audio may be recorded at one time. However, this "limitation" can actually be used as an advantage by educators as they can use the time limit to better help students deal with economy and pacing, two of the Seven Elements of Digital Storytelling described at the beginning of this chapter. Additionally, a series of recorded segments may be edited together using a digital audio editing software program such as Audacity, a free application that may be downloaded from, http://audacity.sourceforge.net/

On Location Interviews with a Microphone and Laptop Computer

Microphones can also be plugged into most laptop computers, and this is an excellent way to record interviews "on location" for times when those being interviewed are not able to come to where a desktop computer recording station is set up.

Digital Voice Recorders

Digital voice recorders can be a wonderful tool for students who want to interview people in the community. One good option is the Olympus WS-100, a portable device that is easy to use, records high-quality audio, and is reasonably priced. This particular model will operate for many hours, long enough to conduct lengthy interviews on a single AAA battery. An optional tie-clip microphone is also available and this accessory will improve the sound quality of the interview, since it places the microphone closer to the interviewee than by just using the recorder's built-in microphone.

StoryCorps (http://storycorps.net), a national project developed by the American Folklife Center at the Library of Congress, is seeking to "instruct and inspire Americans to record one another's stories in sound." The Web site contains a Do-It-Yourself guide that outlines recording equipment basics, a section on how to conduct an interview and an interview checklist that will help students think about the steps involved before, during, and after the interview takes place. The StoryCorps Web site also includes a Question Generator (located at: http://storycorps.net/participate/question_generator/) that students and teachers will find helpful in creating the questions to be used in an audio interview. This Web-based resource not only creates a printable version of the questions that have been selected for the interview, but also will email a copy of the list to the user.

GETTING STARTED WITH DIGITAL STORYTELLING

One of the easiest ways to get started with Digital Storytelling is to create a digital story using materials found on the Internet by using a Web search engine. A list of useful Web-search tools may be found at: http://www.coe.uh.edu/digitalstorytelling/tools.htm

The process for creating a digital story can be divided into four major parts, as follows:

Part One: Define, Collect, and Decide

The first and most important step in the process is to define what the story will be about. Once a preliminary topic is selected, Web search tools may be used to locate visual resources for the story, such as pictures, drawings, photographs, maps, and charts. When they are collected, they should be saved to a location on a computer where they can be easily found. Audio resources such as music, speeches, and interviews may also be located on the Web and, like the visual resources, should be saved in the selected location on the computer. Search tools might then be used to look for informational content, which might come from Web sites, word-processed documents, PDF documents, or PowerPoint slides. For all types of materials collected, more is definitely better, since not all materials will be usable in the final story. However, in this early stage, collecting an abundance of material is recommended. Finally, begin thinking of the purpose of the story. Will it be used to inform, convince, provoke, question? That decision can be made at this point in the process or it can be deferred until later.

Part Two: Select, Import, Begin to Create

It is in this second phase of the digital storytelling process that an attempt should be made to select the specific images that will be used in the story. The use of audio resources, if any, should also be determined at this time. Some developers incorporate a storyboard at this point in the process. A storyboard is a series of rough sketches or diagrams that show a visual outline of a proposed story. Storyboards may be simple or complex, but either way, they can be a valuable step in the digital storytelling process. This is especially true in the classroom, as storyboards help students organize their ideas and plans for how images, text, and audio will be used in the creation of the story and can also inspire new ideas as the student begins to see any gaps in the story that need to be filled. Storyboards can be drawn on paper or constructed on the computer using specialized storyboard software or just a word processing program. A storyboarding tutorial using Microsoft Word is online at, http://www.coe.uh.edu/digital-storytelling/PhotoStory3-Tutorials/Tutorial_Storyboard.pdf

Once the initial plans for the story's content are made, a decision will also need to be made about which software program to use to create the story, such as PowerPoint, iMovie, Photo Story 3 or another of the many applications that are available. When a particular program is selected, the collected images, text, and audio should be imported into the program and an initial version of the story should be created.

Part Three: Write, Record, Modify, Finalize

When the first two parts of the process have been completed, a rough version of the story will be available. If audio narration is going to be included, a script needs to be written that will work with the selected images and support the purpose and point of view of the story. A microphone will be needed to record the narration and audio will need to be imported into the program. It is especially important at this point in the process that students involved in creating digital stories critically review their work and look for ways that their story can be modified and improved. These modifications might include technical adjustments to the number of images used in the story, the length of time certain images are displayed on the screen, the sound level and quality of audio (narration and music), and most importantly, the effectiveness of the story itself. When all of these steps have been completed, it's time to finalize the digital story.

Part Four: Demonstrate, Evaluate, Replicate

The last part of the digital storytelling process actually has little to due with the production itself, but is still an essential component of the process, particularly when students and teachers are developing digital stories in their classrooms. When the digital story is complete, it should be shared with others. By demonstrating these multimedia-rich resources to other students as well as other teachers, interest in digital storytelling can easily be spread. One of the reasons that digital storytelling is such a powerful educational tool is because just about everyone who sees a story immediately starts to think of stories they might create on a variety of topics in which they have an interest. And, as with the evaluation component in the previous phase, soliciting feedback from others who view the stories but who have not been part of the design and development process can provide additional suggestions for making the stories even stronger and more useful. The final recommendation is to teach someone else how to create their own digital story. In this way, new stories based on new ideas will be developed, new opportunities for creativity will be promoted, and the excitement of digital storytelling will reach a wider audience.

HOW DO COPYRIGHT RESTRICTIONS AFFECT THE EDUCATIONAL USE OF DIGITAL STORYTELLING?

Respect for copyright and the intellectual property of others is an important issue for students and teachers. It is always tempting for students of all ages to use the Internet to find images, music, and other material for inclusion in their digital stories. In some classrooms, the concept of educational fair use may be openly discussed, giving students some latitude in what materials they may use, while in other classrooms, the teacher or the school may have restrictions on what type of content may be used by students.

One useful strategy for using copyright-free content in their digital stories is for students to create their own content. This might include taking pictures with a digital camera and recording audio narration with an inexpensive computer microphone. However, personally created content is not the only source of usable materials. A variety of Web sites allow users to access content in the public domain. This includes sites such as the American Memory Collection from the United States Library of Congress (http://memory.loc.gov/ammem/), the New York Public Library Picture Collection Online (http://memory.loc.gov/ammem/), and the Free Kids Music Web site (http://freekidsmusic.com/music). Many other Web sites let students and teachers use their content royalty-free for educational purposes.

A list of Web sites that provide access to resources that students and instructors can use for free may be found in the Tools section of the Educational Uses of Digital Storytelling Web site, at, http://www.coe.uh.edu/digitalstorytelling/tools.htm. When searching the Internet, students should learn to check on the usage rights for the site, and be sure the site specifically states that the material can freely be shared.

WHAT ARE SOME OTHER CONSIDERATIONS FOR EDUCATORS WHO WANT TO TEACH DIGITAL STORYTELLING TO THEIR STUDENTS?

One of the first issues to consider is whether the students have access to the technology they need to create digital stories. Do they have digital cameras available so that they can take photographs for their stories? And, what about microphones for recording their narrations and/or interviews?

Since many schools use filtering programs and have restrictions on what students are allowed to do on the Internet, are they able to use search engines to find images for their stories and download and can the school provide them with a location on a computer or server where they can save their work?

Another consideration is that digital storytelling can be very time consuming. It can take many hours, several days, or even weeks to work on all of the digital storytelling components described in this chapter. Educators who wish to incorporate digital storytelling in their classrooms should also be aware that it might take students several attempts at creating digital stories before they demonstrate technological proficiency and an understanding of their selected topic. As with all new instructional methods, students will need time to learn what is expected of them as they begin using digital storytelling in their classrooms. One option for educators who wish to begin using digital storytelling with their students is to use peer review and reflection where students and teachers together have an opportunity to discuss student work and the learning process.

WHAT RESEARCH HAS BEEN DONE AND/OR NEEDS TO BE DONE TO DEMONSTRATE THE IMPACT OF DIGITAL STORYTELLING ON TEACHING AND LEARNING?

Since 2005, educators and graduate students at the University of Houston's Laboratory for Innovative Technology in Education (LITE) have been conducting a series of research projects to evaluate the effectiveness of digital storytelling. In one case, three groups of public-school teachers are being tracked following their participation in an intensive digital storytelling workshop offered at the University of Houston campus. The three groups, composed of elementary, middle-, and high-school teachers, were shown examples of different types of digital stories and then learned to create digital stories that they could use in their own classrooms. The teachers are completing surveys that will be used to measure and evaluate whether or not they have continued to use digital storytelling as a component of their instructional practice, the impact of such use and in cases where there is no use of digital storytelling, what are the barriers to its use. Table 43.3 Illustrates the specific research questions that are being investigated.

Researchers in early childhood education and multimedia technology at the University of Texas at El Paso are conducting a research study on digital storytelling with elementary and middle school students and teachers from the border region of Texas, New Mexico and Mexico. In the study, the students are using multimedia software tools to create digital stories based on multicultural folktales and myths (Giza & Ainsa, in press). The study seeks to measure the effectiveness of the digital storytelling activity by examining the students' understanding of the major points in the folktales as well as their technology skills in creating the stories. Also, because many of the students in the study are second language learners of English, the effectiveness of digital storytelling to enhance both graphics-based technology tools and communication will undoubtedly lead to further research.

Barrett (2005) has proposed a research design to collect data about digital storytelling in education. In part, Barrett suggested that if digital storytelling is to become an accepted practice in today's schools, it will be necessary to collect data about its impact on student learning, motivation, and engagement as well as teaching practices and strategies. She suggested that the following key research questions be investigated:

- How do digital stories provide evidence of deep learning?
- Under what conditions can digital stories be successfully used to support assessment for learning?
- Under what conditions do students take ownership of their digital stories?
- What are the benefits of developing digital stories as perceived by students, teachers, administrators, and/or parents?
- What are perceived obstacles to implementing digital storytelling with P–12 students and how can they be overcome?
- How does the quality of paper-based reflection differ from digital stories?

Aligning Digital Storytelling with Statewide and National Education Standards

Another fertile area for research deals with aligning digital storytelling with specific learning outcomes as measured by statewide and/or national education standards. The U.S. Department of Education's No Child Left Behind Act (2001) mandates that students be proficient in the use of technology and further encourages individual states to set performance goals to measure how federal funding for technology is being used to improve student achievement. A variety of research studies are needed to examine whether digital storytelling can measurably increase student achievement by improving written, oral, visual, and technological communication skills, as well as demonstrating mastery of content.

In Texas, statewide education standards are called the Texas Essential Knowledge and Skills (TEKS, 1998) and technology infusion is a key area for students at all grade levels. And like many other states, the Texas standards mandate that students begin early since kindergarten through second-grade students are expected to know how to,

- select appropriate strategies to navigate and access information for research and resource sharing;
- acquire information including text, audio, video, and graphics;
- use electronic tools and research skills to build a knowledge base regarding a topic, task, or assignment; and
- use appropriate software, including the use of word processing and multimedia, to express ideas and solve problems.

Many practitioners of digital storytelling are just beginning to understand the need for both qualitative and quantitative research studies that measure the effectiveness of digital storytelling to support these educational expectations. Testimonials from teachers, students, parents, and organizations that praise the use of digital storytelling are helpful, but in today's climate of educational performance indicators and accountability, research including empirical studies, surveys, observations, and case studies must be designed and conducted. This research must be rigorous and draw upon established literature in the field as well as accepted conceptual frameworks and theoretical foundations. The challenge is clear. A large amount of data on the use of digital storytelling by educators and their students must be collected and analyzed, and teaching and learning must be evaluated in order to understand and maximize the usefulness of digital storytelling as a sound instructional practice.

WHERE ELSE CAN EDUCATORS FIND GOOD EXAMPLES OF DIGITAL STORYTELLING?

In addition to the Educational Uses of Digital Storytelling Web site created at the University of Houston, many other locations on the World Wide Web feature good examples of digital stories. Some of the most useful sites include,

- A History of Digital Storytelling Through Story from the Center for Digital Storytelling http://www.storycenter.org/movies/
- **Capture Wales** http://www.bbc.co.uk/wales/capturewales/
- **Coming to California** (a digital storytelling contest for students sponsored by San Francisco public television station, KQED) http://www.dsi.kqed.org/index.php/contest
- **DigiTales—The Art of Telling Digital Stories**
  - Living Memories http://www.digitales.us/gallery/gallery_living_memories.php
  - Beyond Words http://www.digitales.us/gallery/gallery_beyond_words.php
  - The Path of Me http://www.digitales.us/gallery/gallery_pathofme.php

TABLE 43.2 Research Questions for Teachers Who Completed a Digital Storytelling Workshop

Teachers who ARE Using Digital Storytelling	Teachers who are NOT Using Digital Storytelling
How are you using Digital Storytelling?	Why are you not using Digital Storytelling? What are the obstacles?
Are you creating digital stories to show to your students?	Do you have questions about how to use Digital Storytelling in your instruction?
Are you teaching your students to create their own digital stories?	Are you experiencing technical problems? If so, what problems are you having?
If students are using Digital Storytelling, what are the outcomes?	Are you interested in additional Digital Storytelling training sessions?
Have you demonstrated Digital Storytelling to others? If so, to other teachers? Who else?	Are there other issues that are preventing you from using Digital Storytelling in your instruction?
Do you feel that Digital Storytelling has changed your teaching practice?	Are you planning to use Digital Storytelling in the future?

- **Digital Stories Created by Students in Scott County, Kentucky** http://www.scott.k12.ky.us/technology/digitalstorytelling/studentstories.html
- **Digital Stories Created by Teachers in Scott County, Kentucky** http://www.scott.k12.ky.us/technology/digitalstorytelling/teacherstories.html
- **Maricopa Center for Learning and Instruction** http://www.mcli.dist.maricopa.edu/learnshops/digital/examples.php
- **Sample Digital Stories from the Digital Storytelling Network** http://www.groups.edna.edu.au/mod/resource/view.php?id=3714
- **Telling Lives** http://www.bbc.co.uk/tellinglives/

THE FUTURE OF DIGITAL STORYTELLING

As computer technology evolves, new digital tools and resources will have a dramatic effect on how we deal with digital information and in turn, how digital storytelling will evolve. Some of the more promising new resources that are already being used by innovative educators and their students include,

Blogging—the practice of recording one's personal thoughts and observations on a Web site. Short for "Weblog," a blog can become an online journal that is shared by a large number of like-minded individuals and can include comments, personal reflections, and opinions. Several blogs are available online that deal with digital storytelling. One that deserves attention is *Moving at the Speed of Creativity* (http://www.speedofcreativity.org/category/edtech/digital storytelling/), created by Wesley Fryer, a teacher and doctoral student at Texas Tech University.

Del.icio.us (http://del.icio.us/)—has been called a social bookmarking manager where Web users can find someone else's favorite sites on the Web. This deceptively simple resource may sound like nothing more than another search engine like Yahoo or Google; however, after exploring its contents for just a few minutes, users will quickly understand that visiting a preselected group of someone's favorite Web sites on a topic such as digital storytelling, will yield a much more useful set of resources to explore than a typical search engine, which collects so much information that going through it all can be so time consuming that it becomes overwhelming.

Flickr (http://flickr.com/)—a digital photo-sharing Web site that can be used to find images that can be used in digital storytelling.

Podcasting—takes its name from Apple Computer's ubiquitous music player, the iPod. Podcasts are audio broadcasts available on the Web that can be downloaded to a music player or even listened to through a computer that has speakers attached.

Wikipedias—free online encyclopedias that are written, evaluated, and modified collaboratively, by Web users from around the world. The original Wikipedia (http://en.wikipedia.org/wiki/Main_Page) began in 2001 and now contains more than 800,000 articles that may provide content that can be used in the development of digital stories.

Even traditional technology companies are beginning to offer tools that support and facilitate digital storytelling. **Picasa** (http://picasa.google.com/index.html) is a software program that can be used to edit and organize digital images. Originally for sale, but now offered for free, Picasa has captured the imagination of educators, not only for its innovative tools and potential for using digital images in interesting and interactive ways, but also for the fact that their students can freely obtain their own copy of the program for use on computers away from school.

We are also certain to see more applications such as **StoryCast**, an experimental program from technology giant, Hewlett Packard (http://www.hpl.hp.com/research/storycast/) that will allow users of cellular telephones equipped with cameras to create digital stories from the pictures they take. By using the phone's handset, users will also be able to record their voice and add an accompanying narration for their digital stories as well as share them with other cell-phone users.

What these technologies have in common is that they represent a turning point in access to new applications that can be used in digital storytelling. A dizzying array of Web-based tools with new interfaces, new interactivity options, and new capabilities are already being used in the creation and delivery of digital stories with more on the way. Also, many of these applications are free, so the digital divide between information haves and information have-nots is rapidly dissipating. Digital storytelling is undergoing a growth spurt in education as more teachers and their students are learning about it and are finding ways to add it to their classroom activities. The research opportunities in this area are just beginning to be seen, and new investigations will surely provide greater insights and understanding in how digital storytelling can engage, inform, and enlighten new generations of students and educators to come.

ACKNOWLEDGMENTS

This chapter is about digital storytelling and how it is being used by educators and teachers as an effective tool for teaching and learning. As the name implies, digital storytelling revolves around the use of computers and computer-based technologies, and a good deal of information in this chapter focuses on technology and digital media tools and resources. Consequently, the chapter contains numerous links to additional material on the Web that can help clarify some of the more technical aspects of digital storytelling. A companion Web site has been created for those who wish to access more of the digital storytelling materials described in the narrative and view many examples of the digital stories that are described. To visit the Web site, please go to, http://fp.coe.uh.edu/brobin/digital-storytelling/chapter-companion/index.html

REFERENCES

American Library Association. Presidential Committee on Information Literacy. (1989). *Final report*. Chicago: American Library Association.

Apple Computer. (2005). *An effecting performance: Video effects and transitions*. Retrieved November 9, 2005, from http://www.apple.com/ilife/imovie/videoeffects.html

Ausubel, D. P. (1978). In defense of advance organizers: A reply to the critics. *Review of Educational Research, 48*, 251–257.

Banaszewski, T. M. (2005, May). *Digital Storytelling: Supporting digital literacy in grades 4–12*. (Master's Thesis Defense, Georgia Institute of Technology). Retrieved from http://techszewski.blogs.com/techszewski/files/TBanaszewski_DS_thesis.pdf

Barish, S., & Daley, E. (2005). *Multimedia scholarship for the 21st century*. Retrieved, April 20, 2007, from http://www.educause.edu/ir/library/pdf/FFP0509S.pdf

Barrett, H. (2005). *Digital storytelling research design.* Retrieved November 18, 2005, from http://electronicportfolios.com/digistory/ResearchDesign.pdf

Boster, F. J., Meyer, G. S., Roberto, A. J., Lindsey, L., Smith, R. A., Inge, C., & Strom, R. E. (2007). The impact of video streaming on mathematics performance. *Communication Education,* 56, 134–144.

Brown, J., Bryan, J., & Brown, T. (2005). Twenty-first century literacy and technology in K–8 classrooms. *Innovate, 1*(3). Retrieved October 13, 2005, from http://www.innovateonline.info/index.php?view=article&id=17

Burmark, L. (2004, May/June). Visual presentations that prompt, flash & transform. *Media and Methods, 40*(6), 4.

Center for Digital Storytelling Web site. (2005). Retrieved November 4, 2005, from http://www.storycenter.org/history.html

Edutopia. (2002). *Marco Torres on empowering students through multimedia.* Retrieved November 4, 2005, from http://www.edutopia.org/php/interview.php?id=Art_994&key=188#paragraph4

Giza, B., & Ainsa, P. (in press). *Children's digital storytelling with open source tools.*

Hibbing, A. N., & Rankin-Erikson, J. L. (2003). A picture is worth a thousand words: Using visual images to improve comprehension for middle school struggling readers. *Reading Teacher, 56*(8), 758.

Hicks, L., & Woodburn, R. (2004). *A story about teaching digital storytelling at Scottsdale Community College.* Retrieved November 9, 2005, from http://www.mcli.dist.maricopa.edu/forum/spr04/dstory.html

Interview with John Seely Brown. (2003). Retrieved November 26, 2005, from http://www.sethkahan.com/Kahan_John_Seely_Brown_intrvw.pdf

Lambert, J. (2003). *Digital storytelling cookbook and traveling companion.* Berkeley, CA: Digital Diner Press. Available at http://www.storycenter.org/cookbook.pdf

Levin, H. (2003). Making history come alive. *Learning & Leading with Technology, 31*(3), 22–27.

Meadows, D. (2005). *What is digital storytelling?* Retrieved November 9, 2005, from http://www.photobus.co.uk/dstory_pages/what_dstory.html

No Child Left Behind Act. (2001). (P. L. 107–110). Retrieved November 27, 2005, from http://www.ed.gov/nclb/landing.jhtml

Ohler, J., & Dillingham, B. (2004). *Telling your story: A handbook for putting the story into digital (and traditional) storytelling.* Retrieved November 25, 2005, from http://www.jasonohler.com/pdfs/storybook11-v2.pdf

Ormrod, J. E. (2004). *Human learning* (4th ed.). Upper Saddle River, NJ: Pearson Educational, Inc.

Rafferty, C. D. (1999). Literacy in the information age. *Educational Leadership, 57,* 22–25.

Riesland, E. (2005). Visual literacy in the classroom. *New Horizons for Learning.* Retrieved October 17, 2005, from http://www.newhorizons.org/strategies/literacy/riesland.htm

Sherman, E. (2005). *Vision of Vincent Sherman: A director's life.* Retrieved November 9, 2005, from http://www.moviemaker.com/issues/21/21_vincent.html

Texas Education Association. (1998). *Texas Essential Knowledge and Skills for Technology Applications.* Retrieved November 27, 2005, from http://www.tea.state.tx.us/rules/tac/ch126.html

Theodosakis, N. (2001). *The director in the classroom: How filmmaking inspires learning.* San Diego, CA: Tech4Learning Publishing.

Wilder, S. (2005). Information literacy makes all the wrong assumptions. *The Chronicle of Higher Education, 51*(18), B13. Retrieved January 7, 2005, from http://chronicle.com/weekly/v51/i18/18b01301.htm

•44•

TEACHER LEARNING FOR NEW TIMES: REPURPOSING NEW MULTIMODAL LITERACIES AND DIGITAL-VIDEO COMPOSING FOR SCHOOLS

Suzanne M. Miller
UNIVERSITY AT BUFFALO, SUNY

NEEDED: NEW LITERACIES FOR NEW TIMES

In the technological and cultural contexts of the past two decades, the notion of literacy has significantly shifted from the conventional sense of reading and writing *only* print text *to* an expanded sense of reading and writing multiple forms of nonprint "texts," as well (IRA, 2001; NCTE, 2003). In this broadened view, more than ever, literacy is plural: "reading" and "writing" include literacies or *multiliteracies* (New London Group, 1996), that is, producing and understanding multiple, representational print and nonprint forms deeply embedded in new social practices and contexts.

New Multimodal Literacies

The field of New Literacy Studies (NLS) brings together interdisciplinary thinking to describe a sociocultural approach to literacy as constructed through visible events and underlying practices which vary across time and place (Gee, 2003; Kress, 1999, 2000, 2003; Lankshear & Knobel, 2003; Street, 1995). In 21st century social and cultural contexts, meanings are more and more represented multimodally, including "the performative, visual, aural, and semiotic understandings necessary for constructing and reconstructing print- and nonprint-based texts" (Alvermann, 2002, viii). Computer-based digital technologies provide new (and quick) access to these multiple modes of representation, creating "digitally afforded multimodality" (Hull & Nelson, 2005).

As a "once in several centuries" innovation (diSessa, 2000), the computer has been transforming our world and shaping these new textual and social practices. The computer offers a dazzling array of digital forms/texts—electronically processed images and video, hypertext, Web pages, spreadsheets, game interfaces, simulations, interactive stories, multiform narratives, Facebooks, music videos, blogs, video blogs (vlogs), zines, and other print-mixed assemblages. These forms have extended not just the material basis for literacy, but also its social processes and cultural contexts. The digital affordances and dynamics of the wired world have influenced how all of us work, think, and live; daily life most often includes use of e-mail, instant messaging, voicemail, and Internet Web pages with images, voices, music mixed with print. The "new landscape of communication" (Kress, 2000, p. 183) is marked by the emergence of domains besides language at the center of everyday communication—particularly multimodalities such as images, music, and bodily movements—which, unlike print language, are created and need to be "read" with nonlinear logic. As print-mixed texts are now widely constituted through more than one mode or means of representation, the literacy practices needed for functioning in the world have been and still are rapidly transforming (Leu, 2002).

Especially for the "millennial generation" (Hagood, Stevens, & Reinking, 2002)—youth born after 1981—reality includes new literacies embedded in these new technologies (Alvermann, 2002; Lankshear & Knobel, 2003). They have grown up surrounded and shaped by practices related to computers, the Internet, and mobile phones (arguably a portable computing device for communicating, taking pictures, playing music and games, word processing, storing information). As a significant part of youth culture, these everyday tools and artifacts bind adolescents in a social culture through communication and meaning making. Increasingly, the millennial generation, immersed in popular and online cultures, thinks of messages and meanings multimodally—not just in terms of printed words, but also in terms of images and music.

In all, we live in new times of digitally accessible multimodality for designing texts as part of evolving social purposes and practices. Theorists and researchers have reached a clear consensus: facility with interpreting and designing new multimodal literacies will increasingly be required by human beings to communicate, work, and thrive in the digital, global world of the 21st century (Alvermann, 2002; Buckingham, 2003; Cope & Kalantzis, 2000; Gee, 2003; Jewitt & Kress, 2003; Kress, 2003; Lankshear & Knobel, 2003; New London Group, 1996; Street, 1995). These scholars agree, also, that significant changes will be needed in schooling, in teachers, and, especially, in educational beliefs about the status/design of nonprint modes as ways of knowing and communicating.

Needed in Schools/By Teachers: Performance Knowledge and Design

One important consequence of the intense proliferation of knowledge in the digital age is the transformation of what counts as *knowing* (Lankshear & Knobel, 2003). The status of propositional knowledge, or knowledge that already "exists" in statements, has changed: in the context of a superabundance of digitally accessible informational "texts," no one can "know" all there is of importance to know in the world. What's essential is performance knowledge—knowing *how* to find, gather, use, communicate, and imagine new ways of envisioning assemblages of knowledge.

This dramatic change to "knowing as an ability of perform" (Lankshear & Knobel, 2003, p. 173) reflects the rethinking of knowing in an age of "digital epistemologies" where emergent social practices are aimed at garnering attention to one's point of view on collected resources. These "practices of knowing. . . . reflect a range of strategies for assembling, editing, processing, receiving, sending, and working on information and data to transform diverse resources of 'digitalia' into 'things that work'" (p. 173)—that is, into new digital resources and multimodal texts with representational meaning and communicative purpose.

Many argue that if these essential new literacies are to enter classrooms as powerful learning tools and enable practices for social futures, schools must change from the current approaches of "institutions of old learning" that prepare students for life and work in the print-only industrialized world of the past (O'Brien & Bauer, 2005). Because of the "social and cultural revolution" ushered in by new technologies (Grabill & Hicks, 2005), more and more students arrive at school more competent in these new multimodal literacies than their teachers (Chandler-Olcott, & Mahar, 2003; Leu, Kinzer, Coiro, & Cammack, 2004, p. 1599). This gap between new multimodal literacy practices and print-based schooling has been called "the digital divide and disconnect" (O'Brien & Bauer, 2005, p. 126). Critiques of existing schooling point to the "more compelling and motivating" multimodal learning that students engage in outside of school (Gee, 2004) as an explanation for increasing student disengagement in classrooms.

Some argue that the problem is that teachers are largely "outsiders" who have grown up and work in a print-based space, while students are largely "insiders" who have grown up in a digital world of new literacies (Lankshear & Knobel, 2003). Others claim that the problem is educational policy and the structure of schools, "not just teacher generational resistance" (Luke, 2002, p. 197). Most agree, however, that traditional schooling and literacy are not adequate for the 21st-century public, private, and workplace spheres. Integrating the dramatic broadening of purposeful literacy to include multimodal meaning-making systems beyond printed text for all students is an essential—if not *the* essential—task for schools in the 21st century (Miller & Borowicz, 2006).

The needed sea change in schooling should begin by providing opportunities for teachers to transform their roles, knowledge, and beliefs—especially their views on what counts as literacy and evidence of learning (Koehler & Mishra, 2005; Leu et al., 2004). For the most part, instead of drawing on millennial students' facility with new literacies in school learning, the school "preference for print may preclude teachers from even noticing their students' competence with multi- and digital literacies" (King & O'Brien, 2002, p. 41). Restrictive school practices of literacy are characterized by a bias for printed propositional knowledge, recitation, the structured expository essay, and the student practice of scanning for textbook answers (King & O'Brien; also Anyon, 1997; Finn, 1999). This "deep grammar of schooling" (Lankshear & Knobel, 2003) foregrounds the view of knowledge as a propositional commodity held by the teacher and supplied to the student and helps account for the relatively superficial changes technologies have brought to schools (e.g., word processing and presentation tools). To integrate new beliefs about knowledge and literacies into classrooms, the notion of "teachers first" is important for guiding efforts: teachers need opportunities to learn how to use new multimodal literacies for their own authentic purposes with support for their ongoing needs—before they can effectively use them in their teaching (Lankshear & Knobel, 2003, p. 67). The necessary initial step, then, is for teachers to develop performance knowledge through design themselves and, thereby, develop understanding of the wired world of the digital age, where knowledge is multimodal, coconstructed and performed or represented—not absorbed.

Finally, central to this changed view of knowledge in new times is the concept of design. Arguing for an urgent change in school curriculum, Kress (2003) explained that since language is a time-based, sequentially organized mode, while images are space-based and simultaneously organized, competence with mixing these modes involves design. The multimodal meaning-making systems available in digital multimedia texts include the potential of designing linguistic, visual, gestural, audio, and spatial elements dynamically to communicate (New London Group, 2000, p. 26). Facility with *design*—the process of orchestrating representational modes and their interconnection—is therefore vital for composing a text that can meet the communication demands of new and future multimodal environments. "Design refers to how people make use of the resources that are available at a given moment in a specific communicational environment to realize their interests as makers of a message/text" (Jewitt & Kress, 2003, p. 17). In short, in the digital age "the task of text-makers is that of complex orchestration" for authentic purposes (Kress, 2000, p. 160). As the reviewed research illustrates, a recurring problem with teachers' uses of technologies in classrooms is inattention to such multimodal design and to new ways of knowing (Leu et al., 2004, p. 1600).

Chapter Outline

This chapter discusses next what research suggests about professional development aimed at transforming teachers' classroom uses of new multimodal literacies. I argue here that digital-video (DV) composing is a quintessential multimodal literacy that can play a key role in those professional experiences and have positive influences on students and classrooms. The term DV composing aims to conceptualize and emphasize the knowledge-assembling and communicative functions of this multimodal literacy practice.

The following first reviews the work on teacher professional development for integrating new literacies into the curriculum and then focuses on what research says about what does not work and what seems to be promising. In the remainder of the article, teacher professional development for learning to integrate DV composing into the curriculum as a new multimodal literacy practice is reviewed, followed by an overview of a growing body of work situated in a DV composing program that examines both teacher learning and subsequent changes in student engagement, learning, and school performance.

TEACHER PROFESSIONAL DEVELOPMENT ON NEW LITERACIES

What does research suggest about what works and what does not, in teacher professional development for integrating new literacies into the curriculum?

Problems With Assumptions and Epistemologies

Schools *have* attended to what they perceive as the need for technology in classrooms. The profusion of technology standards at the state and national levels suggest that training teachers to use technology (both hardware and software) will allow them to apply that knowledge to unlock "the power and potential of technology" in their classrooms (Mishra & Koehler, 2004). However, this perspective positions teachers as consumers of technological knowledge in stand-alone workshops and courses and has not led to their effectively integrating technology into teaching (e.g., Miliken Exchange on Educational Technology, 1999). The consensus is clear about what does not work to develop the deep understanding that teachers need: focus on basic technological skills, short-term workshops, stand-alone instructional technology coursework, decontextualized training on software, and lack of focus on authentic practices of designing (Apple Classrooms of Tomorrow [ACOT], 1995; Brand, 1997; Koehler & Mishra, 2005; Milliken Exchange on Education Technology). Increases in hardware, software, and Internet connections in schools have not led to widespread technology integration, and teacher professional development for learning technology has generally not produced changes in teaching and learning (e.g., Brand, 1997; Leu et al., 2004).

From the multimodal literacy practices theoretical perspective, key problems in much professional development include focusing only on technological knowledge, excluding authentic literacy practices, and failing to provide opportunities for teachers to learn how to support student design of multimodal texts. In their study of literacy learning and technology in 20 classrooms, Lankshear and Knobel, (2003) found problems with teachers appropriating new technologies for "schoolish practices" (p. 67) that were very unlike authentic social practices for meaningful purposes in the world. In part, teachers had not experienced uses of technology that were socially meaningful in their own lives, so they focused on the operational aspects of technologies, adapting them to status quo teaching practices. With traditional mindsets about knowledge—like teacher as final knowledge authority—technology integration was largely "reduced to teaching [students] how to drive the new technologies," (p. 31), instead of expanding possibilities with new literacy practices for communicative purposes.

When millennial students meet old-school technology, research evidence suggests that students are familiar enough with meaningful new multimodal literacies in their lives that they manage to stay under the radar of teachers instructing in artificial practice on technology or software (e.g., typing tutorials, Excel, Internet scavenger hunt): these students spend their computer time purposefully writing fan-fiction, creating Zines, and designing Web sites (Chandler-Olcott & Mahar, 2003; Thompson, 2005). This secretive work of students represents authentic new multimodal literacies—with students bringing their out-of-school design capabilities into classrooms—but quite apart from the school technology agenda.

Promising Insights on Teachers Making the "Cultural Jump"

Developing through support over time. From such experiences, Lankshear and Knobel, (2003) concluded that the first issue in any effort to integrate new literacies in schools requires ongoing support for teachers to use new literacy practices "for their own authentic purposes" (p. 67), before attempting to integrate practices into classrooms. In short, they argued that teachers need experiences as insiders in new literacies as social practices to prompt a change to a mindset more congruent with "digital epistemologies" (p. 172).

Next is the transformation of teaching practices. According to findings from Apple's longitudinal study of professional development in 100 classrooms in three schools, effective integration aimed at changes in teaching and learning (not just access to technologies) occurs over the course of several years (ACOT, 1995). Teachers need time and support to move through a developmental progression from initial adoption of technologies for maintaining existing traditional instruction to more advanced levels of appropriating technologies for developing new approaches to teaching or innovating with new uses for technologies. Supporting teachers' "evolution of thought and practice" (Apple Education, 2004) does not happen in a few workshop sessions. Similar conclusions appeared in reviews of research on professional development for meaningful technology and literacy integration (e.g., Coiro, 2005): to learn best, teachers need ongoing support, time for interaction and reflection with other teachers, and effective models of teaching and learning literacies with technology for authentic communicative purposes and audiences.

Situating new literacies in context. A natural forum for developing such effective models would arise during courses in teacher preparation. Through a 5-year design experiment for studying teacher development in rich uses of technologies in university courses, Mishra and Koehler (2004), also Koehler and Mishra (2005), created a conceptual framework to break down the perceived dichotomy between technology and subject-matter knowledge that has hindered some approaches to professional development. They drew on Shulman's concept of "pedagogical content knowledge" (PCK), the relationship between subject matter and teaching, particularly "the ways of representing and formulating the subject that make it comprehensible to others" (Shulman, 1986, p. 9). Their contribution is an emerging concept called *technological PCK* or TPCK, which refers to situated understandings of how to use technologies to represent and teach concepts difficult for students and to build on their existing knowledge and ways of knowing. Attending to these transactions through this complex, relational form of knowledge, they argued, leads teachers to "appropriate, context-specific strategies and representations" of technology for potential use with specific students in the teacher's specific content-area (Koehler & Mishra, 2005, p. 95).

Teaching here is appropriately viewed as complex performative practice, which helps to explain the problem with professional-development approaches that construct teachers as mechanically "applying" and "implementing" knowledge from their technology "training." What teachers need, instead, is engagement in design-based activities in their content area with technologies and opportunities to develop the deep professional knowledge needed for integrating them into the complex performance of teaching students in a subject (Koehler & Mishra, 2005).

Using this strategy, the researchers studied teachers as they collaboratively pursued educational problems in specific contexts by designing technology solutions (e.g., designing an online course, a Web site, a digital video). This "learning by design" worked: educational technology majors in their master's classes successfully learned the affordances and constraints of technologies, the processes of purposeful design, and the power of engaged, active learning. It is not clear whether their class experiences later influenced their teaching: researchers concluded with the "hope that this view of learning and teaching" would carry into classrooms (Koehler & Mishra, 2005, p. 99).

Foregrounding multimodal affordances. Although TPCK is helpful in representing the complexity and situatedness of teacher knowledge, it may still underrepresent what teachers need to know to integrate new multimodal literacies in classrooms. In a case study of a fifth-grade teacher who completed school district professional development on technology integration, for instance, Shanahan (2006) found that the teacher adapted technologies over the school year through student hypermedia projects to engage them in understanding science concepts. Analysis of the social and cultural context of the classroom revealed the copresence of both traditional and new literacy skills and strategies, and students incorporated nonprint elements into print-based projects as they made sense of ecosystems and acid rain. This seems to be an appropriate multimodal strategy for young students learning to represent complex concepts.

However, the findings showed that in the instructional space "the focus on print as the valued information medium constrained the development of the students' new literacy skills and strategies. Students rarely thought strategically about the use of visual and auditory design elements" (Shanahan, 2006, p. 231). The teacher represented only print text as an information medium, and this assumption constrained how students used visual and auditory modes for understanding. This under use of the affordances or resources of multimodality because of the teacher's unconscious print bias suggested another needed focus for new literacies professional development—direct attention to the orchestration of multiple modes. More explicitly foregrounding multimodality as a theoretical framework (e.g., Kress, 2003)—to merge multimodality to new literacies as its essential affordance—is a promising approach to this problem (Miller & Borowicz, 2006).

Foregrounding a multimodal perspective, a teacher educator in a class for preservice English teachers (PSTs) engaged students in design of curriculum as a recursive, multimodal inquiry (Albers, 2006). Beginning with one major fiction text, students sought out related "multimodal expressions" (e.g., video, digital texts, photos, drama, painting, music, sculpture), and focused attention to the meaning potentials that choices in modes of expression afforded, for example, in a Tupac printed poem, as sung by his mother, and as a PowerPoint interpretation with images, music, and written text. PSTs learn to move away from textbooks and teacher guides to focus on how students represent their understanding, retranslate it from one mode to another ("transmediation"), and multimodally connect their lives and experiences with literature. This broad focus on meaning making through multimodal arts provides a model for English teaching afforded by digital texts and technologies. The teacher educator ended on a hopeful note, suggesting that her PSTs would be more likely to support their future students to "imagine expression in a variety of modes" in the context of schools (Albers, 2006, p. 97).

Scaffolding reflections on knowledge and multimodal design. A somewhat similar focus on multimodality occurred in a graduate course in literacy and technology taught by a group of teacher educators studying their emerging pedagogies at the same time they explored their K–12 in and preservice teachers' learning (McVee, Bailey, & Shanahan, 2006). For them, new literacies integration did not mean acquiring computing skills, but self-reflexive examination of "multimodal and multisemiotic reading and composition with the grammars and conventions that each modality requires" (p. 4). Multiple online and in-class forums for reflection on readings, collaborative design activities, and ongoing scaffolding of metacognitive strategies in the class created a context for critical reflection on "the role of digital technologies in literacy instruction." The initial "fear and loathing" (p. 12) that emerged among teachers and PSTs in the class highlighted the complexities of this undertaking. Fear of losing control, of failure, of the unknown surfaced in reflective responses. These real tensions mediated by shared problem solving in design/redesign experiences and reflections led to struggles and to growth in teacher knowledge and thinking.

However, did these teachers take their emerging knowledge into their own classrooms? A collective case study of two teachers from this class (Bailey, 2006) provided an interesting opportunity to examine this question. The teachers were both ninth-grade English teachers from the same suburban high school who shared their lesson plans and said they desired new literacies integration into their curriculum. Yet the outcomes in their classes were quite different. Terry Martin's use of new multimodal literacy activities was impeded primarily by her teacher-centered pedagogy. Using the same assignments and activities as the successful teacher, the purpose she constructed orally for student tasks was monologic—merely covering authoritative content, not orchestrating modes in meaningful representation and communication. Student response generally was "mock participation and procedural display" (Bloome, 1986). Terry did not develop in her teaching of new literacies over the year.

In contrast, the other teacher, Carol Smith, orchestrated many opportunities for her students to learn the curriculum by creating opportunities to read and compose multimodal texts. Through her ongoing reflection on her experiences in the university class, her own teaching, and her students' experiences, Carol moved from using new literacies as a motivational hook for students to developing a "new literacies stance" that included (a) enacting literacy as a social practice with the capacity to draw on students' connections and out of school knowledge and (b) making multimodal design a priority that included "explicit instruction in new, as well as traditional, forms of representation and communication" (Bailey, 2006). Successfully integrating new multimodal literacies into this classroom allowed students to design dialogically, use local knowledge, and over time develop metacognitive strategies for designing multimodally. Here is evidence, then, that the pedagogy of the teacher-education class did successfully induce a change in Carol that put her on the road to transforming her teaching.

In the findings from Bailey's (2006) inadvertent naturalistic experiment, two necessary elements for professional development on new literacies surfaced: (a) explicit attention to scaffolding reflection on digital epistemologies to promote dialogic beliefs about knowing and (b) metacognitive strategies for multimodal design.

The study also made clear that following teachers into their classrooms after professional-development opportunities to examine impacts on teaching and learning is indispensable for uncovering potentials for and negative drags on *teachers'* design of new literacies pedagogies and students' design-based learning in the contexts of schools. If we accept the consensus notion that new literacies are emerging social practices in "synergistic, reciprocal, and constantly evolving relationship with older literacies" (Swenson, Rozema, Young, McGrail, & Whitin, 2006, p. 355), then the education field urgently needs such research on the challenges and supports for teachers attempting to sustain students' authentic new multimodal literacies for learning subject-matter in institutions of old learning (i.e., schools). And educators need additional strategies for assisting the teachers like Terry Martin who completed the same class as Carol, but did not develop along the same path to make the profound "cultural jump" (Cope & Kalantzis, 2000, p. 223) to new multimodal literacies.

Mediating change through collaborative talk and activity. Another component at play in the Bailey (2006) study was an emerging role for the researcher as a collaborator in Carol's class. Due to personal, family, and scheduling issues, Terry was not available for informal conversation with Bailey, which Carol had before and after every visit. Carol used those times to voice what she had noticed about her students' work and her concerns, reflecting aloud about what changes she might make. Bailey used some of those times to member check her emerging findings about the class. Carol appropriated the researcher's language. For example, she began talking about her students bringing in "local knowledge." She regularly talked to Bailey about the importance of "integrating technology into her lessons to create multimodal experiences" for students. Then Carol asked Bailey to coteach the multimodal poetry interpretation with her, providing opportunities for collaborative planning and debriefing conversations. In short, the collaborative talk served as another mediator for Carol's transformation.

Other research provides evidence that close-at-hand collaboration situated in the teacher's classroom can lead to rapid teacher transition to new literacies. In mutually respectful relationships, these partnerships prompted changes in curriculum, pedagogies, and teacher identities, as classes moved toward student use and design of new multimodal literacies (Borowicz, 2003; Ikpeze, 2006; McMaster, 2004).

In an intentional collaboration on infusing multimodal literacies into a fifth-grade curriculum, Ikpeze (2006) found that through joint planning of new literacies activities (Web quests, PowerPoints, discussion boards), teaching, and review of student multimodal work, the teacher developed an understanding of purposeful integration of new literacies for inquiry, moving away from computer use as reward for completing class work. Through writing and discussion eliciting students' interests, what had been out-of-school literacies for students became teacher-sanctioned topics and tools for inquiry for class (e.g., a child doing research on his favorite kind of video game; a self-sponsored magazine published by a small group becoming a whole-class magazine).

In this class, the teacher learned how to allow youth culture and day-to-day literacies from home into the classroom as an accepted part of the process of inquiry argued that the changes the teacher made to invite students' out-of-school new literacies into this classroom constituted culturally responsive teaching (Ladson-Billings, 1995; Wlodkowski & Ginsberg, 1995). Appropriating this concept from its origin as response to values and attitudes based on students' ethnicity and race, she expanded it to teachers' inclusion of youth culture and out-of-school literacies to create conditions for motivation, meaning making, and student competence. Whether this teacher continued these new pedagogies after the collaboration ended, though, is not known.

A planned collaboration on multimodal arts-based curriculum and assessment in an 11th-grade classroom (McMaster, 2004) documented the careful negotiation between researcher and teacher to build trust and balance power relations. Case studies of focal students in the class revealed the strengths of their differing visual/spatial, musical/rhythmic, bodily/kinesthetic, and verbal/linguistic modes of understanding literature, evident in their DV productions on *The Girl Who Loved Tom Gordon.* In the context of this English class, which had to take the 6-hour graduation test in June, the teaching-inquiry collaboration was key to sustaining changes toward new multimodal literacies by the teacher and her students. Seeing the deep understanding exhibited by students, the teacher developed a strong belief in the value of multimodal productions as authentic assessments. Her students did very well on the state test, too, with all focal students choosing to write an essay about *The Girl Who Loved Tom Gordon.*

In 2005, the teacher and researcher continued their collaboration by presenting their work together at a national conference. The teacher also took on other new roles, as technology coordinator for a Writing Project site. In 2006, she presented in a university Teaching of Literature class with her new collaborator from a local college: her students and their preservice teachers were blogging about the books on war they were reading in common (e.g., *The Things They Carried*) before they met face to face in book groups. The multimodality, the layers of collaboration, the new professional roles, the authentic social practices—everything seems to be in place for a continuing productive path for this new innovator.

Long-term, face-to-face collaboration can be very effective in promoting teachers' more rapid move to new multimodal literacies in schools. However, this is a time- and resource-intensive strategy. If "print literacy is not enough" for teachers and students in new times (Gee, 2003, p. 19), then teacher educators and others who seek school change need to create additional sturdy strategies for teacher transformation. Elements of the collaborative approach and of the other promising approaches just reviewed coalesce in a DV-composing project in an urban school district. In the next section, an overview of a growing body of work situated in this DV-composing program examines both teacher learning and subsequent changes in student engagement, learning, and school performance.

TEACHER PROFESSIONAL DEVELOPMENT FOR DIGITAL-VIDEO COMPOSING

Over the past 6 years a school-based DV composing program called City Voices, City Visions (CVCV) has provided professional development for urban teachers. While there were many reasons for focusing on DV composing, two are important here.

First, DV composing provides a potential solution to the problem of teachers' under-using affordances of new multimodal literacies: DV production requires integration of many modes—what some call "an integrative, combinatorial assemblage of modes" (Burnes & Parker, 2003, p. 59). In that sense, DV is a quintessential multimodal literacy, integrating visual, aural, kinetic, and verbal modes electronically—making it difficult to stay in the comfort zone of print-only texts, as editing DV footage requires working with a visual and two audio tracks (often music and narration). Teachers need to engage in design-based performances so that they have the embodied experience of engaging in purposeful orchestration of modes to create meaning. DV composing provides that experience.

In addition, Cope and Kalantzis (2000) recommended situated (contextual) practice through immersion in experiences with designs of meaning that make "intuitive sense" to learners because they appear in realms outside of school (p. 244). DV composing is a high-status social and cultural practice with powerful attention-getting qualities and expert versions in the real world. The connection to youth-media culture (music videos, movies, vlogs, clip culture[1]) is strong, making it a high-interest endeavor that draws on student (explicit and implicit) out-of-school knowledge. Use of familiar media genres in DV composing creates another school connection to the mediasphere.

This section summarizes the research examining the impact on teacher and student learning of participation in a DV-composing program. First, an overview of the project in which this research was embedded is provided

Overview of an Urban-School Digital-Video Composing Program

Through the CVCV partnership between the University at Buffalo Graduate School of Education and the Buffalo Public Schools (BPS)[2], over 120 urban teachers[3] have participated in CVCV professional development institutes aimed at preparing subject-area teachers to use DV composing as a new multimodal literacies tool for their 6th- to 12th-grade urban students. Summer and spring (Saturday) institutes (for a total of 28 hours) are taught by experienced CVCV teachers, who have helped develop and infuse genre-based DV composing with their lived teaching experience in BPS classrooms. The CVCV university team[4] collaborates with the lead BPS team in teaching and providing one-one-one support for teachers at the point of need.

Using the Internet, hand-sized DV cameras and movie-editing software as creative research tools, teachers learn to make sequences of DV projects in media genres familiar to them and to students: poetry videos (based on music videos); public-service announcements, uncommercials (using a TV ad format to sell a concept—the First Amendment- Priceless); movie trailers ("coming soon to a science class near you"); and news-segment/interview TV shows (based on *20/20, 60 Minutes,* E!True Hollywood, or other news inquiries). During DV production/workshop time, new teacher cohorts work in subject-matter teams across schools or on in-school teams (same-subject or interdisciplinary).

The institute instructors support teachers' inquiries into which units of study and subject-matter concepts pose difficulties for their students' learning, and then assist with developing usable curricular materials to solve their pedagogical problems by creating new multimodal literacies solutions. As teachers create assignments, evaluation rubrics, and sample videos for DV-composing projects in their own classrooms, they consider how they will engage their students in design and production of DV-projects like the ones they are creating. These DV-composing activities are aimed at helping teachers and then students in classrooms develop multimodal design strategies, which at the same time support student achievement of new higher-level state learning standards in English, social science, science, math, languages, and other school subjects.

Continued support for teacher participants occurs through the university team collaborators working side-by-side with teachers in regular school visits to classrooms. A project Web site provides

[1] Clip culture refers to an emergent new literacy, "an internet activity of sharing and viewing a short video." It was made possible by broadband networks, but has boomed since 2005 when Web sites for uploading clips emerged on the market, including youtube, Google Video, MSN Video. Sources for clips include news, movies, music video and amateur video shot with DV, digital cameras, webcams and mobile phones. (Adapted from http://en.wikipedia.org/wiki/Clip_culture.)

[2] The Buffalo Public Schools system has 70 schools which serve predominantly high-poverty communities. Seventy-four percent of Buffalo Public School students are eligible for free or reduced-priced lunch (compared to 38% of students statewide). Once a thriving industrial city, a stop on the Erie Canal, Buffalo slipped into economic decline in recent decades as the steel mills and aircraft manufacturers closed. The median household income is $28, 544, a little over half of the state median (U.S. Census Bureau, 2004). According to their NYS District Report Card (2003), the multiethnic community is reflected in the school population of 41,600 students with a Black majority, both African Americans and African immigrants (57%); with Whites of western European origin—especially German, Irish, Polish (26.9%); Hispanic (12.4%); and American Indian, Alaskan, Asian, or Pacific Islander (2.7%). Students for whom English is a second language comprise 6.4% of the district.

[3] Sixty percent of the CVCV teachers are in middle grades. Sixty percent teach English and social studies; the rest teach special education, science, languages, arts, ESL, and math. One third of the teachers are male, and one fourth are African American and Latino. Teaching experience ranges from 2 years to over 20 years.

[4] Miller, as CVCV Director, and two CVCV graduate associates—in 2006 Monica Blondell and Jonathan Federick. Previous associates included Suzanne Borowicz, Gary Huber, and Kara Olidge.

a publication space for DV curriculum projects and products. Bimonthly reunions provide a forum with multiple purposes: teachers share their experiences of teaching with DV composing, their teaching materials, and their students' completed DV products; present successful DV-composing activities, stories, strategies; and raise issues and questions with other CVCV teachers. Research shows that teachers have been inspired by the examples and work of other teachers in the project (Blondell, 2006). DVs highlighting teachers explaining their practice and students in action in classroom DV workshops are also featured at reunions and published on the project Web site. The aim is to literally provide strong images of what is possible in this urban school district and to help evolve a larger, supportive community of practice.

In all, this ongoing professional development is aimed at (a) providing teachers with multimodal design experiences in DV composing as a means of understanding its power as a social practice and learning tool; (b) creating engaging, purposeful activities for student DV composing embedded in the curriculum; (c) developing strong pedagogical and design strategies for use at the point of need in classroom DV composing; (d) creating a professional community to support teacher efforts to change; and (e) ultimately, prompting the cultural jump necessary for enacting changes in teaching and what counts as knowing/learning in classrooms.

It is important to note that the model for professional development in the CVCV program emerged over time through ongoing cycles of collaboration and reflection with all the partners. For example, the initial purpose for the university team visiting classrooms was to provide any needed technical support and to document cycles of DV composing. However, when enthusiastic teachers from the institute hit the realities of their urban classrooms, DV composing diminished as a priority. Research (Borowicz, 2003) revealed the essential need for in-school collaboration with individual teachers when they began trying to integrate DV composing as a learning tool for students. These collaborations then became a planned and central part of the program.

Currently funded by the New York State Education Department and the John R. Oishei Foundation,[5] CVCV ultimately aims to foster achievement in urban schools and social futures (New London Group, 1996) by empowering students with new multimodal literacies. (See Miller & Borowicz [2006] for a summary of the teacher and student learning documented in the program. Access the Web site at www.cityvoicescityvisions.org).

Studies of DV Composing in Classrooms

The research suggesting the power of youth digital video authoring has been conducted largely outside of schools in community centers (e.g., Goodman, 2003; Hull, 2003; Hull & Nelson, 2005; Hull & James, 2007). In school-based research, the CVCV university team and colleagues have examined the situated learning through DV composing in urban classrooms (Miller & Borowicz, 2005, 2006, 2007; Blondell, 2006; Borowicz, 2005; Costello, 2006; Lauricella, 2006). Employing grounded theory, ethnographic, and case-study methods, these studies taken together provide evidence that DV composing can be a potent new literacy-learning tool that leads to increased student engagement and achievement. Learning to use and to teach DV composing can induce the changes in epistemology and social practice that promote changes in teachers' pedagogies and students' learning (Miller & Borowicz, 2006).

At the same time, teacher and school traditional beliefs about knowledge, teaching, and learning and constraints in urban schools create tensions. In this section, an overview of findings from these studies focuses on how these promises and challenges played out in schools. Three stories of classrooms will serve to illustrate the range of tensions and impacts. (To assure anonymity, pseudonyms are used throughout for the names of teachers, students, and school buildings.)

Multimodal composing as embodied learning—or not. DV composing often interrupted the limited print-only mode of schools. In her ethnographic case study of an 11th-grade English class, Borowicz (2005) found that student engagement changed dramatically when the teacher introduced DV composing. One focal student, Darrius, who was perceived in school as nonresponsive and a troublemaker, created a DV story in response to a novel to depict his vision of the importance of loyalty among friends based on his own lived experiences. In an impressive change, he came to class early and often stayed late, sometimes giving up his lunch period to work on his movie. He orchestrated a tragic scene, demonstrating to the actor her language and movements before filming, then edited the footage using quick cuts and dramatic music to amplify the shock. He watched his movie over and over, sometimes talking to himself, sometimes singing along with the music he had imported, sometimes turning to a fellow student for assistance. On one occasion, he announced, "Man, I love this. I could stay here and work on this all day."

Much like the adolescent artists Heath (2004) studied, Darrius called this intensive work "fun," a stance Heath explains by the concept of "flow" (Csikzentmihalyi, 1990), a state "when action and awareness merge, consciousness narrows to focus attention on what is most relevant for the role of participation one is intending" (Heath, 2004, p. 340) and time slips by ("class is over already?"). The shift in role and stance, like Heath's artists, seems to come from a similar focus on creation: "The arts encircle learning with meaning and thereby make comprehension and engagement fundamental for participation" (p. 339). For the first time in school, Darrius felt what it was like "being connected in a social space with resources for expressive productivity" (Borowicz, 2005). This connectedness to tools, peers, and the multimodal world outside is key to purposeful, embodied learning through all the senses (Gee, 2004).

However, this embodied meaning making was not teacher Nate Russel's main purpose for using DV composing with his students. Nate felt that DV was a motivation that "forces kids to study." After students created a DV poetry interpretation, Nate abruptly turned to 6 weeks of rote test preparation—drill, practice and recitation for the end-of-year state test. During these 6 weeks, student attendance in this class dropped dramatically. Those who came were disengaged, adopting their familiar student tableaux of sitting perfectly still staring out the window (Borowicz, 2005).

Nate Russel, it seems clear, had not broadened his concept of literacy and knowledge and did not feel an authentic purpose for new multimodal literacies. He did not see the fun of flow among his students as productive, just as a distraction from the necessary

[5] The New Literacies Group (NLG) at the University at Buffalo is committed to preparing teachers, researchers, and future professors in theoretical, empirical, and practical, understanding of why and how to access students' rich funds of knowledge and multimodal literacy practices developed outside of school as multimodal tools for mediating in-schooling learning.

drudgery of regular school work. He felt responsible for bringing his students out of poverty by giving them what the school said they needed—passing scores on the graduation test. It is interesting to note that even when the teacher did not construct an authentic purpose for DV composing as a social practice, students like Darrius did. In this class and others, research findings demonstrated that opportunities for students to make multimodal meaning of classroom content through the embodied experiences of DV composing helps students move out of passivity, alienation, and powerlessness (Miller & Borowicz, 2005, 2006).

Wholeheartedness and achievement. In her case study of two eighth-grade English classes taught by the same teacher, Costello (2006) found that integrating process drama with DV composing in the classrooms "created opportunities for a synergy through which student interpretation thrived." During DV production, the classroom space changed as Dylan Bradley left his position at the front of the class and moved around the room to support student groups. In DV productions to dramatize vocabulary words, develop a newscast on a novel, and create a poetry interpretation, students deeply engaged with each other and grappled with ideas and meanings.

In the final process drama/confessional DV, students in small groups enacted a new DV genre, representing each chapter from *The Outsiders* with a tableau, using body placement, gestures, and facial expressions to capture a significant aspect of the text. These students added a reality-show confessional, with students speaking in character, to construct motives, pose questions, and sound themes central to the printed text—in a social space for "wholehearted literature study."

What seemed to be "brilliant successes" in this class contrasted with the second class, which had only "small moments of beauty." There was the moment when Mr. Bradley wanted students to write out their confessionals in "standard English," but asked them to perform, not read. Only Curtis understood and offered this translation to the class, "It's like you freestylin'." The class then got it, too: "Yeah! Freestylin'! Yeah, it's like a rap." Costello concluded, "Drawing on their implicit media and performance knowledge seemed to energize the activity for students like Curtis." This class read *Freak the Mighty* as the basis for their DV confessionals, and it was there that the complex "challenges and tensions surrounding the integration of new literacies" erupted.

The urban school context and the resulting coconstruction of teacher and student identities undermined the innovative use of DV composing in this class. Although Dylan Bradley wanted to engage students and help them "to overcome oppositional identity," at Neighborhood School, he focused mostly "on managing student behavior." The school was a "tight ship," with students in straight lines in hallways and straight rows in classrooms. In this culture of "rigid order," Dylan had warned the *Freak the Mighty* class about not following directions: "not every class gets the privilege of participating in iMovie . . . and if you can't behave yourselves, I will cut off the project completely." In the middle of a class period in the middle of DV production, Dylan did stop the project due to a conflict with Curtis and another student, both of whom were known in the school and teachers' lounge as "troublemakers" or "thugs." When faced with what he perceived as challenge, Dylan "defaulted to the discourse of the lunchroom–the identity of the exasperated disciplinarian."

It seems accurate that "Dylan's willingness to disrupt the traditional paradigm of teaching quiet students in straight rows with the student-centered, multimodal endeavor of DV is admirable." At the same time, though, shutting down the project had academic consequences. The six focal students from *The Outsiders* homeroom passed the end of year school district exam. The most challenging section was a "critical lens" essay, requiring students to interpret any piece of literature from the perspective of a supplied quotation. Analysis of those essays revealed that they all incorporated "either the pivotal moments in the story that they focused on for the DV project or the thematic issues explored." The two students in the *Freak the Mighty* homeroom who finished their video on their own time also wrote about *Freak the Mighty* for that essay, whereas one focal student in that class who did not finish the DV did not pass the exam.

Students developed deep understanding of these texts from the DV composing, which provided support for their thinking in timed essays of academic writing. This finding argues against a dichotomy between new multimodal literacies and print academic literacies: the embodied experience of multimodal design "may be the basis for achievement on high-stakes essay assessments about literature" (Costello, 2006).

Implications from this study include the need in teacher professional development to foreground potential tensions and politics in schools and professional strategies for working in those spaces. A vital implication is the need to explicitly support teachers' deep understanding of the positive influences of DV composing on interpretive strategies and reflective dispositions engendered by embodied learning. Developing such understanding of how and what students learn in DV composing may help to work against notions that DV composing is a privilege for a special class and promote the idea that it is a "pedagogical necessity" to support achievement for all students.

DV composing as inquiry, voice, vision. In her ethnographic case study of an 11th-grade social studies class, Lauricella (2006) traced events and developing ways of thinking as teacher Robert Williams provided students opportunities to use primary sources to investigate historical events and compose DV products. Findings revealed that Mr. Williams enacted a stance toward history as an ongoing inquiry that needed to be open to new evidence. This consistent attitude toward historical knowledge as not fixed, but evolving, created a "felt need" for inquiry among his students. The authentic purpose for students to engage in DV composing, then, was to make sense of their inquiries into multimodal historical texts and represent their historical analyses.

Williams' pedagogy reflected his stance on history: instead of linear chronology, he posed big questions and themes to get at underlying conceptual issues. Through supportive talk, he helped students pose questions for their inquiries. Particularly when the inquiries surfaced student-initiated questions, students drew the world into the classroom through a variety of multimodal texts as they were impelled to find a solution to their perplexity (Dewey, 1933; Miller, 2003). When a DV project was in process, students worked in teams with cameras and computers as mediating tools, focused by the larger inquiry purpose of the class and the immediate purpose of creating a political commercial for a past election or a movie trailer on Jim Crow laws of the Reconstruction Era. Students interacted with each other around the content of textbooks and other curricular texts (posters, teacher-made materials), but also around the multimodal texts students generated through the camera and designed using movie-editing software. Students turned to and taught each other, drawing on knowledge distributed among the team and from outside sources on the Internet. This "affinity space" (Gee, 2004) that developed was a social space where students interacted face to face and learned while they pursued their common endeavor to design a DV.

In all, Williams engaged students in "doing history" as collaborative inquiry through DV composing. For example, Paige and Nicole designed their DV *For Coloreds Only* through their inquiry into multimodal texts (e.g., newspaper accounts, advertisements, photographs, literacy tests, music, vernacular history from their community, enacted scenes), using historical skills to "read" them, and negotiate a story in the genre of a movie trailer set to Billie Holiday's singing of "Strange Fruit." At the screening, the class was stunned. As Lauricella (2006) concluded, "The orchestration of these multimodal texts capture the auditory and visual senses and work to encompass a holistic understanding of lynching as a horrific event in America's history."

Robert Williams was pleased with his students' learning and achievement, including their performance on the end-of-year state graduation test. One of the assessments was a document-based question (DBQ), which asked students to read primary historical documents (excerpts from speeches, essays, graphs, political cartoons, laws) related to an historical issue (e.g., Progressive Reform) and compose a well-argued essay. This *timed* inquiry required students to draw on these multimodal texts and their knowledge of U.S. history to compose an interpretation for an audience. This is the kind of thinking they had been doing all year as they composed DVs related to the curriculum.

Lauricella (2006) heard about Williams' student pass rate from an administrator and then confirmed with Williams: for the previous five years his students had a "100% pass rate on the New York State U.S. History Regents Exam, the social studies graduation test for all students" (p. 112). In the year of the study, all of his more than 120 students engaged in composing six DVs passed this test, which only 73% passed in the rest of the school district. Lauricella concluded that through their embodied learning in these classes, students developed strategies for historical thinking and deeply appropriated historical knowledge, at the same time that they learned to "experience the world with an embedded understanding of what it means to be an active citizen" (p. 161).

TEACHER CHANGE: IMPLICATIONS FROM RESEARCH FOR NEW MULTIMODAL LITERACIES IN SCHOOLS

Taken together, these studies suggest, first of all, that DV composing can provide rich opportunities for students to learn curricular concepts deeply as they draw on tacit knowledge of media, connect curriculum to their lives through embodied experience, learn multimodal design, and create new identities as designers and active learners. These impacts occurred even when teachers were not fully aware of them. Secondly, these studies provide evidence that integrating new media literacies and DV composing in classrooms and schools is quite complex, but quite possible.

As Bransford, Darling-Hammond & LePage (2005) argued, the evidence base is small for how teacher learning influences what teachers do in classrooms and what their students learn—and even smaller for how teachers learn the practices that research shows make a difference for students (p. 23). To contribute to building a professional consensus through "evidence-based practice," the field of education plainly needs more long-term studies of how teachers take up professional development experiences and enact them in classrooms. Looking across the case studies of DV composing in schools helps to illustrate trends in the studies and may contribute to a budding consensus on new literacies pedagogical practice.

A strong sense of integrative purpose. Teacher attention to constructing strong purposes for new multimodal literacies and DV composing in their classrooms is essential. Robert Williams (Lauricella, 2006) and the other teacher *innovators* constructed social contexts and new multimodal literacy practices in their classrooms for strong, conscious purposes that supported their clear goals for teaching their subjects and their students. Robert consistently communicated the need for ongoing inquiry into multimodal media texts in order to understand historical and current issues and to become critical citizens of the 21st century. Carol Smith (Bailey, 2006) began by using new literacies only for student motivation, but through her supported reflection on how and what her students were learning, she developed a purposeful "new literacies stance," treating knowledge as composed from perspectives and learning as represented multimodally. (Both teachers' purposes are quite congruent with digital epistemologies.)

In the classrooms of teachers with such strong integrative purposes, compelling patterns of change emerged for classrooms and students. As students engaged in multimodal design, transformations for them emerged through joint purposeful endeavor or "affinity spaces," where designers drew on knowledge across people, tools, spaces (Gee, 2004; Bailey, 2006; Miller & Borowicz, 2006). Evidence reviewed here shows that students drew on social and cultural funds of knowledge that included youth media practices, home and peer language, vernacular history, and urban life experiences to connect to and make sense of curriculum from what they already knew. This interweaving of modes and knowledges for meaning making mediated student understanding of the school curriculum, and also served social and personal agendas of students, particularly those perceived to be struggling academically.

Student and school learning purposes coalesced in DV composing activities, providing almost total engagement in codesigning and embodied learning. Students' deep engagements and multimodal learning also served them well as mediators and resources for more print-based reading and writing, for example, in passing high-stakes tests (Costello, 2006; Lauricella, 2006; McMaster, 2004), though students' performance went well beyond learning standards and passing tests.

In some classes, these patterns emerged *only* during DV composing. For example, the experience of Darrius in Nate Russel's class (Borowicz, 2005) showed the potential transformation over time that he and other students might have experienced with a more purposeful teacher stance toward new multimodal literacies. With collaborative support, Dylan Bradley (Costello, 2006) sustained a clear purpose for DV composing—deeply understanding literature—in *The Outsiders* homeroom, but not in his second class.

Teachers with conflicted purposes and low-level restrictive purposes for DV composing at times succeeded and at times succumbed to inevitable tensions in schools: Dylan Bradley, to school norms of controlling student behavior; Nate Russel, to testing pressures and the rote learning perceived as needed for students to pass; Terry Martin, to her views of knowledge as authoritative content and teacher as expert. The irony in these instances is that teachers appeared to be cutting students off from embodied learning and new multimodal literacies because they were seen as distractions to learning or only hooks or privileges—when evidence is strong that these were the very means students needed to succeed. Ironic, too, was extensive teacher effort at quieting students for compliance—which cut teachers off from the funds of knowledge active students might bring to teacher/school goals of learning content (e.g., Curtis offering the youth genre of "freestylin" to explain performance in his class). Opening school learning to out-of-school literacies and popular multimodal texts can reposition students in school by redefining their competence (O'Brien, 2003), perhaps even providing Darrius and Curtis spaces for voices and visions for purpose and success in school.

The value of constructing deep integrative purposes for new multimodal literacies in classrooms can be enhanced by relating it to findings from research on impacts of arts involvement on youth (Heath & Smyth, 1999; Heath, 2004). In a 10-year study of 124 youth-based community organizations in poor communities, Heath described how sustained multimodal arts activities—including video production, visual arts, music, drama, and photography—served as "incubators" for purposeful meaning making, joint thinking/problem solving, risk/responsibility, and meaningful connection. Key elements of these programs included engaging youth as resources, producers, cocreators, and mentors in the context of authentic, supported art activities. Participants learned the kinds of language necessary to create projects: joint planning, preparing, critiquing, and debriefing. As these youth developed future scenarios, explained, argued, provided strategies in teams, they developed socially and cognitively in profound ways.

These impacts through purposeful participation in arts affinity spaces resonate with some of the findings from the reviewed research on DV composing, arguably an arts-inspired practice. In their study, Heath and Smyth (1999) found that the kinds of talking and designing in these multimodal learning environments "appeared to accelerate later language development of forms central to academic language and literacy" (p. 338). To the extent that DV composing in classrooms similarly involves "coengagement in designing" (New London Group, 2000, p. 22) for motivating purposes, possibilities are raised for the importance of exploring long-term impacts on students. Like the multimodal arts-production environments described by Heath and Smyth (1999), the purposeful affinity space experiences in DV workshops may develop in students the essential embodied strategies for "the collaborative work projects of the new economy" (p. 67).

Finally, the research in classrooms using DV composing suggests that the guiding purpose constructed by teachers for authentic new literacies in school cannot be for low-level comprehension and remembering, but in some way must be about designing multimodal texts to bring curriculum and youth culture/out-of-school literacies and experiences together. Blondell (2006) traced one facet of the conflict over purpose for DV composing in her interview study of CVCV English teachers. As teachers began to integrate DV composing into their classes, they felt new identities as "innovators" and "nontraditional" and valued "the respect and interest they receive from students and teachers." At the same time, though, they were "conflicted about taking on this new role: handing over responsibility, choice, and aspects of design to students" (p. 18).

Possibly teachers with low-level goals for DV composing faced this conflict. Perhaps they were in transition on their developmental trajectories. In either case, additional strategies are needed for assisting teachers like Terry Martin who had very similar supports as her successful colleague, but had not developed along the same path to integration. Trends in the research on professional development for new literacies provide some guidance.

Strategies from research for new literacies professional development. The reviewed research suggests that some of the teacher professional development strategies tried were effective: ongoing support for learning authentic new literacy practices; for creating curricular activities that meet subject learning standards; for creating knowledge about teaching in work group forums, like DV workshop; for creating visions of teachers successful in classrooms (live and DV); and, where possible, for in-classroom collaboration on planning and inquiry to speed up the process of integration.

These strategies were not sufficient for all teachers, though. The following expansions of approaches for teacher professional development, derived from the previous review of research on new multimodal literacies in classrooms, provide additional trends for successful teacher learning. Professional development in new multimodal literacies also needs to,

- Focus metareflective talk and metacognitive opportunities on critically examining and possibly expanding beliefs about teaching, learning, knowing, and literacy;
- Foreground the classroom-constructed purposes for integrating new multimodal literacies, not just procedural, logistical, and technological knowledge (e.g., Miller & Borowicz, 2006);
- Attend to and develop ways for teachers to describe *what* students are learning through new multimodal literacy design activities;
- Initiate *metacognitive talk* about the planning, thinking, and learning in teachers' own multimodal design activities, what Kist (2002) called "metadialogues," to develop teachers' abilities to provide multimodal and pedagogical strategies at points of need for students in their classrooms (McVee et al., 2006; Miller & Borowicz, 2005, 2006);
- As in all effective preparation of teachers for a changing world (Darling-Hammod & Bransford, (2005) provide strong images of good, committed teaching with new multimodal literacies; and
- Develop collaborative inquiry dispositions to help teachers deal professionally with the complexities of schools and the real-world messiness of all teaching.

Finally, the complexities of developing teachers as "adaptive experts" who can balance routine efficiency and innovation (Bransford, Derry, Berliner,& Hammerness 2005, p. 48) is daunting in teacher education and in school contexts. Building relationships between these contexts is another approach to initiating and sustaining change.

A research-based partnership strategy for teacher learning. In a statewide grounded-theory study, Miller et al. (2003) developed a "promising systems leadership framework" for transforming teaching and teacher preparation through wise integration of new technologies. A key component is long-term partnerships between schools of education and public schools to provide opportunities to jointly create new contextualized knowledge and promising approaches in classrooms, and then to share them with teachers, administrators, teacher educators, and preservice teachers. In this way, for example, perceptions of new multimodal literacies and DV composing as merely privileges or distractions to the business of schools can begin to be transformed by sharing research evidence showing how new literacies can function in classrooms as purposeful, academic learning tools.

Fundamental to substantive change through innovation, the framework suggested, are changes in materials (such as digital technologies), changes in teaching approaches (such as infusion of DV composing as a learning tool), and possible alteration of beliefs (e.g., assumptions about knowledge, teaching, literacies) (Fullan, 2001; Miller et al., 2003). Research linked to the CVCV program suggested that the most serious need is creating new ways to prompt changes in teacher beliefs. To develop professional teachers who are reflective, knowledgeable inquirers, ongoing support of teacher learning across contexts may provide a productive approach.

Finally, the framework called for change to be guided by "the need to make a positive difference in society" (Fullan, 2001; Miller et al., 2003). This "moral purpose" for the CVCV partnership and for the University at Buffalo faculty partnership in the New Literacies Group[6] is transforming schools through new multimodal literacies to create purposeful classrooms where *all* students develop social futures and performance competence for 21st -century life. Ipeze (2006) argued that integrating new multimodal literacies in schools constitutes culturally responsive teaching (Ladson-Billings, 1995; Wlodkowski & Ginsberg, 1995), inasmuch as inclusion of youth culture and out-of-school literacies can create conditions for motivation, meaning making, and student competence. Such changes in student positioning and identity can lead to changes in students' school achievement. Educational scholarship on identity has a central tenet: "identities are crucial to learning" (Sfard & Prusak, 2005, p. 19); "learning is all about identity and identification" (Gee, 2004, p. 37). Evidence from CVCV classrooms suggested that these theories tended to hold true, not just for students, but for teachers as well.

As for the moral purpose for partnerships around new literacies, in particular, the goal of repositioning urban youth as competent and building their performance knowledge with new literacy practices is an issue of equity and social justice. In a recent review of research on and theories of new literacies, Leu et al. (2004) warned of potentially severe consequences of ignoring these needs:

> We believe that implementing a New Literacies Perspective in classrooms is essential if we hope to avoid societies in which economic advantage is sustained by the wealthy and denied to the poor. . . . Such a development presents fundamental challenges to any society that professes egalitarian ideals and equal opportunities for all its citizens. (pp. 1600–1601)

Unfortunately, underfunded urban schools have not often taken up needed transformations, but instead have been bound up by bureaucracy, lack of communication, and disrespect for teachers and students (Weiner, 2000). Ongoing partnerships with schools of education provide possibilities for introducing and supporting change.

In the CVCV school-university partnership, developing contextual knowledge through collaboration remains central to working toward change. Preservice (PST) teachers at the university now take a new multimodal literacies course focusing on DV composing, and it is cotaught with BPS teachers (Miller & Borowicz, 2007). Those PSTs are then paired for student teaching with CVCV teachers in the schools (Huber 2006). CVCV teachers from the schools have become master's students at the university who engage in master's inquiries on their students' DV learning in their classrooms (Malley, 2004). PSTs have graduated, become BPS teachers, and joined the CVCV project. And, university doctoral students partner with CVCV teachers to conduct collaborative research in their classrooms. In this ferment of activity, some of the collaboration is planned; some is serendipity, but all opportunities induce collaborative reflection on beliefs, materials, and approaches, and form seeds of change.

CONCLUSION: TEACHERS FIRST

A startling consensus about the need for schools to integrate advanced technology-afforded multimodal literacy practices has emerged across diverse groups with varying agendas. The perspectives of business/workplace interests (SCANS, 1991), Department of Education assessments (1999), and unique partnerships of education, business, and government leaders (Partnership for 21st Century Skills, 2006) converge with new multimodal literacies scholars and researchers: students urgently need opportunities in schools to develop new literacies, performance knowledge, and multimodal learning strategies required for new times and social futures.

To this end, teacher learning needs to be highlighted as part of the new multimodal literacies school reform agenda. Institutions of old learning have shaped and continue to shape teachers in an era of high-stakes accountability to print texts. Simply urging teachers to change their shaping beliefs about knowing or requiring them to infuse technology in classrooms is undoubtedly inadequate. Teachers need ongoing high-quality professional development activities to help them transform their beliefs about the purposes for schooling, learning, and literacy and to become reflective insiders to the new multimodal literacy practices necessary for new times.

The quintessential multimodality of DV composing provides an entry point for developing new multimodal literacy practices for teachers and students, with the potential to develop the needed performance knowledge, design abilities, and social and cognitive strategies needed for 21st-century literacies. Along the way, it has the potential to transform what goes on in schools.

REFERENCES

Albers, P. (2006). Imagining possibilities in multimodal curriculum design. *English Education*, *38*(2), 75–101.

Alvermann, D. E. (Ed.). (2002). *Adolescents and literacies in a digital world*. New York: Peter Lang.

Apple Classroom of Tomorrow (ACOT). (1995). *Changing the conversation about teaching, learning & technology: A report of 10 years of ACOT research*. Cupertino, CA: Apple Computer. Retrieved May 16, 2006, from http://images.apple.com/edu/education/k12/leadership/acot/pdf/10yr.pdf

Apple Education. (2004). *The evolution of thought and practice. Technology planning guide: Professional development*. Retrieved May 14, 2006, from http://www.apple.com/education/planning/profdev/index4.html

Anyon, J. (1997). *Ghetto schooling*. New York: Teachers College Press.

Bailey, N. (2006). *Designing social futures: Adolescent literacy in and for new times*. Unpublished doctoral dissertation, University at Buffalo, State University of New York.

Blondell, M. (2006). *Teachers' perceptions of DV composing in English classrooms: Blurring boundaries for understanding lives and curriculum*. Unpublished manuscript, University at Buffalo.

Bloome, D. (1986). Building literacy and classroom community. *Theory into Practice, 25*(2), 71–76.

Borowicz, S. (2003). *Poetry in motion: Collaborative inquiry into digital video authoring in an urban school.* Unpublished manuscript, University at Buffalo, State University of New York.

Borowicz, S. (2005). *Embracing lives through the video lens: An exploration of literacy teaching and learning with digital video technology in an urban secondary English classroom.* Unpublished doctoral dissertation, University at Buffalo.

Brand, G. A. (1997). What research says: Training teachers for using technology [Electronic version]. *Journal of Staff Development, 19*(1), 10–13. Retrieved May 20, 2006, from http://www.nsdc.org/library/jsd/brand191.html

Brandsford, J., Darling-Hammond, L., & LePage, P. (2005). Introduction. In L. Darling-Hammond, & J. Bransford (Eds.), *Preparing teachers for a changing world: What teachers should learn and be able to do.* Hoboken, NJ: Jossey-Bass.

Bransford, J., Derry, S., Berliner, D., & Hammerness, K., with Beckett, K. L. (2005). Theories of learning and their roles in teaching. In L. Darling-Hammond, & J. Bransford (Eds.), *Preparing teachers for a changing world: What teachers should learn and be able to do.* Hoboken, NJ: Jossey-Bass.

Buckingham, D. (2003). Digital literacies: Media education and new media technologies. In B. Duncan, & K. Tyner (Eds.), *Visions/revisions: Moving forward with media education.* Madison, WI: National Telemedia Council.

Burnes, A., & Parker, D. (2003). Tiger's big plan: Multimodality and the moving image. In C. Jewitt, & G. Kress (Eds.), *Multimodal literacy.* New York: Peter Lang.

Chandler-Olcott, K., & Mahar, D. (2003). Adolescents' *anime*-inspired "fanfictions": An exploration of multiliteracies. *Journal of Adolescent & Adult Literacy, 46*(7), 556–566.

Coiro, J. (2005). Every teacher a Miss Rumphius: Empowering teachers with effective professional development. In R. A. Karchmer, M. H. Mallette, J. Kara-Soteriou, & D. J. Leu. (Eds.), *Integrating approaches to literacy education: Using the internet to support new literacies* (pp. 199–219). Newark, DE: International Reading Association. Retrieved on May 15, 2006, from http://ctell1.uconn.edu/coiro/missrumphius.pdf

Cope, B., & Kalantzis, M. (2000). Multiliteracies: The beginning of an idea. In B. Cope, & M. Kalantzis (Eds.), *Multiliteracies: Literacy learning and the design of social futures* (pp. 3–8). London: Routledge.

Costello, A. (2006). *Digital video and drama production as literacy learning tools in English classrooms.* Unpublished doctoral dissertation, University at Buffalo, State University of New York.

Csikzentmihalyi, M. (1990). *Flow: The psychology of optimal experiences.* New York: Harper & Row.

Darling-Hammond, L., & Bransford, J. (Eds.) (2005). *Preparing teachers for a changing world: What teachers should learn and be able to do.* Hoboken, NJ: Jossey-Bass.

Dewey, J. (1933). *How we think.* Lexington, MA: D.C. Heath and Company.

diSessa, A. A. (2000). *Changing minds: Computers, learning, and literacy.* Cambridge, Ma: MIT Press.

Finn, P. (1999). *Literacy with an attitude: Educating working class students in their own self-interest.* Albany, NY: SUNY Press.

Fullan, M. (2001). *The new meaning of educational change* (3rd ed.). New York: Teachers College Press.

Gee, J. (2003). *What video games have to teach us about learning and literacy.* New York: Palgrave Macmillan.

Gee, J. P. (2004). *Situated language and learning: A critique of traditional schooling.* New York: Routledge.

Goodman, S. (2003). *Teaching youth media: A critical guide to literacy, video production.* New York: Teachers College Press.

Grabill, J. T., & Hicks, T. (2005). Multiliteracies meet methods: The case for digital writing in English education, *English Education, 37*(4), 301–311.

Hagood, M. C., Stevens, L. P., & Reinking, D. (2002). What do THEY have to teach US? Talkin' 'cross generations! In D. E. Alvermann (Ed.), *Adolescents and literacies in digital world.* New York: Peter Lang.

Heath, S. B. (2004). Learning language and strategic thinking through the arts. *Reading Research Quarterly, 39*(3), 338–342.

Heath, S. B. & Smyth, L. (1999). *ArtShow: Youth and community development.* Washington, DC: Partners for Livable Communities.

Huber, G. (2006). *Popular culture in student digital video production.* Unpublished Reflective Inquiry Project, University at Buffalo.

Hull, G. (2003). Youth culture and digital media: New literacies for new times. *Research in the Teaching of English, 38*(2), 229–233.

Hull, G. A., & Nelson, M. E. (2005) Locating the semiotic power of multimodality. *Written Communication, 22*(2), 224–261.

Hull, G. A., & James, M. A. (in press). Geographies of hope: A study of urban landscapes, digital media, and children's representations of place. In P. O'Neill (Ed.), *Blurring boundaries: Developing writers, researchers and teachers.* Cresskill, NJ: Hampton Press.

Ikpeze, C. (2006). *Bringing together the bits: Web-based literacy learning in a fifth-grade classroom.* Unpublished doctoral dissertation, University at Buffalo, State University of New York.

International Reading Association. (2001). *Integrating literacy and technology in the curriculum: A position statement.* Retrieved May 12, 2006, from http://www.reading.org/resources/issues/positions_technology.html

Jewitt, C., & Kress, G. (Eds.). (2003). *Multimodal literacy.* New York: Peter Lang.

King, J. R., & O'Brien, D. G. (2002). Adolescents' multiliteracies and their teachers' needs to know: Toward a digital détente. In D. E. Alvermann (Ed.), *Adolescents and literacies in a digital world* (pp. 40–50). New York: Peter Lang.

Kist, W. (2002). Finding "new literacy" in action: An interdisciplinary high school western civilization class. *Journal of Adolescent & Adult Literacy*, 45(5), 368–377.

Koehler, M. J., & Mishra, P. (2005). Teachers learning technology by design. *Journal of Computing in Teacher Education, 21*(3), 94–102.

Kress, G. (1999). "English" at the crossroads: Rethinking curricula of communication in the context of the turn to the visual. In G. E. Hawisher & C. L. Selfe (Eds.), *Passions, pedagogies & 21st century technologies.* Urbana-Champaign, IL: NCTE

Kress, G. (2000). Multimodality. In B. Cope & M. Kalantzis (Eds.), *Multiliteracies: Literacy learning and the design of social futures* (pp. 182–202). London: Routledge.

Kress, G. (2003). *Literacy in the new media age.* New York: Routledge

Ladson-Billings, G. (1995). Toward a theory of culturally relevant pedagogy. *American Educational Research Journal, 32*(3), 465–491

Lankshear, C., & Knobel, M. (2003). *New Literacies: Changing knowledge and classroom learning.* Philadelphia: Open University Press.

Lauricella, A. M. (2006). *Digital video production as a tool for learning: Exploring multiple text documents in an urban social studies classroom.* Unpublished doctoral dissertation, University at Buffalo, State University of New York.

Leu, D. J. Jr. (2002). The new literacies: Research on reading instruction with the Internet. In A. E. Farstrup, & S. Samuels (Eds.), *What research has to say about reading instruction* (pp. 310–336). Newark, DE: International Reading Association.

Leu, D. J. Jr., Kinzer, C. K., Coiro, J., & Cammack, D. W. (2004). Toward a theory of new literacies emerging from the Internet and other information and communication technologies. In R. B. Ruddell, & N. J. Unrau (Eds.), *Theoretical models and processes of reading* (pp. 1570–1613). Newark, DE: International Reading Association.

Luke, A. (2002). What happens to literacies old and new when they're turned into policy. In D. Alvermann (Ed.), *Adolescents and literacies in digital world* (pp. 186–203). New York: Peter Lang.

Malley, J. (2004). *Pitch it to me: The role of talk and inquiry in the iMovie classroom.* Unpublished manuscript, University at Buffalo.

McMaster, R. (2004). *Collaborating for curricular change: Arts-based authentic assessments in the English classroom.* Unpublished doctoral dissertation, University at Buffalo, State University of New York.

McVee, M. B., Bailey, N., & Shanahan, L. (2006, February). *Literacy teachers and the (artful) deception of technology integration.* Paper presented at the 27th Annual Ethnography in Education Research Forum, Philadelphia, Pennsylvania.

Miliken Exchange on Education Technology. (1999). *Will new teachers be prepared to teach in a digital age?* Retrieved May 14, 2006, from http://www.mff.org/publications/publications.taf?page=154

Miller, S. M. (2003). How literature discussion shapes thinking: Teaching/learning habits of the heart and mind. In A. Kozulin, V. Ageyev, S. Miller, & B. Gindis (Eds.), *Vygotsky's educational theory in cultural context* (pp. 289–316). Cambridge, U.K.: Cambridge University Press.

Miller, S. M. & Borowicz, S. (2005). City Voices, City Visions: Digital video as literacy/learning supertool in urban classrooms. In L. Johnson, M. Finn & R. Lewis (Eds.), *Urban education with an attitude.* Albany, NY: State University of New York Press.

Miller, S. M. & Borowicz, S. (2006). *Why multimodal literacies? Designing digital bridges to 21st century teaching and learning.* Buffalo, NY: GSE Publications & SUNY Press.

Miller, S. M. & Borowicz, S. (2007). New literacies with an attitude: Transformative teacher education through digital video learning tools. In Finn, M. & Finn, P. (Eds.), *Teacher education with an attitude.* Albany, NY: State University of New York Press.

Miller, S., Meier, E., Payne-Bourcy, L., Shablak, S., Newman, D. L., Wan, T. Y., et al. (2003, October 20). Technology as a catalyst for change: A leadership model for transforming urban teacher preparation (ISSN 1206-9620). *The International Electronic Journal for Leadership in Learning, 7*(12). Retrieved April 25, 2006, from http://www.ucalgary.ca/~iejll/volume7/miller.htm

Mishra, P., & Koehler, M. J. (2004). Technological pedagogical content knowledge: A new framework for teacher knowledge. Retrieved May 1, 2006, from http://punya.educ.msu.edu/PunyaWeb/publications/inpress/MishraKoehler_TPCK.pdf

National Council of Teachers of English (2003). *NCTE position statement: On composing with nonprint media.* Retrieved May 10, 2006, from http://www.ncte.org/about/over/positions/category/media/114919.htm

New London Group. (1996). A pedagogy of multiliteracies: Designing social futures. *Harvard Educational Review, 66*, 60–92.

New London Group. (2000). A pedagogy of multiliteracies: Designing social futures. In B. Cope & M. Kalantzis (Eds.), *Multiliteracies: Literacy learning and the design of social futures.* London: Routledge.

O'Brien, D. G. (2003). Juxtaposing traditional and intermedial literacies to redefine the competence of struggling adolescents. *Reading Online.* Retrieved April 15, 2006, from http://www.readingonline.org/newliteracies/obrien2/

O'Brien, D. G., & Bauer, E. B. (2005). New literacies and the institution of old learning. *Reading Research Quarterly, 40*(1), 120–131.

Partnership for 21st Century Skills. (2006). *Results that matter: 21st century skills and high school reform.* Retrieved May 20, 2006, from http://www.21stcenturyskills.org/documents/RTM2006.pdf

The Secretary's Commission on Achieving Necessary Skills. (1991). *What work requires of schools: A SCANS report for America 2000.* Washington, DC: United States Department of Labor. Retrieved May 20, 2006, from http://wdr.doleta.gov/opr/fulltext/document.cfm?docn=6140

Sfard, A., & Prusak, A. (2005, May). Telling identities: In search of an analytic tool for investigating learning as a culturally shaped activity. *Educational Researcher, 34*(4), 14–22.

Shanahan, L. E. (2006). *Reading and writing multimodal texts through information and communication technologies.* Unpublished doctoral dissertation, State University of New York at Buffalo.

Shulman, L. S. (1986). Those who understand: Knowledge growth in teaching. *Educational Researcher, 15*(2), 4–14.

Street, B. V. (1995). *Social literacies: Critical approaches to literacy in development, ethnography and education.* London: Longman.

Swenson, J., Rozema, R., Young, C. A., McGrail, E., & Whitin, P. (2006). Extending the conversation: New technologies, new Literacies, and English education, *English Education, 38*(4), 349–367.

Thompson, M. (2005). *Slut, warrior, princess: Three gender identities in one students' fan-fiction writing.* Unpublished manuscript State University of New York at Buffalo.

United States Census Bureau. (2004). *State and county quick-facts.* Retrieved June5,2006,fromhttp://quickfacts.census.gov/qfd/states/36/3611000.html

United States Department of Education. (1999). *Getting America's students ready for the 21st century: Meeting the technology literacy challenge.* Retrieved May 12, 2006, from http://www.ed.gov/about/offices/list/os/technology/plan/national/index.html

Weiner, L. (2000). Research in the 90s: Implications for urban teacher preparation. *Review of Education Research, 70*(3), 369–406.

Wlodkowski, R. J. & Ginsberg, M. B. (1995). A framework for culturally responsive teaching. *Educational Leadership, 53*(1), 17–21.

•45•

DRAMATIC PLAY AND DRAMATIC ACTIVITY: LITERATE LANGUAGE AND NARRATIVE UNDERSTANDING

Lee Galda and A. D. *Pellegrini*
UNIVERSITY OF MINNESOTA

In dramatic play, children enact some make-believe theme. This involves their suspension of reality in their interactions with peers, adults, and/or props. While recognized as a hallmark of the preschool period, dramatic play occurs from the toddler period throughout childhood and into adulthood (Fagen, 1981). Researchers, however, have been most interested in the ways in which aspects of young children's dramatic play relate to various educational and developmental outcomes, such as literacy. Dramatic play, like other forms of play (see Fagen, 1981; Pellegrini & Boyd, 1993; Rubin, Fein, & Vandenberg, 1983), follows an inverted developmental U-function, first appearing around 1½ years of age, peaking during the late preschool/early primary-school period, and then declining (Fein, 1981). To this end, a number of integrative reviews have been written on the role of dramatic play in young children's social and cognitive development (e.g., Christie & Johnsen, 1983; Rubin, Fein, & Vandenberg; Smith, 1982), and in oral language and literacy development (Fein, 1981; Garvey, 1984; Pellegrini & Galda, 1993; 2001; Wagner, 1992).

Among other topics, these researchers have explored the influence of aspects of social context on children's development and learning, in this case an examination of the role of social context, as well as physical context, in children's pretend play, language, and literacy (Haight & Miller, 1992; Morrow & Rand, 1991; Neuman & Roskos, 1991; Vukelich, 1991) and social behavior (Howes, 1992). Others have focused on the development of narrative competence through dramatic play (Fein, Ardilla-Rey, & Groth, 2000; Pellegrini, 1985 a & b; Pellegrini & Galda, 1988; Sachs, Goldman, & Chaille, 1985; Sawyer, 2002). Other studies have explored the role of dramatic play in fostering increased story comprehension (Pellegrini, 1984; Pellegrini & Galda, 1982). Additionally, some research has examined the role of drama in extending responses to and understandings about literary narratives in school with older children. (Edmiston, 1993; Edmiston, Enciso, & King, 1987; O'Neill, 1989; Verriour, 1985; Wolf, S., 1994; Wolf, S. & Enciso, 1994). In this chapter, we attempt to explain the role of two kinds of play in the development of literacy through attention to the shared design features of each.

We first review the research on dramatic play in early childhood, focusing on the role of context and the relationship between play and literate language, especially narrative language. Then we turn to an outgrowth of dramatic play, drama as a response to literature, examining what we know about how it relates to narrative understanding.

DRAMATIC PLAY

Although there are differences in types of dramatic play, here we do not differentiate dramatic play from fantasy, pretense, or symbolic play. We define dramatic play as the nonliteral (or symbolic) behavior that children use to transform the identities of objects, actions, and people (Fein, 1981; Garvey & Kramer, 1989). Children engage in dramatic play in many different social configurations: alone, with an adult, or with a peer, and with a variety of physical props, ranging from no props to explicitly defined thematic, or replica, toys, such as Barbie dolls. Dramatic play is also often spontaneous and voluntarily initiated by the child.

ORAL LANGUAGE AND THE ROLE OF PRETENSE

Specific design features of social dramatic play relate to the forms of language that children use in a variety of important situations, such as school-literacy events (Pellegrini, 1985a, b). Social dramatic play is characterized by a very specific sort of oral language. As Halliday (1969–70) noted many years ago, the "Imaginative Function" of language, or that form of language used when children engage in social pretense, is elaborated, or decontextualized language. In this register linguistic meaning is verbally encoded through cohesive ties (Halliday & Hasan, 1976), such as endophora and conjunctions. Others (e.g., Bernstein, 1960; Cook-Gumperz, 1977; Olson, 1977; Snow 1983) have also pointed out that the features of this register are similar to the register of school, and more specifically to the language of literacy. As they engage in social dramatic play, children are learning to use this register while simultaneously learning other pragmatic and discourse level skills; thus, pretense may be a practice or learning venue for these important language skills (Garvey & Kramer, 1989).

Fein (1981) analyzed pretense play in terms of the following design features: (a) decontextualization, (b) object substitution, and (c) role playing. Decontextualization involves framing realistic events in fantasy: for example, pretending to eat dinner. Object substitution involves having one thing (e.g., a prop, gesture, or utterance) to represent something else; for example, a child verbally defines a stick as "my sword." Role playing has players enacting real and pretend roles. These designs features co-occur: Consequently, linguistic forms will also co-occur. For example, decontextualization, role play, and object substitution often co-occur as, for example, when children pretend to build a "fort," each child dramatizes a different role, using pretend tools. Decontextualization is often realized linguistically with temporal (e.g., *and then*) and causal (e.g., *'cause*) conjunctions; thus, decontextualized drama often has a narrative structure (Wolf & Grollman, 1982).

Role play is typically realized through the use of explicit linguistic reference, such as "I'll be the boss." In this case the pronoun "I" is linguistically defined by its tie to "boss," thus minimizing ambiguity. Similarly, such explicit reference is used with object substitutions. Indeed, such explicit definitions as, "Here's my hammer," to transform a real stick into a pretend hammer are not only used referentially in dramatic play, but also to signal other children that the event they are participating in is symbolic. Each of these language forms, in turn, has important implications for children's early school-based literacy (Christie, 1991; Pellegrini, 1985a, b; Pellegrini & Galda, 1993).

Understanding that pretense is being enacted is important to the success of social dramatic play. Garvey and Kramer (1989) analyzed the forms of language that preschoolers used to announce to their partners "This is play." Announcing, "This is play" was labeled metacommunication, by G. Bateson (1972), and has been thoroughly studied (e.g., Auwarter, 1986; Giffin, 1984) since that time. Metacommunication occurs in dramatic play because of the communicative problems inherent in social pretending: Enacting a decontextualized event; coordinating, negotiating, and clarifying the multiple meaning inherent in pretend scenes; and entering and terminating the pretend frame (Garvey & Kramer, 1989). Children use a specific register, marked by specific verb tenses, modal auxiliaries, and sentence/discourse complexity to metacommunicate in pretend play.

Past tense is used to "set the stage," or provide the background for the upcoming play episode, while present tense is used to enact the episode (Garvey & Kramer, 1989); for example, "Once there was a little boy and he lost in the woods." Future tense is often used to plan the upcoming episode (Pellegrini, 1985b). For example, "Let's pretend that you're gonna fall in the hole." Children more frequently use past- and future-tense verbs when they engage in fantasy play compared to nonpretend peer discourse (Pellegrini, 1986). This is commonsensical to the extent that in fantasy, children are talking about things that are not there; past and future tense verbs also mark nonpresence. Further, the planning, assignment, and negotiation of pretend episodes necessitate using past tense. Modal auxiliaries are used to mark mood, such as obligation (e.g., You have'ta), often at the onset of an episode (Garvey & Kramer, 1989).

It is well documented that children use complex language during social pretense. As just noted, verbal explication is necessary in pretend because of its inherent ambiguity. At the utterance level, we know that in children's social pretense, compared with no pretense, language is functionally more diverse (Pellegrini, 1982). Similarly, children's choice of verbs is more diverse (Wolf, Goldfield, Beeghly, & Cardona, 1985, cited in Garvey & Kramer, 1989). The actual verbs used in pretense are often those that encode verbal and mental processes (Pellegrini & Galda, 1993).

By extension, complexity at the discourse level is another characteristic of pretend discourse. Just as sentence-level complexity is realization of explicit meaning, so too, at the discourse level. In social pretense, as just noted, children define potentially ambiguous terms, such as pronouns, with cross-sentential ties and use a variety of conjunctions to organize ideas across the play discourse (Pellegrini, 1982, 1986).

Garvey and Kramer (1989) raised an obvious, but often overlooked, point. The development of these language features in the context of pretense play is also developing in children's nonpretend discourse. However, rather than minimizing the role of pretend play in learning and developing these forms, we argue that pretend play is a vital part of children's everyday life in which they learn and practice all sorts of new behaviors. Pretend, or dramatic, play is one of the most important contexts for learning and development during the early childhood period. What features of the context of dramatic play are important?

THE DIMENSIONS AND ROLE OF CONTEXT

Context is a term very frequently used in educational, psychological, and anthropological research and is often defined in terms of social and physical dimensions (e.g., Caldwell & Bradley, 1984; Wachs, 1990). Social dimensions of context include the number of participants, as in social-network theory (e.g., Cochran & Riley, 1988); the status of the participants, as in peer versus adult interaction (e.g., Tudge & Rogoff, 1989); and the specific relationships between participants, such as friends versus nonfriends (Hartup, 1996). Physical dimensions of context can be proximal, such as the props in the dramatic play center of a classroom; or distal, such as the number of books read to a child across the school year.

Many conceptualizations of contexts, as noted by Bronfenbrenner (1979) and Hinde (1980), share two unfortunate, and interrelated, features. First, many dichotomize social and physical contexts by looking at the ways in which variables in each, independent of the other, relate to children's behavior. Second, context is often conceptualized in unidirectional terms; that is, the environments are sometimes seen as "coercing" (Barker, 1968) behaviors in children. Examples of this sort of work include looking at "effects" of classroom structure on children's behavior (see Minuchin & Shapiro, 1983, for a review) and the role of activity centers on children's pretend play and literate behavior. The assumption behind these conceptions is that social and physical aspects of context shape children's behavior; the child is a passive recipient of environmental stimuli.

Again evoking Bronfenbrenner (1979) and Hinde (1980), we know that contexts and persons are transactional; that is, they affect each other. Specifically, children often self-select themselves into desirable contexts and then interact with the contexts in such a way as to make it most suitable for them. For example, certain children may choose to engage in spontaneous dramatic play on the playground; these children choose other like-minded individuals; individuals' behavior, in turn, influences others' behavior (e.g., cooperative acts are reciprocated). Additionally, individuals influence aspects of the physical context of the playground (e.g., a slide becomes a launching pad). In this latter case, it is important to recognize that individuals also change physical aspects of their environment to suit their needs.

Research has focused on a more specific level of context—social participation in dramatic play. Social participants such as peers, who may be superficially similar, often play differential roles in children's play, depending on their relationships or their shared interactional history (Hinde, 1980). Interactional history is affected in a dialectical way by both individual and situational variables. This, in turn, influences future interactions. For example, children in a classroom may be assigned by their teacher to "play" at the same center. Because of similar interests and repeated interactions, these children become friends: their friendship, in turn, affects their play.

The importance of examining context in terms of relationships is that it specifies more exactly the social arrangements that relate to learning and development. For example, conceptualizing context in terms of peer interaction or adult-child interaction is often too global because there are different sorts of relationships within each of these configurations, each of which relates differentially to children's dramatic play and language (Pellegrini, 2001).

The importance of specifying the relationships that comprise social contexts can be found in descriptions of naturally occurring dramatic play between mother and child, and child and siblings (Haight & Miller, 1992; Dunn, 1988) in which play differed according to the players. Children played differently with their older siblings than they did with their mothers. However, a closer look at play between mother and child, using measures of attachment, or the degree to which children and their mothers have a secure or insecure relationship, points to differences even within the mother-child contest. The pretend play of securely attached children is more frequent and more positive and responsive than that of insecurely attached children (Howes, 1992). Thus, a more specific look at context yields a clearer picture of the effect of context on pretense play.

Peer play has received much attention in the educational and developmental literature. Attachment theorists, for example, have discussed children's peer relations, friendship, and play patterns as an outgrowth of the attachment relationships (Howes, 1992). Other theorists have contrasted peer interaction with adult-child interaction as a venue for stimulating children's social cognitive development. Providing the foundation for the facilitative role of peers on development, Piaget's (1983) theory stressed the role of conceptual conflict and resulting reequilibration that typifies the reciprocal roles that peers take with each other. This is contrasted with the more subordinate, and complementary roles that children assume when interacting with adults. While the contrastive role of peers and adults in children's cognitive development has yielded some very interesting findings and brought us closer to explicating the role of social context in development (e.g., Tudge & Rogoff, 1989), not all peer interactions are alike. Just as attachment history influences the quality of mother-child play, so too with peer interactions.

At a very basic level, it is illustrative to note that children's pretend play differs as a function of their playmates. For example, Kramer, Bukowski, and Garvey (1989) found that the language of preschoolers varied significantly across different triadic partners. By way of explanation for the seemingly unreliable behavior of play behavior, researchers have explored a number of avenues. Doyle (1982), for example, has suggested that preschool children's familiarity with each other has an important impact on their pretend play. When comparing the social and cognitive dimensions of the preschoolers play, Doyle found that children's interactions were more cooperative, active (i.e., involved), and dramatic in familiar dyads, compared to interactions with unfamiliar peers. Familiar children were also more willing to imitate their peers' play than the play of unfamiliar peers.

Familiarity is necessary, but not sufficient, for another important dimension of peer interaction: friendship. By friendship, we mean dyadic groupings that make reciprocal choices of each other; friends would nominate each other as friends and would also be observed interacting with each other. Obviously, children must be familiar with each other before they can be friends. Indeed, the degree to which children are familiar with each other, in terms of spending time in proximity to each other and sharing similar play preferences, is a very good predictor of their becoming friends (Hartup, 1983). Thus, friends like other familiar peers, know, (usually) trust, and reinforce each other.

Not surprisingly, the play between preschoolers who are friends, compared to nonfriends, is longer and more harmonious (Gottman, 1983). When conflicts do arise, friends are more likely to resolve the conflicts and resolve them equitably (Hartup, 1996). Play for friends, because of these features, tends to reinforce the strength of the friendship. Children enjoy playing with their friends and consequently, they exert many cognitive resources to maintain this play, the end result being complex and sustained interaction.

It is clear that particular aspects of context affect the pretend play and accompanying oral language of young children. Examining specific relationships enables us to more clearly understand the actual process of social interaction responsible for learning and development within the context of dramatic play. Close consideration of these relationships continues to be important as children move through school and are increasingly more constrained in selecting the peers with whom they engage. Indeed, researchers who looked at literature discussion groups pointed out the effect of peer relationships on group dynamics and literary understanding (Lewis, 2001).

DRAMATIC PLAY AND NARRATIVE UNDERSTANDING

Much has been written about our penchant for narrative. Humans seem to have a predisposition to make sense of our experiences and to tell others about ourselves through story (Britton, 1970; Bruner,

1986). We seek out narratives to read to ourselves and our children, and these same children voluntarily spend time performing narratives in either sociodramatic play, in which they recreate an aspect of their experience (Smilansky, 1968), or thematic fantasy play, in which they recreate aspects of stories they have encountered in literature, film, video, etc. (Saltz, Dixon, & Johnson, 1977). Further, dramatic play, like storytelling (Applebee, 1978), is marked by borders between the play episode and reality, often realized by an unambiguous beginning and ending, with interruptions to the pretense also clearly marked (Garvey, 1974; Rubin, Fein, & Vandenberg, 1984; Scarlett & Wolf, 1979; Wolf & Pusch, 1985).

Dramatic play is also marked by the presence of narrative structures, beginning with the simple plots that emerge through role playing with other children around familiar situations to plots that are organized temporally, with links between events and a thematic focus. By late preschool, children are differentiating between the voice of the characters, or actors, and that of the narrator in their play episodes (Gardner, 1980), exhibiting a rather sophisticated, albeit unvoiced, understanding of how narratives work. Across the years from preschool to middle childhood play acquires a more complex story-like structure (Wolf & Grollman, 1982).

In explaining the context of successful dramatic play, French, Lucariello, Seidman, and Nelson (1985) argued that successful dramatic play is "scripted," that is, based on knowledge of the roles, organization, and content of familiar events, such as serving and eating breakfast or going to the doctor's office. These familiar social scripts, along with scripts that come from interactions with books and films, help children to build coherent narratives during social dramatic play. By building on familiar scripts in a pretense play context, children gain practice at analyzing and reconstructing the temporal and causal structure of these narrative-like events. Sawyer (1997, 2002) argued that these scripts help children manage the improvisational nature of play. Play narratives, like improvisational theatre, are collaborative, jointly constructed oral narratives; the structure evolves as individuals contribute to the construction, and the outcome is unpredictable (Sawyer, 2002).

Heath (1982) found that children who enacted a variety of events and story themes were often successful at school-based literacy tasks. Children who have a variety of well-developed play scripts for both everyday and fantasy events usually come to school with a well-developed sense of narrative. Both symbolic play and narrative production involve creating stories, suspending reality, and ascribing fictional features to everyday objects (Heath, 1982). As children mature, this is accomplished increasingly through the use of decontextualized language.

From its origins in the early years through its peak in the primary grades, dramatic play consists of increasingly complex narratives, narratives that are based on scripts, or knowledge about the scenes being enacted. These enactments are also distinguished by particular aspects of oral language in that decontextualized language is necessary to successful pretense. It is social, occurring with the collaboration of other players. It is also creative, jointly constructed by the players themselves. These characteristics also describe some forms of classroom dramatic activity in the elementary and later years.

DRAMA IN THE CLASSROOM

Dramatic activity in the classroom takes many forms, such as mime, puppetry, invented dialogue, interpretation, improvisation, and role playing. While both dramatic play and dramatic activity involve narrative, they are not the same. Rather, dramatic activity in the classroom is an outgrowth of dramatic play. Dramatic play is characterized by the following traits:

- Spontaneity, or voluntary engagement by participants
- Control of the activity by the players themselves
- Positive affect displayed in expression and language
- A focus on the activity of play itself rather than any outcomes
- Flexibility, or "novel combinations of ideas and behaviors"
- Transformations of objects, roles, actions through pretense (Christie, 1991, p. 29).

Dramatic activity in the classroom usually does not share all of the traits of dramatic play. Dramatic activities are usually not spontaneous, but rather suggested by a teacher, although over time students can learn to turn to drama as a choice for responding to literature. Nor are dramatic activities without a goal orientation, as the teacher usually has specific goals in mind. Successful dramatic activities in the classroom often demonstrate the positive engagement of students in the act of dramatizing, although even if students are not enjoying themselves they are still expected to engage in the activity.

DRAMA AS RESPONSE TO LITERATURE

When responding to literature through drama, especially in the case of improvisation and role playing, dramatic activity offers opportunities for the use of decontextualized oral language through transformation of objects, roles, and events. It is also social, resulting in a jointly constructed oral narrative that evolves as players respond to each other's verbal cues. Further, dramatic activity is scripted through its ties to a particular story. When done well, dramatic enactment of stories also offers students the opportunity to explore their responses, try on character roles, and work with peers to enlarge their understandings of the story world (Galda, 2005).

When engaged in drama in response to literature, students are involved in the transformation of objects, roles, and actions—they are engaged in pretense. Their language, just as the language of children engaged in spontaneous dramatic play, must be decontextualized to convey their intended meaning. Their language is also collaborative and open ended, as they engage with peers to construct a narrative. Further, as students take on the diction and tone of the characters that they are representing, they are using new and often more formal language than usual. This, like play in young children, offers them opportunities for language development.

Ties to a particular story are the basis of the "scripts" with which students work. These are not written scripts, but rather shared knowledge that can be acted upon, much like the familiar social or fantasy scripts children play about when younger. This requires that students think deeply about the stories they read. In order to dramatize a story, students must think about that story—the event structure, the mood, the characters and their motivation. This has the potential to broaden and deepen their understanding of narratives.

Dramatic activities in the classroom are social. They involve peers as partners and sometimes as audience. When students play about a story with their peers, they have the opportunity to increase their understanding of the story. Edmiston (1993) pointed out that one of the reasons for engaging in dramatic activity in response to literature is that it offers students the opportunity to revisit the story world in the company of others. The social nature of drama allows student to make public their private understandings of characters and events in a story, and offers the possibility of a deepening of their understandings about the same.

CONCLUSION

Vygotsky (1978) linked dramatic play in the early years to imagination in the later years. Play, or the creation of an imaginary situation, he argued, allows a child to "behave beyond his average age, above his daily behavior; in play it is as though he were a head taller than himself" (p. 102). Dramatic play offers young children the opportunity to develop their oral narrative language, increase their understandings of the events of both daily life and the fantasies they encounter, and collaborate with peers to construct an imaginary situation. Dramatic activity in response to literature offers students the opportunity to develop their oral language, collaborate with peers, and develop their understandings of the narratives. Drama asks them to try on new roles, use varied language forms, and explore and enrich their understandings of story. It engages students in talking and thinking about what they have read, helps them connect with books, and allows them to explore their emotional responses to what they have read. When students play about a story, they become part of that story as the story becomes part of them, and part of their repertoire for understanding other stories, themselves, and the world around them.

REFERENCES

Applebee, A. N. (1978). *The child's concept of story.* Chicago: University of Chicago Press.

Auwarter, M. (1986). Development of communicative skills. In J. Cook-Gumperz, W. Corsaro, & J. Streeck (Eds.), *Children's worlds and children's language* (pp. 205–230). Berlin, Germany: DeGruyter.

Barker, R. (1968). *Ecological psychology.* Stanford, CA: Stanford University Press.

Bateson, P. (1972). *Steps to an ecology of mind.* San Francisco: Chandler.

Bernstein, B. (1960). Language and social class. *British Journal of Sociology, 2,* 217–276.

Britton, J. B. (1970). *Language and learning.* London: Penguin.

Bronfenbrenner, U. (1979). *The ecology of human development.* Cambridge, MA: Harvard University Press.

Bruner, J. (1986). *Actual minds, possible worlds.* Cambridge, MA: Harvard University Press.

Caldwell, B., & Bradley, R. (1984). *The HOME inventory-elementary.* Little Rock, AR: Unpublished manuscript.

Christie, J. (Ed.). (1991). *Play and early literacy development.* Albany, NY: State University of New York Press.

Christie, J., & Johnsen, P. (1983). The role of play in social-intellectual development. *Review of Educational Research, 53,* 93–115.

Cochran, M., & Riley, D. (1988). Mother reports of children's personal networks. In S. Salzinger, J. Antrobus, & M. Hammer (Eds.), *Social networks of children* (pp. 13–147). Hillsdale, NJ: Lawrence Erlbaum Associates.

Cook-Gumperz, J. (1977). Situated instructions. In S. Ervin-Tripp & C. Mitchell-Kernan (Eds.), *Child discourse* (pp. 103–124). New York: Academic.

Doyle, A. (1982). Friends, acquaintances, and strangers: The influence of familiarity and ethnolinguistic background on social interaction. In K. Rubin & H. Ross (Eds.), *Peer relationships and social skills in children* (pp. 229–252). New York: Springer.

Dunn, J. (1988). *The beginnings of social understanding.* Cambridge: Harvard University Press.

Edmiston, B. (1993). Going up the beanstalk: Discovering giant possibilities for responding to literature through drama. In K. E. Holland, R. A. Hungerford, & S. B. Ernst (Eds.), *Journeying: Children responding to literature* (pp. 250–266). Portsmouth, NH: Heinemann.

Edmiston, B., Enciso, P., & King, M. L. (1987). Empowering readers and writers through drama: Narrative theater. *Language Arts, 64,* 219–229.

Fagen, R. (1981). *Animal play behavior.* New York: Oxford University Press.

Fein, G. (1981). Pretend play in childhood: An integrative review. *Child Development, 52,* 1095–1118.

Fein, G. G., Ardilla-Rey, A. E., & Groth, L. A. (2000). The narrative connection: Stories and literacy. In K. A. Roskos & J. F. Cristie (Eds.), *Play and literacy in early childhood* (pp. 27–43). Mahwah, NJ: Erlbaum.

French, L., Lucariello, J., Seidman, S., & Nelson, K. (1985). The influence of discourse content and context on preschoolers' use of language. In L. Galda & A. Pellegrini (Eds.), *Play language and stories* (pp. 1–28). Norwood, NJ: Ablex Publishing.

Galda, L. (2005). Exploring characters through drama. In N. L. Roser & M. G. Martinez (Eds.), *What a character! Character study as a guide to literary meaning making in grades K-8* (pp. 83–95). Newark, DE: International Reading Association.

Gardner, H. E. (1980). Children's literary development: The realms of metaphors and stories. In P. McGhee & A. Chapman (Eds.), *Children's humor.* New York: Wiley.

Garvey, C. (1974). Some properties of social play. *Merrill Palmer Quarterly, 20,* 163–180.

Garvey, C. (1984). *Children's talk.* Cambridge: Harvard University Press.

Garvey, C., & Kramer, T. (1989). The language of social pretend play. *Developmental Review, 9,* 364–382.

Giffin, (1984). The coordination of meaning in the creation of shared make-believe reality. In I. Bretherton (Ed.), *Symbolic play* (pp. 73–101). New York: Academic Press.

Gottman, J. (1983). How children become friends. *Monographs of the Society for Research in Child Development, 48,* (Serial No. 201).

Haight, W., & Miller, P. (1992). *The ecology of everyday pretending.* Albany, NY: State University of New York Press.

Halliday, M. A. K. (1969–70). Relevant models of language. *Educational Review, 22,* 26–37.

Halliday, M. A. K., & Hasan, R. (1976). *Cohesion in English.* London: Longman.

Hartup, W. (1983). Peer relations. In E. M. Hetherington (Ed.), *Manual of child psychology* (Vol. 4; pp. 103–196). New York: Wiley.

Hartup, W. (1996). The company they keep. *Child Development, 67,* 1–13.

Heath, S. B. (1982). What no bedtime story means: Narrative skills at home and school. *Language in Society, 11,* 49–76.

Hinde, R. (1980). *Ethology.* London: Fontana.

Howes, C. (1992). *The collaborative construction of play.* Albany, NY: State University of New York Press.

Kramer, T., Bukowski, W., & Garvey, C. (1989). The indulgence of the dyadic context on the conversational and linguistic behavior of its members. *Merrill Palmer Quarterly, 35,* 327–341.

Lewis, C. (2001). *Literacy practices as social acts: Power, status, and cultural norms in the classroom.* Mahwah, NJ: Lawrence Erlbaum Associates.

Minuchin, P., & Shapiro, E. (1983). The school as a context for social development. In E. M. Hetherington (Ed.), *Manual of child psychology* (Vol. 4; pp. 197–274). New York: Wiley.

Morrow, L., & Rand, M. (1991). Preparing the classroom environment to promote literacy during play. In J. Christie (Ed.), *Play and early literacy development* (pp. 141–166). Albany, NY: State University of New York Press.

Neuman, S., & Roskos, K. (1991). The influence of literacy enriched play centers on preschoolers conceptions of the function of print. In J. Christie

(Ed.), *Play and early literacy development* (pp. 167–188). Albany, NY: State University of New York Press.

Olson, D. (1977). From utterance to text. *Harvard Educational Review, 47,* 257–281.

O'Neill, C. (1989). Dialogue and drama: The transformation of events, ideas, and teachers. *Language Arts, 66,* 147–159.

Pellegrini, A. D. (1982). The construction of cohesive text by preschoolers in two play contexts. *Discourse Processes, 5,* 101–108.

Pellegrini, A. D. (1984). The effects of exploration and play on young children's associative fluency. In T. D. Yawkey & A. D. Pellegrini (Eds.), *Child's play: Developmental and applied* (pp. 237–254). Norwood, NJ: Ablex.

Pellegrini, A. D. (1985a). The relations between symbolic play and literate behavior. *Review of Educational Research, 55,* 107–121.

Pellegrini, A. D. (1985b). Relations between preschool children's symbolic play and literate behavior. In L. Galda & A. D. Pellegrini (Eds.), *Play, language and stories* (pp. 79–98). Norwood, NJ: Ablex.

Pellegrini, A. D. (1986). Play centers and the production of imaginative language. *Discourse Processes, 9,* 115–125.

Pellegrini, A. D. (2001). Two social contextual routes to the development of school-based literacy. In S. Neuman & D. Dickinson (Eds.) *Handbook on research in early literacy for the 21st century.* New York: Guilford.

Pellegrini, A. D., & Boyd, B. (1993). The role of play in early childhood development and education: Issues of definition and function. In B. Spodek (Ed.), *Handbook of research on the education of young children* (pp. 105–121). New York: Macmillan.

Pellegrini, A. D., & Galda, L. (1982). The effects of thematic fantasy play training on the development of children's story comprehension. *American Educational Research Journal, 19,* 443–452.

Pellegrini, A. D., & Galda, L. (1988). The effects of age and context on children's use of narrative language. *Research in the Teaching of English, 22,* 183–195.

Pellegrini, A. D., & Galda, L. (1993). Ten years after: A reexamination of symbolic play and literacy research. *Reading Research Quarterly, 28,* 163–175.

Pellegrini, A. D., & Galda, L. (2001). I'm so glad, I'm glad, I'm glad: The role of emotions and close relationships in children's play and narrative language. In A. Goncu & E. Klein (Eds.), *Young children in play, story, and school: Essays in honor of Greta Fein.* New York: Guilford.

Piaget, J. (1983). Piaget's theory. In W. Kessen (Ed.), *Manual of child psychology* (Vol. 1; pp. 103–128). New York: Wiley.

Rubin, K., Fein, G., & Vandenberg, B. (1983). Children's play. In E. M. Hetherington (Ed.) *Manual of child psychology (Vol 4*; pp. 693–774). New York: Wiley.

Sachs, J., Goldman, J., & Chaille, C. (1985). Narratives in preschoolers' sociodramatic play: The role of knowledge and communicative competence. In L. Galda & A.D. Pellegrini (Eds.), *Play, language, and stories: The development of children's literate behavior* (pp. 45–61). Norwood, NJ: Ablex.

Saltz, E., Dixon, D., & Johnson, J. (1977). Training disadvantaged preschoolers on various fantasy activities: Effects on cognitive functioning and impulse control. *Child Development, 48,* 367–380.

Sawyer, R. K. (1997). *Pretend play as improvisation: Conversation in the preschool classroom.* Norwood, NJ: Lawrence Erlbaum Associates.

Sawyer, R. K. (2002). Improvisation and narrative. *Narrative Inquiry, 12,* 319–349.

Scarlett, W. G., & Wolf, D. (1979). Crossing over: The construction of boundaries between fantasy and reality. In E. Winner & H. Gardner (Eds.), *Fact, fiction, and fantasy.* New directions for child development *6,* 29–40.

Smilansky, S. (1968). *The effects of sociodramatic play on disadvantaged preschool children.* New York: John Wiley.

Smith, P. K. (1982). Does play matter? Functional and evolutionary aspects of animal and human play. *The Behavioral and Brain Sciences, 5,* 517–523.

Snow, C. (1983). Literacy and language: Relationships during the preschool years. *Harvard Educational Review, 83,* 165–189.

Tudge, J., & Rogoff, B. (1989). Peer influences on cognitive development. In M. Bornstein & J. Bruner (Eds.), *Interaction in human development* (pp. 17–40). Hillsdale, NJ: Erlbaum.

Verriour, P. (1985). Face to face: Negotiating meaning through drama. *Theory into Practice, 24,* 181–186.

Vukelvich, C. (1991). Materials and modeling: Promoting literacy during play. In J. Christie (Ed.), *Play and early literacy development* (pp. 215–231). Albany: Satte University of New York Press.

Vygotsky, L. S. (1978). *Mind in society.* Cambridge, MA: Harvard University Press.

Wachs, T. (1990). Must the physical environment be mediated by the social environment in order to influence development? *Journal of Applied Developmental Psychology, 11,* 163–178.

Wagner, B. (1992). Imaginative expression. In J. Jensen, J. Flood, D. Lapp (Eds.), *Handbook of research on teaching the English language arts* (pp. 787–804). New York: Macmillan

Wolf, D., & Grollman, S. (1982). Ways of playing. In D. Pepler & K. Rubin (Eds.). *The play of children.* Basel, Switzerland: Karger.

Wolf, D., & Pusch, J. (1985). The origins of autonomous texts in play boundaries. In L. Galda & A. D. Pellegrini (Eds.), *Play, language, and stories: The development of children's literate behavior* (pp. 63–77). Norwood, NJ: Ablex.

Wolf, S. A. (1994). Learning to act/acting to learn: Children as actors, characters, and critics in classroom theatre. *Research in the Teaching of English, 28,* 7–45.

Wolf, S. A., & Enciso, P. E. (1994). Multiple selves in literary interpretation: Engagement and the language of drama. In C. K. Kinzer, D. J. Leu (Eds.), *Multidimensional aspects of literacy research, theory, and practice* (forty-third yearbook) (pp. 351–360). Chicago: The National Reading Conference.

•46•

PLAYING WITH TEXTUAL TOYS: POPULAR CULTURE AND CHILDHOOD WRITING

Anne Haas Dyson

UNIVERSITY OF ILLINOIS AT URBANA-CHAMPAIGN

> The value of a new toy lies not in its material qualities (not "having things that buzz inside you and a stick-out handle,") the Skin Horse explains [to the Velveteen Rabbit], but rather in how the toy is used. . . . The Skin Horse emphasizes, not the deterioration of the original but rather the new meanings that get attached to it and the relationship into which it is inserted. (Jenkins, 1992, p. 50)

The cultural scholar Henry Jenkins uses material from a book media commercial product—*The Velveteen Rabbit* (Williams, 1975)—to help explain how *Star Trek* fans use material from a loved television series for social connection and symbolic activity. Fans talk about, enact, and recreate that old show, even merging bits of its symbolic stuff with other media fare. As the *Star Trek* shows fragment, get reworked, become almost unrecognizable, they grow in meaningfulness; that is, they become the "real" stuff of collective meaning-making—of popular culture.

In very similar ways, children, as active participants in popular culture, may treat the commercial media as a shared toy box; among its prized toys are communicative practices and their attendant forms, memorable characters, bits of dialogue, elements of plots, striking images, and appealing themes (Dyson, 2003a). Children transform these textual toys as they use them in their conversations, collaborative play, group singing, and, potentially, in forms of written participation in official classroom, and unofficial childhood, worlds. Indeed, across the globe, children and youth appropriate and transform commercial media to their local systems of symbolic meanings and social relations (Hall, 1981; Massey, 1998). In this way, they produce shared cultural practices and, thereby, friendships, expressive practices, and imaginative worlds (Dyson, 1993, 1997; Fisherkeller, 2002; Garvey, 1990; Jenkins, 1988; Newkirk, 2002; Opie & Opie, 1959).

In this chapter, I consider how young children's participation in popular culture may influence the nature and processes of learning to write. To begin, however, some terms and phrases must be defined. What is this "popular culture," which, in truth, is not so popular in school curricula? How is "writing" defined in studies informed by popular culture? After all, the commercial media themselves often intermingle sounds, images, movement . . . and very little written text if any.

Responses to the above questions provide a kind of foundational playground upon which to consider studies of child writers and their engagement with popular culture. In discussing that engagement, I emphasize the recontextualization processes through which children—even without any official encouragement—appropriate and transform "popular" materials into potential resources for learning to write. These processes are not idyllic, by any means. However, the social, symbolic, and, indeed ideological tensions that may arise are, potentially, productive of individual and classroom learning. I consider as well studies that describe children's responses to educators' efforts to incorporate aspects of popular culture into the writing curriculum; such incorporation raises its own instructional possibilities and challenges. Through the chapter as a whole, I aim to address yet another foundational question: What is the educational point of allowing children to bring those toys, those *popular* toys, into the classroom?

As is usual for me, I call on the children I have met in my own studies over the years to help me exemplify ideas. All of these studies have been in U.S. urban schools, serving economically limited households (i.e., families qualifying for the school lunch program) and societal groups traditionally not well served by our schools (i.e., "minority" children, herein, all African American in heritage, except for Ezekial, who was Mexican American). As I discuss in the closing section, it may be children so categorized for whom a theoretically informed consideration of popular culture and schooling is most critical.

PREPARING THE PLAYGROUND: THE CONCEPTUAL EQUIPMENT

The Nature of Popular Culture

In Fig. 46.1, 6-year-old Ezekial has drawn himself and his friend Joshua sitting on the couch playing a video game (note the *PS 2* [Play Station 2, a video-game console that works with a television set]). He's written what readers might assume is an actual plan for his friend to come to his house and play a game (*Spyro: Year of the Dragon* [2002]). The question to be raised is, What and where is "popular culture" in this piece?

The answer is not so straightforward. Popular culture is not a video game, a radio program, a movie (profitable or not), nor any other particular media text. It could not be so defined, in part simply because the cultural products deemed low or "popular" (and thus, distinguished from the elite or "high") have shifted over time; hence Dickens and Shakespeare are no longer "popular" (so to speak) but the stuff of high-school English classes (Levine, 1988). Indeed, fans of varied forms of commercial media themselves defy attempts to associate categories of cultural texts with categories of people (i.e., "the educated" versus "the masses" [Grossberg, 1997; Jenkins, McPherson, & Shattuc, 2002]; I myself would have finished this chapter more quickly if I could have resisted a television series [or two]).

Popular culture is also not a textual genre, like superhero comics, televised sports reports, or rap songs. If popular culture were, in fact, easily objectified and neatly contained, it would not pose such complex challenges for educators. Rather, curricular experts and instructional leaders could simply designate the acceptable forms of popular "culture" and the unacceptable ones. Although publishing a classroom newspaper or designing a quiz show (for social studies) might be deemed appropriate given particular learning objectives, reconstructing a "save-the-world" plot from a superhero cartoon or crafting a "hook" appropriate for a hip-hop CD would be less likely to be included on an objectives-based unit plan.

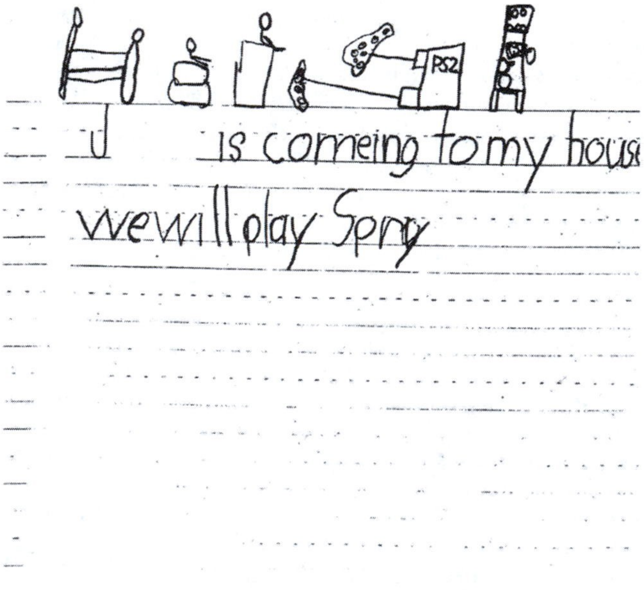

FIGURE 1. Ezekial and Joshua's planned get-together.

However, to revoice the teachings of the Skin Horse, the power of any such commercial material—its meaningfulness—does not come from the institution of schooling. People use the products of corporate culture—or whatever symbolic material is in hand—to produce meanings within their historical and sociopolitical contexts; those meaning-making practices produce the popular culture of everyday life (for a review of this cultural studies perspective, see Storey, 2001; for a discussion of the history of the concept of popular culture, see Jenkins, McPherson, & Shattuc, 2002).

Indeed, media figures (including those of canonical children's literature [Hade & Edmondson, 2003]) themselves defy containment, as they, and their plot lines, increasingly cross symbolic and technological lines (Kinder, 1991; Schlosser, 2002). Imagine the Velveteen Rabbit (already the subject of a made-for-television movie) hops from his book into a PBS cartoon series and onto a Web site, and then ventures into a video game, becomes a side kick of the Nursery Magic Fairy in a superhero cartoon, and, finally, an actual (if not yet "real") stuffed toy accompanying a McDonald's meal. Once acceptable in academic circles, as the rabbit hops about he becomes a more complex figure—less controlled by the school, more embedded in the global economy and more subject to corporate interests and, yet, also more accessible to children and more subject to them too (not every rabbit who hops into his own series becomes "real"—appropriated for use by the young).

In their own participation in popular culture as family members and playful peers, children both enjoy themselves and negotiate with the cultural storylines that "sell" well, so to speak, in our society (Dyson, 1997; Jenkins et al., 2002; Mitchell & Reid-Walsh, 2002). As such, commercial texts become deeply implicated in questions of identity, including those of gender, race, and class. They are the material stuff by which children and adults may situate themselves amongst others, conforming, mocking, resisting, or otherwise negotiating with available identities.

To return now to Ezekial's text and to his planned get-together with his friend Joshua, consider once again the location of popular culture. It does not reside in the appropriated commercial media, from which Ezekial took a label and a design. Rather, it is located in—or, more accurately, produced through—the meaning-making practices that allow Ezekial and Joshua a shared, interpreted world. During the daily writing time, the children sometimes coordinated their individual texts, as, in fact, Ezekial and Joshua had done on this day; through those coordinated texts, they planned imagined get-togethers (see Dyson, in press). Within this practice, a prime planned activity for the boys was playing video games. Boys could appropriate from a shared toy box of game names (even if they did not own the games, were not allowed to play a named game, had a dated console, or no console at all). Planning to get together to play video games was gendered—a cool thing for the guys to do (and something the girls never planned).

Thus, the children's plans for a fun time were influenced by the corporate media and, indeed, contextualized within the socioeconomic circumstances of their distressed community (heavily influenced by the city's deindustrialization [cf. Chin, 2001]). At the same time, the children used their media appropriations to go beyond their present circumstances as small children with limited power over time, space, and money. Through their contextualized use of media materials, they participated in the production of popular culture and, thereby, in their identities as friends and boys (not to mention as students doing their "work").

In related ways, media materials—the stuff of cartoons, superhero movies, music, sports shows, and on and on—become all wrapped up with children's sense of themselves and others. It is not so easy to keep commercial media out of the classroom without keeping the children themselves out. It comes "in" in the imaginations, social sensibilities, and textual experiences of the students. In addition, because it is linked to production, to symbol making, it is not surprising that, in school, children's participation in popular culture becomes particularly visible and audible during writing time.

The Nature of Writing

Ezekial's production in Fig. 46.2 mediated another "planning-a-get-together" event between himself and Joshua. In this event, Ezekial entered the video screen itself, becoming a player in an invented football video game (note the goal posts labeled "Lions," the region's professional football team). For the bulk of this long, complex event, Ezekial talked, dramatized, and drew an unfolding scene; at one point, he transformed himself and Joshua from playful opponents (their usual roles in planned get-togethers) to male teammates, as his female classmates took (a unisex, stick shape) on his screen.

"It's the girls versus the boys," Ezekial told a curious Joshua, as the video display seemed to transition to the school playground, where girls-versus-boys games were burgeoning. In the on-screen play, the boys were more than holding their own. Ezekial escaped his peer Janette's tackle (I wasn't to tell Janette this, Ezekial told me), and the final score was the boys 106, the girls 0.

FIGURE 2. Ezekial's imagined (and re-imagined) game for a planned get-together.

When Ezekial turned to his letter graphics, though, he was guided by the textual routines of the unofficial or child-governed getting-together practice. Joshua was coming to his house to play a video game; the boys would be friendly competitors. Ezekial originally wrote the boys' final score as "106 to 0," consistent with his narrated drawing. However, since such a trouncing was inconsistent with the way Ezekial and Joshua regularly imagined their play, I asked Ezekial if this indeed was the score for his game with Joshua. Ezekial hesitated and then revised the score to "106 to 105," commenting, "I'm right behind him one point."

The question to be raised here is, given Ezekial's actions and reactions, what is the nature of his writing? Does it involve written words alone? Does it incorporate images? Narrated action? Spoken words? Moreover, how many "texts" has Ezekial produced? One? More?

To begin with the question of writing, children's appropriation and use of shared media toys suggests, first, a conception of writing as rewriting. That is, writing involves crafting already circulating words and images. This notion of writing is most fully articulated by the language philosopher Bakhtin (1981, 1986); for this reason, his "dialogic" theory has been important to the study of popular culture. Jenkins and his colleagues explained,

> We can write only through borrowed terms . All acts of writing, Bakhtin argues, bear the traces of the previous contexts in which our words and images have circulated [i.e., have become "real"]. The writer struggles to inflect the meaning of these pre-circulated materials, to shape the ways they are understood by viewers. (Jenkins, McPherson, & Shattuc, 2002, p. 161)

Authors must use words and images in ways that are recognizable to their addressees, or they will not be able to communicate with them. At the same time, in order to invest their own intentions into those symbols, authors have to adapt, resist, or stretch them to make them do their will.

Second, even if the meaning of writing is confined to the social and representational use of print (see also Kress, 2003; Newkirk, 2002), child writers' participation in popular culture links their writing to multiple channels of communication. In composing their own texts (i.e., their own configurations of signs), be they multimodal productions or purely print, children appropriate discursive material from the varied voices of their everyday lives. Ways of telling stories and enacting dramas, of participating in sport and game, of reporting local and national news, of advertising products and services, of celebrating, communicating, or praying through song—all are kinds of voices enacted through different technologies (e.g., video, radio, animation), using different kinds of symbol systems (e.g., written language, drawing, music), and implicating different ideologies about how the world works (e.g., about what is a "good" story, a "worthwhile" use of one's time, an "appropriate" way to play). To produce their own texts, composers transform the symbolic stuff of these voices for their own communicative ends.

To return now to Ezekial's event, he made ample use of the cultural stuff of sports and video games. They provided the names of teams, roles, actions, and goals—the substance of plots (e.g., in his talk and drawing he identified "defenders," "runners," and escapes from "tacklers," and, of course, "goal posts" and "scoreboards"). Within that cultural material, he also found social roles (teammates, opponents), interpretive common ground with peers, and a sense of male affiliation. Like others in the class, Ezekial used this material to forge classroom relationships and (with a conversational nudge from me) even revised imagined scores to fit relational conditions.

Still, the multimodal text—drawn, enacted, and minimally written—on the top of Ezekial's page seemed disjointed, rather than blended with, the written one on the bottom. Ezekial was a just-beginning writer, benefiting from interactional support to orchestrate his diverse modes. Nonetheless, he was sensitive to the delicacy of his position, given his friend Janette and the nature of the "secret" game on the top of his page.

In sum, understanding popular culture and child composing entails, in part, a perspective on writing as rewriting, as appropriating and adapting representational materials to the social demands of the present encounter. Moreover, writing itself must be understood in relationship to other channels of communication.

These concepts, then, are the foundation for this consideration of "popular culture" and childhood "writing." In the sections ahead, I discuss research both on children's self-initiated use of the stuff of popular culture during school writing activities and on curricular efforts to channel that use. In the process, I consider the political and pedagogical dilemmas revealed by this research, dilemmas posed by the official use of material so intimately connected with children's sense of power and pleasure.

LEARNING TO WRITE IN SCHOOL: THE INTERPLAY OF THE ACADEMIC AND THE POPULAR

Children's use of cultural material (e.g., characters, plots, themes) from the popular media is not uncommon during daily writing periods, a mainstay of writing curricula. During this time, children have a relatively open-ended assignment, a stretch of time and material space (e.g., an empty paper, marking implements), and the companionship of peers.

My own research in popular culture originated in these rather mundane school contexts, which children themselves infused with unexpected cultural material—those textual toys. Through a series of ethnographic studies of childhood peer groups within urban primary schools, I have examined official school writing activities from the perspective of unofficial childhood practices (e.g., Dyson, 1989, 1993, 1997, 2003a). The work has yielded a conceptualization of young children's composing as, at least potentially, shaped by this interplay of unofficial practices, like Ezekial's planning of get-togethers, and official ones, like the daily composing practices.

Children may initially rely on drawing and talking to mediate the bulk of their communicative efforts, and that symbolic and intentional activity may be organized primarily by familiar childhood play practices and their symbolic stuff (including their popular toys). As children begin to take control of the written medium, these unofficial frames may guide children's writing decisions. In recontextualizing the stuff of unofficial childhood play into official composing times, children potentially cross borders of symbolic media, social expectations, and governing ideologies. The particular nature of these border-crossing challenges depends on the symbolic and social resources, and demands, of the practices from which material is being appropriated and the ones in which it is being recontextualized.

For example, given an educational goal of a written text, any images child writers appropriate from an audiovisual source must be translated, at least in part, to linear graphics of pencil-formed written symbols (Dyson, 1989); any social expectations for, let us say, "fun" superhero play with peers during recess (e.g., good guys and bad guys chasing each other wildly about) may prove "boring" in written form and lacking in character motivation or plot detail; even the goodness of "good guys" and their actions may be deemed bad or "violent" by members of the official classroom audience (which may include children with no interest in such play [Dyson, 1997]). Through experiencing the sort of tensions engendered by recontextualization, children may learn about the symbolic, social, and ideological "options, limits, and blends" of practices (Miller & Goodnow, 1995, p. 12), which is one way to envision literacy development within a sociocultural frame (Dyson, 2003a).

These tensions are most salient when children are deliberately orchestrating multiple modes (e.g., talk, drawing, and writing) within a familiar practice; such practices might include composing a picture book (allowing a narrative interrelationship between images and print), writing and directing a play (allowing the incorporation of "animated" characters and their actions), or producing a comic (allowing verbal dialogue to enter the spatial relations of a visual display).

Sampling a Popular Production

Consider, for example, the remarkable singing fish (see Fig. 46.3), a production of 6-year-old Jameel, who lived in a shelter in a dense urban area. (Jameel was a focal child in Dyson [1993]—a study of the ways children used writing to manage their relationships with other children.) Jameel's approach to the daily composing time was primarily as a performer, as someone whose goal was to entertain an audience—a goal in some tension with the classic "workshop" practice of sharing work with colleagues who ask questions seeking clarity (Graves, 1983/2003). Jameel frequently appropriated material from out-of-school cartoons; those cartoons, and their graphic ver-

FIGURE 3. Jameel's singing fish.

sion (the comics), provided a visual frame for the production of a fish singing an original song. Jameel's piece had designated "parts," but it was a coherent hybrid—a multivoiced text.

The representation of the singing fish was itself a visual pun, merging cartoon dialogue bubbles and drawn air bubbles for a fish. That fish was given to the crooning of Jameel's favorite music (R & B love songs) and to the operatic singing ("me me me") of cartoon fame—and of the children's surreptitious and silly singing during morning song routines. Underneath the singing fish, on a stapled-on paper strip, were the words of an announcer who would take the singing fish to the streets (the stapled strip was actually a "pocket" for the money donations that would surely follow). The text as a whole was performed for his first-grade class, who sat mesmerized as Jameel switched voices from a crooning fish to a fast-talking salesman; they clapped heartily and then many wrote their own "me-me-me" songs. His teacher, impressed too, invited a music composer to talk with the class about writing music, and also had the children search their library for storybooks that included written songs.

Jameel had differentiated, appropriated, and recontextualized from a diversity of typified voices (e.g., cartoon opera stars, misbehaving children, televised salespeople, comic characters, street performers, and radio crooners). The very fact that Jameel's classmates found his "singing fish" both admirable and amusing suggests that they recognized the voices he had appropriated; their recognition contributed, not only to their collective pleasure, but also to a social connection that generated an emerging practice (of peer composed "me me me" songs) and even permeated the official curriculum.

In composing his singing fish, Jameel had negotiated varied semiotic challenges, particularly those entailed in translating operatic singing to the visual display of a written page. Using the tools he controlled, he adapted punctuation marks, which, along with repetition, infused a sense of rhythm and melody into his letters and words. For example, he placed periods after individual letters to indicate that the name of each should be sung; he repeated the words *I* and *you* to suggest that they stretched over time (although that use differed from his initial repetition—to a beat of 3—of the words *me, you,* and *my*).

This is but one example—and a particularly vivid one—of the semiotic and social work entailed in recontextualization processes (e.g., appropriation, translation across modes, reframing in new practices, and hybridization or merging of material from differing social spheres). These recontextualization processes are amenable to a diversity of official and unofficial practices and to a range of popular materials (e.g., sports media, radio singing, cartoon animation); such a child "sampling" and "remixing" of material should further the use of the written system in symbolically flexible and sociopolitically astute ways (Dyson, 2003a).

The examples throughout this chapter illustrate how children's experiences as participants in popular culture may yield substantial resources for their entry into the written language demands of school. However, that participation also poses challenges. As Marsh (in press) discussed in her interview study of preservice teachers in England, educators may prefer that children simply leave most popular toys at home.

Problematizing the Toy Box

If children's textual toy boxes were filled with the stuff of velveteen rabbits, sweet and lovable as they are, they would pose no problems in the classroom. However, the content of those toy boxes appeals to children, at least in part, for precisely the same reason it may disconcert some educators: it features dominant images and storylines about power, wealth, and beauty, which themselves are all tangled up with the complexities of age, gender, race, and class (Buckingham, 1993; Grace & Tobin, 1998; Newkirk, 2002; Willis, 1990). Out on the playground, children's play with identities is fluid, both assuming and mocking relationships of, for example, power or gender. However, in official spaces, children's texts may become fixed indicators of individuals' minds and souls, so to speak (Zumwalt, 1995).

Ultimately, teachers are responsible for classrooms in which children are not subject to material viewed as abusive or bigoted. At the very least, though, children's written texts about ideologically charged matters present opportunities to talk about the construction of represented worlds in ways that are at once pedagogical (i.e., about the construction of a textual world) and ideological (i.e., cognizant that words and represented worlds mean differently, dependent on one's position, power, and evaluative stance in the society).

Newkirk (2002) himself engaged in such discussions with about 100 intermediate-grade children attending five New Hampshire elementary schools. He focused on the children's talk about their written stories constructed from cinematic ones; he was particularly interested in boys' stories featuring what adults might deem "violence" but the children deemed "action," "excitement," or "suspense."

Generally, the children had genre-specific and nuanced views of violence and were able, at least in conversation, to link compositional decisions about violence to genre and audience. Indeed, their very terminology—"action," "suspense"—suggested that physical force must serve some narrative function. The children discussed the limits of violence in cinema and text—what was too graphic, too threatening—and how it was made safe, for example, by being clearly "fake" or mitigated with humor.

I observed a skilled classroom teacher guide her second and third graders through just these sorts of reflections in an ethnographic study focused on superhero play (Dyson, 1997). The key instructional tool used by the teacher was an Author's Theater—an option for sharing one's writing that involved the child author choosing peers to enact a written story. In making use of the textual toys of superhero media, children assumed (and assigned) identities within their written and enacted texts, and those identities revealed dominant ideological assumptions about relations between people (e.g., between males and females, between people of varied physical and societal powers, between people constructed as of different races). These assumptions reflected the immediate values and interests of some children—and antagonized others.

Perhaps because the classroom's children had strikingly diverse identities themselves (e.g., of gender, race, culture, class), the children's superhero productions elicited intense responses about how "fun," "fair," and "nice" each other's stories were. In her responses to these ideological conflicts surrounding Author's Theater, the teacher produced a larger, critical drama; its central theme was that there were social and ideological consequences to their authorial choices about "plot," "character," and "motivation," for example, and those consequences were central to written language use in the public of the classroom.

In the superheroes story, the children's unofficial participation in popular culture intersected the official curriculum, and, in the process, both the unofficial and official world were changed. In a sense, and to varying degrees, this is true of most teachers I have observed.

They have not taught popular culture, but they have made their curricula permeable by engaging with the textual toys the children have brought. Next, I turn to studies with more interventionist aims.

FINDING OLD TOYS IN NEW PLACES: "POPULAR" INTERVENTIONS

In language arts education, there has been an increased recognition of the centrality of media to childhood and youth identities and the changing nature of communicative practices (i.e., their multimodal nature and potential links to new media [e.g., Cope & Kalantzis, 2000; Fisher, 2005; Hull & Nelson, 2005; Kress, 2003; Marsh, 2005; Pahl, in press; Short, Schroeder, Kauffman, & Kaser, 2003]). Thus, there have been educational efforts to incorporate children's experiences with popular culture and new technological media into the formal school curriculum (as evidenced by the newly appearing chapter topics in this handbook).

Intervention efforts are often collaborations between classroom teachers and university-based researchers, who analytically describe "what happened" when the children responded to newly offered possibilities. The educational point of this work is, in general, to build on children's experiences with popular culture and, thereby, further their understanding of writing practices and multimodal texts (e.g., the narrative and expository structure of movies, Web pages, and more traditional picture books). The projects often include a critical dimension, in which children produce their own texts, at least in part, by mobilizing their localized knowledge and experience to write the world differently than do the commercial media themselves.

Popular culture, though, is "popular" because it is produced in the everyday meaning making of families, communities, and peer groups. Whatever their common sociocultural heritage, members draw in varied ways on diverse cultural systems, including those of the commercial media, to produce meaningful lives (Gonzalez, 2005). For example, family pleasures may include being sports fans or cooking aficionados (for which the television may be a major mediator of participation), following soap operas, singing along with radio stars, watching a favorite video, or playing video games (indeed, as in Ezekial's class, any games may themselves belong to "dad" or older brothers).

Such pleasures may enact varied cultural memberships and entail diverse languages and, even, different written language scripts (Comber & Nixon, 2004; Kenner, 2000, 2005; Mercado, 2005; Pahl, in press; Seiter, 2005). The particular cultural materials may be passing fads but also may be linked to longstanding family or community interests. An understanding of the role of the media in children's lives out of school is thus critically important, as illustrated by Seiter. She organized a school-university sponsored computer journalism class for 8–12-year-olds; her goals included: using children's experience with popular culture as a basis for their engagement with writing and talk about community issues; allowing low-income children access to, and support in the savvy use of, the Internet (more "mall than library" given its ads and its appealing distractions [Seiter, p. 38]). She had some notable successes; for example, the boys' intense interest in video games—and their frustration at the costs involved—fueled an investigation of the business of video gaming. The boys used a social-class discourse to compose a detailed critique of the local manifestations (i.e., the prices at stores) of the planned obsolescence of expensive consoles.

However, Seiter had some challenges too, including the socioeconomic, cultural, and ideological gaps between the largely Mexican-heritage children at one site and the university students who helped teach the class. These conflicts were exemplified by a group of boys' interest in Worldwide Wrestling Entertainment (the WWE). That interest was an avenue for self-expression, group affiliation, and cultural identification, given its links to wrestling performance traditions in Mexico (and to their own fathers, who shared their interest). The WWE generated a rare discursive space in which the children talked about racial and ethnic typecasting in the media. The boys' eagerness to develop reports and examine sites on this topic was derailed by university students' own eagerness to "lead" the boys to understand the WWE as a "fake" sport inappropriate for children.

Thus, on the one hand, experience with popular culture may provide potentially rich "funds of knowledge" (Gonzalez, Moll, & Amanti, 2005)—and of textual toys—for children's entry into, and transformation of, school composing. On the other hand, within school curricula, popular pleasures (if they gain admittance at all) may mutate into "correct" forms of commercial texts or become fodder for official critiques and thereby no longer popular, so to speak (Luke, 1998). It is an educator's responsibility to widen children's literacy experiences and to deepen their critical response to represented worlds, but one cannot widen or deepen experiences denied classroom admission.

Linking Official and Unofficial Worlds Through Textual Toys

The following are illustrative projects that both allow children considerable agency for participation and control and, at the same time, guide children into a newly imagined writing curriculum. In other words, the projects work toward the interplay of official and unofficial (or nonacademic) worlds. Collectively, they portray the varied dimensions of such interplay, encompassing families, peers, and communities. (For extended discussions of popular culture and pedagogy, see Alverman, Moon, & Hagood, 1999; Evans, 2004, and Marsh & Millard, 2000).

Family connections. The rich array of potential linkages between families and schools is suggested by Kenner (2000, 2005). She collaborated with teachers in a South London nursery school to develop links between children's multilingual communities, their families, and their school-literacy learning. The parents were invited to bring to school texts in different languages that their children enjoyed. The material that they brought in captured the complex cultural and linguistic worlds of children in these globally mediated times: a Chinese cartoon, a Bollywood movie, a Thai karaoke video, newspapers in different languages, travel brochures, and materials linked to local and international sports teams and popular singers. On the initiative of varied classroom participants—children, parents, teachers—the materials gave rise to children's exploratory and collective writing of different languages and scripts and of varied multimodal texts (e.g., movie posters, travel brochures, newspapers).

To the extent that material was appropriated for talk and play, children's engagement with popular culture continued. At the same time, teachers and parents organized the environment, paid attention to children's efforts, and talked with them about symbolic and graphic features and about visual and textual design; in these ways, they helped children recontextualize the stuff of popular culture within explicitly instructional practices.

Peer relations. Popular culture sometimes evokes images of undifferentiated mass audiences, mesmerized by one media form or another, but this is not accurate. As already suggested, popular culture *is* culture, it's a part of the meaning-making practices of everyday life. Participation in ethnic cultures, for example, is linked to participation in popular cultures (Smitherman, 2000). Nonetheless, observant educators and researchers may be attuned to potential textual toys that, in the local setting, may intrigue children across linguistic and cultural boundaries (Hong & Genishi, 2005).

For example, Marsh (1999) has been particularly concerned about the ways in which young children's out-of-school literacy practices, often steeped in popular culture, have not been recognized as useful in early childhood curricula. She has designed varied projects to examine children's responses to such inclusion. In one such project in a linguistically, socio-economically, and ethnically diverse inner-city, she instigated a situational context that was ripe for primary grade children's dramatic and literate activity: a "Bat Cave." The teachers discussed with the children a wide range of writing practices that Batman and Batwoman might need, stressing that the two superheroes shared that cave.

In response, the children "clamor[ed] to enter [the cave] on first sight" (Marsh, 1999, p. 121); even those who had avoided writing took to that symbolic mode, among others, as they situated writing within the appropriated roles and discourse of gendered-but-active superheroes. The textual productions may not always have been extensive but they provided children opportunities to be, and to be seen by their peers as, writers, that is, to use the dramatic narratives of popular play to enact a diversity of literacy practices (e.g., maps, lists, reports, comics). Those productions also allowed teachers to observe child knowledge and skills on which they could explicitly build in other writing activities.

Community transformations. Finally, participation in popular culture through writing can be a site of participation and power and, thus, serve as an avenue of community transformation (Dolby, 2003). The very concept of popular culture, as discussed in this chapter, entails some notion of agency—of the appropriation and social use of available symbolic material (Willis, 1977, 1990). Even in the studies previously discussed, there was the potential for young children's popular rewriting to engender critical public discussions that themselves could fuel further rewriting (e.g., the gender and racial identity of superheroes and other popular figures were rendered open for discussion and rewriting [Dyson, 1997]; the entertainment business, particularly video-game production, gave rise to class-based critiques based on issues of access [Seiter, 2005]).

Future handbooks will be able to offer detailed analyses of the classroom dynamics, instructional challenges, and contextual conditions that influence localized efforts to further such critical and popular participation through writing. Still, the descriptive accounts of such efforts to date document pedagogical possibilities.

The accounts feature teachers familiar with the sociocultural nature of their school's neighborhoods and with the popular pleasures of their children. The teachers' stance might be described as one of critical alertness to the issues important to, or embedded in, children's lives. The "critical" aspect of the curriculum does not entail abandoning any mandated lessons, but it does require time and space for teacher agency. In a sense, teachers acknowledge, extend, and formalize children's common alertness to issues of what's "fair," "nice," or "bossy" (e.g., to quote Vasquez's [2004, p. 26] kindergarteners, "McDonalds and [media texts] can make you think their way"). Finally, the process of writing itself entails a critical reading, as it were, of media texts and then a rewriting, to include one's world.

A project described by Comber and Nixon (2004) is a suitable one with which to end this discussion, as it captures, in gentle detail, the interplay of official and unofficial lives. The writing project itself was situated in a larger curricular endeavor in an Australian classroom of culturally diverse 8–10 year olds. The children's teacher, Marg Wells, had been part of a collaborative effort to involve her students in an urban renewal project; as part of that work, the children had closely studied the places of their everyday lives and imagined the projects that would improve their economically stressed but richly diverse community.

The writing project of interest herein was inspired by an alphabet book, a book in which one does not expect to find narratives of community life. The picture book was about the places important to an Aboriginal child. The children collectively wrote their own alphabet book, to be shared in the community and with a partner school in South Africa. For our purposes here, what matters is the way in which popular culture was woven throughout the children's own narrated childhoods. The picture book itself is called A is for Arndale; Arndale is a shopping mall where the child author likes to look at CDs and puppies, among other pleasures. Children recount getting to go to McDonald's, waiting for the ice-cream van, and going to the movies (and having to be separated from a sibling so as to not fight over popcorn). In writing a picture book, the children in effect wrote an ethnography of everyday life, of the pleasures they had and too what they hoped for (e.g., quieter streets, more trees and flowers, better houses). Their popular pleasures were written into their detailed narratives of friendships, family, and community. They were integral to their childhoods, and this is why they could not be simplistically dismissed without dismissing children themselves.

MAKING SCHOOL "REAL"

Years ago, in the late seventies, I met 5-year-old Ashley, who could spell his name but mainly liked to make S's, the letter he shared with Superman. Legible S's and invented letters were written alongside (and on) his narrated and drawn adventures of Superman rescuing women, defying piranhas, and generally being quite heroic. For Ashley, the connection to letters, and to the textual production of stories, was mightily aided by Superman.

In the educational politics of current times, children who could be categorized as "poor," "minority," and/or "English-Language Learners"—including Ashley and all the children featured herein—are conceptualized as having no resources for literacy learning and, thus, needing a tightly scripted, linear march through basic skills (Dyson, 2003b). In this attempt to provide a solid foundation for "all" children, the actual foundation of many children is not used; that foundation is the experience they have manipulating symbolic material for social and representational purposes. And, as noted throughout this chapter, a significant proportion of that material is rooted in popular culture.

That material is not without troubling content (nor is the so-called cannon of children's literature, for that matter [Fox & Short, 2003]). However, for children, the material is "real" because it is subject (to at least some extent) to their own agency as they engage with others. It is, in this sense, material amenable to the recontextualization processes that are integral to learning to write.

The metaphor of "realness" has undergirded this chapter's consideration of popular culture and children's writing. This emphasis is compatible with new literacy studies (Street, 1993), in that it emphasizes the contextualized nature of literacy use. However, it also suggests that educators distinguish popular literacies from the related concept of new media literacies. The latter concept has arisen with the importance of new technologies in the changing capitalistic world, technologies differentially available to children, particularly given socioeconomic differences (Seiter, 2005). If popular culture enters into the hierarchical ordering of school knowledge, whose popular culture will that be and with what consequences? Will popular literacies most amenable to the school's use (like participating in electronic mail or contributing to interactive Web sites) become an assumed part of children's experience and, thus, an assumed resource for school learning? What would happen, then, to children without computers in the home, like Ezekial and his peers? Would the writing entailed in popular culture become a new way to identify lacks in those at risk, rather than new practices with which to engage children's agency and symbolic resources?

Children's intense engagement with popular culture in their everyday lives is a rich resource for their education as composers of multiple media, and writers of the written word And, in spite of, or maybe because of, the societal complexities popular culture brings into focus (e.g., authority, power, class, race), it is an essential resource if school itself is to stay real to young children in their present and allow them to assume agency in a rich diversity of practices in their unfolding futures.

AUTHOR'S NOTE

The ongoing project in Ezekial's classroom proceeds with the much appreciated support of the Spencer Foundation. The findings and opinions expressed are, of course, my sole responsibility . I thank my research assistant, Yanan Fan.

REFERENCES

Alvermann, D., Moon, J. S., & Hagood, M. C. (1999). *Popular culture in the classroom: Teaching and researching critical media literacy.* Newark, DE: International Reading Association.

Bakhtin, M. (1981). Discourse in the novel. In C. Emerson & M. Holquist (Eds.), *The dialogic imagination: Four essays by M. Bakhtin* (pp. 254–422). Austin: University of Texas Press.

Bakhtin, M. (1986). *Speech genres and other late essays.* Austin: University of Texas Press.

Buckingham, D. (1993). *Children talking television: The making of television literacy.* London: Falmer Press.

Chin, E. (2001). *Purchasing power: Black kids and American consumer culture.* Minneapolis: University of Minnesota Press.

Comber, B., & Nixon, H. (2004). Children reread and rewrite their local neighborhoods: Critical literacies and identity work. In J. Evans (Ed.), *Literacy moves on: Using popular culture, new technologies and critical literacy in the primary classroom* (pp. 115–133). London: Fulton.

Cope, B., & Kalantzis, M. (Eds.). (2000). *Multiliteracies: Literacy learning and the design of social futures.* London: Routledge.

Dolby, N. (2003). Popular culture and democratic practice. *Harvard Educational Review, 73*, 258–284.

Dyson, A. H. (1989). *Multiple worlds of child writers: Friends learning to write.* New York: Teachers College Press.

Dyson, A. H. (1993). *Social worlds of children learning to write in an urban primary school.* New York: Teachers College Press.

Dyson, A. H. (1997). *Writing superheroes: Contemporary childhood, popular culture, and classroom literacy.* New York: Teachers College Press.

Dyson, A. H. (2003a). *The brothers and sisters learn to write: Popular literacies in childhood and school cultures.* New York: Teachers College Press.

Dyson, A. H. (2003b). Popular literacies and the "all" children: Rethinking literacy development for contemporary childhoods. *Language Arts, 81*, 100–109.

Dyson, A. H. (in press). School literacy and the development of a child culture: Written remnants of the "gusto of life". In D. Thiessen & A. Cook-Sather (Eds.), *International handbook of student experience in elementary and secondary school.* Dordrecht, The Netherlands: Kluwer Academic Publishers.

Evans, J. (Ed.). (2004). *Literacy moves on: Using popular culture, new technologies and critical literacy in the primary classroom.* London: Fulton.

Fisher, M. (Ed.). (2005). Literocracy: A new way of thinking about literacy and democracy [Special issue]. *English Education, 37*, 91–164.

Fisherkeller, J. (2002). *Growing up with television: Everyday life among urban adolescents.* Philadelphia, PA: Temple University Press.

Fox, D., & Short , K. (Eds.). (2003). *Stories matter: The complexity of cultural authenticity in children's literature.* Urbana, IL: National Council of Teachers of English.

Garvey, C. (1990). *Play* (enl. ed.). Cambridge, MA: Harvard University Press.

Gonzalez, N. (2005). Beyond culture: The hybridity of funds of knowledge. In N. Gonzales, L. Moll, & C. Armanti (Eds.), *Funds of knowledge* (pp. 19–46). Mahwah, NJ: Erlbaum.

Gonzalez, N., Moll, L., & Amanti, C. (Eds.). (2005). *Funds of knowledge: Theorizing practices in households, communities, and classrooms.* Mahwah, NJ: Erlbaum.

Grace, D. J., & Tobin, J. (1998). Butt jokes and mean-teacher parodies: Video production in the elementary classroom. In D. Buckingham (Ed.), *Teaching popular culture: Beyond radical pedagogy* (pp. 42–62). London: University College London Press.

Graves, D. (2003/1983). *Writing: Teachers and children at work.* Exeter, NH: Heinemann.

Grossberg, L. (1997). *Dancing in spite of myself: Essays on popular culture.* Durham, NC: Duke University Press.

Hade, D., & Edmondson, J. (2003). Children's book publishing in neoliberal times. *Language Arts, 81*, 135–144.

Hall, S. (1981). Notes on deconstructing the popular. In R. Samuel (Ed.), *People's history and socialist theory* (pp. 227–239). London: Routledge & Kegan Paul.

Hong, M., & Genishi, C. (2005). Voices of English language learners. In L. D. Soto & B. B. Swadener (Eds.), *Power & voice in research with children* (pp. 165–176). New York: Peter Lang.

Hull, G. A., & Nelson, M. E. (2005). Locating the semiotic power of multimodality. *Written Communication, 22*, 224–261.

Jenkins, H. (1988). "Going Bonkers!": Children, play and Pee-wee. *Camera Obscura, 17*, 169–193.

Jenkins, H. (1992). *Textual poachers: Television fans and participatory culture.* New York: Routledge.

Jenkins, H., McPherson, T., & Shattuc, J. (2002). Defining popular culture. In H. Jenkins, T. McPherson, & J. Shattuc (Eds.), *Hop on Pop: The politics and pleasures of popular culture* (pp. 26–42). Durham, NC: Duke University.

Kenner, C. (2000). *Home pages: Literacy links for bilingual children.* Staffordshire, England: Trentham Books Limited.

Kenner, C. (2005). Bilingual children's uses of popular culture in text-making. In J. Marsh (Ed.), *Popular culture, new media, and digital literacy in early childhood* (pp. 73–88). London: Routledge.

Kinder, M. (1991). *Playing with power in movies: Television and video games from muppet babies to teenage mutant ninja turtles.* Berkeley: University of California Press.

Kress, G. (2003). *Literacy in the new media age.* London: Routledge.

Levine, L. (1988). *Highbrow/Lowbrow: The emergence of cultural hierarchy in America.* Cambridge, MA: Harvard University Press.

Luke, C. (1998). Pedagogy and authority: Lessons from feminist and cultural studies, postmodernism and feminist pedagogy. In D. Buckingham (Ed.), *Teaching popular culture: Beyond radical pedagogy* (pp. 18–41). London: University College London Press.

Marsh, J. (1999). Batman and Batwoman go to school: Popular culture in the literacy curriculum. *International Journal of Early Years Education, 7,* 117–131.

Marsh, J. (2005). Moving stories: Digital editing in the nursery. In J. Evans (Ed.), *Literacy moves on: Using popular culture, new technologies, and critical literacy in the primary classroom* (pp. 31–47). London: Fulton.

Marsh, J. (in press). Tightropes, tactics, and taboos: Pre-service teachers' beliefs and practices in relation to popular culture and literacy. In J. Marsh & E. Millard (Eds.), *Popular literacies, childhood, and schooling.* London: Routledge.

Marsh, J., & Millard, E. (2000). *Literacy and popular culture.* London: Sage.

Massey, D. (1998). The spatial construction of youth cultures. In T. Skelton & G. Valentine (Eds.), *Cool places: Geographies of youth cultures* (pp. 121–129). London: Routledge.

Mercado, C. I. (2005). Reflections on the study of households in New York City and Long Island: A different route, a common destination. In N. Gonzales, L. Moll, & C. Armanti (Eds.), *Funds of knowledge: Theorizing practices in households, communities, and classrooms* (pp. 233–256). Mahwah, NJ: Erlbaum.

Miller, P., & Goodnow, J. J. (1995). Cultural practices: Toward an integration of culture and development. In J. J. Goodnow, P. J. Miller, & F. Kessel (Eds.), *Cultural practices as contexts for development: No. 67. New directions in child development* (pp. 5–16). San Francisco: Jossey Bass.

Mitchell, C., & Reid-Walsh, J. (2002). *Researching children's popular culture: The cultural spaces of childhood.* London: Routledge.

Newkirk, T. (2002). *Misreading masculinity: Boys, literacy, and popular culture.* Portsmouth, NH: Heinemann.

Opie, I., & Opie, P. (1959). *The lore and language of school children.* London: Oxford University Press.

Pahl, K. (in press). Children's popular culture in the home: Tracing cultural practices in texts. In J. Marsh & E. Millard (Eds.), *Popular literacies, childhood, and schooling* (pp. 45–76). London: Routledge.

Schlosser, E. (2002). *Fast food nation.* New York: Houghton Mifflin.

Seiter, E. (2005). *The Internet playground: Children's access, entertainment, and mis-education.* New York: Peter Lang.

Short, K. G., Schroeder, J., Kauffman, G., & Kaser, S. (Eds.). (2003). *Language Arts: Popular Culture and Media Literacy* [Entire issue]. (Vol. 81).

Smitherman, G. (2000). *Talkin' that talk: Language, culture, and education in African America.* New York: Routledge.

Spyro: Year of the Dragon [PlayStation]. (2002). Sony Computer Entertainment.

Storey, J. (2001). *An introductory guide to cultural theory and popular culture* (3rd ed.). Essex: Pearson Education Limited.

Street, B. V. (Ed.). (1993). *Cross-cultural approaches to literacy.* Cambridge, U.K.: Cambridge University Press.

Vasquez, V. M. (2004). *Negotiating critical literacies with young children.* Mahwah, NJ: Erlbaum.

Williams, M. (1975). *The velveteen rabbit or how toys become real.* New York: Avon Books.

Willis, P. (1977). *Learning to labor: How working class kids get working class jobs.* London: Saxon House.

Willis, P. (1990). *Common culture: Symbolic work at play in the everyday culture of the young.* Boulder, CO: Westview Press.

Zumwalt, R. (1995). The complexity of children's folklore. In B. Sutton-Smith, J. Mechling, T. W. Johnson, & F. R. McMahon (Eds.), *Children's folklore: A source book* (pp. 23–47). New York: Garland Publishing.

•47•

PROMOTING SELF-KNOWLEDGE: ADOLESCENTS ENGAGED IN EDUCATING

Marino C. Alvarez
TENNESSEE STATE UNIVERSITY

Victoria J. Risko
VANDERBILT UNIVERSITY

Bobby and Addie wrote,

> "Abandon hope, all ye, who enter here." This quote by Dante was referring to the gates of Hell, but it also applies to entering the dark abyss of a black hole. The theory of black holes is one of the most mysterious and intriguing concepts in science. These monstrous anomalies are believed to have many terrifying qualities and are usually identified with science fiction and horror stories. A scientist's definition of a black hole is this: A black hole is a theoretical region of space with gravitational forces so strong that not even light can escape. Resulting from the collapse of a high-mass star, these astounding phenomena are believed to contain infinite mass and zero volume. This paper will explore the clues to a black hole's existence, its reactions with matter, and will end with a hypothetical journey into a black hole. Get ready for the ride of a lifetime! Saddle up; lock and load!

The quote above is taken from a peer collaborative writing of two students who have two goals for their writing: to explain what they are learning about "black holes" and to develop a narrative using their imaginations to communicate their interpretation of how "black holes" could affect life, such as the lives of two astronauts. In their paper, they explain scientific concepts they are learning in their high school astronomy class. These include *event horizon*, *gravitational lensing*, *x-ray radiation*, *gravitational redshift*, and the role of *tidal force* on the effect of matter. In the telling of their story, they coin a new term, *spaghettifcation,* to describe the effect of tidal forces on an astronaut, representing matter, as he enters a black hole (e.g., the astronaut is stretched into what looks like spaghetti). This writing activity, typical of activities within the Exploring Minds project, engages the students in self-directed learning projects and integrates the language arts curriculum with disciplines across the curriculum to foster application of content to new contexts (e.g., in their writing, Addie and Bobby are applying their newly acquired science learning to a plausible real life event).

In this chapter, we describe two projects: the Gallatin High School "To Kill A Mockingbird" project and the Exploring Minds project. In both projects, language arts and content disciplines are integrated and learning is supported with electronic tools. We present examples of students' learning and productions taken from over 15 years of research examining how adolescents directed their own learning within meaningful learning environments designed to promote curiosity and build self-knowledge. The Gallatin High School project portrays the use of self-directed case-based instruction and connections to students' societal curriculum skills while studying the novel *To Kill a Mockingbird* in a ninth grade English classroom. Emerging from that five-year project were instructional principles supported by theory and our observations of teaching practices that were applied for further examination in the Exploring Minds project.

The high school astronomy class, in which Addie and Bobby were members, is a hub for communication of ideas that are learned across the curriculum. It is one of several high school classes in four states participating in a scientific literacy educational project called Exploring Minds, funded partially by NASA Tennessee Space Grant Consortium, and the Center of Excellence in Information Systems, Tennessee State University (Alvarez, 1995). In these classrooms, students are reading multiple texts, including those accessed on the Internet; collaborating with two astronomers via automatic photoelectric telescopes to collect and analyze data; using electronic formats for note taking, journal writing, peer-collaborative compositions, threaded discussions about course content; and, using electronic tools, such as concept maps and interactive V diagrams, to make sense of their discoveries. Communication occurs within and beyond the physical classroom walls as students collaborate electronically with their peers—both local peers and those across sites—teachers, and scientists (e.g., University and NASA astronomers, mathematicians, and other community experts). Students' thinking *in process* and final writings and productions are shared on the Internet and at state, national, and international conference presentations

A theory of educating that is grounded in the belief that educating comes about through self-educating guides our research and curriculum development (see Gowin, 1981; Gowin & Alvarez, 2005). In this theory of educating, making sense of educative events is paramount. The teacher initiates the event; the materials (curriculum) are guides to the event; the students use their prior knowledge and world experience to take part in the event; the event has distinctive qualities governing it; and, the societal environment is an important consideration that encompasses the event. Educating is a process of deliberate intervention in the lives of students in order to *change* the meaning of experience, and begins in midstream of important events in their lives. The change educating makes empowers students to become self-educating; they learn to take charge of their own experience. Educating occurs when students grasp the meaning of the materials they are using and "get the point" of the facts and concepts that they are studying. Thus, the overarching goal of these projects is to facilitate students' self-knowledge building. Across the two projects, we identified and refined the following five instructional principles:

- Assemblage of relevant texts initiates the learning process.
- Critical and imaginative thinking enhances intellectual power of learning events.
- Posing and seeking answers to self-directed questions contribute to self-educating.
- Developing and using metacognitive tools for demonstrating how meaning is changed.
- Producing and voicing findings provide deliberate use of information and creative thought.

We elaborate on each by describing how they developed within the two projects. We then discuss the importance of educational questions and offer recommendations for implementation and for further investigations.

In the two projects described, student and teacher data were collected quantitatively and qualitatively to document characteristics of the learning environments in these two projects—both at the respective school sites and through virtual communication that engaged these students in their investigations.

Background

The educational aim of both the Gallatin High School and Exploring Minds projects is to involve students in meaningful and self-directed learning activities using a variety of methods and authentic problem situations and circumstances that meet the standards of the academies and promote critical and imaginative thinking, conceptual learning, and application of written discourse and scientific inquiry across disciplines using innovative technology.

The literacy and science strategies and skills needed to learn, make connections within and among disciplines, and communicate with others are vital to learners who are expected to achieve educational goals espoused by the academies (e.g., American Association for the Advancement of Science, 1989; International Reading Association, 1992; National Council of Teachers of Mathematics, 2000; National Science and Technology Council, 1995; Science Council of Canada, 1984; Royal Society, 1985). So, too, are the specific ways in which these learners use language and instructional tools, and technology for literacy learning and applying scientific and mathematical concepts (National Aeronautics and Space Administration, 1999–2003).

The goals shared by these academies are clear: *to promote a quality education plan that meets scientific, mathematical, literacy, and technology standards, by providing challenging opportunities for both teachers and students to think and construct knowledge generated in meaningful contexts.* For us, providing learning environments that take into account a theory of educating (Gowin, 1981; Gowin & Alvarez, 2005) that provide opportunities for students to "show" new meaning of experiences is crucial.

Researchers during the last decade in particular, have pushed for reforms in science education and the integration of interactive technologies within the science curriculum and across other disciplines. Project-based science learning that requires access to multiple sources of information via the Internet and use of multimedia to display projects has been highly successful in urban schools to enhance students' science learning and promoting equity among diverse learners (Hug, Krajcik, & Marx, 2005). Such projects are guided by funds of knowledge beliefs about learners (Hammond, 2001; Moll, 1997), models of teaching across the curriculum (Beane, 1991)) and coteaching, including the advantage of peers as coteachers (Tobin, Roth, & Zimmermann, 2001), and cultural views of learning that describe how taking on the practices of schooling or scientists or writers *produces* these attributes for learners engaged in such practices (Levinson & Holland, 1996). Students cross boundaries of identities as they begin to think and act like scientists, novelists, and so on (Buxton, Carlone, H. B., & Carlone, D., 2005).

Emphasizing the importance of self-directed learning projects that build on students' own questions and knowledge and apply to understanding world phenomenon is viewed by some researchers as the only tenable way to reform education within middle and high school classrooms (Penner, 2001; Roth & Barton, 2004). Norris and Philips (2003) described the learning espoused by the academies as "fundamental" where students are learning in and about science, as distinguished from, "derived" learning where students learn, understand, and apply overarching concepts to solve authentic problems in real-world settings. Tinker and Thornton (1992) described science not as a set of ideas to be learned but as a "process, a set of activities, a way of proceeding and thinking" (p. 155). The goal of this process, though, is not only to learn new facts or replace earlier naïve understandings of disciplinary content, but more importantly, to engage in activities that require examination and refinement of ideas (Penner, 2001; White & Frederiksen, 1998) and justifying explanations and arguments (Holland, 1998). Accessing information via the Internet and use of computer tools to represent knowledge can support students' exploration, productions, and evaluation of information. Students need to be able to find pertinent information that enhances their ability to construct new knowledge in the process (see Kuiper, Volman, & Terwel, 2005). Yet typical school science instruction is not *scientific literacy* at its best—dealing with uncertainties and questioning findings—but instead is impoverished when presented as a body of factual knowledge and unproblematic practices quite removed from students' lived experiences and events in their global world.

Both projects include aspects of project-based science learning; peers as coteachers; collaboration among educators, researchers, and peers; interactions with technology; and, learning practices associated with experts, authentic data collection, analysis, and representation of findings. Grounded in a sound theory of educating (see Gowin, 1981; Gowin & Alvarez, 2005) and multiple forms of data (e.g., students' writings, analyses and representations of variable star data, etc.), we have traced specific changes in expectations for living. At first students mistakenly believe that success in school is equated with "knowing" a given body of knowledge of a subject based on "right" answers, and then come to believe that "learning" how new knowledge can be related to their experiences and other subject disciplines both in and out of school is more meaningful and enduring—even more interesting.

GALLATIN HIGH SCHOOL INTERDISCIPLINARY PROJECT

Gallatin High School is located in a rural community where industry and agriculture (e.g., dairy and tobacco farming) are the primary sources of revenue. A needs assessment conducted by the principal and faculty of this high school initiated this project and identified a recommendation to improve students' critical thinking and writing skills. An overview of this experimental case-based instruction investigation and observations relevant to this initial six-week interdisciplinary project with ninth grade students are reported to describe how case-based instruction can be implemented and used to activate and refine existing knowledge and build new knowledge (Alvarez, 1993; Alvarez, Binkley, et al., 1991).

The context of the literature unit, *To Kill a Mockingbird* (Lee, 1960), served as the anchor upon which the cases were written. A flyer requesting donations or loans of various categorized memorabilia that related to the time period of the story (e.g., music, architecture, history, photographs, publications, fashions, etc.) was devised by the English teachers and librarians and circulated to faculty members and to the local newspaper that invited these items to be included as part of the case information. After receiving a variety of items, students sorted these materials according to style and format advocated by Newmann and Oliver (1967): journalistic-historical narratives, documents, research data, interpretive essay, oral statements, story, vignette, and text. Students added four additional categories: oral history (video tapes of invited speakers from the community), visuals and illustrations, propaganda, and recordings.

Cases were developed to help students reason about multiple major concepts expressed in the novel and to help students apply these concepts to other contexts and subject areas. Each case (a) identified a major text concept (e.g., a jury of peers) which was examined within the context of the narrative, and (b) contained a problem situation that required students to analyze this concept according to a different perspective or within a different situation (e.g., the analysis of a peer jury's verdict in a more recent court case to decide whether the verdict compromised the role and function of the court). Each case required students to apply information to authentic problem situations that required students to think critically for obtaining a plausible and defensible resolution.

The case method of teaching used in this project differs from whole class deliberations that involve a discussion of the same concept by all class members. Instead, students individually selected one case from an array of cases that appealed to their interest. Each case was unique because different reading, research, and writing skills were needed to problem solve and complete the task of the particular case. For example, some cases asked students to keep a written journal of their thoughts in working out the case problem, list sources consulted and materials referenced, make hierarchical concept maps as their case progressed, and then write a report containing illustrations, maps, mathematical principles and examples to support their position. Other cases required students to present a portion of their findings in a videotape. This required them to write and act out the script for the videotape that they produced and edited. These cases allowed students to bridge the gap of the happenings in the 1930s by comparing and contrasting these events to the present. All students were required to write a final report of their findings. Students' performance was evaluated on their ability to analyze various positions, take a stance and to justify it rationally. Students engaged in group and class discussions as they studied their respective cases. For example, students who had selected the same case formed groups, consulted with each other as they gathered information, and discussed their approaches and resources. Class discussions of the novel gave students the opportunity to share what they were investigating as they pertained to the structural elements (e.g., setting, plot, characters, and theme) of the novel. These discussions raised questions that encouraged students to seek additional information in reaching a resolution to their case of inquiry.

Faculty members from other subject areas served as resource persons for these students in this interdisciplinary project as they investigated their cases. Some teachers included the historical context and themes of the novel into their subject area. For example, the art teacher discussed the artists and their paintings of the 1930s. From these discussions, the geometry teacher was asked to use a painting of Picasso, *Guernica* (1937), from which she made photocopies for her ninth-grade students and devised mathematical problems that could be discerned from the painting. The librarians played a crucial role in this undertaking by teaching library/research skills, gathering research materials, co-ordinating interdisciplinary studies (e.g., communicating with all teachers concerning materials available, working with interested teachers concerning interdisciplinary units), and archiving materials (videotapes were made of teachers and students collaborating with these cases using concept maps, thematic organizers, etc., oral histories of invited community members who gave testimony of the conditions of the community during the 1930s, artifacts—paintings, letters, pictures, etc. of this historical period). The societal curriculum was evident in these archived materials.

For example, students used interview techniques explained and shown to them by a TV news anchor who was invited to their class by conducting video histories through interviews with a lawyer who talked about the court proceedings affecting the character Tom Robinson, an African American teacher in the then segregated Union High School which later integrated with Gallatin High School and who later became an administer at this school, and an African American woman, who was student at the time of this integration process. These archives were housed in a special collection of the library holdings for faculty, students, and interested personnel to review.

Self-selected cases served to activate and expand their knowledge using thematically organized and cross-disciplinary cases and facilitated students' abilities to generate explanations for new information that were plausible and meaningful. In working through these cases, students were given opportunities to demonstrate the variety of abilities and interests they possessed by revealing in-school and out-of-school knowledge. Students were most articulate when they were confronted with meaningful tasks that required thinking and active participation in situations that: (a) incorporated knowledge from other disciplines and contexts, (b) were relevant to the experiences of their community; and, (c) allowed them to formulate and pursue their own interests to the related topics; thereby, allowing them to create their own learning contexts. Examples of some of these cases included the Fishing Boat case, where students designed and built model boats, calculated weights and floatation based on Archimedes Principle, and compared prices of the building materials of the 1930s to current prices; the Uncle Finch case where students determined routes and constructed a map that Uncle Finch would have taken from Nashville, Tennessee to Macomb, Alabama and calculated the mileage costs of fuel used in the mileage of this route; the Jury of Peers case where students compared the court case of Tom Robinson and the social climate of the 1930s that prevailed to those that have been decided in the 1990s; and, the Dixie Howell: Fact or Fiction case that students searched to find if Howell was a real person, and if so, why Harper Lee mentioned him in the novel. This case led to students making videos based on an event in his football career and writing papers of their interpretations based on his football accomplishments.

The teacher and her students became active participants in the learning process by creating an environment that was mutually adaptable rather than one that was arbitrary and teacher dominated. Genuine questions were raised without preconceived answers. These kinds of questions were asked by both the teacher and students not to seek right answers, but to gather information or clarify ambiguities. Concepts identified in the novel were used to construct questions about pertinent ideas with other related contexts that included their personal life and community. Self-selected cases allowed students to proceed on their own individual path and reduced their chances to fail. During this six-week project, time was not imposed by fractured units (all students on a given page, completing the same exercises), but on personal time schedules driven by curiosity and interest.

Evident in these self-selected case findings were that students assembled information that pertained to the case they selected and became involved in determining which materials were relevant and pertinent to their case and which materials were to be discarded. Students thought about the events being portrayed in the novel with the case they had selected and made connections by thinking about how these circumstances could be made compatible through reasonable interpretations of documents and applications to life experiences. The learning process was initiated by selecting their own case for study, posing, and seeking answers to their own questions. While the teacher facilitated the process, the student chose pathways to resolving the selected case. During this excursion, it was the student who took charge of their own learning and became self-educated in the end product. Our findings indicated that authentic cases seem to spur curiosity and invite students to initiate critical thinking. Case-based instruction and learning provide students with a forum by which to take an active role in structuring and creating their own meaning. Students were presented with a thematic organizer developed by the teacher to aid them in activating their schema with target concepts of the novel and their own life experiences. Another metacognitive tool was the development of hierarchical concept maps that students created and shared with each other and the teacher. Finally, each student produced a paper that gave a voice to their thoughts and feelings about an event of the novel, and their individual perceptions of its context.

EXPLORING MINDS NETWORK

Like the Gallatin High School (GHS) project, the primary goal of the Exploring Minds educational project is to involve teachers and their students in interdisciplinary study that is grounded in literacy and communication activity (Alvarez, 2001a, 2001b, 1995, 1996; Alvarez & Rodriguez, 1995). Students are engaged in problem-solving inquiries that involve authentic tasks, such as collaborating with their teachers and peers, university educators and scientists and NASA astronomers to analyze star data or water levels on Mars. Like the GHS Project, students pursue individual paths guided by their own questions that actively engage them in writing and reflecting on ideas gathered from conversations and readings (electronic and conventionally). Our quest in this project was to document systematically instructional characteristics that enabled self-knowledge production. Schools that participated in this project are located in inner city (e.g., Nashville, Tennessee, New York City, and Columbus, Ohio) and suburban environments (e.g., Alexandria, Virginia).

Exploring minds network. Exploring Minds (http://exploringminds.tsuniv.edu) is an interactive electronic password protected network that was developed for the project to facilitate communication and language activities among teachers, professors, researchers, and students (Alvarez, 1997). This network has the usual management functions, but is unique in that it contains several interactive metacognitive tools for posting notebook entries, constructing hierarchical concept maps and V diagrams, and contains an electronic version of the Cornell note taking procedure. Physical spaces, referred to as the teacher library and the teacher/student study are present for teachers and students to assemble or store information in a variety of electronic formats, such as video clips, musical renditions, art work, works in progress, primary documents, relevant articles, and so forth.

Promoting Self-Knowledge: The Goal of Educating Is Self-Educating

Again, our guiding premise for these projects is the belief that self-knowledge comes about from our own individual experiences and the experiences that we glean from others. During this process, ideas are shared and meaning is negotiated in ways that go beyond simple listings or incoherent thoughts. Instead, ideas are critically scrutinized for value and educational significance. The meaning that is transacted in the process involves the receptive acts of reading and listening and the expressive acts of writing and speaking. Within this process, language is not free of ambiguity. Language is *alive*, ever changing, as one becomes more precise or more elaborative as the human mind manipulates and explores the ambiguities that lie in every general idea and in every word; such scrutiny prevents the closure of ideas and fosters critical and imaginative thinking.

Promoting scrutiny of ideas for mindful learning lies at the heart of the Exploring Minds project signaling a *process* where meaning is given to outcomes rather than as a means of achieving desired outcomes. Being mindful requires us to be more observant, to evaluate, to ask more questions, to take into consideration the context in which events take place, and to be more cognizant of knowledge as assertions rather than knowledge as absolutes. As part of this mindful learning process, we describe a couple of instances that indicate how students advance their own knowledge with a topic of study by the processes of assemblage, critical and imaginative thinking, posing and seeking answers to their own questions, use of metacognitive tools to monitor their understanding, and producing and voicing their findings.

Assemblage: Initiates Learning

Assemblage, as a concept, is a vital part of the educating process. It takes place as learning begins and consists of exploring ways of thinking about novel content without abandoning one's own experiences and knowledge in the process (Whitehead, 1938). Within a language arts curriculum, assemblage requires a gathering of multilevel written materials, documents, video, musical renditions, and so forth predicated on personal knowledge and world experience rather than following a prescribed set of procedural steps devised by others when asking questions, solving problems, and delving into inquiry. Students choose materials that are of interest, or are determined by them, as being relevant. Choice of materials affords students the opportunity to plan their own path of inquiry.

The process of assemblage, because it is not prescribed ahead of time, is not an easy task. Teachers must facilitate the process by asking guiding questions that foster an identification of clear goals that match to appropriate materials, and they should help students make connections across resources that may initially appear to be disparate. When Bobby H and Addie G began their project, they had difficulty gathering relevant sources for their topic on "black holes" (Alvarez, Burks, King, Hulan, & Graham, 2000). This resulted in two problems requiring mediation by Terry King, their teacher, and Dr. Geoff Burks, a university astronomer. One immediate barrier was the fact that their learned concept of *black holes* did not have a straightforward definition: a practice that is common in science texts that serve to promote conceptual ambiguity rather than clarity. As Bobby and Addie began gathering materials and reading about the topic, the more overwhelmed they became due to the conceptual density of the text writings. Dr. Burks commented that these two students "seem to have been frustrated that they could not understand everything in the sources" they gathered. Although they assembled books containing more and more information about their topic, the books varied in conceptual difficulty and posed barriers to establishing a clear path of inquiry. This resulted in Dr. Burks working with the students to limit their search based on their own questions and background knowledge.

The role of the content teacher becomes important in *guiding students* in the assemblage process. Dr. Burks helped them focus their questions:

> I knew that some of the topics could not be well-understood with previous work with calculus and general relativity. So it became my job to help the students pare down their list of topics to a few questions that were appropriate to their educational background and could be addressed in a research paper as opposed to a book. When we focused on three questions of interest to the students, they were able to obtain the information they needed through focused search.

The second problem relates to the need to see conceptual relationships across texts. Bobby H and Addie G were asked to construct a series of four concept maps on their topic of "black holes." A concept map is a visual representation of an individual's thought processes, is a word diagram portrayed visually in a *hierarchical* fashion, and represents concepts and their relationships. Both the teacher and students need to have a starting place from which to facilitate the process of relating new information to prior knowledge and experience and to share these ideas. Concept maps provide a starting point from which to determine what the learner already knows about a given topic and new learning *in process*. For example, by asking a student to make a concept map of a topic the teacher is able to determine: (a) the students' general knowledge with the topic; (b) how the student represents embedded concepts and connections across these concepts; and (c) if there are any misconceptions the student has about the topic to be studied. A hierarchical concept map progresses from most inclusive (general) ideas to least inclusive (specific) ones, and students have many opportunities to represent and refine their use of concept maps to represent their thinking.

For the "black hole" study, each map was sent to Dr. Burks who provided feedback on parts that were unclear or needed to be elaborated. In Fig. 47.1, comments are portrayed on a map sent for review and sent back to Bobby and Addie.

Notice that one comment refers to changing the linking word from "and" to "include" giving new meaning to this relationship between Reactions with Matter that "includes" Time. Ideas were then reconceptualized and a final version of Bobby and Addie's map is shown in Fig. 47.2.

Critical and Imaginative Thinking

As we observed our students, mindful learning involved various aspects of thinking when making connections across facts and concepts. Critical thinking involves the analysis of ideas and their

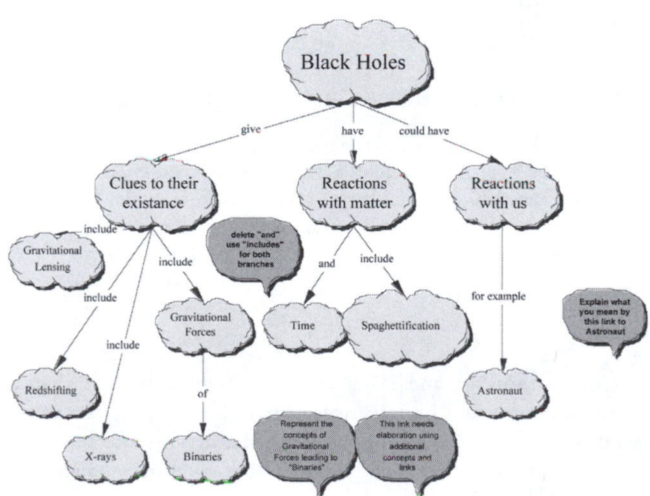

FIGURE 47.1 Bobby and Addie's concept map with Dr Burk's comments.

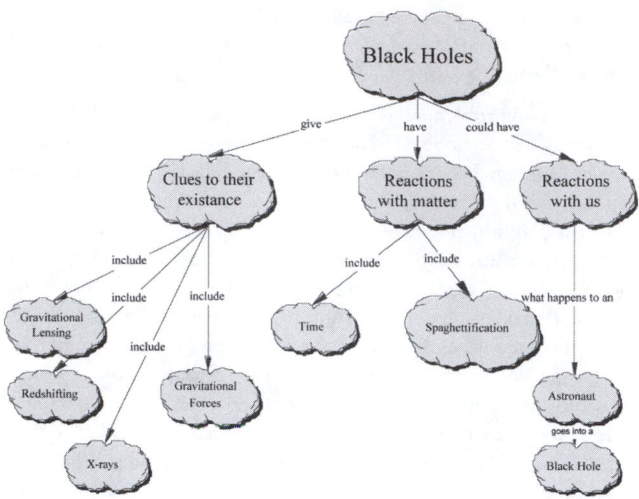

FIGURE 47.2 Bobby and Addie's revised concept map on "Black Holes".

degree of relationship. Imaginative thinking involves application of newly learned information to what can be imagined in a new world of ideas and/or what is plausible to real world events. Both types of this thinking are displayed in the writing quoted at the beginning of this chapter.

Teacher mediation through electronic journaling, e-mail correspondence, sharing of concept map analyses, or other forms of interactive transactions provides means for negotiating meaning outside of the walls of the classroom. The following e-mail exchange between Bobby and Katie provide another example of how students use both critical thinking (thinking about thinking in ways to bring about change in one's experience) and imaginative thinking (exploring future possibilities with existing ideas, Alvarez, 1996, 1997) as they pursue their case on "Water on Mars."

> Dr. Stockman
>
> We had a couple of questions that we were not able to ask you when you here. One was what are the reasons that some of the craters have plateaus in the middle?
>
> From Stephanie Stockman
>
> Hi Bobby and Katie,
>
> I think you need to do a little research on cratering and mass wasting . . . but here are a few hints: The plateau in the middle of some craters is called a central peak and has to do with crater formation (imagine a raindrop or rock falling into a pond). Mass wasting is related to erosion and landslides.
>
> Glad to hear from you!
>
> Steph

Critical thinking and using one's imagination is more than a worthy notion; it is a prominent feature of our project. This statement asked that they imagine what can be because of their findings. Stephanie explained her thought processes when responding to Bobby and Katie's message:

> Cratering and mass wasting are both processes that significantly shaped the surface of Mars. I hoped to encourage Bobby and Katie to do additional research in these areas. There are a number of good references on Cratering that are targeted for middle/high school students. Mass wasting is covered in High School earth science classes and texts.

Stephanie Stockman provided a visualization in her e-mail response to Bobby and Katie's question about crater formation: "Imagine a raindrop or rock falling into a pond." In this instance, a reference is made to an event that takes place in their societal environment that resembles features with the new information being studied. Making connections between what is known to new information enables students to understand new ideas meaningfully instead of resorting to memorization.

Our scientists do not give direct answers to questions; rather they guide them toward other sources so that they can read and decipher for themselves relevant and pertinent information. These ideas are shared and responses to questions are given, not as answers, but in circumstances that guide the students to other sources where information can be accessed and reviewed by them to make judgments about their relevance to their case study (e.g., other journals, books, documents, persons, Internet sites with simulations, etc.).

Posing and Seeking Answers to Self-Directed Questions

When students are first asked to formulate their own questions, many become uncertain about how to do this task. Not only have they not had many opportunities to do so, once they begin their questions, they are typically too global to be helpful for a focused inquiry. However, once they have completed their study, many students have commented how much they enjoyed finding knowledge claims to the questions that they had posed. Self-questioning raises their level of consciousness with a topic and stimulates their curiosity that leads to active engagement with their case.

By engaging in the processes of assemblage and critical and imaginative thinking, students begin to formulate questions that arouse their curiosity and interest with a given topic. These questions are shared with their teacher and peers, who provide feedback to the degree that they *focus* on a particular aspect of the topic they wish to study.

Yet even when more focused, these generated questions are sometimes perplexing for students. In one case, a student was encouraged to seek answers to his own questions, sort through electronic and print mediums, make judgments, and synthesize facts and ideas as he progressed in his case research. At first, he was unsure how to formulate his own questions. As he progressed in his study, he found that a resolution was not forthcoming to one of his questions. This created a sense of anxiety for him in that he was sure that there must be a "right" answer since this had been his experience in lessons and assignments throughout his formal schooling. Once assured, after several probes, that there was not yet an answer to the question asked he began to ask how this would affect his grade. The teacher asked him what he thought would be needed in order to answer the question. The student then thought about the dilemma and wrote a paper that he believed would be needed in terms of background knowledge of the topic, level of mathematical aptitude, and the use of a new science of inquiry. This thought-provoking writing enabled him to better understand the structure of knowledge and how advanced knowledge with the target concept needed further investigation by scientists that were more sophisticated in theoretical mathematics and knowledge of variable stars. He made a hypothesis of what it would take to resolve the question; the same type of mindful learning and analysis that engage researchers everyday in their quest for discovery of new information.

Using Metacognitive Tools for Self-Understanding

Students monitor their learning with adjunct aids developed by the teacher, and in our projects, these are provided in electronic formats. We list three adjunct aids that have been so transformed from a paper-and-pencil format.

Thematic Organizers. A thematic organizer (see Alvarez, 1983; Alvarez & Risko, 1989, 2002; Risko & Alvarez, 1986) is a preview strategy intended to activate students' prior knowledge, relate this knowledge to the central theme of a passage, define the theme by explaining its attributes, and ask students to predict what will occur in reading and viewing passages. As part of a process to activate schema with novel concepts, several thematic organizers were developed to accommodate various electronic texts via the Internet. For example, a thematic organizer with hyperlinks to pertinent data sources was constructed as part of the CD "Water on Mars" study. The first paragraph of this thematic organizer makes the Earth and Mars connection by describing an event that created mass hysteria. This was a reenactment of a radio broadcast by Mercury Theater based on H. G. Wells, *The War of the Worlds*. A hyperlink to this Web site connects the reader/viewer with this radio broadcast. The paragraphs that follow describe the target concept (Water on Mars) and provide the reader with an opportunity to record their thoughts via an electronic notebook. Statements are written to guide the student to make informed judgments with the electronic sources. This process of alerting students to common elements between their prior knowledge and concepts presented in varied contexts can reduce confusion and encourage the generalizability of knowledge.

Concept Maps. In our project, students send their maps for review electronically via the Exploring Minds Network. Students can use a software program, such as Inspiration 6.0 or CMap, to construct their concept maps. This software enables students to construct a map, to save it as a file, and to submit the map to a teacher or peer and can be printed as a hard copy. These maps are very helpful for negotiating ideas not only with the teacher but also with one's peers. The connections shown on the map together with the linking words determine the extent to which ideas are meaningfully represented. Cross-links (broken lines showing relationships between ideas portrayed on one part of a map with another) provide valuable insight into the visual display. Using the maps as a template, students are able to write coherent and cogent paragraphs that explain their reasoning processes with each phase of their study.

Interactive V Diagrams. The V heuristic was developed by Gowin (1981; Gowin & Alvarez, 2005) to enable students to understand the structure of knowledge (e.g., relational networks, hierarchies, combinations) and to understand the process of knowledge construction. Gowin's fundamental assumption is that knowledge is not absolute, but rather it is dependent upon the concepts, theories, and methodologies by which we view the world. To learn meaningfully, individuals relate new knowledge to relevant concepts and propositions they already know. The V diagram aids students in this linking process by acting as a metacognitive tool that requires students to make explicit connections between previously learned and newly acquired information.

The V diagram is shaped like a "V" and elements are arrayed around it (see Fig. 47.3).

The left side, the conceptual or thinking side, of the V displays *world view, philosophy, theory*, and *concepts*. The right side, the methodological or doing side, has *value claims, knowledge claims, transformations*, and *records. Events and/or objects* are at the point of the V. Both sides are interactive, not exclusive (see Gowin, 1981; Gowin & Alvarez, 2005; Novak & Gowin, 1984).

An *Interactive V Diagram* has been designed to be used electronically on the Internet (Alvarez, 1998; Gowin & Alvarez, 2005). The Interactive V Diagrams appearing on the Exploring Minds Network aids high school students to plan, organize, and carry out research investigations meaningfully. These students used this metacognitive tool in two ways—first, to evaluate documents; second, to plan, carry out, and report their research investigations.

These students submitted their V Diagrams electronically and their teacher and researcher reviewed them. Feedback was written and transmitted to the student. The student reviewed, read, and printed the comments of the reviewer. If more than one reviewer responds, the names appear and the color-coded check marks of different colors are next to their names. The user is then able to distinguish who made the comments and to whom the responses are to be sent. When the user reconstructs the V incorporating the ideas of the reviewers, the reconceptualization process begins and ideas begin to be negotiated, concepts and facts are clarified, and the precision and validity of knowledge claims are enhanced.

Producing and voicing their findings. Teachers and their students present findings from their self-designed inquiry projects at scientific, mathematical, literacy, and technology conferences so their voices can be heard about their research endeavors (e.g., Alvarez, Burks, & Sotoohi, 2002; Alvarez, Busby, Burks, et al., 2000; Alvarez & Hennig, 2000; Alvarez, Rodriguez, Capp, et al, 1999; Alvarez, Busby, Henry, et al, 1995; Alvarez, Rodriguez, Hennig, et al., 1998; Alvarez, Stockman, Rodriguez, et al., 1999; Alvarez, & Rodriguez, 1995, 1997; Stockman, Alvarez, & Albert, Jr., 1998). They also develop manuals that contain examples of variable star data and steps using least squares analysis to compute these data that aid other teachers and their students to record, analyze, and report the data received from the missions (Rodriguez & Hennig, 1997). Students field-test these manuals and provide input. Once they are field-tested, these manuals are placed on the school's Web site for public access.

High school physics and astronomy students have published their papers electronically on the Web (Alvarez, 1996). At first, the papers were written and posted on the school Web site. However, after receiving comments from faraway readers who were faceless and unknown concerning content and the use of inappropriate grammar, these students became more conscious of their writing style and presentation format. In a significant sense, this feedback from readers whom they did not know raised their level of awareness about their research investigation and how the findings needed to be clearly written for consumption by readers who may not have the necessary background knowledge and/or who wanted to read a coherent paper. As a result of these inquiries, students in the astronomy class shared their draft revisions of their papers with students who were not members of their class, and asked them if they understood their ideas and to make

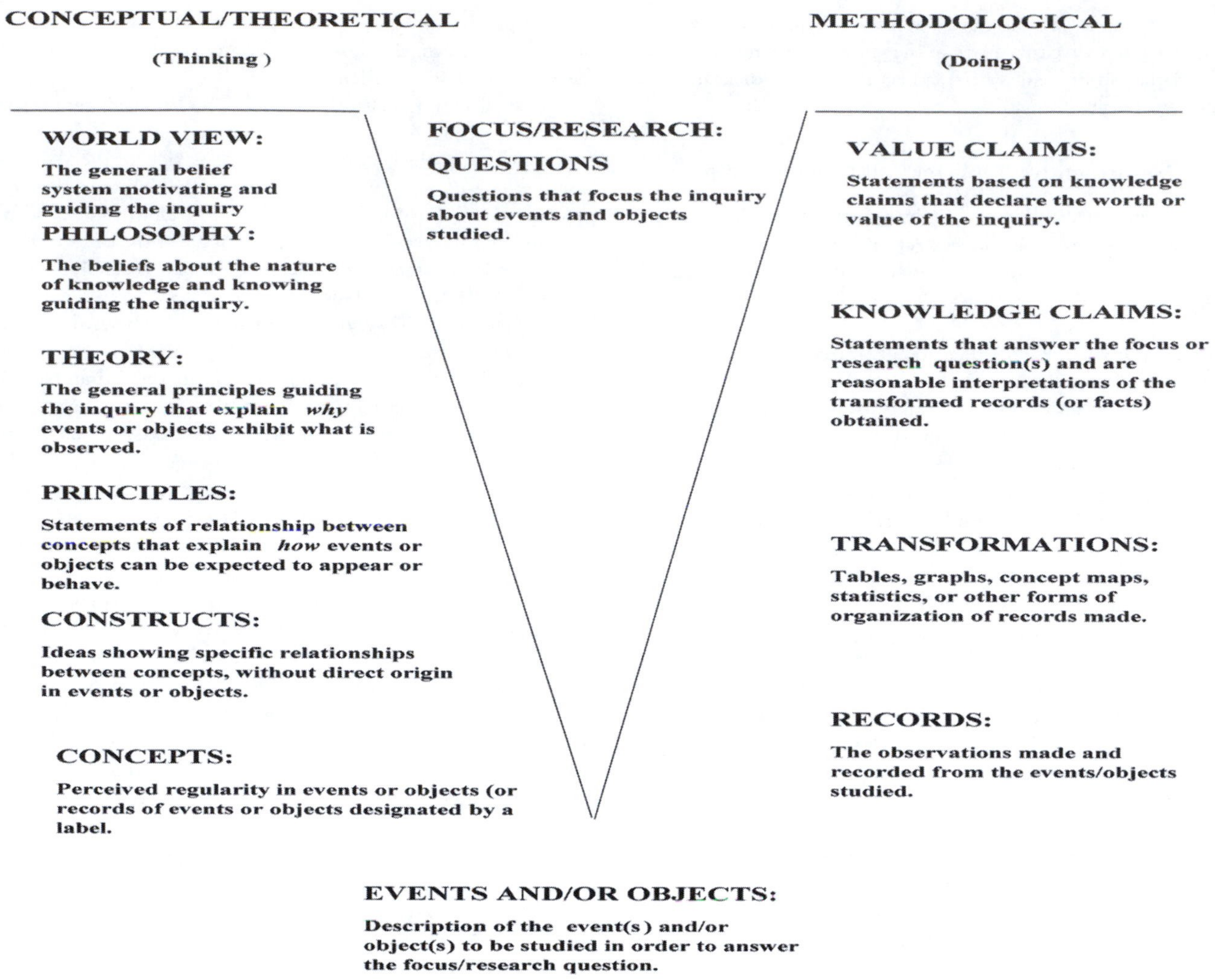

CONCEPTUAL/THEORETICAL

(Thinking)

METHODOLOGICAL

(Doing)

WORLD VIEW:

The general belief system motivating and guiding the inquiry

PHILOSOPHY:

The beliefs about the nature of knowledge and knowing guiding the inquiry.

THEORY:

The general principles guiding the inquiry that explain *why* events or objects exhibit what is observed.

PRINCIPLES:

Statements of relationship between concepts that explain *how* events or objects can be expected to appear or behave.

CONSTRUCTS:

Ideas showing specific relationships between concepts, without direct origin in events or objects.

CONCEPTS:

Perceived regularity in events or objects (or records of events or objects designated by a label.

FOCUS/RESEARCH: QUESTIONS

Questions that focus the inquiry about events and objects studied.

VALUE CLAIMS:

Statements based on knowledge claims that declare the worth or value of the inquiry.

KNOWLEDGE CLAIMS:

Statements that answer the focus or research question(s) and are reasonable interpretations of the transformed records (or facts) obtained.

TRANSFORMATIONS:

Tables, graphs, concept maps, statistics, or other forms of organization of records made.

RECORDS:

The observations made and recorded from the events/objects studied.

EVENTS AND/OR OBJECTS:

Description of the event(s) and/or object(s) to be studied in order to answer the focus/research question.

FIGURE 47.3 Knowledge V diagram.

comments where they felt needed clarification or elaboration. This was peer review at its best. Based on these student comments, the papers were then rewritten and published on the school's Web site.

This incident calls to mind an interesting aspect of the classroom environment and its relationship to learning. When a student is asked by the teacher to write a paper or prepare a visual presentation is one circumstance that occurs in a familiar setting for one's own peers; however, preparing these documents for unfamiliar faces such as publishing papers and/or visual presentations on the Internet for others demands greater scrutiny, coherence of ideas, and exactness of information. Students came to realize that they needed to become more pensive and deliberate in their writings notwithstanding the audience.

CD Reports. Students display their reports on CDs that incorporate animations, video, simulations, music, graphs, charts, illustrations, figures, and hyperlinks to other related sources that enrich knowledge and understanding and make available opportunities for them to make new knowledge. For example, high school students designed CDs to represent their case investigations (Alvarez & Busby, 1999). First, they planned the contents by creating a semantic web of the components that was included in the CD (see Fig. 47.4). Next, they organized their materials to fit their conceptual framework. This included the developing of subdirectories. Then, they decided if they would include music, photographs, video clips, audio clips, simulated models, and so forth to better compliment their CD presentation. Finally, they produced a final product that can be shared with, and used by, others to extend the research findings reported.

CONCLUSION

Educational value arises out of the construction of meanings that tie ideas together and thus create our world. Students are experiencing these kinds of educational values when they are asked to self-direct their own learning in contexts that are guided and facilitated by their teachers in meaningful learning practices.

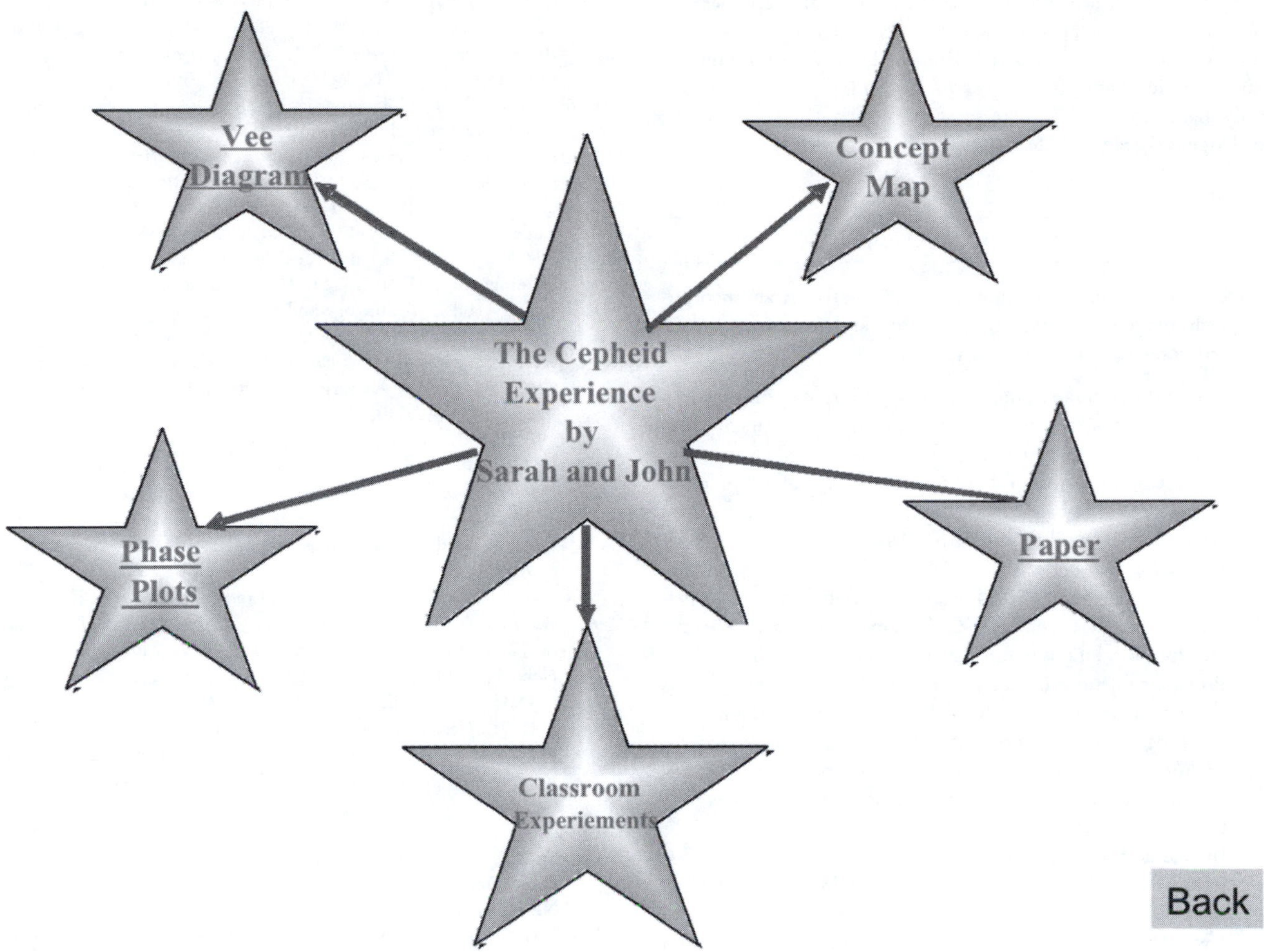

FIGURE 47.4. Sarah and John's case report on CD.

Students also begin to view their textbooks in a different light. Questions are being raised that are interesting and demonstrates how these students think about their own work. For example, they paraphrased their questions and formulated opinions about textbooks: "Why do astronomy books assume knowledge about terms when they are supposed to be introductory texts?" "Much of the information in the texts is superficial and rote in nature. There doesn't seem to be good explanations, examples, or pictures of the information." In a documentary that appeared on public television (Public Television Corporation, 1999), a section highlighted two of our high school students in Mr. Rodriguez's physics class viewing data from NASA's site on the Mars Orbital Laser Altimeter (MOLA) flight. Students did "think alouds" about their use of concept maps, the interpretation of the data, and how they were comparing and contrasting the physical features of Mars and the planet Earth. A comment made by Kati, one of these students, was echoed by high school students in other studies that we have conducted: "In other classes, we are given the questions, find the answers, and are told if we are either correct or incorrect. In this project, we get to ask our own questions, form hypotheses, and search for our own answers. We are out there with the scientists."

Our role as educators, administrators, and policy makers is to provide opportunities for students to use the components of reading, writing, listening, speaking, and viewing by providing them with meaningful lessons and assignments that actively engage them with making meaning of new information. The value of a lesson is crucial not only in its preparation but also in its process to culmination. The issue of value is significant in the educative process.

In such a curriculum, questions are valued and encouraged by the teacher as students engage in inquiries that go beyond the minimum required in a *fixed* curriculum. In our forum, the teacher and student are both involved in the learning process. Both are engaged in an *emergent* curriculum through reciprocal questioning, discussing, and seeking resolutions that go beyond a text or a curriculum guide. In our project, students and teachers are a community of thinkers (Alvarez, 1996). Teachers are thinking and learning more about their subject area as they (a) prepare topics for study; (b) analyze their students' concept maps, V diagrams, and working portfolios portrayed on interactive computer text files; and (c) negotiate the curriculum by guiding and encouraging students to engage in imaginative and critical thinking. Likewise, students are thinking and learning about the world by relating their formal in-school experiences to their informal out-of-school experiences. As they research their cases and study assigned or self-selected topics, they are invited to know more about the process of learning. Together students and teachers become a community of thinkers: a community where knowledge is shared and ideas are valued.

RECOMMENDATIONS

We offer several recommendations for consideration when incorporating technology in language arts programs and the writing of language arts content literacy curricula.

1. Use of different assessment procedures for analyzing reading comprehension in an electronic literacy environment from those used in print mediums.
2. Provide opportunities for students to engage in active learning, such as case-based instruction, where they generate their own questions and follow paths of inquiry that may or may not lead to a resolution.
3. Abandon the notion of total reliance on "right" answers, by permitting students to come to a *dead end* and posit what they believe are possible solutions to unknown or ambiguous findings.
4. Provide students with interactive metacognitive tools such as concept mapping, interactive V diagrams, to promote and share thinking and the anchoring of ideas with new information.
5. Meld the societal curriculum with the formal school curriculum so that connections and sense making with new ideas can be discussed and learned.
6. Invoke a theory of educating that promotes self-knowledge by changing the meaning of experience for each individual by enabling them to take charge of their own experience as a way to guide and evaluate the planning, carrying out, and finalization of lessons and learning of new ideas (see Gowin & Alvarez, 2005).
7. Engage in the process of "assemblage" as a prelude to initiating and learning new information.
8. Ensure the language arts curriculum serve as a codependent with the content disciplines in the communicative and visual arts.

ACKNOWLEDGMENTS

This chapter is supported by the Center of Excellence in Information Systems at Tennessee State University and by NASA through the Tennessee Space Grant Consortium NGT-40021, Network Resources Training Site (NRTS) NCC5-96, and NASA Center for Automated Space Science NCC5-511.

REFERENCES

Alvarez, M. C. (1983). Using a thematic pre-organizer and guided instruction as aids to concept learning. *Reading Horizons, 24*(1), 51–58.

Alvarez, M. C. (1993). Imaginative uses of self-selected cases. *Reading Research and Instruction, 32*(2), 1–18.

Alvarez, M. C. (1995). Explorers of the universe: An action research scientific literacy project. In K. Camperell, B. L. Hayes, & R. Telfer (Eds.), *American reading forum: Vol. 15. Linking literacy: Past, present, and future* (pp. 55–62). Logan UT: Utah State University.

Alvarez, M. C. (1996). A community of thinkers: Literacy environments with interactive technology. In K. Camperell & B. L. Hayes (Eds.), *American reading forum: Vol 16. Literacy: The information highway to success* (pp. 17–29). Logan, UT: Utah State University.

Alvarez, M. C. (1997). Thinking and learning with technology: Helping students construct meaning. *NASSP Bulletin, 81*(592), 66–72.

Alvarez, M. C. (1998). Interactive Vee diagrams as a metacognitive tool for learning. In S. McNeil, J. D. Price, S. Boger-Mehall, B. Robin, & J. Willis (Eds.), Technology and Teacher Education Annual, Vol. 2. (pp. 1245–1248). *Proceedings of SITE 98. 9th International Conference of the Society for Information Technology and Teacher Education (SITE).* Charlottesville, VA: Association for the Advancement of Computing in Education (AACE).

Alvarez, M. C. (2001a). Exploring minds: Revealing ideas electronically. In N. Callaos, Y. Ohsawa, Y. Zhang, R. Szabo, & M. Aveledo (Eds.), *Proceedings of the World Multiconference on Systemics, Cybernetics and Informatics: Vol. VIII. Human information and education systems* (pp. 1–6). Orlando, FL: International Institute of Informatics and Systemics.

Alvarez, M. C. (2001b). Developing critical and imaginative thinking within electronic literacy. In J. A. Rycik & J. L. Irvin (Eds.), *What adolescents deserve: A commitment to students' literacy learning* (pp. 191–197). Newark, DE: International Reading Association.

Alvarez, M. C., Binkley, E., Bivens, J., Highers, P., Poole, C., & Walker, P. (1991). Case-based instruction and learning: An interdisciplinary project. In T. V. Rasinski, N. D. Padak & J. Logan (Eds.), *College Reading Association Yearbook: Vol. 13. Reading is knowledge* (pp. 53–62). Pittsburg, KS: College Reading Association.

Alvarez, M. C., Burks, G., King, T., Hulan, B., & Graham, A. (2000, April). *Students creating their own thinking-learning contexts.* Paper presented at the American Educational Research Association Annual Meeting, New Orleans, LA. ERIC Document ED 441 037.

Alvarez, M. C., Burks, G., & Sotoohi, G. (2002, April). *High school students using action research in science investigations.* Paper presented at the annual meeting of the American Educational Research Association, New Orleans, LA.

Alvarez, M. C., & Busby, M. R. (1999). Interactive literacy: A forum for thinking. In J. Price, J. Willis, D. A. Willis, M. Jost, & S. Boger-Mehall (Eds.), *Technology and Teacher Education Annual, 1999* (pp. 760–765, vol. 1.) Proceedings of SITE 99. 10th International Conference of the Society for Information Tchnology and Teacher Education (SITE), Charlottesville, VA: Association for the Advancement of Computing in Education (AACE).

Alvarez, M. C., Busby, M. R., Burks, G., Sotoohi, G., Wade, M., & Brooks, K. (2000, September). *Negotiating the learning process electronically.* Paper presented at the MU-SPIN Tenth Anniversary Users' Conference and MURED Second Annual Education Conference, Morris Brown College and Renaissance Atlanta Hotel, Atlanta, GA.

Alvarez, M. C., Busby, M. R., Henry, G., Rodriguez, W. J., & Silver, I. (1995, March). *Creating a multimedia environment in your classroom.* Paper presented at the Tennessee Educational Technology Conference, Nashville, TN.

Alvarez, M. C., & Hennig, L. A. (2000, February). *Electronic literacy in the content areas: Teachers and students informing their practice.* Forum on Adolescent Literacy, George Mason University, Fairfax, VA. Co-Sponsored by the International Reading Association, George Mason University Graduate School of Education, the Virginia State Reading Association, & the Greater Washington Reading Council. Program developed by the Adolescent Literacy Commission of the International Reading Association.

Alvarez, M. C., & Risko, V. J. (1989). Using a thematic organizer to facilitate transfer learning with college developmental studies students. *Reading Research and Instruction*, *28*(2), 1–15.

Alvarez, M. C., & Risko, V. J. (2002). Thematic organizers. In B. J. Guzzetti (Ed.), *Literacy in America: An encyclopedia of history, theory, and practice: Vols. I & II* (pp. 653–655). Santa Barbara, CA: ABC-CLIO.

Alvarez, M. C., & Rodriguez, W. J. (1995). Explorers of the universe: A pilot study. In W. M. Linek & E. G. Sturtevant (Eds.), *College Reading Association Yearbook: Vol. 17. Generation of literacy* (pp. 221–236). Commerce, Texas: Texas A&M-Commerce.

Alvarez, M. C., & Rodriguez, W. J. (1996, April–May). *Exploring the stars and the universe: Using multimedia for literacy and scientific learning.* Paper presented at the 41st Annual Convention of the International Reading Association, New Orleans, LA.

Alvarez, M. C., & Busby, M. R. (1999). Interactive literacy: A forum for thinking. In J. Price, J. Willis, D. A. Willis, M. Jost, & S. Boger-Mehall (Eds.), *Technology and Teacher Education Annual, 1999* (pp. 760–765, vol. 1). Proceedings of SITE 99. 10th International Conference of the Society for Information Technology and Teacher Education (SITE), Charlottesville, VA: Association for the Advancement of Computing in Education (AACE).

Alvarez, M. C., & Rodriguez, W. J. (1997, March). *Explorers of the universe: Forecasting interactive learning environments.* Paper presented at the Satellites and Education Conference X - A Forum for Teachers, West Chester University, West Chester, PA.

Alvarez, M. C., Rodriguez, W. J., Capp, C., Mayne, B., Stein, B. J., Wilson, A., et al. (1999, March). *Explorers of the universe: Intermingling technology, research, and metacognitive tools.* Paper presented at the Satellites and Education Conference XII, West Chester University, West Chester, PA.

Alvarez, M. C., Rodriguez, W. J., Hennig, L. A., Berenty, J., King, T., Grener, D., et al. (1998, February). *Explorers of the universe.* Paper presented at the NASA Research Center Technical Advances in Aeronautic Space Sciences, Global Hydrology, and Education Conference, Huntsville, AL.

Alvarez, M. C., Stockman, S. A., Rodriguez, W. J., Davidson, B., & Swartz, K. (1999, April). *Informing practice through collaborative partnerships.* Paper presented at the American Educational Research Association Annual Meeting, Montreal, Canada.

American Association for the Advancement of Science. (1989). *Science for all Americans.* Washington, DC: Author.

Beane, J. A. (1997). *Curriculum integration: Designing the core of democratic education.* New York: Teachers College press.

Buxton, C. A., Carlone, H. B., & Carlone, D. (2005). Boundary spanners as bridges of student and school discourses in an urban science and mathematics high school. *School Science and Mathematics*, *105*(6), 302–311.

Gowin, D. B. (1981). *Educating.* Ithaca, NY: Cornell University Press.

Gowin, D. B., & Alvarez, M. C. (2005). *The art of educating with V diagrams.* New York and Cambridge, UK: Cambridge University Press.

Hammond, L. (2001). Notes from California: An anthropological approach to urban science education for language minority families. *Journal of Research in Science Teaching, 38*(9), 983–999.

Holland, J. H. (1998). *Emergence: From chaos to order.* Reading, MA: Helix Books.

Hug, B., Krajcik, J. S., & Marx, R. W. (2005). Using innovative learning technologies to promote learning and engagement in an urban science classroom. *Urban Education, 40*(4), 446–472.

International Reading Association. (1992). *Standards for reading professionals.* Newark, DE: Author.

Kuiper, E., Volman, M., & Terwel, J. (2005). The web as an information resource in K–12 education: Strategies for supporting students in searching and processing information. *Review of Educational Research, 75*(3), 285–328.

Lee, H. (1960). *To kill a mockingbird.* Philadelphia: Lippincott.

Levinson, B. A., & Holland, D. (1996). The cultural production of the educated person: An introduction. In B. A. Levinson, D. E. Foley, & D. Holland (Eds.), *The cultural production of the educated person: Critical ethnographies of schooling and local practice* (pp. 1–54). Albany: State University of New York Press.

Moll, L. C. (1997). The creation of mediating settings. *Mind, Culture, and Activity, 4*(3), 191–199.

National Aeronautics and Space Administration. (1999–2003.) *NASA implementation program for education.* www.hq.nasa.gov/office/codef/education/ed_implmt_plan/exec.htm

National Council of Teachers of Mathematics. (2000). *Principles and standards for school mathematics.* Reston, VA: Author.

National Science and Technology Council, Committee on Education and Training. (1995). *A strategic planning document for meeting the 21st century.* Washington, DC: U.S. Department of Education.

Newmann, F. M., & Oliver, D. W. (1967). Case study approaches in social studies. *Social Education, 31*, 108–113.

Norris, S. P., & Phillips, L. M. (2003). How literacy in its fundamental sense is central to scientific literacy. *Science Education, 87*, 221–240.

Novak, J. D., & Gowin, D. B. (1984). *Learning how to learn.* New York: Cambridge University Press.

Penner, D. E. (2001). Cognition, computers, and synthetic science: Building knowledge and learning through modeling. In W. G. Secada (Ed.), *Review of research in education: Vol. 25* (pp. 1–35). Washington, DC: AERA.

Public Television Corporation. (1999). *Thinking Connections: The Scientific Revolution.* Nashville, TN: WDCN Channel 8. Public Broadcasting Service.

Risko, V. J., & Alvarez, M. C. (1986). An investigation of poor readers' use of a thematic strategy to comprehend text. *Reading Research Quarterly, 21*(3), 298–316.

Rodriguez, W. J., & Hennig, L. A. (1997). *Finding periods in variable star data.* Technical Manual 101-97. Nashville, TN: Tennessee State University.

Roth, W. M. & Barton, A. C. (2004). *Rethinking scientific literacy.* New York: Routledge.

Royal Society. (1985). *The public understanding of science.* London: Author.

Science Council of Canada. (1984). *Science for every student: Educating Canadians for tomorrow's world* (Report No. 36). Ottawa: Author.

Stockman, S. A., Alvarez, M. C., & Albert, T. J., Jr. (1998, March). *Bringing Mars exploration into the K–12 classroom: The Mars orbiter laser altimeter.* Education program at the 29th Lunar and Planetary Science Conference, Houston, TX.

Tinker, R. F., & Thornton, R. K. (1992). Constructing student knowledge in science. In E. Scanlon & T. O'Shea (Eds.), *New directions in educational technology* (pp. 153–170). Berlin: Springer-Verlag.

Tobin, K., Roth, W. M., & Zimmermann, A. (2001). Learning to teach science in urban schools. *Journal of Research in Science Teaching, 38*(8), 941–964.

White, B. Y., & Frederiksen, J. R. (1998). Inquiry, modeling, and metacognition: Making science accessible to all students. *Cognition and Instruction, 16*, 3–118.

Whitehead, A. N. (1938). *Modes of thought.* New York: Macmillan Company.

48

CRITICAL MEDIA LITERACY IN SECONDARY SCHOOLS

Pamela U. Brown
OKLAHOMA STATE UNIVERSITY

Gretchen Schwarz
OKLAHOMA STATE UNIVERSITY

Middle-school and high-school students and their teachers need to develop an ability to analyze critically the media with which they are bombarded through television, magazines, radio, the Internet, advertisements inside and outside school settings, and even curriculum materials with which they are presented. Arguing otherwise seems counterintuitive to the generally accepted educational aim of creating citizens capable of "fulfilling the duties of citizenship in a participatory democracy" (National Council for the Social Studies, 1994) or able "to pursue life's goals and to participate fully as informed, productive members of society" (National Council of Teachers of English, 1996).

The state of critical media literacy in U.S. secondary schools is difficult to determine, largely because what happens in individual classrooms, schools, and districts across the country is quiet. Perhaps thousands of teachers, committed to the notion that their students should be able to read media texts as well as traditional texts, are incorporating the tenets of media literacy into instruction; perhaps not. Helping students determine purpose, point of view, and attention-getting techniques in media messages from a variety of sources can have many positive effects, including enlivening the teaching and learning process and helping students gain skills to be actively engaged in the democratic process. Teachers who use media literacy elements in class may or may not name what they do *media literacy*, and very few teachers publicly share their work through presentations or publication. However, there is no better way to describe media literacy practices in secondary schools than to look to existing literature, though what we find here can be only an approximation of what is actually happening in schools.

Goodman (2003) decried accepted practices and attitudes of media producers, school personnel, and the larger society that seek to make youth—especially poor and minority youth—passive observers who are easy to control rather than active participants empowered to make an impact (pp. 2–3). He went on to define critical media literacy as,

> The ability to analyze, evaluate, and produce print, aural, and visual forms of communication. A critical literacy empowers low-income, urban teenagers to understand how media is made to convey particular messages and how they can use electronic and print technologies themselves to document and publicly voice their ideas and concerns regarding the most important issues in their lives. (Goodman, 2003, p. 3)

Critical media literacy in schools, presented through both professional development for teachers and classroom activities for students, is one vehicle that "helps students access, analyze, evaluate, and create messages using media in various forms" (Hobbs, 2005b, p. 58), skills necessary to full democratic participation. However, the documented presence of critical media literacy curricula in U.S. schools is not widespread. This chapter will examine the state of critical media literacy in U.S. secondary schools by presenting the history of the media literacy movement, the need for media literacy in secondary schools, research in media literacy, and examples of how students become critical through media creation, concluding with recommendations for further research.

A BRIEF HISTORY OF MEDIA LITERACY IN SECONDARY SCHOOLS

The state of media literacy in America's secondary schools has been and remains more precarious than in some other countries such as England, Norway, and Australia (Ferrington & Anderson-Inman, 1996). Interest has emerged as new media have emerged over time, evident from the National Society for the Study of Education yearbook, Part I, of 1954, *Mass Media and Education*, which "acknowledged the growing impact of movies and newspapers on American society and thus on schooling" (Schwarz, G., 2005, pp. 6, 8–9), to the short-lived burst of interest shown in the critical viewing skills approach of the 1970s, which focused almost solely on television. With the rise of the personal computer and concern about the media-dominated environment, media literacy has again been making inroads into the curriculum, at least on paper, since the 1990s.

The implementation of media literacy has been strengthened by such documents as the *Standards for English Language Arts* (National Council of Teachers of English, 1996) and the report of the Carnegie Council on Adolescent Development (1995), *Great Transitions: Preparing Youth for the 21st Century*, which urges the adoption of media literacy in middle schools. Kubey and Baker (1999) reported that 48 states included elements of media literacy in their state curriculum frameworks; six years later, McBrien (2005) noted that all 50 states included media literacy in state standards.

The extent of these objectives varies widely. California, for example, goes into detail, including for grades 11 and 12 under language arts: "Recognize strategies used by media to inform, persuade, entertain, and transmit culture (e.g., advertising, perpetuation of stereotypes, use of visual representations, special effects, language)" (California State Board of Education, 2005). As reported by the Media Literacy Clearinghouse (2005), however, the media literacy objectives in Missouri are brief and vague, such as the grades 9–12 language/communication arts objective: "Analyze and evaluate print and nonprint advertising." State curriculum frameworks vary widely in their emphasis on media literacy, and few districts offer stand-alone courses in media literacy at the secondary level. Media literacy is more likely to be integrated into existing content areas, and Hobbs (2004) noted the variety of places media literacy appears, "including English language arts, social studies, fine arts, library-skills and educational technology, vocational education, and health education" (p. 44).

Moreover, actual teaching of media literacy remains spotty despite state guidelines. Hobbs (2005a), who has studied media literacy across the secondary curriculum widely in the United States, concluded,

> Media literacy in the United States is not emerging primarily from statewide or school district initiatives, but from the bottom-up energy of individual teachers who value the way using media, technology, and popular culture improves the quality of their interaction with students or who are passionate about helping young people understand, challenge, and transform media culture's dominance. (p. 92)

Even in Canada, where media literacy has been mandated nationally for a number of years, Pungente, Duncan, and Andersen (2005) observed that "at the classroom level the implementation of media education skills has been uneven from school to school and district to district" (p. 155). In addition, media literacy is not tested on college entrance exams or standardized tests mandated by *No Child Left Behind Act* in the United States, so there is no powerful national drive for media literacy.

One other issue is the approach taken to media literacy. Media literacy in the United States remains largely motivated by anxiety over bad effects such as violence and body image problems for the young (see the curriculum products available through the New Mexico Media Literacy Project at http://www.nmmlp.org.). This approach is called *protectionist* or the *inoculation* approach, and the research that exists is devoted to showing that media literacy can reduce smoking or improve eating habits (e.g., Davies, 1993; Strasburger, 1995; Wade, Davidson, & O'Dea, 2003). Generally, practice and research in other countries has moved beyond these concerns. Buckingham (2003), for example, claimed for the United Kingdom and similar countries that,

> While protectionist views have been far from superseded, there has been a gradual evolution towards a less defensive approach. In general, the countries with the most "mature" forms of practice in media education—that is, those which have the longest history and most consistent pattern of development—have moved well beyond protectionism. (p. 12)

In these countries, research has included such topics as audience interaction with media and cultural representation. Classroom studies in media literacy are taking new directions abroad.

THE NEED FOR CRITICAL MEDIA LITERACY IN THE SECONDARY CURRICULUM

The importance of making critical media literacy part of what happens in secondary classrooms is summarized by Semali (2005):

> Once parents worried about the effect of the peer group; now they worry about the effect of the media . . . .The media are powerful teachers; their lessons should not be ignored if schools want to live up to the presumed ideals of American schooling—the ideals of democracy, increased opportunity (economic, educational, etc.) for each American, honoring the diversity of the population (old and new), and responsible world citizenship. The media curricula should be examined and questioned in schools . . . because media goals and purposes do not necessarily support the highest ideals America has to offer its children. (p. 35)

However, compared with the longevity, complexity, and officially acknowledged status of the media literacy movement in countries such as Canada (Pungente et al., 2005), media literacy in the United States is a relatively recent notion. As is often the case with new ideas in school reform, the professional literature on critical media literacy in schools is heavily weighted with pieces devoted to recommending best practices. Hart (2001) commented about media literacy that "unlike other academic disciplines, it cannot yet claim to draw on a body of systematic published research. There is no shortage of enthusiasm or accounts of practice, but little solid research that can act as a basis for curriculum development" (p. 28).

Among the best practice literature in media literacy are writings describing basic media literacy practices (Eken, 2002; Hobbs, 2005b; Kruger, 1998; Thoman, 1999; Thoman & Jolls, 2005), writings describing particular recommended practices (Maness, 2004; Schiebe, 2004; Schwarz, G., 2000), and writings focusing on encouraging social critique on the part of adolescents (Goodman, 2003; Morrell, 2004; Silverblatt, 2004). Other media literacy advocacy pieces examine and recommend specific areas of focus within content areas or within the field of media literacy itself. For example, Thier (2005) described media literacy activities for secondary science, and G. E. Schwarz (2002) proposed using graphic novels in secondary classrooms to engage students and promote literacy events.

MEDIA LITERACY RESEARCH WITH SECONDARY STUDENTS AND TEACHERS

The line between best practice literature and research literature is somewhat blurred, and several pieces combine recommendations for classroom activities with action research studies that describe implementation and results in particular settings (Eken, 2002; Frey & Fisher, 2004; Hoffman & Brecklin, 1996; Zill, 2002). Though the research examples presented in these articles were limited in scope, they provided rich detail of classroom practice and student work and presented intriguing possibilities for further research. Hoffman and Brecklin (1996) described in some detail their work with 550 middle school students, using tools of semantics to implement a media literacy program. For example, students in a suburban Milwaukee middle school learned about the decision making and abstracting process engaged in by all media producers by creating their own "maps," bringing three pictures or mementos and using them to present themselves to several classmates. Hoffman and Brecklin noted, "What they chose to bring, and what they chose to tell about the item, put each student in the role of mapmaker." The authors described in detail much of their work with the middle school students, so that other teachers could implement the activities in their own settings. However, they were not willing to overgeneralize their results; they wrote, "It would be an overstatement to say we have created a group of young general semanticists or even a group of students capable of sophisticated media analysis. We have, in the limited time allotted to us, raised some consciousness about the codes and conventions of the media."

Frey and Fisher (2004) used graphic novels with 32 ninth graders from the poorest part of San Diego. Their struggling readers and writers, 72% of whom were English language learners, increased the quantity and quality of their literacy events in school, apparently because of their engagement with graphic novels as opposed to more traditional texts. The researchers, both of whom are high school teachers and college instructors, found their ninth grade students using more complex, longer sentences as they wrote their own graphic novel texts. Frey and Fisher (2004) specified carefully several individual lessons and activities and maintained, "Using graphic novels to scaffold writing instruction helped students practice the craft of writing and gain necessary skills to become competent readers" (p. 23).

Several studies with formal research designs, some with large numbers of participants and some with very few, add to the existing literature on media literacy in secondary settings, including research by Hobbs and Frost (2003), Fox (1996), Chandler-Olcott and Mahar (2003), Hobbs (1999), and Feuerstein (1999). The methodologies represented range from large-scale experimental designs to co-operatively designed narrative interpretations of qualitative data.

Looking at the effect of media literacy integration across the curriculum on grade 11 students' reading comprehension, writing skills, and message-analysis skills, Hobbs and Frost (2003) used a quasi-experimental pretest and posttest design in matching control group and research groups according to demographic variables. The treatment group consisted of 293 high school juniors enrolled in a school whose teachers are trained in media literacy in all content areas, and the control group was made up of 89 students from a second high school in the area whose teachers are not trained in media literacy strategies. Students whose teachers integrated media literacy for a school year had significantly higher scores in reading comprehension, listening comprehension, and viewing comprehension, and students who spent time on media literacy wrote longer samples. Essentially, Hobbs and Frost's (2003) results demonstrated "that media-literacy instruction embedded in a secondary-level English language arts course can be effective in meeting traditional academic goals" (p. 350). They continued, "Teachers need to be less fearful of making use of a wider range of multimedia fiction and nonfiction texts as study objects when their primary goal remains the development of students' skills of reading, comprehension, interpretation, message analysis, and writing" (p. 350).

Fox's (1996) book, *Harvesting Minds: How TV Commercials Control Kids*, detailed his qualitative study of 200 rural high school students' responses to commercials. Specifically, he observed and interviewed students who watched commercials aired in Missouri schools with Channel One contracts requiring daily viewing of a 12-minute Channel One news broadcast in all classrooms, including two minutes of commercials (Channel One, 2004). Arguably, the most striking finding was that student after student reported noticing no point of view in commercials (such as those broadcast by soft drink companies) beyond the youthful actors who appeared in the ads (Fox, 1996). Concomitantly, these students with no identified school-media-literacy experiences apparently believed the merchants constructed and broadcast the ads as a public service. Fox (1996) summarized that "kids in this study consistently judged commercials in positive, benign ways" (p. 61). This study emphasized the need for critical media literacy, both for students who are the audience for Channel One and other mandated curriculum materials and for teachers and administrators who make decisions about what resources to use in secondary schools.

One 14-year-old boy's experience in an after-school media club is at the heart of a research study by Alvermann, Hagood, and Williams (2001). Ned, an eighth grader who scored in the bottom quartile of the school district's standardized reading test, was particularly interested in rap music. The researchers highlighted Ned's decision making processes in deciding what media texts he liked, and they stated, "Youth can know more or less what they like about such texts; they frequently know and can articulate why they like what they like; however, as we contend in this article, it is quite another thing for us adults to claim to know what they like does in terms of our understanding of how they make meaning of popular culture texts." Though this is not named as a study of media literacy, the data analysis of Ned's interaction with media texts should be useful to proponents of media literacy in secondary schools.

Using the out-of-school literacy practices of eighth-grade girls as a research focus, Chandler-Olcott and Maher (2003) collaborated to explore the students' use of technology outside school and its impact on identity formation. Out-of-school literacy practices of secondary students are increasingly of interest to educational researchers (e.g., Gee, 2003; Redmon, 2000; Wilhelm & Smith, 2002) as they grapple with the divide between what is expected of students in school settings and what they are capable of accomplishing as evidenced by their out-of-school activities. A complex case study design enabled them to eventually narrow focus to only two girls, one who was technologically advanced, and one whose technology use typified that of the 12 girls who participated in the study. Rhiannon taught herself HTML programming in order to design Web pages devoted to her original anime fan fiction pieces, but she found no support at school for this work. Eileen's technology use was more typical of adolescent girls in the United States as she was "more concerned with what a technology could *do* rather than how it worked" (Chandler-Olcott & Maher, 2003, p. 366). Eileen's time on the computer was often spent e-mailing friends or scanning in her own anime art for critique by an online community of anime artists. Though this study is not specifically about critical media literacy, it does describe in detail these adolescent girls' use of media technology and the gap between their knowledge and that of their classroom teachers, who had little interest in or understanding of such technology applications.

Several research studies examine the need for critical media literacy on the part of teachers. Yates (2002) surveyed 350 teachers, finding very strong support for media literacy. However, over two-thirds of his respondents reported having no time to address media literacy in their own classrooms. Based on a three-year observation of two schools, Hobbs (1999) listed several "misuses" of media such as passive viewing of videos with no opportunities for student dialogue, using videos as a reward, and teachers doing paperwork while students view videos. She wrote, "Simply using media in the classroom does not mean that teachers are helping the development of students' media literacy skills" (Hobbs, 1999, p. 5). Sparked by this information, Hobbs surveyed 130 teachers about the ways media such as videos, newspapers, magazines, computers, and camcorders are used in schools and teacher attitudes toward that use. Her nonrandom sample was obtained by asking undergraduate students to conduct phone interviews with two of their own former high school teachers. Of the teachers interviewed, 85% indicated an awareness of teachers in their buildings using media for noneducational purposes. Three-fourths of the respondents had heard of the term *media literacy,* but only one teacher included the ability to create media as a facet of being media literate. Hobbs contended that most teachers do not interrogate the purpose or point of view of documentary filmmakers, "Perhaps because documentary and nonfiction programs are perceived by teachers to be believable and trustworthy . . . " (Hobbs, 1999, p. 17).

Engaging in a text analysis of the marketing of curriculum packages, Brown (2005) also called for critical media literacy not just for students, but for teachers. Adapting Thoman and Jolls' (2005) key questions in media literacy, she analyzed the marketing presentations (via catalog and Web site) of Saxon Math and Great Expectations of Oklahoma, a curriculum package promoting a school-wide character development program. Framing questions used were, "*Apparent purpose*—why was this package created? *Attention-getting techniques*—what means are used by the designers to draw the attention of teachers and administrators? *Point of view*—what perspectives are represented (or left out) about teaching and learning?" (Brown, 2005, p. 126). Those who produce and market any particular curriculum package are not without a stance, and teachers and administrators can use these framing questions to "bring their unconscious reactions to media texts and messages into the forefront of their own thinking, through examining the texts themselves along with information about their creation and their creators" (Brown, 2005, p. 126). She concluded, "Teachers should not just ask students critically to interrogate the cultural messages surrounding them, but teachers should themselves engage in such critical interrogation" (Brown, 2005, p. 137).

Several other studies, through text-based analysis rather than research with students or teachers, also point out the need for critical media literacy in secondary schools. Cortés (2005) used the term *data smog* to refer to the deluge of information presented by the media. He analyzed various popular media sources and the way they organized and disseminated their ideas regarding many types of events and situations of interest to students, such as the portrayal in the popular press of the current war in Iraq. He concluded simply, "Media teach," (Cortés, 2005, p. 71), making a case for the need for students to have opportunities to learn to read these texts, too.

TWO CRITICAL MEDIA LITERACY EDUCATORS: ERNEST MORRELL AND STEVEN GOODMAN

Rich work in media literacy is present within some classrooms and in some extracurricular opportunities offered to youth. Examples of the latter include the work of Ernest Morrell (2004) in Los Angeles and Steven Goodman (2003, 2005) in New York.

Morrell (2004) presented several action research studies in critical literacy based on students' interactions with and interpretations of the texts of popular culture, without calling upon the typical tools of media literacy. Instead, he sought from the beginning to encourage students to voice their connections to popular media (including films, mass media, sports broadcasts, and product tie-ins) in a critique of the media. His work examined students' abilities to use media critique as a vehicle for a larger critique of social norms and practice. Without naming his work as research in media literacy education, Morrell (2004) asked questions of his students as they viewed *The Godfather*: "Who is hidden in the shadows? Who is captured in full light? To whom does the camera defer? Who does the camera subordinate? . . . Who has the power? Who wants it?" (p. 78).

Describing his work with a high school research institute during the summer, Morrell (2004) wrote of apprenticing "urban youth as critical researchers of urban issues" (p. 94). In 2000, the research institute centered on the Democratic National Convention held in Los Angeles. After settling on their research questions, one student inquiry group surveyed convention participants and shadow (alternative) convention participants, conducted a single-day text analysis of newspaper coverage of the convention, and interviewed media personnel. Morrell (2004) reported that analysis of their data led the student researchers to conclude that,

> Many students have a tendency to read and interact with mainstream media without questioning the perspective, the experience, the truth, the author's positionality, and the expertise of others, let alone how it might affect students in the process of identity formation to determine how they saw themselves and how they interact with others. . . . Students, they argued, need to be trained in critical media literacy and seen as experts on youth to be empowered to change the future for the better. (p. 99)

At the Educational Video Center (EVC) in New York City, Goodman (2003, 2005) also worked with inner city youth as researchers. However, EVC students' work focused on creating media as a means to engage in critique. The 22 year history of the EVC is reported by Goodman in narrative fashion rather than framed as a report of longitudinal research. The short documentary films are available for sale through a catalog and the organization's Web site as a way to report findings to a larger mainstream audience. Films address topics that are close to the students' experiences, such as the effects of unequal funding for public schools, youth suicide, gang violence, and why so many inner city youth enlist in the military.

Though the work of the EVC is usually extracurricular with students working after school in a community workshop, Goodman (2003) also imported EVC methods into a high school classroom. Using case study methodology, his research questions included, "What, then, does it look like when students in the classroom practice this kind of community-based and learner-centered media work? . . . Which practices change, and which ones remain the same? And how do the students experience the lesson?" (Goodman, 2003, p. 63). As he reported the results of this classroom research through transcripts of dialogue and contextual descriptions based on observations over time, the data revealed many examples of growth in student literacy skills. However, Goodman (2003) focused instead on the way media literacy pedagogy transforms students' self-perceptions, concluding, "By sharing and listening to the stories of despair that so many teens carry inside every day in school, the students learned to explore deeper levels of truth and hope" (p. 98).

CONCLUDING THOUGHTS

Clearly, there is a great deal of interest in critical media literacy among teachers and students who have engaged in the process of analyzing and creating media texts. Unfortunately, the existing media literacy research in and about secondary schools is spotty, leaving many avenues open for future research. To date, Hobbs and Frost (2003) conducted the only large-scale quantitative study in the United States devoted to examining the impact of media literacy instruction on student communication skills. There is certainly a need for more such studies if advocates of critical media literacy are to make inroads toward broad acceptance and deep implementation in secondary schools within the current climate of "scientifically proven" reforms called for by *No Child Left Behind Act.*

However, the thick description and student voice characteristic of qualitative research in the field is persuasive. Fox (2005) made a case for the aptness of qualitative designs to the study of critical media literacy, even while acknowledging that federal funding to support qualitative research has disappeared. He pointed out both possibilities and pitfalls of further research in the area. Among his list of 11 questions for future research in media literacy are some particularly intriguing thoughts:

> How do media affect the development of students' voices? How do students respond to rapid, brief, fragmented, and decontextualized media messages, such as those delivered in television commercials and in 'news headlines' programs? What are teachers' perceptions of the barriers they face in teaching about media? What are the ethical issues within the media literacy movement itself, and how are they resolved? (Fox, 2005, pp. 252–253)

As Rogow (2005) averred, "The critical next step is media literacy efficacy research" (p. 286). Secondary teachers are using media literacy, but we know little about to what extent and in what way. Media literacy makes so much sense, as a means of using personal relevance to help connect school with students' lived experience, as a way to give voice to teachers and students as they create their own media messages, and as a vehicle for social transformation. It is up to teachers and researchers to *just do it*—and to publicize what they have done.

REFERENCES

Alvermann, D., Hagood, M. C., & Williams, K. H. (2001). Image, language, and sound: Making meaning with popular culture texts. *Reading Online, 4*(11). Retrieved May 13, 2005, from http://www.readingonline.org/newliteracies/action/alvermann/index.html

Brown, P. U. (2005). The shadow curriculum. In G. Schwarz & P. U. Brown (Eds.), *Media literacy: Transforming curriculum and teaching. The 104th Yearbook of the National Society for the Study of Education, Part I* (pp. 119–139). Malden, MA: Blackwell Publishing.

Buckingham, D. (2003). *Media education: Literacy, learning, and contemporary culture.* Malden, MA: Blackwell.

California State Board of Education. (2005). *Grades eleven and twelve: English language arts content standards.* Retrieved September 10, 2005, from http://www.cde.ca.gov/be/st/ss/enggrades11-12.asp

Carnegie Council on Adolescent Development. (1995). *Great transitions: Preparing adolescents for a new century.* New York: Carnegie Corporation.

Chandler-Olcott, K., & Mahar, D. (2003). "Tech-savviness" meets multiliteracies: Exploring adolescent girls' technology-mediated literacy practices. *Reading Research Quarterly, 38,* 356–385.

Channel One. (2004). *About Channel One.* Retrieved September 4, 2004, from http://www.channelone.com/common_about/

Cortés, C. (2005). How the media teach. In G. Schwarz & P. U. Brown (Eds.), *Media literacy: Transforming curriculum and teaching. The 104th Yearbook of the National Society for the Study of Education, Part I* (pp. 55–73). Malden, MA: Blackwell Publishing.

Davies, J. (1993). The impact of the mass media upon the health of early adolescents. *Journal of Health Education, Supplement to 24,* 28–S35.

Eken, A. N. (2002). The third eye. *Journal of Adolescent & Adult Literacy, 46,* 220–230.

Ferrington, G., & Anderson-Inman, L. (1996). Media literacy: Upfront and on-line. *Journal of Adolescent & Adult Literacy, 39,* 666–670.

Feuerstein, M. (1999). Media literacy in support of critical thinking. *Journal of Educational Media, 24*(1), 43–54.

Fox, R. F. (1996). *Harvesting minds: How TV commercials control kids.* Westport, CT: Praeger.

Fox, R. F. (2005). Researching media literacy: Pitfalls and possibilities. In G. Schwarz, & P. U. Brown (Eds.), *Media literacy: Transforming curriculum and teaching. The 104th Yearbook of the National Society for the Study of Education, Part I* (pp. 251–259). Malden, MA: Blackwell Publishing.

Frey, N., & Fisher, D. (2004). Using graphic novels, anime, and the Internet in an urban high school. *English Journal, 93*(3), 19–25.

Gee, J. P. (2003). *What video games have to teach us about learning and literacy.* New York: Palgrave Macmillan.

Goodman, S. (2003). *Teaching youth media: A critical guide to literacy, video production, and social change.* New York: Teachers College Press.

Goodman, S. (2005). The practice and principles of teaching critical literacy at the Educational Video Center. In G. Schwarz & P. U. Brown (Eds.), *Media literacy: Transforming curriculum and teaching. The 104th Yearbook of the National Society for the Study of Education, Part I* (pp. 206–228). Malden, MA: Blackwell Publishing.

Hart, A. (2001). Researching media education in English. *Research in Education, 66,* 28–39.

Hobbs, R. (1999). *The uses (and misuses) of mass media resources in secondary schools.* Unpublished manuscript. (ERIC Document Reproduction Services No. ED439452)

Hobbs, R. (2004). A review of school-based initiatives in media literacy education. *American Behavioral Scientist, 48*(1), 42–59.

Hobbs, R. (2005a). Media literacy and the K–12 content areas. In G. Schwarz & P. U. Brown (Eds.), *Media literacy: Transforming curriculum and teaching. The 104th Yearbook of the National Society for the Study of Education, Part I* (pp. 74–99). Malden, MA: Blackwell Publishing.

Hobbs, R. (2005b). What's news? *Educational Leadership, 63*(2), 58–61.

Hobbs, R., & Frost, R. (2003). Measuring the acquisition of media-literacy skills. *Reading Research Quarterly, 38*, 330–355.

Hoffman, G., & Brecklin, T. (1996). A media literacy course for middle school students [Electronic version]. *ETC: A Review of General Semantics, 53*(1), 39–47.

Kruger, E. (1998). Media literacy does work, trust me. *English Journal, 87*(1), 17–20.

Kubey, R, & Baker, F. (1999). Has media literacy found a curricular foothold? *Education Week, 19*(9), 56–57.

Maness, K. (2004). Teaching media-savvy students about the popular media. *English Journal, 93*(3), 46–51.

McBrien, J. L. (2005). Uninformed in the information age: Why media necessitate critical thinking education. In G. Schwarz & P. U. Brown (Eds.), *Media literacy: Transforming curriculum and teaching. The 104th Yearbook of the National Society for the Study of Education, Part I* (pp. 18–34). Malden, MA: Blackwell Publishing.

Media Literacy Clearinghouse. (2005). *State standards which include elements of media literacy.* Retrieved September 9, 2005, from http://medialit.med.sc.edu/missouri.htm

Morrell, E. (2004). *Linking literacy and popular culture: Finding connections for lifelong learning.* Norwood, MA: Christopher-Gordon Publishers, Inc.

National Council for the Social Studies. (1994). *Mission statement.* Retrieved November 30, 2005, from http://www.socialstudies.org/about/

National Council of Teachers of English. (1996). *Standards for English language arts.* Retrieved November 30, 2005, from http://www.ncte.org/about/over/standards/110846.htm

Pungente, J. J., Duncan, B., & Andersen, N. (2005). The Canadian experience: Leading the way. In G. Schwarz & P. U. Brown (Eds.), *Media literacy: Transforming curriculum and teaching. The 104th Yearbook of the National Society for the Study of Education, Part I* (pp. 140–160). Malden, MA: Blackwell Publishing.

Redmon, R. J. (2000). *Vernacular literacies of adolescent boys: A multi-case qualitative inquiry.* Unpublished doctoral dissertation, Oklahoma State University, Oklahoma..

Rogow, F. (2005). Terrain in transition: Reflecting on the pedagogy of media literacy education. In G. Schwarz, & P. U. Brown (Eds.), *Media literacy: Transforming curriculum and teaching. The 104th Yearbook of the National Society for the Study of Education, Part I* (pp. 282–287). Malden, MA: Blackwell Publishing.

Schiebe, C. L. (2004). A deeper sense of literacy: Curriculum-driven approaches to media literacy in the K–12 classroom. *American Behavioral Scientist, 48*(1), 60–68.

Schwarz, G. (2000). Exploring media literacy with young adults. *The ALAN Review, 28*(1). Retrieved on May 16, 2005, from http://scholar.lib.vt.edu/ejournals/ALAN/v28n1/schwarz.html

Schwarz, G. (2005). Overview: What is media literacy, who cares, and why? In G. Schwarz, & P. U. Brown (Eds.), *Media literacy: Transforming curriculum and teaching. The 104th Yearbook of the National Society for the Study of Education, Part I* (pp. 5–17). Malden, MA: Blackwell Publishing.

Schwarz, G. E. (2002). Graphic novels for multiple literacies. *Journal of Adolescent & Adult Literacy, 46*, 262–265.

Semali, L. (2005). Why media literacy matters in American schools. In G. Schwarz & P. U. Brown (Eds.), *Media literacy: Transforming curriculum and teaching. The 104th Yearbook of the National Society for the Study of Education, Part I* (pp. 35–54). Malden, MA: Blackwell Publishing.

Silverblatt, A. (2004). Media as social institution. *American Behavioral Scientist, 48*(1), 35–41.

Strasburger, V. C. (1995). *Adolescents and the media: Medical and psychological impact.* Thousand Oaks, CA: Sage.

Thier, M. (2005). Merging media and science: Learning to weigh sources and not just evidence. In G. Schwarz & P. U. Brown (Eds.), *Media literacy: Transforming curriculum and teaching. The 104th Yearbook of the National Society for the Study of Education, Part I* (pp. 260–268). Malden, MA: Blackwell Publishing.

Thoman, E. (1999). Skills and strategies for media education. *Educational Leadership, 56*(5), 50–54.

Thoman, E., & Jolls, T. (2005). Media literacy education: Lessons from the Center for Media Literacy. In G. Schwarz & P. U. Brown (Eds.), *Media literacy: Transforming curriculum and teaching. The 104th Yearbook of the National Society for the Study of Education, Part I* (pp. 180–205). Malden, MA: Blackwell Publishing.

Wade, T. D., Davidson, S., & O'Dea, J. A. (2003). A preliminary controlled evaluation of a school-based media literacy program and self-esteem program for reducing eating disorder risk factors. *Internationalljournal of Eating Disorders, 33*, 371–383.

Wilhelm, J. D., & Smith, M. W. (2002). *"Reading don't fix no chevys": Literacy in the lives of young men.* Portsmouth, NH: Heinemann.

Yates, B. L. (2002). *Media education's present and future: A survey of teachers.* Retrieved on May 16, 2005, from http://www.westga.edu/~byates/teacher.htm

Zill, K. (2002). Media literacy: Television meets the internet [Electronic version]. *Multimedia Schools, 9*(2), 24–28.

49

WANTING TO LOOK A THOUSAND TIMES: BLENDING VISUAL AND TEXTUAL ELEMENTS IN THE CONTEMPORARY YOUNG ADULT NOVEL

Jennifer Lynn Wolf
STANFORD UNIVERSITY

In "Reading Lessons: Graphic Novels 101," Rudiger (2006) described her technique for introducing graphic novels to English teachers: She distributed a page from a graphic novel, one that arranged the elements of picture, text, and symbol in a variety of panel combinations and directions and asked for a volunteer to read the page aloud. Ensuing discussions inevitably center around what it means to read, what do we look at when we are reading, how do we know what it means, and how do we express it? I was eager to try Rudiger's method with contemporary young adult (YA) novels, especially those that blend visual and textual elements between their covers.

For the exercise, I selected *Monster* (Myers, 1999), the first YA novel to be awarded the Printz Award in 2000. The book is an urban crime novel incorporating a variety of genres, text types, design formats, and illustrations. In fact, it is a novel with both an author (Walter Dean Myers) and an illustrator (his son, Christopher Myers). For the read-aloud passage, I chose a two-page spread that college students in my YA literature class have often focused on when we read the book together.

Multiple questions presented themselves as I tried to read these pages aloud. Because the bulk of the printed text looks on the page like a play script, I readied myself for a dramatic reading, though I did not know if I should read what was labeled as a voice over differently than I would a standard play line. As I tried to create voices for each of two inmate characters, I realized that they are introduced to the novel for the first time on the two pages I had chosen, so I knew nothing about them other than the words they spoke here. Flipping back one page, I found the following passage, but it raised more questions than it answered: "FADE IN: INTERIOR: CELL at nighttime: We barely see the outlines of the two inmates, 2 of whom are sleeping on the floor." What exactly is a "FADE IN" and should it influence how I read the ensuing lines? What about the visual image of the two inmates sleeping on the floor, and should that affect my reading? Why is Steve, the protagonist, given dialogue in the scene if he is not physically present, and how should I read the words of someone not there? Should I read any of the character labels, or just their lines? What about the faded questions offered as handwritten marginalia? Should I read them aloud, and if so, how? Who is speaking these words, and how should I represent their faded quality? And, finally, what about the photographs—is there any way to read those aloud? Do they need to be included, and if not, why are they there in the first place?

Reading young adult novels is not what it used to be. This statement is true for many reasons—the sheer number of novels written for teens, the reading ages to which these novels are geared, the subject matters treated, the authors who cross over (both media and genre) to write them, and the variety of characters and settings included in them. But the changing feature that is the focus of this chapter is the *visual* nature of the YA novel.

The American Library Association has long given out two major annual words for literature for young readers: the Caldecott, awarded on the merits of the illustration in picture books, and the Newbery, awarded on the merits of the story presented in chapter books. Traditionally, visual and narrative aspects of young people's literature have been treated distinctly. This chapter explores how the contemporary YA novel incorporates visual elements into its textual narrative to create a challenging and aesthetic literary genre for teen readers. YA novels that make use of spot illustrations, graphic design techniques, the visual arts, and multiple narrative perspectives display understanding and respect for the multiple ways teens can and do read in their daily lives beyond the classroom. YA novels also make use of our growing recognition that learning through today's literacies calls upon our ability to read across modes and beyond the printed word in new ways.

VISUAL LEARNING

In the past 25 years, educators have focused our attention on the role of the visual in teaching and learning. In the early 1980s, Howard Gardner (1993) reconceptualized intelligence—away from the notion of a single, general, countable ability, and toward the notion of multiple abilities that support the wide range of adult roles that we find across time and cultures (Kornhaber, Fierros, & Veenema, 2004). Among other things, Gardner asked us to consider spatial thinking as a form of intelligence, specifically "the ability that allows people to perceive visual or spatial information, to transform this information, and to recreate visual images from memory" (Gardner, 1993). The 1980s also witnessed a steep rise in societal screen time, and as some teachers felt the influence of television, movies, and the computer, they began paying attention to *visual literacy*, a concept posited by those studying the screen arts to refer to the ability to read, produce, and understand visually imbued communication (Burmark, 2002). Advocates for the study of visual literacy recognize that those who live in postindustrial societies find themselves inundated with visual images, hence the need to examine image meanings in terms of truth value, action potential, and much more. Visual literacy advocates also point out that as image readers, we must constantly consider how we should or can interpret the images that surround us and ask what is happening when pictures move us emotionally. These questions lead us then to consider the processes that take place in our minds as we respond to visual devices (Messaris, 1994).

In 1981, Roger Speery won the Nobel Prize in Medicine for his work in split-brain research, demonstrating that the right and left hemispheres of the brain execute distinct functions and identifying the functions of each hemisphere. Educators took permission from hemispheracy studies to use pictures, images, and visuals (purview of the right brain) along with words and numbers (purview of the left brain) in learning and embraced the notion that students can be taught to search their minds for and select appropriate images to enhance their learning (Sousa, 2001). Also in the 1980s, economic shifts in how we fund public education led in part to a renewed interest in, and advocacy of, the role of the arts in education, including attention paid to visual arts. In an attempt to continue funding arts education, some who rose to advocate for the arts argued for their abilities to help students learn other subjects (Fowler, 1996). Still other advocates examined the power of the arts for art's sake and for learning's sake. To this end, Eisner (2002) offered four cognitive benefits of engaging in the visual arts: (a) Engagement in visual arts helps us learn to notice the world; (b) they offer us permission to engage the imagination as a means for exploring new possibilities. Moreover, (c) they invite the development of disposition to tolerate ambiguity, and (d) they are a means through which we may explore our own interior landscapes.

Together, these four cognitive benefits reflect in turn four aspects of visual learning: spatial intelligence, visual literacy, visualization, and the visual arts. Taken together, all these expand our thinking about what it takes to acquire knowledge conveyed through multiple modes simultaneously. Research approaches to visual learning begin from some key principles: Images communicate meaning and deepen our understanding of the symbolic; there is more than one way to approach the learning of something new or complex, and the more ways we approach something the better. Most fundamental is perhaps the tenet that the more meaningful practice learners gain with multimodal materials, the more they dig deeper for meaning, compare facts across contexts, and see themselves as cocreators with authors and artists. YA novels bring into evidence all these principles at work for readers and enable researchers and practitioners (whether in education, arts, industry, or medicine) to see ways to use these principles in their own materials and communication practices.

THE CONTEMPORARY YA NOVEL

In the year 2000, the American Library Association added a third major annual award to the Caldecott and the Newbery—the Printz Award, for the best Young Adult novel. The Printz Award is, among other things, the American Library Association's attempt to acknowledge and define the genre of the YA novel as something separate and distinct from pictures books for the very young and chapter books for readers in middle childhood. The making of this distinction is still a work in progress (for example, one year Nancy Farmer's, 2002, science fiction novel *The House of the Scorpion* was nominated for both the Newbery and the Printz awards). Even so, the YA novel is clearly moving up in recognition as a genre of its own. One feature that makes this genre unique is its incorporation of visual elements—both the *types* of visual elements the YA novel incorporates and the *ways* it incorporates them. The remainder of this chapter explores the YA novel's use of four of these visual elements.

Beyond its growth in literary attention and accolades, contemporary YA literature has grown dramatically in sales and popularity. Tipped off by the Harry Potter effect, YA novels have been written, published, and sold at record rates since the last half of the 1990s. Every major publishing house in the United States has at least one YA imprint, and international YA titles have traveled onto best-seller lists in the United States. For the purposes of this chapter, I have examined a collection of award-winning (nominated for either the Printz Award or the National Book Award for Young Readers) and best-selling (as determined by the *New York Times* and *Publishers Weekly*) YA novels published since the year 2000. Some titles in this collection are both award winners and best sellers, some are titles in larger series, and among the 60 resulting titles, a wide variety of subgenres is represented.

ILLUSTRATION

Illustrated literature for young readers is nothing new. As early as 1658, we have published proof of the belief that illustration could either help children learn to read, make their reading more pleasurable, or both. (Educational reformer John Amos Comenius wrote and illustrated *Orbis Sensualium Pictus* "The Visible World in Pictures" specifically for children. This volume remained popular in Europe for more than two centuries (Burlingame, 1997).) Today, wordless picture books tell their stories with no text at all, picture books combine text and pictures in a wide variety of ratios, and chapter books employ occasional illustrations within and through their chapters. Pictures in these works take the place of words, repeat words, define words, and illuminate the mechanics of plot, character, and setting: They translate the literal. Illustration also carries the power to communicate the figurative, the literary, and the aesthetic. An impressive literature has developed to explore the many reading experiences that children's literature creates by combining words with pictures. Artists, teachers, librarians, literary scholars, and literary critics have all added their experiences and perspectives to this question, and they demonstrate for us how picture books communicate from a grammar of images (Nodelman, 1988); emphasize the relationship between shape, form; and emotion (Bang, 2000); tap deep issues of emotional significance (Spitz, 1999); and offer guidance with the sophisticated demands of decision making (Wolf, 2004) to name just a few.

Much less explored is how the genre of the young adult novel makes use of illustration and how it combines text and pictures to create a literary reading experience for adolescents. Illustration is not the required element in YA literature that is in children's literature. Of the 60 award-winning and best-selling YA novels written in the past six years, about 20% use illustration in some way. And, setting aside graphic novels and comic books as separate genres, the percentage of pictures in relation to text in illustrated young adult novels is much smaller than it is for children's literature. Illustrated YA novels employ spot and occasional illustrations that are small in size, nearly always black and white, line drawings and photographs, as well as collaged multimedia pictures.

The most conventional use of spot illustrations grows out of chapter books for children. Small pictures regularly highlight important events, settings, or characters to follow. The American hardback editions of the Harry Potter novels use illustration in this way. The fourth novel in the series, *Harry Potter and the Goblet of Fire* (Rowling, 2000), like its predecessors, offered Mary GrandPré's shades of black and grey pastel drawings, each roughly the size of a dollar coin placed between the chapter numbers and titles. Chapter 1, titled "The Riddle House," shows such a picture of a room in a house, specifically the back of an arm chair facing a fire, with a diamond-eyed snake undulating behind the chair legs—the very scene Harry will dream about as the book opens. Each chapter follows suit with a different picture. These illustrations are not necessary, in the strict sense of the word, for reading and understanding the novel; indeed, the paperback and British editions do not even offer them. However, they serve important purposes.

Spot illustrations like these whet the reading appetite by previewing the story to come (readers can enjoy feeling knowledgeable recognition when they arrive at the illustrated points within the chapters; they can also link the pictures together to form a kind of pictorial preview of the entire novel). Pictures used in this way pose questions of foreshadowing and prediction (Who might be sitting in the armchair? Accompanied by a snake? And fire?). At the same time, spot illustrations highlight key happenings of the novel (the snake is mentioned briefly in this first chapter where his picture appears, but he goes on to serve an important role later in the novel). Though offered only once per chapter, spot illustrations like these encourage connections between and among chapters as well as activate background knowledge (series readers know that Harry's archenemy Voldemort can speak to snakes, so the question of just who is sitting in that arm chair anyway becomes especially critical.). These pictures invite and reward careful consideration of detail by offering up discreet bits of information not revealed in the text (chapter 1 describes the snake as having a diamond-shaped tail and scales on its skin, but the picture adds the further detail of its diamond-shaped eyes); and they communicate emotional affect through shape, color, and form (the thin, pointed diamond patterns combined with the smoky, waving shadows in the picture communicate a sharp, suffocating, and dangerous presence).

YA fantasy novels have taken occasional illustrations in another direction, but one that also encourages deep reading. YA fantasy novels carry a devoted readership (25% of the best-selling and award-winning novels written since 2000 are fantasy or science fiction, and most of these titles belong to larger series). They carry their readership into complex, imaginary worlds constructed of invented cities, countries and planets, languages, laws, and technologies. Many of these novels turn to occasional illustrations to help their readers organize and track information, with maps, family trees, battle charts, blue prints, schematics, pictographs, and illustrated glossaries. These illustrations are typically placed on the book's frontispiece, end papers, or perhaps as a centerfold. The content and placement of these illustrations encourages bidirectional, recursive reading with repeated and frequent movement between text and illustrations. In this way, fantasy novels encourage their readers to clarify relationships and make connections within a story, and thus offer their readers visual props for carrying information between and among volumes in a series. Occasional pictures also aid the reader in visualizing the invented and fantastical—an especially important reading move when the subject at hand exists nowhere else but in the author's mind. Spatial intelligence will serve the fantasy reader well, and YA fantasy novels encourage the exercising of this intelligence with their marriage of text and pictures.

The best-selling *Artemis Fowl* series (Colfer, 2001) adorns the bottoms of its pages with lines of fairy code—an invented pictograph language used by the novel's fairy characters. Readers are challenged to "crack the code." To do so, readers must carefully inspect the small shapes and designs used to construct the code, collect clues from the text concerning the shapes and objects pictured, and decode the meaning of the pictographs. For these efforts by readers, the author offers the general enjoyment that comes from working and solving puzzles plus the sense of mastery of a new language and membership in the club of fellow fairy speakers. Moreover, such readers gain exclusive information that answers questions embedded in the novel. As the series' popularity has grown, the author wrote (and drew) a companion volume to the series, *The Artemis Fowl Files* (Colfer, 2004), which along with diagrams of the more complex physics concepts used in the novel (using heat from the earth's core for space travel, for example), also provides textual and pictorial instructions of how to understand and communicate in the fairy language.

Contemporary YA novels also use spot illustration to inject crucial information into a story that is nowhere contained in written words. Walter Myers' (1999) novel *Monster* introduces its protagonist, Steve Harmon, as he begins to stand trial for a robbery. The novel spans the length of the trial, and throughout the protagonist shares with readers the journal he keeps in prison, as well as a film script he writes of his own trial, but, noticeably, he never tells the reader whether or not he committed the robbery. To determine Steve's innocence or guilt for themselves, readers can read back over the novel's texts looking for clues; they may also read back over 10 photographs carefully placed throughout the text. The passage just discussed includes two such photographs as illustrations. Readers will likely notice the picture's grainy quality, the camera's angle above Steve's head, and the shelves of merchandise in the background. Young people will be especially inclined to deduce that these are photographs made by surveillance cameras. Yet these photographic images are never entered as evidence in the trial portions of the novel. They are not labeled or written about in the text in any way; in fact, they are placed on pages of written dialogue between prison inmates discussing the meaning of truth. If readers want the resolution normally promised by a novel's end, they must read the images into and beyond the text themselves.

The mystery *The Gospel According to Larry* (Tashjian, 2001) presents numbered photographs of items important in the protagonist's life as clues to his identity and whereabouts. Ellen Wittlinger's (1999) novel *Hard Love* about teens who publish underground personal magazines includes fictional zines (complete with sketches, cartoons, photographs, and collaged items) that characters in the novel then critique, analyze, copy, and question. Carolyn Coman's novel *Many Stones* offers one portion of a photograph in each chapter; by the end of the novel the reader has been given all of the pieces of the photograph, puzzle style, and the reader is then left to assemble these pieces in the "right" order. The completed photograph gives some reward, to be sure, for it illuminates the meaning of the novel's title. In *Criss Cross*, author and illustrator Lynn Rae Perkins (2005) scatters quirky line drawings and tiny, altered photographs throughout her text. Sometimes her illustrations match the adjoining text, but sometimes the match is metaphorical rather than literal (such as when the narrator is describing the emotional confusion in a complicated relationship but the illustration offers a picture of electrons colliding with one another inside a smoky spiral). With the forms of spot illustration described here, a reader cannot skip the pictures and still completely understand the text, nor can she understand the full meaning of the text by looking at the pictures alone. The reader shoulders the responsibility of connecting the visual with the textual to complete the reading experience.

GRAPHIC DESIGN

In addition to considering the shape of illustrations and pictures in YA novels, readers can also read the shape of words in YA novels. Former United States Poet Laureate Billy Collins (2006) talked about poets as architects who build their poems with shape, giving them a physicality, contour, and body on the page. Contemporary YA novels display evidence of taking this same architectural approach to the construction of their genre. While many of the recent YA best sellers and award winners elect the uniform look of a conventional novel—single, standard type font, spelling out each of the words that make up the traditional paragraphs and chapters that extend throughout the novel—others do not. Over 40% of the 60 novels considered for this chapter use multiple font types and point sizes, punctuation marks and forms of emphases, margins and spaces, and symbols and numbers—any symbol or function available via a keyboard—to style their content for visual consideration. Some graphically designed YA novels highlight accepted conventions of text images; teen readers can see that bolded words demand emphasis, for example, or that words written altogether with no separating spaces are to be read in one breath. In other cases, the genre models for its readers how to communicate meaning through visual invention.

YA literature enthusiastically welcomes multiple genres into its fold, and it uses graphic design to signal the inclusion of these genres to readers. A list of all the genres found within the pages of the 60 novels considered for this chapter is too long to print here, but a representative sampling includes: dictionary entries, instant messages, poems, song lyrics, advertisements, lists, scripts, Bible verses, dairy entries, notes passed between friends, pages from instruction manuals, and recipes. Some novels select and weave a single additional genre into their texts for thematic reasons, while other novels collage together five, six, seven, or more genres and use little or no traditional novel-like prose to bind them together. To make sense of these novels, teen readers first must activate prior visual knowledge (What does the print in a newspaper look like? How do advertisements make use of space? What emotions show up in emails?). Next readers must recognize and track which visual cues signal which genres, since such graphic transitions are not explicitly labeled for readers. The best-selling and award- winning confessional romance, *Angus Thongs and Full Frontal Snogging* (Rennison, 2000), (as well as its five sequels) is an example of an epistolary novel exponentially expanded by genres. The text of the novel is formed out of Georgia Nicholson's diary entries, which in turn incorporate others' notes, letters, post cards, and memos to her, in addition to her notes, letters, essays, and cards written to others. To signal textually each of these genre transitions would be a cumbersome impediment to the compulsive reading quality prized by teen readers of these novels. Instead, the text assumes and builds on the complex back-and-forth, up-and-down visual reading capacity of its audience.

In the futuristic world of M.T. Anderson's (2003) novel *Feed*, characters are implanted at birth with electronic brain feeds that track their every desire and then instantly market products to satisfy their needs. Untitled pages between the novel's early chapters interject white space peppered with snippets of text separated from one another by design symbols. Each snippet is a portion of script from a different feed commercial broadcast; each looks different from the others in its font, lettering, or punctuation style and arranges itself in a different shape appropriate to its topic. As the novel progresses and the protagonist becomes increasingly critical of the feed, these interjection pages slowly respond by displaying shorter and shorter snippets of commercial text, presented in increasingly similar scripts, all composed in single lines across the page. The words of the advertisements are not the same, but their visual display is. The novel's prose explains in detail how the protagonist changes his thinking about the feed, but the novel also shows how it feels to be dazzled, entertained, hypnotized, bored, and ultimately unmoved by the feed.

One subgenre of YA that warrants particular attention in a discussion of graphic design is the novel in verse. Beyond the YA novels that include or allude to individual poems are those written entirely or largely in verse, their words laid out on the page in stanzas or blank verse rather than in paragraphs. Though at first glance, a novel in verse appears as a shorter read than one in prose, the reality is that the former requires the reader to take in fewer words offered in multiple ways. Readers must also "hear" the words for their diction and sound, and they must perceive the figurative content conveyed through multiple layers of meaning, including the intertextual links to other poems. Visually, the physical forms that the words of these novels assume on the page also carry meanings. When one literary critic praised YA author Virginia Euwer Wolff (2001) for her poetic novel *True Believer*, Wolff rebutted that she had not set out to write a novel in formal verse. Instead, she tried to write the novel in such as a way that the words look on the page the way they sound when you hear them (*Children's Literature Review*, 2003).

Readers are then expected to form mental images as they read from the sound of the protagonist LaVaughn's words and, further, to use the physical shape of the words to suggest the sounds that in turn carry within them mental pictures. Here is a passage from *True Believer* as the author shaped it on the page, describing how LaVaughn feels as she grows apart from old friends, or perhaps as they grow apart from her:

> Folders on my floor
> a bird nest on my ceiling,
> my room is almost how I want it.
> I think of how Myrtle and Annie are slipping away from me
> and I keep remembering
> us three were laying on my bed
> admiring my birds and the leaves on my ceiling tree
> and Myrtle said she wanted me to paint a picture on her ceiling
> only she never decided exactly what she wanted,
> maybe a beach but I didn't think I could do good waves,
> and I never painted her a picture at all. (Wolff, 2001, p. 77)

How does the visual appearance of these words assist a reader? Do the line breaks come where we would expect a person to take a pause when speaking? What does pausing communicate about personality and intention? How does it feel as the reader to be pulled back and forth between the longer and shorter lines? Do the words—in shape, sound, and meaning—communicate the feeling of waves? Ocean waves? Waves of emotion? Wave lengths? Imagining these words written in traditional paragraph form emphasizes the multiple kinds of meanings created by the author's choice to shape the words on the page.

THE VISUAL ARTS

The contemporary YA novel often includes a thematic element that simultaneously honors the interests of its teen audience while affording these readers opportunities to practice visual learning. This may be thought of as the heart of the visual arts. In fact, arts of all kinds surface in YA novels, from performing to industrial to literary to homemaking to visual and musical. It is also often the case that the teenaged protagonists of YA novels pursue the arts, and mastery of their chosen art forms parallel their mastery of the process of growing up, as well as the achievement of claiming their own voices as they enter adulthood. Art making necessitates trial and error, audience and performance, subversion and conformity, critique and praise, and accomplishment—all recognizable ingredients in coming-of-age stories. In the case of the visual arts, YA readers typically get to read through protagonists' construction of their works of art from start to finish, meeting art teachers and mentors along the way and listening in on conversations about the arts, always replete with references to the vocabulary and materials of the arts.

The protagonist of L. H. Anderson's (1999) novel *Speak* enrolled in a high school art class in chapter 1 and worked on a visual arts representation of a tree until the last page, when she handed it in as the final product for her class. Unlike authors who provide narrative spot illustrations for key or complex images in YA novels, Anderson offered no such graphic representations of Melissa's tree; she offered only the narrative. One of the readers' tasks with this novel, then, is to construct for themselves the novel's core visual image by understanding how its creator saw this image—both when she was a novice artist and when she was more experienced. Moreover, readers have to "see" how the art teacher saw the tree and how its critics and admirers viewed it as well. Readers also learn to envision this piece of art in its various draft stages, constructed out of various media. They come to empathize with young artists who feel both the triumphs and the pains of learning that all art forms come from mistakes, accidents, failures, and losses as well as sustained effort, knowledge, and supportive guidance. One third of the 60 award-winning and best-selling YA novels considered for this chapter feature a main character engaged in the visual arts (the percentage climbs to nearly 45% when all art forms are included). Yet, as with *Speak*, only two of these 19 novels offer readers visual images of the art work that figures so centrally in the literary genre. YA novels are about the practice of viewing the visual arts in the *real* world, but they are also very much about envisioning worlds within the eye of the mind.

Because the process of artistic creation holds such a central place within many YA novels, we find that the visual arts parallel the adolescent characters' genre-defining journeys of learning and growth. YA literature highlights the metaphoric and symbolic powers of the arts. Melinda, the protagonist of *Speak* (Anderson, 1999), enters high school paralyzed with silence, and she struggles through the novel to find her voice. Her attempts to learn how to speak up for herself parallel her attempts to create an artistic representation of a tree that will satisfy herself and others. The tandem story lines encourage readers to pay attention to details of similarity, the building blocks of figurative communication, as they showcase the visual arts' power to represent particular experiences in ways that are communal to all who view them. Consumers of the genre see the visual arts used as a tool of intrapersonal learning, and they see it used as a means of intensifying interpersonal experiences. Teens in art-themed novels offer, exchange, and cocreate their art with one another; they examine and read one another's art with care and come to conclusions about artist's fears, priorities, and desires. The teens of *Hard Love* (Whittlinger, 1999) compose and publish their own zines (self-styled compendia of essays, stories, poems, paintings, drawings, and comic strips). They also belong to a zine exchange, whereby they read one another's art: for inspiration, for insight into the authors' life and philosophies, for allusions to yet more art work, and for artistic ideas against which to push and pull as they create their next works of art.

YA novels also explore the visual arts as a means of question asking, as a means of learning within the boundaries of a genre's rules. Steve Harmon, the protagonist of *Monster* (Myers, 1999), records his trial as a movie script in part because he was taking a high school class in movie making at the time of his arrest. He draws on his knowledge of the art form to organize the chaos of his situation (writing the words and actions of others into a script) and to reformat it in a way that is bounded and aesthetic (writing out scene shots, directions for how to construct the filming of the scenes). These actions, in turn, allow him to examine his own struggles from a removed omnipotent stance (as both the director and the audience for a film about his own life). At the conclusion of the novel, when he has been released from prison and returns home, he spends his time making movies with a handheld video camera, filming himself again and again. He does so because, he says, "I want to know who I am. I want to know the road . . . that I took. I want to look at myself a thousand times to look for one true image" (Myers, 1999, p. 281). YA characters and readers alike learn to hold the visual arts up as mirrors, to reflect their images to others to promote introspection and recognition of what has gone before and may open the path ahead.

POINTS OF VIEW

In addition to using illustrative, graphic, and thematic elements to link readers to visual ways of knowing, the contemporary YA novel also employs narrative access to visual practices. Less immediately linked to the visual realm, perhaps, than the link from pictures or design features, narrative point-of-view structures nonetheless offer teens valuable practice in visualizing what they read from multiple perspectives. The first-person narrative point of view is a feature that has defined the genre of YA literature since its first appearance in the 1960s. With first-person narration, readers of YA novels are allowed, invited or required (depending on your own point of view) to enter into the mind of the adolescent. Readers of S. E. Hinton's (1967) "mother of all YA books" (Cart, 1996), *The Outsiders*, hear about life though protagonist Ponyboy's own brand of greaser slang, and readers see it through the eyes of an urban, long-haired, poor gang member. Readers feel life as someone who rebels against the authority of his older brother, who shows unfailing allegiance to his friends, and who senses the impact of the poetry introduced to him by his high school English teacher. This intimate narrative invitation to walk in the shoes of an adolescent was met with immediate enthusiasm by readers young and old, and the vast majority of YA novels written in the next half century have reflected this same point of view.

Since the middle of the 1990s, YA authors have experimented and improvised in various ways with the first-person narrative structure of the YA novel. They have told novels in combinations of first- and third-person points of view, and even from the second-person point of view. Additionally, an increasingly common technique presents a novel narrated in the first-person point of view but through multiple narrators. Or even one narrator at multiple points in his or her life. Of the award-winning and best-selling books, 14 offer experiments or variations on the traditional formula of first- or third-person narrative perspective.

One strategy employed by successful, engaged readers is that of visualizing, creating clear, detailed mental images out of text, and playing these images inside one's mind to track and organize the story (Wilhelm, 1997; Schoenbach, Greenleaf, Cziko, & Hurwitz, 1999). When YA novels offer their text from multiple first-person points of view, they enhance (and complexify) the visualization process for readers. Take Ann Brashares' (2001) best-selling, sequel-spawning, movie-generating girlfriend novel *The Sisterhood of the Traveling Pants*. Instead of the voice of a single protagonist, this novel's narration is shared by four main characters, all of whom fit into one nearly magical pair of thrift-store jeans. The novel is divided into four sections, each of which is told from the point of view of the character in possession of the pants at that time. Readers of this book, not once, but four times, must try on mental images of the pants, like the other girls in the novel, and thereby take on the challenges of coming of age as several different adolescent females.

Reading YA novels from multiple points of view has much in common with another visual task—assembling a jigsaw puzzle composed of many pieces. Each point of view submitted by the author accesses some of the pieces of the puzzle, but many of these do not make complete sense until the alternate points of view create the context into which they will fit. While reading these novels, readers must hold visual images or even partial images in the mind, returning to them to add, delete, reassess, and refocus details as they become useful or not for the larger picture. *The First Part Last* (Johnson, 2003) offers a narrative perspective seldom heard in YA (or any) novels: that of a teenaged father raising his baby. Johnson has the teenager narrate the novel in the first person, but alternating chapters are told from his point of view from before he becomes a father and after he becomes a father. Readers must continually shift. Everything looks different to the character because of this one event, and everything looks different to the reader as well: the personality of the supporting characters in his life; his interests, values, and pastimes; and even his physical body and thus, his sense of self. Reading back and forth through dramatic change, gradual maturing, and shifts of self-perception means running two or more visualizations simultaneously, comparing them, contrasting them, and ultimately, splicing them together to arrive at something that the reader can perceive as the "complete" picture.

WANTING TO LOOK A THOUSAND TIMES

Steve Harmon, the protagonist of *Monster* we met at the beginning of this chapter, confides that he "wants to look at (himself) a thousand times for one true image" (Myers, 1999, p. 281). By blending visual devices with written text, contemporary YA novels create reasons for teens to look again and again as they read for pleasure and pursue depths of meaning. Using illustration, design, art forms, and multiple narrative points of view, YA novels make as transparent as any medium we have the intricacies and the interdependent skills that visual learning depends upon. Moreover, this genre reflects in almost unending ways incentives for increasing short-term memory and drawing deeply from long-term memory to reach in the moment conclusions or to build hypotheses about possible developments to come. They tell us in no uncertain terms that we must think carefully and openly about the similarities of mental processes called for in reading these novels (as well as comics, graphic novels, films, and photographs) and the cognitive demands of interpreting and creating digital imaging and images—certain to become the primary literacy of professional fields in medicine, engineering, and the entertainment world. In developmental and comparative terms, YA novels remind us of what is to come.

REFERENCES

Anderson, L. H. (1999). *Speak*. New York: Farrar Strauss Giroux.

Anderson, M. T. (2003). *Feed*. New York: Candlewick Press.

Bang, M. (2000). *Picture this: How pictures work*. San Francisco: Chronicle Books.

Brashares, A. (2001). *The sisterhood of the traveling pants*. NY: Delacorte.

Burmark, L. (2002). *Visual literacy: Learn to see, see to learn*. Alexandria, VA: ASCD.

Burlingame, C. (1997). *Picturing childhood: The evolution of the children's pictures book*. Oakland, CA: The Regents of the University of California. Retrieved May 20, 2006, from http://www.library.ucla.edu/special/childhood/pictur.htm

Cart, M. (1996). *From romance to realism: 50 years of growth and change in young adult literature*. New York: Harper Collins.

Colfer, E. (2001). *Artemis Fowl*. New York: Hyperion.

Colfer, E. (2004). *The Artemis Fowl files: The ultimate guide to the best selling series*. New York: Hyperion.

Collins, B. (2006, May 17). Poetry on record [Radio series episode]. On T. Gross, & D. Miller (Executive producers), *Fresh Air with Terry Gross*. Philadelphia, PA: WHYY-FM.

Coman, C. (2002). *Many stones*. NY: Puffin.

Children's Literature Review. (2003). *Interview with Virginia Euwer Wolff* (Vol. 90). Farmington Hills, MI: Author.

Eisner, E. (2002). *Arts and the creation of the mind*. New Haven, CT: Yale University Press.

Farmer, N. (2002). *The house of the scorpion*. New York: Antheneum.

Fowler, A. (1996). *Strong arts, strong schools: The promising potential and shortsighted disregard of the arts in American schooling*. Oxford, U.K.: Oxford University Press.

Gardner, H. (1993). *Frames of mind: The theory of multiple intelligences*. New York: Basic Books.

Hinton, S. E. (1967). *The outsiders*. New York: Puffin.

Johnson, A. (2003). *The first part last*. New York: Simon Schuster.

Kornhaber, M. L., Fierros, E. G., & Veenema, S. A. (2004). *Multiple intelligences: Best ideas from research and practice*. San Francisco: Pearson.

Messaris, P. (1994). *Visual "literacy:" Image, mind, and reality*. San Francisco: Westview Press.

Myers, W. D. (1999). *Monster*. New York: HarperCollins, Amistad Imprint.

Nodleman, P. (1988). *Words about pictures: The narrative art of children's picture books*. Athens, GA: Athens University Press.

Perkins, L. R. (2005). *Criss cross*. New York: HarperCollins, Willowbooks Imprint.

Rennison, L. (2000). *Angus, thongs, and full frontal snogging: The confessions of Georgia Nicholson*. New York: Harper Collins.

Rowling, J. K. (2000). *Harry Potter and the goblet of fire*. New York: Scholastic.

Rudiger, H. M. (2006, March/April). Reading lessons: graphic novels 101. *The Horn Book Magazine*, 126.

Schoenbach, R., Greenleaf, C., Cziko, C., & Hurwitz, L. (1999). *Reading for understanding: A guide to improving reading and middle school classrooms*. San Francisco: Jossey-Bass.

Sousa, D. (2001). *How the brain learns* (2nd ed.). Thousand Oaks, CA: Sage.

Spitz, E. (1999). *Inside picture books*. New Haven, CT: Yale University Press.

Tashjian, J. (2001). *The gospel according to Larry*. NY: Henry Holt.

Wilhelm, J. D. (1997). *"You Gotta BE the Book": Teaching engaged and reflective reading with adolescents*. New York: Teachers College Press.

Whittlinger, E. (1999). *Hard love*. New York: Simon Schuster.

Wolf, S. (2004). *Interpreting literature with children*. Mahwah, NJ: Lawrence Erlbaum Associates.

Wolff, V. E. (2001). *True believer*. New York: Antheneum.

50

SHAKESPEARE AND GAIMAN: STRANGE BEDFELLOWS ATTAIN IMMORTALITY

Jacqueline T. Pham and Andrea A. Lunsford[1]
STANFORD UNIVERSITY

> I would give *anything* to have your gifts. Or more than anything to give men dreams that would live on long after I am dead.
>
> —the character of Will Shakespeare in "Men of Fortune," Issue 13 of *The Sandman* (Gaiman, 1990a)

With words reminiscent of Marlowe's (2003) Faustus, the character of William Shakespeare makes a pact with Morpheus, the Lord of Dreams, in Neil Gaiman's (1990a) "Men of Fortune" (an issue in Gaiman's graphic novel series, *The Sandman*) to create dreams that would guide men's imaginations for centuries to come. Both William Shakespeare and Neil Gaiman mastered the art of bringing words to life, each in his own fashion. Shakespeare had a rare gift for writing enthralling plays that helped lift the genre out of the pits of common folks' entertainment to the pinnacle of English literature. Four hundred years later, comics rose from low-brow children's fare to a serious art form capable of charting new territory, thanks to artists such as Art Spiegelman, Chris Ware, Michael Chabon, Lynda Barry, Marjane Satrapi—and Neil Gaiman.

HISTORY OF COMICS/GRAPHIC NOVELS

Until fairly recently, linking the name of Shakespeare with a comic artist would have been nearly impossible—seen, at best, as an insult to the bard. But the technological revolution of the last 30 years, the rise in importance of images,[2] and the ease with which images can be created, have led to an outpouring of works that link words and images and that are—like Shakespeare's plays—meant to be experienced as performances. Works that link words and images are not entirely new, to be sure: some artists, such as Scott McCloud (1994), traced the origins of comics and graphic novels as far back as the cave paintings of Lescaux, the Bayeux tapestry, or the great satirical works of William Hogarth ("A Harlot's Progress") and Thomas Rowlandson ("The Tours of Dr. Syntax"), especially since the latter engravings were designed to be viewed side by side, in narrative sequence, thus fitting McCloud's definition of *comics* as "sequential art" (p. 7). Most, however, would agree with Brian Walker (2004), who chronicled the rise of comics in the United States, from the cartoons that began appearing in American newspapers in the 1860s to the Yellow Kid, Richard Outcault's star of his *Hogan's Alley* series, which ran throughout the 1890s. Eventually, most newspapers carried "funnies," and strips such as Crazy Kat, The Gumps, and Mutt and Jeff enjoyed huge popularity.

Even in their heyday, however, such comic strips were rarely regarded as art, much less as "literature." With the 1978 publication of Will Eisner's (2001) *A Contract with God and Other Tenement Stories: A Graphic Novel*—often cited as one of the first of the new genre—comics took a serious leap, and the last 30 years have witnessed huge growth in numbers of graphic novels published and increasing attention to them as a major art form. To date, two graphic novels have been recognized with prestigious Pulitzer Prizes (Art Spiegelman won the award in 1992 for *Maus*, and Michael Chabon won in 2001 for *The Amazing Adventures of Kavalier and Klay*), and they are increasingly taught in schools and colleges. Today, from North America to Japan, comics and graphic novels (and the movies that often grow out of or accompany them) are hailing young audiences, who not only respond powerfully to the word/image narratives performed in their pages but often go on to create their own, thus participating actively in this form of literacy.

[1] Jackie Pham wrote this essay for her Stanford University sophomore seminar, The Graphic Novel, taken during 2006 winter term and taught by Andrea Lunsford. While they have worked together to revise the text for this volume, Jackie is the primary author of this piece.

[2] Michael Stephens's (1998) *The Rise of the Image, the Fall of the Word,* is one book that traces this sweeping change.

So we know that "funnies" began to appear regularly in North American newspapers in the last quarter of the 19th century and that these evolved into enormously popular comic strips, which the *Columbia Encyclopedia* (Columbia University, 2001–05) defined as "The combination of cartoon with a story line, laid out in a series of pictorial panels across a page and concerning a continuous character or set of characters, whose thoughts and dialogues are indicated by means of 'balloons' containing written speech." We also know that these comic strips—from the 1897 *Katzenjammer Kids* to the 1906 *Little Nemo in Slumberland,* 1930s *Tintin,* and the current *Doonesbury*—were soon joined by the comic books (think of superheroes such as Spider-Man, Captain America, Superman, and Wonder Woman) marketed so successfully by Marvel Comics and DC Comics. However, the medium has not stopped expanding and developing, giving rise most recently to new forms of expression such as the Web comic. Without the physical boundaries of a book's page, Web comics can go on indefinitely, making the comic a more cohesive whole, and breaking out of the traditional linear progression of panels into a network of images.

However, the graphic novel trumps nearly all other comic forms in its ability to reach both young and adult readers. What, then, is the graphic novel? Put most simply, a graphic novel (*graphic* indicates images, drawings, pictures, and *novel* indicates a word narrative) is a book-length comic that treats a serious theme, what Art Spiegelman (2006) once referred to as a comic long enough to need a bookmark. As Will Eisner explains in an interview with *Time*, in writing *A Contract with God,* he "sat down and tried to do a book that would physically look like a 'legitimate' book and at the same time write about a subject matter that would never have been addressed in comic form, which is man's relationship with God" (Arnold, 2003). While the term *graphic novel* has stuck—you can now find graphic novel sections in most bookstores and many libraries—many are dissatisfied with it, some seeing it as a pretentious bid for respectability and others as a misnomer that would be better replaced with "graphic literature" or "graphic story" or even "book-length comic."

In any event, the range of popular comics to the most serious graphic novels is very wide indeed, encompassing everything from Neil Gaiman's (2004) *The Sandman: Endless Nights* or Spiegelman's haunting Holocaust memoir *(Maus)* (Spiegelman, 2004) to Superhero adventures and the hottest item of all, manga (Japanese comics). Moreover, graphic novels and comics are increasingly making their way into movies (e.g., *American Splendor, Sin City,* and *The League of Extraordinary Gentlemen*) and other forms of communication (e.g., Charles Schwab's recent television advertisements that feature a comic-character Schwab dispensing advice via the traditional comic speech balloon). The merging of word and image—the hallmark of both comics and graphic novels—is now a major literate form. And whatever new terms emerge to capture these forms, teachers will most likely favor the most ambitious and serious of the graphic novels, those characterized not just by a merging of words and images but by intensive creativity and quality of thought as well.

ENTER NEIL GAIMAN

Gaiman, a prolific author of comics and graphic novels, has an enormous following of readers, who enter enthusiastically into the world he creates in *The Sandman* series. Although he appeals to younger readers, he enjoys introducing them to works of high quality but low "hipness"—as in his decision to integrate Shakespeare and two of his most popular plays into *The Sandman.* "A Midsummer Night's Dream" and "The Tempest" appeared in Issues 19 and 75 of *The Sandman* after Gaiman introduced Shakespeare in Issue 13. The Bard's plays carry the heart of *The Sandman* in their comic book reincarnation, lending Gaiman's work greater depth and sophistication. Instead of merely repeating Shakespeare's works, Gaiman reworked it so that it kept the essence of the plot but also had a patina distinctive of the Sandman.

Gaiman established a dialogue between the plays and their comic forms so that neither Shakespeare nor *The Sandman* dominated these sequences. Even though they lived in different times, both Shakespeare and Gaiman wrestled with the tenacity of dreams. Gaiman used the dialogue between their works as presented in *The Sandman* to prove that true immortality does not entail the permanence of an individual's body but of his dreams and ideas. Exploration of the public's perception of each writer's medium, the content of the common stories, and their styles of visual presentation, all in the context of Gaiman's stories, reveals a common message with different interpretations.

BACKGROUND AND HISTORY

Neil Gaiman was born on November 10, 1960, in Portchester, Hampshire, England. By attending several Church of England schools, he acquired a broad knowledge of Christian theology that he incorporated into his works alongside other influences, such as his Jewish heritage. He went on to pursue journalism in order to learn more of

FIGURE 50.1 Neil Gaiman has written several novels and screenplays, but is best known for his stunning and collaborative graphic novels.

the world and published several books. Gaiman broke into the world of comics after collaborating with Dave McKean on *Violent Cases: Words and Pictures* (Gaiman, 1998) and *Black Orchid* (McKean & Gaiman, 1991), followed by his best-known work, *The Sandman* series (HarperCollins Publishers, 2006).

The Sandman, serialized into 10 graphic novels in the early 1990s, chronicles the reign of Morpheus, the Lord of Dreams, who watches over humanity with his six siblings. These seven personifications of life's aspects—Destiny, Death, Dream, Destruction, Desire, Despair, and Delirium—form an assembly known as the Endless, reflecting their presence before life arose in this universe. They exist as aspects of reality, "ideas cloaked in the semblance of flesh," and can never be destroyed so long as this universe exists (Gaiman, 2004).

However, the Endless can change over the course of time, as Morpheus discovers as he rebuilds his kingdom after 72 years of captivity. He realizes the world never existed in the stark black and white terms he had assumed and that either he must change with the times or die, for his past methods no longer apply to humanity's changing relationship with its dreams. *The Sandman's* first issues portray Morpheus as an implacable arbiter of justice, exercising sternness rather than compassion. His imprisonment gives him time to reflect and the need to repair his downtrodden realm, the Dreaming, forces Morpheus to revisit and right past injustices. He ultimately embraces his limited capacity for change and dies so another aspect of Dream can take his place.

In Issue 13, "Men of Fortune" (Gaiman, 1990a), Morpheus encounters a young Will Shakespeare who wishes he could write as well as his friend, Christopher Marlowe, and give men dreams that will survive long after he has died. Morpheus makes a pact with him: Morpheus will give him the inspiration he craves and Shakespeare will write two plays in return. These two plays make their appearances in Issue 19, "A Midsummer Night's Dream," and Issue 75, "The Tempest."

William Shakespeare was supposedly born on April 23, 1564, and definitely baptized three days later in Stratford-upon-Avon, Warwickshire, England. Due to the inconsistency of Elizabethan record keeping, no one knows the exact dates of his birth or of his plays' publications. Shakespeare's first plays appeared in the mid-1580s, beginning with light comedies and histories, and progressed on to his great tragedies before finishing his career with romances. *A Midsummer Night's Dream* (Bloom, 1987) falls into the earlier category of light comedies, with its two pairs of confused lovers, fairies, intrigues, and enchantment. On the other hand, Shakespeare wrote *The Tempest* (Shakespeare, 2003) at the very end of his life as a play of romance and redemption. Both plays, though, toy with dreams and their central role in their characters' lives.

In bringing Shakespeare's plays to life in a different medium, Gaiman gave them a more human edge by allowing the reader behind the scenes of their production. He focused on the birth and performance of these two plays while drawing parallels between his stories and Shakespeare's stories. The intertextuality of Gaiman's work—embedding Shakespeare's stories within his own—not only enlivens the original text but also challenges readers to stretch their minds. Gaiman expected them to be familiar with different cultures, myths, and texts across various media. He does not cater to the superhero comic reader, nor does he choose to hobnob with only the scholars of Norse mythology or Shakespeare buffs; Gaiman expected all these elements, and more, to play with each other in novel ways. To fully enjoy a Gaiman story, a reader cannot rest in one sole niche, such as comics or novels, because Gaiman is equally adept in both and expects his readers to be the same.

PARALLEL DEVELOPMENT OF MEDIA

Before examining the contents of Gaiman's stories, tracing the parallel development of Shakespearean plays and comics or graphic novels as a medium will establish the viability of their comparison. Both plays and graphic novels traversed the long path from cheap entertainment lacking credibility to serious art forms.

Plays written during Shakespeare's time began to acquire a greater degree of prestige. People living in the Elizabethan era considered plays the entertainment of the common folk or groundlings, but public perception changed. Shakespeare's plays now hold a revered place in the annals of "quality" English literature; most students have studied his plays in school and theatre troupes continue to perform his works. The ascendancy of graphic novels closely mirrors that of the theatrical play in that both genres overcame their respective stigmas by redefining their boundaries (Mabillard, 2000).

Alongside other now famous comic artists, Gaiman helped bring the comics genre out of the obscurity of juvenile, disposable literature. Adults once considered comic books and other illustrated literature kid fare, full of one-dimensional characters, trite story lines, and gaudy cartoons. Through the work of pioneering artists, they have risen to a status of greater respect as graphic novels. The term *graphic novel* still smacks of pretension and attempts at respectability, but more adults have accepted the medium's potential for serious as well as entertaining narratives (McCloud, 1994).

Both Shakespeare and Gaiman drew inspiration from myths and stories that came before them. Shakespeare's *Romeo and Juliet* retold the Greek tale of the ill-fated lovers, Pyramus and Thisbe and *Hamlet* most likely sprang from a lost story of a Scandinavian prince. Gaiman also drew heavily from Greek and Norse mythologies, Christianity, Judaism, as well as pop culture. However, it is important to remember that Shakespeare and Gaiman's successes stemmed from their abilities to adapt old tales, which had once enthralled people, to please modern audiences.

Shakespeare's plays deftly combined light elements to please the masses while maintaining more refined aspects in order to reach the nobility's level of sophistication. For the groundlings, he used humorous actions, puns, and prose to inject humor into his plays and distinguish those comedic interludes from the main story. In *A Midsummer Night's Dream* (Bloom, 1987), Nick Bottom supplies the comedy by inadvertently wooing Titania, Queen of Faerie, after awaking to find his head turned into that of an ass. Likewise, Stephano and Trinculo provide the scatterbrained slapstick in *The Tempest* (Shakespeare, 2003) as they ineptly plot to wrest control of the island from Prospero. Although these characters try to deal with their situations as normally as possible, nonsense and hilarity take over without fail.

On the other hand, Shakespeare employed more serious, dramatic sequences for the benefit of the nobility. These scenes reflect courtly behavior and Shakespeare's characters that are more serious speak in iambic pentameter to express their nobility and sweeping emotions, for example, when Hermia and Lysander profess their love for each other (*Midsummer,* I, 1). While Shakespeare wrote duels to satisfy the groundlings, he wrote eloquent soliloquies and masques, such as the one performed at Ferdinand and Miranda's wedding (*Tempest,* IV, 1).

Similarly, Gaiman strived to please a broad range of readers by incorporating elements to please both children and adults. For younger audiences, Gaiman enjoyed the addition of classic DC Comics characters, such as Batman, Robin, the Martian Manhunter, and the Fury. Children immediately recognize most of these characters, which provides them with a sense of comfort and familiarity. One of Gaiman's important characters, Hippolyta, actually dresses up in her mother's uniform and attempts to take her place as the Fury. The appearance of old DC Comics characters can tickle young and old readers, even as Gaiman reshapes them. Under his guidance, they become fallen heroes with emotions, problems, and greater complexity. These characters may appear to remain the same, giving children what they expect, but they also address more serious themes and issues of interest to an older audience.

The integration of religions and cultures from around the world makes an even greater appeal to Gaiman's older audiences. The 75 issues of *The Sandman* weave together cultural influences ranging from Greek and Norse mythologies to Shakespeare's fairies to American pop culture. Younger readers who have not been exposed to such mythologies or the cultures of foreign countries can still enjoy his tales, but those who understand the multifaceted background can appreciate even more the craft involved in meshing them with Gaiman's stories. The more erudite the reader, the more likely he or she will see Gaiman's allusions to other works, adding another layer of interpretation to the explicit story.

Both Gaiman and Shakespeare wrote their works with a broad audience in mind. Although they worked in different media, they used the same technique of casting the net wide and touched upon similar themes in the process. Art constantly changes, yet the core ideas of Shakespeare's and Gaiman's masterpieces will live on despite the vacillating popularity of plays and comics. The presentations may change, but the messages remain the same. The development of one medium from childish recreation to sophisticated literature mirrors that of the other.

ANALYSIS OF CONTENT

Adapting Shakespeare's plays to comic book form necessitated some alterations to the actual presentation of the story. Gaiman cut out portions of the story but retained and augmented other parts. He kept enough of the major events of the play within the retelling so that the story remains coherent, but the fairies fill in a large portion of the story by narrating the action concerning them. The rest of the space allotted to "A Midsummer Night's Dream" goes to behind-the-scenes sequences where Gaiman reveals the gritty inner workings of the troupe. Actors haggle over parts and Hamnet, the Shakespeare character's son, bemoans his father's estrangement from him due to working on the plays. This technique allowed Gaiman to shorten the story while preserving the essence of the tale itself.

"The Tempest" treated its namesake play in a similar fashion, opening with lines from the play itself. Unlike "Midsummer," though, "Tempest" sharply delineates between *The Tempest,* with its lush drawings and beautiful calligraphy, and the world of Gaiman's Shakespeare, drawn in a style more pertinent to comics. This schism between Shakespeare's inner and outer worlds sharply reflects his estrangement from his family. For all his great works, Gaiman's Shakespeare wishes to run away from the very gift that he bargained for so long ago with Morpheus. He realizes that fame and power cannot mend everything; like Prospero and Gaiman himself, Shakespeare understands that it is time to leave behind his power over the dominion of imagination.

Gaiman's decision to set his Shakespeare stories in the proper times, as opposed to adapting them to modern times, allowed them to develop in their own fashion, untainted by modern conventions. Yet the depth and complexity in the stories reveal Gaiman's hand in their creation, from the pain of being forgotten in "Midsummer" to the bittersweet ending of "The Tempest." Setting these two episodes in Elizabethan times makes more apparent the constancy of man's struggle to live a happy life when the definition of one constantly changes.

Several themes unite Gaiman's work with that of Shakespeare, who came before him. Both men wrote of love, hate, redemption, and dreams as the creative force behind life. Yet they also latched onto very contemporary themes and issues, namely discrimination against seemingly foreign races. Shakespeare's plays consistently reflected the racism of his times. For example, despite Caliban's right to rule the island, Prospero continues to keep him under magical restraint until it comes time for him to face his past mistakes. Shakespeare reflected Englishmen's inhumane treatment of new peoples simply because they differed from the European norm. Gaiman voiced the same concerns in *The Sandman,* highlighting modern prejudices against homosexuality, AIDS, and those struggling to form their own identities. Not only did their works entertain people, they provided social and political commentary. These issues never change; they merely resurface in a new form, so Shakespeare's work, and probably Gaiman's too, will always be relevant and insightful.

Furthermore, the progression of Shakespeare's talent mirrors the progression of *The Sandman* series itself as well as Morpheus' dawning realization that he must change. As Gaiman's story strengthened, so did the complexity of Shakespeare's life according to Gaiman. The Bard first appears in Issue 13, called "Men of Fortune," around the same time that Morpheus rebuilds his kingdom. "Midsummer" appears a little bit later on, but still earlier in both Gaiman's series and Shakespeare's actual life. "The Tempest" elegantly finishes *The Sandman* series, just as it finished Shakespeare's real career. Gaiman deliberately chose to end his series with "The Tempest" because it brings the story of dreams full circle. Dreams begin in the minds of men, walk the earth for a short time, and ultimately return to the mind, where they will always reside.

ANALYSIS OF VISUAL PRESENTATION

The audience and its expectations shape the visual presentation of a work. Shakespeare and Gaiman knew for whom they were writing and thus set out to meet the expectations set before them, but not without demanding some level of involvement in return. Both men required their audiences to practice different forms of what Scott McCloud (1994) termed as *closure.*

McCloud's closure referred to the reader's active completion of information omitted by the artist, which is solely used in the context of comics (McCloud, 1994). Although Gaiman's comics undoubtedly require the reader to fill in actions and movements between cels on the page, Shakespeare's audience also practiced closure. The traditional Shakespearean set actually contained very few pieces. There were surely costumes and perhaps a few props, but the Shakespearean stage was quite spartan, forcing the viewer to imagine the background of the action and the movement between settings (Kernan, 1987, p. 43). Gaiman's readers faced the opposite challenge: He gave them the images and words, but the reader had to fill in the sound and the action.

The use of caricatures in Shakespeare's plays and Gaiman's comics also facilitated the process of making the story one's own. Shakespeare's buffoons made the audience laugh but also endeared themselves to them. Gaiman's comedic characters, such as Matthew, the raven, or Merv, the talking pumpkin head, lightened the deep philosophical questions raised by Morpheus and gave the reader an inviting aspect of Morpheus' world with which they could empathize. In the ninth serialized volume, *The Kindly Ones* (Gaiman, 1996), Gaiman "wanted a sense of form . . . a sense of everything reducing to light and shadow, of everything reducing to simple shape" (McCabe, 2004). Marc Hempel's visual style reflected Gaiman's direction, filling the pages with thick black lines filled with luminous, vibrant color. The artwork's simplification eased sympathizing with characters even as it radiated a harsh intensity previously unseen in *The Sandman*.

Unlike Hempel, Charles Vess brought a much more traditional, refined style to Gaiman's Shakespeare stories. Vess mostly worked in book illustration and brought the same "curvilinear, rhythmic forms of nature" to Issues 13, 19, and 75 that he used in his noncomic work (McCabe, 2004). His figures exuded an organic, fairy tale quality, which complements Gaiman's fanciful script. Alternating between realism and impressionism, Vess's artwork captured the dreamy, nostalgic mood of "Midsummer" and "Tempest" better than any live performance. The abridged nature of these Shakespeare stories also pushed Vess to invest more nonverbal language into his illustrations, so that together, script and cel could convey more information (McCabe, 2004).

The techniques and images used by Shakespeare and Gaiman matched the tastes of their times, but the same methods may not work in the future. Perhaps comic books and graphic novels will become obsolete in the next 50 years—though we doubt it. Rather, we expect such works to play increasingly important roles in the development of literacy and in bringing new generations of students to reading and writing in new genres and forms. Certainly, despite different presentation styles, the themes covered by Shakespeare and Gaiman will survive in whatever new forms arise. The dreamer's body may disintegrate, but the dreams and ideas will endure.

CONCLUSION

Despite a separation of 400 years, Neil Gaiman successfully united his vision with a small part of William Shakespeare's extensive body of work by incorporating *A Midsummer Night's Dream* and *The Tempest* into *The Sandman*. Gaiman proved humanity's quest for corporeal immortality futile, for the only true immortality is that of dreams and ideas. Examining the rise in popularity of plays and comics revealed the ever-changing nature of art's significance in the face of the constancy of ideas. A comparison of Gaiman's comic with Shakespeare's text clearly showed differing treatments of the same stories, but the essence of the stories passed down from generation to generation intact. Finally, scrutiny of Shakespeare's and Gaiman's different visual presentations of the material, in the form of a performance and of printed media, showed the staying power of central beliefs, such as true love and redemption.

The stories told by Shakespeare and Gaiman attested to the endurance of dreams. Their tales changed slightly with every generation, since every generation reinterprets the meaning of every work of art. Yet in this way, stories continue to resonate with new listeners and readers. The staying power of Shakespeare's plays lies in his ability to voice basic human emotions and desires. Gaiman used the comic book form to show readers their own psyche in vibrant, new images, reawakening them to their own potential. They comfort the reader with the reassurance that

> Nothing of him that doth fade,
> But doth suffer a sea-change
> Into something rich and strange.
>
> (*The Tempest*, I, 2, ll 402–404)

REFERENCES

Arnold, A. (2003, November 14). *The graphic novel silver anniversary. Time.* Retrieved June 10, 2006, from http://www.time.com/time/columnist/arnold/article/0,9565,542579,00.html

Bloom, H. (Ed.). (1987). *William Shakespeare's a midsummer night's dream.* New York: Chelsea House Publishers.

Columbia University. *The Columbia Encyclopedia.* 6th ed. Gale, 2001–05.

Eisner, W. (2001). *A contract with god and other tenement stories: A graphic novel.* New York: DC Comics.

Gaiman, N. (1990a). *The sandman: The doll's house.* New York: DC Comics.

Gaiman, N. *The sandman: Endless nights.* Vertigo Press, 2004.

Gaiman, N. *The sandman: The kindly ones.* Vertigo Press, 1996.

Gaiman, N. *The sandman: Season of mists.* Vertigo Press, 1994.

Gaiman, N. (1998). *Violent cases: Words and pictures.* New York: Kitchen Sink Press.

HarperCollins Publishers. (2006). *Biography.* Retrieved February 12, 2006, from http://www.neilgaiman.com/

Kernan, A. (1987). "A little o'erparted": Actors and audiences in a midsummer night's dream. In H. Bloom (Ed.), *William Shakespeare's a midsummer night's dream.* New York: Chelsea House Publishers.

Mabillard, A. (2000). FAQ. *Shakespeare online.* Retrieved February 1, 2006, from http://www.shakespeare-online.com

Marlowe, Christopher. *Christopher Marlowe: The complete plays.* Ed. Frank Romany and Robert Lindsey. Penguin, 2003.

McCabe, J. (2004). *Hanging out with the dream king.* Seattle, WA: Fantagraphics.

McCloud, S. (1994). *Understanding comics: The invisible art.* New York: Harper.

McKean, D., & Gaiman, N. (1991). *Black orchid.* New York: Vertigo.

Shakespeare, William. *The tempest.* Ed. Peter Hulme and William H. Sherman. W. W. Norton, 2003.

Spiegelman, Art. "*Comix 101.*" Lecture. Jewish Community Center, San Mateo, CA, February 21, 2006.

Spiegelman, Art. *The complete maus.* Penguin, 2004.

Stephens, M. (1998). *The rise of the image, the fall of the word.* New York: Oxford University Press.

Walker, B. (2004). *The comics before 1945.* New York: Harry Abrams.

51

FILM, LITERATURE, AND LANGUAGE

Lawrence Baines
UNIVERSITY OF TOLEDO

"The cinema is not a slice of life, but a piece of cake."

Alfred Hitchcock

The same year that Michael Moore's *Fahrenheit 9/11* (2004) became a flash point with regard to politics, terrorism, and the military, the Pope was purported to have commented, "It is as it was," after viewing a special premiere of Mel Gibson's *The Passion of the Christ* (Marcus, 2005; Rutten, 2004). Shortly after news of the Pope's comment reached the more than a billion Catholics around the world, the Vatican issued a formal statement denying the comment. However, the retraction only added to the brouhaha of publicity enveloping the film. A month later, the actor who played Christ, Jim Caviezel, was issued a personal invitation for a private audience with the Pope. Eventually, *The Passion of the Christ* became the most lucrative R-rated film of all time.

Undeniably, film is a powerful medium that can foster intense emotional responses (Cantor, 1991; Cox, Garrett, & Graham, 2005; Durgnat, 1967; Lacey, 1972; Zillmann & Bryant, 1986). Film has been integral in electing government officials, determining the success or failure of a business, and helping shape world opinion. Experts (Hinton, 2000; Welch, 2001) are still debating the extent to which the films of Leni Reifenstahl, *Triumph of the Will* (1935) and *Olympiad* (1938), helped propel Hitler and Nazism to power in 1930s Germany. Some speculate that the Berlin Wall may never have fallen if it were not for the impact of film (Murray-Brown, 1991). Because the image seems to offer irrefutable evidence, film can provide a pictorial representation of lived experience (Langsdorf, 1991; Rosenblatt, 1978). When tragedy strikes (e.g., Hurricane Katrina, the tsunami that hit Thailand in December 2004), it is the moving image that becomes the *lingua franca* of the moment; words often serve as nothing more than elaborations on the images.

The poet Richard Wilbur (1970) wrote, "Even the worst movie has much of the authority of the actual, and quite without knowing it one comes out of the theater brainwashed into scanning the world through the norms of the camera" (p. 167). Kraft, Cantor, & Gottdiener (1991) hypothesized that one reason film seems so much like actual experience is that film's structure mimics human interaction with the natural world. Viewers understand that when a scene cuts to a high angle camera shot, the characters being filmed will appear small and insignificant because they have previously looked down upon people from an elevated position (such as a tall building) and seen the same kind of image.

The evidence that images shape thought and influence behavior is well documented. Consider the effects of films such as *Jaws* (1975), *Easy Rider* (1969), *Boyz 'n the Hood* (1992), and the Harry Potter films (*Goblet of Fire,* 2006) on American attitudes toward sharks, hippies, urban neighborhoods, witches, and wizards (who were considered less genial in Salem in the 17th century).

The trend in research on media effects has been away from the concept of viewer as passive agent to the reformulation of the viewer as active communicator (Clément, Baker, Josephson, & Noels, 2005; Anderson & Anderson, 1993; Rubin, 1993; Scholle, 1991). The uses and gratifications model, substantiated through more than three decades of research (Blumler & Katz, 1974; Greene & Krcmar, 2005; Rosengren, Wenner, & Palmgreen, 1985; Sherry, 2004), posits that certain human behaviors are motivated by the satisfaction of perceived needs. According to the uses and gratifications model, a young man who has become disconcerted when he notices that he is gradually losing hair, will be receptive to products that he perceives as remedies for his baldness.

The uses and gratifications model is often used in combination with audience activity research to ascertain why individuals think and behave in certain ways (Kellerman, 1985; Ko, Cho, & Roberts, 2005; Levy & Windahl, 1984; Metzger & Flanagin, 2002; Slater, 2003; Wenner, 1986). For example, say the balding young man mentioned earlier happened to see a product advertised on television that promised to grow back his hair, and he immediately went to the drug store to purchase it. Audience activity research would examine the mental processes of the young man during different phases of the process from the factors that contributed to his receptiveness to the advertisement to his selection of the product at the drugstore.

The analyses of uses and gratifications and audience activity research, one begins to understand the complexities involved in determining how a film might affect human behavior. The Payne Fund studies, a series of 12 experiments carried out between 1929 and 1932, represent one of the first important investigations into the effects of watching movies on the behavior and attitudes of children. Some film scholars have justly criticized the Payne Studies for the lack of rigor in some experiments, for using a strong moralistic tone in reporting the results of the experiments, and for the conception of children as passive receivers of information. Yet, few media educators today would quarrel with the three major conclusions from the studies: (a) Motion pictures serve as a potent medium of education; (b) the subject matter of many motion pictures may not be appropriate for children; and (c) the motion picture is only one influence in the complicated, ever-changing worlds of children (Charters, 1933; Holaday & Stoddard, 1933).

In the 1960s, Bandura (1968) studied how children responded to watching certain violent images on television and found that prolonged exposure to images of violence "tends to reduce the child's inhibitions against acting in a violent, aggressive manner" (p. 126). Greeson and Williams (1986) found that junior and senior high school students were less inhibited about violence after viewing selected videos from MTV. A host of studies (Bandura, 1986; Hansen, C., & Hansen, R., 1990a, 1990b, 1991; Sherman & Dominick, 1986) found exposure to videos with extreme amounts of sex or violence may affect the social judgments and the personal value systems of viewers.

Eisenman, Girdner, Burroughs, and Routman (1993) found that even showing a single, short film could alter human perceptions and behavior. In their experiment, 211 college students in Mississippi were shown a film *Who is David Duke?* (1992) which provided evidence that Duke was anti-Black, anti-Semitic, and pro-Nazi. Before the film was shown, 35 of the 211 students perceived Duke as anti-Semitic. After the film, 129 students perceived Duke as anti-Semitic.

The viewing of specific films has also been linked experimentally with childhood phobias, traumas, and nightmares (Cantor, 1991; Cantor & Reilly, 1982; Sarafino, 1986); sensual arousal (Hansen, C., & Krygowski, 1994); empathy (Davis, Hull, Young, & Warren, 1987; Tamborini, Salomonson, & Bahk, 1993); the use of preventive measures to combat AIDS (Maibach & Flora, 1993); desensitization to portrayals of women (Stam & Raengo, 2005; Linz, 1989; Linz, Donnerstein, & Penrod, 1988; Oliver, M., 1993) and other effects.

In a study of the role of the cinema in urban poor areas of Southern India, Dickey (1993) found that films served as powerful factors in the shaping of moral codes of viewers and that much of the structure of social interaction in the Indian urban community under study revolved around attending and discussing movies. In the city of Madurai (Tamil Nadu, India), where "cinema is everywhere" (p. 3), 85% of adults went to the movies at least three times a month and the state's last five Chief Ministers have been either film actors or directors.

Schneller (1988) found that small town youth in Israel spent large amounts of time watching film as compared with their central city peers. Schneller suggested that watching films at home in this particular rural community had become so prevalent among small town youth that it greatly reduced the time spent in person-to-person socializing activities. New patterns of behavior (students either watched videos alone or at each other's houses) had deleterious consequences on the amount of business done by coffee shops, entertainment venues, and other local businesses.

Media researchers and public relations professionals have come to realize that film has an impact on audiences not only at the moment of exposure, but also potentially in any subsequent interaction (Alexander, 1993; Fry, V., Alexander, & Fry, D., 1990). Unsurprisingly, in the wake of the killings at Columbine, legislative fingers pointed to the motion picture studios as being in part culpable. The film *Basketball Diaries* (1995) contains a dream/drug sequence in which the character played by Leonardo DiCaprio imagines that, while wearing a black trench coat and toting numerous assault weapons, he walks into school and methodically murders his classmates, thereby earning the applause of his best friend. Similarly, in one scene in *The Matrix* (1999), the character played by Keanu Reeves, who is also wearing a black trench coat, walks into an office building while armed with a dozen or so weapons strapped to his body and one rather large bomb tucked into a briefcase. In slow motion, Reeves and his leather-clad girlfriend walk through the corridor, blowing the heads off of the dozen or so police officers unfortunate enough to have been in the lobby when they arrived. Even academics who readily dismiss the persuasive powers of film cannot deny the eerie similarity between these commercial offerings and the Columbine High murders.

The act of viewing a film—moving into a dark room where other stimuli do not intervene and becoming engrossed in an expertly photographed and carefully orchestrated, auditorially enhanced multimedia experience—can have a profound effect (consciously or subconsciously) upon how one views the world. Over the past 20 years, the American Educational Research Association, the American Psychological Association, and other organizations have issued policy statements acknowledging the power of film to influence human behavior. Although the topic of discussion post-Columbine placed the focus upon the ways that film can steer adolescents toward acts of violence, there is also substantial evidence attesting to the influence of film upon cultural sensitivity, voting behavior, history, perceptions of gender roles, and other phenomena.

Despite a century of research attesting to the power of film to inform, educate, and influence behavior, film has yet to receive widespread adoption as a teaching tool in the secondary classroom.

FILMS IN THE CLASSROOM

The National Council of Teachers of English and International Reading Association included "visual language" alongside spoken and written language in their declaration of standards for English and reading (Bazalgette, Sevoty, & Savino, 1993; Smagorinsky, 1996; Wilhelm, 2006). Robert Neal (1913) was perhaps the first to suggest that the study of film be integrated into the language arts curriculum, though he did so with much ambivalence. Neal wrote, "The moving picture is not an invention of the devil. There is a great deal in it, at the present stage of its development, that we have to think of with all the optimistic faith summonable, in order not to regard it as excessively satanic" (p. 68).

Once film was established as a mass medium, a small contingent of educators has seemingly always been around to lobby on its behalf (Hoban, 1942; Meierhenry, 1952; Miller, H., 1979; Nichols, 1992; Usher, 1985). But, these groups have never been large enough or organized enough to affect permanent alterations in the school curriculum. The film study movement enjoyed the peak of its popularity during two periods—the 1930s and the late 1960s. In 1930, movie houses sold almost five billion tickets in the United Sates (compared to 1.1 billion in 1993; Golenpaul, 1994). In the 1930s, the sheer popularity of cinema helped propel the film study movement into prominence for a period before it was abruptly cut off by the beginning of World War II. In the 1970s, the "Back to Basics" movement eventually drove most of the film study movement's contributions to the curriculum, evident in many American schools in the late 1960s, into quiet oblivion.

The passages below will give a brief idea of the dialogue that has ensued over the years regarding the study and use of film in school.

1915

> Moving pictures everywhere will become a valuable adjunct in the mastery of skill in English composition. (Gerrish, 1915, p. 230)

1923

> It is useless to condemn moving pictures; we may as well condemn all novels . . . Why not bring the movies into the schoolroom? (Cunningham, 1923, p. 490)

1936

> I submit now that motion-picture appreciation is here to stay. The momentum it has created will insure its adoption, gradually but surely, not only into the high schools, but also into teacher- training institutions. (Dale, 1936, p. 113)

1948

> The next ten years should show a great increase in the intelligent use of films and in the establishing of motion picture appreciation units by English teachers. (Elliot, 1948, p. 170)

1952

> It may properly be said that virtually every state supports to some degree a film program because every state has one or more libraries which provide films on a rental basis to the schools. (Meierhenry, 1952, p. 188)

> In motion pictures the spurt of interest that occurred about fifteen years ago has died down. (Boutwell, 1952, p. 131)

1964

> One believes that with the continually growing enthusiasm for film among young intellectuals, good film teachers will be easier to find in the future . . . One concludes that the future is bright for the study of film. (Selby, 1968, p. 226, 227)

1970

> Movies are moving into the high school. The proliferation of film societies on the college level is now commonplace. (Carrico, 1970, p. 97)

1978

> [In retrospect regarding his 1964 study] Looking backward, I would say that my optimism for the importance of the film as an art form in secondary school was unfounded. (Selby, 1978, p. viii)

1981

> No one doubts that language, reading, and writing are central to school programs or that they are the proper business of English language arts teachers; but most people, teachers included, have strong reservations about media studies. (Karl, 1981, p. 139)

1992

> With research that suggests how effective film can be, why does the medium continue to be regarded critically by school administrators, school board members, and the general public? (Lankford, 1992, p. 3)

2001

> Today's classroom is less than ever insulated from the cultural environment, and we cannot ignore the pervasiveness of electronic mass media. . . . We should acknowledge film and television as the great history educators of our time. (Weinstein, 2001, p. 27)

Perhaps some teachers eschew film out of a misunderstanding of "fair use" under copyright law. Section 110 of the Copyright Revision Act of 1976 authorizes the use of copyrighted work, such as videotapes, for use in educational settings (Miller, J., 1988). A teacher may use films provided certain criteria are met:

- The film is shown in a face-to-face teaching situation.
- A teacher, student, or guest speaker shows the film in an educational setting (such as a classroom or an auditorium) as part of an instructional plan.
- The film is shown only to students, the teacher, and the guest speaker.
- The copy of the film or videotape is a legal one.

The courts have been especially forgiving of school districts and teachers, even when they flagrantly abuse the liberal guidelines for using film in the classroom. When one school district openly admitted that personnel copied noneducational programs from a cable station and distributed multiple copies to employees and friends, it was assessed a modest fine of $63,000 (Resch & Schicker, 1992, p. 134).

FILM AS A TEACHING TOOL

Many studies since the 1940s, including a good deal of research performed by the offices of the U.S. armed forces, have tested the effectiveness of film in helping to educate students, workers, and soldiers. The results of such tests often yielded bold praise for the medium of film as a tool for instruction. However, as Clark (1983; 1985; 1991; 1992) repeatedly pointed out, media comparison studies that find greater learning gains in the newer media often fail to consider "novelty effects." In addition, the failure of researchers to maintain adequate control over aspects of the instructional design sometimes translates into unequal presentation of content to participants. Thus, when Clark (1992) wrote, "During the early days of the motion picture, studies tended to favor movies over teachers" (p. 806), he meant that the superiority shown by films was due to an infatuation with a new medium, not due to some mystical powers of film.

Conversely, Ullmer (1994) and Kay (1991) contended that the differential content in studies that find superior achievement in newer media might instead be the result of a natural propensity of the newer medium. That is, each medium possesses its own strengths, some of which make it more appropriate than other media for particular kinds of learning (Krendl, 1986). In the medium-driven configuration, results are thought to be traceable to the inherent advantages and appeals of the delivery systems themselves. Such a philosophical stance would seem to substantiate McLuhan's (1962; 1964; 1967) famous dictum that "the medium is the message."

Film has proven effective in teaching students about myriad topics, including mental illness (Kerber, Clemens, & Medina, 2004; Livingston, 2004; Fleming, Piedmont, & Hiam, 1990); mathematics (Beckmann, Austin, & Thompson, 2004; Kelly, Wiebe, & Hynes, 1993); critical thinking skills (Guista, 1992; Remender, 1992; Weerts, 2005); German language and culture (Flippo, 1993); psychological development (Boyatzis, 1994; Calich, 2001); law (Anderson, D., 1992), civil rights (Christopher, Marek, & Walter, 2004; Loewen, 1991; Manley, 1994); popular culture (Groce, 1992); sociology (Berg, 1992); propaganda (Rhiel, 1993); attitude toward the elderly (Cross, 1989); biology (Faulkner, 1993) and, of course, literature.

FILM AND LITERATURE

A teacher of English is most likely to use a film when it relates directly to a literary work covered in class (Amelio, 1972; Lynch, 1983, 1986). Larsson (2001) found that 98% of English teachers reported using film at least once over the past five years. The most popular techniques of teachers who use film with literature involve either asking students to compare a film with a recently completed novel or showing the film as a sort of reward for getting through the book. Although students tend to enjoy watching films without teacher intervention, allowing the student to remain passive viewers has probably drawn the strongest criticism in the literature (Considine & Haley, 1992; Gardner, P., 1992; Golden, 2005; Watson, 1990).

A student who has difficulty understanding the context of *Grapes of Wrath* (1939) could immensely benefit from documentaries about the Dust Bowl and The Great Depression. Showing select clips from John Ford's 1940 film adaptation might help bring to life parts of the book for weak readers who otherwise might miss important details or inferences. Indeed, a growing segment of educators has shown interest in the use of filmed adaptations as a device for improving the comprehension skills of low-achieving students. Goldman (1990), McKenzie (1993), Shiring (1990), and Squires (1990) found filmed adaptations effective in filling in gaps for reluctant readers or special populations, such as students designated as "at risk." Vetrie (2005) and McDonald (1983) suggested using film to improve literacy skills. Bottge and Hasselbring (1993, as cited in Skolnik & Smith, C., 1993) argued that film might help low-achieving students to construct mental models that are richer than those derived solely from text (p. 23).

The differences and similarities between film and the novel have been debated at length (e.g., Admussen, 1978; Aycock & Schoenecke, 1988; Beja, 1979; Biro, 1982; Bluestone, 1957; Boyum, 1985; Cohen, 1979; Costanzo, 1985, 1992, 2004; Cox & Many, 1989; Ely & Minor, 1993; Eidsvik, 1978; Fadiman, 1978; Gardner, P., 1991; Giddings, Selby, & Wensley, 1990; Harrington, 1977; Hulesberg, 1978; Jinks, 1974; Kawin, 1977; Kittridge & Krauzer, 1979; Klein & Parker, 1981; Knight, 1972; Magill, 1976; Magney, 1972; Manchel, 1990; Marcus, F., 1971, 1977; Maynard, 1971; McConnell, 1979; McDougal, 1985; Miller, G., 1980; Miller, J., 1986; Millichap, 1983; Murray, 1972; Oliver, 1989; Peary & Shatzkin, 1977, 1978; Richardson, 1969; Ross, 1991; Self, 1987; Sheridan, Owen, Macrorie, & Marcus, 1965; Sinyard, 1986; Sohn, 1970; Speigel, 1976; Street, 1983; Wagner, 1975; Weinberg, 1973; and others).

When discussing the similarities in the two media (film and the novel), scholars usually conclude that both film and literature are narrative arts—both exist to tell a story. J. Miller (1986) asserted that the two media share the capability to create an invisible structure to which the viewer or reader responds. Like a reader who must ignore the construction of the text in order to continually derive meaning from it (Iser, 1989), the viewer is rarely conscious of every cut or change in camera angle. Yet, it is the cut and the angle of the camera that give much of film its meaning (Kraft, 1986, 1987).

A third similarity is that much of the jargon of literary criticism is equally applicable to film. *Plot, symbolism, theme, tone, characterization, foreshadowing,* and *setting* are terms as applicable to film as text.

Despite the similarities, most writers agree with Bluestone (1957): "The film and the novel remain separate institutions, each achieving its best results by exploring unique and specific properties" (p. 218). The differences between the film and the novel noted often in the literature (Baines, 1993) are these:

- Film is dominated by the image, while literature is bound by the word.
- Time constraints limit what films can do.
- Novels are usually produced by an individual working alone for a limited audience, while films are made by an assemblage of technicians and dramatists for a widespread audience.
- With film, star power usually trumps story line if the two should ever collide.

An intriguing area of exploration is the degree to which writers of novels have been influenced by film. Hamilton (1990) chronicled the efforts of Faulkner, Fitzgerald, Chandler, and others who dabbled in screenwriting for Hollywood. Hamilton found that the lure of money and steady work was irresistible to writers, famous or not, who usually had to eke out a living on the paltry royalties from books. Millichap (1983) asserted that Steinbeck drew his documentary style "from the . . . films of the period" (p. 176) and often wrote with future film adaptations in mind. Early filmmaker D.W. Griffith is said to have often consulted the work of Charles Dickens in the making of his films. It was also through Dickens' novels that Russian director Eisenstein (1949) was inspired to develop montage, dissolve, and close up.

As with Steinbeck, popular novelists such as John Grisham, Michael Crichton, and J. K. Rowling likely entertain how ideas and characters might be manifested in film as they write. Certainly, a writer would find it difficult to ignore the huge sums given to authors whose books have been optioned for film and the millions of dollars generated by popular films. For example, J. K. Rowling's *Harry Potter and the Prisoner of Azkaban* was only a minor hit in 2004, yet it earned $250,000,000, not including foreign sales.

To fully grasp the influence of electronic media on the sales of books, recall that sales of Hawthorne's canonical *The Scarlet Letter* in a single year exceeded the sum total of sales of the book since 1850 after release of the adaptation starring Demi Moore (1995). A perusal of the best selling children's books for 2004 finds not authors E. B. White or Judy Blume, but Irene Trimble and Louise Gilkow, who write novelizations based upon films. Indeed, it has become rare for any of the best selling children's books *not* to be tied to electronic media in some way. According to the Infoplease Web site (2006), the best-selling children's books in 2004 were as follows (in order):

1. *Harry Potter and the Order of the Phoenix*, J. K. Rowling
2. *Disney/Pixar's The Incredibles* by Irene Trimble
3. *Spider-Man 2: Spider-Man Versus Doc Ock*, by Acton Figueroa; illustrated by Jesus Redondo

4. *Shark Tale: The Movie Novel*, by Louise Gikow
5. *My Little Pony: Pony Party*, by Kate Egan; illustrated by Carlo LoRaso
6. *Spider-Man 2: Everyday Hero*, by Acton Figueroa; illustrated by Ivan Vasquez
7. *Spider-Man 2: Doc Around the Clock*, by Jacob Ben Gunter
8. *The Sisterhood of the Traveling Pants* (trade paper and mass market), by Ann Brashares
9. *The Polar Express, the Movie: The Journey Begins*, by Kitty Richards
10. *The Polar Express, the Movie: The Magic Journey*, by Tracy West

Five of the best selling children's books are novelizations based upon films (*Incredibles*, 3 books based upon *Spider-Man*, and *Shark's Tale*). One book is based upon a television series (*My Little Pony*). Only *Harry Potter and the Order of the Phoenix* and *The Sisterhood of the Traveling Pants* were books from the inception, though both were made into films in 2004 (helping to explain their appearance on the top 10 list). *The Polar Express* has the distinction of debuting as a book by Chris Van Allsburg in 1985, becoming a film directed by Robert Zemeckis in 2004, and finally turning into best-selling novelizations written by Kitty Richards and Tracy West.

LANGUAGE

Initially, one might suppose that one way to create an engaging, language-rich environment would be to use book/film combinations that have both contemporary themes and complex language. However, even the adaptations of difficult and complex texts are greatly simplified in terms of plot, characterization, themes, and language when they are translated for the screen. Film communicates predominantly on the basis of images, with music and even sound effects more pertinent than words to the holistic effect.

To get a sense of the superfluity of dialogue in film, compare the chapter from Ray Bradbury's science-fiction classic *Something Wicked This Way Comes* (1983) in which the father first meets Mr. Dark in the town's library. In the book, while his son attempts to hide in the book stacks from Dr. Dark (the incarnation of the devil), the father attempts to fend off Dark's attack with wit and a belief in the power of good. Dark threatens the father and attempts to bribe him by offering him the chance to be young again in exchange for turning over his son. After some crisp dialogue heavy with allusions to Shakespeare and the Bible, Dark threatens the father, then leaves. The chapter ends with some subtle, menacing remarks about the bargains humans strike with themselves to cope with their unresolved longings and inevitable frailties.

In the film version, instead of merely asking the father to trade his youth for the life of his son, director Jack Clayton has Dark literally tear out pages from a *Bible* during their conversation. He teases the father by offering him the chance to relive life as a 20-year-old. When the father does not agree to the bribe, Dark rips out a page, it magically catches fire, and then Dark exclaims, "Twenty—gone!" then "twenty-five—gone!" until there is no more youth with which to bargain. When his repeated appeals to the father go unheeded, Dark grabs the father by the wrist and gives him "a taste of death." Using some remarkable special effects, the father's arm begins to wrinkle then to petrify.

After seeing the five-minute film clip, most viewers will readily note that little of the initial text was kept for the film. In fact, in recollections of *Something Wicked this Way Comes*, most readers/viewers will be unable to recall any part of the original text at all. Instead, they will remember from the film the withering arm and the pages of the Bible going up in flames.

However gripping a movie might be, a close analysis of the language of the screenplay reveals that few scripts ever achieve a level of difficulty above that which a fourth grader could comprehend. Regardless of the readability index used, most contemporary scripts have a level of difficulty between 1.0 and 4.0 (a level of language that a first to fourth grader would understand).

For example, the scripts of film critic favorites such as *She's Gotta Have It* (1986, directed and written by Spike Lee) is written at a grade level of 2.6, *LaStrada* (1954, directed and written by Federico Fellini) is at a grade level of 1.7, *Rashomon* (1950, directed by Akira Kurosawa and written by Shinobu Hashimoto and Akira Kurosawa) is at a grade level of 2.2, and even *Seventh Seal* (1957), the wordy, cerebral film of director/writer Ingmar Bergman is at the grade level of 3.6. The scripts of renowned American authors, such as William Faulkner (who worked on several Hollywood movies, among them *Road to Glory*, 1936) and F. Scott Fitzgerald (*Three Comrades*, 1938) score similarly (2.5 and 3.2 respectively).

To assess differences in lexical diversity, Baines (1997) analyzed specific passages from scenes in texts and compared them to the dialogue used in the film adaptation. Using two 250-word excerpts from the film *The African Queen* (1951) and the 1935 book of the same name by C. S. Forester, Baines found that the film used only three polysyllabic words—*cataracts, different, impossible*—compared to 23 polysyllabic words from the passage in the book—*appearance, astonishment, backwater, beginning, dangerous, decision, easily, enabled, equally, expatiate, fluency, garrulity, implication, jocularity, jumpiness, nervousness, obvious, provided, remotest, replying, sufficient, suggesting, volubility.*

Obviously, in its current manifestation, film does not come close to the richness of the language of books. Critics of nonprint media are correct when they note that entrance into undergraduate or graduate study at the postsecondary level still requires satisfactory scores on standard tests such as the Scholastic Aptitude Test (SAT) and Graduate Record Exam (GRE), which lean heavily on linguistic and logical assessments of intelligence. However, film's strong points are not words, but accessibility and immediacy. Only the most bookish of us would rather read a five-page description of a sunset than view its Technicolor glory on the big screen while listening to Mozart's *Symphony #40 in G minor*.

Many educational reformers (among the most prominent, Gardner, H., 1983; 1991; 1993) have recommended that schools broaden their concept of literacy. Whether or not schools will undertake such a transformative view of literacy remains to be seen. Two things are indisputable—film cannot do what books can; books cannot do what film can.

FILM AS ART AND ARTIFACT

One of the strengths of film is its ability to capture and preserve moments in time (Byrne, 1971). Most of us remember certain events, places, and persons with more clarity if we have photographs or movies to help jar the recollection. With film, as with literature, newer works do not replace older works, but are annexed into the domain's cumulative archives. Michael Almereyda's *Hamlet* (2005; starring Ethan Hawke) does not supplant Branagh's Hamlet (1996; with Branagh, Kate Winslet, and numerous other stars), nor Zefferelli's *Hamlet* (1990; starring Mel Gibson), Kline's *Hamlet* (1990; starring Kevin Kline), Richardson's *Hamlet* (196; starring an elderly Nicol Williamson), Kozintsev's *Hamlet* (1964; a Russian film starring Innokenti Smoktunovsky), Gielgud's *Hamlet* (1964; starring Richard Burton), Kurosawa's The *Bad Sleep Well* (1960; an adaptation of Hamlet set in modern Japan; starring Tohiro Mifune), Olivier's Hamlet (1948; starring Laurence Olivier), or any of the myriad other versions *of Hamlet* that seem to debut from year to year (McMurtry, 1994).

The body of work that is "film" is continually expanding. Kaes (1992) wrote, "Film constitutes a collective memory that, however much it splinters into innumerable individually remembered images, forgets nothing" (p. 317).

Since film is generally accepted as an authentic record of events, some anthropologists argued against the use of film in describing customs or cultures. The fear is that documenting events by using film may actually inhibit objective discussion and analysis (Raymond, 1991). Certainly, there is a grain of truth in the statement that film is an unwitting part "of and ideological conspiracy in which we are invited to look back at our past through the distortions of our present culture" (Giddings, Selby, & Wensley, 1990, p. xi).

Semiotics, or the science of signs, allows scholars to examine the ways in which media images represent reality and ideology (Gibson, 1979; McArthur, 1992; McGinty, 1987; Rank, 1991; Scholes, 1982). In studying the semiotics of the mass media, critics such as Gerbner (1988, 1992), asserted that the film presented by personalities of the mass media often reinforces stereotypes and reduces the complexities of real life. Truly, the mass media are often blamed for creating conflict, fabricating (or prefabricating) history, and manipulating interpretation of world events in such a manner as to bolster its audience share. It is not uncommon for contemporary analysis of media to hold film responsible for oppressing or suppressing a particular segment of society. One study (Everett, 1994) blamed the American mass media for damaging the self-esteem of all minority children through a conspiratorial, uniform portrayal of a unicultural, White world.

Works such as *Past Imperfect* (Carnes, 1996), *Teaching the Sixties* (Workman, 1992), *Projections of War* (Doherty, 1999), *Hollywood as Historian* (Rollins, 1983), and *American History/American Film* (O'Connor & Jackson, 1980) advocated analysis of film as a document of social history as well as its value as an artistic creation. Knight (1972) claimed, "The most interesting use of film in English teaching is its use to increase an understanding of the formal qualities of art" (p. 36). In an earlier study of film at the secondary level, Selby (1968) found that schools rarely, if ever, considered the aesthetic properties of film.

Jean Cocteau once called film "a petrified fountain of thought." In terms of diversity and ubiquity, film offers semioticians and aesthetes a resource for analysis unrivaled in the world of art.

FILM AS STUDENT PROJECT

The portability and affordability of the motion picture camera has democraticized film and allowed teachers and students the luxury of considering its use for the classroom. Steinman (1993) described how a camera might be used in a science class to monitor experiments, and Baines and Kunkel (2003) explicated several ways to teach philosophy, history, biography, and writing through film. Beasley (1994), Berwick (1994), Brown (1993), Catron (1991), Faulkner (1993), Hannafin (1991), Lang (1986), Turner (1989), and others discussed the advantages of using video camcorders to enhance the student's learning experience in a variety of fields.

Using film for creative endeavors by students would seem to be an obvious match with some educational reform efforts aimed at "empowering students" and getting the teacher "off the stage as a sage." Higgins (1991) viewed the camcorder as an opportunity to implement the philosophies of Freire in the classroom. Higgins wrote, "If one does not work actively against the canons of visual representation, or at a minimum question them, one is working to support the existing methods of shaping reality . . . The education of students in video production is a political activity" (p. 26). However, in a survey of Minnesota teachers, Larsson (2001) found that of those teachers who use film in the classroom, only 8% ever assign film projects.

Some states, such as Vermont, already advocate the inclusion of film in the state-mandated portfolio for each student in public school. As well, the National Board for Teacher Certification mandates that a teacher record and analyze a series of filmed teaching episodes.

The success of Morgan Spurlock's *Super-Size Me* (2004), a film whose total production costs were $65,000 and earned almost 20 million dollars at the box office, would seem to substantiate filmmaking as an entrepreneurial activity as well as a vehicle for media literacy (Baines, 1995; Lasky, 1990). Today, an entrepreneur in film would seem to have a better chance to make a living at his craft than a poet. For serving as the most esteemed poet in the country, Poet Laureate Ted Kooser earns a whopping $35,000, or about the starting salary of a public school teacher.

THE FUTURE OF FILM

The motion picture, now with a history of more than 100 years, is in the unique position of being the most established electronic communications medium of the day still in widespread use. As Culkin (1972) noted, "A lot of things have happened since 1900 and most of them plug into the wall" (p. 88). Knowledge of how and why we create meaning through viewing a film is the kind of literacy that is transferable to the real world, a world inundated with visual and aural stimuli (Auld & Pantelidis, 1994).

Currently, more films are being produced and shot in America than at any other time in history. The number of movies will continue to escalate as emerging computer technologies bring down the costs of making and distributing films (Valenti, 1999; Veronis Suhler Stevenson Communications Group, 2005). While studio products represent a significant portion of new releases, independent films account for two thirds of all new releases, 95% of the direct to video market (Independent Film and Television Alliance, 2005), and about half of the winners of Oscars over the past few years.

Theaters with stadium seating, sophisticated sound systems, and 20 or more screens are the cinemas of the moment, while the single screen repertory theater playing classic and foreign films has become passé. Since the 1920s, attendance at movie theaters per capita has been declining, though ticket prices and revenues have continued to rise. Films are available on DVD and videotape (though tape is definitely on its way out); cable, network, and public television; and over the Internet via digitized computer files. Short films premiering at the Sundance Film Festival are routinely posted at the Sundance Web site before, during, and after the festival, where they can be downloaded and viewed at leisure. At a seminar on the future of movies at the Telluride Film Festival (2005), experts noted that future delivery methods for film would rarely involve celluloid. In the future, films will be deliverable to consumers irrespective of time and place. Already the Sprint Corporation is launching a mobile film service for cell phones (Kharif, 2005).

CONCLUSIONS

Unlike elementary and secondary schools, many factions of American society have shown a genuine willingness to work with film. Today, police officers use film to record evidence at the scene of a crime; doctors probe with tiny cameras to observe and record the workings of a patient's internal organs; and parents film the development of a child over time, beginning with the baby's first movements in utero.

Yet, the view of film as "trash culture" persists among teachers and administrators who still view film as taking time away from other areas of "more serious study" (Cennamo, 1993a, 1993b; Perry & Gluckman, 1990). It is not uncommon for a teacher who uses film often to be viewed as lazy or incompetent by administrators, regardless of the benefit students may reap. When the Education Secretary for England, John Patten, was asked why he was considering the elimination of media studies in English schools, Patten replied that media studies were a "cultural Disneyland for the weaker-minded" *(Clipboard,* 1994, p. 15).

One of the greatest obstacles to the use of film in school has always been its identification with "light entertainment." Gutenberg created movable type so mankind could read and understand the Word of God (the *Bible*). On the other hand, the Lumiere brothers created film to astound and entertain a paying audience (Brower, 1994). Perhaps the circumstances that gave birth to print and film help account for some of our lingering sentiments about them.

REFERENCES

Admussen, R. (1978). Novel into film: An experimental course. *Literature/Film Quarterly, 6*(1), 66–72.

Alexander, A. (1993, March). Exploring media in everyday life. *Communication Monographs*, 55–61.

Amelio, R. (1972). *Film in the classroom.* Cincinnati, OH: Standard Publishing.

Anderson, D. (1992). Using feature films as tools for analysis in a psychology and law course. *Teaching of Psychology, 19*(3), 155–158.

Anderson, J., & Anderson, B. (1993). The myth of persistence of vision revisited. *Journal of Film and Video, 45*(1), 3–12.

Auld, L., & Pantelidis, V. (1994, January/February). Exploring virtual reality for classroom use. *Tech Trends*, 29–31.

Aycock, W., & Schoenecke, M. (Eds.). (1988). *Film and literature: A comparative approach to adaptation.* Lubbock: Texas Tech.

Baines, L. (1993). Aspects of language in literature and film (Doctoral dissertation, The University of Texas, 1993). *Dissertation Abstracts International, 54*(4), 1268.

Baines, L. (1995, February). Scripting screenplays. An idea for integrating reading, writing, and media literacy. *English Journal*, 86–91.

Baines, L. (1997, February). Dispensing with intellect. *Journal of Adolescent and Adult Literacy*, 385–386.

Baines, L., & Kunkel, T. (2003). *Teaching adolescents to write.* New York: Allyn & Bacon.

Bandura, A. (1968). What TV violence can do to your child. In O. Larsen (Ed.), *Violence and the mass media.* New York: Harper & Row, pp. 123–39.

Bandura, A. (1986). *Social foundations of thought and action.* Englewood Cliffs, NJ: Prentice-Hall.

Bazalgette, C., Sevoty, E., & Savino, J. (1993). *New directions: Media education worldwide.* London: British Film Institute.

Beasley, A. (1994). The camcorder revolution. *School Library Media Activities Monthly, 10*(5), 38–39.

Becker, P., McGehee, S., Cenceros, C. & Tipton, D. (2005, September 5). *Seminar: The future of movies.* Presented at the Telluride Film Festival. Telluride, CO.

Beckmann, C., Austin, R., & Thompson, D. (2004). Exploring proportional reasoning through movies and literature. *Mathematics Teaching in the Middle School, 9*(5), 256–262.

Beja, M. (1979). *Film and literature: An introduction.* New York: Longman.

Berg, E. (1992, October). An introduction to sociology using short stories and films. *Teaching Sociology*, 265–269.

Berwick, B. (1994, April). Kids behind the camera: Education for the video age. *Educational Leadership*, 52–54.

Biro, Y. (1982). *Profane mythology.* Bloomington: Indiana University Press.

Bluestone, G. (1957). *Novels into film.* Los Angeles: University of California Press.

Blumler, J., & Katz, E. (Eds.). (1974). *The uses of mass communications: Current perspectives on gratifications research.* Beverly Hills, CA: Sage.

Boutwell, W. (1952, March). What can we do about movies, radio, television? *English Journal*, 131–136.

Boyatzis, C. (1994, April). Using feature films to teach social development. *Teaching of Psychology*, 99–101.

Boyum, J. (1985). *Double exposure: Fiction into film.* New York: Universe Books.

Brower, A. (1994, June 6). Home technology key to the future. *Brandweek*, 17.

Brown, K. (1993). Video production in the classroom. *Tech Trends, 38*(3), 32–35.

Byrne, R. (1971). Study of film. In L. Deighton (Ed.), *The encyclopedia of education*: *Vol. 4* (pp. 1–9). New York: Macmillan.

Calich, A. (2001). From reel to real: Use of video as a therapeutic tool. *Afterimage, 29*(3), 22–24.

Cantor, J. (1991). Fright responses to mass media productions. In J. Bryant & D. Zillmann (Eds.), *Responding to the screen: Reception and reaction processes* (pp. 169–197). Hillsdale, NJ: Erlbaum.

Cantor, J., & Reilly, S. (1982). Adolescents' fright reactions to television and films. *Journal of Communication, 32*(1), 87–99.

Carnes, M. (1996). *Past imperfect : History according to the movies.* New York: Owl Paperbacks.

Carrico, J. (1970). Film and the teaching of English. In A. Schillari & J. Culkin (Eds.), *Films deliver* (pp. 97–115). New York: Citation.

Catron, L. (1991). Camcorder 101: Buying and using video cameras. *Teaching Theatre, 2*(2), 5–8.

Cennamo, K. (1993a). Students' perceptions of the ease of learning from computers and interactive video: An exploratory study. *Journal of Educational Technology Systems, 21*(3), 251–263.

Cennamo, K. (1993b). Learning from video. Factors influencing learners' preconceptions and invested mental effort. *Educational Technology Research and Development, 41*(3), 33–45.

Charters, W. (1933). *Motion pictures and youth. A summary.* New York: Macmillan.

Christopher, A., Walter, J., Marek, P., & Koening, C. (2004). Using a "new classic" film to teach about stereotyping and prejudice. *Teaching of Psychology, 31*(3), 199–202.

Clark, R. (1983). Reconsidering research on learning from media. *Review of Educational Research, 53*, 445–459.

Clark, R. (1985). Confounding in educational computing research. *Journal of Educational Computing Research, 1*(2), 28–42.

Clark, R. (1991, February). When researchers swim upstream. Reflections on an unpopular argument about learning from media. *Educational Technology,* 34–38.

Clark, R. (1992). Media use in education. In M. Allen (Ed.), *Encyclopedia of educational research: Vol. 3* (pp. 805–814). New York: Macmillan.

Clément, R., Baker, S., Josephson, G., & Noels, K (2005). Media effects on ethnic identity among linguistic majorities and minorities: A longitudinal study of a bilingual setting. *Human Communication Research, 31*(3), 399–422.

Clipboard (1994, Summer). International clippings, p. 15.

Cocteau, J. (1989). In G. Plimpton (Ed.), *The writer's chapbook* (p. 248). New York: Viking.

Cohen, K. (1979). *Film and fiction. The dynamics of exchange.* New Haven, CT: Yale University.

Considine, D., & Haley, G. (1992). *Visual images.* Englewood, CO: Teacher Ideas Press.

Costanzo, W. (1985). *Double exposure. Composing through writing and film.* Upper Montclair, NJ: Boynton/Cook.

Costanzo, W. (1992). *Reading the movies.* Urbana, IL: National Council of Teachers of English Press.

Costanzo, W. (2004). *Great films and how to teach them.* Urbana, IL: National Council of Teachers of English Press.

Coughlan, S. (1993, April 23). Battle of the books. Media's removal as a required component of English. *Times Educational Supplement.*

Cox, C. & Many, J. (1989). World of possibilities in response to literature, film, and life. *Language Arts, 66*(3), 287–294.

Cox, M., Garrett, E., & Graham, J. (2005). Death in Disney films: Implications for children's understanding of death. *Omega, 50*(4), 267–270.

Cross, C. (1989). *The influence of a positive portrayal of specific elderly individuals in a film series on the cognitive, affective, and behavioral components of children's attitudes toward the elderly.* (Doctoral dissertation, The University of Maryland at College Park, 1989). *Dissertation Abstracts International, 50,* 3799A.

Culkin, J. (1972). A schoolman's guide to Marshall McLuhan. In T. Giblin (Ed.), *Popular media & the teaching of English* (pp. 82–90). Pacific Palisades, CA: Goodyear.

Cunningham, A. (1923, September). Teaching English with the movies. *English Journal,* 488–490.

Dale, E. (1936, February). Teaching motion picture appreciation. *English Journal,* 113–120.

Davis, M., Hull, J., Young, R., & Warren, G. (1987). Emotional reactions to dramatic film stimuli. *Journal of Personality and Social Psychology, 17,* 616–640.

Dickey, S. (1993). *Cinema and the urban poor in South India.* New York: Cambridge University Press.

Doherty, T. (1999). *Projections of war.* New York: Columbia University Press.

Durgnat, R. (1967). *Films and feelings.* Cambridge, MA: MIT Press.

Eidsvik, C. (1978). *Cineliteracy.* New York: Horizon.

Eisenman, R., Girdner, E., Burroughs, R., & Routman, M. (1993, Fall). Attitudes of Mississippi college students toward David duyke before and after seeing the film *Who is David Duke*? *Adolescence,* 527–532.

Eisenstein, S. (1949). *Film form: Essays in film theory.* New York: Harcourt, Brace and Jovanovich.

Elliot, G. (Ed.) (1948). *Film and education.* New York: Philosophical Library.

Ely, D. & Minor, B. (Eds.). (1993). *Educational media and technology yearbook.* New York: Macmillan.

Everett, S. (1994). The endangered post-modern childhood. *Intermedia, 22*(2), 30–33.

Fadiman,·R. (1978). *Faulkner's intruder in the dust. Novel into film.* Knoxville: University of Tennessee Press.

Faulkner, S. (1993). Videomicroscopy using a home camcorder. *American Biology Teacher, 55*(5), 304–306.

Fleming, M., Piedmont, R., & Hiam, C. (1990). Images of madness: Feature films in teaching psychology. *Teaching of Psychology, 17*(3), 185–187.

Flippo, H. (1993, Fall). Marlene Dietrich in the German classroom. *Die Unterrichtspraxis,* 132–139.

Fry, V., Alexander, A., & Fry, D. (1990). Textual status, the stigmatized self, and media consumption. In J. Anderson (Ed.), *Communication yearbook 13* (pp. 519–544). Newbury Park, CA: Sage.

Gardner, H. (1983). *Frames of mind.* New York: Basic Books.

Gardner, H. (1991). *The unschooled mind.* New York: Basic Books.

Gardner, H. (1993). *Multiple intelligences. The theory in practice.* New York: Basic Books.

Gardner, P. (1991, October). Narrative crossings: Film adaptations in the literature class. *Teaching English in the Two-Year College,* 217–224.

Gerbner, G. (1988). *Violence and terror in the mass media.* Paris: Unesco.

Gerbner, G. (1992). Persian Gulf War, the movie. In H. Mowlana, G. Gerbner, & H. Schiller (Eds.), *Triumph of the image* (pp. 243–265). Boulder, CO: Westview Press.

Gerrish, C. (1915, April). The relation of moving pictures to English composition. *English Journal,* 226–230.

Gibson, J. (1979). *The ecological approach to visual perception.* Boston: Houghton Mifflin.

Giddings, R., Selby, K., & Wensley, C. (1990). *Screening the novel.* London: Macmillan.

Golden, J. (2005). *Reading in the dark.* Urbana, IL: National Council of Teachers of English.

Goldman, M. (1990, November). American fiction for reluctant readers. *English Journal,* 78–79.

Golenpaul, D. (Ed.). (1994). *Information please almanac.* New York: McGraw-Hill.

Greene, K., & Krcmar, M. (2005). Predicting exposure to and liking of media violence: A uses and gratifications approach. *Communication Studies, 56*(1), 71–93.

Greeson, L., & Williams, R. (1986). Social implications of music videos for youth. *Youth & Society, 18,* 177–189.

Groce, S. (1992, January). Teaching the sociology of popular music with the help of feature films. *Teaching Sociology,* 80–84.

Guista, M. (1992, October). Siskel and Ebert, move over. *Teaching English in the Two Year College,* 206–209.

Hamilton, I. (1990). *Writers in Hollywood.* New York: Harper & Row.

Hannafin, K. (1991). Technology and the support of at-risk students. *Journal of General Education, 40,* 163–179.

Hansen, C., & Hansen, R. (1990a). Rock music videos and antisocial behavior. *Basic and Applied Social Psychology, 11,* 357–370.

Hansen, C., & Hansen, R. (1990b). The influence of sex and violence on the appeal of rock music videos. *Communication Research, 17,* 212–234.

Hansen, C., & Hansen, R. (1991). Schematic information processing of heavy metal lyrics. *Communication Research, 18,* 373–411.

Hansen, C., & Krygowski, W. (1994, February). Arousal-augmented priming effects: Rock music videos and sex object schemas. *Communication Research,* 24–47.

Harrington, J. (1977). *Film as literature.* Englewood Clilts, NJ: Prentice-Hall.

Higgins, J. (1991, Fall). Video pedagogy as political activity. *Journal of Film and Video,* 18–29.

Hinton, D. (2000). *The films of Leni Riefenstahl.* Lanham, MD: Scarecrow Trade.

Hoban, C. (1942). *Focus on learning. Motion pictures in the school.* Washington, DC: American Council on Education.

Holaday, P., & Stoddard, G. (1933). *Getting ideas from the movies.* New York: Macmillan.

Hulesberg, R. (1978, Winter). Novels and films. A limited inquiry. *Literature Film Quarterly,* 57–65.

Independent Film and Television Alliance (IFTA). (2005). *About IFTA.* Retrieved October 13, 2005, from http://www.iftaonline.org/aboutafma/about_afma.asp

Infoplease Web site. (2006). *Best-selling children's books, 2004.* Retrieved June 26, 2006, from http://www.infoplease.com/ipea/A0933506.html

Iser, W. (1989). *Prospecting: From reader response to literary anthropology.* Baltimore, MD: Johns Hopkins University Press.

Jinks, W. (1974). *The celluloid literature.* Beverly Hills, CA: Glencoe.

Kaes, A. (1992). History and film. In B. Murray & C. Wickham (Eds.), *Framing the Past* (pp. 298–324). Carbondale, IL: Southern Illinois University Press.

Karl, H. (1981). What it means to be media competent. In C. Cooper (Ed.), *The nature and measurement of competency in English* (pp. 139–163). Urbana, IL: National Council of Teachers of English.

Kawin, B. (1977). *Faulkner and film.* New York: Ungar.

Kay, A. (1991, September). Computers, networks, and education. *Scientific American,* 138–148.

Kellerman, K. (1985). Memory processes in media effects. *Communication Research, 12,* 83–121.

Kelly, M., Wiebe, J., & Hynes, M. (1993, September). Teaching mathematics with technology. *Arithmetic Teacher,* 41–43.

Kerber, C., Clemens, D., & Medina, W. (2004). Seeing is believing. *Journal of Nursing Education, 43*(10), 479.

Kharif, O. (2004, June 22). The movie theater in your pocket. *Business Week Online.* Retrieved October 7, 2005, from http://www.businessweek.com

Kittridge, W. & Krauzer, S. (Eds.). (1979). *Stories into film.* New York: Harper & Row.

Klein, M. & Parker, G. (Eds.). (1981). *The English novel and the movies.* New York: Ungar.

Knight, R. (1972). *Film in English teaching.* London: Hutchinson Educational.

Ko, H., Cho, C., & Roberts, M. (2005). Internet uses and gratifications. *Journal of Advertising, 34*(2), 57–70.

Kraft, R. (1986). The role of cutting in the evaluation and retention of film. *Journal of Experimental Psychology, 12*(1), 155–163.

Kraft, R. (1987). The influence of camera angle on comprehension and retention of pictorial events. *Memory & Cognition, 15,* 291–307.

Kraft, R., Cantor, P., & Gottdiener, C. (1991). The coherence of visual narratives. *Communication Research 18*(5), 601–616.

Krendl, K. (1986). Media influence on learning. *Educational Communications Technology Journal, 34,* 223–234.

Lacey, R. (1972). *Seeing with feeling. Film in the classroom.* Philadelphia: W. B. Saunders.

Lang, F. (1986). Shooting essays. *Teaching English in the Two-Year College, 13(4),* 281–289.

Langsdorf, L. (1991). The emperor has only clothes: Toward a hermeneutic of the video text. In A. Olson, C. Parr, & D. Parr (Eds.), *Video: Icons and values* (pp. 45–62). Albany, NY: State University of New York Press.

Lankford, M. (1992). *Films for learning, thinking, and doing.* Englewood, CO: Libraries Unlimited.

Larsson, D. (2001). *Survey: Use of film in Minnesota high schools: Results.* Retrieved October 10, 2005, from http://www.english.mnsu.edu/larsson/scs/mnsurvey.html

Lasky, K. (1990). Perceptions of television programming among college students with varying degrees of video production experience. *Educational Research Quarterly, 14*(2), 48–52.

Levy, M. & Windahl, S. (1984). Audience activity and gratifications: A conceptual clarification and exploration. *Communication Research, 11,* 51–77.

Linz, D. (1989). Exposure to sexually explicit materials and attitudes toward rape: A comparison of study results. *Journal of Sex Research, 26*(1), 50–84.

Linz, D., Donnerstein, E., & Penrod, S. (1988). Effects of long-term exposure to violent and sexually degrading depictions of women. *Journal of Personality and Social Psychology, 55,* 758–768.

Livingston, K. (2004). Viewing popular films about mental illness through a sociological lens. *Teaching Sociology, 32*(1), 199–28.

Loewen, J. (1991, January). Teaching race relations from feature films. *Teaching Sociology,* 82–86.

Lynch, J. (1983). *Film education in secondary schools.* New York: Garland.

Lynch, J. (1986). Film education research: An overview. *Teaching English in the Two-Year College, 13*(4), 245–253.

Magill, F. (Ed.). (1976). *Cinema: The novel into film.* Pasadena, CA: Salem Softbacks.

Magney, C. (1972). *The age of the American novel: The film aesthetic of fiction between the two wars.* New York: Ungar.

Maibach, E., & Flora, J. (1993, August). Symbolic modeling and cognitive rehearsal. *Communication Research,* 517–545.

Manchel, F. (1990). *Film study: An analytical bibliography: Vols. 1–4.* Cranbury, NJ: Associated University Press.

Manley, T. (1994). Teaching race and ethnic relations. *Ethnic and Racial Studies, 17*(1), 135.

Marcus, A. (2005, March/April). It is as it was: Feature film in the history classroom. *The Social Studies,* 61–67.

Marcus, F. (Ed.). (1971). *Film and literature: Contrast in media.* London: Chandler.

Marcus F. (Ed.). (1977). *Short story, short film.* Englewood Cliffs, NJ: Prentice-Hail.

Maynard, R. (1971). *The celluloid curriculum: How to use movies in the classroom.* Rochelle Park, NJ: Hayden.

McArthur, D. (1992). Sign function and potential of the printed word. *Visible Language, 26*(3), 282–297.

McConnell, F. (1979). *Storytelling and mythmaking: Images for film and literature.* New York: Oxford University Press.

McDonald, B. (1983). *Basic language skills through films.* Littleton, CO: Libraries Unlimited.

McDougal, S. (1985). *Made into movies: From literature to film.* New York: Holt, Rinehart, & Winston.

McGinty, S. (1987, January). Deconstructing "Citizen Kane." *English Journal,* 46–50.

McKenzie, B. (1993). Ten innovative uses of video with at-risk students. *The Clearing House, 66*(1), 238–240.

McLuhan, M. (1962). *The Gutenberg galaxy.* Toronto, Canada: The University of Toronto Press.

McLuhan, M. (1964). *Understanding media: The extensions of man.* New York: Signet.

McLuhan, M. (1967). *The medium is the message.* New York: Bantam Books.

McMurtry, J. (1994). *Shakespeare films in the classroom.* Hamden, CT: Archon.

Meierhenry, W. (1952). *Enriching the curriculum through motion pictures.* Lincoln, NE: University of Nebraska Press.

Metzger, M. & Flanagin, A. (2002). Cultural representations of gender and science. *Communication Research Reports, 19*(4), 338–351.

Miller, G. (1980). *Screening the novel: Rediscovered American fiction in film.* New York: Ungar.

Miller, H. (1979). *Films in the classroom: A practical guide.* Metuchen, NJ: Scarecrow.

Miller, J. (1986). *Subsequent performances.* London: Faber.

Miller, J. (1988). *Using copyrighted videocassettes.* Friday Harbor, WA: Copyright Information Services.

Millichap. J. (1983). *Steinbeck and film.* New York: Ungar.

Murray, E. (1972). *The cinematic imagination: Writers and the motion pictures.* New York: Ungar.

Murray-Brown, J. (1991). Video ergo sum. In A. Olson, C. Parr, & D. Parr (Eds.), *Video: Icons and values* (pp.17–32). Albany, NY: State University of New York Press.

Neal, R. (1913, December). Making the devil useful. *English Journal*, 658–660.

Nichols, B. (1992). Film studies. In E. Laskin (Ed.), *The American Film Institute guide to setting started in film* (pp. xi–xiii). New York: Prentice-Hall.

O'Connor, J., & Jackson, M. (Eds.). (1980). *American history, American film*. New York: Ungar.

Oliver, C. (Ed.). (1989). *A moving picture feast: The filmgoer's Hemingway*. New York: Praeger.

Oliver, M. (1993, February). Adolescents' enjoyment of graphic horror. *Communication Research*, 30–50.

Peary, G., & Shatzkin, R. (Eds.). (1977). *The classic American novel and the movies*. New York: Ungar.

Peary, G., & Shatzkin, R. (Eds.). (1978). *The modern American novel and the movies*. NewYork: Ungar.

Perry, A., & Gluckman, I. (1990). Using (and misusing) movies. *Principal, 70,* 59–61.

Rank, H. (1991). *The pitch*. Park Forest, IL: Counter-propaganda Press.

Raymond, C. (1991). Increasing use of film by visually oriented anthropologists stirs debate over ways scholars describe other cultures. *Chronicle of Higher Education, 37*(28), A5.

Remender, P. (1992). Using feature films to encourage critical thinking. *Southern Social Studies Journal, 17*(2), 33–44.

Resch, K., & Schicker, V. (1992). *Using film in the high school curriculum*. Jefferson, NC: McFarland.

Rhiel, M. (1993, Spring). Teaching Arturo Ui: Triumph of whose will? *Die Unterrichtspraxis*, 67–69.

Richardson, R. (1969). *Literature and film*. Bloomington, IN: Indiana University Press.

Rollins, P. (Ed.). (1983). *Hollywood as historian*. Lexington, KY: University Press of Kentucky.

Rosenblatt, L. (1978). *The reader, the text, the poem*. Carbondale, IL: Southern Illinois University Press.

Rosengren, K., Wenner, L., & Palmgreen, P. (1985). *Media gratifications research: Current perspectives*. Beverly Hills, CA: Sage.

Ross, N. (1991). Literature and film. *ELTJournal, 45*(2), 147–155.

Rubin, A. (1993, March). Audience activity and media use. *Communication Monographs*, 98–105.

Rutten, T. (2004, January 21). Passions are swirling anew. *Los Angeles Times*, E1.

Sarafino, E. (1986). *The fears of childhood*. New York: Human Sciences Press.

Schneller, R. (1988, June). Video watching and its societal functions for small-town adolescents in Israel. *Youth and Society*, 441–459.

Scholes, R. (1982). *Semiotics and interpretation*. New Haven, CT: Yale University Press.

Scholle, D. (1991, Spring/Summer). Reading the audience, reading resistance. *Journal of Film and Video*, 80–90.

Selby, S. (1968). *The study of film as an art form in American secondary schools* (Doctoral dissertation, Columbia University, 1968). *Dissertation Abstracts International, 24*(12), 5098.

Selby, S. (1978). *The study of film as an art form in American secondary schools*. New York: Arno Press.

Self, R. (1987). Film and literature: Parameters of a discipline. *Literature Film Quarterly, 15*(1), 15–21.

Sheridan, M., Owen, H., Macrorie, K., & Marcus, F. (1965). *The motion picture and the teaching of English*. New York: Appleton-Century-Crofts.

Sherman, B., & Dominick, J. (1986). Violence and sex in music videos: TV and rock 'n' roll. *Journal of Communication, 36*, 70–93

Sherry, J. (2004). Flow and media enjoyment. *Communication Theory, 14*(4), 328–347.

Shiring, J. (1990, October). Free reading and film. *English Journal*, 37–40.

Sinyard, N.(1986). *Filming literature: The art of screen adaptation*. London: Croon Helm.

Skolnik, R., & Smith, C. (1993). Utilizing video technology to serve the needs of at risk students. *The Journal for Vocational and Special Needs Education, 16*(1), 23–31.

Slater, M. (2003). Alienation, aggression, and sensation seeking as predictors of adolescent use of violent film, computer, and website content. *Journal of Communication, 53*(1), 105–121.

Smagorinsky, P. (1996). *Standards in practice, 9–12*. Urbana, IL: National Council of Teachers of English.

Sohn, D. (1970). *Film: The creative eye*. Dayton, OH: Pflaum.

Speigel, A. (1976). *Fiction and the camera eye*. Charlottesville: University Press of Virginia.

Squires. N. (1990). A Freireian-inspired video curriculum for at-risk high school students. *English Journal, 79*(2), 49–56.

Stam, R. & Raengo, A. (Eds.) (2005). *Literature and film: A guide to the theory and practice of film adaptation*. Malden, MA: Blackwell.

Steinman, R. (1993, April). Cameras in the classroom. *Science Teacher*, 16–19.

Street, D. (Ed.). (1983). *Children's novels and the movies*. New York: Ungar.

Tamborini, R., Salomonson, K., & Bahk, C. (1993, October). The relationship of empathy to comforting behavior following film exposure. *Communication Research*, 723–738.

Turner, D. (1989). The art teachers' new tool: The video camcorder. *School Arts, 89*(4), 27–28.

Ullmer, E. (1994). Media and learning: Are there two kinds of truth? *Educational Technology Research and Development, 42*(1), 21–32.

Usher, A. (1985). *Filmed books and plays*. Lexington, MA: Lexington Books.

Valenti, J. (1999, May 4). *C-Span broadcast of the congressional hearings on youth and violence*. C-Span.

Veronis Suhler Stevenson Communications Group. (2005). *Communications industry forecast and report*. New York: Author.

Vetrie, M. (2004). Using film to increase literacy skills. *English Journal, 93*(3), 39–45.

Wagner, G. (1975). *The novel and the cinema*. Cranbury, NJ: Associated University Presses.

Watson, R. (1990). *Film and television in education: An aesthetic approach to the moving image*. London: Falmer Press.

Weinberg, H. (1973, Spring). Novel into film. *Literature Film Quarterly*, 98–102.

Weinstein, P. (2001). Movies as the gateway to history. *History Teacher, 35*(1), 27.

Welch, D. (2001). *Propaganda and the German cinema, 1933–1945*. New York: I. B. Tauris.

Wenner, L. (1986). Model specification and theoretical development in gratifications sought and obtained research. *Communication Monographs, 53*, 160–179.

Weerts, S. (2005). Use of films to teach critical thinking. *Journal of Nutrition Education and Behavior, 37*(2), 100–101.

Wilbur, R. (1970). A poet at the movies. In T. Ross (Ed.), *Film and the liberal arts* (pp. 167–170). New York: Holt, Rinehart, & Winston.

Wilhelm, J. (1996). *Standards in practice, 4–8*. Urbana, IL: National Council of Teachers of English.

Workman, B. (1992). *Teaching the sixties*. Urbana, IL: National Council of Teachers of English.

Zillmann, D., & Bryant, J. (1986). Exploring the entertainment experience. In D. Zillmann & J. Bryant (Eds.), *Perspectives on media effects* (pp. 303–324). Hillsdale, NJ: Erlbaum.

•52•

MEDIA OVER THE DECADES: FROM RADIO [FAST-FORWARD] TO PODCASTING AND THE iPOD

James Trier
UNIVERSITY OF NORTH CAROLINA AT CHAPEL HILL

INTRODUCTION

Twin Curiosities

"Video Killed the Radio Star" was the first music video played on MTV during the then radical network's debut broadcast on August 1, 1981. The video (by a group called The Buggles) can be easily accessed via the Wikipedia Web site and searching with the video's name. On that same page, there is also an accompanying link to an animated satire of the Buggle's music video titled "The Internet Killed the Video Star," created by eStudio in 2000. The titles (and narrative contents) of these two music videos refer to how the popularity of a new medium can eclipse the influence of a predecessor, usually by being able to do what the previously popular medium did, but much more. The titles also, however, overstate just what happens in this process of media competition—a new medium does not really *kill off* an older one. Rather, the older medium is somewhat displaced but continues to live on, though typically in the shadows of reigning newer media.

While thinking about the contribution that I wanted to make to this section of the *Handbook* about the role that the visual and communicative arts have played in the English and language arts classroom (hereafter, I will just use the single term *English*), I found myself thinking about both of these music videos. "Video Killed the Radio Star" got me curious about the "starring" roles that radio, film, and television ("video" signifies both film and television) have each played in English classrooms over the decades, and "The Internet Killed the Video Star" satire got me thinking about what the future holds for these media forms as the influence of the Internet continues to rapidly and radically transform education.

To pursue these twin curiosities, I initially decided to research what has been published in *English Journal (EJ)* about the relation between teaching English and the electronic media of radio, film, and television over the decades. Why *EJ*? One reason is that *EJ* is devoted exclusively to publishing articles relevant to the teaching of English. Another reason is that the main contributors to *EJ* are English teachers, along with professors interested in the teaching of English, and the articles are typically about a teaching practice or a specific activity or unit that a teacher has designed and enacted with students. A third reason is that *EJ* has been in business since 1912, publishing between 8–10 issues a year, so it provides a rich historical record of articles about the teaching of English for nine decades.

During the initial phase of researching *EJ*, I knew that I would have to drastically narrow my topic because I was dealing with almost 95 years of a journal's total output of thousands of articles, *and* I was also still dealing with the three media—with an eye out for a section about the Internet, in particular podcasting and the iPod. I eventually decided that I would focus primarily on radio (this is the only chapter in the *Handbook* that does so) because I wanted to explore the connections—*if any*—between how the "old" medium of radio had been taken up in English classrooms and what the new technology of the iPod (radio's descendant) makes possible.[1]

[1] It is important to point out that I also decided not to include for analysis the many *EJ* articles that recommended for pedagogical use various radio programs that were available as phonograph records during the 1930s and 1940s. Most of these articles took the form of short annotated bibliographies compiled by a writer as part of a column that recommended other kinds of media "resources," such as film reels and filmstrips, along with books about films and radio, print texts such as radio scripts, listings of scheduled radio broadcasts coming up, and so on. Such articles can be found in regular columns that ran in *EJ*, such as "The Public Arts," whose editor and main contributor in the late 1950s and early 1960s was Patrick Hazard. I decided not to include these short articles because they were informational rather than conceptual (e.g., they did not discuss pedagogical uses of these audio-visual materials as much as they simply made the reader aware of newly available resources). Instead, I focused on more detailed accounts of teachers conceptualizing how to engage students in thinking about the medium of radio.

Most of the *EJ* articles about radio appeared in the 1930s and 1940s, when radio shared center stage with film as an important focus of study in *EJ*. Through my analysis of approximately 70 articles about radio during this period, I discovered two main approaches of engaging with radio that emerged. I begin my discussion by explaining these different approaches and giving many examples of each. I then briefly summarize why, from the early 1950s up to the present, very few articles were published in *EJ* that were exclusively about radio. Finally, I fast forward to the present and discuss how radio is making a comeback through podcasting and the iPod.

THE GOOD, THE BAD, AND THE RADIO

The first *EJ* article written about radio was titled "A Radio Contract in English" by a teacher named Ruth Batten (1931). Batten described a project in which a group of students (all boys) was asked if they would like to broadcast a radio program on the air. The boys enthusiastically agreed to the idea and underwent a process of developing, in Batten's words, a full radio "program of speeches, plays, music, and jokes" (p. 158). This involved everything from holding tryouts for an announcer, taking turns reading a speech by "saying it through a megaphone," seeking out the help of "a public speaking 'major' from among the practice teachers to coach them in their speeches," enlisting the aid of a member of the school orchestra to provide music for the program, and arranging "with the local broadcasting station for the particular hour and day that the program would be given" (Batten, 1931, p. 158). One problem that arose was a lack of radio material for the program: "One boy wrote a letter to KDKA," a local radio station, "for suitable plays, another went to the library, and still another interviewed the dramatic instructor at the university. It seemed that the plays available were too long or that the company asked a royalty" (pp. 158–159). This problem was solved when one of the boys in the radio group wrote an original play, which the group "immediately accepted" (p. 158). Along with music, speeches, and a play, the boys also culled some jokes from "a library copy of *Old Cracks*" as well as some jokes they had heard on their own. The boys also rehearsed many times for the broadcast. They eventually went on the air and performed the radio program, which was a success and left them with a feeling of accomplishment. In Batten's words, "The boys agreed that they had enjoyed this [radio] contract more than the average lesson even though it had been more difficult than most of them" (p. 160).

So this first *EJ* article about radio, which recounted how a teacher engaged students in the compositional, communicative, and organizational processes involved in writing for and speaking on radio, envisioned radio *in an exclusively positive light*.

A countervailing view of radio, however, was first articulated just two years later by Carlton Larrabee (1933). Larrabee opened with the following observation: "The possibilities and problems of radio entertainment have not as yet been sufficiently recognized. The radio is a new branch of human endeavor which the English teacher must carefully study so that he can guide his pupils toward an intelligent selection of the best in current broadcasting" (p. 824). He then noted how influential radio was in the lives of students, and how the teacher "must be willing to use and direct this powerful interest" (p. 824). The first step is to discover the students' favorite radio programs through a questionnaire. What the teacher will inevitably discover is the students' varying "levels of appreciation" (p. 824). Larrabee then outlined a series of radio lessons to raise the levels of appreciation of students' listening habits. For example, one lesson titled "Listening to a New Program" should lead students "one further step toward the recognition and choice of better programs," and a lesson titled "Comparison of Two Dramatic Programs" should lead students "cautiously toward a recognition of inferior judgments and a rejection of poorer programs" (pp. 826–827). And in a culminating lesson, "The pupils are asked to write and send letters of approval and gratitude to radio stations or to sponsors of programs which the class has found to be culturally worthy" (p. 827). What made Larrabee's orientation toward radio different from that of Batten's (1931) was that his vision was much more fixed on the content of radio programs—particularly on what he deemed negative content—and he called for teachers to engage students in radio lessons for the purpose of helping them to discern the "culturally worthy" and "best" programs from the "poorer programs." So, compared with Batten (1931), Larrabee envisioned radio *in a more skeptical light*.

DIALECTICS OF THE ETHER[2]

Over a 20-year period (1931–1951), the two main visions of radio described in the previous section played themselves out in almost seventy articles. Approximately two thirds of the articles were similar to that of Ruth Batten's (1931) in that they were primarily concerned with discovering imaginative, creative ways to articulate radio with English practices, such as writing, listening, speaking, and performing. About one third of the articles were similar to that of Larrabee's (1933) in that they were mainly concerned with discovering the radio listening habits and "tastes" of students and then engaging in pedagogical activities to alter what were considered the students' problematic listening choices. Of the two types, the former reveals much more variety and experimentation than does the latter. In fact, it's fair to say that, with a couple of exceptions, nearly all the "cultivating taste" articles present the same basic (and rather simple) argument, so that nothing really new in either the argument or the pedagogical approach appeared in 20 years.

In what follows, I discuss these two types of articles, but it is important to point out that though I discuss each type separately, the publication dates reveal that the articles actually formed a dialectical conversation with one another throughout the two decades (the reference list for *EJ* radio articles also impressionistically reveals this, as well).

RADIO PEDAGOGY (OR, RADIO IS GOOD FOR YOU!)

As mentioned, many of the articles that articulate English and radio described activities and units designed to involve students in composing a variety of forms (plays, advertisements, interviews, etc.) for radio, even if what was written was likely never to air on an actual

[2] It was once believed that radio waves traveled through space via a mysterious atmospheric substance called "ether," and in some of the articles in *EJ*, the authors humorously refer to "the ether" when discussing radio (e.g., Batten, 1931).

broadcast For example, following Batten (1931), Tanner (1934) discussed relating canonical literature to radio:

> We first tried the idea of putting on what we called a 'Radio Presentation' in a tenth-grade English class during the study of Shakespeare's *Merchant of Venice*. We divided the class into two parts, one half presenting its radio program in the classroom, the remaining group criticizing and writing its comments to "the artists of the ether." On a later day we reversed the procedure. (p. 678)

Cothrin (1935) involved her students in writing "radio plays" based on magazine advertisements. Phillips (1937) organized a theater group and a five-week speech unit "given over to the study and production of radio plays," during which students studied "voice and interpretation" (p. 33). Duff (1936) described a "literary allusions" project she designed:

> For two months my advanced juniors were asked to note all literary allusions heard over the air. I wished them to listen to programs definitely characterized as literary . . . and to glean the rather subtle references such as Shakespearean lines, quotations from famous poems, essays, and short stories, titular quotations, and ideational content. (p. 867)

Flynt (1937) was inspired to invigorate the routine oral composition lessons he was putting his (quite bored) students through by encouraging them to give their oral compositions "as though they were radio announcers" (p. 237). Carson (1939) involved her students in writing radio adaptations of short stories such as "The Fall of the House of Usher" and "To Build a Fire" (p. 480). Orndorff (1939a) also recommended that teachers have students "browse" the airwaves to discover the variety of programming available to listen to. She argued that, given the plethora of literary "classics" that were being adapted and aired on radio, teachers should take advantage of this windfall: "Why not be an opportunist and take what the gods offer?" Along with "high culture" programs, she also suggested tuning in to more popular forms, such as "comedians of the ether" like Jack Benny and Charlie McCarthy (p. 623). She also saw advertising as a content to have students attend to:

> One of the outstanding qualities of much of the advertising programs on the air is the invitation to do something—engage in a contest, contribute a question, send in a [cereal] box top. Audience participation is intended to stimulate buying a product, but it also enhances enjoyment and thereby the popularity of the program by providing an outlet for reactions set going. And this principle of participation or creative expression should be allowed to take its way in the schoolroom as a result of radio listening. (Orndorff, 1939a, pp. 624–625)

These kinds of articles continued to appear throughout the 1940s. For example, Drinkwater (1941) explained that after her students heard a radio program that featured a contest in which people found grammar and usage errors in each other's way of talking, they wanted to write such speech quizzes and perform them: "The dramatic sketches were written portraying young people in typical situations, and in all the conversations there were to be violations of good usage" (p. 580). Russell (1941) used her students' interests in their favorite radio programs to liven up their writing by having students choose the format and content of a radio program as a model for their own essays. For example, one group of students used a program called "Hobby Lobby" to develop a unit in which "they gave 'radio' talks on their individual hobbies, wrote clever and voluntary paragraphs explaining these hobbies, and planned and arranged a hobby display" (p. 588). Tomlinson (1941) involved her students in writing radio interviews by having them interview "people in school outside their own classes and in the community" and then shaping the interviews "into radio scripts and broadcast over the school public address set" (p. 64). M. Kaplan (1945) used radio programs to introduce students to fundamental features of a stage drama by having students adapt radio plays so they appealed in both aural and visual ways. Golding (1947) had students listen to radio commentaries and then study the backgrounds of the commentators and the companies that sponsored the commentaries, all of which led students to begin to see the "propaganda" elements of commentaries. Golding noted, "I found that this study of commentators and commentaries gave the class excellent material for the study of propaganda" (p. 48). Cullimore (1948) described how the revision process of making writing a radio script, though frustrating, proved worthwhile: "We studied scripts as models, and we evaluated many; in fact, we ate, we dreamed, we wrote, we tore up and re-wrote scripts constantly, but the students grew and finally achieved their goal" (p. 318).

DISTINGUISHING EXCELLENCE FROM TRASH (OR, LISTEN UP: RADIO CAN BE BAD FOR YOU!)

Max Herzberg (1935), then chairman of the Radio Committee of NCTE (and future president of NCTE), explained that teachers should develop units of radio "appreciation" that would bring about "the establishment of a critical attitude, in which the good" in radio programming "will be properly praised and the bad perceived and—perhaps—avoided." More directly, Herzberg observed that teachers should help "show young people how to distinguish excellence from trash" (p. 546).

The main torchbearer of this call to improve the radio-listening habits and tastes of students was K. Tyler (1936), an assistant professor at Ohio State University, who published many articles on this subject. In the first article to appear, K. Tyler discussed a study he had conducted in Oakland, California about the radio listening practices of 700 students, and he explained that his study revealed "a relatively low level of taste in radio programs on the part of high-school students and their lack of critical judgment." He added, "All in all, the programs which were popular were not good programs; many of them were pure Hokum and slapstick." Among the students, he added, "Taste in drama seemed relatively undeveloped, and the musical preferences were not so much bad as they were narrow. Much needs to be done to develop in high-school students the ability to bring critical judgment to bear upon the radio fare which is offered to them" (p. 213).

A year later, K. Tyler (1937) wrote another article, this one titled "Developing Discrimination with Regard to Radio" in which he called for teachers to engage in pedagogical activities that would "enable young people to interpret properly their experience with radio" (p. 122). K. Tyler observed that "an intelligent interpretation of radio programs demands a more mature discrimination," and to develop this, students "must examine the good, the mediocre, and the bad" in radio programming "so that differences may be clearly revealed." Speaking in a collective "we" that identified himself and teachers of English as a community of teachers, K. Tyler imagined addressing students with the following advice: "'Gorge yourselves for a time,' we shall say, 'with radio programs. You may get a bit of indigestion, but gradually you will find out what elements in your listening are responsible for it.'" Then, addressing English teachers,

K. Tyler predicted that by allowing students to "gorge" themselves on all kinds of radio programming, "The students will come to your classrooms full of ill-digested material, but through frequent and heated discussion they will learn to sort out the good and the bad, even to the point of discovering, perhaps, a radio diet which, for them at least, will have its merits" (p. 124).

A year later, K. Tyler (1938) published another article. He observed of the time, "This is the age of radio. All of us are radio-minded. The youth now in our high schools is truly a radio generation. They were born with the birth of radio, and the two have grown up together"—they are "boys and girls who have been raised to accept radio as the most natural thing in the world" (p. 557). K. Tyler then makes a rhetorical move that he had not done before, equating the development of good taste and critical appreciation in radio listening in youth with the act of protecting democracy itself: "Increasingly it becomes clear that democracy's only defense" against the dictatorial forces that have taken over Europe through propagandistic uses of radio "is the critical capacities of its citizens" (p. 565).

Many others, along with K. Tyler, argued for the teaching of higher listening standards for students. One was T. Tyler (no relation to K. Tyler), a professor at the University of Minnesota. In an article titled "The Place of Radio in the Teaching of English," T. Tyler (1940) wrote the following about the effect of radio on students: "Radio has a somewhat dulling effect on the higher mental processes of the listener; he is definitely less critical, less analytical, and more passively receptive when listening to the radio than when he is face to face with the speaker" (p. 395). Tyler then argued that English teachers should engage in "the raising of appreciational standards" (p. 397) among students so that they can come to recognize the "varying degrees of excellence" (p. 398) in the radio programs to which they listen.

Throughout the 1940s, many similar articles appeared. For example, Gilburt (1943) argued that teachers "must start educating the present generation now to select and appreciate better programs" and "to evolve higher artistic standards for the various types of programs" (p. 433) that students listen to. Tallman (1948) recommended specific radio projects that included one that "was intended to introduce all children to the best types of dramatic productions and to make an effort to show them the inanities of soap operas and murder-detective thrillers (p. 410). Larrabee (1949) made another contribution to match his 1933 article—this one titled "Radio, A Public Servant," in which he observed: "For 20 years we have been struggling, against time and space and against a host of lesser but more tangible opponents, to bring our classrooms appropriate programs and transcriptions and thus to make of radio an assistant to the teacher." He also noted, "Because we have realized that our students' listening tastes and habits are usually naïve and unguided, we have tried to help them develop more critical and discriminative attitudes" (p. 92) (For other such articles, see T. Tyler, 1935; Noyes, 1937; Hurley, 1937; K. Tyler, 1939; Rachford, 1944; Novotny, 1946b; T. Tyler, 1946; Stratton, 1948; Saunders, 1949; Anderson, 1949; Gruber, 1950; Roody, 1952).

"VIDEO KILLED THE RADIO STAR"

Though "Video Killed the Radio Star" aired in 1981, radio as a "star" medium in *EJ* actually burned out by the early 1950s with the rapid mass proliferation of television sets in nearly every home. The sudden dominance of television as the new star medium in society was reflected in *EJ*, which began publishing articles that were either exclusively about television or about television as the main medium among the "mass media" to be studied. The last articles of this period that took radio as a main focus were Allen's (1949) "Mass Pressure on Radio and Journalism," Grey's (1951) "Radio—a Means, Not an End," and Hood's (1951) "Canadian Broadcasting." Each of these articles, however, framed radio within a more general discussion of "communication" and "mass media." Each one also elaborated the theme from the 1930s and 1940s about the necessity of developing the critical sensibilities of students toward the mass media. For example, Allen wrote, "We who are concerned with the teaching of communication, then, cannot ignore our responsibility to prepare our students as well as we can to become critical users of the mass mediums of communication" (p. 453).

Because my main focus in this chapter is radio, I will not develop a discussion about how dominant television became in *EJ* throughout the 1950s and 1960s, nor about how film, which was already a "star" well before radio appeared on the scene, rivaled radio as a popular medium in English classrooms, and continued to be the main focus of *EJ* articles long after radio disappeared from the spotlight—in fact, film still remains so today. What is important to state here, however, is that radio all but disappeared from the discourse on media with the mass proliferation of television in the early 1950s. And when radio did remain in the discursive picture in the 1950s and 1960s, it typically got a sort of respectful "honorable mention" reference but was then passed by for a fuller discussion of television and film. Boutwell (1952) provided an example of this kind of superficial reference when he asked, "Should English teachers pay any attention to movies, television, and radio? Perhaps we should ask, 'Can we afford to neglect them?'" (p. 133). Though radio is mentioned (last) in the title, the article is about television. (For other examples of this, see Boutwell, 1958; Lewin, R., 1960; Nevi & Hoffine, 1962; Rowland, 1964).

This absence of radio as the focus in *EJ* articles continued, with some exceptions, throughout the 1970s, 1980s, 1990s, up to the present. The exceptions include about a dozen articles (out of hundreds that appeared during these decades). Interestingly, some of these exceptions read like throwbacks to those of the 1930s and 1940s in how they suggest that teachers take up radio programs in order to improve students' composition skills. One example is Cushman's (1973) article "'Old Radio' in the English Class: It Can't Miss!" Cushman described how she engaged her students in listening to radio programs from decades earlier (such as "The Lone Ranger") and then had them "create their own radio shows" (p. 244), a process that Cushman summed up as follows:

> An "old radio" unit has everything to do with the contemporary English class. Students found a need for creating imaginative situations, dialog, and narrative. To produce an effective show, they needed to work on affectation of speech patterns to get across a character's personality, on clarity of speech, on timing and on vocal variety. Students worked in a medium that emphasizes audio skills only. The visual focus that our young people have been brought up with is absent for once. They listened to music—classical even! They learned to plan, to anticipate, and to analyze their efforts as they went along. Many students learned to operate AV equipment for the first time and to produce desired effects with volume and fading. All students learned a little more about the times that produced the radio era. (p. 248)

Other examples of articles that discuss similar "old radio" activities are Hollister (1974), Alley (1979), Miller (1982), and Gillespie (1990). (For similar "writing radio plays" articles, see Danielson, 1981; Jackson, 1994; Orfanella, 1998.)

A few articles appeared that discussed projects that engaged students in learning radio as a medium. For example, Barrett (1973) described an apprenticeship program that taught students various broadcasting skills, which students then used to give actual broadcasts at a local radio station. Another example is Daniels' (1976) article "Breaker, Break, Broke: Citizens Band [Radio] in the Classroom." Written during the heyday of CB radio—when the film *Smokey and the Bandit* and the song "Convoy" ("10-4, Good Buddy") were all the rage—this article optimistically argued for teaching students how to use "the important new medium" (p. 53) of Citizens Band radio, "the fastest-growing consumer electronics product *in history*" (p. 55). Daniels described in detail a quite sophisticated project that articulates the CB with English: "There are, it seems to me, two broad areas of English instruction in which CB radio can be a useful tool: These are the study of language itself (up to and including "grammar") and the broader study of communication as/and culture" (p. 53). The article, though, reads like a last gasp, of sorts: The fascination with CB radio would eventually disappear when the new "electronics product" hit the market in the late 1970s and early 1980s—videocassette recorders. "Video Killed the Radio Star," indeed (at least in English).

FAST FORWARD TO PODCASTING AND THE IPOD IN EDUCATION

A survey of new media in *The Economist* (2006) appeared under the title "Among the Audience." The thesis of the survey was that we are at "the beginning of a very gradual transition to a new era, which might be called the age of personal or participatory media," which means, "the boundaries between audiences and creators become blurred and often invisible" (p. 4). The survey included sections on Web logs (blogs, personal online journals), "citizen journalism" (where "amateurs"—e.g., everyday citizens—contribute journalistic articles and videos to online newspapers and magazines), the "Wiki principle" ("Wiki" is Hawaiian for "quick" and means a Web page that can be accessed *and* altered by anyone, such as those found at Wikipedia.com), satellite radio (e.g., Clear Channel Communications), and podcasting and the iPod. In this section, I will explain what podcasting is and then discuss some roles that podcasting and the iPod have recently played in education.

As *The Economist* (2006) noted, the "podfather" of podcasting is Adam Curry, a former MTV V-Jay who in 2004 "used his own celebrity and the underlying technologies of blogging to popularize yet another big thing: 'podcasting.'" About the term *podcast, The Economist* explained that it is a "hip but not helpful" term: "The 'pod' comes from Apple's iPod, a fashionable portable music player—a stroke of marketing luck for Apple, which initially had nothing to do with podcasting. The 'casting' comes from broadcasting." *The Economist* also explained how podcasting works:

> A podcaster records something—anything from music to philosophical ramblings, professional news or snorting noises—into a computer with the aid of a microphone, then posts this audio file onto the internet. There, people can listen to it and, more importantly, subscribe to a "feed" from the same podcaster, so that all new audio files from that source are automatically pulled down as soon as they are published. Whenever listeners dock their iPods or other music players for charging, the feeds that have newly arrived on the computers are transferred to the portable devices. People can then listen in their car, while jogging, or wherever and whenever they please. (p. 15)

The Economist added, "Podcasting is about 'time-shifting' (listening offline to something at a time of one's own choosing, as opposed to a broadcaster's)." How has podcasting taken off since its advent? *The Economist* reports that "Apple's iTunes, the software application and online music store that makes iPods work, currently lists 20,000 free podcasts and is adding them at a fast clip, all before podcasting's second birthday." In addition, "Podcasting is even expanding from audio to video, although this trend is as yet so new that several words ('vodcasting,' 'vidcasting,' 'vlogging') are still vying for the honour." The great appeal of podcasting is that all a person needs to do it "is a microphone, a computer and an internet connection, and most people already have those" (p. 16).

Perhaps the most widely reported educational experiment involving podcasting and iPods took place at Duke University during the 2004–2005 academic year. A final report (June 2005) of the experiment, titled "Duke University iPod First Year Experience Final Evaluation Report" (and referenced hereafter as *Duke iPod*) can be accessed at http://cit.duke.edu/pdf/ipod_initiative_04_05.pdf. The study involved almost 50 courses, as many professors, and over 600 students. Faculty used the iPod to disseminate course content "such as lectures, songs, historical speeches, and foreign language content distributed via the Duke iPod content server, iTunes, Blackboard course management tool, and podcasts." Generally, students used the iPod to capture lectures, class discussions, and verbal feedback on papers; to capture "field notes, interviews, environmental sounds and audio data"; to support their studying, through repeated listening to "commercial and original audio content, such as music, audiobooks, rehearsals and vocabulary lists"; and to store large multimedia files (Duke iPod, pp. 1–2). Some specific examples of how the iPod played out in particular classes include the following: Students in an English course "downloaded music, radio plays, and other sounds from early 20th century Europe to analyze how the rise of technology in the era affected literature and communication"; students in an Asian/African American Language and Literature course "recorded natural sounds in various cultural environments to help examine subjective experience as well as ideas about mysticism and human potential"; students in a music class "used iTunes to acquire recordings of selected Bach chorales"; students in a Turkish Language course "used the iPod to listen and become accustomed to a wide range of authentic Turkish language materials such as songs, news broadcasts, and poems"; and many more examples (see Duke iPod, pp. 14–15). Overall, The Duke Digital Initiative reported the experiment as being successful, and it planned during the 2005–2006 academic year to continue using the iPod as a teaching and learning tool for faculty and students.

Podcasting and the iPod have also been part of many other educational projects, as Jeffrey Selingo (2006) reported in a *New York Times* article titled "Students and Teachers, from K to 12, Hit the Podcasts." Selingo noted, "Currently, iTunes [http://www.apple.com/itunes] lists more than 400 podcasts from kindergarten through 12th grade classes, while Yahoo [http://podcasts.yahoo.com] has nearly 900 education-related podcasts." Along with these

Web locations, here are some other links that have a plethora of educational podcasts:

- The Education Podcast Network: http://epnweb.org/index.php
- Podcast Alley: http://www.podcastalley.com/
- Podcast.net: http://www.podcast.net/
- Podcastingnews: http://www.podcastingnews.com/forum/link_6.htm
- PodcastPickle: http://www.podcastpickle.com/

CONCLUSION: BACK TO THE FUTURE

In the introduction to this chapter, I made the point that in the clash of media competition, a new medium does not really *kill off* an older one. Rather, the older medium is somewhat displaced but continues to live on, though typically in the shadows of the reigning newer media. I think of radio as having lived on well enough as a mainstream medium competing with film, television, and the Internet in the broader societal context, though within the discourse of teaching English and language arts, radio's one-time dominance faded and it has been on the margins, watching other media play central roles. But podcasting might radically change radio's long absence from the scene of the English classroom. As more educators become familiar with podcasting, they are likely to recognize its great pedagogical potential, as those involved in the Duke study did, but also as the teachers and professors from the 1930s and 1940s saw the great potential that radio held for teaching students about composition, speech, organization, working collaboratively, researching, drama, media use, critical thinking, and so on. In fact, the eventual journal articles that will be published by teachers about how they have engaged students in designing and making podcasts will perhaps bear striking similarities to those from the 1930s and 1940s (and perhaps those earlier articles might even serve as quite rich models for engaging students in pre-podcast activities).

REFERENCES

This reference list is atypical because the "Radio" list is arranged chronologically rather than alphabetically. Also, it includes references not only to the articles that I discuss and refer to in the chapter, but also to many other articles that I found about radio in my research into the topic in *English Journal*. My reason for presenting the references in this way is to enable the reader to get an immediate, impressionistic glimpse of how the radio discourse played out in *EJ* during radio's 20-year heyday, and how it began to fade in the 1950s and reappeared only occasionally during the 1960s through to the present. Another reason for arranging the radio references chronologically is that this format will also be very useful for anyone who plans to "go to the stacks," as I did, and begin pulling dusty volumes of *EJ* off the shelves to read the articles in the order that they appeared.

General References (not to *English Journal* articles)

A survey of new media: Among the audience. (2006, April 22). *The Economist*, pp. 3–30.

Duke university iPod first year experience final evaluation report. (2005, June). See at: http://cit.duke.edu/pdf/ipod_initiative_04_05.pdf.

Selingo, J. (2006, JANUARY 25). Students and teachers, from K to 12, hit the podcasts. *New York Times*, Section G1, p. 4.

References for EJ "Radio" articles

Batten, R. (1931). A radio contract in English. *English Journal, 20*(2), 158–160.

Newlin, J. (1933). Broadcasting. *English Journal, 22*(8), 643–647.

Larrabee, C. (1933). Ten radio lessons. *English Journal, 22*(8), 824–829.

Lumley, R. (1934). The English teacher and radio broadcasts. *English Journal, 23*(6), 478–485.

Knight, R. (1934). Radio and the English teacher. *English Journal, 23*(6), 504–506.

Tanner, V. (1934). Broadcasting Shakespeare. *English Journal, 33*(8), 677–679.

Cothrin, L. (1935). Advertisements and radio plays. *English Journal, 24*(2), 133–134.

Tyler, T. (1935). What English teachers should know about the broadcasting situation in the United States. *English Journal, 24*(4), 316–318.

Herzberg, M. (1935). Tentative units in radio program appreciation. *English Journal, 24*(7), 545–555.

Tyler, K. (1936). The listening habits of Oakland pupils. *English Journal, 25*(3), 206–215.

Duff, H. (1936). Literary aspects of the air. *English Journal, 25*(10), 867.

Phillips, D. (1937). A unit on the use of radio. *English Journal, 26*(1), 33–38.

Noyes, E. (1937). Balanced diet in radio. *English Journal, 26*(1), 60–61.

Larrabee, C. (1937). The school newspaper on the air. *English Journal, 26*(1), 64.

Tyler, K. (1937). Developing discrimination with regard to radio. *English Journal, 26*(2), 120–126.

Hurley, R. (1937). Movie and radio—friend and foe. *English Journal, 26*(3), 205–211.

Flynt, W. (1937). The oral composition class broadcasts. *English Journal, 26*(3), 235–237.

Mersand, J. (1938). Radio makes readers. *English Journal, 27*(6), 469–475.

Tyler, K. (1938). What can we do about the radio? *English Journal, 27*(7), 556–566.

Tyler, K. (1939). Recent developments in radio education. *English Journal, 28*(3), 193–199.

Nelson, D. (1939). Radio work at Hammond. *English Journal, 28*(3), 228–230.

Parker, L. (1939). British school broadcasting. *English Journal, 28*(4), 296–302.

Lumsden, F. (1939). The newspaper and radio in journalism. *English Journal, 28*(4), 305–308.

Pease, K. (1939). Experiment in movie-radio appreciation. *English Journal, 28*(5), 391–393.

Carson, M. (1939). Students like radio writing. *English Journal, 28*(6), 479–481.

Orndorff, B. (1939a). English via the air waves. *English Journal, 28*(8), 619–628.

Orndorff, B. (1939b). Radio humor: A unit for grades VII-XII. *English Journal, 28*(7), 526–534.

Ginsberg, W. (1939). Radio programs for high-school English. *English Journal, 28*(10), 835–839.

Hanford, E. (1940). Radio club activities. *English Journal, 29*(2), 148–151.

Tyler, T. (1940). The place of the radio in the teaching of English. *English Journal, 29*(5), 394–399.

Cook, M. (1940). The why is plain. *English Journal, 29*(7), 577–581.

Mescall, H. (1941). A radio reading project. *English Journal, 30*(3), 236–238.

Crawford, A. (1941). A radio drama festival. *English Journal, 30*(5), 403–404.

Brock, P. (1941). Radio and speech personality. *English Journal, 30*(6), 468–472.

Drinkwater, P. (1941). A radio project. *English Journal, 30*(7), 580–581.
Russell, E. (1941). C. B. S. English. *English Journal, 30*(7), 588–590.
Brown, R. (1941). The "town crier" in the English classroom. *English Journal, 30*(9), 769–771.
Tomlinson, E. (1941). So we went on the air. *English Journal, 31*(1), 63–66.
Conklin, E. (1942). Using the radio method of presentation. *English Journal, 31*(4), 320–322.
O'Hara, V. (1943). We broadcast the Sohrab-Rustrum fight. *English Journal, 32*(1), 41–42.
Finch, H. (1943). The radio aid to English. *English Journal, 32*(3), 171–172.
Gilburt, S. (1943). Radio appreciation: A plea and a program. *English Journal, 32*(8), 431–435.
Rachford, H. (1944). Developing discrimination in radio listening. *English Journal, 33*(6), 315–317.
Kaplan, M. (1945). Radio technique in high-school dramatics. *English Journal, 34*(2), 88–93.
Horn, G. (1945). Radio journalism. *English Journal, 34*(5), 257–260.
Novotny, L. (1946a). NCTE radio awards project. *English Journal, 35*(3), 149–152.
Novotny, L. (1946b). Radio and the school. *English Journal, 35*(3), 170–171.
Kirk, M. (1946). Newark goes to school. *English Journal, 35*(5), 260–264.
Tyler, T. (1946). English and radio play. *English Journal, 35*(5), 272.
Herzberg, M. (1947). NCTE radio awards. *English Journal, 36*(2), 80–81.
Golding, M. (1947). The radio commentary in the English class. *English Journal, 36*(4), 203.
Cullimore, C. (1948). A radio workshop club. *English Journal, 37*(6), 318–320.
Tallman, M. (1948). Teaching discriminating radio listening. *English Journal, 37*(8), 408–412,
Stratton, O. (1948). Technique for literate listening. *English Journal, 37*(10), 542–544.
Saunders, K. (1949). Among ourselves. *English Journal, 38*(1), 33–37.
Larrabee, C. (1949). Radio, a public servant. *English Journal, 38*(2), 92–94.
Dunn, A. (1949). Experimental teaching in radio listening. *English Journal, 38*(4), 194–197.
Anderson, B. (1949). Are good radio listeners made? *English Journal, 38*(7), 391–394.
Allen, H. (1949). Mass pressure on radio and journalism. *English Journal, 38*(8), 447–453.
Boutwell, W. (1949). Radio—"industry" or "art"? *English Journal, 38*(9), 525–526.
Raymond, J., & Frazier, A. (1949). Daytime serials as laboratory material. *English Journal, 38*(10), 563–567.
Kaplan, M. (1950). The radio play as an introduction to drama. English Journal, *39*(1), 23–26.
Gruber, F. (1950). Out-of-school radio listening habits of high school students. *English Journal, 39*(6), 325–327.
Grey, L. (1951). Radio—a means, not an end. *English Journal, 40*(3), 144–149.
Hood, L. (1951). Canadian broadcasting. *English Journal, 40*(6), 329–332.
Boutwell, W. (1952). What can we do about movies, radio, television? *English Journal, 41*(3), 131–136.
Roody, S. (1952). Effect of radio, television, and motion pictures on the development of maturity. *English Journal, 41*(5), 245–250.
Boutwell, W. (1958). Education for the age of communication. *English Journal, 47*(3), 138–143.
Lewin, R. (1960). A course in communication for high school seniors. *English Journal, 49*(2), 108–112.
Maloney, H. (1960). Stepsisters of print: The public arts in the high school English class. *English Journal, 49*(8), 570–579.
Nevi, C., & Hoffine, L. (1962). We can't ignore the mass media. *English Journal, 51*(8), 560–564.
Rowland, H. (1964). Journalism vs. the mass media. *English Journal, 53*(5), 345–348, 353–355.
Ringler, D. (1964). Mass media and the humanities. *English Journal, 53*(9), 674–678.
Smith, J. (1968). Simultaneousness. *English Journal, 57*(5), 696–699.
Newman, J. (1972). Multi-media in high school journalism—it really works. *English Journal, 61*(3), 381–384, 388.
Cushman, J. (1973). "Old Radio" in the English classroom: It can't miss! *English Journal, 62*(2), 244–249.
Barrett, D. (1973). In the lion's den of media: Living up to the rhetoric. *English Journal, 62*(8), 1136–1138.
Hollister, B. (1974). Tune in yesterday. *English Journal, 63*(7), 77–80.
Daniels, H. (1976). Breaker, break, broke: Citizens band in the classroom. *English Journal, 65*(9), 52–57.
Alley, D. (1979). Radio tapes: A resource for English teachers. *English Journal, 68*(7), 40-41.
Douglas, A. (1979). Radio tapes: A resource for English teachers. *English Journal, 68*(7), 40–41.
Danielson, H. (1981). Radio plays in the classroom: Another way to teach writing. *English Journal,* 70(6), 84–85.
Miller, D. (1982). Who's afraid of Orson Welles? *English Journal, 71*(5), 84–86.
Burmeister, D. (1983). Mainstreaming media: 101 ways to use media in the English classroom. *English Journal, 72*(2), 109–111.
Lyon, R. (1986). Using television and radio in English classes. *English Journal, 75*(8), 62–63.
Gillespie, J. (1990). Reliving the Depression: Integrating English and social studies. *English Journal, 79*(6), 64–69.
Jackson, T. (1994). Writing on the air: Television, radio, and the classroom. *English Journal, 83*(1), 47–56.
McShane, T. (1994). Language art: The radio play's the thing. *English Journal, 83*(1), 52–56.
Orfanella, L. (1998). Radio: The intimate medium. *English Journal, 87*(1), 53–55.

•53•

FILM AND VIDEO IN THE CLASSROOM: BACK TO THE FUTURE

William Kist
KENT STATE UNIVERSITY

During the drafting of this chapter, I attended a national literacy conference. I am amazed at the number of sessions dealing in some way with "new" media. I have raced from session to session trying to see as many as I could. As I hopped between sessions, I began to write down selected quotes from the presenters and their handouts:

- "blogging extends classwork guiding principles" including promotion of the school motto
- "using students' online literacy to encourage and extend literary discussion"
- "how film can help students who are visual read literature"
- "using hip-hop to prepare students for the new SAT"
- "one out of four two-year-olds has a TV in his or her bedroom."

The last speaker was practically wringing his hands as he depicted the plight of two-year-olds already held captive by the boob tube. I felt that I was in a time warp—again! Each time a new medium develops, it seems, we have this kind of hand wringing. Scribner and Cole (1981) described the fears that existed even about print as it first became available to the masses:

> Socrates pointed out that . . . letters might weaken memory and lead to forgetfulness as learners came to rely on external aids for "reminiscence." Would the knowledge available in books help to make men wise? Socrates feared that disciples of the written word would have the show of wisdom (they would know the letters) without the reality (they would not necessarily grasp the true ideas). (p. 5)

As the centuries went by, print became a dominant method of control. The catechism in church settings, Resnick (1991) argued, has worked its way into our schools, with the catechism format infusing the early primers. Reading became the most important subject in early American schools, mainly due to the Protestant bent of the colonial 1600s and the desire on the part of Protestant leaders for the general public to have personal contact with the Bible (Smith, 1934/1986). As the colonial period ended and the new country was formed, the aim of the lessons became less overtly religious and more in the vein of teaching moral principles (Smith, 1934/1986). Indeed, it has been pointed out that it is surprising that writing instruction has existed at all in American classrooms given the challenges of measuring it (Monaghan & Saul, 1987). The Committee of Fifteen in 1895 recommended grammar as one of the core subjects to be taught (along with reading, math, history, and geography), but not writing (Kliebard, 1986).

All new media apparently have to prove themselves or be "fit in" before they can coexist with the dominant media, and this is no different with the medium of film (the focus of this chapter)—a medium that is now more than one hundred years old. From the beginning of the development of the medium, writers and thinkers have been mesmerized by the qualities of this new art form and just what exactly makes this new medium so different from preceding media (Metz, 1974/1991; Monaco, 2000). Sergei Eisenstein, for example, posited that the film montage "has as its aim the creation of ideas, of a new reality, rather than the support of narrative, the old reality of experience" (Monaco, 2000, p. 402).

Over the years, film and video have served many different masters in the classroom. (In this chapter, I am going to be referring to "film" and "video" interchangeably and defining film/video to be "motion pictures whether captured via the medium of film or via the medium of video.") In the previous edition of this *Handbook,* Baines (1997) documented that there have been people advocating on both sides of the issue of whether film or video should even be used in our classrooms. Here are some of the quotes that Baines listed (p. 548):

> Moving pictures everywhere will become a valuable adjunct in the mastery of skill in English composition. (Gerrish, 1915, p. 230)

> It is useless to condemn moving pictures; we may as well condemn all novels. . . . Why not bring the movies into the schoolroom? (Cunningham, 1923, p. 490)

> I submit now that motion-picture appreciation is here to stay. The momentum it has created will insure its adoption, gradually but surely, not only into the high schools, but also into teacher-training institutions. (Dale, 1936, p. 113)

> Movies are moving into the high school. The proliferation of film societies on the college level is now commonplace. (Carrico, 1970, p. 97)

> No one doubts that language, reading, and writing are central to school programs or that they are the proper business of English language arts teachers; but most people, teachers included, have strong reservations about media studies. (Karl, 1981, p. 139)

> With research that suggests how effective film can be, why does the medium continue to be regarded critically by school administrators, school board members, and the general public? (Lankford, 1992, p. 3)

And here we were at the conference, a bunch of English teachers at the cold end of the year and at the beginning of a new century, trying to figure out how these new media are just like the old, how the new media can be used to teach the conventions of print (or oral) storytelling, and, above all, how the new media can be assessed. I suppose, if there had been a discussion of how film is truly a different medium from print, it would have been viewed as "too theoretical" or "not practical enough." But I thought that theory was supposed to inform practice! If we could get a handle on how these new media are different (and film is not even that new anymore), would this not influence a new kind of "English/Language Arts" teaching? But no, at this conference, we were all about using blogging to teach synecdoche.

At least the argument over whether film should be a part of our classrooms is beyond moot at this point. Motion pictures are here to stay in our classrooms. Good thing, since we are fast moving from a page-based to a screen-based society (Kress, 2003). Clicking on many Web sites today will lead the "reader" to options to view film as part of the "reading" experience. The Internet has irrevocably brought elements of film/video as well as graphic design and music and sound design to the experience of "reading." And so, educators who are committed to bringing their students into this 21st century of "reading" must make their English/Language Arts/ Reading classrooms ones that embrace media such as film in addition to print.

But, in taking a quick overview of how film and video have been used in our classrooms, one could make the argument that motion pictures in the classroom are still seen as the spoonful of sugar that helps the medicine go down, or at best a kind of "special" or extracurricular activity that exists only to serve the print-centric curriculum "standards." What follows is an overview of some of the ways film is used in our classrooms.

USING FILM TO TEACH AND/OR ENRICH PRINT LITERACY AND TO TEACH CONTENT

For some teachers, the most intense debate about film in the classroom surrounds whether to show the movie version of a book before or after reading the book with the class. Or some teachers advocate breaking the film up and showing them portions of the movie as the class reads the book. This is particularly advocated for struggling readers. A common assignment would be to compare and contrast the printed text with the filmed interpretations of that text (Martin, 2002).

But beyond using films to accompany the reading of a print text, a common strain in the writing about films in the classroom is how they can be used to teach literary elements such as plot transitions, mood, and setting (see Golden, 2001; Hobbs, 1998; Krueger & Christel, 2001).

An example of this use of film in the English classroom can be found in Krueger & Christel's (2001) discussion of using Hitchcock to teach point of view:

> It is hard to avoid discussing Hitchcock when it comes to examining the use of the camera to achieve a compelling point-of-view shot. His film *Notorious* is filled with examples of subjective and authorial shots. The film opens with a group of reporters waiting outside a Miami courtroom. One of the shots in that sequence visually implies that the viewer is someone, ostensibly one of those reporters, peering through a crack in the courtroom door to hear the final words of a man being tried for treason . . . Examining the manipulation of point of view helps students to recognize that elements of literature are also present in film texts. (p. 65)

By showing kids a flashback in a film, some teachers think, they will be able to understand the literary device of a flashback when they are reading a print text. But beyond helping kids understand literary devices, using moving images in the classroom can even help improve student reading comprehension (Hibbing & Rankin-Erickson, 2003).

This can come in very handy when teaching such difficult concepts as the uses of the number zero or how a bill becomes law. One can see the power of using film in this way anytime one teaches the parts of speech and gets to conjunctions and half the class begins to sing, "Conjunction, junction, what's your function?" (Yohe & Newall, 1996). This chapter does not have the space to go into the uses of various television programs in the classroom. But certainly teachers have long used the moving image via television to help students understand content. I often think of one of my former students who told me that, when she was in high school, one of her social studies teachers showed her class the entire miniseries *Roots* (Chomsky, Erman, Greene, & Moses, 1977), all 573 minutes of it! It took them weeks to get through it all, she said, and watching *Roots* was all they did in class each day.

Other more appropriate examples of using film to teach content would be using the film *Inherit the Wind* (Kramer, 1960) to teach evolution (Benen, 2000) or using *Places in the Heart* (Benton, 1984) to teach the Depression era (Roquemore, 1999). (On the other hand, Carnes, 1996, pointed out that using Hollywood films to teach history can be dangerous.)

Often, film is used as a motivator to reach kids that have not been served by print-dominated curriculum. One teacher who I studied, Lee Rother, described a breakthrough moment he had with an at-risk student:

> But this one kid named Ron, 17 or 18, reading at a grade 4 level, and he was the switcher, and he came back to school one day after being the switcher for maybe a week, he came to me and said, "I can't watch TV anymore." And I thought maybe he got in trouble or something at home, and he said, "No, no, it just doesn't make any sense." And I didn't know what he was talking about. So he went on to describe to me (that) he was watching this program, and he saw this woman was crying or something in it, and they had a medium shot or whatever and I asked him, what

should they have had, and he said, "A close-up." And he went into this whole thing, and I didn't care if he was right or wrong. But this kid was "reading" it and he was making this whole language out of it, and I remember getting all excited and talking with the other kids and sure enough, they were saying the same things, and I haven't been able to let go of that whole thing since. (Kist, 2005, p. 97)

It is clear that film has long been seen as a medium that helps many students make meaning of their print literacy experiences and of content in general (Greene, 1997; Leland & Harste, 1994).

USING FILM TO TEACH MORALS/ VALUES OR SOCIAL CONTROL

As Smith (1999) illuminated in his hilarious *Mental Hygiene*, films have often been used to teach moral behavior and safety. His overview of this genre subdivides the genre into such subgenres as "Fitting in," "Cautionary Tales," "Dating," and "Bloody Highways." As Smith pointed out, the development of the 16mm film format as a standard width for nontheatrical films made possible the mass distribution of titles and projectors (p. 19). His book is filled with hilarious capsule reviews of some of the most famous of these types of films:

Are You Popular?

Coronet Instructional Films, 1947

This was the first social guidance dating film. Caroline Ames—"the kind of girl you'd like to know"—is popular with the gang because, among other reasons, "they've heard no scandal about her." On the other side is Ginny—"a crude looking and acting girl," . . . who "dates all the boys" and is shunned even by those who take advantage of her generosity. "Girls who park in cars are not really popular," the narrator explains, as a table of teens in the lunchroom ignore Ginny and instead invite Caroline to sit with them. (Smith, 1999, p. 118)

Ironically, Smith made at least two tours of the Film Festival circuit playing these films to packed houses of baby boomers and younger viewers who are entertained by these films that originally could be seen only at school.

USING FILM AS A REWARD

Recently, I was presenting to a group of teachers who told me that they must now get permission from their superintendent before showing any film at all in their classrooms. This was because the superintendent was upset that they were using films as rewards on Fridays for good behavior. Class time was being taken up to show Disney films, and so now, all films would be banned without prior permission granted by the superintendent. (Interestingly, many teachers still issue writing as a punishment. What does this say about the way these media are perceived? Can one imagine being punished by having to create a video on "Why I won't misbehave?") Films and videos are seen as desirable rewards.

Perhaps because teachers see the value of films in their classrooms, these kind of blanket bans have not been well received as is described in this recent news item from Maryland:

The regulations require a more stringent review of classroom materials, including using the Motion Picture Association of America's rating scale. Movies rated "R" are out. Movies rated "PG-13" no longer can be shown in middle schools. Teachers wonder if the regulations are going too far by banning films that have long had a place in their classes. (Sedam, 2005)

TEACHING FILM APPRECIATION

Teaching film as an art form tends to take place in some kind of elective or "film studies" class, although increasingly English teachers are taking time out of English class to teach film grammar (for the main purpose of teaching literary elements, as previously described). In classes where students are taught film appreciation, classic films are shown, and any number of printed texts is available for help in sorting out the characteristics of this medium (Bogdanovich, 1997; Costanzo, 2004; Foster, 2002; Giannetti, 2001; Kerr, 1975; Krueger & Christel, 2001; Metz, 1974/1991; Monaco, 2000). There are also resources on the Internet to teach this kind of film appreciation including The Independent Film Channel Film School (http://www.ifc.com/filmschool), The Film Foundation (http://storyofmovies.org/), and The British Film Institute (http://www.bfi.org.uk/education/), to name a few.

Such film appreciation classes might fall under the umbrella of "media literacy" (Buckingham, 1993, 2003; Buckingham & Sefton-Green, 1994; Lusted, 1991). Or they might fall under the umbrella of helping kids become more visually literate (Gombrich, 1960; Messaris, 1994). Often, it seems, there is an intense personal interest on the part of the teacher him- or herself in film that prompts this diversionary path from print texts.

Regardless of the motive behind teaching film appreciation, there is often a component of these activities that includes a criticism of existing power dynamics (Fairclough, 1989, 1995), whether it be a study of the way a film positions the viewer in terms of gender, race, or any number of categories (Ellsworth, 1997). This kind of thinking fits into a critical literacy perspective that seeks to help kids develop these kinds of critical skills (Delpit, 1995; McLaren, 1989; Willinsky, 1990).

The printed texts that are often used to accompany "film appreciation" classes often attempt to cover a very large amount of ground. Costanzo's (2004) text has chapters covering such film-related areas as "The Languages of Film," "The Technology of Film," "A Brief History of Film," "The Business of Film," "Theories of Film," and "Film Genres." The remainder of his text includes study guides for 14 classic films with accompanying questions such as this one to use with *Casablanca:* "How does the film measure up to your criteria for a good story? What features of successful storytelling does it have or need? How can you account for its enduring popularity?" (Costanzo, 2004, p. 137).

Similarly, Monaco's (2000) text begins with an overview of "The Nature of Art" and goes on to cover the technology of films (including sections on film stock, the camera, and the lens), the language of films, the history of films, and an overview of film theory.

Increasingly, as the technology for filmmaking becomes more and more accessible, such film appreciation classes may include a component of "writing" in motion pictures—in other words, having students make their own films or videos. There have been calls for making film/video production (or "writing") as important as "reading" (Buckingham, 2003; Hobbs & Frost, 2003), with several models, including the "pedagogy of multiliteracies" (New London Group, 1996; Cope & Kalantzis, 2000); Green's (1988) 3-D model;

and the model of Freebody & Luke (1990) including both functional and operational levels. Of course, often one of the underlying agendas for teaching students to "write" through video production is so that students will make the jump to print writing—for example, having students use their knowledge of audience and genre derived from their experiences with film/video to improve their print writing (Williams, 2003). Video production has been seen as a medium of choice for educators such as Marco Torres in San Fernando City Schools (Kist, 2005) and Steve Goodman, (2003) who get kids using video production to make pieces that inform social justice.

Teachers have described using video production as a substitute for a research paper on a famous author or literary period (Shafer, 2000). Of course, Romano (1995, 2000) has espoused the multigenre paper (which may include elements of film/video) as a wholesale replacement of the print research paper.

SEEING FILM AS ONE TEXT AVAILABLE TO STUDENTS IN A NEW LITERACIES ERA

A more progressive view of film sees film as just one text available to students for reading and writing. In such a new literacies classroom, film would no longer be viewed as just a tool to teach content, to reward kids, or to teach as a separate "extra" art form in an after-school film club. In such a new literacies environment, film, and print would coexist as nonhierarchical text forms (along with music, graphic design, dance and all other modes of expression.) Being "literate" in such a classroom would mean knowing how to "read" and "write" in a multimedia world. Whether we call it "multiliteracies" (New London Group, 1996), "new literacies" (Kist, 2005; Luke & Elkins, 1998), or "intermediality" (Semali & Watts Pailliotet, 1999) or we simply lump it in under the umbrella of "media literacy," or "arts-based education," it is clear that we must move beyond our conception of literacy as print centric. If we do not allow for "cognitive pluralism" (John-Steiner, 1997) in our classrooms, we will be limiting the literacy of future generations and, so, human thought (Eisner, 1992, 1994, 1997, 2002; Gardner, 1983, 1993, 1995; Tishman & Perkins, 1997).

As many continue to see literacy as not just situated in cognition, but also in the everyday discourses of people's lives (Barton & Hamilton, 1998; Street, 1995; Gee, 1996), and as people are moving daily through hybrid online and offline spaces (Chandler-Olcott & Mahar, 2003; Gee, 2003; Leander, 2003), to continue to separate out film/video as an "other" form of literacy, for an increasing number of educators, seems to be not only a colossal waste of time, but practically impossible. Dyson (2003) demonstrated how these new literacies are inextricably wound up in young students' literacy development.

Indeed, Ellsworth (1997) suggested that film theory can profoundly inform our pedagogy. Film scholars have been asking the question, "How does the way a film address its audience position viewers within relations of power, knowledge, and desire?" Ellsworth (1997) asked if this concept of "mode of address" could be used to think about how each classroom positions our students: "What might a teacher make of the eventful and volatile space of difference or 'misfit' between who a curriculum thinks its students are or should be and how students actually use a curriculum's address to constitute themselves and to act on and within history?" (p. 37).

In fact, some teachers are using such "new" media as film to engage their students in these kinds of essential dialogues. In my study of new literacies classrooms (Kist, 2005), I found one English department, in Calgary, Alberta, Canada, in which film is seen as just one text of many worth "reading," "writing," and discussing. Within the system they developed, in their English classes,

> Students are to select between four and six of these texts to read on their own and write a response to. These are entitled "First Looks." The students are then placed in heterogenous small groups of four to six students, and they each discuss their First Looks in the small group. This is called the First Seminar. During this First Seminar, the group decides upon three of the texts that they feel best help them to understand the essential question. Students in the group who have not read these three texts are then expected to read them on their own and provide First Looks to these texts. Then, the group reconvenes for its Second Seminar, in which students discuss the three texts further, either starting with details found in the texts and then going to the larger essential question, or starting with the essential question and going to the details found in the texts. By the end of this process, students are expected to understand the text creator's intention and how it has addressed the essential question; what purposeful strategies the text creator has used to address the essential question; and what further essential questions are suggested by these works. They do this in the form of a Second Look around all three of the texts which students do independently, and they may do this in any format. If students compose this Second Look in a nonprint medium, they must write a print rationale for the choices they made as they were creating their Second Look. Finally, each group selects one of their three texts and presents it to the entire class. This presentation may be in any text form in which they choose, again demonstrating how the text author has dealt with the essential question. All during the process, students are graded on both their individual work and their collaborative work. (Kist, 2005, pp. 112–113)

In the English classrooms of Bowness High School, film and video are seen on an equal plane with print texts. And the students at the school use the word "text" to talk about any form of communication. One student, describing how she had reacted to *Edward Scissorhands* (Burton, 1990), said,

> In every society that you can think of, people are trying to squeeze themselves into that definition of what is normal. Men and women are already affected by this growing pressure. In *Edward Scissorhands,* Edward is rescued by Peg and introduced to society. What was once considered acceptable is no longer considered acceptable by society. He sees things differently, and because of that, he is looked down on. "He is the devil; he is not one of us." ("Amy" personal communication, May 22, 2003)

As I walked in and out of classrooms at Bowness, I saw students "reading" and "writing" all kinds of media, everything from *Edward Scissorhands* to an Amy Lowell poem to a painting by Frida Kahlo. I was chatting with a student who said that her favorite texts to respond to are poetry. But she frequently responded to poetry in a medium that did not include print. She looked at me and said, "We don't live in a written world."

One of the teachers at Bowness, Heather Harrigan, commented that the transition to this kind of text-neutral teaching is not easy.

> I think that the most difficult task we have as educators now is to figure out . . . what is the role of the teacher in this new kind of educational learning design, knowing what we know about learning that we didn't know before. I think the role of the teacher is to provide an environment in which learning is valued, to provide opportunities for deconstructing texts so that they can understand it, to provide them strategies and

choices to demonstrate what they understand, and for making sure that they intervene at a moment when learning is stalled, and that they intervene at a metacognitive level, that they intervene not to do it, but to facilitate it. And that's really hard, that's really hard. Teaching is hard! It's hard, because it would just be so much easier to do it yourself! (Heather Harrigan, personal communication, May 22, 2003)

EPILOGUE

Early humans used pictorial representations to communicate. Danesi (1993) described "the earliest precursor of modern writing systems [as] the symbols found on clay tokens discovered in western Asia that belong to the Neolithic era. Made out of elemental shapes, these tokens were used as image-making objects. They were obviously employed to express something concretely in visual mimetic form" (p. 27). Danesi pointed out that we still have "residues" of this iconic form of communication in the nonverbal gestures that humans use.

So, our early "literacy" depended on paintings and sculpture, not print. Writing is a relatively new device of human communication (Scribner & Cole, 1981). Danesi (1993) described the development of writing: "As the hand movements used to make . . . works of art became more abbreviated, the figures made by Homo sapiens became more condensed and abstract. This led to the invention of writing. The earliest form of writing was vastly different from the alphabetic or syllabic writing systems that came to be based on vocal language" (pp. 26–27). Literacy, as in the ancient world (Harris, 1989), continues to be a product of complex political, economic, and cultural forces.

So print literacy is, relatively speaking, the "new kid on the block." But, like James Cagney in *White Heat* (Walsh, 1949), it has reached the "top of the world, ma!" Of course, I see the irony in the fact that I am communicating my thoughts on this subject via print in this article, even though I really feel like the protagonist of Umberto Eco's (2004/2005) novel, *The Mysterious Flame of Queen Loana,* whose memory of his personal life has been lost except for texts of all kinds he has encountered throughout his life: "I woke up in a place and murmured that it resembled the cabin of a spaceship, like in movies. (What movies [the doctor] asked; all of them, I said, in general; then I named *Star Trek*.)" (p. 9). I feel this especially as I am overwhelmed by the national literacy conference I am attending and as I wander out into the downtown area surrounding the conference which, even in November, is filled with holiday decorations and lights. Certainly, of all times of the year, the holiday season always seems ripe for the creation of an Eisenstein-like montage.

Still, have I got to get back to print? As Fischman (2001) pointed out, people like Mark Twain have long said that a picture cannot be understood without a label attached to it. But I am having trouble shaking the wordless holiday images and the music out of my mind. (Still, you may say, those images and that music are not attempting to communicate the kind of ideas that one does in a chapter such as this.) OK, but Lois Lowry (1993) used holiday images in *The Giver*, did she not? (Yes, but those images were still described using print.)

Little snowflakes are falling outside as I look past the shoppers and see a display of holiday books and DVDs in a bookstore window. One of the items displayed is the film *Holiday Inn* (Sandrich, 1942), and I am suddenly transported to my senior year of high school. I had been working a lot as a pianist during the season, performing at parties and as an accompanist at concerts. My final performance of the year had occurred just two days before Christmas, and I came home to find no one home. I turned on the Christmas tree lights, collapsed on the couch, and started to channel surf. One of the stations was playing *Holiday Inn*, a film I had never heard of before. I had seen the more well-known *White Christmas* (Curtiz, 1954), but never *Holiday Inn*. The scenes of the rustic inn in the middle of nowhere lulled me to sleep. It is a peaceful memory I have. And a wordless one.

The memory is one of feeling satisfied, yet somehow lonely as I watched the lonely Bing Crosby finding comfort and joy with the now forgotten Marjorie Reynolds. It is difficult for me to adequately put into words how the creamy black and white images of a Christmas that no longer exists affected me, as I watched Fred Astaire and all the other guests in black tie and tails come through the night and the manufactured snow into the idealized stage set that was the Holiday Inn.

Metz (1974/1991), among others, suggested that films are so powerful, because they are so real, albeit in the same way a dream is real. Metz suggested that live theater, for example, cannot begin to approach this dream state because we are distracted by the reality of a living/breathing human in the room with us acting. If film/video has this characteristic, why are we not doing a better job of celebrating this difference in our schools, instead of making everything always go back to print? Yes, a jump cut is a transitional device, but is it not much more than that?

My *Holiday Inn* and *Manhattan* (Kist, 2000) experiences took place outside of school and are consigned to the category of "nice memories," (perhaps) legitimized only at this moment as I translate these experiences into print for this chapter (and only if the editors see this part as relevant). But the work of new literacies scholars makes a persuasive argument that students need to be taught the "grammars" of a variety of semiotic systems so that they have an extensive reservoir of systems upon which to draw when thinking and communicating (New London Group, 1996) and that these should not be consistently consigned to "extras," "specials," "the spoonful of sugar that helps the medicine go down." Allowing students to have some control over the symbol systems they are able to use in various situations, and helping students achieve proficiency in these symbol systems may serve to aid our students in their overall thought processes. "The language of thinking does more than help us communicate. It shapes and regulates thought by providing concepts to guide our thinking" (Tishman & Perkins, 1997, p. 371).

Allowing for more uses of multiple forms of representation in all of our classrooms, no matter the subject area, would allow children to draw on a richer "capital of childhood" over the course of their entire lives. In allowing such a possibility, it would seem that literacy educators will play a crucial role for the entire school, as the "new literacy" informs the overall school mission to lead children to this kind of "cognitive pluralism" (John-Steiner, 1997).

REFERENCES

Baines, L. (1997). Film, video, and books: Some considerations for learning and teaching. In J. Flood, S. B. Heath, & D. Lapp (Eds.), *Handbook of research on teaching literacy through the communicative and visual arts* (pp. 545–557). New York: Simon & Schuster Macmillan.

Barton, D., & Hamilton, M. (1998). *Local literacies: Reading and writing in one community*. London: Routledge.

Benen, S. (2000). Inherit the wind monkeys with the Scopes trial on teaching evolution. *The Education Digest, 66*(2), 60–63.

Benton, R. (Director). (1984). *Places in the heart* [Motion picture]. United States: TriStar Pictures.

Bogdanovich, P. (1997). *Who the devil made it*. New York: Knopf.

Buckingham, D. (1993). *Reading audiences: Young people and the media*. Manchester, U.K.: Manchester University Press.

Buckingham, D. (2003). *Media education: literacy, learning and contemporary culture*. Cambridge, U.K.: Polity.

Buckingham, D., & Sefton-Green, J. (1994). *Cultural studies goes to school: Reading and teaching popular media*. London: Taylor & Francis.

Carnes, M. (1996). *Past imperfect: History according to the movies*. New York: Owl Books.

Burton, T. (Director). (1990). *Edward scissorhands*. [Motion picture]. United States: Twentieth Century Fox.

Carrico, J. (1970). Film and the teaching of English. In A. Schillari & J. Culkin (Eds.), *Films deliver* (pp. 97–115). New York: Citation.

Chandler-Olcott, K., & Mahar, D. (2003). "Tech-savviness" meets multiliteracies: Exploring adolescent girls' technology-mediated literacy practices. *Reading Research Quarterly, 38*, 356–385.

Chomsky, M., Erman, J., Greene, D., & Moses, G. (Directors). (1977). *Roots* [Motion picture]. United States: David Wolper Productions/Warner Brothers.

Cope, B., & Kalantzis, M. (Eds.). (2000). *Multiliteracies: Literacy learning and the design of social futures*. London: Routledge.

Costanzo, W. (2004). *Great films and how to teach them*. Urbana, IL: National Council of Teachers of English.

Cunningham, A. (1923, September). Teaching English with the movies. *English Journal*, 488–490.

Curtiz, M. (Director). (1954). *White Christmas* [Motion picture]. United States: Paramount.

Dale, E. (1936, February). Teaching motion picture appreciation. *English Journal*, 113–120.

Danesi, M. (1993). *Messages and meanings: An introduction to semiotics*. Toronto, Canada: Canadian Scholars' Press, Inc.

Delpit, L. (1995). *Other people's children: Cultural conflict in the classroom*. New York: The New Press.

Dyson, A. H. (2003). *The brothers and sisters learn to write: Popular literacies in childhood and school cultures*. New York: Teachers College Press.

Eco, U. (2005). *The mysterious flame of Queen Loana* (G. Brock, Trans.). New York: Harcourt. (Original work published 2004)

Eisner, E. (1992). The misunderstood role of the arts in human development. *Phi Delta Kappan, 73*, 591–595.

Eisner, E. (1994). *Cognition and curriculum reconsidered* (2nd ed.). New York: Teachers College Press.

Eisner, E. (1997). Cognition and representation: A way to pursue the American dream? *Phi Delta Kappan, 78*, 349–353.

Eisner, E. (2002). *The arts and the creation of mind*. New Haven, CT: Yale University Press.

Ellsworth, E. (1997). *Teaching positions: Difference, pedagogy, and the power of address*. New York: Teachers College Press.

Fairclough, N. (1989). *Language and power*. London: Longman.

Fairclough, N. (1995). *Critical discourse analysis: The critical study of language*. New York: Longman.

Fischman, G. E. (2001). Reflections about images, visual culture, and educational research. *Educational Researcher, 30*(8), 28–33.

Foster, H. M. (2002). *Crossing over: Teaching meaning-centered secondary English language arts* (2nd ed.). Mahwah, NJ: Lawrence Erlbaum Associates.

Freebody, P., & Luke, A. (1990). "Literacies" programs: Debates and demands in cultural context. *Prospect, 5*, 7–16.

Gardner, H. (1983). *Frames of mind: The theory of multiple intelligences*. New York: Basic Books.

Gardner, H. (1993). *Multiple intelligences: The theory into practice*. New York: Basic Books.

Gardner, H. (1995). Reflections on multiple intelligences. *Phi Delta Kappan, 76*, 200–209.

Gee, J. P. (1996). *Social linguistics and literacies: Ideology in discourses* (2nd ed.). London: The Falmer Press.

Gee, J. P. (2003). *What video games have to teach us about learning and literacy*. New York: Palgrave Macmillan.

Gerrish, C. (1915, April). The relation of moving pictures to English composition. *English Journal*, 226–230.

Giannetti, L. (2001). *Understanding movies* (9th ed.). Columbus, OH: Prentice Hall.

Golden, J. (2001). *Reading in the dark: Using film as a tool in the English classroom*. Urbana, IL: National Council of Teachers of English.

Gombrich, E. H. (1960). *Art and illusion: A study in the psychology of pictorial representation*. Princeton, NJ: Princeton University Press.

Goodman, S. (2003). *Teaching youth media: A critical guide to literacy, video production, and social change*. New York: Teachers College Press.

Green, B. (1988). Subject-specific literacy and school learning: A focus on writing. *Australian Journal of Education, 32*, 156–179.

Greene, M. (1997). Metaphors and multiples: Representation, the arts, and history. *Phi Delta Kappan, 78*, 387–394.

Harris, W. V. (1989). *Ancient literacy*. Cambridge, MA: Harvard University Press.

Hibbing, A. N., & Rankin-Erickson, J. L. (2003). A picture is worth a thousand words: Using visual images to improve comprehension for middle school struggling readers. *The Reading Teacher, 56*, 758–770.

Hobbs, R. (1998). The Simpsons meet Mark Twain: Analyzing popular media texts in the classroom. *English Journal, 87*, 49–51.

Hobbs, R., & Frost, R. (2003). Measuring the acquisition of media-literacy skills. *Reading Research Quarterly, 38*, 330–355.

John-Steiner, V. (1997). *Notebooks of the mind: Explorations of thinking* (Rev. ed.). New York: Oxford University Press.

Karl, H. (1981). What it means to be media competent. In C. Cooper (Ed.), *The nature and measurement of competency in English* (pp. 139–163). Urbana, IL: National Council of Teachers of English.

Kerr, W. (1975). *The silent clowns*. New York: Knopf.

Kist, W. (2000). Beginning to create the new literacy classroom: What does the new literacy look like? *Journal of Adolescent and Adult Literacy, 43*, 710–718.

Kist, W. (2005). *New literacies in action: Teaching and learning in multiple media*. New York: Teachers College Press.

Kliebard, H. M. (1986). *The struggle for the american curriculum 1893–1958*. New York: Routledge.

Kramer, S. (Director). (1960). *Inherit the wind* [Motion picture]. United States: United Artists.

Kress, G. (2003). *Literacy in the new media age*. London: Routledge.

Krueger, E., & Christel, M. T. (2001). *Seeing and believing: How to teach media literacy in the English classroom*. Portsmouth, NH: Heinemann.

Lankford, M. (1992). *Films for learning, thinking, and doing*. Englewood, CO: Libraries Unlimited.

Leander, K. (2003). Writing travelers' tales on new literacyscapes. *Reading Research Quarterly, 38*, 392–397.

Leland, C. H., & Harste, J. C. (1994). Multiple ways of knowing: Curriculum in a new key. *Language Arts, 71*, 337–345.

Lowry, L. (1993). *The giver*. New York: Doubleday.

Luke, A., & Elkins, J. (1998). Reinventing literacy in "new times." *Journal of Adolescent & Adult Literacy, 42*, 4–7.

Lusted, D. (Ed.). (1991). *The media studies book: A guide for teachers*. London: Routledge.

Martin, J. L. (2002). Tights vs. tattoos: Filmic interpretations of Romeo and Juliet. *English Journal, 92*(1), 41–46.

McLaren, P. (1989). *Life in schools: An introduction to critical pedagogy in the foundations of education*. New York: Longman.

Metz, C. (1991). *Film language: A semiotics of the cinema* (M. Taylor, Trans.). Chicago: University of Chicago Press. (Original work published 1974)

Messaris, P. (1994). *Visual literacy: Image, mind & reality*. Boulder, CO: Westview Press.

Monaco, J. (2000). *How to read a film: The world of movies, media, and multimedia* (3rd ed.). New York: Oxford University Press.

Monaghan, E. J., & Saul, E. W. (1987). The reader, the scribe, the thinker: A critical look at the history of American reading and writing instruction. In T. S. Popkewitz (Ed.), *The formation of the school subjects: The struggle for creating an American institution* (pp. 85–122). Philadelphia: Falmer.

New London Group. (1996). A pedagogy of multiliteracies: Designing social futures. *Harvard Education Review, 66*(1), 60–92.

Resnick, D. P. (1991). Historical perspectives on literacy and schooling. In S. R. Graubard (Ed.), *Literacy: An overview by fourteen experts* (pp. 15–32). New York: Hill and Wang.

Romano, T. (1995). *Writing with passion: Life stories, multiple genres.* Portsmouth, NH: Boynton/Cook.

Romano, T. (2000). *Blending genre, altering style: Writing multigenre papers.* Portsmouth, NH: Boynton/Cook.

Roquemore, J. H. (1999). *History goes to the movies: A viewer's guide to the best (and some of the worst) historical films ever made.* New York: Main Street Books.

Sandrich, M. (Director). (1942). *Holiday inn* [Motion Picture]. United States: Paramount.

Scribner, S., & Cole, M. (1981). *The psychology of literacy.* Cambridge, MA: Harvard University Press.

Shafer, G. (2000). Prime time literature in the high school. *English Journal, 90*(2), 93–96.

Sedam, S. R. (2005, December 7). *Schools remove movies from class instruction.* Retrieved December 14, 2005, from http://www.gazette.net

Semali, L. M., & Watts Pailliotet, A. (1999). Introduction: What is intermediality and why study it in U.S. schools? In L. M. Semali, & A. Watts Pailliotet (Eds.), *Intermediality: The teachers' handbook of critical media literacy* (pp. 1–30). Boulder, CO: Westview.

Smith, K. (1999). *Mental hygiene: Classroom films 1945–1970.* New York: Blast Books.

Smith, N. B. (1986). *American reading instruction.* Newark, DE: International Reading Association. (Original work published 1934)

Street, B. (1995). *Social literacies: Critical approaches to literacy in development, ethnography and education.* New York: Longman.

Tishman, S., & Perkins, D. (1997). The language of thinking. *Phi Delta Kappan, 78,* 368–374.

Walsh, R. (Director). (1949). *White heat* [Motion picture]. United States: Warner Brothers.

Williams, B. T. (2003). What they see is what we get: Television and middle school writers. *Journal of Adolescent & Adult Literacy, 46,* 546–554.

Willinsky, J. (1990). *The new literacy: Redefining reading and writing in the schools.* New York: Routledge.

Yohe, T., & Newall, G. (1996). *Schoolhouse rock! The official guide.* New York: Hyperion.

•54•

POPULAR CULTURE IN THE LANGUAGE ARTS CLASSROOM

Jackie Marsh
UNIVERSITY OF SHEFFIELD

In this chapter, I offer an overview of issues relating to the use of popular culture in the language and literacy curriculum. In the first part of the chapter, the concept of popular culture is explored and approaches to its use in educational settings analyzed. In the second part of the chapter, I review research studies that have illustrated how popular culture can inform the language arts curriculum, looking separately at oracy, reading, and writing, whilst acknowledging that these areas are interrelated. In the third part of the chapter, consideration is given to the factors that need to be in place if such work is to be successful. Finally, the chapter looks to the future. Given the rich diversity of research and practice that has informed the development of this field so far, this section identifies the key issues that need consideration in the future.

POPULAR CULTURE AND LITERACY

"Culture" is a concept that is so complex that it resists simplistic attempts to provide conclusive definitions. Indeed, Raymond Williams (1979), one of the most significant cultural theorists of the 21st century, became so irritated by such attempts that he stated, "I don't know how many times I've wished that I'd never heard the damned word" (p. 154). Nevertheless, Williams did offer a number of important insights into the nature of culture, one of which was his focus on its "ordinariness." Whilst previous incarnations of the concept had focused on it as a cerebral category, or as a marker for high arts (see Jenks, 1993, for an overview), Williams insisted that culture was about the ordinary stuff of everyday life (1965).

The concept of "popular culture" has similarly been subject to competing and conflicting attempts to define it. Popular cultural forms are those consumed and created by groups of people and are not regarded as having the properties and values associated with "high" cultural forms. Decisions about which cultural forms are popular and which elite are shaped by notions of class and social, cultural, and economic capital (Bourdieu, 1984). In relation to children's popular culture, there are cultural icons, artefacts, and texts, enjoyed on a mass scale, that form the bedrock of children's cultural lives. These are often embedded in global "mediascapes" (Appadurai, 1996): flows of information, images, and narratives relating to media such as film, television, and computer games that cross national boundaries.

This globalization of children's culture has led, inevitably, to concerns about the relationship between children's culture and commercial interests (Kenway & Bullen, 2001). Indeed, it is clear that the producers of popular films and games do develop strategic marketing plans in order to ensure maximum take-up of products, with some companies employing "localisers" whose task it is to shape a cultural product originating in one country to the cultural climate of another (Tobin, 2004). However, children are not passive dupes of this process; they have considerable agency in the consumption of these products. In addition, popular culture is both consumed and produced. This means that we need to move beyond the binary of global/local to a recognition that popular culture is glocal (Robertson, 1992, 1995); children localize globalized products, and they fashion them to their particular contexts. Similarly, popular culture can be consumed and produced on both a mass and a small scale. Some popular cultural forms are distinct to specific social and cultural groups. For example, Kenner (2005) described the popular cultural interests of the bilingual children she studied in projects that focused on the literacy experiences of children in minority ethnic communities in Britain and these interests included "Bollywood" films, Thai karaoke videos, and community-language newspapers.

A further binary divide that needs to be challenged is that of the positioning of popular cultural texts as either submissive or resistant to dominant ideologies. Whilst some popular cultural texts, such as adverts, are shaped by particular commercial or political interests, many are not. In addition, popular culture is not always transgressive in nature. Some forms can be (e.g., rap music or Web "zines") but other popular narratives are more conformist in nature and some contain both oppositional and compliant elements. As Bennett (1998) suggested, popular culture

> consists not simply of an imposed mass culture that is coincident with dominant ideology, nor simply of spontaneously oppositional cultures, but is rather an area of negotiation between the two within which—in different types of popular culture—dominant, subordinate and oppositional cultural and ideological values and elements are "mixed" in different permutations (p. 221).

The complexity of the concept of popular culture, therefore, resists modernist attempts to confine it to a set of specific characteristics and this suggests that literacy educators should be sensitive to its plurality and its need to be considered in the light of particular social and cultural contexts.

The question regarding why literacy educators should concern themselves with popular culture at all has been addressed in various ways. Over the last decade, research in this field has been concerned to establish the ideological rationale for the inclusion of popular culture within literacy curricula. An analysis of the key themes of this work suggests that there are four main lines of argument, sometimes distinct, and at other times overlapping. These have been summarized in Table 54.1.

In the following section, these four models will be outlined briefly.

The Utilitarian Model

In the utilitarian model, popular culture is seen to offer a means of encouraging children to become engaged in the schooled literacy curriculum. Whilst the value of children's cultural forms are recognized, the emphasis in this strand of research and scholarly activity has been on promoting the merit of such forms for the purpose of orienting children to schooled literacy practices (Marsh, 2000). This model is open to criticism because of its potentially narrow focus on the perceived benefits of the use of popular culture for goals that are not primarily related to the cultural experiences themselves. This may lead some to worry about the colonization of children's culture. However, there is no evidence that this is the key message of texts that seek to promote the use of popular culture in schools, nor is there any convincing evidence that when popular cultural texts are used in the curriculum, children feel that their interests are being ruthlessly adopted by educators for their own ends.

The Cultural Capital Model

Research in this strand draws upon the concept of "cultural capital" (Bourdieu, 1977) in its articulation of the place of popular culture in the literacy curriculum. The model starts with the recognition that popular culture plays a central role in contemporary childhoods and thus the driving force for its use is not appropriation for curriculum-focused goals, but respect for the cultural experiences and knowledge of children (Dyson, 1997; 2002). It embodies an acknowledgement that popular culture plays an integral part in many young children's lives and can provide a means of exploring and constructing identities (Marsh, 2005). Whilst popular cultural forms are enjoyed by children in all socioeconomic groups, for working-class children these texts and artefacts may be the primary source of out-of-school literacy practices. In this model, therefore, it is incumbent upon literacy educators to recognize and value such experiences, as not to do so means that the worlds of home and school continue to offer very different experiences for some groups of children. Integral to this model is Moll, Amanti, Neff, & Gonzalez 's (1992) notion of "funds of knowledge," the knowledge store that learners acquire from their experiences in everyday life. Using these funds of knowledge as a starting point for classroom practice is important in the development of "culturally-relevant pedagogy" (Ladson-Billings, 1995).

TABLE 54.1 Theoretical Models for the Use of Popular Culture in the Language Arts Curriculum

Model	Underpinning Philosophy	Indicative Studies
Utilitarian model	Using popular culture can provide a means of orienting children to schooled literacy practices.	Marsh (2000)
Cultural capital model	Popular culture can provide a means of bridging the gap between home and school for children whose "cultural capital" (Bourdieu, 1990) is not normally recognized in educational institutions.	Dyson (1997; 2002) Marsh (2000) Marsh & Millard (2000) Nagle (1999) Xu (2000a; 2000b; 2001)
Critical model	Popular cultural texts have integral value and can be studied in their own right, as part of a critical literacy curriculum in which texts of all kinds, both popular and canonical, are subject to critical analysis.	Alvermann, Moon, & Hagood (2001) Alvermann & Xu (2003) Dyson (1997; 2002) Marsh & Millard (2005) Nixon & Comber (2005) Vasquez (2004; 2005)
Recontextualisation/ "third space" model	The use of popular culture in the language arts curriculum transforms the knowledge developed in both out-of-school and schooled locations and creates new knowledge and understandings.	Davies & Pahl (2007) Dyson (1997; 2002) Millard (2003) Gutierrez et al. (1999) Moje et al. (2004) Willett (2005)

The Critical Model

This approach to the use of popular culture places emphasis on the development of learners as critical readers and writers. The pedagogical focus is on the critical examination of all kinds of texts, both canonical texts and texts located within learners' popular cultural worlds. Because children are engaged with popular cultural texts from the earliest years of life, they acquire a wide range of critical skills that need to be acknowledged and developed further in the classroom (Alvermann, Moon, & Hagood, 1999). Alvermann & Xu (2003) emphasized the need to ensure that children have opportunities to explore the pleasure they experience in interacting with popular texts and not just examine them in terms of identifying how they are positioned by the ideological stances of the texts.

The Recontextualisation or "Third Space" Model

In this model, popular cultural worlds meet the textual worlds of the classroom and in this process, the texts themselves are transformed and new types of knowledge generated. Dyson (2002) has described how, in her ethnographic studies of classrooms

> when children translated cultural material . . . across the boundaries of different practices involving different semiotic technologies, they could be stopped short, as the textual and conceptual knowledge embedded in their everyday and playful practices was disrupted and brought into reflective awareness. (p. 93)

The concept of "third space" has also been utilized in an attempt to understand what happens in this cultural remixing. The concept of "third space" was first developed in depth by Bhabha (1994) as a metaphor for the space in which cultures meet. It is a space in which colonial authority is challenged and hybrid identities are created. This space is not a cohesive one; Bhabha (1994) stressed that it is a site of tension, competing powers, and insurmountable differences: "The non-synchronous temporality of global and national cultures opens up a cultural space—a third space—where the negotiation of incommensurable differences creates a tension peculiar to borderline existences . . ." (p. 218).

This nexus of cultural identities is, therefore, a shifting space, a space which is always in flux. This notion of hybridity occurring through cultural border-crossing has a long history, as Heidegger (1975) argued, and was strongly articulated in the work of Bakhtin (1986), who suggested that the "most intense and productive life of culture takes place on the boundaries of its individual areas and not in places where these areas have become enclosed in their own specificity" (p. 2). Therefore, in this articulation of the notion of "third-space," both Bakhtin and Bhabha emphasized how the process of cultural production is dependent on interactions between previously quite separate, even dichotomous, spaces.

The concept of third-space has also been used to explore how the diverse worlds of home and nursery or school can be brought together in educational settings. In relation to literacy education, Gutiérrez, Baquedano-Lopez, Alvarez, & Chiu (1999) have used third-space theory to explore how the different cultural spaces children inhabit can be brought together in the classroom, rather than these domains remaining distinct. Moje, Ciechanowski, Kramer, Ellis, Carrillo, & Collazzo (2004), however, argued that this position emphasizes the importance of the third space as a site for introducing children to the discourses of power, rather than seeing it as a metaphor for a space in which new, hybrid, and challenging discourses are created. Instead, Moje et al. (2004) suggested that the third space of classrooms should be perceived as a place in which academic discourses are challenged and reshaped, but also give rise to the reconstitution of the everyday, out-of-school knowledge of learners. These two uses of "third space," the first to describe the cultural hybridity that occurs when border-crossing (Bhabha, 1994) and the second as a metaphor for curricula and pedagogical practice that treats all knowledge, whether schooled or out-of-school, as open to challenge and change, are not mutually exclusive, and both can usefully inform studies of the use of popular culture in the language arts curriculum.

However, the concept of third space is not without its limitations. The worlds of educational institutions and homes/communities cannot be seen as two entirely distinct and separate domains; there is seepage between them. In addition, children's social and cultural worlds are constructed of numerous domains and discourses that overlap in complex ways. As Richardson (2000) suggested is the case in relation to the triadization model within research which focuses on the notion of "triangulation" as a means of enhancing validity, "in postmodernist mixed-genre texts, we do not triangulate; we crystallize. We recognise that there are far more than "three sides" from which to approach the world." (p. 934)

There are, indeed, more than three dimensions (school, out-of-school, and the interface between these) in children's lives and thus the concept of "third space" faces the same constraints. Nevertheless, it is a useful metaphor when considering what happens when the different discourses embedded within contemporary childhoods meet and it can provide a tool for imagining innovative educational spaces that offer children opportunities to engage in transformative practices in which new kinds of knowledge are produced. This process has also been referred to as a "transformative pedagogy of literacy fusion" by Millard (2003, p. 6), who suggested that children's out-of-school interests can be fused with schooled literacy in classroom practice that pays attention to what happens when the two textual worlds collide.

There is overlap between all of the models outlined earlier. For example, the very act of recontextualizing knowledge is a critical one and, therefore, these two models share many underlying principles. Nevertheless, examining the research conducted so far on the use of popular culture in the language arts curriculum in the light of these models enables reflection on the way in which the theoretical rationale for the use of popular culture in the language arts curriculum has developed over the last decade. With the justification for the use of popular texts in schools established, it is now timely to turn to a review of research that has explored its impact on the various strands of the language arts curriculum—oracy, reading, and writing.

Popular Culture in the Language Arts Classroom

In the following section, I will provide an overview of the key issues that have emerged in research so far into the role and nature of popular culture in the language arts curriculum. The areas of oracy, reading, and writing will be addressed separately, although it is recognized that they interrelate. For the purposes of this analysis, I have not distinguished between particular elements of children's popular culture (e.g., superheroes and other cultural icons, toys, television and film, books, comics and magazines, computer games, and the Internet), although each of these deserves examination in its own right. However, as the emphasis in this chapter is on the impact that the use of popular culture can have on children's experience of the language arts curriculum, the discussion will move between these cultural forms.

Oracy

The language and lore of popular culture permeate children's use of language at both home and school. For bilingual children, popular cultural narratives as experienced in the home can be powerful sources of learning about English as an additional language. Orellana (1994) studied three bilingual preschool children's language use in superhero play and suggested that American popular culture was a useful tool in developing English. This was also the case in Xu's (1999) study of six Chinese-American children aged between 5 and 6 and Rodriguez's (1999) study of three Dominican preschool children aged 2 1/2 to 5 years. In both of these studies, bilingual children interacted extensively with television and media and these texts had a positive impact on their language development. Similarly, in studies conducted in England (Kenner, 2005; Marsh, Brooks, Hughes, Ritchie, Roberts, & Wright, 2005), bilingual parents have commented on the value of media engagement for their children's acquisition of English as an additional language.

The fact that popular culture can provide a common discourse amongst children from disparate cultural and linguistic groups has been noted by cultural theorists such as Ellen Seiter (1993), who has suggested that popular culture forms the "lingua franca" of playgrounds. This theme has permeated the work of Grugeon (1999; 2001; 2005). In a number of research projects that have explored the playground games of contemporary children, she has outlined how many are based on popular cultural themes and suggested that "the playground is a richly intertextual and creative site where children play out narratives of their own devising" (Grugeon, 2005, p. 8). It is clear that the language developed in this type of playground play has much potential to inform classroom practice.

Despite this work, the use of popular culture in classrooms to promote oracy has not been a central focus for much of the research in the field. Rather, it is normally commented upon almost in passing as a positive feature of the introduction of such work. For example, in a recent study in England, "Digital Beginnings" (Marsh et al., 2005), nine early-years settings incorporated aspects of popular culture, media, and/ or new technologies in the curriculum. Practitioners reported that this had a strong impact on children who would not normally talk extensively in the classroom. One setting in the study planned its whole curriculum on the theme of "Balamory", a popular television program in the United Kingdom. Role-play areas, puppet-making, story-telling, music, and arts and craft activities were all related to the program. The teacher, Beth, stated,

> A lot of what we did was speaking and listening. Once we'd done the puppet show and invented the puppets, one day I walked around the corner and they'd put all the big blocks and made a puppet theatre and they were acting puppet stories. One of the little boys from the project, he's very hard to get on side, and he was PC Plum and I could hear him say, "One day, PC Plum . . ." and he's just, he has never used that story language before, at all. (Marsh et al., 2005, p. 69)

This was a strongly recurrent theme in the data. Children who had previously not spoken much in the setting were finding a voice through the projects, as reported by another practitioner:

> Shafeeq, who doesn't particularly talk a lot unless it's, "I'm gonna shoot you," that kind of thing, he really got into it and he wanted to tell us a story. His story came alive and it was alive for him and everyone was listening to his story. Well usually it's, "Come on, don't talk about guns, don't talk about that." So he really found a vessel to tell his story . . . I think he's got more friends now through it. (Marsh et al., 2005, p. 69)

It would appear that popular culture has an important role to play in the acquisition and use of language. However, there is a need for specific research studies that focus on this area of the language arts curriculum in order to determine the conditions that best support the development of oracy through the use of popular culture.

Reading

Surveys of children's out-of-school reading habits invariably identify popular cultural texts as being central to children's reading choices (Hall & Coles, 1999). Children's interests in popular culture do impact upon their reading choices and practices. In the "Digital Beginnings" project (Marsh et al., 2005), in which 1,852 parents of children aged from birth to six were surveyed about their children's media-related literacy practices, a total of 82% of all children spent time with books at home on a typical day. Parents reported that children read, or engaged in early reading behaviors, for an average of 30 minutes on a typical day. They were read to by someone else for an average of 32 minutes. Engaging with books either as an individual or with others was the third most frequent activity for children (after playing inside with toys and watching television). There were no significant differences in relation to socioeconomic status in terms of children being read to by someone else. Not surprisingly, older children were more likely to read than younger children, and girls were more likely to spend longer periods than boys doing this.

Eighty-one percent of children owned books related to their favorite television programs or characters. Sixty percent of parents in the survey felt that these books motivated their child to read or write, and this was supported by data from the interviews with parents, in which many parents felt that this was the case for their child:

> He's got the monsters book, he's got the "Bug's Life" book, "Toy Story" book and they are the ones he always goes for. If I say, "Go and choose a book", he will choose generally one of his favourite films. It motivates him to pick a book up in the first place, certainly. (Marsh et al., 2005, p. 42)

Some parents noted that children deliberately related the books to the film/television program, drawing on the language experienced with the moving image to retell the stories:

> I mean, he'll sit there and he'll watch the "Jungle Book" on the DVD and then maybe the next couple of days he'll get his books and he'll look at the pictures and say, "Oh, I've seen that bit on the telly". He does sit there and he makes up his own words, do you know what I mean, like he's reading the book. (Marsh et al., 2005, p. 43)

Children were also motivated to read comics and magazines that were related to their media interests. In addition, they visited Web sites that focused on their favorite television characters and films. Studies of older children have indicated that online reading is an important element of their out-of-school reading practices (Atkinson & Nixon, 2005; Burnett & Wilkinson, 2005).

Despite this evidence that popular culture plays an important role in children's reading practices, there is limited research on the use of popular culture in the reading curriculum. Millard and Marsh (2001) described a home-school comic lending library, set up in one primary school in England. Children were allowed to take home a comic along with their usual reading book on a weekly basis. Findings suggested that the scheme motivated reluctant readers to engage in reading and involved family members in reading alongside children.

Writing

It is this area of the language arts curriculum that has received most of the attention in research relating to popular culture and schooling. This is, perhaps, not surprising, as it is the area in which children can draw from their own cultural experiences as they complete classroom activities. Even if teachers do not actively promote the use of popular culture, children weave in their own out-of-school experiences into the complex tapestry of classroom life.

Anne Haas Dyson's work (1994, 1996, 1997, 1999a, 1999b, 2001, 2002) has provided a series of insightful glimpses into the social discourses informing children's writing and has illuminated the way in which popular culture permeates childhood worlds. Her work has informed much of the research in this field and her analysis provides a conceptual framework for analysis that draws on Bakhtin's (1986) concept of heteroglossia. Children reshape and rework the media culture in which they are immersed into their writing and the result is a heady mix of complex, intertextual products. For example, in *Brothers and Sisters Learn to Write* (2002), Dyson referred to the rich and varied range of texts and artefacts from which children draw as a "shared textual toybox" into which children dip and she describes six purposes to which these texts are put. These materials were, in her studies: a source of pleasure; material for personal expression and performance; a context for dramatic play; a source of displayed knowledge and expertise; a resource for both social affiliation and differentiation; and, finally, resources for participation in school literacy events. Thus, the textual toys of home and community were powerful tools that children used to forge entry into the official discourses of schooling and, as toys, they ensured that this entry was playful and inventive in nature.

Some studies have focused on examining the impact of the introduction of popular cultural texts on children's attainment in writing. In a study that involved three local education authorities in England, teachers used films and cartoons to stimulate writing (PNS/UKLA, 2004). The study found that this work was highly motivating for children and raised attainment in writing. The study also had a positive impact on children's attitudes toward writing and enhanced their self-perceptions as writers. This positive effect on attainment when incorporating popular forms into the curriculum has also been noted by Parker (1999).

A close analysis of children's writing in which popular cultural forms are embedded would suggest that children do not just adopt these narratives in an unreflective manner. They build on and develop these narratives in interesting, creative ways. For example, Willet (2005) outlined how a group of six eight- to nine-year-olds drew from film narratives in the development of written stories and creatively extended them through the use of techniques such as parody and pastiche. Bearne and Wolstencroft (2005) discussed the impact of children's understanding of computer-game narratives on their story writing. They suggest that children's "knowledge of game narratives of different kinds adds significantly to their potential for constructing written narrative texts" (p. 73) in that they are able to create complex, multilayered narratives that draw on some of the features of games such as multiple-choice of pathways through the narrative and the use of sound and visual effects to enhance meaning.

There has been less extensive research on the impact of other popular forms of writing, such as e-mailing, blogging, and texting, on classroom practice. Merchant (in press) offers a review of research in this emergent field and states that "a relatively small amount of work on digital literacy has been published in journals that address the development of reading and writing in educational contexts." Some may feel that such digital literacy practices may have little relevance to children in the earliest stages of schooling. However, the "Digital Beginnings" project (Marsh et al., 2005) indicated that very young children were aware of "digitextual" (Everett, 2003) practices and engaged in literacy practices such as writing e-mails and instant messages (with parents acting as scribe) and pretending to send text-messages. Indeed, there are some interesting accounts from parents which indicate that, in technically-advanced families, children are already being introduced to more complex forms of communication. Web logs (blogs), for example, are online diaries in which bloggers create an account of their everyday lives, or outline their interests and current thinking. Readers can post comments on blogs and, therefore, the writing has the potential to become dialogic in nature. One blogger, Beth Kantor, has described in her blog how her 5-year-old son, Harry, became interested in the concept of blogging. In a blog post, Beth explained how they worked by suggesting to her son that they were very much like Harry's journal, which he completed each week in his kindergarten class:

> Tonight, I showed them how I can "put their drawings into the computer" and add them to mommy's blog. Harry asked, "Mommy, what's a blog . . . ?" I told him it was a web site that is similar to the journal that he writes in paper but the blog is on the computer/ internet so other people can read it. (He writes a journal in Kindergarten, so he made the connection.) He then asked me, "Does that mean other people will see my drawing and tell us what they think about it?" I said yes, people do that, but not all the time. (Kantor, 2005, n.p.)

This is an interesting example of how parents are scaffolding children's understanding of digital literacy practices in much the same way as they have always scaffolded children's understanding of paper-based texts. Given the potential for this form of online writing, it may not be too long before we see blogging as an integral practice in many language arts classrooms, and blogging replacing journal writing as a tool for recording ongoing events, thoughts, and experiences. However, in adopting popular cultural forms such as this, it will be important to recognize the integral features of such practices in order to ensure that they retain integrity and validity in the children's eyes (Merchant, in press).

From the work reviewed in this section, it is clear that the use of popular cultural texts in the classroom to develop reading, writing, and oracy can have a strong impact on motivation and engagement and, in some cases, attainment. However, such work has to be planned effectively in order for it to be successful. The simple adoption of popular cultural forms in order to enliven the language arts curriculum will not lead to meaningful work. Instead, teachers need to plan such activities carefully and take into account a number of factors in order to ensure that the use of popular culture fosters innovative and creative practice. In the next section, the factors that contribute to the successful use of popular culture in the language arts curriculum will be considered.

SUCCESS FACTORS WHEN USING POPULAR CULTURE IN THE LANGUAGE ARTS CURRICULUM

In the "Digital Beginnings" study (Marsh et al., 2005), nine early-years settings in England conducted action research projects in which an aspect of popular culture, media, and/or new technologies was introduced into the communications, language, and literacy curriculum. A number of factors were identified as contributing to the success of the projects. These were as follows:

1. Projects started with the interests of children. In the most successful projects, practitioners had spent time prior to the project identifying the interests of children through discussions in group time. They did not introduce topics and characters they assumed to be of interest; instead, the subjects emerged from the stated preferences of children.
2. Parents were closely involved with the projects from their inception. Where projects were most successful, parents had been fully informed from the beginning and invited to participate in aspects of them (e.g., through taking home media boxes, being asked to bring in particular items). Given the wealth of knowledge parents demonstrated of their children's interest in popular culture, media, and new technologies, it is clear that they have a valuable role to play in projects which focus on these aspects of children's lives. Children's popular culture is also a part of the families' "cultural capital" (Bourdieu, 1977), and provides a valuable means of building bridges between homes and educational settings for both children and parents.
3. The projects involved all members of staff. The projects worked successfully because practitioners reported that all members of staff were involved and committed to them. In all cases, if senior managers were not the representatives of the setting directly involved in the project, they were highly supportive of it.
4. Settings were supported by "critical friends."Practitioners suggested that being part of the project had offered them support for new initiatives, support which was important because it provided new ideas and resources and the opportunity to work with a group of others with whom they could discuss progress. Being part of an externally monitored research project also meant that practitioners were encouraged and supported in collecting data systematically. Although collecting data on children is an integral part of early-years practice, the project did impose additional demands and the advice and support offered by the project team in relation to the research methods was valued.
5. Activities were sustained and integrated. Settings did not plan "one-off" activities or events, but carefully planned integrated units of work that offered development and progression. One highly successful project had developed the themes from a children's television program and had planned the curriculum in all six areas of learning from this program. Practitioners felt that this enhanced the project further, as it enabled children to integrate aspects of their learning across the curriculum.
6. Activities drew on a range of modes and media. The most successful projects drew on a wide range of modes and media in their planning. Children enjoyed encountering, playing with and producing narratives across a broad range of multimodal texts, as this reflected their encounters with media texts outside of schools and early-years settings.

These factors have implications for the planning and implementation of projects that intend to draw from children's popular cultural worlds in order to develop the language arts curriculum. It may not be realistic for schools to have all of these factors in place; for example, links with external research projects are not easy to establish and, therefore, teachers might have to look elsewhere for "critical friends," such as education authority advisers or practitioners from local schools. However, what the factors illustrate is that the development of a "culturally relevant curriculum" (Ladson-Billings, 1995) is a complex and considered process requiring careful planning and implementation, and is also a rich site for the development of professional expertise.

CONCLUSION

The research reviewed in this chapter indicates that popular culture can inform the language arts curriculum in a range of exciting and innovative ways, if used in a respectful and reflective manner. Popular culture can motivate children and engage them in sustained curriculum activities; it can provide rich material for imaginative play, talk, and writing and can be seen to raise achievement in some contexts. However, there are still many areas that remain relatively unexplored and, in this final section, I will outline a few themes that deserve further attention from literacy educators in the years ahead.

First, whilst there has been a wealth of research into the relationship between popular culture and writing, there is less extensive evidence of studies that have focused on oracy and reading. It would be useful, for example, to explore how far children's reading of popular online texts outside of school could be harnessed in the classroom in order to develop further their critical-reading skills (Burnett & Wilkinson, 2005). Given the recognition of the way in which popular culture permeates oral interactions in playgrounds (Grugeon, 2004), we could usefully explore how popular culture could be used in the classroom to promote oracy (e.g., to inform work on specific oral genres such as speeches and arguments). Second, there are a few studies that have indicated the very positive response of parents and carers to classroom work on popular culture (Arthur, 2005; Makin, Hayden, Holland, Arthur, Beecher, Jones Diaz, & McNaught, 1999; Marsh et al., 2005). Many parents appreciate the interest their children have in these cultural forms and support their use in the language arts curriculum. As there is now a wealth of evidence that parental involvement in children's education is vital to their achievement (Desforges & Abouchaar, 2003; Sylva, Melhusish, Sammons, Siraj-Blatchford, & Taggart, 2004), it would seem that introducing work on popular culture into family literacy and learning programs could offer a means of effectively engaging a range of parents in activities that are meaningful to them (Marsh & Thompson, 2001; Pahl & Rowsell, 2005). Third, there are some popular cultural forms that have been the focus of study to the exclusion of other forms. Television, films, and computer games appear to dominate much of the research in the field. Yet it is evident that popular music and the radio, for example, are very important to children and young people (Alvermann, Moon, & Hagood, 2001; Davies & Pahl, 2007; Dyson, 2002; Marsh et al., 2005). Future research could focus in more depth on this area, particularly given the rich potential that some forms of music have because of their exceptional uses of language. For example, work at the Sheffield College in England has engaged learners in comparing and contrasting the lyrics of the rapper Nas and the poet William Blake, given the overlap in conceptual themes both artists address (Hooper, 2004). This model could be usefully extended to earlier stages of schooling, if the lyrics used were age-appropriate.

Finally, given the extent to which the media permeate children's encounters with popular culture, there is much work to be done on developing children's understanding of different forms of media and their affordances (Kress, 2003). Whether or not this aspect of the language arts curriculum should be defined as "media literacy" is a key question (Marsh, 2004), but one that should not get in the way of developing a curriculum that offers children spaces to analyze and produce a wide range of media forms, utilizing their extensive knowledge of digital technologies and drawing from their out-of-school repertoires of practice (Carrington, 2004, 2005; Davies, 2005; Knobel, 2005; Merchant, in press). The agenda outlined here is one that will require some risk-taking by literacy educators and will challenge traditional notions of what it means to be literate, but it is one that is essential if classrooms are to offer children meaningful experiences with communicational modes and practices that are central to contemporary lives. Popular culture is not extraneous to the central needs of the language arts curriculum; it is, as Raymond Williams (1965) emphasized, the stuff of everyday life and, therefore, should form the stuff of everyday classrooms.

REFERENCES

Alvermann, D., Moon, J. S., & Hagood, M. C. (1999). *Popular culture in the classroom: Teaching and researching critical media literacy*. Newark, Delaware: IRA/ NRC.

Alvermann, D. E., & Xu, S. H. (2003). Children's everyday literacies: Intersections of popular culture and language arts instruction. *Language Arts, 81*, 145–154.

Appadurai, A. (1996). *Modernity at large: Cultural dimensions of globalisation*. Minneapolis: University of Minnesota Press.

Arthur, L. (2005). Popular culture: Views of parents and educators. In J. Marsh (Ed.), *Popular culture, new media and digital literacy in early childhood*. (pp. 165–182) London: RoutledgeFalmer.

Atkinson, S., & Nixon, H. (2005). Locating the subject: Teens online @ ninemsn, *Discourse: Studies in the cultural politics of education, 26*, 387–409.

Bakhtin, M. (1986). *Speech genres and other late essays* (V. W. McGee, Trans.). Austin: University of Texas.

Bearne, E., & Wolstencroft, H. (2005). Playing with texts: The contribution of children's knowledge of computer narratives to their story writing. In J. Marsh & E. Millard (Eds.), *Popular literacies, childhood and schooling*. (pp. 72–92). London: RoutledgeFalmer.

Bennett, T. (1998). Popular Culture and "turn to Gramsci." In J. Storey (Ed.), *Cultural theory and popular culture: A reader* (2nd ed.) (pp. 217–224). Hemel Hempstead, England: Prentice Hall.

Bhabha, H. K. (1994). *The location of culture*. London: Routledge.

Bourdieu, P. (1977). *Outline of a theory of practice*. Cambridge: Cambridge University Press.

Bourdieu, P. (1984). *Distinction: A social critique of the judgement of taste*. (R. Nice, Trans.). London: Routledge & Kegan Paul.

Burnett, C., & Wilkinson, J. (2005). Holy Lemons! Learning from children's use of the Internet in out-of-school contexts. *Literacy, 39*, 158–165.

Carrington, V. (2004). Texts and literacies of the Shi Jinrui. *British Journal of Sociology of Education, 25*, 215–228.

Carrington, V. (2005). New textual landscapes, information and early literacy. In J. Marsh (Ed.), *Popular culture, new media and digital literacy in early childhood*. London: RoutledgeFalmer.

Davies, J. (2005). Nomads and tribes: Online meaning making and the development of new literacies. In J. Marsh & E. Millard (Eds.), *Popular literacies, childhood and schooling*. London: RoutledgeFalmer.

Davies, J., & Pahl, K. (2007) Blended voices, blended learning: Lessons in pedagogy from a post-16 classroom. In E. Bearne & J. Marsh (Eds.) *Literacy and social inclusion: Closing the gap*. Stoke on Trent, Staffs: Trentham Books.

Desforges, C., & Abouchaar, A. (2003). *The impact of parental involvement, parental support and family education on pupil achievement and adjustment: A review of literature*. London: HMSO.

Dyson, A. H. (1994). "The Ninjas, the X-Men, and the Ladies": Playing with power and identity in an urban primary school. *Teachers College Record, 96*, 219–239.

Dyson, A. H. (1996). "Cultural constellations and childhood identities: on Greek gods, cartoon heroes, and the social lives of schoolchildren". *Harvard Educational Review, 66*, 471–495.

Dyson, A. H. (1997). *Writing superheroes: Contemporary childhood, popular culture, and classroom literacy*. New York: Teachers College Press.

Dyson, A. H. (1999a). Coach Bombay's kids learn to write: Children's appropriation of media material for school literacy. *Research in the Teaching of English, 33*, 367–402.

Dyson, A. H. (1999b). "Transforming transfer: unruly children, contrary texts and the persistence of the pedagogical order." In A. Iran-Nejad & P. D. Pearson (Eds.), *Review of Research in Education, 24*. Washington, DC: American Educational Research Association.

Dyson, A. H. (2001). Where are the childhoods in childhood literacy? An exploration in outer (school) space. *Journal of Early Childhood Literacy, 1*, 9–39.

Dyson, A. H. (2002). *Brothers and sisters learn to write: Popular literacies in childhood and school cultures*. New York: Teachers College Press.

Everett, A. (2003). Digitextuality and click theory: Theses on convergence media in the digital age. In A. Everett & Jon T. Caldwell (Eds.), *New media: Theories and practices of digitextuality*. (pp. 3–28). New York: Routledge.

Grugeon, E. (1999). The state of play: Children's oral culture, literacy and learning. *Reading, 33*(1), 13–16.

Grugeon, E. (2001). "We like singing the Spice Girls' songs . . . and we like Tig and Stuck in the Mud": Girls' traditional play in two playgrounds. In J. C. Bishop & M. Curtis (Eds.), *Play today in the primary school playground: Life, learning and creativity*. Buckingham: Open University Press.

Grugeon, E. (2005). Listening to learning outside the classroom: Student teachers study playground literacies. *Literacy, 39*(3), 3–9

Gutierrez, K. D., Baquedano-Lopez, P., Alvarez, H., & Chiu, M. M. (1999). Building a culture of collaboration through hybrid language practices. *Theory into Practice, 38*, 87–93.

Hall, C., & Coles, C. (1999). *Children's reading choices*. London: Routledge.

Heidegger, M. (1975). *Poetry, language, thought*. London, New York: Harper & Row.

Hooper, J. (April, 2004) *Hip-hop and high stakes testing in GCSE English at the Sheffield College, UK*. Paper presented at the American Educational Research Association, Montreal, April 2004. Sheffield: Sheffield College.

Jenks, C. (1993). *Culture*. London: Routledge.

Kantor, B. (2005). *Blog post*. Retrieved November, 2005, from http://beth.typepad.com/beths_blog/ed_tech_and_early_childhood/index.html

Kenner, C. (2005). Bilingual children's uses of popular culture in text-making. In J. Marsh (Ed.), *Popular culture, new media and digital literacy in early childhood*. (pp. 28–50) London: RoutledgeFalmer.

Kenway, J., & Bullen, E. (2001). *Consuming children: Education—entertainment—advertising*. Buckingham: Open University Press.

Knobel, M. (2005). Technokids, Koala Trouble and Pokémon: Literacy, new technologies and popular culture in children's everyday lives. In J. Marsh & E. Millard (Eds.), *Popular literacies, childhood and schooling.* London: RoutledgeFalmer.

Kress, G. (2003). *Literacy in the new media age.* London: Routledge.

Ladson-Billings, G. (1995). Towards a theory of culturally relevant pedagogy. *American Educational Research Journal, 32,* 465–491.

Makin, L., Hayden, J., Holland, A., Arthur, L., Beecher, B., Jones Diaz, C., & McNaught, M. (1999). *Mapping literacy practices in early childhood services.* Sydney: NSW Department of Education and Training and NSW Department of Community Services.

Marsh, J. (2000). Teletubby Tales: Popular culture in the early years language and literacy curriculum. *Contemporary Issues in Early Childhood, 1,* 119–133.

Marsh, J. (2004). The primary canon: A critical review. *British Journal of Educational Studies, 52*(3), 249–262.

Marsh, J. (Ed.). (2005). *Popular culture, new media and digital literacy in early childhood.* London: RoutledgeFalmer.

Marsh, J., Brooks, G., Hughes, J., Ritchie, L., Roberts, S., & Wright, K. (2005). *Digital beginnings: Young children's use of popular culture, media and new technologies.* Sheffield: University of Sheffield. Retrieved November, 2005, from Digital Beginnings Project Web site: http://www.digitalbeginnings.shef.ac.uk/

Marsh, J., & Millard, E. (2000). *Literacy and popular culture: Using children's culture in the classroom.* London: Paul Chapman.

Marsh, J., & Millard, E. (2005). *Popular literacies, childhood and schooling.* London: RoutledgeFalmer.

Marsh, J. & Thompson, P. (2001). Parental involvement in literacy development: Using media texts. *Journal of Research in Reading, 24,* 266–278.

Merchant, G. (in press). Digital writing in the early years. In D. J. Leu, Jr., C. Lankshear, M. Knoble, & J. Coiro, (Eds.), *Handbook of research on new literacies.* Mahwah, NJ: Lawrence Erlbaum.

Millard, E. (2003). Transformative pedagogy: Towards a literacy of fusion. *Reading, Literacy and Language, 37*(1), 3–9.

Millard, E., & Marsh, J. (2001) Sending Minnie the Minx home: Comics and reading choices. *Cambridge Journal of Education, 31*(1), 25–38.

Moje, E. B., Ciechanowski, K. M., Kramer, K., Ellis, L., Carrillo, R., & Collazzo, T. (2004). Working towards third space in content area literacy: An examination of everyday funds of knowledge and Discourse. *Reading Research Quarterly, 39,* 38–70.

Moll, L., Amanti, C., Neff, D., & Gonzalez, N. (1992). Funds of knowledge for teaching: Using a qualitative approach to connect homes and classrooms. *Theory into Practice, 31,* 132–141.

Nagle, J. P. (1999). Histories of success and failure: working class students' literacy experiences. *Journal of Adolescent and Adult Literacy, 43,* 172–185.

Nixon, H., & Comber, B. (2005). Behind the scenes: Making movies in early years classrooms. In J. Marsh (Ed.), *Popular culture, new media and digital literacy in early childhood.* London: RoutledgeFalmer.

Orellana, M. F. (1994). Appropriating the voice of the superheroes: Three preschoolers' bilingual language uses in play. *Early Childhood Research Quarterly, 9,* 171–193.

Pahl, K., & Rowsell, J. (2005). *Literacy and education: Understanding the new literacy studies in the classroom.* London: Sage.

Parker, J. (1999). You've read the book, now make the film: Moving image media, print literacy and narrative. *English in Education, 33,* 24–35.

Primary National Strategy (PNS)/ United Kingdom Literacy Association (UKLA) (2004). *Raising boys' achievement in writing.* London: PNS/ UKLA.

Richardson, L. (2000). Writing: A method of inquiry. In N. K. Denzin & Y. S. Lincoln (Eds.), *Handbook of Qualitative Research* (2nd ed.). Thousand Oaks, CA: Sage.

Robertson, R. (1992). *Globalization: Social theory and global culture.* London: Sage.

Robertson, R. (1995). Globalization: Time-space and homogeneity-heterogeneity. In M. Featherstone, S. Lash, & R. Robertson (Eds.), *Global modernities.* London. Sage.

Rodriguez, M. V. (1999). Home literacy experiences of three young Dominican children in New York City. *Educators for Urban Minorities, 1,* 19–31.

Seiter, E. (1993). *Sold separately: Children and parents in consumer culture.* New York: Rutgers University Press.

Sylva, K., Melhusish, E., Sammons, P., Siraj-Blatchford, I., & Taggart, B. (2004). *Effective provision of pre-school education (EPPE) project: Final report.* London: DfES.

Tobin, J. (2004). Introduction. In J. Tobin (Ed.), *Pikachu's global adventure: The rise and fall of Pokemon.* Durham and London: Duke University Press.

Vasquez, V. M. (2004). *Negotiating critical literacies with young children.* Mahwah, NJ: Lawrence Erlbaum.

Vasquez, V. M. (2005). Resistance, power-tricky and colorless energy: What engagement with everyday popular cultural texts can tell us about learning, and literacy. In J. Marsh (Ed.), *Popular culture, new media and digital literacy in early childhood.* London: RoutledgeFalmer.

Willet, R. (2005). "Baddies" in the classroom: Media education and narrative writing. *Literacy, 39,* 142–148.

Williams, R. (1965). *The long revolution.* Harmonsworth, England: Penguin.

Williams, R. (1979). *Politics and letters: Interviews with "New Left Review".* London: New Left Books.

Xu, S. H. (1999) Young Chinese ESL children's home literacy experiences. *Reading Horizons, 40*(1), 47–64.

Xu, S. H. (2000a). Pre-service teachers integrate understanding of diversity into literacy instruction: An adaptation of the ABC's model. *Journal of Teacher Education, 51,* 135–142.

Xu, S. H. (2000b). Pre-service teachers in a literacy methods course consider issues of diversity. *Journal of Literacy Research, 32,* 505–531.

Xu, S. H. (2001). *Exploring diversity issues in teacher education* [Electronic version]. Reading Online, 5, 1. Retrieved December, 2001, from http://wwww.readingonline/org/newliteracies/lit_index.asp?HREF=action/xu/index.html

•55•

DIFFERENTIATING VISUAL, COMMUNICATIVE, AND PERFORMATIVE ARTS INSTRUCTION IN WELL-MANAGED CLASSROOMS

Diane Lapp
SAN DIEGO STATE UNIVERSITY

James Flood
SAN DIEGO STATE UNIVERSITY

Kelly Moore
SAN DIEGO UNIFIED SCHOOL DISTRICT

We have all become increasingly aware that students are learning through out-of-school experiences at a rate that may exceed in-class learning (see Preface to this volume), but we also know classrooms provide a critical space for most students' literacy development. Classrooms are the major place of in-school learning, and, as such, need to be organized to create ongoing opportunities for practicing the visual, communicative, and performative arts in an integrated way.

The visual arts are at play through the architectural design of the room from the classroom library display, the tables, desks, chairs, nooks for silent reading, writing slates, painting easels, computer stations, video/CD production centers to platforms for orations, readings, plays, and Readers Theater productions. Viewers in the classroom (students, teachers, parents, aides, the school management team) need to be awed by the aesthetics of the room through pictures, posters, and mobiles, to student's art and artifacts. The design must be interpretable to students whether it a simple, slick design or an ornate, decorative design. Architectural and design features need to motivate students and teachers, helping them to imagine the unimaginable.

The communicative arts are at play throughout the room all day long. The room must announce that "reading, writing, listening, speaking, and viewing happen here." Discussion tables and student-teacher conference tables must be available, as well as nooks where students can discuss their learning with one another.

We've already alluded to the role of the performative arts in the classroom: stages; platforms; video/CD production centers; and high-tech computer applications like blogs, Wikis, and vPod broadcasting opportunities that will be available at the technology station so that children can bring their out-of-school experiences to the classroom to inform their learning.

Every classroom must be stunning to meet all of the needs of very diverse student populations. Stunning as they might become, we also have to remember that all architectural design theories and practices change, so we need to be ready to change our classroom structures at a moment's notice if our students' needs are not being met. Beyond the physical aspects of the classroom, great attention has to be given to the organization of the classroom and the instruction that occurs within. Issues like routines, rituals, and grouping must be considered if we are to establish settings where our students will be learning by using the visual, communicative, and performative arts. We have to ask ourselves: "What philosophy of classroom instruction can accommodate all of the differences that our students bring to our classroom?" We propose a theory of differentiated instruction in well-managed classrooms which promotes individual student learning while supporting each child's growth toward literate independence.

DIFFERENTIATED INSTRUCTION

Differentiated instruction, with philosophical roots in Dewey's (1915, 1916) concepts of progressive education, Vygotsky's (1986) theory of proximal development, and Gardner's (1993) theory of multiple intelligences, has emerged as a 21st century mandate for educators (Lapp & Flood, 2004; Popkewitz, 1998; Tomlinson, 1996, 1999). While effective teachers have long been aware of cultural, linguistic, motivational, and knowledge differences that exist among their students, and while they have regularly crafted instruction to individualize their instruction to cultivate the strengths embedded in these differences (Allington & Johnston, 2002; Bond & Dykstra, 1997; Brophy & Evertson, 1976; Haycock, 1998; Lapp, 1980; Marzano, Marzano, & Pickering, 2003; Vaughn, Moody, & Schumm, 1998; Wright, Horn, Sanders, 1997), their attempts at universal individualization have often fallen short of the mark due to management issues within classrooms (Tomlinson, 1999). To put it succinctly, teachers have found it extremely difficult to have 20 to 30 or more individual lessons occurring at one time.

Four principles that define differentiated instruction as noted by Lapp and Flood (2004) included,

1. All students are unique and their differences do not necessarily remain constant. Their strengths and needs change as their literacy develops and as their knowledge grows.
2. Instruction that attempts to meet the needs of all students must be flexible and adaptable for each individual.
3. Assessment of students' strengths and needs must be continuous to ensure that each learns all he/she can.
4. Instruction must be multisensory with learning opportunities that rely on all of the senses, and it must be scaffolded for each student's learning differences.

Differentiated instruction differs from individualized instruction most significantly in the area of management (Evertson & Weinstein, 2006). While individualized instruction attempts to meet the needs of children through unique lessons for each child it does not rely on the use of an effective management system to ensure the efficient use of time during the school day (Tomlinson, 1999). In contrast, Butler, Elaschuk, and Poole (2000) have argued that well implemented differentiated instruction takes full advantage of all we know about the principles of effective instruction, especially in the areas of pacing, choice, and grouping.

Teachers who implement differentiated instruction begin where students are when they arrive in their classroom. They accept and act on the premise that they must be ready to engage students through different learning modalities, by appealing to differing interests, and by using varied rates of instruction along with varied degrees of complexity (Tomlinson, 1996, 1999).

A major goal in differentiated classrooms is to provide specific ways for each individual to learn as deeply as possible. Teachers in differentiated classes use time flexibly; they call upon a range of instructional strategies and become partners with their students to see that both what is learned and the learning environment are shaped to the learner. They begin with a clear sense of what constitutes powerful curriculum and engaging instruction. Then they modify that instruction so that each learner comes away with understandings and skills that offer guidance to the next phase of their learning. Essentially, teachers in differentiated classrooms accept and plan for the fact that learners bring many commonalities to school, but that they also bring critical differences (Lapp & Flood, 2004).

When thinking about differentiated curriculum and instruction, there are crucial questions to consider. What is the teacher differentiating? How is the teacher differentiating? Why is the teacher differentiating? (Tomlinson, 1996, 1999). If differentiation is effective it must include the modification of curricular elements that the teacher alters in response to students' learning needs including content (what students will learn and the materials used); process (activities through which students make sense of key ideas using essential skills); product (how students demonstrate and extend what they understand and can do as a result of a span of learning); and environment (e.g., the classroom conditions that set the tone and expectation of learning) (Flood & Lapp, 2004).

DESIGNING AND MANAGING EFFECTIVE DIFFERENTIATED INSTRUCTION

One of the most important roles assumed by the effective teacher is that of classroom manager (Evertson & Weinstein, 2006). As the classroom manager the teacher designs curriculum and instruction that is implemented in an environment offering many differentiated and varied language and literacy learning experiences. The better managed the classroom the greater success students will have (Wang, Haertel, & Wahlberg, 1993) and the more powerful will be the relationships which occur among students and their teacher and students among themselves (Marzano, Marzano, & Pickering, 2003).

Effective learning occurs in differentiated classrooms where there are no misconceptions about expectations, responsibilities, and consequences regarding classroom rules and goals for student/teacher behaviors; independent and group work practices; procedures for beginning and ending the day; routines for transitioning between and during lessons and activities; and procedures when using materials and equipment (Evertson & Emmer, 1982; Evertson & Weinstein, 2006; Glasser, 1969, 1990, 1998, 2000).

Throughout the history of literacy education, scholars have aligned themselves with Dewey (1938), who suggested that students' learning of skills and concepts should occur through experience based on instruction that supports their meaning-making (Brooks, 2002; Gage, 1978; Graves, 1983; Langer & Allington, 1992; Lapp & Flood, 1978, 2005; Nystrand & Gamoran, 1997; Pearson, 1984) or other scholars who supported the notions of Hume (1963) that students' mastery of decontextualized information should occur through practice (Bloom, 1971; Hirsch, 1996; Rosenshine, 1971; Skinner, 1974; Torgensen, 1998). Regardless of where scholars place themselves in this discussion they all agree that the learner grows in a supportive environment while engaging in substantive, collaborative interactions with other students and with the teacher (Barnes, 1976; Johnston, 2004; Langer, 1995, 2004; Larsen, 1998; Nystrand, Gamoran, & Heck, 1992; Ornish, 1997; Raphael & McMahon, 1994; Roser & Martinez, 1995; Slavin, 1983; Swing & Peterson, 1982).

Pressley, Wharton-McDonald, Allington, Block, Morrow, et al. in their *Effective Teacher* studies (2001) noted that effective teachers of literacy engaged in a diverse array of instructional practices within an environment of differentiated instruction that fostered the development of visual, communicative and performative arts learning for all. They maintained that effective teachers always establish a complex yet transparent set of management routines, which they use to ensure minimal disruption in their classrooms and maximal amounts of time spent on learning. In the classrooms of effective teachers, who are differentiating their instruction, almost all of their time is spent on instruction in an atmosphere of support and encouragement and a visual environment where developing learners feel comfortable to take risks (Cochran & Lytle, 1999; Shulman, 1986).

Flexible Grouping Patterns Supported by Continuous Evaluation

Differentiated instruction has proven to be most effective when it incorporates effective instructional and grouping practices, appropriate materials, and differential pacing practices (Doyle, 1986; Evertson & Weinstein, 2006; Good & Brophy, 2003; Nastasi & Clements, 1991; Slavin, 1996).

Accommodating individual learning differences occurs when teachers focus on each student's strengths and needs through instruction occurring in a variety of grouping patterns (individual, partner, small and whole-class groups) with a range of materials. Instruction which is designed to acknowledge and support student differences is situated in Bakhtin's (1981) notion of heteroglossia which noted that all learning occurs through the personal expansions of one's experiences while engaging in encounters that require the individual to view a situation from the perspective of the learner, the teacher, and the investigator. Through dialogue with others who have a wide array of different cultural, personal, and knowledge perspectives to bring to the situation, the learner is able to expand his own perspective (Kozminsky & Kozminsky, 2003).

In order to accommodate these differences teachers need to implement flexible grouping practices. A major rationale for implementing flexible grouping is that no single type of classroom arrangement can be entirely conducive for meeting the needs of every student. This has recently been documented by many teachers who have witnessed the ill effects of long-term ability grouping on students that did not allow time for focused teacher-directed interactions with individuals and with small groups of students with similar needs or strengths (Allington, 1983; Hiebert, 1983; Pallas, Entwisle, Alexander, & Stluka, 1994). These flexible grouping practices include but are not exclusive to

1. One-to-one teaching events in which teachers tailor instruction to meet individual needs. This occurs as the teacher confers individually with one student while the other students are working independently on assignments;
2. Partner time in which students talk and work together on a designated topic, and the teacher may be near the two students and able to engage in uninterrupted dialogue and problem solving;
3. Small-group instruction in which the teacher works with students who have similar instructional strengths or needs. Effective groups require the teacher to be in close proximity with students so that quick, supportive responses can be immediate and exact;
4. Whole-class instruction that provides general input and information that is needed by all students as they practice and review content information.

Continuous evaluation of each student's instructional needs supports a classroom with flexible learning formats such as whole group, small group (homogeneous and heterogeneous), partners (homogeneous and heterogeneous), one-to-one (student & teacher), and peer tutoring (older and younger students), in which explicit, direct, and indirect instruction can occur.

Flexible grouping formats provide the means through which teachers can offer the most effective teaching and learning experiences for each child (DeVries & Edwards, 1974; Lapp, Fisher, & Flood, 1999; Slavin, 1996). Students who grasp a concept that is introduced through a whole group format may become bored and unchallenged as the information is retaught in a different manner in an attempt to ensure mastery for those who did not totally understand it during the first presentation. The next steps in their instruction should accommodate such variability (Roller, 1996).

Materials

While striving to help children acquire meaning in their learning, effective teachers use a wide variety of instructional materials and practices as they work with their students to develop their language and knowledge bases. They continually ask high-level questions that require their students to draw inferences and think beyond the text. Effective teachers help students make connections from many different materials at their appropriate reading levels, and they use flexible grouping to share instruction that meets the individual needs while supporting the strengths of each of their students. A wide array of materials written at different levels makes information accessible to students. This range of materials should include,

Pacing. Depending upon prior content knowledge, students require different levels of pacing when material is presented. Differentiated instruction requires that lessons be accelerated for some students and decelerated for others. It often requires the repetition of a lesson for students who are struggling with the content or the language of the lesson.

Components of Effective Differentiated Instruction

Effective differentiated instruction is an individualized instructional program that contains a complex management system which enables the learning program to function for all students in a classroom. In order to more fully understand the concept of differentiated instruction, it is imperative to jointly analyze the effectiveness of its requisite components: (a) the learner, and (b) the types of instruction necessary for inclusion as an example of effective differentiated instruction.

Differentiated instruction researchers who build models of effective instruction examine the role of learners and teachers within the contexts of instructional variables that impact on the success of the models (Butler & Winne, 1995). The primary characteristic of effective learners in differentiated classrooms is their ability and willingness to self regulate. The variables that are critical to differentiated instruction are a self-regulated learner, types of instruction, and instructional strategies.

Self-regulated, motivated, and engaged learners. Self-regulated learners recursively engage in a cycle of learning activities as they work through visual, communicative, and performative tasks (Butler and Winne, 1995; Zimmerman, 1994). Self-regulated learners analyze task demands and draw upon prior knowledge as they go about completing the tasks. They base their subsequent decisions about the most effective strategies to use to complete the task on their perception of the task demands.

Based on the requirements for a particular task, self-regulated learners select, adapt, and even invent strategic approaches to achieve task objectives. Once self-regulated learners implement strategies, they can consistently monitor outcomes associated with strategy use. Effective learners self-evaluate by comparing progress against task criteria. They monitor themselves and generate judgments about progress.

To promote self-regulation in students, teachers must assist them in engaging flexibly and adaptively in a cycle of cognitive activities (e.g., task analysis, strategy selection and use, and self-monitoring). The teacher's goals include promoting students' instruction of metacognitive knowledge about academic work; strategies for analyzing tasks; metacognitive knowledge about task-specific strategies; skills for implanting strategies; and strategies for self-monitoring and strategic use of feedback. Strategy instruction alone is not sufficient. Instead what is required is explicit attention to how students adapt strategies reflectively within recursive cycles of task analysis, strategy-use and, monitoring (Butler & Winne, 1995; Harris & Graham, 1996).

For differentiated instruction to be effective student's positive self-perceptions of confidence and motivational beliefs must be fostered (Borkowski, 1992; Schunk, 1994). Student's perceptions of self-efficacy, which has been defined as "beliefs about their capabilities to exercise control over their own level of functioning and over events that affect their lives" are critical to engagement (Bandura, 1993, p. 118). Students' perception of self-efficacy influences the goals they set, their commitment to these goals, and the learning strategies they use to complete these goals (Schunk, 1994). Low perceptions of self-efficacy undermine students' willingness to invest in academic tasks.

Attributions are student's causal explanations for success or failure (Borkowski, 1992; Schunk, 1994.) Productive attributional beliefs, which support strategic performance, link outcomes to controllable factors such as applying effort and using strategies. Unproductive attributional patterns reflect low perceptions of control and undermine student engagement and learning.

Types of learning in effective differentiated instructional classrooms. Keefe and Jenkins (2000) maintained that personalized instruction is the hallmark of differentiated instruction and the following types of learning, which are all designed around personalized instruction principles, are requisite elements. Each of these types of learning must be evident in a differentiated instruction classroom in order for or it to be classified as an example of effective differentiated instruction (Lapp and Flood, 2004; Flood and Lapp, 2004): individualized instruction, accelerated learning, technology assisted instruction, contract learning, authentic pedagogy, guided practice, cooperative learning, independent study, independent learning centers, complex questions, and tiered activities.

DIFFERENTIATED INSTRUCTION IN ACTION

While there is no one system that will meet everyone's needs, Lapp and Flood (2004) have demonstrated the effectiveness of an instructional model for implementing effective differentiated instruction. The model, *Center Activity Rotation System* (CARS), emphasizes how well-researched principles of effective differentiated instruction can be implemented in elementary classrooms. In their 2004 paper, the researchers described schools and classrooms in which CARS had been used effectively with students in the primary and intermediate grades (Lapp & Flood, 2004).

CARS is a system that supports teachers' attempts to meet the instructional needs of all of their students through flexible grouping practices. As shown in Fig. 55.1, predetermined, intact, heterogeneous student groups rotate through all centers, except the teacher center, for a specified amount of time, which is decided by the teacher. As the heterogeneous groups rotate, individuals who have similar strengths or needs are called from each group to visit the Teacher Center for specific instruction. A makeup period allows all students to visit the center they missed during the times when they were meeting with the teacher at the Teacher Center.

Students at the regular centers work in heterogeneous groups on specific tasks/activities associated with the targeted content area or skills development that students need. While these activities are topically related and often culminate in shared group discussion they are leveled to accommodate the individual differences of the children working at each center. Meanwhile, students with similar instructional needs or strengths meet at the Teacher Center for focused instruction. This allows the teacher to target the learning development of individuals in the classroom while providing a rich learning environment for the entire classroom community. CARS may be used with students at any grade who are studying any curriculum area.

ENVISIONING MULTIMODAL CLASSROOMS THAT FOSTER THE INTEGRATION OF THE VISUAL, COMMUNICATIVE, AND PERFORMATIVE ARTS

While we are all anxious for classrooms to reflect what we know about the visual, communicative, and performative arts in schools throughout the world, we still need a philosophical base for the type of instruction that we will use to guide the transition from classrooms of today to effective multimodal classrooms of the future. The philosophy that we recommend is differentiated instruction through classroom organization and management.

Differentiation instruction, with its complex philosophical constructs, detailed attention to learner and learning variables, and its requirement for a technologically advanced management system to implement the instruction, is a new mandate for educators in the same way as is the editors of this *Handbook* call for teacher development in new understandings about the relationships among literacy and the visual, communicative, and performative arts. In the past, educators have given considerable attention to the concept of individualized instruction, but they have always been constrained in implementation by a lack of management theory and procedures. As we have suggested in this chapter, differentiated instruction, with its requisite management system, provides a clear path for meeting

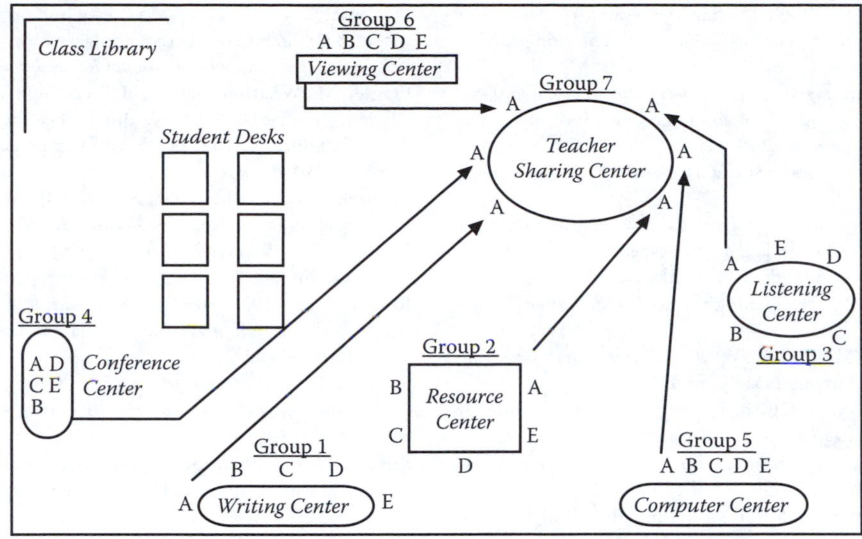

FIGURE 55.1. Center Activity Rotation System (CARS).

the needs of all students as they use the visual, communicative, and performative arts as the critical cores of their learning.

REFERENCES

Allington, R. L. (1983). The reading instruction provided readers of differing reading abilities. *Elementary School Journal, 83*, 548–559.

Allington, R. L., & Johnston, P. (2002). *Reading to learn: Lessons from exemplary fourth-grade classrooms*. New York: Guilford Press.

Bakhtin, M. M. (1981). *The dialogic imagination*. Austin: University of Texas Press.

Bandura, A. (1993). Perceived self-efficacy in cognitive development and functioning. *Educational Psychologist, 28*, 117–148.

Barnes, D. (1976). *Communication and curriculum*. London: Penguin.

Bloom, B. S. (1971). Master learning and its implications for curriculum development. In E. W. Eisner (Ed.), *Confronting curriculum reform*. Boston: Little, Brown.

Bond, G. L., & Dykstra, R. (1997). The cooperative research program in first-grade reading instruction. *Reading Research Quarterly, 32*, 348–427.

Borkowski, J. G. (1992). Metacognitive theory: A framework for teaching literacy, writing, and math skills. *Journal of Learning Disabilities, 25*, 253–257.

Brooks, J. G. (2002). *Schooling for life: Reclaiming the essence of learning*. Alexandria, VA: Association for Supervision and Curriculum Development.

Brophy, J. E., & Evertson, C. M. (1976). *Learning from teaching: A developmental perspective*. Boston: Allyn & Bacon.

Butler, D. L., Elaschuk, C. L., & Poole, S. L. (2000). Promoting strategic writing by postsecondary students with learning disabilities: A report of three case studies. *Learning Disability Quarterly, 23*, 196–213.

Butler, D. L., & Winne, P. H. (1995). Feedback and self-regulated learning; A theoretical synthesis. *Review of Educational Research, 65*, 245–281.

Cochran, M., & Lytle, S. (1999). Relationship of knowledge and practice: Teacher learning in communities. In A. Iran-Nejad & P. D. Pearson (Eds.), *Review of research in education* (pp. 249–306). Washington, DC: American Educational Research Association.

DeVries, D., & Edwards, K. (1974). Student teams and learning groups. Their effects on cross-race and cross-sex interaction. *Journal of Educational Psychology, 66*, 741–749.

Dewey, J. (1915). *The school and society*. Chicago: University of Chicago Press.

Dewey, J. (1916). *Democracy and education: An introduction to the philosophy of education*. New York: Macmillan.

Dewey, J. (1938). *Experience and education*. New York: Macmillan.

Doyle, W. (1986). Classroom organization and management. In M. C. Wittrock (Ed.), *Handbook of research on teaching* (pp. 392–431). New York: Macmillan.

Evertson, C. M., & Emmer, E. T. (1982). Preventive classroom management. In D. Duke (Ed.), *Helping teachers manage classrooms* (pp. 2–31). Alexandria, VA: Association for Supervision of Curriculum Development.

Evertson, C. M., & Weinstein, C. S. (Eds.) (2006). *Handbook of classroom management: Research, practice, and contemporary issues*. Hillsdale, NJ: Erlbaum.

Flood, J., & Lapp, D. (2004). *Differentiated instruction: Research and practice*. Paper presented at the California Reading Association, San Jose, CA.

Gage, N. L. (1978). *The scientific basis of the art of teaching*. New York: Teachers College Press.

Gardner, H. (1993). *Multiple intelligences: The theory in practice*. New York: Basic Books.

Glasser, W. (1969). *Schools without failure*. New York: Harper & Row.

Glasser, W. (1990). *The quality school: Managing students without coercion*. New York: Harper & Row.

Glasser, W. (1998). *Choice theory*. New York, Harper Collins.

Glasser, W. (2000). *Every student can succeed*. Chula Vista, CA: Black Forest Press.

Good, T. L., & Brophy, J. E. (2003). *Looking in classrooms*. Boston: Allyn & Bacon.

Graves, D. (1983). *Writing: Teachers and children at work*. Exeter, NH: Heinemann.

Harris, K. R., & Graham, S. (1996). Making the writing process work: Strategies for composition and self-regulation. Cambridge, MA: Brookline.

Haycock, K. (1998). *Good teaching matters . . . a lot. Thinking K–16, 3,* 1–4.

Hiebert, E. H. (1983). An examination of ability grouping for instruction. *Reading Research Quarterly, 18,* 231–235.

Hirsch, E. D. (1996). *The schools we need and why we don't have them.* New York: Doubleday.

Hume, D. (1963). *An enquiry concerning human understanding and selections from a treatise of human nature.* LaSalle, IL: Open Court.

Johnston, P. (2004). *Choice words.* York, MN: Stenhouse Publishers.

Joyce, B., & Showers, B. (1982). The coaching of teaching. *Educational Leadership, 40*(1), 4–10.

Keefe, J. W., & Jenkins, J. M. (2000). *Personalized instruction: Changing classroom practice.* Larchmont, NY: Eye on Education.

Kozminsky, E., & Kozminsky, L. (2003). Improving motivation through dialogue. *Educational Leadership, 61,* 50–53.

Langer, J. A. (1995). *Envisioning literature: Literary understanding and literature instruction.* New York: Teachers College Press.

Langer, J. A. (2004). Beating the odds: Teaching middle and high school students to read and write well. *American Educational Research Journal, 38,* 837–880.

Langer, J. A., & Allington, R. L. (1992). Curriculum research in writing and reading. In P. W. Jackson (Ed.), *Handbook on research on curriculum* (pp. 687–725). New York: Macmillan.

Lapp, D. (1980). (Ed.). *Making reading possible through effective classroom management.* Newark, DE: International Reading Association.

Lapp, D., Fisher, D., & Flood, J. (1999). Does it matter how you're grouped for instruction? YES! Flexible grouping patterns promote student learning. *California Reader, 33*(1), 28–32.

Lapp, D., & Flood, J. (1978). *Teaching reading to every child.* New York: Macmillan.

Lapp, D., & Flood, J. (2004). *Differentiated instruction.* Paper presented at International Reading Association Conference, Reno, NV.

Lapp, D., & Flood, J. (2005). Exemplary reading instruction in the elementary school: How reading develops, how students learn and how teachers teach. In J. Flood & P. Anders (Eds.), *Literacy development of students in urban schools.* Newark, DE: International Reading Association.

Larsen, J. (1998). Managing student aggression in high schools: Implications for practice. *Psychology in the Schools, 35,* 283–295.

Marzano, R. J., Marzano, J. S., & Pickering, D. J. (2003). *Classroom management that works.* Alexandria,VA: Association for Supervision and Curriculum Development.

Nastasi, B. K., & Clements, D. H. (1991). Research on cooperative learning: Implications for practice. *School Psychology Review, 20,* 110–131.

Nystrand, M., & Gamoran, A. (1997). *Opening dialogue.* New York: Teacher's College Press.

Nystrand, M., Gamoran, A., & Heck, M. J. (1992). Using small groups for response to and thinking about literature. *English Journal, 83,* 14–22.

Ornish, D. (1997). *Love and survival.* New York: Harper Collins.

Pallas, A. M., Entwisle, D. R., Alexander, K. L., & Stluka, M. F. (1994). Ability-group effects: Instructional, social or institutional? *Sociology of Education, 67,* 27–46.

Pearson, P. D. (1984). Direct explicit teaching of reading comprehension. In G. G. Duffy, L. R. Roehler, & J. Mason (Eds.), *Comprehension instruction: Perspectives and suggestions* (pp. 222–233). New York: Longman.

Popkewitz, T. (1998). Dewey, Vygotsky, and the social administration of the individual: Constructivist pedagogy as systems of ideas in historical spaces. *American Educational Research Journal, 35,* 535–570.

Pressley, M., Wharton-McDonald, R., Allington, R., Block, C. C., Morrow, L., Tracey, D., Baker, K., Brooks, G., Cronin, J., Nelson, E., & Woo, D. (2001). A study of effective first-grade literacy instruction. *Scientific Studies of Reading, 5,* 35–58.

Raphael, T. E., & McMahon, S. I. (1994). An alternative framework for reading instruction. *The Reading Teacher, 48,* 102–116.

Roller, C. M. (1996). *Variability not disability.* Newark, DE: International Reading Association.

Rosenshine, B. (1971). *Teaching behaviours and student achievement.* Windsor, England: National Foundation for Educational Research in England and Wales.

Roser, N. L., & Martinez, M. G. (Eds.) (1995). *Booktalk and beyond: Children and teachers respond to literature.* Newark, DE: International Reading Association.

Schunk, D. H. (1994). Self-regulation of self-efficacy and attributions in academic settings. In D. H. Schunk & B. J. Zimmerman (Eds.), *Self-regulation of learning and performance: Issues and educational application* (pp. 75–99). Hillsdale, NJ: Erlbaum.

Shulman, L. S. (1986). Paradigms and research programs in the study of teaching: A contemporary perspective. In M. C. Wittrock (Ed.), *Handbook of research on teaching (3rd ed.).* (pp. 3–36). New York: Macmillan.

Skinner, B. F. (1974). *About behaviorism.* New York: Vintage Books.

Slavin, R. E. (1983). *Cooperative learning.* New York: Longman.

Slavin, R. E. (1996). A cooperative learning approach to content area teaching. In D. Lapp, J. Flood, & N. Farnan (Eds.), *Content area reading and learning: Instructional strategies* (pp. 369–382). Needham Heights, MA: Allyn & Bacon.

Swing, S. R., & Peterson, P. L. (1982). The relationship of student ability and small group interaction to student achievement. *American Educational Research Journal, 19,* 259–274.

Tomlinson, C. A. (1996). *How to differentiate instruction in mixed-ability classrooms.* Alexandria: VA: Association for Supervision and Curriculum Development.

Tomlinson, C. A. (1999). Leadership for a differentiated classroom. *School Administrator, 56*(9), 11.

Torgensen, J. K. (1998). Instructional interventions for children with reading disabilities. In B. K. Shapiro, P. J. Accardo, & A. J. Capute (Eds.), *Specific reading disability: A view of the spectrum* (pp. 197–200). Parkton, MD: York.

Vaughn, S., Moody, S. W., & Schumm, J. S. (1998). Broken promises: Reading instruction in the resource room. *Exceptional Children, 64,* 211–225.

Vygotsky, L. (1986). *Thought and language.* Cambridge, MA: MIT Press.

Wang, M. C., Haertel, G. D., & Wahlberg, H. J. (1993). Toward a knowledge base for school learning. *Review of Educational Research, 63,* 249–294.

Wright, S. P., Horn, S. P., & Sanders, W. L. (1997). Teacher and classroom contexts on student achievement: Implications for teacher evaluation. *Journal of Personnel Evaluation in Education, 11,* 57–67.

Zimmerman, B. J. (1994). Dimensions of academic self-regulation. A conceptual framework for education. In D. H. Schunk & B. J. Zimmerman (Eds.), *Self-regulation of learning and performance; Issues and educational applications* (pp. 3–21). Hillsdale, NJ: Erlbaum.

IV

VOICES FROM THE FIELD

PICTURES AS PART OF A NORMAL SCHOOL DAY: THIRD GRADE

Molly Bang
SCHOLASTIC BLUE SKY PRESS

I am exploring with children what it is to make pictures because I want to find out what children are interested in and what they are capable of doing with the picture form as they mature. I earn a living as a writer/illustrator of children's books and have been working as a volunteer in the Falmouth public schools when my schedule and the teachers' permit.

I had noticed that most second graders still consider themselves capable artists. It is usually by about the third grade that children decide that Sasha and Juan are the artists of the class and everybody else is not. Because of this, I decided to begin working with third graders to see if all the children in a class could know that they are artists. I also wanted to see whether I could figure out ways to use art that any third-grade teacher, regardless of his or her art background, could use with a class.

I asked a third-grade teacher, Bob Schuman, if I might work in his class for about an hour or so every day for 8 weeks to see what we could do with art. He was intrigued with the idea, he said, because of all the classes he had had in some 30 years of teaching, these children as a group seemed the least artistically inclined. "They are wonderful kids," he said, "but they just aren't artists. It will be a challenge to bring it out of them." I could not have been happier. I had no idea what I was going to do. I had done some reading and had lived with a growing child for 13 years, but I had no ideas about developmental theory or about what third graders are capable of. What I did have was some sense of what pictures are about, and I loved to use them to play. I also felt that each child has something special and important to say. I hoped that this would be enough to work with.

I needed to find out what the children were doing already, so I began by watching them. They had all written book reports on biographies of famous people, and they were in the process of drawing a portrait of their chosen person.

I looked over the pictures. The pictures were all on large sheets of Manila paper, but there was a wide variety in their choices of the size of the figure, in whether or not there was a background, and in their use of pencils, crayons, and magic markers. There was certainly plenty to work with here. I began on a cold wet day in March.

We sat in a group and went over the pictures one by one. I asked five questions, which we listed on the board.

1. What was this person famous for?
2. How might this be shown?
3. What DOES work in this picture?
4. What is unusual in this picture?
5. How might the empty space be used?

This took about 20 minutes, but by the end of the short session, the children had seen each other's work, had analyzed it, and had gotten new ideas for their own pictures. Several cut out their central figure and pasted it onto a new sheet so they could do more with the background. Most of them referred to their books for details of dress or background, and the inevitable question came up, "Can I copy?"

There seems to be a horror of copying in U.S. education, especially where "art" is concerned, and I think it is one of the most peculiar misconceptions we could have. We **live** by copying. I asked the children how we learned to talk: Did we invent the words ourselves? How did we learn to walk? I described the wild boy of Avedon, and how he had been unable to talk, and could only talk and run like the wolves that had raised him, but could not walk upright like a human. The children thought of everything we do and how we learn it: We learn to eat with utensils, ride a bike, brush our teeth, and read and write, all by copying. Any human activity, including art, is learned all largely (we do seem to eat, cry, and excrete instinctually) by copying others and building on this mimicry. The best artists have painted copies of the works of artists they most admire, because they know this is the best way to learn just how they painted. Only when a copy is made that looks **exactly** like the original and the artist pretends that he or she came up with the idea first is it not advisable. I told them that in art, this is called forgery and in writing or ideas, it is called plagiarism, and we get arrested for it. Otherwise, copy, copy, copy! Two precepts came out of this discussion: Copying is the highest form of flattery, and when you do copy something, give credit to the person who first thought of it.

The children finished their pictures by the next day. We looked at them again and noticed the changes each student had made and how they changes had affected the picture. We also looked at what we noticed first in the pictures and why. Bob put the pictures up around the room, and I returned the next day full of enthusiasm for my new project: Since our hands were the tools we were using to make our pictures, we could begin by drawing our hands. "Can we trace?" they asked? "No way. Try to look, and put down what you see." Dutifully they set to work. In about 3 minutes, their hands were done and they started getting bored and restless. We looked at their work.

On these great sheets of manila paper where they had made large portraits, they now had only made the most miniscule, stiff, and pitiful scratchings I had ever seen. I asked them to make their hands BIG, so big they would take up the whole page. They turned the paper over and in about 3 minutes they had redone the same hands. One child had colored in his bracelet, another added wrinkles, and a third had drawn a large shadow cast by his hand. Otherwise, they were pitiful.

We sat and discussed what was going on. I said it looked to me like they hated this project. They said it was stupid, that somebody might see their picture and think it was stupid, that it was boring to draw your hand, that they were embarrassed, that it was too hard, and that they might make a mistake. I agreed with them that it is hard, and that we are embarrassed when people look at our work. I asked them what sort of pictures **they** wanted to draw. They said they wanted to draw things so these things looked **real**. I said I would do what I could to help them do this, but I made one request: if they were going to make mistakes, I did not want to see scrinchy little mistakes but GREAT BIG ones, and the only way to make GREAT BIG MISTAKES was to make GREAT BIG PICTURES.

I could not think of anything to suggest at the moment as a project except that, since we all found the picture of the hand with the shadow the most interesting, we try drawing our hands a third time, but this time look at shadows like in the one picture. We went to the window and saw what shapes the hands cast; we turned on two small desk lamps sitting on one table. Again, the children drew, but this time their pictures were truly awful and they themselves were wild. It was not a successful day. As I sat at home trying to figure out what I could do next, the only thing that came to mind was that they had not seemed to LOOK at their hands. They had all drawn the way a hand SHOULD look—flat, with five fingers. They had drawn the shadows they way they SHOULD look, but I had rarely seen a child really LOOKING at the shadows, or at his or her hand. I wondered what I might do to help them slow down, help them LOOK, and also help them to play with the whole page.

The following day, I had them work in pairs. One person in the pair was to choose a color of magic marker. (These were the big markers, with squared nibs.) The second child then chose a color that complemented it—a color the first color seemed to want. Directions: The first person make a shape. The second person make a shape that answers it or goes with it, for example, one person might make a blob and the second make a curve around it, or another similar blob on the other side of the picture. We brainstormed about various shapes they might make. They were to take turns back and forth until the whole picture was filled. The children loved this exercise, and for the most part they worked enthusiastically. After about 15 minutes, we brought our pictures over to the rug to discuss them.

Now the pictures were quite different from what I was expecting. I was expecting simple abstract SHAPES. The children drew THINGS. I did not say anything about this; I wanted to see what they noticed on their own.

The children noticed that two of the boys had not made a picture; they looked like they were trying to **destroy** each other. (This had been the case. They had scribbled over each other's work.) They noticed that two girls had things floating all over the page and needed to fill it up more. They noticed that one girl had put shadows in her picture, using what we had done the day before. One picture had little blobs floating in the air with balloons coming out of their mouths that said, "Hi!" This is what these children had thought that I had meant by "having the shapes answer each other." For the most part, they seemed to be noticing details without having any sense of the overall picture. I asked them to finish their pictures, and to try and use something they had noticed in someone else's picture. Again they worked. I walked around the room, asking questions like, "How did you get that great purple? It looks good when you overlay the two like that; you get a third color." "How else could use red?" or "What are you going to do with this space up here?" and "You look like you've come to a standstill; would you get more ideas if you traded colors with each other?" After about 10 minutes, we came back once again to the rug.

I told the class that I had had them play with this exercise so they could work on looking, which they seem to need to play with some more, and that looking is the core of what an artist does. Look, paint, look, analyze, paint, and on and on. We looked at the pictures again. This time I led the discussion more.

I held up two pictures by boys and asked the artists to describe what they had done. One was of a hockey game, and the boys described how each color had been a different team, but then they had mixed them up for some details, and they described what had happened in the game. The other pair of boys had made a battle scene, and they told us blow by blow about the fight with the dragon and the enemies. I asked how these were different from the other pictures. The class saw very clearly that these children had set up a game with their pictures. As one girl put it, "They weren't making a picture, they were playing games." I said yes, but they were making a picture, too. The girls did very different things. Either they had made designs, usually of hearts and squiggles, or they had worked out a little play in the picture: "now she is leaving the house and she says . . . and this one gives her . . ."

This to me points out the whole peculiarity of pictures. We see only the finished product, but the delight of making pictures is in the process. It is the process, the unfolding, that is the game. The children could become very involved in the game, but they did not seem to have a clear idea of the picture as picture. My problem as their teacher is that I think the process is easily as important as the finished product, and I did not want to lose this sense of involvement, but I also wanted them so start seeing how pictures work as pictures.

The next day there was an odd number of children, so I became Jonathan's partner. He chose chartreuse. I chose orange. He made a shape, and I drew a pattern out of it. He drew another pattern; I filled in the space he had made. We worked back and forth, and in about 5 or 10 minutes I called the children to the rug. We looked at several pictures and discussed them, but they wanted to see what I (the Teacher, the Artist) had done. I showed them, and asked Jonathan to describe what we had done. He said he had drawn a bog, but I had made zigzags on it so then he made another shape growing out of it, and we kept going like that. We turned it upside down. The children were intrigued. They thought it looked weird, but they also wanted to try it.

This time, I set them up as boy-girl partners. I told them there were two reasons I was doing this: one, many of them were talking too much, not about pictures, and I wanted them to talk with their markers, not with their mouths. Two, that I wanted them to stretch their minds here, and that since, as we had all noticed, the boys and girls tended to do different things, I wanted to see what they might do as mixed partners. They made faces and objected strenuously. I put my foot down here.

> All our lives we have to work with other people. Some we'll like and some we won't. I don't want to stop you from having your feelings. Feelings are part of being a person: happy, sad, angry, calm. But I want each of you to treat each other with respect, no matter what you feel. If you have violent feelings, put those feelings into your hand and let them out of the magic marker onto the paper. This is a new and strange job we're doing, and a lot of us feel a little scared and hesitant about it. We need to support each other here, to help each other. Put your feelings in your pictures.

In grandly suppressed distaste, the children set to work. At the beginning, they tended to each work in their own corner of the page, but they gradually came out more and more toward each other. I asked them if there were spaces they might not want to color in. I asked them to work on the whole page, and not just one corner. Two of the couples were still avoiding each other after 5 minutes, so I asked them to see what would happen if they turned the paper around. This helped them integrate the pieces better.

When we sat on the rug and looked at them, they were delighted, and so was I. We discussed what some different children had done, but I noticed that in most of the pictures the pieces were floating around in space. There were no connections. I told them this, and we brainstormed about what sorts of connections they might make. They went back to work and we returned in another 10 or 15 minutes.

Their connections, both with lines and colors, made the pictures real delights.

> "Their connections are like roads and they go the things."
> "That looks like God's face and this is like a ladder through the sky."

The most triumphant pair was Heather and Glenn. Halfway through, Glenn had become furious with the picture and had crumpled it up and thrown it in the trash. I took it out and looked at it, and it looked fine to me. Glenn tearfully told me everything that was wrong with it; I told him what I liked about it, and I suggested that they see what connections might do. When we looked at their picture, Glenn said proudly, "We took our mistake and fixed it!" The others agreed that it was "awesome."

I saw that the children could begin to analyze pictures in a group, but I wanted to have a way of doing it on their own as well. I decided to see whether Donald Grave's method of using notebooks with writing as they worked might help in the same way with pictures, and might enhance their writing and thinking at the same time.

The following day I distributed the notebooks and told the class that these were for writing whatever they wanted to about picture making. For the first day, I asked them to write something in their partner's book, about how they had worked, and then to write in their own books whatever they wanted. I said I would collect them all at the end of the week and write things back to them, that they wouldn't be graded, but it would be a way for me to talk with them each in private.

I told them that tomorrow we would be starting a new project but that today I wanted them to finish up their "together" pictures, this time trying to fill in some of the blank areas with color and to look at the corners to see what they might do with them. We could all see from their pictures that they had enough of this project. They did fill in some spaces, but they did not understand why they were doing it, and they did "do something" to the corners: They quickly made the same design in each corner. I made a mental note not to force them to do things they didn't understand and that I hadn't explored with them first. One child still felt very uncomfortable about the whole process. "These pictures are all weird," she said.

I wanted to help them make pictures with "real things," but after looking through their notebooks, I decided to work on emotions first. Most of the notebooks were rather restrained and polite, but there were others that were not.

"S. likes to destroy my dezines. Because he likes to." "I didn't think I would work good with him because he's messy. But we made a good picture." "Today me and R. worken together and it was hard because each person has a different opinion. He said we were done but I said we was not." "C. sometimes destroys my things . . . she is lieing." "I disliked being R's partner because I hate him." They clearly had VERY strong feelings about their work and about their classmates, and I wondered if I might be able to channel these emotions and help them deal with them, but without smashing their neighbors in the process.

The next day the children named some feelings, and I wrote them on the board as they suggested them. They came up with a much wider variety than I was expecting—frustrated, angry, happy, sad, awesome, glorious, hurt, broken-hearted, stressed, embarrassed, shy, disgusted, and so forth. I asked them to choose ONE feeling and ONE marker that went with the feeling and to draw shapes that would show it. They could not tell us what their feelings were, but we would have to guess it.

Again, this was hard for many of them. One child tried to draw objects that made him happy. One girl could only draw hearts and houses, and another just watched her marker trace across the page. She was "figuring out." I walked around, sympathized with their difficulties, and watched. They were much more thoughtful and concentrated than usual. We brought the pictures to the rug and discussed them. Bryan had jagged red points. "That's ANGRY," the others said. "He is angry." I asked them how they could tell. "Because it has all those points." "Because it is red." "It looks like a mouth with teeth." Brunel had made a purple broken heart, arrows, and drippy blobs. He explained, "Sometimes when I feel hurt, I think of things that are purple like this because it's my favorite color, and it makes me feel better." The other children agreed that it did look sad.

They seemed to be getting the idea, so I suggested they pick a second color that would help express the feeling, but that they concentrate on abstract shapes rather than the symbols for feelings. This got into a discussion of the difference between symbols, for example, Brunel's arrows and broken heart, and abstract shapes, for example, his drippy blobs.

That night I talked to a friend who has had years of experience teaching children of all levels. I told her I was amazed at how tractable third graders were compared to seventh and eighth graders, at how much they wanted to be shown what was "right," rather than look on their own. "That's third grade," she said. "And so when your teacher says that blue rose looks like THIS—and not like THAT . . ." I wondered if this might not be the reason so many children stop making pictures around this time. They want to do it "right," but their pictures always look "wrong." I hoped I was not going to do this to the children I was working with. I just wanted to LOOK, and experiment, analyze, discuss, and keep looking.

When the course was over and we were showing our work to the parents, I asked the adults about their own experiences with art. Four out of the 20 or 30 parents who came remembered very clearly specific instances when, in second, third, or fourth grade, they had had a teacher who had said their fish or boat was not "right." That had been the last time they had made a picture.

When we began work the next day, several children asked if they could work together; others preferred to work alone. Fine. This day, I could see them finally beginning to work with pictures. Liz used Brunel's idea about purple drips to make her picture look sadder. "I started with those diamonds and tears," she said, "but his purple drippy things looked sadder." Two boys working together realized on their own that when they had started making "crazy," it had turned into "destroying," so they decided on "awesome" and calmed each other down. The children added a third color, overlaid colors, and kept visiting each other to see what was happening.

This was not a quiet class. There were a few times when I asked them to talk with their markers, not with their mouths, but for the most part, their talking and visiting was part of looking at pictures and sharing ideas. They were excited. And their pictures were exciting. We were onto something here.

After we had exulted in our "feeling" pictures, I told them it was time to work on something real at last. It was March, and gray and dreary. And I had recently seen an exhibit of the art of preschoolers in Reggio Emilia, Italy, full of the most extraordinary pictures of poppies. I told them I was going to have them draw flowers.

Now I do not know how many children of any age or gender would really get excited about drawing flowers, but for the boys this was truly like asking them to get excited about emptying the garbage. The girls were less vocal. I did have some idea of the reaction I was going to get, so I ignored it and just asked them to draw the best pictures they could think up of flowers. Their works were not inspired.

They next day I brought in a bouquet of the most varied flowers I could buy at the market. One child brought in a paper cup with crocuses. Another brought in a geranium plant. We looked at them, we smelled them, we touched them, and discussed them and named them, and then they drew, with whatever they wanted—pencils, markers, or crayons. The children looked, and they worked, and they tried, but their pictures were still tight and squinched, no matter how much I asked, urged, and begged them to make them BIG.

The next day, I brought in a large book of paintings by Georgia O'Keefe, and we looked at her flower paintings one by one. The children were amazed. They told me they thought that now they understood what I meant by BIG.

They did. But it wasn't just that they began to make their flowers BIG, and to look at them carefully, but they began to both apply the things they had done in other pictures and to apply what they saw in each other's work. One boy began coloring in his background. We looked at it and discussed what happened to the picture when he did this. "The flower pops out at you!" Then most of the others worked on backgrounds, not just solid colors, but they saw what was behind the flower in the room and drew that—the chalkboard, bookcases, the edge of the table. When a child was having trouble or was sick of coloring in, another would help. All I did was look at their pictures with them and go over the parts of the flowers to see how closely their picture resembled the way the stem ended on the stalk or where the leaves came out. When they were stuck, I asked them what shape the object was—round or squarish—or how they would describe how the pieces fit together. Heather could draw her geranium leaves once she described them as clouds. Brunel. said the lily leaves looked like long pointy bananas. Then he could draw them.

There was one odd gender difference: None of the girls chose the orange lily, but several boys did. The boy who drew the "anger" picture first drew the lily as almost an exact reproduction of that feeling. He saw this himself when I was looking at it with him. "It doesn't have all those petals. They look like spikes. It doesn't look like the flower. I want to do it over again." His second picture was quiet, searching, and thoughtful, and he was much more pleased with it. I was happy with both pictures and with the process.

The only thing I was adamant about with the children was that their work be carefully and thoroughly done. I would not accept pictures in which the background was only partially colored in, sloppily done, or scribbled. I would help them fill in, or hold their paper or hold them, but no shoddy work. This took a solid week, and the flowers drooped, but the pictures were wonderful. They were drawing real things.

The art project was beginning to take up more time than either Bob Schuman or I had anticipated, and although he was delighted with what was going on, he was worried that we were elbowing out other subjects the children should be learning. He said that luckily feelings were one of the subjects the curriculum wanted covered and we had certainly explored that, and he was also worried that the parents would begin to object that so much time was spent on art—a "nonserious" subject.

Now I feel that the children were benefiting in several ways from their work with art. First, they were more in touch with their feelings, and they were expressing them and working them through in their pictures rather than either keeping them inside or exploring onto the other children. Second, they were dealing with real, concrete things just when the school curriculum is steering them into more and more abstract learning: reading, math, social studies, and the like. They were looking carefully, concentrating, experimenting, discussing, and analyzing their work and learning from ach other, which for me is what learning is all about. Lastly, they were excited about what they were doing, and they obviously felt confident and capable. On the other hand, I know what the general public feels about art: that it requires "inspiration" and takes an unusual, slightly illogical person to relate to it. I also agreed that it would be more cohesive for the children if we could "integrate it with the curriculum." We reviewed what the children were learning in their various subjects, and we came up with the idea of using the different food groups as subjects for their pictures. The children thought the idea was fine, but they also said they wanted their pictures to look still "more real" than they were. I told them that we would have to look at the most simple, basic shapes and learn to represent them first, because all things can be seen as combinations of these shapes.

I put three or four shapes on each table: a cube (Cuisinart blocks the class was using for math), a cylinder (rolls of paper towels), spheres (tennis balls) and for some reason I cannot remember, bananas. The children drew these in pencil. I asked them to look carefully at the outside edge of each object, and also to look at shadows: both the shadows that were on the object and the shadows that they cast on the table. We noticed that different faces of the cubes were darker or lighter than others were.

The children arranged the objects themselves, in ways I never would have done. They preferred the tennis balls on top of the paper towels, for example, which for me defiled some order. As I watched them and watched my own reactions, I realized that this arrangement made the tennis balls look ridiculous to me—as well as to them. Didn't they realize that this was serious, that this was still life they were doing? They were making it fun, when it should be serious. I breathed a great sigh of relief that they DID think it was fun and they COULD make it look absurd, and they could also look, think, and delight in their activity. This was still a frustrating task for them, especially with the cube. They could see that their cubes did not "look right," but they did not know why. We practiced making those cubes on the board in which one makes two squares and then joins three or four of the corners with diagonal lines. Some children already knew how to do this and showed others. This is a nice gimmick, and fun to learn, but I was more interested to see something else—the children could see parallel lines and distinguish parallel lines from those that were not, but they had great difficulty drawing parallel lines themselves. This is a developmental stage; in a year or two or three, parallel lines are a breeze. When I realized what was going on, I told Bob that I could see I was asking them to do something they were not ready for yet. He said,

> Don't worry. . . . It's a little beyond them, but it won't hurt them to get a taste of it now and to grapple with it a bit. This will come back to them when they're doing it next time, and they'll realize how easy it is, and they'll be happy at how "smart" they've become.

As some children finished their "basic shapes," their eyes moved back to what was behind them, and they saw their classmates and drew them, filling up their pictures. This gave great delight to everybody, and several pictures soon had the "background" filled with human figures with details like ribbons and sweater patterns and freckles carefully delineated. The models were not always pleased to see how they were represented, but I was very happy. They were playing, and they were playing with whole pictures.

I brought in milk cartons, cylindrical yogurt, ice-cream containers, and triangular wedges or cheese, and gave a set to each table along with a colored cloth to put them on. They arranged them, we discussed the shapes, and they drew. All I asked was the usual request: that the objects be BIG so we could all see them, and that they LOOK.

When we first brought them to the rug to look at, one of the first things we noticed was the enormous size of several of them. One child whom I had thought of as unusually delicate had made a milk carton so tall and bold it looked like a skyscraper. We noticed that one student had drawn the background in pencil and the foreground lines with magic marker, which gave the picture a great sense of depth. Several of the pictures used the bottom of the page as a baseline, which gave an odd quality of flatness turning to three-dimensionality as our eyes went up the page. One child did a rather extraordinary thing with his picture. When I first came around to see what the children were doing, I saw that he had begun the picture so far over to the right that he had run off the page, so he decided to finish it by coming back around from the left like a map. I asked him whether he wanted another piece of paper so he could begin again, and he said he did, upon which he repeated the same structure over again. It was only then that I realized how delightful it was, and told him I made a mistake in trying to stop him. He continued, and soon noticed that there was space at the top and bottom of the page, so he repeated the idea there, and then united the picture with the plaid of the lining of Bob's hood, which we had used for the base material.

The cheese, of course, was the most difficult for them. Again, they could "see" that it was made of a square, a "slanted rectangle" and a triangle, but they couldn't put the three shapes together. I was more impressed with what they **could** do.

Our last classroom project was vegetables and fruits. The children said that they were sick of magic markers and wanted to use paints, chalks, or something else. I agreed.

I brought in two bags full of the most varied and nonspoiling vegetables I could find, and again they arranged them on color cloths, and again they set to work.

It was odd to see, and to watch them notice when we looked at them together, how their objects suddenly shrank as soon as they used a new medium. I also noticed that they were drawing an orange ball for an orange, a yellow curve for a banana, because they "knew" this was how they looked. They needed to LOOK again. I brought in paintings of fruit by Manet, Cezanne, Matisse, and Gauguin. The children noticed the backgrounds, and they noticed how the fruit stood out from the backgrounds. I asked them how many colors were in an apple by Cezanne: green, red, orange, and yellow. A painting of asparagus had all the colors of the palette.

Almost all of them decided to start over again, BIG this time, shaking their heads at themselves. They had a bit of trouble with the chalk smudging, but as soon as we admitted it was indeed a problem, and we could cover up the part of the picture that had chalk on it with a blank sheet of paper, it was fine. One child made a shiny spot on the orange; when the others noticed it, she explained how she had done it, and soon all the other oranges had shiny spots. I noticed how the children had lost interest in shadows in their "milk" still life, but this time one of the children wanted to draw them again, and was upset when he found there was no black. I told him I wanted to stay away from black because it tends to take over a picture, but to look again to see if there was another color he might use. Again the other children saw what he had done and became intrigued with how to put shadows in their own work. I took a big white pitcher and held it against first a blue cloth then a red one. The children could see that the darkness at the bottom of the pitcher was the same color as the cloth, but no one applied this, thank you very much.

They worked on their picture for several days. Colors that had begun as pale and tentative became richer as they pressed down harder on the chalk. Some children centered their pictures; others had the fruits and vegetables far off to the side. Some made very delicate drawings; others made grand, bold work. Some finished before the others and then went and helped to color in backgrounds or whatever they were asked to do. I think what impressed me most as I walked around and watched was the air of competence and confidence in the room. These children knew they were good. They knew they were artists.

We were finished. We arranged all their pictures in individual folders in the order in which they had made them, and we looked at them to see how they had changed. The notebooks had not been used nearly as well as I had wanted. Some of the children had begun to LOOK and EXPLORE less in their final chalk pictures, and follow the rules more. I regretted that I had not spent much more time on both having children work together and on going further with the emotion pictures.

But overall, I was overjoyed with what the children had done. They seemed to be almost as happy with each other's pictures as they were with their own. They could see, and their parents could see when they came into the exhibit, that these children knew how to make pictures and how to think about pictures. They were not only comfortable and confident (and angry and frustrated and happy) with the process of making pictures, but they had made something exciting and beautiful. I think I was happiest not only to see what they had accomplished, but also to see how proud they were of **each other's** accomplishments. As I walked around the room where their work was exhibited, I could hear them say, "I got that from Jeff!" or "That's awesome!" or "You really CHANGED!" They had indeed.

AN ERUPTION OF POPPIES: A MEDITATION ON WRITING LANDSCAPE

Jane Yolen

> The ultimate concern of the artist is not to paint mountains and clouds and trees but the air between them. (Wang Wei)

Too many writers ignore landscape, to their peril. Perhaps the problem is their lack of visual acuity. We are unpracticed in the art of looking.

Nobody has taught us to *see*. Except in art courses, we are never told the value of looking at what is all around us. Oh, if something big moves—a bear, a truck, a train, a moose—we will notice and get out of the way. But most of us miss the little things or the immovable objects. Or if we notice, it is a fleeting moment, then gone.

For the majority of people, landscape is simply just *there*. It exerts no gravitational pull on our senses. We walk through it, slap at it, step over it, or break off a piece. However, to observe it carefully takes too long.

Many authors know this about landscape: that it can be a simple setting or a background for their characters. But the better authors realize much more. Place can be shorthand (or longhand) to explain a hero or villain: think of the difference between the living green forest of ents and the orc-made desert of Mordor in *Lord of the Rings*.

Better writers also know that landscape can be metaphor, can be a parallel to their characters' lives, can become central to the action, can even be a character in itself.

Think of R. L. Stevenson's Davey Balfour, striding across the harsh Highland countryside, becoming a man. The territory he treads helps shape him.

Think of the uncompromising sea through which Captain Ahab plows and how it defines him and creates him just as the whale Moby Dick "tasks" him and "heaps" him.

Or how the rough island on which Robinson Crusoe is marooned is the making of his soul.

How Mary Lennox is changed by her secret garden, how she blossoms and grows strong within its stone walls.

Think of the cozy familiarity of the March girls' landscape, how the careful plantings, the warm comfortable house, emphasizes their domesticity as they grow from little women into mature ones.

Then consider Catherine Earnshaw and Heathcliff, as wild and untamable as their wind-swept moors.

Sometimes, as in the *Dune* books, the arid desert through which the sand worms tunnel, becomes a metaphor for the life lived. Sometimes, as in the island on which Ratty and Mole find the living Pan in *Wind in the Willows*, landscape is the beating heart of the book. And just see what the variety of landscapes do to poor Gulliver in his travels or Alice in her Wonderland.

In the stories written about King Arthur, there are many characters: Arthur, who is the king despite himself, valourous, trusting, and true; Merlin, the magic maker, who unmakes himself through love; Guinevere, married to a king, loved by a knight, trying to remain true to both and to herself as well; Lancelot, the perfect knight, whose perfection is a trap for all. And there are others: Morgan le Fey, Mordred, Bors, Gawaine, the Green Knight, the Lady of the Lake, and Elaine—characters who live on and on.

But the character that interests me the most is Camelot itself. Whether it is a place of turrets and ballrooms shining on a hill, or a rough turf-and-timbered fortress surrounded by a stone shell wall; whether we call it Camelot, Camlann, or something else entirely, that castle focuses our attention. It tells us that within this place magic, mystery, adventure, and romance will happen. It is a spot that is both within and without time. So, when I wrote my YA novel about King Arthur—*Sword of the Rightful King*—the castle became a character on its own.

However, it is not just Arthurian stories that demand that kind of landscape. All novels work best when they have a landscape that seems real, alive, purposeful, and important.

In her lovely fantasy novel for children, *Tom's Midnight Garden,* Phillipa Pearce wrote: "There is a time, between night and day, when landscapes sleep." It is a lovely line, full of the promise of magic. And magic is what happens. Tom goes through the back door of the flat, though he has been told it leads only to an alley strewn with garbage cans. And there, magically, a garden appears, a Victorian garden from the 1880s, with broad sweeps of lawn and yew hedges, and a water tank filled with the flash of goldfish.

Pearce's description of the garden echoed her own love of landscape, and her words truly were magical:

> At first <Tom> took the outermost paths, gravelled and box-edged, intending to map for himself their farthest extent. Then he broke away impatiently on a cross-path. It tunneled through the gloom of yew-trees arching overhead from one side, and hazel nut stubs from the other: ahead was a grey-green triangle of light where the path must come out into the open again. Underfoot the earth was soft with the humus of last year's rotted leaves . . . . and a few sentences later . . .
>
> His path came out by the asparagus beds of the kitchen-garden—so he found them later to be. Beyond their long, grave-like mounds was a dark oblong—a pond. At one end of the pond, and overlooking it, stood an octagonal summer-house with an arcaded base and stone steps up to it door. The summer-house, like the rest of the garden, was asleep on its feet.

Already the reader is as enchanted as Tom. But the description of the garden—walled on three sides, a lawn, a fir tree wound with ivy, a hedge with a hole in it just the size for a boy to squeeze through, then a meadow with cows, and geese in the long grasses—goes on for another three pages.

Just so lovingly, Robin McKinley described the Beast's garden in *Beauty.* A keen gardener herself, McKinley's visual sense of the garden is word perfect.

She wrote,

> Beauty's father was distracted from his pleasant musings by a walled garden opening off the path to his right; the wall was waist-high, and covered with the largest and most beautiful climbing roses that he had ever seen. The garden was full of them; inside the rose-covered wall were rows of bushes: white roses, red roses, yellow, pink, flame-colour, maroon; and a red so dark it was almost black.
>
> This arbor of roses seemed somehow different from the great gardens that lay all around the castle, but different in some fashion he could not define. The castle and its gardens were everywhere silent and beautifully kept; but there was a self-containment, even almost a self-awareness here, that was reflected in the petals of each and every rose, and drew his eyes from the path.
>
> He dismounted and walked in through a gap in the wall, the reins in his hand; the smell of these flowers was wilder and sweeter than that of poppies. The ground was carpeted with petals, and yet none of the flowers were dead or dying; they ranged from buds to the fullest bloom, but all were fresh and lovely. The petals he and the horse trampled underfoot took no bruise.

In Alice Hoffman's *The Probable Future,* the Sparrow family of magical women are all intimate with the landscape. Hoffman, too, knew such things, describing spring this way: "The smell of the laurel, so spicy just before blooming, the way everything turned green, all at once, as though winter itself were a dream, a fleeting nightmare made up of ice and heartlessness and sorrow." As well as this: "The yearly flight of returning cowbirds and blackbirds and sparrows, flocks whose great numbers blocked out the sun for an entire day every year, a winged and breathing eclipse of the pale, untrustworthy sky."

The generous literary landscape—whether garden or mountainside, forest or copse, moor or plain—is as much a part of these stories as the plot, characters, and theme.

Still, the problem comes down to this: how to visualize a landscape well enough that the reader is truly there. I can take a friend by the hand and lead him around my garden in Massachusetts or along the St. Andrews coastline in Fife. But how does a writer lead a reader?

Perhaps it would be helpful to think of landscape as coming in three parts.

First, find the large shapes. Some are immovable and, in human terms, immutable. Ask yourself how the mountains are defined against the sky. Are they so far away that they are fuzzy and muzzy around the edges? Are they lumpy, which makes them older, or sharp and pointed, which means they are younger and have not yet been worn away? Read some good books on geology and construct your mountain ranges accordingly, because a mountain landscape made by volcanic action will be different from one that has been carved out by eons of rivers meandering down their sides.

Water—rivers, streams, oceans—certainly move within their banks and sometimes in fierce storms or in the aftermath of runoffs even break over those banks. How does one describe them so that the reader actually sees the shifting blues and greens, the foaming spume of white water, the tumble of waves? What about the shadows of fingerlings darting along the sandy bottoms, or the whale that humps out of the blue-black water?

Some large shapes are mobile and shifting. What about the clouds? Are they streamers or plump cumulus? Are they white as ibis feathers or gray as stone? (And by the way, do you see a difference in the colors gray and grey?)

Do the trees rise up like fists or spread out like fingers? Does the mountain wear a stubble of small trees on its face?

With such depictions of landscape, the writer can set a mood, background music for the eye. Or can set up the landscape to act contrapuntally against (or with) the hero.

Second, there are singular features: a rock, flower, vine, bird against the slate of sky. These individuals are punctuations of landscape, used instead of an exclamation point.

Perhaps you could place a solitary gnarled tree to stand defiantly upon a hill. Or place a blood-colored flower near the outstretched hand of a dead knight. As your hero treads up a hill, heedless of the pine needles underfoot or the wuthering of the wind tangling his or her hair, the reader sees the character in motion. By watching his or her actions upon the landscape or in concert with it, the reader does not need to be told how they are feeling.

Third, know that landscape well enough to individualize the features: grey porous rock, spikes of yew, eruptions of red poppies in a green field, blue morning glories straining for the sun, and a hawk in a perilous stoop taking its living from the sky.

Go outside and walk about. Do not take notes, but let yourself truly see what is in front of you, above you, and below you. Sit still for a half of an hour, or for an hour, and watch what goes on around you. Life happens—busy, mobile life. If you do not move, you will not affect it. You will be only an eye—a careful, studious, sometimes startled eye.

What might you see—Ants and beetles scurrying by your boots, a woodpecker flecking the bark behind you, a squirrel stopping to gaze at you with its black button eyes, or a butterfly resting on your shoulder with a tremor of wings?

If you are luckier, a rabbit will skitter by your feet, a fox with its flagged tail will stalk by, a deer might find its way to a stream and stand drinking with its long tongue, a flash of trout might ripple the water.

In the city, though the buildings take the place of the large shapes of mountains, there is still a great deal to see: birds, beetles, green shoots springing up through the cracks in the pavement, wallflowers perching precariously atop stone abutments, gargoyles that wink in the rain, the changing shape of shadows gray on gray.

The trick is that the details of the landscape must be precise. It is as if the author has been there, not just as a visitor but also as a native of the place.

Some authors get to that specificity by making lists, writing out travelogues, drawing maps, researching seasons/flora/fauna in books. But first, the author must become an observer: of nature as well as of character.

If you do not look, you cannot see. If you cannot see, how can you write well enough to make others see? How can you write well enough to keep your characters from floating?

And then you see, you must learn to hear: unseen frogs chorusing in the fading light, the weeping cry of a screech owl, the long fall of a coyote's voice.

After that, you must learn the smells: the sharp brine of ocean, the pong of rotting seaweed, the crisp mountain air scented lightly with pine.

And how—I hear you ask—do you keep all of this in your head? The answer is simple: You do not, unless you are a wildlife expert, a rare gardener, a butterfly fancier as fine as Nabokov, a fly fisherman extraordinaire, or live (as I did) with a birding expert. Actually, none of us can keep it all in our heads. I bet even Peter Matthiesen has to do his homework.

So, on your research shelves, close at hand, you will store bird books and mushroom identification books, books about animal tracks and seashells and the changing face of forests. Buy second-hand Audubon guides and when you go on vacation bring home all the pamphlets you can find. These go right next to your thesaurus, dictionary, books of time lines, rhyming dictionaries, encyclopedias, and Strunk & White.

But first and most important, go outside. Sit in a shadow. Become part of the tree. Watch the world. Drink it in.

Then write it—all of it—as much as you can get down. Write the landscape as character, as metaphor, as background and foreground, as counterpoint to your hero, as villain, as friend. Become that better writer who knows the worth of landscape and can set down what is seen to illuminate what is not seen. Draw that world with your words and you will draw the readers in.

REFERENCES

Burnett, Francis Hodgson. (1911; 1988; Reissue). *The Secret Garden*. New York: Viking.

Defoe, Daniel. (1719; 2001). *Robinson Crusoe*. Penguin Publishers

Grahame, Kenneth. (1908; 1940; 1961). *The Wind in the Willows*. New York: Scribner's.

Hoffman, Alice. (2004). *The Probable Future*. Ballantine Books.

McKinley, Robin. (1978). *Beauty: A Retelling of the Story of Beauty and the Beast*. Harper Collins.

Melville, Herman. (1851). *Moby Dick*. Harper and Brothers.

Melville, Herman. (1992). *Moby-Dick*. Wordsworth editions. (1st ed. in 1851)

Stevenson, R. L. (1886) *Kidnapped*. Classic Publishers.

Tolkien, J. R. R. (1965). *The Fellowship of the Ring. The Two Towers. The Return of the King* (The Lord of the Rings trilogy). Houghton Mifflin.

White, William & Strunk E. B. (1979*). The Elements of Style*, 3rd edition. Allyn & Bacon.

THE TRUTH ABOUT NONFICTION

Edward T. Sullivan
SCARECROW PRESS

Informational books do not get the respect they deserve. Lists teachers compile for supplemental and summer reading rarely include nonfiction titles. In the shelves of paperbacks teachers have in their classrooms for self-selected reading, there are few, if any, nonfiction titles. Betty Carter and Richard F. Abrahamson (1998) conducted many notable studies over the years documenting the fact that middle and high school students not only enjoy reading nonfiction; they prefer it. Despite that evidence, Carter and Abrahamson noted, "It is still one of the best-kept secrets in education."

It does not occur to many teachers that nonfiction can simply be a "good read:" something entertaining, fun, enjoyable, or just plain interesting. In a study of the reading preferences of middle and high school students, Carter and Abrahamson (1990) noted, "Much of the nonfiction read by young adults is read for pleasure, diversion, and entertainment." Teachers need to remember that nonfiction is the preferred reading choice of many of their students. In another study of young adult reading preferences, Abrahamson and Carter (1993) observed, "What we know is that young adults in the middle and high schools of America make nonfiction books a substantial part of their self-selected reading. . . . Educators must first of all recognize and reward the nonfiction reading that teens do just as they praise their reading of fiction." Teachers can capitalize on this interest in nonfiction and get their students really excited about reading.

Boys, in particular, tend to prefer reading nonfiction to fiction. Many boy readers have what Smith and Wilhelm (2002) described as an *information-driven orientation*. These readers are less interested in an engagement with the story world. Fictional elements like character development and plot are not appealing to them. In his study of adolescent literacy development, Brozo (2002) observed the enthusiasm adolescent boys have for nonfiction and informational books but is troubled by the lack of access and exposure students have to these texts. "For most boys," Brozo noted, "reading nonfiction consists almost exclusively of reading textbooks, which has been found to be a principal culprit in creating disaffection with reading for both boys and girls." In his interactions with students in the classroom, Brozo found that adolescents who were previously complacent and disengaged became curious and involved when he passed around nonfiction written specifically for them.

Teachers are missing many excellent opportunities and inviting some potentially serious problems by not providing students access and encouragement to read nonfiction. Students are left with the unfortunate impression that the types of books they find appealing and interesting are trivial or inferior. If the only informational text to which they are exposed is from a textbook, they will be led to believe that nonfiction is dry, uninteresting, and strictly utilitarian. Students who have an information-driven reading orientation will have whatever initial enthusiasm they have for reading quickly extinguished. Teachers must also consider the fact that much of the reading adolescents encounter in standardized tests is nonfiction material.

There are several reasons why teachers tend to be "fictioncentric?" Penny Colman (1999), a distinguished author of many nonfiction books for children and young adults, lamented at how many librarians and teachers told her that reading nonfiction is not "real reading." Educators think of nonfiction as informational: something to be used for homework assignments. In other words, little or no literary value is accorded to nonfiction books. Colman believed there are at least three reasons why negative perceptions of nonfiction persist. The first is that in the world of publishing for youth, the personal preferences influential editors, educators, librarians, and reviewers have for fiction has a profound impact. The second is the romanticized image adults have for children's and young adult fiction. The third reason is Zena Sutherland's coining of the term *informational books* for nonfiction, which unfortunately caught on and continues to shape how people in education, librarianship, and publishing view it. The very name given to the books is problematic. Describing a book as not fiction does nothing to explain what it is. It is like calling 7-Up the "uncola." The term *informational books* is not terribly helpful either. Nonfiction is not just about information. Nonfiction needs a name that is positive and wide ranging. Perhaps the answer lies with children. They come into libraries asking for "true books." Although that term too can be problematic, it does sound more affirming.

One reason why teachers have a narrow view of nonfiction is a gender gap. Most school librarians and teachers are female. Boys tend to prefer nonfiction. Girls tend to be drawn to fiction. Female teachers and librarians presume that all of their students will find fiction as appealing as they do. If teachers have little experience reading nonfiction, they will not have an appreciation of the genre as literature.

Abrahamson and Carter (1993) observed that educators are uncomfortable with nonfiction because they do not know how to approach it. "There are many reasons why educators do not value the nonfiction reading their students do as much as they value their fiction reading. Perhaps teachers and librarians unconsciously perpetuate a bias toward fiction because nonfiction was not stressed in their own course of study" (Abrahamson & Carter, 1993, p. 168). Student teachers take classes in which nonfiction is given short shrift. Most curricula for courses in children's and young adult literature are heavily slanted toward fiction. This is also true of the literature courses secondary teachers take as English majors. At best, nonfiction in these courses is accorded only token attention, if it receives any at all. Teachers do not value nonfiction and do not understand how to use it with their students. Unrecognized is the potential nonfiction has to stimulate the analytical and critical thinking skills they see in fiction.

Teachers know how to ask questions of fiction readers dealing with such elements as characterization, conflict, point of view, setting, theme, and so on, but they are often at a loss as to what to do with nonfiction. Carter and Abrahamson (1990) suggested 10 questions educators can use as a basis for designing strategies to elicit student responses about nonfiction. The questions address such factors as the context of the time in which the book was written; the role illustrations play in the book and how they do or do not successfully complement the text; the quality of the book as compared to others written on the same topic; which part, if any, of the book might make a good documentary film; the depth of research the author employed to write the book; the success of the book in speaking to its intended audience and how it would be altered to speak to a different audience; how the author succeeds in teaching the reader about his or her subject; what the reader would ask the author about the book in an interview; what facts or ideas found in the book would the reader want to further investigate; and how the cover art and title of the book effectively represent its contents. Good nonfiction books are as rich in possibilities for deep, thoughtful discussion as any good novel.

Unfortunately, a lot of poor quality nonfiction is published that perpetuates the misconception that nonfiction is just about information. Many series publishers are in the business of cranking out nonfiction in assembly like fashion for school libraries and classrooms. What these publishers typically do is find a subject that they can milk for all it is worth, producing brief, superficial, poorly designed, cheaply made, and outrageously overpriced books. These types of series nonfiction books consistently feature sensational cover designs; didactic and dull writing; unimaginative layout, design of text, and illustrations; and repetitive use of stock photographs that do little to complement the text. Information in these books is "dumbed down" for the reader, in the same way that textbooks manage to strip facts down to the most unappealing presentation imaginable. These books may indeed inform the reader, often condescendingly, but they do nothing to engage the mind or spark the imagination. They certainly do not reflect a respect for their audience. They succeed only in reducing reading to a boring, laborious chore. There is no reason why series publishers cannot produce books of quality and substance, but the sad reality is that many publishers are concerned more with profit than with quality and substance. It is these types of books that help perpetuate the perception of nonfiction as only "informational" books—products only to be used, not enjoyed.

Reviews of nonfiction books in education and library journals are also to blame for reinforcing the perception that nonfiction is only to be used, not enjoyed. These reviews typically comment upon the author's thoroughness in addressing the subject, the organization and layout of the information, the ease with which the information is accessible, if there is a glossary and index, and other observations about the book's overall usefulness. There is little or no commentary upon the aesthetic qualities of the book: the author's ability to craft an engaging narrative, its structure, point of view, pace, tone, voice, and other literary qualities. Nonfiction is regarded in purely utilitarian terms. A book's merits are judged exclusively upon its usefulness to the reader.

The truth is that, for many young adult readers, nonfiction serves the same purposes as fiction does for other readers: It entertains, provides escape, sparks the imagination, and indulges curiosity. There is a lot more to a good nonfiction book than mere information. Teachers need to acknowledge this fact about nonfiction and start giving their students more opportunities where they can be encouraged to read what will be more enjoyable and meaningful to them.

REFERENCES

Abrahamson, R. F. & Carter, B. (1993). What we know about nonfiction and young adult readers and what we need to do about it. In S. Sebesta & K. Donelson (Eds.) *Inspiring literacy: Literature for children and young adults* (pp. 159–172). New Brunswick, NJ: Transaction.

Brozo, W. G. (2002). *To be a boy, to be a reader: Engaging teen and preteen boys in active literacy.* Newark, DE: International Reading Association.

Carter, B., & Abrahamson, R. F. (1990). *Nonfiction for young adults: From delight to wisdom.* Phoenix, AZ: Oryx.

Carter, B., & Abrahamson, R. F. (1998). Castles to Colin Powell: The truth about nonfiction. In K. Beers & B. G. Samuels (Eds.), *Into focus: Understanding and creating middle school readers.* Norwood, MA: Christopher-Gordon.

Colman, P. (1990). Nonfiction is literature, too. *The New Advocate, 12,* 215–223.

Smith, M. W., & Wilhelm, J. D. (2002). *"Reading don't fix no chevys:" Literacy in the lives of young men.* Portsmouth, NH: Heinemann.

APPENDIX

Nonfiction Authors Every Teacher Should Know and Read

Jim Arnosky
Marc Aronson
Susan Bartoletti Campbell
Penny Colman

Michael L. Cooper
Demi
Dennis Fradin
Russell Freedman
Jean Fritz
James Cross Giblin
Joyce Hansen
Jim Haskins
Philip Hoose
Steven Jenkins
Kathleen Krull
Susan Kuklin
Ellen Levine
David Macaulay
Albert Marrin
Patricia and Frederick McKissack
Milton Meltzer
Jim Murphy
Judith St. George
Seymor Simon
Diane Stanley

TIMELESS TIMELINE: VISUALIZING THE PAST AND THE FUTURE

Deborah A. Wooten
UNIVERSITY OF TENNESSEE

Most of us who teach or have taught in the elementary classroom have experienced with amusement a student sharing the story of a personal experience that happened "a long time ago." The funny part is when we discover that the student's definition of "a long time ago" is 2 months, maybe even 2 weeks ago.

Observations like these from elementary students reveal one of the main impediments to teaching history at the elementary level: a limited ability to deal with time and time relationships, which causes difficulty in learning to "think historically" (Zaccaria, 1978). After reviewing the psychological literature on children's time perception, Zaccaria (1978) found that the first grade pupil's time span for thinking about events is only a week. The span widens by the third grade to nearly a month, and by the sixth grade, it is closer to a year. It is not until adolescence, however, that most students become capable of dealing with the periods of time typically used in the chronological account of U.S. history.

Nevertheless, in the national standards for education in America's public schools, the benchmarks for kindergarten through grade 2 students include,

- Understanding broad categories of historical time (e.g., long ago, yesterday, today, tomorrow)

Moreover, the grades 3–5 benchmarks include,

- Knowing significant people and the chronological order of major events in U.S. history
- Interpreting historical data to determine cause-effect and time-order relationships
- Knowing how to develop picture timelines of their own lives or their family history (Kendall, J. S. & Marzano, R. J. 1997)

Broadening an elementary student's time perception is a difficult but necessary task. Almost every state depends on its elementary classrooms to implant in students the foundational knowledge (schema) upon which their upper grade history/social studies curriculum is built. As a result, students encounter their first social studies textbooks at the elementary level, usually by the third grade.

The Student-Driven Class Timeline is an easy to implement tool that addresses this challenge. I developed this timeline idea as part of the Writing and Sharing Connections teaching and learning methodology I constructed as an elementary classroom teacher/researcher and I continue to research today (Wooten, 2000; Wooten & Cullinan, 2004).

A timeline is a two-dimensional graphic organizer that permits the student "to see" time relations quickly and easily that are otherwise obscured in one-dimensional displays, such as text (Larkin & Simon, 1987). One dimension is revealed in the horizontal display of events in time sequence. The other is the vertical display of events that occurred in the same time frame. Of course, there is nothing new about a timeline. What is unique about the Student-Driven Class Timeline is,

- We "timeline" everything we learn in the classroom for the entire year
- The students take charge of the building process
- The students begin to voluntarily scrutinize the timeline and write about what they discover

Mechanics

One-eighth-inch nylon cord is used for the timeline, stretched tightly between screw hooks along the full length of at least two adjoining walls in the classroom. Additional cord is added as needed. Most research classrooms have timelines encircling the room on all four walls by year's end.

Folding a blank sheet of 8 1/2" × 11" paper in half and writing the name and date of the event on one side with a black indelible marker creates a timeline entry. People entries include the name and birth and death years. All writing is as large as the folded paper will allow. Timeline entries are easily read from any point in the classroom.

Entries are placed on the timeline by hanging them over the end of a yardstick or broom and then lifting them over the timeline string. As the timeline grows, slide entries left and right to make room for additional entries and keep the chronology correct. Entries for events that occurred or began in the same year are simply hung one beneath another with scotch tape.

Introduction, Student Involvement, and Strategy

Every person and event presented in every subject through the school year that can be realistically associated with a date is added to the timeline. The well-developed timeline brims with explorers, discoveries, scientists, wars, artists, composers, writers, "firsts", kings, queens, presidents, inventions, and more. Books read aloud to the class are added to the timeline by date of publication.

Before each timeline entry is displayed, a student is selected to decorate (personalize) it with artwork. Creating visuals is a form of elaboration in which the learner creates some type of symbol and, in doing so, engages in deeper processing of text, which, in turn, leads to better memory for the information (Holley & Dansereau, 1984). Students are selected on a rotating basis so that all have artwork on display. Students are encouraged to make the illustration somehow relevant to the event. Artwork is finished and the entry is added to the timeline no more than two days after the event was taught for immediate reinforcement of learning. The teacher has the students applaud as each finished timeline entry is put in place. By these means, the students actually assume the duty of building the graphic organizer (Bean, Singer, & Frasee, 1986).

The Student-Driven Class Timeline offers immediate reinforcement of new learning, organization/categorization of information which aids in building schema, strong visual illustration of horizontal and vertical time relationships, and year-long reinforcement of learned concepts. However, how do we entice students to view the timeline and use its information? With Writing and Sharing Connections sessions in which the teacher reads aloud content related literature.

The Connections Session

The teacher reads aloud a selection of content related literature. In our research classrooms, we supply a list of suggested children's books that are pertinent to the curriculum, but we encourage the teacher to deviate from the list as the dynamics of the classroom are recognized. After the reading, the students are asked to write a response to that literature by answering the question, "What did that book remind you of?" Students are then called on to read what they have written before the class (sharing).

Connections sessions are conducted once per week. An atmosphere of freedom to take chances is vital in connections sessions. Although we want students to make as many connections to content on the timeline as possible, students are never actually told to do so. Instead, the teacher models the process by writing connections to timeline items and reading them aloud in the first two or three Connections sessions. As students begin to connect to information on the timeline, they receive much praise from the teacher, which invariably spawns more timeline connections. Connections are never graded and students are encouraged to take risks with the fact that there are no wrong answers.

Research Results

Let us go inside our latest research classroom and look at students' written Connections. This third grade class of 19 students is in an inner-city elementary school in the southeast. The class is racially mixed and most students fall into the low to moderate socioeconomic category. Thirty percent of the students qualify for the reduced price or free lunch program. The class contains no students who are considered gifted and talented, and five students who qualify for the school's special education offerings. They are studying American history with their first social studies textbook.

During this school year, there were 23 Connections sessions conducted and a total of 415 connections written. Of those connections, 168 (40.48%) contained mention of items that were displayed on the timeline indicating that students may have had visual interaction with timeline content in those cases and did connect two or more items of varying time relationships 168 times.

Here are some of their actual connections:

Connections Session #1 (10/11)

Book: *The Man Who Walked Between the Towers* (Gerstein, 2003). The story of Philip Petit, an aerialist who walked a cable between the twin towers of the World Trade Center in 1974.

Student N: "This story reminds me of the great Houdini."
Student S: "This reminds me of Wilma Unlimited."

Note: Harry Houdini was born in 1874. This connection covers a time span of 100 years. Wilma Rudolph was born in 1940, a time span of 34 years. Connections written in the first 2 or 3 sessions are invariably simple, one-thought sentences or phrases.

Connections Session #3 (10/25)

Book: *Starry Messenger* (Sis, 1996). This book is about the astronomer Galileo.

Student P: "This book reminded me of Neil Armstrong because Neil went to the moon and Galileo looked through the telescope at the moon.

Note: Galileo was born in 1564. Neil Armstrong was born in 1930. This is a time span of 366 years. Three students made the Neil Armstrong connection in this session.

Connections Session #10 (1/12)

Book: *How Ben Franklin Stole the Lightning* (Schanzer, 2003).

Student R: "This book reminds me of storms because the title is how Ben Franklin stole the lightning and because in most of the pictures it was raining. Ben was born in 1706 and died in 1790 and lived for 84 years."

Note: We feel it is significant that Student R seems to have established a connection to the 1700s at the third-grade level. Equally significant is the fact that he or she did the subtraction and reported that Franklyn lived for 84 years. After this connection was read aloud and the teacher praised R for the mathematical discovery, other students began to use math and report time spans frequently. This has been typical in all of our research classrooms.

Connections Session #23 (4/27)

Book: *Satchel Paige* (Cline-Ransome, 2003). The story of the groundbreaking baseball player.

Student L: "This book reminds me of Jackie Robinson because he was a famous baseball player and he was born 14 years later."

Note: It is true that Jackie Robinson was born 14 years after the birth of Satchel Paige. This is another of the many examples of students voluntarily doing the math and reporting time relationships with the visual aid of the Student Driven Class Timeline.

REFERENCES

Bean, T. W., Singer, H., K., & Frasee, C. (1986). The effect of metacognitive instruction in outlining and graphic organizer construction on students' comprehension in a tenth grade world history class. *Journal of Reading Behavior, 18,* 153–169. (ERIC Document Reproduction Service No. 393 484)

Holley, C. D., & Dansereau, D. F. (1984). *Spatial learning strategies: Techniques, applications and related issues.* New York: Academic Press.

Kendall, J. S. & Marzano, R. J. (1997). *Content knowledge: A compendium of standards and benchmarks for K–12 education* (2nd ed.). Alexandria, VA: Association for Supervision and Curriculum Development.

Larkin, J. H. & Simon, H. A. (1987). Why a diagram is (sometimes) worth ten thousand words. *Cognitive Science, 11,* 65–99.

Peterson, R. L. (1992). *Life in a crowded place: Making a learning community.* Portsmouth, NH. Heinemann.

Wooten, D. A. (2000). *Valued voices: An interdisciplinary approach to teaching and learning.* Newark, DE: International Reading Association.

Wooten, D. A. & Cullinan, B. (2004). Metacognition through writing and sharing connections. In D. Lapp, C. Block, E. Cooper, J. Flood, N. Roser, & J. Tinajero (Eds.), *Teaching all the children: Strategies for developing literacy in urban settings* (pp. 294–305). New York: Guilford Publication.

Zaccaria, M. A. (1978). The development of historical thinking implications for the teaching of history. *The History Teacher, 11,* 323–340.

LITERATURE READ ALOUD IN RESEARCH CLASSROOM

Cline-Ransome, L. (2003). *Satchel Paige.* New York: Aladdin Paperbacks.

Gerstein, M. (2003). *The man who walked between the towers.* New York: Roaring Brook.

Hilliard, R. (2005). *Neil, Buzz, and Mike go the moon.* Honesdale, PA: Boyds Mills Press.

Krull, K. (2000). *Wilma unlimited: How Wilma Rudolph became the world's fastest woman.* New York: Voyager.

Krull, K. (2005). *Houdini: World's greatest mystery man and escape king.* New York: Walker.

Schanzer, R. (2003). *How Ben Franklin stole the lightning.* New York: HarperCollins.

Sis, P. (1996). *Starry messenger.* New York: Harper Collins.

STANDARDS IN THE ARTS AND ARTS WITHIN LITERACY INSTRUCTION

Nan L. McDonald
SAN DIEGO STATE UNIVERSITY

Arts activities connected in purposeful ways to other learning at hand (including literacy) do not take the place of what the arts standards define as a sequential education in the arts or disciplined-based learning in the arts. All students need and deserve an education in the arts. Rather than to be thought of as a poor substitution for discipline-based arts education, valid arts activity and instruction infused into the general curriculum (and particularly literacy instruction) may serve to provide more students opportunities for increased involvement, engagement in, synthesis, and memory of the learning at hand (e.g., Cornett, 2003; Hancock, 2000; Jacobs, 1989, 1997; McDonald & Fisher, 2002, 2006).

Inquiry about the arts in the general curriculum (particularly within literacy instructional contexts) might begin by first looking at the arts disciplines themselves. This paper begins by defining the arts discipline areas and their content area standards (music, dance, theatre, and the visual arts). Various challenges faced with the delivery of arts content standards to all students will be discussed. Research assessing the affect of arts activity on student achievement within literacy contexts will be summarized. Finally, resources for arts integration within literacy instruction will be offered.

WHAT ARE THE FOUR ARTS AND WHAT ARE THE ARTS STANDARDS?

The Arts Standards are a statement of what grades K–12 students are to be able to do and know about all four arts (music, dance, theatre, and the visual arts) and describe both content and achievement levels student should know and be able to do by the end of grades 4, 8, and 12. These standards have been adopted and/or adapted in 47 states and have been endorsed or supported by 80 national arts and arts education organizations. "The National Standards for Arts Education articulate goals for accomplishment long sought by teachers of the arts at all levels of education" (Consortium of National Arts Education Associations, 1994, p. 1).

According to the Consortium of National Arts Education Associations (1994), an education in the arts is not to be confused with the visual arts education (one of the four arts). Instead, the word *arts* is a composite term encompassing *all four* of the arts disciplines. The writers of this document comment on the breadth of the content of the *arts* by "recognizing that each of these encompasses a wide variety of forms and sub-disciplines" (Consortium of National Arts Education Associations, 1994, preface). Therefore, an education in the arts includes education and experiences in the panorama of all four arts disciplines (e.g., Consortium of National Arts Education Associations, 1994; Gelineau, 2004; Jensen, 2001; Snyder, 2001).

National education goals were announced in 1990 and "with the passage of the *Goals 2000: Educate America Act*, the national goals are written into law naming the arts as a core academic subject—as important to education as English, mathematics, history, civics and government, geography, science and foreign language" (Consortium of National Arts Education Associations, 1994, p. 131). Therefore, by law, an education in the arts should be available for all our students.

Each of the separate disciplines of the four arts contains many subdisciplines and forms of that art and art-making processes. In music, these areas may include singing, listening, playing of instruments, performance, composition, improvisation, analysis, aesthetic judgment, involvement in the music of many cultures and historical periods, songs in connection with other subjects, and so forth. In the visual arts, we can add sculpture, drawing, photography, painting, computer-based graphics, fabric design, ceramics, history, analysis and critique, connections to other arts and subjects, and more. Dance and theatre also contain performance, choreography, characterization, improvisation, critique and analysis, costuming, stagecraft, readers theatre, scriptwriting, and more (McDonald & Fisher, 2002, 2006).

According to interview information obtained from Dr. Carolynn A. Lindeman (Past President of MENC and a member of the writing team for the National Arts Standards), the Arts Standards are designed to encourage achievement in each of the arts and provide benchmarks for how well students are learning and performing in the arts. They are to inspire excellence in teaching practices, goals, comprehensive planning, implementation, and assessment (e.g., Burz & Marshall, 1999; MENC, 1995, 1996). They give breadth to each of the disciplines and offer a comprehensive guide for teaching and learning. They also (through achievement standards within each content standard) clearly spell out levels of achievement students should reach throughout the grade levels. As such, they are rigorous in both design and content.

Specific content standards (without achievement level standards listed) in each of the four arts (also known compositely as the instructional content area of visual and performing arts) include the following:

Music Content Standards

1. Singing, alone and with others, a varied repertoire of music
2. Performing on instruments, alone and with others, a varied repertoire of music
3. Improvising melodies, variations, and accompaniments
4. Composing and arranging music within specified guidelines
5. Reading and notating music
6. Listening to, analyzing, and describing music
7. Evaluating music and music performances
8. Understanding relationships between music, the other arts, and disciplines outside the arts
9. Understanding music in relation to history and culture

Dance Content Standards

1. Identifying and demonstrating movement elements and skills in performing dance
2. Understanding choreographic principles, processes, and structures
3. Understanding dance as a way to create and communicate meaning
4. Applying and demonstrating critical and creative thinking skills in dance
5. Demonstrating and understanding dance in various cultures and historical periods
6. Making connections between dance and healthful living
7. Making connections between dance and other disciplines.

Drama (Theatre) Content Standards

1. Script writing by planning and recording improvisations based on personal experience and heritage, imagination, literature, and history
2. Acting by assuming roles and interacting in improvisations
3. Designing by visualizing and arranging environments for classroom dramatizations
4. Directing by planning classroom dramatizations
5. Researching by finding information to support classroom dramatizations
6. Comparing and connecting art forms by describing theatre, dramatic media (such as film, television, and electronic media, and other forms)
7. Analyzing and explaining personal preferences and constructing meanings from classroom dramatizations and from theatre, film, television, and electronic media productions
8. Understanding context by recognizing the role of theatre, film, television, and electronic media in daily life

Visual Arts Content Standards

1. Understanding and applying media, techniques, and processes
2. Using knowledge of structures and functions
3. Choosing and evaluating a range of subject matter, symbols, and ideas
4. Understanding the visual arts in relation to history and cultures
5. Reflecting upon and assessing the characteristics and merits of their work and the work of others
6. Making connections between visual arts and other disciplines

(Consortium of National Art Education Associations. (1994). National standards for arts education: Dance, music, theatre, visual arts: What every young American should know and be able to do in the arts. *Proceedings of the American Alliance for Theatre & Education, Music Educators National conference, National Art Education Association, National Dance Association, Reston, Virginia* pp. 23–72)

Important to our discussion of standards in the arts is the defining premise that these standards are deeply rooted in distinct, *specialized* areas (disciplines) of study. Within each area of the arts, the writers of the standards intended that *all students* have the opportunity to develop competence (doing and knowing) in each of the arts. This requires specialized arts instruction by teachers who are specialists in the arts. There are many ways for students to actually learn about and do the arts, and study in the arts may take place at different times, in different ways, and at different levels.

That being said, the writers of the standards in the arts also importantly acknowledge, "A basic intent of the Standards is that the arts be taught for their intrinsic value. Beyond their significance in this arena, however, one of the most important goals the Standards can achieve is to help students make connections between concepts and across subjects" (Consortium of National Art Education Associations, 1994, p. 13). Herein lies the beginning of further inquiry into the role of the arts (both specialized and nonspecialized instruction) within grades K–12 general curriculum.

WHAT ARE SOME CHALLENGES FACED IN THE DELIVERY OF ARTS EDUCATION TO ALL STUDENTS?

Although the standards clearly define the need for specialized instruction in the arts for all students grades K–12, the reality of meeting that goal seems illusive, if not impossible. We are faced with the situation that core curriculum in all four arts is frequently not available or is delivered in a marginalized, nonsupported manner to our school children (e.g., Leonhard, 1991; McDonald & Fisher, 2002, 2006; Stake, Bresler, & Mabry, 1991). If schools have arts specialists, they are usually music and art teachers. Therefore, in many instances, the delivery of arts education becomes the responsibility of classroom teachers under the nonspecialist instructional umbrella of arts *within* general education (McDonald & Fisher, 2002, 2006).

While we may believe and legislate that the arts are essential to the development of a fully educated child, the delivery of arts education is threatened. Is there a way out for the benefit of all our students and teachers? What about arts in *connection* to other content areas? What about arts activities *within* literacy instruction as a natural way to enhance teaching and learning? We will turn our attention to integrated formats where arts activities are infused into literacy instruction taught by nonarts specialists, classroom teachers. By doing so, we will review evidence that arts activities positively impact student achievement, particularly within the context of literacy instruction.

HOW DO INTEGRATED ARTS ACTIVITIES INFUSED WITHIN LITERACY INSTRUCTION IMPACT OVERALL STUDENT ACHIEVEMENT AND SATISFACTION?

Classroom teachers can choose to design interdisciplinary curriculum in which students experience deeper understanding of the arts through "the intersections and interactions of the disciplines" (Barrett, 2001, p. 27). Vygotsky (1962, 1978) proposed that human language is developed through multiple signs, both verbal and nonverbal, during which students connect learning to what they already know. The arts are full of nonverbal and verbal communication systems and thus provide students with opportunities for a wider range of literacy development beyond reading, writing, speaking and listening (McDonald & Fisher, 2006). "Synthesis takes place through a child's active involvement with the meanings of language. Furthermore, we know the centrality of human language toward thinking and that a child's learning depends on language, cutting across learning within all subject matter and school activity" (McDonald & Fisher, 2002, p. 16).

Purposeful cross-disciplinary arts teaching (e.g., arts activity within or connected to literacy instruction) may involve many active avenues toward the literacy development of young readers (Hancock, 2000). In other words, literacy instruction and student learning can benefit by connecting arts activities within literacy instruction. By these kinds of active learning, important opportunities for creative student involvement in language development can be found. Students may actively and expressively participate in dramatic read alouds and reader's theatre, move to poetic text, write about artists' lives and work, illustrate and perform original poetry, set poetry to music and dance, create three-dimensional art projects exploring text meanings, and so forth (e.g., Cornett, 2003; Hancock, 2000; McDonald & Fisher, 2002, 2006). They may also use today's latest technologies and various forms of everyday and created media as artistic avenues for literacy skill development (e.g., Lapp, Fisher, & Flood, 1999a, 1999b; Morrison, Bryan, & Chilcoat, 2002).

Within a pivotal summary collection of recent academic research about the affect of the arts on learning, *Critical Links: Learning in the Arts and Student Academic and Social Development* (Arts Education Partnership, 2002), the following connections are established linking specific arts activity to literacy skill development in the following areas (for a complete listing of specific research studies, refer to the complete version of *Critical Links*; reference the specific art to locate supporting studies connected to literacy within the areas designated below):

1. Visual arts
   Drawing is linked to content and organization of writing.
   Visualization training is linked to sophisticated reading skills/interpretation of text.
   Instruction in visual art is linked to reading readiness.
2. Music
   Early childhood music training is linked to cognitive development.
   Musical listening is linked to quality and prolixity of writing.
   Instrument training is linked to reading and SAT verbal scores.
   Music with language learning is linked to English skills for ESL learners.
3. Classroom drama
   Dramatic enactment is linked to story comprehension (oral and written), character identification, character motivation, increased peer interaction, writing proficiency and prolixity, conflict resolution skills, skills with subsequently read, unrelated texts, problem-solving dispositions/strategies, and general self-concept.
4. Dance
   Traditional dance is linked to self-confidence, persistence, reading skills, nonverbal reasoning, expressive skills, creativity in poetry, social tolerance, and appreciation of individual/group social development.
   Creative dance is linked to creative thinking and fluency as well as general creative thinking, originality, elaboration, flexibility.
5. Integrated arts/academics are linked to the following:
   reading, verbal, and mathematics skills, creative thinking, achievement motivation, cognitive engagement, instructional practice in the school, professional culture of the school, school climate, and community engagement and identity.
6. Arts-rich school environment is linked to the following:
   creativity, engagement/attendance, range of personal and social developments, and higher-order thinking skills. (Arts Education Partnership, 2002)

Other research indicates that when diverse students are asked to be an audience or present their work to others, they readily construct meanings of their worlds with others through dialogue about texts and through involvement in the arts (Many & Henderson, 2005). Having an audience is at the heart of many arts activities and experiences and has an important impact on the literacy development and learning of students involved (e.g., Bloodgood, 1995; Dyson, 1991; Rowe, 1989; Wollman-Bonilla, 2001). Audiences can also become an inspiration and motivator for increasing student writing skills and performance (e.g., Britton, Burgess, Martin, McLeod, & Rosen, 1975; Rowe, 1989) and reading skills (Dixon-Krauss, 1995). According to Many & Henderson (2005),

> The importance of developing a sense of audience and providing and audience for students is grounded in the recognition of the role social interactions play in literacy learning. Social interactions are viewed as an integral part of the learning process (Vygotsky, 1978) and thus help define literacy concepts (Cook-Gumperz, 1986; Dixon-Krauss, 1995; Rowe, 1989) Through social contexts in which literacy experiences such as reading and writing occur, students develop richer understandings of literacy processes which may be reflected in future reading and writing opportunities. (p. 1)

In summary, research clearly indicates that arts activities and experiences positively impact student literacy skill development. With this knowledge in mind, general educators may wish to explore what resources are available to begin or continue their curriculum development in this area.

WHAT RESOURCES ARE AVAILABLE FOR TEACHERS TO INFUSE ARTS ACTIVITIES WITHIN LITERACY INSTRUCTION IN THE GENERAL CLASSROOM?

Jensen (2001), Cornett (2003), Gelineau (2004), and Hancock (2000) provided compelling research about the value of arts within literacy instruction. These sources also provide many detailed lesson examples, comprehensive resources and materials lists for classroom teaching as well as a great deal of background information about the arts and their role in literacy development. McDonald and Fisher's (2006) qualitative research offered numerous cross-disciplinary, arts within literacy curriculum units and reflections from real-life K–12 classroom teachers and students. Over 50 teacher-created units were taught in three underserved, inclusive urban school settings with English language learners. Reflections from both students and classroom teachers provide a compelling case for the importance of the arts within literacy instruction.

What follows is a list of teacher resources toward developing lessons and curriculum in this area:

Multiarts

Blecher, S., & Jaffee, K. (1998). *Weaving in the arts.* Portsmouth, NH: Heinemann.

Brady, M. (1997). *Dancing hearts: Creative arts with books kids love.* Golden, CO: Fulcrum Publishing.

Burnaford, G., Arnold, A., & Weiss, C. (Eds.). (2001). *Renaissance in the classroom: Arts integration and meaningful learning.* Mahwah, NJ: Lawrence Erlbaum Associates.

Dodge, D., Colker, L., & Heroman, C. (2002). *The creative curriculum: Connecting content, teaching and learning.* Washington, DC: Teaching Strategies, Inc.

Gust, J. & McChesney, J. (1995). *Learning about cultures: Literature, celebrations, games and art activities.* Carthage, IL: Teaching and Learning Company.

Piazza, C. (1999). *Multiple forms of literacy: Teaching literacy and the arts.* Upper Saddle River, NJ: Prentice-Hall.

Remer, J. (1996). *Beyond enrichment: Building effective arts partnerships with schools and your community.* Washington, DC: American Council for the Arts.

Teaching Artist Journal. Mahwah, NJ: Lawrence Erlbaum Associates.

Music

Beall, P. & Nipp, S. (1994). *Wee-sing songbooks and CD's.* New York: Price Stern Sloan.

Blevins, W. (1999). *Phonemic awareness songs & rhymes.* New York: Scholastic.

Burz, H. & Marshall, K. (1999). *Performance-based curriculum for music and the visual arts: From knowing to showing.* Thousand Oaks, CA: Sage Publications.

Fitzpatrick, J. (1997). *Phonemic awareness: Playing with sounds to strengthen beginning reading skills.* Cypress, CA: Creative Teaching Press.

Hansen, D., Bernstorf, E., & Stuber, G. (2004). *The music and literacy connection.* Reston, VA: MENC: The National Association for Music Education.

Levene, D. (1993). *Music through children's literature: Theme and variations.* Englewood, CO: Teacher Ideas Press.

Longden, S. & Taucher, W. (2005). *Making music with movement and dance.* Parsippany, NJ: Scott Foresman.

Rooyackers, P. (1998). *101 dance games for children: Fun and creativity with movement.* Alameda, CA: Hunter House.

Rooyackers, P. (2003). *101 more dance games for children: New fun and creativity with movement.* Alameda, CA: Hunter House.

Visual art

Chambers, J., Hood, M., & Peake, M. (1995). *A work of art: Creative activities inspired by famous artists.* Nashville, TN: Incentive Publications.

Chambers, J., & Hood, M. (1997). *Art for writing: Creative ideas to stimulate written activities.* Nashville, TN: Incentive Publications.

Frohardt, D. (1999). *Teaching art with books kids love: Art elements, appreciation, and design with award-winning books.* Golden, CO: Fulcrum Publishing.

Henry, S. (1999). *Kids' art works: Creating with color, design, texture and more.* Charlotte, VT: Williamson Publishing.

Hierstein, J. (1995). *Art activities from award-winning picture books.* Carthage, IL: Teaching and Learning Company.

Johnson, P. (1997). *Pictures and words together: Children illustrating and writing their own books.* Portsmouth, NH: Heinemann.

Kohl, M. & Solga, K. (1996). *Discovering great artists: Hands-on art for children in the styles of the great masters.* Bellingham, WA: Bright Ring Publishing.

Ritter, D. (1991). *Literature-based art activities: Creative art projects inspired by 45 popular children's books: PreK-3.* Cypress, CA: Creative Teaching Press.

Schecter, D. (1997). *Science art: Projects and activities that teach science concepts and develop process skills.* New York: Scholastic.

Sterling, M. (1994). *Focus on artists.* Huntington Beach, CA: Teacher Created Materials.

Welton, J. (1992). *Eyewitness art: Monet.* New York: Dorling Kindersley.

Drama/theater

Balwin, P. & Fleming, K. (2003). *Teaching literacy through drama: Creative approaches.* London: Routledge Falmer.

Barchers, S. (1993). *Reader's theatre for beginning readers.* Englewood, CO: Teacher Ideas.

Bray, E. (1995). *Playbuilding: A guide for group creation of plays with young people.* Portsmouth, NH: Heinemann.

Caruso, S. & Kosoff, S. (1998). *The young actor's book of improvisation: Dramatic situations from Shakespeare to Spielberg* (Vol.1). Portsmouth, NH: Heinemann.

Cornett, C. (2003). *Creating meaning through literature and the arts* (2nd ed.). Upper Saddle River, NJ: Merrill Prentice Hall.

Heinig, R. (1993). *Creative drama for the classroom teacher.* Upper Saddle River, NJ: Merrill Prentice Hall.

Kohl, M. (1999). *Making make-believe: Fun props, costumes and creative play ideas.* New York: Gryphon House.

Larrick, N. (1991). *Let's do a poem! Introducing poetry through listening, singing, chanting, impromptu choral reading, body movement, dance, and dramatization.* New York: Delacort Press.

Laughlin, M. & Latrobe, K. (1990). *Reader's theatre for children.* Englewood, CO: Teacher's Ideas.

Martinez. M. (1993, May). Motivating dramatic story reenactments. *The Reading Teacher, 46,* 682–688.

McCaslin, N. (1990). *Creative drama in the classroom* (5th ed.). New York: Longman.

Rosenberg, H. (1987). *Creative drama and imagination: Transforming ideas into action.* New York: Rinehart & Winston.

Ross, E. & Roe, B. (1997). Creative drama builds proficiency in reading. *The Reading Teacher,* 383–387.

Spolin, V. (1996). *Theater games for the classroom: A teacher's handbook.* Evanston, IL: Northwestern University Press.

Tarlow, E. (1998). *Teaching story elements with favorite books: Creative and engaging activities to explore character, plot, setting, and theme: Grades 1–3.* New York: Scholastic.

Wolf, A. (1993). *It's show time! Poetry from the page to the stage.* Asheville, NC: Poetry Alive!

Dance

Benzwie, T. (1987). *A moving experience: Dance for lovers of children and the child within.* Tuscon, AZ: Zephyr Press.

Fraser, D. (2000). *Danceplay: Creative movement for very young children.* Lincoln, NE: Author's Choice Press.

Joyce, M. (1993). *First steps in teaching creative dance to children.* New York: McGraw Hill.

Web Sites

The Art Geek
www.dhc.net/-artgeek

The Art Room
www.arts.ufl.edu/art/rt_room/

Arts Edge: *lesson plans and other resources provided by the Kennedy Center for the Arts artsedge.kennedy-center.org*

Arts Resource Connection: *Arts education resource provided by Minnesota's Center for Arts Education*
www.mcae.k12.mn.us/art_connection/art_connection.html

ArtsEdNet: *Extensive curriculum, lesson plans, and resources provided by the Getty Center*
artsednet.getty.edu/

Crayola Arts Education: *Teachers and others share ideas, lessons, and arts advocacy*
www.crayola.com

Culturefinder: The Internet Address for the Performing Arts: *Large database of cultural events around the country, schedules and information, reviews, and news.*
culturefinder.mediapolis.com/

eWorld: Learning Museum: *Virtual tours of 24 art, history, and science museums*
www.eworld.com/learning/museum.html

The Foundation Center: *provides guides to grant and research writing*
www.fdcenter.org

GeoCities the Tropics: *lots of information on museums, arts styles and periods, and art education*
www.geocities.com/thetropics/1009/index.html

Learning in Motion's Top Ten List
www.learn.motion.com/lim/links/linkman

On Broadway: *summaries of the season, many resources*
artsnet.Heinz.cmu.edu:80/OnBroadway/

Storytelling, etc.
falcon.jmu.edu/-ramseyil/drama.htm

Virtual Museums
www.icom.org/vlmp

Visual Art and Writing
www.picturingwriting.org

World Wide Arts Resources: *Over a thousand types of resources and links to websites.*
www.wwar.com

World Wide Web Virtual Library
www.icom.org

REFERENCES

Arts Education Partnership. (2002). *Critical links: Learning in the arts and student academic and social development.* Washington, DC: Council of Chief State School Officers. May 1, 2006 http://www.aep-arts.org/cllinkspage.html

Barrett, J. (2001). Interdisciplinary work and musical integrity. *Music Educators Journal, 87*(5), 27–31.

Bloodgood, J. (1995, December). *Exploring a model of reading proficiency.* Paper presented at the Annual Meeting of the National Reading Conference, New Orleans, Louisiana.

Britton, F., Burgess, T., Martin, N., McLeod, A., & Rosen, H. (1975). *The development of writing abilities.* London: Schools Council Publications.

Burz, H. & Marshall, K. (1999). *Performance-based curriculum for music and the visual arts: From knowing to showing.* Thousand Oaks, CA: Corwin Press.

Consortium of National Art Education Associations. (1994). National standards for arts education: Dance, music, theatre, visual arts: What every young American should know and be able to do in the arts. *Proceedings of the American Alliance for Theatre & Education, Music Educators National Conference, National Art Education Association, National Dance Association,* Reston, Virginia.

Consortium of National Arts Education Associations, International Council of Fine Arts Deans, Council of Arts Accrediting Associations. (2001). *To move forward: An affirmation of continuing commitment to arts education.* Reston, VA: Music Educators National Conference. Retrieved date, from http://146.186.186.119/ToMove.html

Cook-Gumperz, J. (1986). *The social construction of literacy.* Cambridge, U.K.: Cambridge University Press.

Cornett, C. (2003). *Creating meaning through literature and the arts: An integration resource for classroom teachers* (2nd ed.). Upper Saddle River, NJ: Merrill Prentice Hall.

Dixon-Kraus, L. (1995). Partner reading and writing: Peer social dialogue and the zone of proximal development. *Journal of Reading Behavior, 17,* 45–63.

Dyson, A. (1991). Viewpoints: The word and the world: Reconceptualizing written language development or "Do rainbows mean a lot to little girls?" In R. Ruddell, M. Ruddell, & H Singer (Eds.), *Theoretical models and processes of reading* (pp. 297–322). Newark, DE: International Reading Association.

Gelineau, R. (2004). *Integrating the arts across the elementary school curriculum.* Belmont, CA.: Wadsworth.

Hancock, M. (2000). *A celebration of literature and response: Children, books, and teachers in K–8 classrooms.* Upper Saddle River, NJ: Prentice Hall.

Jacobs, H. H. (1989). *Interdisciplinary curriculum: Design and implementation.* Alexandria, VA: Association for Supervision and Curriculum Development.

Jacobs, H. H. (1997). *Mapping the big picture: Integrating curriculum and assessment K–12.* Alexandria, VA: Association for Supervision and Curriculum Development.

Jensen, E. (2001). *Arts with the brain in mind.* Alexandria, VA: Association for Supervision and Curriculum Development.

Lapp, D., Fisher, D., & Flood, J. (1999a). Integrating the language arts and content areas: Effective research-based strategies. *The California Reader, 32*(4), 35–38.

Lapp, D., Flood, J., & Fisher, D. (1999b). Intermediality: How the use of multiple media enhances learning. *The Reading Teacher, 52,* 776–780.

Leonhard, C. (1991). *The status of arts education in American public schools.* Urbana, IL: National Arts Education Resarch Center at the University of Illinois.

Many, J. & Henderson, S. (2005). Developing a sense of audience: An examination of one school's instructional contexts. *Reading Horizons, 45*(4), 321–348.

McDonald, N. & Fisher, D. (2002). *Developing arts-loving readers: Top 10 questions teachers are asking about integrated arts education.* Latham, MD: Scarecrow.

McDonald, N. & Fisher, D. (2006). *Teaching literacy through the arts: A guidebook for teachers.* New York: Guilford.

MENC. (1995). In C. Lindeman (Ed.), *Strategies for teaching, 13 Vols.* Reston, VA: Music Educators National Conference.

MENC. (1996). *Performance standards for music grades preK–12: Strategies and benchmarks for assessing progress toward the national standards.* Reston, VA: Music Educators National Conference.

Morrison, T., Bryan, G., & Chilcoat, G. (2002). Using student generated comic books in the classroom. *Journal of Adolescent and Adult Literacy, 45*(8), 758–767.

Rowe, D. (1989). Author/audience interaction in the preschool: The role of social interaction in literacy learning. *Journal of Reading Behavior, 27,* 311–349.

Snyder, S. (2001). Connection, correlation, and integration. *Music Educators Journal, 87*(5), 32–39.

Stake, R., Bresler, L., & Mabry, L., (1991). *Custom and cherishing: The arts in elementary schools.* Urbana, IL: National Arts Education Research Center at the University of Illinois.

Vygotsky, L. S. (1962). *Thought and language* (E. Hanfmann, & G. Vakar, Eds. & Trans.). Cambridge, MA: MIT.

Vygotsky, L. S. (1978). *Mind in society: The development of higher mental psychological processes.* Cambridge, MA: Harvard University Press.

Wollman-Bonilla, J. (2001). Can first-grade writers demonstrate audience awareness? *Reading Research Quarterly, 36,* 184–201.

Wright, G. & Sherman, R. (1999). Let's create a comic strip. *Reading Improvement, 36*(2), 66–72.

ENCOUNTERS WITH ART IN AND OUT OF THE CLASSROOM

Jan Greenberg
ST. LOUIS, MISSOURI

A group of sixth graders sat in a circle, staring at a slide projected on the wall of the library. The image was an abstract painting by the American artist Marc Rothko.

> "What do you see? Can you describe this painting?" I asked them.
> "It's a blob," said the boy in the middle.
> "I don't like it," said the girl next to him. "It's not about anything."
> "Actually there are two blobs. One sort of yellow, the other orange," said a boy in the back row.
> "What shapes are they?" I asked. "Do you see other colors?"

And so began a dialogue with art, viewing an artwork with no recognizable image. My goal was to help these young viewers find ways to describe this mysterious painting and to understand what the artist was trying to achieve. Art history could come later. Now we would confront a single image and talk about it one part at a time. "It's like taking apart a jigsaw puzzle and putting it back together again," I said. "Think of it as a mystery, collecting facts and clues, until we finally discover the answer." I stressed there were no right or wrong answers as long as we could defend our opinion in the language of art.

I ran through some other questions, a method of inquiry Sandra Jordan and I had developed in writing The Painter's Eye: Learning to Look at Contemporary American Art.

> Let's make a list of sensory words to describe the painting. These are words that remind us of what we can see, hear, taste, smell, or touch. Bright, soft, misty, translucent, airy were some of the descriptive words we wrote on the blackboard. If you could step inside this painting and walk around, how would you move? Would you dance or tiptoe carefully? How would the atmosphere of the painting feel against your skin? Like velvet or perhaps like water? How does the artist use shape, color, and texture to pull us in to another world? And finally, the most important question. What is the feeling expressed through his use of color, line, shape and texture?
>
> "Like sunshine. A happy feeling," said my friend in the middle.
> "If the artist had used dark colors, blacks and gray," I asked, "would the mood be different?"
> "Maybe what it's about," someone said, "is a feeling." Yes!

There have been studies from the Getty Center and other educational labs that demonstrate that discussing artworks in a classroom setting (other than the art room) improves critical and abstract thinking skills. Looking at a painting or a sculpture, analyzing, interpreting, and making judgments teaches students to think metaphorically, to develop a critical language, and to defend their opinions beyond "I like it" or "I don't like it."

Along with analyzing artwork, there are many other ways to bring children into the experience of art. Using sensory images provides one method, making art another. But sometimes in the library, there are no supplies and no room to experiment with art materials. However, we can experiment creatively with artworks through storytelling, poetry, music and movement.

One of my favorite memories from childhood took place outside the St. Louis Art Museum, standing with my mother in front of a stabile by Alexander Calder and watching the colored discs dip and sway in the wind. I was not much of an athlete, but I loved to dance. My mother encouraged me to imitate the rhythm and line of the sculpture through movement and gesture.

Each time Sandra Jordan and I write a book about art for young people, we bring the text to the classroom and try it out with the students. Beginning with a story, such as a vivid anecdote from the artist's biography or a quote from the artist, is the most effective approach, capturing students' attention immediately. Talking about *Vincent van Gogh: Portrait of an Artist* (cowritten with Sandra Jordan) at schools offered an interesting challenge. Most young people are familiar with van Gogh's story. But what do they think they know about him? When asked, many students said he was the famous artist who painted sunflowers and cut off his ear. The myth surrounding van Gogh's life and work, spurred on by hundreds of souvenirs from coffee mugs to posters emblazoned with his *Self-Portrait with Bandaged Ear* disregards the most important questions. Could a madman have painted such monumental paintings? Were his works the result of hallucinatory visions or the result of carefully worked out compositions?

Our goal as biographers lay in getting beyond the myth without losing touch with the power of its appeal. The stories and discussions that followed in classrooms gave students an opportunity to rethink some popularly held assumptions. To set the tone for a conversation, I begin by reading the prologue of the book. It describes van Gogh painting on a hot summer's day in Arles. I pointed out that some phrases in the text come from van Gogh's own words written in letters to his brother Theo. The class can refer to chapter notes in the back of the book that document this material. As a follow-up activity, this literary device can be recreated, using another artist's quotes and asking the class to fit his or her words into a story of their own.

Along with introducing the language of art and telling stories, I enjoy showing the connections between art forms. Often I share a poem about a painting or sculpture and then work with students on writing a poem of their own. Poems enhance the artwork and help young readers appreciate it in a new way.

Here is a poem called "Diamante for Chuck" from my anthology *Heart to Heart: New Poems Inspired by Twentieth Century American Art,* in which poets wrote poems about specific artwork. I wrote a diamond shaped poem to describe *Self-Portrait* by the painter Chuck Close.

Ovals
Luminous, Hot
Popping, Pulsing, Swirling
Curlicues of color, A Kaleidoscope
Blurring, Blending, Focusing
Immense, Intense
Self

This poem and others in the collection follow a simple pattern for young readers to imitate. Students can select a painting from *Heart to Heart* and experiment with word play in their own poems. The class can try to write a concrete poem that imitates the shape of the painting or sculpture. Or they can step inside the canvas and speak in the voice of the person or object depicted there.

Children respond to art through a number of different learning styles. From stories to analysis, from poetry to theatre and dance, from discussion about social issues to philosophy, we can satisfy our students' individual learning styles and open them up to new possibilities. These encounters with art will inspire their creativity and help them come to all artworks, spanning centuries and cultures, with a fresh eye. By looking at art, young people get a better understanding of their own culture, as well other cultures. They are encouraged to be open to fresh ideas and to come to new art with an open mind. They become better appreciators. In other words, they experience the pleasure that comes from responding to an aesthetic object art for its own sake,—if you will, the sensory enjoyment of color line shape and texture organized into a pleasing and satisfying whole, the challenge of the bewildering artwork, and the discussion of what is beauty and what is art?

When I was a junior in high school, a woman from the St. Louis Art Museum came to assembly to show us a movie about an artist named Jackson Pollock. This was in the late 1950s, and I remember how shocked, even amused, everyone was by the way he worked. The film showed the artist unrolling a canvas on the ground and dancing around it, dripping paint from a brush, and pouring paint from a can. I was excited by what I saw. Here was someone flying in the face of tradition, daring to follow his own instincts to do something different. The images of Pollock painting have stayed with me. Writing Action Jackson, I found myself remembering those days when doing something different seemed both alien and appealing at the same time. Over 40 years have gone by. Now Pollock is recognized as one of the most important artists of post-WWII American art. Who would have believed it then? Action Jackson (Greenberg & Jordan, 2002) deals with Pollock's creative process and gave us an opportunity to consider a particular artist's methods, how he thinks, what he does to make a painting.

When Sandra Jordan and I started working together in 1991, almost no books for children focused on contemporary artists. That was the gap in the bookshelf. It was exciting to meet artists such as Chuck Close and Louise Bourgeois and the architect Frank Gehry in their studios, watch them work, and interview them for new anecdotes, and, in the case of Andy Warhol, who died in 1987, to talk to many people who knew him well.

Why did we choose Andy Warhol as a subject? Both Sandra and I have to agree that we like the artist's work. He or she has to be historically important, which means widely collected by museums and accepted by artists, museum curators, art historians, and critics. In Andy's case, he was not only deemed a significant artist by that guild but he also influenced the culture. Films, advertising, product packaging, fashion, and art were forever changed by his methods and subject matter. He was the ultimate pop artist, as well as celebrity icon of the 1960s, 1970s, and 1980s here in the United States as well as in Europe and Japan. But his is also a poignant story. I am always drawn to biographies of people who have had to overcome great odds to succeed. I think young people are drawn to those kinds of real life stories, as well. We ask ourselves what a young reader will find compelling about this artist's life. Andy's is a rags to riches story. He was the sickly, odd son of poor immigrant parents. His mother was overly protective and believed he was special. After art school in Pittsburgh, he moved to New York City and became a successful commercial artist, winning awards for his shoe advertisements. But he wanted to be a serious artist and eventually his paintings of commercial objects, Campbell's Soups, Dollar Bills, and cartoon imagery made him famous.

What are we trying to show our readers? We ask why the artist was important. How did his or her childhood influence the work? How does the artist's life and art intertwine? We want to inspire the reader to look at real works of art. We do this, in part, by weaving the language of art into the text with lively discussions of the artwork without seeming to interject our opinions or interfere with the rhythms of the narrative. We look for themes in their lives that inform their work and we question the myths that surround the artists' lives. In van Gogh's case, the myth that he painted in an hallucinatory state driven by madness, or in Warhol's case, that he was an idiot savant, a jokester who fooled the art world with his soup cans and movie star paintings. Falsely held common beliefs are interesting to dispute and disprove.

REFERENCE

Greenberg, Jan & Jordan, Sandra. (2002). *Action Jackson*. Roaring Book Press.

AUTHOR INDEX

Page references followed by *f* indicate figure.
Page references followed by *t* indicate table.
Page references followed by *n* indicate footnote.

A

B

C

D

E

F

G

H

I

J

K

M

N

O

P

R

S

T

U

V

W

X

Y

Z

SUBJECT INDEX

A

B

C

D

E

F

G

H

I

J

L

M

N

O

P

R

S

T

U

V

W

Y

Z